Bowhunting Big Game Records

OF NORTH AMERICA

Third Edition

BIG GAME   PORE AND YOUNG CLUB   RECORDS

Bowhunting
Big Game Records

OF NORTH AMERICA

Third Edition

Book Editorial Committee

Lee Kline, Editor

G. Fred Asbell
C. Randall Byers
Marvin Clyncke
Jim Dougherty
Harv Ebers
Rick Grooms
Frank "Rit" Heller
M. R. James
George Moerlein
Scott Showalter
Naomi Torrey

Bowhunting Big Game Records of North America

Library of Congress Catalog Card Number: 86-63628
ISBN Number: 0-9617966-0-X
Published March, 1987

Produced and Published in the United States of America by the
Pope and Young Club®
6471 Richard Avenue
Placerville, California 95667

Dedication

This book is dedicated to the small number of you in each state who are directly involved, year in and year out, with our bowhunting seasons. You deal with the never ending, tough political process to assure that bowhunters may hunt a fair share of the wildlife resource.

You are little noticed by most of us. You ask nothing of us other than moral support, discretion in our hunting stories, and genuine respect for all hunters regardless of weapon. Largely through your efforts, bowhunting and all facets of archery have flourished. You provide our lifeline to the world of hunting and the great outdoors.

Dedicating this book to all of you is our way of saying thank you.

Glenn St. Charles
August 20, 1986
Seattle, Washington

Printed by Arcata Graphics/Kingsport
Kingsport, Tennessee 37660

PAGE	CONTENTS

ACKNOWLEDGEMENTS

"Timing is everything," and those words could not be more applicable than when describing the preparation and production of this book. The Pope and Young Club is deeply indebted to the very talented team of contributors who made this publication a reality.

From the outset, the goals of the Book Committee were very ambitious and brimming with challenge: make the third edition of the *Bowhunting Big Game Records of North America* the best records book ever produced, have it done in time for the 1987 awards banquet, and include all trophies entered through December 31, 1986. And do it within budget. This was a tall order that required the dedication and teamwork of a sizable number of individuals.

One of the stickiest jobs belonged to the Records Chairman, Dr. Randall Byers, and the Records Office staff. Over 10,000 entries had to be reviewed for accuracy and prepared for the typesetter. This, in itself, was a monumental effort. Then, consider that panel certification of the top entries for the 15th Recording Period would not be completed until just **five days** before the printer's deadline. Throw in the fact that over thirty entries—in twelve categories—exceeded current world records during this recording period, and the true magnitude of their accomplishments comes into focus. Our sincerest gratitude goes to Dr. Byers, Shirley Gaskill, Joyce Kaecher, Kim McDonald, and Melvin Jolly for making this all happen on schedule.

The efforts of the Records Office would have gone for naught if a typographer hadn't been found who was willing to work with the compressed time table. We are profoundly grateful to the staff of Colorado TypoGraphics in Loveland, Colorado, for meeting this challenge. Not only did Chris Baker, Dolores Highfield, Tina M. Hillman, and Lynn and Paul Schmidt provide top-notch typesetting services, but they helped immeasurably with proofreading and designing the layout of the book.

Proofreading assistance also came from Kenneth Jessen and Jim and Helen Widmier. Their comments and suggestions helped to improve the manuscript and our thanks go to each of them.

The records are a substantial element of this volume, but the attendant written material is of equal significance. We believe it is a rare blend of historical and contemporary reading that is pertinent, thought-provoking, and a credit to its respective authors. The Book Committee is genuinely obliged to the fine group of writers who's names appear on each title page.

Throughout the book, over 100 photographs and illustrations help to convey the message of the text. Additional kudos go to Maurice Carlisle, Doug Walker, Kyla Wood, and Charles Young for the fine photographs they have provided. Also, we salute Dr. Dave Samuel, Bill Wadsworth, and the National Bowhunter Education Foundation for graciously allowing the use of several of that organization's illustrations.

For the first time, a section of original color art has been included in the *Bowhunting Big Game Records of North America.* The beautifully designed dust jacket and preparation of the color pages display the fine graphics talent of Thomas Watson. A very special thank you goes to re-nowned wildlife artists, Michael Sieve and Dave Wade, who each generously offered eight exquisite paintings to enhance this volume. Courtesy of Outdoor Life and Dave Wade, several of his outstanding pencil drawings are also presented.

Our gratitude is also due the Boone and Crockett Club for permission to reproduce their scoring forms for use by the Pope and Young Club.

The Book Committee is confident that all of the original objectives for this book have been met. However, we are not the final judges on whether it is the "best" records book yet done. That decision is reserved for you, the readers, to make.

FOREWORD

This is the third edition of *Bowhunting Big Game Records of North America.* It represents twenty-six years of measuring, collecting, recording, and disseminating data on trophy-sized North American big game taken with bow and arrow. It was preceded by our first book in 1975, and then the second edition in 1981. Each in its own way was a milestone, not only for the Pope and Young Club, but also for bowhunting. Each, larger than the one before, is an indicator of the rapid growth of trophy hunting with the bow and arrow. Each is a visual, silent chronicle of the evolution of the Pope and Young Club.

This edition of *Bowhunting Big Game Records* is the Pope and Young Club's most ambitious effort. The larger format, inside and out, and the inclusion of color are immediately obvious to the eye. The quality of the text, the presentation of the records, and the very printing itself, are testimony to the Club's desire to present to the hunting world the finest records book ever assembled. The various contributors and the book committee deserve much credit. The efforts of

book editor, Lee Kline, have been monumental. There were hunting trips that couldn't be, and many seven-day weeks during the two years of this project. Those personal sacrifices cannot be repaid. We can only offer our sincere gratitude and appreciation for a job well done.

But, this book is more than just a listing of successes . . . the biggest and the best animals ever taken with bow and arrow. Buried within these pages lie thousands of tales of unsuccessful hunts, of near misses, of personal sacrifice, exhiliration, self-denial, achievement, sorrow, elation, and just plain old gut-wrenching effort. The story of trophy hunting is a tale of challenge, pursuit, attitude, and occasional success. It cannot be contained in a single line of data. It is so very much more. This book contains a million camp fires and as many moments of frustration. You may have noted the faint aroma of wood smoke when you first opened these pages . . . it's real . . . it's here.

G. Fred Asbell
President
Pope and Young Club

BOOK I

THE TRADITION

Art Young (l) and Saxton Pope (r) relax during a California bear hunt (1918).

THE LEGACY

by Jim Dougherty

*To you who would follow us into the land of Robin Hood, let me say that
what you need most is a great longing to come, and perseverance.*
—Saxton Pope

Perseverance: no better word describes what bowhunting is. Those that want to enter into the land of Robin Hood need be well armed with it, for they have chosen to take up the chase in a manner that demands it. Those who do not have it will not long stick to the trail.

Perseverance: no better word describes the history of the growth of bowhunting, for the original supporters of bowhunting—and those that followed—had to have a stick-to-it philosophy in the long struggle for acceptance that is the very epitome of the word.

We have persevered to a point where bowhunting has a following of millions. More importantly, we have persevered to a point where bowhunting has its place.

Our sport did not just come about but was fought for over a long period of time. It was born centuries ago, but it did not have its beginning for quite some time. For all things there is a point past birth that seems to be the real beginning. A young bird, for instance, begins not on emerging from the egg but at the moment when it attempts its first flight. So it was with our sport.

Archery—bowhunting, actually—was born eons ago when a man, somewhere, fashioned a method of projecting a smallish spear by means other that his throwing arm. It is interesting to reflect that in the milleniums that have passed, man reached outer space before the basic design of that very first bow was significantly altered.

Bowhunting, as we have come to recognize it, had its beginning on January 27, 1961 when the Pope and Young Club became an organization unto itself, separating from the N.F.A.A. and embarking on a course filled with an earnest purpose. All of us, whether we are bowhunters with decades under our belts, or aficionados who have but recently joined the fraternity, are obligated to recognize the debt we owe those who formed the Club, charging themselves with the responsibility to foster and nourish our chosen sport. That they did so with dedicated good taste and a considerable amount of sense has been proven tenfold. We only have to look around to see and enjoy the fruits of those efforts.

Many individuals have been responsible for creating a public interest in archery and bowhunting; men like Howard Hill, Ben Pearson, our namesakes Saxton T. Pope and Arthur H. Young, and of course the renowned Fred Bear, come immediately to mind as true bowhunting pioneer-promoters. While these men drew much attention to hunting with the bow and arrow, there have been many others less well-known to the spotlight that have had an equal if not superior impact on the development of bowhunting.

At the beginning of the Pope and Young Club in 1961, bowhunting was not much understood or well treated. Many of you are aware of this, but there are thousands of new participants in our sport who do not realize just how far we have come in the past twenty-six years, or how difficult it was to get here. For them it has always been here, full grown, available, with lengthy seasons and comfortable bag limits. It has not always been so.

Glenn St. Charles, the initiator and founding father of the Club, stated it succinctly with a message to the membership in June of 1986: "The Club was born out of adversity." Thus, a relatively small group of hard-core bowhunting enthusiasts—many of whom you have never heard of, save the mention of their efforts in the first two volumes of *Bowhunting Big Game Records of North America*—dug in their heels and began to advance, chipping away at that adversity. They positioned bowhunting as a fair, honorable, and efficient hunting method. The expanding records program supported their position that the bow and arrow was a formidable hunting arm. Game departments started to take interested notice, and our peers in the hunting world began to take bowhunting seriously. Bowhunting was emerging from the shadows into the sunlight. The ranks began to swell and with that swelling came increasing opportunities.

To suggest that the Pope and Young Club was solely responsible for this advance is not the intent. There have been many other worthy, hardworking organizations, clubs, companies, and individuals that put their shoulders to the wheel. But the Club was that all-important catalyst that provided the "beginning."

In the quarter-century that has passed, the Club has grown in many ways, not the least of which is the size of its membership. On the occasion of the third meeting and awards banquet in 1962 there were thirty individuals present representing a total membership of ninety-two (twenty-five regular members and sixty-seven associates) to celebrate world records and a total record listing of 227 trophies. This has

evolved into biennial conventions that draw thousands and records listings totaling over 10,000 entries as of December 31, 1986.

It is perhaps safe to say that bowhunting has come of age. The practice and its followers form a strong coalition to be considered in today's game management programs and objectives. Reaching this plateau took time. It was not easy. However, maintaining the position may be much more difficult than the arriving.

Competition for our wildlife resources is keen, not just for the game but for our woods and waters as well. Indeed, the entire environment reels under a variety of negative impacts ranging from overdone commercial exploitation, to consumption, to pollution. Hunter-use, or consumption, is primarily considered to be recreational use of the resource and oftentimes is at odds with commercial interests.

Of course, it's always at odds with those that feel hunting in general—and bowhunting in particular—is totally unnecessary, immoral, and disgusting. People of this persuasion do not readily accept proven techniques of game management, nor do they agree that hunting is vital to the well-being or the very survival of certain wildlife species. They decry hunting. They vilify bowhunting, and they would take it away. In fact, they strive to that end as dilligently as we strove to obtain its stature today.

This is not a new condition. Saxton Pope recognized and discussed it as far back as 1923 in his classic work, *Hunting With the Bow and Arrow,* and his perspective remains completely accurate:

> Of course, there are those who say that all hunting should cease, and that photography and nature study alone should be directed toward wildlife. That sweet day may come, but at least no man can consistently decry hunting who eats meat, wears furs or leather, or uses any vestige of animal tissue; for he is party to the crime of animal murder, and murder more brutal and ignoble than that of the chase. And those who think the bullet is more certain and humane than the arrow have no accurate knowledge on which to base their comparison.

The founders of the Pope and Young Club, of course, recognized this at the onset. It was the nucleus of the adversity. The Club has con-

The future of all hunting depends on how well we teach our children wildlife values and the *Rules of Fair Chase*.

tinued to be extremely aware that while bow-hunting has come a long way, bowhunters are in the minority in the hunting community. We are, therefore, the weakest link in the chain politically. But, we have been tempered of a very fine steel. The link has bent on occasion but not broken. One of the Club's foremost purposes for existence is to help maintain the strength of the chain. Few bowhunters today are unaware of the Pope and Young Club's records— "The Book." Too few, however, are aware of what the Club has done, what it continues to do, and for what it stands. Obviously it does not stand for the book alone, yet the book has become the backbone of the Club, and "making the book" has perhaps become entirely too important.

Trophy hunting or the selective seeking out of a mature animal of majestic proportions, then succeeding in its conquest with the bow and arrow, is the pinnacle of the chase. It comes about through hard work, dedication, perseverance, and an ample helping of luck. There are those who go afield with no other purpose than to hunt such an animal. When it is accomplished honorably, there is justifiable pride in the victory. But, to feel that there is failure in the taking of something less is wrong. Fortunately bowhunting, and this Club, are not predicated solely on the taking of record-class animals. Just as unfortunately, however, there are those for whom making the book becomes an obsession, for all the wrong reasons. They will go to any length, any expense and worse, any method, to obtain that objective. In so doing they cheat the sport, the game, the book—themselves.

It's not necessary to make the record book to be a good bowhunter. But to be a good bow-hunter in today's social climate, it is necessary to adopt the Pope and Young Club philosophy to be a sportsman. Anyone can be a killer of game, by any method. There are too many ways to shortcut the chase and get to the final act. To do so sours the purpose, and the final result means nothing.

Bowhunting is a romantic, exciting, and honorable pursuit. For many it is more than a way of life; it is life itself. The code, the tradition of bowhunting, has been established. We have an exciting and interesting heritage to pass on to new and future generations of hunting archers. We have obtained the rights and the seasons to protect for them, and they must be properly tutored to maintain them for their sons and daughters.

They must be made to understand and ad-here to the *Rules of Fair Chase* in their adventures afield; to recognize the value of the game and its environment; to cherish it as they use it. Indeed, there are some of our own generations that need to learn these values also.

The Pope and Young Club books represent the tradition, the heritage, and the history of bowhunting. As the volumes emerge they are the increasing culmination of an objective that began over a quarter of a century ago. Embracing the principles and philosophy of the Club is to accept the highest traditions of the hunt and good sportsmanship. Living by them and passing them on is to ensure that bowhunting will always be here. This is the only way bowhunters of today can prove our worthiness as guardians of the legacy handed down to us by our foregoers. We can do that. We must do it, and we will.

A Look Back

by Frank "Rit" Heller

Hunting with a bow and arrows has roots steeped in an interesting, captivating history. It's history that goes back to a time shortly after the Civil War, to a time of two Georgia brothers, Maurice and Will Thompson. From their adventures in the Florida swamps, we have what are most likely the first "bowhunting stories" in the book entitled, *The Witchery of Archery,* published nearly a century before the first volume of *Bowhunter Magazine* came off the press.

Fact is, there have been literally hundreds of fine books, periodicals, and stories written on bowhunting that many of today's bowbenders probably don't even know exist. Some of these writings are truly classic works! Many of them provide a fascinating insight to the history of archery and the emergence of bowhunting, on through the growth of our sport well into the twentieth century.

Before modern technology takes archery and bowhunting too far off into the future, many of you might find it interesting to take a look at some very fine articles and books written on hunting with the bow and arrow in a time gone by—before treestands, buck lure, camo clothes, compounds, sights, aluminum shafts, string-trackers, and the like.

Add a new dimension to your off-season by spending a little time searching out some of these old titles. See what hunting was like before bowhunting had guides and outfitters, booking agents, and hunter referral services; before any form of commercialization existed in our sport; in an era when traveling somewhere for a two-week big game hunt could mean another week of your time to get there and a week to get back again!

There were no guarantees and no past reports to go by in most instances. Much more trial and error with equipment and clothing was necessary. There were few motels, hardly any restaurants, no planes, phones, or archery stores to purchase exactly what you wanted or needed. Back then, archers would spend many hours making most of their equipment before they could begin to enjoy shooting it or hunting with it. The hunts were often much longer in duration and less game was bagged, but there are still some success pictures of bowhunters from back then showing people like Walt Wilhelm, Howard Hill, Fred Bear, Roy Case, Chester Stevenson, and Grover Gouthier.

Reading these old books will provide many hours of pure enjoyment. Finding some of them is not going to be easy, but I can guarantee you'll appreciate them when you do. I'll also bet you will come away with a greater appreciation of our sport and gain a much better understanding of what we take for granted today.

There are a number of ways to track down some of these old books and articles: visit your

The beginning of a bowhunt some seventy years ago. Note the camera case the lead rider is carrying.

local library; use a book search company, of which there are many; check out flea markets and old book stores. Talk with archers older than yourself—either in person, over the phone, or through letter writing—to see if they have saved something you're trying to find.

Here is a list of titles you might want to look for. By no means should this be considered a complete listing, but it does provide a good starting point. So have at it and enjoy the off-season with some truly fine reading.

The Witchery of Archery
by J. Maurice Thompson (1878)

Brothers Maurice and Will Thompson describe their adventures with the bow and arrow. Their hunting tales in the Florida swamps after the Civil War are masterpieces. During the Civil War, the brothers fought for the Confederate Army. After the war, firearms were denied them because of their Confederate allegiance, so they took to the woods for about two years, living chiefly on game they shot with their bows and arrows. This book is truly a classic.

Bows and Arrows
by Saxton T. Pope (1923)

A small hardback of only 114 pages, this book contains some interesting information on testing bows and arrows as they existed at that time. Bows tested include American Indian, English, Turkish, etc., with various arrow weights and lengths.

Hunting With the Bow and Arrow
by Saxton T. Pope (1923)

A *must read,* to get the great feeling of hunting our native North American big game with the bow and arrow. This book tells us how Saxton Pope got to meet and know Ishi, how Art Young met "Chief" Will Compton, and how all four men got acquainted and participated in hunts together. It contains plenty of photos and illustrations. I feel this book represents our Club's roots. "The Principles of Hunting" chapter is well worth reading, perhaps even more today than when it was written.

Courtesy of Charles Young

Many of these old books are illustrated with fine photographs such as this one of Art Young and coyotes brought to bag with bow and arrow.

Lions in the Path
by Stewart Edward White (1926)

This volume is one version of Pope and Young's hunting expedition into Africa. Stewart Edward White accompanied them and acted as a backup rifleman. During the hunt, White and his guide were attacked and mauled by a leopard, but lived through it. These hunts occur during some of the last days of the truly grand old safaris.

The Adventurous Bowmen
by Saxton T. Pope (1926)

Again, more adventures of Pope and Young in their heyday. Feeling very confident with their ability and homemade equipment on big game in the western United States, they wanted to test their skill, nerve, and archery tackle on truly dangerous big game animals in Africa. Aside from all the other adventures in this book, the lion hunting excerpts are outstanding; there's plenty of good photos to make you feel as though you are sharing in their experiences. The hunters took a half-dozen bows apiece, 100 finished arrows each, plus enough shafts, feathers, arrowhead silk, and glue to make 2,000 more arrows! The trip—including sailing time over and back—took over seven months!

David Goes to Greenland
by David Binney Putnam (1926)

Most archers don't realize this book exists, and if they do, they don't know it has anything to do with bowhunting. In reality, it is about the trip made to Greenland where Art Young hunted polar bear and walrus with his bow. Young and his companions lived among Eskimos and learned their primitive ways. Though not totally about archery, it's nevertheless worth reading and having in your library.

Courtesy of Charles Young

This photo of Saxton Pope and Art Young from their 1925 African adventure is one of the last of these two bowhunting pioneers together. A few months after returning from this trip, Pope died from pneumonia.

The Bow and Arrow for Big Game
by Forrest Nagler (1931)

Here's a truly excellent book on bowhunting for moose and caribou in the British Columbia Rockies. It covers the adventures of two friends, Forrest Nagler and Bill Tefft. Roy Case hunts with them on one trip. They traveled by train into the backwoods of the timbered north, making three-week hunts at a time, camping wherever they were at dark. It's exciting reading.

The Flat Bow
by Hunt and Matz (1936)

Only seventy pages, this book is very informative on equipment and hunting methods during that period. It includes several rare pictures of Howard Hill and many very good sketches and drawings of bows, arrows, quivers, and other equipment. The book also tells how archers made equipment in the 1930s. It should be extremely interesting to longbow shooters.

The New Archery Hobby-Sport-Craft
by Paul H. Gordon (1939)

Here's a well-written book for its time with lots of information on many areas of archery. Of special interest to the longbow shooter, it is very informative about making archery tackle such as footed arrows, feather trimming, arm guards, bows, strings, and quivers. There's also some hunting information and instruction on how to make broadheads by hand.

Hunting the Hard Way
by Howard Hill (1953)

This book chronicles the exploits of this great archer from 1928 to the 1950s. Hill hunts all sorts of North American big game with bow and arrow. He tells how he hunted buffalo Indian-style (shooting from a running horse), alligators in Florida, mule deer in Nevada, sheep, and he includes many more colorful hunting tales. Also, Hill covers how he made his equipment and how he used it.

Archery Handbook
by Edmund H. Burke (1954)

This is a good 142-page how-to-do-it kind of book that was very useful in its time. There's plenty of good hunting photos, participation-type photos, and equipment illustrations. This volume describes how hunting with the bow and arrow was looked upon in those days, the different seasons, and what was available to hunt in each state.

Wild Adventures
by Howard Hill (1955)

This book contains additional hunting tales by Howard Hill, mostly of his African hunt with plenty of pictures. It features good adventure yarns. He tells of his preparation to go to Africa, the equipment he used, and his thoughts on how to hunt animals such as lions, leopards, and elephants.

Field Archery and Bowhunting
by Arnold O. Haugen
and Harlan C. Metcalf (1963)

This is a favorite of many archers and hunters of the 1960s. It presents a cross section of information, much of which is still very good and useful today. Included are comparisons of 1930s equipment and methods to those of the 1960s. A well-illustrated book with many excellent old-time photographs, it is truly one of my favorite books for reading during a long, winter evening.

"Ishi," Last of His Tribe
by Theodora Kroeber (1964)

Detailing the life and times of the Indian that we have come to know as the bowhunting mentor of Pope and Young, this book covers the struggle of a small band of Indians trying to survive; how they made their own tools, grew food, their hunting methods, and how they stayed hidden from the white man until only Ishi was left.

Maurice Thompson
by George A. Schumacher (1968)

As the title implies, this is a biography of the man responsible for starting the National Archery Association of the United States. This book will be of interest to those wanting to know more about this fascinating archer and writer, his Civil War days, and his involvement in archery.

Courtesy of Doug Walker

Ishi coming down the trail in Deer Canyon, California (1914).

"Ishi" in Two Worlds
by Theodora Kroeber (1969)

This book provides a more detailed look at the life of Ishi, the last survivor of a California Indian tribe, who emerged from the Stone Age into the modern world in 1911. It compares his lifestyles before and after his discovery. It tells how his life changed and discusses his thoughts about many things, including his life with the white man from 1911 until his death in 1916.

The Archer's Bible
by Fred Bear (1976)

The fundamentals of good shooting, archery safety, and equipment care are covered by the master. It's good reading. He covers making and using equipment as well as many stories of his hunts. This book also talks about "how-to-hunt" various species of big game and bowfishing instruction.

Fred Bear's Field Notes
by Fred Bear (1976)

Fred Bear shares many of his memorable hunts, told in diary-form from his field notes. Featured are many outstanding photographs of Africa, Alaska, British Columbia, Yukon Territory, Brazil, and India. Whether it's hunting African lions or Alaskan moose, mountain goats or caribou, mountain sheep, grizzly bear, polar bear, or tiger, the stories are all very interesting and entertaining.

Some additional books on archery and bowhunting you may be interested in trying to locate are:

American Archery
    by Robert Elmer (1917)
Archery
    by Robert Elmer (1926)
Archery Handbook
    by National Field Archery Association (1945)
Archery Handbook
    by G. Howard Gillelan and William Stump (1958)
Archery From Golds to Big Game
    by Keith C. Schuyler (1970)
Bows and Arrows
    by James Duff (1927)
Bow and Arrow Archer's Digest
    by Jack Lewis (early 70's)
Bowhunting for Deer
    by H. R. "Dutch" Wambold (1964)
Bow Hunting for Big Game
    by Keith C. Schuyler (1974)
Bowhunter's Digest
    by C.R. Learn (1975)
Bow Hunter's Guide
    by Russell Tinsley (1975)
Bowhunting for Whitetail and Mule Deer
    by M. R. James (1976)
Bucks and Bows
    by Walter Perry (1953)
Complete Book of the Bow and Arrow
    by G. Howard Gillelan (1971)
Field Archery Technique
    by Albert J. Love (1956)

Field and Target Archery
by Edmund Burke (1961)

Fred Bear's World of Archery
by Fred Bear (1979)

Guide to Better Archery
by Thomas A. Forbes (1955)

In Africa
by Bob Swinehart (1967)

How to Train in Archery
by Maurice and Will Thompson (1879)

Modern Archery
by Arthur W. Lambert, Jr. (1929)

Modern Bowhunting
by Hiram Grogan (1958)

Pocket Guide to Archery
by Howard T. Sigler (1960)

Sagittarius
by Bob Swinehart (1970)

Shooting the Bow
by Larry C. Whiffen (1946)

Spencer System of Shooting the Bow
by Stanley F. Spencer (1933)

The Complete Archery Book
by Lou Hochman (1957)

The Complete Book of Archery
by Robert Gannon (1964)

The Encyclopedia of Archery
by Paul Hougham (1958)

Illustration by Dave Wade — Courtesy of Outdoor Life

A PERSPECTIVE ADJUSTMENT

History is a short word for the chronicles that describe events of the past. One sure fact applies to history and that is it can't be changed. History can be repeated, studied, enjoyed, learned from, or ignored. It can also be interpreted, criticized, misunderstood, or accepted depending upon the perceptions and standards or "values set" invoked by the person doing the reading. Approach a piece of history from the wrong perspective and invariably your judgement and understanding of the event will be off the mark.

The next two chapters are historical accounts of bowhunting adventures by the Club's namesakes, Dr. Saxton T. Pope and Arthur H. Young. The stories are presented in their entirety, unedited, as they appeared when first published. "Killing Grizzly Bear with the Bow and Arrow," by Saxton Pope, was extracted from his classic book *Hunting with the Bow and Arrow,* published in 1923. "Hunting Moose with the Bow and Arrow," by Art Young, appeared in the June 1924 issue of *Outdoor Life.*

Things were very different back then. Hunting with the bow and arrow was still being pioneered in those days, as were game laws and management philosophies. Much of what we know and accept today about bowhunting equipment, methods, hunting seasons—even ethics— were but experiments or as yet untried in the 1920s. Indeed, society's values were considerably different than those we subscribe to today.

So, as you read these stories, it's important to remember the events took place over sixty years ago, during an extraordinary period in our history. By no means should this preface be even remotely considered an apology for anything you will read. It's only a reminder to adjust your perspective a bit as you enjoy the stories.

The Editor

Arthur H. Young

Courtesy of Charles Young

Hunting Moose With the Bow and Arrow

by Arthur H. Young (1924)

A reminder of the days when a man's prowess as a hunter was measured not by the ballistics of the weapon he used, but by his ability to pull a strong bow.

During our recent five-months trip in Alaska taking motion pictures, we covered the moose flats on the Kenai Peninsula, where the largest moose are to be found. The world's record head which came from this district may be seen in the Field Museum in Chicago.

While we were making our preparations for the expedition I was asked by several people if I should attempt to kill a moose with the bow and arrow and I always answered in the affirmative.

So many question the ability of a present-day archer to kill anything larger than a house cat that I realized that those from whom these questions came knew not just what the killing of a moose with the bow and arrow meant. For when one has a moose down and starts to carve—he gets a fair idea of what a hunk of meat this animal represents.

However, as I have been very successful with kills made with the arrow on big game, including grizzly bear, there was not the least doubt in my mind as to what the outcome would be when the moose and arrow met.

The game laws of Alaska call for a licensed guide to accompany a hunting party entering this particular district to hunt moose, and altho there is some objection to such a law, it is undoubtedly a good thing that this requirement is compulsory, for it does prevent the indiscriminate killing of many moose. Were a guide not at hand to determine the approximate spread and symmetry of the palmated antlers some hunters might be inclined to kill more moose than the law allows before obtaining a head to suit his fancy. A good guide can practically guarantee a satisfactory head with the first kill.

After leaving Seward, we got off the train at Roosevelt, which is situated on Kenai Lake—a trip of twenty-three miles. There we loaded our equipment on Lou Bell's powerboat and made for Charlie Lein's place on the Kenai River, where Henry Lucas, our guide, was to meet us. From there we made a portage of eighteen miles to Skilak Lake, where Lucas has a comfortable cabin on this uncomfortable lake.

After a good night's sleep our party, which consisted of Jack Robertson, my partner, Henry Lucas and me—not to mention our moving picture machine and our grub—started down Skilak Lake with our kicker sending the boat along at good speed, making pop-pop-pop rhythm that one likes to hear.

17

We landed near our cache on the lake, and after adjusting our packs made the last portage of eight miles to our camp on the Killey River. Here we took a number of pictures before the weather settled down to a condition not conducive to the best results along this line.

I decided to make preparations for a moose hunt, and during the evening sharpened up some broadhead arrows, also circled a birch tree with my pocket knife and peeled off the necessary bark for a moose horn. Trying it out in camp that night I was kidded somewhat regarding the quality of the challenge I wrung from this instrument. My two companions said that it sounded awful. I said it was good, but what I thought about it they never really knew.

The following morning I buckled over my shoulder a quiver containing a dozen good arrows, a pair of field glasses, some food and my eighty-pound bow (i.e., a pull of eighty pounds to draw the arrow to the head), and off I started.

I was making good time and out of camp about a quarter of a mile when I discovered that I had failed to bring the moose call. I immediately returned to camp, feeling no great guilt, as I was not accustomed to taking along such a contrivance when going out for game. As I entered the camp and picked up the horn, I caught a smile from Jack.

Once again on my way with this supposedly unnecessary, unmusical piece, I was headed for the moose flats and happy. Reaching the top of a hill I combed the low country below with the field glasses, endeavoring to pick up a moose.

A grouse flew up from the grass and lighted on an overhanging spruce limb, about fifty feet from where I stood. I hesitated to shoot and risk the loss of an arrow or two, as my supply was limited.

We had no meat in camp and our food supply had been considerably lessened the previous day by a bear which had paid us a visit. He had not only amused himself by walking over

Courtesy of Doug Walker

Young admires his 60-inch Alaska moose with the arrow still imbedded in the left antler.

and flattening our tent, but had eaten heartily. I shot an arrow through the grouse, which fell dead into a nearby clump of bushes. (I lost the arrow.)

As I walked over to pick up the bird, a small hawk of a variety unknown to me flew up from where the grouse lay and perched upon a dead snag. When I was within six feet of my game the hawk, realizing the danger of losing his find, uttered a loud screech. As I stooped down to pick up the bird there was an awful protest, but when he saw it dropped into my lunch bag that was too much, and a fearful tongue lashing he gave me. I chuckled aloud with amusement.

Again I scanned the flats for moose, but without success, so I sat down and planned my hunt. In half-an-hour I saw a bull with two cows and one of the latter saw me. They were about 200 yards away and I was in such a position that I could not safely move about.

After challenging my bull a few times, then slapping my horn against some sticks to imitate horns thrashing brush, the bull answered the challenge. With lowered head he started to circle so as to pick up the scent of his challenger. He got my wind at a distance too great to attempt a shot, so this particular case was closed.

I hunted for some time, then decided to cross over into a strip of country which looked more promising. I had not gone far before I stopped suddenly at the sight of a moose horn palm showing above the scant grassy growth and fallen sticks. The animal was lying down about 185 yards away, and in order to approach him for a better shot it was necessary to make nearly a half-circle around him, for the nose of a moose is his best protection. As we imagine a giraffe deriving great pleasure from a drink, so have we good reasons to believe a moose makes the best of his long nose to avoid danger.

Progress was slow at best, but when I came to a heap of deadfalls, it looked as tho it would be impossible to go any farther without being seen, for if I went around the barrier I would be detected, as the moose was lying with his head toward me. Climbing over the top was not feasible on account of the many dry, unbroken twigs, which would make too much noise—and, too, it would raise me above my only protection, which

was a small, scrawny spruce tree about four feet high.

After pondering the situation for a few minutes, I examined the moss-covered ground where I was standing, and finding it favorable for digging I tunneled under the debris. This brought me out in perfect line with the moose and still afforded me the spruce tree as a protection.

When I was within seventy-five yards of the animal he rose to his feet, and as he did so I went from a low crouching position to one flat on my stomach.

Then I challenged him.

Before I had taken the horn from my lips he answered me and came moving forward and around me with a slow, swinging gait, lowered head and apparently looking straight ahead. Had he made any effort to locate the animal which he suspected of having issued the challenge he would have seen no moose, but with little effort he could have seen me, even in my prone position.

As he continued his slow, swaying stride he was continually returning his challenges with a peculiar throaty, grunting noise. Only occasionally did I answer him.

When he had reached a position where it seemed that any second he would get my scent, I raised to a kneeling position with an arrow nocked on the string. He was walking and sixty yards away. I drew my bow until the three-inch steel head on the twenty-eight-inch arrow touched my finger, then released. The flight of the arrow seemed perfect for a good hit.

With a thud it landed in his ribs and I saw the feathers disappear as the shaft buried itself. He ran for forty yards from where he was struck, then, after coming to a sudden stop, stood quartering away for me.

I released another arrow, which just grazed his shoulders and struck squarely in the palm of his left horn, producing a crack like a pistol shot. Watching closely, I could observe nothing but absolute indifference on the part of the moose as the arrow landed. Before I could get another shot he had moved into a thicket of small, dead, standing timber.

By this time it was much after sundown and fast growing dark, so I decided if there was

Courtesy of Doug Walker

Returning to camp with the cape and antlers.

to be a chase lasting even for a short time and any driving to be done it would be toward camp and not away from it.

I quickly got around the moose and pressed him rather hard for a short distance, endeavoring to obtain another shot, but this chance did not come until just as he lay down. Working into a shooting position and obtaining this shot resulted in the deflection of the arrow by a small stick.

At the shot he rose, looked squarely at me, bristled and seemed to be having business in my direction, while I, unconsciously, felt to see if I still had my hunting knife (I never carry any firearms while shooting a bow) and glanced about for a good standing snag for what little protection it might offer, provided I could not stop him with an arrow.

I have been unable to understand what possessed this bull, for he stopped, then turned from me, and as he did so I again started after

him, trying to find an opening through the sticks for another shot.

Darkness seemed to close in all of a sudden and I lost sight of the moose in the dim light. Occasionally I would stop to listen, and when I had about decided to give up the chase for that night I came upon him down about fifty feet from me. Looking closely, I could see one of his amber-colored palms, but it was too dark to make out his body. The idea of going in any closer did not exactly appeal to me, for his threatening attitude of just a few minutes before was still fresh in my mind, so I slowly worked my way in toward him, and when close enough that I could make out his head and body he gave the appearance of being a dead animal and I walked up and claimed him. This was on September 29, 1923.

I could see little on account of the darkness, yet enough light remained that I could partially admire the fine spread and symmetry of the animal's horns.

A hunter knows the limitations of dressing or skinning out the cape of an animal under such light conditions, so will in a measure realize the situation that confronted me. Taking one last admiring look at my trophy, I started that slow, painful trip back to camp about two-and-a-half miles away—to return in the morning. Slow and painful, I mean, on account of the fallen trees, standing snags, overhanging limbs and hidden ditches that I encountered as I started for the high ground that lay in the direction of camp.

One minute I would walk straight into a standing tree and find myself the next sprawled out on the ground. In the darkness, somehow, the wrong thing seemed to be in the right place. Upon reaching the ridge I had traveled nearly a mile, but had somewhat lost my sense of direction. However, the river rapids near camp gave me my bearings and my up and down trip continued until finally I saw a flicker of our camp fire far below me on the banks of the Killey River.

I arrived at camp about midnight and received a rousing welcome and enthusiastic congratulations as I told them of my success. It was a comfortable-looking camp with the boys around the fire and enough beans in the pot for a dozen hungry moose hunters. As I went into detail and took particular pains to describe just how the moose walked right into trouble all on account of that horn that "sounded awful," I could not get a peep out of the boys. They told me, tho, that the beans had been shifted and the fire poked up a dozen times, mistaking a noise in the brush for my return.

The few remaining hours until daylight soon passed; then we all set out with our cameras to complete my last evening's work with the moose.

Upon examining the wound, I found that the arrow had gone between the third and fourth ribs, passed thru the stomach and had penetrated the hide on the opposite side. It had struck farther back than I had intended that it should.

I was rather surprised to find my other arrow still fast in the horn, for more than once I had seen it vibrate violently as it came in contact with sticks and snags. The head was so firmly embedded that I could not extract it. Entering at an angle of about forty-five degrees, it had penetrated one-and-one-half inches of solid horn. A tape showed a sixty-inch spread of symmetrical, heavy antlers, and the bull himself a fine specimen of the fleshy, bulbous prehensile muzzle family.

To date, I may state that out of the many large animals I have shot with the arrow, only one has ever escaped after having been hit.

In a couple of days we broke camp, after having spent about three pleasant weeks, outside of some bad weather.

On our return trip to Skilak Lake we encountered rough weather and were forced to seek shelter two different times, finally walking some two miles to our cabin.

Lucas is a valuable man and is worthy of the consideration of any hunter who contemplates a moose hunt on the Kenai. He is reliable and knows his business, in addition to being a credit to the hunting fraternity, and is a strong advocate for the protection of game. But he can't play craps for beans worth a darn. Jack's cheerful disposition, while struggling to grow a respectable-looking moustache and beard, brought forth our profound admiration.

I was well satisfied with my trophy, for I had made my own weapon and moose call, had called and killed my animal, skinned out the cape and brought the head into camp. This is what I had desired to do.

Dr. Saxton Temple Pope   *Courtesy of Doug Walker*

KILLING GRIZZLY BEAR WITH THE BOW AND ARROW

by Dr. Saxton T. Pope (1923)

The very idea of shooting grizzly bears with the bow and arrow strikes most people as so absurd that they laugh at the mention of it. The mental picture of the puny little archery implements of their childhood, opposed to that of the largest and most fearsome beast of the Western world, produces merriment and incredulity.

Because it seemed so impossible, I presume, this added to our desire to accomplish it.

Ever since we began hunting with the bow, we had talked of shooting grizzlies. We thought of an Alaskan trip as a remotely attainable adventure, and planned murderous arrows of various ingenious spring devices to increase our cutting qualities. We estimated the power of formidable bows necessary to pierce the hides of these monsters. In fact, it was the acme of our hunting desires.

We read the biography of John Capen Adams and his adventures with the California grizzlies, and Roosevelt's admirable descriptions of these animals. They filled out our dreams with details. And after killing black bears we needed only the opportunity to make our wish become an exploit.

The opportunity to do this arrived unexpectedly, as many opportunities seem to, when the want and the preparedness coincide.

The California Academy of Sciences has in its museum in Golden Gate Park, San Francisco, a collection of very fine animal habitat groups, among which are deer, antelope, mountain sheep, cougars, and brown bear. While an elk group was being installed, it happened that the taxidermist, Mr. Paul Fair, said to me that the next and final setting would be one of grizzly bears. In surprise, I asked him if it were not a fact that the California grizzly was extinct. He said this was true, but the silver-tip bear of Wyoming was a grizzly and its range extended westward to the Sierra Nevada Mountains; so it could properly be classified as a Pacific Coast variety. He cited Professor Merriam's monograph on the classification of grizzlies to prove his statements. He also informed me that permit might be obtained from Washington to secure these specimens in Yellowstone National Park.

Immediately I perceived an opportunity and interviewed Dr. Barton Everman, curator of the museum, concerning the feasibility of offering our services in taking these bears at no expense to the academy. Incidentally, we proposed to shoot them with the bow and arrow, and thereby answer a moot question in anthropology. The proposition appealed to him, and he wrote to Washington for a permit to secure specimens in this National Park, stating that the

23

bow and arrow would be used. I insisted upon this latter stipulation, so that there should be no misunderstanding if, in the future, any objection was raised to this method of hunting.

In a very short time permit was given to the academy, and we started our preparations for the expedition. This was late in the fall of 1919, and bear were at their best in the spring, just after hibernation; so we had ample time.

It was planned that Mr. Compton, Mr. Young, and I should be the hunters, and such other assistance would be obtained as seemed necessary. We began reviewing our experience and formulating the principles of the campaign.

Our weapons we now considered adequate in light of our contact with black bears. We had found that our bows were as strong as we could handle, and ample to drive a good arrow through a horse, a fact which we had demonstrated upon the carcasses of recently dead animals.

But we decided to add to the length of our arrowheads, and use tempered instead of soft steel as heretofore. We took particular pains to have them perfect in every detail.

Then we undertook the study of the anatomy of the bears and the location and size of their vital organs. In the work of William Wright on the grizzly, we found valuable data concerning the habits and nature of these animals.

In spite of the reputation of this bear for ferocity and tenacity of life, we felt that, after all, he was only made of flesh and bone, and our arrows were capable of solving the problem.

We also began preparing ourselves for the contest. Although habitually in good physical condition, we undertook special training for the big event. By running, the use of dumbbells and other gymnastic practices, we strengthened our muscles and increased our endurance. Our field shooting was also directed toward rapid delivery and the quick judgement of distances on level, uphill, and falling ground. In fact, we planned to leave no factor for success untried.

My brother, G. D. Pope, of Detroit, being a hunter of big game with the gun, was invited to join the party, and his advice was asked concerning a reliable guide. He gladly consented to come with us and share the expenses. At the same time he suggested Ned Frost, of Cody,

Wyoming, as the most experienced hunter of grizzly bears in America.

About this time one of my professional friends visited the Smithsonian Institute at Washington, where he met a member of the staff, who inquired if he knew Doctor Pope, of San Francisco, a man that was contemplating shooting grizzlies with the bow and arrow. The doctor replied that he did, whereat the sage laughed and said that the feat was impossible, most dangerous and foolhardy; it could not be done. We fully appreciated the danger involved—therein lay some of the zest. But we also knew that even should we succeed in killing them in Yellowstone Park, the glory would be sullied by the popular belief that all park bears were hotel pets, live upon garbage, and that it was a cruel shame to torment them with arrows.

So in my early correspondence with Frost, I assured him that we did not want to shoot any tame bears and that we would not consider the trip at all if this were necessary. He assured us that this was not necessary, and reminded us that Yellowstone Park was fifty miles wide by sixty miles long, and that some of the highest portions of the Rocky Mountains lay in it. The animals in this preserve, he said, were far from tame and the bears were divided into two distinct groups, one mostly composed of black and brown with a few inferior specimens of grizzlies that frequent the dumps back of the camps and hotels, and another group of bears that never came near civilization, but lived entirely up in the rugged mountains and were as dangerous and wary as those in Alaska or any other wild country. These bears wander outside the park and furnish hunting material throughout the neighboring state. He promised to put us in communication with grizzlies that were as unspoiled and unafraid as those first seen by Lewis and Clark in their early explorations.

After explaining the purposes of our trip and the use of the bow, Ned Frost agreed that it was a real sporting proposition and took up the plan with enthusiasm. I sent him a sample arrow we used in hunting, and his letter in reply I take liberty of printing. It is typical of the frontier spirit and comes, not only from the foremost grizzly hunter of all times, but discloses the man's bigness of heart:

My dear Doctor:

Your letter of the 18th was received a day or so ago, and last night I received "Good Medicine" (a hunting arrow) on the evening train, and I feel better away down deep about this hunt after a good examination of this little Grizzly Tickler than I have at any time before. I have, by mistake, let it simmer out in a quiet way that I was going to see what a grizzly would really do if he had a few sticks stuck in his innerds, and my friends have been giving the Mrs. and me a regular line of farewell parties. Really, I think it has been a splendid paying thing to do; pork chops are high, you know, and I really feel I am off to the good about nine dollars and six bits worth of bacon and flour right now on this deal. Maybe I'll be in debt to you before green-grass if I don't look out.

Well, anyway, here is hoping we will all live through it and have a dandy time. Don't worry about coming to blows with the bear; I have noticed from long experience that it is not the times that you think a bear is going to give you trouble that it happens, but always when least expected. I have trailed wounded grizzlies time and time again, and was more or less worried all the while, but never had one turn on me yet. Then, too, I have had about three experiences with them that made my hair stand straight up, and when it finally settled, it had more frost in it than ever before; and let me add right here, that one of the worst places I ever got into was when I had sixteen of the best bear dogs that were ever gotten together I believe, after an old she grizzly, and I was like you, thought they would hold the bear's attention. But, don't let any notion like this get you into trouble. Now, I am not running down dogs as a means of getting bear; I love them and would now have a pack if it was possible to run them in the game fields of this state, but you don't want to think that they can handle a grizzly like they do a black bear. In fact, I would place no value on them whatsoever as a safeguard in case a grizzly got on the pack, and I am speaking from experience, mind you. No, a good little shepherd would do more than a dozen regular bear dogs, but there is only about one little shepherd like I speak of in a lifetime.

If you can use the bow from horseback, here is a safe proposition, and I believe a practical one, too. But I don't feel that there is really so much danger in the game after all, as it is only once in a great while that any bear will go up against the human animal, and then is most likely to be when you are not expecting it at all. Don't worry about it. What I am thinking about most is to get the opportunity to get the first arrow into some good big worthy old boy that will be a credit to the expedition.

There are lots of grizzlies in the park all right, and some of them are not very wild, but if you get out away from the hotels a few miles, they are not going to come up and present their broadsides to you at thirty yards. So, as I say, I am thinking mostly about the chances of getting the opportunities. I don't know, of course, just how close you can place your arrows at thirty yards, and it is getting the first hole into them that I am most interested in now. I feel that we ought to get some good chances, as I have seen so many bear in the park; but, of course, have never hunted them and don't know just how keen they will be when it comes right down to getting their hides. There are some scattered all over the park that will rob a camp at night, and some of them will even put up a fight for it, but most of them will beat it as soon as one gets after them.

It would be impossible, I believe, to keep dogs still while watching a bait, as they would get the scent of any approaching bear, and then you would not be able to keep them quiet, and they would most likely scare the bear out of the country. I can rustle up a few dogs to take along if you want them, and pretty good dogs, too; but I am not strong for them myself only in this way, to put them on the trail of a bear and take a good horse apiece, so that we could get up to the chase and have a chance to land on him. This might be a good thing to try if all others failed.

I know how you feel about killing clean with the bow and not having any shooting, and I can assure you that I would let 'em get just as close as you want them, and not feel any concern about their getting the best of anybody, and you would have a chance to use the bow well in this case; but I am more prone to think they will beat it off with a lot of your perfectly good arrows than anything else.

Yours Truly,
Ned Frost

It was apparent from the first that dogs were of little use in taking grizzly. It would be necessary to shoot from blinds set conveniently near bait. Frost assured us that bears of this variety, when just out of hibernation and lean, would run out of the country if chased by a pack of dogs, and incidentally kill all that they could catch. In the fall of the year, when the bears are fat, they refuse to run, but wade through the pack, which is unable to keep him from attacking the hunter.

As an example of this, he related an instance where he started a grizzly with eight or ten Russian bear hounds, and chased the bear about thirty miles. As he followed on horseback, he found one after the other of his dogs torn to pieces, disemboweled, and dismembered. At last, he came upon the bear at bay in deep snow, against a high cliff. Only two of his hounds were left, and one of these had a broken leg. Mad with vengeance, Frost shot the grizzly. It charged him at forty yards. In quick succession he fired five bullets in the oncoming bear, seemingly with no effect. Up to his waist in the snow, he was unable to avoid its rush. It came on and fell dead on his chest, with the faithful hound hanging to it in a desparate effort to save his master.

This is one of the three or four maulings that Ned has received in his hunting experiences, which, he says, "have added frost to my golden locks." The dog became a cherished pet in the family for many years.

Frost killed his first bear when fourteen years of age, and has added nearly five hundred to this number since that time.

It is characteristic of the grizzly that he will charge upon the slightest provocation, and that nothing will turn him aside from his purpose. Later we found this particularly true where the female with cubs is concerned.

Instances of this are too well-known to recount, but one coming under our own experience was related to me by Tom Murphy, the bear hunter of California.

In early days in Humboldt County, there lived an old settler named Pete Bluford, who was a squaw man. He shot a female grizzly with cubs within a quarter of a mile of what are now the town limits of Blocksburg. The beast charged and struck him to the ground. At the same time she ripped open the man's abdomen. Bluford dropped under a fallen tree, where the bear repeatedly assaulted him, tearing at his body. By rolling back and forth as the grizzly leaped over the log to reach him from the other side, he escaped further injury. Worried by the hunter's dog, she finally ceased her efforts and wandered off. The man was able to reach home in spite of a large open wound in his abdomen, with protruding intestines. This was roughly sewed together by his friend, Beany Powell. He recovered from the experience and lived many years with the Indians of that locality. As an example of Western humor, it is related that Beany Powell, when sewing up the wound with twine and a sack needle, found a large lump of fat protruding from the incision of which he was unable to dispose; so he cut it off, tried out the grease in the frying pan and used it to grease his boots.

Old Bluford became a character in the country. He was, in fact, what is colloquially known as "an old poison oaker." This is an individual who sinks so low in the scale of civilization that he lives out in the backwoods or poison oak brush and becomes animal in type. His hair grew to his shoulders, his beard was unkempt, his fingernails were as long as claws and filthy with dirt. Rags of unknown antiquity partially covered his limbs, vermin infested his body and he stayed with the most degraded remnants of the Indians.

One cold winter they found him dead in his dilapidated cabin. He lay on the dirt floor, his ragged coat over his face, his hands beneath his head, and two house cats lay frozen, one beneath each arm. These old pioneers were strange people and died strange deaths.

In our plans to capture grizzlies we took into consideration the proclivity of this beast to attack. We knew his speed was tremendous. He is able to catch a horse or a dog on the run. Therefore, it is useless for a man to try to run away from him. There is no such thing as being able to climb a tree if the animal is at close quarters. Adams has shown that it is a mistake to attempt it. One only stretches himself out inviting evisceration in the effort.

We decided if cornered either to dodge or to lie flat and feign death. So we practiced dodging, our running being more for the purpose of gaining endurance and to follow the bear if necessary.

Ishi, the Yana Indian, said that grizzlies were to be overcome with arrows and if they charged, they were to be met with the spear and fire. So we constructed spears having well-tempered blades more than a foot in length set upon heavy iron tubing and riveted to strong ash handles six feet in length. Back of the blades we fashioned quick-lighting torches of cotton waste saturated with turpentine. These could be ignited by jerking a lanyard fastened to a spring faced with sandpaper. The spring rested on the ends of several matches. It was an ingenious and reliable device.

The Esquimaux used a long spear in hunting the polar bear. It was ten or twelve feet in length. After being shot with an arrow, if the bear charged, they rested the butt of the spear on the ground, lowered the point and let the bear impale himself on it.

When the time came to use our weapons, Ned Frost dissuaded us from the attempt. He said that he once owned a pet grizzly and kept it fast with a long chain in the backyard. This bear was so quick that it could lie in its kennel, apparently asleep, and if a chicken passed within proper distance, with incredible quickness she reached out a paw and seized the chicken without the slightest semblance of effort. And when at play, the boys tried to stick the bear with a pitchfork, she would parry the thrusts and protect herself like a boxer. It was impossible to touch her.

The fire, Frost thought, might serve at night, but in the daylight it would lose its effect. So he insisted that he would carry a gun to be used in case of attack. On our part, we stipulated that he was to resort to it only to prevent disaster and protested that such an exigency must be looked upon by us as a complete failure of our plans. We knew we could not stop the mad rush of a bear with our arrows, but we hoped to kill at least one by this means and compromise on the rest if necessary.

Frost's bear proof? Cabin at the Lake.

The tree Frost climbed when the grizzly dragged him out of the tent. 1916.

Young sharpening arrows — in spite of the mosquitoes.

Taken from a page in Saxton Pope's personal scrapbook.   *Courtesy of Doug Walker*

Indians, besides employing the spear, poisoned arrows, and fire, also used protected positions, or shot from horseback. We scorned to shoot from a tree and were told that few horses could be ridden close enough, or fast enough, to get within bowshot of a grizzly.

Inquiry among those qualified to know, led to the estimate of the number of all bears in the Park to be between five hundred and one thousand. Considering that there are some three thousand square miles of land, that there were nearly sixty thousand elk, besides hundreds of bison, antelope, mountain sheep, and similar animals, this does not seem improbable. I am aware that recent statements are to the effect that there were only forty grizzlies there. This is palpably an underestimate, and probably takes into account only those that frequent the dumps. Frost believes that there are several hundred grizzlies in the Park, many of which range out in the adjacent country. So we felt no fear of decimating their ranks, and had every hope of seeing many. In fact, their numbers has so increased in recent years that they have become a menace and require killing off.

During the past five years four persons have either been mauled or killed by grizzlies in Yellowstone. One of these was a teamster by the name of Jack Walsh. He was sleeping under his wagon at Cold Springs when a large bear seized him by the arm, dragged him forth and ripped open his abdomen. Walsh died of blood poison and peritonitis a few days later.

Frost himself was attacked. He was conducting a party of tourists through the preserve and had just been explaining to them around the camp fire that there was no danger of bears. He slept in the tent with a horse wrangler by the name of Phonograph Jones. In the middle of the night a huge grizzly entered his tent and stepped on the head of Jones, peeling the skin off his face by the rough pressure of his paw. The man waked with a yell, whereupon the bear clawed out his lower ribs. The cry roused Frost, who having no firearms, hurled his pillow at the bear.

With a roar, the grizzly leaped upon Ned, who dived into his sleeping bag. The animal grasped him by the thighs and dragged him from the tent out into the forest, sleeping bag and all. As he carried off his victim, he shook him from side to side as a dog shakes a rat. Frost felt the great teeth settle down on his thigh bones and expected momentarily to have them crushed in the powerful jaws. In a thicket of jack pines over a hundred yards from camp, the bear shook him so violently that the muscles of the man's thighs tore out and he was hurled free from the bag. He landed half-naked in the undergrowth several yards away.

While the frenzied bear still worried the bedding, Frost dragged himself to a nearby pine and pulled himself up in its branches by the strength of his arms.

The camp was in an uproar; a huge fire was kindled; tin pans were beaten; one of the helpers mounted a horse and by circling around the bear, succeeded in driving him away.

After first aid measures were administered, Frost was successfully nursed back to health and usefulness by his wife. But since that time he has an inveterate hatred for grizzlies, hunting them with grim persistency.

It is said that nearly forty obnoxious grizzlies were shot by the Park rangers after this episode and Frost was given a permit to carry a weapon. We found later that he always went to sleep with a Colt automatic pistol strapped to his wrist.

We planned to enter the Park in two parties. One, comprised of Frost, the cook, horse wrangler, my brother, and his friend, Judge Henry Hulbert, of Detroit, was to proceed from Cody and come with a pack train across Sylvan Pass. Our party consisted of Arthur Young and myself; Mr. Compton was unexpectedly prevented from joining us by sickness in his family. We were to journey by rail to Ashton. This was the nearest point to Yellowstone Station on the boundary of the reservation that could be reached by railroad in winter.

We arrived at this point near the last of May, 1920. The roads beyond were blocked with snow, but by good fortune, we were taken in by one of the first work trains entering the region through the personal interest and courtesy of the superintendent of the Pocatello division.

We had shipped ahead of us a quantity of provisions and came outfitted only with sleeping bags, extra clothing, and our archery equipment. This latter consisted of two bows apiece and a carrying case containing one hundred and forty-four broadheads, the finest assembly of bows and arrows since the battle of Crecy.

Young had one newly made bow weighing eighty-five pounds and his well-tried companion of many hunts, Old Grizzly, weighing seventy-five pounds. He later found the heavier weapon too strong for him in the cold weather of the mountains, where a man's muscles stiffen and lose their power, while his bow grows stronger.

My own bows were seventy-five pounds apiece—"Old Horrible," my favorite, a hard hitter and sweet to shoot, and "Bear Slayer," the fine-grained, crooked-limbed stave with which I helped to kill our first bear. Our arrows were the usual three-eighths birch shafts, carefully selected, straight and true. Their heads were tempered steel, as sharp as daggers. We had, of course, a few blunts and eagle arrows in the lot.

In the Park we found snow deep on the ground and the roads but recently cleared with snow plows and caterpillar tractors. We traveled by auto to Mammoth Hot Springs and paid our respects to Superintendent Albright, and ultimately settled in a vacant ranger's cabin near the Canyon. Here we awaited the coming of the second party.

Our entrance into the Park was well-known to the rangers, who were instructed to give us all the assistance possible. This cabin soon became a rendezvous for them and our evenings were spent very pleasantly with stories and fireside music.

After several days, word was sent by telephone that Frost and his caravan were unable to cross Sylvan Pass because of fifty feet of snow in the defile, and that he had returned to Cody, where he would take an auto truck and come around to the northern entrance to the Park, through Gardiner, Montana.

At the expiration of three days he drove up to our cabin in a flurry of snow. This was about the last day in May.

Frost himself is one of the finest of Western types; born and raised in the sage brush country, a hunter of big game ever since he was large enough to hold a gun. He was in the prime of life, a man of infinite resource, courage, and fortitude. We admired him immensely.

With him he had a full camp outfit, selected after years of experience, and suited to any kind of weather.

The party consisted of Art Cunningham, the cook; G. D. Pope, and Judge Henry Hulbert. Art came equipped with a vast amount of camp craft and cookery wisdom. My brother came to see the fun, the Judge to take pictures and add dignity to the occasion. All were seasoned woodsmen and hunters.

We moved to more commodious quarters, a log cabin in the vicinity, made ourselves comfortable, and let the wind-driven snow pile deep drifts about our warm shelter while we planned a campaign against the grizzlies.

So far, we had met few bears, and these were of the tourist variety. They had stolen bacon from the elevated meat safe, and one we found in the woods sitting on his haunches calmly eating the contents of a box of soda crackers. These were the hotel pets and were nothing more than of passing interest to us.

Contrary to the usual condition, no grizzlies were to be seen. The only animals in evidence were a few half-starved elk that had wintered in the Park, marmots, and the Canadian jay birds.

We began our hunts on foot, exploring Hayden Valley, the Sour Creek region, Mt. Washburn, and the headwaters of Cascade Creek.

The ground was very wet in places and heavy with snow in the woods. It was necessary, therefore, to wear rubber pacs, a type of shoe well suited to this sort of travel.

Our party divided into two groups, usually my brother and the Judge exploring in one direction while Young and I kept close at the heels of Frost. We climbed all the high ridges and swept the country with our binocular glasses. From eight to fourteen hours a day we walked and combed the country for bear signs.

Our original plan was to bring in several decrepit old horses with the pack train and sacrifice them for bait. But because of the failure of this part of our program, we were forced to find dead elk for this purpose. We came across a number of old carcasses, but no signs that bear had visited them recently. Our first encounter with grizzly came on the fourth day. We were scouting over the country near Sulphur Mountain, when Frost saw a grizzly a mile off, feeding

Young studies his practice shot as Pope looks on.

Courtesy of Doug Walker

in a little valley. The snow had melted here and he was calmly digging roots in the soft ground. We signalled to our party and drew together as we advanced on our first bear, keeping out of sight as we did so.

We planned to go rapidly down a little cut in the hills and intercept him as he came around the turn. Progressing at a rapid pace, Indian file, we five hunters went down the draw, when suddenly our bear, who had taken an unexpected cut-off, came walking up the ravine. At a sign from Ned, we dropped to our knees and awaited developments. The bear had not seen us and the faint breeze blew from him to us. He was about two hundred yards off. We were all in a direct line, Frost ahead, I next, Young behind me, and the others in the rear. Our bows were braced and arrows nocked.

Slowly the bear came feeding toward us. He dug the roots of white violets, he sniffed, he meandered back and forth, wholly unconcious of our presence. We hardly breathed. He was

not a good specimen, rather scrawny, long-nosed, male adolescent, but a real grizzly and would do as a starter.

At last he came within fifty yards, stopped, pawed a patch of snow, and still we did not shoot. We could not without changing our position because we were all in one line. So we waited for his next move, hoping that he would advance laterally and possibly give us a broad-side exposure.

But he came onward, directly for us, and at thirty yards stopped to root in the ground again. I thought, "Now we must shoot or he will walk over us!" Just then he lifted his head and seemed to take an eyeful of Young's blue shirt. For one second he half reared and stared. I drew my bow and as the arrow left the string, he bounded up the hill. The flying shaft just grazed his shoulder, parting the fur in its course. Quick as a bouncing rubber ball, he leaped over the ground and as Young's belated arrow whizzed past him, he disappeared over the hill crest.

We rose with a deep breath and shouted with laughter. Ned said that if it had not been for that blue shirt, the bear would have bumped into us. Well, we were glad we missed him, because after all, he was not the one we were looking for. It is a hard thing to pick grizzlies in order. You can't go up and inspect them ahead of time.

This fiasco was just an encouragement to us, and we continued to rise by candle light and hunt till dark. The weather turned warmer, and the snow began to melt.

At the end of the first week we saw five grizzlies way off in the distance at the head of Hayden Valley. They were three or four miles from us and evening was approaching, so we postponed an attack on them. Next morning, bright and early, we were on the ground again, hoping to see them. Sure enough, there they were! Ned, Art and I were together; my brother and the Judge were off scouting on the other side of the ridge. It was about half past eight in the morning. The bears, four in number this time, were feeding in the grassy marshland, about three miles up the valley. Ned's motto has always been: "When you see 'em, go and get 'em."

We decided to attack immediately. Down the river bank, through the draws, up into the timber we circled at a trot. It was hard going, but we were pressed for time. At last we came out on a wooded point a quarter of a mile above the bears, and rested. We knew they were about to finish their morning feeding and go up into the forest to lay up for the day. So we watched them in seclusion.

We waxed our bowstrings and put the finishing touches on our arrowheads with a file.

Slowly the bears mounted the foothills, heading for a large patch of snow, where Frost thought they would lie down to cool before entering the woods. It seems that their winter coat makes them very susceptible to heat, and though the sun had come out pleasantly for us, it was too hot for them. There was an old female and three half-grown cubs in their third year, all looking big enough for any museum group.

At last they settled down and began to nuzzle the snow. The time had come for action. We proposed to slip down the little ravine at the edge of the timber, cross the stream, ascend the hill on the opposite side, and come up on our quarry over the crest. We should thus be within shooting distance. The wind was right for this maneuver, so we started at once.

Now as I write my muscles quiver, my heart thumps and I flush with a strange feeling, thinking of that moment. Like a soldier before a battle, we waded into an uncharted experience. What does a man think of as he is about to enter his first grizzly encounter? I remember well what passed through my head: "Can we get there without alarming the brutes?" "How close will they be?" "Can we hit them?" "What will happen then?"

Ned Frost, Young and I were to sneak up on four healthy grizzlies in the open, and pit our nerve against their savage reaction. Ned had his rifle, but this was to be used only as a last resort, and that might easily fail at such short range.

As we walked rapidly, stepping with utmost caution, I answered all the questions of my subconscious fears. "Hit them? Why, we will sock them in the gizzard; wreck them!" "Charge? Let them come on and may the best man win!" "Die? There never was a fairer, brighter, better day to die on." In fact, "Lead on!" I felt absolutely gay. A little profanity or a little intellectual detachment at these times is of material help in the process of auto-suggestion. As for Young, he was silent, and possibly was thinking of camp flapjacks.

Halfway up the hill, on the opposite side of which lay our grizzlies, we stopped, braced our bows, took three arrows apiece from our quivers, and proceeded in a more stealthy approach.

Young and I arranged ourselves on each side of Frost, abreast with him. Near the top, Ned took out a green silk handkerchief and floated it in the gentle breeze to see if the wind had changed. If it had, we might find the bears coming over the top to meet us. Everything was perfect, so far! Now, stooping low we crept to the very ridge itself, to a spot directly above which we believed the bears to be. Laying our hats on the grass and sticking our extra arrows in the ground before us, we rose up, bows half drawn, ready to shoot.

There on the snow, not over twenty-five yards off, lay four grizzly bears, just like so many hearth rugs.

Instantly, I selected the farthest bear for my mark and at a signal of the eye we drew our great bows to their uttermost and loosed two deadly arrows.

We struck! There was a roar, they rose, but instead of charging us, they rushed together and began such a fight as few men have seen. My bear, pinioned with an arrow in the shoulder, threw himself on his mother, biting her with savage fury. She in turn bit him in the bloody shoulder and snapped my arrow off short. Then all the cubs attacked her. The growls and bellowing were terrific.

Quickly I nocked another arrow. The beasts were milling around together, pawing, biting, mad with rage. I shot at my bear and missed him. I nocked again. The old she-bear reared on her haunches, stood high above the circling bunch, cuffing and roaring, the blood running

from her mouth and nostrils in frothy streams. Young's arrow was deep in her chest. I drove a feathered shaft below her foreleg.

The confusion and bellowing increased, and, as I drew a fourth arrow from my quiver, I glanced up just in time to see the old female's hair rise on the back of her neck. She steadied herself in her wild hurtling and looked directly at us with red glaring eyes. She saw us for the first time! Instinctively I knew she would charge and she did.

Quick as thought, she bounded toward us. Two great leaps and she was on us. A gun went off at my ear. The bear was literally knocked head over heels and fell in backward somersaults down the steep snowbank. At some fifty yards she checked her course, gathered herself, and attempted to charge again, but her right foreleg failed her. She rose on her haunches in an effort to advance, when, like a flash, two arrows flew at her and disappeared through her heaving sides. She faltered, wilted, and as we drew to

Courtesy of Doug Walker

Taking a break in their search for grizzly bear are (left to right) Saxton Pope (standing), G. D. Pope (putting on socks), Art Young, and Ned Frost (seated).

shoot again, she sprawled out on the ground, a convulsed, quivering mass of fur and muscle—she was dead.

The half-grown cubs had disappeared at the boom of the gun. We saw one making off at a gallop three hundred yards away. The glittering snowbank before us was vacant.

The air seemed strangely still; the silence was oppressive. Our nervous tension exploded in a wave of laughter and exclamations of wonderment. Frost declared he had never seen such a spectacle in all his life; four grizzly bears in deadly combat; the din of battle; the wild bellowing; and two bowmen shooting arrow after arrow into the jumble of struggling beasts.

The snow was trampled and soaked with blood as though there had been an Indian massacre. We paced off the distance at which the charging female had been stopped. It was exactly eight yards. A mighty handy shot!

We went down to review the remains. Young had three arrows in the old bear, one deep in her neck, its point emerging back of the shoulder. He shot that as she came at us. His first arrow struck anterior to her shoulder, entered her chest, and cut her left lung from top to bottom. His third arrow pierced her thorax, through and through, and lay on the ground beside her with only its feathers in the wound.

My first arrow cut below the diaphragm, penetrated the stomach and liver, severed the gall ducts and portal vein. My second arrow passed completely through her abdomen and lay on the ground several yards beyond her. It had cut the intestines in a dozen places and opened large branches of the mesenteric artery.

The bullet from Frost's gun had entered at the right shoulder, fractured the humerus, blown a hole an inch in diameter in the chest wall, opened up a jagged hole in the trachea, and dissipated its energy in the left lung. No wound of exit was found, the soft nose copper-jacketed bullet apparently having gone to pieces after striking the bone.

Anatomically speaking, it was an effective shot, knocked the bear down and crippled her, but was not an immediately fatal wound. We had her killed with arrows, but she did not know it. She undoubtedly would have been right on us in another second. The outcome of

this hypothetical encounter I leave to those with vivid imaginations.

We hereby express our gratitude to Ned Frost.

Now one of us had to rush off and get the rest of the party. Judge Hulbert and my brother were in another valley in quest of bear. So Ned set off at a rapid tramp across the bogs, streams, and hills to find them. Within an hour they returned together to view the wreckage. Photographs were taken, the skinning and autopsy were performed. Then we looked around for the wounded cub. Frost trailed him by almost invisible blood stains and tracks, and found him less than a quarter of a mile away, huddled up as if asleep on the hillside, my arrow nestled to his breast. The broken shaft with its blade deep in the thorax had completely severed the head of the humerus, cut two ribs, and killed him by hemorrhage from the pulmonary arteries. Half grown as he was, he would have made an ugly antagonist for any man.

His mother, a fine mature lady of the old school, showed by her teeth and other lineaments her age and respectability. In autumn she would have weighed four or five hundred pounds. She was in poor condition and her pelt was not suitable for museum purposes. But these features could not be determined readily beforehand. The juvenile Ursus weighed 135 pounds. We measured them, gathered their bones for the museum, shouldered their hides, and turned back to camp.

That night Ned Frost said, "Boys, when you proposed shooting grizzly bears with the bow and arrow, I thought it a fine sporting proposition, but I had my doubts about its success. Now I know that you can shoot through and kill the biggest grizzly in Wyoming!"

Our instructions on leaving California were to secure a large male *Ursus Horribilis Imperator,* a good representative female, and two or three cubs. The female we had shot filled the requirements fairly well, but the two-year-old cub was at the high school age and hardly cute enough to be admired. Moreover, no sooner had we sent the news of our first success to the museum than we were informed that this size cub was not wanted and that we must secure little ones.

So we set out to get some of this year's vintage in small bears. Ordinarily, there is no difficulty in coming in contact with bears in Yellowstone; in fact, it is more common to try to keep some of the hotel variety from eating at the same table with you. But not a single bear, black, brown, or silver-tipped, now called upon us. We travelled all over that beautiful Park, from Mammoth Hot Springs to the Lake. We hunted over every well-known bear district. Tower Falls, Specimen Ridge, Buffalo Corrals, Mt. Washburn, Dunraven Pass (under twenty-five feet of snow), Antelope Creek, Pelican Meadows, Cub Creek, Steamboat Point, and kept the rangers busy on the lookout for bear. From eight to fifteen hours a day we hunted. We walked over endless miles of mountains, climbed over countless logs, plowed through snow and slush, and raked the valleys with our field glasses.

But bears were as scarce as hen's teeth. We saw a few tracks but nothing compared to those seen in other years.

We began to have a sneaking idea that the bear had all been killed off. We knew they had been a pest to campers and were becoming a menace to human life. We suspected the Park authorities of quiet extermination. Several of the rangers admitted that a selective killing was carried out yearly to rid the preserve of the more dangerous individuals.

Then the elk began to pour back into the Park; singly, in couples, and in droves they returned, lean and scraggly. A few began to drop their calves. Then we began to see bear signs. The grizzly follow the elk, and after they come out of hibernation and get their fill of green grass, they naturally take to elk calves. Occasionally they include the mother in the menu.

We also began to follow the elk. We watched at bait. We sat up nights and days at a time, seeing only a few unfavorable specimens and these were as wild and as wary as deer. We found the mosquitos more deadly than the bear. We tracked big worthy old boys around in circles and had various frustrated encounters with she-bears and cubs.

Upon one occasion we were tracking a prospective specimen through woods, proceeding with great caution, when evidently the beast heard us. Suddenly, he turned on his tracks and came on a dead run for us. I was in advance and instantly drew my bow, holding it for the right moment to shoot. The bear came directly in our front, not more than twenty yards away and being startled by the sight of us, threw his locomotive mechanism into reverse and skidded towards us in a cloud of snow and forest leaves. In the fraction of a second, I perceived that he was afraid and not a proper specimen for our use. I held my arrow and the bear with an indignant and disgusted look, made a precipitous retreat. It was an unexpected surprise on both sides.

They say that the Indians avoided the Yellowstone region, thinking it a land of evil spirits. In our wanderings, however, we picked up on Steamboat Point a beautiful red chert arrowhead, undoubtedly shot by an Indian at elk years before Columbus burst in upon these good people. In Hayden Valley we found an obsidian spearhead, another sign that the Indian knew good hunting grounds.

But no Indian was ever so anxious to meet grizzly as we were. We hunted continually, but found none that suited us; we had to have the best. Frost assured us that we had made a mistake in ever trying to get grizzlies in the Park—and that in the time we spent there we could have secured all our required specimens in the game fields of Wyoming or Montana.

A month passed; the bears were beginning to lose their winter coats; our party began to disintegrate. My brother and the Judge were compelled to return to Detroit. A week or so later Ned Frost and the cook were scheduled to take out another party of hunters from Cody and prepared to leave us. Young and I were determined to stick it out until the last chance was exhausted. We just had to get those specimens.

Before Frost left us, however, he packed us up to the head of Cascade Creek with our bows and arrows, bed rolls, a tarpaulin, and a couple of boxes of provisions.

We had received word from a ranger that a big old grizzly had been seen at Soda Butte and we prepared to go after him. At the last moment before departure, a second word came that probably this same bear had moved down to Tower Falls and was killing elk around Dunraven Pass.

Young and I scouted over this area and found diggings and his tracks.

A good-sized bear will have a nine-inch track. This monster's was eleven inches long. We saw where he made his kills and used certain fixed trails going up and down the canyons.

Frost gave us some parting advice and his blessing, consigned us to our fate, and went home.

Left to ourselves, we two archers inspected our tackle and put everything in prime condition. Our bows had stood the many wettings well, but we oiled them again. New strings were put on and thoroughly waxed. Our arrows were straightened, their feathers dried and preened in the sun. The broadheads were set on straight and sharpened to the last degree, and so prepared we determined to do our utmost. We were ready for the big fellow.

In our reconnaissance we found that he was a real killer. His trail was marked by many bloody episodes. It seemed quite probable that he was the bear that two years before burst in upon a party of surveyors in the mountains and kept them treed all night. It is not unlikely that he was the same bear that caused the death of Jack Walsh. He seemed too expert in planning murder. We saw by his tracks how he lay in ambush watching a herd of elk, how he sneaked up on a mother elk and her recently born calf on the outskirts of the band, and with a great leap threw himself upon the two and killed them.

In several places we saw the skins of these little wapiti licked clean and empty of bodily structure. No other male grizzly was permitted to enter his domain. He was, in fact, the monarch of the mountain, the great bear of Dunraven Pass.

We pitched our little tent in a secluded wood some three miles from the lake at the head of Cascade Creek, and began to lay our plan of attack. We were by this time inured to fatigue and disappointment. Weariness and loss of sleep had produced a dogged determination that knew no relaxation. And yet we were cheerful. Young has that fine quality so essential to a hunting companion, imperturbable good nature, never complaining, no matter how heavy the load, how long the trail, how late or how early

the hour, how cold, how hot, how little, or how poor the food.

We were there to win and nothing else mattered. If it rained and we must wait, we took out our musical instruments, built up the fire and soothed our troubled souls with harmony. This is better than tobacco or whiskey for the purpose. In fact, Young is so abstemious that even tea or coffee seem a bit intemperate to him, and are only to be used under great physical strain; and as for profanity, why, I had to do all the swearing for the two of us.

We were trained down to rawhide and sinew, keyed to alertness and ready for any emergency.

Often in our wanderings at night we ran unexpectedly upon wild beasts in the dark. Some of these were bears. Our pocket flashlights were used as defensive weapons. A snort, a crashing retreat through the brush told us that our visitant had departed in haste, unable to stand the glaring light of modern science.

We soon found that our big fellow was a night rover also, and visited his various kills under the cloak of darkness. In one particularly steep and rugged canyon, he crossed a little creek at a set place. Up on the side of this canyon he mounted to the plateau above by one of three possible trails. At the top within forty yards of one of these was a small promontory of rock upon which we decided to form a blind and await his coming. We fashioned a shelter of young jack pines, constructed like a miniature corral, less than three by six feet in area, but very natural in appearance. Between us and the trail was a quantity of down timber which we hoped would act as an impediment to an onrushing bear. And the perpendicular face of our outcropping elevated us some twelve or thirteen feet above the steep hillside. A small tree stood near our position and offered a possibility in case of attack. But we had long ago decided that no man can clamber up a tree in time to escape a grizzly charging at a distance less than fifty yards. We could be approached from the rear, but altogether it was an ideal ambush.

The wind blew steadily up the canyon all night long and carried our scent away from the trail. Above us on the plateau was a recently killed elk which acted as a perpetual invitation to bears and other prowlers of the night.

So we started watching in this blind, coming soon after dusk and remaining until sunrise. The nights were cold, the ground pitiless, and the moon, nearly at its full, crept low through a maze of mist.

Dressed in our warmest clothing and permitting ourselves one blanket and a small piece of canvas, we huddled together in a cramped posture and kept vigil through the long hours. Neither of us smoked anyway, and of course, this was absolutely taboo; we hardly whispered, and even shifted our positions with utmost caution. Before us lay our bows ready strung, and arrows, both in the quiver belted upright to the screen and standing free close at hand.

The first evening we saw an old she-bear and her two-year-old cubs come up the path. They passed us with that soft shuffling gait so uncanny to hear in the dark. We were delighted that they showed no sign of having detected us. But they were not suited to our purpose and we let them go. The female was homely, fretful and nervous. The cubs were yellow and ungainly. We looked for better things.

Bears have personality, as obvious as humans. Some are lazy, some alert, surly, or timid. Nearly all the females we saw showed that irritability and irascible disposition that go with the cares of maternity. This family was decidedly commonplace.

They disappeared in the gloom, and we waited and waited for the big fellow that some time must appear.

But morning came first; we stole from our blind, chilled and stiffened, and wandered back to camp to breakfast and sleep. The former was a fairly successful event, but the latter was made almost impossible by the swarms of mosquitos that beset us. A smudge fire and canvas head-coverings gave us only a partial immunity. By sundown we were on our way again to the blind, but another cold dreary night passed without adventure.

On our way to camp in the dim light of early dawn, a land fog hung low in the valley. As we came up a rough path there suddenly appeared out of the obscurity three little bear cubs, not thirty-five yards away. They winded

us, squeaked and stood on their hind legs, peering in our direction. We dropped like stones in our tracks, scarcely breathing, figuratively frozen to the ground, for instantly the fiercest-looking grizzly we ever saw bounded over the cubs and straddled them between her forelegs. Nothing could stop her if she came on. A little bush intervened and she could not locate us plainly for we could see her eyes wander in search of us; but her trembling muscles, the vicious champing of her jaws, and the guttural growls, all spoke of immediate attack. We were petrified. She wavered in her intent, turned, cuffed her cubs down the hill, snorted and finally departed with her family.

We heaved a deep sigh of relief. But she was wonderful, she was the most beautiful bear we had ever seen; large, well proportioned, with dark brown hair having just a touch of silver. She was a patrician, the aristocrat of the species. We marked her well.

Next day, just at sunset, we got our first view of the great bear of Dunraven Pass. He was coming down a distant canyon trail. He looked like a giant in the twilight. With long swinging strides he threw himself impetuously down the mountainside. Great power was in every movement. He was magnificent! He seemed as large as a horse, and had that grand supple strength given to no other predatory animal. Though we were used to bears, a strange misgiving came over me. We proposed to slay this monster with the bow and arrow. It seemed preposterous!

In the blind another long cold night passed. The moon drifted slowly across the heavens and sank in a haze of clouds at daybreak. Just at the hush of dawn, the homely female and her tow-headed progeny came shuffling by. We were desperate for specimens, and one of these would match that which we already had. I drew up my bow and let fly a broadhead at one of the cubs. It struck him in the ribs. Precipitately, the whole band took flight. My quarry fell against an obstructing log and died. His mother stopped, came back several times, gazed at him pensively, then disappeared. We got out, carried him to a distant spot and skinned him. He weighed 120 pounds. My arrow had shaved a piece of his heart. Death was instantaneous.

We packed home the hind quarters and made a fine grizzly stew. Before this we had found the old bears were tough and rancid, but the little ones were as sweet and tender as suckling pigs. This stew was particularly good, well seasoned with canned tomatoes and the last of our potatoes and onions. Sad to relate the better part of this savory pot next day was eaten by a wandering vagabond of the *Ursus* family. Not content with our stew, he devoured all our sugar, bacon, and other foodstuffs not in cans, and wound up his debauch by wiping his feet on our beds and generally messing up the camp. Probably he was a regular camp thief.

That night, early in the watch, we heard the worthy old boy come down the canyon, hot in pursuit of a large brown bear. As he ran, the great animal made quite a noise. His claws clattered on the rocks, and the ground seemed to shake beneath us. We shifted our bows ready for action, and felt the keen edge of our arrows. Way off in the forest we heard him tree the cowardly intruder with such growls and ripping of bark that one would imagine he was about to tear the tree down.

After a long time he desisted and, grunting and wheezing, came slowly up the canyon. With the night glasses we could see him. He seemed to be considerably heated with his exercise and scratched himself against a young fir tree. As he stood on his hind legs with his back to the trunk and rubbed himself to and fro, the tree swayed like a reed; and as he lifted his nose I observed that it just touched one of the lower branches. In the morning, after he had gone and we were on our way to camp, we passed this very fir and stretching up on my tip toes, I could just touch the limb with my fingers. Having been a pole vaulter in my youth, I knew by experience that this measurement was over seven feet six inches. He was a real he-bear! We wanted him more than ever.

The following day it rained—in fact it rained nearly every day near the end of our stay; but this was a drenching that stopped at sunset, leaving all the world sweet and fragrant. The moon came out full and beautiful, everything seemed propitious.

We went to the blind about an hour before midnight, feeling that surely this evening the big fellow would come. After two hours of frigidity and immobility, we heard the velvet footfalls of bear coming up the canyon. There came our patrician and her royal family. The little fellows pattered up the trail before their mother. They came within range. I signalled Young and we shot together at the cubs. We struck. There was a squeak, a roar, a jumble of shadowy figures and the entire flock of bears came tumbling in our direction.

At that very moment the big grizzly appeared on the scene. There were five bears in sight. Turning her head from side to side, trying to find her enemy, the she-bear came towards us. I whispered to Young, "Shoot the big fellow." At the same time, I drew an arrow to the head, and drove it at the oncoming female. It struck her full in the chest. She reared; threw herself sidewise, bellowed with rage, staggered and fell to the ground. She rose again, weakened, stumbled forward, and with great gasps she died. In less than half a minute it was all over. The little ones ran up the hill past us, one later returned and sat up at its mother's head, then disappeared in the dark forever.

While all this transpired, the monster grizzly was romping back and forth in the shaded forest not more than sixty-five yards away. With deep booming growls like distant thunder, he voiced his anger and intent to kill. As he flitted between the shadows of the trees, the moonlight glinted on his massive body; he was enormous.

Young discharged three arrows at him. I shot two. We should have landed, he was so large. But he galloped off and I saw my last arrow at the point blank range of seventy-five yards, fall between his legs. He was gone. We thought we had missed the beast and grief descended heavy upon us. The thought of all the weary days and nights of hunting and waiting, and now to have lost him, was very painful.

After our palpitating hearts were quiet and the world seemed peaceful, we got out of our blind and skinned the female by flashlight. She was a magnificent specimen, just right in color and size for the Museum, not fat, but weighing a trifle over five hundred pounds. My arrow had severed a rib and buried its head in her heart. We measured her and saved her skull and long bones for the taxidermist.

Young and the old female.   *Courtesy of Doug Walker*

At daybreak we searched for the cubs and found one dead under a log with an arrow through his brain. The others had disappeared.

We had no idea that we hit the great bear, but just to gather up our shafts, we went over the ground where he had been.

One of Young's arrows was missing!

That gave us a thrill; perhaps we had hit him after all! We went further in the direction he had gone; there was a trace of blood.

We trailed him. We knew it was dangerous business. Through clumps of jack pines we cautiously followed, peering under every pile of brush and fallen tree. Deep into the forest we tracked him, where his bloody smear was left upon fallen logs. Soon we found where he had rested. Then we discovered the fore part of Young's arrow. It had gone through him. There was a pool of blood. Then we found the feathered butt which he had drawn out with his teeth.

Four times he wallowed down in the mud or soft earth to rest and cool his wound. Then

beneath a great fir he had made a bed in the soft loam and left it. Past this we could not track him. We hunted high and low, but no trace of him could we find. Apparently he had ceased bleeding and his footprints were not recorded on the stony ground about. We made wide circles, hoping to pick up his trail. We searched up and down the creek. We crosscut every forest path and runway, but no vestige remained.

He was gone. We even looked up in the tree and down in the ground where he had wallowed. For five hours we searched in vain, and at last, worn with disappointment and fatigue, we lay down and slept on the very spot where he last stopped.

Near sundown we awoke, ate a little food, and started all over again to find the great bear. We retraced our steps and followed the fading evidence till it brought us again to the pit beneath the fir tree. He must be near. It was absolutely impossible for any animal to have lost so much blood and travel more than a few hundred yards past this spot. We had explored the creek

Courtesy of Doug Walker

Art Young with the Monarch of Dunraven Pass—nearly 1,000 pounds of grizzly bear.

bottom and the cliffs above from below, and we now determined to traverse every foot of the rim of the canyon from above. As we climbed over the face of the rock we saw a clot of dried blood. We let ourselves down the sheer descent, came upon a narrow little ledge, and there below us lay the huge monster on his back, against a boulder, cold and stiff, as dead as Caesar. Our hearts nearly burst with happiness.

There lay the largest grizzly bear in Wyoming, dead at our feet. His rugged coat was matted with blood. Well back in his chest the arrow wound showed clear. I measured him; twenty-six inches of bear had been pierced through and through. One arrow had killed him. He was tremendous. His great wide head; his worn, glistening teeth; his massive arms; his vast, ponderous feet and long curved claws; all were there. He was a wonderful beast. It seemed incredible. I thumped Young on the shoulder: "My, that was a marvelous shot!"

We started to skin our quarry. It was a stupendous job, as he weighed nearly one thou-sand pounds, and lay on the steep canyon side ready to roll on and crush us. But with ropes we lashed him by the neck to a tree and split him up the back, later box-skinning the legs according to the method required by the museum.

By flashlight, acetylene lamp, candlelight, firelight and moonlight, we labored. We used up all our knives, and having neglected to bring our whetstones, sharpened our blades on the volcanic boulders about us. By assiduous industry for nine straight hours, we finished him after a fashion. His skin was thick and like scar tissue. His meat was all tendons and gristle. The hide was as tight as if glued on.

In the middle of the night we stopped long enough to broil some grizzly cub steaks and brew a pot of tea; then we went at it again.

As we dismembered him we weighed the parts. The veins were absolutely dry of blood, and without this substance, which represents a loss of nearly 10 percent of his weight, he was 916 pounds. There was hardly an inch of fat on his back. At the end of the autumn this adipose layer would be nearly six inches thick. He would have weighed over fourteen hundred pounds. He stood nearly four feet high at the shoulders, while his skull measured 18½ inches long; his entire body length was seven feet four inches.

As we cleaned his bones we hurled great slabs of muscle down the canyon, knowing from experience that this would be a sign for all other bears to leave the vicinity. Only the wolves and jays will eat grizzly meat.

At last we finished him, as the sun rose over the mountain ridges and gilded all the canyon with glory.

We cleaned and salted the pelts, packed them on our backs, and dripping with salt brine and bear grease, staggered to the nearest wagon trail. The hide of the big bear, with unskinned paws and skull, weighed nearly 150 pounds.

We cached our trophies, tramped the weary miles back to camp, cleaned up, packed and wandered to the nearest station, from which we ordered a machine. When this arrived we gathered our belongings, turned our various specimens over to a park ranger to be given the final treatments, and started on our homeward trip.

We were so exhausted from loss of sleep, exertion and excitement, that we sank into a stupor that lasted almost the entire way home.

The California Academy of Sciences now has a handsome representative group of *Ursus Horribilis Imperator*. We have the extremely satisfactory feeling that we killed five of the finest grizzly bear in Wyoming. The sport was fair and clean, and we did it all with the bow and arrow.

Illustration by Dave Wade — Courtesy of Outdoor Life

POPE AND YOUNG, THE MEN, THE CAUSE, AND THE ART

by Max Greiner, Jr.

The creation process for the "Pope and Young" art mentally began many years ago when I first learned of the men's significance in archery and bowhunting. However, it wasn't until 1984 that I made the decision to create special edition archery art to raise funds for the sport which has given me so much enjoyment and so many friends. My first archery composition was of Ishi, the patron saint of bowhunters. The second is of Pope and Young, the founding fathers of modern day bowhunting.

After the "Ishi" art was released in 1985 to benefit the National Bowhunter Education Foundation, Pope and Young director, Frank "Rit" Heller, approached me about a fund-raising project for the Pope and Young Club. The wheels were officially set in motion at the 1985 banquet in Bismarck, North Dakota.

The composition of my art focuses on perhaps the most exciting bowhunting adventure shared by Saxton Pope and Art Young. In May of 1920, these two men packed into Yellowstone Park with a special permit to harvest a family of grizzly bears for the California Academy of Sciences Golden Gate Park Museum in San Francisco. They were determined to accomplish this feat with the bow and arrow, something which had never been done before by a white man (the complete story of that fascinating hunt precedes these pages).

Even though many of their archery accomplishments are still considered truly remarkable today, Dr. Saxton Temple Pope and Arthur H. Young were not foolhardy men. It would probably be more accurate to say they were sensitive intellectuals. Dr. Pope, forty-five years old at the time of the Wyoming hunt, was Head of Surgery at the University of California in San Francisco. It was there in 1911 that he first met Ishi, North America's last wild Indian. During the five years prior to Ishi's death from tuberculosis, Pope learned from Ishi how to make and hunt with the bow and arrow and became Ishi's closest friend. Through Pope, Ishi's bowhunting ethics and knowledge would be passed on to future generations.

Art Young, thirty-seven years old in 1920, was a violinist who learned archery and bowhunting from Pope. The two became the closest of friends during their bowhunts across America and Africa. Young's movie about bowhunting in Alaska and Pope's books and articles on the subject were the primary means by which the sport was introduced to the world.

Ironically, both men died fairly young; Pope at age fifty-one from pneumonia and Young at

"POPE & YOUNG"
FATHERS OF MODERN BOWHUNTING
SPECIAL EDITION FOR THE
POPE & YOUNG CLUB

MAX GREINER JR.   © 1986

"Pope and Young" drawing (pen and ink, 22″ x 30″). The drawing print, 15½″ x 19½″, is issued in a signed and numbered edition limited to 950.

fifty-two from a ruptured appendix. However, the interest they created in hunting with the bow and arrow continued to grow. In the years that followed, modern bowhunting was born with a foundation based primarily on the hunting philosophy and inspiration provided by these two unique pioneers.

It was with these facts in mind that I determined historical accuracy, as well as aesthetic power, were of utmost importance in the creation of the "Pope and Young" art. The drawing and bronze sculpture I have created depicts the exciting moment when a big female grizzly charged the two archers, the second such confrontation on the trip. Pope is shown at full draw, focused on the charging female. Young is nocking his arrow, preparing to shoot at a large male—the Monarch of Dunraven Pass. The painting depicts the moment of jubilation when the two archers recovered the giant bear.

Thanks to the help of friends like Fred Bear, Rit Heller, Chuck Young, Buck Lewis, and Glenn and Joe St. Charles, I was able to secure all the information, artifacts, and old photographs I needed to create the art accurately. Preliminary sketches and a clay model were presented to the Pope and Young Club directors to obtain their constructive criticism, ideas, and approval. Back at the studio I created 1:10 scale drawings of the men, their archery equipment, and the bear. From these, precise wire skeletons were made over which wax would be sculpted. Live models, dressed and positioned like Pope and Young, were photographed as additional reference. The study of two hours of video tape on grizzlies was necessary to obtain the ideal body position for the charging bear. The total creation process took over a year and a half.

I wanted my art to remain totally honest to the actual historic event. Even subtle differences between the men's clothing, shooting form, and archery tackle are depicted. Art wore a pullover shirt on the hunt, while Saxton wore his typical jacket and tie. Pope drew his bowstring in the standard split-fingered fashion, while Young used three fingers under the arrow. I have even

"Pope and Young" painting (oil/canvas, 24″ x 30″). The painting print, 22″ x 28″, is issued in a signed and numbered edition limited to 950.

"Pope and Young" bronze sculpture, 15″ x 21″ x 10″. A limited edition of 100 signed and numbered pieces with matching numbered prints. Also included is a copy of *Bowhunting Big Game Records of North America*, third edition.

tried to reflect the slight differences in their arrow fletchings and broadheads. Fortunately, the old photographs and detailed descriptions in Pope's book, *Hunting With the Bow and Arrow,* allowed me to do this with great accuracy.

The "Pope and Young" pen and ink drawing and oil painting have been reproduced in a signed and numbered limited edition of 950 offset lithograph prints, with fifty Artist Proofs. The bronze sculpture has been issued in an edition of 100 castings. The bronze includes a copy of this book, the third edition of *Bowhunting Big Game Records of North America,* fitted into the sculpture's walnut base. Both the drawing and the painting prints are numbered to match the bronze. As a special touch, each bronze incorporates authentic reproductions of each man's individual broadhead—those actually

used on the Yellowstone grizzly hunt. Molds were made from these rare heads supplied from the collection of Buck Lewis. Below each man's broadhead his signature is inscribed in the bronze.

Bowhunting is fortunate to have had Dr. Saxton Pope and Art Young as its founders. Hopefully, my "Pope and Young" art and the contributions generated for bowhunting through this project would please those two pioneers.

EDITOR'S NOTE:

Each time a print or bronze is purchased, a contribution is directed to the Club. To receive more information on the "Pope and Young" art, contact Max directly at:

Greiner Art Gallery
P.O. Box 552
Kerrville, TX 78029

A CONSERVATION ETHIC

by Charles Kroll

The Board of Directors of the Pope and Young Club is given the power to appoint any committee it deems necessary to assist in the proper functioning of the organization. The Conservation Committee is one such appointment, charged with interpreting and implementing Article II, Section 4 of the Club Bylaws, which states:

> *The objectives and purposes of the Club shall be to promote the welfare and conservation of North American big game and their habitat.*

The present Pope and Young Conservation Committee was formed in 1977 when the club president, Jim Dougherty, with approval of the board members, asked me to chair the committee. As my first assignment, I selected a slate of committee members and our task of choosing worthy projects for funding grants was begun.

In addition to myself, present members of the Conservation Committee are: George Moerlein of Anchorage, Alaska; Billy Ellis, III of Lexington, Mississippi; Marvin Clyncke of Boulder, Colorado; Paul Brunner of Ovando, Montana; Fred Wallace of Lebanon, Ohio.

This geographic spread insures that all regions of America can be monitored for projects worthy of consideration for grants by the committee.

Total grants by the committee to the present date are well in excess of $50,000—a respectable contribution to North American wildlife management for an organization of the Club's size.

Since its formation, the Conservation Committee's funding support has covered a diverse and carefully selected scope of activities, ranging from field research grants for various wildlife species through support of wildlife symposiums, big game relocation projects, emergency winter feeding programs, and wildlife habitat preservation. The committee has also provided funding to national educational programs such as the International Association of Fish and Wildlife Agencies' "Project W.I.L.D." and the National Shooting Sports Foundation's "Unendangered Species."

Field research programs supported by Pope and Young grants have mainly been those carried on by biologists in the various state and provincial game and fish commissions. The committee strongly believes that from research comes the knowledge and understanding to better manage our wildlife resources for the future. One such project receiving major support from the committee was a whitetail deer *(Odocoileus virginianus)* study carried on by the Minnesota Department of Natural Resources.

Figure 1, Whitewater WMA Minnesota

In July of 1981, the Conservation Committee was contacted by John Ludwig, Minnesota Wildlife Biologist, concerning a proposed research project. After reviewing a synopsis of the planned study, and upon approval from the board of directors, the committee awarded a grant of $1,200 to Mr. Ludwig's research unit. Additional grants of $1,200 and $1,000 respectively were awarded during the project's continuation through 1982 and 1983. The field research, carried out in southeastern Minnesota's Whitewater Wildlife Management Area, was completed at the end of that period. The results, later published in the *Journal of Wildlife Management,* produced some new and extremely interesting findings on the lives of whitetail deer.

For many years northern Minnesota had been thought of as fine deer country. Activities there around the turn of the century (logging, homesteading, and fires) created conditions in the mid-1900s conducive to a high deer population. At the same time, unregulated shooting and loss of habitat due to settlements almost eliminated the deer in the southern part of the state.

In recent years, however, the situation has been reversing itself. The harsh winters, habitat maturation, and timber wolves have all taken their toll on the deer in the north. But with a new hunting season framework in place, providing a basis for sensible game management, the deer population of southern Minnesota has been making a remarkable comeback.

From 1976–1979, the farmland area provided between 45 to 48 percent of the annual firearms harvest in the state. By 1980 that number rose to 50 percent. Incidently, this region also accounted for over 75 percent of the Minnesota archery harvest during the same period.

One premise of any successful wildlife management program is to have a reasonably accurate estimate of the population to be managed. Although deer populations could be estimated by counting pellets in the northern areas of the state, that method didn't work in farmland Minnesota due to agricultural practices such as plowing. The primary censusing method used in this part of the state had been aerial counts. It's known that not all of the deer are seen with this

method, but a larger problem is trying to determine the percentage that are missed.

Ludwig's research plan called for attaching radio transmitters and visible collars to a number of deer. Then, by using normal census flights, it would be possible to ascertain how many of these deer were alive and where they were during each count. From this data it was hoped that the proportion of animals missed during an aerial census could be more precisely determined. Also, tracking of the marked deer throughout the year would provide information on movements, behavior, mortality rates, and habitat preferences of the whitetails in the semi-open terrain of the study area.

Another important aspect of the project was to determine the value of a refuge for deer within a large wildlife management area. Refuges—whether designated as such, or created by natural barriers—are existent on most large management units, but their value was basically unknown. If they really did contribute to deer populations, perhaps more of them should be added. If, on the other hand, whitetail populations could be maintained and managed just as well without them, perhaps the refuges could be eliminated, thus providing more land open to public hunting. Radio marking deer on and off such a refuge, and determining movements, recruitment, and mortality, in relation to hunting pressure, could shed light on the value of such refuges.

The Whitewater Wildlife Management Area covers a little over 26,000 acres of the study area east of Rochester. A portion of the management area had been set aside as a sanctuary in 1968. Part of the study would help to determine whether this refuge was causing a problem similar to a situation in Wisconsin. A deer herd bunched in a large tamarack swamp (essentially a refuge due to its inaccessibility) overpopulated the area to a critical point. Deer that migrated out of the area during hunting season were killed, but deer that "stayed home" were not being harvested. Through *differential selection*—harvesting deer that moved and not harvesting those that didn't move—the herd ended up not migrating at all and serious density problems developed.

In such a case, the population slowly builds up because the non-migratory females survive. They reproduce and their offspring learn through association and imprinting to use the home range. Conversely, many of the animals that have a tendency to move get shot each year and thus their offspring don't learn to migrate. Problems with overpopulation and depredation of local crops usually are the result of this behavior.

The research team wanted to find out if the deer in the refuge part of the study area migrated. They needed to know not only if they moved, but when and where they moved, and if they returned. They also wanted to know if these animals, whether migratory or not, were available for hunting.

To begin the study, biologists from the Farmland Wildlife Populations and Research Group, under Ludwig's direction, captured deer with rocket nets and clover traps. Once captured, the animals were sexed, field aged by incisor tooth wear, hair and blood sampled, and ear tagged. Some 179 deer were tagged. Fifty-nine does were fitted with radio collars allowing telemetry tracking to aid in monitoring their movements. The rest of the animals were fitted with highly visible, breakaway collars and numbered ear tags.

"We were interested in how the refuge was related to heavy hunting pressure in the Whitewater Management Area," says Dennis Simon, DNR research biologist who worked on the project. "With trespass laws and increased hunting pressure, most of that pressure is being directed at these larger management blocks. We needed to know how this was affecting movement patterns in whitetails."

Previous findings had shown that whitetail bucks displayed much more random dispersal patterns from refuge areas. Therefore, only does were radio-collared. "Does are the really important part of the population," Ludwig says. "You need to know what's happening to them. Because of their polygamous nature, a good share of the bucks are considered expendable." If bucks had been radio-collared, the high harvest rate on males in the region could also jeopardize the project, through the loss of study animals, long before meaningful data could be collected. At least 50 percent of the males never see their

second birthday and most bucks don't live to their fourth year. A three-year-old is a good, old buck in this area.

When the final results of the three-year research project were tabulated and analyzed, several interesting and important conclusions could be drawn about whitetail behavior; some were rather astonishing in light of what had previously been thought.

For instance, it was determined that the home ranges of adult deer in the type of country studied (mainly semi-open prairie and farmland) varied considerably by season; winter and spring home ranges being larger than those of summer, increasing again in the fall. The straight-line distance between winter and summer ranges for the radio-collared deer averaged about five miles and ranged up to 49.5 miles! This is in complete contrast to much of the "folklore" about whitetails living out their lifetime in a relatively small area.

There was a wide range of behavior patterns among the sampled deer. Their individualistic nature didn't allow them to be easily grouped into categories. Some went straight from one seasonal range to another, while others did considerable wandering before settling down.

Most of the deer that moved out of the refuge had a tendency to make occasional exploratory trips from their normal summer range. Throughout the year, many deer made erratic movements of 1¼ to over 3 miles in just a few days, before returning to their starting point. Two deer made at least one round trip from summer range to winter range and back, prior to settling into their wintering area in the fall.

Of the deer that did migrate from the refuge, three of them regularly swam the main shipping channel in the Mississippi River into Wisconsin. With the approach of fall, they turned around and came back to winter in the refuge. This proved to be the annual migration pattern for these deer.

In the summer of 1982, several deer traveled more than twenty miles from the Whitewater refuge into Wisconsin. During the opening week of archery season, one of them returned the entire distance in just two days.

A significant determination made as a result of this extended research program was that deer herds living in or adjacent to agricultural lands are extremely vulnerable to over-harvest. Cautious hunting season structures are necessary to guard against that. However, it was also determined that the presence of a sizeable refuge in a region could serve as a "repopulation center" for the surrounding area.

Yet, perhaps the most important conclusion of the research was that home ranges of whitetails not only vary considerably by season, but that many of these deer travel a great deal more than was previously thought. With whitetails moving twenty miles or more, twice each year, doubt is cast on the age-old theory that these animals "stay at home" and live out their entire lives in a space of a square mile or so.

The entire membership of the Pope and Young Club can take pride in being associated with such significant wildlife research. So long as the Club exists, the Conservation Committee will continue to function. For only by rational management, increased knowledge, and protection will the fascinating realm of the bowhunter be preserved.

Our earnest desire is to leave a legacy to those who follow after us, which will include the opportunity to experience the joy of wandering through lonely, *game-inhabited lands* with a trusty bow and straight-flying shafts.

Illustration by Dave Wade — Courtesy of Outdoor Life

BOOK II

THE CHASE

Illustration by Dave Wade — Courtesy of Outdoor Life

ANTLERS

by Kathy Etling

I don't remember how old I was when I first realized the strange, magical effect that antlers have on me. Whenever I'd see a deer, I'd pause to watch a little closer. A deer sneaking silently along in the woods is something special. But when that deer has antlers, it's the stuff dreams are made of.

Antlers have cast their spell on mankind since time began. Ancient tribes were fascinated by them. They ground them into powders for use in potions, a practice that continues even today in our mind-boggling, high-tech world. Four thousand years ago, the Greeks tried to explain the why and what of antlers. And while we know *what* they are, we still don't know *why* they are. At least not for certain. But that is part of their mystery. As always, the things we hold most miraculous are those we can least explain.

Hunters everywhere fall victims to the allure of antlers. No one has ever called it "Doe Fever." No, *Buck Fever* it is, and so it will remain until the end of time. And while most of us have taken docs for one reason or another, the respect we feel when we take one can't compare to the awe that strikes us as we walk up on a downed buck.

Antlers, more precisely, huge bucks are the reason why many of us stalk the woods today. A mere glimpse of glistening white "bone" through the grays and blacks of a hardwood forest sets many a heart to thumping within a chest that is suddenly too small; and then the damn bow is trembling, and the arrow skitters off its rest, and the buck walks away unscathed! Know the feeling?

Maybe the problem isn't with the antlers high atop the buck's head, but what goes on inside *the hunter's skull*. I know. I've imagined myself the deserving object of much envy when I bring my mythical record book deer into the check station. The daydream runs rampant as other hunters crowd around, wanting to know how and where I got the monster of the county. News columns are devoted to my incredible hunting skill and the fantastic archery technique that took the hulking grey monster with the oak-like beams. Long tines, like ivory daggers, flash in my mind as I pursue this dangerous pastime; and, when I ultimately see such a trophy, I freeze.

"My God, there he is," I breathe raggedly to myself as I try to remember just where in the heck my anchor point is. "How shall I get him mounted? Alert? Sneak pose? Turned left? Right?" Sure, . . . Right! By this time I'm so worked up that I couldn't hit the ground at my feet, much less a buck worthy of listing with Pope and Young.

Typical and non-typical, tines—forked, drop, and all others, eyeguards, main beams, inside spread, circumferences, and number of points—they all add up to the glory that is antlers. Taxidermists can earn a living largely because of the artistry they possess in preserving antlers as they existed—on a lifelike model of the animal that bore them.

The various systems used to measure antlers and the organizations involved—like Pope and Young—are, in themselves, tributes to the complexities of antlers and all their different shapes.

What do we know about antlers? To begin with, while they're in the velvet stage, they are the fastest form of bone growth known to science. A mature bull elk, for example, is capable of adding several *cubic inches* of antler each and every day during the peak growing season. Growth like this can result in a rack of solid bone, weighing well over sixty pounds, being produced *in less than four months!* A rack that size is equivalent to an adult human male's entire skeletal structure.

A buck fawn or juvenile bull is preprogrammed while still in utero to someday develop antlers. This is when the pedicles (pronounced ped-i-kals) begin to develop.

Pedicles are the antlers' growth platforms. They're the mysterious link between the living bone of the animal's skull and the antler. While the antler is growing, nourishment in the form of blood is provided to the living tissue in two ways: from the capillary-rich outer skin or velvet which is the only regenerating skin found among mammals; and, through the core of the pedicle. The pedicle is a direct source of the blood needed by the osteocytes or true bone cells in the growing antler. But once the message "stop growing" is given, the pedicle cuts off the blood supply and the antlers harden.

This is when the most intriguing part of the entire antler story comes to light. Even though the buck's skull is living bone and the antler is dead bone, the pedicle acts as a connector to hold the living to the dead. Nowhere else in the animal kingdom does this kind of relationship exist. Normally, a living organism will do everything in its power to rid itself of dead tissue. Not so with antlers.

Because of the virility associated with prime bucks, stags and bulls, dried antler velvet is thought to be a cure for impotence and infertility. Even now there is a thriving market for harvested velvet from nearly every species of the deer family. This market is greatest in the Far East, China, and the U.S.S.R. All over the world, venison and velvet farms are springing up to supply the market existing in these countries.

Velvet is also used for other medicinal reasons, primarily by women during the third trimester of pregnancy and while nursing. Menopausal disorders are treated with velvet, and it's also effective as a blood vessel dilator and for stimulating red blood cell production. Unlocking the considerable secrets of antler growth and development might one day lead to some of the most significant medical breakthroughs of mankind.

All bucks or bulls (from here on called bucks for simplicity) need three things to grow a set of trophy antlers: age, nutrition, and genetic potential. A buck is usually in his prime at 4½ years of age. Barring any sickness or injury, he'll maintain this prime condition for about three seasons, or until he's 6½ years old. The next season is generally the start of a gradual decline.

It's also true that deer can and do grow record-class racks at 2½ and 3½ years of age, *if it's their genetic potential to do so.* But generally a trophy buck at these tender ages would only be more magnificent once he reached his prime.

Many record book bucks are taken from areas that are underpopulated by deer. Food supplies in such an area are usually very good since the range hasn't been overbrowsed. But even in his prime and on the best range around, a buck won't grow a trophy-sized rack if his *genes* aren't programmed to do so.

Not every buck is born a potential Boone and Crockett record. That would be roughly equivalent to every thoroughbred foal growing up to be a Secretariat; it just doesn't happen. Far more bucks have the ability to become Pope and Young candidates because of the lower minimum scores. These lower minimums are necessary because of the increased hunting skills required to take a qualifying buck.

Photo by Lee Kline

In their velvet stage, antlers are the fastest form of bone growth known. They are also very sensitive and easily injured. Note the damage to the budding brow tine of this young bull elk.

Even a lowly spike more than likely has the genetic potential to become a trophy. A spike may be considered an eighteen-month-old deer—normal age for the first antler-bearing season—while in reality being less than fifteen months old. Here in Missouri, conservation officers have documented fawn births in late August and September—way past the normal birthing month of May. These little fellows will be three or four months behind their cousins in every way, including antler development.

So, now that we've determined what it takes to grow a record-class rack, let's see exactly how this growth takes place.

Zbigniew Jaczewski, a Polish researcher, started the ball rolling when he showed that the antler growth cycle was controlled by light. Dr. Robert Brown, of the Caesar Kleberg Wildlife Research Institute in Kingsville, Texas explains:

The pineal gland is the receptor of messages from the eye. As the days get longer it's theorized that the pineal gland, a pea-sized gland near the base of the brain, releases a hormone called melatonin. The stimulus for the release of this hormone is the gradually lengthening daylight. The light strikes the eye and nerves transmit the information to the pineal gland. When enough melatonin is coursing through the deer's system it is time for the pituitary—the Master Gland—to do its part. Again, it is thought that LH, the luteinizing hormone which is produced by the pituitary, actually triggers the production of testosterone—the male sex hormone—in the testicles. As the testosterone level rises, the antlers start to grow.

If the pineal gland is surgically removed, the antler cycle is altered. The buck may then grow his antlers during the winter and rub them out in the spring—a complete reversal of the normal growth cycle.

If the pituitary gland is removed, the deer won't ever develop antlers—even if artificially injected with testosterone. The pituitary is so complex and performs so many different functions that researchers still aren't able to duplicate its periodic releases of various hormones.

The antler cycle is irreparably altered when the testes are removed. Aristotle, the Greek philosopher who lived thousands of years before Christ, was the first to discover this fact. But just how the antler cycle is altered depends on the age of the deer when it is castrated.

A fawn that's been castrated will never grow antlers. Pedicle development is a once-in-a-lifetime event. If this event is prevented from occurring by early castration, which disrupts testosterone production, no antlers will ever develop.

When an adult buck is castrated he will grow velvet antlers during each growing season. However, the velvet will *never* be rubbed off and the antlers *never* cast or shed. Why? The testes aren't the only glands that manufacture

testosterone. While a fawn needs the concentrated testosterone boost of the testes for pedicle development, an adult male deer will get enough of the hormone to grow antlers each spring *from the adrenal glands*. But there isn't enough testosterone for a complete antler growth cycle; one that includes shedding of velvet and antlers. A buck like this, with continuous springtime growth of velvet antlers, is called a "cactus" buck because of the weird and rather bizarre shapes the antlers take.

Hypogonadism—undescended or undeveloped testicles—is another reason that bucks become "cactus" bucks. One area in Texas, the Central Mineral Region, has an unusually high ratio of deer with hypogonadism. Scientist suspect that certain plants growing on granite soils cause this condition.

Should a buck be castrated while he has hardened antlers, he'll lose those antlers within

Photos by Lee Kline

"Cactus" bucks like these never shed their antlers or rub off the velvet. This bizarre antler growth is most probably the result of damage to the reproductive organs of these bucks.

two weeks. Then he will grow his "cactus" set the next spring.

Does can grow antlers, too, when given shots of testosterone. When a twenty-four-point *doe* was recently shot in Kentucky, biologists found that she had undescended testicles in addition to normal female reproductive organs. An animal like this is called a "hemaphrodite"—Greek for "of both sexes." The doe's undescended testicles released testosterone and were the reason why the doe had developed antlers.

Dr. Richard Goss, of Brown University in Providence, Rhode Island, researched how light affects antler cycles. Dr. Goss knew North American deer have definite antler cycles; antlers cast in the late winter, new growth through the spring and summer, with velvet shedded and antlers hardened in the fall. South American deer have antler cycles the exact reverse of their northern cousins. But at the Equator, *where day and night are always equal,* bucks have no definite antler cycle. Some bucks keep their antlers for longer than a year; others shed them twice a year. However, when these same bucks were relocated in the northern hemisphere, their antler cycles became identical to those of our native deer.

Dr. Goss kept study deer indoors where he could regulate light and how its pattern affected them. He discovered that a year's worth of daytime could be compressed into six months by "skipping" every other day. When he did this, his study deer grew *two complete sets of antlers each year.*

Sitka bucks grew three sets of antlers in a calendar year when the amount of daylight was altered to make it appear as if three years had elapsed. Bucks need at least three to four months to grow a set of antlers, but then they can rub the velvet off and shed the antlers immediately.

If artificial daylight compresses a year into two-month increments, deer will grow no antlers at all. They simply can't keep up with the breakneck growth required. However, Dr. Goss discovered that the following year when it was spring outside, his study deer *on the inside*—and still subjected to the fabricated two-month year—grew new antlers as though they, too, were outside. This was the first evidence supporting the theory that deer may have a physio-

logical mechanism *within* to let them know when a year has passed, *if all other indicators are absent.* In other words, deer seem to have a built-in indicator of how long a year is.

Temperature, which may have some influence on rutting behavior, has no bearing whatsoever on antler growth or hardening.

An antler develops as a lengthening of the buck's skull and it is similar to skeletal bone. However, while they're growing, antlers are cartilage—the pliable substance you can feel in your nose and ears.

Dr. Brown says:

> The outside of a growing antler is covered with velvet, a skin rich with veins and arteries which supply blood to the antler. And the pedicle also acts like a conduit that carries blood to the interior of the antler. If you could touch a velvet antler it would be quite warm because of all the blood. The velvet is also a network of nerves and very sensitive to touch.

As antlers grow they gradually start to harden, from the inside out. Minerals, like calcium and phosphorus, are deposited to form a bony core. Much has been written about supplementing a deer's feed with minerals to help the animal grow larger antlers.

Dr. Brown continues:

> A deer can't possibly get all the minerals he needs for the development of his rack from his food. So buck deer take minerals from their own skeletons, especially from the ribs and sternum, and deposit them in their antlers. The stress to a buck's system is enormous since antlers grow at a tremendous rate.
>
> When a deer is growing antlers, his ribs become brittle and can break fairly easily, but wild deer take this in stride—and every year, too. Even if a deer breaks a bone while growing antlers, the break will usually heal smoothly. And when antler growth is complete, the minerals are then restored to the temporarily depleted bones.

Research has developed many other interesting theories about deer and their antlers. For example, Dr. Anthony Bubenik of Thornhill, Ontario, Canada writes that every year of a buck's life he'll go through three separate stages of sexual development. When a buck casts his antlers, he loses all aggressive tendencies. He becomes timid and parallels a human's infancy. During this period, the pedicles are healing.

When the days begin to lengthen, a buck enters the adolescent stage. Buck puberty has two phases. The touch-sensitive phase, when he is extremely careful with his antlers, lasts about 75 percent of the antler growth period. The second, desensitizing phase occurs when the antlers "point," harden, and the velvet dies. The velvet dies when the blood supply dries up. This stage ends when the velvet is shed.

When the buck enters annual maturity, hardened antlers show that the buck is ready to breed. Maturity is the most important portion of the buck's year. Until the buck rubs out his antlers, he doesn't act macho at all. His testosterone level is low and estrogen, the female hormone, is also present in his system. Dr. Anthony Bubenik explains:

> During this time the buck's facial expressions are meek and doe-like. The males fight like females, standing on hind legs and flailing with forelegs at the opponents' heads. I feel that it's at this time when dominance is decided, not later on when bucks have hardened antlers.

So, when deer start the rut they already know who the head honcho is. Perhaps instinctively they realize dominance battles with pointed antlers could be dangerous. Because of this, Bubenik feels battles with hardened antlers are more a ritual than a determination of rank.

Deer will use their antlers to fight in deadly earnest for three reasons. First, if one buck wants another buck's doe. This is rare in a population where bucks are aware of rank before the onset of the rut. Second, a fight may result if a stranger wanders through the area. Fights like this don't last long. They end once status is determined.

The third type of fight occurs when a young, inexperienced buck enters a prime male's mating area and challenges him with no regard to

Photos by Lee Kline

These captive bull elk cast their 1985 antlers between March 25-29, 1986. The photos were taken six weeks later on May 11th.

Photos by Lee Kline

The same bulls on July 1, 1986, about twelve weeks after shedding their 1985 antlers.

threats and warnings. If the prime male is fit, this can spell doom to the challenger. But late in the rut, when dominant bucks are worn out, an aggressive younger buck can be real trouble. Because of exhaustion, a prime buck could be accidently killed. If the younger buck wounds the dominant buck, it will make the challenger even more bloodthirsty. He'll attack relentlessly, often killing the older buck in the process.

When deer spar, Dr. Bubenik feels it's for one of two reasons; first, to gain necessary fighting skills for the future while determining the shape of their antlers. It's apparently very difficult for a buck to decide just how large his rack is until antler growth stabilizes during his prime. Sparring or play-fighting is common among deer that hang out in bachelor bands.

Demonstration sparring, the second type, allows bucks to test each other to verify dominance. In other words, if a buck has any doubts about who's the boss after the foreleg flailing, this is the time to settle the issue once and for all.

Dr. Bubenik thinks bucks start soliciting for rank during the rut while they're still in velvet. He says,

> They rub the pheromones from their velvet secretion on vegetation as a sort of pre-rut advertising campaign. They make sure that everyone else makes the connection by rubbing the velvet on their bodies and gently scratching it with their hooves so that they'll track their scent all over the countryside.

When deer shed their antler velvet, this means of communication is lost. Dr. Bubenik feels they compensate by coating their newly hardened antlers with pheromones from their urine which is deposited either directly on the antlers or on vegetation which is rubbed.

Non-typical antlers can be the result of genetics or of injuries—either to the antler itself or

Photo by Lee Kline

Researchers believe bucks and bulls begin soliciting for rank during the rut while their antlers are still in velvet. By gently scratching the antlers with their hooves, they then track their scent all over the countryside as sort of a pre-rut ad campaign.

to the buck, particularly his legs. For example, if a buck injures a rear leg while still in the velvet, the antler on the *opposite* side will be stunted. Scientists think this is what happens:

A deer injures his left rear leg. Since deer walk by raising and lowering legs on the diagonal, the right foreleg and the *injured* left hind leg support the body's weight half of the time. To compensate, the "Antler Growth Center" slows down the right antler's development. This way less weight bears on the affected limb. If a front leg is injured, the antler on the *same side* will be smaller because it bears directly on the injured limb with each step.

Should an antler suffer trauma (injury) during growth, it overdevelops; but, the greatest growth occurs the year *following* the injury. The antler appears to remember the injury for years. It's for this reason that the response is called "trophical memory." If the right antler is injured, *only the right antler* will develop excessively. This verifies the theory that each antler develops independently of the other. Antlers injured early in the growth cycle experience the most damage and result in the most spectacular deformations.

Once the days grow shorter, antlers start to harden. When the antlers are fully ossified—turned to bone—the velvet's blood supply dries up. The velvet starts to itch. Ossification occurs throughout the final third of the velvet stage and begins from the inside out. Once complete, the buck looks for trees where he can rub the velvet off. Velvet shedding within a three-week period, by all normal bucks, is a common occurrence.

Light is apparently the only outside factor governing the antler cycle. Temperature plays no part at all. Food affects size, not the cycle. However, undernourished bucks will shed their antlers early.

A buck with hardened antlers is ready to fulfill his biological calling by fathering the next crop of fawns. Most breeding in a well-balanced population is done by prime males.

Deer, like people, fake each other out at times. Dr. Anthony Bubenik has watched white-tails, muleys, and elk use what he calls "deception strategy."

> In deception strategy, the animal actually alters his antlers' shape by attacking vegetation but leaving moss, leaves, or grass hanging on them instead of shaking it off. The buck purposely parades around with the extra matter on his antlers as if he knows it will intimidate other bucks by making his antlers look larger than they are. Deception strategy is practiced during long-lasting contests. When a buck resorts to deception strategy, the other male *will give up and retreat*. He'll be totally fooled by the deception.

The final portion of the antler cycle is called casting (commonly referred to as "shedding"). Casting dates, unlike velvet shedding, are highly individual and vary greatly. In one study it was found that antlers were shed over a three-month period. However, when kept under identical conditions from year to year, each buck shed his antlers on an uncanny schedule. That is, if Buck No. 1 casts his antlers on December 22 and Buck No. 2 casts his antlers on January 31, evidence is great that each year they'll cast their antlers *on almost the same date.*

Dr. Harry Jacobson said, "This possibly shows that bucks have a pre-programmed rhythm within their system which causes them to cast their antlers."

Dr. Brown sums it up when he says,

> Casting is truly amazing. One day you can't knock a buck's antlers off, and the next day they just fall off—and usually within a day of each other. When the buck's testosterone level drops below the minimum needed to maintain antlers, the pedicle demineralizes. And that's when casting occurs.

After shedding, the pedicle looks like an open sore but soon heals.

Antlers—no matter how much we learn, they'll always be one of nature's miracles. And, as long as hunters roam the forests and plains in search of bigger and better bucks, antlers will remain—*the stuff that dreams are made of.*

FIELD JUDGING AND TROPHY HUNTING

by William C. Shuster

Fifty yards away was a bowhunter's dream. In fact, there were five of them—big four-by-four muley bucks—busily feeding in the tall grass. I'd be happy with any one of them, but which one would score the highest? Would any of them make the record book? How could I tell? The bucks were slowly feeding my way, and I'd have to make a decision pretty quick.

Although many bowmen dream of taking a record-class buck, it's surprising the number of hunters who don't know what to look for when field judging big game. Granted, there are many people who don't really care; they'll hunt for a trophy until the first legal animal comes into range. If it happens to be a record book animal, so much the better. For these hunters, it probably isn't worth the trouble to study mounted heads and photos of trophy animals, or the records books. I have no problem with that, but then I don't have too much sympathy for them when they say, ". . . wish I'd get a chance to shoot a record book deer."

The cardinal rule for a trophy hunter is to *decide what a trophy is and settle for nothing else.* There are a few more rules to keep in mind further on, but this is the main one and by far the hardest to keep. If you do any trophy hunting at all, you'll soon have to come to grips with the fact that this means letting a lot of legal animals walk on by. Of course, the first time the rookie trophy hunter has to do this, all kinds of emotional and physical discomfort can be the result. It's a rude shock to the system for someone who has only seen a couple of record book animals ever.

I suppose just about everyone would like to get a record-class animal, but it takes a lot of dedication and self-control to hold out while that first animal walks by in easy bow range. Like those life/death situations where your life supposedly flashes in front of you, in panic, you reevaluate your decision to shoot only a trophy animal as that young bighorn walks by.

A typical scenerio might go, "I don't know if this ram will make the book, but he's the first one I've ever gotten close to. I may not get another chance! Did I set my goals too high? Should I shoot? I've got to decide quickly. He's going to be out of range!" If you don't think a decision like this is hard, then you've never had to make it before.

One thing that I do which helps to keep me from changing my mind is to tell my hunting buddies what my goals are. A word of warning, though, don't tell anyone unless you really mean it. Imagine the razzing you'll get coming into camp with a spike buck the day after telling your buddies how you're going to hold out for a record book candidate. A little peer pressure, and encouragement, can go a long way toward strengthening your resolve in your quest for a trophy.

Now, there's absolutely nothing wrong with a hunter deciding just to hunt fairly and take whatever comes along. The same goes for the hunter who decides only to take a buck and let the does go by, or the hunter who will only shoot a six-point bull or better. All of these goals are honorable, and when accomplished fairly, the hunter can take great satisfaction in the endeavor. A trophy to one person may not be one to anyone else. Of course, that's the way it should be. However, there is significant difference in some definitions of a trophy, and what it takes to be a record-class animal.

In my opinion, a trophy animal is one significantly larger than what an average hunter takes. Being a bowhunter, I set my standards at the Pope and Young Club minimum scores. I'm not saying this is right or wrong—these are merely my standards. Each person can form their own idea of a trophy.

Once you have decided what a trophy is, you should start doing your homework and find out where your best bets of taking that trophy are. This book is the best place to start. Some areas consistently produce big animals year after year. This is usually because of a combination of genetics in the herd, the quality of the habitat, and the game management program for the area. Winter range conditions can also contribute to the trophy potential of an area.

A person hunting in these spots will stand a greater chance of getting a trophy simply because there is a greater proportion of big animals in the area. By studying this book, you can start to identify these hot spots. A list of the top counties won't tell you the whole story, however. There are several excellent areas for each big game species that are just now being discovered, while other areas are cooling off—perhaps because of a series of harsh winters or major changes in land-use policies in the area.

Take for example, mule deer. According to the record book, Colorado seems to be the best state, while New Mexico is tenth on the list of entries. *Apparently,* New Mexico is not that hot a

spot to hunt. If you look in the Boone and Crockett record book, however, you'll find New Mexico is second for rifle records. In addition, the place where the vast majority of these huge deer came from, the northwest section of the state, only has two Pope and Young heads listed. Bowhunters just haven't discovered this area yet, or very few of them bother to hunt it, or the buster bucks aren't in that area during the bow season. Research is the only way you'll be able to find out the real reason.

Once you've decided on a certain area to hunt, a letter to the local Game and Fish Department would be in order. You need to know the present status of the herds and, of course, the game regulations. Perhaps there's no bowhunting season in that area!

The next step involves scouting the area. As you well know, within a county there are the good hunting areas and the awful areas. Preseason scouting can let you concentrate on the good areas when the season begins and allow you to put in as much high quality hunting time as possible.

The last point in trophy hunting is that you will need to spend every spare minute you can *hunting.* Your odds become much better the more time you spend in the field. It may be easier and a whole lot more comfortable sitting in camp than plodding through the wet brush on a dreary day, but "you can't catch fish if your line ain't wet," as the old saying goes. This is when your dedication becomes important.

If you are trophy hunting, you'll find you will spend much more time hunting per animal taken. This is simply because it takes much more time to find and get within range of that "one-in-a-hundred" animal.

Field Judging

So what does it take to make the book, anyway? Obviously, that bull elk or buck deer isn't going to stand around and let you throw a tape on his antlers. How can you tell how big an animal is from several hundred yards away?

First of all, it takes an understanding of how an animal is measured and scored. Elsewhere in this book you'll find the scoring forms and brief instructions on how to score each species of North American big game. By studying those forms and the listings in this book, I've found patterns emerging for each species. These indicators can be used by a trophy hunter—provided the hunter has the opportunity and time—to help decide from a distance whether an animal will make the record book.

The rules change for each species, as does the scoring criteria. Knowing and understanding these "rules-of-thumb" will be a big help to field judging trophies.

TYPICAL MULE DEER

For those hunters used to looking at whitetails, a big muley buck's rack is an awesome sight. Indeed, an average-sized mule deer is substantially larger than an average whitetail. If this weren't the case, the twenty-point difference in the minimum scores for entry in the records couldn't be justified.

According to the records, only eight muley bucks with three points on either or both antlers have made the book. From this comes the first rule of hunting trophy muleys. *Unless extraordinarily tall or wide, a buck with a three-point side will most likely not make the recording minimum.*

Looking at another statistic from the records will show only thirty bucks had an inside spread of seventeen inches or less. And, there is only one of these in the top 240 heads listed in the 1981 edition of the Pope and Young records! The problem obviously is just how to determine this seventeen inches on a buck that is 100 yards or more away.

On an alert muley buck, the distance from ear-tip to ear-tip is normally about 18 to 22 inches. Now this width will vary, depending on whether the buck has his ears cupped forward, laid back, or laying relaxed and nearly flat. Try to get a look at the ear spread, and compare this distance to the inside spread of the main beams. *The inside spread of the main beams should equal, or extend beyond the tips of*

Photo by William C. Shuster

With an inside spread of around 19 inches, four well-matched long points, and average mass, this mule deer buck will easily make the Pope and Young minimum.

This old buck has well-developed, symmetrical points and what appears to be a good spread—certain book material. But you'd better hurry. His ears indicate he's detected you.

the buck's ears when the ears are in the alert position. This will ensure the buck has enough spread to help the scoring.

A record-class mule deer rack must also have enough "height" to score well. This quality actually is the length of the major points on the head, particularly the second typical point that forms the back fork. This will be the hardest criteria to judge. The reason for this is that some mule deer main beams are almost lyre-shaped, swinging out and up high, instead of the typical forward sweep with a more modest rise. These bucks will have a very high-looking rack, but the points may actually be short. Bucks with this kind of headgear will sometimes score quite a bit lower than a hunter might at first guess.

For the typical shaped racks, *the "height" of the antlers should equal or exceed one-half of the inside spread.* Make this comparison with the back fork of the antlers from its junction with the main beam to the longest point tip of the fork. In many cases, this will be readily apparent.

If this comparison is a "close call," the buck should have other attributes that will help the scoring, or you might want to consider passing him up.

If the points, particularly the main beams, do not have this "height," you may end up with a deduction because inside spread will be more than the length of the main beam. Inside Spread Credit cannot exceed the length of the longest main beam. Bucks that have this deduction typically look very wide in relation to the height of their rack. On a borderline buck, this could be the difference in making the minimum score for entry.

Rule Four is *don't make a big deal over massiveness when sizing up a mule deer.* Mass will not make up for the lack of point length or spread and therefore is a relatively low priority. Most muleys that have grown big enough to be record book candidates by the other criteria will usually have adequate circumference measurements; but, don't count on mass to help borderline bucks. Also, be especially careful when the bucks are in velvet. All antler dimensions are exaggerated by the fuzzy membrane.

TYPICAL WHITETAIL DEER

As with mule deer, inside spread is very important on whitetails. Fewer than 5 percent of the typical entries have an inside spread of fifteen inches or less. *The inside spread of the main beams should equal or extend beyond the tips of the buck's ears when the ears are in the alert position.* This will insure the inside spread is better than fifteen inches.

The current record book shows only three three-by-four bucks and no three-by-three bucks have made the listings. This fact is the basis for my second rule. *A whitetail must have at least four points on each antler to make the book.*

The needed length of the points varies according to the inside spread and number of points the buck has. A ten-point need not have points as long as an eight-point will require. As

a general rule, however, *the buck must have at least two points on each antler that are six inches or longer.* A whitetail's ears are about six inches long, providing a ready-made gauge for determining the length of the points.

As with mule deer, adequate mass is usually present on whitetail bucks that have the other characteristics necessary to meet the minimum score.

YELLOWSTONE ELK

The first thing to consider when trying to field judge elk is to count the number of points on each antler. The record book shows quite clearly a bull must be at least a five-by-five to make the book. As it is, only twelve bulls that were five-by-five managed to make the new minimum score of 260. Therefore, Rule Number One is easy to formulate; *the bull must have at least five points on each antler.*

When trying to count points on an elk, you will often have trouble distinguishing the brow

Photo by William C. Shuster

Even in this early stage of development, the rack on this whitetail shows excellent record book potential.

Excellent main beam and point lengths, plus good spread and symmetry make this 6 x 6 bull a real dandy. He'll probably score near 340.

tines and bez tines from each other. These first two points on each side are often mirror images of each other and side views can be very confusing. One neat trick I've learned is to ignore these points and count back from the sword point on each antler. The sword point is always the fourth typical point and is usually the longest point. Count back from the fourth point and you can determine the number of points very quickly.

Elk are given credit for inside spread, as with mule deer and whitetails. Elk very seldom incur deductions due to having too wide a spread. Only thirteen elk in the book show any deductions due to spread, and the greatest deduction is only 4⅜ inches. This is rather insignificant on an animal scoring 300 points.

In analyzing the records, it was apparent that *a bull must have an inside spread of thirty inches or more to make the book.* The narrowest

spread in the book is 26⅝ inches. An average mature bull is about twenty-two inches across at the shoulders, so if you can mentally add four inches to the outside of each shoulder, you can use that as a guide.

The third criteria to look for is length of antlers. The shortest main beam listed in the 1981 book is 32⅝ inches. A good rule of thumb would be to look for a bull with antlers at least a yard long. When viewing an elk of this size walking broadside, you will see the tips of his antlers reaching to the end of his rib cage. When he is grazing and his head is down, the antler tips will be level to the top of the shoulder.

Elk rarely have abnormal or freak points. These abnormal points will subtract from the total score, but I wouldn't worry too much about them. Elk seem to have fewer deductions due to abnormal points than any other antlered big game species.

BLACK BEAR

This species is one of the most difficult animals to judge. Bears, like mountain lions, are scored by the combined measurements of the length and width of the skull. The problem is determining if a bruin's head is big enough. A bear's skull continues to grow throughout the animal's life. Consequently, the older a bear is, the better the chances it will be of record class. Now, aging live black bears is remarkably hazardous. Therefore, I've developed a few rules a hunter can use in sizing up a bear at a safe distance.

Young bears seem to have dog-like features; these are a long snout and prominent, pointed ears with little distance between them. These youngsters also seem to be "all legs," with plenty of space between their belly and the ground. Their lanky appearance and seemingly ungainly stride are other indicators of immaturity. Females will re-

tain the doggy look longer, sometimes throughout their lives. Very few females will qualify for Pope and Young listing and serious bowhunters will usually pass on them.

Male bears develop the classical "bruin-look" at about 3½ years of age. Full-bodied, blocky, muscular, these are the bears most likely to make the book. Their ears will appear smaller and come from the side of the head instead of standing straight up; their snout is broader, reflecting maturity. Older adult bears also seem to move in a more deliberate, measured gait, with big males appearing a bit pigeon-toed and bowlegged in the front.

If the bear's shoulders and chest look large, but the rear end seems too small for the body, then he's probably a candidate for the record book. In late spring and early summer, this physical characteristic can be exaggerated by the shedding of winter hair, so some care must

Photo by William C. Shuster

Recently out of hibernation, this black bear is feeding on grasses and has a fine pelt. His general physique and heavy head make him a definite record book candidate.

be used in applying this rule. However, the good part of this rule is that it doesn't depend on the hunter having to accurately judge size or weight of the bear.

Many inexperienced bear hunters talk about 500-pound bears. The simple fact is that 500-pound bear are few and far between; and, in the springtime, they are practically nonexistent.

Trophy-class black bears will stand 30 to 36 inches at the shoulders and measure five feet or more from their nose to their stubby tail. Weights can vary all over the place, with the average for a mature male somewhere near 200 to 225 pounds in the spring. Sows will average about 25 to 30 percent less. Bears are very deceptive to judge, and when it starts to get dark, *they all look huge!*

Quite often a hunter set up over bait will get a chance to examine bear sign long before he ever sees a bear. Tracks are good indicators, but again, they are no guarantee of an animal's size. There are lots of small bears with big feet, just as there are plenty of small-footed "busters" prowling the woods. Wildlife researchers have studied foot size to weight and found width of the front foot to have the strongest correlation to body size. *A trophy bear will have at least a five-inch-wide front pad.*

I used to use the hind tracks as an indicator for sizing up a bruin but not anymore. One spring, I watched a small bear come to my bait, leaving nine-inch hind tracks in the snow. A friend of mine later shot that bear, and she weighed 150 pounds—at most—and only scored seventeen. She made big hind tracks, but her front pad was barely 4½ inches across!

PRONGHORN ANTELOPE

There are three main considerations in judging an antelope: length of horn, massiveness, and the size and location of the prong. Unlike the antlered species, spread credit isn't added to an antelope's score. More on this later.

When sizing up the length of a buck's horns, I use the ears as a point of reference. Ear length is usually 5½ to 6 inches. The shortest horn length in the record book is 10⅛ inches, so the horn must be at least double the length of the ears. Keep in mind the length of the horn is measured along the outer curve from the tip to

Photo by William C. Shuster

At first glance, this buck appears to be rather short-horned. However, when you consider the "hook," the horns are more than adequate in length. The buck scored 67⅞.

the lowest edge of the base. The length includes the curve at the tip. The horn does not have to be twice as high as the ears, just twice as long.

Massiveness is the second point to consider when sizing up an antelope. This will be the hardest measurement to determine in the field. If you look at the scoring form, you will note circumference (massiveness) is measured at four places on each horn. The score of these four measurements is often one-half of the total score for a pronghorn. You will need to view the buck from the side as the horns are laterally compressed and the front views will not show you much. Again, compare the horn with the ears. *When viewed from the side, the base of each horn should be nearly as wide as the width of the ear at its widest point.*

If the base is thick enough, then usually the other three measurements will be sufficient. The one thing to watch out for, however, is when the prong is very low on the horn. When this happens, the second circumference will be made immediately below the swelling and the third will be well above the prong. This third measurement can end up being relatively small as the horn tapers quickly after the prong. Therefore, a high prong location is desirable.

To be sure the prong is high enough, consider the third rule: *The top of the prong should be higher than the tip of the ears.*

Prong length is the next point to consider. You need a prong at least four inches long to score well. A prong of this length will look well developed and not just look like a knob. This is the fourth rule: *The prong should extend at least two inches beyond the front edge of the horn.*

The final thing to look for is to be sure the horns do not have too great a spread. Note: Inside spread is not added to your score. In fact, if the spread exceeds the length of the longer horn, the difference will be deducted. If the horns spread out at an angle of 90 degrees or greater, you will probably have some subtraction. On an animal which scores in the 60s or 70s, this can be devastating. Therefore, the serious trophy hunter should pay particular attention to horn symmetry and configuration on pronghorns.

Selective hunting for record-class animals is not for every bowhunter, just as bowhunting isn't the right pastime for every hunter. The reward-to-effort ratio is mighty low for the serious trophy hunter; but, when it all works right, the personal satisfaction of tagging that sought-after specimen is all the recompense you'll ever want.

Proper Shot Placement

by Bill Krenz

Bowhunting carries with it a weighty set of responsibilities. One of the heaviest of these is the outright obligation to take only those shots that will result in the precise placement of every arrow. A single *razor sharp* broadhead attached to a modern hunting arrow—*when properly placed*—will bring down the largest and hardiest of big game animals with remarkable speed and effectiveness. For the bowhunter, nearly everything depends on proper shot placement.

Bowhunters have practiced and hunted for years with the words "pick a spot" as their shooting catchphrase. Without a doubt, picking a single, tiny aiming spot—really trying to split a hair—is extremely important. This is a point that can't be overemphasized. If you fail to pick a spot, you'll probably miss the whole animal or worse, hit it in the wrong place.

Picking a spot is a means of improving your bowhunting accuracy. *But simply picking a spot is not necessarily the same thing as proper shot placement.* Actually, in the mind of the bowhunter, proper shot placement considerations must come before thoughts on choosing an aiming spot. It's proper shot placement fundamentals that determines just exactly where the precise and correct aiming spot lies.

Proper shot placement is the attempt by the bowhunter to preselect the path of the arrow as it strikes cleanly and quickly through the game animal. Proper shot placement allows the *sharp* broadhead to sever a maximum of vital organs, vessels, and tissues. The result is the efficient and speedy dispatch of the game animal and a short, easy-to-follow recovery trail.

Except in the rare instances of a brain or spinal cord hit, a modern hunting arrow kills by hemorrhage. The *razor sharp* broadhead induces such massive hemorrhage that the animal's blood pressure drops rapidly; the wound bleeds so freely that the blood isn't able to coagulate and the lungs fail to receive sufficient lifeblood to supply oxygen to the brain. The real key to such rapid and efficient bowhunting results is placing that arrow in the right spot. To that end, all serious bowhunters should find themselves deeply concerned with all facets of correct shot placement on big game animals.

The preliminary steps toward fully understanding precisely *where* to pick that spot begins with a comprehensive knowledge of the internal anatomy of big game animals. The emphasis should be placed on the location and function of all especially vital organs. By far the largest concentration of vital internal organs lies within

Internal Anatomy

Whitetail Deer

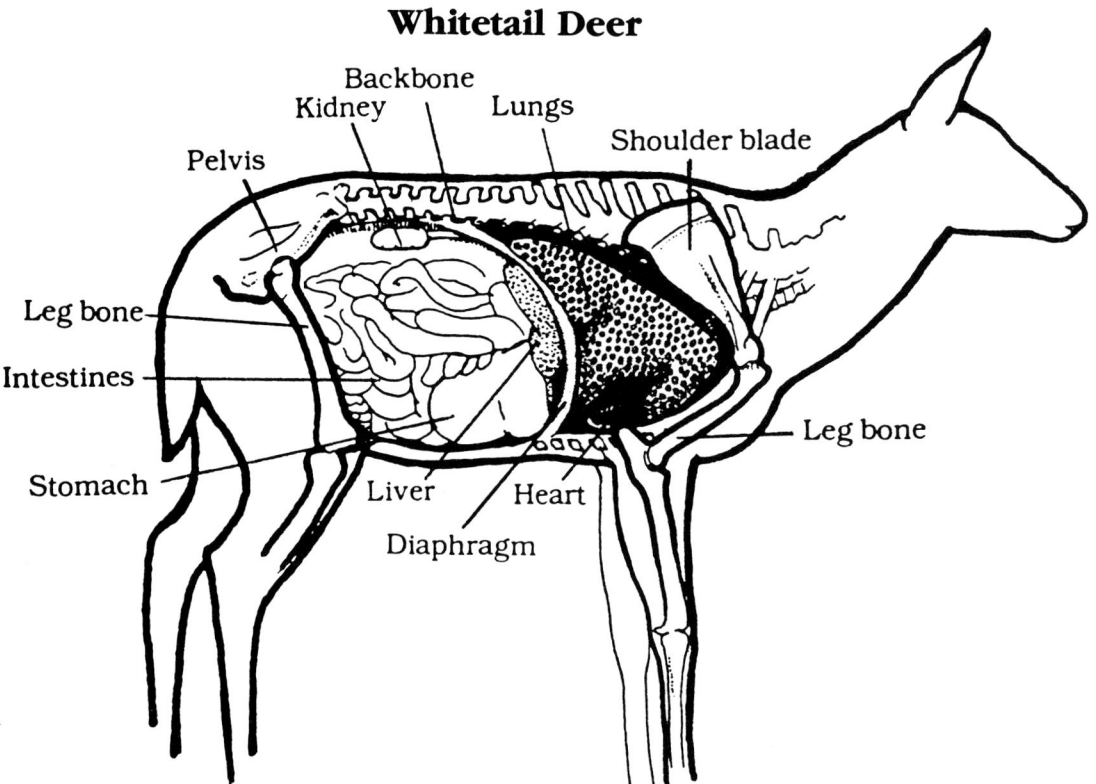

Black Bear

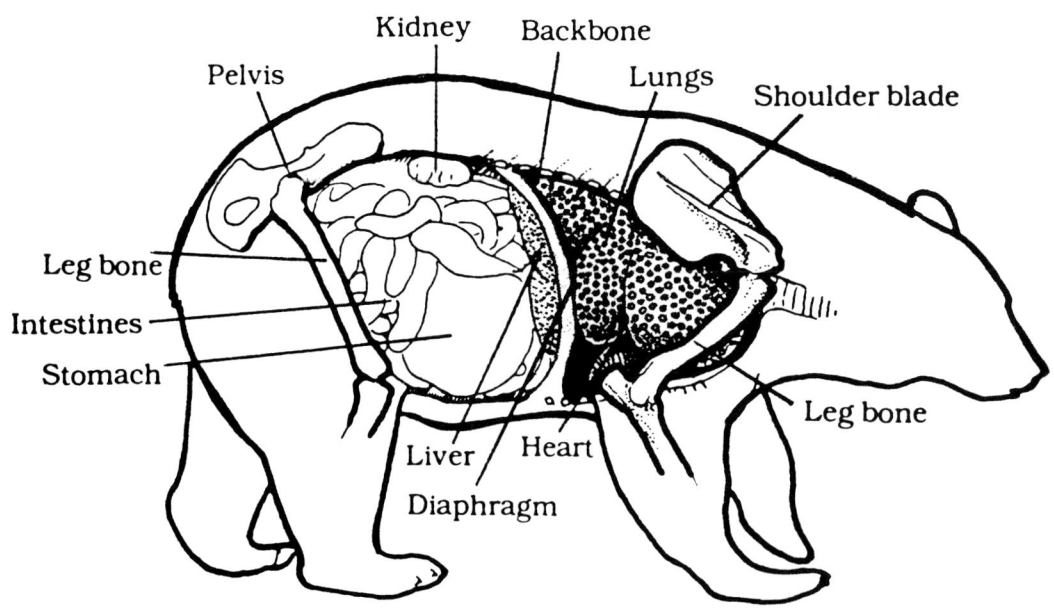

Courtesy of National Bowhunter Education Foundation

A detailed study of the internal anatomy of big game animals is crucial to knowing where to "pick that spot."

the animal's chest cavity. For that reason it is to the chest area, and specifically the heart, lungs, and liver, the bowhunter looks to "pick that spot."

Located low and forward in the animal's chest cavity sits the heart. In the case of a deer, the heart is approximately the size of a man's fist. The heart serves as the muscular pump for the entire blood circulatory system. To be sure, an arrow shot to the heart is extremely effective in downing any animal. The circulatory pump is closed down, blood pressure drops alarmingly and blood-loss shock is transmitted throughout the entire body.

However, as deadly as a heart shot may be, the heart all by itself is quite a small target. It must be remembered that proper shot placement is the attempt to preselect the *very best* path for the arrow. The heart is good shot placement, but maybe not the very best shot placement. In addition to being relatively small, the heart is located so that a shot just slightly forward or barely low will result in either a little-damaging, nonfatal hit, or a complete miss. That leaves precious little room for error. Sometimes, heart-shot big game can leave a meager recovery trail. With the heart pump shut down, blood pressure drops so rapidly that most bleeding occurs internally. Most times, however, the entry and exit wounds are low enough in the chest walls to allow for an adequate blood trail.

Located just behind the chest cavity, snug against the diaphragm, a bit above center and immediately in front of the paunch or stomach area, is the liver. Like the heart, the liver is a major, vital, internal organ of prime interest to the bowhunter. The liver's function is one of filtration for the animal's complete blood supply. A *sharp* broadhead through the liver is quickly fatal and usually results in an excellent recovery trail. But, also like the heart, the liver leaves something to be desired as an ideal intended point of aim. While larger than the heart, the liver still leaves little room for shooting error.

Courtesy of National Bowhunter Education Foundation

Choosing when to shoot is almost as important as picking the right aiming spot. Obstructions can easily turn a perfect shot into a disasterous hit.

From the diagrams it can be seen that even a slight miss toward either of three directions spells disaster. There are better spots to aim for than the liver.

In the approximate center of the chest cavity, side by side, lie the lungs—two of them. Each lung consists of a light, spongy tissue containing millions of minute blood vessels. As the animal breathes in air and fills the bellows-like lungs, oxygen is taken from the air and transferred to the blood through the tiny cellular sponges. Then the newly oxygen-charged blood is pumped to all parts of the body through the arterial circulatory system. The body uses the vital oxygen and returns the depleted blood through the veinous circulatory system to again be recharged by the lungs.

Years of big game bowhunting experiences has shown me that the most consistently effective and most desired predetermined shot placement is one in which a single, *razor sharp* broadhead passes directly through *BOTH* lungs. No other single type of shot placement seems as consistently deadly. Even the biggest of animals neither lives long nor travels far when both lungs are hit. In most cases, even the hardiest of trophies is down within seconds.

The amazing effectiveness of the double-lung shot is easily explained. With such a shot, massive hemorrhage occurs within each lung and speedy failure of the overall blood circulatory system ensues. In addition, bilateral pneumothorax—entrance of air into the thoracic cavity—causes the collapse of the lungs and the immediate failure of the respiratory system as well. With a single, carefully placed shot, both vital systems are knocked out and the animal is downed with remarkable speed and efficiency.

As the ideal choice for proper shot placement, the lungs also have other hidden advantages. In addition to simply being the largest in size of the vital organs, the lungs are conveniently surrounded by other vital organs. Below the lungs lies the heart; to the rear sits the liver;

Courtesy of National Bowhunter Education Foundation

Shots at moving animals, regardless of angle, are always risky and should be passed up in favor of a stationary animal.

and, directly above rests the spinal cord and the spinal (aortic) artery. With the lungs as a selected target, some shooting error may be forgiven as the other vital organs take up the slack. Blood trails resulting from double-lung hits are also generally excellent and easily followed.

But a complete understanding of proper shot placement must progress even beyond vital organ location and function. The bowhunter need also be fully aware of the effects of varying shot angles and the animal's body postures and positions.

With an animal standing perfectly broadside to the hunter, a shot angle of 90 degrees is presented. This is the ideal shot placement angle for the bowhunter. At this position and angle, shot placement becomes a simple matter of directing the arrow straight through the approximate center of the chest cavity. On basically all big game this is represented on the outside of the animal by an aiming spot nearly halfway between the bottom of the chest and the back line and about one hand's width behind the hollow of the shoulder. Such a broadside, chest-centered arrow drives cleanly through both lungs and encounters little resistance.

But what happens when the animal is not at a perfect broadside shooting angle to the hunter? Again, refer to the diagrams. Note that as the shooting angle increases or decreases, shot placement problems develop. As the angle changes—the animal is increasingly quartering toward or quartering away from the hunter—it becomes increasingly more difficult and eventually impossible for a single arrow to pass solidly through both lungs. Herein lies an excellent key for guiding all bowhunters to positioning their shot correctly and effectively. When the shooting angle becomes such that a single arrow cannot be expected to pass solidly through both lungs, the shot should probably be passed up in favor of an opportunity at a more desirable angle.

This is not to say that a perfectly broadside shot is the only one to be taken. A slight amount of angling away by the animal, and even a bit of angling toward the hunter, is often acceptable. In these cases, the bowhunter must, however, ask himself or herself whether the arrow can be angled through both lungs. If the answer is no, it may be wise to wait for a better shot angle.

Courtesy of National Bowhunter Education Foundation

Shooting from elevated stands presents the bowhunter with a whole new set of varying shooting angles. Knowledge of animal anatomy from all angles and perspectives is your responsibility.

Many seasoned bowhunters find it helpful when shooting to mentally picture the lungs as two slightly flattened, water-filled balloons lying side by side in the center of the chest cavity. In a large deer each "balloon" would appear about the size and shape of a football in the placekick position. The objective is to burst both "balloons" with a single arrow. It's quickly apparent that only certain, rather shallow shot angles will indeed provide that both "balloons," and not just one, will be broken. Balloons or lungs, whitetail deer or Alaska brown bear, the shot placement principle is the same.

And, there are additional shot angle problems. As the shooting angle changes, the bowhunter must also consider, along with the problem of hitting both lungs, the problem of skeletal obstructions to arrow penetration. As the shooting angle decreases, such as it does when the animal pivots toward the archer, heavy front leg and shoulder bones can quite effectively block arrows aimed to angle back into the chest cavity. Hard quartering-to-the-hunter shot angles are rarely advisable. On some quartering-away animals, where the shot angle increases, somewhat less of a potential penetration problem usually exists.

However, in all angling away bowhunting shots, rib bones are now presented in such a manner that some arrow deflection may occur and increased amounts of tissue must be penetrated before the chest cavity is reached by the arrow. This is the case on all big game, but becomes particularly important with extremely large animals like elk or moose. As a general rule, a slight amount of angling away is acceptable, but drastic angling away shots are as unadvisable as all but the slightest of quartering-to shots. Of course, at all times the bowhunter must continue to ponder whether the arrow will angle solidly through both lungs. Above all else, this is the primary key for proper shot placement.

To this point, the shot angles discussed have all been horizontal angles—the game angles toward or away from the hunter standing on approximately the same horizontal level. But much of today's bowhunting is done from elevated stands of one sort or another. When a bowhunter climbs up to an elevated shooting position, quite suddenly another set of varying shooting angles emerges. These new angles are vertical angles and must be considered right along with the regular horizontal shooting angles for proper shot placement.

As the bowhunter climbs further off the ground, the resulting "vertical shooting angle" down to the game steepens. The further a bowhunter climbs off the ground, the greater the vertical shooting angle becomes; and, the problem of placing the arrow becomes more acute. See the diagram. It is quite obvious that relatively high tree stand placement causes the most problems. From a tree stand, or any other high stand such as a windmill or whatever, it becomes increasingly difficult to shoot an arrow that will

angle solidly through both lungs. In this sense, elevated stand placement can become a preliminary part of correct shot placement. A relatively high stand may be wonderful for getting your scent, sight, and sound above the game hunted, but is proper shot positioning still possible?

In most cases a stand height in which the bowhunter's feet are eight to fifteen feet off the ground is reasonable. More than that may cause some shooting angle problems.

Probably no other situation better illustrates the vertical shot placement point than does the one in which black bears are hunted from tree stands. Black bears can be tenacious customers when less than perfect shot placement is adhered to. In typical dense black bear cover, unless the shot placement is perfect, recovery trailing can be extremely difficult. Perfect shot placement is a double-lung hit with a *razor sharp* broadhead; and, that is best made possible with a relatively low tree stand. With such a hit even the ruggedest bear rarely travels farther than a few dozen yards and is downed within seconds. Proper shot placement, aided by careful stand selection, is the ultimate tip for quick and easy game recovery.

Shot placement holds more than just an interesting study for all bowhunters. Without a doubt, proper shot placement is the single most important factor in hunting arrow performance. A single, properly placed hunting arrow will down the toughest trophy with amazing efficiency and remarkable speed.

In 1923, at the dawn of modern bowhunting, Saxton Pope wrote of himself and Art Young, "It is surprising even to us to see the extreme facility with which an arrow can interrupt the essential physical processes of life and destroy it. We have come to the belief that no beast is too tough or too large to be slain by an arrow."

Proper shot placement, coupled with *razor sharp broadheads:* If it isn't everything in bowhunting, it's as close as one single thing can come. As such, it is the ethical responsibility and obligation of every bowhunter to fully understand its principles and stringently adhere to them in the field.

MAKE YOUR HUNT LAST A LIFETIME

by Judd Cooney

Nothing raises my hackles more than to be visiting a fellow bowhunter and have him or her hand me a thick stack of three-by-five prints of their last bowhunt, only to find nothing in the photos but a trophy buck or bear or whatever laying on the tailgate of a pickup with its tongue sticking out and blood all over its muzzle. For variety, to go with the rear of the pickup and the miserable looking trophy, they may have a fuzzy shot or two of themselves holding up the head so that you can get a good look at the other side of the bloody face and a better view of the lolling tongue.

What a great way to show off the trophy of a lifetime, impress your bowhunting buddies and non-hunting friends, right? YUCK!!!

I've never been able to fathom why a bow-hunter will spend hundreds of dollars on the best archery tackle, invest hours and hours in learning how to use it properly, spend more money and time on scouting and getting prepared for the hunt, then spend virtually nothing in time or money to make the memories of that hunt last forever.

Good photography is certainly no deep dark secret known only to a few gifted people. With the proliferation of excellent camera equipment on the market today, taking good photographs is now easier to accomplish than ever before.

There is absolutely no reason a bowhunter can't return from a hunt with a set of photos that will provide many hours of enjoyment for friends and family through the ensuing years.

Fine pictures—like trophy bucks—generally don't just happen to fall into your lap. They take a minimal investment in dollars and cents and a substantial investment in time and planning; but not any more than you put into planning and carrying out a good bowhunt. Photography has an advantage over bowhunting in the sense that you will never come back from your hunt "skunked" on photos, if you carry through with your picture taking.

Most of the time a bowhunter doesn't take his camera out of his pack until he makes a kill. If he fails to get his trophy he has nothing to show for his time, effort, and money when he returns home. Your hunt might end without that trophy buck or bear. But with good photos, you will have all the elements of the hunt on film for you and others to enjoy.

The real key to coming home from a two-week bowhunt with some good photos is PLAN-NING. Sit down before your hunt and make a checklist of photos that you think will document your total hunt. By planning a photo "shot" list and carrying through on it with the camera, you will have a complete picture log of your trip

Photo by Judd Cooney

Like finding the right place for a tree stand, planning is the real key to coming home with good photographs of your hunt.

when you return. I can guarantee when you see the results you'll be darn glad you took the time and effort.

If you are going with a group of bow-hunters, the best bet might be to single out one of your party to shoot the basic photos for the whole group, then have each individual add their own shots for the final trip photo story. Regardless of who or how many of you take photos, sit down and make up a list of pictures you think will be needed for complete coverage of your hunt. Your photos should tell the entire story of your hunt from the time you start planning it at home until you return with your trophy and take it to the taxidermist. A good set of photos will need very little narrative to capture and hold the attention of your audience, whether it's your local bowhunting club or the neighborhood kids wanting to hear about your bowhunting trip.

A typical shot list I would make up for a bowhunting trip would look something like the following, but I would be making additions as I went and not limit myself to shooting just what was on the list. It's a lot better to shoot too many photos, then weed out the bad and un-needed ones, than to get home and find that you don't have all the photos you really wanted.

BOWHUNT PHOTO LIST
- Studying maps at home and hunt planning
- Fletching arrows, preparing equipment
- Packing gear, loading vehicles
- Driving away or loading the plane
- Scenery shots while traveling to and around hunting area
- Arrival at camp, greeting guides, cabins, general area
- Camp scenes, around the campfire, inside lodge, cooking, fixing bed, etc.
- Setting up equipment, bows, sharpening broadheads, arranging daypack
- Practice shooting at camp or backyard
- Checking area for game signs—scrapes, rubs, wallows, waterholes, etc.
- Putting up tree stands, setting baits, digging pits, etc.
- Putting on camo gear, face paint, scent pads
- General shots in hunting area
- Getting set in blind, pit, etc.
- Glassing area for game, drawing bow from stand, other bowhunting action shots
- General animal or game shots from stand or blind
- Bloodtrailing, blood trail, tracks, etc.
- Trophy shots of game taken
- Packing game out, backpacking, etc.
- Success photos with you, hunting partner, guide, etc.
- Preparing trophy in camp, caping, skinning, butchering
- Breaking camp, loading truck or plane
- Driving out
- General return trip shots, loaded truck, etc.
- Taking trophy to taxidermist
- Mounted head or rug

This is just a partial list to give you some idea of the photos needed to make a complete picture story of your bowhunt. I try to make a list of photos needed on all of my outings so that I don't forget something and leave gaps in the story. Many of the shots will stay the same from trip to trip with only fill-in shots needed to establish the time and place of your hunt.

A good photo record of your trip does not require that you spend thousands of dollars on the finest camera gear such as the pros use. Today's market is loaded with simple, yet adequate cameras that with a modest investment will fill the bill for most of you. The automatic exposure cameras, like the instamatics, disk film type and such, will do an adequate job but there are better choices. Photography is much like bowhunting in that the better equipment you have, the higher degree of proficiency you can attain with it.

Photo by Judd Cooney

A complete picture story of a hunt includes more than just trophy photos. Make a photo "shots" list and carry through on it with your camera.

A book could be written on the proper camera gear for your field ventures, but the most important part of getting good photo coverage of your hunts is a thorough working knowledge of your equipment whatever it is. Learn to get the very best out of the camera gear you have or can afford. As you learn more, you can upgrade your equipment as you see fit.

Almost all of your photography can be done with any camera on the market today. However, to get results that will be worth the effort there are a few things to know about film and cameras. First off, you should stay with the 35mm film format. In my opinion, the half-frame, 110 film formats, and the new highly advertised disc-type camera systems are a waste of your valuable time and money. Stick with a 35mm SLR and your results will be much better and far more useable.

Another recommendation I will make—that some won't agree with—is to shoot color transparencies (slide film) instead of color print film. Color prints and negatives are much more expensive to have processed. Rather than getting thirty-six prints where about thirty of them are "throwaways"—that you have paid good money for—shoot slide film. After the slides are processed, screen them with a slide viewer or by running them through a projector. Weed out the junk, and have only the better pictures made into prints. Only your best photos will then be viewed by your friends, and you'll have saved money at the same time.

Most professional wildlife photographers depend on Kodak Kodachrome (ASA 64) transparency film for the bulk of their color work. This film produces excellent results in good daylight but leaves much to be desired in the poor light conditions that bowhunters usually encounter during much of their hunting. Kodak's Ektachrome 100, 200, and 400 are "faster" films and will render completely satisfactory results for most of your general picture taking. The higher ASA ratings of the Ektachrome films permit the use of faster shutter speeds, which will help to minimize the single greatest threat to photo sharpness—camera movement! These films can also be processed by most small color labs in your hometown, where Kodachrome must be sent to Kodak labs for processing. While this processing is by far the safest and best, it does take more time. And there is nothing worse than waiting a couple of weeks to see the results of your photo efforts.

There is one segment of your bowhunting adventures where decent pictures will be almost impossible to obtain with a fixed-lens camera, or even a normal 50mm lens on your trusty 35mm SLR; that is taking good photos of wildlife. Photographing critters in the wild is a very demanding field, requiring some pretty sophisticated equipment and the patience, knowledge, and ability to utilize it.

No doubt most of you at one time or another have been shown a photograph with a little brownish spot in the center and had to be told what a huge old bull or buck it was. It could have been your photo, and you were trying to convince the viewer that it *really* was a bull elk in the picture and not the blurry image of a ant! It's a hell of a lot tougher to get a GOOD photograph of an antelope buck, bull elk, or black bear than it is to simply arrow one and have it mounted. It is not impossible or even improbable, to get good photos of the game animals and birds you hunt. But it will require different equipment than I've covered to this point, and a whole lot more effort on your part. One thing's for certain, learning to get good wildlife photos is darn sure going to make you a better bowhunter.

Equipment-wise, you are going to need a good 35mm camera with interchangeable lenses so you can add a telephoto to your equipment list. If I had to choose one lens for wildlife it would be a high quality 300mm lens. With its six-power magnification, this lens is powerful enough for most wildlife photography, if you get within bow range. A 300mm lens can be hand held if you work at squeezing off your shots with the same gentle release you use for turning your arrow loose. Keep in mind, however, that the slightest wiggle in the camera will be amplified six times on the film. A steady rest and gentle shutter finger will be necessary for sharp photo results.

One factor that really makes photographing an animal a lot tougher proposition than simply bowhunting one is that you have to work with

Photo by Judd Cooney

A moment like this can be vividly re-lived, if you capture it on film. Most bowhunters don't use their camera near enough on a hunt.

the available daylight and make it work for you. The best times for bowhunting—early morning and late evening—are the worst light conditions for good photography. Trying to work the wind and light conditions both to your advantage really adds a whole new dimension to your hunting but one that is ultimately rewarding when you succeed.

Many excellent books covering general photography and wildlife photography are available on bookstore shelves. I can assure you from my own experience that the time spent in studying all that is written about this intriguing game is going to pay you back a thousand times over during your outings.

For the bowhunter, and gun-hunter alike, there are stringent bag limits and season dates. You can't hunt in national parks or refuges and many farms and ranches harboring some trophy game animals simply are not open to hunting. With a camera and a little knowledge, there are

Photo by Judd Cooney

Although a fine bowhunting trophy, the focus here is on a very special moment shared by a father and his daughter. The memories will last a lifetime.

no closed seasons, no bag limits, and all the national parks and refuges are open. With some finesse and friendliness, you might even find yourself photographing trophy critters on private lands closed to all other hunting.

The thrill and excitement of stalking and capturing that record book buck on film will equal getting him with an arrow, I can assure you. With a camera in hand, your preseason scouting will take on a whole new dimension because you just might come back with a trophy or two on film that will show your bowhunting friends what's really out in the woods. By getting good equipment, and taking the time to learn how to use it, you can soon be adding some good wildlife shots to your photo album and slide programs, plus a whole new outlook on your bowhunting.

In my estimation, one of the most abused segments of the usual bowhunter photo story, and one of the most important, is the trophy photos. I have seen some really gross photos of

bowkills; pictures that offend me, and I am completely on the bowhunting side of the fence! Imagine what pictures like that do to women and kids as well as anti-hunters. There is absolutely no reason—or sense—in taking a photo of a dead animal that is offensive to anyone.

When you set up for a trophy photo, try to get the photo as soon after the kill as possible and in a natural setting. Take the time to clean the animal up. Remove as much blood and dirt, *and above all*, get the arrow out of the animal. Move the animal around until it looks as natural as possible and try to show the animal with as much dignity and respect as you can. If possible, try to get a "catch-light" in the animal's eyes. This is a little glint of light that is very important in any wildlife photograph. It gives the critter a live look and is a must in almost all good wildlife photos, whether the animal is dead or alive. Wiping the eye with a handkerchief and then adding a dab of saliva or water will restore the glisten and do wonders for your trophy pictures.

Photo by Judd Cooney

Wildlife photography will require telephoto lenses and the knowledge, patience, and ability to use them. Making a good photograph of a trophy on the hoof is a lot tougher than just getting to within bow range for a shot.

Make sure the tongue is not hanging out! Either tuck it into the mouth or amputate it on the spot.

To me, the worst trophy photo possible is one of God's beautiful creatures crammed in the back of a pickup with its head hanging over the tailgate, tongue hanging out, and a proud hunter sitting on top of it. Showing this type of photo to as many people as possible is probably the best way I can think of to help the anti-hunting fraternity.

Try to show the animal with the same respect and dignity that you gave it in life and you will be just as proud showing your trophy photos to friends and acquaintances as you would the mounted head on the wall.

Good photos don't happen by accident. There is a tremendous difference between "taking" a photo and "making" a picture. To come home from a hunting trip with a set of photos that will tell the story of the whole adventure is going to require some expenditure in time, effort, and money, if you are going to do it right. But then you didn't take up bowhunting because it was the easiest way to hunt, did you?

With a camera in your hand and a little knowledge and perseverance, I can guarantee you won't ever come back from a bowhunt without something worthwhile to show for your trip. Who could ask for anything better than that?

ONE MISSTEP TO DANGER

by Mike Shane

Every year there are numerous accounts of hunting trips that end in tragedy. The news media usually describe the cause of death as "exposure." But the technical term is *hypothermia.* Hypothermia, which can commonly occur in air temperatures from 35 to 50 degrees Fahrenheit, is caused by losing body heat faster than it can be produced.

A few years ago, three bowhunters found themselves stranded on a vertical rock face without food or proper clothing. They were pursuing mountain goats and found, as many mountain bowhunters ultimately do, it is sometimes much easier to *climb up* than it is to *come down.* Often a route that is fairly easy to climb, is impossible to descend without sophisticated rock climbing gear.

These bowhunters had to spend the night on that rock face because they could not get off it without the assistance of a mountain rescue team. The daytime temperature had reached the mid-40s, but the nighttime temperature plummetted to 20 degrees. By rescue time the next morning, two of the cotton-clad bowhunters were suffering from mild hypothermia. The third was in much more serious condition.

It took the rescue team more than four hours just to stabilize the third victim so he could be moved to a hospital intensive care ward. Luckily, all three recovered from their ordeal.

Another incident that comes to mind are the experiences of Kelly and Larry.

It is just past noon. Kelly and Larry have completed setting up camp for their ten-day mountainous bowhunt for elk and whitetails. The blue, cloudless sky has warmed the landscape to a relatively balmy 50 degrees, and the timbered ridge above camp is beckoning. Skipping lunch, Larry grabs his bow and sets out dressed in a cotton camo shirt, jeans, and tennis shoes. His fanny pack, with survival gear, is left lying against the tent.

The climb to the ridgetop is physically demanding and perspiration floods Larry's cotton shirt. At ridgecrest a slight breeze shunts cold drafts through the wet shirt. But, all is forgotten as each turn of the binocular finger knob brings a magnificent whitetail buck into sharper focus; 150, or maybe, a 160-incher! Oblivious to the cold breeze, Larry plots his course to the buck and begins his stalk.

This buck is a veteran of the chase and is very wily; three ridges and four stalks later, Larry has yet to get within shooting range. The buck finally tires of the game and runs for distance.

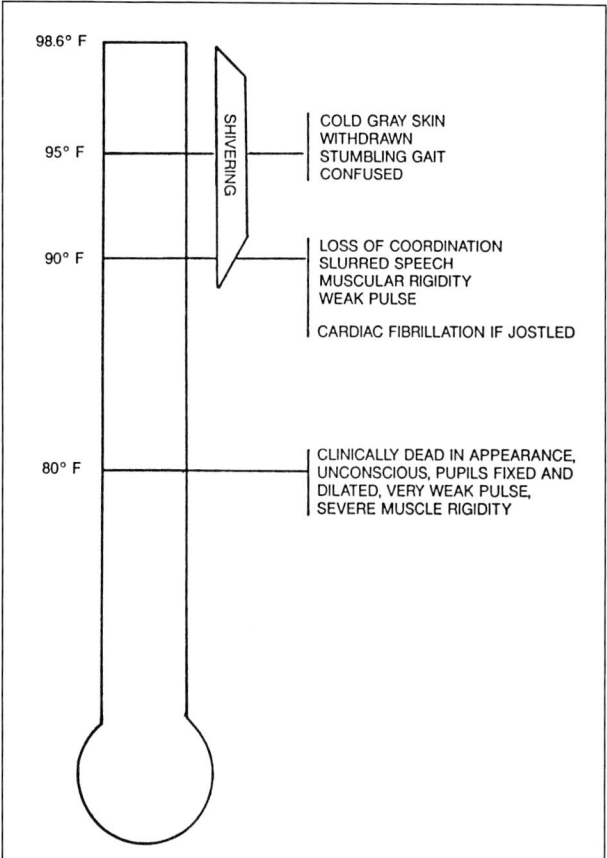

Body Core Temperature and the associated effects of Hypothermia.

Larry now finds himself some distance from camp and not entirely certain of its true direction. While pursuing the buck, Larry hadn't noticed the large thunderhead building on the horizon. The storm cloud rolls in, turning the sky black and filling the air with its splattering missiles. Larry runs for shelter under a large conifer, but the old evergreen finally succumbs to the watery torrent and he is soaked to the bone in an instant. Within minutes, our bowhunter has "goose bumps" and he starts to shiver.

An hour later, the shivering has become violent and Larry is questioning the direction he has chosen to hike. He begins moving faster until he finds himself frantically running through the timber, jumping logs, dodging between trees, and careening through brush. Finally, with great effort, his mind takes control of his erratic actions and he stops running.

What is happening? Where have all those years of experience and preparation gone?

Nerves in orbit as the adrenaline continues to flow, Larry breathes deeply in an effort to calm himself; the violent shivering continues to intensify. The danger of his dilemma begins to sink in.

It will be dark soon, the pleasant afternoon having turned into a raw struggle for survival. Larry begins walking again, retracing his path back to camp. His muscles are now stiffening, his gait stumbling and thoughts clouded. A warming sensation washes over him and Larry resists an incredibly strong urge to sleep.

Shortly, a noise rams through the shroud enveloping Larry's consciousness and his ears echo from the blasting of the auto horn. He is only slightly aware of the blinding lights in his face. Now, semiconscious, he follows his partner's instructions as he is carefully loaded into the truck. Larry has made it by the barest of margins.

Both of these near-tragedies could easily have been avoided. Although hypothermia gives little warning, the body's initial reactions to exposure are *"goose pimples" and uncontrollable shivering.*

Shivering is a reflex mechanism used by the body to produce heat. It becomes increasingly violent and unmanageable as the body's core temperature drops from a normal of 98.6 degrees Fahrenheit down to about 92 degrees Fahrenheit. However, the shivering steadily diminishes between 92 degrees and 88 degrees. At this point, shivering is replaced by muscle rigidity.

The general appearance of a hypothermic victim is pale, cold, usually grayish skin coloring. The pulse is generally slow and often irregular. It may be difficult to locate a pulse in the extremities because of blood vessel constriction. In this case, the best location for measuring the heart rate is on the neck near the angle of the jaw, at the carotid arteries.

Victims of hypothermia follow a fairly consistent pattern of mental and physical changes. Affected persons will drop out of conversation and appear discouraged or depressed. They will become uncoordinated with slow, labored movements; simple tasks such as fastening a button become difficult. They will be lethargic, confused, and sleepy. Some people may even become combative and refuse care. These conditions will continue to deteriorate if the body temperature drops below 90 degrees Fahrenheit. The heart and lungs start to falter, muscles become rigid, and unconsciousness may occur.

Treatment procedures in the field are critical to the victim's survival. When confronted with a hypothermic victim, the first consideration is to determine the extent of hypothermia present, mild or severe.

Body core temperatures above 92 degrees are characterized by violent shivering, loss of coordination, confusion, lethargy, and the inability to speak sensibly. Treatment is straightforward and simple; provide the victim with shelter from the elements and an external heat source.

Passive, slow warming seems to be the best approach. Remove wet clothing, dry the victim and re-dress with dry clothing; or, place the person in a sleeping bag. In more urgent cases, it may be necessary for you to get in the bag with them or huddle closely so the victim can benefit from your body heat. Keep them calm and quiet until they begin to show signs of improvement (usually thirty minutes to an hour). Warm liquids or food should not be given to a hypothermic person until the victim has stabilized. As soon as possible, get the victim to the nearest professional medical care.

Alcoholic beverages are *absolutely forbidden* for people in hypothermic distress. The old saw of "just a nip, to warm me bones" could in fact prove fatal for a victim of hypothermia. Alcohol dilates blood vessels, causing accelerated body heat loss.

Victims with body temperatures below 92 degrees are a different story altogether. As the core temperature falls, shivering is progressively replaced with muscle rigidity, weakening pulse,

Photo by Mike Shane

Going prepared with survival gear can prevent emergencies. The author's personal kit includes a fanny pack, hunting knife, pack-saw, plastic for shelter, water container, medications (if necessary), candles, matches, extra socks, extra gloves, trail food, lantern, nylon cord, first aid pack, web belting, and a space blanket; total weight less than six pounds.

total loss of coordination, and finally uncon-sciousness. Rescue attempts and field treatment must be made in such a manner as to minimize the amount of exertion by the victim. **This is very important.** Even small amounts of heat loss at this stage can trigger a fatal drop in core temperature.

Handle the victim very gently. **Do not jos-tle!** Rough movement can cause cardiac fibrilla-tion and death. Wet clothing should be removed immediately to permit rewarming to begin. If dry clothing is not available, wring out the wet clothes and put them back on the victim; damp clothing is better than no clothing in severe hypothermic cases.

This is no time for modesty. Wrap yourself with the victim in a space blanket, plastic, or some of your own garments to reduce further heat loss. It is imperative that the victim receive immediate professional medical attention; either get help to the victim, or transport the victim to the nearest emergency treatment. If you have to transport a person in hypothermic distress, do it very carefully and keep the victim still.

Of course the old axiom, "an ounce of pre-vention is worth a pound of cure," could never be more true than when applied to hypothermia. The best way to prevent hypothermia is to be prepared for cold and wet conditions when ven-turing afield, whether for half a day or several weeks. Subfreezing temperatures are not neces-sary for hypothermia to strike. Even in the late summer or early fall, a tired bowhunter exposed to wind and rain may develop hypothermic symptoms.

To prevent heat loss, protect yourself against not just cold, but also moisture and wind. Water—whether from rain, snow, or perspira-tion—draws heat away from the body many many times faster than air temperature. The wind has a marked effect on heat loss. If the temperature reads 40 degrees and the wind is blowing twenty miles per hour, the resultant exposure (windchill factor) is comparable to an air temperature of 18 degrees Fahrenheit.

Proper hunting clothes will offer insulation from cold, ventilation of perspiration, and pro-tection against wind, rain, or snow. Rather than one bulky garment, wear several layers of loose

clothing that will trap air, insulate, and provide adequate circulation and ventilation.

Wool, polyproplene, and polyester retain various warmth values even when wet; cotton and goose or duck down do not. Be sure the high heat loss areas such as the head and neck are covered. A person exposed to cold tempera-tures, without any head covering, may lose up to half their total heat production through the scalp and face.

Staying warm is the name of the game when you venture out-of-doors. Learn to layer your clothing. The layering system helps you do just that by keeping your body core temperature on an even keel.

FIRST LAYER: The underwear layer main-tains a micro-climate next to your skin. When you are perspiring, moisture-transferring poly-propylene can keep your skin drier and in turn cut heat loss.

SECOND LAYER: The clothing layer includes the shirt and pants you wear over your first layer. This second layer provides insulation and perspiration ventilation. The "dead-air" space between the first and second layers creates an insulating buffer against temperature. Wool works best. Remember, the fit and closures of the garment are important for temperature control.

THIRD LAYER: The insulation layer adds the most obvious protection from foul weather. Synthetics tend to retain more of their loft and in turn their insulation value.

FOURTH LAYER: A temporary shell layer protects you from wind and rain. Wind shells add 10 to 25 degrees to the warmth of layering, and in windy weather, can increase warmth by 50 percent or more. Breathable fabrics like Gore-Tex are excellent.

Finally, wet clothing will conduct heat from the body to the environment some 20 to 30 times faster than dry clothing.

Also of significance is an individual's general physical condition. Proper rest and adequate food, including plenty of carbohydrates and water, are very important to warding off hypo-thermic symptoms. Make sure you maintain your water intake at all times; dehydration can lead to serious trouble in any temperature, whether hot or cold.

Traveling lightly and silently through the woods is an unequaled experience, but a safe and enjoyable hunt is always the result of careful preparation. Always carry emergency gear which includes a compass, dry socks, gloves, plastic bags, waterproof matches, candles, flashlight, rain poncho, trail food, space blanket, necessary medication, and water, even on half-day trips afield.

Finally, always have a complete change of extra clothes in your camp or rig. It is hard to imagine a day spent scouting, photographing, or bowhunting as a threatening excursion. But lack of sensible preparation could lead to danger. A few minutes of forethought will go a long way toward keeping your outdoor experiences pleasant and safe.

Illustration by Dave Wade — Courtesy of Outdoor Life

MICHAEL SIEVE

by Rick Grooms

The clear northern California sky half turned from blue to pink and gold, and the distant hills had become purple, when mother nature began to unfold one of the greatest spectacles before me. I had crawled up an irrigation ditch to a flock of about 5,000 geese which were in a barley field. The group was a mixed flock; several species of Canadas, Snows, Ross's geese, and White Fronts.

Suddenly, half-a-mile to the north, the main body of geese—approximately 130,000—lifted off of the lake and headed my way. I have seen larger flocks of geese, but never this close or in such great light. For two hours they swarmed around, some as close as thirty feet. Several large flocks of pintails and mallards flew in to join them. Occasionally, swans would pass over, their powerful voices lost in the clamor of the geese. Right then and there I knew that some day I would paint that flock of geese.

Over the years, I have relied on experiences such as this as the inspiration for my paintings. Perhaps it is a rutting battle between bull elk or moose; or, a chance encounter in the woods with a wolf or bobcat; perhaps the memory of a past hunting trip. In any case, it is the experience that is the important starting point to a successful painting.

It is these types of experiences and this kind of inspiration that has made Michael Sieve a very prominent name in the wildlife art world. Mike is known as one of the best big game artists in the United States, and he is becoming equally well-known for his renderings of birds and waterfowl.

Since Mike's college years, his dedication to his art career has brought him considerable satisfaction, as well as recognition. His painting, *Dusky Canadians,* in 1984, won him the "First of State" honors for the Oregon Duck Stamp Print competition. He also designed the 1985 Oregon Duck Stamp Print. This was quite an honor, as it was the first time the same artist had won with back-to-back entries in any state competition.

Mike's painting, *Edge of the Forest,* a bald eagle, received national as well as international acclaim. This painting was chosen for world tour, and it now hangs in the permanent collection of the Leigh Yawkey Woodson Museum in Wausau, Wisconsin. When this painting was published in print form, it was almost an immediate sellout.

To date, nineteen of Mike's paintings have been published in limited edition print form. Most of these are big game animals, and all but a couple of them are sold-out editions.

The list of Mike's accomplishments with a pallet and brush are many, but when you ask him if there is any one particular painting which stands out from the others, he says, "No, not really."

When I am painting, I try to put the subject in its natural setting with the correct habitat. I back up the paintings I do with as much scientific knowledge as possible. That means, getting the correct plants and animals in the correct geographical and geological setting; and, in their proper condition for the time of year. It also includes an understanding of atmospheric conditions.

I have made it my goal to study and understand both the physical and aesthetic qualities of color and light as much as possible; especially their relationship with paints and painting. I believe that this research and study is the only way to do top quality art.

These days, Mike devotes up to four months a year to hunting, backpacking, traveling, and canoeing. These travels provide the experiences

Mike translates to paint. He reinforces these with a lot of photographs, field sketches, color notes, and collected samples, all of which are taken to his studio and contribute to the accurate re-creation of those experiences. The medium that Mike works with is oils; usually on canvas, but sometimes on board.

I do a relatively small number of paintings per year; about eight to ten on the average, but they are fairly large in size. In doing this few paintings and with so many experiences to choose from, there is never a loss of ideas.

On the contrary, I'll never paint all of the things I want to; nor will I ever have to turn to others for my inspiration. There is no room in my book for the kind of uninspired art that is a result of the purchased or stolen magazine photos, or of another artist's ideas.

The people that I would most like to reach with my work are those who already know what I paint. Individuals who know and understand both anatomy and habitat and the behavior of a particular bird or

Michael Sieve

animal. People who will form their own opinions, rather than the opinions of some "art expert."

I am not really interested in painting simple portraits of animals with every hair and feather defined, with little or no background or behavior shown. I want people to see my paintings and go away with a little greater appreciation, or deeper understanding, about that particular place.

In the many years that I have bowhunted, I have been able to better understand wildlife and its relationship with nature; the animals' dependency upon its instincts and its environment. I have observed their behavior patterns and their relationship to man. These experiences have benefited me in developing better hunting skills, and it has enhanced my understanding of animals' anatomies and muscle structures.

In my opinion, bowhunters as a group are the most knowledgeable and highest skilled hunters around. They see more keenly and understand and appreciate more deeply than many others. This is reflected in their preference for longer seasons and more intimate contact with wildlife which is offered by bowhunting. Most bowhunters are also fine sportsmen. I believe the Pope and Young Club members are the cream of an already elite group. They have and hold themselves to the highest standards.

Creating a painting for the Pope and Young Club is a very high honor for me. It is my hope that they will hold me and my art to their high standards, and that my painting will be in harmony with what we, as bowhunters, do; and, that the future generations will have an opportunity to hunt and enjoy this land as you and I know it today.

Mike's bowhunting is as unique as his art. He has hunted whitetail deer with a bow and arrow for seventeen years; and, he has tagged seventeen deer. He prefers to hunt from the ground, using a still-hunting method. He also prefers to get close. Most of his deer have been shot at about ten yards, although some have been taken at less than ten feet. There have been occasions when he has spent the entire day stalking one particular whitetail buck.

Mike is a member of many conservation organizations, one of which is the Pope and Young Club. Most of his hunting is done in his home state of Minnesota where he resides with his wife, Debbie, and a recent addition, son, Eric Teal Sieve.

DAVE WADE

by Lee Kline

The Salt Lake Valley had much to offer in the late 1950s. Its rural culture and abundant wildlife made it a perfect place to grow up for an inquisitive young boy with an unquenchable passion for the outdoors. Whether it was catching lizards with a friend or stealing a glimpse of a mule deer doe and fawn along a creek, the experiences of Dave Wade's youth provided the foundation for a career as one of today's finest wildlife artists.

"I was always outside it seemed like. I mean *always*," Wade recalls of his childhood. "The outdoors has always been everything to me from the time I was real little." It's still that way. Dave explains:

> Getting into nature rejuvenates me. The excitement of hunting—with both rifle and bow—never ceases for me. No one appreciates animals more than hunters; a good one is selective and might wait several years to bag the right trophy. I love the camaraderie, the swapping of stories and animal lore with other hunters, but I most enjoy going out alone. There is a deep satisfaction in reasserting my self-reliance, especially in adverse weather conditions. I feel an increased respect for the animals I paint as I struggle to stay warm in the middle of a blizzard or try to light a fire in wet snow.

> Without the distraction of other human voices, all my senses become more keen and more aware of the sound of the wind or the smell of the pine trees. I find I develop an actual sixth sense, a heightened awareness that only comes from a profound closeness to nature. It is a soul-cleansing experience.

It is this fascination with—and love for—the outdoor world that nourished an artistic desire in Wade. As a youth seven or eight years old, he had a "feeling" for creating wildlife experiences with drawings and paintings. By the time he was a junior high school student, Dave knew he would become a wildlife artist.

As time went on, Wade focused his educational preparation toward that end, eventually enrolling at the University of Utah as a first-year art student. "The University art program was pretty broad and it didn't really fit my needs," Wade says today. "I never wanted to paint anything but wildlife—then or now." He moved on to the Los Angeles Art Center where he further developed his comprehension of fine art basics.

But after one term at the Art Center, the allure of the Wasatch Range and a strong desire to develop his own style drew Wade back to the Salt Lake Valley. Nearly six months later he completed his first wildlife painting of a mule deer during a winter moment. It sold the same day and Dave Wade's career as a full-time wildlife artist was underway.

Wade's style has developed into a distinctive, authentic portrayal of nature's wonderments. He strives to capture the *feelings* of an outdoor moment, the spirit and individual character of the setting and the animal or animals. "I try to convey these feelings, not by imitating nature," Wade expresses, "but by re-creating the emotional texture of an experience in nature."

> Most of my paintings depict the fall of the year. I know that comes from my hunting. A lot of people think the mountains are their prettiest in the summer, but I like the hunting season time of year. It's a time when the weather is unsettled, the storms rolling in . . . it brings out the spirit and changing character or mood of the mountains.
>
> I don't know quite how to say it. You *feel* the mountains more when the storms are coming in. You're at home with them, but you don't really trust them. It's a time when you yourself seem to become insig-

nificant in the whole scheme of things. I like to paint the approaching storms rather than the "bluebird" days.

Dave's hunting background has also contributed much to his paintings in another way. It's from these experiences that he has been able to capture the sheer awe-inspiring magnificence of our native wildlife, particularly truly large mule deer bucks.

> I've always had a special excitement for mule deer hunting and especially for huge bucks. The times that I've seen really big bucks, way up high in the snow, have always stuck with me. I suppose that mule deer are my favorite subject to paint, but my most favorite thing in any painting is when I start doing the horns or antlers. Few things get me as excited as good antlers. Each one is unique. I like designing them—the symmetry, extra points, palmation—just everything about them.

Those who have never seen truly large specimens occasionally have trouble relating to the size of some of the muley bucks painted by

Dave Wade

Wade. Veteran mule deer hunters, however, recognize that deer of those proportions do exist; they provide the justification for many remote camps, rough hours hunting steep ridges, and the very motive to do it all over again next season just to see one of those magnificent specimens. Wade feels that *good* hunters make up an important segment of those who appreciate his work.

> There are three degrees of art appreciation in collectors of my work. Some people want a painting solely for the emotional link it gives them to the wildlife, and that feeling must be there if the painting is to be successful. Then there are those who have "been there" and know if the painting is true to the animal's nature. This is where total accuracy concerning the animal and its environment is important. On the highest level are the people for whom the elements of good art—mood, accuracy, lighting, application of paint, composition—all come together. Painting for these people is essentially like painting for other artists. To please myself, I must paint for this last group.

Another by-product of this 34-year-old artist's hunting experiences don't readily appear in his brush strokes, but perhaps says more about the man than anything written to this point. His appreciation and love for wildlife are easily apparent in his paintings, but Dave Wade's deep concern over the future of our natural resources—and hunting as a pastime—are not so observable on canvas or board.

> Just in general, the bigger the population of people becomes, the more we encroach on the winter range of the animals and the less habitat they have. Some animals can adapt. Coyotes will always be here. Whitetail deer actually seem to do better with man's presence, but mule deer and some other species don't.
>
> It's not just the growth in numbers of people and the encroachment though. Progression from a rural to suburban culture has stripped many people of the ability to appreciate and understand the outdoors and our wildlife. Today, many people can't relate to the outdoors. They intrude on it, then return to their homes. It's like they have lost the feel for the land and the animals. Many of them are too far removed from the outdoor world to really comprehend it, to feel it.
>
> These attitudes also show up in some of the hunting ranks . . . the lack of ethics, the poaching, disrespect for the animals and other hunters. I don't know how you feel, but sometimes I don't want to be associated with some kinds of hunters. The best hunters I know don't just go out to kill something but really appreciate the animals, other people's rights, and understand the outdoors.

When asked what he would say if he had to write this, Dave responded:

> Let's just say I'm someone who was born with some talent, and I've been fortunate enough to have had the opportunity to develop it to the extent that I have. I've got a long way to go. I love the outdoors and the animals, and I love painting them. What sums it all up is that if I were independently weathly, I would still be doing exactly what I'm doing now. My greatest interests are in wildlife, nature, and art. The three of them just go together naturally for me.

oil/canvas

"COTTON-GRASS MEADOW"
Michael Sieve

28x38

"RIVERBOTTOM BUCK"
Michael Sieve

oil/canvas

26x42

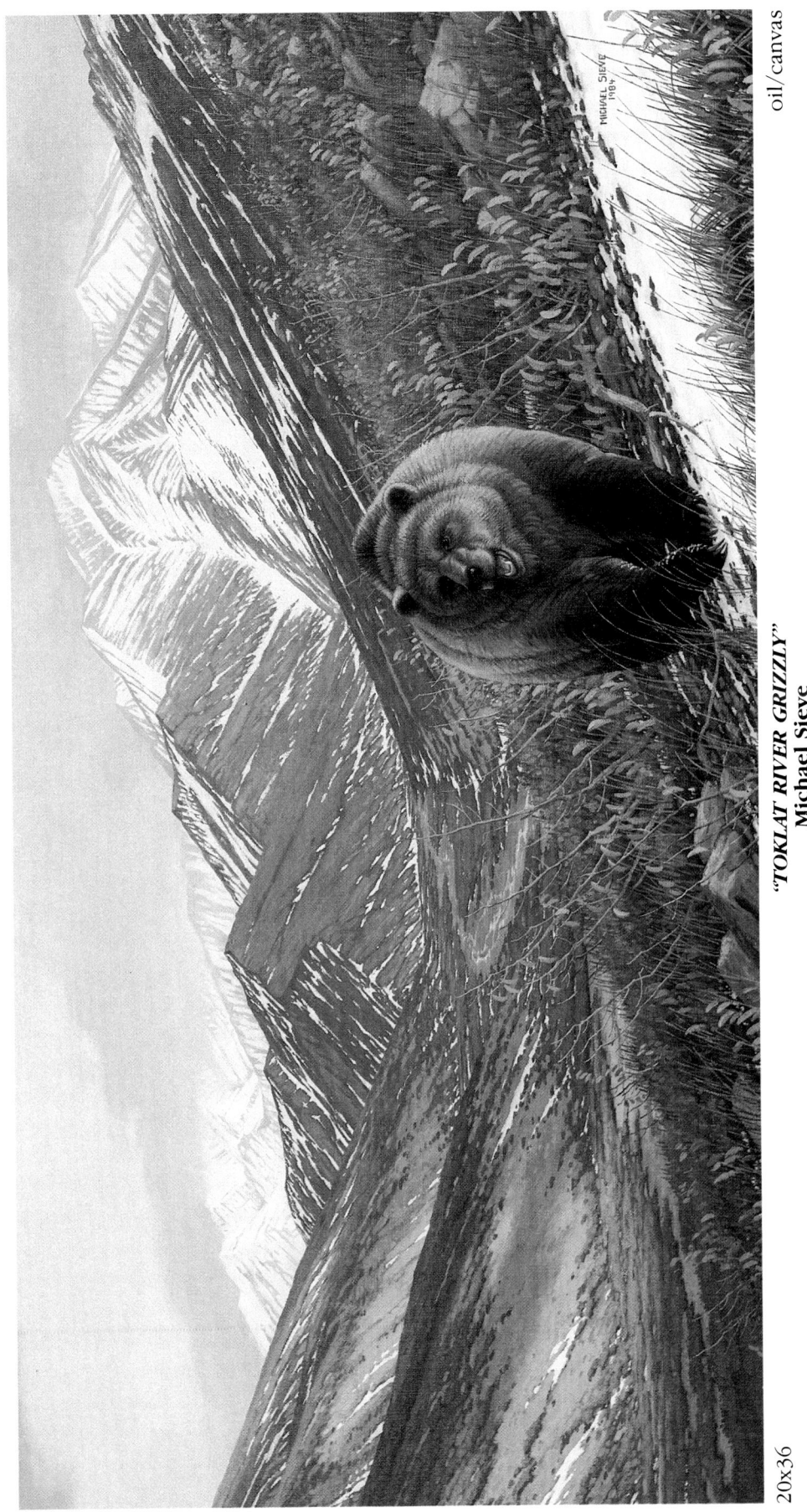

oil/canvas

"TOKLAT RIVER GRIZZLY"
Michael Sieve

20x36

103

oil/board

"CLEAR CUT"
Michael Sieve

24x36

105

oil/canvas

"MAJESTIC MONARCHS"
Michael Sieve

26x42

"SEASON'S END"
Michael Sieve

oil/canvas

30x48

109

"ATHABASCA RIVER BATTLE"
Michael Sieve

26x48

oil/canvas

111

oil/canvas

"EVENING STAND"
Michael Sieve

26x42

113

oil/canvas

"COUGAR KILL"
Dave Wade

30x40

115

"ANTELOPE"
Dave Wade

oil/canvas

16x20

117

oil/canvas

"NON-TYPICAL"
Dave Wade

24x36

119

oil/canvas

"DALL RAMS ON A RIDGE"
Dave Wade

24x36

121

oil/board

"MORNING REVELRY"
Dave Wade

24x36

oil/canvas

"STONES"
Dave Wade

24x36

125

"LA SALS"
Dave Wade

oil/board

30x48

127

oil/board

"THREE RAMS"
Dave Wade

24x36

129

BOOK III

THE RECORDS

BOWHUNTING RECORDS
How to Enter a Trophy

by Dr. C. Randall Byers

The moment of truth has arrived. You slowly draw the arrow back to the corner of your mouth, make the last mental calculation of the distance, and visualize the path of the arrow to the animal. The release is smooth, the arrow flight is true, and the trophy is yours. Your planning, hours of practice, and efforts toward the hunt have paid off in a well-earned trophy, one in which you can be proud.

Later, after the initial elation subsides and you have properly cared for your trophy, you begin to wonder how it compares with other bow-killed trophies taken in North America. Maybe a friend asks, "Will it make 'the book'?" What does this question mean and how do you go about answering it?

When someone refers to making "the book," or to a Pope and Young trophy, they are referring to the listings in this very publication. The Pope and Young Club maintains these records and at regular intervals publishes updated editions of the records. The first edition appeared in 1975 and contained 2,367 entries; the second volume was printed in 1981, with 4,577 entries. This edition now lists over 10,000 trophies, including all record entries through December 31, 1986.

Does every big game animal harvested by means of bow and arrow make "the book"? Hardly! In order to qualify for listing in the *Bowhunting Big Game Records of North America,* the trophy must have been taken in compliance with the game laws for the area where the animal was killed and the *Rules of Fair Chase* set forth by the Pope and Young Club. The trophy must also meet the minimum score established for that particular species. From time to time, these qualifying minimums are adjusted.

Even though the minimum scores may be raised later, every animal that meets the minimum score in effect at the time of its entry will be published in at least one edition of the records book. For example, the minimum score for a Pronghorn entry is currently 64. As you look at the Pronghorn records in this edition, you'll note some trophies with scores of less than 64. The minimum for this species was raised January 1, 1983, and all properly completed entries received prior to that date are listed. However, in the next edition of the book, those entries below 64 will be dropped. This practice insures that trophies taken between book publications will appear in at least one edition of *Bowhunting Big Game Records.*

Similar changes have occurred with other species since the last book was published; Yellowstone Elk (240 to 260), Bighorn Sheep (130 to 140), and Desert Sheep (125 to 140), all effective January 1, 1985. The next edition of

BOWHUNTING

Big Game   Records

POPE AND YOUNG CLUB   **FAIR CHASE AFFIDAVIT**

To be entered into the Pope & Young Club Records, the animal must meet the minimum scoring requirements, and must be taken in complete compliance with the controlling game laws and the Rules of Fair Chase. The term "Fair Chase" shall not include the taking of animals under the following conditions:

1. Helpless in a trap, deep snow or water, or on ice.
2. From any power vehicle or power boat.
3. While confined behind fences as on game farms, etc.
4. By "Jacklighting" or shining at night.
5. By the use of any tranquilizers or poisons.
6. By the use of any power vehicles or power boat for herding or driving animals, including use of aircraft to land alongside animal or to communicate with or direct a hunter on the ground.
7. Use of electronic devices for attracting, locating or pursuing game, or guiding the hunter to such game.
8. Any other condition considered by the Board of Directors as unsportsmanlike.

SPECIAL NOTE: For the purpose of the Pope & Young Club, a bow shall be defined as a longbow, recurve bow or compound bow that is hand-held and hand-drawn, and that has no mechanical device to enable the hunter to lock the bow at full or partial draw. Other than energy stored by the drawn bow, no device to propel the arrow will be permitted.

SEARCH & RECOVERY: Was animal recoverd on same day as hit? _____ YES _____ NO
                                                                        (check one)

If "NO" give **COMPLETE DETAILS** of recovery on separate sheet.

Falsification of the Fair Chase Affidavit is grounds for dismissal from the Pope & Young Club. Falsification will cause the entry to be rejected, no future entries accepted, and all past entries dropped from the Pope & Young Club records for the individual falsifying the affidavit. In addition to the requirements of this affidavit, by submitting this entry the applicant agrees that the sole decision of acceptance of this entry belongs to the Board of Directors and its discretionary decision is in all respects final.

I, _____ attest that my _____
                                         (print)
was taken entirely by means of BOW & ARROW, and in complete compliance with the controlling game laws and the rules of Fair Chase.

_____   _____
          Hunter's Signature   Date

WE THE UNDERSIGNED, DECLARE THAT THE FOREGOING STATEMENTS ARE TRUE TO THE BEST OF OUR KNOWLEDGE AND BELIEF:

_____   _____
Signature of witness to verification of bow kill   Address of witness   Zip
(Does not have to be Eye Witness)

_____   _____
Signature of Guide   Address of Guide   Zip
(if none, write 'None')

THIS FORM MUST BE COMPLETELY FILLED OUT!
REVISED SEPTEMBER, 1986

Fair Chase Affidavit

Please complete the following form as it relates the harvest of this trophy. This information is used by the Pope & Young Club to provide an overall view of the nature of hunts for the various North American big game animals for which we maintain records.

1. **SPECIES** _____ SEX _____

2. **HUNTER INFORMATION:** Age _____ Sex _____ Years of Bowhunting Experience _____

3. **HUNT INFORMATION:** Guide _____ _____ Date of Kill _____
                                 yes   no   month   day   year

   WEATHER CONDITIONS AT TIME OF KILL: Clear _____ Cloudy _____ Rain _____

   Snow _____

   Other _____

   Time _____ a.m. p.m. Temperature _____

4. **DISTANCE OF SHOT:** (If more than one shot, write distance of each arrow in appropriate box).

   #1 _____ yds. #2 _____ yds. #3 _____ yds. #4 _____ yds.

   For the next four questions, place an X in the space corresponding to each arrow, e.g., if arrows #1 and #3 were both broadside, record your entry as follows: Broadside
                                                     ☒ ☐ ☒ ☐
                                                     1   2   3   4

   ANGLE OF THE SHOT:

Broadside	Rear Quartering	Front Quartering	Rear	Front	Above
☐ ☐ ☐ ☐	☐ ☐ ☐ ☐	☐ ☐ ☐ ☐	☐ ☐ ☐ ☐	☐ ☐ ☐ ☐	☐ ☐ ☐ ☐
1 2 3 4	1 2 3 4	1 2 3 4	1 2 3 4	1 2 3 4	1 2 3 4

   WHERE ARROW STRUCK ANIMAL:

Chest	Paunch	Rump	Leg	Head	Other _____
☐ ☐ ☐ ☐	☐ ☐ ☐ ☐	☐ ☐ ☐ ☐	☐ ☐ ☐ ☐	☐ ☐ ☐ ☐	☐ ☐ ☐ ☐
1 2 3 4	1 2 3 4	1 2 3 4	1 2 3 4	1 2 3 4	1 2 3 4

5. **STYLE OF HUNTING:** Bait _____ Stalk _____ Still _____ Tree Stand _____ Ground Blind _____

   Calling _____ Dogs _____

   (Stalk - spotting animal first then moving in: Still - locating animal by moving.)

6. **NUMBER OF MEMBERS** IN HUNTING PARTY WHEN ANIMAL WAS HARVESTED _____

7. **NUMBER OF DAYS** HUNTING DURING THE SEASON FOR THIS SPECIES _____

8. **NUMBER OF ARROWS** SHOT DURING THE SEASON AT THIS SPECIES _____

9. **NUMBER OF ANIMALS** OF THIS SPECIES SEEN DURING SEASON _____

10. **TYPE OF BOW:** Longbow _____ Recurve _____ Compound _____ Draw Weight _____ lbs.

   TYPE OF QUIVER: Hip _____ Back _____ Other (specify) _____ _____ **Quiver Size** (number of arrows) _____

   TYPE OF BROADHEAD: Fixed Blade (no insert) _____ Fixed Blade (with inserts) _____

   Replaceable Blade _____ Other _____ **Number of Blades** _____

   TYPE OF ARROWS: Wood ____ Glass ____ Aluminum ____ Other (specify) _____ Length _____

11. **COMMENTS:**

Fair Chase Affidavit

the book will reflect these changes, and any others that might be take place during the interim.

Does this mean an animal that fails to make "the book" is any less a trophy? NO, absolutely not! It just turns out that some animals are bigger than others. The purpose of the records is to list those bow-harvested animals that exhibit certain size and structural characteristics that distinguish them as above average for their species; thus, the distinction between a bowhunting trophy and a record-class animal. Many fine *trophies* are not included simply because they aren't large enough, are the wrong sex, or exhibit non-standard antler, horn, or skull development. Yet in many instances they required the same effort, dedication, luck, and skill to harvest as the larger members of the species.

Many bowhunters ask if they have to be a member of the Pope and Young Club to enter an animal? Again, the answer is no. The Club accepts all animals that meet the qualifying standards. No check is made to see if the lucky hunter is a club member or not. While we would like you to join the organization, it certainly is not a requirement for entry of an animal in the records. Many, if not most, of the animals listed in this book have been taken by non-members.

Now, back to that trophy you've just put your tag on. How will you find out if it qualifies for entry? First, you might look at the score charts for each of the record book categories. These charts are printed in *Appendix A* of this book. From these charts, you may be able to estimate the approximate score of your trophy. If you think it exceeds—or is even close to—the required minimum score, then you should contact an official measurer.

The Pope and Young Club currently has over 600 individuals who serve the Club in a voluntary capacity as official measurers. There are measurers from Alaska to Florida; from Hawaii to Maine; from Canada to Mexico. A listing of these individuals appears in *Appendix B.*

You might contact the local office of your game and fish department, sporting goods stores, or taxidermists. In many cases, individuals at these places may be familiar with the scoring system or may be able to put you in contact with an official measurer. *Appendix C* to this

edition includes a listing of all game and fish departments in North America.

The Pope and Young Club also accepts scores from certified Boone and Crockett measurers. To obtain names of B&C measurers in your area, contact the Boone and Crockett Club, 241 South Fraley Blvd., Dumfries, VA 22026.

Of course, you can always contact the Pope and Young Club Records Office directly. While this address may change from time to time, the current one can generally be found in various bowhunting publications. The Records Office will provide you with a current list of measurers in your vicinity. If there isn't a measurer near your location, it may be possible for you to arrange shipment of your trophy to the nearest measurer. There have even been instances where trophy owners have shipped their trophy to the Records Office for measurement.

Once you locate the nearest measurer, you should make an appointment with him or her to have your trophy scored. There is no charge for having a trophy measured. Remember this as you try to arrange a mutually convenient time to have the animal scored. Since the official measurers are volunteers, they must meet their schedules as well as yours.

Before a trophy can be officially measured, a sixty-day period *MUST* pass from the date of kill. This sixty days gives you the opportunity to put together some material the measurer will need. The Records Office requires that three photographs of the trophy be submitted with each antlered or horned entry. The required photos include one of each side view, plus a frontal view. The purpose for these photos is to show the antler or horn development and configuration as well as the structure of the various points. On heads with abnormal development or non-typical points, another photo from a rear view of the trophy may be requested by the Records Office.

Three photos are also required for bear and cat entries. These pictures should include one of each side of the cleaned skull and a top view taken from the front at a 45 degree angle. The photos should show the skull clearly so the entry can be reviewed for possible abnormalities. It is important to note that bear and cat skulls *must be completely cleaned of all flesh and cartilage*

NORTH AMERICAN

Big Game Competition

_____

SPECIES

_____   _____

SCORE   WHERE TAKEN

_____   _____

DATE   BOW HUNTER

THE POPE AND YOUNG CLUB

_____   _____

PRESIDENT   CHAIRMAN, RECORDS COMMITTEE

material. Your photos should be taken after the skull has been cleaned.

All required photographs can be taken at any time before the entry is submitted. Oftentimes, the photos are of the mounted trophy. Black and white or color prints are acceptable for entry but slides are not.

The Records Office also requests that a site-of-kill photo be included. Although not mandatory—for obvious reasons—we request such photos whenever it's possible for the hunter to provide them. When you take the head to be scored, take the photos along. Then you and the measurer can generally complete the entire entry procedure as he or she finishes the scoring form. All photos are retained by the Records Office and become part of the permanent entry for that trophy.

There is an entry fee required for each animal submitted for the record book. Currently, the fee is twenty-five dollars. The entry fee helps to cover the cost of processing the entry and maintaining the Records Office. Personal checks or money orders are fine. Make them out to the Pope and Young Club. Please, do not send cash through the mail.

You will also need to complete a *Fair Chase Affidavit.* It is important to complete all portions of this statement, including the Search and Recovery section (many hunters miss seeing this question, forcing us to return the entry for this information).

Also note that if you used a guide on the hunt for this trophy, you must have the guide's signature on the Fair Chase Form. In many cases, it is handy to have the form along when on a guided hunt. If you contact the Records Office, we'll provide you the *Fair Chase Affidavit* prior to your hunt. Likewise, these forms can be obtained from any official Pope and Young measurers.

One of the required signatures on the *Fair Chase Affidavit* is that of an individual who is willing to attest that the animal was harvested legally, with bow and arrow, under conditions of fair chase. That person does not actually have to witness the shot or retrieval of the animal. However, if you are hunting with someone who witnessed the shot, it's best to have that person sign the form. If no one was present, then verification can be obtained from a friend, spouse, or fellow bowhunter who is willing to state that you took the animal appropriately. On guided hunts, the guide may also serve as the witness to the authenticity of the kill.

The head now needs to be measured. Pope and Young will accept the entry of mounted heads so long as the skullplate between the antlers or horns has not been broken. However, it is much easier to measure the head before it's mounted. Since most taxidermists require more than two months to complete their work, you can generally arrange to have the antlers or horns measured without upsetting the taxidermist's schedule.

Once the head has been scored, the entry is ready to be sent to the Records Office. A complete entry will include:

1. Completed scoring form
2. Completed *Fair Chase Affidavit*
3. Three required photographs
4. Entry fee ($25.00)
5. Site of kill photo, if available

Be sure all blanks on the scoring form are filled in. Your name should be spelled as you would like it to appear in the next edition of the *Bowhunting Big Game Records.* This information is sent (original documents, not copies) to the Pope and Young Records Office. The address is currently:

Pope and Young Records Office
1804 Borah
Moscow, Idaho 83843

After this information is received, it's checked for completeness and accuracy. Once the entry is verified, it is entered into the records listings. The Records Office then sends a distinctive color certificate for each qualified entry to the trophy owner. This certificate lists the Recording Period as well as information about the trophy and the bowhunter. In addition to the certificate, the hunter receives a copy of the completed scoring form for his or her personal records, plus some general information on the Pope and Young Club.

Although record entries are accepted the year around, the Club operates on two-year recording periods. Currently, the Club is accepting entries for the Sixteenth Recording Period (January 1, 1987 through December 31, 1988). At the end of each recording period, the Club hosts a banquet to honor the top heads entered during the biennium and to recognize new world records.

Each animal entered during a particular recording period is eligible for recognition at the biennial awards banquet. Owners of these top heads are notified of the awards program agenda in early January. Also, the Club publishes a supplemental listing of all trophies entered during those recording periods that fall in between editions of the book. These supplements prove to be valuable updates for the *Bowhunting Big Game Records.*

Since the Pope and Young Club came into existence in 1961, there has been tremendous growth in bowhunting and in the number of trophy entries in the records system. If you should be fortunate enough to harvest an animal that qualifies, you should strongly consider having it entered in the records. Whether the trophy just exceeds the qualifying score or is a potential world record, it joins a select few animals that meet the standards set forth by the Pope and Young Club for listing in the official bowhunting records.

The records serve as a source of pertinent biological information for the serious bowhunter and professional wildlife researcher as well as providing interesting facts for the casual reader. Your trophy, and the information related to it, will be a welcome addition to this data base.

Illustration by Dave Wade

STORIES BEHIND
THE WORLD RECORDS

Many of us have dreamed of that moment when all of our planning and effort culminated in a chance at taking a world-record animal. Some of us will go on dreaming forever. It's the nature of the game, some of the spice that keeps us going back, time and again, just to see an animal of those magnificent proportions. But to actually succeed . . . In this chapter, are the stories behind some of the world records as told by the bowhunters whose skill, determination, and good fortune led to their listing in this book. There's a whole lot more to these stories than could be presented here, but the exciting moments and feelings of each hunt have been captured for your enjoyment—and to fuel your dreams.

ALASKA BROWN BEAR

by Jack Frost

I had been very fortunate to draw a brown bear permit for the 1985 spring season on Unimak Island, just off the tip of the Alaskan Peninsula. A severe spring storm with 60–70 knot winds in Cold Bay delayed the start of my hunt by a couple of days, but undoubtedly contributed to its ultimate sucess. After the storm, my friend, Tony Oney, and I flew our Piper Cubs from Anchorage to Cold Bay, then on to Unimak the next day.

We flew the entire circumference of the island looking for sheltered camping areas and spotted a dead whale that had been beached by the storm. It was just below a fifty-foot bluff and appeared to be an ideal setup for stalking a brown bear. About two miles from the whale, we located a relatively sheltered place where we could land and set up camp.

The next morning we hiked up to the bluff for a look at the whale. On the way, we spotted

two bears about a mile or so from the beach. Directly inland, about 100 yards from where the whale was, we encountered a sow with two cubs sleeping on the tundra. We carefully slipped past them and eased up to the lip of the bluff.

A huge brown bear was standing on top of the whale. At first glance he seemed to have something in his mouth. Further inspection with binoculars showed it was a lower canine tooth jutting out at such an angle that he couldn't get his lip closed over it. At this point, a second large bear came walking down the beach. I really couldn't tell which was larger, but after a quick conference with Tony, I decided to try for the snaggle-toothed bear since he was closest.

The snaggle-toothed bear stepped off the whale to meet the advancing second bear, and I chose that moment to shoot. Hit behind the shoulder, the bear ran down the beach about 200 yards and turned onto the tundra where he layed down in plain view.

Tony and I circled to get straight downwind and slowly stalked to within twenty yards. My final arrow hit him squarely through the heart. The bear spun to charge but couldn't make it happen and was dead within five seconds.

Although I knew that he was big, I never dreamed that he might replace a twenty-five-year-old world record.

BARREN GROUND CARIBOU
by Dennis Burdick

My first trip to Alaska in September of 1981 was a cold and snowy ordeal. I saw only one caribou in a two-week period, and he wasn't close enough for a shot. Taking a bull caribou with my bow had been a lifelong dream, so I returned in August of 1984.

Since we did not have a guide my hunting partners, Keith Hymas and his sons Neil and Troy, and I decided to drop camp on a small lake and hunt a group of high rocky ridges above timberline.

It was about 10:00 a.m. when we spotted a large caribou grazing across an open area about 400 yards below us. We were amazed at the size of his antlers.

Being the senior members of the hunting party, Keith and I were elected to try a stalk. We carefully descended the ridge down a steep rockslide, trying very hard not to dislodge loose rocks and spook the animal.

We had to move fast to intercept the bull as he was feeding at a quick walk. We worked our way to a patch of bushes, about thirty yards in diameter, between us and the caribou. Once there, we paused for a moment and decided Keith would circle the lower side and I the upper. As I crept along the edge of the bushes, my heart began to pound and I began to shake, realizing that any second I might get a shot at my first caribou.

As I reached the far end of the brush, my heart sank. Nothing was in sight, and I thought he had given us the slip. Suddenly, the bull trotted into sight at about fifty yards and stood quartering toward me. The arrow from my eighty-five-pound bow struck him perfectly. He ran about 200 yards and went down.

I have always been a do-it-yourself hunter and feel very fortunate to have taken such an outstanding trophy.

SITKA BLACKTAIL DEER
by Chuck Adams

Bowhunting blacktail deer is my all-time favorite sport. I've matched wits with these animals since I was a kid, and the thrill has never worn off. What blacktails lack in antler size, they make up for in first-class hunting challenge.

For this reason, it was no accident when I shouldered my seventy-pound backpack, clawed several hours through doghair-dense alder brush, and finally reached a remote canyon on Alaska's Kodiak Island. From my research, places like this were remote enough, and of the correct habitat type to harbor giant sitka blacktail bucks.

After pitching my backpack tent, I crawled inside to rest my weary bones. Next morning, I was busy glassing for deer. By sundown, I had seen over fifty animals, including several nice bucks through my 30X spotting scope. Since I was holding out for an oversized trophy, I was thrilled when a standout buck appeared on a distant hillside. Light was fading fast, but I could count five distinct points on each massive antler. Since the deer was across a large brushy canyon, I headed back to camp with high hopes for the next day.

It rained all night—a steady downpour driven by gale-force winds; typical Kodiak weather. At daylight, the winds dropped but a light drizzle continued. I waded through wet brush to a vantage point, set up the scope, and glassed for six hours without seeing so much as one doe! The wind and rain had driven the animals into head-high alder brush.

About 3:00 p.m., things began to hop. The rain had stopped, and patches of blue started showing overhead. In the next forty-five minutes, I counted over two dozen animals. I kept watching the area where the big buck had been the night before, sweeping the brushfield time after time. Suddenly, there he was framed by deep alder brush. As I watched, the old boy strolled downhill, crossed a grassy knoll, and bedded in a shallow depression with only his antlers showing. One look told me the deer was a trophy of a lifetime.

After testing the wind, I trotted off the hillside fighting alders every step of the way. I finally crossed the canyon bottom, slowed to a snail's pace, and eased crosswind 200 yards toward where the buck should be.

Half-an-hour later, I peeked around a bush and was startled to see antlers and eartips only twenty-five yards away! There was no mistaking the massive five-by-five rack, nor what those stiff, alertly cupped ears implied. I drew my eighty-four-pound bow as the buck stood up, and let fly as he whirled to leave. The aluminum shaft flickered and hit him chest-on with a solid thump. The buck lunged, staggered uphill fifty yards, and collapsed like a heart-shot pheasant.

Never mind the tedious field dressing, skinning, and meat boning chores that followed in the pitch-black Alaskan night. And never mind the torturous backpacking trip to base camp. My buck was a fat, heavy-racked five-by-five with incredibly symmetrical antlers—the best-scoring sitka blacktail ever taken with bow and arrow.

TYPICAL COUES DEER
by Harlon J. Wilson

My family and I live in the Bonnie Blink Housing Area on Fort Huachuca, Arizona where I am stationed. My home is located at the base of the mountains on the post which are a haven for the little Arizona whitetails. My neighbor, Ted Dustman, and I would often sit on the patio with binoculars and watch deer in the hunting areas. Ted and I had been seeing the same big buck for about two months. I decided to try my luck on him during the bow season.

When bow season arrived, the buck had changed his habits and was feeding in a new area. I finally located him and on the final day of bow season I got my chance.

The buck was walking and feeding towards me about 300 yards away. When he was about 125 yards from me he decided to turn around and feed the other way. I quickly chose a stalking route that would take me to within fifty yards of him, if he stayed where he was. When the buck put his head down to feed, I began to crawl toward some high grass between me and the deer. When I reached the two-foot-tall grass, I estimated the buck to be about thirty-five yards away. Slowly, I came to my feet, drew, and placed my forty-yard pin about halfway down his body as he quartered away from me. I re-

leased the string and the arrow hit the deer exactly where I wanted it to, or so I thought. The buck jumped straight up and came down running, quickly disappearing in the mesquite.

As it turned out, the hit wasn't as good as I thought, and it took a long, hard trailing job to find the buck. With the help of my friend, Eddie Greene, we recovered the deer the next morning.

When we got him back home, Randy Breland, the post game manager, saw the deer and told me that he was a world record or at least in the top three. A couple of months later, with Randy's urging, I removed the velvet from the rack and sent it to Tom Dalrymple in Tucson. He called me a couple of weeks later all excited and told me I had the new world record.

NON-TYPICAL COUES DEER
by Dave Snyder

In 1984, Bill Hardy and I wanted to improve our chances with coues deer, so Bill had spent hours prescouting for respectable bucks. Upon my arrival for the archery hunt, he told me that he had located at least five bucks that might exceed 100 inches. This renewed my excitement for the hunt.

We hunted and glassed several different areas near Tucson, seeing deer every day. Finally we went back to an area that was one of Bill's favorites. We had been glassing for two or three hours when all at once Bill said, "I got him, there's a new world record coues!" I can't remember ever being more excited or impressed by a single animal before. His massive five-point rack had me shaking.

My first stalk was a miserable failure. Bill had to return to work the next day, but I returned to the same area for the next several days. Glassing the big buck daily, I attempted stalk after stalk without success.

On the fifth morning, I found myself at the same spot earlier than usual and within a short time I located the big buck. There were eight other deer with him, including a very fine four-point. Unlike the previous days, when I let the deer bed, I decided to go after him immediately. Reaching the ridgetop, I couldn't find any deer and wasn't sure if they had gone over or were still below me.

I went about another forty-five yards and heard a loud snort. Carefully, I moved a bit farther and saw the four-point and the larger buck facing one another, with the other deer watching the display. I stalked about ten yards closer when a small, hidden deer jumped up and ran straight away from me.

The two big bucks seemed confused and began moving in my direction. I turned my attention to the bigger deer. He had turned and was walking quickly, angling away.

When I released the arrow, he exploded down the mountain and disappeared behind a large tree about thirty yards from where I had hit him. A few moments later I found the magnificent buck.

TYPICAL MULE DEER
by Bill Barcus

I made my first bowhunt in 1972. It took five seasons before I managed to arrow my first deer—a muley doe. By the time the 1979 Colorado archery season rolled around, I had bowhunted seven consecutive years with just that one deer to show for it. That season, I wanted to fill my tag with a buck. In fact, my first buck EVER.

The season had been open a week before I could get away for a two-week hunt. My parents joined me a few days later, after checking out the fishing in some of the nearby lakes.

Dawn was still more than an hour away as I started the climb up the ridge. Just at daylight, I reached a small clearing on the crest where I began hunting. Almost instantly I saw four bucks feeding along the fringe of aspens on the other side of the clearing, about eighty yards away. Any one of them would make a great "first buck," but two of them carried awesome antlers! After they moved into the aspen, I made a try at getting close enough for a shot but blew it. The rest of the morning passed uneventfully.

I had been moving easterly most of the morning and decided to cut over a small saddle to the north and hunt my way back to the clearing. On a particularly steep part of the hill, I came to a game trail that paralleled the ridgetop. Turning west on the trail, I began still-hunting again.

It was more of a "I thought I saw it" than real movement that drew my attention to some thick weeds and grass on the lip of a small terrace about eighty-five yards below. Through my binoculars, I finally picked out the dark, fuzzy tine of an antler, then a second. At first, I thought there were two bucks bedded together; the portions of antler I could make out were too far apart to belong to the same animal. But that impression didn't last long as the antler pieces moved in unison! The longer I looked, the more obvious it became that one buck belonged to both antlers!!

An hour—maybe more—passed before I found myself fifteen yards slightly uphill from the unsuspecting deer. I had to force myself not to look at the buck's awesome headgear. As the sight pin hovered on the aiming point, I was a bit startled to see the feathers of an arrow magically appear, then vanish in the spot. I had completed the shot without really knowing it.

As I reached the lip of the terrace, I saw the giant—down for the count—thirty yards lower on the slope. The "hunting" part of the season was over and the "work" part was about to begin.

Even with the help of my parents, getting the deer two miles back to camp was all of the ordeal I knew it would be. As incredible as it may sound, I actually thought about leaving the cumbersome antlers behind!!

"That's nonsense! I'll carry them," Mom insisted.

Taking the saw, she removed the antlers from the skull and patiently steered them through the brush, trees, and downfall all the way back to camp. To think, if it hadn't been for my mother, the seven-by-seven antlers might have been left behind on that ridgetop.

QUEBEC-LABRADOR CARIBOU
by Carol Ann Mauch

My husband, Dick, and I had enjoyed such a good time and successful hunt with Bobby Snowball on the Tunulik River in 1982, that we had returned for a second hunt in 1984.

Dick had chosen the area we were hunting because of the way the ridges worked to funnel a series of worn and rutted trails into a single "caribou highway" to a river-crossing area. It was the second day of the hunt and Dick had gone upstream to glass for moving animals. Elijah, my guide, had taken me to a high point overlooking the river.

The crossing site was a mile or more wide at this spot. There was a very long, narrow, and rocky island about a third of the way out from the far shore. From our vantage point, Elijah soon spotted three bulls headed for the crossing and motioned for me to get in the boat. He took me to the far end of the rough island, out of sight of the caribou that were now in the water, and took the boat back across the river to wait and see what developed.

I was able to situate myself amidst the brush and rocks in the middle of the island. I could shoot either to the right or left without moving from my hide, should the bulls come ashore at my end of the island. Just as I had hoped, they came ambling down the beach to my left. I was excited, but ready. The two smaller bulls came by first with the big herd-master trailing behind. I waited until he was nearly broadside and passing before I drew my bow and let fly.

All the caribou broke into a run and I lost sight of them quickly in the rough and rocky terrain. I followed the tracks and the blood trail down the beach until I could see the end of the island, but no caribou. I ran back toward my hiding spot because the wind was now at my back and I didn't want to alert the caribou to my position.

Climbing to the crest and crossing over, I saw the big bull facing me. I shot another arrow that went straight into his chest. I knew then that he was mine.

DALL SHEEP
by Gary Laya

Wow! What a trip this was going to be. In August of 1986, I was headed for parts unknown on a Beaver float plane, somewhere over the Northwest Territories. It was my first hunt this far north—a backpack hunt with outfitter, Greg Williams.

The first day out we hiked for nine hours with ten days of provisions on our backs. As we unzipped the tent on the second morning, and peered out across a canyon, there on the next ridge over stood two good dall rams. Out came the spotting scope and my guide, Al Barvir, said one of the rams was exceptional. For the next seven days, we chased that ram from one end of the mountain range to the other and back.

The first day I saw the ram, I got within forty yards of him, but he offered me no shot. The third day brought a near vertical shot at twenty-five yards that just went over his back. The ram was definitely a world-class sheep, and I had little interest in any other. I guess that's the only reason why I looked over twenty-five other rams and passed up a dozen of them. But after the sixth day of hunting that old ram, I was beginning to believe he was truly a white ghost.

On the seventh day out, I decided to go after him just one more time. If things didn't work this time, I would try for another sheep. I spotted him in a small drainage and watched him for over two hours before he bedded down where I could stalk him.

When I was well within good bow range, he saw me and bolted up the other side of the ravine. As he came to a stop, my arrow was on its way and found the spot I had been hoping for. The beautiful white trophy ram was finally mine.

COUGAR
by Michael J. McCall

It was early December 21, 1985 when my best friend, Drex Schilling and his two boys, an old high school friend, Joe Saxon, and I, with my son, began our slow tedious search for a track in the crystalline snow. We were traveling a favorite road in north-central Idaho.

We rounded a corner that presented a full view of a sidehill clearcut often used by wintering elk. A couple dozen ravens exploded into flight, crackling and cawing as they scattered. Our spirits elevated immediately since this often indicates a cougar kill may be nearby.

Searching the lower part of the hillside, we found nothing. As I climbed to the ridgecrest, lion tracks materialized all about me. The first track was a small cat, probably a female. I followed its trail down a steep ridge toward some heavy timber where another cougar had crossed the track. It was the biggest cat track I'd ever seen. The pad mark was palm sized, each toe mark larger than a man's thumbprint. Some cat!

Just as Drex arrived back on the road across the canyon from me, I yelled what I had found. Drex sent Joe with two dogs to join me. Butkus, a Plott hound with an exceptionally good nose, and a young Walker pup, Stringer, were selected to get the tracks started.

Drex decided to come across and help, bringing Willy, his most dependable hound. Willy's uncanny sixth sense has turned many a poor track into pay dirt. As we worked down the ridge, Willy and Butkus opened simultaneously. It was the hot track of the big cat. Fifteen to twenty minutes later both dogs were barking treed.

The cougar was slung low in the branches of a big pine, peering down with cold steel eyes at his tormentors below. I estimated him at eight feet or more, approximately 180 pounds, and with a head like a basketball.

I had waited many years for a trophy like this. I was elated with satisfaction.

COUGAR
by Jerry J. James

It was a long trail to bagging my cougar. I had hunted two years unsuccessfully due to the lack of snow for tracking. On my third hunt, however, snow conditions were ideal, but hard luck continued to shadow my effort.

I was hunting with Bob Smith of Kooskia, Idaho. The majority of our hunt was spent in the Selway River area. During the first six days, we found three different cougar tracks but none of them were fresh enough to run. With two inches of fresh snow, the seventh day was perfect for hunting.

We spent part of the morning in an area where a cougar was sighted by a truck driver, but the track was too old to follow. After looking and listening for ravens that might indicate a kill in the area, we started to drive our usual route looking for sign.

After some time, we found the track of a large cat that had crossed the road and headed up the mountain. The track was filled with snow, but we knew that it had been made during the night. Bob decided to take the track with his two best dogs, Chief and Ralph. Ralph was kept

on a leash, while Chief was allowed to run ahead. Chief is half-Airedale and half-Bluetick hound. He will only run a track if given the command or he jumps the cougar.

All of a sudden, Chief's barking indicated he had jumped the cat and was following the trail. Bob turned Ralph loose and soon both dogs were sounding their "treed" bark. Bob and I hurried over to the tree, and there was the most beautiful sight that I've ever seen. The big tom looked golden brown against the green of the pine trees.

Bob tied up the dogs as I positioned myself for the shot. The arrow hit him right behind the front leg and the cat died before he could go twenty yards. Later, when we had laid his hide on the floor, it measured eight feet, seven inches and we estimated his weight at 160 pounds.

ROOSEVELT ELK
by Dale F. Baumgartner

The big bull was working a drainage only a couple of miles from my house. It was an area I knew well, and I'd seen the bull two times before the season opened. In an old homestead clearing in the drainage, I had previously built a tree stand. The nearest logging road was about a mile away, and I had cleared a trail for access to the meadow. During the season, I made many trips into the canyon to see if the elk were using the clearing. There wasn't much sign until the day before the season was to close.

When I arrived that day I knew the elk were close by, and I went directly to the tree stand. Before long I could hear elk back in the timber working toward the meadow.

Two cows, two spikes, and a forked-horn entered the meadow cautiously. Just then the big bull bugled from somewhere behind them. Minutes later, he came trotting out into the meadow herding six more cows. He went directly after the lesser bulls and drove them out of the clearing. On his way back toward the cows, which were directly below my tree stand by then, he stopped and tore the heck out of a ten-foot fir tree.

My arrow hit him hard in the chest as he walked directly past my stand. The bull bolted about ten yards before a second arrow hit him in the hindquarter. I hadn't lead him enough.

From the stand, I could see the bull standing back in timber for a few minutes. After waiting for what seemed a long time, I got out of the tree and went over to where I'd last seen the bull. Finding a big pool of blood and a good blood trail, I started after him. Using my flashlight, I followed the trail down toward the bottom of the canyon. It seemed as though he was just staying ahead of me. I could hear him but it was too dark to see him. Finally, I decided to head home and get help.

Picking up the blood trail at first light the next day, I recovered the bull farther down the canyon. With the help of two friends, it still took a day and a half to get him out.

YELLOWSTONE ELK
by Wayne Bradley

I had been invited to join a group of Orange County, Texas bowhunters for a deer and elk hunting trip to Colorado during the 1986 season. The party included Todd Soape, Todd's dad, Willie Joe, Jerry Pearson, Larry Melancon, J. T. Richard, Don Dunaway, and T. Joe Kraut. We were joined in camp later by Von Evans, Herb York, and Don Jones.

I was really excited about my first bowhunting trip and was probably the least likely success candidate in the group. You see, I'd never fired an arrow at an animal in my life.

Three days before we were to head home, I managed to bag a mule deer doe, my first anything with a bow. Todd also bagged a deer. That was quite a feat for both of us, but we still wanted to have a chance at elk. We had heard about a canyon so rugged and inpenetrable that most hunters wouldn't even try to hunt it. Todd and I decided to give it a try.

The next day, we were well within the canyon at daylight and split up to scout the area. I heard Todd blow his call, and a bull answered immediately. Within seconds, another bull bugled. Todd and I got back together and began stalking the nearest bull through a dense aspen thicket.

While we were sneaking toward the nearest elk, three more bulls sounded off. As Todd cut loose a challenge, a big bull elk charged in and stopped on a ledge overlooking us. Todd had the best angle, but his arrow ricocheted off his bow and sailed to the left. He was shooting an overdraw setup and the broadhead had twisted on the shaft, striking the face of the bow when he shot.

About then we heard him! Just from the volume and sound of his bugle, we knew he was huge. Also, the other bulls got real quiet, fast.

We circled to get the wind in our favor, then set up to bugle near a well-used game trail. When I was ready, Todd moved about fifteen yards down the trail, dropping some scent along the way. He waited a few minutes and began breaking limbs, stomping the ground, and rubbing limbs on trees. Then Todd bugled, following it with three or four grunts.

A monsterous bull came charging down the hill. All I could see at first were huge antlers coming at me above the brush. The bull trotted up to where Todd was hidden and stopped less than fifteen feet from him, slobber flying from his mouth and obviously worked up. Even from that close, Todd couldn't shoot because of the brush. When the bull stopped, I shot and heard the arrow hit but didn't see it.

Moments later, I eased over to Todd. "Did you see that? He doggone near ran over me when you shot him!" Todd exclaimed. He had also heard the twang of my bow and saw the arrow strike the bull behind the shoulder. Todd was sure he'd heard the animal fall. We started down the blood trail but didn't have far to go. The huge bull was dead no more than sixty yards away.

Todd's first reaction was, "Oh my God! It's a world record!" He was right.

PRONGHORN
by Judd Cooney

The herd buck, now leisurely following the seven does and fawns toward the water hole, was a good one by any standards. His horns were shiny black and heavy at the bases, with wide prongs. I estimated the horns to be about fifteen inches or a bit more. This started me to having a one-sided mental debate with myself, attempting to calmly decide whether or not I should try to take this buck.

I had been sitting patiently in the pit blind since before daylight, and this was the first bunch of pronghorns that I'd seen. From past years of hunting this particular water hole, I knew it wasn't the most popular antelope hangout, but the bucks that did come to it were always very respectable and some were downright huge. The buck that was getting closer with each step was not in the huge category, but he would probably shade the one that I had taken a year ago—which made him qualify for some serious consideration.

My mental gymnastics were brought to a screeching halt when I caught movement on the skyline where the approaching herd had first appeared. Even without my binoculars, I could make out what was obviously a very good buck standing on the ridgetop. But when I got the glasses focused on him, my heart gave a bit of a jump and my brainstorming started all over again. The herd buck, which by this time was standing some thirty-five yards away eyeing the water, was all but forgotten.

My first thought was that the buck was really odd looking and too skinny-horned to be a real trophy, but those horns had the height to make me forget about their shape. By this time, the new arrival was headed my way, following the exact trail the herd had taken to the water hole. I noticed, but only for an instant, that the first buck was broadside and in perfect position for a shot.

I turned my total concentration to the loner now approaching the water hole. "If he gives me a chance," I thought, "I'm going to try and fill my license with this buck."

I was surprisingly calm as I drew my bow and sent the 2117 flashing toward the big buck. The fluorescent orange cresting and bright yellow vanes stopped just behind his front shoulder. The buck bolted off the dam and headed back for the ridge. He lost his momentum after thirty yards and piled up in the sagebrush.

I felt he was a darn respectable buck until I walked up and got a close look at his horns. It was then that the realization of just how huge he was hit me! The horns were not only long but extremely massive, both below and above

the prong. The upper horn tips seemed to extend forever above the prong, giving him the tall, skinny look. I said a little prayer of thanks to the gods of the hunt and began field dressing him.

ROCKY MOUNTAIN GOAT
by Dave Ramsay

For several years I had been interested in a small creek valley not far from my home in western British Columbia. A good-sized chunk of the north side of this drainage is ideal goat range and my hunting partner and I have spotted several nice trophy-class goats there in past years. We chose this area for our winter goat hunt in 1981/82.

Although we only saw six or seven animals a day, we soon came to recognize three outstanding billies. One of them had large dirt stains on his hindquarters.

As the snow piled up, snowshoes became necessary to reach the hunting area. We decided that too much time was being wasted making the five-mile round-trip from the nearest road. The days were short, and the goats were at least a two-hour climb up from the creek bottom. On February 15, 1982, I worked my way up over our trail with a three-day supply of camping gear tied to my pack board.

That night it snowed another foot. The new snow was blowing and drifting the next morning when I set up my spotting scope. After two hours of glassing, I picked out the old boy with the stained hair bedded under a small ledge.

The knee-deep powder and gusting winds muffled my approach almost completely. Three-and-a-half hours after leaving camp, I was ready for the final stalk. Reaching the edge of a little draw opposite where the goat had been bedded, I could see another animal about 200 yards away across the cliff. Sixty yards above me stood yet another goat. Although he was looking right at me, I think my white camouflage seemed to reassure him.

I had just gotten my mitts off and an arrow nocked when the old boy stepped into view thirty-five yards away. The 2216 arched up and thumped into his left side. The goat turned to the right, disappearing, only to reappear cartwheeling down a slide chute in a cloud of snow.

Backtracking to my pack, I scrambled down off the cliffs and worked my way over to the path the goat had taken. I found him only a few hundred feet from the creek and my tent. Luckily, the horns were undamaged after having tumbled down nearly 400 yards.

BIGHORN SHEEP
by Gene Moore

It was the first day of the 1983 sheep hunting season. Not having scouted the area at all that year, I wasn't mentally prepared for the hunt. But I knew that Colorado's Rampart Range held several large rams, and I'd located a dandy two seasons before.

As daylight approached, I started for where that ram usually beds down. By 8:35, I was thirty yards from the bedded ram. As I moved to get in shooting position, I kicked some rocks loose. The ram got up, turned toward me, then bounded out of sight.

Monday morning I walked across two ridges to where I thought the ram had gone. About 10:15, I got on a rock outcropping and began to scan the area. Some six hundred yards below me, I spotted the ram. He was looking right at me. Satisfied I wasn't a threat, the ram got up from his bed and started feeding.

I stepped off the rocks and planned my stalk. By putting a heavy pair of wool socks over my boots, I silenced my footsteps considerably. It took me one-and-a-half hours to get within twenty-five yards of the ram. As I scanned the area, I now counted seven more sheep with him. With that many rams present, I would have to be extra careful to get a shot at the big one.

Finally, after three-and-a-half hours, he got up and the rest of the sheep followed. They were feeding to my right at the same elevation. I was able to see a small hole through the timber about fifteen yards ahead of them. As I impatiently waited, he stepped into the opening. Instinctively, I let the string go. The arrow was flying perfect, but it was too high! I shot just over his back. The ram ran about thirty yards and stopped broadside out in the open. I nocked

another arrow and started to draw when the ram began feeding back toward me.

Within a few minutes, he was in the same opening. This time, the arrow passed right through him. I was surprised he didn't run. He just turned around, walked twenty feet and layed down.

Only one larger ram has ever been killed in Colorado. It was taken with a rifle and had a Boone and Crocket score of 193.

MUSKOX
by David Collis

As I left my Florida home for a muskox hunt on Banks Island, NWT, I didn't quite realize that I would be experiencing a 118-degree difference in outside temperature. The temperature was −35 degrees when I was met in Inuvik by the hunt coordinator, Jessie Ames. She took me to my hotel and later in the day outfitted me with my special arctic survival clothing.

The next day's air service took me to Banks Island where I was given the choice of staying in the lodge or living with my guide and his family. I opted to stay with my guide. We enjoyed an evening of visiting and story telling about our previous hunting adventures. Quite a few Eskimos came over to inspect my archery equipment, as I was the only bowhunter in the group of seven hunters.

The next morning we packed our sleds with provisions and headed northeast, planning to stay out for three or four days. The trip to the hunting area took us about twelve hours. At night, we slept in a double-walled tent very adequately heated by a fuel oil heater which also served as a cook stove.

The first day we spent hunting muskox, we had a good chance to look over quite a few. Also on the first day, I was able to shoot an arctic hare and a ptarmigan, making for a successful start and a great supper.

On the third day, we spotted a small group of muskox containing two fine bulls. We stalked closer to the group and I decided to take the largest bull. They were feeding on a small wind-swept bluff where the snow was not so deep. A little canyon nearby gave me the cover I needed to stalk. I shot the largest bull twice at twenty yards. Although one shot would have been sufficient, two made for a quicker kill, and he was mine to claim in less a minute or so.

Now the Eskimos had their work cut out for them. Skinning and cutting up the meat took about three hours. After a seven-hour ride back to town, there was a great celebration, for mine was the largest muskox taken on the hunt.

DESERT BIGHORN SHEEP
by Peter C. Knagge

In Arizona, the odds of drawing a desert bighorn sheep tag are overwhelming. However, prior to the 1985 drawing, I had the intuitive feeling that I would draw a license. The day permits arrive in the mail, the real surprise came when my wife called to tell me she too had drawn one of the coveted permits.

I had spent years studying my unit and knew of several large rams including "Old Yellow Horns," an affectionate name given to one ugly, scar-faced old ram, and "The Stove Pipe" ram, so-called because he was well broomed with extremely heavy bases.

During the summer and early fall, I watched these two rams on numerous occasions and felt confident that I'd get a shot at one of them. Once the season began, I spent twelve days in a different unit helping my wife collect a nice ram.

With five days of the season left, I went with a friend to my unit, but we could not locate the large rams. Since the terrain is such that it is next to impossible to miss the sheep in the small mountain ranges that dot the unit, I concluded they were no longer in the area. I would have to settle for another ram.

Most of my fifteen-mile daily jaunts resulted in no sign of sheep. Occasionally, I found bands of ewes, and once I passed up an elephant-tusked-type ram at thirty yards since I estimated him to be below my goal. Finally, nearing the end of my hunt, I found a band of seventeen sheep, including a ram I thought would score high enough to meet my personal minimum.

The next morning the wind was wrong for an approach, so I had to back off and circle around a few ridges to get in position. The herd moved west, but I saw the big ram bed down. The strong wind covered my final stalk. The 2219 hit the ram solidly. At first I thought I had missed, but then the ram slowly stepped off the rock and disappeared except for the top of his horns. He traveled just a few yards.

The ram was not "Old Yellow Horns," but I was more than happy with the largest desert sheep taken with a bow.

Ishi Award

ISHI AWARD

The Ishi Award is the highest award given by the Pope and Young Club. Only one may be presented for any Recording Period and then only when a truly outstanding North American trophy animal is judged to be deserving of the recognition. There have been nine presentations of the Ishi Award during the history of the Pope and Young Club records program. They are the following:

ISHI AWARD PRESENTATIONS

4th Recording Period (1963–1964)
Non-Typical Whitetail Deer
Score: 279 7/8
taken in Nebraska by Del Austin.

6th Recording Period (1967–1968)
Typical Whitetail Deer
Score: 204 4/8
taken in Illinois by Mel Johnson.

7th Recording Period (1969–1970)
Bighorn Sheep
Score: 176 3/8
taken in Montana by Ray Alt.

8th Recording Period (1971–1972)
Barren Ground Caribou
Score: 446 6/8
taken in Alaska by Art Kragness.

9th Recording Period (1973–1974)
Alaska-Yukon Moose
Score: 248 0/8
taken in Alaska by Dr. Michael Cusack.

11th Recording Period (1977–1978)
Columbian Blacktail Deer
Score: 172 2/8
taken in Oregon by B. G. Shurtleff.

12th Recording Period (1979–1980)
Black Bear
Score: 22 4/16
taken in Colorado by Ray Cox.

13th Recording Period (1981–1982)
Cougar
Score: 15 11/16
taken in Idaho by Jerry James.

14th Recording Period (1983–1984)
Typical Mule Deer
Score: 201 4/8
taken in Colorado by Bill Barcus.

Photo by Judd Cooney

WORLD RECORD ALASKA BROWN BEAR
Score: 28 7/16
Unimak Island, Alaska – 1985
Hunter: John D. Frost

ALASKA BROWN BEAR
Ursus arctos middendorffi and certain related subspecies

Minimum Score 20

Score	Greatest Length	Greatest Width	Sex	Area	State/ Province	Hunter's Name	Date	Rank
28-07/16	17-11/16	10-12/16	M	Unimak Island	AK	John D. "Jack" Frost	1985	1
28-00/16	17-15/16	10-01/16	M	Wide Bay, AK Pen.	AK	Fred Bear	1960	2
27-01/16	16-15/16	10-02/16	M	Bear Bay, AK Pen.	AK	Fred Bear	1962	3
25-02/16	16-02/16	9-00/16	M	Chichagof Island	AK	Kenneth T. Wotring	1982	4
23-06/16	14-06/16	9-00/16	M	Kodiak Island	AK	Gordon Longville	1961	5
23-04/16	14-11/16	8-09/16	M	Admiralty Island	AK	John R. Thiele	1984	6
23-04/16	15-03/16	8-01/16	F	Joshua Green River	AK	John Koldeway	1985	6
22-15/16	14-02/16	8-13/16	F	Sheepcreek-Valdez	AK	Gerald R. Gold	1966	8
22-07/16	14-02/16	8-05/16	F	Merrill Pass	AK	Ralph Ertz	1975	9
22-06/16	14-04/16	8-02/16	M	Kodiak Island	AK	Buddy Watson	1965	10
21-15/16	14-07/16	7-08/16	M	Kajulik Bay	AK	Thomas J. Hoffman	1983	11
21-13/16	13-15/16	7-14/16	F	Merrill Pass	AK	Dan Hollingsworth	1975	12
21-13/16	13-04/16	8-09/16	F	Dana Glacier	AK	Dan W. Morrison	1975	12
21-10/16	13-14/16	7-12/16	F	Allantack Bay, AK Pen.	AK	Bill Van Houten	1961	14
21-08/16	13-09/16	7-15/16	M	Hoonah	AK	Len Cardinale	1979	15
21-07/16	13-08/16	7-15/16	F	Fidalgo Bay	AK	Joseph West	1966	16
21-07/16	14-01/16	7-06/16	M	Chichagof Island	AK	Ray Keenan	1984	16
21-02/16	13-14/16	7-04/16	M	Anachuck R., AK Pen.	AK	Martin Hanson	1958	18
21-01/16	13-12/16	7-05/16	F	Mat-Su Borough	AK	Rickie D. Snell	1985	19
20-15/16	13-04/16	7-11/16	M	Admiralty Island	AK	Allen L. Grierson	1985	20
20-12/16	13-08/16	7-04/16	F	King Salmon	AK	Rhonda Baker	1977	21
20-11/16	13-09/16	7-02/16	M	Talketna Mountains	AK	L.M. Peppers	1983	22
20-01/16	12-14/16	7-03/16	M	Fog Lakes	AK	Dennis L. Lattery	1984	23

WORLD RECORD BLACK BEAR
Photo by Lee Kline
Score: 22 4/16
Sinbad Ridge, Colorado – 1978
Hunter: Ray Cox

BLACK BEAR
Ursus americanus americanus and related subspecies

Minimum Score 18

Score	Greatest Length	Greatest Width	Sex	Area	State/ Province	Hunter's Name	Date	Rank
22-04/16	13-07/16	8-13/16	M	Sinbad Ridge	CO	Ray Cox	1978	1
22-00/16	13-11/16	8-05/16	M	Lincoln County	WI	Bob Faufau	1981	2
21-13/16	13-09/16	8-04/16	M	Kooskia	ID	Harold Boyack	1976	3
21-12/16	13-05/16	8-07/16	M	Price County	WI	Robert Brotske	1981	4
21-12/16	13-06/16	8-06/16	M	Big River	SAS	Bill Dear	1985	4
21-11/16	13-09/16	8-02/16	M	Nipawin	SAS	Ray Mastel	1974	6
21-11/16	13-07/16	8-04/16	M	Sevier County	UT	Robert F. Fitzgerald	1984	6
21-10/16	13-06/16	8-04/16	M	Hudson Bay	SAS	Craig Richardson	1985	8
21-09/16	13-05/16	8-04/16	M	Iron County	WI	Gary Johnson	1982	9
21-08/16	13-06/16	8-02/16	M	Hudson Bay	SAS	Garry Benson	1976	10
21-08/16	13-02/16	8-06/16	M	Kern County	CA	Dean M. Lutge	1981	10
21-07/16	13-07/16	8-00/16	M	Nipawin	SAS	Don Adams	1975	12
21-07/16	13-07/16	8-00/16	M	Mendocino County	CA	Jim Oliver	1984	12
21-07/16	13-00/16	8-07/16	M	Garfield County	CO	Norman J. O'Bryan	1985	12
21-06/16	13-02/16	8-04/16	M	Walland	TN	William M. Lyell	1967	15
21-06/16	13-06/16	8-00/16	M	Drummond	WI	Larry L. Frye	1975	15
21-05/16	13-05/16	8-00/16	M	Ministikwan	SAS	Gary Mutter	1985	17
21-05/16	13-00/16	8-05/16	M	Kenora	ONT	Robert Svoboda	1986	17
21-04/16	13-07/16	7-13/16	M	Flournoy	CA	Jim Cox	1980	19
21-04/16	13-05/16	7-15/16	M	Cass County	MN	Myles Keller	1980	19
21-04/16	13-04/16	8-00/16	M	Duck Mountain	MAN	Dave Cordes	1984	19
21-04/16	13-08/16	7-12/16	M	Spiritwood	SAS	Ron Schira	1985	19
21-02/16	13-02/16	8-00/16	M	Mammoth Mountain	CA	Clarke Merrill	1963	23
21-02/16	13-07/16	7-12/16	M	Hubbard County	MN	Dean Como	1974	23
21-02/16	13-04/16	7-14/16	M	Hudson Bay	SAS	Sam Qualls	1981	23
21-02/16	13-10/16	7-08/16	M	Langlade County	WI	Mike Steliga	1981	23
21-02/16	13-06/16	7-12/16	M	Rockingham	VA	Roger O. Wyant	1984	23
21-02/16	12-14/16	8-04/16	M	Herkimer County	NY	John Palmer	1986	23
21-01/16	13-01/16	8-00/16	M	Hubbard County	MN	Darrell Magnussen	1974	29
21-01/16	13-02/16	7-15/16	M	Quetico Provincial Park	ONT	Robert Filbrandt	1981	29
21-00/16	12-13/16	8-03/16	M	Sioux Narrows	ONT	R. B. Cooley	1960	31
21-00/16	12-14/16	8-02/16	M	Uncompahgre N. F.	CO	Dr. James Emerson	1974	31
21-00/16	13-03/16	7-13/16	M	Shasta County	CA	Norman Mallonee	1974	31
21-00/16	13-03/16	7-13/16	M	Ashland County	WI	Bryan C. Anderson	1980	31
21-00/16	13-02/16	7-14/16	M	Yavapai County	AZ	Mike Whelan	1981	31
21-00/16	13-02/16	7-14/16	M	Riding Mountain	MAN	James A. Carson	1982	31
21-00/16	13-02/16	7-14/16	M	Sawyer County	WI	John G. Bohmann	1982	31
21-00/16	12-15/16	8-01/16	M	Kosciusko Island	AK	Michael C. Fezatte	1982	31
21-00/16	13-03/16	7-13/16	M	Langlade County	WI	Michael Steliga	1982	31
21-00/16	13-04/16	7-12/16	M	Hudson Bay	SAS	Archie Lovelace	1983	31
21-00/16	12-10/16	8-06/16	M	Echouani Lake	QUE	Collins F. Kellogg	1985	31
21-00/16	13-03/16	7-13/16	M	Debden	SAS	Allan Sykes	1986	31
20-15/16	13-04/16	7-11/16	M	Sequoia National Forest	CA	Robert Shilling	1971	43
20-15/16	12-12/16	8-03/16	M	Lincoln County	WI	Jay Manthei	1980	43
20-15/16	13-01/16	7-14/16	M	Nipiwan	SAS	Glen Sellsted	1981	43
20-15/16	12-14/16	8-01/16	M	Goodsoil	SAS	Ralph Clarke	1982	43
20-15/16	12-11/16	8-04/16	M	Routt County	CO	Mark A. Chapman	1982	43
20-15/16	13-00/16	7-15/16	M	Monominto	MAN	Erik Thienpondt	1983	43
20-15/16	12-15/16	8-00/16	M	Meadow Lake	SAS	Bruce Stieber	1986	43
20-14/16	12-10/16	8-06/16	M	Unit 61	CO	Richard A. Schreiber	1973	50
20-14/16	13-00/16	7-14/16	M	Prince of Wales Island	AK	Gary G. Smith	1978	50
20-14/16	12-08/16	8-06/16	M	Red Lake	ONT	George Law	1981	50
20-14/16	13-02/16	7-12/16	M	Cass County	MN	Craig Enervold	1982	50
20-14/16	13-06/16	7-08/16	M	Duck Mountain	MAN	John "Jack" Cordes	1984	50
20-14/16	12-09/16	8-05/16	M	Routt County	CO	Lonny Vanatta	1984	50
20-14/16	12-12/16	8-02/16	M	Thunder Bay	ONT	Tim Walters	1985	50
20-14/16	12-15/16	7-15/16	M	Camas County	ID	Ed Cushman	1986	50
20-13/16	12-12/16	8-01/16	M	Marrns Creek	ID	Joe Schreideler	1977	58
20-13/16	12-11/16	8-02/16	M	Langlade County	WI	Eugene Strong	1978	58
20-13/16	12-14/16	7-15/16	M	Humboldt County	CA	Calvin Farner	1983	58
20-12/16	12-12/16	8-00/16	?	Black River	AZ	Dr. C. G. Clare	1967	61
20-12/16	12-05/16	8-07/16	M	Carp Lake	MI	Hawley H. Rhew	1974	61
20-12/16	12-12/16	8-00/16	M	Douglas County	WI	Robert J. Schmidt	1975	61
20-12/16	12-15/16	7-13/16	M	Armstrong	ONT	Paul Mahaney	1977	61

BLACK BEAR

(continued)

Score	Greatest Length	Greatest Width	Sex	Area	State/ Province	Hunter's Name	Date	Rank
20-12/16	13-00/16	7-12/16	M	San Miguel County	CO	John W. Rowe	1978	61
20-12/16	12-15/16	7-13/16	M	Bonneville County	ID	John Hill	1983	61
20-12/16	12-11/16	8-01/16	M	Prince of Wales Island	AK	Jack Williams	1985	61
20-12/16	12-11/16	8-01/16	M	Plumas County	CA	Kevin Hull	1986	61
20-11/16	12-13/16	7-14/16	M	Thunder Bay	ONT	Mel Johnson	1974	69
20-11/16	12-14/16	7-13/16	M	Red Stone	CO	Dale W. Gray	1975	69
20-11/16	13-02/16	7-09/16	M	Burro Mountain	CO	Walter Krom	1976	69
20-11/16	13-02/16	7-09/16	M	Rockingham County	VA	Roger O. Wyant	1982	69
20-10/16	13-01/16	7-09/16	M	Burro Mountain	CO	Frank "Rit" Heller	1969	73
20-10/16	12-10/16	8-00/16	M	Sierra County	CA	Ervin K. McMakin	1971	73
20-10/16	12-14/16	7-12/16	M	Ft. Francis	ONT	George Geisert	1973	73
20-10/16	12-10/16	8-00/16	M	Crawford Park	MAN	Brent Mills	1981	73
20-10/16	12-10/16	8-00/16	M	Tweed District	ONT	John E. Lawson	1983	73
20-09/16	12-12/16	7-13/16	M	Ely	MN	Art A. Heinze	1970	78
20-09/16	12-12/16	7-13/16	M	Prince of Wales Island	AK	Roy C. Ewen	1973	78
20-09/16	12-07/16	8-02/16	M	Grand County	CO	Curt Lynn	1973	78
20-09/16	12-12/16	7-13/16	M	Wawa	ONT	Robert C. McGuire	1975	78
20-09/16	12-11/16	7-14/16	M	Aitkin County	MN	Myles Keller	1977	78
20-09/16	13-01/16	7-08/16	M	Thunder Bay	ONT	Lester W. Jass	1979	78
20-09/16	12-13/16	7-12/16	M	Delta County	CO	Steve McCarthy	1982	78
20-09/16	12-09/16	8-00/16	M	Franklin County	NY	Edward M. Odell	1982	78
20-09/16	12-11/16	7-14/16	M	Missaukee County	MI	Gregory Korkoske	1983	78
20-09/16	12-10/16	7-15/16	M	Northwest of Dryden	ONT	Larry Bauman	1984	78
20-09/16	13-01/16	7-08/16	M	Durban	MAN	David H. Boland	1985	78
20-09/16	12-07/16	8-02/16	M	Thunder Bay	ONT	Daniel Schuttler	1985	78
20-08/16	12-13/16	7-11/16	M	Queen Charlotte Island	BC	Peter Halbig	1960	90
20-08/16	12-14/16	7-10/16	M	Shawano County	WI	Bud Wiesman	1974	90
20-08/16	12-14/16	7-10/16	M	Kamsack	SAS	Steve Boychuk	1977	90
20-08/16	12-14/16	7-10/16	M	Tehama County	CA	Anthony P. Davi	1980	90
20-08/16	12-11/16	7-13/16	M	Strathnarer	BC	Dan Wicks	1981	90
20-08/16	12-13/16	7-11/16	M	Valley County	ID	David S. Scott	1982	90
20-08/16	12-01/16	8-07/16	M	Ignace	ONT	Jerry Klinesmith	1983	90
20-07/16	13-09/16	6-14/16	M	Nenana	AK	Robert Dunn	1968	97
20-07/16	12-10/16	7-13/16	M	Price County	WI	Bob Eckarot	1974	97
20-07/16	12-14/16	7-09/16	M	Montezuma County	CO	Bryan C. Neeley	1974	97
20-07/16	12-07/16	8-00/16	M	Whiteshell	MAN	Ken Warkentin	1978	97
20-07/16	12-11/16	7-12/16	M	Mille Lacs County	MN	Milt Zernechel	1980	97
20-07/16	12-06/16	8-01/16	M	Marquette County	MI	Thomas Benak	1982	97
20-07/16	12-11/16	7-12/16	M	Mat-Su Borough	AK	Jack V. Rouse	1983	97
20-07/16	12-10/16	7-13/16	M	St. Louis County	MN	Ken Lenk	1983	97
20-07/16	12-12/16	7-11/16	M	Garfield County	CO	Roger Bolander	1985	97
20-07/16	12-14/16	7-09/16	M	Arran	SAS	Bill Clink	1986	97
20-06/16	12-11/16	7-11/16	M	Tulare County	CA	Quentin M. Boutch	1967	107
20-06/16	12-11/16	7-11/16	M	Baxter Pass, Mack	CO	Steve Bergman	1970	107
20-06/16	12-15/16	7-07/16	M	Kern County	CA	Leo Farley	1973	107
20-06/16	12-08/16	7-14/16	M	Shasta County	CA	Susan Mallonee	1974	107
20-06/16	12-06/16	8-00/16	M	Saguache County	CO	Ed Wiseman	1975	107
20-06/16	12-11/16	7-11/16	M	Reindeer Lake	SAS	James Buchanan	1976	107
20-06/16	12-12/16	7-10/16	M	Flower Station	ONT	Richard H. Shoup	1977	107
20-06/16	12-09/16	7-13/16	M	Ear Falls	ONT	Terry R. Fletcher	1978	107
20-06/16	12-11/16	7-11/16	M	St. Louis County	MN	Russell Wimberly	1979	107
20-06/16	12-11/16	7-11/16	M	Reserve	SAS	Richard Loffler	1984	107
20-06/16	12-14/16	7-08/16	M	Bayfield County	WI	Paul Deckert	1984	107
20-06/16	12-09/16	7-13/16	M	Ignace	ONT	Randy J. Tylke	1985	107
20-05/16	12-14/16	7-07/16	M	Shasta County	CA	Harv Ebers	1964	119
20-05/16	12-12/16	7-09/16	M	St. Louis County	MN	Jay Deones	1970	119
20-05/16	12-13/16	7-08/16	M	Avery's Creek	NC	Robert T. Austin	1971	119
20-05/16	13-00/16	7-05/16	M	Emma Lake	SAS	Ernie Johnston	1972	119
20-05/16	12-04/16	8-01/16	M	Montezuma County	CO	Stanley A. Coval	1975	119
20-05/16	12-11/16	7-10/16	M	Montrose County	CO	Jack Cassidy	1976	119
20-05/16	12-11/16	7-10/16	M	Lemhi County	ID	Richard R. Smith	1977	119
20-05/16	12-10/16	7-11/16	M	White Mountain Wild.	NM	Tom Mitchell	1978	119
20-05/16	12-12/16	7-09/16	M	Marquette County	MI	Bernard E. Stiritz	1980	119
20-05/16	12-09/16	7-12/16	M	Hudson Bay	SAS	Sam Qualls	1981	119

BLACK BEAR

Minimum Score 18

Score	Greatest Length	Greatest Width	Sex	Area	State/ Province	Hunter's Name	Date	Rank
20-05/16	12-13/16	7-08/16	M	McCoy Creek	ID	Michael Ferraro	1981	119
20-05/16	12-03/16	8-02/16	M	Presque Isle County	MI	William C. Green III	1981	119
20-05/16	12-09/16	7-12/16	M	Lake Devlin	ONT	J. E. Abhold	1982	119
20-05/16	12-05/16	8-00/16	M	Meagher County	MT	Richard M. Campbell	1982	119
20-05/16	12-12/16	7-09/16	M	Otero County	NM	Michael Crebb	1984	119
20-05/16	12-07/16	7-14/16	M	Atikokan	ONT	Greg Morehead	1985	119
20-05/16	12-08/16	7-13/16	M	Archuleta County	CO	Ronald J. Murphy	1985	119
20-05/16,	12-06/16	7-15/16	M	Jackson County	OR	David Greisen, Jr.	1985	119
20-04/16	12-06/16	7-14/16	M	Silver Lake	MI	William Benson	1967	137
20-04/16	12-11/16	7-09/16	M	Somerset County	ME	Felix Nosewicz	1968	137
20-04/16	12-10/16	7-10/16	M	Grand Junction	CO	M. R. James	1971	137
20-04/16	12-12/16	7-08/16	M	Los Alamos	NM	Kenneth A. Meyer	1971	137
20-04/16	12-12/16	7-08/16	M	Hayward	WI	George Geisert	1972	137
20-04/16	12-07/16	7-13/16	M	Madison County	MT	Bob Savage	1977	137
20-04/16	12-05/16	7-15/16	M	Kashabowie	ONT	Hans C. Forssell	1978	137
20-04/16	12-07/16	7-13/16	M	Valora	ONT	Elmer R. Luse, Jr.	1981	137
20-04/16	12-08/16	7-12/16	M	Siskiyou County	CA	Bill Waters	1981	137
20-04/16	12-08/16	7-12/16	M	Mesa County	CO	Larry A. McIntosh	1982	137
20-04/16	12-05/16	7-15/16	M	Nez Perce	ID	Hubert M. Sims, Jr.	1982	137
20-04/16	12-07/16	7-13/16	M	Trinity County	CA	Rodney A. York	1983	137
20-04/16	12-12/16	7-08/16	M	Carrot River	SAS	William Jorgensen	1985	137
20-04/16	12-08/16	7-12/16	M	Swan River	MAN	Marc N. Shaft	1985	137
20-04/16	12-11/16	7-09/16	M	Water Hen River	SAS	Pink Atkins	1986	137
20-03/16	12-13/16	7-06/16	M	Prince Rupert	BC	Frank Huneck	1960	152
20-03/16	12-06/16	7-13/16	M	Ignace	ONT	Jerry Ulrich	1968	152
20-03/16	12-04/16	7-15/16	M	Little Fall Creek	ID	Joe Adams	1971	152
20-03/16	12-08/16	7-11/16	M	Lakeside	OR	Robert L. Wegand	1971	152
20-03/16	12-03/16	8-00/16	M	Payette River	ID	Mark W. Powell	1975	152
20-03/16	12-12/16	7-07/16	M	Smoke Lake	ALB	Kenneth Szgatti	1975	152
20-03/16	12-06/16	7-13/16	M	Dolores County	CO	Randy E. Dossey	1979	152
20-03/16	12-05/16	7-14/16	M	Dolores County	CO	Marvin Reichenau	1979	152
20-03/16	12-10/16	7-09/16	M	Itasca County	MN	Gerald N. Rivetts, Jr.	1980	152
20-03/16	12-08/16	7-11/16	M	Foxford	SAS	Brian Acton	1982	152
20-03/16	12-13/16	7-06/16	M	Catron County	NM	John R. Caminiti	1984	152
20-03/16	12-03/16	8-00/16	M	Marquette County	MI	Kurt Funk	1985	152
20-03/16	12-13/16	7-06/16	M	Red Lake	ONT	Gerald Dykin	1986	152
20-03/16	12-12/16	7-07/16	M	Sioux Lookout	ONT	Tom Rosenthal	1986	152
20-02/16	12-09/16	7-09/16	M	Virginia	MN	James Harwood	1966	166
20-02/16	12-09/16	7-09/16	M	St. Louis County	MN	Ron Johnson	1968	166
20-02/16	12-06/16	7-12/16	M	Bayfield County	WI	Clarence J. Biddle	1973	166
20-02/16	12-06/16	7-12/16	M	Iron County	WI	Chuck Ramsay	1973	166
20-02/16	12-09/16	7-09/16	M	Delta County	CO	Bill Izon	1976	166
20-02/16	12-10/16	7-08/16	M	Montrose County	CO	John Brandt	1978	166
20-02/16	12-01/16	8-01/16	M	Del Norte County	CA	Fred D. Davis, Jr.	1978	166
20-02/16	12-12/16	7-06/16	M	Montezuma County	CO	Floyd H. Hicks	1978	166
20-02/16	12-08/16	7-10/16	M	Grand Junction	CO	Dennis Behn	1979	166
20-02/16	12-09/16	7-09/16	M	Delta County	CO	Scott Dillon	1981	166
20-02/16	12-06/16	7-12/16	M	Mendocino County	CA	Kenneth Marquardt	1981	166
20-02/16	12-12/16	7-06/16	M	Tehama County	CA	Randy Rehse	1981	166
20-02/16	12-02/16	7-06/16	M	Hudson Bay	SAS	Randy Lorenz	1982	166
20-02/16	12-07/16	7-11/16	M	Iron County	MI	George J. Hronkin III	1982	166
20-02/16	12-10/16	7-08/16	M	Douglas County	WI	Ron Ekstrand	1983	166
20-02/16	12-06/16	7-12/16	M	Kuiu Island	AK	William F. Burgess	1984	166
20-02/16	12-07/16	7-11/16	M	Meadow Lake	SAS	Richard W. Theurer	1984	166
20-02/16	12-08/16	7-10/16	M	Nipigon	ONT	Richard Scorzafava	1985	166
20-02/16	13-01/16	7-01/16	M	Sudberry	ONT	Frank Calabro	1986	166
20-02/16	12-13/16	7-05/16	M	Chisago County	MN	Mark Piel	1986	166
20-01/16	12-09/16	7-08/16	?	Shasta County	CA	Robert G. Sinclair	1967	186
20-01/16	12-05/16	7-12/16	M	Nipigon	ONT	Wilfred J. Ritchie, Jr.	1968	186
20-01/16	12-06/16	7-11/16	M	Vilas County	WI	Ben Jones	1972	186
20-01/16	11-15/16	8-02/16	M	Deep Creek, Ruby	AK	Harry Copeland	1976	186
20-01/16	12-10/16	7-07/16	M	Cowlitz County	WA	Smokey Crews	1976	186
20-01/16	12-10/16	7-07/16	M	Kitsap County	WA	Bud Jones	1977	186
20-01/16	12-04/16	7-13/16	M	San Miguel River	CO	Mike Barber	1978	186

BLACK BEAR

(continued)   Minimum Score 18

Score	Greatest Length	Greatest Width	Sex	Area	State/ Province	Hunter's Name	Date	Rank
20-01/16	12-10/16	7-07/16	M	E. Braintree	MAN	Ed Beamish	1979	186
20-01/16	12-00/16	8-01/16	M	Presque Isle	WI	Peter J. Leder	1979	186
20-01/16	12-10/16	7-07/16	M	Grand County	UT	Thomas W. Newman	1979	186
20-01/16	12-04/16	7-13/16	M	Pagosa Springs	CO	Len Cardinale	1980	186
20-01/16	12-03/16	7-14/16	M	Archuleta County	CO	Judd Cooney	1980	186
20-01/16	12-10/16	7-07/16	M	Mistatim	SAS	Gregory Simoneau	1980	186
20-01/16	12-05/16	7-12/16	M	Fremont County	ID	Nancy Atwood	1981	186
20-01/16	12-06/16	7-11/16	M	Clark County	ID	Garry James Kite	1981	186
20-01/16	12-06/16	7-11/16	M	Hudson Bay	SAS	Jerry Bien	1982	186
20-01/16	12-09/16	7-08/16	M	Glenn County	CA	Ron Fonseca	1982	186
20-01/16	12-06/16	7-11/16	M	Hudson Bay	SAS	Craig Richardson	1982	186
20-01/16	13-00/16	7-01/16	M	Bladen County	NC	R. G. Harris	1983	186
20-01/16	12-08/16	7-09/16	M	Fergus County	MT	Tom Storm	1984	186
20-01/16	12-01/16	8-00/16	M	Powell County	MT	Gene Coughlin	1984	186
20-01/16	12-04/16	7-13/16	M	Lost Lake	ONT	Gunter Lemke	1985	186
20-01/16	12-07/16	7-10/16	M	Lewis County	WA	Keith Heldreth	1985	186
20-01/16	12-05/16	7-12/16	M	Siskiyou County	CA	Stan Allison	1985	186
20-00/16	12-10/16	7-06/16	?	Rhinelander	WI	Fred Felbab	1964	210
20-00/16	12-04/16	7-12/16	M	Shasta County	CA	Jim Dougherty	1970	210
20-00/16	13-04/16	6-12/16	M	Cumberland County	TN	Louis Wix	1970	210
20-00/16	12-04/16	7-12/16	M	Kalkaska	MI	Doug Daniels	1978	210
20-00/16	12-11/16	7-05/16	M	Fremont County	ID	Earl Peterson	1978	210
20-00/16	12-09/16	7-07/16	M	Adams County	ID	Jack Arbaugh	1979	210
20-00/16	12-10/16	7-06/16	M	Tehama County	CA	Jim Dueval	1980	210
20-00/16	12-07/16	7-09/16	M	Prince George	BC	Ron F. McKay	1980	210
20-00/16	12-10/16	7-06/16	M	Ear Falls	ONT	Richard Eldridge	1981	210
20-00/16	12-06/16	7-10/16	M	Red Lake	ONT	Donald Schram	1981	210
20-00/16	12-05/16	7-11/16	M	Grand County	CO	Randy O. Vineyard	1981	210
20-00/16	12-06/16	7-10/16	M	Bobcaygeon	ONT	Arthur H. Whitney	1982	210
20-00/16	12-07/16	7-09/16	M	Sierra County	NM	Ray Hatfield	1983	210
20-00/16	12-05/16	7-11/16	M	Otter Lake	QUE	C. Roger Jerzerick	1983	210
20-00/16	12-03/16	7-13/16	M	Wallowa County	OR	Bill Lancaster	1983	210
20-00/16	12-07/16	7-09/16	M	Itaska County	MN	Roger Millard	1984	210
20-00/16	12-06/16	7-10/16	M	Apache County	AZ	Robert E. David	1984	210
20-00/16	12-08/16	7-08/16	M	Langlade County	WI	Jeff Traska	1984	210
20-00/16	12-02/16	7-14/16	M	Cowlitz County	WA	Annette Crews	1985	210
20-00/16	12-12/16	7-04/16	M	Meadow Lake	SAS	Robert Bain	1986	210
20-00/16	12-03/16	7-13/16	M	Thunder Bay	ONT	Bob Vrbsky	1986	210
20-00/16	12-08/16	7-08/16	M	Caribou County	ID	Coby Tigert	1986	210
20-00/16	12-15/16	7-01/16	M	Aitkin County	MN	Scott H. Mogen	1986	210
20-00/16	12-12/16	7-04/16	M	Rockingham County	VA	Roger Wyant	1986	210
19-15/16	11-15/16	8-00/16	F	Mercer	WI	Robert W. Blair	1967	234
19-15/16	12-00/16	7-15/16	M	Bayfield County	WI	Gary P. Kalal	1973	234
19-15/16	12-07/16	7-08/16	M	Blino River	ONT	John Lee	1973	234
19-15/16	12-08/16	7-07/16	M	Dryden	ONT	Robert C. Kirschner	1974	234
19-15/16	12-03/16	7-12/16	M	Trujillo Meadows	CO	Joseph Strasser, Jr.	1978	234
19-15/16	12-01/16	7-14/16	M	Sommerset	CO	Arthur Pace	1980	234
19-15/16	12-08/16	7-07/16	M	Florence County	WI	Peter H. Kortenhorn	1981	234
19-15/16	12-07/16	7-08/16	M	Dolores County	CO	Stanley A. Coval	1981	234
19-15/16	12-02/16	7-13/16	M	Ear Falls	ONT	Mike Woolman	1981	234
19-15/16	11-14/16	8-01/16	M	Penobscot County	ME	Henry C. Williams III	1983	234
19-15/16	12-03/16	7-12/16	M	Sandoval	NM	James M. Finn	1984	234
19-15/16	12-09/16	7-06/16	M	Burnett County	WI	Jerry Strese	1984	234
19-14/16	12-02/16	7-12/16	M	Columbine	CO	Ronald C. Gravenkemper	1962	246
19-14/16	12-02/16	7-12/16	M	Colcord Mountain	AZ	Hugh Pearson	1963	246
19-14/16	12-05/16	7-09/16	M	Burro Mountain, Meeker	CO	H. R. "Dutch" Wambold	1969	246
19-14/16	12-04/16	7-10/16	M	LaPlata County	CO	Wayne E. Knisley	1971	246
19-14/16	12-12/16	7-02/16	M	Tulare County	CA	Ronald J. Wade	1972	246
19-14/16	12-00/16	7-14/16	M	Grand Mesa	CO	Clint Johnston	1973	246
19-14/16	12-04/16	7-10/16	M	Ignace	ONT	Thomas Tietz	1977	246
19-14/16	12-06/16	7-08/16	M	Missoula County	MT	Dwayne Garner	1978	246
19-14/16	12-03/16	7-11/16	M	Thunder Bay	ONT	Lester W. Jass	1978	246
19-14/16	12-04/16	7-10/16	M	Routt County	CO	Mark Chapman	1979	246
19-14/16	12-02/16	7-12/16	M	Gunnison County	CO	Robert Feller	1979	246

BLACK BEAR

(continued)

Minimum Score 18

Score	Greatest Length	Greatest Width	Sex	Area	State/ Province	Hunter's Name	Date	Rank
19-14/16	12-05/16	7-09/16	M	Marinette County	WI	Paul B. Pelzek	1979	246
19-14/16	12-12/16	7-02/16	M	Hudson Bay	SAS	Jerry Bien	1980	246
19-14/16	12-07/16	7-07/16	M	Jemez Springs	NM	Mark Johnson	1980	246
19-14/16	12-06/16	7-08/16	M	Baraga County	MI	Thomas G. Young	1981	246
19-14/16	12-06/16	7-08/16	M	Glenn County	CA	Guy W. Foster	1982	246
19-14/16	12-08/16	7-06/16	M	Duck Mountain	MAN	John "Jack" Cordes	1983	246
19-14/16	12-05/16	7-09/16	M	Mesa County	CO	Raymond Roussett, Jr.	1983	246
19-14/16	12-05/16	7-09/16	M	Ear Falls	ONT	Brent Allen Poindexter	1985	246
19-14/16	12-11/16	7-03/16	M	Kootenai County	ID	John S. Thomson, Jr.	1986	246
19-14/16	12-04/16	7-10/16	M	Boise County	ID	Scott Privette	1986	246
19-14/16	12-08/16	7-06/16	M	Little Susitna River	AK	Brett Blessing	1986	246
19-13/16	12-07/16	7-06/16	M	Shasta County	CA	Stan L. McIntyre	1968	268
19-13/16	12-04/16	7-09/16	M	Dolores County	CO	Daryl Tieben	1976	268
19-13/16	12-11/16	7-02/16	M	Wawa	ONT	Robert C. McGuire	1977	268
19-13/16	12-07/16	7-06/16	M	Estaire	ONT	David L. Roose	1980	268
19-13/16	12-05/16	7-08/16	M	Jackknife Creek	ID	Tom Edwards	1981	268
19-13/16	12-06/16	7-07/16	M	Marble Mt. Wilderness	CA	Bill Hofferber	1981	268
19-13/16	12-09/16	7-04/16	M	Tucker County	WV	Robert B. Golightly	1982	268
19-13/16	12-02/16	7-11/16	M	Beardmore	ONT	Mike Mooney	1984	268
19-13/16	12-11/16	7-02/16	M	Hudson Bay	SAS	Craig Richardson	1985	268
19-13/16	12-04/16	7-09/16	M	Graham	ONT	Todd Henck	1985	268
19-13/16	12-06/16	7-07/16	M	Calvin Twp.	ONT	Bob Foulkrod	1986	268
19-12/16	12-04/16	7-08/16	M	Kenora	ONT	Noel Feather	1964	279
19-12/16	12-02/16	7-10/16	M	Chapleau	ONT	Lawrence Gallagher	1966	279
19-12/16	11-14/16	7-14/16	M	Swan Lake	MT	Joe Lawrence	1966	279
19-12/16	12-07/16	7-05/16	M	Book Cliff Mountains	UT	Edmund H. Auffhammer	1968	279
19-12/16	12-03/16	7-09/16	M	Chapleau	ONT	Anne M. Fiaschetti	1971	279
19-12/16	12-07/16	7-05/16	M	Reserve	NM	Joe E. Stroube	1971	279
19-12/16	12-04/16	7-08/16	F	Colfax County	NM	Bill Conn, Jr.	1973	279
19-12/16	12-04/16	7-08/16	M	Grand Rapids	MN	James R. Kroupa	1973	279
19-12/16	12-02/16	7-10/16	M	Cumbres Pass	CO	Michael Miller	1974	279
19-12/16	12-03/16	7-09/16	M	Siskiyou County	CA	Wayne Haley	1975	279
19-12/16	12-06/16	7-06/16	M	Douglass Pass	CO	David Freeman	1976	279
19-12/16	12-01/16	7-11/16	M	Killarney	ONT	Ken Barnhart	1979	279
19-12/16	12-13/16	6-15/16	M	Crow Wing County	MN	Dave A. Engholm	1980	279
19-12/16	12-08/16	7-04/16	M	Riding Mountain	MAN	James Carson	1980	279
19-12/16	12-00/16	7-12/16	M	North Bay	ONT	Ronald Gerrits	1980	279
19-12/16	12-05/16	7-07/16	M	Lewis & Clark County	MT	James L. Marlen	1980	279
19-12/16	12-08/16	7-04/16	M	Beluga	AK	John Moline	1980	279
19-12/16	12-04/16	7-08/16	M	Georgetown Canyon	ID	Alan G. Smith	1981	279
19-12/16	11-14/16	7-14/16	M	San Juan County	UT	Rick Collard	1982	279
19-12/16	12-07/16	7-05/16	M	The Pas	MAN	Ken Evenson	1983	279
19-12/16	12-03/16	7-09/16	M	Koochiching County	MN	Mike Little	1983	279
19-12/16	12-08/16	7-04/16	M	Gogebic County	MI	Steven D. Baker	1983	279
19-12/16	12-04/16	7-08/16	M	Madison County	MT	John Lantow	1984	279
19-12/16	12-10/16	7-02/16	M	Game Area #23	MAN	Gary Kaluzniak	1984	279
19-12/16	12-01/16	7-11/16	M	St. Louis County	MN	Clancy Lindvall	1984	279
19-12/16	12-08/16	7-04/16	M	Union County	OR	Brad Hathaway	1984	279
19-12/16	12-05/16	7-07/16	M	Ignace	ONT	Raymond Nowak, Jr.	1986	279
19-12/16	12-05/16	7-07/16	M	Cass County	MN	Lauren Brorby	1986	279
19-11/16	12-03/16	7-08/16	M	Atikokan	ONT	Dennis Gregory	1967	307
19-11/16	12-02/16	7-09/16	M	Montezuma County	CO	Marvin Reichenau	1972	307
19-11/16	12-03/16	7-08/16	M	LaPlata County	CO	Robert L. Everett	1973	307
19-11/16	12-04/16	7-07/16	M	Larimer County	CO	Lee Kline	1974	307
19-11/16	11-15/16	7-12/16	M	Chapleau	ONT	Donald E. Meushaw	1975	307
19-11/16	12-09/16	7-02/16	M	Montezuma County	CO	Marvin Reichenau	1976	307
19-11/16	12-11/16	7-00/16	M	Roan Creek	CO	C. David Wlx	1976	307
19-11/16	12-04/16	7-07/16	M	Bingham	ME	Anthony Carratura	1977	307
19-11/16	12-04/16	7-07/16	M	Grand Lake Stream	ME	Charles Hardish	1977	307
19-11/16	12-00/16	7-11/16	M	Ignace	ONT	John Dmytryka	1978	307
19-11/16	12-06/16	7-05/16	M	Itasca County	MN	Daniel O. Bell	1979	307
19-11/16	11-11/16	8-00/16	M	Calais	ME	Gary Farquhar	1979	307
19-11/16	12-01/16	7-10/16	M	Boise County	ID	Michael Sherer	1981	307
19-11/16	12-05/16	7-06/16	M	Prince of Wales Island	AK	Doug Miller	1982	307

BLACK BEAR

(continued)

Score	Greatest Length	Greatest Width	Sex	Area	State/ Province	Hunter's Name	Date	Rank
19-11/16	12-03/16	7-08/16	M	Gunflint Lake	ONT	Kelly Wilhelmi	1982	307
19-11/16	12-01/16	7-10/16	M	Routt County	CO	Guenter Hackl	1983	307
19-11/16	12-11/16	7-00/16	M	Boise County	ID	L. Dean Goodner	1983	307
19-11/16	12-05/16	7-06/16	M	Dickinson County	MI	Mike Vandeven	1983	307
19-11/16	12-00/16	7-11/16	M	Archuleta County	CO	Britton F. Kelley, Jr.	1984	307
19-11/16	12-00/16	7-11/16	M	Sioux Lookout	ONT	James E. Tiefenthaler	1984	307
19-11/16	11-07/16	8-04/16	M	Gogama	ONT	Frank E. Brinton IV	1985	307
19-11/16	11-15/16	7-12/16	M	Cascadden	ONT	Ronnie Long	1985	307
19-10/16	12-00/16	7-10/16	M	Lincoln National Forest	NM	David B. Terk	1964	329
19-10/16	12-06/16	7-04/16	M	Iron County	WI	William Tutt	1966	329
19-10/16	12-10/16	7-00/16	M	Madera County	CA	John D. Faulconer	1971	329
19-10/16	12-02/16	7-08/16	M	Nez Perce County	ID	Bob Gulman	1972	329
19-10/16	12-04/16	7-06/16	M	Forest County	WI	James L. Rablin	1972	329
19-10/16	12-07/16	7-03/16	M	Boise County	ID	Jimmie DeSaro, Jr.	1975	329
19-10/16	12-04/16	7-06/16	M	LaRonge	SAS	David L. Miller	1976	329
19-10/16	11-13/16	7-13/16	M	Manitou	CO	Billy Mulholland	1976	329
19-10/16	12-06/16	7-04/16	M	Sandilands Prov.	MAN	Jerry Parizek	1976	329
19-10/16	12-04/16	7-06/16	M	Gunnison County	CO	Travis L. Wakefield	1977	329
19-10/16	12-02/16	7-08/16	M	St. Louis County	MN	Richard G. Butters	1979	329
19-10/16	12-06/16	7-04/16	M	Book Cliffs	UT	Sam Nesi, Jr.	1979	329
19-10/16	12-12/16	6-14/16	M	Itasca County	MN	Gordon Steffen	1979	329
19-10/16	12-03/16	7-07/16	M	Trinity County	CA	Willis Duhon	1981	329
19-10/16	11-12/16	7-14/16	M	Fort Francis	ONT	Ron Carlson	1982	329
19-10/16	12-02/16	7-08/16	M	Siskiyou County	CA	Jerry Martinez	1983	329
19-10/16	12-11/16	6-15/16	M	Iron County	MI	Leslie Vorpahl	1983	329
19-10/16	12-06/16	7-04/16	M	Langley County	WI	Thomas Radtke	1984	329
19-10/16	12-05/16	7-05/16	M	Archuleta County	CO	Joel L. Duncan	1986	329
19-10/16	12-01/16	7-09/16	M	Lanark	ONT	Elmer M. Hagood, Jr.	1986	329
19-09/16	12-10/16	6-15/16	M	Douglas County	WI	Edwin Fitzgerald	1966	349
19-09/16	12-06/16	7-03/16	M	Grand County	CO	Judd Cooney	1967	349
19-09/16	12-00/16	7-09/16	M	Ignace	ONT	Gordon Bentley	1968	349
19-09/16	11-15/16	7-10/16	M	Kooskia	ID	Kenneth Wallenberg	1970	349
19-09/16	11-09/16	8-00/16	M	Boise County	ID	Ron Sherer	1971	349
19-09/16	12-01/16	7-08/16	M	Walland	TN	Gary Jordan	1973	349
19-09/16	12-05/16	7-04/16	M	Stratton	ME	Ralph Pfister	1977	349
19-09/16	11-09/16	8-00/16	M	Boise County	ID	Susan D. Sherer	1978	349
19-09/16	12-04/16	7-05/16	M	Valley County	ID	L. Dean Goodner	1979	349
19-09/16	11-11/16	7-14/16	M	Sandilands	MAN	Ron Derlago	1979	349
19-09/16	12-04/16	7-05/16	M	Kooskia	ID	Bob Jacobsen	1979	349
19-09/16	12-04/16	7-05/16	M	Kremmling	CO	Leonard L. Kohan	1980	349
19-09/16	12-00/16	7-09/16	M	Pitkin County	CO	Judy Nielsen	1981	349
19-09/16	11-11/16	7-14/16	M	Bobcaygeon	ONT	Dale W. Gray	1982	349
19-09/16	12-04/16	7-05/16	M	Ear Falls	ONT	Grant A. Poindexter	1982	349
19-09/16	12-00/16	7-09/16	M	Ft. Wainwright	AK	Gregory Dean Royse	1983	349
19-09/16	12-04/16	7-05/16	M	Coconino County	AZ	Dale H. Long	1983	349
19-09/16	12-05/16	7-04/16	M	Sawyer County	WI	Richard Carolfi	1983	349
19-09/16	12-03/16	7-06/16	M	Mesa County	CO	Jeff Tedore	1984	349
19-09/16	12-08/16	7-01/16	M	Beluga River	AK	Chad Burris	1984	349
19-09/16	12-06/16	7-03/16	M	Uintah County	UT	John C. Matejov	1985	349
19-09/16	12-06/16	7-03/16	M	La Tuque	QUE	John C. Hutchinson	1986	349
19-09/16	12-05/16	7-04/16	M	Bonneville County	ID	Larry Cross	1986	349
19-09/16	12-07/16	7-02/16	M	Washington County	ME	Cliff Wiseman	1986	349
19-08/16	12-03/16	7-05/16	M	Chapleau	ONT	Bob Sharpe	1959	373
19-08/16	12-04/16	7-04/16	M	Presque Isle County	MI	Eugene W. McKechnie	1964	373
19-08/16	12-06/16	7-02/16	M	Argonne	WI	Jerad Dittrich	1965	373
19-08/16	12-01/16	7-07/16	M	Greenville	ME	James Matulis	1967	373
19-08/16	12-06/16	7-02/16	M	Crow Wing County	MN	James L. Beard	1975	373
19-08/16	11-12/16	7-12/16	M	Payette River	ID	Jack Arbaugh	1976	373
19-08/16	11-11/16	7-13/16	M	Atikokan	ONT	David Graves	1978	373
19-08/16	12-02/16	7-06/16	M	Ear Falls	ONT	Grant Poindexter	1978	373
19-08/16	12-05/16	7-03/16	M	Pagosa Springs	CO	Robert Hoague	1981	373
19-08/16	12-03/16	7-05/16	M	Broadwater County	MT	Jan Hamer	1982	373
19-08/16	12-03/16	7-05/16	M	Remigny	QUE	Joe Hopwood	1982	373
19-08/16	11-15/16	7-09/16	M	Madison County	MT	Shep Lantow	1982	373

BLACK BEAR

(continued)

Minimum Score 18

Score	Greatest Length	Greatest Width	Sex	Area	State/ Province	Hunter's Name	Date	Rank
19-08/16	12-07/16	7-01/16	M	Loon Lake	SAS	Brian Acton	1984	373
19-08/16	12-06/16	7-02/16	M	Hudson Bay	SAS	Bill Zahradka	1984	373
19-08/16	12-00/16	7-08/16	M	Las Animas County	CO	Sam Durham	1984	373
19-08/16	11-11/16	7-13/16	M	Converse County	WY	Neil Hymas	1984	373
19-08/16	12-08/16	7-00/16	M	Sioux Narrows	ONT	Kenneth E. Krahn	1985	373
19-08/16	12-02/16	7-06/16	M	Grant County	OR	Mike E. Billman	1985	373
19-08/16	11-14/16	7-10/16	M	Siskiyou County	CA	Richard L. Westervelt	1985	373
19-08/16	12-08/16	7-00/16	M	Lincoln County	MT	Jim Eff	1986	373
19-07/16	12-03/16	7-04/16	M	Kenora	ONT	Norman Pint	1964	393
19-07/16	12-05/16	7-02/16	M	Crow Creek	ID	Ronald S. Curtis	1969	393
19-07/16	11-10/16	7-13/16	M	Birch Lake	MN	Don Dvoroznak	1970	393
19-07/16	11-15/16	7-08/16	M	Rangely	CO	Louis Preba	1972	393
19-07/16	12-00/16	7-07/16	M	Nestor Falls	ONT	Dennis Bartness	1974	393
19-07/16	12-00/16	7-07/16	M	Haddo Township	ONT	Paul Sorke	1974	393
19-07/16	12-00/16	7-07/16	M	LaPlata County	CO	Mike Dunaway	1975	393
19-07/16	12-07/16	7-00/16	M	Somme	SAS	Phil Patchin	1975	393
19-07/16	12-03/16	7-04/16	M	Boulder Mountain	UT	Lee G. Stoddard	1975	393
19-07/16	12-07/16	7-00/16	M	Snohomish County	WA	Charles J. Bartlett	1976	393
19-07/16	12-01/16	7-06/16	M	Roscommon County	MI	Roger Maeder	1976	393
19-07/16	12-00/16	7-07/16	M	Larimer County	CO	Ron Breitsprecher	1977	393
19-07/16	12-02/16	7-05/16	M	San Luis	CO	Dr. Thomas I. LaValle	1978	393
19-07/16	12-05/16	7-02/16	M	Byers Lake	AK	Eugene Smith, Jr.	1978	393
19-07/16	11-11/16	7-12/16	M	Fremont County	CO	Ronald E. Sniff	1978	393
19-07/16	12-04/16	7-03/16	M	Kooskia	ID	Ray Koenig	1979	393
19-07/16	12-11/16	6-12/16	M	Tehama County	CA	Roy B. Cartwright	1980	393
19-07/16	12-07/16	7-00/16	M	Cass County	MN	Wayne Enger	1980	393
19-07/16	12-02/16	7-05/16	M	Starkey Unit	OR	Bill Lancaster	1980	393
19-07/16	11-15/16	7-08/16	M	Wolf Lake Road	ONT	Gary Johnston	1981	393
19-07/16	12-00/16	7-07/16	M	Huerfano County	CO	Kent Connally	1983	393
19-07/16	11-14/16	7-09/16	M	Bayfield County	WI	Steve Finn	1983	393
19-07/16	12-00/16	7-07/16	M	Dryden	ONT	Alan Koester	1984	393
19-07/16	11-08/16	7-15/16	M	Carmat	ONT	Robert D. DuBois	1984	393
19-07/16	11-08/16	7-15/16	M	Sioux Narrows	ONT	Richard Sapp	1986	393
19-06/16	12-07/16	6-15/16	M	Shasta County	CA	L. Dale Towery	1965	418
19-06/16	11-14/16	7-08/16	M	Atikokan	ONT	Dennis Gregory	1969	418
19-06/16	11-14/16	7-08/16	M	Uncompahgre Area	CO	Charles Leidheiser	1971	418
19-06/16	12-02/16	7-04/16	M	Stratton	ME	Walter Seville	1971	418
19-06/16	12-06/16	7-00/16	F	Sawyer County	WI	Ronald Curry, Jr.	1972	418
19-06/16	12-03/16	7-03/16	M	Uncompahgre N.F.	CO	Thomas J. Hentrick	1975	418
19-06/16	12-02/16	7-04/16	M	Butternut	WI	Jim Keim	1977	418
19-06/16	12-02/16	7-04/16	M	Atikokan	ONT	Earle K. Gray	1979	418
19-06/16	11-14/16	7-08/16	M	Lake Wabigoon	ONT	Gary W. Shaffer	1979	418
19-06/16	11-13/16	7-09/16	M	Great Falls	MT	H. Richard Long	1981	418
19-06/16	12-04/16	7-02/16	M	Lewis & Clark County	MT	Donald K. MacCallum	1982	418
19-06/16	12-00/16	7-06/16	M	Aroostook County	ME	Frank "Rit" Heller	1982	418
19-06/16	12-02/16	7-04/16	M	Hampshire County	MA	James "Boomer" Hayden	1982	418
19-06/16	12-04/16	7-02/16	M	Hudson Bay	SAS	David Tofte	1983	418
19-06/16	12-04/16	7-02/16	M	Sioux Lookout	ONT	Ray Ryan	1983	418
19-06/16	12-02/16	7-04/16	M	Beluga River	AK	Christine Koldeway	1984	418
19-06/16	12-09/16	6-13/16	M	Kitsap County	WA	Betty Jones	1984	418
19-06/16	11-15/16	7-07/16	M	Lemhi County	ID	Ron Scherer	1985	418
19-06/16	11-14/16	7-08/16	M	Heathcote Lake	ONT	Joseph A. Lasch	1985	418
19-06/16	11-14/16	7-08/16	M	Drury Township	ONT	John Wyszynski	1985	418
19-06/16	11-10/16	7-12/16	M	Kenora Dist.	ONT	Mark D. Moss	1985	418
19-06/16	12-00/16	7-06/16	M	Shasta County	CA	Larry Mork	1985	418
19-06/16	12-01/16	7-05/16	M	Teton County	ID	Marc S. Johnson	1986	418
19-06/16	11-12/16	7-10/16	M	Herkimer County	NY	Patrick Niznik	1986	418
19-05/16	11-13/16	7-08/16	M	Pierce	ID	W. R. Vanderhoef	1959	442
19-05/16	11-12/16	7-09/16	M	Upper Peninsula	MI	Donald Schram	1961	442
19-05/16	12-00/16	7-05/16	M	Almont	CO	James Jarvis	1976	442
19-05/16	11-12/16	7-09/16	M	Gulnare	CO	Barry Powell	1976	442
19-05/16	12-03/16	7-02/16	M	Raith	ONT	Jon K. Young	1976	442
19-05/16	11-11/16	7-10/16	M	Stratton	ME	Al Del Greco	1978	442
19-05/16	11-11/16	7-10/16	M	Ear Falls	ONT	Michael Mealey	1978	442
19-05/16	12-00/16	7-05/16	M	Wesley	ME	Dan Paugh	1978	442

BLACK BEAR
(continued)

Score	Greatest Length	Greatest Width	Sex	Area	State/ Province	Hunter's Name	Date	Rank
19-05/16	12-06/16	6-15/16	M	Dolores County	CO	Marv Reichenau	1979	442
19-05/16	12-01/16	7-04/16	M	Hinckley	NY	Ronald J. Beerhalter	1980	442
19-05/16	12-02/16	7-03/16	M	Tulare County	CA	Fred R. Cisneros	1981	442
19-05/16	11-14/16	7-07/16	M	White Lake	ONT	Daniel B. Johnson	1981	442
19-05/16	11-15/16	7-06/16	M	Bonneville County	ID	Richard K. Russell	1981	442
19-05/16	12-02/16	7-03/16	M	Dryden	ONT	Craig A. Swenson	1982	442
19-05/16	12-01/16	7-04/16	M	Sudbury County	ONT	William Doczy	1983	442
19-05/16	12-04/16	7-01/16	M	St. Louis County	MN	Kimberley Anne McGurren	1983	442
19-05/16	11-14/16	7-07/16	M	Caribou County	ID	Coby Tigert	1984	442
19-05/16	12-01/16	7-04/16	M	Snohomish County	WA	Mathew Hayvaz	1984	442
19-05/16	12-01/16	7-04/16	M	Plumas County	CA	Dr. Ronald H. Thole	1984	442
19-05/16	12-01/16	7-04/16	M	Parry Sound	ONT	Ronald D. Lundy	1985	442
19-05/16	12-04/16	7-01/16	M	Cass County	MN	Brad Blanchard	1985	442
19-05/16	12-08/16	6-13/16	M	Caldwell County	NC	Danny K. Adams	1986	442
19-05/16	12-08/16	6-13/16	M	Grand County	UT	David Snyder	1986	442
19-05/16	12-05/16	7-00/16	M	Valley County	ID	Brian Hunter Heck	1986	442
19-04/16	12-04/16	7-00/16	M	Ashland	WI	Herbert H. Lange	1961	466
19-04/16	12-04/16	7-00/16	?	Murphy Dome	AK	Thomas Clark	1963	466
19-04/16	11-15/16	7-05/16	M	Butte Falls	OR	Bob Jacobs	1964	466
19-04/16	12-00/16	7-04/16	M	Sutter Creek	ID	Dick Gulman	1967	466
19-04/16	12-03/16	7-01/16	M	L'Ascension	QUE	Michael L. Kaluszka	1971	466
19-04/16	11-08/16	7-12/16	M	Kooskia	ID	Harold Boyack	1973	466
19-04/16	11-12/16	7-08/16	M	Wasco Unit	OR	John Higgins	1974	466
19-04/16	11-11/16	7-09/16	M	Wanapitei	ONT	Ken Barnhart	1976	466
19-04/16	11-11/16	7-09/16	M	Cimmaron	CO	Roger Reinbold	1976	466
19-04/16	12-01/16	7-03/16	M	Saguache County	CO	Richard Baumfalk	1977	466
19-04/16	11-14/16	7-06/16	M	Pigeon Mountain	ALB	David R. Coupland	1977	466
19-04/16	12-04/16	7-00/16	M	Bayfield County	WI	Bruce Eggenberger	1977	466
19-04/16	11-15/16	7-05/16	M	Caperol	ONT	Bobby Clenney	1978	466
19-04/16	12-00/16	7-04/16	M	Stratton	ME	Harry Feaster	1978	466
19-04/16	11-13/16	7-07/16	M	Thessalon	ONT	Robert R. Rider	1979	466
19-04/16	12-04/16	7-00/16	M	Ontonagon County	MI	Daniel F. Stiltner	1979	466
19-04/16	11-12/16	7-08/16	M	Bayfield County	WI	Dave Tabbert	1979	466
19-04/16	12-01/16	7-03/16	M	Price County	WI	Glenn E. Gaulke	1980	466
19-04/16	11-12/16	7-08/16	M	Shoshone County	ID	Bill Hoffman, Sr.	1980	466
19-04/16	11-14/16	7-06/16	M	Dryden	ONT	Gerald T. Flynn	1981	466
19-04/16	11-12/16	7-08/16	M	Kooskia	ID	Ray Koenig	1981	466
19-04/16	12-02/16	7-02/16	M	Pagosa Springs	CO	Denny Lane Williamson	1981	466
19-04/16	11-14/16	7-06/16	M	Colton	NY	Henry P. Bouchard	1982	466
19-04/16	12-01/16	7-03/16	M	Park County	MT	Gary Hartman	1982	466
19-04/16	12-08/16	6-12/16	M	Burnett County	WI	David Hess	1982	466
19-04/16	12-04/16	7-00/16	M	Mackinaw County	MI	Dale H. Betcher	1983	466
19-04/16	11-14/16	7-06/16	M	Emo	ONT	Hal McClelland	1983	466
19-04/16	12-05/16	6-15/16	M	Game Area #23	MAN	Gary Kaluzniak	1984	466
19-04/16	12-00/16	7-04/16	M	Susitina River	AK	Patricia A. Stewart	1984	466
19-04/16	11-14/16	7-06/16	M	Touchwood Lake	ALB	Warren Witherspoon	1984	466
19-04/16	12-00/16	7-04/16	M	Game Area #23	MAN	Gary Kaluzniak	1984	466
19-04/16	11-12/16	7-08/16	M	Rollet	QUE	George Ollert	1984	466
19-04/16	11-11/16	7-09/16	M	Siskiyou County	CA	Greg Nichols	1984	466
19-04/16	11-14/16	7-06/16	M	Wawa	ONT	James C. Hicks	1984	466
19-04/16	12-01/16	7-03/16	M	Archuleta County	CO	Lisa Cooney	1985	466
19-04/16	12-02/16	7-02/16	M	Cheboygan County	MI	Steve E. Hutchinson	1985	466
19-04/16	12-04/16	7-00/16	M	Madison County	MT	John Ralph	1985	466
19-04/16	12-02/16	7-02/16	M	Siskiyou County	CA	Bruce Kipley	1985	466
19-04/16	12-02/16	7-02/16	M	Archuleta County	CO	David Swanson	1986	466
19-04/16	12-01/16	7-03/16	M	Keeley Lake	SAS	Bruce E. Menz	1986	466
19-04/16	12-00/16	7-04/16	M	Delay River	QUE	Benjamin O. Brookhart III	1986	466
19-03/16	11-12/16	7-07/16	M	Wagon Wheel Gap	CO	Edward Wintz	1960	507
19-03/16	12-02/16	7-01/16	M	Rio Arriba County	NM	Dan Ward	1964	507
19-03/16	11-13/16	7-06/16	M	Iron Bridge	ONT	Philip L. Hawkins	1965	507
19-03/16	11-12/16	7-07/16	M	Shasta County	CA	Michael D. Combs	1967	507
19-03/16	11-11/16	7-08/16	M	Sudbury District	ONT	Floyd Eccleston	1970	507
19-03/16	11-13/16	7-06/16	M	Uncompahgre N.F.	CO	Charles Bojarski	1971	507
19-03/16	11-14/16	7-05/16	M	Sequoia National Forest	CA	Martin Szekeresh, Jr.	1973	507

BLACK BEAR

Minimum Score 18

Score	Greatest Length	Greatest Width	Sex	Area	State/ Province	Hunter's Name	Date	Rank
19-03/16	11-11/16	7-08/16	M	Ovando	MT	Gary L. Wilson	1975	507
19-03/16	11-13/16	7-06/16	M	Fremont County	ID	Roger Atwood	1977	507
19-03/16	12-03/16	7-00/16	M	Dryden	ONT	Bill Rose	1978	507
19-03/16	11-14/16	7-05/16	M	Crestone	CO	Ross M. Clark	1979	507
19-03/16	11-13/16	7-06/16	M	Roscommon County	MI	Roger J. Maeder	1979	507
19-03/16	11-15/16	7-04/16	M	Bonneville County	ID	Fred Huffman	1980	507
19-03/16	11-14/16	7-05/16	M	Conejos County	CO	Frank Scott	1980	507
19-03/16	12-01/16	7-02/16	M	Iron County	WI	Frank Rasch	1982	507
19-03/16	11-15/16	7-04/16	M	Las Animas County	CO	Tom Nelson	1983	507
19-03/16	12-01/16	7-02/16	M	Delta County	CO	Doug McCauley	1983	507
19-03/16	12-01/16	7-02/16	M	Graham	ONT	Michael Perrott	1983	507
19-03/16	11-12/16	7-07/16	M	Grand County	CO	Jim Williams	1983	507
19-03/16	11-14/16	7-05/16	M	Kenora	ONT	Kenneth Gilb	1983	507
19-03/16	12-02/16	7-01/16	M	Hubbard County	MN	Omar Maggard	1984	507
19-03/16	11-13/16	7-06/16	M	Black Sturgeon Lake	ONT	Clarence "Bud" Mrozek	1985	507
19-03/16	12-02/16	7-01/16	M	Durban	MAN	Bill Clink	1985	507
19-03/16	12-02/16	7-01/16	M	Whitemud Creek	ALB	Paul St. Laurent	1986	507
19-03/16	11-15/16	7-04/16	M	Thunder Bay	ONT	Ron K. Serwa	1986	507
19-03/16	11-15/16	7-04/16	M	Bending Lake	ONT	John Lamp	1986	507
19-02/16	11-09/16	7-09/16	M	Sudbury	ONT	Clarence Grandt	1963	533
19-02/16	11-12/16	7-06/16	M	Blount County	TN	Don Dvoroznak	1968	533
19-02/16	11-13/16	7-05/16	M	Chapleau	ONT	Gerald E. Taft	1968	533
19-02/16	11-12/16	7-06/16	M	Trinity County	CA	Fred M. Frakes	1970	533
19-02/16	12-03/16	6-15/16	M	Shasta County	CA	Gerald P. Doyle	1971	533
19-02/16	11-14/16	7-04/16	M	Vilas County	WI	William L. Yessa	1971	533
19-02/16	11-11/16	7-07/16	M	Kormak	ONT	Marvin E. Davis	1972	533
19-02/16	11-15/16	7-03/16	M	Uncompahgre N. F.	CO	Ed Bonardi	1973	533
19-02/16	11-13/16	7-05/16	M	Lemhi County	ID	Curley Keadle	1973	533
19-02/16	12-00/16	7-02/16	M	Dolores	CO	Marvin Reichenau	1973	533
19-02/16	11-14/16	7-04/16	M	Blanco River Basin	CO	Judd Cooney	1974	533
19-02/16	11-13/16	7-05/16	M	Vancouver Island	BC	F. Guillon/A. Klopfenstein	1974	533
19-02/16	12-01/16	7-01/16	M	Dryden	ONT	Ken Horton	1977	533
19-02/16	12-04/16	6-14/16	M	Vilas County	WI	Michael Gapa	1979	533
19-02/16	11-14/16	7-04/16	M	Skamania County	WA	John H. Wahl	1979	533
19-02/16	11-11/16	7-07/16	M	Shasta County	CA	Mark David Broadhead	1980	533
19-02/16	11-14/16	7-04/16	M	Castle Rock	CO	Thomas P. Grainger	1980	533
19-02/16	12-01/16	7-01/16	M	Chetwyrnd	BC	Ron F. McKay	1980	533
19-02/16	12-00/16	7-02/16	M	Bayfield County	WI	William F. Schutte	1980	533
19-02/16	11-15/16	7-03/16	M	Trinidad	CO	David S. Bunce	1981	533
19-02/16	12-04/16	6-14/16	M	Whitecourt	ALB	Wade Johnson	1981	533
19-02/16	12-04/16	6-14/16	M	Makinen	MN	Charlie Paine	1981	533
19-02/16	12-02/16	7-00/16	M	Flathead City	MT	Owen Weaver	1981	533
19-02/16	12-00/16	7-02/16	M	Boise County	ID	Larry Hoff	1982	533
19-02/16	11-12/16	7-06/16	M	Trinchera	CO	Bill R. Lopatta	1982	533
19-02/16	11-10/16	7-08/16	M	Gallatin County	MT	Pat Sinclair	1983	533
19-02/16	11-14/16	7-04/16	M	Lake Savant	ONT	Mark Milford	1983	533
19-02/16	12-04/16	6-14/16	M	Grassy Narrows	ONT	Mike Jacobs	1983	533
19-02/16	11-12/16	7-06/16	M	Carmet	ONT	Thomas Hlinka	1983	533
19-02/16	12-03/16	6-15/16	M	Aulneau Peninsula	ONT	Mike Koska	1984	533
19-02/16	11-14/16	7-04/16	M	Atikokan	ONT	Roger L. Hensley	1984	533
19-02/16	11-12/16	7-06/16	M	Mackinac County	MI	Carson D. McMullen	1984	533
19-02/16	12-02/16	7-00/16	M	Grand County	UT	Diane Snyder	1985	533
19-02/16	12-03/16	6-15/16	M	Sanpete County	UT	Terry Casper	1986	533
19-02/16	12-01/16	7-01/16	M	Rocky Lake	MAN	Dennis Jacobson	1986	533
19-02/16	12-00/16	7-02/16	M	French River	ONT	Mike Bishop	1986	533
19-02/16	11-14/16	7-04/16	M	Boise County	ID	Gary Titus	1986	533
19-02/16	12-00/16	7-02/16	M	Durban	MAN	David H. Boland	1986	533
19-01/16	11-01/16	8-00/16	M	Rogue River	OR	Leander Lowel	1959	571
19-01/16	11-12/16	7-05/16	M	Wagon Wheel Gap	CO	Ed Wintz	1959	571
19-01/16	11-15/16	7-02/16	M	Lake Gogebic	MI	Margaret R. Cooley	1961	571
19-01/16	11-05/16	7-12/16	M	Upper Peninsula	MI	Jerry D. Anderson	1967	571
19-01/16	12-01/16	7-00/16	M	Red Lake	ONT	Don Ellett	1969	571
19-01/16	11-15/16	7-02/16	M	Antigo	WI	Roland Mantzke	1969	571
19-01/16	11-14/16	7-03/16	M	Pagosa Springs	CO	Maurice Chambers	1973	571

BLACK BEAR

(continued)   Minimum Score 18

Score	Greatest Length	Greatest Width	Sex	Area	State/ Province	Hunter's Name	Date	Rank
19-01/16	11-15/16	7-02/16	M	Marquette County	MI	Pete Hillesheim	1974	571
19-01/16	11-04/16	7-13/16	M	Vancouver Island	BC	Klaus Schultz	1974	571
19-01/16	12-01/16	7-00/16	M	Itasca County	MN	William Biggs	1976	571
19-01/16	12-03/16	6-14/16	M	Rifle	CO	Michael D. Dickess	1976	571
19-01/16	11-11/16	7-06/16	M	St. Louis County	MN	Gerry Benson	1977	571
19-01/16	12-00/16	7-01/16	M	Kitsap County	WA	Larry A. Martin	1977	571
19-01/16	11-10/16	7-07/16	M	Oxford County	ME	James P. Wellever	1978	571
19-01/16	12-02/16	6-15/16	M	Oneida County	WI	Douglas A. Severson	1979	571
19-01/16	12-01/16	7-00/16	M	Grover	WY	Ronell Skinner	1979	571
19-01/16	11-12/16	7-05/16	M	Marquette County	MI	Jeff Apel	1980	571
19-01/16	12-02/16	6-15/16	M	Remer	MN	Robert M. Burtch	1980	571
19-01/16	11-13/16	7-04/16	M	Groveton	NH	James "Boomer" Hayden	1980	571
19-01/16	12-00/16	7-01/16	M	Terrace	BC	Bill Coburn	1981	571
19-01/16	11-12/16	7-05/16	M	Caribou Snare Creek	AK	Bill Krenz	1981	571
19-01/16	11-14/16	7-03/16	M	Franklin County	ME	Albert J. Kolatac	1982	571
19-01/16	12-02/16	6-15/16	M	Bayfield County	WI	Larry Frye	1982	571
19-01/16	11-15/16	7-02/16	M	Kenora	ONT	Ray Hawver	1982	571
19-01/16	11-14/16	7-03/16	M	Nester Falls	ONT	Larry Streiff	1982	571
19-01/16	11-12/16	7-05/16	M	Espanola	ONT	Donald W. Taylor	1982	571
19-01/16	11-15/16	7-02/16	M	Bonneville County	ID	Ronnel J. Stacey	1983	571
19-01/16	11-15/16	7-02/16	M	Jellico	ONT	Ed Herzog	1983	571
19-01/16	12-01/16	7-00/16	M	Pitkin County	CO	Perry Smith	1983	571
19-01/16	12-04/16	6-13/16	M	Rockingham County	VA	Roger O. Wyant	1983	571
19-01/16	12-03/16	6-14/16	M	Hudson Bay	SAS	Warren Buss	1984	571
19-01/16	11-15/16	7-02/16	M	Plumas County	CA	Mike Holley	1984	571
19-01/16	11-14/16	7-03/16	M	Redditt	ONT	Jim Christman	1985	571
19-01/16	11-15/16	7-02/16	F	Sanpete County	UT	Judy Hallman	1986	571
19-01/16	12-02/16	6-15/16	M	Plumas County	CA	Mike Holley	1986	571
19-01/16	12-03/16	6-14/16	M	Alpine County	CA	Rick Lund	1986	571
19-00/16	12-06/16	6-10/16	M	Mercer	WI	Charles Kroll	1966	607
19-00/16	11-09/16	7-07/16	M	Sioux Narrows	ONT	Walter J. Sawicki	1967	607
19-00/16	11-13/16	7-03/16	M	?	BC	Terry J. Haines	1968	607
19-00/16	11-12/16	7-04/16	M	Chapleau	ONT	Kenneth R. Larson	1968	607
19-00/16	11-15/16	7-01/16	M	Ignace	ONT	Stanley Olson	1968	607
19-00/16	11-10/16	7-06/16	M	Kenora	ONT	Barry Englehardt	1969	607
19-00/16	11-12/16	7-04/16	M	Armstrong	ONT	James Mahoney	1969	607
19-00/16	11-08/16	7-08/16	M	Shasta County	CA	Patrick J. Marley	1969	607
19-00/16	11-07/16	7-09/16	M	Book Cliff Mountains	UT	C. Donald Lechner	1970	607
19-00/16	11-09/16	7-07/16	M	Lemhi County	ID	Douglas Kittredge	1971	607
19-00/16	11-11/16	7-05/16	M	Saguache County	CO	Gary Ginther	1973	607
19-00/16	11-14/16	7-02/16	M	Cloyne	ONT	Tom Erkinger	1976	607
19-00/16	11-14/16	7-02/16	M	Lanark	ONT	Guy Pointer	1977	607
19-00/16	11-14/16	7-02/16	M	Ash Lake	MN	Jimmy F. Rogers	1978	607
19-00/16	11-08/16	7-08/16	M	Wawa	ONT	Don LaDuke	1980	607
19-00/16	12-05/16	6-11/16	M	Sullivan County	NY	John Nasuta	1980	607
19-00/16	11-14/16	7-02/16	M	North Bay	ONT	Grant R. Beattie	1981	607
19-00/16	12-01/16	6-15/16	M	Fort St. John	BC	Duane Hicks	1981	607
19-00/16	11-09/16	7-07/16	M	Boise County	ID	Richard C. Nichols	1981	607
19-00/16	11-11/16	7-05/16	M	Ravalli County	MT	Rod Osburn	1981	607
19-00/16	11-08/16	7-08/16	M	Whitefield	NH	Edward Silva	1981	607
19-00/16	11-14/16	7-02/16	F	San Juan County	UT	Sheldon Anderson	1982	607
19-00/16	12-01/16	6-15/16	M	Trinchera	CO	Bob Lopatta	1982	607
19-00/16	11-14/16	7-02/16	M	Pacific County	WA	Annette Crews	1983	607
19-00/16	11-13/16	7-03/16	M	Siskiyou County	CA	Fred Searle	1983	607
19-00/16	11-09/16	7-07/16	M	Chapeau	QUE	Joseph D. Maddock	1984	607
19-00/16	11-13/16	7-03/16	M	Meadow Lake	SAS	Gary Bauer	1984	607
19-00/16	12-01/16	6-15/16	M	Fremont County	ID	Joe Bronson	1984	607
19-00/16	11-15/16	7-01/16	M	York County	NBW	Daniel L. Shaffer	1984	607
19-00/16	11-13/16	7-03/16	M	Bingham County	ID	Mike Lee Wohlschlegel	1984	607
19-00/16	12-01/16	6-15/16	M	Lincoln County	WI	Jim Wurster	1984	607
19-00/16	11-14/16	7-02/16	M	Vilas County	WI	Mike Eidson	1984	607
19-00/16	11-13/16	7-03/16	M	Mine Centre	ONT	Bob Roulet	1985	607
19-00/16	12-02/16	6-14/16	M	Ear Falls	ONT	Brent Allen Poindexter	1985	607
19-00/16	11-08/16	7-08/16	M	Chelan County	WA	Leroy E. House	1986	607

BLACK BEAR

Minimum Score 18

Score	Greatest Length	Greatest Width	Sex	Area	State/ Province	Hunter's Name	Date	Rank
18-15/16	11-09/16	7-06/16	M	King George IV Lake	NFL	Frank M. Davis	1958	642
18-15/16	11-15/16	7-00/16	M	Flathead County	MT	Danny Moore	1976	642
18-15/16	12-01/16	6-14/16	M	Redstone	CO	Sharon Payne	1976	642
18-15/16	12-00/16	6-15/16	M	St. Louis County	MN	Roy Kahabka	1978	642
18-15/16	12-02/16	6-13/16	M	Hubbard County	MN	Dr. James Schubert	1978	642
18-15/16	11-14/16	7-01/16	M	Delta County	CO	Bob Gulman, Jr.	1979	642
18-15/16	11-04/16	7-11/16	M	Kalkaska	MI	Gregory Korkoske	1979	642
18-15/16	12-00/16	6-15/16	M	Pough Lake	ONT	Jozset Vass	1979	642
18-15/16	11-15/16	7-00/16	M	Sandilands Prov. Park	MAN	Fred Hay	1981	642
18-15/16	12-01/16	6-14/16	M	Boise County	ID	Jack Arbaugh	1981	642
18-15/16	12-00/16	6-15/16	M	San Miguel County	NM	Dick McClain	1981	642
18-15/16	12-01/16	6-14/16	M	Espanola	ONT	Martin Masek	1982	642
18-15/16	12-00/16	6-15/16	M	Valley County	ID	Bob Dawson	1982	642
18-15/16	11-15/16	7-00/16	M	Larimer County	CO	Douglas Beck	1982	642
18-15/16	11-09/16	7-06/16	M	Pontiac	QUE	Chuck Wade	1983	642
18-15/16	11-10/16	7-05/16	M	Warren	ONT	Clarence Keaton	1983	642
18-15/16	11-14/16	7-01/16	M	Coos County	NH	Greg White	1984	642
18-15/16	12-02/16	6-13/16	M	Little Sturge Lake	ONT	David F. Martinek	1985	642
18-15/16	11-15/16	7-00/16	M	Delta County	CO	Terry Bridgman	1985	642
18-15/16	11-09/16	7-06/16	M	Renfrew	ONT	Jeffrey Tucker	1985	642
18-15/16	11-14/16	7-01/16	M	Timiscoming	ONT	Gary F. Greene	1985	642
18-15/16	11-08/16	7-07/16	M	Poitras	ONT	Robert H. Pavlovic	1985	642
18-15/16	11-12/16	7-03/16	M	Hudson Bay	SAS	Bruce Balerud	1986	642
18-15/16	12-04/16	6-11/16	M	Espanola	ONT	Terry J. Gerber	1986	642
18-15/16	11-14/16	7-01/16	M	Cygnet Lake	ONT	Greg Roufs	1986	642
18-15/16	12-00/16	6-15/16	M	Sioux Lookout	ONT	Dr. Joe Nilsson	1986	642
18-15/16	11-12/16	7-03/16	M	Findly Lake	QUE	Paul Bertrand	1986	642
18-15/16	11-13/16	7-02/16	M	King County	WA	Steven Jackl	1986	642
18-14/16	11-06/16	7-08/16	M	Vermillion Bay	ONT	Wayne I. Munkel	1966	670
18-14/16	12-07/16	6-07/16	?	Vanderhoof	BC	Cecil Raphael	1967	670
18-14/16	11-02/16	7-12/16	M	Cranberry Portage	MAN	Carl Anderson	1968	670
18-14/16	11-11/16	7-03/16	M	Barton	VT	James Gilman	1969	670
18-14/16	11-12/16	7-02/16	M	Kooskia	ID	Peter Eremo	1970	670
18-14/16	12-02/16	6-12/16	M	Collbran	CO	Jerry Cunningham	1972	670
18-14/16	12-03/16	6-11/16	M	Madera County	CA	Duane A. Whittle	1973	670
18-14/16	11-12/16	7-02/16	M	Ely	MN	Art Heinze	1974	670
18-14/16	12-02/16	6-12/16	M	Vermillion Bay	ONT	Myles Keller	1974	670
18-14/16	11-13/16	7-01/16	M	Lincoln County	OR	Stanley D. Miles	1974	670
18-14/16	12-00/16	6-14/16	M	Wabigoon	ONT	Keith Olson	1975	670
18-14/16	11-14/16	7-00/16	M	Minaki	ONT	Greg Stezenski	1975	670
18-14/16	11-10/16	7-04/16	M	Nipigon	ONT	Vickery Frederick	1976	670
18-14/16	11-13/16	7-01/16	M	Prince George	BC	Jim Jackson	1976	670
18-14/16	11-14/16	7-00/16	M	Bingham	ME	John J. Sweeney	1976	670
18-14/16	11-13/16	7-01/16	M	Custer County	CO	William Henderson	1978	670
18-14/16	11-12/16	7-02/16	M	Bighorn Mountains	WY	David M. Nahrgang	1978	670
18-14/16	12-00/16	6-14/16	M	Grand Lake Stream	ME	Raymond Olson	1979	670
18-14/16	11-14/16	7-00/16	M	Bob Marshall Wilderness	MT	James Dean	1980	670
18-14/16	11-10/16	7-04/16	M	Sandilands	MAN	Larry Kraynyk	1980	670
18-14/16	11-11/16	7-03/16	M	Marquette County	MI	William Robert Baltrip	1981	670
18-14/16	11-09/16	7-05/16	M	Grant County	NM	Ross Johnson	1981	670
18-14/16	12-00/16	6-14/16	M	Ignace	ONT	Robert I. Mussey	1981	670
18-14/16	11-14/16	7-00/16	M	Dryden	ONT	Gary J. O'Donnell	1981	670
18-14/16	11-09/16	7-05/16	M	Kootenai County	ID	Stanley Leake	1982	670
18-14/16	11-12/16	7-02/16	M	Chapleau	ONT	Robert J. Davis	1982	670
18-14/16	11-15/16	6-15/16	M	Souix Lookout	ONT	Michael R. Traub	1982	670
18-14/16	11-14/16	7-00/16	M	Montezuma County	CO	William C. Shuster	1983	670
18-14/16	11-09/16	7-05/16	M	Aulneav Peninsula	ONT	Michael F. Koska	1983	670
18-14/16	11-13/16	7-01/16	M	Thunder Bay	ONT	Todd Gilb	1983	670
18-14/16	11-13/16	7-01/16	M	Park County	MT	Cecil Hendricks	1983	670
18-14/16	11-09/16	7-05/16	M	Jackson County	CO	Kurt Keskimaki	1984	670
18-14/16	11-06/16	7-08/16	M	Fort Francis	ONT	Lloyd R. Branchcomb	1984	670
18-14/16	11-13/16	7-01/16	M	Wallowa County	OR	Jerry Jensen	1984	670
18-14/16	11-12/16	7-02/16	M	Scoop Lake	BC	Ronald Montross	1984	670
18-14/16	11-08/16	7-06/16	M	Mine Centre	ONT	Gary Schuler	1985	670

BLACK BEAR

(continued)   Minimum Score 18

Score	Greatest Length	Greatest Width	Sex	Area	State/Province	Hunter's Name	Date	Rank
18-14/16	11-12/16	7-02/16	M	Fremont County	CO	Leroy Miller	1985	670
18-14/16	12-01/16	6-13/16	M	Ignace	ONT	Ken Terry	1985	670
18-14/16	11-10/16	7-04/16	M	Atikokaw	ONT	Eugene Francisco	1985	670
18-14/16	12-00/16	6-14/16	M	Grant County	OR	Don D. Litts	1986	670
18-13/16	11-11/16	7-02/16	M	Iron County	MI	John E. Lawson	1971	710
18-13/16	11-08/16	7-05/16	M	Grand Lake Stream	ME	Norman Jolliffe	1973	710
18-13/16	11-06/16	7-07/16	M	Jefferson County	CO	Chuck Hutton	1974	710
18-13/16	11-11/16	7-02/16	M	Colfax County	NM	Jerry R. Wood	1974	710
18-13/16	11-10/16	7-03/16	M	?	ONT	Lee Murphy	1975	710
18-13/16	11-08/16	7-05/16	M	Pemberton	BC	Dr. Michael R. Cummings	1976	710
18-13/16	11-08/16	7-05/16	M	Sanders County	MT	Jay Gunter	1976	710
18-13/16	11-07/16	7-06/16	M	Messines	QUE	Larry R. Scott, Sr.	1977	710
18-13/16	11-12/16	7-01/16	M	Dryden	ONT	Dr. Bill Young	1977	710
18-13/16	12-00/16	6-13/16	M	Gem County	ID	DeLoy Desaro	1978	710
18-13/16	11-10/16	7-03/16	M	Bingham	ME	Ray King	1978	710
18-13/16	11-14/16	6-15/16	M	Chapleau	ONT	Maurice Perrault	1978	710
18-13/16	11-13/16	7-00/16	M	Koochiching County	MN	Mark A. Andrist	1979	710
18-13/16	11-11/16	7-02/16	M	Smokey Mountain	WA	Ronald D. Hopkins	1979	710
18-13/16	11-12/16	7-01/16	M	Wawa	ONT	Robert C. McGuire	1979	710
18-13/16	12-04/16	6-09/16	M	Lincoln County	WI	Bob Faufau	1980	710
18-13/16	11-11/16	7-02/16	M	Thunder Bay	ONT	David Manthei	1980	710
18-13/16	11-14/16	6-15/16	M	Armistice Lake	ONT	Cliff Buland, Jr.	1982	710
18-13/16	12-04/16	6-09/16	M	Price County	WI	Gary Berg	1982	710
18-13/16	11-15/16	6-14/16	M	Kenora	ONT	John L. Angel	1982	710
18-13/16	12-01/16	6-12/16	M	Hudson Bay	SAS	Mark Hughes	1982	710
18-13/16	12-00/16	6-13/16	M	The Pas	MAN	Scott Lang	1983	710
18-13/16	11-12/16	7-01/16	M	Iron County	MI	John O. Cowell	1983	710
18-13/16	11-05/16	7-08/16	M	Caramat	ONT	Robert A. Boyer	1984	710
18-13/16	12-01/16	6-12/16	M	Sunbury Co.	NBW	Burchel Blevins	1984	710
18-13/16	12-01/16	6-12/16	M	Dist. 21	ONT	Ron Harger	1985	710
18-13/16	11-07/16	7-06/16	M	Otter Lake	QUE	Dana P. Calhoun	1985	710
18-13/16	12-02/16	6-11/16	M	St. James Bay	AK	John Gary Price	1985	710
18-13/16	12-00/16	6-13/16	M	Sierra County	NM	Kendall Doyle	1985	710
18-13/16	11-11/16	7-02/16	M	Thunder Bay	ONT	Howard Leopold	1985	710
18-13/16	11-14/16	6-15/16	M	Kenora	ONT	Ron Books	1986	710
18-13/16	11-08/16	7-05/16	M	Gallatin County	MT	Stephen Lockington	1986	710
18-13/16	11-11/16	7-02/16	M	Archuleta County	CO	Lonnie Draper	1986	710
18-13/16	12-03/16	6-10/16	M	Wasilla	AK	Ted Grover	1986	710
18-12/16	12-01/16	6-11/16	M	Shasta County	CA	Harv Ebers	1964	744
18-12/16	11-11/16	7-01/16	M	Carbon County	UT	Marvin Tye	1965	744
18-12/16	11-09/16	7-03/16	M	Manowam Lake	QUE	Dennis H. Driscoll	1969	744
18-12/16	11-05/16	7-07/16	M	Calahan	CA	W. E. Cates	1972	744
18-12/16	11-13/16	6-15/16	M	Stratton	ME	Bob Kuhar	1973	744
18-12/16	11-14/16	6-14/16	M	Trinity County	CA	Daniel Higuera	1974	744
18-12/16	11-13/16	6-15/16	M	Uncompahgre N. F.	CO	Anthony Keeling	1975	744
18-12/16	12-01/16	6-11/16	M	Hubbard County	NM	Jack Smythe	1977	744
18-12/16	12-02/16	6-10/16	M	Lesser Slave Lake	ALB	Gene Solyntjes	1978	744
18-12/16	11-14/16	6-14/16	M	Fremont County	ID	Dennis L. Shirley	1979	744
18-12/16	11-10/16	7-02/16	M	Stratton	ME	Len Cardinale	1980	744
18-12/16	12-02/16	6-10/16	M	Gunnison National Forest	CO	James F. Dougherty	1980	744
18-12/16	11-03/16	7-09/16	M	Madrid	ME	John Janelli	1980	744
18-12/16	11-14/16	6-14/16	M	Washington Island	MN	Herbert O. Lundberg	1980	744
18-12/16	11-15/16	6-13/16	M	Sandy Bar Creek	CA	Dale H. Bracken	1981	744
18-12/16	11-12/16	7-00/16	M	Warren County	VA	Joseph A. Ramey	1981	744
18-12/16	11-12/16	7-00/16	M	Clear Creek	CO	David L. Skiff	1981	744
18-12/16	12-00/16	6-12/16	M	Lemhi County	ID	Bob Ulshafer	1981	744
18-12/16	11-14/16	6-14/16	M	Remingy	QUE	Richard L. Jackson	1982	744
18-12/16	12-01/16	6-11/16	M	Idaho County	ID	Robert Dale Evans	1982	744
18-12/16	11-14/16	6-14/16	M	Madoc	ONT	Mel Johnson	1982	744
18-12/16	11-06/16	7-06/16	M	Archuleta County	CO	Steve Vittetow	1982	744
18-12/16	12-00/16	6-12/16	M	Kenmount	ONT	James D. Murray	1983	744
18-12/16	11-08/16	7-04/16	M	McAdam	NBW	David W. Peltier	1983	744
18-12/16	12-03/16	6-09/16	M	Langlade County	WI	Michael Steliga	1983	744
18-12/16	12-02/16	6-10/16	M	Langlade County	WI	Larry Petts	1983	744

BLACK BEAR

Minimum Score 18

Score	Greatest Length	Greatest Width	Sex	Area	State/ Province	Hunter's Name	Date	Rank
18-12/16	11-05/16	7-07/16	M	Capreol	ONT	P. W. "Bill" Meyer	1984	744
18-12/16	11-13/16	6-15/16	M	Graham County	ONT	Joe Neal Walters	1984	744
18-12/16	11-06/16	7-06/16	M	Boise County	ID	Gary Kinney	1984	744
18-12/16	11-14/16	6-14/16	M	Koochiching County	MN	Daniel Krasean	1984	744
18-12/16	12-00/16	6-12/16	M	Dryden	ONT	Mark Guelzow	1985	744
18-12/16	12-00/16	6-12/16	M	Riverside County	CA	Paul Persano	1985	744
18-12/16	11-11/16	7-01/16	M	Capreol	ONT	Lawrence M. Sowders	1986	744
18-12/16	11-09/16	7-03/16	M	Pitkin County	CO	Gary B. McClure	1986	744
18-11/16	11-12/16	6-15/16	M	Presque Isle	MI	Herbert Miller	1957	778
18-11/16	11-08/16	7-03/16	M	Chirvakum Creek	WA	Joe Zuend	1962	778
18-11/16	11-13/16	6-14/16	M	Iron County	MI	Donald Schram	1965	778
18-11/16	11-07/16	7-04/16	M	Shawano County	WI	Kenneth Karbon	1970	778
18-11/16	11-10/16	7-01/16	M	Lac Cayamant	QUE	Charles Shaffner	1971	778
18-11/16	11-09/16	7-02/16	M	Book Cliff Mountains	UT	Dennis Schoenick	1972	778
18-11/16	11-07/16	7-04/16	M	Las Vegas	NM	Dr. Rick H. Jackson	1975	778
18-11/16	11-12/16	6-15/16	M	Nestor Falls	ONT	Greg Roach	1977	778
18-11/16	11-11/16	7-00/16	M	Estaire	ONT	Donnie Evans	1978	778
18-11/16	11-10/16	7-01/16	M	Lake Nipigon	ONT	Gary L. Smith	1978	778
18-11/16	11-07/16	7-04/16	M	Orofino	ID	John Wagner	1978	778
18-11/16	11-15/16	6-12/16	M	Itasca County	MN	Harold Whitt	1979	778
18-11/16	11-09/16	7-02/16	M	Huerfano County	CO	Patricia J. Matarazzo	1980	778
18-11/16	11-10/16	7-01/16	M	Oquossoc	ME	Jeff Roberts	1980	778
18-11/16	11-11/16	7-00/16	M	Bessemer	MI	Edward Burley	1981	778
18-11/16	11-10/16	7-01/16	M	Itasca County	MN	Tom Brudeli	1981	778
18-11/16	11-11/16	7-00/16	M	Iron County	MI	Tom A. Longnecker	1981	778
18-11/16	11-12/16	6-15/16	M	Wesley	ME	Lincoln Michaud	1981	778
18-11/16	11-11/16	7-00/16	M	Dryden	ONT	Harry L. Stalter	1981	778
18-11/16	11-08/16	7-03/16	M	Franklin County	MA	George Holmes, Jr.	1982	778
18-11/16	11-09/16	7-02/16	M	Chapleau	ONT	Jim Grooters	1982	778
18-11/16	10-11/16	7-00/16	M	Atikokan	ONT	Al Taylor	1983	778
18-11/16	11-15/16	6-12/16	M	Dorsett	ONT	Daryll E. Smith	1983	778
18-11/16	11-05/16	7-06/16	M	Lynn Lake	MAN	Gord Monteath	1983	778
18-11/16	11-12/16	6-15/16	M	Valley County	ID	George Wadsworth	1983	778
18-11/16	11-06/16	7-05/16	M	Kiamath County	OR	Jeffery K. Russell	1983	778
18-11/16	11-13/16	6-14/16	M	Rio Arriba County	NM	William Rule	1983	778
18-11/16	11-10/16	7-01/16	M	North of Fort Frances	ONT	Kerry Ella	1984	778
18-11/16	11-07/16	7-04/16	M	Muskoka	ONT	Alexander Button	1984	778
18-11/16	11-09/16	7-02/16	M	Bonner County	ID	Brian T. Farley	1984	778
18-11/16	11-14/16	6-13/16	M	Franklin County	ME	Harold Osborne	1984	778
18-11/16	11-15/16	6-12/16	M	Spokane County	WA	David Lossett, Sr.	1984	778
18-11/16	11-09/16	7-02/16	M	Opasatika	ONT	Rob J. Smith	1985	778
18-11/16	11-12/16	6-15/16	M	Huerfano County	CO	Jerry Barth	1985	778
18-11/16	11-13/16	6-14/16	M	Sioux Lookout	ONT	Todd Koelzer	1986	778
18-11/16	11-15/16	6-12/16	M	Lost Lake	ONT	Richard Martin	1986	778
18-11/16	11-10/16	7-01/16	M	Fort Coulonge	QUE	Kevin Ball	1986	778
18-11/16	12-02/16	6-09/16	M	Duck Mtns.	MAN	Terry Schar	1986	778
18-10/16	11-08/16	7-02/16	M	Iron County	WI	Carl Hulbert	1963	816
18-10/16	11-08/16	7-02/16	M	Montreal River	ONT	S. Robinson/J. Beach	1966	816
18-10/16	11-07/16	7-03/16	M	Rio Grande R.	CO	Ron Wintz	1967	816
18-10/16	11-11/16	6-15/16	M	Vermillion Bay	ONT	Thomas L. A. Pucci	1968	816
18-10/16	11-12/16	6-14/16	M	Kooskia	ID	Randolph Coleman	1970	816
18-10/16	12-02/16	6-08/16	M	McLeod Lake	BC	Ron McKay	1973	816
18-10/16	11-08/16	7-02/16	M	Las Animas County	CO	Dr. John Adams	1974	816
18-10/16	11-05/16	7-05/16	M	Madison County	ID	Bruce W. Baird	1974	816
18-10/16	11-00/16	7-10/16	M	Goodman	WI	Dan Stencel	1974	816
18-10/16	11-08/16	7-02/16	M	Madrid	ME	Mark Checki	1976	816
18-10/16	11-13/16	6-13/16	M	Starkey Unit	OR	Timothy D. Palmore	1976	816
18-10/16	11-05/16	7-05/16	M	Grand County	CO	Lyle Willmarth	1976	816
18-10/16	11-10/16	7-00/16	M	Orofino Circle	ID	Tom Cummings	1977	816
18-10/16	11-11/16	6-15/16	M	Lewis & Clark County	MT	Scott Koelzer	1977	816
18-10/16	12-01/16	6-09/16	M	Palmer	AK	John F. Sumrall	1977	816
18-10/16	11-08/16	7-02/16	M	Uncompahgre N.F.	CO	William Hendricks	1978	816
18-10/16	11-12/16	6-14/16	M	Stone Creek	BC	Larry McKay	1978	816
18-10/16	11-10/16	7-00/16	M	Chaffee County	CO	Frank A. Morminello	1978	816

BLACK BEAR

(continued)   Minimum Score 18

Score	Greatest Length	Greatest Width	Sex	Area	State/ Province	Hunter's Name	Date	Rank
18-10/16	11-10/16	7-00/16	M	Mendocino County	CA	Russell L. Browning	1979	816
18-10/16	11-14/16	6-12/16	M	Dolores County	CO	Stanley A. Coval	1979	816
18-10/16	11-02/16	7-08/16	M	Judith Basin County	MT	Don Davidson	1981	816
18-10/16	11-05/16	7-05/16	M	Boise County	ID	Richard C. Nichols	1981	816
18-10/16	11-07/16	7-03/16	M	Thunder Bay	ONT	Roberta Byerly	1982	816
18-10/16	11-07/16	7-03/16	M	Warren County	NY	Ernie Ahr	1982	816
18-10/16	12-00/16	6-10/16	M	Susitna Valley	AK	Matt Jones	1982	816
18-10/16	11-12/16	6-14/16	M	Gunnison County	CO	Mike Miller	1982	816
18-10/16	11-10/16	7-00/16	M	Meagher County	AZ	John Levison	1983	816
18-10/16	11-14/16	6-12/16	M	Clearwater County	ID	Tim Newbold	1983	816
18-10/16	11-09/16	7-01/16	M	Ear Falls	ONT	Ron Marion	1983	816
18-10/16	11-14/16	6-12/16	M	Douglas County	OR	Ralph Burt	1983	816
18-10/16	11-02/16	7-08/16	M	Rouyn Noranda	QUE	Claude St. Amour	1983	816
18-10/16	12-00/16	6-10/16	M	Mine Centre	ONT	Edwin John Durushia	1984	816
18-10/16	11-13/16	6-13/16	M	Lemhi County	ID	Clint Bevins	1984	816
18-10/16	11-13/16	6-13/16	M	Beluga River	AK	Dennis Redden	1984	816
18-10/16	12-01/16	6-09/16	M	Valley County	ID	Gary Angell	1985	816
18-10/16	11-11/16	6-15/16	M	Hudson Bay	SAS	Warren Buss	1985	816
18-10/16	11-06/16	7-04/16	M	Huerfano County	CO	Michael Beckwith	1985	816
18-10/16	11-07/16	7-03/16	M	Jellico	ONT	John Paul McKown	1985	816
18-10/16	11-13/16	6-13/16	M	Las Animas County	CO	Tom Storr	1985	816
18-10/16	11-10/16	7-00/16	F	Sanpete County	UT	C. Danny Butler	1986	816
18-10/16	11-04/16	7-06/16	M	Papineau	ONT	Fred Law	1986	816
18-09/16	11-08/16	7-01/16	M	Sudbury	ONT	Vinnie Pisani	1985	857
18-09/16	11-05/16	7-04/16	M	Chelan County	WA	Wayne Hathaway	1960	858
18-09/16	11-06/16	7-03/16	M	Olsen Bay	AK	Don Daniels	1963	858
18-09/16	11-10/16	6-15/16	M	Iron County	MI	Don Schram	1964	858
18-09/16	11-10/16	6-15/16	M	Mattawa	ONT	Dr. Max G. Menefee	1966	858
18-09/16	11-05/16	7-04/16	M	St. Louis County	MN	Ron Johnson	1967	858
18-09/16	11-05/16	7-04/16	M	Blue Jay Ridge	CA	Delbert Allmon	1972	858
18-09/16	11-06/16	7-03/16	M	Nez Perce County	ID	Betty Gulman	1972	858
18-09/16	11-12/16	6-13/16	M	Lake Hopewell	NM	Curtis W. McClahan	1973	858
18-09/16	12-00/16	6-09/16	M	Swan Hills	ALB	Gerald L. Egbert	1976	858
18-09/16	11-07/16	7-02/16	M	Stratton	ME	John G. Morningstar	1977	858
18-09/16	11-09/16	7-00/16	M	Ottawa River	QUE	Roger D. Davis	1978	858
18-09/16	11-13/16	6-12/16	M	Wabigoon	ONT	Jon Helgason	1979	858
18-09/16	11-04/16	7-05/16	M	Caramat	ONT	John LaForge	1979	858
18-09/16	11-12/16	6-13/16	M	Fremont County	ID	Tom Savage	1979	858
18-09/16	11-13/16	6-12/16	M	Sawyer County	WI	Joe Gohres	1980	858
18-09/16	11-05/16	7-04/16	M	Idaho County	ID	Darrel Howard	1980	858
18-09/16	11-06/16	7-03/16	M	Nels Lake	NM	Cornie P. Intveld	1980	858
18-09/16	11-11/16	6-14/16	M	Ravalli County	MT	Mike F. Bartz	1981	858
18-09/16	11-09/16	7-00/16	M	Marquette County	MI	Gary Lohman	1981	858
18-09/16	11-07/16	7-02/16	M	Idaho County	ID	Darrell Howard	1982	858
18-09/16	11-11/16	6-14/16	M	Marquette County	MI	Keith B. Putnam	1982	858
18-09/16	11-13/16	6-12/16	M	Dryden	ONT	Dennis L. Havey	1982	858
18-09/16	11-07/16	7-02/16	M	Nipigon	ONT	James P. Kina	1982	858
18-09/16	11-08/16	7-01/16	M	Susitna Valley	AK	Patrick McKay	1982	858
18-09/16	12-03/16	6-06/16	M	Game Area #23	MAN	Gary Kaluzniak	1983	858
18-09/16	12-05/16	6-04/16	M	Carlton County	MN	Larry H. Hoyt	1983	858
18-09/16	11-10/16	6-15/16	M	Ear Falls	ONT	Scott J. Strook	1984	858
18-09/16	11-08/16	7-01/16	M	Temiscaminque	QUE	Joe G. Hopwood	1984	858
18-09/16	11-09/16	7-00/16	M	Cedar Lake	ONT	Brad Wiehr	1984	858
18-09/16	11-09/16	7-00/16	M	Idaho County	ID	Ronald J. Larson	1984	858
18-09/16	11-09/16	7-00/16	M	Shasta County	CA	Peter Esposito	1984	858
18-09/16	11-10/16	6-15/16	M	Pancake Bay	ONT	Brad L. Rogers	1985	858
18-09/16	11-10/16	6-15/16	M	Mendocino County	CA	Charles Verne	1985	858
18-09/16	11-07/16	7-02/16	M	Lemhi County	ID	Thomas Fuller	1985	858
18-09/16	11-12/16	6-13/16	M	Cass County	MN	Larry Fischer	1985	858
18-09/16	11-06/16	7-03/16	M	Missoula County	MT	Terry See	1985	858
18-09/16	11-11/16	6-14/16	M	Boundary County	ID	Walt Dinning	1986	858
18-09/16	11-11/16	6-14/16	M	Clearwater County	ID	Ronnie Larson	1986	858
18-09/16	11-09/16	7-00/16	M	Fort Coulonge	QUE	Westley Keller	1986	858
18-08/16	11-08/16	7-00/16	M	Bellingham	WA	Jack Fish	1961	897

BLACK BEAR

Minimum Score 18

Score	Greatest Length	Greatest Width	Sex	Area	State/ Province	Hunter's Name	Date	Rank
18-08/16	11-13/16	6-11/16	M	Prince William Sound	AK	Bob Snelson	1962	897
18-08/16	11-08/16	7-00/16	M	Cedar	WI	Maynard Peck	1963	897
18-08/16	11-06/16	7-02/16	M	Elk River	ID	Robert J. Kreisher	1965	897
18-08/16	11-11/16	6-13/16	M	Sapawe	ONT	Dennis Gregory	1967	897
18-08/16	11-04/16	7-04/16	M	Creede	CO	Ron Wintz	1967	897
18-08/16	11-12/16	6-12/16	M	McCloud	CA	Lyle L. Stroble	1968	897
18-08/16	11-07/16	7-01/16	M	Stratton	ME	John Miterko	1970	897
18-08/16	12-00/16	6-08/16	M	Forest County	WI	Vilas Backhaus	1972	897
18-08/16	11-04/16	7-04/16	M	Messines	QUE	John W. Redmond	1973	897
18-08/16	11-10/16	6-14/16	M	Athens	ME	John D. Bonargo	1974	897
18-08/16	11-07/16	7-01/16	M	LaPlata County	CO	Ronald C. Gaines	1975	897
18-08/16	11-00/16	7-08/16	M	Messines	QUE	Arthur R. Litschewski	1975	897
18-08/16	11-07/16	7-01/16	M	Hopetown	ONT	Dale Bailey	1976	897
18-08/16	11-06/16	7-02/16	M	Dryden	ONT	Jim Dyer	1977	897
18-08/16	11-06/16	7-02/16	M	Sioux Narrows	ONT	David Bailey	1978	897
18-08/16	11-08/16	7-00/16	M	Cook County	MN	Paul Smith	1978	897
18-08/16	11-06/16	7-02/16	M	Jemez Mountain	NM	Johnny R. Trujillo	1978	897
18-08/16	11-04/16	7-04/16	M	Kingston	ME	John Janelli	1979	897
18-08/16	11-13/16	6-11/16	M	Lincoln County	WI	James Lechleitner	1981	897
18-08/16	12-00/16	6-08/16	M	Burnett County	WI	Gary K. Roholt	1981	897
18-08/16	11-06/16	7-02/16	M	Atikokan	ONT	Larry Stewart	1982	897
18-08/16	11-12/16	6-12/16	M	Kanabec County	MN	Raymond J. Altman	1982	897
18-08/16	11-10/16	6-14/16	M	Bancroft	ONT	Dean J. Farkas	1982	897
18-08/16	11-03/16	7-05/16	M	Love	SAS	David M. Tofte	1982	897
18-08/16	11-07/16	7-01/16	M	Terrace Bay	ONT	William J. Ernst	1983	897
18-08/16	11-07/16	7-01/16	M	McAdams	NBW	David Baldwin	1983	897
18-08/16	12-01/16	6-07/16	M	Ear Falls	ONT	Ernest C. Boser	1983	897
18-08/16	11-12/16	6-12/16	M	Langlade County	WI	Raymond Juedes	1983	897
18-08/16	11-11/16	6-13/16	M	Vilas County	WI	Alan L. Black	1983	897
18-08/16	11-08/16	7-00/16	M	Park County	CO	Larry A. Welchlen	1984	897
18-08/16	11-02/16	7-06/16	M	Carbon County	WY	Vaughn Cross	1984	897
18-08/16	11-10/16	6-14/16	M	Swan River	MAN	Kevin Hisey	1984	897
18-08/16	11-06/16	7-02/16	M	Spokane County	WA	Kenneth R. Wengert	1984	897
18-08/16	11-11/16	6-13/16	M	Iron County	WI	Gary Johnson	1984	897
18-08/16	11-12/16	6-12/16	M	Kootenai County	ID	Kenneth R. Wengert	1985	897
18-08/16	11-10/16	6-14/16	M	Susitna River	AK	Roger Stewart	1985	897
18-08/16	11-09/16	6-15/16	M	Fremont County	ID	Doug Burkman	1985	897
18-08/16	11-14/16	6-10/16	M	Shasta County	CA	Larry Walkley	1985	897
18-08/16	11-06/16	7-02/16	M	Pitkin County	CO	Richard E. Davis	1986	897
18-08/16	11-04/16	7-04/16	M	Lemhi County	ID	Art Hrabec	1986	897
18-08/16	11-06/16	7-02/16	M	White River	ONT	Daniel B. Meece	1986	897
18-08/16	11-05/16	7-03/16	M	Palfrey Lake	NBW	Lou Probo	1986	897
18-08/16	12-00/16	6-08/16	M	Siskiyou County	CA	Larry Holmes	1986	897
18-07/16	11-05/16	7-02/16	M	Stratton	ME	Ed Hall	1968	941
18-07/16	11-11/16	6-12/16	M	Larimer County	CO	Ronald M. Breitsprecher	1975	941
18-07/16	11-08/16	6-15/16	M	Greenville	ME	John Kuhar	1975	941
18-07/16	11-12/16	6-11/16	M	Cass Lake	MN	Walter L. Lash	1976	941
18-07/16	11-13/16	6-10/16	M	Albemarle County	VA	J. C. Locke	1976	941
18-07/16	11-09/16	6-14/16	M	Clearwater County	ID	Edward Russell	1976	941
18-07/16	11-11/16	6-12/16	M	Atikokan	ONT	John Carlson	1977	941
18-07/16	11-09/16	6-14/16	M	Lake County	MN	W. Dan Williams, Jr.	1977	941
18-07/16	11-07/16	7-00/16	M	English Bay	AK	Roger Stewart	1978	941
18-07/16	12-01/16	6-06/16	M	Iron County	WI	Douglas R. Parrott	1979	941
18-07/16	11-01/16	7-06/16	M	Phelps Twp.	ONT	Robert C. Precious	1979	941
18-07/16	11-10/16	6-13/16	M	Almonte	ONT	Thomas S. Gerstner	1980	941
18-07/16	11-09/16	6-14/16	M	Madrid	ME	Bob Spano	1980	941
18-07/16	11-06/16	7-01/16	M	Little Belt Mountains	MT	Gary H. Thompson	1980	941
18-07/16	11-12/16	6-11/16	M	Beluga	AK	Tom Atkins	1981	941
18-07/16	11-04/16	7-03/16	M	El Paso County	CO	Max Tallent	1981	941
18-07/16	11-15/16	6-08/16	M	Archuleta County	CO	James P. Mitchell	1982	941
18-07/16	11-08/16	6-15/16	M	Kenora	ONT	Floyd McDanell	1982	941
18-07/16	11-10/16	6-13/16	M	?	ONT	Bill Stonebraker	1982	941
18-07/16	11-10/16	6-13/16	M	Kirkland Lake	ONT	Michael Hogan	1983	941
18-07/16	11-07/16	7-00/16	M	Nipigon	ONT	Wayne Beltz, Jr.	1983	941

BLACK BEAR

(continued)   Minimum Score 18

Score	Greatest Length	Greatest Width	Sex	Area	State/ Province	Hunter's Name	Date	Rank
18-07/16	11-09/16	6-14/16	M	Timmins	ONT	Paul Eldridge	1983	941
18-07/16	11-10/16	6-13/16	M	Tatalina River	AK	Timothy J. Barber	1983	941
18-07/16	11-06/16	7-01/16	M	Clackamas County	OR	Robert L. Smitherman	1983	941
18-07/16	11-01/16	7-06/16	M	Sioux Lookout	ONT	Steve Sherry	1984	941
18-07/16	11-09/16	6-14/16	M	Skeleton Lake	ALB	Dwayne Alton	1984	941
18-07/16	11-08/16	6-15/16	M	Devlin	ONT	Jim Leqve	1984	941
18-07/16	11-11/16	6-12/16	M	Luce County	MI	Terry L. Cook	1984	941
18-07/16	11-02/16	7-05/16	M	Lemhi County	ID	Dennis Derrer	1985	941
18-07/16	11-07/16	7-00/16	M	Kenora	ONT	Steven Duerksen	1985	941
18-07/16	11-02/16	7-05/16	M	Adams County	ID	Rick Clinton	1985	941
18-07/16	11-13/16	6-10/16	M	Las Animas County	CO	Kelly Williams	1985	941
18-07/16	11-09/16	6-14/16	M	Douglas County	OR	Jim Nielsen	1985	941
18-07/16	11-07/16	7-00/16	M	Gallatin County	MT	Terry L. Anderson	1985	941
18-07/16	11-09/16	6-14/16	M	Mine Centre	ONT	Bob Roulet	1986	941
18-07/16	11-12/16	6-11/16	M	Savant Lake	ONT	Daniel J. Gartner	1986	941
18-07/16	11-09/16	6-14/16	F	Smith	ALB	Dave Gerber	1986	941
18-06/16	11-09/16	6-13/16	M	Mariposa County	CA	Douglas Walker	1965	978
18-06/16	11-08/16	6-14/16	M	Fulton County	NY	Peter Mertens	1966	978
18-06/16	11-08/16	6-14/16	M	Chicago Creek	CO	Jim Dougherty	1970	978
18-06/16	11-12/16	6-10/16	M	Stratton	ME	Joe Melchiore	1970	978
18-06/16	11-10/16	6-12/16	M	Mt. Mitchell	NC	Jerry Rushing	1970	978
18-06/16	11-02/16	7-04/16	M	Chetwyn	BC	Lee E. Hansel	1973	978
18-06/16	11-04/16	7-02/16	M	Valley County	ID	Charles F. Maloney	1973	978
18-06/16	11-08/16	6-14/16	M	Becker County	MN	Gordon Swenson	1973	978
18-06/16	11-06/16	7-00/16	M	Dryden	ONT	John L. Dykes	1974	978
18-06/16	11-12/16	6-10/16	M	Flathead County	MT	Dr. Barry Wensel	1974	978
18-06/16	11-08/16	6-14/16	M	Blanco R. Basin	CO	Judd Cooney	1975	978
18-06/16	12-00/16	6-06/16	M	Snohomish County	WA	Jim Gregory	1975	978
18-06/16	11-00/16	7-06/16	M	Larimer County	CO	Michael Lewis	1975	978
18-06/16	11-10/16	6-12/16	M	Saguache County	CO	Sandra Scheid	1975	978
18-06/16	11-06/16	7-00/16	M	Bingham	ME	Anthony Ciletti	1976	978
18-06/16	11-12/16	6-10/16	M	Meeker	CO	Brad Cook	1978	978
18-06/16	11-05/16	7-01/16	M	Lemhi County	ID	Roy Auwen	1979	978
18-06/16	11-08/16	6-14/16	M	Marinette County	WI	William Brunette	1979	978
18-06/16	11-14/16	6-08/16	M	Thunder Bay	ONT	Neil E. Gilles	1980	978
18-06/16	11-10/16	6-12/16	M	Red Lake	ONT	Leon L. Miller	1981	978
18-06/16	11-04/16	7-02/16	M	Espanola	ONT	Ronald E. Hergott	1982	978
18-06/16	11-05/16	7-01/16	M	Siskiyou County	CA	Dave S. Semple	1982	978
18-06/16	11-07/16	6-15/16	M	Diamond Canyon	UT	Bill Dunstan IV	1982	978
18-06/16	11-14/16	6-08/16	M	Game Area #23	MAN	Gary Kaluzniak	1983	978
18-06/16	11-08/16	6-14/16	M	McAdams	NBW	Donald R. Shipley	1983	978
18-06/16	11-05/16	7-01/16	M	Ramsey	ONT	Robert H. Pavlovic	1983	978
18-06/16	11-12/16	6-10/16	M	Cheboygan County	MI	Roger A. Greve	1983	978
18-06/16	11-15/16	6-07/16	M	Sawyer County	WI	Kevin Capelle	1983	978
18-06/16	11-08/16	6-14/16	M	Chelan County	WA	Edward M. Beitner	1983	978
18-06/16	11-15/16	6-07/16	M	Green County	NY	Bob Spina	1983	978
18-06/16	11-04/16	7-02/16	M	Douglas County	OR	Tim O'Kelly	1984	978
18-06/16	11-15/16	6-07/16	M	Cass County	MN	James D. Zahalka	1984	978
18-06/16	11-08/16	6-14/16	M	Marquette County	MI	George M. Barosko	1984	978
18-06/16	11-10/16	6-12/16	M	Luce County	MI	Norman E. Bell	1984	978
18-06/16	11-02/16	7-04/16	M	Bathurst	NBW	Daryl Labarron	1985	978
18-06/16	11-04/16	7-02/16	M	Pontiac	QUE	Loren L. Fish	1985	978
18-06/16	11-08/16	6-14/16	F	Spirtwood	SAS	Kent W. Brigham	1986	978
18-06/16	11-10/16	6-12/16	M	Rio Arriba County	NM	Terry Sanders	1986	978
18-06/16	11-08/16	6-14/16	M	Thunder Bay	ONT	Gene Anderson	1986	978
18-06/16	11-03/16	7-03/16	M	Valley County	ID	Larry Hoff	1986	978
18-05/16	11-03/16	7-02/16	M	Iron Bridge	ONT	Philip L. Hawkins	1965	1018
18-05/16	11-09/16	6-12/16	M	Thomaston	MI	LaVern Miller	1971	1018
18-05/16	11-06/16	6-15/16	M	Florence County	WI	Jim Thimmig	1971	1018
18-05/16	11-03/16	7-02/16	M	Pine Lake	WI	Ernie V. Hutchinson	1972	1018
18-05/16	11-04/16	7-01/16	M	Duluth	MN	Art Heinze	1973	1018
18-05/16	11-09/16	6-12/16	M	Hutch Mountain	AZ	Stan Nordell	1975	1018
18-05/16	11-07/16	6-14/16	M	Cimarron	CO	Rick Hunckler	1976	1018
18-05/16	11-07/16	6-14/16	M	Montezuma County	CO	Stanley A. Coval	1977	1018

Minimum Score 18

Score	Greatest Length	Greatest Width	Sex	Area	State/ Province	Hunter's Name	Date	Rank
18-05/16	11-07/16	6-14/16	M	Ear Falls	ONT	John Brandt	1980	1018
18-05/16	11-09/16	6-12/16	M	Park County	MT	Charles Burdette	1980	1018
18-05/16	11-03/16	7-02/16	M	E. Braintree	MAN	Chester Surma	1980	1018
18-05/16	11-02/16	7-03/16	M	Abbott Butte	OR	Dan Viles	1980	1018
18-05/16	11-05/16	7-00/16	M	Gogebic County	MI	Donald E. Thompson, Jr.	1981	1018
18-05/16	11-07/16	6-14/16	M	Blind River	ONT	Cleve Roush	1982	1018
18-05/16	11-11/16	6-10/16	M	Iron County	WI	Keith Kaat	1982	1018
18-05/16	11-11/16	6-10/16	M	Alatna River	AK	John D. "Jack" Frost	1982	1018
18-05/16	11-04/16	7-01/16	M	Missoula County	MT	Tom Storm	1983	1018
18-05/16	11-09/16	6-12/16	M	Sundridge	ONT	Abby Lape	1983	1018
18-05/16	11-08/16	6-13/16	M	Thunder Bay	ONT	Bob Kraus	1985	1018
18-05/16	11-11/16	6-10/16	M	Hudson Bay	SAS	Clark Jenner	1985	1018
18-05/16	11-08/16	6-13/16	M	Cold Lake	ALB	Orest Popil	1985	1018
18-05/16	11-06/16	6-15/16	M	Atikokan	ONT	Bruce Wynn	1985	1018
18-05/16	11-14/16	6-07/16	M	Grand County	CO	Lyle Willmarth	1986	1018
18-05/16	11-08/16	6-13/16	M	Massey	ONT	Jim Hunsaker	1986	1018
18-05/16	11-11/16	6-10/16	M	Sudbury	ONT	Richard Dohm	1986	1018
18-05/16	11-13/16	6-08/16	M	Rocky Lake	MAN	Tim Finley	1986	1018
18-05/16	11-05/16	7-00/16	M	Blaine County	ID	Larry R. Newton	1986	1018
18-04/16	10-14/16	7-06/16	M	Deary	ID	Don Lawrence	1962	1045
18-04/16	11-07/16	6-13/16	M	Mt. Emley	OR	Gerald Rimbey	1962	1045
18-04/16	11-04/16	7-00/16	M	Shawano County	WI	Peter Erickson	1967	1045
18-04/16	11-12/16	6-08/16	M	Ft. Frances	ONT	Wayne Keefer	1968	1045
18-04/16	11-06/16	6-14/16	M	Kooskia	ID	Larry W. Gehre	1972	1045
18-04/16	11-12/16	6-08/16	M	Itasca County	MN	Lonny Herrick	1973	1045
18-04/16	11-10/16	6-10/16	M	LaPlata County	CO	Kenneth L. Biegel	1974	1045
18-04/16	11-07/16	6-13/16	M	Tuolumne County	CA	Willis Chapman	1974	1045
18-04/16	11-06/16	6-14/16	M	Harcourt	ONT	Robert M. Sweisthal	1977	1045
18-04/16	11-07/16	6-13/16	M	Boise County	ID	Richard C. Nichols	1978	1045
18-04/16	11-12/16	6-08/16	M	Caribou County	ID	Randy J. Stephens	1978	1045
18-04/16	11-07/16	6-13/16	M	Vermillion Bay	ONT	Daniel D. Carlson	1979	1045
18-04/16	11-06/16	6-14/16	M	Lily Lake	BC	Stanley Moore	1979	1045
18-04/16	11-08/16	6-12/16	M	DeBeque	CO	David E. Samuel	1979	1045
18-04/16	11-09/16	6-11/16	M	Beltrami County	MN	Greg Siekaniec	1979	1045
18-04/16	11-07/16	6-13/16	M	Dover-Foxcroft	ME	Mark Sutherly	1979	1045
18-04/16	11-07/16	6-13/16	M	Lunenburg	VT	James "Boomer" Hayden	1980	1045
18-04/16	11-12/16	6-08/16	M	Tehama County	CA	Gerald McKenzie	1980	1045
18-04/16	11-07/16	6-13/16	M	St. Louis County	MN	Mike Schullo	1981	1045
18-04/16	11-12/16	6-08/16	M	Susitna River	AK	Mel Hein	1983	1045
18-04/16	11-06/16	6-14/16	M	Seine River	ONT	George David Shelton	1983	1045
18-04/16	11-04/16	7-00/16	M	Cloud Bay	ONT	Ronald C. Maikranz	1983	1045
18-04/16	11-10/16	6-10/16	M	Iron County	MI	Jim Johnson	1983	1045
18-04/16	11-10/16	6-10/16	M	Mistatim	SAS	Jeff Grewe	1984	1045
18-04/16	11-08/16	6-12/16	M	Saguache County	CO	Jerry Barth	1984	1045
18-04/16	10-14/16	7-06/16	M	Idaho County	ID	James Jay Hill	1984	1045
18-04/16	11-04/16	7-00/16	M	Langlade County	WI	Edward R. Jenelewicz	1984	1045
18-04/16	11-08/16	6-12/16	M	Oxford County	ME	Gary Russell	1984	1045
18-04/16	11-12/16	6-08/16	M	Sudbury	ONT	Nancy A. Guisbert	1985	1045
18-04/16	11-10/16	6-10/16	M	Fawcett Lake	ALB	David R. Coupland	1985	1045
18-04/16	11-00/16	7-04/16	M	Oxford County	VA	Allen Baker	1985	1045
18-04/16	11-06/16	6-14/16	M	Lemhi County	ID	Mark Neer	1985	1045
18-04/16	12-00/16	6-04/16	M	Ft. Assiniboine	ALB	Jim Dahlberg	1985	1045
18-04/16	11-10/16	6-10/16	M	Siskiyou County	CA	Arthur M. Cain	1985	1045
18-04/16	11-08/16	6-12/16	M	Standard Creek	AK	William B. Childress	1986	1045
18-04/16	11-10/16	6-10/16	M	Beaconfield	NBW	William Clark	1986	1045
18-04/16	11-08/16	6-12/16	M	Fergus	ONT	David L. Reeves	1986	1045
18-03/16	11-01/16	7-02/16	M	Penobscot County	ME	Charles A. Kronyak	1965	1082
18-03/16	11-00/16	7-03/16	M	Stanley	ID	C. Randall Byers	1967	1082
18-03/16	11-04/16	6-15/16	M	Franklin County	ME	Philip Copp	1967	1082
18-03/16	11-06/16	6-13/16	M	Florence County	WI	Elaine S. Peck	1967	1082
18-03/16	11-15/16	6-04/16	M	Roan Cliff Mtns	CO	Bob Swinehart	1967	1082
18-03/16	11-03/16	7-00/16	M	Larkspur	CO	Larry Baker	1975	1082
18-03/16	11-08/16	6-11/16	M	Penobscot County	ME	Neil Zullo	1975	1082
18-03/16	11-06/16	6-13/16	M	Slave Lake	ALB	Gordon Roline	1976	1082

BLACK BEAR
(continued)

Minimum Score 18

Score	Greatest Length	Greatest Width	Sex	Area	State/ Province	Hunter's Name	Date	Rank
18-03/16	11-08/16	6-11/16	M	Targhee National Forest	ID	Thomas Pinkston	1978	1082
18-03/16	11-03/16	7-00/16	M	Sudbury	ONT	Alvin Lybarger	1979	1082
18-03/16	10-15/16	7-04/16	M	St. Louis County	MN	George Sheets	1979	1082
18-03/16	11-09/16	6-10/16	M	Anchorage	AK	Ronald Arch	1980	1082
18-03/16	11-10/16	6-09/16	M	Renfrew	ONT	Walter Cymbal	1980	1082
18-03/16	11-11/16	6-08/16	M	Fremont County	ID	Doug M. Chase	1981	1082
18-03/16	11-06/16	6-13/16	M	Thunder Bay	ONT	Sharon Larsen	1981	1082
18-03/16	11-07/16	6-12/16	M	Fort Frances	ONT	Pam Baird	1982	1082
18-03/16	11-03/16	7-00/16	M	Baraga County	MI	Jim Humber III	1982	1082
18-03/16	11-02/16	7-01/16	M	Meagher County	MT	Chuck Adams	1982	1082
18-03/16	11-06/16	6-13/16	M	Sierraville	CA	Robert Smith	1982	1082
18-03/16	11-08/16	6-11/16	M	Dryden	ONT	Richard Stock	1983	1082
18-03/16	11-06/16	6-13/16	M	Coaldale	CO	Al Weaver	1983	1082
18-03/16	11-01/16	7-02/16	M	Echouani Lake	QUE	Collins F. Kellogg	1983	1082
18-03/16	11-12/16	6-07/16	M	Burnett County	WI	Daniel D. Clayton	1983	1082
18-03/16	11-10/16	6-09/16	M	Otter Lake	QUE	Dana P. Calhoun	1984	1082
18-03/16	11-10/16	6-09/16	M	Moose River	ONT	Bob Duncan	1984	1082
18-03/16	11-05/16	6-14/16	M	Standard Creek	AK	James A. Jones	1984	1082
18-03/16	11-02/16	7-01/16	M	Idaho County	ID	David Gename	1984	1082
18-03/16	11-11/16	6-08/16	M	Langlade County	WI	Dan Buss	1984	1082
18-03/16	11-02/16	7-01/16	M	Wallowa County	OR	Mike Tyrholm	1984	1082
18-03/16	11-03/16	7-00/16	M	Valley County	ID	Douglas Bunch	1984	1082
18-03/16	11-06/16	6-13/16	M	Douglas County	WI	Dennis Plantenberg	1984	1082
18-03/16	11-03/16	7-00/16	M	Larimer County	CO	Doug O'Herron	1985	1082
18-03/16	11-07/16	6-12/16	M	English River	ONT	Richard Nielsen	1985	1082
18-03/16	11-03/16	7-00/16	M	Ignace	ONT	Walter E. Hammerling	1985	1082
18-03/16	12-01/16	6-02/16	M	Durban	MAN	Bill Wright, Jr.	1985	1082
18-03/16	11-15/16	6-04/16	M	Loon Lake	SAS	Harvey McNalley	1986	1082
18-03/16	11-04/16	6-15/16	M	Idaho County	ID	David Gename	1986	1082
18-02/16	11-08/16	6-10/16	M	Murphy Dome	AK	Richard Cooper	1955	1119
18-02/16	11-02/16	7-00/16	M	Sudbury	ONT	Floyd Eccleston	1961	1119
18-02/16	11-04/16	6-14/16	M	Patten	ME	Bill L. Carlos	1963	1119
18-02/16	11-08/16	6-10/16	M	Patten	ME	Dennis H. Driscoll	1967	1119
18-02/16	11-08/16	6-10/16	M	Franklin County	ME	Kenneth Rapp	1969	1119
18-02/16	11-05/16	6-13/16	M	Chapleau	ONT	Ed Helgason	1970	1119
18-02/16	11-06/16	6-12/16	M	Chetwyn	BC	Lee E. Hansel	1973	1119
18-02/16	11-09/16	6-09/16	M	LaPlata County	CO	Rose Neeley	1975	1119
18-02/16	11-06/16	6-12/16	M	Waupaca County	WI	Neil Pietenpol	1975	1119
18-02/16	10-14/16	7-04/16	M	Flathead County	MT	Paul P. Schafer	1976	1119
18-02/16	11-12/16	6-06/16	M	Iron County	MI	Harry W. Squibb	1976	1119
18-02/16	11-06/16	6-12/16	M	Madison County	ID	Paul Beesley	1977	1119
18-02/16	11-10/16	6-08/16	M	Skykomish	WA	Stephen C. Zabransky	1978	1119
18-02/16	11-08/16	6-10/16	M	Ovando	MT	Paul Brunner	1979	1119
18-02/16	11-09/16	6-09/16	M	Orr	MN	James D. Coakley	1979	1119
18-02/16	11-07/16	6-11/16	M	Kootenai County	ID	Stanley Leake	1979	1119
18-02/16	11-04/16	6-14/16	M	Whitney	ONT	Doug Merkel	1979	1119
18-02/16	11-11/16	6-07/16	F	Freemont County	ID	Paul Phillips	1979	1119
18-02/16	11-07/16	6-11/16	M	Boise County	ID	Larry Spiva	1979	1119
18-02/16	11-14/16	6-04/16	M	Boise County	ID	Larry Hoff	1980	1119
18-02/16	11-10/16	6-08/16	M	Gunnison	CO	Holt Dougherty	1980	1119
18-02/16	11-11/16	6-07/16	M	Chichester	QUE	Don Marin	1981	1119
18-02/16	11-04/16	6-14/16	M	Piscataquis Cty	ME	Daniel E. Reznik	1981	1119
18-02/16	11-04/16	6-14/16	M	Ear Falls	ONT	Robert J. Roach	1981	1119
18-02/16	10-15/16	7-03/16	M	North Cumberland	NH	Phillip E. Williams	1981	1119
18-02/16	11-08/16	6-10/16	M	Ignace	ONT	Elmer R. Luce, Jr.	1982	1119
18-02/16	11-04/16	6-14/16	M	Brookton	ME	Richard Manchur	1982	1119
18-02/16	11-10/16	6-08/16	M	Clearwater Cty	ID	Dan J. Martin	1983	1119
18-02/16	11-10/16	6-08/16	M	Algonquin	ONT	Walter F. Dotson, Jr.	1983	1119
18-02/16	11-05/16	6-13/16	M	Sundridge	ONT	Jack Lape	1983	1119
18-02/16	11-02/16	7-00/16	M	Haliburton	ONT	John Dawson	1983	1119
18-02/16	11-01/16	7-01/16	M	Boise County	ID	Larry Spiva	1983	1119
18-02/16	11-08/16	6-10/16	M	Oneida County	WI	Don Ries	1983	1119
18-02/16	11-04/16	6-14/16	M	Latah County	ID	Marcus B. Caudill	1984	1119

BLACK BEAR

Minimum Score 18

Score	Greatest Length	Greatest Width	Sex	Area	State/ Province	Hunter's Name	Date	Rank
18-02/16	11-02/16	7-00/16	M	Cumberland House	SAS	Wayne Muth	1984	1119
18-02/16	11-06/16	6-12/16	M	Latah County	ID	Robert Walter Brooks	1984	1119
18-02/16	11-10/16	6-08/16	M	Clearwater Cty	ID	Mark McMurray	1984	1119
18-02/16	11-06/16	6-12/16	M	Pontiac County	QUE	Russ Kay	1984	1119
18-02/16	11-08/16	6-10/16	M	Fiddler Township	ONT	Mike Johnson	1984	1119
18-02/16	11-09/16	6-09/16	M	Valley County	ID	Kenneth Hyde	1984	1119
18-02/16	11-07/16	6-11/16	M	Sunbury	NBW	Mike Lamade	1985	1119
18-02/16	11-04/16	6-14/16	M	Ft. Coulonge	QUE	Wm. Fred Stone	1985	1119
18-02/16	11-06/16	6-12/16	M	Penobscot County	ME	Gary Thorne	1985	1119
18-02/16	11-06/16	6-12/16	M	Riverside County	CA	Jim Wagner	1985	1119
18-02/16	11-06/16	6-12/16	M	Jackson County	OR	Lou Probo	1985	1119
18-02/16	11-08/16	6-10/16	M	Eagle Lake	ONT	Paul Sieg	1986	1119
18-02/16	11-07/16	6-11/16	M	Fort Francis	ONT	Randy Durushia	1986	1119
18-02/16	11-09/16	6-09/16	M	Wabagoon	ONT	Robert Barrie	1986	1119
18-02/16	11-15/16	6-03/16	M	Duck Mountains	MAN	Bill Clink	1986	1119
18-02/16	11-10/16	6-08/16	M	Grant County	NM	Dr. Douglas R. Hahn	1986	1119
18-02/16	11-01/16	7-01/16	M	Siskiyou County	CA	Kirk Westervelt	1986	1119
18-01/16	11-08/16	6-09/16	M	Nason Creek	WA	Dick Smethvrst	1965	1170
18-01/16	11-04/16	6-13/16	M	Magic Creek	ID	Jess Stinichcome	1965	1170
18-01/16	11-00/16	7-01/16	M	N. New Portland	ME	Raymond Benedetto	1970	1170
18-01/16	11-07/16	6-10/16	M	Chama Basin	CO	A. H. Gutierrez, Jr.	1971	1170
18-01/16	11-07/16	6-10/16	M	Stratton	ME	Walter Krom	1972	1170
18-01/16	11-03/16	6-14/16	M	Black Water River	BC	Ron McKay	1974	1170
18-01/16	11-11/16	6-06/16	M	Shasta County	CA	P. W. "Bill" Meyer	1975	1170
18-01/16	11-03/16	6-14/16	M	Cornell	MI	Rick Moudry	1975	1170
18-01/16	11-12/16	6-05/16	M	Itasca County	MN	Charles W. Schultz	1976	1170
18-01/16	11-04/16	6-13/16	M	Stratton	ME	Bernard Caruso	1977	1170
18-01/16	11-01/16	7-00/16	M	Saguache County	CO	Robert Faris II	1977	1170
18-01/16	11-03/16	6-14/16	M	Fremont County	CO	Robert Andrew	1978	1170
18-01/16	11-09/16	6-08/16	M	Cooper Landing	AK	Richard A. Hoag	1979	1170
18-01/16	11-06/16	6-11/16	M	Clearwater	ID	George P. Mann	1980	1170
18-01/16	11-00/16	7-01/16	M	Oxford County	ME	Michael Matoushek	1980	1170
18-01/16	11-10/16	6-07/16	M	Kenora	ONT	Ervin Wagner	1980	1170
18-01/16	11-08/16	6-09/16	M	Iron County	MI	George Hronkin III	1981	1170
18-01/16	11-09/16	6-08/16	M	Dryden	ONT	Anne M. Fancher	1982	1170
18-01/16	11-05/16	6-12/16	M	Lochsa River	ID	Brad L. Johnson	1982	1170
18-01/16	11-09/16	6-08/16	M	Archuleta County	CO	Stephen E. Kennedy	1982	1170
18-01/16	11-08/16	6-09/16	M	Mineral County	MT	Greg L. Munther	1982	1170
18-01/16	11-08/16	6-09/16	M	Dwight	ONT	Michael D. Moore	1983	1170
18-01/16	10-10/16	7-07/16	M	Fort Coulonge	QUE	Curtis A. Peterman	1983	1170
18-01/16	11-05/16	6-12/16	M	Park County	CO	Dan Tekavec	1983	1170
18-01/16	11-02/16	6-15/16	M	Colfax County	NM	Dean Oatman	1983	1170
18-01/16	11-03/16	6-14/16	M	Clearwater Cty	ID	J. David Powers	1983	1170
18-01/16	11-10/16	6-07/16	M	Ignace	ONT	Kenneth C. Kaufmann	1984	1170
18-01/16	11-13/16	6-04/16	M	Price County	WI	Tom Gouger	1984	1170
18-01/16	11-05/16	6-12/16	M	Clackamas County	OR	Bob Smitherman	1984	1170
18-01/16	11-08/16	6-09/16	M	Marinette County	WI	James L. Behn	1984	1170
18-01/16	11-03/16	6-14/16	M	Ashland County	WI	Tony D. Snow	1984	1170
18-01/16	11-09/16	6-08/16	M	McBride Lake	SAS	John Rook	1985	1170
18-01/16	11-03/16	6-14/16	M	Clearwater Cty	ID	Gene Kiele	1985	1170
18-01/16	11-11/16	6-06/16	M	Nass River	BC	John Jones	1985	1170
18-01/16	11-06/16	6-11/16	M	Payette County	ID	Gary Kinney	1986	1170
18-01/16	11-06/16	6-11/16	M	Lemhi County	ID	Anthony S. Winterer	1986	1170
18-01/16	11-05/16	6-12/16	M	Bird River	MAN	Dale Selby	1986	1170
18-01/16	11-02/16	6-15/16	M	Lemhi County	ID	Cathy Lee Jordan	1986	1170
18-01/16	11-09/16	6-08/16	M	Becker County	MN	Richard Enger	1986	1170
18-01/16	11-09/16	6-08/16	M	Wallowa County	OR	Michael Crawford	1986	1170
18-00/16	11-00/16	7-00/16	M	Dallas	OR	H. Dale Overholser	1959	1210
18-00/16	11-09/16	6-07/16	M	Prince William Sound	AK	Bob Snelson	1962	1210
18-00/16	11-12/16	6-04/16	M	Tim Pond	ME	John Iannuzzo	1966	1210
18-00/16	11-06/16	6-10/16	M	Medford	OR	Pat Mastan	1970	1210
18-00/16	11-02/16	6-14/16	M	Stratton	ME	Donald R. Pyne	1970	1210
18-00/16	11-00/16	7-00/16	M	Stratton	ME	John Fedor	1973	1210
18-00/16	11-08/16	6-08/16	M	Igitna River	AK	George Faerber	1974	1210

BLACK BEAR

(continued)

Score	Greatest Length	Greatest Width	Sex	Area	State/ Province	Hunter's Name	Date	Rank
18-00/16	11-04/16	6-12/16	M	?	ONT	Larry Kuskie	1974	1210
18-00/16	11-10/16	6-06/16	M	Stratton	ME	Michael P. Murphy	1974	1210
18-00/16	11-06/16	6-10/16	F	Taylor County	WI	Christopher A. Jeffords	1976	1210
18-00/16	11-09/16	6-07/16	M	Marathon County	WI	Jay Schultz	1977	1210
18-00/16	11-12/16	6-04/16	M	Boise County	ID	Clae Kress	1978	1210
18-00/16	11-06/16	6-10/16	M	Stratton	ME	James E. Roy	1978	1210
18-00/16	11-08/16	6-08/16	F	Hubbard County	MN	George Arimond	1979	1210
18-00/16	11-06/16	6-10/16	M	Callahan	CA	John Grochowski, Jr.	1979	1210
18-00/16	11-10/16	6-06/16	M	Bonneville Cty	ID	Paul M. Kniss	1980	1210
18-00/16	11-01/16	6-15/16	M	Bingham	ME	Albert Buonanno	1980	1210
18-00/16	11-05/16	6-11/16	M	Colton	NY	Richard Hurteau	1981	1210
18-00/16	11-04/16	6-12/16	M	Custer County	CO	Leonard Moore	1981	1210
18-00/16	11-07/16	6-09/16	M	Thunder Bay	ONT	Rob J. Smith	1981	1210
18-00/16	11-08/16	6-08/16	M	Hatcher Pass	AK	Roger Stewart	1981	1210
18-00/16	11-06/16	6-10/16	M	Susitina River	AK	Roger G. Stewart	1984	1210
18-00/16	11-07/16	6-09/16	M	Archuleta County	CO	Roy S. Marlow III	1984	1210
18-00/16	11-10/16	6-06/16	M	Little Susitna River	AK	Gary G. Wall	1984	1210
18-00/16	11-05/16	6-11/16	M	Beluga Mtn.	AK	Dick Carlson	1984	1210
18-00/16	11-06/16	6-10/16	M	Sublette County	WY	Randy Erye	1984	1210
18-00/16	11-06/16	6-10/16	M	Messines	QUE	Howard "Butch" Malone	1984	1210
18-00/16	11-01/16	6-15/16	M	North Bay	ONT	John R. Rexroad	1984	1210
18-00/16	11-02/16	6-14/16	M	Kechika Range	BC	Wase L. Carstens	1984	1210
18-00/16	11-07/16	6-09/16	M	Iron County	WI	Floyd J. Vancil	1984	1210
18-00/16	11-07/16	6-09/16	M	Gilpin County	CO	Bryon Scott Johnson	1985	1210
18-00/16	11-03/16	6-13/16	M	Anchorage	AK	Ronald D. Mills	1985	1210
18-00/16	11-05/16	6-11/16	M	Idaho County	ID	Ed Vallee	1985	1210
18-00/16	11-07/16	6-09/16	M	Wayne County	PA	Mike B. Lamade	1985	1210
18-00/16	11-10/16	6-06/16	M	Brandon	MAN	Gary Kaluzniak	1986	1210
18-00/16	11-01/16	6-15/16	M	Missoula County	MT	John L. Wozniak	1986	1210
18-00/16	11-06/16	6-10/16	F	Rouyn-Noramda	QUE	Roy Cucuzza	1986	1210
18-00/16	11-02/16	6-14/16	M	Breckenridge	ONT	John A. Bogucki	1986	1210
18-00/16	11-08/16	6-08/16	M	Duck Mtns.	MAN	Marty Stubstad	1986	1210
18-00/16	11-05/16	6-11/16	M	Idaho County	ID	Jay J. Bowman	1986	1210
18-00/16	11-08/16	6-08/16	M	Durban	MAN	Jerry V. Finley	1986	1210
18-00/16	11-07/16	6-09/16	M	Cook County	MN	Richard P. Smith	1986	1210

WORLD RECORD GRIZZLY BEAR
Score: 25 6/16
Anzac River, British Columbia – 1972
Hunter: Harley Tison

Photo by Maurice Carlisle

GRIZZLY BEAR
Ursus arctos horribilis

Minimum Score 19

Score	Greatest Length	Greatest Width	Sex	Area	State/ Province	Hunter's Name	Date	Rank
25-06/16	16-00/16	9-06/16	M	Anzac River	BC	Harley Tison	1972	1
25-03/16	15-13/16	9-06/16	M	Stevens Lake	BC	Dr. Rex Hancock	1968	2
24-14/16	15-10/16	9-04/16	M	Yellowstone National Park	WY	Art Young	1920	3
24-11/16	15-02/16	9-09/16	M	Stevens Lake	BC	Dr. R. L. Hambrick	1965	4
24-09/16	15-13/16	8-12/16	M	Bella Coola	BC	William P. Mastrangel	1956	5
23-13/16	15-06/16	8-07/16	M	Gulkana River	AK	Art Kragness	1973	6
23-12/16	14-15/16	8-13/16	M	Kotzebue	AK	James P. Jacobson	1981	7
23-07/16	14-14/16	8-09/16	M	Kakwa River	ALB	Rick Michalski	1981	8
22-13/16	14-03/16	8-10/16	M	Kingcomb Inlet	BC	Peter Halbig	1982	9
22-12/16	14-06/16	8-06/16	M	Brazua River	ALB	Curt Lynn	1973	10
22-07/16	13-15/16	8-08/16	M	Earn Lake	YUK	Dr. R. D. Keeler	1986	11
20-07/16	13-00/16	7-07/16	F	Kispiox	BC	Dr. Rex Hancock	1965	12
20-06/16	12-14/16	7-08/16	F	Scoop Lake	BC	Ronald Montross	1984	13
20-03/16	13-02/16	7-01/16	M	Galbraith Lake	AK	Maxallen D. Jackson	1981	14
20-01/16	13-01/16	7-00/16	M	Stevens Lake	BC	Fred Bear	1961	15
20-00/16	12-14/16	7-02/16	F	Yellowstone National Park	WY	Saxton T. Pope	1920	16
19-15/16	12-11/16	7-04/16	M	Dalton Hwy.	AK	Thomas Chadwick	1984	17
19-14/16	12-08/16	7-06/16	F	Ptarmigan Creek	AK	Donald O. Smith	1964	18
19-14/16	13-00/16	6-14/16	M	Atigun Pass, N.Slope	AK	Alan Richey	1984	18
19-10/16	12-05/16	7-05/16	F	Stevens Lake	BC	G. Fred Asbell	1969	20
19-08/16	12-08/16	7-00/16	M	Tangle Lakes	AK	John Musacchia	1972	21
19-08/16	12-10/16	6-14/16	M	Whitehorse	YUK	Scott Koelzer	1977	21
19-05/16	11-15/16	7-06/16	F	Stevens Lake	BC	Walter Krom	1968	23
19-00/16	12-10/16	6-06/16	M	Kispiox River	BC	Charles Kroll	1960	24

WORLD RECORD POLAR BEAR
Score: 26 6/16
Cape Lisburne, Alaska – 1958
Hunter: Richard McIntyre

Photo by Maurice Carlisle

POLAR BEAR

Ursus maritimus

Minimum Score 20

Score	Greatest Length	Greatest Width	Sex	Area	State/ Province	Hunter's Name	Date	Rank
26-06/16	16-04/16	10-02/16	M	Cape Lisburne	AK	Richard McIntyre	1958	1
25-14/16	16-03/16	9-11/16	M	Chocki Sea, N. of Siberia	AK	Larry Jones	1965	2
25-01/16	15-05/16	9-12/16	F	Baffin Island	NWT	Arthur Young	1926	3
24-04/16	15-05/16	8-15/16	F	Baffin Island	NWT	Arthur Young	1926	4

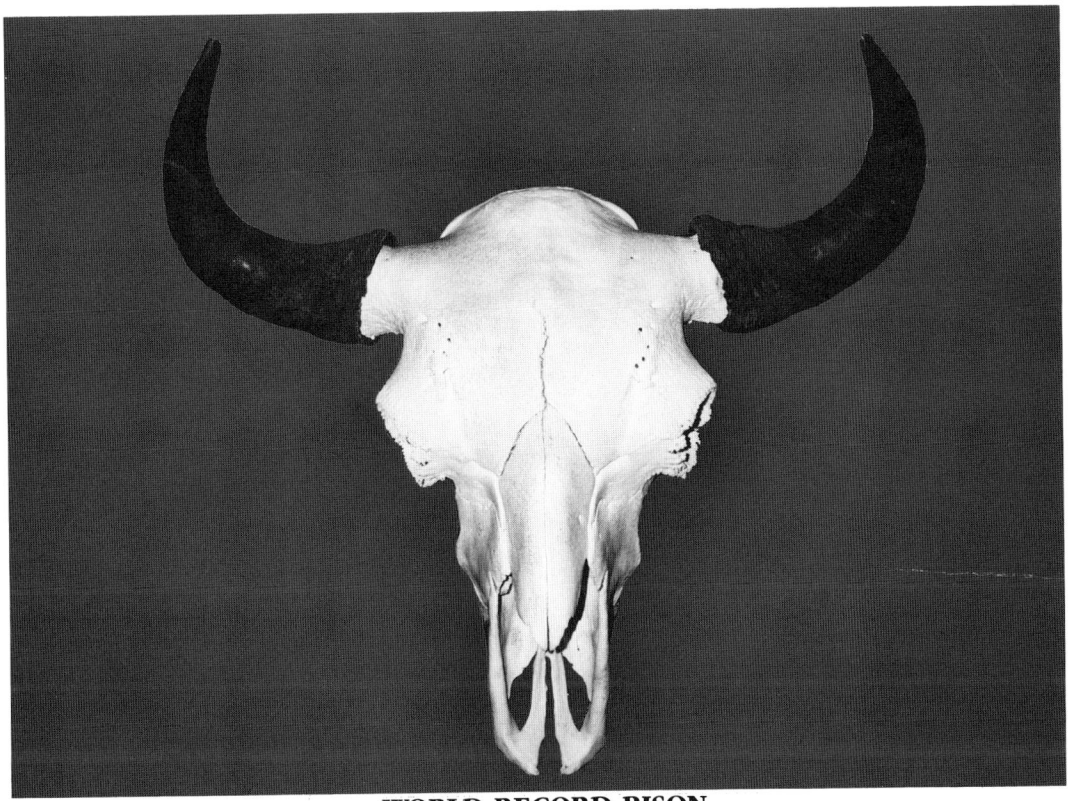

WORLD RECORD BISON
Score: 112 2/8
Farewell Lake, Alaska – 1972
Hunter: George A. Moerlein

BISON

Bison bison bison and *Bison bison athabascae*

Minimum Score 80

Score	Length of Horn		Circumference of Base		Greatest Spread	Area	State/ Province	Hunter's Name	Date	Rank
	R	L	R	L						
112-2/8	18-4/8	18-0/8	14-1/8	14-1/8	29-6/8	Farewell Lake	AK	George A. Moerlein	1972	1
111-0/8	18-0/8	17-6/8	13-3/8	13-4/8	27-2/8	Garfield County	UT	Craig Bonham	1983	2
110-4/8	16-2/8	15-2/8	14-1/8	14-1/8	26-7/8	Henry Mountains	UT	Paul B. Brunner	1979	3
106-6/8	17-2/8	16-4/8	13-0/8	12-7/8	25-0/8	Garfield County	UT	Chuck Adams	1986	4

WORLD RECORD BARREN GROUND CARIBOU
Score: 448 6/8
Lake Clark Region, Alaska – 1984
Hunter: Dennis Burdick

BARREN GROUND CARIBOU
Rangifer tarandus granti and *Rangifer tarandus groenlandicus*

Minimum Score 300

Score	Length of Main Beam R	L	Inside Spread	Number of Points R	L	Area	State/ Province	Hunter's Name	Date	Rank
448-6/8	48-4/8	48-5/8	40-3/8	17	20	Lake Clark Region	AK	Dennis Burdick	1984	1
446-6/8	55-0/8	55-6/8	40-5/8	23	19	Meshik River, AK Pen.	AK	Art Kragness	1970	2
424-0/8	52-7/8	51-1/8	41-6/8	21	12	Delta River	AK	Bill Brown	1960	3
417-0/8	50-5/8	52-3/8	33-6/8	13	17	Little Delta River	AK	Fred Bear	1959	4
414-6/8	48-3/8	47-1/8	39-7/8	13	12	Aleutian Range	AK	Robert Smith	1983	5
414-3/8	62-1/8	63-6/8	51-7/8	14	10	King Salmon	AK	Larry Spiva	1983	6
412-5/8	53-3/8	54-3/8	37-3/8	15	21	Lake Iliamna	AK	Don Wells	1982	7
407-4/8	54-3/8	55-3/8	51-4/8	20	14	Lake Becharof	AK	Larry Jones	1969	8
407-4/8	57-3/8	52-6/8	29-3/8	10	15	White Fish Lake	AK	Ron Lehmann	1984	8
406-2/8	56-5/8	58-2/8	37-3/8	11	23	Port Heiden	AK	Art Heinze	1973	10
405-0/8	61-4/8	62-5/8	47-0/8	13	13	Bonanza Hills	AK	Dan Hollingsworth	1982	11
401-3/8	53-4/8	52-6/8	42-0/8	14	16	Glenn Highway	AK	Harv Ebers	1959	12
400-0/8	53-1/8	53-1/8	37-0/8	9	19	Lake Louise	AK	George Moerlein	1962	13
399-0/8	50-5/8	51-2/8	40-2/8	16	14	Clemmons	AK	Bob Lee	1960	14
397-4/8	46-4/8	46-3/8	34-2/8	15	15	Telaquana Lake	AK	John Moline	1971	15
396-6/8	50-1/8	49-5/8	49-1/8	12	15	Aleutian Range	AK	Chuck Adams	1984	16
396-5/8	57-7/8	55-1/8	49-4/8	13	11	Tyone Lake	AK	James Moline	1961	17
396-5/8	50-0/8	46-6/8	40-5/8	13	16	Telaquana Lake	AK	Eldon W. Zeller	1972	17
396-2/8	55-3/8	53-0/8	33-3/8	18	19	Little Delta River	AK	Keith R. Clemmons	1958	19
394-5/8	51-0/8	48-7/8	27-6/8	13	19	Susitna	AK	Ron Mason	1980	20
392-2/8	51-3/8	55-4/8	32-6/8	13	15	Aleutian Range	AK	Chuck Adams	1983	21
391-7/8	53-6/8	50-5/8	45-6/8	11	14	Glenn Highway	AK	Joe West	1965	22
391-7/8	57-0/8	56-3/8	31-4/8	11	14	Lake Clark	AK	Jim Jarvis	1982	22
391-0/8	49-3/8	53-0/8	41-6/8	11	13	Ugashik River	AK	Dr. Robert Roland-Smith	1986	24
389-4/8	48-0/8	49-2/8	34-0/8	22	19	Mother Goose Lake	AK	Dennis L. Smythe	1975	25
388-5/8	52-0/8	53-2/8	32-6/8	18	18	Delta River	AK	Dick Bolding	1957	26
388-2/8	56-5/8	57-1/8	47-2/8	18	16	Ugashik River	AK	George Moerlein	1972	27
388-2/8	50-7/8	55-7/8	30-5/8	14	15	Atigun Pass	AK	Alan Richey	1984	27
388-1/8	48-0/8	46-0/8	41-0/8	16	13	Mulchatna River	AK	Calvin Coziah	1986	29
387-7/8	42-0/8	40-6/8	31-5/8	23	25	McGrath	AK	Robert Barrie	1975	30
387-1/8	53-2/8	55-6/8	36-3/8	13	13	Baffin Island	NWT	Randall J. Kiessel	1986	31
387-0/8	52-2/8	62-4/8	51-3/8	10	10	Lake Iliamna	AK	Jon Vanderhoef	1983	32
386-7/8	48-4/8	44-5/8	43-4/8	19	18	Little Delta	AK	Dale K. Marcy	1964	33
385-3/8	51-2/8	53-5/8	40-0/8	13	11	King Salmon	AK	Tom Daley	1984	34
385-2/8	58-5/8	57-0/8	38-0/8	14	17	Talkeetna Range	AK	Harvey Matz	1959	35
384-5/8	47-2/8	47-5/8	37-5/8	16	15	Talkeetna Mountains	AK	Dr. Rex Hancock	1962	36
384-3/8	49-2/8	49-1/8	34-6/8	15	18	Alaska Peninsula	AK	Betty Gulman	1968	37
383-5/8	40-1/8	37-5/8	41-2/8	19	21	Yanert River	AK	E. Donnall Thomas, Jr.	1984	38
382-4/8	50-2/8	51-3/8	39-2/8	17	27	King Salmon River	AK	Eugene Smith, Jr.	1978	39
381-5/8	51-1/8	47-1/8	39-1/8	14	19	Ugu River	AK	Stanley J. Rogers, Jr.	1974	40
381-1/8	52-4/8	50-7/8	43-2/8	12	17	Galbraith Lake	AK	Edward L. Russell	1981	41
380-7/8	46-1/8	47-7/8	36-7/8	13	15	Delta Creek	AK	Wayne Trimm	1960	42
380-5/8	61-2/8	62-2/8	36-5/8	8	9	King Salmon	AK	Glenn Hisey	1984	43
379-5/8	46-2/8	48-4/8	33-2/8	20	19	Alatna River	AK	Don D. Seward	1975	44
378-1/8	47-3/8	47-3/8	40-4/8	10	10	Lake Clark	AK	Neil K. Hymas	1984	45
377-7/8	55-7/8	57-0/8	40-0/8	11	11	Ugashik River	AK	Douglas A. Smythe	1986	46
377-6/8	52-0/8	51-4/8	35-6/8	13	19	Dawn Lake	AK	Bob Kroll	1963	47
376-7/8	50-2/8	45-4/8	40-2/8	14	13	Alaska Peninsula	AK	Bob Gulman	1968	48
376-7/8	52-6/8	50-5/8	49-4/8	16	14	Alaska Peninsula	AK	Roger O. Iveson	1976	48
376-0/8	58-3/8	52-3/8	44-0/8	9	10	Lake Clark	AK	Joe Ball	1986	50
374-3/8	57-2/8	51-4/8	33-4/8	11	12	Holitna River	AK	Rick Tollison	1978	51
373-6/8	47-5/8	47-5/8	40-2/8	11	17	Delta Creek	AK	Dwight Guynn	1980	52
373-5/8	46-6/8	46-7/8	39-5/8	18	15	Devil Creek	AK	Douglas Walker	1966	53
371-6/8	46-4/8	48-6/8	33-0/8	12	13	Cutler River	AK	Randy Doyle	1985	54
371-5/8	40-1/8	40-1/8	34-1/8	17	28	McLaren River	AK	Dick Cooley	1962	55
371-5/8	48-5/8	49-1/8	41-6/8	20	15	Port Heiden	AK	Jim Dougherty	1968	55
371-3/8	51-5/8	51-6/8	39-5/8	11	17	Cinder River	AK	Keith Pilz	1976	57
370-5/8	45-3/8	48-3/8	39-2/8	11	15	Lake Iliamna	AK	John Meschko	1981	58
370-3/8	48-7/8	49-7/8	32-3/8	10	12	Shenjek Lake	AK	J. Keith Chastain	1984	59
370-2/8	55-3/8	54-5/8	38-5/8	9	9	Mulchatna River	AK	William A. Sheka, Jr.	1984	60
370-1/8	54-0/8	52-6/8	34-5/8	10	13	North Slope	AK	Ronald L. Sherer	1983	61
369-1/8	52-0/8	51-4/8	34-1/8	12	9	Fairbanks	AK	Keith Jensen	1986	62
368-7/8	46-6/8	47-1/8	40-7/8	16	17	Prudhoe Bay	AK	Calvin Farner	1985	63

BARREN GROUND CARIBOU
(continued)

Score	Length of Main Beam R	L	Inside Spread	Number of Points R	L	Area	State/ Province	Hunter's Name	Date	Rank
368-4/8	58-2/8	55-6/8	40-1/8	12	11	Ambler	AK	Richard A. Kimmon	1983	64
368-2/8	51-1/8	53-6/8	44-1/8	12	12	Swift River	AK	Rolf J. Sandberg	1986	65
368-0/8	51-5/8	46-4/8	36-3/8	14	19	Port Heiden	AK	John E. Lawson	1970	66
368-0/8	55-1/8	54-5/8	38-3/8	14	10	King Salmon River	AK	Rick Grooms	1979	66
364-6/8	53-5/8	51-5/8	26-3/8	12	19	Sagavanirktok River	AK	Judd Cooney	1982	68
363-0/8	53-4/8	52-6/8	37-5/8	10	9	King Salmon	AK	Kent D. Keenlyne	1982	69
363-0/8	47-0/8	47-0/8	39-5/8	8	10	Aleutian Range	AK	H. Richard Long	1984	69
362-4/8	44-3/8	47-2/8	34-4/8	17	18	Egegik River	AK	Walter Eslinger	1970	71
362-2/8	51-1/8	51-1/8	36-0/8	14	11	Sourdough	AK	Dan Jordan	1965	72
361-7/8	57-4/8	57-0/8	34-1/8	13	13	White Hills	AK	Dick Carlson	1984	73
361-3/8	54-4/8	54-0/8	46-1/8	9	10	Kajulik Bay	AK	Thomas J. Hoffman	1983	74
361-3/8	51-6/8	52-5/8	44-2/8	13	12	Brooks Range	AK	John Ribic	1986	74
361-0/8	49-2/8	48-4/8	41-2/8	11	11	Mulchatna Valley	AK	James W. Southworth	1983	76
360-6/8	52-7/8	52-3/8	36-4/8	10	8	Lake Clark	AK	John W. Rose	1986	77
359-6/8	45-5/8	46-3/8	43-7/8	17	16	Mulchatna River	AK	Ralph Ertz	1982	78
359-3/8	52-7/8	53-4/8	29-7/8	10	9	Lake Clark	AK	Mark Buehrer	1985	79
358-4/8	50-0/8	51-0/8	34-1/8	13	12	Alaska Peninsula	AK	Chris Cassidy	1982	80
358-2/8	54-7/8	57-1/8	35-5/8	13	10	Tyone Lake	AK	Jake Sonnentag	1961	81
358-2/8	53-5/8	54-5/8	41-0/8	13	13	McLaren River	AK	George Moerlein	1963	81
358-0/8	48-4/8	49-3/8	36-5/8	9	11	King Salmon	AK	Norm Epperson	1983	83
357-5/8	48-6/8	49-0/8	45-3/8	11	12	Deadhorse	AK	George P. Mann	1986	84
357-3/8	48-0/8	48-3/8	39-7/8	11	13	King Salmon	AK	Gerry C. Stinski	1986	85
355-6/8	43-5/8	42-4/8	28-2/8	12	14	Deadhorse	AK	Jim Hodson	1985	86
355-5/8	57-0/8	56-0/8	44-0/8	15	16	Sag River	AK	David D. Bestul	1986	87
354-7/8	46-0/8	46-0/8	36-0/8	10	10	Sag River	AK	Kevin R. Wiley	1986	88
354-6/8	49-4/8	51-4/8	44-6/8	10	14	Kuktuli River	AK	Neil Summers	1982	89
354-6/8	47-1/8	45-0/8	44-1/8	12	13	Mulchatna River	AK	Richard LeBlond	1985	89
354-1/8	49-0/8	50-6/8	39-1/8	10	9	Alaskan Range	AK	Roger Wintle	1985	91
353-3/8	48-2/8	46-6/8	36-7/8	17	13	Caribou Creek	AK	H. R. "Dutch" Wambold	1964	92
353-3/8	54-4/8	53-7/8	43-2/8	11	12	Telaquana Lake	AK	Jake Sonnentag	1971	92
353-1/8	45-4/8	46-2/8	37-4/8	13	14	Richardson Highway	AK	Donald O. Smith	1963	94
352-2/8	54-1/8	54-0/8	45-1/8	9	10	Pilot Point, AK Pen.	AK	John D. "Jack" Frost	1980	95
351-5/8	48-4/8	52-6/8	38-5/8	10	11	Ugashik Lake	AK	Diane Snyder	1984	96
351-2/8	62-4/8	59-5/8	36-2/8	13	12	Ugashik Lake	AK	John Amundson	1986	97
350-7/8	51-3/8	49-0/8	27-2/8	20	21	Big Delta	AK	Bill Brown	1958	98
350-6/8	55-1/8	56-0/8	31-4/8	9	8	Lake Clark	AK	Stacy M. Tompkinson	1986	99
350-5/8	51-1/8	47-6/8	43-4/8	9	11	Selawik River	AK	Kirk Westervelt	1985	100
350-3/8	51-3/8	44-0/8	41-3/8	11	14	Meshik River, AK Pen.	AK	Art Kragness	1970	101
349-7/8	52-2/8	45-3/8	35-1/8	15	11	Pilot Point, AK Pen.	AK	Rolf J. Sandberg	1976	102
349-7/8	48-1/8	49-3/8	28-7/8	10	12	Frankling Bluff	AK	Craig Kulchak	1982	102
349-4/8	55-7/8	57-3/8	39-2/8	9	11	Prudhoe Bay	AK	Rick Grooms	1986	104
349-2/8	52-4/8	51-5/8	36-4/8	13	8	Kobuk River Valley	AK	Richard A. Kinmon	1986	105
348-3/8	43-6/8	44-6/8	42-0/8	13	14	Putilick Mt.	AK	Gary B. Gingerich	1986	106
348-0/8	51-1/8	49-2/8	37-3/8	10	13	Anchorage	AK	Salvatore J. Scaltrito	1983	107
347-5/8	46-4/8	47-6/8	37-6/8	20	16	Colville River	AK	John D. "Jack" Frost	1982	108
347-4/8	46-2/8	45-2/8	41-7/8	12	14	Ogilby Range	YUK	Emile Gele	1965	109
347-3/8	46-7/8	52-4/8	37-0/8	9	9	Mulchatna River	AK	Ray Roussett, Jr.	1986	110
346-7/8	50-4/8	50-2/8	32-0/8	10	19	Telaquana Lake	AK	Gary Wall	1974	111
346-5/8	50-0/8	48-6/8	36-5/8	10	12	Little Delta	AK	Herb Lindsay	1964	112
346-5/8	49-1/8	48-2/8	35-2/8	17	17	Sagavanirktok River	AK	Judd Cooney	1982	112
345-3/8	47-5/8	49-0/8	37-4/8	16	22	Anchorage	AK	Robert K. Paulson	1977	114
345-2/8	47-3/8	48-6/8	32-4/8	11	10	Port Heiden	AK	Dennis G. Goldbach	1979	115
345-1/8	51-4/8	53-4/8	43-1/8	9	8	Lake Lach Buna	AK	Bob Ebert	1983	116
345-1/8	47-2/8	45-5/8	42-1/8	10	12	Mulchatna River	AK	E. Donnall Thomas, Jr.	1985	116
344-7/8	51-4/8	50-4/8	34-0/8	13	12	Lake Clark	AK	Troy Hymas	1984	118
344-6/8	52-5/8	51-1/8	29-4/8	15	11	Susitna Valley	AK	Ronald D. Hopkins	1974	119
343-1/8	51-6/8	53-2/8	38-6/8	8	13	Taylor Highway	AK	Jae Beardon	1961	120
341-6/8	58-2/8	56-3/8	39-6/8	11	14	McGrath	AK	Jim Holdenried	1982	121
341-5/8	48-5/8	47-6/8	33-4/8	12	13	Alaska Peninsula	AK	Edward L. Russell	1980	122
341-4/8	53-3/8	52-2/8	43-4/8	14	12	Franklin Bluffs	AK	Dr. Jack Harvey	1984	123
341-0/8	49-2/8	49-0/8	37-2/8	14	13	King Salmon	AK	Reggie Callender	1971	124
340-6/8	49-2/8	49-3/8	27-1/8	12	13	Brooks Range	AK	Roger G. Stewart	1983	125
340-0/8	49-0/8	51-0/8	36-2/8	14	14	Franklin Bluffs	AK	John T. Toenes	1985	126

BARREN GROUND CARIBOU

Minimum Score 300   (continued)

Score	Length of Main Beam R	L	Inside Spread	Number of Points R	L	Area	State/ Province	Hunter's Name	Date	Rank
339-7/8	48-3/8	43-4/8	36-3/8	14	12	Prudhoe Bay	AK	John Bilek	1986	127
339-4/8	46-0/8	45-0/8	29-0/8	12	13	Port Heiden	AK	Dennis G. Goldbach	1980	128
339-4/8	49-5/8	51-7/8	41-0/8	12	10	Franklin Bluffs	AK	Roger E. Wheelock	1982	128
339-1/8	52-5/8	53-4/8	38-4/8	10	12	Little Delta	AK	Dr. Judd Grindell	1959	130
339-0/8	45-3/8	51-5/8	34-4/8	18	13	Tyone Lake	AK	Jake Sonnentag	1963	131
338-4/8	49-4/8	47-7/8	35-1/8	11	16	Bonanza Hills	AK	Larry Langston	1974	132
338-4/8	46-6/8	47-2/8	30-7/8	14	12	Brooks Range	AK	Lyle Willmarth	1984	132
337-7/8	50-7/8	51-7/8	39-6/8	16	11	Cold Bay	AK	John Sarvis	1985	134
337-5/8	49-7/8	49-1/8	41-6/8	12	14	Cinder River	AK	Francis Hosch	1966	135
337-3/8	47-4/8	47-3/8	32-2/8	13	14	McLaren River	AK	George Moerlein	1963	136
337-1/8	50-6/8	51-2/8	29-1/8	19	18	Dry Creek	AK	Russell Kucinski	1983	137
335-7/8	50-2/8	47-1/8	42-0/8	12	16	Port Heiden	AK	Noel Feather	1973	138
335-1/8	47-3/8	48-3/8	22-5/8	9	10	Colville River	AK	Bob Gulman	1984	139
333-7/8	54-4/8	56-0/8	47-2/8	10	8	Selawik River	AK	Kirk Westervelt	1985	140
333-5/8	47-2/8	47-2/8	32-5/8	15	11	Ugashik	AK	Stanley Winslow	1973	141
332-7/8	53-0/8	54-3/8	36-2/8	18	15	Denali Highway	AK	Junie Moll	1961	142
332-5/8	48-1/8	47-2/8	35-7/8	18	13	Caribou River Drainage	AK	Al Reay	1981	143
332-4/8	47-2/8	47-3/8	40-3/8	10	11	Mulchatna Drainage	AK	Skip Koske	1986	144
331-7/8	54-3/8	55-0/8	35-6/8	9	16	Port Heiden	AK	John E. Lawson	1970	145
331-5/8	45-5/8	48-1/8	35-6/8	12	11	High Lakes	AK	Doug Walker	1970	146
330-5/8	51-1/8	51-5/8	35-6/8	15	10	Tangle Lakes	AK	R. Glen Williams	1966	147
330-0/8	54-2/8	55-0/8	37-7/8	13	12	Atigun Pass	AK	Keith K. Appel	1984	148
329-7/8	47-4/8	47-3/8	31-0/8	10	15	Dawn Lake	AK	Chuck Kroll	1963	149
329-7/8	56-4/8	53-7/8	40-3/8	9	12	Little Delta	AK	Bill Tutt	1964	149
329-6/8	49-6/8	49-4/8	33-1/8	6	8	Sagavanirktok River	AK	Patricia A. Stewart	1983	151
329-4/8	57-6/8	53-2/8	41-3/8	8	9	Chandler River	AK	Chuck Roady	1986	152
329-1/8	49-0/8	48-4/8	40-2/8	11	8	Ambler	AK	Dean Bergman	1986	153
328-4/8	42-6/8	44-3/8	31-5/8	18	12	Little Delta	AK	Roy Bryan	1964	154
328-4/8	47-6/8	47-7/8	35-3/8	11	13	Sagavanirktok River	AK	Paul G. Barclay	1981	154
328-3/8	50-2/8	49-1/8	30-3/8	9	9	Prudhoe Bay	AK	Denver Perry	1981	156
328-2/8	42-0/8	39-7/8	27-2/8	8	9	Prudhoe Bay	AK	Gene Barcak	1985	157
327-6/8	40-7/8	41-3/8	36-7/8	15	12	Galbraith Lake	AK	G. Stevens Abdoe	1983	158
327-5/8	47-3/8	49-3/8	40-0/8	13	13	North Slope	AK	Susan D. Sherer	1983	159
327-3/8	46-1/8	47-0/8	40-0/8	8	9	Selawik River	AK	Richard L. Westervelt	1985	160
326-7/8	47-6/8	51-2/8	27-3/8	15	13	Dago Creek	AK	Don Davidson	1980	161
326-6/8	49-1/8	47-3/8	41-0/8	12	18	Anchorage	AK	Roy Bryan	1964	162
326-4/8	47-7/8	49-7/8	31-7/8	10	11	Brooks Range	AK	Roger Stewart	1985	163
326-3/8	47-6/8	49-0/8	39-0/8	11	13	King Salmon	AK	Glenn Hisey	1983	164
325-6/8	49-0/8	46-1/8	21-1/8	14	13	Atigun Pass	AK	Maxallen D. Jackson	1980	165
325-4/8	52-4/8	52-3/8	31-0/8	13	15	Galbraith Lake	AK	Maxallen D. Jackson	1981	166
325-2/8	48-4/8	48-2/8	33-3/8	11	14	Happy Valley	AK	Troy Graziadei	1984	167
324-1/8	51-1/8	44-6/8	24-0/8	11	10	Brooks Range	AK	Robert D. Warpack	1985	168
323-7/8	47-4/8	51-2/8	38-7/8	13	8	Squirrel River	AK	Larry Spiva	1985	169
323-2/8	46-7/8	46-5/8	40-3/8	13	13	King Salmon	AK	Howard Wille	1972	170
323-1/8	42-0/8	45-0/8	31-2/8	8	9	High Lake	AK	Clarence Bowers, Jr.	1970	171
322-5/8	48-6/8	49-3/8	35-1/8	13	14	King Salmon River	AK	Harold Stam	1976	172
322-4/8	48-0/8	48-2/8	35-5/8	10	17	Brooks Range	AK	Patricia Stewart	1982	173
321-7/8	50-7/8	50-1/8	32-3/8	11	8	Squirrel River	AK	Timothy J. Conrads	1986	174
321-6/8	48-5/8	48-4/8	30-3/8	7	11	Delong Mtns.	AK	Dan White	1981	175
321-3/8	60-6/8	60-6/8	38-4/8	9	10	Toolik River	AK	Bill Krenz	1984	176
321-2/8	45-0/8	45-6/8	34-1/8	11	12	Alaska Peninsula	AK	Curt Lynn	1977	177
321-2/8	48-5/8	47-3/8	40-0/8	13	14	Selawick River	AK	Kirk Westervelt	1984	177
320-4/8	45-7/8	42-4/8	29-1/8	11	11	Lime Village	AK	Dale Drilling	1979	179
320-2/8	38-4/8	38-4/8	34-6/8	8	10	Ugashik Lake	AK	Richard E. Davis	1986	180
320-0/8	46-5/8	46-2/8	29-5/8	13	11	Ugashik Narrows	AK	Richard D. Thomas	1983	181
319-5/8	43-7/8	44-1/8	43-4/8	7	8	Franklin Bluffs	AK	Keith K. Appel	1984	182
319-4/8	46-3/8	44-5/8	35-6/8	11	15	Chulitna	AK	Keith Johnson	1964	183
318-5/8	51-4/8	52-0/8	34-2/8	9	12	Crosswinds Lake	AK	Ray Uhl, Sr.	1964	184
318-5/8	54-6/8	50-0/8	39-6/8	11	8	Last Lake	AK	Donald Gansch	1983	184
318-4/8	42-6/8	43-1/8	37-0/8	16	14	Meshik River	AK	Scott M. Showalter	1974	186
316-7/8	44-6/8	44-0/8	31-2/8	16	15	Delta River	AK	Glenn St. Charles	1957	187
316-5/8	46-6/8	47-4/8	46-0/8	10	13	Alaska Peninsula	AK	David G. Snyder	1979	188
315-5/8	45-7/8	48-6/8	33-6/8	8	7	Mulchatua River	AK	Michael J. Schneider	1984	189

BARREN GROUND CARIBOU

(continued)   Minimum Score 300

Score	Length of Main Beam R	L	Inside Spread	Number of Points R	L	Area	State/ Province	Hunter's Name	Date	Rank
314-6/8	48-0/8	48-4/8	34-4/8	15	10	Nueman Creek	AK	Paul Brunner	1973	190
314-3/8	43-1/8	39-4/8	36-1/8	10	11	Lake Clark	AK	Michael D. Lewis	1986	191
314-2/8	46-7/8	48-7/8	35-5/8	19	12	Stoney River	AK	Bruce D. Kipley	1981	192
314-1/8	45-2/8	45-7/8	38-6/8	12	11	Sagavanirktok River	AK	Judd Cooney	1982	193
313-0/8	46-0/8	46-0/8	24-4/8	15	14	Atigun Pass	AK	Maxallen D. Jackson	1980	194
312-6/8	45-7/8	42-1/8	36-5/8	9	10	Lake Clark	AK	Art Cracraft	1977	195
312-6/8	54-2/8	50-2/8	37-2/8	9	10	Needle Lake	AK	Daniel T. Bertalan	1986	195
312-5/8	41-0/8	41-7/8	28-6/8	13	12	Whitehorse	YUK	Scott Koelzer	1977	197
311-6/8	44-2/8	49-5/8	36-0/8	9	10	David River	AK	Melvin E. Putnam	1983	198
310-5/8	38-6/8	47-3/8	41-4/8	9	12	Port Heiden	AK	Paul R. Shannon	1974	199
309-7/8	47-0/8	49-0/8	32-3/8	10	13	Sagavanirktok River	AK	Jack V. Rouse	1984	200
309-3/8	46-4/8	47-0/8	38-3/8	11	11	Chandler River	AK	Walt Dinning	1986	201
308-7/8	34-2/8	37-1/8	26-0/8	15	14	Unit 13D	AK	Dayle Paulson	1971	202
308-7/8	48-1/8	46-7/8	39-4/8	10	10	Prudhoe Bay	AK	Daniel D. Bestul	1984	202
308-1/8	54-0/8	54-0/8	30-5/8	13	10	Little Delta River	AK	Dr. Judd Grindell	1959	204
308-1/8	48-2/8	46-2/8	29-1/8	12	15	Lake Chandalar	AK	George Moerlein	1966	204
308-0/8	47-4/8	47-3/8	36-3/8	8	8	White Fish Lake	AK	David Fowler	1984	206
305-1/8	48-7/8	50-7/8	28-5/8	8	6	Cold Bay	AK	John Sarvis	1983	207
305-0/8	40-7/8	41-6/8	35-4/8	10	14	Brooks Range	AK	John Hale	1980	208
304-5/8	44-5/8	49-6/8	38-3/8	11	10	Toolik River	AK	Bill Krenz	1984	209
303-4/8	45-5/8	45-0/8	37-6/8	13	14	Port Heiden	AK	Jon G. Koshell	1964	210
302-2/8	53-2/8	50-2/8	34-4/8	14	16	Sagwon	AK	Stephen E. Russell	1986	211
300-3/8	48-2/8	45-5/8	34-0/8	10	9	Tangle Lakes	AK	R. Glen Williams	1966	212
300-3/8	38-2/8	38-3/8	30-0/8	19	16	Alaska Peninsula	AK	Curt Lynn	1977	212

WORLD RECORD MOUNTAIN CARIBOU
Score: 410 2/8
Cassiar Mountains, British Columbia – 1978
Hunter: Thomas B. Frye

MOUNTAIN CARIBOU
Rangifer tarandus caribou

Minimum Score 265

Score	Length of Main Beam R	L	Inside Spread	Number of Points R	L	Area	State/ Province	Hunter's Name	Date	Rank
410-2/8	54-0/8	55-6/8	46-0/8	15	12	Cassiar Mts.	BC	Thomas B. Frye	1978	1
390-1/8	55-2/8	51-6/8	34-1/8	15	11	Firesteel Lake	BC	Melvin K. Wolf	1970	2
387-6/8	44-3/8	42-7/8	36-0/8	15	14	Cold Fish Lake	BC	Steve Gorr	1976	3
374-6/8	55-4/8	55-6/8	40-2/8	10	8	Thutade Lake	BC	Edward C. Pawinski	1984	4
374-1/8	43-6/8	47-1/8	35-0/8	16	16	Duti River	BC	Dr. Lowell Eddy	1967	5
371-7/8	48-1/8	47-1/8	39-1/8	15	13	Tatlatui Lake	BC	Larry Alma	1979	6
371-3/8	38-7/8	39-3/8	30-3/8	16	15	Thutade Lake	BC	Bob Brill	1980	7
370-0/8	46-4/8	44-5/8	30-4/8	14	14	Mackenzie Mountains	NWT	Janice J. Traub	1985	8
351-6/8	46-4/8	45-0/8	37-4/8	11	11	Watson Lake	YUK	Pete Shepley	1985	9
345-0/8	51-5/8	49-1/8	33-7/8	13	11	Mackenzie Mountains	NWT	Al Reay	1982	10
343-3/8	48-2/8	50-6/8	35-4/8	15	11	Serpentine Mt.	BC	Randolph P. Wilson	1976	11
339-6/8	42-7/8	44-6/8	20-0/8	20	18	Tatlatui Lake	BC	G. Fred Asbell	1975	12
334-1/8	40-4/8	41-1/8	33-7/8	13	17	Firesteel River	BC	Walter Krom	1971	13
333-5/8	45-1/8	47-2/8	31-0/8	12	11	Firesteel River	BC	Jay Deones	1978	14
332-1/8	40-0/8	40-4/8	32-5/8	10	12	Firesteel River	BC	Larry Alma	1984	15
321-7/8	48-4/8	47-3/8	32-4/8	13	14	Kitchener Lake	BC	Stephen E. Mitchell	1970	16
320-6/8	43-6/8	44-4/8	31-7/8	11	12	Thutade Lake	BC	Jack W. Kriener	1974	17
319-1/8	44-3/8	48-5/8	24-7/8	13	10	Cold Fish Lake	BC	Steve Gorr	1975	18
315-5/8	43-3/8	44-3/8	29-1/8	11	12	Kitchener Lake	BC	Dick Crowder	1976	19
314-5/8	44-7/8	47-6/8	32-7/8	10	9	Ittlemit Lake	YUK	Chuck Buchanan	1979	20
313-4/8	40-2/8	45-1/8	32-7/8	10	8	MacKenzie Mountain	NWT	John "Jack" Cordes	1985	21
309-2/8	43-3/8	41-2/8	27-2/8	10	13	Thutade Lake	BC	Harold H. Vander Horst	1974	22
307-7/8	46-6/8	47-4/8	29-7/8	9	9	Thutade Lake	BC	Kim S. Ades	1984	23
306-2/8	43-4/8	43-2/8	29-2/8	11	10	Tatlatui Lake	BC	Robert Pitt	1975	24
303-6/8	42-4/8	42-4/8	25-2/8	9	12	Tatlatui Lake	BC	Rick Gilley	1983	25
298-4/8	40-5/8	41-2/8	24-2/8	12	15	Lake Tatlatui	BC	Curtis W. Lynn	1974	26
297-6/8	38-2/8	37-7/8	21-5/8	13	12	Whitehorse	YUK	A. M. Oakes, Jr.	1980	27
292-3/8	42-2/8	41-4/8	35-7/8	12	9	Area 21	BC	Harold H. Vander Horst	1972	28
290-0/8	42-3/8	45-2/8	25-0/8	10	9	Cotty Plateau	BC	Pink Atkins	1984	29
289-3/8	47-0/8	49-6/8	25-6/8	10	7	Stalk Lake	BC	Chester J. Thompson	1977	30
288-2/8	37-1/8	36-7/8	27-0/8	10	11	Stony Pass	BC	Peter L. Halbig	1968	31
288-1/8	36-3/8	39-3/8	27-0/8	11	12	Cold Fish Lake	BC	Dennis Behn	1976	32
278-3/8	36-0/8	40-2/8	27-0/8	11	9	Cold Fish Lake	BC	Fred Bear	1957	33
272-2/8	39-4/8	44-2/8	36-0/8	13	9	Kechika River	BC	Scott L. Koelzer	1976	34

WORLD RECORD QUEBEC-LABRADOR CARIBOU
Score: 434 0/8
Tunulik River, Quebec – 1984
Hunter: Carol Ann Mauch

QUEBEC-LABRADOR CARIBOU

Rangifer tarandus caribou from Quebec and Labrador   Minimum Score 300

Score	Length of Main Beam R	L	Inside Spread	Number of Points R	L	Area	State/ Province	Hunter's Name	Date	Rank
434-0/8	53-6/8	56-1/8	46-1/8	17	12	Tunilik River	QUE	Carol Ann Mauch	1984	1
429-1/8	52-2/8	52-1/8	45-1/8	15	17	Delay River	QUE	Bob Foulkrod	1985	2
416-5/8	45-3/8	47-7/8	47-4/8	28	27	George River	QUE	Collins F. Kellogg	1978	3
415-7/8	51-5/8	55-3/8	53-0/8	16	16	Unagava Bay	QUE	Dr. Woodallen G. Snyder	1984	4
411-4/8	56-4/8	57-0/8	52-0/8	16	14	Ungava Region	QUE	Richard S. Neely	1977	5
399-7/8	52-3/8	53-1/8	49-6/8	12	12	Whiskey Lake	QUE	D.F.Baldwin & T. Barta	1985	6
398-5/8	52-2/8	54-2/8	51-1/8	20	17	George River	QUE	Richard Mielke	1981	7
395-6/8	59-4/8	55-4/8	47-7/8	18	16	George River	QUE	Paul Brunner	1980	8
392-0/8	51-4/8	50-6/8	48-2/8	18	27	Lac Cananee	QUE	Brad L. Johnson	1981	9
391-0/8	55-6/8	56-2/8	39-4/8	17	15	George River	QUE	Jim McCrory	1980	10
390-7/8	51-6/8	51-2/8	48-1/8	14	15	Weymouth Inlet	QUE	Tink Nathan	1986	11
387-1/8	52-0/8	53-5/8	48-4/8	9	12	Shefferville	QUE	Tom Kayser	1986	12
384-7/8	56-2/8	54-4/8	57-7/8	15	20	George River	QUE	John Kuhar	1972	13
384-0/8	46-0/8	44-3/8	43-0/8	17	13	Weymouth Inlet	QUE	Jules Pacheco	1986	14
381-4/8	51-0/8	51-6/8	41-2/8	17	19	Wedge Hill Lodge	QUE	John Janelli	1980	15
381-2/8	48-3/8	50-4/8	39-1/8	13	14	Caniapiscau River	QUE	David C. Arndt	1986	16
380-6/8	56-0/8	52-1/8	40-4/8	12	12	Oltanook Lake	QUE	Ken Mowerson	1986	17
380-5/8	57-6/8	53-5/8	56-7/8	11	16	Ungava Region	QUE	Donald Schram	1982	18
379-6/8	49-4/8	49-2/8	42-5/8	11	12	Shefferville	QUE	Ted Jaycox	1986	19
378-6/8	54-2/8	54-2/8	54-3/8	11	12	Tunulik	QUE	Jay G. St. Charles	1986	20
377-3/8	51-6/8	55-2/8	52-4/8	12	13	Schefferville	QUE	Frank "Rit" Heller	1978	21
375-7/8	46-2/8	47-6/8	37-2/8	24	25	Ungava Region	QUE	Jose Rivero	1979	22
375-1/8	60-3/8	59-6/8	42-0/8	15	16	George River	QUE	Robert M. Sweisthal, Jr.	1980	23
374-3/8	60-2/8	59-0/8	52-5/8	14	13	Schefferville	QUE	Bill Heather	1979	24
373-3/8	53-2/8	51-1/8	40-0/8	15	13	Fort Chimo	QUE	Scott M. Showalter	1982	25
372-7/8	44-2/8	45-2/8	37-7/8	17	17	Delay River	QUE	Ray Moulton	1986	26
372-4/8	55-7/8	53-1/8	43-2/8	13	13	Ungava Bay	QUE	David Dunnigan	1984	27
370-7/8	46-6/8	44-5/8	41-2/8	5	6	Schefferville	QUE	Elmer R. Luce, Jr.	1986	28
370-1/8	50-4/8	50-4/8	57-0/8	13	11	Ungava Bay	QUE	Ed Riley	1985	29
367-6/8	49-5/8	52-1/8	59-2/8	11	15	Ungava Region	QUE	Bob Frank	1979	30
367-4/8	54-7/8	52-0/8	43-3/8	11	14	George River	QUE	Lee Kline	1980	31
366-1/8	54-7/8	52-3/8	55-0/8	20	16	Ungava Region	QUE	Joe Caruso	1979	32
366-1/8	48-0/8	48-2/8	38-2/8	21	14	Mistinibi Lake	QUE	Dieter Foerst	1981	32
364-5/8	49-0/8	51-0/8	34-4/8	13	11	George River	QUE	Gary L. Fritzler	1983	34
364-3/8	53-4/8	53-1/8	48-0/8	12	10	George River	QUE	Billy Ellis	1980	35
364-2/8	49-5/8	47-3/8	41-0/8	16	16	Big Island Lake	QUE	Jim Ponciano	1985	36
363-0/8	48-6/8	47-5/8	48-6/8	13	14	Tunulik	QUE	Rick Morgan	1986	37
362-7/8	44-2/8	44-3/8	46-2/8	15	14	Kuujjuac	QUE	Phillip B. Grable	1985	38
362-4/8	53-7/8	47-1/8	53-1/8	10	16	River De Paz	QUE	David F. Baldwin	1981	39
362-3/8	47-6/8	48-3/8	41-4/8	13	12	Tunulik	QUE	David J. Hell	1986	40
361-3/8	54-4/8	55-6/8	42-0/8	12	11	Schefferville	QUE	Elmer R. Luce, Jr.	1986	41
359-7/8	50-4/8	51-2/8	47-0/8	15	17	George River	QUE	Cecil Tharp	1982	42
358-6/8	50-6/8	53-1/8	42-2/8	18	23	George River	QUE	Dale Selby	1980	43
358-2/8	41-5/8	42-1/8	34-7/8	15	18	Delay River	QUE	Ray Moulton	1986	44
358-0/8	52-4/8	52-0/8	41-7/8	15	17	Ungava Region	QUE	Carl G. Esterly	1983	45
356-4/8	51-5/8	53-3/8	44-6/8	11	10	Ungava	QUE	Larry Nirk	1983	46
356-0/8	55-4/8	56-4/8	49-4/8	17	23	Schefferville	QUE	Gregory G. Justus	1980	47
356-0/8	54-3/8	54-0/8	45-6/8	10	8	Schefferville	QUE	Nicholas J. Gray	1981	47
355-5/8	55-6/8	58-0/8	50-4/8	10	14	George River	QUE	Charles E. Spreeman	1985	49
354-2/8	50-2/8	50-1/8	41-5/8	9	10	Big Island	QUE	Fred C. Church	1985	50
354-1/8	59-2/8	61-5/8	51-4/8	13	7	Ungava Bay	QUE	Joe Prinzi	1985	51
354-1/8	44-3/8	45-2/8	40-1/8	10	12	Schefferville	QUE	Robert Pyne	1985	51
353-4/8	52-7/8	51-2/8	39-6/8	14	12	Schefferville	QUE	Robert J. Lewis	1986	53
353-2/8	61-5/8	58-2/8	47-5/8	12	10	Tunalik River	QUE	Jon Vanderhoef	1984	54
353-0/8	50-4/8	49-2/8	46-2/8	13	9	Ungava Region	QUE	Casimir Leknius	1977	55
352-0/8	55-4/8	54-6/8	44-3/8	11	11	Ungava Bay	QUE	Tink Nathan	1984	56
351-5/8	51-4/8	49-1/8	48-1/8	15	14	George River	QUE	Frank Charette	1982	57
351-0/8	53-2/8	52-7/8	36-6/8	20	15	Dihourse Lake	QUE	Kenneth W. Lohr	1982	58
350-6/8	55-5/8	56-2/8	45-3/8	14	12	Tunulik River	QUE	Henry F. Rauch	1982	59
349-6/8	47-0/8	44-1/8	37-4/8	20	15	George River	QUE	Charlie Kroll	1980	60
349-0/8	49-3/8	49-1/8	35-7/8	12	9	Tunulik River	QUE	Ty Martin	1986	61
348-1/8	52-4/8	55-3/8	28-7/8	18	14	George River	QUE	Bob Goodall	1980	62
348-1/8	49-0/8	50-2/8	44-2/8	14	9	George River	QUE	Phillip J. Taylor	1984	62
347-5/8	52-3/8	52-2/8	49-0/8	12	12	Ungava Region	QUE	Charles R. Leidheiser	1977	64

QUEBEC-LABRADOR CARIBOU

(continued)

Minimum Score 300

Score	Length of Main Beam R	L	Inside Spread	Number of Points R	L	Area	State/ Province	Hunter's Name	Date	Rank
347-1/8	51-4/8	53-6/8	47-1/8	11	11	Shefferville	QUE	Ronnie Everett	1986	65
346-7/8	54-4/8	58-4/8	41-0/8	10	11	Akuliak Camp	QUE	Lauri Johnson	1985	66
346-0/8	48-6/8	50-6/8	45-7/8	13	14	George River	QUE	William E. Bullock	1982	67
345-7/8	52-6/8	54-1/8	45-2/8	11	13	Ungava Bay	QUE	John Musacchia	1978	68
345-2/8	47-2/8	48-7/8	41-5/8	11	18	Fort Chimo	QUE	Bob Jensen	1982	69
344-6/8	51-0/8	50-5/8	38-6/8	10	11	Schefferville	QUE	Gregg Tanner	1985	70
344-4/8	45-6/8	46-7/8	45-0/8	12	13	Ungava	QUE	David Baldwin	1986	71
343-6/8	48-0/8	48-0/8	38-4/8	11	14	Akuliak Camp	QUE	Barry Dyar	1985	72
343-3/8	48-0/8	47-0/8	44-7/8	14	12	George River	QUE	Leonard L. Kohan	1981	73
342-7/8	53-4/8	52-6/8	39-5/8	14	14	George River	QUE	Frank Hogan	1980	74
342-5/8	47-4/8	50-3/8	46-1/8	15	10	Tuktu Camp	QUE	Martin G. Billeri	1977	75
341-3/8	48-5/8	48-6/8	47-4/8	14	15	George River	QUE	William B. Bullock, Jr.	1982	76
341-0/8	51-3/8	45-7/8	44-4/8	14	12	Ungava Region	QUE	Glenn Reno	1980	77
340-5/8	54-7/8	57-7/8	51-0/8	14	13	Tunulik River	QUE	Jean-Claude Duff	1985	78
340-3/8	39-2/8	48-7/8	31-5/8	18	15	George River	QUE	Craig Richardson	1982	79
339-6/8	45-4/8	47-3/8	43-3/8	15	13	Ungava	QUE	Dean M. Westby	1986	80
339-4/8	47-7/8	48-2/8	44-6/8	13	15	Audipure Lake	QUE	Stan Godfrey	1983	81
339-0/8	56-4/8	55-0/8	45-5/8	12	11	Tuktu Camp	QUE	John C. Mitchell	1984	82
338-3/8	47-1/8	46-1/8	38-0/8	19	20	George River	QUE	Len Cardinale	1971	83
337-7/8	48-3/8	47-2/8	45-5/8	14	12	DePas & George River	QUE	Fred F. Potts	1974	84
337-6/8	52-0/8	51-7/8	45-4/8	9	10	Tunulik River	QUE	Jay E. Johnson	1985	85
337-6/8	51-0/8	51-5/8	48-4/8	8	9	Pons River	QUE	Bradford Higson	1986	85
336-4/8	53-4/8	52-2/8	41-0/8	10	10	George River	QUE	David Tofte	1982	87
336-1/8	53-0/8	52-0/8	51-0/8	15	19	Twin River	QUE	Jon P. Thomas	1982	88
333-5/8	53-2/8	52-7/8	41-6/8	12	13	Tunulik River	QUE	Gregory G. Kilby	1985	89
333-2/8	55-4/8	52-6/8	47-5/8	13	15	Schefferville	QUE	Al Reay	1978	90
333-2/8	51-6/8	53-1/8	46-1/8	11	10	Whiskey Lake	QUE	Glenn R. Kuklick	1986	90
332-4/8	51-6/8	51-1/8	36-3/8	10	11	Tunulik River	QUE	Glenn St. Charles	1984	92
331-6/8	52-0/8	52-6/8	45-4/8	15	14	Schefferville	QUE	Thomas E. Smith	1981	93
331-5/8	55-5/8	55-4/8	39-1/8	14	9	Pons River	QUE	Robert Amaral	1986	94
331-3/8	47-0/8	47-1/8	47-1/8	9	9	Whiskey Lake	QUE	Peter L. Halbig	1986	95
330-2/8	49-1/8	49-4/8	37-5/8	16	16	Delay River	QUE	Roy Goodwin	1986	96
330-0/8	49-5/8	45-6/8	31-0/8	12	10	Fort Chimo	QUE	Larry Hayes	1986	97
329-1/8	52-5/8	48-7/8	43-7/8	16	13	George River	QUE	Jerry V. Finley	1981	98
328-6/8	55-4/8	56-7/8	42-3/8	9	11	Ungava Region	QUE	David L. Cook	1982	99
328-5/8	49-1/8	52-4/8	45-2/8	13	12	Pons River	QUE	Jim Ellis	1986	100
327-6/8	52-0/8	53-0/8	45-3/8	15	19	Schefferville	QUE	Irv Plotz	1981	101
326-6/8	53-6/8	54-3/8	44-0/8	8	10	Tunulik River	QUE	Ty Martin	1986	102
326-1/8	59-3/8	57-0/8	43-6/8	10	17	Ungava Region	QUE	Gary L. Snyder	1977	103
325-1/8	60-1/8	60-5/8	49-3/8	7	4	Tunulik River	QUE	Ron Carpenter	1982	104
324-5/8	51-4/8	53-4/8	44-3/8	13	15	George River	QUE	Emanuele Baron	1972	105
323-3/8	44-4/8	43-1/8	37-6/8	19	22	DePas & George River	QUE	Walter L. Seville	1971	106
319-6/8	48-1/8	48-2/8	48-0/8	8	8	Tunulik River	QUE	Glenn St. Charles	1982	107
319-5/8	54-0/8	53-0/8	46-2/8	13	11	Schefferville	QUE	Dennis Groebner	1981	108
318-7/8	47-6/8	46-6/8	38-2/8	11	11	George River	QUE	P. W. "Bill" Meyer	1983	109
317-4/8	58-5/8	56-4/8	55-4/8	7	7	Tunulik River	QUE	Jack Joseph	1984	110
316-1/8	48-1/8	47-3/8	38-7/8	10	13	George River	QUE	Michael Shaughnessy	1980	111
315-6/8	44-6/8	46-0/8	43-3/8	11	10	Ungava	QUE	John M. McAteer	1986	112
314-7/8	50-6/8	51-2/8	44-4/8	5	10	George River	QUE	Stanley Skorch	1980	113
314-0/8	51-1/8	50-4/8	41-0/8	7	9	Audipere Lake	QUE	Ryk Visscher	1983	114
311-7/8	46-3/8	47-6/8	42-6/8	14	15	George River	QUE	Hayden Allen, Jr.	1980	115
310-7/8	46-6/8	44-5/8	41-2/8	5	6	Schefferville	QUE	Elmer R. Luce, Jr.	1986	116
309-7/8	48-3/8	43-7/8	53-0/8	9	13	George River	QUE	Dean Farkas	1980	117
309-7/8	49-3/8	46-4/8	40-3/8	13	12	Delay River	QUE	Roy Goodwin	1986	117
309-5/8	45-0/8	44-2/8	41-0/8	10	10	Tunulik River	QUE	Kenneth Bean	1982	119
309-3/8	54-7/8	56-1/8	41-6/8	13	11	George River	QUE	John "Jack" Cordes	1981	120
308-2/8	44-2/8	44-4/8	39-2/8	12	15	Ungava Region	QUE	James Dobay	1974	121
308-2/8	44-3/8	47-7/8	51-3/8	12	16	DePas & George River	QUE	William L. Winter	1974	121
308-2/8	47-6/8	46-0/8	38-3/8	9	9	Weymouth Inlet	QUE	Denise Laux	1986	121
305-4/8	49-3/8	47-3/8	47-6/8	6	8	Weymouth Inlet	QUE	Denise Laux	1986	124
305-1/8	48-4/8	49-5/8	43-7/8	10	11	Fort Chimo	QUE	George R. Garman	1985	125
304-7/8	55-1/8	52-3/8	40-6/8	13	8	George River	QUE	Byron Knutson	1980	126
303-4/8	38-4/8	37-2/8	28-5/8	18	18	Tunulik River	QUE	Larry Hoff	1984	127
302-6/8	47-4/8	47-0/8	48-3/8	10	9	George River	QUE	George A. Kearns	1985	128
300-1/8	44-1/8	44-0/8	35-7/8	7	8	Whiskey Lake	QUE	Ronald J. Watt	1986	129

WORLD RECORD WOODLAND CARIBOU
Score: 345 2/8
Victorian River, Newfoundland – 1966
Hunter: Demsey Cape

WOODLAND CARIBOU

Rangifer tarandus caribou from Nova Scotia, New Brunswick, and Newfoundland

Minimum Score 220

Score	Length of Main Beam R	L	Inside Spread	Number of Points R	L	Area	State/ Province	Hunter's Name	Date	Rank
345-2/8	46-6/8	46-4/8	27-3/8	11	12	Victorian River	NFL	Dempsey Cape	1966	1
324-0/8	42-7/8	42-3/8	26-6/8	10	11	SitDown Pond	NFL	Ed J. Bowser	1966	2
310-1/8	41-0/8	41-0/8	29-2/8	10	12	Millertown	NFL	Gerhart Huber	1966	3
276-7/8	42-3/8	43-0/8	25-2/8	10	9	King George IV Pond	NFL	Mark McCarty	1966	4
270-6/8	33-4/8	33-6/8	34-2/8	9	10	Lake Atikonak	NFL	Dr. James L. Emerson	1973	5
269-1/8	37-1/8	37-4/8	23-4/8	15	13	Corner Brook	NFL	Al Reay	1980	6
262-6/8	39-4/8	41-6/8	34-4/8	6	7	Buchans Plateau	NFL	Fred A. Turner	1984	7
260-3/8	35-2/8	35-3/8	27-5/8	9	11	Buchans Plateau	NFL	Wm. R. Vanderhoef	1986	8
259-5/8	37-6/8	32-2/8	34-7/8	10	11	Buchans Plateau	NFL	John "Jack" Cordes	1982	9
258-7/8	40-4/8	37-6/8	33-1/8	6	7	Lloyds River	NFL	Harold A. Hill	1964	10
258-1/8	36-7/8	33-6/8	25-4/8	10	11	Atikonak Lake	NFL	Bill L. Carlos	1972	11
249-3/8	36-5/8	37-2/8	26-4/8	9	9	Millertown	NFL	Cliff Wiseman	1962	12
248-0/8	40-7/8	36-7/8	34-0/8	7	7	SitDown Pond	NFL	Dr. Ed Bowser	1965	13
247-3/8	34-5/8	37-4/8	28-4/8	7	7	King George IV Pond	NFL	Bill Hirst	1966	14
241-6/8	33-2/8	30-6/8	29-2/8	9	11	Buchans Plateau	NFL	Glenn Hisey	1982	15
241-2/8	33-2/8	34-6/8	25-1/8	11	11	Interior District	NFL	Bill Goff	1965	16
236-3/8	36-0/8	35-0/8	25-3/8	12	9	Princess Lake	NFL	John Musacchia	1967	17
233-2/8	38-0/8	37-0/8	27-5/8	7	4	Gull Lake	NFL	M. W. Bowser	1958	18
232-5/8	33-3/8	35-0/8	24-5/8	6	7	Deer Lake	NFL	Douglas L. Buchler	1984	19
232-4/8	35-5/8	34-7/8	26-7/8	6	6	Buchans Plateau	NFL	Terrence H. Estes	1984	20
227-7/8	36-1/8	33-0/8	27-1/8	10	9	Princess Lake	NFL	Ken Rapp	1966	21
225-0/8	38-0/8	40-3/8	25-1/8	5	8	Victorian River	NFL	Clarence Bowers, Jr.	1966	22
224-1/8	36-0/8	35-0/8	27-4/8	8	9	Lloyds River	NFL	Harold A. Hill	1965	23
221-0/8	32-6/8	30-2/8	27-2/8	11	8	Saddler Pond	NFL	Paul Locey	1982	24
220-2/8	37-6/8	40-7/8	24-0/8	7	14	Alex Lake	NFL	Dr. James J. Schubert	1980	25

Photo by Judd Cooney

WORLD RECORD COUGAR *(TIE)*
Score: 15 11/16
Idaho County, Idaho – 1982
Hunter: Jerry J. James

WORLD RECORD COUGAR *(TIE)*
Score: 15 11/16
Idaho County, Idaho – 1985
Hunter: Mike McCall

COUGAR (MOUNTAIN LION)

Felis concolor hippolestes

Minimum Score 13

Score	Greatest Length	Greatest Width	Sex	Area	State/ Province	Hunter's Name	Date	Rank
15-11/16	9-02/16	6-09/16	M	Idaho County	ID	Jerry J. James	1982	1
15-11/16	9-04/16	6-07/16	M	Idaho County	ID	Mike McCall	1985	1
15-10/16	9-00/16	6-10/16	M	Unit 5-5	BC	Harold J. Coult	1986	3
15-08/16	9-01/16	6-07/16	M	Salmon River	ID	Doug Kittredge	1971	4
15-07/16	9-02/16	6-05/16	M	Green Horn Mountains	CO	J. D. Dodge	1971	5
15-07/16	9-00/16	6-07/16	M	Bitterroot Mountains	ID	William Egner	1972	5
15-07/16	9-04/16	6-03/16	M	Cuba	NM	Tom David	1980	5
15-07/16	9-02/16	6-05/16	M	Rio Arriba County	NM	Dick Ray	1985	5
15-07/16	9-02/16	6-05/16	M	Uintah County	UT	John M McAteer	1985	5
15-06/16	9-04/16	6-02/16	M	Book Cliff Mountains	UT	Art Kragness	1969	10
15-06/16	8-11/16	6-11/16	M	Costilla	NM	George P. Mann	1981	10
15-06/16	9-02/16	6-04/16	M	Water Valley	ALB	Don Ferguson	1983	10
15-05/16	8-15/16	6-06/16	M	Grand Junction	CO	John Lamicq, Jr.	1969	13
15-05/16	8-15/16	6-06/16	M	Mineral County	MT	Dennis Moos	1976	13
15-05/16	8-15/16	6-06/16	M	Larimer County	CO	Glenn Schmidt	1976	13
15-05/16	8-13/16	6-08/16	M	Madison County	MT	Don Schaufler	1982	13
15-05/16	9-00/16	6-05/16	M	Idaho County	ID	A. M. Oakes, Jr.	1985	13
15-05/16	9-02/16	6-03/16	M	Rio Blanco County	CO	Rob Raley	1985	13
15-05/16	9-00/16	6-05/16	M	Clearwater County	ID	Daniel J. Greve	1985	13
15-04/16	9-00/16	6-04/16	M	Young	AZ	Dr. James L. Smith	1958	20
15-04/16	8-15/16	6-05/16	M	Ogden County	UT	Royce Ross	1971	20
15-04/16	9-02/16	6-02/16	M	San Juan County	UT	Diane Snyder	1986	20
15-03/16	8-13/16	6-06/16	M	Ojai	CA	Warren C. Johnston	1953	23
15-03/16	9-00/16	6-03/16	M	Texas Creek	CO	Art Heinze	1976	23
15-03/16	8-14/16	6-05/16	M	Douglas COunty	CO	Donald R. Looper	1977	23
15-03/16	8-13/16	6-06/16	M	Jicarilla Indian Reservation	NM	Anderson Bakewell, S.J.	1978	23
15-03/16	8-04/16	6-15/16	M	Cassia County	ID	Ronald C. Ward	1984	23
15-03/16	8-13/16	6-06/16	M	Clallam County	WA	Ron W. Cram	1984	23
15-02/16	8-15/16	6-03/16	M	Rio Blanco County	CO	Leonard Cardinale	1963	29
15-02/16	9-00/16	6-02/16	M	Bitter Creek	UT	Richard Oakleaf	1967	29
15-02/16	8-12/16	6-06/16	M	Flathead County	MT	Jerry Almos	1971	29
15-02/16	8-14/16	6-04/16	M	Wallowa County	OR	Terrell Buchanan	1973	29
15-02/16	9-00/16	6-02/16	M	Utah County	UT	Max F. Park	1975	29
15-02/16	8-14/16	6-04/16	M	Sanders County	MT	Conrad Anderson	1984	29
15-02/16	8-14/16	6-04/16	M	Meagher County	MT	Gene Clark	1985	29
15-01/16	8-13/16	6-04/16	M	Parawan	UT	William P. Mastrangel	1964	36
15-01/16	8-12/16	6-05/16	M	Nez Perce County	ID	Pete Baughman, Jr.	1979	36
15-01/16	8-15/16	6-02/16	M	Lindrith	NM	Joe Strasser, Jr.	1980	36
15-01/16	8-13/16	6-04/16	M	Archuleta County	CO	Judd Cooney	1982	36
15-01/16	9-01/16	6-00/16	M	Lincoln County	MT	Gary C. Cargill	1986	36
15-00/16	8-11/16	6-05/16	M	Elko County	NV	Earl Dudley	1959	41
15-00/16	8-13/16	6-03/16	M	Spanish Fork Canyon	UT	Richard C. Smith	1968	41
15-00/16	8-11/16	6-05/16	M	Mizzezula Mountains	BC	Bengt G. Bjalme	1969	41
15-00/16	8-12/16	6-04/16	M	Columbia Lake	BC	Ray Lundstrom	1979	41
15-00/16	8-14/16	6-02/16	M	Madison County	MT	George A. Dieruf	1980	41
15-00/16	8-12/16	6-04/16	M	Lemhi County	ID	Roy Auwen	1981	41
15-00/16	8-11/16	6-05/16	M	Cuba	NM	Ernest C. Torres	1981	41
15-00/16	8-11/16	6-05/16	M	Rio Arriba County	NM	Mike Ray	1982	41
15-00/16	8-11/16	6-05/16	M	Mineral County	MT	Grover L. Hedrick	1983	41
15-00/16	8-10/16	6-06/16	M	Sanders County	MT	Joe Schaefer	1984	41
14-15/16	8-12/16	6-03/16	M	Lincoln County	MT	Allen Apling	1959	51
14-15/16	8-11/16	6-04/16	M	Bonners Ferry	ID	Rick Furniss	1968	51
14-15/16	8-14/16	6-01/16	M	Rio Blanco County	CO	Jack Pawlak	1971	51
14-15/16	8-13/16	6-02/16	M	Rio Blanco County	CO	Stanley R. Winslow	1971	51
14-15/16	8-14/16	6-01/16	M	Price	UT	Larry Wright	1975	51
14-15/16	8-11/16	6-04/16	M	Kooskia	ID	Dick Gulman	1976	51
14-15/16	8-12/16	6-03/16	M	Piute County	UT	Douglas Wagner	1976	51
14-15/16	8-11/16	6-04/16	M	Anaconda	MT	Scott Koelzer	1979	51
14-15/16	8-15/16	6-00/16	M	Montezuma County	CO	Roy Keefer	1984	51
14-15/16	8-14/16	6-01/16	M	Cascade County	MT	Charles A. Vande Hei	1984	51
14-14/16	8-14/16	6-00/16	?	Libby	MT	Dr. B. L. Lundberg	1958	61
14-14/16	8-11/16	6-03/16	M	Flathead County	MT	Jack Whitney	1967	61
14-14/16	8-10/16	6-04/16	M	Lemhi County	ID	Ray Torrey	1969	61
14-14/16	8-10/16	6-04/16	M	Granite County	MT	John Lawler	1972	61

COUGAR (MOUNTAIN LION)

(continued)

Minimum Score 13

Score	Greatest Length	Greatest Width	Sex	Area	State/ Province	Hunter's Name	Date	Rank
14-14/16	8-13/16	6-01/16	M	Elmore County	ID	Dan F. Hackney	1973	61
14-14/16	8-15/16	5-15/16	M	Lemhi County	ID	Jim Dougherty	1980	61
14-14/16	8-11/16	6-03/16	M	Utah County	UT	Kelly R. Clements	1981	61
14-14/16	8-12/16	6-02/16	M	Lemhi County	ID	Jay Meyers	1982	61
14-14/16	8-12/16	6-02/16	M	Clearwater County	ID	J. David Powers	1982	61
14-14/16	8-12/16	6-02/16	M	Iron County	UT	Craig R. White	1983	61
14-14/16	8-12/16	6-02/16	M	Montezuma County	CO	Ms. Charlie White	1983	61
14-14/16	8-12/16	6-02/16	M	Madison County	MT	Cecil I. Tharp	1984	61
14-13/16	8-11/16	6-02/16	M	Entiat River	WA	Dr. R. Congdon	1951	73
14-13/16	8-11/16	6-02/16	M	Ferry County	WA	R. O. Hilderbrant	1965	73
14-13/16	8-12/16	6-01/16	F	Duchesne County	UT	Larry Jones	1967	73
14-13/16	8-13/16	6-00/16	M	Garfield County	CO	Albert L. Heise	1971	73
14-13/16	8-13/16	6-00/16	M	Buena Vista	CO	Phillip B. Grable	1973	73
14-13/16	8-10/16	6-03/16	M	Walsenburg	CO	William F. Eikleberry	1974	73
14-13/16	8-12/16	6-01/16	M	Ferron	UT	Rex Peterson	1975	73
14-13/16	8-11/16	6-02/16	M	Vernal	UT	Ronald D. Shank	1976	73
14-13/16	8-12/16	6-01/16	M	Warner	BC	John "Jack" Cordes	1977	73
14-13/16	8-10/16	6-03/16	M	Stevens County	WA	Tim C. Boyd	1979	73
14-13/16	8-10/16	6-03/16	M	Elmore County	ID	Dr. Robert T. Laughery	1979	73
14-13/16	8-14/16	5-15/16	M	Mesa County	CO	Jim R. Lewis	1981	73
14-13/16	8-13/16	6-00/16	M	Idaho County	ID	Ray Keenan	1982	73
14-13/16	8-12/16	6-01/16	M	Moffat County	CO	John A. Lee	1982	73
14-13/16	8-11/16	6-02/16	M	McGuire Creek	BC	William Morley	1983	73
14-13/16	8-12/16	6-01/16	M	Sanders County	MT	Gil Gilbertson	1984	73
14-13/16	8-11/16	6-02/16	M	San Miguel County	CO	David E. Smith	1985	73
14-13/16	8-12/16	6-01/16	M	Albany County	WY	R.D. Keeler, D.C.	1985	73
14-12/16	8-14/16	5-14/16	M	Preston Creek	WA	Dr. R. Congdon	1952	91
14-12/16	8-12/16	6-00/16	M	Clallam County	WA	Lloyd Beebe	1953	91
14-12/16	8-11/16	6-03/16	M	Rio Blanco County	CO	LeRoy Wood	1965	91
14-12/16	8-12/16	6-00/16	M	?	CO	Clyde Hector	1967	91
14-12/16	8-13/16	5-15/16	M	Henry Mountain	UT	Harold Boyack	1968	91
14-12/16	8-11/16	6-01/16	M	McCall	ID	John Buford Reese	1976	91
14-12/16	8-10/16	6-02/16	M	Maguire Creek	BC	William Morley	1979	91
14-12/16	8-10/16	6-02/16	M	Boulder County	CO	Doug Beck	1984	91
14-12/16	8-10/16	6-02/16	M	Larimer County	CO	Jim Johnson	1985	91
14-12/16	8-14/16	5-14/16	M	Moffat County	CO	Michael B. Moline	1985	91
14-12/16	8-11/16	6-01/16	M	Cache County	UT	Ed Lawlor	1985	91
14-12/16	8-09/16	6-03/16	M	Madison County	MT	Ken Hoehn	1985	91
14-12/16	9-00/16	5-12/16	M	Custer County	CO	David Waldrop	1986	91
14-11/16	8-10/16	6-01/16	M	Sundre	ALB	Tom Decker	1966	104
14-11/16	8-08/16	6-03/16	M	Custer County	ID	Ralph V. Pehrson	1969	104
14-11/16	8-09/16	6-02/16	M	Cottonwood Creek	ID	Harlow D. Austad	1971	104
14-11/16	8-08/16	6-03/16	M	Kettle River	BC	Irvin Plotz	1976	104
14-11/16	8-12/16	5-15/16	M	Bull Lake	MT	Ronald J. Wade	1976	104
14-11/16	8-10/16	6-01/16	M	Boulder Mountain	UT	Bradford L. Sheltrown	1977	104
14-11/16	8-10/16	6-01/16	M	Middle Fork	ID	Robert Frank	1978	104
14-11/16	8-10/16	6-01/16	M	Flathead County	MT	Dr. James J. Shubert	1978	104
14-11/16	8-14/16	5-13/16	M	Westcliffe	CO	Philip Stegenga	1979	104
14-11/16	8-12/16	5-15/16	M	Tucannon	WA	John Wahl	1979	104
14-11/16	8-09/16	6-02/16	M	Ravalli County	MT	Bill Mitchell	1980	104
14-11/16	8-10/16	6-01/16	M	Norwood	CO	Judd Cooney	1981	104
14-11/16	8-12/16	5-15/16	M	Utah County	UT	Fred Tarran	1982	104
14-11/16	8-08/16	6-03/16	M	Chaffee County	CO	Reggie Spiegelberg	1983	104
14-10/16	8-10/16	6-00/16	M	Lincoln County	MT	Dr. Lowell L. Eddy	1967	118
14-10/16	8-10/16	6-00/16	M	Idaho County	ID	C. Bruce Peeples, Jr.	1970	118
14-10/16	8-09/16	6-01/16	M	Carbon County	UT	Paul F. Nottingham	1972	118
14-10/16	8-08/16	6-02/16	M	Meeker	CO	Paul Janke	1976	118
14-10/16	8-10/16	6-00/16	M	Flathead County	MT	Jerry Karsky	1976	118
14-10/16	8-10/16	6-00/16	M	Pincher Creek	ALB	Theo Mitchell	1977	118
14-10/16	8-08/16	6-02/16	M	Madison County	MT	Don Schaufler	1977	118
14-10/16	8-10/16	6-00/16	M	Salina	UT	Harold Hugelen	1979	118
14-10/16	8-10/16	6-00/16	M	Cotopaxi	CO	Pete J. Santi	1979	118
14-10/16	8-11/16	5-15/16	M	Trinidad	CO	Glenn R. Kuklick	1980	118
14-10/16	8-09/16	6-01/16	M	Elmore County	ID	L. Dean Goodner	1981	118

COUGAR (MOUNTAIN LION)
(continued)

Score	Greatest Length	Greatest Width	Sex	Area	State/ Province	Hunter's Name	Date	Rank
14-10/16	8-13/16	5-13/16	M	Fremont County	CO	Carolyn E. Lama	1981	118
14-10/16	8-10/16	6-00/16	M	Fremont County	CO	Johnny J. Lama	1981	118
14-10/16	8-10/16	6-00/16	M	Carbon County	UT	Claude A. Flippin	1982	118
14-10/16	8-08/16	6-02/16	M	Sanders County	MT	Scott Lennard	1982	118
14-10/16	8-09/16	6-01/16	M	Boxelder County	UT	Jerry Mason	1982	118
14-10/16	8-13/16	5-13/16	M	San Miguel County	CO	James Yuds	1982	118
14-10/16	8-10/16	6-00/16	M	Montezuma County	CO	Mike Morgan	1983	118
14-10/16	8-10/16	6-00/16	M	Piute County	UT	James C. Hicks	1983	118
14-10/16	8-15/16	5-11/16	M	Chaffee County	CO	Tom Bowman	1983	118
14-10/16	8-09/16	6-01/16	M	San Juan County	NM	Gary Weber	1984	118
14-10/16	8-09/16	6-01/16	M	Douglas County	NV	Kirk Westervelt	1986	118
14-09/16	8-05/16	6-04/16	M	Young	AZ	Ben Pearson	1958	140
14-09/16	8-10/16	5-15/16	M	Salmon River	ID	Keith N. Johnson	1966	140
14-09/16	8-08/16	6-01/16	M	Grand County	UT	Henry "Hank" Frey	1974	140
14-09/16	8-08/16	6-01/16	M	Lemhi County	ID	Richard E. Vail	1974	140
14-09/16	8-08/16	6-01/16	M	Jemez Mountain	NM	John W. Rose	1979	140
14-09/16	8-11/16	5-14/16	M	Henry Mountain	UT	Al Schweitzer	1979	140
14-09/16	8-08/16	6-01/16	M	Santa Fe National Forest	NM	Richard McClain	1980	140
14-09/16	8-09/16	6-00/16	M	Jefferson County	CO	Lee Veldhouse	1984	140
14-09/16	8-06/16	6-03/16	M	Idaho County	ID	LeRoy West	1984	140
14-09/16	8-07/16	6-02/16	M	Elmore County	ID	Susan D. Sherer	1984	140
14-09/16	8-10/16	5-15/16	M	Rio Blanco County	CO	Don Waechtler	1984	140
14-09/16	8-09/16	6-00/16	M	Douglas County	CO	Wayne Kraft	1986	140
14-09/16	8-09/16	6-00/16	F	Wheatland County	MT	Jim Bouchard	1986	140
14-09/16	8-10/16	5-15/16	M	Fremont County	CO	Bill Goodspeed	1986	140
14-08/16	8-09/16	5-15/16	F	Bovill	ID	Charles Kelso	1965	154
14-08/16	8-08/16	6-00/16	M	Ventura County	CA	Betty Gulman	1967	154
14-08/16	8-10/16	5-14/16	M	Luna	NM	Ed Schaub	1970	154
14-08/16	8-08/16	6-00/16	M	Ogden Canyon	UT	Norm Goodwin	1971	154
14-08/16	8-09/16	5-15/16	M	Lemhi County	ID	Dr. Henry C. McDonald	1971	154
14-08/16	8-09/16	5-15/16	M	Emery County	UT	Terry Molneux	1972	154
14-08/16	8-09/16	5-15/16	M	Kane County	UT	Charles F. Maloney, Jr.	1973	154
14-08/16	8-08/16	6-00/16	F	Texas Creek	CO	P. W. "Bill" Meyer	1974	154
14-08/16	8-06/16	6-02/16	M	Lincoln County	MT	Jerry Brown	1975	154
14-08/16	8-06/16	6-02/16	M	Duchesne County	UT	Roland Mantzke	1976	154
14-08/16	8-10/16	5-14/16	M	Boise County	ID	Ronald L. Sherer	1979	154
14-08/16	8-09/16	5-15/16	M	Boise County	ID	Richard C. Nichols	1981	154
14-08/16	8-12/16	5-12/16	M	Saguache County	CO	J. Keith Chastain	1982	154
14-08/16	8-07/16	6-01/16	M	Utah County	UT	Dell J. Christensen	1982	154
14-08/16	8-08/16	6-00/16	M	Eagle County	CO	Stephen W. Nottingham	1982	154
14-08/16	8-08/16	6-00/16	M	Sheep River	ALB	Bob Toothill	1984	154
14-08/16	8-10/16	5-14/16	M	Grand County	UT	Harold Lee Schuerman	1984	154
14-08/16	8-10/16	5-14/16	M	Washoe County	NV	Jerry Pennington	1984	154
14-08/16	8-08/16	6-00/16	M	Garfield County	CO	Douglas Starks	1984	154
14-08/16	8-10/16	5-14/16	M	Union County	OR	Ken Richter	1984	154
14-08/16	8-09/16	5-15/16	M	Archuleta County	CO	Howard Payne	1985	154
14-08/16	8-07/16	6-01/16	M	Idaho County	ID	William A.S. Hever, Sr.	1985	154
14-08/16	8-09/16	5-15/16	M	Fremont County	CO	Oney Cole	1985	154
14-08/16	8-09/16	5-15/16	M	Iron County	UT	Patrick Barwick	1985	154
14-08/16	8-07/16	6-01/16	M	Elmore County	ID	Chris Koldeway	1985	154
14-07/16	8-09/16	5-14/16	M	Elmore County	ID	William Vanderhoef	1966	179
14-07/16	8-11/16	5-12/16	M	Range Creek	UT	Gordy J. Longville	1967	179
14-07/16	8-06/16	6-01/16	M	Ely	NV	Barry L. May	1975	179
14-07/16	8-08/16	5-15/16	M	Lemhi County	ID	Wally Rueger	1975	179
14-07/16	8-09/16	5-14/16	M	Wellington	UT	Rick Hunckler	1977	179
14-07/16	8-09/16	5-14/16	M	Duffy Lake	BC	Wilfred Klingsat	1977	179
14-07/16	8-09/16	5-14/16	M	Ravalli County	MT	Kim Engelbert	1978	179
14-07/16	8-06/16	6-01/16	M	Challis	ID	Jim L. McCrory	1978	179
14-07/16	8-07/16	6-00/16	M	San Miguel County	CO	Bob Mays, Sr.	1979	179
14-07/16	8-06/16	6-01/16	M	Sevier County	UT	Lee Jernigan	1980	179
14-07/16	8-10/16	5-13/16	M	Lemhi County	ID	Daniel M. Alegre	1983	179
14-07/16	8-09/16	5-14/16	M	Saunders County	MT	Jerry V. Finley	1983	179
14-07/16	8-08/16	5-15/16	M	Franklin County	ID	Clair J. Buxton	1983	179
14-07/16	8-09/16	5-14/16	M	Judith Basin County	MT	Kay Davidson	1984	179

COUGAR (MOUNTAIN LION)
(continued)

Minimum Score 13

Score	Greatest Length	Greatest Width	Sex	Area	State/ Province	Hunter's Name	Date	Rank
14-07/16	8-09/16	5-14/16	M	Duchesne County	UT	Jerry Ippolito	1984	179
14-07/16	8-08/16	5-15/16	M	Lemhi County	ID	Dennis N. Minnich	1984	179
14-07/16	8-06/16	6-01/16	M	Dolores County	CO	Ms. Charlie White	1984	179
14-07/16	8-08/16	5-15/16	M	Lander County	NV	David P. Lindman	1985	179
14-07/16	8-09/16	5-14/16	M	Catron County	NM	Stan Rauch	1986	179
14-06/16	8-07/16	5-15/16	M	Sequoia National Forest	CA	Douglas Walker	1960	198
14-06/16	8-07/16	5-15/16	M	Elmore County	ID	C. Randall Byers	1966	198
14-06/16	8-08/16	5-14/16	M	Missoula	MT	John Hershey	1969	198
14-06/16	8-07/16	5-15/16	M	Lemhi County	ID	Ray Torrey	1971	198
14-06/16	8-06/16	6-00/16	M	Falkland	BC	W. Klingsat	1974	198
14-06/16	8-07/16	5-15/16	M	Cimarron	NM	Richard A. Meyer	1974	198
14-06/16	8-08/16	5-14/16	M	Spanish Peaks	CO	Douglas E. Miller	1974	198
14-06/16	8-07/16	5-15/16	M	Clearwater County	ID	Oscar Levingston	1975	198
14-06/16	8-07/16	5-15/16	M	Coal Creek	UT	Thomas W. Pinkston	1977	198
14-06/16	8-08/16	5-14/16	M	Uintas County	UT	Donald Redfox	1978	198
14-06/16	8-05/16	6-01/16	M	Fremont County	CO	Russell Hull	1979	198
14-06/16	8-09/16	5-13/16	M	Dry Wash Creek	UT	Mark J. Checki	1981	198
14-06/16	8-06/16	6-00/16	M	Chaffee County	CO	Judy Clyncke	1981	198
14-06/16	8-08/16	5-14/16	M	Ravalli County	MT	Dean Irwin	1982	198
14-06/16	8-06/16	6-00/16	M	Colfax County	NM	Joseph Wambach	1982	198
14-06/16	8-08/16	5-14/16	M	San Juan County	NM	Mike Ray	1983	198
14-06/16	8-08/16	5-14/16	M	Wasatch County	UT	Kendall Julander	1983	198
14-06/16	8-07/16	5-15/16	M	Clearwater County	ID	Tim Newbold	1983	198
14-06/16	8-09/16	5-13/16	M	Walla Walla County	WA	Winford Bradford	1983	198
14-06/16	8-03/16	6-03/16	M	Caribou County	ID	Rhett Bradford	1984	198
14-06/16	8-06/16	6-00/16	M	Lemhi County	ID	Donald L. Minnich	1984	198
14-06/16	8-08/16	5-14/16	M	Lemhi County	ID	Phil R. Ginochio	1985	198
14-06/16	8-05/16	6-01/16	M	Boise County	ID	David W. Peltier	1985	198
14-06/16	8-08/16	5-14/16	M	Cochise County	AZ	John Holcomb	1985	198
14-05/16	8-06/16	5-15/16	M	Lida	NV	Don Schram	1965	222
14-05/16	8-09/16	5-12/16	M	Tatla Lake	BC	William L. Nickerson	1966	222
14-05/16	8-08/16	5-13/16	M	Henry Mountains	UT	H. R. "Dutch" Wambold	1966	222
14-05/16	8-08/16	5-13/16	M	Henry Mountains	UT	Robert K. Paulson	1968	222
14-05/16	8-10/16	5-11/16	M	Carbon County	UT	M. R. James	1970	222
14-05/16	8-08/16	5-13/16	M	Chaffee County	CO	Michael Ballard	1975	222
14-05/16	8-07/16	5-14/16	M	Ely	NV	James L. Beard	1975	222
14-05/16	8-08/16	5-13/16	M	Beaver County	UT	Bruce Post	1975	222
14-05/16	8-07/16	5-14/16	M	Gulnare	CO	Barry L. Powell	1975	222
14-05/16	8-08/16	5-13/16	M	Daggett County	UT	Bob Butler	1976	222
14-05/16	8-09/16	5-12/16	M	Elmore County	ID	L. Dean Goodner	1978	222
14-05/16	8-10/16	5-11/16	M	Grand County	UT	Terry L. Benzine	1978	222
14-05/16	8-09/16	5-12/16	M	Fir Mt.	BC	John "Jack" Cordes	1978	222
14-05/16	8-07/16	5-14/16	M	Custer County	CO	William Henderson	1979	222
14-05/16	8-07/16	5-14/16	M	Judith Basin County	MT	Don Davidson	1981	222
14-05/16	8-07/16	5-14/16	M	Mancos	CO	Marvin Reichenau	1981	222
14-05/16	8-10/16	5-11/16	M	Dolores County	CO	Mike Gleason	1982	222
14-05/16	8-06/16	5-15/16	M	Lemhi County	ID	Stephen N. Bean	1983	222
14-05/16	8-08/16	5-13/16	M	Custer County	ID	Robert L. Hudman	1984	222
14-05/16	8-05/16	6-00/16	M	Jefferson County	CO	Jeff Fulkner	1984	222
14-05/16	8-08/16	5-13/16	M	Meeker County	CO	Michael Ingold	1984	222
14-05/16	8-08/16	5-13/16	M	Sanpete County	UT	Judy Hallman	1985	222
14-05/16	8-05/16	6-00/16	M	Colfax County	NM	Jim Stauft	1985	222
14-05/16	8-07/16	5-14/16	M	Idaho County	ID	Jay D. Stringer	1985	222
14-05/16	8-08/16	5-13/16	M	Judith Basin County	MT	Joseph R. "Bob" Fabian	1986	222
14-05/16	8-09/16	5-12/16	M	Dona Anna County	NM	Larry M. Sellers	1986	222
14-05/16	8-09/16	5-12/16	M	Kane County	UT	Allan Dangerfield	1986	222
14-04/16	8-08/16	5-12/16	M	Stoneman Lake	AZ	Dr. C. L. Clare	1962	249
14-04/16	8-08/16	5-12/16	M	Troy	MT	Dale McNutt	1964	249
14-04/16	8-10/16	5-10/16	M	Elmore County	ID	Don Bennett	1968	249
14-04/16	8-04/16	6-00/16	M	Missoula County	MT	Tony Dumay	1968	249
14-04/16	8-06/16	5-14/16	M	Boise County	ID	John E. Anderson	1972	249
14-04/16	8-06/16	5-14/16	M	Lemhi	ID	Kenneth Anselmi	1972	249
14-04/16	8-06/16	5-14/16	M	Big Smokey Valley	NV	Ken Viles	1972	249
14-04/16	8-04/16	6-00/16	M	Salmon River	ID	Bob Tucker	1974	249

COUGAR (MOUNTAIN LION)
(continued)   Minimum Score 13

Score	Greatest Length	Greatest Width	Sex	Area	State/Province	Hunter's Name	Date	Rank
14-04/16	8-06/16	5-14/16	M	Lemhi County	ID	H. R. "Rusty" Neely	1975	249
14-04/16	8-04/16	6-00/16	M	Gateway	CO	Robert Tobias	1975	249
14-04/16	8-06/16	5-14/16	M	Challis	ID	Gerald Conway	1978	249
14-04/16	8-08/16	5-12/16	M	McMullen County	TX	James E. Jordan	1978	249
14-04/16	8-04/16	6-00/16	M	Enterprise	UT	Richard L. Mobilio	1979	249
14-04/16	8-08/16	5-12/16	M	Boulder Mountain	UT	George Holfeltz	1980	249
14-04/16	8-03/16	6-01/16	M	Colfax County	NM	Stephen "Don" Hornady	1980	249
14-04/16	8-04/16	6-00/16	M	Garfield County	CO	T. Michael Casey	1982	249
14-04/16	8-06/16	5-14/16	M	Riverton	UT	William L. Randles	1982	249
14-04/16	8-08/16	5-12/16	M	Pioche	NV	David A. Widby	1982	249
14-04/16	8-06/16	5-14/16	M	Clearwater County	ID	Ralph Ertz	1983	249
14-04/16	8-05/16	5-15/16	M	Elmore County	ID	Brad L. Johnson	1983	249
14-04/16	8-06/16	5-14/16	M	Lemhi County	ID	Bob Hudson	1984	249
14-04/16	8-06/16	5-14/16	M	Spokane County	WA	Kenneth R. Wengert	1984	249
14-04/16	8-07/16	5-13/16	M	Austin County	NV	Peter Esposito	1984	249
14-04/16	8-08/16	5-12/16	M	Sanpete County	UT	C. Danny Butler	1985	249
14-04/16	8-07/16	5-13/16	M	Lander County	NV	Leonard Ruimveld	1985	249
14-04/16	8-05/16	5-15/16	M	Montrose County	CO	Tony Hoza	1986	249
14-04/16	8-06/16	5-14/16	M	Colfax County	NM	John L. Chapman	1986	249
14-04/16	8-08/16	5-12/16	M	Eureka County	NV	Marty Pawelek	1986	249
14-03/16	8-06/16	5-13/16	M	Tonopah	NV	Dick Gulman	1968	277
14-03/16	8-07/16	5-12/16	?	Republic	WA	Tom Smith	1968	277
14-03/16	8-05/16	5-14/16	M	Book Cliff Mountains	UT	John B. Baughman	1969	277
14-03/16	8-06/16	5-13/16	M	Douglas County	NV	Bill Fuller	1972	277
14-03/16	8-07/16	5-12/16	M	Walsenburg	CO	Marvin C. Clyncke	1973	277
14-03/16	8-09/16	5-10/16	M	Calleo	UT	Samuel McCarty	1975	277
14-03/16	8-07/16	5-12/16	M	Stevens County	WA	Ronald A. Carpenter	1977	277
14-03/16	8-08/16	5-11/16	M	Poncha Springs	CO	John C. Dekker	1977	277
14-03/16	8-08/16	5-11/16	M	Richfield	UT	Claude Flippin	1980	277
14-03/16	8-07/16	5-12/16	M	Adams County	ID	Rube Powell	1982	277
14-03/16	8-04/16	5-15/16	M	Mesa County	CO	William G. Padilla	1982	277
14-03/16	8-06/16	5-13/16	M	Judith Basin County	MT	Stan Colton	1983	277
14-03/16	8-05/16	5-14/16	M	Madison County	MT	Tony Schaufler	1983	277
14-03/16	8-04/16	5-15/16	M	Flathead County	MT	Gary A. Crowe	1983	277
14-03/16	8-06/16	5-13/16	M	Sierra County	NM	Kendall Doyle	1985	277
14-03/16	8-04/16	5-15/16	M	Montezuma County	CO	Duain Morton	1985	277
14-03/16	8-05/16	5-14/16	F	Shuswap River	BC	Mark Siegmueller	1985	277
14-03/16	8-05/16	5-14/16	M	Sanders County	MT	Jim Clark	1985	277
14-03/16	8-04/16	5-15/16	M	Clearwater County	ID	Dexter Siler	1986	277
14-02/16	8-06/16	5-12/16	M	Fish Lake	WA	Dr. Russell Congdon	1950	296
14-02/16	8-06/16	5-12/16	M	Glendale	UT	William P. Mastrangel	1957	296
14-02/16	8-04/16	5-14/16	M	Fresno County	CA	John Faulconer	1964	296
14-02/16	8-06/16	5-12/16	M	Rifle	CO	Phillip C. Durr	1970	296
14-02/16	8-04/16	5-14/16	M	Willow Creek	UT	Larry Jones	1970	296
14-02/16	8-05/16	5-13/16	M	Texas Creek	CO	Noel Feather	1975	296
14-02/16	8-06/16	5-12/16	M	Book Cliffs	CO	James L. Emerson	1976	296
14-02/16	8-04/16	5-14/16	M	Lane County	OR	Eugene W. Gramzow	1978	296
14-02/16	8-05/16	5-13/16	M	Saguache County	CO	John T. Rauch	1979	296
14-02/16	8-04/16	5-14/16	M	Ravalli County	MT	Dean Irwin	1980	296
14-02/16	8-03/16	5-15/16	M	Montrose County	CO	Hoyte Driggers	1981	296
14-02/16	8-04/16	5-14/16	M	Greenlee County	AZ	Fred L. Smith	1982	296
14-02/16	8-08/16	5-10/16	M	Duchesne County	UT	Bill Painter	1982	296
14-02/16	8-09/16	5-09/16	M	Duchesne County	UT	Michael Wieck	1983	296
14-02/16	8-06/16	5-12/16	M	Color County	UT	Carl D. Winton	1984	296
14-02/16	8-04/16	5-14/16	M	Sweetgrass County	MT	David W. Sorensen	1984	296
14-02/16	8-08/16	5-10/16	M	Ravalli County	MT	John L Wozniak	1985	296
14-02/16	8-03/16	5-15/16	M	Mesa County	CO	David A. Schroeder	1986	296
14-02/16	8-06/16	5-12/16	M	Sanpete County	UT	Joe Johnston	1986	296
14-01/16	8-14/16	5-03/16	M	Garfield County	CO	Jack Peters	1964	315
14-01/16	8-07/16	5-10/16	M	Rio Blanco	CO	Charles Kohler	1969	315
14-01/16	8-07/16	5-10/16	?	Buena Vista	CO	Frank B. Parrish	1969	315
14-01/16	8-06/16	5-11/16	M	Boise County	ID	Jerry E. Burt	1971	315
14-01/16	8-03/16	5-14/16	M	Fruita	CO	Cary E. Weldon	1972	315
14-01/16	8-05/16	5-12/16	M	Carbon County	UT	David K. Elliot	1973	315
14-01/16	8-05/16	5-12/16	M	Little Lost River	ID	Ken Anselmi	1975	315

COUGAR (MOUNTAIN LION)

Minimum Score 13

(continued)

Score	Greatest Length	Greatest Width	Sex	Area	State/ Province	Hunter's Name	Date	Rank
14-01/16	8-05/16	5-12/16	M	Book Cliff Mountains	CO	Chris Christian	1976	315
14-01/16	8-05/16	5-12/16	M	Bicknell	UT	C. Duane Kerr	1979	315
14-01/16	8-05/16	5-12/16	M	Cache County	UT	Val D. Larsen	1980	315
14-01/16	8-05/16	5-12/16	M	Williams	AZ	Fred McDonald	1980	315
14-01/16	8-05/16	5-12/16	M	Elko County	NV	Don Tripp	1980	315
14-01/16	8-05/16	5-12/16	M	Lemhi County	ID	Jim Jungk	1981	315
14-01/16	8-04/16	5-13/16	M	Adams County	ID	Dennis Atwater	1982	315
14-01/16	8-09/16	5-08/16	M	Coconino County	AZ	Dale Tasa	1982	315
14-01/16	8-05/16	5-12/16	M	Douglas County	CO	Gary James Morrow	1982	315
14-01/16	8-04/16	5-13/16	M	Madison County	MT	Dick Curtis	1983	315
14-01/16	8-06/16	5-11/16	M	Madison County	MT	John E. Larsen	1984	315
14-01/16	8-05/16	5-12/16	M	Tooele County	UT	Dennis L. Shirley	1984	315
14-01/16	8-06/16	5-11/16	M	Flathead County	MT	Dean F. Bergman	1984	315
14-01/16	8-05/16	5-12/16	M	Austin County	NV	Louis Probo	1984	315
14-01/16	8-04/16	5-13/16	M	Gilpin County	CO	Kurt W. Keskimaki	1985	315
14-00/16	8-04/16	5-12/16	M	Tavaputs Plateau	UT	Dr. Quentin F. Mangion	1962	337
14-00/16	8-04/16	5-12/16	M	Salt Lick Canyon	AZ	Hugh Pearson	1963	337
14-00/16	8-04/16	5-12/16	M	Flathead County	MT	Dorn L. Brinker	1969	337
14-00/16	8-03/16	5-13/16	M	Cascade Mountains	ID	Ronald N. Kolpin	1972	337
14-00/16	8-01/16	5-15/16	M	Skull Valley	AZ	Louis A. Vohs	1973	337
14-00/16	8-05/16	5-11/16	M	Lemhi County	ID	T. A. Low IV	1977	337
14-00/16	8-02/16	5-14/16	M	Duchesne	UT	James Sot	1977	337
14-00/16	8-04/16	5-12/16	M	Blacktail Mountain	UT	Jerry Dittrich	1978	337
14-00/16	8-05/16	5-11/16	M	Fremont County	CO	Gary Fisher	1979	337
14-00/16	8-04/16	5-12/16	M	Blanding	UT	Gary Paluszcyk	1979	337
14-00/16	8-04/16	5-12/16	M	Payette River	ID	Paul Anderson	1980	337
14-00/16	8-03/16	5-13/16	M	Flagstaff	AZ	Larry Almaraz	1981	337
14-00/16	8-03/16	5-13/16	M	Norwood	CO	Robert Finelli	1981	337
14-00/16	8-05/16	5-11/16	M	Madison County	MT	Leland S. Speakes, Jr.	1984	337
14-00/16	8-02/16	5-14/16	M	Madison County	MT	Pat Sinclair	1985	337
14-00/16	8-08/16	5-08/16	M	Rio Grande County	CO	Tom Tietz	1985	337
13-15/16	8-03/16	5-12/16	M	Gila County	AZ	Hugh Pearson	1963	353
13-15/16	8-05/16	5-10/16	M	Baxter Pass	CO	Joel Hogan	1967	353
13-15/16	8-06/16	5-09/16	M	Okanogan County	WA	Stuart Irwin	1971	353
13-15/16	8-05/16	5-10/16	M	Lehmi County	ID	John Mascellino	1972	353
13-15/16	8-03/16	5-12/16	M	San Miguel County	CO	Ken Grandow	1979	353
13-15/16	8-06/16	5-09/16	M	Lowman	ID	Richard C. Nichols	1980	353
13-15/16	8-03/16	5-12/16	M	Judith Basin County	MT	Ed Evans	1981	353
13-15/16	8-05/16	5-10/16	M	Las Animas County	CO	David S. Bunce	1982	353
13-15/16	8-05/16	5-10/16	M	Piute County	UT	Lynn Kuhlmann	1984	353
13-15/16	8-03/16	5-12/16	M	Boise County	ID	William Atkinson, Jr.	1985	353
13-14/16	8-04/16	5-10/16	M	Flathead County	MT	Jerry Almos	1970	363
13-14/16	8-06/16	5-08/16	F	Flagstaff	AZ	Midge Dandridge	1972	363
13-14/16	8-01/16	5-13/16	M	Grand Junction	CO	Stan Bocian	1974	363
13-14/16	8-05/16	5-09/16	M	Buena Vista	CO	Ben Cuadra	1975	363
13-14/16	8-02/16	5-12/16	M	Boise County	ID	Robert L. Bevan	1976	363
13-14/16	8-06/16	5-08/16	M	Lemhi County	ID	James C. Costopoulos	1976	363
13-14/16	8-04/16	5-10/16	M	Lemhi County	ID	Dan E. Hershberger	1979	363
13-14/16	8-04/16	5-10/16	M	Book Cliff Mountains	CO	Wayne Watson, Sr.	1979	363
13-14/16	8-03/16	5-11/16	M	Vernal	UT	Dan Darrell Boy	1980	363
13-14/16	8-09/16	5-05/16	M	Washington County	UT	Scott Petersen	1982	363
13-14/16	8-03/16	5-11/16	M	Indian Spring Ridge	UT	Henry "Hank" Frey	1982	363
13-14/16	8-03/16	5-11/16	M	Pagosa Springs	CO	Ronald Murphy	1983	363
13-14/16	8-01/16	5-13/16	M	Lemhi County	ID	Wendell L. Seelig	1983	363
13-14/16	8-03/16	5-11/16	M	Sanpete County	UT	Bob Fitzgerald	1984	363
13-14/16	8-05/16	5-09/16	M	Chaffe County	CO	Raymond Roussett, Jr.	1985	363
13-14/16	8-05/16	5-09/16	M	Elmore County	ID	John Koldeway	1985	363
13-14/16	8-02/16	5-12/16	M	Gilpin County	CO	Lyle Willmarth	1986	363
13-13/16	8-02/16	5-11/16	M	Lida	NV	George Hooker	1961	380
13-13/16	7-15/16	5-14/16	M	Lemhi County	ID	Vern Herman	1969	380
13-13/16	8-02/16	5-11/16	M	EL Paso County	CO	L. Clark Kiser	1984	380
13-13/16	8-04/16	5-09/16	M	Mesa County	CO	Edgar Bobo	1984	380
13-13/16	8-01/16	5-12/16	M	Sandoval County	NM	David Taylor	1985	380
13-13/16	8-01/16	5-12/16	M	San Juan County	UT	David Snyder	1985	380

COUGAR (MOUNTAIN LION)

(continued)   Minimum Score 13

Score	Greatest Length	Greatest Width	Sex	Area	State/ Province	Hunter's Name	Date	Rank
13-13/16	8-03/16	5-10/16	M	Johnson County	WY	Terry Krahn	1986	380
13-12/16	8-04/16	5-08/16	M	Shasta National Forest	CA	Harv Ebers	1963	387
13-12/16	8-00/16	5-12/16	M	Swan R. Valley	MT	Joe Lawrence	1965	387
13-12/16	7-11/16	6-01/16	M	Henry Mountains	UT	Robert E. Todd	1969	387
13-12/16	8-02/16	5-10/16	M	Baboquivari Mountains	AZ	Sherwin Lipsitz	1976	387
13-12/16	8-03/16	5-09/16	M	Lemhi County	ID	Ray Torrey	1978	387
13-12/16	8-03/16	5-09/16	M	Custer County	ID	Larry Bonetti	1979	387
13-12/16	8-04/16	5-08/16	M	Lemhi County	ID	Buck Farni	1979	387
13-12/16	8-03/16	5-09/16	M	Carbon County	UT	Claude Flippin	1981	387
13-12/16	8-02/16	5-10/16	M	Grand County	UT	Robert Jacobsen	1986	387
13-11/16	8-03/16	5-08/16	M	McCall	ID	Clarence Grandt	1972	396
13-11/16	8-03/16	5-08/16	M	Mack	CO	William J. Vincent	1972	396
13-11/16	8-02/16	5-09/16	M	Price	UT	Bernard R. Giacoletto	1975	396
13-11/16	8-06/16	5-05/16	M	Manti-LaSal N.F.	UT	James Karlovec	1975	396
13-11/16	7-15/16	5-12/16	M	Cisco	UT	David Seidelman	1975	396
13-11/16	8-00/16	5-11/16	M	Cathedral Mountains	CO	Darlene Frye	1976	396
13-11/16	8-04/16	5-07/16	M	Boise County	ID	Fred Sanders	1981	396
13-11/16	7-15/16	5-12/16	M	Missoula County	MT	Blair Hamer	1983	396
13-11/16	8-03/16	5-08/16	M	Gilpin County	CO	John Rhine	1984	396
13-11/16	8-03/16	5-08/16	M	Clearwater County	ID	Mike I. Powers	1984	396
13-11/16	8-03/16	5-08/16	F	Socorro County	NM	Paul Persano	1986	396
13-10/16	8-02/16	5-08/16	F	Greystone	CO	Roland C. Gravenkemper	1959	407
13-10/16	8-00/16	5-10/16	F	Sana Arroya Canyon	UT	Edward Collins	1967	407
13-10/16	7-14/16	5-12/16	M	Texas Creek	CO	Jeffrey D. McKnight	1970	407
13-10/16	7-15/16	5-11/16	M	Boise County	ID	Robert B. Braswell	1971	407
13-10/16	7-12/16	5-14/16	M	Lemhi County	ID	Richard R. Smith	1976	407
13-10/16	8-02/16	5-08/16	M	Grand County	UT	Karen Jacobsen	1980	407
13-10/16	8-03/16	5-07/16	M	Salina County	UT	Robert C. McGuire	1980	407
13-10/16	8-02/16	5-08/16	M	Garfield County	UT	William B. McGuire, Jr.	1983	407
13-10/16	8-02/16	5-08/16	M	Seveir County	UT	Kenneth L. Jackson	1984	407
13-10/16	8-00/16	5-10/16	M	Flathead County	MT	Charles J. Williams	1986	407
13-10/16	8-04/16	5-06/16	M	Colfax County	NM	I. Lionel Kelley	1986	407
13-09/16	8-00/16	5-09/16	M	Dragerton	UT	Tom Kludy	1965	418
13-09/16	8-01/16	5-08/16	M	Boise County	ID	Larry Bergmann	1972	418
13-09/16	8-00/16	5-09/16	F	Challis	ID	John Kuhar	1975	418
13-09/16	7-15/16	5-10/16	M	Rio Blanco County	CO	John Horstman	1977	418
13-09/16	8-00/16	5-09/16	M	Saguache County	CO	Ed R. Wiseman	1977	418
13-09/16	8-03/16	5-06/16	M	Peachland	BC	Roger Gipple	1983	418
13-09/16	7-15/16	5-10/16	M	Hot Springs County	WY	John Backs	1983	418
13-09/16	8-05/16	5-04/16	M	Monroe County	UT	Peter Esposito	1984	418
13-09/16	7-14/16	5-11/16	M	Sanders County	MT	Fred J. Hoppe	1984	418
13-09/16	8-03/16	5-06/16	M	Beaver County	UT	Joseph Drover	1985	418
13-09/16	8-02/16	5-07/16	M	San Juan County	UT	Charles R. Horvath	1985	418
13-09/16	8-00/16	5-09/16	M	Lemhi County	ID	Ed Montouri	1985	418
13-09/16	8-00/16	5-09/16	M	Sanders County	MT	Gene Altiere	1985	418
13-09/16	8-01/16	5-08/16	M	Juab County	UT	Kirt Prestwich	1986	418
13-08/16	8-00/16	5-08/16	M	Wilcox Range Valley	UT	Creetie Kerr	1964	432
13-08/16	8-02/16	5-06/16	M	Wilcox Range Valley	UT	Dr. George A. Waldriff	1965	432
13-08/16	7-12/16	5-12/16	F	Lincoln County	MT	G. H. Malinoski	1967	432
13-08/16	8-08/16	5-00/16	F	Fallon	NV	Quentin P. Nightingale	1971	432
13-08/16	8-01/16	5-07/16	M	Coconino County	AZ	Tim Kennedy	1974	432
13-08/16	8-02/16	5-06/16	M	Coconino County	AZ	Robert West	1974	432
13-08/16	8-00/16	5-08/16	M	Price	UT	John Brandt	1978	432
13-08/16	8-00/16	5-08/16	M	Cassia County	ID	Leon Peterson	1978	432
13-08/16	8-02/16	5-06/16	M	Penticton	BC	Dale W. Gray	1979	432
13-08/16	8-00/16	5-08/16	M	Lemhi County	ID	John A. McCarthy	1979	432
13-08/16	8-01/16	5-07/16	M	Fremont County	CO	Steve Byerly	1981	432
13-08/16	8-02/16	5-06/16	M	Clearwater County	ID	Donita K. Powers	1982	432
13-08/16	8-01/16	5-07/16	F	Wallowa County	OR	Jim Turcke	1983	432
13-08/16	8-01/16	5-07/16	M	Washington County	UT	Nic Blake	1984	432
13-08/16	8-00/16	5-08/16	M	Yavapai County	AZ	Pat Henley	1984	432
13-08/16	8-01/16	5-07/16	M	Alimosa County	CO	Barry J. Smith	1985	432
13-08/16	7-13/16	5-11/16	M	Madison County	MT	Jim Ellis	1985	432
13-07/16	8-00/16	5-07/16	M	Navajo County	AZ	John Spriggs	1976	449
13-07/16	7-15/16	5-08/16	M	Fish Lake National Forest	UT	Robert W. Fritz	1979	449

COUGAR (MOUNTAIN LION)

Minimum Score 13   (continued)

Score	Greatest Length	Greatest Width	Sex	Area	State/ Province	Hunter's Name	Date	Rank
13-07/16	8-02/16	5-05/16	M	Gem County	ID	Deloy Desaro	1980	449
13-07/16	8-02/16	5-05/16	M	Glade Park	CO	Charles C. Pacheco	1980	449
13-07/16	7-14/16	5-09/16	F	Delta County	CO	Ron Berlier	1982	449
13-07/16	7-15/16	5-08/16	F	Books Cliffs	UT	Jon P. Thomas	1984	449
13-07/16	8-02/16	5-05/16	M	Idaho County	ID	William A.S. Hever, Jr.	1985	449
13-07/16	7-15/16	5-08/16	F	Idaho County	ID	David Gename	1985	449
13-07/16	7-14/16	5-09/16	M	Cochise County	AZ	Charles Lee Marsh III	1985	449
13-06/16	8-00/16	5-06/16	M	Boise County	ID	Ronald L. Sherer	1969	458
13-06/16	7-14/16	5-08/16	M	Globe	AZ	Jack Steppe	1970	458
13-06/16	7-14/16	5-08/16	M	Caroline	ALB	Daniel E. Littleton	1975	458
13-06/16	7-13/16	5-09/16	F	Idaho County	ID	Glenn Hisey	1977	458
13-06/16	7-14/16	5-08/16	M	Judith Basin County	MT	Larry Schweitzer	1983	458
13-06/16	7-12/16	5-10/16	F	Garfield County	CO	Dan Liccardi	1984	458
13-06/16	8-00/16	5-06/16	M	Lewis and Clark County	MT	Rich Fait	1985	458
13-06/16	8-00/16	5-06/16	M	Shoshone County	ID	Lyle C. Kelley	1985	458
13-05/16	7-13/16	5-08/16	F	Clinton	BC	Dr. Charles Raab	1968	466
13-05/16	8-01/16	5-04/16	M	Santa Barbara County	CA	Patrick J. Marley	1970	466
13-05/16	8-00/16	5-05/16	M	Cathedral Mountain	CO	Thomas B. Frye	1976	466
13-05/16	7-15/16	5-06/16	M	Fremont County	CO	Doug Burwell	1977	466
13-05/16	7-13/16	5-08/16	M	Robie Creek	ID	Richard C. Nichols	1977	466
13-05/16	7-15/16	5-06/16	F	LaVerkin Creek	UT	John Janelli	1980	466
13-05/16	7-13/16	5-08/16	F	Sanpete County	UT	Stanley R. Smith	1981	466
13-05/16	7-14/16	5-07/16	M	Sanders County	MT	Richard M. Mielke	1984	466
13-05/16	7-14/16	5-07/16	F	Owyhee County	ID	Robert Pyne	1984	466
13-05/16	8-00/16	5-05/16	M	Carbon County	UT	Tom Paluso	1986	466
13-04/16	8-02/16	5-02/16	M	Lake County	MT	Jack Whitney	1962	476
13-04/16	7-12/16	5-08/16	M	Book Cliff Mountains	UT	Don Dvoroznak	1970	476
13-04/16	7-14/16	5-06/16	M	Lemhi County	ID	Lowell E. Ganger	1972	476
13-04/16	7-13/16	5-07/16	M	Lincoln County	NV	Fred Searle	1972	476
13-04/16	7-10/16	5-10/16	F	Tay River	ALB	Joseph W. Waters	1973	476
13-04/16	7-15/16	5-05/16	M	Clark's Valley	UT	Kenny E. Leo	1976	476
13-04/16	7-13/16	5-07/16	F	?	UT	Toby Johnson	1977	476
13-04/16	7-15/16	5-05/16	M	Monroe County	UT	Louis Probo	1983	476
13-04/16	7-14/16	5-06/16	M	Richfield County	UT	Louis Probo	1984	476
13-04/16	7-14/16	5-06/16	M	Sheridan County	WY	Marshall Powers	1984	476
13-04/16	7-12/16	5-08/16	F	Powell County	MT	Karen Brunner	1986	476
13-03/16	8-02/16	5-01/16	M	Manzano Mountains	NM	Joe B. Matthews	1970	487
13-03/16	7-14/16	5-05/16	M	Rifle	CO	Leroy Lake	1975	487
13-03/16	8-00/16	5-03/16	M	Buena Vista	CO	Ron McKnight	1975	487
13-03/16	7-13/16	5-06/16	F	Caroline	ALB	Martin Merkel	1975	487
13-03/16	7-14/16	5-05/16	M	Flathead County	MT	Don Davidson	1979	487
13-03/16	7-12/16	5-07/16	F	Huerfano County	CO	Kenneth D. Allen	1982	487
13-03/16	7-12/16	5-07/16	F	Uintah County	UT	Wesley W. Moulton	1984	487
13-03/16	7-15/16	5-04/16	M	San Miguel County	CO	G. Merrill Jones	1984	487
13-03/16	7-12/16	5-07/16	F	Boise County	ID	Eldon D. Hagen	1985	487
13-03/16	7-11/16	5-08/16	F	Missoula County	MT	Dyrk Eddie	1986	487
13-02/16	7-13/16	5-05/16	F	Emery County	UT	Carolyn Siebrasse	1966	497
13-02/16	7-15/16	5-03/16	M	Phantom Canyon	CO	Lawrence O. Streeter	1968	497
13-02/16	7-12/16	5-06/16	M	Carbon County	UT	Paul K. Thompson, Sr.	1971	497
13-02/16	7-12/16	5-06/16	F	Salina Canyon	UT	Danny C. Lloyd	1974	497
13-02/16	7-12/16	5-06/16	M	E. Douglas Pass	CO	John D. Rook	1976	497
13-02/16	7-12/16	5-06/16	F	Book Cliffs	CO	John W. Ellas	1977	497
13-02/16	7-11/16	5-07/16	M	'Las Animas County	CO	Max Tallent	1978	497
13-02/16	7-12/16	5-06/16	F	Jicarilla Reservation	NM	Ralph Ertz	1982	497
13-02/16	7-15/16	5-03/16	M	Norwood	CO	David E. Smith	1983	497
13-02/16	7-12/16	5-06/16	F	Sheridan County	WY	David V. Collis	1983	497
13-02/16	7-13/16	5-05/16	F	Beaver County	UT	David Drover	1985	497
13-02/16	7-10/16	5-08/16	F	Tooele County	UT	Cleve Roush	1985	497
13-02/16	7-12/16	5-06/16	M	Sanpete County	UT	James Saunoris	1985	497
13-02/16	7-13/16	5-05/16	F	Chelan County	WA	Vaughn Cross	1986	497
13-01/16	7-13/16	5-04/16	M	New Harmony	UT	William P. Mastrangel	1958	511
13-01/16	7-11/16	5-06/16	?	Henry Mountains	UT	Michael Bowser	1966	511
13-01/16	7-12/16	5-05/16	F	Canon City	CO	Jim Pederson	1968	511
13-01/16	7-11/16	5-06/16	F	?	UT	Philip Copp	1969	511

COUGAR (MOUNTAIN LION)

(continued)   Minimum Score 13

Score	Greatest Length	Greatest Width	Sex	Area	State/ Province	Hunter's Name	Date	Rank
13-01/16	7-13/16	5-04/16	F	Kooskia	ID	Dick Gulman	1969	511
13-01/16	7-11/16	5-06/16	F	Carbon County	UT	Leonard E. Scarborough	1971	511
13-01/16	7-08/16	5-09/16	F	Price	UT	James V. Golightly	1974	511
13-01/16	7-13/16	5-04/16	F	Waterton Canyon	CO	James L. Morrow	1974	511
13-01/16	7-10/16	5-07/16	F	Challis	ID	Billy Ellis	1977	511
13-01/16	7-12/16	5-05/16	F	Mineral County	MT	Larry L. Streiff	1977	511
13-01/16	7-10/16	5-07/16	F	Vernal	UT	John D. Sandor	1979	511
13-01/16	7-14/16	5-03/16	M	Iron County	UT	Roy Cucuzza	1983	511
13-01/16	8-00/16	5-01/16	F	Brewster County	TX	William Holt	1984	511
13-01/16	7-10/16	5-07/16	F	Sanders County	MT	Matthew R. Pedrotte	1985	511
13-01/16	7-13/16	5-04/16	M	Clearwater County	ID	Steven Garnell Grandy	1985	511
13-00/16	7-14/16	5-02/16	M	Libby	MT	Robert Arbine	1961	526
13-00/16	7-11/16	5-05/16	?	LacHache	BC	Vic Clarkson	1964	526
13-00/16	7-12/16	5-04/16	F	Beryl	UT	George Moerlein	1965	526
13-00/16	7-08/16	5-08/16	F	Bear Lake County	ID	Joseph W. DeClark	1966	526
13-00/16	7-12/16	5-04/16	M	Monitor Valley	NV	Michael D. Perry	1968	526
13-00/16	7-11/16	5-05/16	F	Book Cliffs	CO	Jerry Putnam	1970	526
13-00/16	7-12/16	5-04/16	F	Nye County	NV	Fred Perry	1974	526
13-00/16	7-12/16	5-04/16	F	Wellington	UT	Tim Good	1975	526
13-00/16	7-09/16	5-07/16	F	Rifle	CO	Mike Dickess	1976	526
13-00/16	7-08/16	5-08/16	F	Grand Junction	CO	Robert Kirschner	1977	526
13-00/16	7-09/16	5-07/16	F	Lowman	ID	Jerry E. Burt	1978	526
13-00/16	7-09/16	5-07/16	F	Salinas	UT	Warren Buss	1979	526
13-00/16	7-10/16	5-06/16	F	Monticello	UT	Vaughn Ballard	1980	526
13-00/16	7-12/16	5-04/16	F	Dixie National Park	UT	Mike Murphy	1982	526
13-00/16	7-10/16	5-06/16	F	Garfield County	CO	Norman J. O'Bryan	1985	526
13-00/16	7-11/16	5-05/16	F	Boise County	ID	Richard Larrivee	1985	526

WORLD RECORD COLUMBIAN BLACKTAIL DEER
Score: 172 2/8
Marion County, Oregon – 1969
Hunter: B. G. Shurtleff

COLUMBIAN BLACKTAIL DEER
Odocoileus hemionus columbianus   Minimum Score 90

Score	Length of Main Beam R	Length of Main Beam L	Inside Spread	Number of Points R	Number of Points L	Area	State/ Province	Hunter's Name	Date	Rank
172-2/8	26-3/8	25-7/8	20-4/8	7	7	Marion County	OR	B. G. Shurtleff	1969	1
172-0/8	26-4/8	25-5/8	22-6/8	4	4	Multnomah County	OR	Dave Brill	1985	2
164-7/8	23-6/8	23-3/8	19-7/8	5	5	Marion County	OR	B. G. Shurtleff	1977	3
160-7/8	23-0/8	23-4/8	19-4/8	6	5	Jackson County	OR	Dr. G. Scott Jennings	1972	4
156-7/8	23-5/8	24-1/8	23-1/8	5	5	Trinity County	CA	Steve Bradford	1986	5
150-4/8	23-4/8	23-1/8	20-2/8	5	5	Jackson County	OR	E. C. Brittsan	1976	6
144-5/8	21-2/8	20-3/8	16-6/8	6	7	Jackson County	OR	Leroy Bedingfield	1970	7
143-7/8	21-0/8	20-6/8	21-0/8	5	5	Shasta County	CA	Dave Swenson	1968	8
142-2/8	19-1/8	19-7/8	19-0/8	5	5	Round Mountain	OR	Don Chandler	1968	9
141-7/8	20-7/8	21-0/8	17-3/8	5	5	Jackson County	OR	Chester Stevenson	1917	10
140-6/8	21-3/8	20-4/8	16-2/8	3	3	Jackson County	OR	Art W. Lee	1965	11
140-6/8	22-6/8	22-5/8	15-4/8	4	5	Jackson County	OR	Dr. G. Scott Jennings	1973	11
138-4/8	22-5/8	22-4/8	18-5/8	5	5	Siskiyou County	CA	John Bridgewater	1980	13
137-2/8	20-2/8	19-7/8	16-1/8	6	5	Jackson County	OR	Steve Wirth	1983	14
137-0/8	20-3/8	20-1/8	14-5/8	4	4	Ukiah	CA	Russell L. Browning	1980	15
137-0/8	21-1/8	21-2/8	15-7/8	4	5	Linn County	OR	Charlie Endicott	1985	15
135-0/8	22-0/8	21-2/8	18-7/8	6	4	Jackson County	OR	Bob Staten	1964	17
134-5/8	21-0/8	16-0/8	16-2/8	5	4	Butte Falls	OR	Milton L. Cady	1968	18
134-5/8	21-7/8	21-7/8	17-0/8	7	5	Trinity County	CA	Bob Auser	1981	18
133-7/8	20-6/8	20-6/8	18-7/8	4	4	Jackson County	OR	Donald R. Pritchett	1966	20
133-7/8	19-4/8	21-6/8	13-7/8	7	7	Linn County	OR	J. C. James	1984	20
133-2/8	20-1/8	20-2/8	17-0/8	5	5	Jackson County	OR	Chester Stevenson	1921	22
133-0/8	20-5/8	21-0/8	14-6/8	5	5	Benton County	OR	Robert W. Worthean	1982	23
132-6/8	20-1/8	20-6/8	18-0/8	4	5	Jackson County	OR	Stanley Moore	1962	24
132-5/8	22-0/8	21-0/8	16-1/8	7	7	Clackamas County	OR	Charlie Medlicott	1983	25
132-3/8	18-6/8	19-4/8	16-7/8	5	5	Jackson County	OR	Donald R. Pritchett	1966	26
132-1/8	20-2/8	19-6/8	18-4/8	5	7	Jackson County	OR	John Schauble	1985	27
131-4/8	21-5/8	22-0/8	17-3/8	6	4	Multnomah County	OR	Dennis Thorud	1985	28
131-3/8	20-0/8	20-0/8	15-5/8	5	5	Jackson County	OR	Joe Williamson	1965	29
131-2/8	21-2/8	21-4/8	18-2/8	5	4	Clatsop County	OR	B. G. Shurtleff	1979	30
131-1/8	19-4/8	19-4/8	14-5/8	5	5	Bangor Naval Base	WA	Dale Axtman	1983	31
130-1/8	19-0/8	18-7/8	15-1/8	5	5	Linn County	OR	Duane Etherington	1983	32
129-3/8	26-1/8	25-3/8	19-2/8	5	3	W. Parker Mountain	OR	Troy Fennel	1964	33
128-7/8	18-2/8	18-2/8	16-3/8	5	5	Lane County	OR	Dave E. Jarrett	1982	34
128-6/8	19-6/8	19-3/8	22-2/8	5	5	Linn County	OR	David F. Scheid	1968	35
128-2/8	19-3/8	19-4/8	14-4/8	8	5	Clackamas County	OR	John Christiansen	1981	36
128-2/8	20-1/8	20-3/8	15-2/8	6	5	Linn County	OR	Steve Richards	1983	36
127-4/8	21-3/8	21-1/8	19-6/8	5	5	Linn County	OR	John Stone	1981	38
127-2/8	20-2/8	19-6/8	14-6/8	5	5	Trinity County	CA	George Flournoy, Jr.	1986	39
127-1/8	18-7/8	19-5/8	16-1/8	6	5	Mendocino County	CA	James Buffum	1965	40
126-4/8	17-1/8	18-5/8	14-6/8	5	5	Linn County	OR	Dennis H. Wessels	1985	41
125-7/8	19-1/8	19-4/8	13-7/8	5	5	Marion County	OR	Doug Harris	1985	42
125-6/8	19-3/8	18-5/8	14-2/8	4	4	Siskiyou County	CA	Cliff Dewell	1969	43
125-4/8	19-7/8	21-6/8	19-6/8	6	6	Josephine County	OR	Dave Hall	1983	44
124-6/8	20-7/8	19-0/8	16-6/8	4	5	Clackamas County	OR	Joseph Suire	1983	45
124-2/8	20-0/8	20-6/8	16-4/8	4	5	Capital Forest	WA	Sandy Tyler	1957	46
123-7/8	17-3/8	17-4/8	15-1/8	5	5	Siskiyou County	CA	Bill Collinsworth	1983	47
123-0/8	20-0/8	21-0/8	14-4/8	6	5	White Salmon River	WA	Larry Ramsey	1977	48
123-0/8	18-6/8	18-7/8	14-6/8	6	6	Jackson County	OR	Larry Frost	1984	48
122-7/8	19-1/8	20-4/8	16-1/8	4	5	Trinity County	CA	Loran G. August	1981	50
122-5/8	17-7/8	18-1/8	15-3/8	5	5	Trinity County	CA	Ted Lohse	1985	51
122-1/8	19-5/8	19-5/8	17-4/8	5	6	Jackson County	OR	Richard G. Speer	1965	52
121-3/8	15-5/8	15-2/8	14-0/8	5	5	Humboldt County	CA	Doug Walker	1965	53
121-3/8	19-7/8	18-7/8	16-4/8	7	5	Trinity County	CA	Mark Greving	1982	53
121-1/8	20-3/8	20-6/8	18-2/8	4	3	Yamhill County	OR	Ray Kelton	1981	55
121-0/8	18-0/8	17-0/8	14-4/8	5	5	Benton County	OR	Larry D. Jones	1966	56
120-6/8	18-5/8	19-0/8	15-4/8	5	5	Humboldt County	CA	Joe Henry	1980	57
119-6/8	20-0/8	20-3/8	16-2/8	4	4	Long Island	WA	John Higgins	1973	58
119-5/8	21-2/8	21-2/8	19-6/8	6	7	Wasco County	OR	Cecil Shuler	1967	59
119-3/8	21-5/8	21-4/8	17-3/8	4	3	Humboldt County	CA	Art Young	1918	60
118-6/8	20-4/8	20-2/8	14-6/8	4	5	Skamania County	WA	Frank Adkins	1967	61
117-4/8	18-0/8	18-2/8	14-1/8	5	5	Benton County	OR	Chris Reed	1970	62

COLUMBIAN BLACKTAIL DEER

Minimum Score 90   (continued)

Score	Length of Main Beam R	L	Inside Spread	Number of Points R	L	Area	State/ Province	Hunter's Name	Date	Rank
116-7/8	17-6/8	18-2/8	15-6/8	6	8	Siskiyou County	CA	Kurt Case	1980	63
116-5/8	19-5/8	20-3/8	12-5/8	4	5	Long Island	WA	Smokey Crews	1969	64
116-2/8	18-7/8	19-7/8	19-0/8	4	4	Jackson County	OR	Ray Gibson	1962	65
116-2/8	18-6/8	18-4/8	16-6/8	5	4	Trinity County	CA	Mike Lindley	1983	65
116-1/8	19-0/8	19-4/8	15-3/8	5	4	King County	WA	John Martin	1983	67
115-6/8	19-6/8	19-6/8	16-6/8	5	4	Clackamas County	OR	Jack Smith	1981	68
115-6/8	19-2/8	18-2/8	18-0/8	5	5	Siskiyou County	CA	Fred Searle	1983	68
115-4/8	17-4/8	17-4/8	13-7/8	5	5	Hilt	CA	Mike Garretson	1981	70
115-5/8	17-0/8	17-1/8	14-5/8	5	5	Polk County	OR	Randy Gunn	1981	70
115-2/8	19-4/8	19-4/8	16-2/8	4	4	Humboldt County	CA	J. E. Grundman	1963	72
115-1/8	16-6/8	16-3/8	15-7/8	5	5	Sumas Mtn.	BC	Peter L. Halbig	1985	73
114-0/8	17-3/8	16-6/8	16-0/8	5	4	Clackamas County	OR	Dave Showerman	1982	74
113-6/8	17-3/8	15-6/8	15-0/8	5	5	Benton County	OR	Gregory M. McHuron	1966	75
113-4/8	18-1/8	17-5/8	15-2/8	4	4	Mendocino County	CA	Jeff S. Spangler	1982	76
113-2/8	18-2/8	17-5/8	16-0/8	4	4	King County	WA	Vick Stevens	1984	77
112-7/8	19-1/8	17-6/8	14-1/8	4	4	Skagit County	WA	J. B. Bright	1986	78
112-5/8	21-2/8	20-4/8	14-1/8	5	5	King County	WA	Greg Tedlund	1984	79
112-4/8	16-0/8	15-1/8	13-4/8	5	5	Trinity County	CA	Dennis Schroer	1982	80
112-3/8	16-7/8	16-3/8	13-7/8	5	5	Snohomish County	WA	Jack Davis	1975	81
112-3/8	17-4/8	19-2/8	13-6/8	4	5	Douglas County	OR	Ken French	1980	81
112-2/8	18-5/8	19-1/8	15-2/8	4	4	Long Island	WA	Leon Poindexter	1968	83
112-1/8	17-1/8	17-4/8	13-3/8	5	5	Benton County	OR	Gary Nyden	1986	84
111-7/8	17-7/8	17-0/8	14-5/8	4	4	Long Island	WA	Smokey Crews	1967	85
110-7/8	18-3/8	17-0/8	16-3/8	4	4	Jackson County	OR	Dale K. Marcy	1966	86
110-6/8	18-4/8	17-7/8	17-0/8	4	4	Del Norte County	CA	Michael Penn	1979	87
110-5/8	19-7/8	20-3/8	13-4/8	4	6	Jackson County	OR	Dr. G. Scott Jennings	1979	88
110-4/8	17-1/8	17-3/8	13-6/8	4	4	Clark County	WA	Larry D. Nahrstedt	1968	89
110-4/8	17-0/8	18-7/8	17-4/8	4	4	Marin County	CA	Howard C. Gold	1976	89
110-3/8	16-1/8	16-1/8	15-7/8	5	5	Wild Deer Lake	BC	Guy Anttila	1970	91
110-3/8	19-3/8	20-0/8	13-6/8	6	5	North Vancouver	BC	Fred Day	1970	91
110-2/8	19-6/8	20-0/8	17-4/8	5	5	Lane County	OR	Richard M. Cook	1982	93
109-7/8	22-0/8	21-3/8	14-5/8	5	5	Linn County	OR	Steve Gilbert	1982	94
109-6/8	21-1/8	20-7/8	16-4/8	3	4	Winston Creek	WA	Barney Johnson	1974	95
109-5/8	20-4/8	19-4/8	15-3/8	5	4	Douglas County	OR	Teddy Rainville	1980	96
109-5/8	19-1/8	21-0/8	14-5/8	3	3	Lake County	CA	Paul W. Farina	1983	96
109-5/8	16-2/8	16-2/8	14-5/8	4	4	Siskiyou County	CA	Ralph Atkinson	1984	96
109-5/8	17-1/8	17-2/8	15-7/8	4	4	Clackamas County	OR	Randy Teeney	1985	96
109-5/8	18-4/8	18-6/8	15-5/8	4	4	Lane County	OR	Wm E. Sweetland	1985	96
109-3/8	17-0/8	17-5/8	14-4/8	6	5	Lane County	OR	Mark Klein	1982	101
108-7/8	17-6/8	19-1/8	13-7/8	5	5	Jackson County	OR	Joe Williamson	1963	102
108-7/8	16-7/8	17-0/8	13-5/8	5	5	Chetco Unit	OR	Michael Penn	1983	102
108-4/8	16-1/8	16-2/8	11-6/8	5	4	Clackamas County	OR	Ed Franzen	1985	104
107-5/8	17-5/8	18-5/8	14-1/8	5	4	Clackamas County	OR	Bob Manley	1982	105
107-1/8	15-7/8	15-4/8	13-7/8	4	4	Lincoln County	OR	Ray Kelton	1982	106
106-7/8	18-3/8	18-2/8	16-3/8	4	3	Skamania County	WA	Steve Shipp	1984	107
106-5/8	18-2/8	18-4/8	19-3/8	3	4	Trinity County	CA	Dennis Alan Betts	1980	108
106-2/8	17-1/8	16-3/8	13-6/8	5	4	Lewis County	WA	Mike Mussman	1984	109
106-1/8	19-4/8	19-0/8	12-7/8	3	4	Trinity County	CA	Mike Lindley	1981	110
105-7/8	17-4/8	17-6/8	17-7/8	4	5	Trinity County	CA	Chuck Adams	1982	111
105-3/8	17-3/8	17-3/8	15-5/8	3	4	Coos County	OR	Gary Scorby	1971	112
105-1/8	18-6/8	19-2/8	15-7/8	3	3	Stanislaus County	CA	Harold Arnold	1970	113
105-0/8	23-3/8	22-4/8	18-1/8	7	4	Douglas County	OR	Jerry R. DeLoach	1975	114
104-6/8	18-1/8	18-1/8	18-4/8	3	3	San Mateo County	CA	John Grochowski	1985	115
104-0/8	18-6/8	21-6/8	15-1/8	5	5	Trinity County	CA	Chuck Adams	1982	116
103-5/8	17-7/8	18-3/8	15-5/8	3	3	Linn County	OR	Gary Burns	1981	117
103-2/8	16-7/8	16-6/8	17-0/8	3	4	Sonoma County	CA	Arnie Dado	1986	118
103-0/8	15-5/8	15-0/8	14-0/8	5	5	Mendocino County	CA	Gregg L. Welch	1982	119
102-6/8	17-4/8	17-4/8	17-4/8	3	3	Polk County	OR	Robert L. Ball	1975	120
102-5/8	16-7/8	16-6/8	14-5/8	4	4	Cline Mountain	OR	Steve L. Stilwell	1976	121
102-2/8	17-7/8	16-5/8	12-0/8	3	4	Clackamas County	OR	A. Corey Heath	1980	122
102-0/8	17-2/8	17-0/8	13-6/8	4	4	Jackson County	OR	George Miller	1966	123
101-6/8	20-4/8	19-2/8	16-0/8	4	7	Douglas County	OR	Thomas E. Tipton	1983	124
101-3/8	17-0/8	17-4/8	15-3/8	4	3	Rogue River	OR	Dr. G. Scott Jennings	1959	125

COLUMBIAN BLACKTAIL DEER

(continued)   Minimum Score 90

Score	Length of Main Beam R	L	Inside Spread	Number of Points R	L	Area	State/ Province	Hunter's Name	Date	Rank
100-6/8	15-6/8	15-5/8	15-4/8	4	5	Parker Mountain	OR	Dr. George Miller	1964	126
99-6/8	20-6/8	20-0/8	14-0/8	2	2	Long Island	WA	Robert A. Brown	1965	127
99-3/8	17-5/8	18-0/8	15-1/8	3	3	Siskiyou County	CA	Dave S. Semple	1984	128
99-0/8	16-3/8	16-5/8	14-0/8	5	5	Logsden	OR	Charles M. Roeser	1974	129
99-0/8	21-2/8	19-7/8	15-6/8	4	5	Santa Clara County	CA	Mike Walker	1979	129
99-0/8	16-6/8	16-6/8	12-6/8	4	4	Mendocino County	CA	Russell L. Browning	1983	129
99-0/8	17-0/8	16-3/8	13-2/8	4	4	Contra Costa County	CA	Richard L. Westervelt	1985	129
98-7/8	20-2/8	19-4/8	14-1/8	3	2	Long Island	WA	William V. Mishler	1968	133
98-3/8	16-1/8	16-3/8	14-3/8	4	4	Sonoma County	CA	Ray Torrey	1967	134
98-1/8	16-0/8	16-3/8	12-7/8	4	4	Rogue Unit	OR	Barbara Richardson	1964	135
98-0/8	19-7/8	19-6/8	14-6/8	4	2	Long Island	WA	Morris Wolters	1967	136
97-7/8	16-3/8	15-5/8	16-1/8	5	5	Benton County	OR	Harold Stice	1957	137
97-5/8	20-2/8	19-7/8	16-7/8	3	3	Marin County	CA	Mike Taylor	1985	138
97-4/8	18-6/8	18-2/8	18-6/8	3	3	Glacier	WA	Steve Holland	1963	139
97-2/8	16-7/8	17-0/8	12-2/8	4	3	Pacific County	WA	Todd Hubble	1980	140
97-2/8	17-4/8	17-4/8	13-4/8	4	4	King County	WA	Jay E. Tinker	1986	140
97-0/8	16-7/8	16-4/8	12-0/8	4	4	Long Island	WA	Lawrence Rogers	1972	142
96-7/8	17-2/8	17-2/8	14-7/8	4	4	Glenn County	CA	Joe Williams	1977	143
96-4/8	19-1/8	18-4/8	20-0/8	3	3	Marin County	CA	Joe Checchio	1985	144
96-1/8	15-4/8	15-0/8	13-3/8	4	4	Long Island	WA	Lynne Sharp	1965	145
96-0/8	16-0/8	15-7/8	12-6/8	4	4	Soda Springs	OR	Harold Benson	1961	146
95-5/8	17-5/8	15-2/8	14-3/8	5	5	Klamath	CA	Thomas V. Sieverding	1971	147
95-5/8	16-1/8	17-2/8	12-1/8	4	4	Humboldt County	CA	Calvin Farner	1983	147
94-5/8	15-6/8	15-3/8	10-7/8	4	4	Alsea	OR	Raymond E. Root	1970	149
94-4/8	18-0/8	17-5/8	13-2/8	4	3	Mendocino County	CA	Chuck Adams	1983	150
94-3/8	18-0/8	16-2/8	16-5/8	2	4	Parker Mountain	OR	Don Pritchett	1964	151
94-3/8	15-7/8	15-5/8	16-1/8	4	4	Sonoma County	CA	Russell L. Browning	1980	151
94-0/8	16-7/8	18-4/8	12-0/8	4	4	Capitol Forest	WA	C. N. Pickle	1960	153
94-0/8	17-6/8	17-5/8	11-4/8	3	4	Alsea	OR	Edward U. Tobler	1970	153
93-6/8	18-3/8	18-5/8	13-6/8	2	4	Cougar Mountain	WA	Floyd Gregg	1962	155
93-6/8	15-6/8	15-5/8	12-6/8	4	4	Mendocino County	CA	Chuck Adams	1979	155
93-2/8	17-0/8	16-7/8	12-4/8	4	3	Linn County	OR	Joe Mengore	1983	157
93-1/8	16-2/8	17-2/8	17-3/8	3	3	Humboldt County	CA	Monty Clemmer	1986	158
92-3/8	18-0/8	18-2/8	15-1/8	3	2	Mendocino County	CA	Wilfred Willis	1982	159
91-2/8	18-4/8	18-4/8	19-2/8	2	2	Josephine County	OR	Joe White	1986	160
91-1/8	17-1/8	18-0/8	13-1/8	3	3	Benton County	OR	Jim Nielsen	1981	161
90-4/8	14-6/8	14-3/8	12-3/8	4	4	Glacier	WA	Jack Fish	1956	162
90-4/8	16-4/8	16-7/8	15-0/8	2	2	Los Banos	CA	Jim Walton	1980	162
90-2/8	14-5/8	15-1/8	12-0/8	4	4	Long Island	WA	Leonard Bray	1965	164

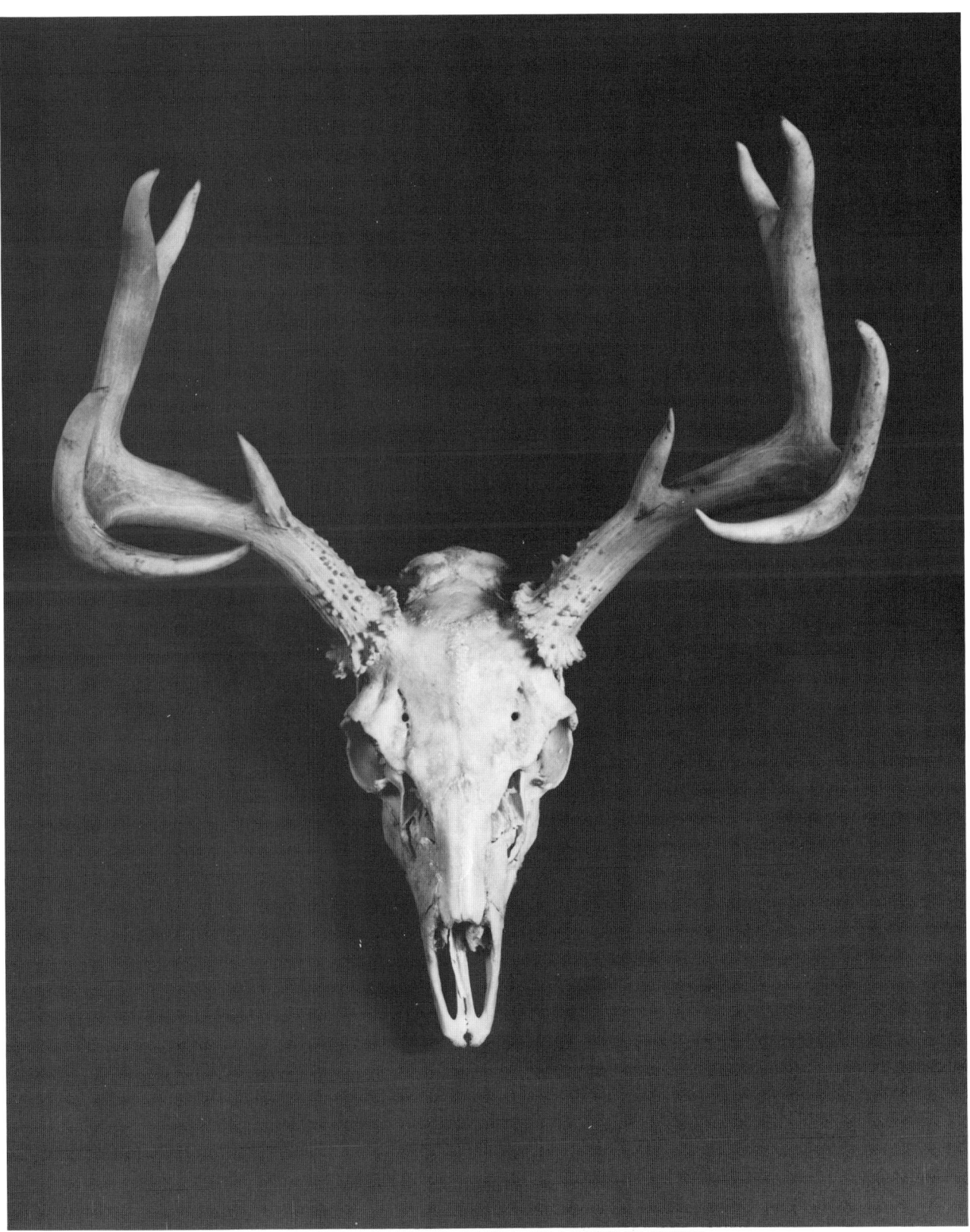

WORLD RECORD SITKA BLACKTAIL DEER
Score: 108 4/8
Kodiak Island, Alaska – 1986
Hunter: Chuck Adams

SITKA BLACKTAIL DEER
Odocoileus hemionus sitkensis

Minimum Score 65

Score	Length of Main Beam R	L	Inside Spread	Number of Points R	L	Area	State/ Province	Hunter's Name	Date	Rank
108-4/8	16-4/8	15-6/8	15-0/8	5	5	Kodiak Island	AK	Chuck Adams	1986	1
107-6/8	17-2/8	16-2/8	14-2/8	5	5	Kodiak Island	AK	Chuck Adams	1986	2
106-4/8	17-3/8	16-6/8	16-5/8	5	6	Kodiak Island	AK	Douglas G. Bonetti	1985	3
102-0/8	18-0/8	18-0/8	16-2/8	5	4	Kodiak Island	AK	John D. "Jack" Frost	1986	4
101-0/8	19-0/8	19-0/8	17-0/8	5	5	Kodiak Island	AK	Gene Coughlin	1984	5
101-0/8	18-1/8	17-7/8	16-4/8	5	4	Kodiak Island	AK	Danny Moore	1986	5
99-4/8	17-4/8	17-7/8	16-0/8	4	5	Kodiak Island	AK	Danny Moore	1984	7
99-0/8	14-1/8	15-5/8	13-4/8	5	5	Kodiak Island	AK	Al Besch	1984	8
98-4/8	16-4/8	14-2/8	14-0/8	4	5	Kodiak Island	AK	Michael L. Nunn	1984	9
98-3/8	14-4/8	17-0/8	17-1/8	5	4	Kodiak Island	AK	Tom Chadwick	1985	10
98-2/8	14-7/8	14-7/8	13-4/8	5	5	Kodiak Island	AK	Philip F. Nuechterlein	1985	11
97-6/8	18-1/8	18-0/8	18-0/8	4	3	Kodiak Island	AK	Patricia A. Stewart	1983	12
97-2/8	15-0/8	13-6/8	13-0/8	5	5	Kodiak Island	AK	Chuck Adams	1986	13
94-7/8	16-7/8	16-7/8	13-1/8	5	6	Kodiak Island	AK	Chuck Adams	1984	14
93-3/8	15-2/8	15-4/8	13-3/8	5	5	Kodiak Island	AK	Herman J. Griese	1982	15
92-0/8	16-5/8	16-0/8	13-4/8	4	4	Kodiak Island	AK	Chuck Adams	1986	16
91-7/8	16-1/8	16-5/8	14-7/8	4	4	Afognak Island	AK	Edward L. Russell	1980	17
91-5/8	14-4/8	15-1/8	12-7/8	5	5	Kodiak Island	AK	Danny Moore	1986	18
91-4/8	14-6/8	14-4/8	13-0/8	5	5	Kodiak Island	AK	Chuck Adams	1986	19
91-2/8	12-4/8	16-2/8	13-2/8	5	4	Kodiak Island	AK	Randy Mannix	1984	20
89-6/8	15-1/8	14-3/8	12-4/8	5	4	Kodiak Island	AK	John Sarvis	1984	21
89-1/8	17-2/8	16-4/8	16-3/8	3	2	Kiliuda Bay	AK	Rick Tollison	1978	22
88-5/8	14-5/8	15-2/8	12-7/8	4	4	Queen Charlotte Islands	BC	Atley Lovelace	1984	23
88-4/8	14-3/8	14-0/8	14-2/8	5	4	Afognak Island	AK	Edward L. Russell	1983	24
86-7/8	15-0/8	14-4/8	14-3/8	4	4	Kodiak Island	AK	Jim Hodson	1985	25
86-6/8	16-2/8	14-7/8	14-2/8	4	4	Kodiak Island	AK	Matt Jones	1985	26
86-3/8	16-1/8	15-5/8	16-3/8	4	3	Admiralty Island	AK	Charles R. Hakari	1983	27
85-3/8	16-3/8	16-0/8	15-5/8	3	3	Afognak Island	AK	Roger Stewart	1980	28
85-2/8	15-4/8	15-0/8	14-0/8	3	4	Afognak Island	AK	Ralph Ertz	1983	29
84-1/8	16-2/8	16-6/8	15-1/8	4	3	Kodiak Island	AK	Ralph Ertz	1984	30
83-7/8	14-6/8	14-5/8	15-7/8	4	4	Kodiak Island	AK	John Sarvis	1985	31
83-2/8	14-4/8	14-0/8	13-2/8	6	6	Afognak Island	AK	Ralph Ertz	1981	32
82-4/8	12-6/8	14-0/8	12-6/8	5	5	Afognak Island	AK	Ralph Ertz	1980	33
82-4/8	14-4/8	15-4/8	14-6/8	3	3	Kodiak Island	AK	Kirk Westervelt	1986	33
82-3/8	14-4/8	13-7/8	14-5/8	4	4	Kodiak Island	AK	Richard L. Westervelt	1986	35
82-0/8	15-4/8	15-2/8	15-4/8	3	3	Montague Island	AK	Ray Uhl	1978	36
81-2/8	15-0/8	11-7/8	13-4/8	4	4	Kodiak Island	AK	Richard L. Westervelt	1986	37
80-1/8	13-2/8	13-1/8	13-1/8	4	4	Kodiak Island	AK	Jim Hodson	1985	38
80-0/8	15-6/8	14-5/8	14-2/8	3	4	Afognak Island	AK	Charlie Kroll	1984	39
78-1/8	14-3/8	15-1/8	12-3/8	3	3	Kodiak Island	AK	Danny Moore	1984	40
77-2/8	15-2/8	15-2/8	13-2/8	3	3	Kodiak Island	AK	Chuck Adams	1984	41
75-6/8	13-5/8	13-7/8	12-0/8	3	4	Afognak Island	AK	H. Richard Long	1984	42
75-2/8	13-5/8	13-1/8	12-6/8	3	4	Kodiak Island	AK	Gary G. Wall	1985	43
73-6/8	13-2/8	13-1/8	13-4/8	3	3	Kodiak Island	AK	Dennis L. Smythe	1980	44
71-4/8	13-1/8	13-0/8	12-0/8	3	3	Kodiak Island	AK	Ralph Ertz	1982	45
71-3/8	13-0/8	12-6/8	10-5/8	3	4	Kodiak Island	AK	Chuck Adams	1984	46
71-2/8	12-4/8	13-2/8	13-6/8	3	4	Kodiak Island	AK	Donald R. Rossiter	1984	47
69-5/8	12-2/8	13-3/8	11-7/8	3	4	Kodiak Island	AK	Kirk Westervelt	1986	48
66-6/8	13-2/8	12-7/8	11-6/8	4	2	Kodiak Island	AK	Roger Stewart	1983	49
66-1/8	13-5/8	12-4/8	13-5/8	3	2	Kodiak Island	AK	Kirk Westervelt	1986	50

WORLD RECORD COUES WHITETAIL DEER
(Typical Antlers)
Score: 106 1/8
Cochise County, Arizona – 1982
Hunter: Harlon Wilson

COUES WHITETAIL DEER *(Typical Antlers)*

Odocoileus virginianus couesi   Minimum Score 60

Score	Length of Main Beam R	L	Inside Spread	Number of Points R	L	Area	State/ Province	Hunter's Name	Date	Rank
106-1/8	17-5/8	18-5/8	14-3/8	5	5	Cochise County	AZ	Harlon Wilson	1982	1
105-7/8	17-5/8	17-2/8	11-7/8	4	6	Pima County	AZ	Harold Boyack	1985	2
104-2/8	18-2/8	17-7/8	15-0/8	4	4	Payson	AZ	Larry Peterson	1978	3
100-6/8	16-6/8	16-3/8	12-6/8	4	4	Graham Mountain	AZ	Hugh H. Hamman	1966	4
100-4/8	17-5/8	16-5/8	12-4/8	4	5	Huachuca Mountains	AZ	Dallas Scherck	1971	5
100-2/8	17-0/8	16-0/8	14-5/8	4	5	Cochise County	AZ	Ray Edwards	1984	6
99-6/8	16-6/8	17-0/8	14-0/8	4	4	Catalina Mountains	AZ	Tracy Gene Hardy	1982	7
98-7/8	15-7/8	15-5/8	14-5/8	4	5	Gila County	AZ	Darryl Kessler	1978	8
98-5/8	13-0/8	13-4/8	12-3/8	6	4	Graham County	AZ	John A. Holcomb	1983	9
98-3/8	17-1/8	17-0/8	13-7/8	4	4	Cochise County	AZ	David Schied	1973	10
96-3/8	16-6/8	17-1/8	15-6/8	6	5	Graham County	AZ	Maurice Holthaus	1984	11
95-5/8	15-7/8	16-2/8	13-5/8	4	4	Santa Cruz County	AZ	Bill Krenz	1984	12
94-1/8	15-0/8	16-0/8	13-6/8	5	4	East Eagle Creek	AZ	John T. Skeen	1975	13
94-1/8	14-3/8	15-2/8	13-3/8	4	4	Cochise County	AZ	Daniel Staples	1981	13
94-0/8	16-6/8	16-1/8	14-0/8	4	4	Greenlee County	AZ	Jack Sartain	1983	15
93-1/8	14-3/8	15-0/8	14-3/8	4	4	Catalina Mountains	AZ	Jerry Muir	1982	16
92-2/8	16-1/8	16-2/8	14-2/8	4	5	Santa Cruz County	AZ	Rowland J. Robinson	1985	17
91-6/8	15-1/8	15-4/8	14-4/8	4	4	Cochise County	AZ	Randy Breland	1981	18
91-2/8	15-2/8	14-6/8	12-2/8	4	4	Santa Cruz County	AZ	Perry Schaal	1983	19
91-0/8	16-2/8	15-5/8	12-6/8	4	4	Gila County	AZ	John Radford	1972	20
90-6/8	17-0/8	17-5/8	14-6/8	4	4	Cochise County	AZ	Richard E. "Dick" Johnson	1986	21
86-1/8	14-7/8	15-6/8	14-3/8	4	3	Pinal County	AZ	Steve E. Allen	1979	22
84-7/8	13-0/8	12-2/8	10-3/8	4	4	Huachuca Mountains	AZ	Dave Rhodes	1976	23
84-1/8	13-4/8	13-7/8	12-5/8	4	4	Four Peaks	AZ	Ed Matteson	1963	24
82-6/8	15-3/8	15-7/8	13-3/8	4	4	Coconino County	AZ	Carl Vance	1973	25
82-5/8	14-3/8	15-2/8	13-1/8	4	4	Gila County	AZ	Mike Mahoney	1976	26
81-6/8	13-1/8	13-1/8	12-0/8	4	4	Pima County	AZ	Jack R. Frazier	1984	27
81-0/8	14-5/8	14-0/8	13-2/8	4	4	Silver City	NM	Bob J. Brown	1960	28
80-6/8	12-4/8	12-1/8	13-0/8	4	4	Graham Mountain	AZ	Bill Cross	1967	29
80-1/8	13-4/8	13-4/8	10-3/8	4	4	Pima County	AZ	Dave Snyder	1983	30
77-7/8	15-3/8	14-7/8	12-5/8	3	3	Pine	AZ	Tom Hashem	1964	31
77-6/8	14-2/8	14-1/8	9-6/8	5	5	Pima County	AZ	Richard Dawe, Jr.	1964	32
77-4/8	14-4/8	13-7/8	10-4/8	4	5	Black Range Mountain	NM	Charles E. Franzoy	1972	33
73-6/8	12-6/8	13-1/8	10-4/8	4	4	Santa Rita Mountains	AZ	Howard Cooper	1980	34
73-6/8	12-2/8	13-5/8	11-2/8	4	3	Rincon Mountains	AZ	William E. Dickinson	1982	34
73-4/8	15-0/8	14-4/8	13-2/8	2	4	Pima County	AZ	Michael L. Henrikson	1979	36
73-2/8	13-0/8	13-0/8	10-6/8	4	4	Pinal Mountain	AZ	Jim Mercer	1958	37
73-0/8	12-2/8	12-7/8	13-4/8	5	4	Animas Mountains	NM	Larry Behrends	1969	38
72-4/8	11-6/8	11-6/8	11-4/8	4	4	Young	AZ	Gary H. Behrends	1969	39
71-2/8	13-2/8	12-7/8	13-2/8	4	3	Pima County	AZ	Stephen E. Johnson	1979	40
68-6/8	13-2/8	12-7/8	10-0/8	3	4	Atasco Mountains	AZ	Peter C. Knagge	1978	41
68-6/8	12-5/8	12-7/8	12-0/8	4	4	Cochise County	AZ	Daniel Staples	1980	41
66-4/8	12-3/8	12-4/8	8-6/8	3	3	Pima County	AZ	Larry Rogge	1984	43

WORLD RECORD COUES WHITETAIL DEER
(Non-Typical Antlers)
Score: 112 4/8
Pima County, Arizona – 1984
Hunter: David G. Snyder

COUES WHITETAIL DEER *(Non-Typical Antlers)*

Minimum Score 66

Odocoileus virginianus couesi

Score	Length of Main Beam R	L	Inside Spread	Number of Points R	L	Area	State/ Province	Hunter's Name	Date	Rank
112-4/8	18-4/8	18-6/8	13-2/8	5	5	Pima County	AZ	David G. Snyder	1984	1

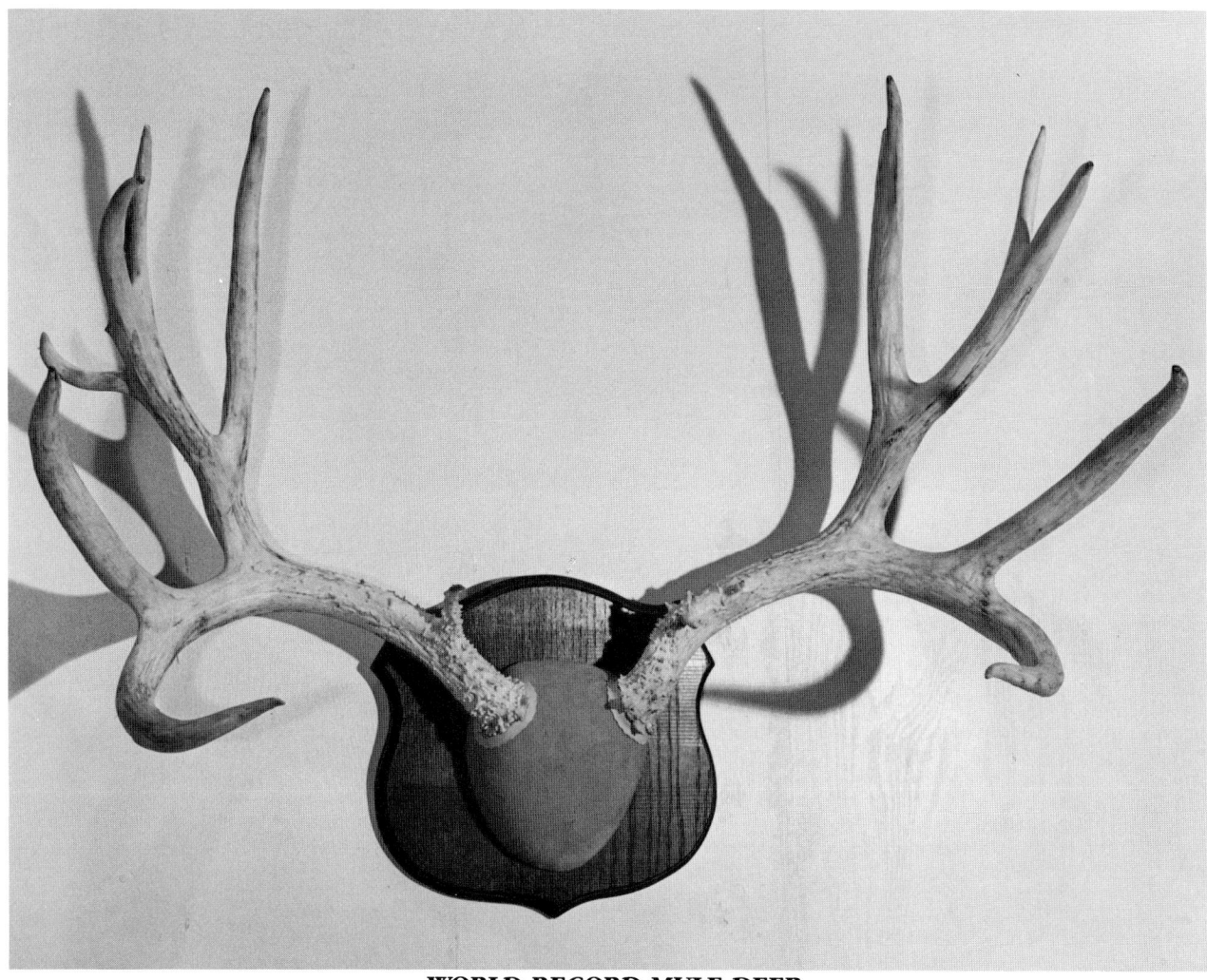

WORLD RECORD MULE DEER
(Typical Antlers)
Score: 201 4/8
White River National Forest, Colorado – 1979
Hunter: Bill Barcus

MULE DEER *(Typical Antlers)*
Odocoileus hemionus hemionus and certain related subspecies

Minimum Score 145

Score	Length of Main Beam R	L	Inside Spread	Number of Points R	L	Area	State/ Province	Hunter's Name	Date	Rank
201-4/8	28-5/8	27-6/8	30-2/8	7	7	White River National Forest	CO	Bill Barcus	1979	1
197-0/8	24-6/8	27-7/8	23-6/8	5	5	Guffy	CO	Ronald E. Sniff	1969	2
196-1/8	24-2/8	22-4/8	21-4/8	6	7	Beaver County	UT	David Snyder	1982	3
194-2/8	28-0/8	26-0/8	32-2/8	7	7	Apache County	AZ	William T. Rose	1985	4
192-7/8	24-6/8	23-3/8	23-0/8	6	5	San Isabel N.F.	CO	Donald D. Garrison	1972	5
192-1/8	25-3/8	26-2/8	23-0/8	6	5	Lemhi County	ID	Mike Nelson	1978	6
192-0/8	25-6/8	26-4/8	22-0/8	7	5	Uncompahgre Plateau	CO	Donald Click	1973	7
190-6/8	27-4/8	27-4/8	25-7/8	9	8	Grand Junction	CO	Allen Personious	1976	8
190-5/8	26-2/8	26-2/8	22-4/8	7	8	Teller County	CO	Dan Mersman	1982	9
190-0/8	25-1/8	23-4/8	24-4/8	5	5	Utah County	UT	John Edwards	1967	10
189-3/8	27-0/8	27-0/8	24-1/8	6	5	Cedar Mountain	UT	Ken Davis	1963	11
189-1/8	23-6/8	23-7/8	23-6/8	5	8	Chelan County	WA	R. Early/D. Davies, Jr.	1983	12
188-7/8	25-2/8	26-3/8	21-1/8	6	6	Settlement Canyon	UT	Derald R. Evans	1965	13
188-6/8	24-5/8	24-6/8	21-2/8	5	5	De Beque	CO	Bob Jensen	1974	14
188-4/8	25-6/8	26-6/8	24-3/8	6	5	Abbey	SAS	Barry Minor	1979	15
188-2/8	24-3/8	24-4/8	23-2/8	6	6	De Beque	CO	John Lamicq, Jr.	1967	16
187-7/8	23-7/8	24-7/8	22-5/8	5	6	Duck Creek	UT	Gerald Clark	1966	17
187-6/8	24-4/8	23-5/8	25-6/8	5	6	Montezuma County	CO	Al Newkirk	1983	18
187-5/8	23-2/8	22-5/8	18-3/8	5	5	Dinosaur	CO	Leonard Jefferson	1971	19
187-0/8	20-1/8	22-1/8	22-0/8	6	5	Boise County	ID	Ricky D. Addison	1984	20
186-7/8	25-3/8	25-0/8	20-1/8	5	6	Eagle County	CO	Dr. J. D. Jones	1963	21
186-7/8	26-3/8	26-0/8	22-0/8	6	8	Uncompahgre Plateau	CO	Jerry Click	1973	21
186-6/8	24-5/8	25-2/8	24-2/8	5	5	Cassia County	ID	Pat Miller	1965	23
186-5/8	25-1/8	25-6/8	19-2/8	5	6	Elbert County	CO	Loren Dellinger	1984	24
186-2/8	24-2/8	23-1/8	24-4/8	5	5	White River N.F.	CO	Walt Seville	1977	25
186-1/8	24-1/8	24-0/8	21-3/8	5	5	Cassia County	ID	Bill Shockey	1965	26
186-0/8	25-3/8	24-0/8	25-4/8	5	5	Humboldt County	NV	Tim Bray	1984	27
185-6/8	24-1/8	24-4/8	24-0/8	5	5	Imperial County	CA	Gilbert Clement	1982	28
185-4/8	22-0/8	22-3/8	20-4/8	5	5	Williams	AZ	Ronald Hollamon	1978	29
185-2/8	26-4/8	26-0/8	27-4/8	6	9	Gunnison	CO	Don E. Lampert	1973	30
184-7/8	26-0/8	26-2/8	26-3/8	5	6	Poudre Canyon	CO	Don Lampert	1969	31
184-7/8	25-7/8	25-4/8	21-7/8	5	5	Mesa County	CO	James L. Peterson	1983	31
184-5/8	23-0/8	23-2/8	23-3/8	5	5	Mesa County	CO	David L. Myers	1976	33
184-1/8	24-2/8	25-4/8	27-0/8	7	6	Glade Park	CO	Art Cook	1962	34
184-1/8	24-3/8	24-6/8	24-6/8	5	6	Delta County	CO	Scott Kolb	1963	34
184-1/8	27-5/8	27-0/8	25-3/8	5	4	Albuquerque	NM	Gregory A. Gwash	1970	34
184-0/8	24-1/8	25-1/8	24-2/8	5	6	Boise County	ID	Joseph Greenley	1984	37
183-7/8	25-0/8	24-3/8	23-7/8	5	5	Blue Mountain	CO	Joel Hogan	1966	38
183-6/8	26-4/8	27-3/8	27-0/8	5	4	Parowan Canyon	UT	Ted Garrett	1963	39
183-5/8	26-6/8	25-7/8	25-5/8	5	5	Manti	UT	Weldon Noland	1965	40
183-5/8	20-2/8	19-3/8	20-2/8	6	6	Rio Arriba County	NM	Billy Terrazas	1985	40
183-3/8	25-7/8	26-1/8	22-4/8	7	5	Fish Lake	UT	Kyle Johnson	1970	42
183-2/8	25-5/8	26-5/8	22-7/8	6	9	Strawberry	UT	Blake Spenser	1963	43
183-1/8	25-0/8	25-1/8	24-5/8	5	6	White Pine County	NV	Robert Price	1986	44
183-0/8	25-1/8	25-5/8	25-2/8	5	6	Lincoln County	MT	John C. Bartlett	1982	45
182-7/8	23-3/8	22-0/8	21-7/8	5	5	Dia Creek Road	ID	Neil Dursteler	1967	46
182-7/8	24-4/8	25-1/8	24-1/8	5	5	Cache County	UT	Robert Bronson	1985	46
182-6/8	22-0/8	22-2/8	20-2/8	5	7	Nason Creek	WA	Glenn St. Charles	1959	48
182-5/8	26-4/8	25-4/8	21-5/8	5	5	Lincoln County	WY	Laei Eddins	1978	49
182-4/8	25-2/8	24-2/8	25-0/8	5	5	Humbolt County	NV	George Rajnus	1985	50
182-4/8	24-5/8	24-3/8	21-4/8	5	5	Mesa County	CO	Charles C. Perry	1985	50
182-4/8	25-0/8	25-5/8	21-2/8	5	5	Mesa County,	CO	David M. Gant	1986	50
182-2/8	25-6/8	24-2/8	25-2/8	6	5	S. Grand Mesa	CO	Robert C. Dawson	1974	53
181-5/8	24-3/8	24-0/8	21-5/8	5	5	Wakely	CO	Lynn Grace	1964	54
181-3/8	26-0/8	26-5/8	26-3/8	5	5	Uncompahgre Plateau	CO	John Lamb	1981	55
181-2/8	22-1/8	22-6/8	20-5/8	5	6	Ft. Collins	CO	Wayne Eberhard	1972	56
181-1/8	24-3/8	25-4/8	19-3/8	6	6	LaGrande	OR	Thomas Mussatto	1968	57
181-0/8	24-7/8	22-7/8	23-0/8	6	6	Chama	NM	Charles Tapia	1965	58
181-0/8	21-7/8	21-1/8	22-6/8	5	5	Arbon Valley	ID	Austin Cummins	1970	58
180-7/8	20-7/8	22-5/8	21-7/8	6	5	Uinta County	WY	Joseph Gilmore	1978	60
180-7/8	25-2/8	24-7/8	22-7/8	5	5	Washoe County	NV	Donald E. Callen	1984	60
180-4/8	24-1/8	25-1/8	21-6/8	4	4	Gateway	CO	Jack Kruckenburg	1958	62
180-4/8	24-0/8	24-7/8	21-0/8	6	6	Fremont County	ID	Steven M. Jones	1979	62

MULE DEER *(Typical Antlers)*

(continued)   Minimum Score 145

Score	Length of Main Beam R	L	Inside Spread	Number of Points R	L	Area	State/ Province	Hunter's Name	Date	Rank
180-4/8	24-6/8	25-3/8	24-0/8	6	5	Ravalli County	MT	Gary Habeck	1984	62
180-3/8	23-6/8	23-3/8	24-7/8	5	5	Little Lost River	ID	Richard A. Southwell	1980	65
180-3/8	24-4/8	23-3/8	28-4/8	6	5	Caribou County	ID	Coby Tigert	1983	65
180-2/8	24-4/8	23-2/8	25-6/8	5	5	Douglas Pass	CO	Henry Wichers	1967	67
180-2/8	23-1/8	24-0/8	23-2/8	5	5	Lincoln County	NV	Fred B. Allen III	1974	67
180-2/8	24-1/8	23-7/8	20-6/8	5	5	Natrona County	WY	Chuck Webster	1979	67
180-2/8	23-2/8	24-2/8	24-0/8	5	5	Onion Lake	NV	Robert A. Ashby	1980	67
180-1/8	22-0/8	22-4/8	19-3/8	5	5	Dawson County	MT	Gordon M. Quilling	1957	71
179-4/8	24-3/8	23-0/8	21-4/8	5	8	Ada County	ID	Vance Gardner	1971	72
179-4/8	22-2/8	24-3/8	19-6/8	5	5	Garfield County	CO	Ed Downard	1984	72
179-2/8	24-5/8	24-7/8	25-7/8	8	5	Rifle	CO	Michael R. Allen	1967	74
179-0/8	23-5/8	24-4/8	22-4/8	5	5	Elko County	NV	Jerry Vega	1986	75
178-7/8	26-6/8	24-6/8	27-6/8	5	5	Alamosa	CO	Joseph Mazurek, Jr.	1978	76
178-6/8	24-2/8	24-1/8	24-6/8	5	4	Illinois Creek Drainage	IL	Gordon E. Scott	1964	77
178-5/8	23-6/8	23-4/8	24-1/8	5	5	Lake City	CO	Sam E. Adkins	1978	78
178-4/8	24-6/8	25-0/8	23-1/8	5	5	Boges	MT	R. C. Tucker	1958	79
178-3/8	28-3/8	27-3/8	28-3/8	5	5	Garden City	KS	Larry Ochs	1968	80
178-3/8	24-0/8	25-5/8	27-5/8	5	5	Mores Creek	ID	Benton K. Wetzel	1970	80
178-0/8	23-4/8	23-7/8	23-4/8	5	6	Hart Mountain	OR	Ronald C. Halpin	1966	82
178-0/8	24-2/8	23-2/8	24-7/8	6	6	Sheep Creek	CO	Rex Schmude	1968	82
178-0/8	25-0/8	24-4/8	24-6/8	7	6	Lincoln County	MT	Jerry Brown	1986	82
177-7/8	23-2/8	23-7/8	23-2/8	4	4	Steamboat Springs	CO	Richard M. Hansen	1964	85
177-7/8	26-1/8	26-2/8	23-1/8	4	4	Gunnison County	CO	Glen Farnum	1978	85
177-7/8	23-6/8	23-0/8	19-3/8	6	6	Mesa County	CO	John D Wood	1984	85
177-6/8	24-4/8	23-6/8	24-6/8	5	5	Garfield County	CO	Larry Santek	1985	88
177-4/8	25-6/8	26-0/8	22-4/8	5	4	Lander	WY	Walter Millhollin	1960	89
177-4/8	23-0/8	22-5/8	22-2/8	5	5	Malad	ID	J. L. Shelton	1980	89
177-2/8	21-5/8	23-2/8	20-6/8	6	5	Malheur County	OR	Bennie B. Simpson	1986	91
177-1/8	23-7/8	24-4/8	22-0/8	4	6	Meagher County	MT	Mike Weitz	1981	92
177-0/8	24-4/8	25-5/8	21-4/8	7	5	Douglas Pass	CO	Steve U'Selis	1967	93
177-0/8	19-1/8	19-4/8	21-4/8	5	6	Jemez	NM	D. J. Heckler, Jr.	1969	93
176-6/8	26-3/8	25-1/8	26-0/8	4	5	Yuma County	CO	Mark Sievers	1985	95
176-4/8	23-4/8	23-5/8	20-0/8	5	5	Ada County	ID	Edward Keeton	1983	96
176-2/8	22-1/8	24-0/8	20-4/8	5	6	North Platte	NE	M. R. Buchtel	1959	97
176-2/8	22-0/8	23-6/8	24-4/8	6	5	White Pine County	NV	Dr. Donald Wicher	1961	97
176-2/8	25-5/8	23-6/8	26-6/8	5	5	Glade Park	CO	Dr. Tom Postel	1975	97
176-1/8	24-3/8	24-3/8	23-1/8	7	6	Duchesne County	UT	M.H. "Bill" Wilkinson, Jr.	1964	100
176-0/8	23-6/8	23-7/8	21-2/8	6	5	Monticello	UT	Charles Farmer	1964	101
176-0/8	22-3/8	21-5/8	18-6/8	5	5	Blue Ridge	AZ	Tom Dennis	1972	101
176-0/8	24-7/8	24-7/8	23-6/8	5	6	Cassia County	ID	Earl Peterson	1981	101
175-6/8	22-6/8	22-5/8	22-6/8	5	5	Uintah County	UT	Merlin L. Killpack	1957	104
175-6/8	24-3/8	25-0/8	22-1/8	4	6	Larimer County	CO	Kevin Vinzant	1986	104
175-5/8	23-6/8	25-0/8	21-1/8	4	4	Grant County	OR	Larry Saunders	1985	106
175-3/8	21-5/8	23-1/8	19-5/8	6	7	Park County	CO	Marvin Clyncke	1981	107
175-3/8	24-4/8	24-0/8	23-1/8	5	5	Billings County	ND	Joe Kytoichuk	1983	107
175-2/8	24-1/8	24-4/8	24-4/8	7	6	Huntington Canyon	UT	Ron Myers	1958	109
175-2/8	24-6/8	25-3/8	23-6/8	6	7	Garfield County	CO	Robert Pitt	1978	109
175-1/8	21-7/8	22-2/8	19-7/8	4	4	Lincoln County	NV	Fred B. Allen III	1975	111
175-1/8	24-1/8	25-4/8	21-5/8	7	8	Delta County	CO	Michael Sturm	1977	111
175-1/8	21-4/8	22-7/8	21-6/8	6	6	Millard County	UT	Jason Woodland	1985	111
174-7/8	23-7/8	23-7/8	18-3/8	5	6	Delta	CO	Paul Dickson	1969	114
174-6/8	24-4/8	24-4/8	25-4/8	6	6	Grand Mesa	CO	Joe Egner	1965	115
174-6/8	26-2/8	26-0/8	26-2/8	5	5	Hart Mountain	OR	Gene Lyons	1969	115
174-6/8	24-0/8	20-5/8	21-2/8	5	6	Rifle	CO	Jewell Petz	1970	115
174-6/8	26-1/8	25-1/8	24-2/8	5	5	San Juan County	CO	Robert C. Dawson	1978	115
174-5/8	25-0/8	25-0/8	23-1/8	4	4	Craig	CO	Roland C. Gravenkemper	1961	119
174-5/8	23-6/8	22-6/8	19-4/8	6	6	Monroe Mountain	UT	Kenneth L. Shirley	1968	119
174-5/8	24-6/8	27-1/8	27-5/8	5	5	Sawlog Creek	KS	Merle Schulte	1974	119
174-4/8	22-5/8	21-7/8	23-0/8	5	5	Gallatin County	MT	Bob Savage	1970	122
174-4/8	24-3/8	24-1/8	22-6/8	4	5	Mesa County	CO	Jay Verzuh	1983	122
174-3/8	21-0/8	23-7/8	23-1/8	6	5	Pima County	AZ	Robert A. Edgar	1982	124
174-2/8	23-3/8	23-3/8	26-2/8	5	6	Logan County	KS	Thomas Standard	1967	125
174-2/8	22-7/8	22-6/8	21-2/8	5	5	Natrona County	WY	Pat McAteer	1982	125

MULE DEER *(Typical Antlers)*

Minimum Score 145

Score	Length of Main Beam R	L	Inside Spread	Number of Points R	L	Area	State/ Province	Hunter's Name	Date	Rank
174-0/8	25-0/8	25-1/8	20-6/8	5	5	Ravalli County	MT	John Schulz	1976	127
174-0/8	26-0/8	23-5/8	26-4/8	6	5	Grand Junction	CO	Douglas D. Watts	1976	127
173-7/8	25-4/8	25-4/8	21-0/8	5	5	Roan Creek	CO	Danny C. Lloyd	1969	129
173-7/8	24-2/8	24-1/8	22-6/8	7	6	Vail	CO	Edward L. Berlier	1970	129
173-7/8	25-0/8	24-5/8	23-5/8	7	7	Okotoks	ALB	Dave Demeter	1981	129
173-6/8	25-3/8	24-4/8	23-5/8	7	6	Fish Lake	UT	Morris Stuart	1972	132
173-6/8	23-6/8	24-0/8	20-4/8	6	5	Boulder County	CO	Floyd Sullivan	1982	132
173-5/8	24-6/8	24-7/8	23-7/8	5	5	Morton County	ND	Pat Sullivan	1957	134
173-5/8	25-1/8	25-5/8	25-2/8	7	5	Tucson Mountains	AZ	Joe Nochta	1959	134
173-5/8	21-4/8	21-1/8	21-0/8	6	7	Cottonwood Creek	CO	Lee Rowe	1966	134
173-4/8	22-1/8	22-1/8	20-4/8	6	7	Ada County	ID	David D. Howard	1971	137
173-4/8	23-5/8	24-4/8	21-0/8	4	6	De Beque	CO	G. Fred Asbell	1974	137
173-4/8	21-5/8	20-4/8	21-2/8	5	5	Montrose	CO	Chip Greene	1978	137
173-3/8	23-0/8	23-5/8	23-5/8	5	5	Fry Canyon	UT	Robert J. Shumway	1969	140
173-3/8	21-5/8	22-6/8	22-0/8	6	5	Caribou County	ID	Jim Walton	1983	140
173-2/8	22-6/8	23-1/8	22-6/8	6	6	Beaver Mountain	UT	George Kendall	1959	142
173-2/8	25-3/8	25-2/8	26-0/8	4	4	Uintah County	UT	Hal Wallentine	1962	142
173-2/8	25-6/8	25-1/8	22-4/8	5	5	Cow Canyon	CO	Jack Acree	1969	142
173-2/8	24-0/8	24-0/8	21-4/8	5	7	Sandia Mountains	NM	Rolland Hanna	1972	142
173-2/8	25-1/8	24-3/8	24-3/8	6	5	Carbon County	UT	Demar Guymon	1982	142
173-2/8	21-4/8	22-0/8	22-4/8	6	5	Humboldt County	NV	Joel C. Lenz	1984	142
173-1/8	26-3/8	25-0/8	21-3/8	5	5	Coconino County	AZ	H. H. Harter	1961	148
173-1/8	23-3/8	24-1/8	20-5/8	5	5	Ryan Peak	ID	Paul Beesley	1976	148
173-1/8	21-5/8	22-1/8	23-7/8	5	5	Rifle	CO	Norman L. Richerson	1978	148
173-1/8	22-1/8	22-5/8	21-6/8	5	6	Bear Lake County	ID	Steven A. Dewey	1985	148
173-0/8	26-6/8	26-5/8	23-5/8	6	6	Edmonton	ALB	Brian Berrecloth	1981	152
173-0/8	22-2/8	22-2/8	18-2/8	5	5	Caribou County	ID	Larry Jaeger	1985	152
172-7/8	23-4/8	24-0/8	24-1/8	5	5	Cimmaron	KS	Bob Barnes	1966	154
172-7/8	23-3/8	23-7/8	24-5/8	5	5	San Juan County	UT	Robert G. Hester	1972	154
172-7/8	22-6/8	22-2/8	20-2/8	6	5	Boise County	ID	Marlin Tullis	1982	154
172-6/8	28-7/8	26-3/8	28-7/8	6	6	Jicarilla Reservation	NM	Kerino H. Revel	1968	157
172-6/8	21-7/8	22-4/8	19-4/8	5	4	Ada County	ID	Ronald B. Jones	1971	157
172-6/8	23-4/8 .	24-0/8	20-7/8	7	5	Blanding	UT	Harold Boyack	1975	157
172-6/8	22-3/8	23-0/8	20-6/8	4	5	Mable Lake	BC	Mark Siegmueller	1984	157
172-5/8	22-4/8	24-1/8	24-7/8	5	5	Kaibab Forest	AZ	Jack Richards	1958	161
172-5/8	23-6/8	24-2/8	22-3/8	5	5	Bernalillo County	NM	Noble Sinclair	1982	161
172-4/8	24-3/8	22-7/8	24-3/8	6	5	Malheur Area	OR	Carl R. Stone	1957	163
172-4/8	25-3/8	25-4/8	24-2/8	5	5	Owyhee County	ID	Don Rosenvall	1961	163
172-4/8	25-6/8	23-6/8	20-3/8	5	5	Chelan County	WA	Timothy E Pflugh	1984	163
172-4/8	25-4/8	25-7/8	22-2/8	6	6	Mesa County	CO	DeWayne Young	1986	163
172-3/8	23-3/8	22-6/8	21-6/8	5	7	Garfield County	CO	Kenneth Rapp	1974	167
172-3/8	22-0/8	22-0/8	20-3/8	5	5	Ouray County	CO	Don Castrup	1975	167
172-3/8	25-3/8	25-4/8	23-0/8	6	6	Shasta County	CA	Russell Browning	1983	167
172-3/8	24-5/8	24-1/8	23-0/8	5	6	Norton County	KS	Greg J. McCall	1985	167
172-2/8	24-4/8	25-3/8	21-0/8	6	7	Rock Creek	CO	Louis Prestridge	1961	171
172-2/8	26-0/8	26-0/8	25-6/8	5	5	Soldier Summit	UT	Bill Dean	1965	171
172-2/8	22-6/8	23-6/8	28-6/8	6	6	Tucson Mountain	AZ	Sherwin Lipsitz	1977	171
172-2/8	25-2/8	25-0/8	25-7/8	6	5	Dolores County	CO	Hulen D. McEntire	1977	171
172-2/8	25-5/8	23-0/8	28-2/8	5	5	Elbert County	CO	Robert D. Olivier	1981	171
172-1/8	24-1/8	24-6/8	24-5/8	5	5	Monte Vista	CO	Marvin Tompkins	1960	176
172-1/8	22-3/8	22-3/8	18-1/8	4	4	Hart Mountain	OR	Ralph Hoover	1964	176
172-1/8	24-0/8	24-4/8	23-7/8	5	6	Sevier County	UT	Bob Covington	1965	176
172-1/8	21-1/8	22-2/8	20-7/8	5	5	Saguache County	CO	Rick Duggan	1984	176
172-0/8	26-1/8	26-3/8	26-1/8	4	5	Baker County	OR	James D. Hanley	1960	180
171-7/8	26-4/8	24-5/8	24-5/8	4	5	Lancer	SAS	Del Erickson	1976	181
171-7/8	20-3/8	20-5/8	17-7/8	5	5	Larimer County	CO	Mike Kolano	1985	181
171-6/8	23-0/8	22-7/8	22-2/8	5	5	Rawlins	WY	Steve Parker	1974	183
171-6/8	24-7/8	25-4/8	21-6/8	5	6	Delta County	CO	Louis A. Brunett	1983	183
171-6/8	23-7/8	22-5/8	24-4/8	5	5	Montrose County	CO	Greg Blackburn	1986	183
171-5/8	24-3/8	24-3/8	23-2/8	6	5	Harney County	OR	Chuck Warner	1977	186
171-5/8	25-4/8	25-4/8	26-7/8	6	5	Carbon County	UT	Tom Riebe	1983	186
171-5/8	23-5/8	24-0/8	19-1/8	4	5	Sweetwater County	WY	Keith Dana	1983	186
171-4/8	24-4/8	24-3/8	21-2/8	5	5	Medina	ND	Harold Hugelen	1977	189

MULE DEER *(Typical Antlers)*

(continued)   Minimum Score 145

Score	Length of Main Beam R	L	Inside Spread	Number of Points R	L	Area	State/ Province	Hunter's Name	Date	Rank
171-4/8	23-0/8	22-6/8	22-3/8	6	5	Clark County	KS	Dan Fenton	1980	189
171-3/8	23-4/8	23-5/8	22-5/8	6	5	Ravalli County	MT	Joe Wandstrath	1980	191
171-2/8	23-2/8	23-6/8	20-2/8	4	5	Weber River	UT	Kent Garfield	1959	192
171-2/8	24-0/8	23-7/8	19-2/8	5	5	Richland County	MT	Dennis Engle	1966	192
171-2/8	21-5/8	22-0/8	16-2/8	5	6	Clark	CO	Joe Mucka	1975	192
171-2/8	22-7/8	21-6/8	23-3/8	8	8	Teton County	MT	James Dean	1977	192
171-1/8	28-0/8	26-4/8	22-4/8	8	7	Wolf Creek	UT	Frank Snyder	1959	196
171-1/8	25-4/8	25-3/8	24-7/8	7	6	Millard County	UT	Shirley B. Pace	1962	196
171-1/8	23-3/8	23-2/8	22-7/8	5	5	Lavan	UT	Farren Anderson	1964	196
171-1/8	20-7/8	22-7/8	22-2/8	6	7	Baxter Pass, Book Cliffs	CO	Curtis Bateman	1983	196
171-1/8	22-7/8	23-2/8	21-5/8	5	5	Garden County	NE	Monte Shaul	1985	196
170-7/8	21-1/8	22-7/8	19-3/8	4	4	Beaver	UT	Richard L. Anderson	1960	201
170-7/8	23-4/8	22-1/8	19-6/8	6	5	Uncompahgre N.F.	CO	Allen G. Hughes	1974	201
170-6/8	22-7/8	22-4/8	22-6/8	5	6	Nason Creek	WA	Gerald Weiss	1967	203
170-6/8	25-2/8	24-5/8	25-0/8	5	5	Wilcox Ranch	UT	Eugene Damron	1974	203
170-5/8	21-5/8	22-2/8	24-5/8	4	5	Gateway	CO	Floyd Kendall	1966	205
170-5/8	24-3/8	24-2/8	27-2/8	5	6	Garfield County	CO	Don Mayen	1966	205
170-5/8	24-7/8	25-6/8	19-7/8	5	6	Garfield County	CO	Robert H. Pitt	1971	205
170-4/8	23-2/8	23-0/8	22-0/8	5	5	Rawlins	WY	James E. Lawrence	1971	208
170-4/8	21-1/8	21-5/8	20-1/8	6	5	Humboldt County	NV	Vic Christison	1982	208
170-3/8	23-6/8	24-5/8	19-7/8	5	5	Chelan County	WA	Dave Johnson	1977	210
170-3/8	21-0/8	21-0/8	20-0/8	5	6	Marney County	OR	Chuck Warner	1979	210
170-3/8	24-5/8	25-5/8	26-5/8	5	5	Chaffee County	CO	Bruce Fish	1981	210
170-2/8	24-7/8	23-7/8	24-2/8	6	6	Amidon	ND	Jim Peters	1954	213
170-2/8	23-1/8	23-1/8	20-1/8	5	7	Fishlake National Forest	UT	Stan Rock	1961	213
170-2/8	23-0/8	23-3/8	20-1/8	7	5	Jicarilla Reservation	NM	Robert H. Keadle	1966	213
170-2/8	21-3/8	20-4/8	20-4/8	7	7	McKenzie County	ND	Don Davidson	1982	213
170-1/8	23-3/8	24-0/8	19-7/8	5	5	Gray County	KS	Dick Masters	1968	217
170-0/8	22-4/8	23-0/8	20-6/8	4	5	Routt National Forest	CO	Robert Syvertson, Jr.	1975	218
170-0/8	23-5/8	22-7/8	19-7/8	5	6	John Day	OR	Timothy D. Palmore	1976	218
169-6/8	23-0/8	23-3/8	23-0/8	5	5	Rifle	CO	C. W. Gilbreath	1967	220
169-6/8	20-7/8	19-4/8	21-4/8	5	5	Moores Creek	ID	Jim Spearman	1970	220
169-6/8	25-0/8	23-0/8	22-2/8	4	4	Platte County	WY	Jerry Bowen	1976	220
169-6/8	22-0/8	23-0/8	22-2/8	5	5	Elbert County	CO	Mike Amendt	1981	220
169-5/8	23-3/8	22-2/8	23-6/8	7	7	Sierrita Mountains	AZ	James M. Fry	1975	224
169-5/8	21-6/8	23-3/8	25-2/8	5	6	Uncompahgre N.F.	CO	Vito Benedetto	1976	224
169-5/8	23-3/8	23-7/8	24-2/8	5	6	Uncompahgre N.F.	CO	Robert Meyler IV	1976	224
169-5/8	24-3/8	24-3/8	22-0/8	5	7	Lincoln County	MT	Harold Leslie	1980	224
169-5/8	26-0/8	25-5/8	19-5/8	9	8	Garfield County	CO	Jay A. Keeler	1984	224
169-3/8	21-4/8	22-3/8	19-5/8	5	5	McKimly County	NM	Hayden Lambson	1979	229
169-3/8	20-4/8	22-3/8	22-3/8	5	5	Elmore County	ID	Steve Bresnahan	1980	229
169-3/8	22-3/8	22-0/8	19-3/8	5	5	Box Elder County	UT	Bob Doutre	1981	229
169-2/8	22-3/8	21-6/8	23-4/8	6	5	Nassin Ridge	WA	Larry Lockhart	1966	232
169-2/8	22-7/8	21-5/8	24-4/8	5	5	Bernalillo County	NM	Dr. E. J. Bowser	1971	232
169-1/8	24-2/8	23-4/8	21-1/8	7	6	Manti-LaSal Range	UT	Dean Wolf	1970	234
169-0/8	22-0/8	21-5/8	20-0/8	5	4	Raton	NM	Gary Ginther	1973	235
169-0/8	23-5/8	24-6/8	22-6/8	5	5	Howard	CO	Bill W. Canterbury	1975	235
169-0/8	23-2/8	24-6/8	24-3/8	6	5	Blanding	UT	Harold Boyack	1978	235
168-7/8	23-3/8	22-7/8	24-3/8	4	5	Caribou County	ID	Chet Hopkins	1968	238
168-7/8	21-6/8	24-3/8	22-7/8	5	6	Park County	CO	Jim Johnson	1980	238
168-7/8	21-3/8	22-3/8	21-5/8	5	5	Union County	OR	Jerry W. Simmons	1982	238
168-6/8	23-1/8	24-2/8	20-6/8	5	4	Sumptor	OR	Joe Williamsen	1959	241
168-6/8	24-7/8	24-3/8	23-4/8	5	5	Little Belt Mountains	MT	James Ployhar	1969	241
168-6/8	21-5/8	21-614	17-6/8	6	5	Darby	MT	Bob Brill	1977	241
168-6/8	20-5/8	19-0/8	19-2/8	5	6	Umatillo County	OR	Donald E. Durland	1983	241
168-6/8	22-4/8	23-0/8	17-4/8	6	5	Mesa County	CO	J.D. "Butch" Shivers	1985	241
168-4/8	24-6/8	24-7/8	21-6/8	5	5	Elk Ridge	UT	Garland Bray	1970	246
168-3/8	23-5/8	23-3/8	17-5/8	5	5	Nason Creek	WA	George Wells	1960	247
168-3/8	22-7/8	22-0/8	19-6/8	5	6	Creede	CO	Richard Kolish	1961	247
168-3/8	24-1/8	23-2/8	22-1/8	5	6	Eureka County	NV	Joel C. Lenz	1986	247
168-2/8	28-6/8	26-5/8	26-0/8	4	5	Uintah County	UT	S. K. Daniels	1908	250
168-2/8	25-0/8	24-0/8	21-7/8	5	5	Glade Park	CO	Jack Kenyon	1965	250
168-2/8	22-6/8	24-0/8	22-6/8	5	5	Durango	CO	Don Putterbaugh	1966	250

MULE DEER *(Typical Antlers)*

Minimum Score 145   (continued)

Score	Length of Main Beam R	L	Inside Spread	Number of Points R	L	Area	State/ Province	Hunter's Name	Date	Rank
168-2/8	23-4/8	23-5/8	27-2/8	5	5	Uintah	UT	Alvin Sisam	1966	250
168-2/8	22-0/8	22-6/8	21-4/8	5	5	Mesa	CO	Joseph Sverak	1968	250
168-2/8	24-1/8	22-1/8	21-4/8	4	4	Nathrop	CO	Frank A. Morminello	1977	250
168-2/8	25-0/8	24-3/8	20-6/8	5	5	Humboldt County	NV	James A. Dallimore	1983	250
168-2/8	22-0/8	21-4/8	18-6/8	6	5	Caribou County	ID	Gene Keller	1985	250
168-1/8	21-4/8	21-5/8	19-7/8	5	5	Bowen Pass	CO	Lenard Boughton	1968	258
168-1/8	21-7/8	22-5/8	22-7/8	5	5	Weber County	UT	Dennis L. Shirley	1972	258
168-1/8	23-4/8	22-4/8	23-7/8	5	5	Uncompahgre N.F.	CO	Paul R. Holmes	1974	258
168-1/8	21-3/8	22-2/8	19-7/8	6	6	McKenzie County	ND	Craig A. Ross	1983	258
168-0/8	25-3/8	24-3/8	23-0/8	4	6	Uncompahgre N.F.	CO	Dick Gulman	1976	262
168-0/8	24-0/8	22-7/8	23-2/8	5	5	Waterton	CO	Robert Anderson	1980	262
167-7/8	24-2/8	24-0/8	26-3/8	5	5	Saguache County	CO	Pat Schambow	1985	264
167-6/8	21-4/8	20-6/8	18-5/8	5	5	N. Minam Meadows	OR	Leonard Brooks	1967	265
167-6/8	22-7/8	23-5/8	23-0/8	5	5	Boise County	ID	Ed Moser	1982	265
167-3/8	21-4/8	21-3/8	19-3/8	5	5	Owyhee County	ID	Eugene R. Mallard	1963	267
167-3/8	25-1/8	26-1/8	25-1/8	6	5	Grand Mesa	CO	Gary R. Haske	1977	267
167-3/8	25-0/8	25-0/8	19-3/8	7	5	Klamath County	OR	V. Kenneth Murdock	1978	267
167-3/8	21-6/8	22-7/8	19-0/8	5	7	Mesa County	CO	Paul H. Dickson	1984	267
167-2/8	20-7/8	21-5/8	20-3/8	5	4	Lincoln County	WY	Ronell Skinner	1980	271
167-2/8	23-0/8	23-0/8	20-6/8	6	5	Pinion Mesa	CO	Jim Bennett	1981	271
167-1/8	21-1/8	19-3/8	18-2/8	6	6	Anahim Lake	BC	Guy Antilla	1965	273
167-1/8	26-3/8	24-4/8	21-2/8	5	4	Denio	NV	Jerry Stout	1965	273
167-1/8	24-1/8	24-2/8	23-7/8	6	7	Gunnison County	CO	Richard L. Geissler	1983	273
167-0/8	23-3/8	24-2/8	22-2/8	4	4	Eagle County	CO	Arvine Routh	1965	276
167-0/8	23-3/8	24-4/8	22-0/8	5	5	De Beque	CO	Mike Gilbert	1973	276
167-0/8	23-2/8	23-1/8	22-1/8	7	8	Grand County	CO	Michael K. Ward	1973	276
167-0/8	21-2/8	19-7/8	18-4/8	5	5	Glade Park	CO	Glen Hitt	1975	276
166-7/8	21-2/8	22-0/8	20-5/8	5	5	Diamond Fork	UT	Orson Stilson	1964	280
166-6/8	25-1/8	25-3/8	24-4/8	5	6	Wilcox Ranch	UT	Doug Walker	1967	281
166-6/8	24-3/8	23-4/8	23-4/8	5	4	Roar Creek	CO	David E. Samuel	1974	281
166-6/8	23-4/8	23-0/8	20-2/8	5	5	Adams County	CO	John C. Schmidt	1974	281
166-6/8	23-0/8	22-7/8	24-2/8	5	4	Lamoille County	NV	James A. Algerio	1980	281
166-5/8	22-6/8	23-0/8	20-1/8	5	5	Borne	OR	Lloyd V. Christensen	1959	285
166-5/8	23-4/8	23-6/8	23-5/8	5	5	Montezuma County	CO	Marvin Reichenau	1983	285
166-5/8	22-0/8	22-1/8	19-7/8	5	5	Grant County	OR	Ray Kelton	1985	285
166-4/8	23-2/8	24-0/8	22-2/8	7	7	Owyhee County	ID	Bill Payne	1958	288
166-4/8	23-5/8	22-6/8	21-6/8	5	5	Owyhee County	ID	Blake Murphy	1961	288
166-4/8	20-3/8	20-5/8	16-6/8	5	5	Adams County	ID	Jack St. Germain	1986	288
166-3/8	21-7/8	22-5/8	21-0/8	6	7	Butte County	SD	L. G. Braun	1957	291
166-2/8	25-2/8	23-1/8	18-0/8	5	5	Buzzard Creek	CO	Lloyd Kell	1967	292
166-1/8	21-4/8	22-1/8	18-1/8	5	5	Saratoga	WY	Duncan G. Weibel	1955	293
166-1/8	20-6/8	21-4/8	19-5/8	5	5	Ada County	ID	M. F. Smith	1968	293
166-1/8	20-4/8	22-4/8	21-3/8	5	5	Calgary	ALB	Dean Reed	1981	293
166-0/8	23-0/8	23-3/8	26-7/8	5	5	Owyhee County	ID	Dwane Marler	1955	296
166-0/8	20-0/8	20-7/8	19-5/8	6	5	Maxwell	NE	M. R. Buchtel	1958	296
166-0/8	19-7/8	21-1/8	17-6/8	5	5	Kaibab	AZ	Norman J. Brown	1966	296
166-0/8	24-4/8	23-0/8	21-6/8	4	4	Rifle	CO	Robert G. Kuper	1966	296
165-7/8	23-4/8	25-0/8	25-0/8	9	6	Silver City	ID	Thomas Eld	1964	300
165-7/8	23-6/8	25-6/8	20-3/8	5	5	Moffat County	CO	Albert A. Adams	1982	300
165-6/8	24-0/8	23-2/8	19-2/8	6	6	Douglas Pass	CO	John Richard	1972	302
165-6/8	21-1/8	21-1/8	24-2/8	5	5	Cache Forest	UT	Carl Roush	1979	302
165-6/8	22-5/8	22-2/8	26-2/8	5	5	Lenora	KS	Joseph E. Schroeder	1979	302
165-6/8	23-4/8	24-0/8	24-2/8	5	4	Lewis and Clark County	MT	Donald Davidson, Jr.	1980	302
165-6/8	23-6/8	23-4/8	17-2/8	5	5	Grand County	CO	Burt Thompson	1983	302
165-5/8	21-1/8	21-0/8	20-5/8	5	5	Elk Ridge	UT	Frank Eicholt	1964	307
165-5/8	21-0/8	21-2/8	18-5/8	5	5	Zone 5	SAS	Ward Minifie	1985	307
165-4/8	22-4/8	23-4/8	19-0/8	5	5	San Miguel County	NM	Louis Baca	1985	309
165-4/8	24-1/8	24-7/8	19-3/8	7	6	Kane County	UT	Richard Jolley	1986	309
165-3/8	27-0/8	26-0/8	19-1/8	7	5	Mesa County	CO	Kent Stumpf	1973	311
165-3/8	23-2/8	21-2/8	20-0/8	5	6	Boise County	ID	Peter Cintorino	1985	311
165-2/8	26-5/8	27-0/8	25-2/8	5	5	Grand Junction	CO	Ray Carpenter	1960	313
165-2/8	20-6/8	20-1/8	18-4/8	5	5	Georgetown	CO	John Marolt III	1967	313
165-1/8	20-5/8	22-3/8	20-2/8	5	6	Fish Lake	UT	Severin Jensen	1959	315

MULE DEER *(Typical Antlers)*

(continued)   Minimum Score 145

Score	Length of Main Beam R	L	Inside Spread	Number of Points R	L	Area	State/ Province	Hunter's Name	Date	Rank
165-1/8	23-1/8	23-6/8	24-1/8	6	5	Mesa County	CO	Bob Woodhouse	1978	315
165-0/8	24-3/8	25-0/8	19-7/8	5	6	Rio Arriba County	NM	David L. Chandler	1967	317
165-0/8	24-3/8	24-0/8	27-2/8	6	6	Book Cliffs	UT	Bob Paulson	1967	317
165-0/8	22-2/8	22-1/8	22-0/8	5	5	Saguache County	CO	Michael Snodgrass	1977	317
165-0/8	26-4/8	25-2/8	25-0/8	4	5	Hart Mountain	OR	Wayne Lamson, Jr.	1981	317
165-0/8	24-6/8	25-6/8	21-4/8	5	5	Los Alamos	NM	Doug Aikin	1985	317
164-7/8	24-0/8	22-7/8	23-5/8	4	4	Uncompaghre Plateau	CO	Richard Rounds	1973	322
164-7/8	22-3/8	21-7/8	19-5/8	5	5	Routt County	CO	Paul Blotz	1974	322
164-7/8	23-4/8	22-6/8	23-5/8	5	6	Huachuca Mountain	AZ	Richard Dawe, Jr.	1976	322
164-6/8	22-4/8	21-3/8	18-2/8	5	5	Skyline Drive	UT	George Heath	1964	325
164-6/8	24-6/8	24-4/8	26-0/8	5	5	Cassia County	ID	Jack B. Watts	1968	325
164-6/8	21-3/8	22-2/8	23-6/8	5	5	Roan Creek	CO	Jim Walters	1975	325
164-5/8	25-6/8	26-1/8	24-4/8	5	5	Fox Valley	SAS	Doug Findlay	1977	328
164-5/8	20-4/8	21-3/8	20-3/8	4	5	LaSal Mountains	UT	Don Dvoroznak	1979	328
164-5/8	23-4/8	25-4/8	26-0/8	5	7	Grand Mesa	CO	George J. Hronkin III	1982	328
164-5/8	20-3/8	22-0/8	22-1/8	4	4	White Pine County	NV	Larry T. Gilbertson	1984	328
164-5/8	22-2/8	23-2/8	19-4/8	5	6	Cassia County	ID	Richard Ponciano	1985	328
164-5/8	19-5/8	20-7/8	16-6/8	6	5	Mesa County	CO	Don Walsh	1986	328
164-3/8	21-7/8	23-0/8	19-7/8	5	5	Siskiyou County	CA	Dale Gatlin	1959	334
164-3/8	24-6/8	23-4/8	24-6/8	8	8	Jarbidge	NV	Dick Woltering	1960	334
164-3/8	20-1/8	21-4/8	19-0/8	7	7	Conejos County	CO	Frank Holloway	1983	334
164-2/8	23-2/8	24-0/8	19-4/8	7	9	Cathedral Bluffs	CO	D. H. Nolting	1956	337
164-2/8	22-6/8	21-6/8	22-0/8	6	5	Clark	CO	John Hale	1975	337
164-2/8	20-6/8	23-1/8	18-4/8	7	6	Dolores County	CO	Tommy C. Jeffcoat	1977	337
164-2/8	21-7/8	22-0/8	21-6/8	5	5	Green Lee County	AZ	Steve E. Allen	1980	337
164-2/8	24-4/8	24-3/8	23-7/8	6	6	Stafford County	KS	Rob Ginest	1982	337
164-2/8	22-0/8	20-4/8	18-4/8	4	4	Cassia County	ID	Bryan Sprauge	1984	337
164-1/8	25-3/8	25-6/8	23-6/8	8	7	Owyhee County	ID	Merlie Hampton	1962	343
164-1/8	24-0/8	24-6/8	24-6/8	6	5	Eagle's Nest Mountain	CO	Russell F. Rider	1964	343
164-1/8	24-4/8	23-1/8	22-7/8	4	4	Roan Creek	CO	Roy Hoff	1968	343
164-1/8	22-3/8	22-1/8	19-3/8	5	5	Tucannon County	WA	Wayne Dickhaut	1983	343
164-0/8	19-4/8	20-1/8	19-6/8	5	5	Roan Creek	CO	Dr. Lowell L. Eddy	1968	347
164-0/8	21-3/8	21-3/8	18-0/8	4	4	Ada County	ID	Richard C. Nichols	1971	347
164-0/8	24-6/8	25-3/8	23-7/8	7	6	White Pine County	NV	Robert Davie	1983	347
163-7/8	20-1/8	21-3/8	17-6/8	5	6	Eustis	NE	Keene Hueftle	1961	350
163-6/8	21-2/8	22-1/8	26-0/8	5	5	Tabernach	CO	Michael A. Contreras	1978	351
163-5/8	24-4/8	24-3/8	21-6/8	8	9	Uncompahgre Plateau	CO	Franklin E. Adams	1971	352
163-5/8	23-3/8	23-2/8	22-3/8	5	5	White Pine County	NV	Joe Marich	1978	352
163-5/8	19-0/8	19-0/8	17-7/8	5	5	Gallatin National Forest	MT	Jim Diercks	1981	352
163-5/8	21-2/8	21-0/8	18-1/8	5	5	Mesa County	CO	Edwin L. Porter	1983	352
163-4/8	23-1/8	23-2/8	20-4/8	5	5	?	UT	Darwin Crawford	1964	356
163-4/8	24-1/8	24-1/8	25-0/8	5	5	Lake County	OR	William P. Petredis	1972	356
163-4/8	22-3/8	22-3/8	23-2/8	5	5	Sheridan County	KS	Kevin J. Ryan	1974	356
163-4/8	24-4/8	24-0/8	22-2/8	9	5	Osborne County	KS	Gary Krier	1984	356
163-3/8	22-5/8	25-4/8	17-6/8	8	7	Kaibab Forest	AZ	Jake Price	1963	360
163-3/8	21-6/8	22-1/8	17-5/8	5	5	Gunnison County	CO	Clark Gallup	1970	360
163-2/8	21-5/8	20-1/8	19-7/8	6	6	Chaffee County	CO	J. Melvin Rose	1973	362
163-2/8	23-7/8	24-3/8	21-2/8	5	4	Coconino County	AZ	Edward R. Allen, Sr.	1974	362
163-1/8	20-0/8	22-6/8	19-5/8	4	4	Routt County	CO	Robert H. Blue	1983	364
163-1/8	21-6/8	21-6/8	20-7/8	4	4	McKenzie County	ND	Mike "Myron" Rosemore	1986	364
163-0/8	24-2/8	23-4/8	24-2/8	5	7	Durango	CO	Bryan B. Owen	1964	366
163-0/8	23-3/8	25-3/8	20-6/8	5	5	Coconino County	AZ	Larry Hayden	1983	366
163-0/8	21-3/8	22-5/8	18-2/8	5	5	Teton County	WY	Al Nelson	1985	366
162-7/8	23-5/8	21-6/8	20-5/8	5	5	Howard	CO	Jerry Tiemeyer	1981	369
162-7/8	22-4/8	22-3/8	23-1/8	5	5	Billings County	ND	Mark Lothspeich	1984	369
162-7/8	22-6/8	22-4/8	25-6/8	6	7	Gray County	KS	Allen D. Bailey	1985	369
162-6/8	21-1/8	23-4/8	23-2/8	5	5	Nason Creek	WA	Les Eide	1954	372
162-6/8	23-2/8	23-6/8	25-4/8	5	5	Calgary	ALB	David Lovo	1979	372
162-6/8	23-5/8	24-2/8	18-5/8	5	6	Chelan County	WA	Brian Kayler	1984	372
162-5/8	23-6/8	23-7/8	24-1/8	5	4	Elko	NV	Orrin M. Owens	1966	375
162-5/8	20-7/8	22-0/8	23-3/8	4	4	West Desert	UT	Myron Adams	1969	375
162-5/8	22-4/8	21-0/8	21-2/8	7	6	Washoe County	NV	Ed Fuller	1984	375
162-4/8	21-3/8	21-0/8	19-2/8	5	5	Orangeville	UT	Kerry Ware	1964	378

MULE DEER *(Typical Antlers)*

Minimum Score 145

(continued)

Score	Length of Main Beam R	L	Inside Spread	Number of Points R	L	Area	State/ Province	Hunter's Name	Date	Rank
162-4/8	22-6/8	22-6/8	23-4/8	5	5	Collbran	CO	Larry D. Tillett	1972	378
162-4/8	21-0/8	21-7/8	17-2/8	5	5	Slope County	ND	Todd Seymonski	1983	378
162-3/8	25-2/8	25-0/8	22-6/8	7	7	Bear Lake County	ID	Marriner Jensen	1957	381
162-3/8	21-6/8	22-6/8	25-7/8	5	5	Hodgeman County	KS	Charles Fuller	1985	381
162-2/8	23-3/8	26-2/8	25-0/8	4	5	Owyhee County	ID	Ralph Collins	1960	383
162-2/8	22-5/8	23-0/8	17-0/8	5	5	Eureka County	NV	Gordon Diehl	1980	383
162-2/8	23-5/8	23-2/8	19-6/8	5	5	Lassen County	CA	Chuck Mazza	1984	383
162-1/8	23-7/8	23-6/8	18-1/8	5	5	Fishlake National Forest	UT	R. E. Kerr	1957	386
162-1/8	23-2/8	22-5/8	22-1/8	5	5	Range Creek	UT	Frank Turner	1965	386
162-1/8	22-4/8	22-5/8	17-2/8	5	6	Grand Mesa	CO	Joel Prickett	1973	386
162-0/8	22-3/8	23-1/8	21-2/8	5	5	Elko County	NV	Larry D Jones	1985	389
161-7/8	21-4/8	21-7/8	20-3/8	4	5	?	CO	Douglas Kenyon	1964	390
161-7/8	22-6/8	21-6/8	21-5/8	5	5	Fish Lake	UT	Clark Richards	1967	390
161-7/8	23-0/8	22-1/8	20-0/8	5	5	Book Cliffs	CO	Leonard Conley	1973	390
161-7/8	20-4/8	22-5/8	20-7/8	6	6	Beaver	UT	Joe Cordonier	1975	390
161-7/8	24-3/8	23-6/8	20-5/8	5	6	Collbran	CO	T. C. Gonyo	1975	390
161-7/8	21-1/8	20-3/8	18-5/8	5	5	Plumas County	CA	John Grochowski, Jr.	1976	390
161-7/8	24-3/8	24-1/8	20-7/8	5	4	Carefree	AZ	Paul N. Rambeau	1981	390
161-7/8	25-4/8	23-6/8	22-5/8	8	5	Catron County	NM	Richard D. Trapp	1986	390
161-6/8	23-2/8	24-0/8	27-3/8	6	6	East Douglas	CO	Dale Slade	1967	398
161-5/8	22-0/8	22-4/8	19-3/8	5	5	Lander County	NV	Paul Q. Lenz	1984	399
161-5/8	20-6/8	20-6/8	22-6/8	6	5	Bear Lake County	ID	Terry Davis	1984	399
161-4/8	24-5/8	24-6/8	24-2/8	7	7	Salt Lake City	UT	Frank M. Davis	1957	401
161-4/8	24-4/8	24-2/8	23-6/8	4	3	Owyhee County	ID	William Vanderhoef	1958	401
161-4/8	22-5/8	23-5/8	19-2/8	5	5	Sheridan County	WY	Mike Barrett	1985	401
161-3/8	22-5/8	21-7/8	19-1/8	5	5	Elko County	NV	Bert W. Fox	1961	404
161-3/8	23-2/8	21-6/8	22-3/8	4	4	Alliance	NE	Fred H. D. Krueger	1970	404
161-2/8	21-0/8	20-6/8	16-7/8	5	6	Ada County	ID	Ed Moser	1971	406
161-2/8	24-6/8	23-5/8	20-4/8	3	3	Glade Park	CO	Billy Ellis	1976	406
161-2/8	23-4/8	22-3/8	17-6/8	5	5	Bighorn County	MT	Mike Barrett	1984	406
161-1/8	25-0/8	24-0/8	25-0/8	5	5	Los Alamos	NM	J. R. McDaniels	1960	409
161-1/8	20-5/8	20-4/8	15-5/8	5	5	Garfield County	CO	John Murray	1963	409
161-1/8	20-3/8	22-0/8	23-0/8	7	5	Mora County	NM	Michael J. Maes	1977	409
161-1/8	25-6/8	26-3/8	27-5/8	4	5	Pima County	AZ	Steve Mikitish	1983	409
161-1/8	23-1/8	21-7/8	18-1/8	5	5	San Juan County	CO	Eddie Claypool	1984	409
161-0/8	21-3/8	21-3/8	21-6/8	5	5	Garfield County	CO	Warren Buss	1978	414
160-7/8	21-7/8	21-7/8	23-1/8	6	6	Dundy County	NE	Jim Lutz	1980	415
160-6/8	22-6/8	22-4/8	21-1/8	7	6	Chelan County	WA	Paul Cohoon	1967	416
160-6/8	20-7/8	20-2/8	22-3/8	6	5	Park County	WY	Jim Patterson	1968	416
160-6/8	22-4/8	22-6/8	15-4/8	5	4	Washoe County	NV	Lawrence Heward	1974	416
160-6/8	20-5/8	20-3/8	19-4/8	5	5	Boise County	ID	Mike McCollum	1975	416
160-6/8	19-6/8	20-1/8	22-0/8	5	5	Santa Rita Mountains	AZ	Jerry Clarno	1978	416
160-6/8	21-0/8	22-4/8	21-4/8	5	5	Kremmling	CO	Terry J. Kramer	1978	416
160-6/8	23-1/8	20-3/8	21-0/8	5	5	Nez Perce County	ID	J. David Powers	1980	416
160-5/8	20-5/8	20-5/8	19-7/8	4	4	Humbolt County	NV	Mike Toone	1961	423
160-5/8	20-6/8	21-4/8	21-5/8	5	5	Colfax County	NM	Carl Osborne	1965	423
160-5/8	21-1/8	21-2/8	20-7/8	5	5	Steamboat Springs	CO	Mark Chapman	1975	423
160-5/8	24-5/8	25-7/8	27-6/8	5	8	Leader	SAS	Don Tourand	1982	423
160-4/8	23-6/8	23-1/8	20-0/8	7	8	Jarbidge	NV	Robert Narrimore	1963	427
160-4/8	23-5/8	23-5/8	18-0/8	5	5	Lemhi County	ID	Robert J. Eckardt	1978	427
160-3/8	22-7/8	22-3/8	18-0/8	5	6	Cedar Mountain	UT	Clair Adams	1958	429
160-3/8	22-4/8	22-4/8	18-2/8	6	6	Collbran	CO	Ed Adkins	1974	429
160-3/8	20-6/8	22-1/8	20-1/8	4	4	Glade Park	CO	Ralph Ertz	1980	429
160-3/8	18-5/8	21-1/8	22-1/8	6	5	Cochrane	ALB	Colby Robison	1982	429
160-3/8	22-0/8	23-4/8	19-1/8	6	6	Jefferson County	CO	Steve Rehm	1984	429
160-2/8	19-2/8	21-2/8	19-0/8	5	5	Lynndyl	UT	Scott Chesley	1962	434
160-2/8	19-6/8	21-2/8	20-6/8	5	5	Lemhi County	ID	Kemper McMaster	1978	434
160-2/8	24-0/8	24-4/8	21-1/8	4	5	Mesa County	CO	Bill Stonebraker	1978	434
160-2/8	20-5/8	21-1/8	17-0/8	5	5	Mesa County	CO	Bill Dunbar	1984	434
160-2/8	25-6/8	24-6/8	23-3/8	6	6	Scott County	KS	Michael E. Woodard	1984	434
160-1/8	20-2/8	20-7/8	19-7/8	5	5	Meagher County	MT	Mickey Anderson, Jr.	1966	439
160-0/8	22-4/8	21-7/8	20-2/8	5	5	Chaffee County	CO	Paul J. Zeisler	1964	440
160-0/8	23-0/8	22-7/8	20-3/8	6	5	Gunnison County	CO	Wayne Depperschmidt	1973	440

MULE DEER *(Typical Antlers)*

(continued)   Minimum Score 145

Score	Length of Main Beam R	L	Inside Spread	Number of Points R	L	Area	State/ Province	Hunter's Name	Date	Rank
160-0/8	24-4/8	23-2/8	24-4/8	4	5	Unit 13	AZ	Bruce McIntyre	1979	440
160-0/8	21-4/8	21-7/8	19-2/8	5	5	Linn County	OR	Mary Cook	1980	440
160-0/8	23-3/8	24-2/8	20-2/8	5	5	Crestone	CO	Russell Hull	1980	440
160-0/8	26-2/8	25-1/8	25-0/8	5	5	LaPlata County	CO	Michael R. Hinson	1986	440
159-7/8	24-2/8	25-0/8	19-4/8	5	6	Raton	NM	James Kelly	1957	446
159-7/8	20-7/8	21-6/8	21-6/8	5	5	Liberty County	MT	Kenneth Aaberge	1960	446
159-7/8	22-5/8	23-0/8	18-7/8	5	5	Sanders County	MT	Walt Borgmann	1968	446
159-7/8	23-6/8	22-2/8	24-0/8	5	5	Dinosaur	CO	Ron Hopkins	1970	446
159-7/8	23-1/8	21-3/8	17-3/8	5	5	Sandia Mountains	NM	Lee Burnett	1972	446
159-7/8	25-4/8	22-4/8	21-0/8	6	6	De Beque	CO	Ronald E. Stull	1974	446
159-6/8	23-4/8	22-7/8	22-3/8	7	7	Owyhee County	ID	Gilbert Martin	1960	452
159-6/8	22-2/8	21-4/8	19-4/8	5	5	Beaver	UT	Joe Cordonier	1974	452
159-6/8	22-0/8	22-0/8	20-6/8	4	4	Kamloops	BC	Barry Anderson	1982	452
159-6/8	23-0/8	22-2/8	23-6/8	5	5	Washoe County	NV	Robert L. Brooks, Jr.	1983	452
159-3/8	21-1/8	20-4/8	16-5/8	4	4	Beaver Mountain	UT	Dean Todd	1956	456
159-3/8	22-4/8	22-7/8	18-4/8	5	5	Pine Grove	OR	Bill Neary	1966	456
159-2/8	21-1/8	20-4/8	17-2/8	5	5	Garfield County	CO	Robert Pitt	1978	458
159-1/8	22-6/8	21-6/8	20-5/8	5	7	Garfield County	CO	Jack Peters	1963	459
159-1/8	23-0/8	23-2/8	18-7/8	4	5	Douglas Pass	CO	Donald J. Walsh	1977	459
159-1/8	21-1/8	22-0/8	20-7/8	5	5	White Pine County	NV	Steve Wood	1978	459
159-0/8	20-6/8	21-1/8	17-1/8	5	6	Montrose County	CO	David M. Gant	1977	462
159-0/8	21-3/8	22-7/8	22-2/8	6	5	San Juan County	CO	Dennis Atwater	1978	462
159-0/8	17-1/8	19-3/8	19-4/8	4	4	Jefferson County	CO	Calvin Farner	1986	462
158-7/8	21-2/8	22-6/8	21-7/8	5	5	Elmore County	ID	Peter J Cintorino	1981	465
158-6/8	21-3/8	22-3/8	22-0/8	5	5	Hart Mountain	OR	Lyle Reeder	1954	466
158-6/8	21-6/8	20-7/8	17-0/8	6	4	Stacy	MT	Dewey Olsen	1960	466
158-5/8	22-2/8	22-5/8	18-1/8	6	6	Ogden Canyon	UT	Bruce N. Moss	1974	468
158-5/8	22-1/8	22-3/8	18-5/8	6	5	Hodgeman County	KS	Ron Adams	1985	468
158-4/8	23-3/8	23-6/8	22-6/8	4	4	Albany County	WY	Nelson W. Brower	1979	470
158-4/8	21-0/8	19-6/8	18-2/8	5	5	Greeley County	KS	Keith Foster	1981	470
158-4/8	20-0/8	20-3/8	15-4/8	5	5	Lane County	KS	Hurley T. Smith	1982	470
158-3/8	25-1/8	21-1/8	20-1/8	6	5	Pine Ridge	NE	Gerald J. McKinney	1974	473
158-3/8	24-5/8	24-2/8	21-3/8	4	6	Ada County	ID	Robert E. Stauts	1979	473
158-2/8	23-4/8	19-3/8	21-4/8	6	4	Tincup Mountain	ID	Gary L. Vaughn	1969	475
158-2/8	23-4/8	22-1/8	20-0/8	6	7	Elwood	NE	Johnny Hemelstrand	1972	475
158-2/8	19-7/8	20-1/8	19-2/8	5	5	Las Animas County	CO	Byron E. Brown	1984	475
158-2/8	21-2/8	21-2/8	20-0/8	6	5	Butte County	ID	Gene Fitzgerald	1985	475
158-1/8	20-7/8	20-0/8	18-3/8	5	5	?	UT	Gordon Young	1963	479
158-1/8	22-3/8	22-1/8	24-7/8	5	5	Blanding	UT	Russell Smith	1971	479
158-1/8	20-6/8	20-3/8	17-7/8	5	4	Texas County	OK	J. Alva Hammond	1981	479
158-0/8	21-4/8	21-0/8	21-4/8	7	7	Beach	ND	Bob Ross	1959	482
158-0/8	22-2/8	23-3/8	21-2/8	5	5	Owyhee County	ID	R. W. McIntire	1961	482
158-0/8	21-7/8	22-6/8	19-2/8	5	5	De Beque	CO	Matt Spohnhauer	1975	482
157-7/8	23-6/8	24-0/8	21-3/8	4	5	Chama	NM	Larry Wright	1972	485
157-7/8	21-6/8	22-0/8	21-4/8	5	6	Mesa County	CO	Jerol W. Vaughn	1985	485
157-6/8	23-7/8	23-4/8	23-7/8	6	5	Owyhee County	ID	Roland Duram	1964	487
157-6/8	22-5/8	23-3/8	21-0/8	5	5	Collbran	CO	Terry J. Gerber	1976	487
157-6/8	25-6/8	26-2/8	27-5/8	5	7	Bartlett Lake	AZ	George Toot	1980	487
157-5/8	19-6/8	20-0/8	18-3/8	5	5	Montezuma County	CO	Marvin Reichenau	1973	490
157-5/8	24-1/8	23-4/8	21-7/8	5	5	Washoe County	NV	Donald J. Taysom	1984	490
157-5/8	23-6/8	24-1/8	20-3/8	9	6	Cheyene County	KS	Chet Gardner	1984	490
157-4/8	23-1/8	23-2/8	23-2/8	6	6	Book Cliff Mountains	UT	Dean Caldwell	1960	493
157-4/8	22-2/8	22-4/8	19-4/8	5	5	Western Colorado	CO	Bob Gulman	1966	493
157-4/8	18-5/8	19-2/8	16-0/8	4	4	Sandia Mountains	NM	William R. Johnson	1969	493
157-4/8	20-1/8	19-4/8	21-4/8	5	6	Carbon County	WY	Daniel S. Christie	1982	493
157-4/8	22-1/8	20-2/8	21-0/8	5	6	Carter County	MT	Edward Susa	1983	493
157-4/8	20-2/8	22-2/8	22-5/8	5	6	Owyhee County	ID	Duane Zemliska	1985	493
157-3/8	26-2/8	26-0/8	21-2/8	7	6	Fish Lake	UT	Dale Gardner	1958	499
157-3/8	21-6/8	20-0/8	20-0/8	6	6	Steamboat Springs	CO	Bing Kemp	1966	499
157-3/8	24-1/8	24-1/8	23-3/8	6	7	Montrose County	CO	James A. Davison	1984	499
157-3/8	17-4/8	19-0/8	16-3/8	5	5	Albany County	WY	Paul Ayotte	1985	499
157-3/8	21-0/8	21-0/8	20-5/8	5	5	Caribou County	ID	Gary Hunt	1986	499
157-2/8	22-5/8	21-4/8	20-6/8	6	6	McKenzie County	ND	Roy Mitten	1956	504

MULE DEER *(Typical Antlers)*
(continued)

Minimum Score 145

Score	Length of Main Beam R	Length of Main Beam L	Inside Spread	Number of Points R	Number of Points L	Area	State/ Province	Hunter's Name	Date	Rank
157-2/8	21-5/8	21-4/8	16-4/8	5	5	Sandia Mountains	NM	Robert F. Knight	1970	504
157-1/8	22-0/8	23-4/8	23-3/8	6	4	Beaty Butte	OR	Gary Soeth	1980	506
157-1/8	23-6/8	23-3/8	20-7/8	6	7	Boise County	ID	Gary Kinney	1981	506
157-0/8	21-4/8	21-5/8	18-0/8	5	5	Collbran	CO	Robert O. Bash	1976	508
157-0/8	22-6/8	21-4/8	16-0/8	5	5	Lassen County	CA	Tom McMurphy	1977	508
157-0/8	21-6/8	20-3/8	18-6/8	5	5	Lane County	KS	Dean Hamilton	1978	508
157-0/8	23-7/8	23-7/8	18-6/8	4	4	Clackamas County	OR	Thomas L. Carter	1984	508
156-7/8	24-3/8	24-0/8	23-4/8	4	4	Roan Creek	CO	John Lamicq, Jr.	1966	512
156-7/8	20-1/8	19-7/8	22-1/8	5	5	Fish Lake	UT	Mike Otten	1973	512
156-7/8	21-2/8	20-6/8	18-3/8	5	5	Mesa County	CO	David H. Boland	1978	512
156-7/8	20-2/8	20-2/8	19-2/8	4	4	Rio Blanco	CO	George David Epperson	1983	512
156-7/8	23-5/8	21-6/8	21-7/8	5	5	McKenzie County	ND	Steve Rehak	1985	512
156-7/8	21-4/8	20-2/8	15-7/8	5	5	Teller County	CO	Butch Smerkonich	1985	512
156-7/8	23-2/8	22-3/8	21-2/8	6	5	Chelan County	WA	Brian Kayler	1985	512
156-6/8	23-6/8	24-2/8	20-0/8	6	5	Diamond Fork Canyon	UT	Terry Peck	1964	519
156-6/8	22-5/8	22-6/8	19-4/8	5	5	Fruita	CO	Ed Meyer	1967	519
156-6/8	21-6/8	21-4/8	22-6/8	5	5	Elmore County	ID	Harold Lefler	1981	519
156-6/8	23-2/8	22-2/8	18-4/8	4	5	Kittitas County	WA	Rich Carnahan	1982	519
156-5/8	21-2/8	21-3/8	20-3/8	5	5	Amidon	ND	Vern R. Keim	1959	523
156-5/8	20-0/8	21-6/8	18-6/8	6	6	Estes Park	CO	Leslie McKenzie	1970	523
156-5/8	22-0/8	22-0/8	22-1/8	5	6	Clark	CO	Moulton Larmay	1981	523
156-5/8	21-7/8	21-0/8	19-3/8	7	6	Lower Arrow Lake	BC	Gerald Bond	1983	523
156-5/8	20-7/8	18-5/8	18-6/8	6	5	Caribou County	ID	Michael Aldrich	1984	523
156-4/8	21-7/8	22-1/8	22-0/8	5	4	Weston County	WY	Thomas L. A. Pucci	1956	528
156-4/8	20-0/8	20-0/8	19-2/8	5	5	Owyhee County	ID	Bill Leisi	1961	528
156-4/8	22-2/8	24-2/8	20-3/8	4	5	Summit County	UT	Richard Douglass	1964	528
156-4/8	23-1/8	21-4/8	20-4/8	4	4	Elko County	NV	Paul Dinan	1968	528
156-4/8	21-0/8	22-3/8	24-0/8	6	6	Meeker	CO	Jerry R. Bowen	1970	528
156-4/8	23-1/8	20-7/8	19-2/8	4	4	Square Butte	MT	Michael R. Buesseler	1971	528
156-4/8	22-5/8	23-6/8	21-4/8	4	5	Campbell County	WY	James P. Smith	1983	528
156-4/8	20-1/8	20-6/8	18-4/8	5	5	Grant County	OR	Jeffrey A. Young	1986	528
156-3/8	25-5/8	24-6/8	23-5/8	3	3	Mt. Trumbull	AZ	Bill Cross	1963	536
156-2/8	21-5/8	20-725	20-0/8	5	5	Collbran	CO	Donald Aaron	1971	537
156-2/8	20-5/8	20-2/8	19-2/8	5	5	Clark County	KS	Rod Lies	1976	537
156-1/8	20-6/8	20-7/8	20-2/8	5	6	Beaver Mountain	UT	Jerry White	1962	539
156-1/8	21-3/8	22-2/8	26-7/8	6	6	Blanding	UT	Dale Warren	1972	539
156-1/8	22-3/8	21-2/8	25-2/8	5	6	Ada County	ID	Deloy Desaro	1973	539
156-1/8	25-1/8	25-6/8	18-5/8	5	5	Rio Arriba County	NM	Gary Isom	1985	539
156-0/8	21-4/8	21-0/8	18-2/8	5	5	Cedar City	UT	Ken McKnight	1966	543
156-0/8	20-0/8	20-1/8	18-2/8	5	6	Nason Creek	WA	Steve Gorr	1975	543
156-0/8	21-6/8	22-6/8	23-4/8	6	6	Eagle Cap	OR	Randy Hopp	1979	543
156-0/8	22-1/8	20-7/8	18-6/8	5	5	Powder River County	MT	Dan Brockman	1986	543
155-7/8	21-3/8	21-6/8	21-0/8	5	6	McKenzie County	ND	Mark E. Ferry	1981	547
155-6/8	24-1/8	24-1/8	22-0/8	3	4	Owyhee County	ID	Lynn Thomas	1960	548
155-6/8	22-2/8	21-3/8	18-4/8	4	5	Roan Cliff Mountains	CO	Henery Jaman	1966	548
155-6/8	24-0/8	22-7/8	25-0/8	6	6	Lane County	KS	Dean Hamilton	1982	548
155-5/8	23-2/8	23-3/8	22-3/8	5	6	Nason Creek	WA	R. F. Kelly	1960	551
155-5/8	21-2/8	24-5/8	25-3/8	7	6	Hart Mountain	OR	Orvil Winters	1965	551
155-5/8	24-0/8	25-725	22-0/8	7	5	North Kaibab	AZ	Robert G. Arcieri	1977	551
155-5/8	21-0/8	20-5/8	18-1/8	4	4	Baggs	WY	Robert K. Paulson	1979	551
155-5/8	21-0/8	20-4/8	18-7/8	5	5	Garfield County	CO	Joe Wiater	1982	551
155-5/8	21-4/8	20-4/8	17-7/8	5	5	Chugwater	WY	James D. Wagner	1982	551
155-5/8	20-5/8	20-5/8	19-1/8	5	5	Carbon County	WY	Andy Lindahl	1984	551
155-4/8	22-2/8	23-6/8	23-2/8	5	4	Millard County	UT	Shirl Pace	1966	558
155-4/8	19-4/8	21-0/8	19-6/8	5	5	Wayne County	UT	Harold Boyack	1968	558
155-3/8	20-1/8	21-1/8	22-3/8	5	5	Rangely	CO	Jim Pickering	1966	560
155-2/8	20-2/8	19-4/8	19-2/8	5	5	Owyhee County	ID	Ralph O. Collins	1957	561
155-2/8	23-6/8	24-2/8	22-4/8	6	6	Ada County	ID	Ronald K. White	1971	561
155-2/8	20-7/8	21-3/8	22-5/8	5	6	Gunnison County	CO	Jim Jarvis	1974	561
155-2/8	21-7/8	22-1/8	17-6/8	5	5	Mesa County	CO	Rudy Wilkison	1984	561
155-2/8	19-1/8	20-6/8	18-5/8	6	5	Colfax County	NM	Dean K. Oatman	1985	561
155-2/8	21-0/8	22-4/8	19-6/8	5	5	Eagle County	CO	Tom Tietz	1985	561
155-1/8	21-2/8	21-3/8	17-7/8	6	5	Fish Lake	UT	Ray Shepard	1965	567

MULE DEER *(Typical Antlers)*

(continued)   Minimum Score 145

Score	Length of Main Beam R	L	Inside Spread	Number of Points R	L	Area	State/ Province	Hunter's Name	Date	Rank
155-0/8	23-2/8	21-4/8	22-0/8	5	4	Hart Mountain	OR	Bill Chahon	1967	568
155-0/8	23-4/8	23-0/8	22-0/8	6	5	Broadwater County	MT	Larry P. Stevens	1968	568
155-0/8	21-6/8	22-3/8	20-0/8	6	7	Garfield County	CO	Toby Johnson	1972	568
155-0/8	19-7/8	22-4/8	17-6/8	4	4	Summit County	CO	Harley Smith	1976	568
155-0/8	22-6/8	23-0/8	21-2/8	6	6	Rio Blanco County	CO	Larry Streiff	1978	568
155-0/8	21-7/8	22-0/8	20-1/8	5	5	Collbran	CO	Clarence Bowers, Jr.	1979	568
155-0/8	21-2/8	22-6/8	21-6/8	4	4	Slope County	ND	Bill Schwendinger	1982	568
155-0/8	20-5/8	19-3/8	18-4/8	5	5	Bernalillo County	NM	Doug Aikin	1983	568
155-0/8	21-2/8	21-6/8	21-4/8	5	5	Boise County	ID	Larry S. Zurgot	1985	568
154-7/8	22-3/8	23-4/8	23-3/8	5	5	Dolores	CO	Oscar A. Harden	1957	577
154-7/8	19-4/8	21-2/8	19-2/8	5	6	Beaver Mountain	UT	Dale Moore	1961	577
154-7/8	21-6/8	21-7/8	16-7/8	4	4	Elko	NV	Jim Cox	1974	577
154-7/8	21-5/8	22-3/8	18-3/8	5	6	Mountain City	NV	John S. Chace, Jr.	1982	577
154-6/8	19-6/8	21-5/8	24-4/8	5	5	Owyhee County	ID	Fred Audette	1960	581
154-6/8	20-7/8	20-4/8	21-6/8	5	5	Elko County	NV	Frank M. Davis	1967	581
154-6/8	21-0/8	21-6/8	22-4/8	5	5	Hart Mountain	OR	Wayne Lamson, Jr.	1980	581
154-6/8	23-1/8	22-7/8	20-2/8	4	5	Montrose County	CO	Dave Reitz	1983	581
154-6/8	17-5/8	20-1/8	13-4/8	5	5	EL Paso County	CO	Michael Thompson	1984	581
154-5/8	20-3/8	21-7/8	21-7/8	5	5	Lincoln County	NV	Larry Gehre	1963	586
154-5/8	21-3/8	19-3/8	16-7/8	4	5	Roan Creek	CO	Tommy Biffle	1975	586
154-5/8	23-6/8	23-2/8	20-0/8	5	8	Manti Range	UT	Bruce Gordon	1980	586
154-5/8	20-1/8	19-5/8	19-5/8	5	5	Lake County	OR	Dale A. Bolin	1983	586
154-4/8	22-3/8	22-5/8	21-0/8	6	6	Hahn's Peak	CO	Douglas J. Peterson	1965	590
154-3/8	21-7/8	23-1/8	20-5/8	4	5	Pawnee County	KS	Robert E. Lagree	1970	591
154-3/8	23-5/8	24-0/8	24-7/8	5	4	Elbert County	CO	Billy Tillotson	1985	591
154-2/8	21-7/8	21-5/8	17-4/8	8	8	Canyon Creek	OR	Lloyd V. Christensen	1960	593
154-2/8	22-5/8	22-3/8	19-5/8	4	4	Mesa County	CO	Jimmy E. Ash	1966	593
154-2/8	22-2/8	21-2/8	21-0/8	7	8	Kirby	WY	Steve Gorr	1970	593
154-2/8	20-5/8	20-0/8	19-2/8	5	5	Moffat County	CO	Mary E. Nussberger	1978	593
154-2/8	21-2/8	23-7/8	22-4/8	5	5	Blaine County	ID	Dean Muchow	1979	593
154-2/8	21-2/8	21-5/8	18-6/8	5	5	Mesa County	CO	Carl Phillips	1980	593
154-2/8	23-4/8	23-0/8	19-1/8	5	6	Chelan County	WA	Daniel S Nelson	1984	593
154-1/8	18-3/8	16-6/8	16-1/8	5	7	Carbon County	UT	Lieb D. Miller	1959	600
154-1/8	21-6/8	22-6/8	25-0/8	5	6	Owyhee County	ID	Bill Kerr	1962	600
154-1/8	21-4/8	21-4/8	20-4/8	4	4	South Rio Grande River	CO	Kenneth G. McCombs	1969	600
154-1/8	24-6/8	24-4/8	29-0/8	5	4	Canyon Creek	OR	Chuck Lynde	1972	600
154-1/8	20-3/8	21-0/8	16-0/8	5	6	Montrose County	CO	Arthur L. Pace	1974	600
154-0/8	22-7/8	22-6/8	20-6/8	7	6	San Francisco Peaks	AZ	Stuart Diehl	1962	605
154-0/8	22-0/8	22-2/8	19-4/8	5	5	Grand Junction	CO	Al Dawson	1964	605
154-0/8	25-2/8	24-4/8	21-2/8	5	4	Unit 41	CO	Dale Anderson	1973	605
154-0/8	23-5/8	21-6/8	23-6/8	4	4	Montrose	CO	Don Allen, Jr.	1979	605
154-0/8	20-4/8	21-4/8	19-3/8	6	5	Calgary	ALB	Manfred Grewe	1981	605
154-0/8	22-7/8	23-6/8	22-5/8	9	7	Lake County	OR	Charles F. Brown	1985	605
153-7/8	19-5/8	19-2/8	19-1/8	6	5	Little Belt Mountains	MT	Leroy Dukes	1972	611
153-7/8	22-6/8	21-7/8	16-6/8	6	6	Baxter Pass	CO	Kevin Jackson	1973	611
153-7/8	22-4/8	19-6/8	17-7/8	5	5	Tavaputs Plateau Ranch	UT	Matt Brooks	1974	611
153-7/8	23-3/8	22-4/8	23-1/8	6	6	Sumpter	OR	Randy Jennings	1981	611
153-6/8	23-0/8	21-7/8	18-0/8	5	5	Dawes County	NE	William W. Plooster	1958	615
153-6/8	20-7/8	21-3/8	22-7/8	6	5	Uncompahgre N.F.	CO	Donald Click	1979	615
153-5/8	22-0/8	22-4/8	20-7/8	4	4	Billings County	ND	Ed Bry, Jr.	1957	617
153-5/8	21-0/8	20-7/8	17-7/8	6	7	Craig	CO	Zenus E. Cozart	1962	617
153-5/8	21-4/8	21-4/8	18-7/8	5	6	Craig	CO	Hugh Cox	1971	617
153-4/8	22-5/8	21-7/8	22-4/8	5	5	Monticello	UT	Roy D. Chesley	1963	620
153-4/8	23-0/8	23-0/8	17-4/8	6	5	Long Pine	NE	Seth Fritzler	1965	620
153-4/8	20-1/8	22-1/8	20-2/8	6	5	Wolf Creek	UT	Don Callister	1967	620
153-4/8	24-2/8	24-4/8	26-0/8	4	3	Mesa County	CO	Duane Beenblossom	1979	620
153-3/8	22-1/8	21-1/8	21-1/8	4	5	Garfield County	CO	John Nottingham	1974	624
153-2/8	21-0/8	21-0/8	20-0/8	5	5	Miles City	MT	Gene T. Buck	1961	625
153-2/8	21-4/8	21-3/8	17-6/8	5	5	Rifle County	CO	Randy Gilmore	1982	625
153-2/8	21-2/8	20-3/8	20-0/8	6	6	Coconino County	AZ	Richard S Jones	1985	625
153-2/8	19-4/8	20-0/8	15-6/8	5	5	Gregory County	SD	Terry Marcukaitis	1985	625
153-2/8	20-1/8	20-6/8	14-6/8	6	5	Washoe County	NV	Ronald W. Lindquist	1986	625
153-1/8	22-0/8	22-3/8	24-0/8	5	4	Delta	UT	Milton F. McQueary	1961	630

MULE DEER *(Typical Antlers)*

Minimum Score 145

Score	Length of Main Beam R	L	Inside Spread	Number of Points R	L	Area	State/ Province	Hunter's Name	Date	Rank
153-1/8	23-5/8	25-2/8	20-2/8	5	4	White River	CO	Thomas Nicholls	1967	630
153-1/8	22-0/8	21-5/8	21-5/8	5	4	Rifle	CO	Lester Meredith	1974	630
153-1/8	21-3/8	22-0/8	24-1/8	6	4	Snowville	UT	Richard Hess	1981	630
153-1/8	21-0/8	22-7/8	18-7/8	7	5	Converse County	WY	Ted Jaycox	1982	630
153-1/8	21-6/8	21-4/8	19-7/8	4	5	Chelan County	WA	Don McNees, Jr.	1983	630
153-0/8	22-3/8	22-7/8	23-4/8	5	5	Tortollita Mountain	AZ	James M. Fry	1974	636
152-7/8	20-7/8	21-7/8	20-1/8	6	6	Gove County	KS	Alan D. Beougher	1970	637
152-7/8	20-4/8	21-7/8	15-3/8	4	4	White River N.F.	CO	Leonard Steiner	1978	637
152-6/8	22-6/8	23-1/8	24-0/8	5	5	Routt County	CO	Lee R. Hoxit	1978	639
152-6/8	20-3/8	20-4/8	22-4/8	5	5	Mesa County	CO	R. L. Harrison III	1985	639
152-5/8	21-3/8	21-5/8	20-3/8	4	4	Elko	NV	Bill Freeman	1961	641
152-5/8	22-0/8	22-3/8	22-3/8	5	5	Lysite	WY	Gene Farley	1964	641
152-5/8	22-4/8	22-1/8	21-6/8	6	6	Mesa County	CO	Don Rogers	1986	641
152-5/8	22-4/8	22-2/8	25-2/8	5	6	Bow River	ALB	Michael D. Coupland	1986	641
152-4/8	21-1/8	20-7/8	17-5/8	5	6	Melrose	MT	Tony Rebich	1982	645
152-3/8	20-6/8	20-7/8	20-2/8	5	6	Price	UT	John C. Culpepper	1969	646
152-3/8	23-0/8	21-7/8	22-4/8	4	4	Montrose County	CO	Viron Barbay	1985	646
152-2/8	21-0/8	21-0/8	19-0/8	5	6	Book Cliff Mountains	UT	Roger Smith	1962	648
152-2/8	19-3/8	20-4/8	20-4/8	5	5	Jarbidge	NV	Jack Konvalin	1963	648
152-2/8	26-0/8	26-0/8	22-0/8	4	4	Roan Creek	CO	Jim Dougherty	1968	648
152-2/8	21-5/8	21-7/8	21-5/8	5	5	Beaver Mountain	UT	David G. Snyder	1968	648
152-2/8	21-0/8	21-0/8	24-6/8	6	6	Ennis	MT	Dave Bonczyk	1972	648
152-1/8	20-1/8	20-1/8	18-1/8	5	5	Winchester Moutains	AZ	John Behrends	1969	653
152-0/8	20-0/8	20-6/8	17-3/8	8	7	Mt. Dutton	UT	Bob Mackinnon	1970	654
152-0/8	19-3/8	19-5/8	18-0/8	5	5	Bowman County	ND	Mark Loutzenhiser	1985	654
152-0/8	20-2/8	22-7/8	18-6/8	6	6	Elko County	NV	LeRoy McQueen	1986	654
151-7/8	22-0/8	22-2/8	20-0/8	6	8	Duchesne County	UT	Rowland S. Enomoto	1965	657
151-7/8	22-0/8	21-2/8	21-7/8	5	4	Chelan County	WA	L. James Bailey	1977	657
151-7/8	19-6/8	21-1/8	22-5/8	5	5	Meagher County	MT	Chuck Adams	1979	657
151-7/8	21-1/8	22-1/8	23-2/8	5	6	Golden Valley County	MT	Tim Ford	1979	657
151-6/8	20-3/8	20-2/8	21-4/8	4	5	Jordan	MT	Herman Hass	1961	661
151-6/8	18-7/8	21-7/8	21-7/8	6	6	Rio Blanco County	CO	Doug Kenyon	1967	661
151-6/8	17-5/8	15-4/8	14-4/8	5	5	Garfield County	CO	Roger Smith	1973	661
151-6/8	22-5/8	21-0/8	20-0/8	5	5	Loma	CO	Steve Fossen	1974	661
151-6/8	19-3/8	21-6/8	16-5/8	5	5	Grand County	CO	Mark Chapman	1978	661
151-6/8	20-3/8	20-4/8	15-7/8	7	7	Mesa County	CO	Jack O. Rothwell	1979	661
151-5/8	21-5/8	20-5/8	20-5/8	5	5	Panquitch	UT	Dick Gulman	1968	667
151-5/8	20-2/8	18-7/8	18-1/8	6	6	Chaffee County	CO	Eugene K. Post	1971	667
151-5/8	20-5/8	20-5/8	18-1/8	5	5	Mesa County	CO	Richard E. Davis, Jr.	1977	667
151-4/8	21-6/8	21-0/8	21-6/8	6	5	Pima City	AZ	Herbert Tom	1981	670
151-3/8	22-4/8	19-2/8	19-1/8	5	5	Dolores County	CO	Dennis Atwater	1979	671
151-3/8	22-0/8	21-5/8	21-7/8	5	5	Washoe County	NV	David J. Fujii	1981	671
151-2/8	22-7/8	19-2/8	16-4/8	5	5	Chelan County	WA	G. H. Malinoski	1959	673
151-2/8	24-5/8	23-1/8	24-5/8	7	6	Montpelier Canyon	ID	Keith V. Hymos	1961	673
151-2/8	23-2/8	22-7/8	22-4/8	5	4	Nason Creek	WA	Ron Carpenter	1973	673
151-2/8	22-4/8	21-4/8	22-4/8	5	5	Harding County	SD	Mike Barrett	1976	673
151-2/8	20-6/8	22-6/8	22-0/8	7	5	Uncompahgre N. F.	CO	Clifford Patterson	1976	673
151-2/8	21-4/8	21-3/8	20-0/8	5	5	Phillips County	MT	Brian Roness	1984	673
151-2/8	21-0/8	20-6/8	17-0/8	7	5	Stanley County	SD	Dale DeBoer	1985	673
151-1/8	21-4/8	22-2/8	20-2/8	6	7	Butte County	SD	John Kirk	1958	680
151-1/8	23-7/8	22-7/8	20-1/8	4	5	Mesa County	CO	Bill Martens	1984	680
151-0/8	22-1/8	22-0/8	20-6/8	5	7	Nason Creek	WA	Deryl E. Bland	1964	682
151-0/8	18-4/8	21-2/8	17-4/8	5	5	Craig	CO	Wayne Liskey	1966	682
151-0/8	20-3/8	21-4/8	19-0/8	5	5	Platte County	WY	Jody Nordin	1984	682
150-7/8	22-3/8	23-4/8	20-0/8	6	6	Hockberry Creek	KS	Dale Redmond	1967	685
150-7/8	22-5/8	19-3/8	25-3/8	5	4	Monticello	UT	Ken Ciarelli	1968	685
150-7/8	22-6/8	22-6/8	20-1/8	6	6	Fremont County	CO	Dave Elliott	1976	685
150-6/8	20-5/8	20-3/8	20-5/8	5	5	Enterprise	UT	Jack Richards	1960	688
150-6/8	20-2/8	20-0/8	18-2/8	5	5	Albuquerque	NM	Lee Braudt	1968	688
150-6/8	21-2/8	20-6/8	18-4/8	5	5	John Day County	OR	Rodney Keenon	1982	688
150-5/8	22-7/8	20-7/8	18-6/8	5	5	Park County	CO	Marvin Clyncke	1978	691
150-5/8	24-2/8	24-7/8	19-6/8	6	5	Bernalillo County	NM	Alan Spitznagle	1982	691
150-4/8	21-6/8	22-0/8	21-649	5	6	Pima County	AZ	Tony Don	1980	693

MULE DEER *(Typical Antlers)*
(continued)

Score	Length of Main Beam R	L	Inside Spread	Number of Points R	L	Area	State/ Province	Hunter's Name	Date	Rank
150-4/8	21-4/8	21-4/8	19-4/8	5	4	Garfield County	CO	Keith Backhaus	1981	693
150-4/8	19-0/8	18-4/8	19-4/8	5	5	Maricopa County	AZ	Dave Barnhart	1986	693
150-3/8	22-6/8	22-7/8	15-5/8	4	5	Summit	UT	Clifton Rees	1962	696
150-3/8	19-6/8	20-3/8	19-7/8	4	5	Grand County	UT	Lowell W. Dobson	1968	696
150-3/8	21-0/8	21-0/8	15-7/8	5	5	Sandia Mountains	NM	Michael M. Emery	1973	696
150-3/8	21-6/8	22-1/8	22-4/8	4	5	Hamilton County	KS	Mike Gilbert	1976	696
150-3/8	21-6/8	21-1/8	19-7/8	5	5	Washoe County	NV	Fred C. Church	1983	696
150-2/8	13-0/8	19-7/8	15-3/8	3	6	Cottonwood R. S.	ID	Ralph Hoobing	1964	701
150-1/8	18-3/8	18-5/8	17-3/8	6	7	Douglas Pass	CO	J. B. Hogan	1961	702
150-1/8	24-7/8	26-2/8	24-0/8	5	5	Deschutes County	OR	Walter M. Graham	1963	702
150-1/8	22-3/8	22-2/8	18-3/8	5	5	Rand	CO	William B. Tutt	1964	702
150-1/8	22-6/8	22-7/8	22-3/8	4	4	Gove County	KS	Merton Ikenberry	1966	702
150-1/8	21-3/8	21-4/8	20-1/8	5	5	Washoe County	NV	Felton Hickman	1970	702
150-1/8	22-5/8	21-2/8	23-2/8	5	6	Box Elder County	UT	Steven B. Perry	1980	702
150-0/8	21-2/8	22-4/8	24-4/8	4	4	Eureka	NV	B. Verlyn Ownes	1963	708
150-0/8	18-7/8	18-6/8	16-3/8	5	6	Panquitch	UT	Dick Gulman	1966	708
150-0/8	19-3/8	21-4/8	20-4/8	5	5	Jarbidge	NV	Dick Woltering	1968	708
150-0/8	20-0/8	20-1/8	18-1/8	6	6	Larimer County	Co	Tom Tietz	1979	708
149-7/8	21-2/8	23-0/8	20-5/8	4	4	Fish Lake	UT	Milt McQueary	1964	712
149-7/8	20-1/8	20-1/8	17-3/8	5	5	Trego County	KS	Larry Pearson	1974	712
149-7/8	21-1/8	21-0/8	22-2/8	6	5	Rio Arriba County	NM	Howard Payne	1984	712
149-6/8	21-3/8	21-1/8	19-6/8	4	4	Douglas Pass	CO	Skip Candahl	1966	715
149-6/8	22-0/8	19-1/8	23-2/8	5	4	Uncompahgre N.F.	CO	Roy Miller	1972	715
149-6/8	26-5/8	27-5/8	25-0/8	7	4	Uncompahgre Plateau	CO	Jim Moan	1976	715
149-5/8	18-1/8	20-7/8	17-7/8	5	5	Black Sulpher Creek	CO	Joseph H. French	1972	718
149-5/8	21-2/8	20-2/8	19-1/8	6	8	Canmore	ALB	Karl Pachonik	1982	718
149-5/8	21-6/8	22-0/8	18-3/8	6	4	Boise County	ID	Tom Weston	1984	718
149-5/8	20-6/8	22-1/8	18-7/8	5	5	Nye County	NV	Ed Fuller	1986	718
149-4/8	22-4/8	22-4/8	19-2/8	4	4	Cimarron	NM	Ed Foster	1966	722
149-3/8	22-4/8	21-6/8	17-1/8	4	4	Okanogan County	WA	Irl Stamps	1939	723
149-3/8	22-4/8	20-4/8	19-1/8	5	7	Bourne	OR	Chuck Brackin	1964	723
149-3/8	21-5/8	22-5/8	20-7/8	5	4	Grand Mesa	CO	John Smith	1964	723
149-3/8	23-0/8	24-0/8	22-4/8	4	4	Baker Creek	NV	Milo W. Burt	1971	723
149-3/8	22-6/8	22-1/8	19-2/8	6	4	San Juan County	UT	Randy Radant	1984	723
149-2/8	22-6/8	22-5/8	21-4/8	4	4	Lake City	CO	Thomas V. Sieverding	1972	728
149-2/8	25-5/8	25-2/8	25-0/8	6	4	Lincoln County	WY	Mike Barrett	1984	728
149-2/8	22-3/8	22-5/8	21-4/8	5	5	Garfield County	CO	James P. Speck	1984	728
149-0/8	24-0/8	22-5/8	22-4/8	4	4	Uncompahgre Plateau	CO	Tom Hentrick	1974	731
148-7/8	22-3/8	23-5/8	20-3/8	6	4	Hodgeman County	KS	James Wiggins	1978	732
148-7/8	22-3/8	23-3/8	21-3/8	4	4	Crook County	OR	Vernon Simpson	1982	732
148-6/8	20-7/8	20-6/8	13-2/8	5	4	Okanogan County	WA	Dennis N. Johnson	1971	734
148-6/8	21-3/8	20-5/8	15-7/8	5	7	Lane County	KS	Vernon L. McBee	1971	734
148-6/8	21-0/8	22-3/8	21-3/8	5	6	Umatilla County	OR	Loren R. Olsen	1981	734
148-6/8	19-4/8	20-7/8	19-4/8	5	5	Converse County	WY	Greg Popie	1982	734
148-6/8	22-6/8	23-4/8	19-6/8	5	4	Siskiyou County	CA	Jim Langley	1984	734
148-6/8	20-6/8	21-1/8	22-1/8	6	6	Mesa County	CO	Parker Leon	1984	734
148-6/8	21-2/8	20-0/8	17-6/8	5	5	Sioux County	NE	Jeffrey Sales	1985	734
148-5/8	24-4/8	23-7/8	23-2/8	6	6	Chelan County	WA	Ted A. Kinsey	1983	741
148-4/8	19-4/8	19-0/8	17-0/8	5	5	Cottonwood R. S.	ID	Floyd Audette	1964	742
148-4/8	21-7/8	19-7/8	19-2/8	7	6	Perkins County	SD	Dr. David W. Schrody	1979	742
148-4/8	21-7/8	22-4/8	20-4/8	5	5	Campbell County	WY	Carrol D. Wert	1979	742
148-4/8	22-2/8	22-6/8	20-4/8	5	5	Bill	WY	James D. Miller	1980	742
148-4/8	21-3/8	22-1/8	23-7/8	4	4	Valley County	MT	Andy Hicks	1981	742
148-4/8	22-0/8	21-7/8	19-6/8	5	4	San Juan County	UT	Bill Clink	1985	742
148-3/8	22-5/8	23-5/8	18-5/8	5	4	LaVeta Pass	CO	Loren Johnson	1966	748
148-3/8	19-4/8	19-6/8	20-2/8	5	6	Silt	CO	Charles E. Whaley	1974	748
148-2/8	20-3/8	21-0/8	17-6/8	5	5	Fergus County	MT	Bob Wanner	1977	750
148-2/8	20-1/8	20-6/8	20-4/8	5	5	Billings County	ND	Thomas Treto	1982	750
148-2/8	21-0/8	23-1/8	21-1/8	4	5	Cochrane	ALB	David Richardson	1983	750
148-1/8	23-0/8	22-3/8	19-5/8	4	4	Basalt	CO	William F. Havel	1962	753
148-1/8	21-7/8	21-7/8	21-5/8	4	5	Hart Moutain	OR	Richard G. Speer	1964	753
148-1/8	20-0/8	21-0/8	21-0/8	4	5	Dodge City	KS	Aubrey Ballard	1966	753
148-1/8	20-7/8	20-1/8	18-5/8	5	4	Kremmling	CO	Judd Cooney	1969	753

MULE DEER *(Typical Antlers)*

Minimum Score 145

Score	Length of Main Beam R	L	Inside Spread	Number of Points R	L	Area	State/ Province	Hunter's Name	Date	Rank
148-1/8	19-0/8	19-3/8	18-5/8	5	5	Carbon County	UT	Leonard Thompson	1973	753
148-1/8	20-3/8	21-5/8	21-2/8	6	5	Hoxie	KS	Tom Reedy	1980	753
148-1/8	21-4/8	19-6/8	18-5/8	4	5	Mesa County	CO	Jay Verzuh	1982	753
148-1/8	21-4/8	22-1/8	19-3/8	5	4	Sheridan County	WY	Mike Barrett	1983	753
148-0/8	21-7/8	21-4/8	21-1/8	6	6	White River N.F.	CO	Paul M. Ramsey	1959	761
147-7/8	22-3/8	24-0/8	23-3/8	3	4	Delta	UT	Milton F. McQueary	1958	762
147-7/8	21-2/8	21-0/8	18-0/8	5	6	Deschutes	OR	Joe Reynolds	1967	762
147-7/8	21-5/8	22-0/8	21-5/8	5	5	Johnson County	WY	Scott L. Koelzer	1978	762
147-7/8	21-1/8	20-4/8	21-5/8	5	5	Carbon County	WY	Rod Schmidt	1984	762
147-7/8	23-7/8	22-7/8	20-7/8	5	4	Mesa County	CO	Richard Kunevicius	1985	762
147-7/8	22-2/8	21-0/8	21-5/8	5	4	Washoe County	NV	Cecil D. Martin	1986	762
147-6/8	20-0/8	20-2/8	20-2/8	5	4	Rifle	CO	Steve Love	1972	768
147-6/8	19-4/8	21-0/8	21-0/8	5	5	Clark	CO	John P. Hale	1974	768
147-6/8	20-5/8	21-6/8	15-6/8	7	5	New Castle	CO	Edwin Hurt	1980	768
147-6/8	22-5/8	22-2/8	20-5/8	5	5	Boise County	ID	Matt March, Jr.	1983	768
147-6/8	17-6/8	22-0/8	20-0/8	4	4	Malheur County	OR	Steve Savage	1985	768
147-5/8	21-6/8	21-4/8	20-1/8	5	5	Fish Lake	UT	Rowland Enomoto	1963	773
147-5/8	23-0/8	23-0/8	24-2/8	5	6	Monticello	UT	Jack Howard	1966	773
147-5/8	21-1/8	18-7/8	17-5/8	5	4	Sevier County	UT	Robert W. Shilling	1974	773
147-5/8	25-2/8	24-2/8	22-1/8	7	5	Garfield County	CO	Terry Bridgman	1978	773
147-4/8	22-1/8	22-2/8	19-4/8	5	5	Albuquerque	NM	Larry W. Johnson	1969	777
147-4/8	21-2/8	22-1/8	19-0/8	5	5	Boulder	CO	Jack Frank	1970	777
147-4/8	21-0/8	21-0/8	18-5/8	5	5	Garfield County	CO	Paul R. Shannon	1975	777
147-4/8	22-3/8	21-5/8	17-4/8	5	5	Guadalupe Canyon	AZ	Stephen C. Christensen	1976	777
147-4/8	20-1/8	20-5/8	19-6/8	5	5	Routt County	CO	Tom N. Garvin	1983	777
147-4/8	23-0/8	24-0/8	24-0/8	6	6	Sweetwater County	WY	Vic Dana	1983	777
147-4/8	24-2/8	22-2/8	20-2/8	4	5	Harney County	OR	Gary D. Nyden	1985	777
147-3/8	23-4/8	23-2/8	20-3/8	5	6	Valentine	NE	Jack E. Joseph	1961	784
147-3/8	19-4/8	20-4/8	16-5/8	4	5	Latah County	ID	Chas. A. McDonald	1965	784
147-2/8	21-3/8	18-7/8	23-6/8	5	5	Park County	CO	Ed Zehner	1972	786
147-2/8	22-7/8	23-2/8	17-0/8	6	6	Wood Lake	NE	Ken Hollpeter	1979	786
147-2/8	23-5/8	22-6/8	26-2/8	4	5	Pima County	AZ	Michael B. Cachero	1985	786
147-1/8	20-4/8	21-7/8	22-7/8	9	4	Emery County	UT	Bob Jacobsen	1961	789
147-1/8	20-5/8	20-1/8	16-7/8	5	5	Tavaputs Plateau	UT	Rolland Esterline	1967	789
147-1/8	19-6/8	23-6/8	17-0/8	6	5	Baker County	OR	Larry Garoutte	1970	789
147-1/8	22-5/8	21-2/8	24-0/8	6	9	Custer County	CO	Kurt Keskimaki	1981	789
147-0/8	20-3/8	20-7/8	20-2/8	5	5	Uintah County	UT	Merlin L. Killpack	1958	793
147-0/8	25-4/8	25-0/8	23-5/8	7	5	Moab	UT	William W. Selby	1974	793
147-0/8	21-6/8	21-7/8	20-6/8	5	5	Glendive	MT	Smucky Mann	1975	793
147-0/8	20-5/8	21-6/8	19-2/8	5	5	Area 57	WY	Ronald J. Wedge	1978	793
147-0/8	20-4/8	20-4/8	17-2/8	5	5	Stanley County	SD	George Hipple	1982	793
146-7/8	19-5/8	20-1/8	20-1/8	5	5	Book Cliff Mountains	UT	Norm Goodwin	1960	798
146-7/8	23-4/8	23-1/8	23-4/8	5	4	Orangeville	UT	Bruce Ware	1961	798
146-7/8	19-2/8	20-0/8	18-5/8	5	5	Sumpter	OR	James E. Hodson	1966	798
146-7/8	21-3/8	20-7/8	21-2/8	4	4	Saratoga	WY	John Swanson	1966	798
146-7/8	20-7/8	21-2/8	21-3/8	5	5	Meade County	SD	Kenneth McNenny	1967	798
146-7/8	21-2/8	21-4/8	18-7/8	5	5	Marshall Pass	CO	Skip Mulso	1974	798
146-7/8	20-3/8	21-5/8	20-3/8	6	5	Sheridan County	WY	David Shoop	1980	798
146-7/8	19-7/8	20-4/8	17-3/8	5	5	Mesa County	CO	Gary L. Hoekman	1986	798
146-6/8	19-6/8	20-3/8	15-7/8	4	4	Owyhee County	ID	Seneth Ward	1960	806
146-6/8	21-1/8	20-2/8	20-3/8	6	5	Glade Park	CO	Dennis Kelly	1981	806
146-6/8	20-4/8	19-7/8	19-0/8	6	7	Elbert County	CO	Donald A. Morgan	1983	806
146-6/8	23-3/8	24-2/8	22-2/8	4	4	Pitkin County	CO	Bill Krenz	1983	806
146-5/8	22-0/8	22-6/8	18-7/8	5	5	Nason Creek	WA	Gerald King	1963	810
146-4/8	23-3/8	23-0/8	21-0/8	4	5	Wayne County	UT	Harold Boyack	1968	811
146-4/8	20-0/8	20-7/8	19-4/8	5	4	Glade Park	CO	Kaye B. McCrory	1978	811
146-4/8	20-5/8	20-3/8	20-6/8	5	5	Johnson County	WY	Gary Olsen	1979	811
146-4/8	24-0/8	26-5/8	23-0/8	7	6	Eagle County	CO	Dave Mendoza	1983	811
146-4/8	23-6/8	21-6/8	24-123	5	9	Pima County	AZ	Stacy Tompkinson	1984	811
146-4/8	22-4/8	22-3/8	20-4/8	5	5	Piute County	UT	Tim Sayer	1984	811
146-4/8	22-3/8	22-1/8	19-6/8	5	4	Rio Grande County	CO	Jerry Woodland	1984	811
146-4/8	21-0/8	23-2/8	22-4/8	5	5	Bowman County	ND	Dwight Eckart	1984	811
146-4/8	21-7/8	22-4/8	16-7/8	5	8	Cache County	UT	Robert Bronson	1985	811

MULE DEER *(Typical Antlers)*

(continued)

Score	Length of Main Beam R	Length of Main Beam L	Inside Spread	Number of Points R	Number of Points L	Area	State/ Province	Hunter's Name	Date	Rank
146-3/8	19-0/8	19-0/8	17-3/8	5	5	Kaibab	AZ	George Kili	1964	820
146-3/8	20-2/8	21-1/8	19-1/8	5	5	Book Cliffs	UT	Bob Paulson	1967	820
146-3/8	21-0/8	21-2/8	19-5/8	5	5	Glade Park	CO	Curtis W. Dorroh	1979	820
146-3/8	19-2/8	21-2/8	19-3/8	4	4	Boulder County	CO	Al Miller	1983	820
146-3/8	20-4/8	21-3/8	19-5/8	5	6	San Miguel County	NM	Ricardo Roybal	1984	820
146-2/8	25-4/8	23-6/8	23-4/8	5	5	Trinidad	CO	Tom Valamdro	1967	825
146-2/8	21-0/8	20-2/8	19-1/8	7	6	Gallatin County	MT	Scott Koelzer	1969	825
146-2/8	21-4/8	21-4/8	20-0/8	5	5	Powder River County	MT	Charles R. Maloney	1973	825
146-2/8	22-4/8	22-0/8	19-0/8	4	5	Powder River County	MT	Mike Barrett	1985	825
146-1/8	20-6/8	19-0/8	15-7/8	5	5	Boise Front	ID	Jim Wenzel	1971	829
146-0/8	20-4/8	20-2/8	18-2/8	5	5	Ruby Mountains	NV	Howard Hill	1944	830
146-0/8	21-2/8	21-3/8	20-2/8	5	5	Grand Mesa	CO	William F. DeEsch	1966	830
146-0/8	18-6/8	19-7/8	17-0/8	5	5	Decatur County	KS	A. E. "Butch" Whelchel	1977	830
146-0/8	20-4/8	19-6/8	23-4/8	5	5	Lincoln County	WY	Vaughn Cross	1978	830
146-0/8	22-1/8	22-2/8	22-5/8	7	6	Lane County	KS	Dean Hamilton	1980	830
146-0/8	21-1/8	19-4/8	21-4/8	5	5	Billings County	ND	Roy Boots	1985	830
145-7/8	21-1/8	20-4/8	20-5/8	5	6	Madera County	CA	Rodney York	1978	836
145-7/8	20-1/8	20-3/8	19-5/8	4	4	Chelan County	WA	Rick Morgan	1984	836
145-6/8	17-0/8	18-3/8	16-0/8	5	5	Hart Mountain	OR	George Rajnus	1961	838
145-6/8	22-2/8	24-3/8	21-4/8	5	3	Fish Lake	UT	James R. Bell	1964	838
145-6/8	19-1/8	17-0/8	21-0/8	6	5	Canyon Creek	OR	Arthur Redinger	1972	838
145-5/8	24-1/8	21-2/8	24-2/8	6	6	Chaffee County	CO	Gary Ginther	1973	841
145-5/8	22-5/8	21-2/8	21-7/8	4	5	Ellis County	KS	Mark A. Murphey	1983	841
145-4/8	20-5/8	18-4/8	19-4/8	6	6	Left Hand Canyon	CO	Bob Byerly	1967	843
145-4/8	19-6/8	14-2/8	18-4/8	7	4	Catalina Mountains	AZ	Peter C. Knagge	1976	843
145-4/8	21-5/8	21-6/8	19-6/8	5	5	Sioux County	NE	Steve Woitaszewski	1983	843
145-4/8	21-7/8	22-4/8	20-4/8	5	4	Converse County	WY	Frank N. Moore	1984	843
145-4/8	18-6/8	18-7/8	21-0/8	5	4	Elbert County	CO	Calvin Farner	1984	843
145-4/8	18-4/8	19-4/8	16-6/8	4	4	Platte County	WY	Dave Hiiva	1985	843
145-4/8	23-3/8	23-5/8	22-4/8	5	5	Lassen County	CA	Wayne Wood	1985	843
145-3/8	27-2/8	26-5/8	26-2/8	5	4	Moffat County	CO	Scott Showalter	1971	850
145-3/8	21-1/8	20-4/8	19-7/8	4	4	Sioux County	NE	William A. Voor Vart	1978	850
145-2/8	24-0/8	24-4/8	19-6/8	4	4	Sandia Mountains	NM	Robert Bulcock, Jr.	1969	852
145-2/8	20-1/8	20-2/8	16-2/8	5	5	Uncompaghre N.F.	CO	Larry Holak	1979	852
145-2/8	21-7/8	22-7/8	25-2/8	3	3	Butte County	SD	Glenn D Priebe	1984	852
145-2/8	22-4/8	23-1/8	17-4/8	5	5	Mesa County	CO	Paul T Brown	1985	852
145-1/8	23-0/8	23-3/8	22-7/8	5	4	Casper	WY	Bill Wade	1970	856
145-1/8	21-6/8	19-3/8	19-1/8	4	5	Eagle County	CO	Rick Duggan	1981	856
145-1/8	19-4/8	20-3/8	17-5/8	5	4	Coconino County	AZ	Dick Tone	1981	856
145-1/8	23-4/8	21-3/8	20-7/8	4	4	Summit County	CO	Mark Anderson	1982	856
145-1/8	18-5/8	19-4/8	17-5/8	5	5	Routt County	CO	Ronald P. Kelley, Sr.	1985	856
145-0/8	22-1/8	21-6/8	17-6/8	5	5	Colorado Springs	CO	Thomas M. Farmer	1961	861
145-0/8	22-1/8	22-2/8	21-0/8	5	6	Trego County	KS	Don Howard	1966	861
145-0/8	22-1/8	22-4/8	21-2/8	5	5	Plumas County	CA	Wayne Ghidossi	1977	861

WORLD RECORD MULE DEER
(Non-Typical Antlers)
Score: 258 2/8
Mesa County, Colorado – 1976
Hunter: David Glick

MULE DEER *(Non-Typical Antlers)*
Odocoileus hemionus hemionus and certain related subspecies   Minimum Score 160

Score	Length of Main Beam R	Length of Main Beam L	Inside Spread	Number of Points R	Number of Points L	Area	State/ Province	Hunter's Name	Date	Rank
258-2/8	26-6/8	26-7/8	24-0/8	13	11	Mesa County	CO	David Glick	1976	1
246-6/8	25-1/8	27-4/8	24-6/8	12	11	Mesa County	CO	Dean Derby II	1976	2
236-1/8	25-5/8	25-2/8	18-3/8	10	11	Kaibab Forest	AZ	Stanley L. McIntyre	1965	3
232-5/8	26-3/8	24-7/8	20-3/8	11	10	Rio Blanco County	CO	Harold Boyack	1979	4
232-3/8	23-2/8	21-2/8	23-0/8	12	14	Arapaho County	CO	James P. Verney	1974	5
229-7/8	27-5/8	28-0/8	25-7/8	6	7	Lambs Canyon	UT	Lee Lindley	1942	6
225-4/8	23-4/8	23-2/8	22-0/8	10	13	Herd Unit 54	UT	John C. Balch	1965	7
225-2/8	24-2/8	24-2/8	23-1/8	12	7	Roan Creek	CO	Dennis Quinn	1972	8
224-6/8	25-5/8	25-5/8	22-4/8	9	9	Ferry County	WA	Romie Hilderbrant	1963	9
224-0/8	25-6/8	23-6/8	25-6/8	8	12	Lake County	OR	Jeff Eggleston	1986	10
223-7/8	27-5/8	26-4/8	24-4/8	12	9	Uncompahgre Mountains	CO	Steve Haynes	1972	11
222-1/8	23-2/8	23-7/8	19-4/8	8	7	Manti Canyon	UT	Louie Arko	1972	12
222-1/8	25-5/8	24-5/8	20-4/8	8	10	Montrose	CO	LaVern Rucker	1975	12
221-1/8	26-4/8	26-1/8	22-6/8	11	11	Bernalillo County	NM	Timothy Dwyer	1985	14
220-6/8	20-4/8	18-4/8	19-0/8	15	12	Coconino County	AZ	Placido Alderette	1978	15
220-3/8	27-3/8	27-1/8	23-1/8	11	7	Manti	UT	I. B. "Blackie" Owen	1964	16
220-2/8	26-6/8	26-0/8	24-7/8	8	9	Uncompahgre Plateau	CO	Michael T. Schwitters	1971	17
218-0/8	27-0/8	27-5/8	27-0/8	7	9	Blanding	UT	Harold Boyack	1974	18
218-0/8	26-1/8	25-0/8	25-0/8	8	9	Garfield County	CO	Bob Hill	1979	18
217-6/8	25-6/8	26-4/8	23-6/8	8	10	Caribou County	ID	James C. Ashley	1977	20
216-6/8	23-4/8	24-4/8	22-0/8	9	12	Rifle	CO	Richard Lepak	1975	21
216-6/8	21-2/8	23-1/8	26-0/8	9	8	Glade Park	CO	Roger Lewis	1980	21
216-2/8	21-7/8	22-5/8	19-4/8	8	9	Mt. Trumbull	AZ	William Cross	1965	23
215-5/8	21-3/8	23-0/8	16-6/8	7	10	Uinta County	UT	Jon E Bingham	1969	24
214-0/8	25-3/8	25-4/8	22-3/8	8	9	Circle	MT	James F. Kosi	1974	25
213-0/8	22-2/8	23-3/8	18-7/8	10	9	Soda Springs	ID	Bob McAteer	1966	26
212-0/8	21-0/8	20-5/8	19-5/8	10	9	Calgary	ALB	Bert Frelink	1985	27
211-6/8	23-4/8	23-3/8	24-4/8	8	8	Ness County	KS	Ralph Stum	1966	28
211-1/8	23-5/8	24-4/8	20-6/8	7	7	Uintah	UT	Vern Hatch	1962	29
210-2/8	22-2/8	27-6/8	27-2/8	4	7	Buzzard Creek	CO	Art Cook	1972	30
208-3/8	23-6/8	26-7/8	23-6/8	10	8	Adams County	ID	Donnie Lee Voss	1986	31
208-1/8	26-5/8	25-5/8	21-7/8	8	8	Grand County	UT	Charles Denver	1986	32
207-0/8	24-2/8	23-0/8	20-6/8	7	5	Boise County	ID	Deloy Desaro	1972	33
206-7/8	22-2/8	24-1/8	22-1/8	7	9	Lemhi County	ID	A. LaVerne Hokanson	1967	34
205-3/8	24-2/8	24-0/8	22-0/8	8	8	Book Cliff Mountains	UT	C. B. "John" Olsen	1958	35
204-4/8	26-2/8	22-6/8	17-5/8	7	9	Fishlake National Forest	UT	Dick Kerr	1955	36
204-3/8	23-6/8	25-3/8	18-1/8	8	8	Collbran	CO	Don Zanow	1976	37
204-1/8	25-3/8	26-2/8	17-2/8	11	10	Umatilla County	OR	Dan Follett	1982	38
203-4/8	19-7/8	20-7/8	18-7/8	11	12	Johnson County	WY	Chuck Webster	1983	39
202-5/8	26-0/8	25-3/8	23-3/8	6	7	Garfield County	CO	A. H. Sandidge	1972	40
202-4/8	22-0/8	21-5/8	16-4/8	9	8	Harrison County	NE	Douglas Buckley	1982	41
201-6/8	21-4/8	22-5/8	22-0/8	9	8	Soda Springs	ID	Dennis Dockstader	1969	42
200-3/8	24-4/8	24-3/8	19-4/8	8	9	Farm Creek	UT	Tex Ross	1966	43
200-2/8	27-5/8	26-2/8	19-1/8	9	8	Montezuma County	CO	Bryon C. Neeley	1971	44
200-1/8	23-7/8	22-1/8	20-2/8	7	8	Pima County	AZ	Jim Johnson	1981	45
199-7/8	26-6/8	23-3/8	22-0/8	10	9	Glade Park	CO	Larry Stewart	1975	46
199-1/8	22-6/8	23-4/8	19-1/8	9	10	Mesa County	CO	James R. Boyles	1971	47
198-5/8	24-1/8	23-3/8	19-2/8	5	11	Teller County	CO	Robert Runkles	1986	48
198-0/8	21-5/8	22-0/8	19-0/8	8	9	Routt County	CO	Bruce F. Davison	1968	49
197-7/8	21-6/8	22-6/8	23-4/8	9	8	Franklin County	KS	John R. Coblentz	1966	50
197-7/8	26-5/8	26-3/8	25-0/8	9	7	Lincoln County	MT	Gary Weber	1978	50
197-5/8	22-0/8	21-1/8	20-5/8	10	8	Pine	ID	Jerry G. Fetters	1970	52
196-5/8	24-6/8	24-4/8	25-5/8	9	7	Morton County	KS	Kevin White	1982	53
195-7/8	25-0/8	24-6/8	22-6/8	6	7	Lemhi County	ID	James Stuart	1982	54
195-6/8	21-2/8	22-6/8	19-3/8	9	9	Weld County	CO	Densel Bolin	1974	55
195-4/8	25-2/8	23-2/8	22-3/8	9	14	?	CO	Douglas Kenyon	1964	56
194-7/8	23-0/8	22-7/8	19-7/8	6	7	Finney County	KS	Jay Sloan	1967	57
194-7/8	26-649	25-3/8	22-3/8	6	7	Mirror Lake	UT	Frank Warburton	1969	57
193-7/8	23-4/8	24-0/8	22-1/8	9	7	Sumpter	OR	B. G. Shurtleff	1980	59
193-6/8	22-5/8	22-6/8	20-0/8	9	9	Spanish Fork Canyon	UT	Ivan B. Henderson, Jr.	1959	60
192-4/8	24-4/8	26-0/8	21-3/8	6	7	Caribou County	ID	Mack Tigert	1985	61
191-7/8	22-2/8	19-1/8	17-6/8	7	12	Bell Marsh Canyon	ID	Loren H. Dunn	1965	62
191-4/8	23-2/8	24-3/8	17-1/8	5	10	Garfield County	CO	J. D. Jones	1971	63

MULE DEER *(Non-Typical Antlers)*

(continued)

Minimum Score 160

Score	Length of Main Beam R	L	Inside Spread	Number of Points R	L	Area	State/ Province	Hunter's Name	Date	Rank
191-4/8	23-6/8	23-6/8	20-6/8	7	8	Grant County	OR	Joe Mengore	1981	63
191-1/8	23-1/8	24-3/8	22-0/8	7	9	Smith County	KS	Linton Haresnape	1981	65
190-6/8	23-5/8	22-4/8	21-3/8	6	7	Laveta Pass	CO	Ron Johnson	1970	66
189-4/8	23-4/8	23-4/8	17-2/8	7	8	Kaycee	WY	Charles Jahnke	1979	67
189-1/8	20-1/8	22-2/8	19-3/8	6	8	Battlement Mountian	CO	Robert C. McCardell	1974	68
189-0/8	20-0/8	22-3/8	16-7/8	8	6	New Castle	CO	Stephen Kennedy	1975	69
188-7/8	25-1/8	24-6/8	25-2/8	12	11	Dawson County	MT	Monte Dassinger	1973	70
187-7/8	17-1/8	22-1/8	16-3/8	12	8	Book Cliffs	UT	Lee Allred	1958	71
187-2/8	22-0/8	22-0/8	21-2/8	6	6	Eagle County	CO	Gary O. Glenn	1978	72
187-2/8	23-2/8	23-7/8	20-6/8	9	7	Ouray County	CO	Roger Wyant	1984	72
186-6/8	25-6/8	22-1/8	24-6/8	8	6	Dolores County	CO	Michael W. Forth	1978	74
186-0/8	23-1/8	21-5/8	21-0/8	8	7	Ravalli County	MT	Ed Barrett	1983	75
185-7/8	22-7/8	22-3/8	18-0/8	11	8	Klamath County	OR	Charles A. Warner	1975	76
184-2/8	20-5/8	21-5/8	19-3/8	8	6	Uintah Basin	UT	Dean Reynolds	1961	77
183-3/8	25-5/8	25-1/8	25-0/8	6	7	Franklin County	ID	Doug Ransom	1985	78
182-0/8	25-0/8	24-4/8	23-7/8	7	8	Farragut St. Park	ID	Rodney W. Willis	1977	79
181-5/8	27-0/8	24-3/8	23-4/8	7	9	Nason Creek	WA	David M. Bartholemew	1967	80
181-4/8	27-5/8	26-3/8	27-4/8	5	7	Como	CO	John Cliff	1967	81
180-4/8	21-1/8	22-5/8	21-3/8	7	5	Spanish Fork Canyon	UT	Frank Warburton	1972	82
177-7/8	21-2/8	18-6/8	20-2/8	6	7	Garfield County	CO	Steve Byerly	1980	83
176-7/8	20-5/8	22-5/8	21-2/8	7	7	Rock Creek	CO	Adolph Kuhns	1961	84
176-0/8	23-3/8	23-5/8	20-4/8	6	6	Scott County	KS	Vince Strickler	1975	85
175-7/8	19-4/8	20-7/8	18-6/8	6	6	Beaver Flattops	CO	Chuck Nemec	1974	86
175-7/8	24-4/8	22-2/8	26-1/8	9	7	Rio Arriba County	NM	Michael D. Bruce	1986	86
175-3/8	24-2/8	23-2/8	17-3/8	7	8	Culberson County	TX	Gary Oden	1985	88
174-7/8	25-1/8	22-4/8	27-0/8	6	5	Grant County	OR	Chuck Warner	1983	89
174-3/8	23-4/8	24-3/8	23-5/8	7	8	Glendive	MT	Richard Harmes	1972	90
174-2/8	23-6/8	23-1/8	22-0/8	9	10	Gateway	CO	Art Cook	1958	91
174-1/8	25-7/8	24-5/8	18-7/8	7	5	Carbon County	UT	B. E. Epperson	1971	92
173-3/8	20-4/8	26-6/8	20-3/8	6	5	Morrow County	OR	Ray Kelton	1976	93
173-1/8	19-7/8	22-1/8	17-1/8	8	7	Ft. Robinson	NE	LaVerne J. Weber	1975	94
173-1/8	21-3/8	21-3/8	21-4/8	8	8	Boise County	ID	Peter J. Cintorino	1980	94
173-0/8	25-3/8	24-6/8	31-0/8	6	7	San Juan County	UT	Guy Gates	1970	96
171-4/8	22-2/8	20-1/8	16-3/8	5	12	Mesa County	CO	Paul H. Dickson	1985	97
171-3/8	21-1/8	22-1/8	21-1/8	8	6	Meade County	KS	Richard A. Nordyke	1971	98
170-7/8	18-4/8	20-0/8	17-1/8	6	6	Wallowa County	OR	Wayne van Zwoll	1977	99
170-6/8	23-6/8	24-1/8	21-2/8	7	7	Jughandle Mountain	ID	John Pyle	1978	100
170-5/8	22-0/8	22-1/8	16-3/8	6	5	Hart Mountain	OR	Bill Hendrick	1964	101
170-5/8	20-6/8	24-2/8	29-0/8	9	9	Ness County	KS	Pete McBee	1969	101
170-4/8	20-3/8	19-5/8	20-4/8	5	7	McCone County	MT	David Tofte	1985	103
170-3/8	25-6/8	26-4/8	29-0/8	6	6	Grant County	OR	Ray Kelton	1980	104
170-0/8	19-5/8	17-5/8	19-5/8	7	5	Pierceville	KS	Rod Lies	1968	105
169-4/8	23-4/8	22-4/8	18-5/8	7	8	Brewster County	TX	Roger Wintle	1986	106
169-0/8	25-2/8	25-4/8	21-0/8	6	7	Lassen County	CA	Wayne Wood	1984	107
168-7/8	25-7/8	25-5/8	22-1/8	8	6	Uncompahgre N.F.	CO	Thomas J. Hentrick	1972	108
166-5/8	20-3/8	20-1/8	20-2/8	7	7	Linn County	OR	Joe Mengore	1980	109
166-3/8	22-4/8	21-7/8	19-4/8	9	10	Grand County	CO	Jim Fitzgerald	1984	110
164-6/8	20-2/8	21-2/8	18-0/8	6	6	Meade County	KS	Kent Davis	1972	111

WORLD RECORD WHITETAIL DEER
(Typical Antlers)
Score: 204 4/8
Peoria County, Illinois – 1965
Hunter: Melvin J. Johnson

WHITETAIL DEER *(Typical Antlers)*

Minimum Score 125

Odocoileus virginianus virginianus and certain related subspecies

Score	Length of Main Beam R	Length of Main Beam L	Inside Spread	Number of Points R	Number of Points L	Area	State/ Province	Hunter's Name	Date	Rank
204-4/8	27-5/8	26-6/8	23-5/8	7	6	Peoria County	IL	M. J. Johnson	1965	1
197-6/8	25-6/8	26-4/8	18-6/8	7	7	Monroe County	IA	Lloyd Goad	1962	2
197-6/8	29-1/8	30-2/8	20-4/8	6	5	Wright County	MN	Curt Van Lith	1986	2
194-2/8	26-5/8	25-0/8	21-0/8	6	6	Jones County	IA	Robert L. Miller	1977	4
194-0/8	25-6/8	25-3/8	23-6/8	6	7	Logan County	CO	Stuart Clodfelder	1981	5
190-5/8	27-0/8	27-1/8	18-0/8	5	7	Warren County	IA	Richard Swim	1981	6
190-4/8	28-6/8	28-3/8	20-0/8	5	6	Parke County	IN	B. Dodd Porter	1985	7
189-1/8	27-3/8	28-6/8	20-1/8	8	7	Kearney County	NE	Robert Vrbsky	1978	8
182-2/8	27-2/8	28-3/8	21-1/8	8	6	Jefferson County	KS	John Welborn	1982	9
182-0/8	26-5/8	28-6/8	22-1/8	6	7	Jefferson County	KS	Michael J. Rose	1982	10
181-7/8	28-6/8	27-0/8	21-6/8	5	7	Greenwood County	KS	Boyd Schneider	1984	11
181-7/8	26-6/8	26-5/8	21-7/8	7	6	Dakota County	MN	Eugene Lengsfeld	1985	11
181-6/8	26-1/8	26-4/8	17-6/8	5	5	Lake City	MN	Lee G. Partington	1971	13
181-4/8	29-6/8	29-5/8	24-2/8	6	5	Keya Paha County	NE	Steve R. Pecsenye	1966	14
181-4/8	26-0/8	28-5/8	18-6/8	9	7	Canton	IL	Arnold Hegele	1968	14
181-4/8	26-5/8	26-7/8	24-4/8	5	6	North Norfolk	MAN	Lloyd Lintott	1986	14
180-1/8	25-4/8	24-2/8	17-5/8	6	6	Lamoille	MN	Kenneth W. Schreiber	1980	17
179-5/8	26-6/8	25-7/8	20-7/8	7	8	Lac Qui Parle County	MN	Mary A. Barvels	1978	18
179-3/8	26-2/8	26-5/8	17-3/8	5	5	Marshal County	SD	Phyllis Roehr	1976	19
179-0/8	25-7/8	25-7/8	22-1/8	6	6	Scotland County	MO	David Smith	1985	20
179-0/8	27-2/8	26-1/8	19-2/8	6	5	Wapello County	IA	Robert L. McDowell	1985	20
178-4/8	26-2/8	25-0/8	21-2/8	5	6	Meade County	KS	Tim Ross	1985	22
178-4/8	25-1/8	25-0/8	18-4/8	5	5	Fulton County	IL	Locie L. Murphy	1985	22
178-3/8	25-6/8	26-4/8	21-2/8	7	8	McPherson County	KS	Larry Daniels	1967	24
177-3/8	28-3/8	28-1/8	18-6/8	6	6	Wayne County	OH	Gary E. Landry	1975	25
177-3/8	27-3/8	26-5/8	20-7/8	5	7	Jones County	IA	Ken Dausener	1984	25
176-6/8	25-2/8	25-0/8	23-4/8	6	6	Frankfort	KS	Ray A. Mosher	1966	27
176-2/8	28-2/8	27-5/8	21-0/8	7	5	Houston County	MN	John Zahrte	1981	28
176-2/8	28-0/8	28-6/8	21-2/8	5	6	Kingman County	KS	Gerald Stroot	1981	28
176-1/8	25-1/8	26-1/8	21-0/8	7	5	Lewis County	KY	Alfred Simms	1985	30
176-0/8	25-5/8	23-6/8	25-5/8	6	5	Clay County	KS	Rayford W. Willingham	1985	31
175-7/8	27-3/8	26-4/8	24-4/8	7	6	Kandiyohi County	MN	Eldon Hauser	1969	32
175-5/8	29-0/8	28-6/8	21-3/8	4	4	Burnett County	WI	Myles Keller	1977	33
175-5/8	25-4/8	25-2/8	22-2/8	7	7	Pratt County	KS	Gary Brehm	1984	33
175-5/8	26-0/8	25-6/8	22-2/8	5	6	Dickinson County	KS	Gary Stroda	1985	33
175-4/8	26-0/8	25-4/8	17-7/8	9	5	Murray County	MN	Steven Wynia	1973	36
175-3/8	25-7/8	26-5/8	19-7/8	5	5	Ottawa County	KS	Gary Gans	1985	37
175-2/8	28-5/8	27-2/8	23-5/8	6	6	Sangamon County	IL	Wm. Richard Olsen	1978	38
175-2/8	26-1/8	25-7/8	20-0/8	6	6	St. Mary County	LA	Shannon Presley	1981	38
175-1/8	24-4/8	24-4/8	21-5/8	5	6	Marion County	IA	Gordon Hayes	1973	40
175-1/8	26-3/8	28-0/8	21-3/8	7	9	Dodge County	MN	Bill Chase	1976	40
174-5/8	25-1/8	25-7/8	18-7/8	5	5	Pickaway County	OH	Hunter R. Certain	1985	42
174-4/8	25-4/8	24-7/8	27-2/8	7	5	Toole County	MT	Dale Farnes	1979	43
173-7/8	24-0/8	24-2/8	19-1/8	5	5	Noble County	OK	Danny McCants	1968	44
173-7/8	27-2/8	26-2/8	25-5/8	5	5	Texas County	MO	Don Belew	1981	44
173-6/8	26-6/8	27-1/8	19-7/8	7	5	Mercer County	IL	Floyd A. Clark	1961	46
173-6/8	26-1/8	25-0/8	21-5/8	6	5	Winneshiek County	IA	Herbert Amundson	1985	46
173-5/8	26-2/8	26-0/8	22-3/8	6	7	Muskingum County	OH	David R. Hatfield	1980	48
173-4/8	26-2/8	27-1/8	23-4/8	6	5	Lac Qui Parle County	MN	Dale W. Shackelford	1981	49
173-3/8	26-4/8	26-5/8	20-1/8	5	6	Warren County	IL	Larry C. Harding	1974	50
173-2/8	26-0/8	26-3/8	22-5/8	5	5	Miami County	KS	Dan R. Moore	1982	51
173-0/8	25-6/8	25-5/8	19-4/8	5	5	White County	IN	Eric L. Mohler	1978	52
172-6/8	26-7/8	27-6/8	19-4/8	5	5	Ripley County	IN	Steve A. Allen	1982	53
172-6/8	25-4/8	25-1/8	19-4/8	5	5	Sullivan County	TN	C. Alan Altizer	1984	53
172-4/8	26-0/8	26-0/8	18-2/8	7	6	Lucas County	IA	Jim Barlow	1985	55
172-3/8	26-3/8	24-0/8	18-6/8	6	7	Clinton County	IL	James D. Rueter	1984	56
172-2/8	26-1/8	25-3/8	19-2/8	5	6	Iowa County	IA	Ardith Lockridge	1965	57
172-2/8	27-3/8	25-1/8	18-4/8	5	5	Clinton County	IA	Robert S. Stankee	1985	57
172-0/8	24-6/8	24-2/8	18-6/8	5	5	Whiteside County	IL	Noel Feather	1977	59
171-7/8	26-2/8	26-4/8	24-1/8	5	5	Scotland County	MO	David Smith	1984	60
171-7/8	28-5/8	28-0/8	20-7/8	8	7	Linn County	IA	Charles Bemer	1985	60
171-6/8	26-7/8	26-6/8	25-2/8	7	8	Richland County	ND	Todd Funfar	1982	62
171-6/8	28-1/8	27-1/8	17-6/8	7	6	Carroll County	OH	Randy S Mulheim	1983	62

WHITETAIL DEER *(Typical Antlers)*

(continued)   Minimum Score 125

Score	Length of Main Beam R	L	Inside Spread	Number of Points R	L	Area	State/ Province	Hunter's Name	Date	Rank
171-5/8	24-6/8	24-0/8	17-3/8	6	6	Calgary	ALB	Scott Simi	1979	64
171-5/8	25-3/8	25-2/8	20-3/8	8	6	Cowley County	KS	Michael L. Snyder	1985	64
171-4/8	24-3/8	23-2/8	16-6/8	6	6	Ellsworth County	KS	Jim Willems	1985	66
171-3/8	23-7/8	24-5/8	18-7/8	5	5	Harrison County	IA	R. A. Cronk	1985	67
171-1/8	23-5/8	24-0/8	16-7/8	6	6	Monticello	IL	Ronald E. Waugh	1971	68
171-1/8	24-3/8	23-2/8	17-4/8	8	7	Mandan	ND	Tony Schatz	1974	68
171-0/8	30-0/8	27-5/8	19-5/8	5	8	Belmont County	OH	Charles J. Wilson	1979	70
171-0/8	27-4/8	27-4/8	22-2/8	5	5	Parke County	IN	Fred Sills	1985	70
170-7/8	27-6/8	27-5/8	18-4/8	6	8	Republic County	KS	Carroll Couture	1986	72
170-6/8	26-1/8	25-3/8	17-4/8	5	5	St. Ansgar	IA	Dan Block	1981	73
170-6/8	26-7/8	28-1/8	19-6/8	5	5	Racine County	WI	Anthony J Wozniak	1985	73
170-5/8	23-6/8	23-4/8	16-5/8	6	6	Teton County	MT	James R. Dean	1983	75
170-4/8	25-1/8	25-4/8	20-2/8	5	4	Des Moines County	IA	Bob Fudge	1966	76
170-3/8	28-5/8	28-2/8	21-6/8	6	4	Hall County	NE	Gust Bergman	1965	77
170-3/8	22-4/8	23-7/8	24-7/8	6	6	Cass County	ND	Warren Buss	1966	77
170-3/8	27-0/8	26-1/8	20-3/8	5	5	Ogle County	IL	John E. Lawson	1985	77
170-2/8	27-1/8	27-2/8	21-0/8	4	4	Opelika	AL	George P. Mann	1980	80
170-1/8	26-1/8	27-1/8	22-1/8	5	5	Edwards County	KS	Jay Schaller	1968	81
170-1/8	25-4/8	25-7/8	22-2/8	6	7	Winona County	MN	Roger Traxler	1980	81
170-1/8	25-6/8	25-2/8	21-3/8	5	5	Mower County	MN	Robert D. Plumb	1984	81
170-0/8	26-1/8	26-6/8	20-0/8	5	5	Scott County	KS	Monte L. Barker	1973	84
170-0/8	29-4/8	29-0/8	20-4/8	6	6	Puslinch Twp.	ONT	Richard Foss	1980	84
169-6/8	26-0/8	27-3/8	20-6/8	4	4	Decatur County	IA	Bruce Jermyn	1979	86
169-6/8	29-6/8	29-2/8	27-0/8	6	6	Coffey County	KS	Jack McCullough	1984	86
169-4/8	23-7/8	25-2/8	17-7/8	6	7	Charles Mix County	SD	Don Carda	1974	88
169-2/8	26-1/8	27-2/8	21-6/8	6	6	Ashland County	OH	Darrell Huff	1985	89
169-1/8	28-6/8	28-2/8	19-3/8	6	5	Lasalle County	IL	Dave Mrowicki	1985	90
169-0/8	25-5/8	25-2/8	20-5/8	5	5	Marion County	KS	Max Williams	1985	91
168-7/8	24-3/8	24-4/8	20-7/8	5	5	Jackson County	IA	Al Weidenbacher	1984	92
168-7/8	27-4/8	27-0/8	19-0/8	5	6	Washington County	MN	Ronald Jacobson	1985	92
168-5/8	26-2/8	26-0/8	18-5/8	5	6	Des Moines County	IA	Michael P. Anderson	1977	94
168-5/8	26-3/8	26-1/8	20-6/8	5	6	Mahoning County	OH	Jeff J Hartman	1984	94
168-5/8	25-0/8	24-5/8	17-1/8	7	7	Calhoun County	IL	Dennis A. Kendall	1985	94
168-4/8	24-0/8	24-7/8	18-6/8	5	5	Lincoln County	KS	Gerald Huehl	1985	97
168-2/8	27-0/8	26-5/8	19-2/8	5	7	Cowley County	KS	Larry G. Gann	1975	98
168-2/8	25-0/8	24-4/8	21-2/8	5	5	Macon County	IL	Larry D. Smith	1985	98
168-2/8	27-2/8	26-7/8	20-4/8	5	6	Lyon County	KS	John R. Clifton	1985	98
168-1/8	27-0/8	27-7/8	20-1/8	6	6	Blue Earth County	MN	Rich Detjen	1984	101
168-0/8	27-2/8	25-7/8	19-0/8	5	5	Vinton	OH	Ronald E. Morgan	1978	102
168-0/8	26-0/8	25-6/8	19-1/8	10	5	Amherst County	VA	William Dixon Morgan	1980	102
168-0/8	25-4/8	23-7/8	15-6/8	7	7	Dewitt County	IL	William R. Henson	1982	102
167-7/8	27-6/8	27-7/8	21-2/8	6	6	Brown County	OH	David Grayson	1976	105
167-6/8	26-4/8	26-2/8	19-6/8	5	5	Monona County	IA	Douglas M. Bonine	1985	106
167-6/8	27-2/8	27-1/8	21-2/8	5	5	Coffey County	KS	Edward L. Bess	1985	106
167-5/8	27-7/8	26-6/8	20-7/8	7	7	Chase County	KS	William E. Drummond	1984	108
167-4/8	22-4/8	23-1/8	18-4/8	5	5	Washington County	KS	Bill R. Mallean	1974	109
167-3/8	25-1/8	25-0/8	20-5/8	5	7	Sauk County	WI	Daniel Kaczmar	1985	110
167-1/8	24-5/8	24-7/8	18-6/8	5	6	Chase County	KS	Ronald E. Rhodes	1985	111
167-0/8	28-0/8	27-6/8	19-0/8	6	5	Clay County	MN	Ryan Hines	1986	112
166-7/8	26-4/8	26-4/8	20-1/8	7	5	Saline County	NE	Scott Theis	1982	113
166-6/8	24-3/8	24-0/8	21-6/8	6	7	Lanigan	SAS	Bob Tempel	1985	114
166-5/8	26-7/8	27-4/8	19-5/8	5	5	Lyon County	MN	Gene Gustafson	1982	115
166-3/8	26-6/8	26-4/8	17-1/8	6	6	Clarke County	IA	Dwight E. Green	1965	116
166-3/8	26-3/8	26-0/8	18-2/8	8	5	Yankton County	SD	Roger Irwin	1985	116
166-2/8	29-3/8	29-4/8	21-5/8	6	4	Monoma County	IA	G. K. Tuttle	1967	118
166-1/8	23-2/8	23-5/8	19-3/8	5	5	Camp River	MN	Corey Loney	1963	119
166-1/8	27-0/8	27-1/8	18-0/8	5	6	Stearns	MN	Bruce C. Meade	1978	119
166-0/8	27-5/8	26-7/8	23-4/8	5	5	Clinton County	IA	Loy J. Brooker	1964	121
166-0/8	23-4/8	23-5/8	18-0/8	5	5	Springfield	SD	Delbert Newman	1964	121
166-0/8	26-1/8	28-4/8	21-6/8	7	6	Shelby County	IL	Ernest D. Richardson	1977	121
166-0/8	26-6/8	24-2/8	22-7/8	6	6	Anoka County	MN	John A. Cardinal	1979	121
166-0/8	24-5/8	25-2/8	20-4/8	6	5	Tazewell County	IL	Jerry W. Kammerer	1981	121
165-7/8	23-4/8	23-4/8	16-3/8	5	5	Wapello County	IA	Richard L. Larsen	1976	126

WHITETAIL DEER *(Typical Antlers)*

(continued)

Minimum Score 125

Score	Length of Main Beam R	L	Inside Spread	Number of Points R	L	Area	State/ Province	Hunter's Name	Date	Rank
165-7/8	25-4/8	26-1/8	17-5/8	7	6	Licking County	OH	Pat Walker	1978	126
165-7/8	27-2/8	27-0/8	19-5/8	5	5	Prowers County	CO	Edward Henson	1980	126
165-6/8	27-0/8	26-1/8	19-0/8	7	6	Pott County	IA	Dan Bowen	1968	129
165-4/8	25-6/8	25-1/8	21-0/8	5	5	Kent County	MD	Kent Price	1962	130
165-4/8	23-2/8	22-5/8	19-4/8	6	6	Peoria County	IL	Larry T Oppe	1984	130
165-3/8	23-7/8	25-6/8	17-1/8	5	7	Owen County	KY	Joseph Caruso	1977	132
165-3/8	27-0/8	27-2/8	22-5/8	7	7	Coal City	IL	Gary R. Kuriger	1978	132
165-2/8	26-5/8	24-6/8	18-1/8	6	6	McPherson County	KS	Daniel Willems	1981	134
165-2/8	25-6/8	24-2/8	18-2/8	5	5	Clermont County	OH	Nick Lung	1985	134
165-1/8	25-3/8	25-5/8	21-7/8	5	5	Barry County	MI	Jim Birmingham	1977	136
165-1/8	24-0/8	24-2/8	20-1/8	6	6	Sawyer County	WI	Robert N. Dale	1980	136
165-1/8	22-1/8	18-1/8	21-7/8	6	6	Iowa County	IA	David Roberts	1980	136
165-0/8	25-2/8	23-5/8	19-0/8	6	6	Srony Plain	ALB	Wayne C. Prier	1983	139
165-0/8	24-1/8	24-2/8	17-6/8	5	5	Doniphan County	KS	Richard Williams	1983	139
164-7/8	28-0/8	25-1/8	20-1/8	4	5	Kane County	IL	James A. Anderson	1980	141
164-7/8	25-4/8	26-2/8	19-3/8	5	5	Peoria County	IL	Joe R. McCord	1983	141
164-7/8	24-7/8	25-0/8	17-1/8	5	5	Elkhart County	IN	Joe Leszczynski	1984	141
164-7/8	25-0/8	25-4/8	19-3/8	6	6	Gray County	KS	Ralph W. Herron	1984	141
164-7/8	26-1/8	25-6/8	21-7/8	6	6	Madison County	MT	Gordan Sampson	1986	141
164-6/8	28-1/8	26-5/8	20-7/8	8	5	Shelby County	OH	Jerry Atkinson	1975	146
164-6/8	26-4/8	28-2/8	22-2/8	5	6	Highland County	OH	Daniel L. Henges	1976	146
164-6/8	27-5/8	26-0/8	15-6/8	5	5	Sanilac County	MI	Michael J. Wines	1981	146
164-6/8	26-0/8	26-2/8	20-6/8	5	5	Macoupin County	IL	John E. Eldred	1985	146
164-5/8	25-2/8	23-5/8	18-5/8	8	6	Sumner County	KS	Archie A. Stralow	1967	150
164-5/8	22-5/8	22-6/8	25-2/8	5	7	Dodge County	MN	Myles Keller	1985	150
164-4/8	23-7/8	24-3/8	18-6/8	5	5	Morton County	ND	Butch Sammons	1985	152
164-4/8	27-5/8	27-0/8	19-3/8	5	6	Trempealeau County	WI	Keith Lynch	1985	152
164-3/8	25-4/8	25-4/8	19-6/8	8	7	Norman County	MN	Gilbert Guttormson	1953	154
164-3/8	21-4/8	21-6/8	16-5/8	6	6	Wibaux County	MT	Gerald Polesky	1959	154
164-3/8	28-4/8	28-0/8	20-4/8	7	8	Trigg County	KY	Charles Stahl	1965	154
164-3/8	25-1/8	25-2/8	18-3/8	5	5	Cottonwood County	MN	Jim Hansen	1972	154
164-3/8	26-4/8	25-5/8	17-3/8	7	8	Madison County	MT	Jim Schilke	1978	154
164-3/8	25-6/8	25-4/8	20-1/8	5	7	Shiawassee N.W.R.	MI	Larry Steinley	1979	154
164-3/8	27-1/8	27-5/8	20-7/8	4	4	Hardin County	OH	Anthony A. Krummrey	1982	154
164-3/8	26-7/8	27-0/8	20-7/8	4	4	Louisa County	IA	Roger Gipple	1984	154
164-2/8	27-2/8	26-2/8	21-0/8	11	9	Coal City	IL	Jerome M. Fris	1972	162
164-1/8	26-5/8	26-3/8	18-2/8	6	5	Ft. Ripley	MN	Lloyd Neuman	1971	163
164-1/8	26-2/8	26-4/8	22-5/8	5	5	Washington County	OH	Roger Pape	1980	163
164-1/8	24-6/8	24-5/8	16-5/8	5	6	Dundy County	NE	John Crump	1983	163
164-0/8	24-3/8	25-0/8	16-6/8	5	5	Olmstead County	MN	Robert Meyer	1969	166
164-0/8	25-1/8	25-5/8	23-3/8	5	7	Morrison County	MN	Bruce Edberg	1977	166
163-6/8	23-6/8	26-5/8	19-2/8	5	5	Fayette County	IA	Bob Nicolay	1981	168
163-6/8	23-5/8	25-4/8	19-4/8	7	8	Porter County	IN	Raymond T. Satterblom	1983	168
163-5/8	25-6/8	25-4/8	21-6/8	5	5	Phillips County	KS	Bill Duncan	1969	170
163-5/8	26-5/8	26-1/8	21-3/8	6	6	Lawrence County	IL	Larry K. Karns	1975	170
163-5/8	25-5/8	25-1/8	19-3/8	5	5	Wright County	MN	Rick Heberling	1978	170
163-4/8	25-4/8	25-5/8	18-0/8	5	7	Swenson Bend	ND	Bobby Triplett	1958	173
163-4/8	23-4/8	23-0/8	17-6/8	5	5	Wright County	MN	Dale Guetzkow	1978	173
163-4/8	28-1/8	30-0/8	23-2/8	5	5	Lawrence County	OH	Berkley Pennington, Sr.	1981	173
163-4/8	27-6/8	27-5/8	19-3/8	7	8	Buffalo County	WI	Patrick Ryan	1985	173
163-3/8	24-4/8	22-7/8	22-1/8	5	5	Linn County	IA	Delmar Phillips	1960	177
163-3/8	24-3/8	23-7/8	17-5/8	8	7	Morrison County	MN	Alvin A. Diemert	1973	177
163-3/8	26-4/8	26-2/8	20-5/8	5	5	Scott County	KY	Garry Hoffman	1982	177
163-3/8	26-1/8	26-7/8	15-3/8	6	7	Chase County	KS	John Moore	1983	177
163-3/8	24-4/8	25-0/8	19-0/8	8	8	Winnebago County	IL	Bradley S. Conrad	1984	177
163-2/8	28-2/8	27-3/8	23-7/8	6	6	Brown County	IL	Keith E. Meiser	1981	182
163-2/8	25-7/8	29-2/8	22-6/8	8	5	Monticello County	AR	Larry Standley	1982	182
163-2/8	25-4/8	25-5/8	19-6/8	5	5	Mason County	KY	R. Kenton Ring	1982	182
163-2/8	26-1/8	24-6/8	16-3/8	5	7	Licking County	OH	Don Conrad	1985	182
163-2/8	24-1/8	24-4/8	21-2/8	5	5	Sumner County	KS	Kevin Disney	1985	182
163-1/8	27-6/8	27-5/8	18-6/8	8	5	Knox County	OH	Robert L. Hammond	1983	187
163-0/8	24-0/8	24-6/8	20-0/8	5	5	Dickinson County	IA	Harold Ehrp	1959	188
163-0/8	25-2/8	25-0/8	15-1/8	6	6	Texas County	OK	Edward F. Bryan, Jr.	1976	188

WHITETAIL DEER *(Typical Antlers)*

(continued)   Minimum Score 125

Score	Length of Main Beam R	L	Inside Spread	Number of Points R	L	Area	State/ Province	Hunter's Name	Date	Rank
163-0/8	26-3/8	25-3/8	22-0/8	7	8	Vevay	IN	Richard W. Keebler	1977	188
162-7/8	29-0/8	30-4/8	19-0/8	6	8	Centerville	MD	L. P. Stephens, Jr.	1962	191
162-7/8	24-6/8	24-6/8	22-4/8	6	7	Cowley County	KS	Kenneth Highfill	1968	191
162-7/8	26-6/8	26-7/8	19-5/8	5	5	Kookuk County	IA	Mike Bentler	1983	191
162-6/8	24-2/8	26-2/8	20-6/8	6	7	Rice County	MN	Ken Bakken	1957	194
162-6/8	26-2/8	26-2/8	19-4/8	5	6	Clayton County	IA	Dale Kartman	1984	194
162-5/8	26-2/8	24-0/8	20-7/8	8	7	Marshall County	KS	Gary W. Tobin	1966	196
162-5/8	26-4/8	27-5/8	20-3/8	4	4	Saunders County	NE	Robert Parkins	1967	196
162-5/8	26-6/8	26-6/8	21-5/8	5	7	Henry County	IL	Lewis E. Burson	1976	196
162-5/8	25-2/8	24-7/8	20-1/8	4	5	Lucas County	IA	Bill Brown	1979	196
162-5/8	25-2/8	25-3/8	15-7/8	5	8	Crawford County	KS	Fred Geier	1981	196
162-5/8	27-2/8	27-4/8	19-7/8	5	5	St. Charles County	MO	Roland Heiliger	1985	196
162-4/8	23-6/8	23-6/8	21-0/8	7	6	Branch County	MI	Randy Massey	1981	202
162-4/8	25-4/8	27-0/8	18-6/8	5	5	Allegheny County	PA	Christopher T. Joyce	1985	202
162-3/8	24-2/8	24-6/8	19-7/8	5	5	Barber County	KS	Glen Snell	1982	204
162-2/8	22-2/8	24-7/8	17-6/8	6	5	Kingsbury County	SD	Dale Peterson	1972	205
162-2/8	24-7/8	24-2/8	19-0/8	5	5	Marion County	KS	Leslie Lalouette	1983	205
162-2/8	25-3/8	24-7/8	17-6/8	5	5	Trego County	KS	Craig Doll	1985	205
162-1/8	23-6/8	24-7/8	17-6/8	6	6	Buffalo County	WI	Bruce Curtis	1983	208
162-1/8	23-4/8	24-2/8	20-4/8	6	5	Winnebago County	IL	Jeffrey A. Saxby	1984	208
162-1/8	25-2/8	26-0/8	16-4/8	8	6	Monroe County	IA	Larry Whitson	1985	208
162-0/8	25-0/8	27-1/8	20-4/8	8	6	Bond County	IL	Larry Nelson	1976	211
162-0/8	24-2/8	24-2/8	17-2/8	5	5	Lancaster	IL	Ron Hawf	1978	211
162-0/8	24-3/8	27-2/8	19-2/8	6	6	Edgar County	IL	John J. Dillon	1985	211
161-7/8	23-4/8	25-4/8	18-3/8	5	5	Leshare	NE	David Strimple	1961	214
161-7/8	24-2/8	24-1/8	20-7/8	5	5	Douglas County	NE	Noel Miller	1970	214
161-7/8	23-5/8	24-0/8	17-6/8	7	7	Fulton County	IL	Bob Neal	1981	214
161-7/8	26-0/8	27-2/8	20-7/8	5	5	Greene County	OH	Charles O. Hill	1982	214
161-7/8	25-3/8	26-0/8	20-6/8	7	7	Tuscarawas County	OH	Gary Stevens	1982	214
161-7/8	23-3/8	22-2/8	16-0/8	6	6	Brandon	MAN	Gary Kaluzniak	1985	214
161-7/8	26-5/8	25-6/8	18-3/8	6	5	Winona County	MN	Tim Rislow	1986	214
161-5/8	23-3/8	23-1/8	14-5/8	6	6	Dunn County	WI	Leonard Hines	1970	221
161-5/8	22-6/8	22-5/8	18-6/8	5	6	Necedah	WI	Harlan Steindl	1971	221
161-5/8	25-0/8	25-5/8	19-1/8	6	6	Jefferson County	IL	Rick Osborn	1982	221
161-5/8	22-5/8	24-3/8	17-7/8	5	5	Butler County	KS	Mike Turner	1982	221
161-5/8	26-3/8	24-4/8	16-4/8	5	6	Butler County	KS	Ronald Tilson	1983	221
161-4/8	26-1/8	26-1/8	19-2/8	5	4	Bond County	IL	Sam White	1974	226
161-4/8	26-0/8	25-6/8	17-4/8	8	6	Jackson	LA	James K. Morgan	1977	226
161-4/8	25-2/8	27-0/8	20-2/8	5	5	Sumner County	KS	Phill Allton	1983	226
161-4/8	28-4/8	28-3/8	22-1/8	5	5	Jones County	IA	David A. Leuchs	1984	226
161-3/8	25-0/8	23-6/8	16-6/8	8	7	Wyandotte County	KS	George F. Bigelow	1967	230
161-3/8	26-4/8	25-4/8	19-1/8	6	6	Sumner County	KS	Larry Wycoff	1980	230
161-3/8	29-1/8	27-2/8	23-4/8	7	8	Clark County	OH	Kenneth Preston	1982	230
161-3/8	27-2/8	25-4/8	22-3/8	4	6	Fayette County	IL	Bill Holman	1983	230
161-3/8	23-1/8	23-0/8	19-1/8	6	5	Augaize County	OH	Lee Atha	1983	230
161-3/8	23-0/8	24-1/8	14-5/8	5	5	Butler County	KS	David R. Rogers	1985	230
161-2/8	24-2/8	24-0/8	20-0/8	5	5	Muskingum County	OH	Lee E Wilson	1984	236
161-2/8	23-3/8	24-7/8	18-7/8	6	5	Graham County	KS	Chris Jolly	1984	236
161-1/8	26-0/8	27-1/8	18-6/8	6	5	Charlestown	IN	Frank Mauk, Jr.	1966	238
161-1/8	24-2/8	25-1/8	16-7/8	5	5	Marinette County	WI	Dale J. Hanson	1985	238
161-0/8	26-2/8	25-1/8	19-4/8	5	5	LaCrosse County	WI	Ray Howell	1977	240
161-0/8	28-0/8	27-3/8	23-4/8	4	4	Jefferson County	IN	Donnie Ball	1984	240
161-0/8	27-7/8	26-4/8	21-3/8	6	5	Morris County	KS	Craig Johnson	1985	240
160-7/8	25-5/8	27-3/8	21-4/8	5	6	?	IA	Everett Reid	1962	243
160-7/8	24-2/8	23-4/8	17-6/8	7	5	Smith County	KS	Ron Sturgeon	1965	243
160-7/8	22-6/8	23-1/8	21-1/8	5	5	Lincoln County	MN	Bernie Ahlberg	1974	243
160-7/8	24-2/8	23-5/8	19-3/8	5	5	Saline County	KS	Ray Peterman	1979	243
160-7/8	25-1/8	26-7/8	18-5/8	4	4	Pike County	IL	Richard Dewey	1981	243
160-7/8	24-5/8	23-4/8	15-3/8	5	6	Leavenworth County	KS	Albert Lyle Karl	1982	243
160-6/8	25-4/8	25-7/8	17-0/8	6	5	Bellevue	NE	Lawrence A. Klabunde	1968	249
160-6/8	26-2/8	27-0/8	21-5/8	5	6	Alleghany County	VA	Roger O. Wyant	1984	249
160-5/8	22-3/8	23-4/8	16-4/8	7	8	Lawrence County	IL	Bob Brian	1971	251
160-5/8	24-4/8	25-5/8	23-4/8	5	6	Murray County	MN	Paul Beech	1974	251

WHITETAIL DEER *(Typical Antlers)*

Minimum Score 125

(continued)

Score	Length of Main Beam R	Length of Main Beam L	Inside Spread	Number of Points R	Number of Points L	Area	State/ Province	Hunter's Name	Date	Rank
160-5/8	25-2/8	25-3/8	14-3/8	6	5	Hubbard County	MN	Myles Keller	1982	251
160-4/8	20-5/8	24-0/8	24-3/8	7	5	Medicine Creek Lake	NE	Vernon Laverack	1959	254
160-4/8	26-6/8	25-4/8	20-7/8	7	7	Williston	ND	John Bloom	1963	254
160-4/8	27-2/8	28-0/8	21-4/8	5	7	Lyon County	IA	Marvin H. Peterson	1970	254
160-4/8	23-1/8	22-4/8	19-0/8	6	7	Keith County	NE	Gil Wilkinson	1970	254
160-4/8	28-5/8	28-2/8	24-2/8	7	7	Fairfield County	OH	Robert A. Fletcher	1977	254
160-4/8	24-2/8	24-7/8	17-6/8	5	6	Dawson County	MT	Frank Legato	1978	254
160-4/8	26-0/8	26-2/8	19-2/8	5	5	Trempealeau County	WI	Duane Kupietz	1981	254
160-4/8	24-2/8	24-7/8	19-2/8	6	5	Waukesha County	WI	Donald T. Lurvey	1982	254
160-3/8	22-2/8	22-4/8	20-7/8	6	6	Rushville	NE	Wayne Krotz	1975	262
160-3/8	24-3/8	24-2/8	17-1/8	5	5	St. Charles County	MO	Dan Schulte	1976	262
160-3/8	23-6/8	24-7/8	20-1/8	7	6	Barber County	KS	Herbie M. Landwehr, Jr.	1980	262
160-3/8	27-5/8	26-0/8	19-7/8	4	4	Clark County	IL	Gerald Shaffner	1983	262
160-2/8	25-6/8	26-3/8	19-2/8	5	5	Nance County	NE	Ralph I. Hansen	1963	266
160-2/8	25-7/8	26-0/8	21-4/8	4	4	Cherokee	IA	Jerry L. Smith	1969	266
160-2/8	22-6/8	23-3/8	19-4/8	5	5	Glasgow	MT	John "Rosey" Roseland	1981	266
160-2/8	23-1/8	23-1/8	18-0/8	6	6	Mills County	IA	Dale R. Clayton	1983	266
160-2/8	24-5/8	24-6/8	18-1/8	6	6	Phelps County	NE	Bruce Nielsen	1984	266
160-1/8	25-7/8	26-2/8	18-5/8	5	6	Polk County	MN	Scott Gullickson	1985	271
160-1/8	25-3/8	25-6/8	17-3/8	6	6	Blue Earth County	MN	Darwin Arndt	1985	271
160-0/8	24-6/8	24-5/8	21-3/8	6	6	Worth County	IA	Terry Lynch	1972	273
160-0/8	26-3/8	24-7/8	21-6/8	8	5	Winona County	MN	James Enderson	1973	273
160-0/8	23-0/8	22-3/8	20-0/8	5	5	Cooper County	MO	Nancy Smith	1984	273
160-0/8	22-7/8	23-0/8	17-2/8	6	5	Morrill County	NE	Michael A. Brening	1985	273
159-7/8	22-7/8	22-5/8	18-2/8	5	6	Clark County	KS	William Rule	1983	277
159-6/8	26-2/8	25-7/8	19-2/8	6	4	Fillmore County	MN	Doyle Tarrence	1974	278
159-6/8	21-2/8	21-2/8	17-0/8	5	5	Hillsdale	IN	Floyd Jackson	1977	278
159-6/8	24-1/8	23-2/8	19-6/8	5	6	Sherburne County	MN	Allen Hugget	1981	278
159-6/8	26-7/8	25-6/8	17-6/8	6	6	Buffalo County	WI	Bill Peterson	1981	278
159-6/8	25-0/8	25-0/8	18-2/8	5	5	Miami County	KS	Tom Wiggin	1982	278
159-6/8	25-6/8	25-1/8	20-6/8	4	4	Washington County	MS	Steve Nichols	1986	278
159-5/8	26-3/8	25-5/8	21-5/8	5	5	Des Moines County	IA	Richard Howard	1964	284
159-5/8	22-4/8	22-3/8	18-1/8	5	5	McAlester Ads	OK	John Baumann	1977	284
159-5/8	23-7/8	23-7/8	15-5/8	6	6	Reno County	KS	Richard A. Swisher	1978	284
159-5/8	24-6/8	23-1/8	18-1/8	5	5	Madison County	IL	Barry Ash	1980	284
159-5/8	24-5/8	26-1/8	18-5/8	6	5	Muskingum County	OH	Brent L. Taylor	1981	284
159-5/8	25-4/8	24-7/8	17-7/8	4	4	Ogle County	IL	Charles L. Martoglio	1982	284
159-5/8	24-6/8	24-6/8	20-7/8	6	5	Watonwan County	MN	Richard Enger	1983	284
159-5/8	26-2/8	26-2/8	23-6/8	6	6	Cochrane	ALB	Edward Defrancesco	1984	284
159-4/8	27-6/8	27-6/8	25-4/8	4	4	Blue Earth County	MN	Harold Tow	1963	292
159-4/8	22-6/8	21-5/8	17-5/8	6	5	Wabash County	IL	Tom J. McRaven	1967	292
159-4/8	24-5/8	24-6/8	21-2/8	5	5	Hocking County	OH	James Allen Downs	1980	292
159-4/8	22-5/8	22-6/8	18-0/8	5	4	Morris County	KS	Kenneth R. Bryant	1983	292
159-4/8	24-4/8	24-6/8	18-0/8	5	6	Dade County	MO	Charles A. Myers	1985	292
159-4/8	24-7/8	27-3/8	18-0/8	6	6	Scott County	IA	Albert Perreault	1985	292
159-4/8	26-0/8	25-2/8	19-0/8	5	4	Goodhue County	MN	Brad C. Nesseth	1986	292
159-3/8	27-6/8	27-1/8	22-3/8	4	4	Pike	OH	Ray C. Pritchett, Jr.	1977	299
159-3/8	25-5/8	25-4/8	18-5/8	4	4	Washington County	KS	Tony Mann	1985	299
159-2/8	22-4/8	24-0/8	20-2/8	6	7	Hamlin County	SD	John R. Gregory	1975	301
159-2/8	25-1/8	27-6/8	20-6/8	4	4	Yankton County	SD	Michael L. Tacke	1983	301
159-2/8	23-2/8	23-0/8	16-2/8	5	5	Anne Arundel County	MD	Jim Roy	1985	301
159-1/8	23-7/8	23-0/8	20-1/8	6	6	Lucas County	OH	Martin Higley	1962	304
159-1/8	22-4/8	24-2/8	16-5/8	7	6	Clayton County	IA	Gary Troester	1978	304
159-1/8	26-2/8	25-6/8	17-4/8	6	6	S.W. Heard County	GA	Howard E. Taylor	1980	304
159-1/8	24-7/8	25-7/8	21-5/8	8	6	Saline County	KS	Raymond Peterman	1984	304
159-0/8	25-7/8	26-1/8	17-6/8	5	5	Shelby County	IL	Gary E. Sievers	1971	308
159-0/8	22-6/8	22-6/8	18-4/8	5	5	Pulaski County	IN	William F. Bean	1977	308
159-0/8	23-3/8	23-7/8	18-3/8	7	7	Sarpy County	NE	Todd W. Steward	1985	308
158-7/8	24-7/8	22-4/8	20-3/8	5	6	Pope County	IL	Gary Thomas	1964	311
158-7/8	27-4/8	25-7/8	18-3/8	8	8	Blue Earth County	MN	Gordon F. Kopischke	1968	311
158-7/8	24-7/8	24-2/8	18-1/8	6	5	Gosport	IN	Steven Collins	1973	311
158-7/8	23-1/8	22-4/8	19-7/8	5	5	Sedgwick County	KS	Marion A. Crumm	1974	311
158-7/8	24-1/8	24-1/8	20-6/8	5	6	Putnam County	IL	David A. Heath	1975	311

WHITETAIL DEER *(Typical Antlers)*

(continued)   Minimum Score 125

Score	Length of Main Beam		Inside Spread	Number of Points		Area	State/ Province	Hunter's Name	Date	Rank
	R	L		R	L					
158-6/8	22-5/8	22-7/8	15-6/8	7	7	Irion County	TX	John K. Watson	1977	316
158-5/8	24-3/8	25-3/8	15-6/8	5	9	Marinette County	WI	Valerie P. Williams	1966	317
158-5/8	24-4/8	23-6/8	18-5/8	5	5	Shelby County	IL	Jim Helm	1977	317
158-4/8	23-5/8	22-3/8	20-0/8	5	6	Cedar	KS	Gordon Reneberg	1965	319
158-4/8	26-4/8	25-2/8	22-6/8	5	5	Des Moines County	IA	Michael P. Anderson	1978	319
158-4/8	23-7/8	24-1/8	16-7/8	6	6	Boone County	IA	Chris W. Doran	1984	319
158-3/8	22-5/8	23-1/8	15-3/8	6	6	Texas County	OK	Edward F. Bryan, Jr.	1980	322
158-3/8	23-2/8	23-3/8	19-5/8	5	5	Jackson County	MI	Donald L. O'Dell	1984	322
158-2/8	26-4/8	24-6/8	22-7/8	5	7	Lee County	IA	Gary Frost	1965	324
158-1/8	25-2/8	25-4/8	16-5/8	5	4	Randolph County	IN	Ron J. Carlin	1973	325
158-1/8	22-4/8	22-5/8	17-6/8	6	5	Algona	IA	Steve Rochleau	1981	325
158-1/8	25-1/8	24-2/8	21-5/8	5	4	King George County	VA	L. M. "Ted" Williams	1981	325
158-1/8	25-2/8	25-4/8	17-7/8	6	6	Jackson County	IA	Jeff W. Ernst	1984	325
158-1/8	25-5/8	24-7/8	18-2/8	6	6	Brown County	OH	Michael W. Babcock	1985	325
158-1/8	26-4/8	26-4/8	18-1/8	6	6	Wyandot County	OH	Michael D Saam	1985	325
158-0/8	24-0/8	23-5/8	18-6/8	6	6	Wayne County	IL	Bill Naney	1981	331
158-0/8	24-0/8	24-0/8	19-1/8	6	6	Lancaster County	NE	Martin Erickson	1983	331
157-7/8	23-0/8	25-0/8	19-5/8	5	5	Meeker County	MN	Russell T. Nelson	1974	333
157-7/8	28-5/8	28-6/8	25-7/8	4	4	Goodhue County	MN	John "Jack" Cordes	1975	333
157-7/8	23-7/8	24-1/8	16-4/8	5	7	Harvey County	KS	P. Bruce Mosiman	1984	333
157-6/8	23-7/8	24-2/8	15-4/8	5	5	Lyon County	MN	M. Dean Holm	1976	336
157-6/8	23-4/8	23-3/8	18-4/8	5	5	Phillips County	KS	Lavern A. Wheaton	1978	336
157-6/8	25-3/8	26-1/8	19-5/8	6	6	Des Moines County	IA	David Bollei	1979	336
157-6/8	24-7/8	25-2/8	21-4/8	4	6	Geauga County	OH	John A. Suszynski	1981	336
157-6/8	24-4/8	24-4/8	16-4/8	4	5	Oconto County	WI	Richard E. Liss	1983	336
157-6/8	23-3/8	23-6/8	17-1/8	6	6	Leavenworth County	KS	John Garrison	1983	336
157-6/8	23-6/8	23-6/8	17-5/8	8	6	DesMoines County	IA	Ken Thorndyke	1984	336
157-5/8	22-4/8	23-2/8	16-5/8	6	7	Marion County	KS	Ron Hershberger	1923	343
157-5/8	22-7/8	24-2/8	18-7/8	5	6	Fulton County	AR	Lynn Luther	1983	343
157-5/8	27-4/8	27-2/8	21-1/8	5	6	Saline County	KS	Richard Cockroft	1985	343
157-4/8	25-7/8	25-7/8	17-2/8	4	4	Marion County	IA	Charles H. Walter	1967	346
157-4/8	22-7/8	23-5/8	18-0/8	5	5	Kalamazoo County	MI	Guy Stutzman	1979	346
157-4/8	24-2/8	24-4/8	13-6/8	5	5	Webster County	IA	Larry K. Fossen	1980	346
157-3/8	23-0/8	23-2/8	22-7/8	5	5	Adams County	IL	John Musolino	1966	349
157-3/8	23-5/8	23-2/8	16-3/8	5	5	Harrison County	KY	Kevin Poe	1984	349
157-3/8	24-4/8	23-1/8	16-1/8	6	5	Yuma County	CO	Chuck Anderson, Sr.	1985	349
157-2/8	23-1/8	22-6/8	16-2/8	6	6	Johnson County	IL	Jim Casey	1963	352
157-2/8	22-3/8	23-2/8	16-4/8	5	5	Mountrail County	ND	Dean A. Rehak	1963	352
157-2/8	22-3/8	22-2/8	21-1/8	8	6	Cottonwood County	MN	Brian Grothe	1978	352
157-2/8	27-6/8	27-6/8	22-3/8	5	6	Jessamine County	KY	David Cartwright	1979	352
157-2/8	25-4/8	25-0/8	17-6/8	5	6	Argyle	MAN	Russ Snell	1982	352
157-2/8	26-2/8	28-0/8	20-4/8	8	5	Westchester County	NY	Ralph Finacchiaro	1983	352
157-1/8	25-3/8	26-1/8	18-5/8	6	6	Puslinch Twp.	ONT	Jeff Sinclair	1977	358
157-0/8	25-7/8	26-0/8	16-5/8	6	7	Medelia	MN	Dave Ellertson	1973	359
157-0/8	25-3/8	26-0/8	15-6/8	7	8	McKenzie County	ND	Donald Olson	1974	359
157-0/8	23-6/8	23-7/8	20-7/8	7	6	McLean County	IL	Daryle W. Tipsord	1985	359
156-7/8	28-7/8	26-6/8	19-7/8	5	5	Chippewa County	MN	Paul D. Lundgren	1969	362
156-7/8	25-2/8	24-5/8	19-7/8	6	5	Johnson County	KS	Jim Laybourne	1979	362
156-7/8	25-6/8	25-4/8	19-7/8	6	5	Kildeer	IL	Dennis P. Schor	1979	362
156-7/8	27-1/8	25-0/8	21-3/8	5	6	Clearwater County	MN	Dennis Engerbretson	1980	362
156-7/8	23-7/8	23-7/8	19-5/8	5	5	Cherokee County	IA	Dan Roberts	1982	362
156-7/8	24-0/8	23-7/8	18-0/8	6	6	Butler County	KS	William D. George	1986	362
156-6/8	27-1/8	26-5/8	20-5/8	5	5	Lincoln County	WV	Gary Smith	1970	368
156-6/8	24-1/8	24-0/8	16-6/8	5	5	Meigs County	OH	Brian Kelley	1982	368
156-5/8	26-1/8	25-2/8	20-2/8	6	6	Grant County	WI	Walter Edge	1957	370
156-5/8	24-6/8	26-3/8	19-5/8	5	4	Traverse County	MN	Roland L. Hausmann	1960	370
156-5/8	22-7/8	25-0/8	19-6/8	7	7	Des Moines County	IA	E. E. Smith	1965	370
156-5/8	23-7/8	24-1/8	18-7/8	7	7	Nicollet County	MN	Thomas J. Merkley	1967	370
156-5/8	27-3/8	26-2/8	21-5/8	5	5	Queen Annes County	MD	Charles Milford Squires	1969	370
156-5/8	24-7/8	24-3/8	21-1/8	6	5	Wabaunsee County	KS	Tom Willard	1983	370
156-5/8	22-0/8	22-2/8	16-1/8	6	8	Koosuth County	IA	Ron Burton	1985	370
156-4/8	26-4/8	25-7/8	22-5/8	4	5	Crab Orchard Lake	IL	Roy Williams	1960	377
156-4/8	26-3/8	24-4/8	17-4/8	5	6	Forest County	WI	Daniel Radder	1968	377

WHITETAIL DEER *(Typical Antlers)*

(continued)

Minimum Score 125

Score	Length of Main Beam R	L	Inside Spread	Number of Points R	L	Area	State/ Province	Hunter's Name	Date	Rank
156-4/8	24-1/8	23-3/8	15-0/8	6	5	Jones County	IA	Gary McCormick	1977	377
156-4/8	23-7/8	24-1/8	18-3/8	6	6	Hill City	KS	Russell Hull	1979	377
156-3/8	27-0/8	25-5/8	20-0/8	8	6	Hamilton County	KS	Mike Gilbert	1977	381
156-3/8	25-0/8	25-2/8	18-4/8	6	8	Russell County	KS	John W. Frost	1983	381
156-2/8	26-1/8	26-4/8	21-0/8	6	6	Butler County	KS	Ralph R. Belt	1967	383
156-2/8	25-0/8	23-2/8	18-0/8	9	6	Palo Alto County	IA	Earl J. Gustafson	1972	383
156-2/8	23-3/8	23-6/8	16-6/8	5	5	Fulton County	IL	Sam Smith	1973	383
156-2/8	25-3/8	25-3/8	23-6/8	5	6	Winona County	MN	Daniel McIntire	1979	383
156-2/8	22-2/8	22-7/8	16-6/8	5	5	Jordan	MT	Larry H. Hoyt	1982	383
156-2/8	25-2/8	26-2/8	18-6/8	6	5	Stevens County	WA	Tom Duffey	1983	383
156-2/8	25-5/8	26-1/8	19-0/8	4	5	Ogle County	IL	Gary D. Shaw	1984	383
156-2/8	25-1/8	26-0/8	19-4/8	5	5	Oakland County	MI	David B. Tater	1984	383
156-2/8	24-2/8	24-6/8	21-0/8	5	4	Cass County	IL	Dale Milstead	1985	383
156-1/8	25-4/8	25-2/8	19-1/8	5	5	Crawford County	IL	Mickie D. Purcell	1972	392
156-1/8	24-3/8	23-7/8	19-7/8	5	5	Ravali County	MT	Vernon L. Cooper	1977	392
156-1/8	22-6/8	23-2/8	17-7/8	5	5	Monroe County	OH	Wendell Newhouse	1982	392
156-1/8	24-3/8	25-0/8	19-7/8	7	8	Douglas County	NE	Oran L. Foxworthy	1984	392
156-1/8	25-5/8	24-6/8	22-1/8	4	4	Sumner County	KS	Ralph Shaver	1984	392
156-1/8	22-1/8	25-7/8	17-1/8	7	5	Cloud County	KS	Richard Bieker	1985	392
156-0/8	26-0/8	27-1/8	16-4/8	4	5	Bertie County	NC	Gordon Gardner	1975	398
156-0/8	23-4/8	23-7/8	19-6/8	5	5	Stark County	OH	Don Cerosky	1979	398
156-0/8	25-5/8	25-6/8	19-6/8	4	4	Louisa County	IA	Roger Gipple	1982	398
156-0/8	22-2/8	22-5/8	19-6/8	7	7	Perry County	IL	Terry Queen	1983	398
155-7/8	24-7/8	24-4/8	19-7/8	5	5	Frontier County	NE	Charles Druse	1963	402
155-7/8	24-3/8	24-5/8	15-5/8	5	5	Modale	IA	Clarence N. Jackson, Jr.	1963	402
155-6/8	25-1/8	24-4/8	18-4/8	4	5	Madison County	NE	Dick Gambill	1967	404
155-6/8	23-0/8	23-6/8	19-2/8	5	6	Monroe County	IA	John Vollmer	1982	404
155-6/8	24-0/8	23-6/8	16-7/8	5	6	Area 28	MAN	Gary Kaluzniak	1983	404
155-6/8	21-6/8	20-5/8	16-4/8	6	6	McHenry County	IL	Michael D. Patrick	1984	404
155-6/8	25-2/8	24-1/8	20-2/8	5	5	Lawrence County	MO	David T. Kail	1984	404
155-5/8	25-5/8	26-0/8	19-1/8	5	6	Rice County	KS	Gordon Leo Rayl	1967	409
155-5/8	22-5/8	23-0/8	18-5/8	5	5	Anne Arundel County	MD	Gene Hyatt	1976	409
155-5/8	25-2/8	23-7/8	17-1/8	5	5	Trempealeau County	WI	Greg Halpern	1982	409
155-4/8	23-2/8	25-4/8	18-6/8	7	7	Westchester County	NY	Bernard J. Crescione	1960	412
155-4/8	25-5/8	25-5/8	16-4/8	5	5	Marion County	IA	Thomas L. Tucker	1967	412
155-4/8	26-2/8	25-4/8	22-3/8	5	6	Dubuque County	IA	Kurt Cable	1973	412
155-4/8	23-6/8	25-4/8	19-5/8	7	7	Flathead County	MT	Ralph Ertz	1977	412
155-4/8	22-3/8	22-3/8	18-1/8	5	6	Lucas County	IA	Lance Brauer	1980	412
155-4/8	23-2/8	23-6/8	16-6/8	5	5	Lyon County	KS	Ronald E. Rhodes	1981	412
155-4/8	27-0/8	26-2/8	20-0/8	4	4	Houston County	MN	Gary L. Maier	1985	412
155-4/8	23-4/8	24-0/8	20-0/8	5	5	Posey County	IN	Duane Daws	1985	412
155-4/8	24-1/8	24-0/8	19-4/8	5	5	Marinette County	WI	John Floriano	1985	412
155-4/8	25-1/8	24-6/8	18-0/8	5	6	Washburn County	WI	Wayne Dahlstrom	1986	412
155-3/8	23-5/8	24-0/8	18-4/8	6	7	Garden City	KS	Wray Decker	1966	422
155-3/8	26-0/8	26-3/8	21-1/8	5	6	Chickasaw County	IA	William A. Harris	1978	422
155-3/8	23-3/8	24-2/8	16-0/8	6	5	Union County	OH	Jerry Faine	1982	422
155-3/8	26-2/8	25-5/8	19-6/8	6	4	Dodge County	MN	Jimmie Donald Hanna	1983	422
155-3/8	29-2/8	28-2/8	19-7/8	6	8	McDonough County	IL	Locie L. Murphy	1983	422
155-3/8	24-4/8	24-5/8	21-3/8	5	5	Suffolk County	NY	John C. Wehrs	1984	422
155-3/8	21-4/8	22-0/8	15-5/8	5	6	McKenzie County	ND	Brent Smith	1985	422
155-3/8	23-7/8	23-6/8	16-5/8	5	5	Cherry County	NE	Gary Galloway	1985	422
155-3/8	25-2/8	26-2/8	23-1/8	5	5	Sabine County	TX	Bobby Brundidge	1986	422
155-2/8	22-0/8	21-6/8	17-4/8	6	5	Benton County	IA	Gene Pollock	1958	431
155-2/8	25-0/8	25-5/8	18-3/8	5	6	Floyd County	IA	Richard G. Long	1967	431
155-2/8	26-4/8	25-4/8	15-2/8	6	6	Scott County	VA	Hugh McConnell	1978	431
155-2/8	21-6/8	21-7/8	20-0/8	5	5	Des Moines County	IA	Brad Entsminger	1980	431
155-2/8	24-5/8	24-2/8	15-4/8	5	6	Knox County	OH	Robert Hammond	1980	431
155-2/8	23-7/8	24-3/8	17-1/8	5	5	Richland County	MT	Wynn Privratsky	1980	431
155-2/8	25-3/8	25-4/8	18-4/8	5	5	Licking County	OH	Richard E Pipes	1984	431
155-2/8	24-4/8	24-1/8	18-0/8	6	6	Lake County	MI	John Mudrovich	1984	431
155-1/8	24-7/8	24-7/8	17-3/8	5	5	Roberts County	SD	Roland L. Hausmann	1959	439
155-1/8	25-2/8	24-7/8	19-3/8	6	6	Madison County	KY	Sonny Barker	1965	439
155-1/8	25-6/8	25-0/8	19-7/8	6	5	Morrison County	MN	Timothy L. Kampa	1984	439

WHITETAIL DEER *(Typical Antlers)*
(continued)   Minimum Score 125

Score	Length of Main Beam R	L	Inside Spread	Number of Points R	L	Area	State/ Province	Hunter's Name	Date	Rank
155-1/8	24-7/8	25-7/8	19-7/8	5	5	Calhoun County	MI	Steve D. Munier	1985	439
155-0/8	23-7/8	24-5/8	18-6/8	7	7	Pope County	MN	John Myhre	1982	443
155-0/8	26-2/8	25-4/8	20-2/8	5	5	Muskingum County	OH	P. W. "Bill" Meyer	1983	443
155-0/8	20-5/8	24-0/8	15-7/8	9	7	Lee County	IA	Ralph D. Zaehringer	1985	443
154-7/8	26-7/8	25-7/8	18-2/8	5	5	Murray County	MN	Craig Cohrs	1968	446
154-7/8	26-5/8	25-6/8	17-6/8	7	8	Pendleton County	KY	Thomas P. Jones	1969	446
154-7/8	22-5/8	23-2/8	23-1/8	6	6	Minster	OH	Gary L. Dues	1979	446
154-7/8	23-4/8	23-5/8	16-4/8	5	4	Kingsbury County	SD	Dan R. Limmer	1981	446
154-7/8	23-0/8	24-0/8	19-5/8	5	6	Henniper County	MN	Harold Greseth	1983	446
154-7/8	23-4/8	23-7/8	16-4/8	10	6	Lincoln County	MN	Paul Erickson	1983	446
154-7/8	24-2/8	23-6/8	19-1/8	4	5	Blue Earth County	MN	Rory Deutchman	1984	446
154-6/8	24-1/8	22-5/8	17-2/8	5	5	Renner	SD	Clifford Sudenga	1962	453
154-6/8	25-1/8	25-1/8	21-0/8	5	4	Cottonwood County	MN	Rodney Bailey	1975	453
154-6/8	24-7/8	25-6/8	20-0/8	5	5	Gray County	KS	Allen D. Bailey	1980	453
154-6/8	24-0/8	23-0/8	18-4/8	5	5	Van Buren County	MI	Rick Reese	1980	453
154-6/8	25-1/8	21-7/8	18-4/8	6	4	Mills County	IA	Doug Roll	1985	453
154-5/8	23-7/8	24-0/8	20-7/8	4	4	Buchanan County	IA	Frank Sanderson	1983	458
154-5/8	24-3/8	25-4/8	17-2/8	7	8	Miami County	KS	Gary Wurdack	1985	458
154-5/8	26-1/8	25-4/8	21-3/8	4	4	Dunnville	ONT	Randy Robins	1985	458
154-4/8	24-0/8	24-3/8	23-2/8	5	5	Allamakee County	IA	Dayton Jones	1968	461
154-4/8	22-6/8	22-6/8	16-6/8	6	5	Fillmore County	MN	James J. Johnston	1974	461
154-4/8	24-4/8	24-0/8	19-3/8	7	8	Waupaca County	WI	Gary L. Hintz	1978	461
154-4/8	25-3/8	24-1/8	18-0/8	5	5	Will County	IL	Fred Lukanc	1978	461
154-4/8	24-4/8	23-6/8	20-0/8	5	5	Phillips County	KS	Dennis Fredrickson	1983	461
154-3/8	23-4/8	24-3/8	18-5/8	7	7	Cripple Creek	VA	C. D. Tarter	1961	466
154-3/8	27-2/8	26-0/8	21-5/8	4	4	Crane	IN	Bill Clark	1967	466
154-3/8	25-3/8	25-2/8	19-1/8	4	4	Jefferson County	IL	Kirby Laur	1981	466
154-3/8	23-1/8	24-0/8	21-1/8	5	5	Sherman County	KS	Keith A. Foster	1984	466
154-2/8	25-4/8	27-0/8	16-6/8	6	6	Waupaca County	WI	Carl Schoenike	1948	470
154-2/8	25-1/8	25-7/8	17-6/8	5	6	Cloud County	KS	Jerrold L. Istas	1981	470
154-2/8	22-3/8	21-7/8	16-6/8	6	6	Clark County	MO	Myles Keller	1981	470
154-2/8	22-6/8	22-6/8	17-4/8	5	5	Burleigh County	ND	Tony Niemann	1984	470
154-2/8	24-6/8	25-1/8	17-0/8	5	5	Pendleton County	WV	Roger O. Wyant	1984	470
154-2/8	23-6/8	23-1/8	17-6/8	6	6	White County	IL	Bruce Masser	1984	470
154-2/8	24-6/8	23-1/8	18-0/8	8	7	Comanche County	KS	Tommie A. Berger	1985	470
154-1/8	24-6/8	23-7/8	15-5/8	5	5	Storey	IN	Glen E. Parton	1970	477
154-1/8	24-6/8	25-5/8	20-4/8	5	7	Noble County	OH	Donald J. Mace	1973	477
154-1/8	23-5/8	23-7/8	19-5/8	5	6	Stoddard County	MO	Gary Barton	1980	477
154-1/8	24-6/8	23-4/8	19-6/8	5	7	Shawano County	WI	John Popp	1980	477
154-1/8	23-0/8	23-1/8	18-7/8	6	7	Faribault County	MN	Carlton Eastvold, Jr.	1982	477
154-1/8	26-5/8	26-2/8	20-1/8	6	7	Nelson County	KY	Tom Bullock	1983	477
154-1/8	23-7/8	23-4/8	18-3/8	5	5	Merrick County	NE	Lauren N Erickson	1985	477
154-0/8	26-5/8	26-5/8	19-1/8	4	5	Guthrie County	IA	Gordon Headlee	1977	484
154-0/8	27-0/8	26-7/8	19-2/8	6	6	Kosciusko County	IN	Charles L. Baker	1979	484
154-0/8	27-2/8	25-7/8	18-4/8	6	4	Knox County	IL	James C. Drake	1979	484
154-0/8	22-4/8	22-1/8	18-2/8	5	5	Price County	WI	Jim Sorensen	1982	484
154-0/8	24-6/8	24-3/8	15-4/8	5	5	Clay County	IN	Terry L. Dewey	1985	484
154-0/8	25-1/8	24-1/8	19-2/8	5	5	Kent County	MD	J. Richard Herr	1985	484
153-7/8	22-6/8	22-2/8	17-5/8	5	5	McLean County	ND	Terry Cossette	1983	490
153-7/8	25-6/8	26-0/8	17-1/8	7	7	Black Hawk County	IA	Gary Schoeberl	1985	490
153-6/8	22-1/8	22-7/8	17-0/8	5	5	Kent County	MD	S. Russell Edie	1966	492
153-6/8	24-5/8	25-1/8	18-2/8	6	5	Lee County	IL	George Nevins	1976	492
153-6/8	23-3/8	24-3/8	18-0/8	5	5	Lincoln County	SD	Mike Pederson	1979	492
153-6/8	24-1/8	23-7/8	16-0/8	5	5	Jasper County	MO	Steve Lewis	1983	492
153-6/8	24-5/8	23-6/8	18-0/8	5	5	Kenosha County	WI	John ny Schnider	1984	492
153-6/8	25-1/8	24-7/8	18-4/8	5	5	Morrison County	MN	John Erdrich	1984	492
153-5/8	23-4/8	23-0/8	22-4/8	5	7	Harris	SAS	Garry Benson	1966	498
153-5/8	26-0/8	25-2/8	18-1/8	7	5	Halton Hills	ONT	Don Lewis	1978	498
153-5/8	23-4/8	24-0/8	18-7/8	5	5	Dorchester County	MD	David Logan White	1983	498
153-5/8	26-0/8	25-5/8	21-1/8	6	5	Will County	IL	John Madonis	1984	498
153-5/8	25-4/8	25-7/8	20-5/8	5	5	Stephenson County	IL	Clarence E. Hille, Jr.	1984	498
153-5/8	23-0/8	23-0/8	19-5/8	5	5	Sauk County	WI	Michael H. Smith	1986	498
153-4/8	25-7/8	25-2/8	19-3/8	7	6	Jackson County	MN	Lyle Babcock	1973	504

WHITETAIL DEER *(Typical Antlers)*

Minimum Score 125

(continued)

Score	Length of Main Beam R	L	Inside Spread	Number of Points R	L	Area	State/ Province	Hunter's Name	Date	Rank
153-4/8	25-1/8	23-6/8	22-0/8	6	5	Knox County	OH	John L. Yarman, Jr.	1975	504
153-4/8	23-5/8	24-1/8	20-6/8	6	5	Billings County	ND	David L. Torkelson	1976	504
153-4/8	26-2/8	26-0/8	23-2/8	6	6	Douglas County	KS	Richard D. Brown	1979	504
153-4/8	25-5/8	25-7/8	23-4/8	6	5	Logan County	KY	Milton O. Gaddie	1979	504
153-4/8	24-4/8	24-2/8	16-2/8	5	6	Columbia County	FL	Robert Ballard	1980	504
153-4/8	22-5/8	22-4/8	14-6/8	5	5	Callaway County	MO	Marvin Giboney	1980	504
153-4/8	25-3/8	25-2/8	17-6/8	6	6	Morrison County	MN	Dennis Midas	1983	504
153-3/8	25-5/8	24-7/8	19-4/8	5	6	Coal City	IL	Ed Vitko, Jr.	1972	512
153-3/8	21-2/8	22-3/8	19-0/8	7	6	Ripley	MN	Robert R. Ganzer	1973	512
153-3/8	25-5/8	27-6/8	21-1/8	4	4	Knox County	IL	Bill Richards	1981	512
153-3/8	25-1/8	24-3/8	19-3/8	4	4	Webster County	WV	Charles P. Green	1982	512
153-3/8	22-7/8	22-7/8	20-6/8	7	7	Macoupin County	IL	Charles M. Woolfolk	1983	512
153-2/8	24-4/8	24-3/8	24-4/8	5	6	Tekahmah	NE	Harold W. Hawkins	1966	517
153-2/8	26-0/8	26-7/8	20-6/8	6	6	Thompson	IA	Ronald Gordon	1972	517
153-2/8	22-5/8	22-3/8	20-4/8	5	5	North Platte	NE	Greg Wingfield	1978	517
153-2/8	21-6/8	21-7/8	15-0/8	5	5	Wood County	WI	James Wilke	1984	517
153-2/8	26-3/8	25-2/8	18-4/8	7	5	Butler County	KS	Larry Womack	1984	517
153-2/8	26-2/8	27-2/8	24-2/8	4	4	Muskingum County	OH	P. W. "Bill" Meyer	1985	517
153-2/8	24-3/8	23-6/8	20-2/8	5	5	Jackson County	MN	Bill Vangsness	1985	517
153-1/8	25-2/8	25-0/8	18-5/8	4	5	Lincoln County	NE	Rich Birch	1965	524
153-1/8	25-6/8	25-1/8	17-1/8	7	6	Moody County	SD	Paul Schlobohm	1983	524
153-0/8	25-0/8	25-2/8	17-4/8	5	5	Cambria County	PA	Andrew J. Getsy	1965	526
153-0/8	21-3/8	21-1/8	16-4/8	5	5	Bismarck	ND	Jim Balzer	1977	526
153-0/8	24-7/8	25-1/8	16-3/8	5	6	Koochiching County	MN	Dr. Thomas Zbaracki	1980	526
153-0/8	23-2/8	23-6/8	16-0/8	5	5	Lawrence County	PA	Wayne Edwards	1981	526
153-0/8	23-5/8	23-6/8	15-7/8	6	6	Shelby County	IL	Bill D. Pesch	1983	526
153-0/8	23-7/8	24-3/8	18-4/8	5	5	Trumbull County	OH	Art Stanton	1985	526
152-7/8	23-2/8	22-2/8	18-4/8	7	5	Morgan County	CO	Stuart Clodfelder	1974	532
152-7/8	22-1/8	23-0/8	17-0/8	6	5	Sullivan County	IN	Kenny Pirtle	1975	532
152-7/8	24-3/8	24-2/8	20-7/8	5	6	Spook Lake	MT	Rick L. Stone	1981	532
152-7/8	23-2/8	23-4/8	19-1/8	6	5	Delaware County	PA	John A. Lashinsky	1984	532
152-7/8	24-2/8.	24-2/8	20-3/8	5	5	Washington County	WI	Lee A. Richard	1984	532
152-6/8	25-6/8	25-1/8	21-2/8	4	5	Jefferson County	IN	Robert Schmidt	1959	537
152-6/8	24-6/8	23-2/8	17-7/8	7	7	Winona County	MN	Donald M. Bzoskie	1978	537
152-6/8	24-7/8	24-1/8	21-0/8	4	4	Randolph County	IL	Steven Wydeck	1979	537
152-6/8	25-2/8	24-3/8	18-4/8	5	5	Saginaw County	MI	Jack W. Bare	1981	537
152-6/8	23-3/8	23-0/8	20-0/8	5	5	Morrison County	MN	Floyd Foslien	1981	537
152-6/8	25-0/8	25-2/8	17-6/8	6	6	Holt County	MO	Frank Berkemeier	1984	537
152-6/8	22-6/8	22-2/8	14-2/8	6	5	Rogers County	OK	Byron Jasper	1984	537
152-5/8	23-2/8	23-0/8	17-2/8	5	6	Paris	MO	Carl T. Peak	1968	544
152-5/8	23-1/8	24-0/8	16-1/8	6	6	Roseau County	MN	Dave Hovda	1982	544
152-5/8	24-5/8	24-0/8	19-4/8	7	7	Delaware County	IA	Chet Goldsberry	1982	544
152-5/8	22-7/8	22-5/8	16-3/8	5	5	Lyon County	MN	Dwight A. Hemme	1984	544
152-4/8	28-7/8	26-2/8	19-2/8	5	5	Somerset County	MD	Burgess Blevins	1974	548
152-4/8	24-3/8	24-0/8	19-2/8	5	5	Scott County	MN	Dean Jansen	1976	548
152-3/8	24-7/8	24-7/8	18-5/8	8	6	Pope County	IL	Dr. H. Neil Becker	1968	550
152-3/8	25-4/8	25-4/8	17-6/8	8	7	Jasper County	IA	Edward L. Stevens	1976	550
152-3/8	24-5/8	24-3/8	19-1/8	4	4	Guthrie County	IA	Barry Chalfant	1979	550
152-3/8	23-2/8	24-7/8	18-3/8	6	5	Schuyler County	IL	Stephen J. McCoy	1979	550
152-3/8	22-5/8	21-6/8	17-3/8	5	5	Butler County	KS	John Schwartz	1981	550
152-3/8	24-6/8	24-6/8	16-3/8	5	5	Oceana County	MI	J. C. Ingram	1982	550
152-3/8	24-7/8	25-3/8	19-7/8	4	4	Yorkton	SAS	Ron Vandermeulen	1983	550
152-3/8	24-0/8	24-4/8	19-5/8	5	5	Jewell County	KS	Rod Rose	1984	550
152-3/8	22-3/8	23-2/8	18-5/8	6	5	Kenosha County	WI	Howard Moore	1984	550
152-3/8	24-3/8	25-0/8	19-7/8	5	5	Logan County	IL	Charles E. Dumire	1984	550
152-3/8	25-0/8	24-3/8	17-2/8	5	8	Franklin County	KS	Joe Maloney	1985	550
152-3/8	23-0/8	22-5/8	17-7/8	5	6	Gasconade County	MO	John R Hawkins	1985	550
152-3/8	25-6/8	24-7/8	17-2/8	8	5	Washington County	KS	Stan Brustowicz	1985	550
152-2/8	24-6/8	24-4/8	18-4/8	5	5	Cowley County	KS	Michael L. Snyder	1978	563
152-2/8	28-4/8	27-4/8	20-2/8	4	4	Winona County	MN	Leonard Anglewitz	1978	563
152-2/8	24-5/8	24-4/8	20-2/8	6	7	Miami County	KS	Brian J. Hammond	1982	563
152-2/8	24-2/8	23-5/8	17-4/8	6	4	Marshall County	KS	Dean C. Bookwalter	1982	563
152-2/8	22-2/8	21-7/8	19-5/8	5	7	Morrison County	MN	Willard L. Voight, Jr.	1984	563

WHITETAIL DEER *(Typical Antlers)*

(continued)   Minimum Score 125

Score	Length of Main Beam R	L	Inside Spread	Number of Points R	L	Area	State/ Province	Hunter's Name	Date	Rank
152-2/8	24-3/8	23-4/8	16-6/8	6	5	Highland County	OH	James Stephens	1984	563
152-2/8	25-6/8	24-2/8	19-2/8	8	7	LaCrosse County	WI	Kenne A. Happel	1985	563
152-2/8	25-3/8	25-3/8	21-6/8	5	5	Middlesex County	CT	Felix Nosewicz	1985	563
152-2/8	24-4/8	25-0/8	18-6/8	4	4	Marathon County	WI	Mark Schneider	1985	563
152-1/8	21-4/8	24-2/8	21-3/8	5	4	Owen County	IN	Edward L. Armstrong	1967	572
152-1/8	25-6/8	26-1/8	20-3/8	6	4	Watonwan County	MN	David Raney	1972	572
152-1/8	22-4/8	22-3/8	18-3/8	5	6	Ogle County	IL	Chuck Bowman	1974	572
152-1/8	25-1/8	25-3/8	17-1/8	6	6	Louisa County	IA	Duane O'Donnell	1979	572
152-1/8	24-1/8	24-5/8	19-3/8	5	5	Schuyler County	NY	Steve Herforth	1981	572
152-1/8	24-4/8	24-4/8	20-7/8	4	4	Iowa County	IA	Rick Ransom	1985	572
152-0/8	24-0/8	24-6/8	20-2/8	5	5	Finney County	KS	Howard Haug, Jr.	1973	578
152-0/8	23-0/8	23-0/8	16-0/8	5	5	Allen Springs	KY	Johnny Upton	1976	578
152-0/8	22-1/8	22-1/8	16-2/8	5	6	Marshall County	SD	Merle Funston	1982	578
152-0/8	26-6/8	26-3/8	17-6/8	5	4	Clay County	MO	Anthony Laddusaw	1985	578
152-0/8	24-6/8	25-6/8	17-6/8	7	6	Dakota County	MN	Tom Esslinger	1985	578
152-0/8	24-6/8	24-3/8	17-6/8	5	5	Itasca County	MN	Thomas A. Leedham	1985	578
152-0/8	22-7/8	23-1/8	17-0/8	5	5	Champaign County	IL	John W. Chumbley	1985	578
151-7/8	27-1/8	28-0/8	18-6/8	5	5	Ripley	MN	Steve Smythe	1968	585
151-7/8	24-3/8	24-7/8	18-3/8	5	5	Davis County	IA	George C. Francis	1979	585
151-7/8	23-7/8	23-7/8	17-6/8	6	6	Tama County	IA	Kirk Lundberg	1980	585
151-7/8	26-1/8	25-6/8	18-0/8	5	7	Brown County	SD	Jan Hinrichs	1981	585
151-7/8	24-6/8	24-4/8	19-1/8	5	5	Will County	IL	Ike Rhodes	1984	585
151-7/8	24-6/8	25-4/8	18-1/8	6	6	McCook County	SD	James C. Perkins	1984	585
151-7/8	24-4/8	23-6/8	15-5/8	5	5	Grant County	WI	William Stetler	1985	585
151-6/8	22-1/8	23-2/8	15-4/8	6	5	Flathead County	MT	Jerry D. Almos	1970	592
151-6/8	25-4/8	24-7/8	21-0/8	8	6	Warren County	OH	Lundy Lewis	1981	592
151-6/8	25-0/8	24-7/8	17-4/8	5	5	Murray County	MN	Dennis Lunderborg	1982	592
151-6/8	25-7/8	22-1/8	20-1/8	5	9	Columbiana County	OH	Bill Lawrence	1983	592
151-6/8	27-6/8	26-6/8	19-7/8	5	5	Champaign County	OH	Thomas R. Weaver	1984	592
151-5/8	26-2/8	24-7/8	20-6/8	6	6	Franklin County	KS	Kenneth Heinitz	1966	597
151-5/8	26-0/8	24-3/8	18-3/8	6	6	Reno County	KS	Dan Ropp	1981	597
151-5/8	26-6/8	26-1/8	17-3/8	4	4	Carter County	KY	Herbie Jackson	1982	597
151-5/8	25-6/8	25-4/8	21-5/8	6	7	Green County	WI	Alex Elkins	1982	597
151-5/8	26-6/8	26-5/8	17-5/8	4	4	Jackson County	OH	Jeffrey L. Walters	1984	597
151-5/8	24-7/8	25-2/8	20-7/8	5	5	Vermilion County	IL	Bill Fitton	1984	597
151-4/8	23-2/8	22-5/8	16-0/8	6	6	Gogebic County	MI	Fred Felbab	1959	603
151-4/8	23-2/8	22-7/8	16-2/8	5	5	Murray County	MN	Jim F. Wyffels	1968	603
151-4/8	21-1/8	21-7/8	18-6/8	6	5	Brown County	SD	Duane Trost	1973	603
151-4/8	24-2/8	24-3/8	19-4/8	5	5	Marshall County	IL	William J. McNutt	1979	603
151-4/8	23-6/8	22-5/8	17-3/8	6	5	Pittsburg County	OK	Harry Milican	1983	603
151-4/8	26-4/8	26-0/8	20-2/8	4	4	Mason County	IL	David C. Gillespie	1984	603
151-4/8	21-3/8	21-5/8	19-0/8	5	6	Lincoln County	MT	Glenn W. Gibson	1985	603
151-4/8	22-7/8	22-4/8	17-0/8	5	5	Buffalo County	WI	Gerald Palmer	1985	603
151-4/8	24-4/8	24-7/8	23-0/8	5	5	Riley County	KS	L. F. Howerton	1985	603
151-4/8	25-1/8	25-1/8	21-2/8	5	4	Pierce County	WI	Dave Clare	1985	603
151-4/8	26-3/8	25-0/8	18-2/8	5	5	Polk County	WI	Todd C. Swenson	1986	603
151-3/8	26-3/8	25-4/8	15-6/8	6	7	Crane	IN	Robert E. Sloan	1968	614
151-3/8	23-2/8	23-7/8	19-1/8	5	5	Amherst County	VA	Jerry Armes	1975	614
151-3/8	23-4/8	24-0/8	18-3/8	5	6	Morris Twp.	NJ	Phil D'Ottavio	1980	614
151-3/8	23-4/8	23-1/8	17-7/8	5	5	Langlade County	WI	Larry Petts	1983	614
151-3/8	26-1/8	26-1/8	18-0/8	5	7	Clay County	MN	Randy Swanson	1984	614
151-3/8	26-2/8	26-4/8	17-7/8	5	5	Osage County	KS	Gene Beam	1984	614
151-3/8	22-3/8	22-4/8	18-5/8	5	5	Trempealeau County	WI	Michael Baer	1984	614
151-3/8	25-2/8	25-4/8	17-3/8	6	5	Sauk County	WI	Casey A. Blum	1985	614
151-2/8	25-5/8	25-6/8	17-2/8	4	4	Fillmore County	MN	David Carson	1967	622
151-2/8	24-1/8	23-4/8	14-1/8	7	5	Blue Earth County	MN	Rory Duetchman	1974	622
151-2/8	22-1/8	22-4/8	18-2/8	6	6	Clark	SD	Dean L. Myers	1975	622
151-2/8	25-0/8	24-4/8	18-0/8	5	5	LaSalle County	IL	John Sullivan	1977	622
151-2/8	25-3/8	24-6/8	18-6/8	4	5	Litchfield County	CT	Donald R. Groody	1982	622
151-2/8	23-4/8	24-4/8	17-6/8	7	6	Warrick County	IN	Thomas Scheucher	1982	622
151-2/8	26-2/8	25-3/8	18-0/8	5	5	Cowley County	KS	Michael L. Snyder	1984	622
151-1/8	22-3/8	23-4/8	18-4/8	7	5	Adair County	MO	Dr. Eddy Transano	1971	629
151-1/8	22-6/8	22-6/8	17-4/8	7	6	Wood County	WI	Scott Arneson	1979	629

WHITETAIL DEER *(Typical Antlers)*

(continued)

Minimum Score 125

Score	Length of Main Beam R	L	Inside Spread	Number of Points R	L	Area	State/ Province	Hunter's Name	Date	Rank
151-1/8	23-4/8	21-4/8	18-3/8	5	5	Minnehaha County	SD	Bradley D. Swier	1982	629
151-1/8	25-2/8	24-0/8	20-7/8	4	5	Franklin County	KS	Don Hrabe	1985	629
151-0/8	25-0/8	26-0/8	16-6/8	5	5	Tennyson	IN	Gerald G. Taylor	1970	633
151-0/8	23-6/8	24-5/8	19-6/8	5	5	Western Polk County	WI	Bryan Anderson	1976	633
151-0/8	30-1/8	29-0/8	20-2/8	7	5	Gray County	KS	Paul Meininger	1980	633
151-0/8	23-2/8	23-5/8	21-2/8	5	5	Grant County	WI	Doug J. Leibfried	1981	633
151-0/8	25-3/8	24-0/8	17-4/8	5	5	Columbia County	WI	Jeffrey M. Ballweg	1984	633
151-0/8	23-7/8	23-3/8	20-0/8	5	5	White County	IL	Eric D. Devore	1985	633
150-7/8	23-2/8	22-2/8	18-1/8	5	5	Trempealeau County	WI	Phillip Lunde	1969	639
150-7/8	22-6/8	22-5/8	20-1/8	5	5	Harlan County	NE	Edwin Witte	1973	639
150-7/8	26-0/8	26-0/8	21-1/8	5	5	Kent County	MI	Robert Ten Eyck	1980	639
150-7/8	22-5/8	23-1/8	18-3/8	6	6	Cumberland County	ME	David C. Smart	1984	639
150-6/8	22-3/8	22-0/8	16-4/8	5	5	Redwood County	MN	Irvin Plotz	1975	643
150-6/8	22-2/8	21-7/8	19-0/8	5	6	Allegan County	MI	Lane Humphreys	1979	643
150-6/8	24-4/8	23-7/8	18-6/8	6	6	Columbia County	WI	Jerry Ulrich	1980	643
150-6/8	25-3/8	25-3/8	20-1/8	4	6	Winnebago County	IL	Fred L. Smith	1985	643
150-5/8	21-0/8	22-7/8	19-3/8	6	5	Madison County	NE	Darwin Heppner	1967	647
150-5/8	22-7/8	22-6/8	22-1/8	5	6	Eaton County	MI	Greg Hoefler	1982	647
150-5/8	22-7/8	22-5/8	18-5/8	5	5	Ashland County	OH	Lyle Bennett	1984	647
150-5/8	24-4/8	23-4/8	18-1/8	7	5	Pratt County	KS	Scott Haworth	1984	647
150-5/8	22-3/8	22-3/8	17-3/8	5	5	Chippewa County	WI	Tim Walters	1985	647
150-4/8	24-4/8	24-4/8	18-6/8	5	4	Scott County	IA	Howard A. Goettsch	1974	652
150-4/8	22-5/8	22-3/8	14-7/8	6	7	Wabasha County	MN	Lee Partington	1975	652
150-4/8	21-4/8	21-6/8	15-6/8	6	6	Dunn County	WI	Mary Nussberger	1976	652
150-4/8	24-7/8	24-7/8	17-6/8	5	5	Guernsey County	OH	Miltos Stefanitais	1979	652
150-4/8	23-6/8	23-4/8	19-0/8	5	5	Schuyler County	NY	Donald L. Lane	1980	652
150-4/8	22-1/8	22-0/8	20-4/8	5	5	Woodford County	IL	Roger Miller	1980	652
150-4/8	24-2/8	25-1/8	19-4/8	4	4	McCoy	WI	Dirk Gillette	1981	652
150-4/8	26-3/8	25-0/8	18-4/8	5	4	Miami County	OH	Richard G. Williamson	1981	652
150-4/8	23-6/8	22-3/8	16-0/8	4	4	Osage County	KS	Bill Senne	1985	652
150-4/8	26-2/8	26-2/8	18-2/8	4	4	Pepin County	WI	Myles Keller	1985	652
150-4/8	26-0/8	26-1/8	20-3/8	7	6	Knox County	MO	Roger Gipple	1986	652
150-3/8	24-5/8	24-5/8	22-5/8	4	4	Oneida County	WI	Philip Hildebrand	1967	663
150-3/8	20-4/8	21-2/8	16-7/8	5	5	Langlade County	WI	Herbert Buettner	1970	663
150-3/8	23-3/8	23-5/8	18-3/8	6	7	Graham County	KS	Russell Hull	1977	663
150-3/8	24-0/8	23-4/8	15-4/8	5	6	Juneau County	WI	Anthony Wulin	1977	663
150-3/8	22-2/8	22-3/8	15-3/8	5	5	Souris River	MAN	Garry William Kaluzniak	1980	663
150-3/8	26-0/8	24-4/8	16-4/8	9	8	Oakland County	MI	Donald J. Fisher	1981	663
150-3/8	25-1/8	25-0/8	17-2/8	5	5	Jackson County	MO	Marvin Thomey	1983	663
150-3/8	23-1/8	22-3/8	16-4/8	5	6	Dakota County	MN	Dave Vomela	1985	663
150-2/8	23-5/8	23-3/8	17-2/8	6	6	Jackson County	WI	Roger Reinart	1972	671
150-2/8	26-0/8	24-2/8	19-0/8	4	5	Spink County	SD	Gerald A. Kettering	1978	671
150-2/8	23-3/8	23-5/8	14-0/8	5	5	Cottonwood County	MN	Leonard P. Thiner	1978	671
150-2/8	25-2/8	27-1/8	19-4/8	4	4	Fulton County	IL	William L. Beaird	1984	671
150-2/8	23-3/8	22-7/8	17-2/8	5	5	Marathon County	WI	Kevin Denzine	1985	671
150-1/8	23-5/8	23-0/8	16-7/8	5	6	Johnson County	IA	Jim Keefer	1969	676
150-1/8	22-5/8	23-7/8	16-1/8	5	5	Stuart	IA	Bill Barringen	1975	676
150-1/8	24-2/8	24-5/8	16-7/8	5	5	Freeborn County	MN	Robert Haney	1977	676
150-1/8	20-6/8	20-2/8	18-1/8	6	6	Richland County	IN	Lyle Fritz	1978	676
150-1/8	26-0/8	26-2/8	19-0/8	4	5	Fairfield	OH	Roger S. Trigg	1979	676
150-1/8	24-7/8	26-2/8	19-7/8	5	6	White Bear	MN	Patricia Barry	1980	676
150-1/8	22-1/8	22-4/8	17-7/8	5	5	Dearborn County	IN	Mike Serio	1982	676
150-1/8	22-7/8	22-5/8	17-1/8	5	4	Oldham County	KY	Phillip Burba	1985	676
150-1/8	23-4/8	24-2/8	17-3/8	4	5	Jefferson County	WI	Patrick Thiede	1985	676
150-1/8	24-4/8	24-3/8	20-1/8	7	8	Lake County	IL	James C. Carlson	1985	676
150-0/8	26-6/8	27-1/8	17-6/8	5	4	Benton County	IA	Robert L. Walker	1961	686
150-0/8	26-4/8	26-4/8	18-4/8	5	5	Shelby County	IA	Einar Leistad	1970	686
150-0/8	22-0/8	23-2/8	17-2/8	5	6	Ozaukee County	WI	Rand Krueger	1980	686
150-0/8	24-5/8	23-0/8	17-4/8	5	5	Kosciusko County	IN	Gil Reed	1981	686
150-0/8	22-3/8	22-4/8	17-1/8	6	6	Carroll County	AR	Larry Gasaway	1984	686
150-0/8	24-4/8	24-1/8	18-1/8	4	6	Penobscot County	ME	Kris T. Saunders	1985	686
150-0/8	21-0/8	21-4/8	15-7/8	4	5	Wabash County	IL	Paul Benham	1985	686
150-0/8	22-5/8	23-4/8	16-5/8	5	7	Tazewell County	IL	William H. Ray	1985	686

WHITETAIL DEER *(Typical Antlers)*

(continued)　　　　　　　　　　　　　　　　　　　　　　　　　　　　Minimum Score 125

Score	Length of Main Beam R	L	Inside Spread	Number of Points R	L	Area	State/ Province	Hunter's Name	Date	Rank
150-0/8	25-4/8	24-7/8	17-5/8	6	6	Livingston County	IL	James B. Smith	1985	686
150-0/8	23-7/8	23-3/8	20-0/8	5	5	White County	IL	Eric D. Devare	1985	686
150-0/8	23-6/8	24-2/8	17-0/8	5	5	Chase County	KS	Dan McClure	1985	686
149-7/8	26-0/8	25-6/8	20-3/8	4	4	Pulaski County	VA	Ray S. Carter	1962	697
149-7/8	21-6/8	21-1/8	17-3/8	5	5	Adams County	IL	Lyndall W. Heyen	1967	697
149-7/8	24-6/8	24-1/8	20-1/8	6	6	Will County	IL	Jerry Yost	1978	697
149-7/8	23-5/8	23-5/8	17-1/8	5	5	Scott County	KY	Mike Northcut	1980	697
149-7/8	25-1/8	24-1/8	18-7/8	6	6	Dauphin County	PA	Larry D. Wiestling	1983	697
149-7/8	25-0/8	25-0/8	17-5/8	5	5	Pittsburg County	OK	Doug Larimer	1985	697
149-6/8	23-4/8	23-5/8	17-1/8	7	6	Gull Lake	SAS	Keith Roney	1978	703
149-6/8	23-6/8	24-7/8	21-6/8	4	4	Branch County	MI	Howard W. Loehr	1983	703
149-6/8	25-0/8	24-5/8	17-4/8	5	5	Lasalle County	IL	Gary Tabor	1984	703
149-6/8	26-1/8	25-7/8	21-5/8	6	6	Anderson County	TN	Daniel W. Chase	1985	703
149-6/8	25-6/8	23-3/8	18-1/8	6	6	Douglas County	KS	Samuel J. Tunget	1985	703
149-5/8	25-6/8	25-3/8	18-5/8	6	6	LaSalle County	IL	Timothy L. Kakara	1975	708
149-5/8	25-4/8	25-2/8	20-1/8	6	5	Chase County	KS	John Moore	1981	708
149-5/8	24-5/8	25-2/8	20-1/8	5	7	Sheboygan County	WI	Leon Schultz	1983	708
149-5/8	24-4/8	23-5/8	20-1/8	5	5	Johnson County	NE	Brad Seitz	1984	708
149-5/8	24-7/8	27-2/8	28-1/8	5	4	Greenwood County	KS	Ray Penner	1984	708
149-5/8	22-4/8	23-1/8	16-5/8	6	5	York County	NE	Harold Bowman	1985	708
149-5/8	25-1/8	23-2/8	17-5/8	6	6	Livingston County	NY	John J. Valle	1985	708
149-4/8	23-3/8	26-0/8	20-2/8	5	5	Anthon	IA	Don Gothier	1962	715
149-4/8	23-2/8	23-2/8	17-1/8	6	5	Newton County	IN	Gerald R. Metros	1973	715
149-4/8	22-5/8	22-3/8	17-4/8	7	5	Ogle County	IL	Jerome Bruns	1983	715
149-4/8	24-5/8	25-2/8	17-0/8	5	5	Sedgewick County	KS	Bob Shull	1984	715
149-4/8	25-3/8	25-0/8	21-4/8	4	4	Shawnee County	KS	Jim Dultmeier	1985	715
149-3/8	24-1/8	25-3/8	19-7/8	5	6	Perry County	IL	Vern Quillman	1981	720
149-3/8	24-2/8	23-3/8	19-3/8	6	7	Charles County	MD	Frank A. Rankin	1981	720
149-3/8	24-0/8	25-2/8	17-4/8	5	4	Washington County	OH	Charles E. Vaughan	1983	720
149-3/8	25-5/8	25-0/8	20-4/8	4	5	Noble County	OK	Bill Hughes	1984	720
149-3/8	22-5/8	22-6/8	15-5/8	5	5	Morgan County	CO	Stan Kingcade	1985	720
149-324	26-6/8	25-4/8	22-1/8	4	4	?	NY	George Ferber	1957	725
149-324	23-4/8	23-3/8	15-7/8	5	5	Madison County	KY	Robert Young	1963	725
149-324	23-4/8	24-4/8	19-3/8	5	5	Newton County	IN	Philip Kozlowski	1968	725
149-324	24-1/8	24-2/8	19-3/8	5	5	Lawrence County	OH	Ronald E. Burnette	1971	725
149-324	23-7/8	23-4/8	17-5/8	5	5	Waushara County	WI	Ronald Anunson	1974	725
149-324	22-2/8	23-1/8	15-7/8	6	6	Lac Qui Parle County	MN	Ron Patzer	1980	725
149-2/8	25-3/8	24-6/8	20-4/8	5	5	Westchester County	NY	Joseph H. Keeler	1957	731
149-2/8	22-0/8	22-1/8	16-6/8	5	5	Will County	IL	Daniel R. Altiery	1973	731
149-2/8	23-0/8	23-7/8	18-2/8	5	5	Muskingum County	OH	P. W. "Bill" Meyer	1976	731
149-2/8	22-7/8	22-6/8	20-6/8	4	5	Auglaize County	OH	Fred Rostorfer	1980	731
149-2/8	23-3/8	23-4/8	15-3/8	5	7	Livingston County	MI	John Richmond	1981	731
149-2/8	23-4/8	22-6/8	18-6/8	6	6	Columbia County	WI	Gene R. Elsing	1981	731
149-2/8	24-0/8	22-1/8	17-4/8	5	5	Washtenaw County	MI	Fred Johnson	1984	731
149-2/8	27-4/8	26-6/8	20-2/8	7	7	Fulton County	IL	Locie L Murphy	1984	731
149-2/8	23-6/8	23-4/8	18-0/8	5	5	Jackson County	MO	Marvin Thomey	1984	731
149-1/8	25-4/8	25-0/8	17-0/8	5	7	Bon Homme County	SD	Terry Gretschman	1974	740
149-1/8	23-3/8	22-0/8	19-6/8	6	5	Coles County	IL	Bill Spaniol	1976	740
149-1/8	25-7/8	23-2/8	19-7/8	5	5	Clark County	IL	Gerald D. Shaffner	1984	740
149-1/8	24-0/8	24-6/8	19-4/8	6	6	Phillips County	KS	Bryan Henry	1984	740
149-1/8	22-3/8	24-2/8	17-2/8	6	5	Traill County	ND	Dale Grindeland	1986	740
149-0/8	25-7/8	23-5/8	19-4/8	6	5	Mitchell County	IA	Elmer Krueger	1961	745
149-0/8	25-0/8	25-0/8	19-4/8	5	4	Black Hawk County	IA	Robert Riggle	1975	745
149-0/8	24-4/8	23-4/8	19-6/8	5	5	Marion County	KS	David C. Hett	1980	745
149-0/8	23-4/8	22-5/8	15-4/8	5	5	Pickaway County	OH	Weldon R. Snyder	1980	745
149-0/8	24-6/8	25-1/8	19-2/8	6	5	Warren County	IA	Grant Poindexter	1981	745
149-0/8	25-5/8	24-5/8	18-6/8	4	5	Kiowa County	KS	Dan Manwarren	1984	745
149-0/8	25-1/8	24-6/8	17-7/8	6	5	Calhoun County	MI	Larry C. Holcomb	1984	745
149-0/8	21-5/8	21-6/8	20-0/8	5	5	Atchison County	KS	Larry Bleier	1985	745
148-7/8	15-4/8	26-0/8	19-4/8	5	7	Lincoln County	WI	Ronald Pond	1961	753
148-7/8	24-6/8	24-0/8	18-7/8	4	5	Grant County	SD	Larry Turbak	1964	753
148-7/8	23-1/8	23-1/8	18-4/8	6	6	Knox County	OH	John E. Bumpus	1971	753
148-7/8	23-1/8	23-1/8	19-3/8	5	4	Clayton County	IA	Ralph Edward Livingston	1984	753

WHITETAIL DEER *(Typical Antlers)*

Minimum Score 125 (continued)

Score	Length of Main Beam R	L	Inside Spread	Number of Points R	L	Area	State/ Province	Hunter's Name	Date	Rank
148-7/8	24-2/8	22-7/8	17-2/8	6	5	Clay County	KS	Larry Reed	1985	753
148-6/8	25-2/8	25-2/8	19-6/8	5	5	Iowa County	IA	Russ Sill	1967	758
148-6/8	23-0/8	23-0/8	18-4/8	5	5	Jefferson County	IN	Jim Coldiron	1969	758
148-6/8	21-3/8	21-1/8	19-1/8	6	6	Columbia	SD	Bill Franklin	1972	758
148-6/8	22-0/8	21-7/8	16-5/8	7	5	Schuylkill County	PA	Scott Bond	1979	758
148-6/8	24-2/8	23-4/8	22-6/8	6	7	Brookings County	SD	Larry Bohls	1982	758
148-6/8	24-1/8	23-6/8	17-2/8	5	5	Boone County	IA	Earl Taylor	1982	758
148-6/8	22-6/8	22-6/8	16-6/8	5	6	Reno County	KS	Davis J. Ediger	1982	758
148-6/8	22-6/8	22-3/8	15-2/8	5	4	Pierce County	ND	James Olson	1983	758
148-6/8	23-2/8	23-3/8	18-0/8	6	5	Kingsbury County	SD	Scott L. Laudenslager	1984	758
148-6/8	23-2/8	23-0/8	16-5/8	7	6	Jefferson County	WI	Steve Behm	1985	758
148-5/8	25-2/8	25-3/8	17-7/8	5	5	Newton County	IN	Larry Boezeman	1971	768
148-5/8	21-7/8	22-0/8	14-7/8	5	6	Ft. Leonard Wood	MO	Ron Poston	1972	768
148-5/8	26-7/8	26-6/8	23-1/8	6	5	Coshocton County	OH	Charles H. Vlasek, Jr.	1979	768
148-5/8	23-0/8	22-6/8	22-1/8	5	5	Marion County	IA	Leonard Grimes	1981	768
148-5/8	23-1/8	24-5/8	18-6/8	5	5	Tuscola County	MI	Patrick C. Lewis	1983	768
148-5/8	25-6/8	25-6/8	19-6/8	6	5	Niobrara County	WY	Kenneth Fluck	1985	768
148-5/8	19-3/8	21-7/8	20-5/8	6	6	Dunn County	WI	Richard Urbaniak	1985	768
148-4/8	23-0/8	22-4/8	20-1/8	4	5	Murray County	MN	Mike Molitor	1968	775
148-4/8	20-7/8	21-4/8	16-6/8	5	5	Milton	WI	Bruce Douglas	1978	775
148-4/8	24-2/8	24-5/8	21-5/8	5	5	Martin County	MN	Dean Roben	1982	775
148-4/8	23-0/8	23-6/8	17-7/8	5	6	Pepin County	WI	Roger Anderson	1984	775
148-4/8	23-7/8	25-2/8	19-4/8	5	4	Jefferson County	OH	Larry C. Riggle	1984	775
148-4/8	24-3/8	24-5/8	20-6/8	7	6	Meade County	KS	Randall J. VanDegrift	1985	775
148-4/8	22-2/8	22-2/8	19-6/8	5	5	Seward County	KS	Stuart G. Hazard III	1985	775
148-3/8	25-6/8	26-7/8	22-2/8	9	5	Belle Plaine	MN	Bob Gregory	1967	782
148-3/8	23-5/8	23-7/8	17-5/8	5	5	Monroe County	NY	Robert J. Ranalletta	1976	782
148-3/8	23-0/8	23-4/8	18-0/8	6	7	Ballard County	KY	Gregory Joles	1978	782
148-3/8	22-5/8	22-1/8	17-5/8	6	6	Watonwan County	MN	Joe Graif	1981	782
148-3/8	22-1/8	22-6/8	18-1/8	5	5	Morrison County	MN	Robert Redmann	1984	782
148-3/8	24-6/8	25-5/8	19-1/8	5	5	Baltimore County	MD	Donald Layne	1985	782
148-3/8	24-3/8	24-2/8	18-1/8	6	6	Phillips County	KS	Julius E. Schoenberger	1985	782
148-3/8	22-2/8	23-6/8	16-7/8	5	5	Ottawa County	KS	Wayne E. Smith	1985	782
148-2/8	22-3/8	21-6/8	16-2/8	5	5	Walworth County	SD	Irvin Guthmiller	1956	790
148-2/8	22-7/8	21-5/8	18-2/8	5	5	Harrison County	IA	James W. Glasscock	1968	790
148-2/8	24-5/8	24-7/8	24-0/8	5	5	Jackson County	IL	Darrell Fritsche	1973	790
148-2/8	20-7/8	22-2/8	16-4/8	5	5	Pittsburg County	OK	Bill Hisle	1975	790
148-2/8	24-2/8	23-4/8	18-0/8	5	7	Latah County	ID	Don A. West	1976	790
148-2/8	26-5/8	24-3/8	19-7/8	6	8	Coshocton County	OH	Charles N. McDonald	1977	790
148-2/8	23-0/8	22-2/8	20-7/8	4	5	Sanford	MAN	Wayne Rodgers	1979	790
148-2/8	24-7/8	25-1/8	18-0/8	5	5	Winnebago County	IL	Fred Kelley	1981	790
148-2/8	24-6/8	23-3/8	16-5/8	4	6	Clark County	KS	Casey V. Rudd	1981	790
148-2/8	23-4/8	23-1/8	22-6/8	6	10	Marion County	IL	Paul Duncan	1982	790
148-2/8	27-3/8	27-0/8	20-7/8	5	6	Washington County	WI	Steve Karoses	1983	790
148-2/8	26-0/8	26-2/8	17-5/8	8	6	Adair County	MO	Tim Richardson	1983	790
148-2/8	23-0/8	23-6/8	17-0/8	5	5	Pierce County	WI	Mitchell C. Nelson	1984	790
148-2/8	21-2/8	21-6/8	18-4/8	5	5	Kenosha County	WI	Marty Daniels	1985	790
148-1/8	24-2/8	24-2/8	20-5/8	4	4	Erie County	NY	William R. Helmich	1975	804
148-1/8	23-0/8	22-5/8	17-2/8	5	6	Wellington County	ONT	Barry Marshall	1975	804
148-1/8	27-3/8	27-5/8	21-6/8	6	6	Tazewell County	IL	David Huser	1980	804
148-1/8	23-5/8	23-7/8	24-1/8	6	5	Fairfield County	OH	Jim Jordan	1982	804
148-1/8	24-2/8	22-5/8	19-3/8	5	5	Uvalde County	TX	Jim Jordan	1986	804
148-0/8	22-1/8	22-2/8	14-6/8	5	5	Ft. Pierre	SD	Brad Taylor	1979	809
148-0/8	23-5/8	23-1/8	18-6/8	5	6	Uvalde County	TX	M.H. "Bill" Wilkinson, Jr.	1980	809
148-0/8	22-6/8	23-1/8	17-6/8	5	5	Green County	WI	E. Dussault	1983	809
148-0/8	25-2/8	25-2/8	18-3/8	5	5	Buffalo County	WI	Daniel Folkedahl	1984	809
148-0/8	24-6/8	25-5/8	23-6/8	4	5	Clay County	MN	Keith J Fischer	1984	809
148-0/8	24-3/8	25-0/8	18-3/8	6	8	McIntosh County	ND	Garnes Ruff	1985	809
148-0/8	22-4/8	22-0/8	15-3/8	5	6	Norman County	MN	Les Krogstad	1985	809
148-0/8	25-7/8	27-7/8	16-7/8	7	6	Madison County	NY	Lloyd Weigel	1985	809
148-0/8	24-1/8	24-4/8	15-6/8	5	6	Vernon County	WI	Harry J. Curtis	1986	809
147-7/8	21-7/8	22-2/8	18-5/8	5	5	Green Lake County	WI	Al Hubbell	1974	818
147-7/8	25-6/8	24-7/8	21-7/8	4	4	Galesville	MD	James E. Roy	1977	818

WHITETAIL DEER *(Typical Antlers)*

(continued)   Minimum Score 125

Score	Length of Main Beam R	L	Inside Spread	Number of Points R	L	Area	State/ Province	Hunter's Name	Date	Rank
147-7/8	22-2/8	22-3/8	18-5/8	5	5	Iron County	MI	David C. Tarsi	1978	818
147-7/8	26-3/8	25-6/8	17-5/8	4	4	Lafayette County	WI	Kim D. Gruenberg	1979	818
147-7/8	20-6/8	21-6/8	18-4/8	6	6	Cass County	NE	David R. Kempnich	1981	818
147-7/8	27-0/8	26-0/8	23-2/8	4	6	Cowley County	KS	Virgil Dwayne Graham	1982	818
147-7/8	24-5/8	24-0/8	19-5/8	5	5	Guthrie County	IA	Vernie W. Grasty	1983	818
147-6/8	23-4/8	23-2/8	16-0/8	5	5	Ripley	MN	John Zwickey	1955	825
147-6/8	23-5/8	24-3/8	16-6/8	6	7	Ripley	MN	Allen E. Farmes	1957	825
147-6/8	25-3/8	24-5/8	19-7/8	6	5	Jo Daviess County	IL	Jerry Fritz	1971	825
147-6/8	24-1/8	25-6/8	19-0/8	5	5	Peary Pond	MI	Myles Keller	1976	825
147-6/8	24-0/8	24-2/8	17-2/8	6	5	Harlan County	NE	Ron Breitsprecher	1978	825
147-6/8	25-2/8	24-4/8	23-3/8	6	8	Texas County	MO	Don Belew	1980	825
147-6/8	22-1/8	22-2/8	19-6/8	5	5	Union County	IL	Karen Mason	1980	825
147-6/8	22-3/8	22-1/8	17-4/8	4	4	Pick City	ND	Steven J. Prock	1980	825
147-6/8	25-6/8	24-6/8	18-0/8	5	5	Jackson County	IA	Carl Severson	1982	825
147-6/8	23-2/8	23-1/8	18-0/8	5	5	Sumner County	KS	Danny S. Holden	1982	825
147-6/8	22-3/8	22-4/8	21-2/8	4	4	Kingsbury County	SD	Mack Butler	1984	825
147-6/8	22-5/8	23-2/8	19-2/8	5	6	Stafford County	KS	Larry E Bowser	1985	825
147-5/8	24-2/8	26-0/8	20-2/8	6	6	Nicollet County	MN	Thomas J. Merkley	1970	837
147-5/8	21-0/8	20-4/8	16-3/8	5	6	Morgan County	TN	Chuck Webster	1976	837
147-5/8	22-7/8	23-2/8	18-1/8	4	4	Wilkin County	MN	Darrel G. Montieth	1978	837
147-5/8	23-5/8	23-4/8	18-3/8	4	5	Morrison County	MN	Leon Fuchs	1981	837
147-5/8	22-2/8	22-7/8	16-6/8	6	5	Merrimack County	NH	Jerry Smith	1982	837
147-5/8	24-7/8	25-3/8	19-5/8	5	6	Peoria County	IL	Joe Shryock, Jr.	1983	837
147-5/8	24-6/8	25-2/8	17-2/8	5	6	Koochiching County	MN	Terrance L. Jaeger	1983	837
147-5/8	23-5/8	22-7/8	18-3/8	5	5	Dewitt County	IL	John H. Piatt	1983	837
147-5/8	25-3/8	24-7/8	17-7/8	5	5	Butler County	PA	David L. Travaglio	1986	837
147-4/8	22-2/8	22-6/8	18-4/8	4	4	Shawano County	WI	John Schoenike	1960	846
147-4/8	23-7/8	23-2/8	16-4/8	7	5	Darke County	OH	Jim Duvall	1977	846
147-4/8	24-0/8	23-3/8	20-6/8	6	6	Fulton County	OH	Gary R. Bailey	1980	846
147-4/8	22-6/8	22-2/8	16-6/8	5	5	Burleigh County	ND	James A. Sauvageau	1980	846
147-4/8	25-3/8	25-6/8	19-0/8	4	5	Blue Earth County	MN	Aaron L. Urke	1981	846
147-4/8	23-7/8	23-7/8	16-5/8	7	5	Trempealeau County	WI	Donald Skaar	1982	846
147-4/8	21-0/8	20-5/8	17-6/8	5	5	Cloud County	KS	Jeff Gerard	1982	846
147-4/8	23-0/8	23-1/8	18-4/8	5	5	St. Charles County	MO	Harry L. Smith	1983	846
147-4/8	24-1/8	26-0/8	18-6/8	4	4	Prairie County	AR	Joe Moody	1984	846
147-4/8	25-0/8	25-1/8	19-4/8	5	5	Dane County	WI	John M. Welke, Jr.	1985	846
147-3/8	22-4/8	22-4/8	17-7/8	5	6	Waushara County	WI	Mike Barth	1977	856
147-3/8	21-5/8	21-5/8	16-3/8	6	5	Lee County	IA	Mark Clemens	1978	856
147-3/8	28-1/8	28-1/8	19-7/8	5	4	Huntingdon County	PA	John A. Williams	1979	856
147-3/8	22-5/8	23-7/8	18-3/8	5	5	Guthrie County	IA	Steve Hunerdosse	1982	856
147-3/8	22-0/8	22-3/8	12-7/8	7	5	Jackson County	MO	Marvin Thomey	1984	856
147-3/8	21-1/8	20-2/8	15-7/8	6	6	Troup County	GA	Eddie D. Martin	1984	856
147-3/8	22-6/8	23-0/8	18-3/8	5	5	Lee County	IA	Glenn E. Wagner	1985	856
147-2/8	23-2/8	25-1/8	20-4/8	9	8	Gillette Grove	IA	Uriah M. Hostetler	1964	863
147-2/8	23-2/8	22-4/8	19-2/8	5	5	Madison	IN	Pat Moreland	1969	863
147-2/8	23-1/8	23-1/8	15-6/8	5	5	Green Lake County	WI	Don Chier	1973	863
147-2/8	25-2/8	25-2/8	20-6/8	5	5	Fayette County	IA	Terry Cannady	1976	863
147-2/8	21-3/8	20-6/8	17-4/8	5	5	Iroquios County	IL	Scott L. Mohler	1979	863
147-2/8	25-7/8	24-3/8	25-4/8	4	4	Parke County	IN	Alan W. Brannan	1980	863
147-2/8	24-6/8	22-7/8	18-4/8	5	6	Hancock	WI	Tim J. Terrell	1980	863
147-2/8	23-2/8	22-6/8	19-2/8	5	7	Pembina County	ND	Roger Furstenau	1983	863
147-2/8	24-7/8	25-0/8	18-7/8	7	8	Clay County	MN	John Randash	1984	863
147-2/8	21-5/8	21-6/8	18-2/8	6	5	Grant County	MN	Harold Forcier	1984	863
147-2/8	24-5/8	24-3/8	18-2/8	6	5	Jackson County	OH	Keith Kuhn	1984	863
147-1/8	25-1/8	25-3/8	16-7/8	5	5	Delaware County	IA	Blair Berens	1963	874
147-1/8	24-7/8	24-4/8	18-4/8	7	7	McCook	NE	Gary Ginther	1967	874
147-1/8	22-6/8	23-1/8	17-5/8	5	6	Iron County	WI	Dr. C. J. Rainaldo	1967	874
147-1/8	21-0/8	21-5/8	16-3/8	6	6	Vilas County	WI	Anthony J. Sahulcik, Jr.	1969	874
147-1/8	25-0/8	24-0/8	18-3/8	4	4	Dodge County	MN	Clark Gallup	1974	874
147-1/8	24-3/8	25-7/8	18-5/8	4	4	Coffey County	KS	Joyce Wilhite	1974	874
147-1/8	20-5/8	20-0/8	19-5/8	5	5	Redwood County	MN	Dennis Groebner	1975	874
147-1/8	22-1/8	22-1/8	19-3/8	5	5	Kiowa County	KS	Ralph A. Brown	1981	874
147-1/8	25-2/8	24-3/8	18-1/8	5	5	Hancock County	OH	Robert E. Ebert	1981	874

WHITETAIL DEER *(Typical Antlers)*

Minimum Score 125

(continued)

Score	Length of Main Beam R	L	Inside Spread	Number of Points R	L	Area	State/ Province	Hunter's Name	Date	Rank
147-1/8	23-2/8	23-6/8	18-1/8	5	5	Teton County	MT	James R. Toms	1984	874
147-1/8	27-5/8	27-5/8	21-1/8	4	5	Highland County	OH	Larry K. Snoddy	1984	874
147-1/8	24-2/8	25-4/8	15-7/8	4	5	Wallace County	KS	Gerry Nix	1985	874
147-0/8	23-6/8	24-0/8	20-3/8	6	5	Hancock County	IL	Ron Paul	1974	886
147-0/8	24-3/8	24-7/8	19-2/8	7	7	Dodge County	NE	Donald W. Robinson	1974	886
147-0/8	28-5/8	26-2/8	19-0/8	5	4	Avon	IL	Bernard Smith	1974	886
147-0/8	19-1/8	20-1/8	19-2/8	5	5	Platte County	WY	Robert V. Kiser	1978	886
147-0/8	25-4/8	24-1/8	21-2/8	6	7	Morrison	MN	Gordon Bayerkohler	1979	886
147-0/8	23-5/8	23-5/8	20-0/8	5	5	Allamakee County	IA	Don Kieler	1979	886
147-0/8	26-4/8	26-2/8	16-0/8	5	7	Beatrice County	NE	Eldon C. Wellman	1981	886
147-0/8	24-4/8	23-7/8	18-6/8	4	5	Osborne County	KS	Mike Kidwell	1981	886
147-0/8	25-1/8	25-2/8	19-6/8	7	6	Charles County	MD	David G. Wilson	1981	886
147-0/8	22-3/8	22-2/8	18-4/8	5	5	Outagamie County	WI	Jim Vorland	1983	886
147-0/8	26-1/8	24-2/8	22-0/8	4	5	Dorchester County	MD	Michael F. Blair	1983	886
147-0/8	23-6/8	24-4/8	17-2/8	5	6	Lee County	IL	Donald E. Moore	1983	886
147-0/8	26-2/8	25-4/8	17-6/8	5	5	Vernon County	MO	Roger L. Hensley	1985	886
146-7/8	24-0/8	24-3/8	22-1/8	5	7	Fargo	ND	Duane H. Olsen	1959	899
146-7/8	24-2/8	24-2/8	15-5/8	4	4	Burns City	IN	Clarence McIntosh	1976	899
146-7/8	22-2/8	21-2/8	19-7/8	5	5	Waushara County	WI	Norman A. Moss	1976	899
146-7/8	23-1/8	21-6/8	16-1/8	5	5	Day County	SD	Cary Gill	1982	899
146-7/8	22-6/8	21-6/8	16-1/8	5	5	Jasper County	IA	Mike Needham	1982	899
146-6/8	23-3/8	23-1/8	17-6/8	7	8	Sisseton	SD	Robert Hendren	1967	904
146-6/8	24-6/8	27-0/8	20-2/8	5	4	Neosho County	KS	Carl Walker	1968	904
146-6/8	26-1/8	25-3/8	18-1/8	4	5	Lee County	IA	Jim Bohenkamp	1970	904
146-6/8	25-6/8	25-5/8	18-0/8	5	5	Robinson Creek	IL	Gary E. Sievers	1972	904
146-6/8	21-5/8	21-5/8	18-3/8	6	7	Will County	IL	Richard Manegold	1976	904
146-6/8	23-0/8	25-6/8	16-3/8	6	5	Lafayette County	WI	Greg Penniston	1977	904
146-6/8	26-1/8	25-3/8	16-0/8	5	4	Waushara County	WI	James L. Reiff, Jr.	1981	904
146-6/8	25-2/8	24-3/8	18-0/8	5	5	Logan County	OH	David Katterheinrich	1984	904
146-5/8	22-5/8	22-5/8	18-7/8	4	3	Brown County	SD	Donald Grote	1963	912
146-5/8	23-2/8	24-1/8	17-3/8	5	6	Buckingham County	VA	Larry D. Baker	1974	912
146-5/8	25-2/8	25-6/8	18-7/8	4	5	Carroll County	IL	Art Heinze	1978	912
146-5/8	24-2/8	24-1/8	18-7/8	6	7	Burlington	IA	Larry R. Booth	1979	912
146-5/8	20-6/8	22-1/8	19-4/8	7	7	Clinton County	IN	Sheldon H. Stoops	1979	912
146-5/8	23-4/8	24-0/8	19-1/8	5	5	Morrison County	MN	Bart Brodt	1984	912
146-5/8	24-3/8	24-4/8	16-5/8	6	5	Cole County	MO	Norman P. Stucky	1984	912
146-4/8	24-4/8	24-0/8	15-0/8	5	5	Amherst County	VA	Garry B. Pruitt	1972	919
146-4/8	22-0/8	23-3/8	18-0/8	5	5	Terre Haute	IN	Richard E. Smith	1973	919
146-4/8	25-0/8	24-7/8	18-6/8	5	5	Summer Hill	NY	John Andrews, Sr.	1974	919
146-4/8	24-2/8	25-2/8	17-6/8	6	5	Christian County	IL	Camron Fitzsimmons	1980	919
146-4/8	26-4/8	25-2/8	17-4/8	4	5	Polk County	MO	James Scott Hogan	1982	919
146-4/8	24-3/8	24-5/8	18-6/8	4	4	Green County	IL	Daniel E. Kallal	1983	919
146-4/8	21-5/8	21-2/8	15-0/8	5	5	Forest County	WI	Eugene A. Pribek	1985	919
146-4/8	22-3/8	22-7/8	16-0/8	5	5	Ritchie County	WV	Tim Jividen	1985	919
146-4/8	24-0/8	23-6/8	16-2/8	4	4	Randolph County	IL	Edward J. Lannon	1985	919
146-4/8	23-4/8	25-3/8	17-0/8	7	7	Washington County	WI	Eric Handeland	1986	919
146-3/8	24-6/8	24-5/8	15-3/8	5	5	Palo Alto County	IA	Kim E. Gustafson	1972	929
146-3/8	24-7/8	25-0/8	24-3/8	4	4	Muskingum County	OH	P. W. "Bill" Meyer	1977	929
146-3/8	23-1/8	23-6/8	19-2/8	6	6	Bafaar	KS	Jim Wilson	1980	929
146-3/8	23-5/8	23-5/8	20-1/8	5	5	Hamilton County	OH	Jerome R. Buschle, Jr.	1981	929
146-3/8	23-1/8	23-1/8	17-5/8	4	5	Cecil County	MD	John M. Martino	1981	929
146-3/8	23-5/8	23-1/8	16-1/8	5	6	Jo Daviess County	IL	David R. Kammerude	1983	929
146-3/8	22-5/8	22-1/8	16-7/8	6	6	Floyd County	IA	Mike Bull	1983	929
146-3/8	24-0/8	22-2/8	19-1/8	5	5	Perry County	IL	Richard Kuhnert	1984	929
146-3/8	24-6/8	25-7/8	20-7/8	5	5	Hamilton County	OH	Bob Miller	1985	929
146-2/8	24-3/8	24-1/8	18-2/8	5	5	Stearns County	MN	Mike Beuning	1945	938
146-2/8	24-6/8	24-1/8	18-2/8	5	5	Butler County	KS	David R. Rogers	1976	938
146-2/8	21-2/8	21-7/8	21-2/8	5	5	Clark County	KS	Danny R. Fenton	1977	938
146-2/8	22-7/8	23-5/8	16-5/8	6	6	Lafayette County	WI	Wayne Gassman	1977	938
146-2/8	24-4/8	24-6/8	15-6/8	4	4	Clark County	IL	Gerald Shaffner	1978	938
146-2/8	24-6/8	24-0/8	19-1/8	5	7	Berkeley County	SC	Hugh Gaskins	1980	938
146-2/8	25-1/8	24-2/8	20-2/8	6	4	Union County	OH	Charles Yoakum	1980	938
146-2/8	25-2/8	25-0/8	17-2/8	5	6	Graham County	KS	Russell Hull	1982	938

WHITETAIL DEER *(Typical Antlers)*

(continued)   Minimum Score 125

Score	Length of Main Beam R	L	Inside Spread	Number of Points R	L	Area	State/ Province	Hunter's Name	Date	Rank
146-2/8	23-6/8	22-5/8	18-0/8	5	5	Brown County	OH	Ronald Akins	1982	938
146-2/8	24-4/8	24-3/8	19-4/8r	5	4	Washington County	WI	J.J. Ziegler	1983	938
146-2/8	24-6/8	24-5/8	19-4/8	5	5	Lafayette County	WI	Roger Wand	1983	938
146-2/8	24-0/8	24-0/8	18-2/8	6	6	Dane County	WI	Roland G. Lettman	1983	938
146-2/8	26-7/8	26-3/8	16-5/8	7	6	Granville County	NC	Bradley Brann	1984	938
146-2/8	22-2/8	21-6/8	16-5/8	5	6	Parkland County	ALB	Michel Carigan	1984	938
146-2/8	26-1/8	25-0/8	18-6/8	5	5	St. Lawrence County	NY	Joseph W. Pudney	1985	938
146-2/8	25-0/8	22-7/8	14-4/8	4	4	Van Buren County	IA	Tom Weigand	1985	938
146-2/8	22-6/8	22-0/8	17-5/8	5	6	Dodge County	MN	David Lyke	1985	938
146-1/8	23-5/8	24-5/8	17-7/8	6	5	Delaware County	IA	Douglas G. Dabroski	1975	955
146-1/8	25-2/8	25-6/8	21-2/8	6	8	Jefferson County	WI	Neil L. Lindemann	1977	955
146-1/8	24-1/8	25-0/8	18-3/8	5	5	Lamar County	GA	Joe A. Medcalf	1977	955
146-1/8	24-2/8	24-2/8	19-3/8	4	4	Chisago County	MN	Richard Brown	1980	955
146-1/8	25-2/8	23-3/8	18-2/8	6	5	Dickinson County	MI	Edward J. Henkel	1980	955
146-1/8	25-3/8	25-2/8	19-1/8	5	5	Darke County	OH	Larry Moore	1980	955
146-1/8	24-3/8	23-4/8	14-7/8	6	5	Chisago County	MN	Clancy Lindvall	1982	955
146-1/8	24-3/8	23-2/8	17-2/8	5	7	Waseca County	MN	Mark Williams	1982	955
146-1/8	23-4/8	21-5/8	16-1/8	5	5	Montcalm County	MI	David Tompsett	1985	955
146-0/8	22-1/8	22-2/8	19-2/8	6	6	Sidney	MT	James L. Kelly	1958	964
146-0/8	21-1/8	20-6/8	17-5/8	5	6	Cass County	IN	William D. Finks	1967	964
146-0/8	24-0/8	25-0/8	18-4/8	5	5	Will County	IL	Terry Marcukaitis	1971	964
146-0/8	25-0/8	24-0/8	22-0/8	5	5	Winona County	MN	Henry Scharmack,Jr.	1973	964
146-0/8	20-5/8	20-5/8	14-3/8	7	8	Murray County	MN	John Stenke	1973	964
146-0/8	24-1/8	24-4/8	16-0/8	6	6	Keith County	NE	Gerald Spurgin	1975	964
146-0/8	23-0/8	22-4/8	18-1/8	6	5	Calgary	ALB	Fred Walker	1981	964
146-0/8	21-6/8	21-5/8	16-2/8	5	5	Saline County	NE	Donald D. Matejka	1982	964
146-0/8	22-0/8	23-0/8	18-2/8	6	6	Kewaunee County	WI	Harold Blahnik	1982	964
146-0/8	21-5/8	22-1/8	18-2/8	5	5	Roberts County	SD	John Fridgen	1984	964
146-0/8	27-0/8	27-2/8	21-6/8	4	4	Little Falls County	MN	John Sobaski	1985	964
145-7/8	25-4/8	24-4/8	19-1/8	4	5	Scotia	NE	Bill W. Surface	1962	975
145-7/8	22-4/8	22-7/8	20-7/8	4	8	Lafayette County	WI	James Goetzke	1972	975
145-7/8	21-4/8	22-0/8	15-2/8	5	6	Chase County	KS	John L. Moore	1982	975
145-7/8	22-6/8	24-4/8	18-7/8	6	5	Lewis and Clark County	MT	Royce Dake	1982	975
145-7/8	22-4/8	22-3/8	20-1/8	5	5	Harvey County	KS	Gregory K. Dirksen	1983	975
145-6/8	20-0/8	20-5/8	17-0/8	5	6	Okmulgee	OK	Pat Giulioli	1973	980
145-6/8	21-5/8	22-4/8	17-0/8	5	5	Camp McCoy	WI	Bob Besch	1980	980
145-6/8	22-0/8	22-0/8	17-2/8	5	5	Millarville	ALB	Richard Freudenberg	1982	980
145-6/8	21-3/8	21-3/8	17-0/8	6	5	Clay County	MN	Darwin Cihak	1986	980
145-5/8	25-1/8	24-4/8	19-7/8	6	5	Waseca County	MN	Robert Barrie	1971	984
145-5/8	23-7/8	24-0/8	21-2/8	4	6	Montgomery County	AL	Rett Kelly	1974	984
145-5/8	23-5/8	23-0/8	18-4/8	6	7	Stearns County	MN	Larry Schwarze	1979	984
145-5/8	23-0/8	23-6/8	17-3/8	5	5	Rich Valley	ALB	Eric Teege	1980	984
145-5/8	24-0/8	24-4/8	18-5/8	6	5	Athens County	OH	Steve Wilkes	1983	984
145-5/8	26-1/8	25-7/8	18-2/8	5	5	Houston County	GA	Issac W. Horne	1985	984
145-5/8	24-1/8	23-4/8	19-2/8	5	6	Black Hawk County	IA	John L. Derifield	1985	984
145-5/8	26-2/8	25-1/8	20-6/8	5	7	Christian County	IL	Carl Tucker	1985	984
145-5/8	23-2/8	24-3/8	20-4/8	6	5	Coffey County	KS	James Bowman	1985	984
145-4/8	23-3/8	24-0/8	17-2/8	6	7	Morton County	ND	Eddy Wallery	1959	993
145-4/8	25-5/8	24-4/8	19-0/8	4	5	Monroe County	WI	Larry Arentz	1977	993
145-4/8	23-2/8	22-0/8	18-2/8	7	6	Mower County	MN	Walter E. Bauer	1977	993
145-4/8	24-3/8	23-0/8	20-4/8	5	4	Marion County	IA	Donald Bennett	1977	993
145-4/8	22-1/8	21-6/8	17-2/8	5	5	Van Buren County	MI	Bob Zedeck	1979	993
145-4/8	24-3/8	22-7/8	18-1/8	5	6	Lawrence County	AL	Richard McClanahan	1980	993
145-4/8	23-7/8	24-3/8	20-2/8	4	4	Kent County	MI	Peter Champnoise	1981	993
145-4/8	24-1/8	24-3/8	21-4/8	7	6	Hamilton County	OH	Jack Ranz	1982	993
145-4/8	24-0/8	24-1/8	18-7/8	5	4	Scott County	KY	Park Tackett	1984	993
145-4/8	23-0/8	24-0/8	19-4/8	4	5	Cass County	MI	Lee Davis	1985	993
145-3/8	24-3/8	25-1/8	20-5/8	5	5	Lyon County	KS	Edward Bess	1967	1003
145-3/8	22-4/8	22-5/8	18-1/8	5	5	Ripley	MN	Gerald A. Young	1971	1003
145-3/8	23-4/8	23-4/8	18-6/8	5	5	Kanawha County	WV	Luther McClure	1973	1003
145-3/8	24-5/8	25-5/8	22-1/8	4	5	Will County	IL	Philip J. Gariboldi	1977	1003
145-3/8	26-7/8	26-3/8	20-2/8	4	4	Jackson County	MI	Scot Gazlay	1977	1003
145-3/8	22-7/8	23-0/8	19-1/8	4	5	Des Moines County	IA	John Jindrich	1979	1003

WHITETAIL DEER *(Typical Antlers)*

Minimum Score 125

Score	Length of Main Beam R	L	Inside Spread	Number of Points R	L	Area	State/ Province	Hunter's Name	Date	Rank
145-3/8	22-6/8	21-3/8	17-4/8	6	6	Marshall County	SD	Tim Johnson	1980	1003
145-3/8	23-7/8	23-7/8	17-5/8	4	4	Pike County	OH	William H. Koehler	1981	1003
145-3/8	23-3/8	23-6/8	17-2/8	5	4	Jackson County	OH	Joe W. Wright	1982	1003
145-3/8	23-4/8	22-2/8	18-1/8	5	4	Osage County	KS	Gary Hunsicker	1985	1003
145-2/8	21-6/8	21-3/8	18-2/8	5	5	Des Moines County	IA	Gary Biles	1973	1013
145-2/8	22-5/8	22-7/8	17-2/8	5	5	Yankton County	SD	Gordon Orton	1976	1013
145-2/8	23-0/8	22-4/8	15-4/8	7	6	Douglas County	KS	Richard D. Brown	1978	1013
145-2/8	23-3/8	23-0/8	16-2/8	5	5	Polk County	IA	Jim Young	1978	1013
145-2/8	23-7/8	24-4/8	17-5/8	5	5	Livingston County	MI	Alan K. Newberry	1979	1013
145-2/8	21-5/8	21-1/8	19-4/8	5	6	Clark County	AR	Thomas E. Taylor	1982	1013
145-2/8	22-7/8	23-6/8	18-6/8	5	5	Madison County	IA	Stephen W. Kent	1982	1013
145-2/8	24-2/8	22-0/8	22-0/8	5	6	Stephenson County	IL	Dwight Pickard	1983	1013
145-2/8	26-2/8	25-7/8	22-1/8	6	6	Grant County	WI	Gary Wiest	1983	1013
145-2/8	26-6/8	25-6/8	21-2/8	4	4	Mercer County	NJ	James E. McCloskey, Jr.	1984	1013
145-2/8	22-6/8	21-0/8	16-4/8	5	5	Hennepin County	MN	Robert L. Halverson	1985	1013
145-2/8	23-0/8	23-0/8	15-6/8	5	5	Holt County	NE	Thomas D. Lanz	1986	1013
145-1/8	24-7/8	25-2/8	22-0/8	5	6	Grundy County	IL	Tony Muhich	1975	1025
145-1/8	23-1/8	22-7/8	17-1/8	7	7	Dearborn County	IN	David Goodwin	1978	1025
145-1/8	22-3/8	22-5/8	15-5/8	5	5	Kent County	MI	Virgil G. Baker, Jr.	1979	1025
145-1/8	23-6/8	23-2/8	18-5/8	5	6	Green County	WI	Dan Behring	1979	1025
145-1/8	24-6/8	24-0/8	18-5/8	6	5	Leavenworth County	KS	Chris Calovich	1982	1025
145-1/8	23-0/8	23-0/8	17-3/8	5	5	Berkshire County	MA	Richard Scorzafava	1984	1025
145-0/8	22-5/8	21-2/8	14-2/8	6	6	Washington County	IA	Doron Whitlock	1966	1031
145-0/8	24-0/8	24-5/8	20-0/8	4	4	Summit	SD	Kevin Bronson	1973	1031
145-0/8	24-0/8	22-2/8	15-2/8	6	6	Trigg County	KY	Donald Powell	1974	1031
145-0/8	23-1/8	22-6/8	15-2/8	5	5	Mahaska County	IA	Randy Randall	1978	1031
145-0/8	21-5/8	22-4/8	15-4/8	5	5	Jones County	IA	Jim H. Dougherty	1979	1031
145-0/8	24-2/8	22-1/8	14-1/8	8	6	St. Genevieve	MO	Dr. Dennis Diaz	1980	1031
145-0/8	23-6/8	24-2/8	19-6/8	5	5	Huntingdon County	PA	John A. Williams	1983	1031
145-0/8	20-4/8	21-4/8	16-4/8	5	5	Polk County	MN	Grant Schultz	1984	1031
145-0/8	23-0/8	23-4/8	19-1/8	9	5	St. Joseph	IN	Monty Layne	1984	1031
144-7/8	23-0/8	23-4/8	19-7/8	6	6	Wyandotte County	KS	George F. Bigelow	1966	1040
144-7/8	21-7/8	22-3/8	17-1/8	5	6	Sussex County	VA	Alvin D. Skinner	1972	1040
144-7/8	25-1/8	25-0/8	18-3/8	5	6	Louisa County	IA	Harold E. Boysen	1978	1040
144-7/8	20-2/8	20-1/8	15-2/8	6	5	Sidney	MT	Garth N. Kallevig	1980	1040
144-7/8	25-7/8	25-4/8	19-3/8	4	4	Sumner County	KS	Dave Baldwin	1982	1040
144-7/8	23-7/8	22-0/8	18-3/8	4	4	Cerro Gordo County	IA	Earl L. Goodman	1983	1040
144-7/8	22-3/8	22-1/8	17-5/8	5	5	Onondaga County	NY	Kim A. Schneider	1985	1040
144-7/8	25-4/8	25-2/8	16-3/8	5	6	Mayes County	OK	John W. Madlock	1985	1040
144-7/8	21-2/8	21-1/8	18-7/8	5	5	Osborne County	KS	Gary L. Ozias	1985	1040
144-6/8	19-6/8	20-0/8	15-2/8	6	7	Powell County	MT	Danny Moore	1974	1049
144-6/8	21-7/8	22-1/8	17-4/8	6	7	Christian County	IL	Scott M. Cassidy	1983	1049
144-6/8	25-2/8	24-6/8	19-2/8	4	5	Deleware County	PA	James Taylor	1984	1049
144-6/8	21-0/8	21-4/8	17-0/8	5	5	Sumner County	KS	Jeffrey L. Nash	1984	1049
144-5/8	24-0/8	24-4/8	21-3/8	4	4	Tulare	SD	Jerald Shantz	1959	1053
144-5/8	23-6/8	23-6/8	19-7/8	4	4	Geauga County	OH	Rudy Grecar	1970	1053
144-5/8	24-7/8	26-3/8	21-7/8	5	6	Valley County	MT	Leith Wimmer	1971	1053
144-5/8	22-2/8	22-7/8	17-7/8	5	6	Vermillion County	IN	Robert McClara	1972	1053
144-5/8	23-6/8	24-2/8	16-5/8	5	5	Will County	IL	Joseph Wyer	1978	1053
144-5/8	23-2/8	23-6/8	18-3/8	5	5	Huntingdon County	PA	John A. Williams	1980	1053
144-5/8	22-2/8	21-2/8	18-1/8	4	5	Oconto County	WI	David Nelsen	1982	1053
144-5/8	24-2/8	23-4/8	15-1/8	5	6	Traill County	ND	Arlin Ingebretson	1983	1053
144-5/8	23-0/8	22-1/8	14-5/8	5	5	Price County	WI	Peter Koenig	1983	1053
144-5/8	22-5/8	21-5/8	16-3/8	6	6	Stanley County	SD	Randy Kleinschmidt	1985	1053
144-4/8	22-6/8	22-6/8	16-3/8	5	7	Wood River	NE	Verne Skow	1958	1063
144-4/8	23-2/8	23-6/8	16-3/8	5	6	Bristol	SD	John E. Sigdestad	1963	1063
144-4/8	25-3/8	26-1/8	16-4/8	5	4	Montgomery County	MD	Victor Ezerski	1975	1063
144-4/8	23-0/8	24-5/8	14-5/8	6	8	Scott	MN	Charlie Abeln	1977	1063
144-4/8	23-1/8	22-2/8	17-2/8	5	5	Winnebago County	IA	Ronald Gorden	1977	1063
144-4/8	23-2/8	22-5/8	18-4/8	5	6	Green County	OH	Don F. Necina	1981	1063
144-4/8	26-2/8	26-1/8	18-3/8	5	6	Jo Daviess County	IL	Kenneth Pluym	1985	1063
144-4/8	25-6/8	26-4/8	19-7/8	7	7	Madison County	NY	John Loveday	1985	1063
144-4/8	25-1/8	24-5/8	19-2/8	4	4	Montgomery County	OH	Anthony W. Miller	1986	1063

WHITETAIL DEER *(Typical Antlers)*

(continued)

Score	Length of Main Beam R	Length of Main Beam L	Inside Spread	Number of Points R	Number of Points L	Area	State/ Province	Hunter's Name	Date	Rank
144-3/8	23-7/8	23-5/8	17-2/8	6	7	Rock County	NE	Dick Mauch	1963	1072
144-3/8	23-7/8	24-5/8	19-5/8	6	4	Delaware	OH	Jack R. Hecker	1975	1072
144-3/8	23-6/8	23-6/8	16-4/8	4	5	Columbia County	WI	Ronald Bordson	1976	1072
144-3/8	22-4/8	23-5/8	16-6/8	6	5	Murray County	MN	John Laundre	1981	1072
144-3/8	23-1/8	22-7/8	17-7/8	6	6	Kingman County	KS	Scott Helmke	1982	1072
144-3/8	23-0/8	23-6/8	19-7/8	5	6	Clayton County	IA	Kenneth Clayton	1982	1072
144-3/8	22-6/8	22-4/8	18-7/8	6	5	Columbia County	WI	Jerry Ulrich	1984	1072
144-3/8	24-1/8	24-4/8	19-5/8	5	6	Morrison County	MN	Rick Hayner	1984	1072
144-3/8	21-6/8	22-1/8	18-3/8	5	5	Ripley County	IN	Dick Gambrel	1984	1072
144-3/8	23-7/8	24-1/8	17-1/8	4	5	Anderson County	TN	Johnny Wayne Jobe	1985	1072
144-2/8	25-7/8	26-2/8	23-0/8	4	4	Bucks County	PA	Robert Weaver	1923	1082
144-2/8	21-5/8	21-4/8	17-2/8	5	5	Miner County	SD	William Hueners	1965	1082
144-2/8	21-7/8	21-7/8	14-2/8	5	5	Brown County	SD	Harold Larson	1966	1082
144-2/8	20-6/8	20-7/8	15-4/8	5	5	Juneau County	WI	Gordon Stittleburg	1966	1082
144-2/8	22-4/8	23-4/8	17-6/8	5	5	Steele Center	MN	Maynard Bauer	1977	1082
144-2/8	24-2/8	22-6/8	19-6/8	5	5	Miami County	OH	Dale Stull	1980	1082
144-2/8	22-7/8	23-2/8	17-0/8	5	5	Coffey County	KS	Marc Chester	1983	1082
144-2/8	20-3/8	20-1/8	15-4/8	5	6	Brown County	KS	Ken Spencer	1983	1082
144-2/8	25-1/8	24-2/8	20-6/8	5	4	Hamilton County	IL	Paul Sebby	1984	1082
144-1/8	21-1/8	21-0/8	17-1/8	5	5	Maverick County	TX	Dean Oatman	1923	1091
144-1/8	21-3/8	21-2/8	17-2/8	5	7	Marshall City	KS	Jack Thornton	1965	1091
144-1/8	25-0/8	24-0/8	17-7/8	5	4	Union County	IL	Pat Mitchell	1974	1091
144-1/8	21-6/8	22-1/8	17-5/8	5	5	Jackson County	IL	Dave Yearian	1979	1091
144-1/8	25-0/8	25-7/8	16-0/8	4	5	Vinton County	OH	Randy Fee	1981	1091
144-1/8	23-7/8	23-1/8	19-1/8	4	4	Defiance County	OH	Alan Stark	1981	1091
144-1/8	22-3/8	21-6/8	14-7/8	7	7	Calumet County	WI	Myron E. Jochmann	1982	1091
144-1/8	26-3/8	26-0/8	20-3/8	3	4	Charles County	MD	Fred Dolinger	1982	1091
144-1/8	21-1/8	21-6/8	17-0/8	7	7	Pittsburg County	OK	Brett Jones	1984	1091
144-1/8	23-1/8	22-7/8	19-4/8	5	4	Des Moines County	IA	Ray Waschkat	1985	1091
144-1/8	22-6/8	22-4/8	17-1/8	5	5	Woodbury County	IA	Ritch A. Stolpe	1985	1091
144-0/8	21-4/8	22-0/8	16-6/8	5	5	Adams County	IL	Gerald Morton	1963	1102
144-0/8	22-4/8	23-0/8	18-6/8	5	5	Fayette County	IA	Kenneth Durnin	1971	1102
144-0/8	24-4/8	23-5/8	17-6/8	5	4	Wayne County	WV	Eddie Mullins	1976	1102
144-0/8	23-4/8	24-0/8	17-2/8	5	5	Hocking County	OH	Greg Bonecutter, Sr.	1979	1102
144-0/8	23-2/8	23-3/8	18-4/8	5	5	Opelika	AL	George P. Mann	1979	1102
144-0/8	24-2/8	24-4/8	18-4/8	5	4	Murray County	MN	Alan Metz	1979	1102
144-0/8	23-5/8	24-4/8	18-6/8	4	4	Juneau County	WI	Kelly Urban	1980	1102
144-0/8	25-6/8	25-6/8	17-5/8	4	5	Jackson County	OH	Thomas Hart	1981	1102
144-0/8	22-4/8	22-3/8	18-2/8	5	5	Logan County	OH	Mark A. Payne	1981	1102
144-0/8	22-0/8	22-1/8	21-7/8	7	8	Hennepin County	MN	Clarence D. Huls	1984	1102
144-0/8	23-5/8	23-6/8	19-2/8	6	4	Franklin County	KS	J. R. Oshel	1985	1102
144-0/8	23-6/8	24-2/8	18-4/8	5	6	Monmouth County	NJ	Cliff Underwood	1985	1102
144-0/8	23-7/8	23-2/8	19-0/8	5	5	Lewis & Clark County	MT	Sonny Templeton	1985	1102
144-0/8	23-7/8	23-0/8	18-0/8	5	5	Hubbard County	MN	Tim Leeseberg	1985	1102
143-7/8	21-5/8	22-2/8	15-7/8	5	5	Oktiabbeha County	MS	Frank Cascio, Jr.	1978	1116
143-7/8	22-5/8	21-6/8	14-7/8	6	5	Traverse County	MN	Gary Anderson	1980	1116
143-7/8	23-1/8	23-0/8	19-1/8	4	5	Monon	IN	Richard Zaring	1980	1116
143-7/8	27-3/8	26-2/8	19-0/8	5	6	Erie County	NY	Mark A. Bennett	1981	1116
143-7/8	22-1/8	23-1/8	17-3/8	5	5	Taylor County	WI	Tony Kliscz	1981	1116
143-7/8	28-6/8	26-3/8	21-1/8	4	5	Ross County	OH	Jack F. Hatton	1982	1116
143-7/8	24-1/8	23-0/8	17-7/8	6	5	Morrill County	NE	Gerry Hrasky	1983	1116
143-7/8	20-4/8	20-3/8	15-3/8	5	5	Macon County	AL	George P. Mann	1984	1116
143-7/8	24-3/8	23-2/8	19-1/8	7	7	Allegheny County	PA	Richard J. Kudranski	1985	1116
143-6/8	22-3/8	21-0/8	18-6/8	6	10	Ionia County	MI	Bob Jones	1966	1125
143-6/8	23-7/8	23-4/8	19-0/8	4	5	Iron County	WI	Lee C. Dix	1968	1125
143-6/8	21-1/8	21-1/8	17-2/8	7	6	Upham	ND	William J. Berg	1978	1125
143-6/8	20-7/8	21-2/8	15-2/8	6	5	Sabine County	TX	Max L. Turner	1982	1125
143-6/8	23-0/8	21-3/8	17-4/8	5	5	Onieda County	WI	Pat Abraham	1983	1125
143-6/8	24-4/8	25-2/8	21-2/8	6	4	Shawnee County	KS	Kevin Hogan	1985	1125
143-6/8	23-3/8	23-2/8	18-6/8	5	5	Ottawa County	OK	Ed Hammons	1986	1125
143-5/8	22-5/8	23-4/8	17-4/8	6	4	Washington County	MN	Keith Christensen	1975	1132
143-5/8	23-5/8	23-5/8	17-3/8	5	6	St. Paul	KS	Hugh B. Woolard	1976	1132
143-5/8	23-3/8	22-4/8	18-6/8	6	8	Houston County	MN	Arden M. Schock	1980	1132

WHITETAIL DEER *(Typical Antlers)*

Minimum Score 125

(continued)

Score	Length of Main Beam R	L	Inside Spread	Number of Points R	L	Area	State/ Province	Hunter's Name	Date	Rank
143-5/8	25-0/8	24-7/8	17-5/8	5	4	Miami County	OH	Philip C. Gudorf	1982	1132
143-5/8	23-7/8	22-7/8	19-7/8	5	5	Randolph County	WV	Charles Byrd	1982	1132
143-5/8	23-6/8	23-4/8	15-3/8	5	5	Union County	OR	Kim Tameris	1983	1132
143-5/8	23-7/8	23-5/8	18-3/8	6	5	Blue Earth County	MN	LeRoy Urban	1983	1132
143-5/8	20-1/8	20-6/8	16-4/8	6	6	Pine County	MN	Mike Stauty	1984	1132
143-5/8	25-1/8	23-6/8	16-3/8	7	8	Fayette County	IA	Roger DeKok	1985	1132
143-5/8	23-4/8	24-4/8	20-1/8	4	4	Pike County	IL	Rick L. Rodhouse	1986	1132
143-4/8	23-7/8	23-0/8	20-0/8	5	7	Traverse County	MN	Roland L. Hausmann	1958	1142
143-4/8	22-5/8	22-7/8	21-4/8	6	6	Hays	KS	Lee Couture	1969	1142
143-4/8	24-3/8	25-0/8	17-2/8	5	5	Miami County	KS	Fred Supulver	1969	1142
143-4/8	23-0/8	22-4/8	16-6/8	5	6	Sheboygan County	WI	Gary Mueller	1971	1142
143-4/8	23-4/8	22-1/8	18-4/8	5	5	Saginaw	MI	Dorm Haskins	1978	1142
143-4/8	23-5/8	22-7/8	19-2/8	4	5	Belmont	OH	Fred Holub	1980	1142
143-4/8	23-4/8	24-0/8	17-2/8	6	5	Baxter Springs	KS	Brett Thomas	1981	1142
143-4/8	24-5/8	23-3/8	17-0/8	5	5	St. Clair County	MI	Art Brown	1981	1142
143-4/8	24-2/8	24-4/8	17-6/8	5	6	Pike County	OH	Billy Ray Jenkins	1981	1142
143-4/8	24-0/8	23-5/8	17-6/8	4	4	Finney County	KS	Wilferd Nichols	1981	1142
143-4/8	23-6/8	23-1/8	18-2/8	7	5	Winona County	MN	Jim Keim	1982	1142
143-4/8	23-6/8	23-1/8	18-6/8	4	4	Stafford County	KS	Larry Hoffman	1982	1142
143-4/8	22-4/8	22-5/8	18-4/8	6	5	Huntingdon County	PA	John A. Williams	1984	1142
143-4/8	24-4/8	23-7/8	17-6/8	5	5	Outertail County	MN	Ross R Grothe	1984	1142
143-4/8	25-5/8	25-6/8	17-2/8	7	6	Sheboygan County	WI	Randy Mavis	1985	1142
143-4/8	24-6/8	24-7/8	21-0/8	4	5	Logan County	IL	Mark E. Humbert	1985	1142
143-4/8	23-3/8	25-4/8	19-0/8	6	4	Clayton County	IA	Paul "Buck" Farni, Jr.	1986	1142
143-3/8	25-0/8	23-6/8	16-3/8	6	5	Ottertail County	MN	J. P. Maurins	1956	1159
143-3/8	23-0/8	23-1/8	15-7/8	5	5	Comanche County	OK	Kenneth D. Cook	1971	1159
143-3/8	22-2/8	22-0/8	17-2/8	7	7	Ripley	MN	Glen Marklowitz	1972	1159
143-3/8	22-3/8	22-4/8	20-1/8	4	6	Allamakee County	IA	Jim Schmidt	1974	1159
143-3/8	24-1/8	25-2/8	17-1/8	5	5	Cass County	MN	Richard J. Schabert	1977	1159
143-3/8	27-0/8	26-0/8	20-1/8	4	4	Charles County	MD	John Allen Williams	1980	1159
143-3/8	24-1/8	24-0/8	15-5/8	4	5	Saginaw County	MI	Paul Mickey	1981	1159
143-3/8	22-0/8	23-4/8	19-0/8	8	8	Pike County	IL	Steve Carlen	1982	1159
143-3/8	24-1/8	23-7/8	17-5/8	5	5	Green County	WI	B. Duane Byrne	1984	1159
143-3/8	23-6/8	24-3/8	18-1/8	4	4	Ogle County	IL	Dr. Juanito E. Delfinado	1984	1159
143-3/8	25-3/8	24-7/8	19-1/8	4	4	Norman County	MN	Bryan Mickelson	1985	1159
143-3/8	22-7/8	24-2/8	17-7/8	4	4	Walworth County	WI	Gary Jordan	1985	1159
143-3/8	18-6/8	21-0/8	16-3/8	5	5	Slope County	ND	Jack Lefor	1985	1159
143-3/8	24-0/8	23-6/8	22-2/8	5	6	Pennington County	MN	John A. Monroe	1986	1159
143-2/8	25-0/8	24-0/8	16-6/8	5	6	Phillips County	AR	Stanley Zellner	1964	1173
143-2/8	25-0/8	23-7/8	19-4/8	5	5	Geauga County	OH	Rudy Grecar	1971	1173
143-2/8	26-0/8	25-0/8	17-4/8	8	7	Ft. Sill	OK	Lloyd Payne III	1976	1173
143-2/8	25-2/8	26-1/8	18-4/8	4	4	E. Bloomington	IN	Mike Webb	1977	1173
143-2/8	22-0/8	23-1/8	16-0/8	5	5	Fond du Lac County	WI	Jim Rickmeyer	1979	1173
143-2/8	25-4/8	25-0/8	19-2/8	5	5	Price County	WI	Todd R. Sorensen	1981	1173
143-2/8	24-6/8	25-0/8	18-4/8	5	5	Marion County	TN	Larry Gravitt	1981	1173
143-2/8	21-7/8	21-6/8	18-4/8	5	5	Jefferson County	MT	Bob Peterson	1983	1173
143-2/8	24-2/8	24-6/8	16-2/8	5	6	Green County	WI	Wellington W. Wert	1983	1173
143-2/8	24-3/8	24-3/8	20-0/8	4	4	Edgar County	IL	Benton B. Caldwell	1983	1173
143-2/8	23-2/8	23-3/8	13-4/8	5	5	Hardin County	IA	Rick McDowell	1983	1173
143-2/8	23-2/8	22-4/8	18-7/8	5	6	Winona County	MN	Bill Clink	1984	1173
143-2/8	24-3/8	24-6/8	15-6/8	6	6	Cooper County	MO	Vaughn Sell	1985	1173
143-2/8	26-0/8	25-6/8	21-4/8	5	4	Montgomery County	MD	Bobby Ray Waters	1985	1173
143-1/8	23-0/8	23-2/8	17-1/8	5	4	Hill City	KS	Russell Hull	1965	1187
143-1/8	21-7/8	23-2/8	21-5/8	5	5	Linn County	IA	Tom Postel	1979	1187
143-1/8	21-2/8	22-7/8	18-3/8	6	7	Lincoln County	MN	David J. Rouge	1981	1187
143-1/8	22-6/8	22-1/8	18-6/8	6	6	Barry County	MI	Jay W. Gaston	1981	1187
143-1/8	21-6/8	21-2/8	19-5/8	6	6	Holmes County	OH	Dale R. Kaufman	1983	1187
143-1/8	22-5/8	22-4/8	19-5/8	5	5	Missoula County	MT	Greg Munther	1983	1187
143-1/8	20-6/8	20-3/8	18-7/8	6	6	Olmsted County	MN	Brian Veloske	1984	1187
143-1/8	24-6/8	25-4/8	17-7/8	6	7	Riley County	KS	Kenneth W. Lynch	1985	1187
143-0/8	23-5/8	22-0/8	19-4/8	5	5	Wright County	IA	Ronald Gorden	1958	1195
143-0/8	24-0/8	24-5/8	20-5/8	5	5	Pope County	IL	Bob E. Sims	1964	1195
143-0/8	25-4/8	21-0/8	14-6/8	5	6	Bennington	KS	Scotty Baugh	1967	1195

WHITETAIL DEER *(Typical Antlers)*

(continued)   Minimum Score 125

Score	Length of Main Beam R	L	Inside Spread	Number of Points R	L	Area	State/ Province	Hunter's Name	Date	Rank
143-0/8	22-7/8	21-7/8	16-2/8	5	5	Edwards County	KS	Gerald L. Schaller	1972	1195
143-0/8	20-2/8	19-6/8	15-4/8	5	5	Madison County	IA	Larry L. Cavanaugh	1979	1195
143-0/8	24-3/8	24-4/8	18-1/8	6	5	Black Hawk County	IA	Richard Minahan	1980	1195
143-0/8	24-3/8	25-0/8	18-2/8	4	4	Sawyer County	WI	Steve Olson	1981	1195
143-0/8	20-5/8	20-5/8	15-4/8	5	5	Seward County	KS	Lynn Leonard	1983	1195
143-0/8	22-1/8	23-0/8	17-4/8	5	6	Montgomery County	PA	Robert J. Bochnak	1983	1195
143-0/8	24-6/8	23-1/8	22-0/8	6	5	Kankakee County	IL	Rick Renzi	1983	1195
142-7/8	23-5/8	23-1/8	27-1/8	5	5	Spencerville	IN	Stanley Bremer	1969	1205
142-7/8	20-4/8	20-6/8	16-3/8	5	5	Brown County	SD	Wayne Miller	1971	1205
142-7/8	21-1/8	22-4/8	16-1/8	5	5	Jackson County	WI	Clark Gallup	1972	1205
142-7/8	24-1/8	24-2/8	20-1/8	4	5	Omaha	NE	Walter Ruff, Jr.	1973	1205
142-7/8	26-2/8	25-6/8	22-7/8	4	4	Carroll County	IL	Donald Lauer	1978	1205
142-7/8	21-0/8	23-5/8	19-6/8	6	5	Fairfield	MT	Richard C. Semrad	1979	1205
142-7/8	22-2/8	21-5/8	13-7/8	4	4	St. Louis County	MN	Dan Tanner	1979	1205
142-7/8	22-7/8	23-0/8	17-1/8	5	6	Redwood County	MN	Kenneth A. Gilb	1980	1205
142-7/8	22-0/8	23-2/8	18-1/8	4	5	Central Warren County	IA	Charly Stills	1980	1205
142-7/8	25-2/8	25-2/8	18-3/8	5	6	Freeborn County	MN	Kermit Askland	1982	1205
142-7/8	21-2/8	21-2/8	16-7/8	5	5	Richland County	MT	Dave McGough	1983	1205
142-7/8	21-0/8	20-4/8	18-0/8	5	6	Jefferson County	NE	Bob Funke	1983	1205
142-7/8	22-3/8	23-1/8	17-7/8	5	4	Shelby County	IL	David Russell	1983	1205
142-7/8	24-4/8	25-5/8	21-1/8	4	4	Will County	IL	Terry Marcukaitis	1984	1205
142-7/8	24-4/8	24-5/8	20-1/8	5	5	Marshall County	KS	Steve Johnson	1984	1205
142-7/8	24-5/8	24-6/8	20-3/8	6	4	Lafayette County	WI	Larry Rose	1985	1205
142-6/8	23-5/8	23-0/8	19-5/8	4	5	Green Lake County	WI	Mark Novitske	1969	1221
142-6/8	22-2/8	21-7/8	18-7/8	6	6	Douglas County	MN	David Koenen	1973	1221
142-6/8	25-3/8	25-4/8	16-6/8	4	4	Darke County	OH	Wayne Goubeaux	1974	1221
142-6/8	25-6/8	25-7/8	16-6/8	4	4	Prairie County	AR	John W. Hogue	1978	1221
142-6/8	21-3/8	21-3/8	18-6/8	5	6	Empress	ALB	Alan R. Francis	1980	1221
142-6/8	22-4/8	21-1/8	19-4/8	4	4	Dekalb County	MO	Mark Garr	1982	1221
142-6/8	23-6/8	24-0/8	19-5/8	6	5	Jefferson County	WI	Jed Kottwitz	1983	1221
142-6/8	24-2/8	23-7/8	19-2/8	6	5	Madison County	AL	Rocky Drake	1983	1221
142-6/8	22-3/8	23-1/8	17-6/8	5	4	Clay County	KS	Larry Reed	1984	1221
142-6/8	21-7/8	22-5/8	15-4/8	5	6	Lycoming County	PA	Kelly J. Cooper	1985	1221
142-6/8	14-4/8	22-0/8	17-4/8	6	6	Waukesha County	WI	John Riehle	1985	1221
142-6/8	22-0/8	22-1/8	17-2/8	5	5	Hamilton County	KS	Scott Showalter	1985	1221
142-5/8	24-2/8	22-7/8	15-5/8	5	5	Fleming County	KY	Dewey Miller	1976	1233
142-5/8	22-2/8	22-3/8	18-5/8	5	5	Richland County	OH	Joey A. Garcia	1980	1233
142-5/8	22-0/8	22-2/8	16-7/8	5	5	Chase County	KS	Lanny Deering	1981	1233
142-5/8	25-6/8	25-4/8	16-4/8	4	6	Darke County	OH	Norbert D. Schlecty	1981	1233
142-5/8	22-5/8	22-2/8	18-1/8	6	6	Waukesha County	WI	Mike Edlebeck	1982	1233
142-5/8	24-7/8	24-1/8	18-1/8	5	5	Dane County	WI	Dean Stolen	1982	1233
142-5/8	24-0/8	24-2/8	20-3/8	5	5	Cochrane	ALB	Kenneth Bills	1982	1233
142-5/8	21-4/8	22-3/8	15-7/8	7	5	Pepin County	WI	James D. Williams	1984	1233
142-5/8	22-6/8	22-5/8	20-3/8	5	4	Berkshire County	MA	Richard Scorzafava	1985	1233
142-4/8	22-5/8	22-4/8	19-0/8	5	5	Newton County	IN	Jim Manes	1963	1242
142-4/8	23-3/8	23-4/8	18-4/8	4	5	Winnebago County	IA	Duane Peterson	1966	1242
142-4/8	22-0/8	21-1/8	14-6/8	6	6	Eau Claire	WI	John J. Logan	1970	1242
142-4/8	24-7/8	24-0/8	19-6/8	4	4	Ballard County	KY	Archie Jacobs	1977	1242
142-4/8	24-7/8	24-3/8	19-3/8	6	5	Campbell Hill	IL	Mark A. Bollman	1979	1242
142-4/8	23-3/8	22-6/8	17-0/8	5	5	Musselshell County	MT	Larry W. Ostermiller	1979	1242
142-4/8	21-0/8	21-5/8	18-4/8	6	5	Jo Daviess County	IL	Kelly John Arnold	1981	1242
142-4/8	24-2/8	24-3/8	20-6/8	5	5	Robertson County	KY	Glen Arnold	1981	1242
142-4/8	23-5/8	24-1/8	15-6/8	5	5	Hysham	MT	Scott Brockway	1981	1242
142-4/8	21-0/8	20-6/8	16-3/8	5	6	Winona County	MN	Ron J. Parks	1981	1242
142-4/8	22-0/8	22-2/8	14-6/8	5	5	McKenzie County	ND	David Tofte	1983	1242
142-4/8	23-7/8	23-6/8	18-2/8	4	4	Bon Homme County	SD	Leon Somsen	1984	1242
142-4/8	20-4/8	20-4/8	16-0/8	5	5	McLean County	ND	Curt Radke	1985	1242
142-3/8	25-4/8	24-3/8	20-7/8	4	5	Mercer County	NJ	John K. Deveney	1975	1255
142-3/8	21-5/8	21-5/8	15-1/8	5	5	Wapello County	IA	Larry Terrell	1977	1255
142-3/8	23-4/8	22-4/8	18-1/8	5	5	Jersey County	IL	Jerry Cover	1979	1255
142-3/8	21-1/8	24-4/8	20-4/8	6	6	St. Charles County	MO	Edward J. Davidson	1980	1255
142-3/8	22-5/8	22-0/8	18-1/8	5	5	Washtenaw County	MI	Philip John Maly	1983	1255
142-3/8	21-4/8	22-5/8	17-5/8	6	7	Barton County	KS	Craig Doll	1984	1255

WHITETAIL DEER *(Typical Antlers)*

Minimum Score 125

(continued)

Score	Length of Main Beam R	L	Inside Spread	Number of Points R	L	Area	State/ Province	Hunter's Name	Date	Rank
142-3/8	20-6/8	21-0/8	17-5/8	5	5	Hardin County	TX	Mike Allen	1985	1255
142-3/8	24-2/8	26-5/8	16-1/8	4	4	Wright County	MN	Donald J. Emons	1985	1255
142-3/8	20-0/8	19-5/8	19-3/8	5	5	Shelby County	MO	Willard Otto	1985	1255
142-2/8	23-3/8	24-0/8	20-0/8	4	5	Riverdale	ND	Robert Loftin	1959	1264
142-2/8	23-2/8	22-6/8	17-6/8	5	6	Grant County	WI	Bob Woods	1962	1264
142-2/8	21-1/8	22-2/8	18-1/8	6	4	Ripley	MN	Dale Nieters	1971	1264
142-2/8	21-2/8	21-1/8	17-1/8	6	5	Bronson	TX	Norman D. Davis	1972	1264
142-2/8	27-3/8	28-5/8	19-6/8	4	5	Harrison County	OH	Joe Cola	1976	1264
142-2/8	24-3/8	23-7/8	19-6/8	4	4	Gallatin County	KY	Thomas W. Roberts	1976	1264
142-2/8	24-1/8	24-1/8	17-0/8	6	5	Le Seuer County	MN	Gene Solyntjes	1976	1264
142-2/8	22-4/8	23-6/8	19-0/8	7	5	Monticello	IA	Donald Bohlken	1978	1264
142-2/8	21-7/8	21-0/8	17-0/8	6	6	Dodge County	MN	Myles Keller	1980	1264
142-2/8	21-1/8	20-3/8	18-2/8	5	5	Edgar County	IL	Rory Steidl	1983	1264
142-2/8	24-7/8	24-3/8	21-4/8	5	5	Jackson County	MI	Russell P. Blair	1983	1264
142-2/8	22-7/8	24-5/8	18-0/8	5	5	Buffalo County	WI	Patrick Myers	1985	1264
142-1/8	23-1/8	22-7/8	18-6/8	5	5	Huron County	OH	Thomas Sheldon	1956	1276
142-1/8	23-6/8	23-1/8	15-3/8	6	6	Morgan County	GA	Jerry Wall	1966	1276
142-1/8	25-1/8	25-2/8	20-3/8	6	6	Blue Earth	MN	Timothy Anderson	1970	1276
142-1/8	24-2/8	25-7/8	22-1/8	5	4	Pope County	AR	Danny L. Mathis	1971	1276
142-1/8	24-2/8	24-0/8	18-3/8	6	5	Buffalo County	WI	Myles Keller	1973	1276
142-1/8	23-4/8	23-4/8	16-7/8	4	4	Ripley County	IN	Dick Gambrel	1981	1276
142-1/8	22-7/8	22-2/8	16-3/8	5	5	McPherson County	KS	James Willems	1981	1276
142-1/8	22-1/8	21-6/8	14-5/8	5	5	Charles County	MD	John L. Penny	1982	1276
142-1/8	20-1/8	20-5/8	13-7/8	5	5	Juneau County	WI	Dennis Dreischmeier	1982	1276
142-1/8	24-6/8	25-3/8	18-1/8	4	4	Lawrence County	OH	Carl G. Coburn	1982	1276
142-1/8	26-0/8	25-0/8	22-1/8	6	6	Medina County	OH	Bruce Hamilton	1983	1276
142-1/8	21-2/8	21-4/8	16-5/8	6	6	Washington County	MD	David M. Kumsher	1985	1276
142-1/8	25-0/8	24-2/8	18-3/8	6	7	Ohio County	IN	Ernest Frady	1985	1276
142-1/8	25-0/8	24-6/8	17-7/8	4	4	Logan County	CO	Kent Sump	1985	1276
142-0/8	22-4/8	23-0/8	17-2/8	6	5	Logan County	IL	Irwin L. Miller	1976	1290
142-0/8	24-1/8	24-1/8	17-6/8	5	6	Winona County	MN	Clayton Bentson	1977	1290
142-0/8	24-0/8	23-7/8	15-5/8	5	6	Bayfield County	WI	James J. Messerschmidt	1979	1290
142-0/8	24-5/8	24-4/8	18-6/8	4	4	Woodford County	IL	Byron L. Davenport	1980	1290
142-0/8	20-7/8	19-5/8	18-2/8	5	5	Shelby County	IL	Richard W. Neumann	1982	1290
142-0/8	23-4/8	21-6/8	19-6/8	5	7	Union County	IL	Randy Cronk	1983	1290
142-0/8	27-0/8	27-0/8	20-0/8	4	4	Ravalli County	MT	Harry Potton	1983	1290
142-0/8	22-2/8	22-5/8	18-5/8	5	7	Will County	IL	Joseph R. Pergram	1983	1290
142-0/8	23-1/8	23-3/8	16-6/8	5	5	Dane County	WI	Joseph A. Radecki	1984	1290
142-0/8	20-6/8	20-6/8	17-0/8	5	5	Shawnee County	KS	Eldon Johnson	1985	1290
141-7/8	24-2/8	24-5/8	23-3/8	4	6	Jackson County	IA	Thomas L. Berkley	1959	1300
141-7/8	23-0/8	22-0/8	20-1/8	5	4	Pottawattamie County	IA	Gary A. Green	1968	1300
141-7/8	21-0/8	19-6/8	15-7/8	5	5	Lincoln County	SD	Kai R. Anderson	1972	1300
141-7/8	23-6/8	22-1/8	17-1/8	5	5	Stoney Plain	ALB	Barry A. Olsen	1979	1300
141-7/8	26-0/8	26-2/8	20-5/8	4	4	Hocking	OH	Paul T. Sater	1979	1300
141-7/8	23-7/8	23-3/8	17-3/8	5	5	Pine County	MN	Jack Pichotta	1980	1300
141-7/8	25-5/8	26-2/8	18-3/8	4	4	Shelby County	OH	Kenneth E. Huffman	1982	1300
141-7/8	26-2/8	26-3/8	21-0/8	5	6	Coshocton County	OH	Mike Stumph	1983	1300
141-7/8	21-2/8	20-6/8	18-3/8	5	5	Dunn County	WI	Bruce Olson	1983	1300
141-7/8	25-1/8	24-7/8	20-5/8	5	5	Kent	ONT	John McGuigan	1984	1300
141-7/8	25-7/8	24-4/8	19-5/8	4	4	Muskingum County	OH	Rick A. Goodin	1984	1300
141-7/8	23-6/8	23-6/8	17-3/8	4	5	Camden County	MO	Steve West	1985	1300
141-7/8	24-7/8	24-4/8	16-1/8	5	5	Anderson County	SC	J. Alan Wilson, Jr.	1985	1300
141-7/8	25-3/8	24-6/8	20-0/8	5	5	Seneca County	NY	Dominic D'Amico	1985	1300
141-6/8	24-3/8	24-2/8	20-0/8	4	4	Morrison County	MN	Rodney W. Olson	1958	1314
141-6/8	23-6/8	23-7/8	17-4/8	5	4	Dodge County	MN	Cy Champa	1969	1314
141-6/8	23-6/8	24-4/8	24-0/8	4	4	Newton County	IN	Denny Raper	1980	1314
141-6/8	26-2/8	25-2/8	22-6/8	4	4	Johnson County	NE	Ronald G. Filip	1981	1314
141-6/8	20-5/8	22-6/8	17-2/8	5	5	Alpena County	MI	Michael E. Kaiser	1981	1314
141-6/8	24-7/8	24-2/8	20-2/8	4	4	Hewitt	MN	Ted Pilgrim	1981	1314
141-6/8	24-4/8	23-2/8	17-2/8	5	6	Pittsburg County	OK	Richard H. Gill	1984	1314
141-6/8	21-4/8	21-4/8	17-2/8	5	7	Hughes County	SD	Kent D. Keenlyne	1984	1314
141-6/8	21-4/8	21-2/8	16-1/8	5	6	Lyon County	MN	Randy S Van Overbeke	1985	1314
141-5/8	24-0/8	24-3/8	21-6/8	6	3	Allegan County	MI	Stan Skorch	1967	1323

WHITETAIL DEER *(Typical Antlers)*

(continued)   Minimum Score 125

Score	Length of Main Beam R	L	Inside Spread	Number of Points R	L	Area	State/ Province	Hunter's Name	Date	Rank
141-5/8	23-3/8	23-5/8	19-5/8	4	5	Crawford County	IL	Jim Earleywine	1978	1323
141-5/8	21-7/8	23-0/8	19-7/8	4	5	Shelby County	IL	Ed Ikemire	1979	1323
141-5/8	24-5/8	24-6/8	17-2/8	5	6	Gallia County	OH	Buck Blankenship	1981	1323
141-5/8	24-7/8	23-7/8	20-1/8	5	4	Roane County	TN	Thomas K. Grause	1981	1323
141-5/8	25-2/8	26-0/8	18-1/8	4	4	Highland County	OH	Douglas Ambroza	1982	1323
141-5/8	23-3/8	22-3/8	19-2/8	5	6	Well County	MT	Bob Jacobsen	1982	1323
141-5/8	25-5/8	26-0/8	18-3/8	5	4	Dane County	WI	Don Magnuson	1983	1323
141-5/8	22-2/8	23-2/8	18-1/8	5	5	Grant County	WI	Randy Dressler	1984	1323
141-5/8	22-0/8	22-1/8	17-1/8	5	5	Yellow Medicine County	MN	Harold Greseth	1985	1323
141-4/8	21-1/8	21-4/8	19-6/8	5	5	Hyde County	SD	Gordon Sampson	1974	1333
141-4/8	22-3/8	22-3/8	17-4/8	5	5	Richland County	OH	Walter A. Bartashus	1976	1333
141-4/8	23-3/8	22-7/8	17-3/8	5	7	Trigg County	KY	Wayne R. Brooks	1978	1333
141-4/8	23-6/8	24-4/8	19-0/8	5	5	Jackson County	IA	Thomas E. Maas	1979	1333
141-4/8	22-2/8	22-1/8	16-0/8	5	4	Stephenson County	IL	John Miller	1983	1333
141-4/8	20-6/8	20-7/8	17-0/8	5	5	Cowley County	KS	George B. Smith	1983	1333
141-4/8	22-2/8	22-2/8	20-0/8	6	5	Pepin County	WI	Brian Berger	1984	1333
141-4/8	25-4/8	21-0/8	21-0/8	10	9	Wyandotte County	KS	Robert A. Bentz	1984	1333
141-4/8	27-4/8	25-3/8	20-4/8	6	5	McNairy County	TN	Arlus Ray Burney	1985	1333
141-3/8	23-3/8	22-4/8	17-1/8	7	6	Harrold	SD	Ross Krull	1969	1342
141-3/8	24-5/8	26-3/8	16-3/8	5	6	Vilas County	WI	Dennis W. Essers	1976	1342
141-3/8	24-6/8	24-5/8	18-2/8	6	10	Seneca County	OH	Bruce R. Stover	1980	1342
141-3/8	24-0/8	23-1/8	19-7/8	5	5	Mitchell County	KS	Charlie Stevens	1981	1342
141-3/8	23-5/8	23-3/8	17-4/8	7	5	Warren County	VA	Ronnie Wines	1981	1342
141-3/8	22-3/8	21-5/8	15-1/8	5	5	Eau Claire County	WI	Terry R. Zich	1982	1342
141-3/8	24-7/8	24-0/8	16-7/8	5	4	Burleigh County	ND	Andrew M. Schneider	1982	1342
141-3/8	24-6/8	24-6/8	19-2/8	5	7	Putnam County	WV	James H. Myers	1983	1342
141-3/8	25-1/8	25-0/8	19-7/8	5	4	Fayette County	IL	Mike Kistler	1983	1342
141-3/8	22-2/8	22-1/8	18-5/8	4	5	Clermont County	OH	Harold A. Thompson, Jr.	1983	1342
141-3/8	27-7/8	26-2/8	18-5/8	7	5	Boone County	IA	Dan A. Dillavou	1984	1342
141-3/8	23-5/8	23-4/8	18-5/8	5	5	Dakota County	MN	Brad Bieber	1984	1342
141-3/8	21-2/8	23-0/8	19-5/8	6	9	Louisa County	IA	Jay Schmelzer	1985	1342
141-3/8	23-5/8	23-2/8	15-2/8	6	5	Kay County	OK	Guy LeMonnier	1985	1342
141-3/8	25-5/8	25-3/8	19-5/8	4	5	Jackson County	MN	Merlin Jurgens	1985	1342
141-3/8	21-7/8	23-0/8	16-2/8	5	7	Jackson County	IA	David Schrody	1985	1342
141-3/8	24-5/8	22-7/8	17-5/8	5	5	Howard Township	ONT	Wm. K. Jamieson	1985	1342
141-2/8	24-4/8	23-1/8	16-6/8	5	5	Lee County	IA	Terry E. Woodworth	1973	1359
141-2/8	22-5/8	23-1/8	22-2/8	4	5	Bon Homme County	SD	Jeff Miedema	1978	1359
141-2/8	25-7/8	25-7/8	20-4/8	5	4	Douglas County	KS	Russell Stevens	1978	1359
141-2/8	23-3/8	23-2/8	17-2/8	5	5	Cottonwood County	MN	Robert K. Vincent	1978	1359
141-2/8	24-2/8	23-4/8	20-2/8	4	5	DeKalb County	IL	Bob Broos	1980	1359
141-2/8	21-6/8	20-2/8	16-0/8	7	6	Grant County	WI	Thomas A. Franseen	1982	1359
141-2/8	22-4/8	22-4/8	20-3/8	5	6	Allamakee County	IA	Glen A. Jones	1983	1359
141-2/8	24-4/8	25-7/8	20-6/8	6	5	Powell County	MT	Steve Pocha	1984	1359
141-2/8	21-6/8	20-5/8	19-2/8	6	5	Green County	WI	Randall A. Schupbach	1984	1359
141-2/8	26-1/8	26-1/8	18-4/8	5	4	Lawrence County	OH	Don Nickles	1985	1359
141-2/8	24-5/8	24-3/8	20-2/8	5	6	Pike County	OH	Harry R. Fite	1985	1359
141-2/8	23-3/8	23-3/8	16-2/8	4	4	Kandiyohi County	MN	Jeffrey L. Danielson	1986	1359
141-1/8	26-2/8	27-6/8	19-0/8	4	5	Dodge County	NE	Gary Trost	1961	1371
141-1/8	22-0/8	24-2/8	18-1/8	4	6	Shelby County	IL	Ron Ragan	1979	1371
141-1/8	21-5/8	22-2/8	17-5/8	5	6	Talbot County	MD	Gary W. Sommers	1979	1371
141-1/8	25-0/8	25-0/8	17-2/8	6	6	Jefferson County	OH	William J. Fedor	1981	1371
141-1/8	24-2/8	24-6/8	17-1/8	5	4	Fosters	AL	Bobby Hemphill	1981	1371
141-1/8	24-0/8	23-1/8	23-3/8	5	5	McAlester Ads	OK	Dave Jilge	1981	1371
141-1/8	22-1/8	22-7/8	19-0/8	6	5	Des Moines County	IA	David R. Bessine	1982	1371
141-1/8	23-7/8	22-1/8	17-7/8	5	5	Stanley County	SD	Jim P. Hallock	1983	1371
141-1/8	22-5/8	21-7/8	15-4/8	8	7	Boone County	MO	Craig S Gemming	1984	1371
141-1/8	27-1/8	26-6/8	18-0/8	4	5	Boone County	MO	Dale Robb	1984	1371
141-1/8	22-4/8	22-2/8	21-0/8	6	6	Wabaunsee County	KS	Charles Bisnette	1985	1371
141-0/8	22-2/8	21-7/8	16-0/8	4	5	Ree Heights	SD	Robert Werdel	1963	1382
141-0/8	21-5/8	22-0/8	16-0/8	4	5	Nobles County	MN	Rod McNab	1974	1382
141-0/8	24-2/8	24-4/8	18-0/8	5	4	Georgetown	IL	Larry Mollet	1974	1382
141-0/8	24-2/8	24-1/8	18-3/8	4	5	Ohio County	IN	Mike Meyer	1979	1382
141-0/8	22-4/8	22-4/8	16-2/8	5	5	Marion County	IA	Steven F. Donnelly, Jr.	1982	1382

WHITETAIL DEER *(Typical Antlers)*

Minimum Score 125

Score	Length of Main Beam R	L	Inside Spread	Number of Points R	L	Area	State/ Province	Hunter's Name	Date	Rank
141-0/8	22-5/8	23-1/8	15-4/8	6	5	Marion County	WV	Samuel E. Clingan	1983	1382
141-0/8	21-2/8	22-0/8	17-1/8	6	5	Floyd County	IA	Dennis Grauerholz	1983	1382
141-0/8	24-3/8	23-5/8	18-1/8	5	4	Pine County	MN	Dave Hartl	1984	1382
141-0/8	23-4/8	23-3/8	21-2/8	5	5	Flathead County	MT	Wes Plummer	1984	1382
141-0/8	23-4/8	23-4/8	19-4/8	5	6	Douglas County	KS	Russell Stevens	1984	1382
141-0/8	24-5/8	23-7/8	17-4/8	5	4	Chatham County	NC	James T. Noonan III	1984	1382
141-0/8	22-3/8	21-5/8	18-6/8	4	4	Cass County	NE	Roger E. Buck	1985	1382
141-0/8	25-1/8	25-1/8	20-6/8	4	4	Prince George County	MD	Robert O. Turner II	1985	1382
140-7/8	21-7/8	21-1/8	16-7/8	5	6	Pierre	SD	Gerald Snyder	1962	1395
140-7/8	24-5/8	24-5/8	17-1/8	4	4	Ripley County	IN	Melvin M. Weddell	1968	1395
140-7/8	24-7/8	24-6/8	17-5/8	5	5	Jackson	OH	Bob McGuire	1975	1395
140-7/8	21-1/8	21-4/8	16-2/8	5	7	Stuart	IA	Dennis Rote	1977	1395
140-7/8	21-7/8	21-6/8	14-3/8	5	6	Dunn County	WI	Douglas G. Clements	1981	1395
140-7/8	22-0/8	21-7/8	19-7/8	6	5	St. Louis County	MO	Jack Repp	1982	1395
140-7/8	21-7/8	23-1/8	17-3/8	4	4	Scott County	KS	Lynn Freese	1983	1395
140-7/8	20-2/8	21-5/8	16-1/8	5	5	Saunders County	NE	David L Prochaska	1984	1395
140-7/8	22-7/8	23-2/8	16-2/8	5	5	Sauk County	WI	Brad J. Luce	1984	1395
140-7/8	22-3/8	22-3/8	16-7/8	5	5	Monroe County	WI	John W. Zahrte	1984	1395
140-7/8	21-1/8	19-7/8	16-3/8	6	6	Claiborne County	MS	John Robert Moon	1985	1395
140-6/8	24-2/8	24-6/8	19-5/8	5	6	Blue Earth County	MN	Earl D. Kopischke	1967	1406
140-6/8	24-0/8	23-3/8	20-0/8	4	4	Cottonwood County	MN	Kerry Ella	1973	1406
140-6/8	22-6/8	23-3/8	18-0/8	5	5	Morrison County	MN	Galen Miller	1973	1406
140-6/8	21-4/8	22-1/8	18-0/8	7	5	Weld County	CO	Roger Bechler	1974	1406
140-6/8	23-6/8	24-2/8	19-6/8	6	6	Grant County	MN	Ronald W. Johnson	1974	1406
140-6/8	24-2/8	24-6/8	16-4/8	5	5	Brant Twp.	ONT	Kent Callen	1979	1406
140-6/8	21-5/8	21-1/8	18-4/8	5	5	Kossuth County	IA	Larry M. Johnson	1979	1406
140-6/8	21-5/8	22-2/8	18-2/8	6	6	Redwood County	MN	Todd Gilb	1981	1406
140-6/8	20-0/8	19-2/8	16-7/8	6	9	Gregory County	SD	Leroy Lamp	1983	1406
140-6/8	23-0/8	24-2/8	18-0/8	6	7	Putnam County	IN	E. Duyane Tucker	1984	1406
140-6/8	23-0/8	23-5/8	18-0/8	4	4	Vinton County	OH	Randy Boggs	1984	1406
140-6/8	23-6/8	24-1/8	18-3/8	5	6	Hancock County	WV	Daniel Salatino	1985	1406
140-6/8	21-1/8	21-1/8	17-2/8	5	5	Hamlin County	SD	Ronald Schoffelman	1985	1406
140-6/8	26-0/8	25-1/8	20-6/8	5	4	Lake County	IL	Carl H. Spaeth	1985	1406
140-5/8	20-7/8	21-0/8	14-2/8	5	5	Horicon	WI	Donald D. Voss	1960	1420
140-5/8	22-7/8	23-1/8	17-4/8	6	5	Sidney	IA	Scott Morris	1972	1420
140-5/8	25-0/8	26-0/8	19-4/8	6	5	Edgar County	IL	Richard Griffin	1973	1420
140-5/8	25-5/8	25-0/8	19-2/8	5	5	Lewis County	WV	David A. Hill	1978	1420
140-5/8	23-5/8	23-1/8	15-6/8	7	6	Morrison County	MN	Joan Morris	1979	1420
140-5/8	23-4/8	23-3/8	19-4/8	6	6	Sargent County	ND	Richard Williams	1980	1420
140-5/8	23-6/8	23-6/8	20-1/8	4	4	Hardin County	IA	Bill Stonebraker	1981	1420
140-5/8	22-4/8	22-6/8	17-1/8	6	6	Kandiyohi County	MN	Mike Hannemann	1982	1420
140-5/8	22-0/8	23-7/8	20-4/8	5	4	Christian County	IL	Richard E. Davis	1983	1420
140-5/8	23-6/8	25-0/8	13-5/8	5	5	Surry County	VA	David W. Huffman	1983	1420
140-5/8	21-2/8	21-6/8	17-5/8	5	5	Jefferson County	IA	Victor Stickels	1983	1420
140-4/8	24-5/8	22-7/8	18-2/8	7	6	Casey	IA	Dale Kromrie	1964	1431
140-4/8	21-1/8	21-1/8	15-5/8	5	5	Dickinson County	MI	Bernard Schmidt	1964	1431
140-4/8	22-4/8	22-4/8	17-2/8	6	6	Pendleton County	KY	Gerald Bezold	1971	1431
140-4/8	24-2/8	24-1/8	20-2/8	5	5	Fairfax County	VA	Daniel C. Holtz	1971	1431
140-4/8	25-4/8	24-7/8	17-0/8	6	5	Berks County	PA	John R. Intelisano	1975	1431
140-4/8	20-0/8	20-0/8	16-2/8	5	5	Osage County	KS	Mike Vandevord	1977	1431
140-4/8	23-3/8	23-7/8	20-2/8	5	5	Claytoh County	IA	Dave White	1977	1431
140-4/8	26-1/8	24-5/8	17-5/8	7	5	Calhoun County	MI	Roger L. Sims	1979	1431
140-4/8	22-2/8	22-1/8	18-4/8	5	5	Bradley County	AR	Barnard Smith	1979	1431
140-4/8	25-0/8	23-5/8	19-0/8	5	4	Marquette County	WI	Ed Shields	1980	1431
140-4/8	23-6/8	24-3/8	18-6/8	5	7	Marion County	KS	Max Williams	1980	1431
140-4/8	21-7/8	22-0/8	17-7/8	6	5	Berkeley County	SC	Hugh Gaskins	1981	1431
140-4/8	21-6/8	22-0/8	16-6/8	5	5	Hemstead County	AR	Dan Moore	1982	1431
140-4/8	24-1/8	23-4/8	17-6/8	6	6	Oconto County	WI	Richard L. Roth	1982	1431
140-4/8	24-3/8	24-6/8	19-0/8	5	4	Logan County	IL	William Edwards	1983	1431
140-4/8	22-2/8	22-3/8	17-4/8	5	5	Jackson County	KY	David A. Cornett	1984	1431
140-4/8	24-2/8	24-0/8	16-6/8	4	4	Waukesha County	WI	Paul B. Kressin	1984	1431
140-4/8	22-3/8	21-5/8	17-6/8	5	5	Harford County	MD	Hank Voigt	1984	1431
140-3/8	23-5/8	23-6/8	16-4/8	6	7	Guthrie County	IA	Leland Purviance	1964	1449

WHITETAIL DEER *(Typical Antlers)*

(continued)   Minimum Score 125

Score	Length of Main Beam R	Length of Main Beam L	Inside Spread	Number of Points R	Number of Points L	Area	State/Province	Hunter's Name	Date	Rank
140-3/8	27-0/8	26-1/8	19-5/8	1	1	Pulaski County	VA	Harold M. Peters	1965	1449
140-3/8	22-6/8	23-5/8	19-0/8	5	4	Ripley	MN	Gary D. Wells	1972	1449
140-3/8	21-3/8	21-4/8	15-1/8	5	5	Essex County	NY	Donald Frazier	1979	1449
140-3/8	23-6/8	23-0/8	20-3/8	5	4	Aitkin County	MN	Lloyd Boelter	1981	1449
140-3/8	27-0/8	27-0/8	21-2/8	5	5	Hardin County	OH	Devere Sams	1984	1449
140-3/8	24-0/8	24-0/8	19-2/8	5	4	Union County	IL	Steve Wilhite	1984	1449
140-3/8	21-6/8	22-1/8	17-6/8	5	5	Chester County	PA	Jess A. Hassinger	1986	1449
140-2/8	23-7/8	23-1/8	18-4/8	4	4	Redwood County	MN	Irvin Plotz	1967	1457
140-2/8	20-4/8	20-7/8	19-4/8	5	5	Ripley	MN	Gary Sutherland	1973	1457
140-2/8	21-2/8	20-4/8	18-0/8	5	5	Walworth County	WI	Michael Stang	1975	1457
140-2/8	22-2/8	21-6/8	12-4/8	5	5	Platte County	MO	Edward D. Johnson	1977	1457
140-2/8	24-5/8	24-2/8	21-4/8	4	4	Buffalo County	WI	Brent Bauer	1978	1457
140-2/8	23-1/8	23-1/8	18-2/8	5	4	Cochrane	ALB	Warren McInenly	1980	1457
140-2/8	23-5/8	23-2/8	17-6/8	6	5	Dunn County	WI	Terry W. Stallman	1981	1457
140-2/8	22-6/8	23-7/8	17-2/8	4	5	Tazewell County	IL	Jim Plemmons	1982	1457
140-2/8	21-2/8	20-6/8	16-2/8	7	8	Jackson County	WI	Gary L. Barneson	1985	1457
140-2/8	21-7/8	22-5/8	16-6/8	5	4	Morrison County	MN	Jeffrey J. Moris	1985	1457
140-2/8	23-1/8	22-3/8	15-6/8	4	4	Saline County	KS	Barry Miller	1985	1457
140-2/8	26-3/8	27-2/8	21-2/8	4	3	Highland County	OH	Floyd Wagers, Jr.	1985	1457
140-2/8	23-7/8	27-1/8	15-4/8	6	5	Butler County	KS	Mark Scott	1985	1457
140-1/8	23-5/8	22-1/8	16-5/8	6	7	Ripley	MN	Bernie Nieters	1971	1470
140-1/8	24-5/8	24-2/8	18-6/8	5	5	Freeborn County	MN	Kent Dugstad	1973	1470
140-1/8	20-5/8	21-3/8	16-7/8	5	5	Jennings County	IN	Fred Hodson	1973	1470
140-1/8	22-4/8	23-2/8	17-1/8	6	5	Omaha	NE	Carl Martin	1973	1470
140-1/8	22-1/8	21-2/8	16-1/8	5	4	Stratten	NE	Roger Stewart	1976	1470
140-1/8	23-4/8	23-6/8	18-3/8	4	4	Coweta County	GA	Doug Miller	1979	1470
140-1/8	24-4/8	24-4/8	19-1/8	6	5	Champaign County	OH	Dave Anders	1980	1470
140-1/8	25-2/8	24-2/8	19-0/8	6	5	McPherson	KS	Daniel R. Koehn	1981	1470
140-1/8	22-7/8	23-1/8	20-1/8	5	5	Hillsdale County	MI	William C. Mittlestat	1982	1470
140-1/8	22-0/8	21-7/8	16-1/8	6	6	Nez Perce County	ID	Mark Deyo	1982	1470
140-1/8	22-0/8	21-6/8	17-1/8	6	7	Barron County	WI	Dave Peterson	1983	1470
140-1/8	23-1/8	22-1/8	15-3/8	4	4	Dane County	WI	Scott J. Maloney	1985	1470
140-1/8	23-7/8	24-0/8	15-1/8	7	6	Henry County	VA	Keith M. Braddock	1986	1470
140-0/8	25-3/8	24-7/8	20-0/8	4	4	Houghton County	MI	Dr. V. R. Graber	1957	1483
140-0/8	27-7/8	27-6/8	19-0/8	6	5	Ford County	KS	Melvin Miller	1973	1483
140-0/8	23-1/8	22-0/8	19-2/8	6	6	Winona County	MN	Robert Fratzke	1974	1483
140-0/8	22-0/8	22-1/8	15-5/8	8	6	Ottawa County	KS	Edward L. Wright	1974	1483
140-0/8	23-3/8	22-3/8	15-0/8	5	5	Jackson County	MO	Marvin Thomey	1977	1483
140-0/8	22-6/8	22-3/8	17-4/8	5	5	Macoupin County	IL	Terry Jenkins	1979	1483
140-0/8	22-1/8	21-7/8	16-0/8	5	5	Brown County	SD	Todd T. Tunby	1980	1483
140-0/8	22-3/8	22-7/8	16-4/8	5	5	Clay County	MN	Joe Lahlum	1981	1483
140-0/8	20-6/8	21-2/8	16-2/8	5	5	Bismarck	ND	Doran D. Alfstad	1982	1483
140-0/8	23-3/8	21-7/8	19-2/8	5	5	Lucas County	IA	Bill Brown	1983	1483
140-0/8	22-4/8	22-4/8	17-0/8	4	4	Washington County	KS	Stanley Brustowicz	1983	1483
140-0/8	21-3/8	21-7/8	14-4/8	5	5	Hill County	MT	Steve Gorr	1984	1483
140-0/8	25-3/8	26-2/8	20-6/8	5	5	Adams County	OH	Harry Tudor, Jr.	1984	1483
140-0/8	21-5/8	21-7/8	16-4/8	5	5	Lake County	IL	Steve M. Andrews	1985	1483
140-0/8	24-6/8	25-2/8	17-2/8	5	4	Pratt County	KS	Shawn M. James	1985	1483
140-0/8	23-6/8	23-1/8	20-0/8	5	7	Brown County	MN	Hap Raabe	1986	1483
140-0/8	20-2/8	21-6/8	14-6/8	5	5	Waupaca County	WI	Brian D. Korb	1986	1483
139-7/8	22-6/8	23-3/8	16-3/8	5	5	Crane Naval Depot	IN	Warren Trinkle	1968	1500
139-7/8	24-2/8	23-1/8	18-2/8	6	7	Spring Port	MI	Alfred A. Brenner	1973	1500
139-7/8	23-7/8	23-6/8	19-4/8	7	4	Goodhue County	MN	Dwight Dankers	1975	1500
139-7/8	24-3/8	23-0/8	19-3/8	5	6	Woodford County	IL	Byron L. Davenport	1977	1500
139-7/8	22-3/8	22-7/8	16-2/8	6	6	Franklin Grove	IL	Charles L. Osborne	1977	1500
139-7/8	23-6/8	22-0/8	14-0/8	5	6	Lyon County	KY	Denny Eubanks	1978	1500
139-7/8	24-6/8	22-1/8	21-5/8	4	4	Perry County	IL	Dennis Vancil	1981	1500
139-7/8	21-4/8	21-1/8	17-5/8	5	5	Roberts County	SD	Brian Sand	1983	1500
139-7/8	23-1/8	23-6/8	18-5/8	4	4	Pike County	IL	Frank Dolbeare	1984	1500
139-7/8	22-7/8	23-3/8	17-5/8	5	5	Walworth County	WI	James Kurth	1986	1500
139-6/8	22-5/8	23-2/8	20-6/8	5	5	Great Bend	KS	Charles Batman	1968	1510
139-6/8	23-4/8	23-0/8	20-4/8	5	5	Morgan	OH	Marion Reed	1978	1510
139-6/8	23-1/8	23-0/8	16-3/8	5	7	Ozaukee County	WI	Steven J. Baumann	1980	1510

WHITETAIL DEER *(Typical Antlers)*

Minimum Score 125   (continued)

Score	Length of Main Beam R	L	Inside Spread	Number of Points R	L	Area	State/ Province	Hunter's Name	Date	Rank
139-6/8	21-6/8	20-6/8	16-4/8	5	5	Arkadelphia	AR	David McLemore	1980	1510
139-6/8	28-0/8	27-4/8	21-3/8	3	5	Buffalo County	WI	Dean Sankey	1981	1510
139-6/8	21-4/8	20-4/8	15-2/8	5	5	Clearwater River	ID	Jim Sherman	1981	1510
139-6/8	22-7/8	22-6/8	16-6/8	8	6	Pierce County	WI	Lee Langer	1982	1510
139-6/8	24-1/8	22-4/8	16-6/8	5	5	Union County	IL	Leon Lane	1983	1510
139-6/8	25-3/8	25-6/8	22-5/8	5	4	Reno County	KS	Wayne Finch	1983	1510
139-6/8	22-5/8	22-3/8	19-0/8	4	4	Richland County	IL	Billy Joe Hicks	1983	1510
139-6/8	23-2/8	23-5/8	19-0/8	4	4	Wabasha County	MN	Myles Keller	1983	1510
139-6/8	22-6/8	22-4/8	16-1/8	6	6	Columbia County	WI	Steve Deminsky	1985	1510
139-6/8	20-0/8	20-5/8	18-2/8	5	5	Campbell County	TN	Harold D. Tackett	1985	1510
139-5/8	22-0/8	22-3/8	18-6/8	6	6	Edinburg	IN	Howard VanSweringer	1961	1523
139-5/8	24-4/8	24-6/8	19-1/8	5	4	Milburn	NE	Paul Ekberg	1974	1523
139-5/8	22-2/8	23-3/8	18-5/8	5	5	Miles City	MT	Dale Drilling	1980	1523
139-5/8	26-7/8	25-1/8	21-7/8	5	6	Westchester County	NY	Michael Iuzzolino	1980	1523
139-5/8	23-2/8	22-3/8	16-5/8	5	5	Lasalle County	IL	Jack Tabor	1983	1523
139-5/8	21-5/8	23-3/8	17-1/8	5	5	Dawson County	MT	Martin P. Weiske	1985	1523
139-4/8	23-5/8	23-0/8	20-0/8	5	4	Hart County	KY	Robert L. Galloway	1967	1529
139-4/8	20-1/8	19-3/8	17-4/8	5	5	Clinton County	MI	Richard H. Wilt	1968	1529
139-4/8	22-4/8	23-4/8	19-0/8	5	5	Fillmore County	MN	Orvis J. Dahl	1971	1529
139-4/8	25-5/8	27-1/8	20-2/8	4	5	Jacksboro	TX	Ray Brewster	1975	1529
139-4/8	22-0/8	21-5/8	16-4/8	6	7	Dane County	WI	Mike Schoenbeck	1981	1529
139-4/8	21-6/8	22-0/8	17-4/8	5	5	Idaho County	ID	Dwight Schuh	1981	1529
139-4/8	23-5/8	23-2/8	20-3/8	6	6	Rock County	WI	Dennis L. Meyer	1981	1529
139-4/8	23-4/8	22-0/8	18-0/8	5	5	Licking County	OH	Richard E Pipes	1983	1529
139-4/8	21-0/8	21-0/8	16-6/8	4	4	Marion County	IA	Tim Pottorff	1985	1529
139-3/8	24-0/8	27-0/8	18-2/8	5	5	Fulton County	IL	Raymond Rumler	1968	1538
139-3/8	21-1/8	21-6/8	17-1/8	5	5	Outagamie County	WI	Thomas L. Haber	1975	1538
139-3/8	21-1/8	21-1/8	16-3/8	6	6	Kalamazoo County	MI	Walter Myers	1977	1538
139-3/8	24-7/8	22-5/8	16-3/8	5	6	Cumberland County	NJ	Winfield Cassaboon	1978	1538
139-3/8	23-0/8	22-2/8	17-5/8	5	4	Des Moines County	IA	Ronald L. Cover	1978	1538
139-3/8	23-0/8	21-2/8	14-7/8	5	5	Chatham County	NC	James Noonan III	1981	1538
139-3/8	22-3/8	21-6/8	16-1/8	6	6	Jackson County	TN	Michael Mitchell	1983	1538
139-3/8	20-1/8	20-3/8	15-5/8	6	6	Dodge County	WI	Lester C. Neuman	1985	1538
139-3/8	23-0/8	21-7/8	17-7/8	5	6	Jefferson County	KS	Robert Ulmer	1985	1538
139-3/8	24-1/8	23-4/8	17-7/8	5	5	Clayton County	IA	Ralph Livingston	1985	1538
139-3/8	21-0/8	21-0/8	15-3/8	5	5	Morrison County	MN	Timothy Droher	1986	1538
139-2/8	21-6/8	22-6/8	16-4/8	6	6	Findlay	IL	David McSchooler	1968	1549
139-2/8	20-2/8	20-7/8	15-2/8	5	5	Wing	ND	Burnell F. Paul	1971	1549
139-2/8	22-1/8	23-2/8	17-2/8	5	5	Buffalo County	WI	Leonard Anglewitz	1972	1549
139-2/8	24-2/8	23-4/8	17-6/8	4	4	McPherson County	KS	Glenn Waggoner	1977	1549
139-2/8	23-1/8	23-1/8	18-2/8	4	4	Bayfield County	WI	Thomas E. Smith	1979	1549
139-2/8	22-3/8	23-6/8	15-6/8	4	5	O'Brien County	IA	Ted Bruning	1980	1549
139-2/8	22-3/8	22-3/8	22-2/8	4	5	Whiteside County	IL	B. J. Higley	1981	1549
139-2/8	24-6/8	23-7/8	17-2/8	5	6	Greenwood County	KS	Ed Tarver	1981	1549
139-2/8	22-7/8	24-3/8	18-4/8	4	4	Richland County	WI	Dennis Kaderavek	1985	1549
139-2/8	21-6/8	22-1/8	18-0/8	6	6	St. Charles County	MO	John Yacup	1985	1549
139-1/8	24-0/8	24-0/8	20-7/8	4	4	Pottawattamie County	IA	James R. Kirlin	1968	1559
139-1/8	21-0/8	20-5/8	17-7/8	6	5	Calumet County	WI	Leo A. Broeckel	1969	1559
139-1/8	20-3/8	21-7/8	18-1/8	5	6	Kalamazoo County	MI	Dr. Ronald L. Mahan	1975	1559
139-1/8	23-2/8	22-4/8	19-7/8	5	5	Johnson County	IL	Billy J. Hillebrand	1977	1559
139-1/8	23-1/8	20-0/8	16-3/8	5	5	Switzerland County	IN	James T. Brent	1979	1559
139-1/8	22-2/8	22-4/8	20-1/8	5	5	Milton	ONT	Ernest Groh	1979	1559
139-1/8	23-0/8	22-6/8	18-2/8	5	5	Monte County	PA	Joseph Maddock	1980	1559
139-1/8	22-4/8	20-1/8	17-3/8	7	5	Green County	WI	Ora Howard	1980	1559
139-1/8	21-4/8	21-3/8	16-4/8	6	5	Finney County	KS	Rodney Stapleton	1980	1559
139-1/8	19-4/8	20-1/8	14-2/8	6	5	Shelby County	MO	Jamie McWilliams	1981	1559
139-1/8	23-6/8	23-3/8	19-1/8	5	5	Boone County	IN	James L. Schenck	1981	1559
139-1/8	22-4/8	23-2/8	18-7/8	5	5	Franklin County	MO	Tom Mitchell	1982	1559
139-1/8	25-1/8	25-4/8	17-7/8	5	5	Tazewell County	IL	Scott A. Knight	1983	1559
139-1/8	22-4/8	22-2/8	19-3/8	5	5	Ogle County	IL	Earl B. Thomas, Jr.	1984	1559
139-1/8	22-4/8	22-2/8	16-4/8	6	5	Montgomery County	MD	Steve Hoffman	1985	1559
139-1/8	22-1/8	23-5/8	18-7/8	4	4	Brown County	KS	Pat Bauman	1985	1559
139-1/8	21-5/8	22-5/8	16-7/8	6	4	Preble County	OH	Jerrol L. Meredith	1985	1559

WHITETAIL DEER *(Typical Antlers)*

(continued)   Minimum Score 125

Score	Length of Main Beam R	L	Inside Spread	Number of Points R	L	Area	State/ Province	Hunter's Name	Date	Rank
139-1/8	19-5/8	23-6/8	17-1/8	5	5	Dakota County	NE	Michael W. McKenna	1986	1559
139-1/8	20-7/8	20-5/8	14-1/8	5	5	Goodhue County	MN	Deick Bridley	1986	1559
139-0/8	23-2/8	23-5/8	18-5/8	5	4	Indianola	IA	Grant A. Poindexter	1964	1578
139-0/8	21-6/8	20-4/8	19-0/8	7	5	Butler County	KS	John Holzrechtes	1967	1578
139-0/8	20-4/8	20-1/8	16-0/8	5	5	Fillmore County	MN	Richard Fryar	1972	1578
139-0/8	24-2/8	24-5/8	15-7/8	7	5	Lewis County	WV	James Cogar	1976	1578
139-0/8	21-3/8	21-0/8	14-2/8	5	5	Saco	MT	Bill Beede	1980	1578
139-0/8	22-3/8	23-1/8	18-6/8	5	5	West Morris	IL	Ronald A. Thompson	1980	1578
139-0/8	25-4/8	25-5/8	19-4/8	5	5	Shelby County	OH	Richard A. Havenar	1981	1578
139-0/8	18-7/8	23-2/8	17-4/8	6	5	Shoals	IN	Jan J. Armour	1981	1578
139-0/8	22-1/8	20-7/8	16-2/8	8	8	Moultrie County	IL	Jim Dallefeld	1981	1578
139-0/8	22-2/8	22-1/8	15-2/8	6	5	Linn County	MO	Robert L. "Bob" Schultz	1981	1578
139-0/8	23-0/8	22-0/8	16-2/8	5	5	Cass County	MI	Allen Welburn	1981	1578
139-0/8	24-2/8	25-1/8	18-2/8	5	6	Cozad County	NE	Randy Wilson	1982	1578
139-0/8	25-1/8	25-7/8	21-1/8	4	5	Morrison County	MN	Pat Mckenzie	1982	1578
139-0/8	20-4/8	23-4/8	18-0/8	5	5	Lake County	IL	Gary S. Rogers	1982	1578
139-0/8	23-4/8	22-5/8	22-4/8	6	4	Clark County	IN	Noble E. McCutcheon	1985	1578
139-0/8	23-2/8	22-4/8	16-2/8	4	4	Morrison County	MN	Doug Schmode	1985	1578
139-0/8	21-4/8	22-1/8	17-6/8	4	4	Racine County	WI	Mark Nelsen	1985	1578
139-0/8	22-7/8	23-1/8	17-0/8	5	6	Monroe County	NY	David Smith	1985	1578
139-0/8	22-4/8	24-0/8	17-2/8	5	5	Adams County	IN	Rick A. Goldner	1985	1578
139-0/8	25-4/8	25-4/8	17-6/8	4	4	Baltimore County	MD	Danny Stivers	1985	1578
139-0/8	21-2/8	23-2/8	16-4/8	5	4	Morgan County	OH	Lynn A. Weingart	1985	1578
138-7/8	22-5/8	21-4/8	16-1/8	5	6	Fairbanks	IN	Mike Burch	1976	1599
138-7/8	24-4/8	23-0/8	18-6/8	6	7	Cedar County	IA	Tom Foley	1978	1599
138-7/8	22-5/8	24-1/8	19-3/8	4	6	Williams County	OH	Gary Bowles	1978	1599
138-7/8	24-1/8	26-1/8	17-3/8	5	4	Delaware County	IA	Tom Wilhelm	1978	1599
138-7/8	23-0/8	23-0/8	15-1/8	5	4	Hamilton County	OH	Donald R. Buehler	1980	1599
138-7/8	27-6/8	25-4/8	21-2/8	6	4	Cowley County	KS	Maloy Rollins	1981	1599
138-7/8	23-5/8	24-1/8	17-1/8	5	4	Clark County	SD	Jerry Comes	1982	1599
138-7/8	23-1/8	26-3/8	19-1/8	6	4	Crawford County	MO	Bill Kaltenbach	1985	1599
138-7/8	21-5/8	19-2/8	18-1/8	5	5	Jackson County	KS	Jimmy Braden	1985	1599
138-6/8	25-0/8	23-7/8	20-4/8	4	4	Phillips County	AR	Everett Foley	1968	1608
138-6/8	22-0/8	20-7/8	20-3/8	6	5	Leavenworth County	KS	Michael Pearce	1977	1608
138-6/8	21-5/8	21-5/8	15-2/8	5	5	Putnam County	GA	Tim S. Doxsey	1978	1608
138-6/8	23-0/8	22-5/8	18-0/8	5	5	Des Moines County	IA	Dennis R. Morgan	1978	1608
138-6/8	23-5/8	23-4/8	18-6/8	4	4	St. Joseph County	MI	Jack R. Menges	1979	1608
138-6/8	24-3/8	24-1/8	17-6/8	6	4	Latah County	ID	Dolan McLean	1980	1608
138-6/8	23-4/8	23-4/8	18-4/8	5	4	Chase County	KS	Jerry D. Keller	1982	1608
138-6/8	25-1/8	24-2/8	18-5/8	5	3	Calgary	ALB	Keith Riddell	1983	1608
138-6/8	22-3/8	23-3/8	18-2/8	5	5	Jefferson County	MT	Jeff Nathan	1986	1608
138-5/8	23-1/8	21-3/8	16-3/8	5	5	Washington County	KS	Stan Brustowicz	1923	1617
138-5/8	24-6/8	23-3/8	17-3/8	5	5	Vilas County	WI	B. C. Roemer	1963	1617
138-5/8	21-0/8	21-3/8	16-7/8	5	5	Martin County	IN	Tom Vieke	1967	1617
138-5/8	24-0/8	24-3/8	17-3/8	4	6	Logan County	IL	Lee Miller	1971	1617
138-5/8	23-0/8	23-4/8	16-2/8	4	5	Hennepin County	MN	Thomas F. Rose	1973	1617
138-5/8	24-0/8	24-0/8	17-7/8	4	4	Chippewa County	WI	Patrick Kohls	1980	1617
138-5/8	25-7/8	24-3/8	19-5/8	4	4	Auglaize County	OH	Bob Moser	1980	1617
138-5/8	23-2/8	23-5/8	16-5/8	5	5	Colquitt County	GA	David A. Carmichael	1981	1617
138-5/8	22-3/8	21-7/8	20-6/8	4	5	Greenwood County	KS	Gary Hughes	1985	1617
138-4/8	24-4/8	25-4/8	18-1/8	5	7	Emmet County	IA	Dr. Jerald T. Waite	1966	1626
138-4/8	21-4/8	21-3/8	18-4/8	5	6	Mackinac County	ME	Terry Konle	1977	1626
138-4/8	20-4/8	20-0/8	19-0/8	5	6	Milford Twp.	WI	Edwin C. Wollin	1978	1626
138-4/8	24-4/8	25-2/8	18-6/8	6	4	Pulaski County	KY	Eddie Howard	1979	1626
138-4/8	24-0/8	23-7/8	21-0/8	4	4	Reno County	KS	Carl L. Gaston	1981	1626
138-4/8	24-1/8	24-0/8	21-6/8	10	6	Lake County	IN	Horace Weaver	1981	1626
138-4/8	24-4/8	23-4/8	19-0/8	5	5	Darke County	OH	Jim H. Duvall	1982	1626
138-4/8	22-2/8	23-0/8	16-4/8	6	6	Hennepin County	MN	Raymen Peterson	1982	1626
138-4/8	22-7/8	23-7/8	21-6/8	5	4	Jones County	IA	Hugh Shaw	1984	1626
138-4/8	21-2/8	21-7/8	15-0/8	5	5	Des Moines County	IA	Brad Entsminger	1984	1626
138-4/8	27-0/8	26-1/8	18-0/8	4	4	Anson County	NC	John Harris	1985	1626
138-4/8	22-7/8	23-5/8	18-1/8	5	7	Greene County	IN	John W. Burks	1985	1626
138-3/8	20-1/8	20-2/8	18-3/8	6	6	Marshall County	SD	Robert Peterson	1962	1638

WHITETAIL DEER *(Typical Antlers)*

Minimum Score 125

(continued)

Score	Length of Main Beam R	L	Inside Spread	Number of Points R	L	Area	State/Province	Hunter's Name	Date	Rank
138-3/8	22-4/8	20-3/8	16-7/8	6	5	Long Island	IL	David DeMoss	1967	1638
138-3/8	22-0/8	21-3/8	16-5/8	5	5	Chase County	KS	Larry Krom	1971	1638
138-3/8	22-1/8	22-7/8	16-7/8	4	4	O'Brien County	IA	Chuck Pemble	1973	1638
138-3/8	20-4/8	21-4/8	17-6/8	5	6	Ferry County	WA	Robert Lantiegne	1980	1638
138-3/8	21-4/8	21-5/8	19-1/8	7	5	Soreven County	GA	John Frankhouser	1982	1638
138-3/8	22-3/8	22-2/8	17-7/8	4	4	Republic County	KS	Carroll W. Couture	1982	1638
138-3/8	22-4/8	22-1/8	16-5/8	6	5	Wilcox County	GA	George L. Haynie	1983	1638
138-3/8	22-4/8	21-5/8	19-5/8	6	5	St. Clair County	MO	LaVern Rucker	1983	1638
138-3/8	25-2/8	25-5/8	16-2/8	5	5	Vernon County	WI	Stan Getter	1984	1638
138-3/8	24-4/8	23-2/8	17-7/8	5	5	Allen County	IN	Robert M. Wallin	1984	1638
138-3/8	21-6/8	22-5/8	16-3/8	5	6	Marquette County	WI	David M. Borzick	1985	1638
138-3/8	22-6/8	22-7/8	17-7/8	5	5	Clark County	WI	James F. Baker	1985	1638
138-2/8	20-6/8	20-6/8	17-0/8	5	5	Kent Narrows	MD	Paul W. Broadhurst	1962	1651
138-2/8	20-4/8	20-2/8	13-6/8	5	5	Adams County	IL	Russ Griffin	1970	1651
138-2/8	23-3/8	21-3/8	18-4/8	5	5	Ripley County	IN	Pat Wolf	1971	1651
138-2/8	23-3/8	22-0/8	16-4/8	5	4	Des Moines County	IA	Cory Dalton	1973	1651
138-2/8	23-5/8	22-1/8	20-2/8	5	6	Crawford County	WI	Jim Ferebee	1976	1651
138-2/8	21-2/8	21-2/8	16-3/8	5	7	Edmonton	ALB	Wilf Hunter	1978	1651
138-2/8	23-4/8	23-2/8	17-2/8	5	5	Huron Township	ONT	Jim McAuley	1980	1651
138-2/8	21-4/8	23-0/8	16-2/8	5	5	Laselle County	IL	Leonard Cochran	1981	1651
138-2/8	21-6/8	22-4/8	17-4/8	5	6	Johnson County	AR	Jeff Adams	1981	1651
138-2/8	25-2/8	25-1/8	19-7/8	4	5	Prebel County	OH	William J. Hahn	1981	1651
138-2/8	24-3/8	24-3/8	18-6/8	4	4	Cass County	IA	Reggie Schuler	1982	1651
138-2/8	22-7/8	23-2/8	17-6/8	4	4	Clark County	OH	David Parrott	1983	1651
138-2/8	24-7/8	26-0/8	16-0/8	7	6	Morgan County	GA	Rod Ayers	1983	1651
138-2/8	22-4/8	23-3/8	20-4/8	4	5	Lenawee County	MI	Kevin S. Zalecki	1983	1651
138-2/8	22-1/8	22-5/8	17-4/8	5	5	Chippewa County	WI	Ty Sweeney	1984	1651
138-2/8	24-6/8	25-4/8	18-4/8	5	4	Berks County	PA	Joseph W. Ruppe	1984	1651
138-2/8	23-1/8	23-0/8	17-4/8	4	5	Waushara County	WI	Michael A. Hale	1984	1651
138-2/8	23-4/8	23-6/8	16-6/8	5	5	Houston County	MN	Richard Crabtree	1985	1651
138-2/8	22-6/8	21-7/8	17-2/8	5	5	Cass County	MO	Rusty Murry	1985	1651
138-2/8	22-4/8	23-1/8	16-2/8	4	4	Morgan County	CO	Rodney Washburn	1985	1651
138-1/8	25-4/8	24-0/8	17-2/8	4	5	Cottonwood County	MN	Rodney Ella	1971	1671
138-1/8	23-1/8	22-5/8	19-7/8	5	5	Greenbank	WV	Jim Manley II	1971	1671
138-1/8	27-3/8	28-1/8	20-0/8	4	7	Nicollet County	MN	Steve Suess	1976	1671
138-1/8	23-0/8	22-4/8	18-3/8	4	4	Blaine	MN	Johnny E. Boatner	1978	1671
138-1/8	22-1/8	21-0/8	19-3/8	5	5	Kalamazoo County	MI	Dale Gray	1978	1671
138-1/8	22-5/8	24-6/8	20-1/8	6	7	Goodhue County	MN	Victor LoPresto	1979	1671
138-1/8	24-0/8	25-4/8	17-3/8	4	5	Grand Traverse County	MI	Roger Kirby	1980	1671
138-1/8	22-4/8	22-5/8	17-1/8	5	5	Huron County	OH	Larry Smith	1980	1671
138-1/8	23-4/8	23-3/8	18-4/8	6	5	Bond County	IL	Donald E. Cruse, Jr.	1981	1671
138-1/8	23-4/8	23-2/8	16-3/8	4	5	Jackson County	MO	Marvin Thomey	1982	1671
138-1/8	20-6/8	20-6/8	18-0/8	5	6	San Augustine	TX	Billy E. Corley	1982	1671
138-1/8	24-1/8	24-4/8	17-3/8	4	4	Harris County	GA	Allan Rovig	1983	1671
138-1/8	22-5/8	24-3/8	15-7/8	5	5	Price County	WI	Allen F. Feltz	1983	1671
138-1/8	23-6/8	23-1/8	19-7/8	4	4	Allegan County	MI	Tim Leslie	1983	1671
138-0/8	24-1/8	23-7/8	19-1/8	8	6	Frederick County	MD	Donald R. Shipley	1962	1685
138-0/8	22-2/8	22-3/8	18-4/8	4	4	Dane County	WI	Ernest Kalar	1966	1685
138-0/8	21-3/8	21-7/8	19-4/8	5	6	Webster	WI	John C. Gehlen	1971	1685
138-0/8	21-4/8	21-6/8	13-0/8	5	5	Taylor County	KY	James Hedgespeth	1978	1685
138-0/8	23-0/8	23-4/8	14-0/8	5	5	Jefferson County	WI	Dennis Roberts	1980	1685
138-0/8	22-6/8	23-6/8	20-4/8	4	5	Traverse County	MN	Danny Hormann	1981	1685
138-0/8	23-1/8	23-7/8	18-4/8	5	5	Langlade County	WI	Mike Plzak	1982	1685
138-0/8	20-3/8	21-6/8	15-5/8	5	7	Payne County	OK	David Ray Beene	1983	1685
138-0/8	22-6/8	22-5/8	16-6/8	5	5	Tyler County	WV	John S McMulley	1984	1685
138-0/8	23-6/8	23-1/8	17-2/8	5	5	Lake County	IL	John R. Love	1984	1685
138-0/8	22-1/8	21-2/8	14-4/8	5	5	Dekalb County	MO	Daniel E. Terry	1985	1685
138-0/8	22-7/8	23-5/8	19-0/8	5	4	Waukesha	WI	Steve Pease	1986	1685
137-7/8	22-3/8	22-7/8	21-1/8	6	8	Williston	ND	Ray Hoveskeland	1959	1697
137-7/8	21-0/8	21-2/8	17-1/8	4	4	Monroe	NE	Lee Rupp	1968	1697
137-7/8	21-5/8	21-3/8	16-3/8	5	5	Roseau County	MN	Terry Wilson	1977	1697
137-7/8	23-0/8	23-4/8	17-5/8	5	5	Chippewa County	MN	Layton Albrecht	1978	1697
137-7/8	21-6/8	22-2/8	19-0/8	5	4	Kay County	OK	Guy L. LeMonnier, Jr.	1979	1697

WHITETAIL DEER *(Typical Antlers)*

(continued)   Minimum Score 125

Score	Length of Main Beam R	L	Inside Spread	Number of Points R	L	Area	State/ Province	Hunter's Name	Date	Rank
137-6/8	24-5/8	23-7/8	19-2/8	4	5	Adams County	IL	William D. Force	1970	1702
137-6/8	22-1/8	20-1/8	18-1/8	6	5	Watonwan County	MN	Thomas E. Isley	1972	1702
137-6/8	20-7/8	21-1/8	16-4/8	5	5	Polk County	IA	John Dykes	1973	1702
137-6/8	22-7/8	23-6/8	18-4/8	4	5	Roscommon County	MI	James J. Osentoski	1978	1702
137-6/8	21-2/8	21-2/8	18-2/8	5	5	Goodhue County	MN	Tom Nesseth	1979	1702
137-6/8	23-6/8	23-0/8	16-1/8	5	5	Middlesex County	CT	James Matulis	1980	1702
137-6/8	22-0/8	22-6/8	17-6/8	5	5	Walkworth	ONT	Ken McGarrity	1982	1702
137-6/8	21-2/8	21-7/8	19-6/8	5	5	Cowley County	KS	Michael R. Bowlin	1983	1702
137-6/8	23-6/8	24-5/8	20-3/8	6	6	McHenry County	IL	Al Stroh	1983	1702
137-6/8	21-7/8	22-6/8	16-4/8	5	5	Pine County	MN	Pat Riley	1984	1702
137-6/8	23-1/8	23-2/8	16-2/8	4	4	Vernon County	WI	Gary Holcombe	1984	1702
137-6/8	20-7/8	21-4/8	18-4/8	5	5	Crawford County	IL	Todd McDaniel	1985	1702
137-6/8	22-4/8	21-7/8	17-0/8	5	5	Jefferson County	NE	Bob Funke	1985	1702
137-6/8	25-1/8	26-1/8	16-7/8	5	4	Cumberland County	NOV	P. Jeff Comeau	1985	1702
137-6/8	23-7/8	23-3/8	17-6/8	5	4	Grand Forks County	ND	Dan M. Finnie	1986	1702
137-5/8	20-4/8	19-7/8	15-5/8	5	5	Clark County	SD	Delmar Tobey	1959	1717
137-5/8	26-4/8	26-4/8	14-7/8	4	4	Rock County	NE	William Tutt	1963	1717
137-5/8	20-4/8	20-4/8	17-1/8	4	4	Miles City	MT	Dale Drilling	1976	1717
137-5/8	23-3/8	24-1/8	21-5/8	4	4	Hardin County	KY	Thomas R. Abner	1979	1717
137-5/8	21-6/8	22-6/8	16-5/8	5	5	McAlester Ads	OK	John Badger	1979	1717
137-5/8	21-1/8	21-1/8	14-5/8	5	6	Hamilton County	OH	Jack McConnell	1979	1717
137-5/8	23-3/8	22-5/8	15-5/8	4	4	Cloud County	KS	Don Watowa	1982	1717
137-5/8	17-7/8	20-5/8	15-7/8	5	6	Wankesha County	WI	Tom Millane	1982	1717
137-5/8	23-1/8	23-0/8	20-5/8	4	4	Prince Georges Co.	MD	Dave Williams	1982	1717
137-5/8	24-5/8	24-0/8	16-5/8	6	5	Suffolk County	VA	Mark T. Smith	1984	1717
137-4/8	23-4/8	23-6/8	18-2/8	5	4	Rice County	MN	Robert W. Berg	1965	1727
137-4/8	23-6/8	22-0/8	21-4/8	5	5	Spink County	SD	Ray McIntyre	1967	1727
137-4/8	25-4/8	24-0/8	18-6/8	4	4	Berrien County	MI	Lawrence C. Ford	1981	1727
137-4/8	21-5/8	20-7/8	14-2/8	5	6	Pope County	MN	Roger Tollefson	1982	1727
137-4/8	22-6/8	22-6/8	18-2/8	4	4	Newaygo County	MI	David Davis	1982	1727
137-4/8	23-3/8	23-0/8	16-4/8	4	5	Vernon County	WI	Jerry Willer	1983	1727
137-4/8	21-2/8	20-3/8	15-4/8	6	5	Pierson	MAN	Brad Minshull	1984	1727
137-4/8	23-5/8	23-1/8	18-6/8	5	5	Nelson County	KY	James H. Stiles	1984	1727
137-4/8	21-2/8	20-4/8	19-0/8	5	5	Sauk County	WI	Jimmie S Gluth	1984	1727
137-4/8	22-5/8	20-4/8	16-4/8	5	5	Albany County	NY	James O'Connor	1984	1727
137-4/8	22-3/8	22-7/8	16-6/8	5	5	Rogers County	OK	Ernie Merydith	1986	1727
137-3/8	22-0/8	21-4/8	19-7/8	5	4	Ft. Sill	OK	Edward J. Baumlin, Jr.	1960	1738
137-3/8	20-6/8	20-2/8	12-6/8	5	10	Farragut	ID	John Ruthuen	1961	1738
137-3/8	23-5/8	23-3/8	16-6/8	4	5	Allegan County	MI	Clayton Foster	1964	1738
137-3/8	25-6/8	23-1/8	15-7/8	4	4	Madison	IN	Lee Middleton	1966	1738
137-3/8	25-1/8	24-4/8	20-7/8	4	4	Trempealeau County	WI	Randall J. Van Vleet	1966	1738
137-3/8	20-2/8	19-7/8	16-5/8	5	5	Stone County	MO	Charles A. Myers	1974	1738
137-3/8	22-2/8	23-3/8	19-7/8	4	5	Dane County	WI	Donald W. Pache	1980	1738
137-3/8	20-7/8	21-2/8	15-4/8	6	5	Jo Daviess County	IL	Herb Imbus	1981	1738
137-3/8	21-4/8	20-6/8	15-3/8	5	5	St. Croix County	WI	Daniel A. Score	1982	1738
137-3/8	23-1/8	25-2/8	20-3/8	4	5	Meeker County	MN	Thomas Wylie	1983	1738
137-3/8	22-5/8	22-5/8	16-6/8	6	4	Marion County	IL	Joseph B. Smith III	1983	1738
137-3/8	23-6/8	20-7/8	19-7/8	5	5	Stephenson County	IL	Jeff S. Olsen	1986	1738
137-2/8	23-2/8	24-7/8	18-5/8	8	5	Phelps County	NE	Dick Cepel	1959	1750
137-2/8	21-1/8	20-0/8	17-4/8	6	5	Sand Lake Refuge	SD	Richard Felch	1966	1750
137-2/8	23-1/8	24-1/8	16-4/8	5	5	Marion County	IA	David Hedgecock	1973	1750
137-2/8	21-4/8	21-1/8	17-2/8	7	7	Laramie River	WY	Mark A. Brant	1976	1750
137-2/8	23-2/8	23-6/8	17-4/8	5	5	Brown County	OH	Howard Ayers	1977	1750
137-2/8	22-4/8	22-6/8	19-0/8	5	5	Sanders County	MT	Dyrk Eddie	1980	1750
137-2/8	25-0/8	24-4/8	16-6/8	4	4	Putnam County	TN	Doyle B. Wilmoth	1980	1750
137-2/8	20-6/8	20-7/8	15-2/8	5	5	Rock County	WI	Ronald S. Pulcine	1981	1750
137-2/8	21-4/8	22-5/8	16-6/8	5	5	Teton County	MT	William McRae	1982	1750
137-2/8	21-7/8	18-5/8	16-4/8	7	6	St. Charles County	MO	Donald L. Hauser	1982	1750
137-2/8	21-6/8	21-4/8	17-6/8	7	5	Linn County	IA	Dennis W. Frye	1983	1750
137-2/8	23-6/8	23-5/8	20-0/8	4	4	Jo Davies County	IL	Kenneth Scharfenorth	1983	1750
137-2/8	23-1/8	22-4/8	16-2/8	4	5	Hughes County	SD	Alvin Truax	1983	1750
137-2/8	22-1/8	20-2/8	17-2/8	5	5	Deleware County	OH	David Orndorf	1983	1750
137-2/8	24-1/8	24-2/8	17-0/8	5	4	Arkansas County	AR	Sam Snowden	1984	1750

WHITETAIL DEER *(Typical Antlers)*

Minimum Score 125   (continued)

Score	Length of Main Beam R	L	Inside Spread	Number of Points R	L	Area	State/ Province	Hunter's Name	Date	Rank
137-2/8	22-1/8	21-7/8	18-0/8	4	4	Belmont County	OH	Walter Kapiskovsky	1984	1750
137-2/8	22-0/8	21-4/8	17-0/8	5	5	Rock County	WI	Ronald S. Pulcine	1984	1750
137-2/8	25-4/8	25-1/8	18-6/8	5	5	Sauk County	WI	Daniel A. Mundth	1985	1750
137-1/8	26-5/8	24-7/8	18-5/8	4	4	Bartholomew County	IN	Jimmy Middleton	1963	1768
137-1/8	26-6/8	24-2/8	17-3/8	4	5	Muskingum County	OH	William H. Archer	1976	1768
137-1/8	25-2/8	24-2/8	19-7/8	5	5	Newton County	IN	James Manes	1976	1768
137-1/8	22-6/8	22-4/8	16-1/8	5	5	Itasca County	MN	Donald Kenneth Kress	1977	1768
137-1/8	21-0/8	21-5/8	16-1/8	6	5	Tompkins County	NY	Carlo Troise	1978	1768
137-1/8	23-7/8	23-3/8	18-0/8	6	5	Grant County	WI	Lloyd J. Hach	1982	1768
137-1/8	21-6/8	20-0/8	18-2/8	6	6	Fairfield County	OH	Paul R. Baker	1982	1768
137-1/8	24-0/8	23-4/8	18-7/8	5	4	Hardin County	IA	Tom Herold	1982	1768
137-1/8	26-4/8	24-1/8	22-1/8	4	4	Christian County	IL	Daniel Hinds	1983	1768
137-1/8	21-7/8	22-1/8	14-7/8	4	5	Evensville	TN	Leland H. Rothwell, Sr.	1983	1768
137-1/8	22-5/8	22-7/8	18-7/8	4	4	Carroll County	IL	Gary R. Schneider	1983	1768
137-1/8	20-7/8	20-5/8	16-3/8	5	6	Jasper County	IA	Kevin Lynn Patterson	1984	1768
137-0/8	26-0/8	24-0/8	19-6/8	5	4	Pierre	SD	Gerald Snyder	1963	1780
137-0/8	22-0/8	22-3/8	20-4/8	4	5	Blandon	PA	Frank "Rit" Heller	1971	1780
137-0/8	21-4/8	22-3/8	18-2/8	4	7	Black Hawk County	IA	Bob Wood	1971	1780
137-0/8	23-5/8	23-6/8	22-4/8	4	4	Freeborn County	MN	Brian Johnson	1978	1780
137-0/8	24-5/8	25-7/8	20-2/8	5	4	Iroquois County	IL	Terry D. McDaniel	1978	1780
137-0/8	22-1/8	22-3/8	17-0/8	5	4	Miles City	MN	Jim Walters	1978	1780
137-0/8	21-5/8	22-2/8	14-6/8	4	4	Blue Earth County	MN	Stanley Defries	1980	1780
137-0/8	22-2/8	23-1/8	15-5/8	5	6	Drew County	AR	Herman S. Fleming	1980	1780
137-0/8	23-3/8	22-7/8	16-4/8	4	4	Walworth	WI	Robert Mereness	1980	1780
137-0/8	21-5/8	21-6/8	16-6/8	5	5	Scott County	KY	Milton Lee Pribble	1980	1780
137-0/8	21-5/8	20-3/8	17-2/8	5	5	Randolph County	MO	Ronald Chirillo	1982	1780
137-0/8	20-0/8	20-3/8	17-0/8	5	5	Douglas County	WI	Carl Ellison	1983	1780
137-0/8	24-0/8	23-3/8	18-0/8	5	5	Crawford County	WI	Ken Fernette	1984	1780
137-0/8	22-3/8	24-1/8	15-0/8	4	5	Green County	WI	William H. Holt	1986	1780
137-0/8	22-3/8	20-7/8	17-6/8	5	5	Litchfield County	CT	John C. Murphy, Sr.	1986	1780
136-7/8	20-5/8	21-5/8	25-0/8	6	6	Missouri Valley	IA	Larry Vaughn	1961	1795
136-7/8	20-2/8	19-1/8	15-2/8	8	7	Ashland County	WI	Jim McGarvey	1965	1795
136-7/8	23-5/8,	23-6/8	18-1/8	4	5	Jefferson County	IN	James Coldiron	1972	1795
136-7/8	22-3/8	22-6/8	17-0/8	6	5	Dugger	IN	John Chesterfield	1977	1795
136-7/8	21-2/8	21-4/8	18-7/8	5	5	Fulton County	IL	Jeffrey L. Keefauver	1979	1795
136-7/8	23-2/8	23-7/8	20-1/8	5	4	Muskingum County	OH	Larry Shoop	1979	1795
136-7/8	23-5/8	24-0/8	19-3/8	5	5	Montgomery County	IN	Derrick Kidd	1980	1795
136-7/8	24-6/8	23-7/8	21-1/8	4	4	Union County	IL	Carl E. Cronk	1983	1795
136-7/8	20-7/8	19-5/8	15-3/8	5	5	Ozaukee County	WI	Scott T. Frank	1983	1795
136-7/8	19-7/8	20-1/8	17-5/8	5	5	Kingsbury County	SD	Joe Jensen	1983	1795
136-7/8	22-3/8	22-2/8	18-3/8	4	5	Montgomery County	PA	Robert Pyne	1985	1795
136-7/8	22-4/8	21-4/8	17-7/8	5	5	Woodson County	KS	Jerry Ramshaw	1985	1795
136-7/8	25-1/8	25-1/8	17-6/8	6	5	Coshocton County	OH	Keith Duncan	1985	1795
136-7/8	23-6/8	24-0/8	16-2/8	7	7	Door County	WI	Daniel W. Herrbold	1986	1795
136-6/8	23-2/8	22-4/8	15-4/8	4	5	Ogle County	IL	Edwin Fitzgerald	1963	1809
136-6/8	22-0/8	20-6/8	16-5/8	5	6	Hayti	SD	James Larson	1963	1809
136-6/8	23-5/8	24-2/8	17-4/8	4	4	Mower County	MN	Robert Meyer	1965	1809
136-6/8	21-4/8	20-6/8	18-2/8	5	6	St. James	MN	Gary G. Miest	1969	1809
136-6/8	22-1/8	20-6/8	17-4/8	5	5	Lake County	SD	Dennis DeBoer	1974	1809
136-6/8	23-3/8	24-5/8	21-1/8	5	5	Whiteside County	IL	Art Heinze	1975	1809
136-6/8	22-4/8	21-2/8	20-5/8	4	5	Centerville	MD	Norman C. Herdegen	1977	1809
136-6/8	27-4/8	24-0/8	18-4/8	6	6	Livingston County	MI	Peter Bolen	1979	1809
136-6/8	22-4/8	23-5/8	17-0/8	6	5	Coahoma County	MS	David Holcomb	1979	1809
136-6/8	22-0/8	20-6/8	16-0/8	5	4	Houston County	MN	Howard Lampert	1979	1809
136-6/8	21-7/8	22-3/8	17-2/8	4	4	Waukesha County	WI	Jeff Dickenson	1984	1809
136-6/8	22-0/8	22-3/8	17-6/8	5	5	Chippewa County	MI	James R. Dreves	1985	1809
136-5/8	24-6/8	24-6/8	18-5/8	4	4	Broxton County	WV	John M. Friend	1965	1821
136-5/8	23-4/8	22-5/8	16-5/8	4	4	Marathon County	WI	Leroy Kazmierczak	1966	1821
136-5/8	20-0/8	22-0/8	18-6/8	5	5	Perry County	IL	Robert P. Berry	1980	1821
136-5/8	21-4/8	20-6/8	14-7/8	5	5	Huron County	MI	John F. Deroche	1981	1821
136-5/8	22-1/8	22-0/8	16-3/8	5	5	Phillips County	AR	Larry Scott	1981	1821
136-5/8	23-1/8	22-0/8	16-1/8	4	4	Crawford County	IL	Brentley D. Smith	1981	1821
136-5/8	21-3/8	20-7/8	17-3/8	5	5	Jackson County	AL	Rocky Drake	1982	1821

WHITETAIL DEER *(Typical Antlers)*

(continued)

Score	Length of Main Beam R	L	Inside Spread	Number of Points R	L	Area	State/ Province	Hunter's Name	Date	Rank
136-5/8	25-2/8	26-1/8	22-2/8	8	4	Champaign County	IL	Carl Park	1982	1821
136-5/8	21-6/8	21-4/8	16-7/8	5	5	Jackson County	IA	Gregory L. Schulte	1982	1821
136-5/8	23-5/8	23-1/8	20-1/8	4	4	Ripley County	IN	Steve A. Allen	1983	1821
136-5/8	21-1/8	22-0/8	14-6/8	6	6	Oneida County	WI	Jeff Aulik	1983	1821
136-5/8	22-0/8	22-2/8	18-1/8	5	5	Bryn-Athyn County	PA	Glenn Kuklick	1983	1821
136-5/8	22-1/8	22-1/8	18-7/8	4	4	Cowley County	KS	Don Smith	1984	1821
136-5/8	20-4/8	20-4/8	16-1/8	5	5	Pierce County	WI	Lester Clare	1985	1821
136-5/8	21-4/8	21-1/8	18-7/8	5	4	Pine County	MN	Ron Ekstrand	1986	1821
136-4/8	25-3/8	24-4/8	20-4/8	4	4	Roberts County	SD	Byron Siegel	1963	1836
136-4/8	27-4/8	26-2/8	17-3/8	6	6	Wake County	NC	Robert E. Butler	1977	1836
136-4/8	23-1/8	22-3/8	17-0/8	5	5	Brevard County	FL	Mike Field	1979	1836
136-4/8	22-0/8	23-7/8	18-4/8	5	5	Clark County	IL	Gerald Shaffner	1980	1836
136-4/8	21-7/8	22-1/8	17-2/8	5	5	Coweta County	GA	Bobby Edwards	1981	1836
136-4/8	24-0/8	24-0/8	18-3/8	6	7	Hancock County	IN	Paul E. Williams	1982	1836
136-4/8	21-6/8	22-3/8	18-4/8	4	4	Oneida County	WI	Dennis Steinberger	1983	1836
136-4/8	22-0/8	22-0/8	17-6/8	6	5	Livingston County	MI	Thomas E. Shay	1984	1836
136-4/8	22-5/8	22-4/8	16-4/8	5	5	Wyoming County	NY	Ray Minnick	1985	1836
136-4/8	22-3/8	21-7/8	14-4/8	5	5	Clayton County	IA	Betty Jane Jungk	1985	1836
136-4/8	21-7/8	22-7/8	17-2/8	4	4	Washington County	TN	Bobby Davis	1985	1836
136-4/8	21-6/8	21-2/8	17-0/8	5	5	Marshall County	IA	Ed Albee	1985	1836
136-3/8	23-5/8	24-2/8	17-6/8	4	5	Pope County	IL	Murray Schuchardt	1973	1848
136-3/8	23-6/8	23-6/8	18-5/8	5	7	Pope County	MN	Ernie Janish	1976	1848
136-3/8	24-4/8	24-3/8	18-5/8	5	5	Delaware County	OH	Ron E. Murphy	1979	1848
136-3/8	22-7/8	22-1/8	16-3/8	4	5	Des Moines County	IA	John Thompson	1982	1848
136-3/8	21-1/8	21-1/8	15-1/8	5	5	Iron County	WI	John W. Schulz	1983	1848
136-3/8	22-2/8	22-2/8	18-1/8	4	4	Clay County	MO	Kent Robb Waters	1983	1848
136-3/8	22-0/8	22-4/8	18-7/8	4	4	Webster County	KY	John Wayne Elkins	1983	1848
136-3/8	25-0/8	25-6/8	21-3/8	4	4	McPherson County	KS	Dan Koons	1985	1848
136-2/8	21-6/8	21-6/8	16-5/8	6	5	McKenzie County	ND	David Tofte	1923	1856
136-2/8	21-2/8	21-2/8	17-0/8	5	5	Sheridan County	ND	Robert Conklin	1967	1856
136-2/8	22-0/8	22-4/8	17-4/8	5	4	Taylor County	WI	Roger Williams	1968	1856
136-2/8	22-3/8	22-0/8	14-2/8	4	5	Lucas County	IA	Cynthia Squibb	1973	1856
136-2/8	21-1/8	20-6/8	16-4/8	5	5	Montgomery Twp.	NJ	John K. Deveney	1977	1856
136-2/8	21-7/8	21-7/8	14-0/8	5	6	Jefferson County	IA	Scott Dillon	1980	1856
136-2/8	21-4/8	22-0/8	15-3/8	4	7	Cass County	MI	Clark A. Baugher	1981	1856
136-2/8	22-4/8	22-6/8	18-0/8	4	5	Nelson County	KY	Mark Gies	1982	1856
136-2/8	23-0/8	23-2/8	16-4/8	5	5	Loudon County	VA	Larry Clayton Sherertz	1983	1856
136-2/8	22-2/8	23-2/8	18-2/8	4	5	Fairfax County	VA	Frederick Alf, Jr.	1983	1856
136-2/8	22-3/8	22-7/8	16-6/8	5	6	Fairfield County	CT	Paul Fitzgerald	1984	1856
136-2/8	22-7/8	22-4/8	18-5/8	5	5	Crawford County	KS	Don Garritson	1984	1856
136-2/8	21-0/8	23-0/8	20-0/8	6	5	Howard County	NE	Dwayne Berggren	1985	1856
136-2/8	24-5/8	24-4/8	17-2/8	6	6	Gray County	KS	Melvin L. Weber	1985	1856
136-1/8	21-5/8	21-2/8	18-0/8	5	4	Spink County	SD	Louis Smith	1963	1870
136-1/8	23-3/8	23-4/8	19-7/8	6	6	Cornwall	CT	Eugene Clini, Jr.	1970	1870
136-1/8	21-1/8	23-2/8	19-1/8	5	5	Morrison County	MN	Raymond G. Fair	1981	1870
136-1/8	23-2/8	23-5/8	19-1/8	5	5	Jefferson County	IL	Kevin Lisenby	1982	1870
136-1/8	22-2/8	21-6/8	17-3/8	5	4	El Paso County	CO	Michael Thompson	1983	1870
136-1/8	21-4/8	22-1/8	17-3/8	4	4	Fillmore County	MN	Glenn Hisey	1983	1870
136-1/8	20-5/8	21-1/8	15-0/8	8	6	Atchison County	MO	Orville L. Chaslain	1983	1870
136-1/8	23-3/8	23-3/8	18-1/8	5	6	Franklin County	OH	Richard J. Ferguson	1983	1870
136-1/8	24-7/8	23-5/8	19-7/8	4	5	Wayne County	IA	Gary Purvis	1983	1870
136-1/8	26-1/8	24-7/8	21-3/8	4	4	Claiborn Parrish	LA	Joe M. Tuggle	1985	1870
136-1/8	24-4/8	22-4/8	16-7/8	4	4	Washington County	IA	Marc Phelps	1985	1870
136-1/8	20-0/8	21-1/8	17-1/8	5	5	Dickinson County	KS	Donald L. Ackerman	1985	1870
136-1/8	20-1/8	20-1/8	18-5/8	5	5	Lincoln County	MT	Michael F. Shepard	1985	1870
136-1/8	21-3/8	21-5/8	15-3/8	5	6	Adams County	WI	Brad A. Bauer	1986	1870
136-1/8	21-3/8	21-0/8	15-7/8	5	5	Duval County	TX	Peggy Barcak	1986	1870
136-0/8	19-6/8	19-5/8	19-4/8	4	4	Jackson County	IL	Henry Mika	1962	1885
136-0/8	23-2/8	23-4/8	17-2/8	5	5	Brookings	SD	Douglas Tschetter	1964	1885
136-0/8	23-6/8	23-0/8	18-0/8	4	4	Noblesville	IN	Sondra K. Scifres	1975	1885
136-0/8	23-3/8	23-2/8	18-2/8	4	4	Greene County	IN	Guy Aldrich	1977	1885
136-0/8	22-2/8	22-2/8	18-0/8	5	5	Chester	NJ	Len Cardinale	1980	1885
136-0/8	22-7/8	23-3/8	19-4/8	4	4	Delaware County	IA	David Becker	1981	1885

WHITETAIL DEER *(Typical Antlers)*

Minimum Score 125

(continued)

Score	Length of Main Beam R	L	Inside Spread	Number of Points R	L	Area	State/ Province	Hunter's Name	Date	Rank
136-0/8	23-3/8	23-1/8	18-4/8	5	5	Houston County	MN	Roger Giese	1981	1885
136-0/8	20-1/8	20-6/8	16-6/8	5	5	Ottawa County	KS	Rodney Ponton	1981	1885
136-0/8	21-3/8	21-5/8	16-4/8	5	5	Juneau County	WI	Terry Taft	1981	1885
136-0/8	22-1/8	23-5/8	17-2/8	5	5	Berkeley County	SC	Hugh Gaskins	1982	1885
136-0/8	22-5/8	22-0/8	18-0/8	5	5	Red Willow County	NE	Dudley Jackson	1983	1885
136-0/8	23-4/8	21-4/8	18-6/8	4	4	Hancock County	IL	Tim Lee	1983	1885
136-0/8	24-0/8	23-5/8	17-1/8	7	5	Cherokee County	KS	Darren Collins	1983	1885
136-0/8	21-5/8	21-1/8	18-0/8	5	5	Johnson County	IA	Danny Stegall	1983	1885
136-0/8	23-2/8	22-5/8	18-4/8	4	4	Clark County	KS	William Rule	1984	1885
136-0/8	22-4/8	21-6/8	17-4/8	5	5	Wayne County	NY	Eugene Vincent	1984	1885
136-0/8	21-5/8	20-5/8	17-2/8	6	5	Flathead County	MT	Carter Jensen	1985	1885
136-0/8	21-3/8	21-6/8	16-4/8	6	5	Winona County	MN	George McIntire	1985	1885
136-0/8	23-3/8	23-6/8	13-6/8	6	5	Fayette County	OH	Ronnie L. Jenkins	1985	1885
136-0/8	22-0/8	23-0/8	19-0/8	5	5	Jackson County	MI	William D. Burgess	1985	1885
135-7/8	23-6/8	22-2/8	16-7/8	6	8	Long Island	IL	Joe Johnson	1967	1905
135-7/8	24-6/8	21-6/8	20-1/8	4	5	Westchester County	NY	Colin M. Pierson	1967	1905
135-7/8	22-5/8	22-3/8	15-3/8	4	5	Brown County	IN	Junior R. Hutchings	1974	1905
135-7/8	21-4/8	21-6/8	16-3/8	5	5	Argonia	KS	Len Sanders	1980	1905
135-7/8	24-6/8	24-3/8	15-5/8	5	5	Elgin	ONT	Mike Rusnak	1982	1905
135-7/8	24-0/8	25-0/8	23-4/8	6	5	Suffolk County	NY	Richard W. Geminski	1982	1905
135-7/8	24-1/8	23-0/8	21-1/8	4	4	Vermilion County	IL	Frank Palmer	1983	1905
135-7/8	19-7/8	20-0/8	15-7/8	5	5	Renville County	MN	Daniel J. Scharba	1983	1905
135-7/8	20-2/8	20-6/8	16-3/8	5	5	Duval County	TX	John Clinton Manges	1984	1905
135-7/8	23-1/8	23-0/8	19-5/8	5	6	Monroe County	OH	Mark A. Landefeld	1984	1905
135-7/8	22-4/8	22-2/8	18-3/8	4	4	Sauk County	WI	Dan Bauer	1985	1905
135-6/8	24-4/8	22-7/8	19-2/8	5	5	Rockford	IL	Edward Fuller	1963	1916
135-6/8	22-6/8	23-2/8	20-6/8	4	4	Shawano County	WI	Darryl Erdman	1968	1916
135-6/8	25-5/8	24-4/8	19-7/8	6	4	Knox County	IL	Fred E. Miller	1968	1916
135-6/8	22-3/8	22-5/8	15-2/8	6	7	Dodge County	MN	Bradley Blanchard	1973	1916
135-6/8	24-0/8	24-0/8	20-2/8	5	5	Parke County	IN	Charles Loomis	1978	1916
135-6/8	23-0/8	24-1/8	16-0/8	4	4	Pine County	MN	Paul L. Videen	1979	1916
135-6/8	20-7/8	22-7/8	15-0/8	6	6	Fayette	GA	Tom Mann, Jr.	1980	1916
135-6/8	20-2/8	20-2/8	16-0/8	5	5	Rochester	IN	James L. Kerr	1981	1916
135-6/8	22-0/8	23-0/8	15-2/8	5	6	Ozark County	MO	Bruce Webb	1981	1916
135-6/8	20-3/8	21-0/8	15-2/8	5	5	Dubuque County	IA	Harry Bries	1982	1916
135-6/8	22-5/8	21-1/8	15-6/8	5	5	Saline County	KS	Kenneth D. Sterling	1982	1916
135-6/8	23-0/8	22-0/8	18-0/8	5	5	Shawano County	WI	Ron Vander Kelen	1982	1916
135-6/8	22-1/8	22-5/8	16-6/8	5	5	Tompkins County	NY	Michael R. Deschamps	1982	1916
135-6/8	21-4/8	21-6/8	14-2/8	4	4	Watonwan County	MN	Brad Nielsen	1984	1916
135-6/8	21-1/8	21-2/8	15-3/8	7	6	Pope County	IL	Roy L. Arnold	1984	1916
135-6/8	21-5/8	22-4/8	16-4/8	5	4	Oldham County	KY	Garnett B. Morgan, Jr.	1985	1916
135-6/8	23-4/8	23-2/8	19-4/8	6	6	Allamakee County	IA	Mark E. Walleser	1985	1916
135-5/8	22-1/8	23-6/8	19-1/8	6	4	Montgomery County	IN	Derrick W. Kidd	1932	1933
135-5/8	21-4/8	20-0/8	16-1/8	5	5	Sheboygan Marsh	WI	Earl Uhl	1960	1933
135-5/8	22-1/8	22-1/8	19-3/8	5	5	Ringold County	IA	William K. Seitz	1973	1933
135-5/8	23-4/8	23-2/8	14-7/8	4	4	Jasper County	IN	Gary L. Hepler	1980	1933
135-5/8	23-7/8	22-6/8	14-3/8	5	5	Allegheny County	PA	John Camillo	1980	1933
135-5/8	23-5/8	21-2/8	17-5/8	4	5	Winona	MN	Hank Scharmach	1981	1933
135-5/8	22-6/8	22-0/8	18-3/8	4	4	Dodge County	MN	Robert Rhodes, Jr.	1982	1933
135-5/8	22-4/8	23-2/8	14-0/8	4	7	Anderson County	KS	Steve Spangler	1983	1933
135-5/8	24-2/8	23-2/8	17-3/8	4	4	Buffalo County	WI	Edward Brannen	1984	1933
135-5/8	21-3/8	22-2/8	19-7/8	4	4	Tama County	IA	Clyde Bearden	1985	1933
135-5/8	23-7/8	25-4/8	21-5/8	4	4	Charles Mix County	SD	Frank Mingo	1985	1933
135-5/8	22-1/8	22-2/8	17-7/8	4	4	Price County	WI	Leonard J. Stein	1985	1933
135-4/8	21-0/8	23-0/8	18-6/8	6	5	St. Angar	IA	Arthur Cepeda	1962	1945
135-4/8	23-4/8	23-4/8	18-6/8	4	4	Horicon	WI	Daniel J. Rozek	1966	1945
135-4/8	21-6/8	21-4/8	19-4/8	5	5	Mower County	MN	Arthur McKenzie	1972	1945
135-4/8	21-3/8	23-0/8	18-0/8	5	5	Versailles	IN	G. Fred Asbell	1973	1945
135-4/8	20-5/8	20-5/8	13-2/8	5	5	Iron Mountain	MI	Dave Bath	1973	1945
135-4/8	23-0/8	23-6/8	18-0/8	5	5	Lyon County	KY	Kenneth McKay	1973	1945
135-4/8	21-7/8	21-6/8	18-0/8	5	5	Moore County	MN	Clark Gallup	1975	1945
135-4/8	22-7/8	22-6/8	19-0/8	6	5	McAlester	OK	Bill Nelson	1977	1945
135-4/8	23-4/8	23-2/8	17-3/8	5	4	Lincoln County	SD	Merle A. Henry	1980	1945

WHITETAIL DEER *(Typical Antlers)*

(continued)   Minimum Score 125

Score	Length of Main Beam R	L	Inside Spread	Number of Points R	L	Area	State/ Province	Hunter's Name	Date	Rank
135-4/8	21-3/8	22-2/8	16-6/8	5	4	Canton	SD	Eldon D. Hagen	1981	1945
135-4/8	19-0/8	19-0/8	14-3/8	6	8	Lee County	IA	Glenn E. Wagner	1981	1945
135-4/8	24-3/8	25-7/8	18-4/8	5	4	Freeborn County	MN	Richard Rippentrap	1982	1945
135-4/8	25-2/8	23-3/8	19-3/8	5	6	Mercer County	IL	David McCaw	1983	1945
135-4/8	22-0/8	22-4/8	14-3/8	7	6	Adams County	WI	David A. Schmitt	1984	1945
135-4/8	25-0/8	20-5/8	18-0/8	5	6	Tazewell County	IL	Darrell A Lee	1984	1945
135-4/8	23-1/8	22-5/8	17-4/8	5	5	Muskegon County	MI	R. Lawrence Meyers	1985	1945
135-3/8	22-0/8	22-2/8	17-1/8	5	5	Columbia County	WI	Chester Sroka	1936	1961
135-3/8	23-2/8	23-0/8	21-0/8	6	6	Sully County	SD	R. L. Marso	1965	1961
135-3/8	21-6/8	23-2/8	19-1/8	4	5	Brown County	SD	Arnie Goldade	1974	1961
135-3/8	22-6/8	22-6/8	16-5/8	4	4	Iowa County	WI	Jerry Statz	1977	1961
135-3/8	21-0/8	21-0/8	14-7/8	4	4	Richland County	MT	Dan Sturgis	1977	1961
135-3/8	23-7/8	23-0/8	17-5/8	4	4	Barneveld	WI	Paul Klingelhoets	1978	1961
135-3/8	22-3/8	21-5/8	15-5/8	5	5	Charlestown	IN	Robert W. Thompson	1979	1961
135-3/8	23-5/8	24-6/8	16-1/8	5	5	Burnett County	WI	Gene Hill	1980	1961
135-3/8	22-7/8	23-0/8	19-1/8	4	4	Washington County	MN	Rodney P. Bailey	1981	1961
135-3/8	24-1/8	24-1/8	19-7/8	4	4	Phillipsburg	NJ	Bill L. Raub	1982	1961
135-3/8	22-6/8	22-4/8	16-3/8	5	5	Dodge County	WI	George Warden	1983	1961
135-3/8	21-2/8	21-1/8	16-1/8	5	5	Latah County	ID	Jim Frazier	1983	1961
135-3/8	21-7/8	21-4/8	18-2/8	5	4	Champaign County	IL	Gary Ray Varner	1984	1961
135-3/8	23-3/8	23-3/8	21-1/8	4	5	Ottawa County	MI	Ed Diemer	1984	1961
135-3/8	21-7/8	21-3/8	15-3/8	5	5	Strathcona	ALB	Ryk Visscher	1985	1961
135-2/8	25-0/8	24-0/8	18-2/8	5	4	Lucas County	IA	Everett Parsons	1964	1976
135-2/8	21-3/8	22-7/8	16-0/8	5	8	Brown County	SD	Jack Eagleson	1966	1976
135-2/8	23-0/8	23-2/8	20-2/8	4	4	Cedar County	IA	Fred Wesselink	1971	1976
135-2/8	20-6/8	21-2/8	18-0/8	5	5	Edinburg	IN	Thomas J. Brown	1978	1976
135-2/8	17-4/8	16-5/8	13-1/8	7	7	Marshall County	IA	Mike Thomas	1978	1976
135-2/8	24-0/8	23-2/8	17-4/8	5	6	Whitewater	MN	Jim Keim	1979	1976
135-2/8	21-5/8	22-5/8	16-6/8	5	6	Juneau County	WI	Steven Hysell	1983	1976
135-2/8	21-3/8	22-0/8	17-6/8	4	4	Hocking County	OH	Rex Wollett	1983	1976
135-1/8	21-0/8	20-4/8	17-3/8	5	5	Westchester County	NY	Francis E. Hill	1958	1984
135-1/8	21-6/8	21-3/8	19-7/8	6	5	Brookings	SD	Ray Buckley	1961	1984
135-1/8	21-5/8	21-5/8	17-7/8	4	4	Bradley	SD	Jack D. Chesmore	1971	1984
135-1/8	21-7/8	22-0/8	16-3/8	4	4	Bloomfield	IN	Jan J. Armour	1976	1984
135-1/8	22-2/8	22-7/8	17-3/8	4	5	Nodaway County	MO	Larry Davison	1982	1984
135-1/8	23-4/8	22-7/8	18-3/8	5	4	Hamilton County	OH	Jerome Buschle, Jr.	1983	1984
135-1/8	19-4/8	20-1/8	16-1/8	5	4	McLean County	IL	Robert P. Ryburn	1984	1984
135-1/8	22-3/8	21-4/8	16-5/8	5	5	Missoula County	MT	Monty Moravec	1985	1984
135-1/8	20-1/8	19-0/8	15-4/8	6	6	Dawes County	NE	Allen Mintken	1985	1984
135-1/8	23-4/8	22-0/8	19-3/8	5	5	Eaton County	MI	Dr. Daniel C. Gulick	1985	1984
135-1/8	23-1/8	23-6/8	18-3/8	6	5	Iowa County	WI	Joe Esser	1985	1984
135-0/8	22-0/8	20-6/8	17-0/8	4	4	Grant County	MN	Stanley D. Miles	1963	1995
135-0/8	20-1/8	20-2/8	15-4/8	5	5	Dodge County	MN	Clark Gallup	1973	1995
135-0/8	22-6/8	17-7/8	15-6/8	6	6	Butler County	KS	Phil Hamilton	1974	1995
135-0/8	20-7/8	19-2/8	17-3/8	8	7	Peoria County	IL	Harry L. Stalter	1975	1995
135-0/8	24-4/8	24-3/8	14-0/8	5	4	Buffalo County	WI	Steve Segerstrom	1978	1995
135-0/8	20-5/8	20-7/8	18-0/8	6	6	Ripley	MN	Larry Hochmayr	1979	1995
135-0/8	22-0/8	22-4/8	17-0/8	5	5	Perry	OK	Glen Elliott	1981	1995
135-0/8	25-7/8	26-6/8	22-4/8	7	6	Pickaway County	OH	Mouse Bailey	1982	1995
135-0/8	22-3/8	22-1/8	19-4/8	5	5	Linn County	IA	David Padget	1985	1995
135-0/8	23-6/8	23-6/8	17-0/8	4	5	Bayfield County	WI	Charles Wallisch	1985	1995
135-0/8	21-2/8	22-5/8	20-2/8	6	5	Union County	IL	Robert Gordon	1985	1995
134-7/8	20-1/8	21-4/8	16-3/8	5	5	Spokane County	WA	Harold Bratlie	1960	2006
134-7/8	20-6/8	20-6/8	16-7/8	4	4	Lawrence County	SD	Oliver Lewis	1960	2006
134-7/8	20-4/8	21-0/8	17-2/8	6	6	Cherokee County	OK	Addison Harrison	1965	2006
134-7/8	20-7/8	21-6/8	17-7/8	5	5	Morrison County	MN	Thomas Ackerman	1971	2006
134-7/8	24-5/8	24-1/8	21-3/8	7	6	Washington County	OH	Lyle W. Townson, Sr.	1974	2006
134-7/8	19-3/8	20-3/8	14-0/8	7	5	Minneapolis	KS	Michael D. Patterson	1975	2006
134-7/8	21-7/8	20-7/8	21-3/8	4	4	Mercer County	NJ	Jim Vandermark	1978	2006
134-7/8	22-6/8	23-5/8	17-3/8	6	5	Cozad	NE	Randy Wilson	1978	2006
134-7/8	22-1/8	21-0/8	16-1/8	4	4	Morrison County	MN	James G. Hurrle	1980	2006
134-7/8	21-0/8	21-2/8	16-5/8	5	5	Jackson County	MO	Marvin Thomey	1981	2006
134-7/8	22-0/8	22-3/8	18-4/8	5	4	St. Marys County	MD	Samuel H. Wilson, Jr.	1981	2006

WHITETAIL DEER *(Typical Antlers)*

Minimum Score 125

(continued)

Score	Length of Main Beam R	L	Inside Spread	Number of Points R	L	Area	State/ Province	Hunter's Name	Date	Rank
134-7/8	24-4/8	23-4/8	20-4/8	4	5	St. Charles County	MO	T. J. Sorenson	1983	2006
134-7/8	21-3/8	21-1/8	14-5/8	4	4	Polk County	WI	Larry Nicholas	1983	2006
134-7/8	25-3/8	27-4/8	20-1/8	4	4	Morrow County	OH	Tony Burns	1983	2006
134-7/8	22-1/8	19-5/8	17-1/8	4	4	Cass County	ND	David Skjei	1984	2006
134-7/8	21-4/8	20-6/8	17-7/8	5	5	Bayham Township	ONT	Max Ward	1984	2006
134-7/8	21-5/8	22-5/8	18-5/8	5	5	Owen County	KY	James B Bevins	1985	2006
134-6/8	25-2/8	24-7/8	15-6/8	4	4	Newton County	IN	Charles Oliver, Sr.	1967	2023
134-6/8	20-0/8	20-0/8	16-5/8	5	6	LaFramboise Is.	SD	Dean Gretschmann	1970	2023
134-6/8	20-7/8	20-6/8	17-2/8	5	5	St. Charles	MO	James Ronquest	1979	2023
134-6/8	20-3/8	20-5/8	16-4/8	5	5	Ionia County	MI	Barry Jackson	1980	2023
134-6/8	22-6/8	22-1/8	15-4/8	8	5	Johnson County	KS	Richard J. Seidel	1980	2023
134-6/8	21-1/8	20-3/8	15-4/8	5	6	Goodhue County	MN	Dennis Wille	1981	2023
134-6/8	24-3/8	24-3/8	19-6/8	4	4	Vinton County	OH	Patrick D. Kearns	1982	2023
134-6/8	24-4/8	24-1/8	20-2/8	4	4	Johnson County	NE	Michael G. Remund	1982	2023
134-6/8	24-0/8	22-7/8	18-2/8	4	5	Dane County	WI	Daniel J. Gartner	1983	2023
134-6/8	25-6/8	25-7/8	17-3/8	6	4	Killam	ALB	Tim Colwell	1985	2023
134-5/8	20-6/8	22-4/8	18-7/8	7	6	Floyd County	IA	James K. Harris	1972	2033
134-5/8	21-4/8	22-2/8	17-1/8	5	6	Republic County	KS	Don R. Dejmal	1978	2033
134-5/8	24-1/8	24-3/8	18-1/8	5	4	Jasper County	IL	William Dowland	1979	2033
134-5/8	22-2/8	22-0/8	16-2/8	7	6	Randolph County	WV	Robert E. Nace	1979	2033
134-5/8	22-1/8	22-2/8	17-3/8	4	4	Vinton County	OH	Paul Ingram	1980	2033
134-5/8	22-2/8	21-5/8	19-6/8	5	5	Fulton County	IL	Cliff C. Conover	1982	2033
134-5/8	23-0/8	22-3/8	18-0/8	6	6	Clark County	KS	William A. Rule	1982	2033
134-5/8	24-0/8	24-4/8	15-5/8	4	5	Marion County	TN	Paul E. Worley	1983	2033
134-5/8	23-0/8	22-2/8	17-2/8	7	8	Morrison County	MN	Harold "Nook" Blank	1983	2033
134-5/8	22-0/8	22-4/8	14-5/8	5	5	Bedford County	VA	Robert Sutton	1983	2033
134-5/8	21-7/8	21-5/8	17-5/8	5	5	Russell County	AL	Jesse Waldrop	1983	2033
134-5/8	22-7/8	23-4/8	14-1/8	4	5	Brooke County	WV	Myron Rees	1983	2033
134-5/8	21-2/8	22-2/8	17-3/8	6	5	Pulaski County	KY	Glen Whitis, Jr.	1985	2033
134-5/8	19-4/8	19-0/8	18-0/8	5	5	Brown County	KS	Ray Kirk	1985	2033
134-5/8	25-7/8	23-6/8	19-1/8	6	5	Fairfield County	CT	Milan G. Bull	1985	2033
134-4/8	23-5/8	21-1/8	17-2/8	4	4	Fairbault County	MN	Sherwood F. Krosch	1969	2048
134-4/8	19-7/8	19-5/8	17-6/8	5	5	Ripley County	IN	Robert Pitt	1974	2048
134-4/8	22-2/8	21-2/8	18-6/8	5	5	Des Moines County	IA	Ron Cover	1975	2048
134-4/8	23-1/8	23-1/8	18-2/8	4	4	Carroll County	OH	Thomas E. Geibel	1978	2048
134-4/8	25-0/8	24-0/8	15-6/8	4	4	Dane County	WI	Douglas E. Seals	1980	2048
134-4/8	22-3/8	20-7/8	17-6/8	5	5	Carroll County	MD	Thomas Creech	1980	2048
134-4/8	20-7/8	20-2/8	17-6/8	5	5	Lincoln	MT	Sonny Templeton	1980	2048
134-4/8	21-6/8	21-4/8	15-2/8	4	5	Vernon County	MO	Roger Hensley	1981	2048
134-4/8	21-2/8	24-4/8	21-2/8	5	4	Wagoner County	OK	Harold Clay	1982	2048
134-4/8	24-3/8	24-2/8	16-5/8	5	5	Yell County	AR	Gary Worm	1983	2048
134-4/8	19-2/8	23-4/8	17-6/8	5	5	Somerset County	MD	Clint Kelbel	1983	2048
134-4/8	22-6/8	23-0/8	16-6/8	4	5	Chippewa County	WI	Larry Paulsen	1984	2048
134-4/8	21-2/8	24-2/8	22-0/8	4	4	Morris County	NJ	David Paddock	1984	2048
134-4/8	22-7/8	23-5/8	15-6/8	5	5	Morgan County	OH	Dean Spears	1984	2048
134-4/8	21-1/8	21-1/8	17-6/8	4	4	Monroe County	WV	Clarence J Burns	1984	2048
134-4/8	19-4/8	19-6/8	16-4/8	6	5	Kingsbury County	SD	Reginald E. Faber, Jr.	1984	2048
134-4/8	24-2/8	22-5/8	15-7/8	6	6	Hickman County	TN	Stanley Hunt	1985	2048
134-4/8	23-1/8	24-2/8	18-0/8	5	4	Marshall County	MN	Bruce Becklund	1985	2048
134-4/8	24-0/8	23-1/8	17-2/8	5	6	Clay County	IL	Myron Woomer	1985	2048
134-3/8	23-4/8	22-1/8	17-1/8	4	5	Ticheonon	AR	Louis Rush	1959	2067
134-3/8	20-5/8	20-5/8	17-3/8	5	5	Faribault	MN	Gary Roemhildt	1965	2067
134-3/8	19-0/8	20-4/8	20-5/8	5	5	Ripley	MN	Harold A. Walsh	1971	2067
134-3/8	20-5/8	20-4/8	17-1/8	5	5	Powell County	MT	Paul E. Tadlock	1972	2067
134-3/8	22-1/8	23-4/8	18-5/8	4	4	Trumansburg	NY	H. R. Swansbrough, Jr.	1977	2067
134-3/8	24-2/8	24-1/8	22-6/8	5	5	Nicollet County	MN	John Seifert	1978	2067
134-3/8	21-4/8	21-2/8	16-6/8	5	8	Phelps County	NE	Kirk Stroup	1981	2067
134-3/8	22-7/8	22-0/8	17-6/8	5	4	Pike County	IL	Dan Wombles	1981	2067
134-3/8	21-6/8	21-2/8	15-7/8	5	5	Pope County	AR	Danny Bennett	1981	2067
134-3/8	23-4/8	23-7/8	18-5/8	6	3	Morrison County	MN	Arnie Borchert	1982	2067
134-3/8	22-1/8	22-3/8	18-1/8	4	4	Texas County	OK	Curtis Clayton	1982	2067
134-3/8	22-3/8	21-2/8	19-2/8	6	5	Chippewa County	MI	Joe Johnston	1983	2067
134-3/8	23-4/8	22-4/8	18-5/8	4	4	Kingman County	KS	Ken Marsh	1984	2067

WHITETAIL DEER *(Typical Antlers)*

(continued)   Minimum Score 125

Score	Length of Main Beam R	L	Inside Spread	Number of Points R	L	Area	State/ Province	Hunter's Name	Date	Rank
134-3/8	22-7/8	22-3/8	14-4/8	6	5	Dawson County	MT	Alan H. Winkel	1984	2067
134-3/8	25-2/8	25-3/8	18-3/8	4	4	Scioto County	OH	Ed Asbury	1984	2067
134-3/8	24-5/8	24-7/8	16-0/8	5	6	Morrison County	MN	Gary Thomas	1985	2067
134-2/8	21-0/8	21-2/8	16-4/8	5	5	Benton County	IA	Larry Walker	1961	2083
134-2/8	22-2/8	21-4/8	16-0/8	5	5	Derby	IN	Jack E. Hungate	1963	2083
134-2/8	24-2/8	23-4/8	20-4/8	5	5	McLean County	IL	Norman Price, Jr.	1973	2083
134-2/8	23-4/8	22-1/8	21-0/8	5	7	Du Page County	IL	William M. Voight	1973	2083
134-2/8	22-5/8	23-2/8	16-2/8	5	4	Danbury	WI	Severin A. Wanous	1976	2083
134-2/8	24-0/8	24-4/8	17-2/8	5	5	Fond du Lac County	WI	Doug Bilgo	1978	2083
134-2/8	21-4/8	21-0/8	15-4/8	4	5	Morrison County	MN	Rodney Forbrook	1979	2083
134-2/8	22-0/8	22-0/8	18-2/8	4	5	Spink County	SD	Douglas Price	1980	2083
134-2/8	20-4/8	21-4/8	17-4/8	5	5	Muskingum County	OH	Allen R. Smith	1980	2083
134-2/8	25-0/8	25-1/8	20-4/8	8	6	Osborne County	KS	Robert Grabast	1981	2083
134-2/8	22-7/8	23-4/8	16-4/8	4	4	Reno County	KS	Monte Long	1982	2083
134-2/8	23-4/8	23-3/8	17-6/8	5	5	Johnson County	IA	Ken Sovers	1983	2083
134-2/8	22-7/8	23-4/8	21-1/8	6	6	Mclean County	ND	Rich Radke	1984	2083
134-2/8	22-4/8	23-1/8	18-0/8	4	4	Sheboygan County	WI	Randy Kolpin	1984	2083
134-2/8	20-5/8	20-0/8	18-4/8	5	5	Dodge County	MN	Chad A. Lenz	1984	2083
134-2/8	22-4/8	22-3/8	17-6/8	5	5	Monroe County	WI	Steve Heintz	1985	2083
134-2/8	22-7/8	21-7/8	18-2/8	4	5	Columbia County	WI	Brian P. Schepp	1985	2083
134-2/8	22-7/8	22-1/8	15-4/8	4	4	Edwards County	TX	Steve Payne	1985	2083
134-1/8	23-2/8	23-3/8	20-1/8	5	5	Nashville	IN	Jason Thompson	1966	2101
134-1/8	21-2/8	22-6/8	18-2/8	7	5	Hillsdale	IN	William H. Davis	1967	2101
134-1/8	24-7/8	25-4/8	21-3/8	6	5	Morrison County	MN	Vincent Pajak	1973	2101
134-1/8	24-3/8	23-6/8	20-2/8	4	5	Hopkins County	KY	James R. Williams	1978	2101
134-1/8	19-6/8	19-7/8	16-2/8	7	7	Benton County	TN	Robert Blackstock	1978	2101
134-1/8	24-6/8	22-7/8	17-3/8	5	5	Jones County	IA	Harold Erger	1979	2101
134-1/8	22-4/8	22-7/8	16-3/8	4	4	Allen County	IN	Martin C. Yager	1979	2101
134-1/8	23-0/8	21-0/8	16-3/8	4	4	Jackson County	MO	Marvin Thomey	1980	2101
134-1/8	23-4/8	22-2/8	19-1/8	5	5	Allamakee County	IA	Brian Carlson	1981	2101
134-1/8	21-1/8	19-4/8	17-3/8	5	5	Swartz Creek	MI	Richard J. Parkhurst	1982	2101
134-1/8	19-6/8	18-3/8	16-1/8	6	5	Washington County	WI	Christopher J. Dequardo	1982	2101
134-1/8	22-2/8	22-0/8	17-4/8	6	7	Wabaunsee County	KS	Gary Hunsicker	1983	2101
134-1/8	22-3/8	17-3/8	15-3/8	8	5	Crawford County	WI	Randall Nash	1985	2101
134-1/8	23-0/8	21-6/8	19-3/8	4	4	Perry County	IN	Junis S. Ingle	1985	2101
134-0/8	23-7/8	23-7/8	19-0/8	4	5	Grundy County	IL	Henry F. Blaha	1977	2115
134-0/8	23-1/8	22-6/8	15-6/8	7	6	Calhoun County	MI	James D. Warner	1979	2115
134-0/8	23-4/8	24-1/8	17-6/8	6	5	St. Joseph County	MI	Randy A. Gordon	1981	2115
134-0/8	23-6/8	22-7/8	20-4/8	5	6	Coshocton County	OH	William Randles	1981	2115
134-0/8	23-6/8	25-2/8	17-6/8	4	4	Lawrence County	OH	Robert D. Wilson	1981	2115
134-0/8	21-6/8	20-5/8	18-0/8	6	6	Nicollet County	MN	Karsten Severns	1982	2115
134-0/8	22-2/8	21-7/8	20-0/8	5	4	Eau Claire County	WI	Donald E. Moss	1983	2115
134-0/8	21-2/8	21-2/8	15-3/8	5	7	Reno County	KS	Norbert Bechtel	1983	2115
134-0/8	22-2/8	21-6/8	17-0/8	4	5	Miami County	KS	Jackie Bethel	1984	2115
134-0/8	25-0/8	24-4/8	17-3/8	4	5	Fayette County	OH	Don M. Curtin	1984	2115
134-0/8	19-5/8	20-2/8	16-6/8	6	6	Stephenson County	IL	Greg Deutsch	1984	2115
134-0/8	23-3/8	24-0/8	18-6/8	4	4	Crawford County	IL	Robert Loveall	1985	2115
134-0/8	22-1/8	22-0/8	17-4/8	4	4	Waukesha County	WI	James J. Mislang	1985	2115
133-7/8	22-7/8	23-0/8	20-5/8	6	7	Dodge County	MN	Myles Keller	1976	2128
133-7/8	19-5/8	20-2/8	15-6/8	5	6	Newton County	IN	Howard Severs	1976	2128
133-7/8	24-4/8	24-1/8	19-1/8	4	5	Harwich	MA	Randy Fisher	1977	2128
133-7/8	23-5/8	22-1/8	18-1/8	4	4	Homer	MI	Douglas Tasker	1978	2128
133-7/8	20-2/8	20-2/8	16-7/8	5	4	Wabaunsee County	KS	Charles L. Bisnette	1979	2128
133-7/8	22-1/8	21-7/8	21-1/8	4	4	Kalamazoo County	MI	Louis G. Sari	1979	2128
133-7/8	19-7/8	20-2/8	16-5/8	6	7	Cortland County	NY	John S. Cutler	1982	2128
133-7/8	20-4/8	19-6/8	14-5/8	5	6	Hennepin County	MN	Robert Boynton	1982	2128
133-7/8	23-1/8	23-3/8	16-1/8	5	4	Knox County	IL	Dave Emken	1982	2128
133-7/8	19-6/8	20-2/8	17-1/8	5	5	Wood County	WI	David J. Rademan	1983	2128
133-7/8	20-4/8	20-1/8	17-6/8	6	5	Darke County	OH	Richard D. Baird	1983	2128
133-7/8	22-3/8	22-1/8	18-5/8	4	5	Washington County	KS	Bill R. Mallean	1983	2128
133-7/8	20-2/8	19-3/8	15-6/8	5	6	Brookings County	SD	William Gibbons	1983	2128
133-7/8	24-6/8	25-5/8	18-3/8	4	4	Guernsey County	OH	Don Cady	1984	2128
133-7/8	22-3/8	22-0/8	16-6/8	5	5	Brown County	IN	Ronald L. Gish	1984	2128

WHITETAIL DEER *(Typical Antlers)*

Minimum Score 125

Score	Length of Main Beam R	L	Inside Spread	Number of Points R	L	Area	State/ Province	Hunter's Name	Date	Rank
133-7/8	22-1/8	21-4/8	19-5/8	5	5	Morrow County	OH	Mark D. Mann	1984	2128
133-7/8	22-7/8	24-4/8	17-1/8	4	4	Jefferson County	WI	Gilbert Krueger	1985	2128
133-7/8	22-3/8	23-3/8	23-3/8	5	5	Green County	WI	Jeffrey D. Miller	1985	2128
133-7/8	22-7/8	23-3/8	17-4/8	5	4	Hardin County	KY	Phillip Crady	1985	2128
133-6/8	22-6/8	24-7/8	17-2/8	5	4	Iowa River	IA	Chad Sivertsen	1971	2147
133-6/8	19-6/8	20-1/8	15-2/8	5	5	Ft. Pierre	SD	Rick Ray	1972	2147
133-6/8	24-2/8	25-2/8	19-7/8	4	6	McPherson County	KS	Mike Chambers	1975	2147
133-6/8	22-5/8	21-5/8	17-4/8	4	4	St. Mary's	MD	Marvin T. Breeden	1979	2147
133-6/8	22-4/8	22-4/8	17-1/8	6	5	Shawnee County	KS	Frank J. Delci, Jr.	1984	2147
133-6/8	24-2/8	22-7/8	17-4/8	4	4	Rock County	WI	Gary Johnson	1985	2147
133-6/8	23-0/8	23-6/8	18-6/8	4	4	Bon Homme County	SD	David B. Cull	1985	2147
133-5/8	23-3/8	23-2/8	17-1/8	4	4	Tripp County	SD	Larry Diehm	1965	2154
133-5/8	19-6/8	19-4/8	16-5/8	5	5	Brookings	SD	Rodney Foster	1967	2154
133-5/8	26-6/8	25-7/8	19-3/8	3	4	Mankato	MN	Dean Como	1973	2154
133-5/8	21-6/8	21-7/8	17-2/8	5	6	Hastings	MN	Leonard Ellingson	1979	2154
133-5/8	21-6/8	22-2/8	17-3/8	4	4	Republic County	KS	Curtis Klima	1979	2154
133-5/8	21-0/8	21-4/8	16-7/8	4	4	Norton County	KS	Robbie L. Madden	1980	2154
133-5/8	24-1/8	24-7/8	19-5/8	4	4	Shelby County	IL	Walter Lash	1981	2154
133-5/8	24-2/8	23-0/8	17-6/8	4	5	Lincoln County	SD	Robert Souter	1981	2154
133-5/8	20-5/8	21-5/8	17-1/8	5	5	Trout Creek	MT	Justin Hoy	1981	2154
133-5/8	22-4/8	25-6/8	17-7/8	4	5	Dickinson County	IA	Rod M. Sheldon	1981	2154
133-5/8	22-5/8	22-2/8	16-5/8	5	6	Pittsburgh County	OK	William A. Willis	1983	2154
133-5/8	22-6/8	24-4/8	19-1/8	5	4	Struthcona	ALB	David Rose	1983	2154
133-5/8	23-2/8	23-6/8	17-4/8	5	4	Winona County	MN	Dean K. Reidt	1984	2154
133-5/8	23-3/8	24-1/8	19-7/8	5	4	St. Joseph County	MI	Timothy A. Balk	1984	2154
133-5/8	21-4/8	23-1/8	17-5/8	5	5	Buffalo County	WI	Paul M Baures	1985	2154
133-4/8	22-2/8	22-0/8	17-2/8	5	5	Burleigh County	ND	Lyle F. Fischer	1956	2169
133-4/8	23-5/8	23-1/8	19-5/8	4	4	Desota Bend	NE	John Johnson	1958	2169
133-4/8	22-7/8	23-2/8	16-5/8	5	4	Hocking	OH	Ted Schultz	1974	2169
133-4/8	19-5/8	19-3/8	15-0/8	5	5	Tewauken	ND	Frank Pfeifer	1975	2169
133-4/8	24-0/8	23-2/8	19-2/8	5	5	Charlotte County	VA	George A. Orme, Sr.	1976	2169
133-4/8	22-3/8	22-6/8	17-0/8	4	4	Edmonton	ALB	Wilf Hunter	1978	2169
133-4/8	20-3/8	21-5/8	16-0/8	4	5	Ft. Pierre	SD	Patrick Hoing	1979	2169
133-4/8	21-0/8	21-0/8	18-6/8	4	4	Jefferson County	WI	Larry Pohlman	1979	2169
133-4/8	24-7/8	23-5/8	19-1/8	6	8	Pittsburg County	OK	Dwayne Durant	1981	2169
133-4/8	23-7/8	24-6/8	18-6/8	4	4	Green Lake County	WI	Dan Walker	1982	2169
133-4/8	21-1/8	20-7/8	16-5/8	5	7	Waupaca County	WI	Randy Hillskotter	1982	2169
133-4/8	20-7/8	19-5/8	16-4/8	4	5	Portage County	WI	Tom Doyle	1983	2169
133-4/8	25-5/8	24-2/8	19-2/8	5	4	Blackhawk County	IA	Jim Lee	1983	2169
133-4/8	23-3/8	23-6/8	18-3/8	6	5	St. Croix County	WI	Tod Sturgul	1985	2169
133-4/8	21-4/8	20-4/8	16-4/8	6	6	Marshall County	KS	Brian McNulty	1985	2169
133-4/8	22-5/8	23-4/8	14-6/8	5	5	Dodge County	MN	Jimmie Hanna	1985	2169
133-4/8	23-3/8	22-2/8	20-2/8	4	4	Morris County	NJ	Gary Schmitz	1986	2169
133-3/8	21-0/8	21-2/8	19-6/8	5	4	Watonwan County	MN	Issac Davis	1962	2186
133-3/8	24-7/8	24-1/8	23-1/8	6	6	Morrison County	MN	Frank Salisbury	1963	2186
133-3/8	22-6/8	24-0/8	18-0/8	5	5	Dickinson County	IA	Keith F. Ellis	1973	2186
133-3/8	21-0/8	21-3/8	17-1/8	6	6	Juneau County	WI	James M. Carriveau	1977	2186
133-3/8	20-2/8	20-0/8	12-3/8	5	5	McAlester	OK	Richard Gill	1977	2186
133-3/8	19-4/8	20-0/8	15-1/8	5	5	Arkansas County	AR	Dennis Chapman	1980	2186
133-3/8	22-0/8	22-1/8	16-1/8	4	7	Stearns County	MN	Kevin Sabrowsky	1981	2186
133-3/8	23-5/8	22-3/8	16-7/8	4	4	McHenry County	IL	Randy Lehr	1984	2186
133-3/8	21-3/8	20-7/8	16-5/8	6	4	Perry County	MO	Dale Korando	1985	2186
133-3/8	21-6/8	21-6/8	17-5/8	5	5	Winona County	MN	Jim Reidt	1986	2186
133-2/8	23-6/8	22-5/8	18-2/8	8	8	Olmstead County	MN	Roger E. Enderson	1961	2196
133-2/8	24-2/8	23-6/8	18-5/8	4	4	Pittsburg County	OK	Fred Parkison	1968	2196
133-2/8	21-1/8	20-7/8	18-2/8	5	5	Wabasha County	MN	Myles Keller	1977	2196
133-2/8	22-1/8	22-5/8	16-0/8	8	7	Lafayette County	WI	Dave Carey	1979	2196
133-2/8	19-0/8	19-1/8	16-4/8	5	5	Wild Rose	WI	Kenneth A. Wollermann	1979	2196
133-2/8	21-2/8	22-1/8	13-1/8	5	7	Portage County	WI	Alan Carter	1981	2196
133-2/8	20-2/8	20-3/8	15-0/8	5	5	St. Louis County	MN	Greg Opland	1981	2196
133-2/8	24-7/8	24-6/8	20-2/8	4	3	Davis County	IA	Richard Squire	1981	2196
133-2/8	20-4/8	20-4/8	20-0/8	4	5	Nobel County	OH	Elroy Kuhner	1982	2196
133-2/8	24-1/8	23-2/8	17-0/8	6	7	Kingsbury County	SD	Stanley A. Rauch	1982	2196

WHITETAIL DEER *(Typical Antlers)*

(continued)   Minimum Score 125

Score	Length of Main Beam R	L	Inside Spread	Number of Points R	L	Area	State/ Province	Hunter's Name	Date	Rank
133-2/8	23-7/8	24-0/8	18-4/8	4	5	Shelby County	IL	Charles Martin, Jr.	1983	2196
133-2/8	22-7/8	22-5/8	18-1/8	5	6	Harper County	KS	Steven R. Lowe	1983	2196
133-2/8	23-4/8	25-4/8	19-1/8	6	6	Ford County	KS	Melvin Habiger	1983	2196
133-2/8	23-3/8	23-2/8	20-6/8	4	4	Union County	IL	Brad Harris	1984	2196
133-2/8	20-0/8	20-5/8	14-2/8	5	5	Madison County	AL	Tony Robinson	1985	2196
133-1/8	22-2/8	21-5/8	16-1/8	4	4	Roberts County	SD	Roland L. Hausmann	1964	2211
133-1/8	24-5/8	23-7/8	20-1/8	4	4	Perry County	IL	Ron Lay	1974	2211
133-1/8	20-725	20-725	17-2/8	6	6	Cowley County	KS	Dr. Phil L. Bradley	1975	2211
133-1/8	23-2/8	25-2/8	16-3/8	5	5	Carver Rapids	MN	George R. Arimond	1976	2211
133-1/8	26-0/8	26-3/8	19-6/8	5	5	Sharon	CT	Phillip M. Demetri	1976	2211
133-1/8	20-1/8	20-7/8	16-1/8	5	5	Bloomington	IN	Jeffrey S. Finley	1977	2211
133-1/8	22-2/8	22-6/8	17-1/8	5	5	Rome	WI	Dennis E. Dabel	1978	2211
133-1/8	21-6/8	22-6/8	16-5/8	5	6	Hocking County	OH	Ted Schultz	1978	2211
133-1/8	22-3/8	21-6/8	18-7/8	5	5	Muskegon County	OH	Randy Whitehair	1978	2211
133-1/8	23-5/8	23-7/8	16-1/8	4	4	Pike County	MO	Jim Holdenried	1979	2211
133-1/8	23-5/8	23-0/8	15-7/8	4	5	Sauk County	WI	Keith Peetz	1980	2211
133-1/8	20-4/8	21-6/8	16-1/8	4	4	Bullitt County	KY	Dwight Hughes	1981	2211
133-1/8	21-3/8	21-5/8	17-1/8	6	6	Marion County	IL	Paul Duncan	1981	2211
133-1/8	23-6/8	22-6/8	17-7/8	4	5	Morgan County	OH	Milan W. Boone	1981	2211
133-1/8	21-3/8	20-5/8	15-3/8	5	5	Calvert County	MD	Al Sullivan	1982	2211
133-1/8	22-2/8	22-4/8	17-7/8	4	4	Oakland County	MI	Gordon E. Bowser	1982	2211
133-1/8	21-7/8	24-3/8	22-3/8	4	4	Geary County	KS	Mark Junghans	1982	2211
133-1/8	22-4/8	25-4/8	21-1/8	4	5	Green County	WI	James K. Campbell	1984	2211
133-1/8	21-6/8	23-6/8	18-1/8	5	6	Cascade County	MT	Tom Storm	1984	2211
133-1/8	21-4/8	21-3/8	16-5/8	5	5	Leavenworth County	KS	John Garrison	1985	2211
133-0/8	22-2/8	21-3/8	16-4/8	4	4	Luce County	MI	Rondell Bisbee	1953	2231
133-0/8	19-0/8	19-3/8	16-6/8	5	5	Lake Thompson	SD	Arnold Aulner	1970	2231
133-0/8	20-7/8	21-0/8	17-4/8	5	5	New Milford	CT	Dan Ferrara, Jr.	1976	2231
133-0/8	21-0/8	20-7/8	17-4/8	5	5	Far Hill	NJ	Dennis Bailey	1977	2231
133-0/8	22-2/8	21-0/8	18-6/8	4	5	Jackson County	MI	Randy Childs	1977	2231
133-0/8	23-5/8	22-1/8	17-4/8	5	6	Macon County	IL	Frank B. Graham	1977	2231
133-0/8	23-3/8	23-1/8	19-4/8	5	7	Dawson County	MT	Bryant Shurtliff	1977	2231
133-0/8	24-5/8	24-2/8	19-2/8	5	6	Huntingdon County	PA	John A. Williams	1978	2231
133-0/8	23-2/8	22-6/8	18-4/8	4	4	Dane County	WI	Dean Cooper	1981	2231
133-0/8	22-2/8	21-7/8	16-4/8	4	5	Geary County	KS	Mike Ehlebracht	1981	2231
133-0/8	20-6/8	20-2/8	16-6/8	6	5	Burleigh County	ND	Donald Magstadt	1981	2231
133-0/8	21-1/8	21-3/8	15-4/8	5	5	Montgomery County	MS	Harold L. Tutor	1981	2231
133-0/8	22-7/8	22-6/8	15-6/8	4	5	Polk County	IA	Jeff Greider	1982	2231
133-0/8	22-2/8	22-6/8	16-4/8	4	4	Jefferson County	OH	Edward D. Whitmore	1983	2231
133-0/8	24-4/8	24-0/8	18-7/8	6	4	Pepin County	WI	Gerald Berg	1984	2231
132-7/8	21-0/8	21-0/8	15-3/8	5	7	Jefferson County	IN	Jerome Sexton	1962	2246
132-7/8	20-0/8	18-6/8	15-5/8	5	6	Wilson County	KS	Warren Townsend	1970	2246
132-7/8	24-4/8	20-6/8	20-2/8	7	7	Sandstone	MN	Bob Sandwick	1973	2246
132-7/8	21-3/8	22-0/8	18-1/8	5	5	St. Croix County	WI	Randy St. Ores	1978	2246
132-7/8	20-4/8	21-3/8	16-1/8	5	6	Wagoner	OK	Sonny Charboneau	1978	2246
132-7/8	20-3/8	21-0/8	14-5/8	5	5	Gallia County	OH	Gail C. Snyder	1980	2246
132-7/8	21-2/8	21-4/8	16-3/8	6	6	Martin County	MN	James Zanke	1982	2246
132-7/8	20-7/8	21-2/8	14-7/8	5	5	Warren County	MS	Ray Bufkin	1983	2246
132-7/8	21-4/8	21-3/8	14-7/8	5	5	Anoka County	MN	John Cardinal	1983	2246
132-7/8	21-2/8	22-6/8	17-5/8	4	4	Riley County	KS	Mike Huff	1983	2246
132-7/8	23-4/8	23-2/8	17-3/8	5	5	Cherokee County	KS	Samuel F. Lancaster	1983	2246
132-7/8	21-4/8	21-4/8	17-4/8	6	6	Sawyer County	WI	Ronald Lee Fischer	1983	2246
132-7/8	24-3/8	22-6/8	14-1/8	5	4	Butler County	KS	David R. Rogers	1984	2246
132-7/8	19-4/8	21-0/8	18-0/8	7	6	Alexandar County	IL	Daniel Boyd	1985	2246
132-7/8	20-2/8	20-3/8	17-7/8	5	6	Cowley County	KS	David M. Ross	1985	2246
132-6/8	23-0/8	23-4/8	20-0/8	4	4	Summit County	OH	Dana C. Feather	1960	2261
132-6/8	21-0/8	20-1/8	16-4/8	5	5	Pocomoke State Forest	MD	Clifford A. Denney	1972	2261
132-6/8	22-3/8	23-0/8	14-6/8	5	5	Jackson County	OH	Robert C. McGuire	1976	2261
132-6/8	19-7/8	22-7/8	17-4/8	6	6	Union County	IL	Fred W. Achilles	1978	2261
132-6/8	22-0/8	22-0/8	19-4/8	5	4	Waterloo County	ONT	Jim Scoggins	1979	2261
132-6/8	22-2/8	22-0/8	14-6/8	4	5	Lancaster County	PA	Albert A. Swider	1980	2261
132-6/8	21-2/8	23-1/8	20-6/8	7	6	Loup County	NE	Syl Glos	1981	2261
132-6/8	21-3/8	21-1/8	17-4/8	4	4	Clinton County	IA	Kent Hoffmann	1982	2261

WHITETAIL DEER *(Typical Antlers)*

Minimum Score 125

(continued)

Score	Length of Main Beam R	Length of Main Beam L	Inside Spread	Number of Points R	Number of Points L	Area	State/ Province	Hunter's Name	Date	Rank
132-6/8	20-4/8	21-5/8	26-2/8	4	6	Suffolk County	NY	Glenn L. Neuschwender	1982	2261
132-6/8	19-6/8	20-2/8	16-0/8	5	5	Butler County	KS	Mark Scott	1983	2261
132-6/8	21-7/8	22-4/8	17-0/8	4	4	Dawes County	NE	Darrell A. Bendel	1984	2261
132-6/8	24-7/8	23-6/8	17-4/8	4	7	Carroll County	MO	Joe D. Earnest	1984	2261
132-6/8	20-2/8	22-2/8	19-2/8	5	4	Buffalo County	WI	Michael L Gates	1984	2261
132-6/8	20-7/8	20-7/8	18-0/8	5	5	Cherry County	NE	Russell Burge	1984	2261
132-6/8	21-7/8	21-6/8	16-6/8	5	5	Linn County	IA	Jon Klein	1985	2261
132-6/8	19-7/8	19-1/8	16-2/8	5	5	Mason County	TX	Thomas Joseph Hicks	1986	2261
132-5/8	23-3/8	24-4/8	21-5/8	4	6	Tazewell County	IL	Don Lounsberry	1964	2277
132-5/8	21-1/8	21-0/8	16-3/8	5	5	Irion County	TX	James E. Fox III	1977	2277
132-5/8	23-1/8	22-5/8	18-5/8	4	5	Freehold	NJ	William Rusznak	1979	2277
132-5/8	19-4/8	20-0/8	16-1/8	6	6	Brookings County	SD	Timothy Modde	1981	2277
132-5/8	23-4/8	24-1/8	18-1/8	4	4	Clearwater County	ID	Bob Proctor	1981	2277
132-5/8	22-3/8	22-7/8	17-5/8	5	5	Furnas County	NE	Doug Huxoll	1982	2277
132-5/8	20-4/8	20-0/8	16-1/8	5	5	West Baton Rouge Parrish	LA	Jim Thibodeaux	1984	2277
132-5/8	21-5/8	21-2/8	17-1/8	5	5	Genessee County	MI	Jack Iman	1984	2277
132-5/8	19-7/8	20-4/8	16-1/8	5	6	Morrison County	MN	John A. Pennoyer	1985	2277
132-5/8	20-5/8	21-3/8	18-2/8	6	7	Buffalo County	WI	Glen Axness	1985	2277
132-5/8	21-3/8	20-5/8	16-6/8	6	5	Goodhue County	MN	John "Jack" Cordes	1985	2277
132-5/8	20-4/8	20-2/8	15-7/8	5	4	Iowa County	WI	Bill Snelgrove	1985	2277
132-5/8	20-0/8	19-6/8	14-7/8	5	5	Goshen County	WY	Doug Starks	1986	2277
132-4/8	23-4/8	23-0/8	16-3/8	6	5	Jackson County	WI	Howard Knockel	1957	2290
132-4/8	25-4/8	26-0/8	21-0/8	4	4	Valley County	MT	Clare F. Mates	1961	2290
132-4/8	21-5/8	21-7/8	15-6/8	4	4	Iowa County	IA	Mel Berstler	1965	2290
132-4/8	21-6/8	21-6/8	16-0/8	5	5	Arkansas City	KS	William L. Walker	1965	2290
132-4/8	23-2/8	24-2/8	18-0/8	5	6	Morrison County	MN	Jerry James	1971	2290
132-4/8	25-1/8	24-5/8	16-6/8	5	6	Springfield	ME	William R. Dengate	1972	2290
132-4/8	24-6/8	23-7/8	18-3/8	5	5	Carbon County	PA	Frank Jackson	1972	2290
132-4/8	23-2/8	23-1/8	15-2/8	5	5	Giles County	VA	Donald Lee Francis	1979	2290
132-4/8	21-7/8	21-4/8	16-2/8	6	6	Spencer	NY	Floyd Bowman, Jr.	1981	2290
132-4/8	23-2/8	22-0/8	17-6/8	4	5	Medicine Hat	ALB	Warren McInenly	1981	2290
132-4/8	26-0/8	26-6/8	16-6/8	6	6	Lake County	IL	Gary S. Rogers	1981	2290
132-4/8	23-0/8	25-0/8	14-0/8	4	4	Lamar County	GA	David Brown	1982	2290
132-4/8	19-3/8	18-5/8	16-2/8	5	5	Tuscola County	MI	Stanley N. Visniski	1982	2290
132-4/8	20-0/8	20-3/8	17-4/8	4	4	Lyon County	MN	Bruce Londgren	1983	2290
132-4/8	20-6/8	21-1/8	14-2/8	4	4	Live Oak County	TX	Rick Hayley	1983	2290
132-4/8	22-3/8	22-2/8	17-0/8	4	4	Washington County	MD	Ronald D. Shank	1985	2290
132-4/8	20-7/8	21-1/8	14-0/8	5	5	Iowa County	WI	Don Caron	1985	2290
132-4/8	22-1/8	21-6/8	16-6/8	5	6	Columbia County	WI	Wayne Woodstock	1985	2290
132-3/8	20-5/8	20-6/8	14-3/8	4	4	Buffalo County	NE	Al Dawson	1961	2308
132-3/8	21-2/8	21-0/8	14-5/8	4	4	St. Joseph County	IN	Harry Ramsbey, Jr.	1963	2308
132-3/8	22-0/8	21-2/8	17-4/8	4	4	Morrison County	MN	Jay J. Jost	1968	2308
132-3/8	21-6/8	22-6/8	18-7/8	5	6	Spink County	SD	Roger Michels	1968	2308
132-3/8	22-6/8	21-7/8	15-3/8	4	4	Shawano County	WI	Gene M. Waite	1971	2308
132-3/8	22-7/8	22-2/8	17-5/8	4	4	Sarpy County	NE	Doug Bowen	1974	2308
132-3/8	25-4/8	24-3/8	19-3/8	7	7	Davis County	IA	Tommy Thompson	1975	2308
132-3/8	22-0/8	21-7/8	15-5/8	5	4	Pine County	MN	Galen Miller	1982	2308
132-3/8	25-3/8	25-1/8	19-2/8	8	5	Fulton County	IL	Ray Brown	1982	2308
132-3/8	21-4/8	21-2/8	13-6/8	5	5	Otter Tail County	MN	Kelly Shannon	1985	2308
132-3/8	22-4/8	22-4/8	18-6/8	5	4	Kent County	MD	Michael A. Snyder	1985	2308
132-2/8	22-1/8	21-7/8	16-6/8	5	4	Waupaca County	WI	Al Wiltzius	1949	2319
132-2/8	21-7/8	23-2/8	16-6/8	5	8	Cherokee County	IA	Darrell Magnussen	1962	2319
132-2/8	22-0/8	22-4/8	19-2/8	4	4	Shepherdsville	KY	Dell Pack	1962	2319
132-2/8	21-4/8	23-5/8	20-4/8	4	5	Sisseton	SD	Clayton Forrette	1967	2319
132-2/8	24-6/8	25-2/8	23-4/8	3	3	Stoddard County	MO	Ted Denkins	1971	2319
132-2/8	21-3/8	21-7/8	16-4/8	4	4	Westmoreland County	PA	Robert C. Kichner	1971	2319
132-2/8	24-3/8	23-6/8	17-4/8	4	4	Easton	MD	Walter Krom	1976	2319
132-2/8	23-2/8	21-6/8	16-5/8	5	6	Clinton County	IL	James D. Rueter	1980	2319
132-2/8	21-0/8	20-6/8	17-6/8	5	6	Perry County	IL	Bob Clark	1981	2319
132-2/8	24-1/8	23-1/8	18-0/8	7	5	Brown County	SD	Jack Ness	1981	2319
132-2/8	21-5/8	22-5/8	16-1/8	6	5	Adams County	WI	David J. Niesen	1982	2319
132-2/8	22-1/8	21-6/8	19-2/8	4	4	Carroll County	IL	Jeffrey Mathew	1983	2319
132-2/8	23-6/8	22-0/8	15-1/8	4	5	Polk County	TX	James K. Hignett	1984	2319

WHITETAIL DEER *(Typical Antlers)*

(continued)

Score	Length of Main Beam R	Length of Main Beam L	Inside Spread	Number of Points R	Number of Points L	Area	State/ Province	Hunter's Name	Date	Rank
132-2/8	22-6/8	23-4/8	17-1/8	4	5	Phillips County	KS	Rick Chapin	1984	2319
132-2/8	21-7/8	22-5/8	18-2/8	5	4	Montgomery County	PA	Ted Sherk	1985	2319
132-2/8	22-5/8	22-3/8	16-6/8	4	4	Champaign County	OH	Gene Watson	1986	2319
132-1/8	18-1/8	19-7/8	18-3/8	5	5	Elm Creek	NE	Bill Orsborn	1962	2335
132-1/8	20-3/8	20-0/8	17-1/8	5	5	Rice County	KS	Robert Lagree	1967	2335
132-1/8	20-2/8	20-0/8	16-1/8	5	5	Mountain Home County	TX	Randolph Coleman	1972	2335
132-1/8	22-4/8	24-1/8	16-3/8	4	5	Jasper County	IA	Paul Casper	1972	2335
132-1/8	21-6/8	22-0/8	15-3/8	5	5	Pittsburg County	OK	Joe Admire	1975	2335
132-1/8	21-5/8	21-5/8	17-7/8	5	6	Freeborn County	MN	Jerry Christenson	1977	2335
132-1/8	20-5/8	20-2/8	16-5/8	6	5	Olmsted County	MN	Jerry V. Finley	1981	2335
132-1/8	22-1/8	21-4/8	16-0/8	5	4	Black Hawk County	IA	Larry Graham	1981	2335
132-1/8	19-6/8	20-0/8	16-4/8	6	5	Pepin County	WI	Terry A. G. Moline	1981	2335
132-1/8	21-0/8	21-1/8	13-3/8	4	4	Cowley County	KS	Bill E. Wilson	1981	2335
132-1/8	21-5/8	21-5/8	16-7/8	4	4	Mills County	TX	Tony Thomas	1982	2335
132-1/8	22-0/8	20-7/8	15-5/8	5	5	Eau Claire County	WI	Thomas R. Budik	1982	2335
132-1/8	24-1/8	24-1/8	18-7/8	4	4	Dunn County	WI	Richard O'Mara	1983	2335
132-1/8	22-2/8	22-7/8	15-5/8	4	4	Walworth County	WI	Gifford Hisel	1984	2335
132-1/8	22-5/8	24-4/8	17-7/8	4	5	McLean County	KY	Earl Smith	1985	2335
132-1/8	23-3/8	23-4/8	19-0/8	5	4	Carroll County	MD	Herbert Eyler	1985	2335
132-0/8	21-4/8	21-2/8	18-2/8	4	4	Juneau County	WI	Arthur Witz	1966	2351
132-0/8	22-5/8	22-2/8	18-6/8	5	5	Iowa County	IA	Larry King	1967	2351
132-0/8	21-6/8	22-4/8	17-0/8	4	4	Orleans	NE	Edward H. Backes	1969	2351
132-0/8	20-0/8	20-5/8	14-6/8	4	4	Pittsburg County	OK	Fred Parkison	1969	2351
132-0/8	21-4/8	21-1/8	16-4/8	6	5	Dunn County	WI	John R. Bilderback	1970	2351
132-0/8	20-2/8	20-7/8	13-7/8	6	5	Burleigh County	ND	Scott Lang	1976	2351
132-0/8	23-4/8	23-5/8	16-6/8	5	4	Wabasha County	MN	Myles Keller	1978	2351
132-0/8	21-6/8	22-1/8	15-3/8	5	5	Monroe County	NY	Tyler D. Smith	1978	2351
132-0/8	20-6/8	21-3/8	18-5/8	5	5	Cambridge	ONT	Fred Law	1979	2351
132-0/8	20-2/8	20-6/8	16-2/8	5	6	Pope County	MN	Wayne Charles	1980	2351
132-0/8	21-4/8	21-1/8	15-6/8	5	4	Redwood County	MN	June E. Gilb	1980	2351
132-0/8	23-2/8	22-6/8	23-7/8	4	5	Burnett County	WI	James Larrabee	1980	2351
132-0/8	20-0/8	21-6/8	14-0/8	5	5	Polk County	IA	Glenn D. Vondra	1980	2351
132-0/8	21-6/8	22-0/8	20-4/8	4	4	Lee County	IA	Randy Waschkat	1983	2351
132-0/8	23-6/8	22-7/8	17-0/8	5	5	Dubuque County	IA	Richard P. Munz	1983	2351
132-0/8	21-4/8	20-1/8	15-4/8	5	5	Shelby County	IL	Joe Thompson	1984	2351
132-0/8	21-6/8	21-2/8	18-0/8	5	5	Buffalo County	WI	Robert L. Kampen	1984	2351
132-0/8	21-6/8	22-3/8	20-6/8	5	5	Buffalo County	WI	Rex Secrist	1984	2351
132-0/8	21-5/8	22-4/8	17-0/8	4	4	Winnebago County	IL	Glenn A. Johnson	1984	2351
132-0/8	23-4/8	24-399	17-2/8	4	5	Scott County	IA	Bob Hankins	1985	2351
131-7/8	22-0/8	22-7/8	22-2/8	6	4	Nerstand	MN	James Jarvis	1964	2371
131-7/8	22-0/8	23-1/8	15-1/8	4	5	Trempealeau County	WI	Clark Gallup	1967	2371
131-7/8	21-1/8	22-1/8	17-5/8	4	4	Brown County	SD	Barry Smith	1967	2371
131-7/8	20-3/8	20-6/8	14-6/8	6	6	Adams County	IL	David E. DeMoss	1970	2371
131-7/8	22-2/8	21-1/8	20-5/8	4	5	Milton	WI	Richard W. Pieterek	1972	2371
131-7/8	21-3/8	20-4/8	15-7/8	6	5	Fulton County	AR	Larry Luther	1977	2371
131-7/8	21-0/8	20-3/8	16-7/8	4	4	Washington County	KS	Bill R. Mallean	1977	2371
131-7/8	21-3/8	21-2/8	19-7/8	5	4	Washtenaw County	MI	Philip J. Maly	1980	2371
131-7/8	23-5/8	25-3/8	19-1/8	4	4	Logan County	OH	Thomas R. Weaver	1980	2371
131-7/8	21-7/8	21-6/8	15-5/8	4	4	Russell County	KS	Joe Schulte	1982	2371
131-7/8	21-3/8	21-5/8	17-1/8	4	4	Will County	IL	Mike Sheehan	1984	2371
131-7/8	21-7/8	20-6/8	17-1/8	4	4	Lincoln County	KS	Robert Chitty	1985	2371
131-7/8	22-3/8	20-6/8	16-1/8	5	5	Putnam County	OH	Randy Schroeder	1985	2371
131-7/8	19-6/8	20-5/8	15-1/8	5	5	Knox County	OH	Tom Bowman	1985	2371
131-7/8	24-1/8	25-4/8	20-3/8	4	4	Westchester County	NY	Roger Jensen	1985	2371
131-7/8	22-1/8	23-2/8	15-3/8	4	4	Garden County	NE	Reggie Spiegelberg	1985	2371
131-6/8	19-0/8	18-6/8	13-6/8	6	6	Norton	KS	Harold Fisher	1966	2387
131-6/8	22-2/8	21-0/8	18-0/8	5	6	Kalamazoo County	MI	Richard Hettinga	1978	2387
131-6/8	23-2/8	22-3/8	17-6/8	4	4	Randolph County	IL	Kevin Lucht	1981	2387
131-6/8	20-1/8	19-2/8	15-6/8	5	5	Marquette County	WI	Steven McReath	1981	2387
131-6/8	21-4/8	21-1/8	18-6/8	4	4	Hunterdon County	NJ	Chris Jensen	1982	2387
131-6/8	21-3/8	22-7/8	18-0/8	4	5	Walworth County	WI	Mike Jacobs	1983	2387
131-6/8	19-3/8	21-0/8	18-0/8	10	8	Roscommon County	MI	David Lacey	1984	2387
131-6/8	23-4/8	24-2/8	16-6/8	4	4	Saline County	NE	C. Michael Morrow	1984	2387

WHITETAIL DEER *(Typical Antlers)*

Minimum Score 125

Score	Length of Main Beam R	L	Inside Spread	Number of Points R	L	Area	State/ Province	Hunter's Name	Date	Rank
131-6/8	24-0/8	24-1/8	17-6/8	4	5	Sawyer County	WI	Bob Swenson	1985	2387
131-5/8	21-4/8	22-1/8	18-5/8	4	4	Forest County	WI	Max Wisnefske	1950	2396
131-5/8	19-7/8	19-7/8	12-3/8	5	5	Jefferson County	IN	Ted Taylor	1959	2396
131-5/8	23-4/8	22-5/8	14-1/8	4	5	Ottertail County	MN	Gordon Swenson	1964	2396
131-5/8	22-4/8	21-6/8	16-1/8	5	5	Hale County	AL	Bo Bonds	1976	2396
131-5/8	23-4/8	25-0/8	18-4/8	5	5	Carroll County	OH	Charles B. Platt	1977	2396
131-5/8	21-7/8	22-2/8	16-3/8	5	5	Washington County	WI	Steven L. Hoelz	1980	2396
131-5/8	23-4/8	24-0/8	19-3/8	5	5	Marquette County	WI	Bryan Anderson	1982	2396
131-5/8	23-7/8	22-4/8	16-7/8	6	7	Allen County	KS	Larry Robertson	1983	2396
131-5/8	23-1/8	21-7/8	18-2/8	5	6	Kandiohoi County	MN	Mike Dallman	1983	2396
131-5/8	19-5/8	20-2/8	17-3/8	5	5	Jefferson County	WI	Donald L. Zubke	1983	2396
131-5/8	22-0/8	20-5/8	18-7/8	4	4	Gratiot County	MI	Robert Allen Mallory	1984	2396
131-5/8	20-4/8	19-2/8	15-1/8	5	7	Miller County	MO	John Ash	1985	2396
131-5/8	24-3/8	23-3/8	20-0/8	5	8	Lake County	IL	Robert Norman Tropple	1985	2396
131-5/8	25-1/8	25-2/8	16-7/8	4	4	Chatham County	NC	Jimmy Womble	1986	2396
131-4/8	20-4/8	20-1/8	17-2/8	5	5	Benton County	IA	Wayne Keefer	1956	2410
131-4/8	21-2/8	21-7/8	16-2/8	5	5	Johnson County	IN	James E. Thompson	1962	2410
131-4/8	20-2/8	22-1/8	14-2/8	5	5	Fifield	WI	Frank W. Taylor	1964	2410
131-4/8	21-3/8	21-2/8	16-0/8	7	5	Rosholt	SD	Martin Carlson	1966	2410
131-4/8	23-1/8	21-5/8	17-4/8	5	4	Calvert County	MD	William L. Neal	1970	2410
131-4/8	20-7/8	22-5/8	18-3/8	5	5	Allamakee County	IA	Dayton Jones	1971	2410
131-4/8	19-2/8	19-2/8	15-2/8	5	5	Sheboygan County	WI	Donald P. Feidmann	1974	2410
131-4/8	23-3/8	23-4/8	16-4/8	4	4	Clinton County	IA	Gary Olson	1975	2410
131-4/8	21-2/8	21-5/8	15-0/8	5	5	Newton County	IN	Ronnie Styck	1976	2410
131-4/8	22-3/8	22-1/8	19-6/8	5	5	Ft. Belvoir	VA	Dickie R. Powell	1979	2410
131-4/8	21-2/8	21-5/8	15-0/8	5	5	Ward County	ND	Richard Huber	1980	2410
131-4/8	24-2/8	22-6/8	16-6/8	4	4	Shelby County	OH	Wayne L. Goubeaux	1981	2410
131-4/8	21-7/8	21-6/8	15-6/8	4	5	Christin County	IL	Dale W. Simmons	1982	2410
131-4/8	21-6/8	21-1/8	16-6/8	5	4	Clay County	KS	Doug Adams	1982	2410
131-4/8	21-6/8	21-0/8	15-2/8	5	5	Dawson County	MT	James C. Slaska	1984	2410
131-4/8	23-3/8	23-6/8	19-5/8	7	5	Calhoun County	MI	Samuel E. Farrington	1984	2410
131-4/8	20-2/8	21-5/8	17-6/8	4	6	Clay County	MN	Don Pake	1984	2410
131-4/8	21-3/8	21-3/8	20-6/8	4	4	Montgomery County	IN	John R Clark	1984	2410
131-4/8	24-4/8	24-5/8	15-6/8	5	4	McNairy County	TN	Howard Russom	1984	2410
131-4/8	21-4/8	23-1/8	19-0/8	6	5	Yuma County	CO	Greg Mekelburg	1985	2410
131-4/8	22-6/8	21-4/8	14-6/8	5	5	Morrill County	NE	Kurt Gaertner	1985	2410
131-4/8	22-3/8	22-5/8	17-6/8	4	5	Grant County	WI	Gary R. Bald	1985	2410
131-3/8	22-2/8	22-6/8	18-7/8	5	5	Bemidji	MN	Charles R. Bowman	1961	2432
131-3/8	21-7/8	21-6/8	17-7/8	4	4	Waushara County	WI	Reginald Vergin	1967	2432
131-3/8	21-0/8	20-4/8	16-5/8	5	6	Delaware County	OH	Bobby Clenney	1975	2432
131-3/8	21-3/8	21-4/8	18-3/8	4	5	Hollowbend	AR	Tom Quinton	1976	2432
131-3/8	23-0/8	23-3/8	16-7/8	4	4	Trigg County	KY	Bruce E. Hollkamp	1978	2432
131-3/8	22-2/8	20-5/8	13-6/8	5	5	Burleigh County	ND	Robert Baker	1980	2432
131-3/8	21-7/8	21-1/8	15-4/8	5	4	Guernsey County	OH	Jim Conrad	1980	2432
131-3/8	23-1/8	23-1/8	19-7/8	4	5	Morrison County	MN	Tim Deadrick	1981	2432
131-3/8	21-1/8	21-1/8	17-1/8	5	5	Crawford County	WI	Michael G. O'Dair	1983	2432
131-3/8	22-3/8	22-1/8	18-1/8	5	5	Marquette County	WI	Roger L. Abraham	1984	2432
131-2/8	19-2/8	19-4/8	17-0/8	5	5	Auburn Road	KS	Guy C. Michael	1968	2442
131-2/8	20-3/8	19-4/8	14-6/8	5	5	Ripley County	IN	Robert Pitt	1969	2442
131-2/8	20-5/8	22-0/8	17-4/8	5	5	Scott County	KY	Jerry Peavler	1975	2442
131-2/8	20-6/8	22-0/8	16-0/8	4	5	Clearwater County	ID	Edward L. Russell	1978	2442
131-2/8	25-0/8	26-3/8	17-6/8	3	4	Scioto County	OH	Charles E. Stambaugh	1979	2442
131-2/8	21-6/8	21-6/8	18-6/8	4	5	Claiborne County	MS	Mike Parker	1980	2442
131-2/8	19-7/8	22-4/8	16-3/8	4	5	Osage County	MO	Rocky Pointer	1980	2442
131-2/8	24-3/8	24-2/8	20-2/8	5	4	Boyle County	KY	Randy Webb	1980	2442
131-2/8	22-0/8	22-0/8	17-2/8	4	5	Des Moines County	IA	Chuck Hawkins	1981	2442
131-2/8	22-6/8	22-6/8	17-6/8	5	6	Carter County	MT	Jamie Byrne	1981	2442
131-2/8	21-5/8	21-6/8	18-2/8	4	4	Scott County	IA	Robert D. Hankins	1983	2442
131-2/8	22-0/8	22-1/8	19-0/8	4	5	Barren County	KY	Tony Deckard	1983	2442
131-2/8	21-3/8	23-1/8	14-0/8	5	5	Edmondson County	KY	Joe Shereliff	1984	2442
131-2/8	23-4/8	24-4/8	16-5/8	6	5	Allegeny County	NY	Lawrence L Davis	1984	2442
131-2/8	21-7/8	21-1/8	18-0/8	4	4	Ogle County	IL	Jerome F. Bruns	1984	2442
131-1/8	22-2/8	22-1/8	20-1/8	4	5	Lafayette County	WI	Bob Wand	1971	2457

WHITETAIL DEER *(Typical Antlers)*

(continued)

Score	Length of Main Beam R	L	Inside Spread	Number of Points R	L	Area	State/ Province	Hunter's Name	Date	Rank
131-1/8	25-2/8	25-6/8	18-7/8	4	5	Columbiana	OH	Bill Henrich	1976	2457
131-1/8	20-6/8	21-5/8	19-3/8	7	6	Neosho County	KS	Robert E. Willis	1979	2457
131-1/8	23-1/8	21-7/8	19-1/8	4	4	Aberdeen	MD	Ronald D. Anderson	1980	2457
131-1/8	22-7/8	22-6/8	17-7/8	5	4	Jefferson County	WI	Scott Mill	1982	2457
131-1/8	21-6/8	21-0/8	15-7/8	5	5	Frederick County	VA	Steven E Shoemaker	1983	2457
131-1/8	22-2/8	22-4/8	17-1/8	4	4	Sedgwick County	KS	Delbert Antle	1983	2457
131-1/8	24-7/8	23-7/8	18-3/8	5	6	Wright County	MN	John W. Horstman	1984	2457
131-1/8	22-3/8	20-4/8	18-3/8	5	4	Washington County	KS	Bob Funke	1984	2457
131-1/8	22-6/8	23-4/8	20-5/8	4	4	Suffolk County	NY	Conrad Grimm	1984	2457
131-1/8	23-2/8	23-3/8	20-0/8	4	5	Morris County	NJ	Donald Howering	1985	2457
131-1/8	21-5/8	22-4/8	15-3/8	4	5	Outagamie County	WI	Dion R. Heinemey	1985	2477
131-1/8	24-1/8	23-4/8	18-3/8	4	4	Latah County	ID	Howard Holmes	1985	2457
131-0/8	21-3/8	21-5/8	16-6/8	5	5	Flathead County	MT	Jack Whitney	1959	2470
131-0/8	23-5/8	23-5/8	17-0/8	4	5	Scott County	IA	Ron Anderson	1966	2470
131-0/8	21-7/8	22-0/8	14-6/8	4	4	Louisa County	IA	Larry King	1968	2470
131-0/8	19-5/8	20-3/8	18-0/8	5	5	Sheboygan County	WI	Steve Rortvedt	1974	2470
131-0/8	22-0/8	23-5/8	16-0/8	6	6	Union County	OH	Bill Steele	1974	2470
131-0/8	21-7/8	21-4/8	16-2/8	4	5	Benton County	IA	Robert Kerkman	1975	2470
131-0/8	21-3/8	21-0/8	17-0/8	5	5	Litchfield County	CT	Elmer L. Perry, Jr.	1978	2470
131-0/8	23-6/8	23-1/8	18-2/8	5	4	Butler County	PA	John E. Fry	1979	2470
131-0/8	19-7/8	20-3/8	15-5/8	5	6	Sidney	MT	Verne L. Cashman	1980	2470
131-0/8	20-7/8	20-3/8	15-4/8	4	5	La Salle	MN	George Nasman	1980	2470
131-0/8	20-3/8	19-5/8	16-0/8	5	5	Burleigh County	ND	Jerry Schmitcke	1980	2470
131-0/8	19-0/8	20-5/8	16-6/8	5	5	Manitowoc County	WI	Roger B. Schroeder	1981	2470
131-0/8	22-6/8	22-0/8	17-0/8	5	5	Dane County	WI	Jeff Bauer	1981	2470
131-0/8	22-3/8	22-4/8	17-6/8	4	4	Fulton County	PA	John A. Williams	1981	2470
131-0/8	19-1/8	19-1/8	14-4/8	4	4	Codington County	SD	Gerald J. Comes	1981	2470
131-0/8	22-6/8	22-5/8	18-2/8	5	5	Grundy County	IL	Michael Marchio	1981	2470
131-0/8	18-4/8	19-3/8	17-4/8	5	5	Berlseley County	SC	Hugh Gaskins	1982	2470
131-0/8	22-3/8	22-3/8	20-6/8	5	5	Menominee County	MI	Theodore R. Olsen	1982	2470
131-0/8	20-0/8	20-4/8	15-4/8	5	5	Hamilton County	IN	Larry E. Eversole	1982	2470
131-0/8	18-3/8	17-1/8	14-4/8	6	6	Will County	IL	Richard D. Tenute	1982	2470
131-0/8	23-6/8	21-6/8	18-0/8	4	4	Shelby County	MO	Rodney Gander	1984	2470
131-0/8	20-6/8	21-5/8	19-0/8	5	5	Crawford County	MO	Ray Morris	1984	2470
131-0/8	23-4/8	22-0/8	18-0/8	4	4	Ottawa County	MI	Steve Lamberts	1985	2470
130-7/8	22-3/8	23-0/8	14-1/8	4	5	Sarpy County	NE	Ronald Beranek	1966	2493
130-7/8	23-2/8	24-1/8	15-6/8	4	5	Strawberry Point	IA	Bryan Sears	1969	2493
130-7/8	21-4/8	21-4/8	17-1/8	6	5	Trempealeau County	WI	Myles Keller	1975	2493
130-7/8	20-0/8	19-0/8	17-0/8	6	5	Bedford County	VA	Bill Hurley	1977	2493
130-7/8	23-6/8	24-4/8	16-3/8	5	4	Sangamon County	IL	Keith Stigleman	1979	2493
130-7/8	24-6/8	24-4/8	17-5/8	5	5	Coshocton County	OH	Gary L. Fischer	1979	2493
130-7/8	22-3/8	22-6/8	15-7/8	5	5	Princeton	NJ	William P. Krueger	1979	2493
130-7/8	22-2/8	21-5/8	16-5/8	5	4	Chickasaw County	IA	James Harris	1980	2493
130-7/8	24-5/8	24-4/8	18-1/8	4	4	Saginaw County	MI	Tom Perrin	1980	2493
130-7/8	23-1/8	22-5/8	16-5/8	5	4	Waukesha County	WI	Mark Heffner	1981	2493
130-7/8	23-2/8	25-2/8	19-7/8	5	5	Licking County	OH	Thomas Hughes	1981	2493
130-7/8	20-5/8	21-4/8	15-5/8	5	5	Filmore County	MN	Dr. Eugene T. Altiere	1983	2493
130-7/8	19-5/8	20-0/8	14-5/8	5	5	Camden County	MO	Mike Hutton	1983	2493
130-7/8	22-3/8	23-0/8	16-5/8	5	4	Vermilion County	IL	Robert G. Downing	1985	2493
130-6/8	23-2/8	21-1/8	14-2/8	5	4	Eagle Butte	SD	Bill Dunn	1969	2507
130-6/8	20-1/8	20-4/8	15-0/8	7	5	Rock County	WI	Mark Butzler	1978	2507
130-6/8	22-1/8	21-7/8	17-6/8	4	5	Salt Plains	OK	Hal Utsler	1980	2507
130-6/8	21-0/8	21-0/8	16-0/8	5	4	Marshall	MI	Harold Vander Horst	1980	2507
130-6/8	23-4/8	21-7/8	19-6/8	5	4	Washington County	MN	Joe Kohler	1981	2507
130-6/8	22-7/8	22-3/8	18-4/8	4	4	Sullivan County	IN	Ron L. Buchanan	1982	2507
130-6/8	22-1/8	23-0/8	19-4/8	4	4	Hays County	NE	Randy Griffiths	1983	2507
130-6/8	22-5/8	23-7/8	17-4/8	4	5	Shawano County	WI	Patrick G. Shulze	1984	2507
130-6/8	21-4/8	21-7/8	17-0/8	4	4	Clarion County	PA	Gary Alan Bullers	1984	2507
130-6/8	21-6/8	22-0/8	17-6/8	5	4	Stephenson County	IL	Eric Zimmerman	1984	2507
130-6/8	23-4/8	23-4/8	14-6/8	4	4	Owen County	IN	Lanse C. Hale	1985	2507
130-6/8	23-6/8	23-4/8	16-6/8	4	4	Jefferson County	WI	Ernie Turpin	1985	2507
130-6/8	20-1/8	20-1/8	14-4/8	5	5	Ravalli County	MT	Terry See	1985	2507
130-5/8	23-4/8	21-4/8	18-1/8	4	5	Roberts County	SD	Franic W. Sherer, Jr.	1965	2520

WHITETAIL DEER *(Typical Antlers)*

Minimum Score 125

Score	Length of Main Beam R	L	Inside Spread	Number of Points R	L	Area	State/ Province	Hunter's Name	Date	Rank
130-5/8	21-5/8	21-3/8	16-3/8	4	4	Tuscola County	MI	Gary A. Bower	1974	2520
130-5/8	20-7/8	21-4/8	14-5/8	5	6	Marquette County	WI	Tom Murphy	1974	2520
130-5/8	20-6/8	20-3/8	18-1/8	5	4	Fairfield County	CT	Mark Hensel	1979	2520
130-5/8	25-3/8	25-2/8	18-2/8	6	7	Lucas County	OH	Patrick Miller	1979	2520
130-5/8	19-4/8	19-4/8	17-6/8	5	6	Throckmorton County	TX	Steve Fikes	1980	2520
130-5/8	20-4/8	21-0/8	15-1/8	5	5	Montgomery County	AL	Rett Kelly	1980	2520
130-5/8	21-4/8	22-0/8	17-2/8	4	6	Knox County	IL	Fred Miller	1981	2520
130-5/8	21-7/8	21-5/8	18-1/8	4	4	Darlingford	MAN	Robert Hunt	1982	2520
130-5/8	24-2/8	24-3/8	18-7/8	4	4	Orange County	NY	David Babcock	1983	2520
130-5/8	23-4/8	23-0/8	18-5/8	4	4	Chisago County	MN	James Swing	1983	2520
130-5/8	21-4/8	21-7/8	16-3/8	4	4	Graham County	KS	Russell Hull	1983	2520
130-5/8	23-3/8	23-6/8	22-0/8	6	7	Lake County	IL	John Schnider, Jr.	1986	2520
130-4/8	21-2/8	21-3/8	17-0/8	5	5	Allegan County	MI	Jack Yaeger	1942	2533
130-4/8	21-0/8	20-4/8	18-2/8	5	5	Putnam County	WV	Dan Lloyd	1966	2533
130-4/8	23-4/8	22-7/8	19-2/8	5	5	Berry County	MI	Thomas L. Bommersbach	1978	2533
130-4/8	23-3/8	21-1/8	17-6/8	5	5	Marquette County	WI	Gary J. Craig	1978	2533
130-4/8	20-5/8	20-6/8	15-0/8	5	5	Louisa County	IA	Roger Gipple	1979	2533
130-4/8	23-5/8	22-0/8	13-4/8	5	4	Cleveland County	OK	Tom Quinton	1979	2533
130-4/8	23-5/8	22-7/8	18-2/8	6	5	Pittsburgh County	OK	Bill Starry	1981	2533
130-4/8	22-3/8	22-1/8	16-0/8	4	5	Riley County	KS	Dennis Peterson	1982	2533
130-4/8	21-7/8	21-7/8	18-2/8	6	6	Knox County	OH	Mark E. Bretz	1983	2533
130-4/8	22-4/8	22-2/8	17-0/8	4	4	Russell County	AL	Owen Veasey	1983	2533
130-4/8	22-0/8	20-7/8	14-6/8	5	5	Wood County	WV	William G. Smith	1983	2533
130-4/8	22-7/8	22-5/8	19-6/8	4	4	Hawkins County	TN	Johnny Ford	1985	2533
130-3/8	21-2/8	20-6/8	14-1/8	5	5	Jefferson Prov. Grnds.	IN	Larry R. Smith	1966	2545
130-3/8	18-6/8	17-3/8	15-4/8	5	6	Omaha	NE	John Prentis	1978	2545
130-3/8	20-1/8	20-4/8	15-3/8	6	5	Ottertail County	MN	Dick Schmidt	1978	2545
130-3/8	23-6/8	23-1/8	17-7/8	7	6	Adams County	IL	David Shupe	1981	2545
130-3/8	20-2/8	20-4/8	17-7/8	5	5	Monroe County	WI	Tony P. Snow	1982	2545
130-3/8	21-1/8	21-5/8	16-5/8	5	5	Polk County	WI	Russell Lee Johnson	1982	2545
130-3/8	23-4/8	22-4/8	17-1/8	4	5	Garfield County	MT	Mitch Kottas	1983	2545
130-3/8	21-5/8	21-1/8	13-5/8	5	6	Lawrence County	MO	Jim Botts	1983	2545
130-3/8	21-2/8	21-7/8	16-7/8	4	4	Morrison County	MN	Arne Mickelberg	1983	2545
130-3/8	22-0/8	22-0/8	18-3/8	9	8	Brown County	KS	Gerry Hertzel	1983	2545
130-3/8	21-3/8	22-0/8	17-3/8	5	5	Ellsworth County	KS	Jeff Dohrman	1983	2545
130-3/8	19-6/8	19-3/8	14-3/8	5	5	Buffalo County	WI	Roger Harm	1984	2545
130-3/8	21-4/8	22-0/8	17-1/8	5	4	Allegheny County	PA	Richard J. Blauser	1984	2545
130-3/8	22-5/8	22-2/8	15-1/8	5	5	Becker County	MN	David Schiller	1985	2545
130-3/8	25-1/8	23-0/8	21-0/8	4	5	Buffalo County	WI	Jeff Joslin	1985	2545
130-3/8	24-2/8	24-0/8	20-5/8	5	4	Middlesex County	CT	James Boczar	1985	2545
130-2/8	20-3/8	20-6/8	16-2/8	4	4	Yankton County	SD	Jack Begley	1959	2561
130-2/8	26-7/8	26-3/8	17-3/8	8	6	Mankato	MN	Ron Herz	1966	2561
130-2/8	21-4/8	22-5/8	17-4/8	5	5	Montgomery County	AL	Charles D. Robinson	1976	2561
130-2/8	16-0/8	20-3/8	18-6/8	6	6	Carroll County	IL	Arthur Heinze	1977	2561
130-2/8	20-4/8	21-3/8	17-4/8	5	5	St. Croix Park	MN	Ron Larsen	1978	2561
130-2/8	21-5/8	21-7/8	15-0/8	6	5	Johnson County	IN	Ronnie L. Fiesbeck	1979	2561
130-2/8	20-3/8	20-7/8	13-4/8	4	5	Fort Pierre	SD	Richard Ray	1980	2561
130-2/8	21-5/8	21-6/8	17-6/8	4	4	Saginaw County	MI	Charles R. Harper	1980	2561
130-2/8	21-3/8	20-7/8	20-0/8	5	5	Allison Park	PA	Thomas Fitz	1981	2561
130-2/8	21-1/8	21-5/8	14-4/8	6	6	Dane County	WI	Thomas B. Gannon	1982	2561
130-2/8	22-0/8	21-2/8	19-5/8	7	5	St. Louis County	MO	Jack Repp	1982	2561
130-2/8	22-0/8	21-0/8	20-2/8	5	6	Jefferson County	KS	Wayne Wenger	1983	2561
130-2/8	22-1/8	23-1/8	20-2/8	4	5	Cheyenne County	NE	Marvin Clyncke	1983	2561
130-2/8	21-1/8	21-6/8	16-0/8	4	4	Dodge County	WI	Steve Muche	1984	2561
130-2/8	21-6/8	21-7/8	18-6/8	5	4	Jackson County	MI	Bruce A. Andrews	1984	2561
130-2/8	21-7/8	21-2/8	16-4/8	5	6	Baltimore County	MD	Jay Holstein	1984	2561
130-2/8	20-6/8	20-7/8	14-4/8	5	5	Clay County	MN	Randy Blankenship	1985	2561
130-2/8	20-7/8	20-4/8	16-2/8	5	4	Shawnee County	KS	Randy Hildreth	1985	2561
130-1/8	24-4/8	25-7/8	19-7/8	4	3	Waupaca County	WI	John Schoenike	1952	2579
130-1/8	22-5/8	21-6/8	16-7/8	5	5	Oneida County	WI	Fred Felbab	1964	2579
130-1/8	22-6/8	24-4/8	17-4/8	6	5	Ripley	MN	Stephen L. Marklund	1964	2579
130-1/8	25-2/8	25-4/8	16-0/8	5	5	Trousdale	KS	Matthew W. Schartz	1979	2579
130-1/8	19-4/8	19-3/8	15-3/8	5	5	Warren County	MO	David A. Wilson	1980	2579

WHITETAIL DEER *(Typical Antlers)*

(continued)   Minimum Score 125

Score	Length of Main Beam R	L	Inside Spread	Number of Points R	L	Area	State/ Province	Hunter's Name	Date	Rank
130-1/8	23-0/8	21-7/8	17-7/8	4	4	Vernon County	WI	Michael R. Gregory	1981	2579
130-1/8	20-4/8	20-3/8	16-3/8	4	4	Tazewell County	IL	Gary Joe Smith	1982	2579
130-1/8	21-1/8	21-0/8	16-7/8	4	5	Perry County	OH	Michael W. Wintgens	1982	2579
130-1/8	19-3/8	20-6/8	17-5/8	5	4	Muscatine County	IA	Brian Nebergall	1983	2579
130-1/8	23-4/8	21-6/8	15-6/8	6	5	Clay County	MN	Joe Lahlum	1983	2579
130-1/8	22-5/8	24-4/8	21-3/8	4	4	Hamilton County	IL	Richard Phelps	1984	2579
130-1/8	22-5/8	22-5/8	19-1/8	4	5	Powell County	MT	Danny Moore	1984	2579
130-1/8	23-1/8	22-3/8	18-5/8	4	4	Hardin County	OH	John B. Britton	1985	2579
130-1/8	23-7/8	23-4/8	17-6/8	5	6	Montgomery County	MD	Donald Stancil Waters, Jr.	1985	2579
130-1/8	23-0/8	22-6/8	16-3/8	4	4	Anderson County	TN	Harold D. Tackett	1985	2579
130-1/8	24-4/8	23-0/8	16-1/8	5	4	Calhoun County	MI	David K. McWhorter	1985	2579
130-0/8	23-4/8	23-5/8	19-0/8	4	4	Salisbury	MD	Donald J. Brown	1956	2595
130-0/8	21-0/8	19-3/8	17-4/8	5	4	Roberts County	SD	Byron Siegel	1962	2595
130-0/8	22-2/8	22-5/8	18-6/8	4	5	Berrien County	MI	Leon L. Williams	1965	2595
130-0/8	20-2/8	20-6/8	15-0/8	5	5	Bucks County	PA	Don Fitting	1967	2595
130-0/8	21-3/8	21-4/8	19-0/8	5	5	Hillsdale	IN	Scott E. Webster	1973	2595
130-0/8	20-2/8	21-0/8	14-6/8	5	5	Stanly County	NC	Steve Efird	1978	2595
130-0/8	22-4/8	22-2/8	19-0/8	4	4	Licking County	OH	James E. Sorg	1978	2595
130-0/8	22-0/8	21-4/8	17-0/8	4	4	Will County	IL	Terry Marcukaitis	1979	2595
130-0/8	23-2/8	24-2/8	18-0/8	4	4	Onondaga County	NY	Jack Sipfle	1980	2595
130-0/8	21-7/8	21-2/8	16-1/8	6	6	Polk County	WI	Paul Petersen	1981	2595
130-0/8	23-0/8	24-2/8	19-6/8	4	4	Westchester County	NY	Richard T. Burke	1982	2595
130-0/8	23-4/8	23-3/8	15-4/8	5	5	McDonough County	IL	John E. Whalon	1982	2595
130-0/8	24-1/8	23-6/8	13-6/8	5	4	Scott County	VA	Charles William Moore	1983	2595
130-0/8	20-5/8	21-0/8	15-4/8	5	6	Fondulace County	WI	Tom Dickmann	1983	2595
130-0/8	20-0/8	21-4/8	18-0/8	5	5	Kenosha County	WI	Ted Hysell	1983	2595
130-0/8	25-1/8	25-2/8	17-6/8	6	7	Ottawa County	KS	Rod Ponton	1983	2595
130-0/8	20-3/8	18-7/8	17-4/8	6	5	Perkins County	SD	H. Melvin Dutton	1983	2595
130-0/8	22-7/8	21-6/8	18-0/8	6	7	Sauk County	WI	Duane Olson	1984	2595
130-0/8	21-0/8	21-1/8	17-4/8	4	4	Rock County	WI	DaLee E. Applebee	1984	2595
130-0/8	21-3/8	21-5/8	17-0/8	4	4	Marinette County	WI	Tom Hirte	1984	2595
130-0/8	21-1/8	20-5/8	15-4/8	5	5	Shawnee County	KS	Roxie Kelly	1984	2595
130-0/8	22-2/8	24-1/8	19-0/8	4	4	Orange County	NY	Richard F Kaufmann	1985	2595
130-0/8	23-0/8	23-3/8	17-4/8	5	5	Minnehaha County	SD	Rick Rang	1985	2595
129-7/8	23-6/8	21-6/8	18-0/8	5	5	Winnebago County	IL	Leo M. Ruefer, Jr.	1958	2618
129-7/8	21-7/8	22-0/8	16-5/8	4	4	Monroe County	WI	Jeff Skrade	1962	2618
129-7/8	23-3/8	23-2/8	16-5/8	5	6	Allegan County	MI	Clayton Foster	1964	2618
129-7/8	23-0/8	21-7/8	15-1/8	5	5	Jefferson County	KS	Delmar Tucking, Jr.	1966	2618
129-7/8	22-3/8	22-6/8	20-7/8	4	4	Ashland County	WI	William Sutton	1968	2618
129-7/8	19-2/8	19-5/8	15-3/8	5	5	Columbia County	WI	Jay Rosendick	1970	2618
129-7/8	22-4/8	21-7/8	17-1/8	4	4	Ogle County	IL	Henry E. Zimmerman	1970	2618
129-7/8	20-3/8	20-6/8	15-5/8	6	5	Cottonwood County	MN	Gene Gustafson	1977	2618
129-7/8	21-5/8	22-2/8	17-1/8	5	5	Sauk County	WI	Clair E. Keylock	1977	2618
129-7/8	21-6/8	22-4/8	20-5/8	4	4	Tioga County	NY	Arthur Schumacher	1977	2618
129-7/8	19-7/8	20-4/8	16-5/8	5	5	Adair County	IA	Wallace R. Waddell	1980	2618
129-7/8	22-0/8	21-5/8	17-3/8	4	4	Hardin County	IA	Randall Martinson	1980	2618
129-7/8	24-6/8	24-6/8	17-3/8	5	5	Oneida County	WI	Tom Knudsen	1981	2618
129-7/8	20-6/8	21-1/8	18-7/8	6	6	Kingman County	KS	Kevin Wasson	1981	2618
129-7/8	22-5/8	22-4/8	17-2/8	6	5	Berkeley County	SC	Hugh Gaskins	1983	2618
129-7/8	20-5/8	20-7/8	16-1/8	4	5	Calumet County	WI	Bill Mertens	1983	2618
129-7/8	21-5/8	21-2/8	15-7/8	5	5	Waupaca County	WI	William Millard	1984	2618
129-7/8	21-2/8	22-7/8	17-1/8	4	4	Rock County	WI	Richard A. Viken	1984	2618
129-7/8	20-6/8	20-4/8	14-7/8	4	5	Butler County	KS	Clifford Rogers	1984	2618
129-6/8	19-5/8	20-7/8	16-2/8	5	6	Adams County	IL	Mel Powell	1964	2637
129-6/8	20-2/8	18-0/8	17-2/8	5	5	Johnson County	WY	Jim Bartz	1969	2637
129-6/8	22-5/8	22-2/8	20-2/8	7	5	Ripley	MN	Robert E. Nordstrom	1973	2637
129-6/8	22-2/8	21-0/8	17-0/8	5	4	Lee County	IA	Jim Bohenkamp	1974	2637
129-6/8	21-4/8	22-0/8	20-0/8	4	4	Washtenaw County	MI	Richard A. Hollo	1980	2637
129-6/8	21-1/8	22-7/8	17-4/8	6	5	Aquasco	MD	Russell A. Nichols	1980	2637
129-6/8	23-6/8	23-2/8	16-4/8	4	4	Lawrence County	OH	Ronald E. Clark	1981	2637
129-6/8	24-2/8	23-0/8	15-7/8	6	5	Lawrence County	OH	Randy Gilmore	1982	2637
129-6/8	22-1/8	22-1/8	15-6/8	4	4	Gallia County	OH	Jack Satterfield, Jr.	1982	2637
129-6/8	22-5/8	23-1/8	16-6/8	4	4	Jo Daviess County	IL	Tom Smith	1982	2637

WHITETAIL DEER *(Typical Antlers)*

(continued)

Minimum Score 125

Score	Length of Main Beam R	L	Inside Spread	Number of Points R	L	Area	State/ Province	Hunter's Name	Date	Rank
129-6/8	20-5/8	22-2/8	19-0/8	4	4	Juneau County	WI	Larry Southworth	1983	2637
129-6/8	21-4/8	22-1/8	15-4/8	5	5	Calhoun County	MI	Dick Coon	1983	2637
129-6/8	22-1/8	22-0/8	20-2/8	4	4	Will County	IL	Richard "Rick" Gagle	1984	2637
129-6/8	22-3/8	22-0/8	15-2/8	5	5	Morrison County	MN	Richard W. Gamache	1984	2637
129-6/8	23-1/8	23-0/8	16-4/8	7	4	Grant County	WI	Jim Johnson	1985	2637
129-6/8	22-5/8	23-0/8	19-2/8	5	5	Mercer County	NJ	Frank Prato	1986	2637
129-5/8	23-2/8	24-0/8	17-6/8	4	4	Taylor County	WV	Jimmie R. Auvil	1959	2653
129-5/8	22-5/8	22-1/8	20-1/8	5	5	Cowley County	KS	Charles O'Daniel	1966	2653
129-5/8	21-6/8	21-2/8	18-5/8	5	4	Waushara County	WI	Roger D. Johnson	1979	2653
129-5/8	22-4/8	23-5/8	17-3/8	6	5	Ontario County	NY	Richard Rockefeller	1979	2653
129-5/8	20-7/8	20-4/8	17-1/8	4	4	Fillmore County	MN	Robert Meyer	1981	2653
129-5/8	21-7/8	22-0/8	16-5/8	5	5	Muskingum County	OH	P. W. "Bill" Meyer	1981	2653
129-5/8	23-0/8	23-2/8	19-5/8	4	5	Ontario County	NY	Ronald Molinari	1981	2653
129-5/8	22-4/8	22-3/8	18-6/8	4	5	Lucas County	OH	James L. Davies	1982	2653
129-5/8	20-6/8	19-2/8	13-7/8	5	5	Traill County	ND	Willis Mueller	1982	2653
129-5/8	21-0/8	20-2/8	18-7/8	6	5	Scott County	KY	Ronnie Jacobs	1983	2653
129-5/8	23-2/8	23-4/8	21-5/8	5	4	Dourchester County	MD	Thomas R. Pohuski	1984	2653
129-5/8	23-4/8	23-4/8	15-1/8	4	4	Washington County	MN	Patrick F. Dolan	1984	2653
129-5/8	24-4/8	26-0/8	16-5/8	4	4	Livingston County	NY	Christopher D. Walp	1985	2653
129-5/8	22-6/8	20-3/8	17-6/8	4	6	Madison County	IL	Mark A. Thompson	1985	2653
129-5/8	22-3/8	21-5/8	17-1/8	5	4	Pike County	MO	Ray Hatfield	1986	2653
129-4/8	21-5/8	20-2/8	15-4/8	5	5	Fontenelle	NE	Russ Calloway	1962	2668
129-4/8	22-4/8	21-7/8	17-6/8	5	5	Monroe County	GA	Robert S. Carey	1973	2668
129-4/8	23-1/8	23-3/8	19-2/8	4	3	Brodhead	WI	Jerry Amundson	1976	2668
129-4/8	23-4/8	22-0/8	15-4/8	5	5	Newton County	IN	Howard Culbertson	1976	2668
129-4/8	22-2/8	22-1/8	16-4/8	4	5	Chippewa County	WI	John M. Hanzlik	1981	2668
129-4/8	22-6/8	22-2/8	16-0/8	4	5	Lasalle County	IL	Steve Wagner	1984	2668
129-4/8	19-1/8	19-6/8	16-5/8	5	5	Juneau County	WI	Dean Tompkins	1984	2668
129-4/8	21-7/8	22-1/8	16-0/8	5	5	LaSalle County	IL	John Liles	1984	2668
129-4/8	22-6/8	23-7/8	18-2/8	5	5	Sherburne County	MN	Marvin Vogelgesang	1985	2668
129-4/8	19-1/8	19-5/8	15-2/8	4	4	Pike County	IL	Lloyd Bateman	1985	2668
129-3/8	23-2/8	22-5/8	19-0/8	4	5	Carroll County	IL	Noel Feather	1965	2678
129-3/8	25-1/8	24-0/8	21-5/8	4	3	Des Moines County	IA	Jerry Snyder	1978	2678
129-3/8	20-7/8	21-1/8	14-5/8	5	5	Monroe County	WI	Paul Moser	1983	2678
129-3/8	20-6/8	20-7/8	20-2/8	7	9	White County	IN	Mark Mohler	1983	2678
129-3/8	21-3/8	21-4/8	14-7/8	5	5	Carroll County	MD	Herbert Eyler	1984	2678
129-3/8	22-2/8	22-0/8	17-2/8	6	4	Door County	WI	Randy Berndt	1985	2678
129-2/8	19-2/8	20-1/8	16-5/8	7	6	Columbia County	WA	Al Farrell	1956	2684
129-2/8	23-2/8	24-0/8	17-4/8	4	4	Juneau County	WI	Robert E. Schober	1977	2684
129-2/8	21-7/8	21-4/8	16-2/8	5	5	Kendall County	IL	Fred W. Achilles	1979	2684
129-2/8	21-6/8	21-6/8	22-0/8	4	5	Puslinch Township	ONT	Larry Knarr	1980	2684
129-2/8	20-3/8	20-4/8	17-4/8	5	5	Canmore	ALB	J. C. Mackid	1982	2684
129-2/8	22-0/8	22-5/8	16-2/8	5	5	Muskingum County	OH	Dr. Jim Emerson	1982	2684
129-2/8	20-6/8	21-6/8	17-2/8	4	4	Buffalo County	NE	Dan Johnson	1983	2684
129-2/8	20-0/8	19-6/8	15-0/8	5	5	Portage County	WI	Jay W. Torkilsen	1984	2684
129-2/8	19-4/8	19-2/8	14-4/8	5	5	Walsh	ALB	Reg Brooks	1984	2684
129-2/8	24-1/8	23-0/8	15-0/8	5	4	Jasper County	IL	Guy Douglas Page	1984	2684
129-2/8	20-7/8	21-3/8	18-6/8	5	5	Ross County	OH	Steven E Bower	1984	2684
129-2/8	20-4/8	21-0/8	13-6/8	5	6	Pierce County	WI	William Kearns	1984	2684
129-2/8	22-2/8	22-2/8	18-4/8	4	4	Calhoun County	MI	Jerry L. Teller	1984	2684
129-2/8	21-6/8	22-1/8	16-6/8	4	4	Des Moines County	IA	Ray Waschkat	1984	2684
129-2/8	20-1/8	19-7/8	18-4/8	5	5	Hillsdale County	MI	Garry Witfoth	1984	2684
129-2/8	23-3/8	23-0/8	17-6/8	4	4	Hocking County	OH	Donald Webb	1985	2684
129-2/8	20-5/8	21-7/8	16-0/8	4	4	Anderson County	KS	Jerry Howarter	1985	2684
129-1/8	22-4/8	21-4/8	17-5/8	5	5	Lee County	IA	Jim Bohenkamp	1973	2701
129-1/8	20-6/8	21-6/8	16-5/8	5	5	Burnett County	WI	James G. Hurrle	1974	2701
129-1/8	22-2/8	22-1/8	16-5/8	5	8	Wabasha County	MN	Richard H. McKnight	1975	2701
129-1/8	22-0/8	22-4/8	15-5/8	6	6	Holt County	NE	Greg Wetthaufer	1980	2701
129-1/8	22-2/8	22-1/8	17-7/8	5	5	Greene County	MS	Russell Herring	1980	2701
129-1/8	22-1/8	22-0/8	15-7/8	4	4	Hancock County	OH	Kenneth E. Hornick	1980	2701
129-1/8	19-2/8	20-0/8	15-3/8	5	5	Sheboygan County	WI	John Steinbruecker	1980	2701
129-1/8	25-1/8	24-1/8	20-5/8	6	4	Houston County	MN	Gary Maier	1981	2701
129-1/8	19-6/8	19-7/8	14-7/8	5	5	Clark County	SD	Bill Soyland	1981	2701

WHITETAIL DEER *(Typical Antlers)*
(continued)

Score	Length of Main Beam R	L	Inside Spread	Number of Points R	L	Area	State/ Province	Hunter's Name	Date	Rank
129-1/8	21-5/8	21-7/8	17-1/8	4	5	Schuyler County	NY	Scott D. Bond	1982	2701
129-1/8	21-6/8	21-0/8	17-5/8	4	4	Hughes County	SD	Alvin Truax	1984	2701
129-1/8	24-0/8	24-3/8	17-3/8	4	4	Jackson County	MI	Mark D. Bacon	1985	2701
129-1/8	21-0/8	21-6/8	16-6/8	6	6	Walsh County	ND	Tobin L. Welch	1986	2701
129-0/8	22-6/8	22-5/8	17-5/8	5	5	Long Island	IL	Roger W. Seehafer	1964	2714
129-0/8	21-4/8	21-3/8	17-4/8	5	5	Monmouth County	NJ	Joseph N. Lazar	1967	2714
129-0/8	19-6/8	20-6/8	19-0/8	4	4	Oneida County	WI	Gary Bohlman	1970	2714
129-0/8	23-7/8	24-3/8	17-4/8	5	5	Erie County	OH	William G. Hlavin	1973	2714
129-0/8	20-3/8	20-2/8	13-7/8	5	6	Minneapolis	KS	Martin Nunn	1976	2714
129-0/8	20-6/8	21-2/8	15-5/8	6	6	Columbia County	WI	Greg Jacobson	1978	2714
129-0/8	22-1/8	22-6/8	17-4/8	4	5	Moore County	MN	Jim Keim	1978	2714
129-0/8	22-2/8	23-4/8	19-4/8	5	4	Trempealeau County	WI	Brian Skroch	1978	2714
129-0/8	20-2/8	20-2/8	15-4/8	5	5	Washington County	WI	Francis N. Vande Boom	1978	2714
129-0/8	20-3/8	20-4/8	19-0/8	4	4	Hollandale	MS	Dan Hensley	1979	2714
129-0/8	23-2/8	22-5/8	20-4/8	7	6	Carroll County	OH	Chuck Caldwell	1981	2714
129-0/8	20-4/8	20-1/8	15-6/8	5	5	Columbia County	WI	Brent J. Nowak	1982	2714
129-0/8	21-0/8	21-4/8	16-0/8	4	4	Wabaunsee County	KS	Tom Willard	1982	2714
129-0/8	21-1/8	21-0/8	17-6/8	4	4	Grant County	WI	Wayne J. Droessler	1985	2714
129-0/8	22-1/8	22-1/8	16-2/8	5	4	Cass County	ND	Ellery Kundert	1985	2714
129-0/8	21-7/8	22-2/8	15-4/8	4	5	Iowa County	WI	Tim Palzkill	1985	2714
129-0/8	22-2/8	22-7/8	17-2/8	4	4	Woodford County	IL	Bill Salsman	1985	2714
129-0/8	21-2/8	21-3/8	16-2/8	6	6	Bremer County	IA	Martin Culpepper	1985	2714
129-0/8	21-4/8	21-4/8	16-2/8	4	5	Pike County	MO	Richard Dewey	1985	2714
129-0/8	20-0/8	20-4/8	16-5/8	6	6	Fond du Lac County	WI	Jeffrey D. Flitter	1986	2714
128-7/8	19-1/8	20-6/8	13-7/8	5	5	Martin County	IN	J. Steve Albertson	1969	2734
128-7/8	22-4/8	21-1/8	16-3/8	5	5	Hurley	WI	Kevin Freymiller	1975	2734
128-7/8	22-6/8	22-3/8	15-2/8	5	5	Taylor County	WI	Eugene L. Racibowski	1976	2734
128-7/8	21-0/8	20-1/8	18-1/8	5	4	Clark County	WI	Clarence J. Biddle	1977	2734
128-7/8	23-3/8	23-1/8	15-4/8	5	4	Two Harbors	MN	Michael Seeber	1980	2734
128-7/8	22-0/8	23-0/8	15-5/8	5	4	Erie County	NY	David J. Wetzler, Sr.	1980	2734
128-7/8	24-1/8	25-3/8	21-6/8	7	6	Gentry County	MO	Bruce Shisler	1982	2734
128-7/8	20-4/8	20-4/8	16-5/8	4	4	Blue Earth County	MN	Dean Como	1982	2734
128-7/8	19-7/8	20-4/8	16-3/8	5	6	Richland County	MT	Dan Sturgis	1985	2734
128-7/8	20-0/8	21-2/8	15-1/8	7	6	Washtenaw County	MI	Gerald Opsahl, Sr.	1985	2734
128-6/8	23-0/8	25-2/8	16-4/8	4	4	Elm Creek	NE	Bill Orsborn	1963	2744
128-6/8	21-1/8	20-2/8	18-6/8	4	4	Johnson County	IA	Claire Doyle	1971	2744
128-6/8	23-2/8	22-5/8	15-3/8	4	6	Lake County	IN	Bruce R. Prue	1977	2744
128-6/8	19-4/8	20-0/8	18-2/8	6	5	Seward County	NE	Ronald G. Filip	1978	2744
128-6/8	20-6/8	21-2/8	17-0/8	5	5	Brown County	SD	Jerome J. Lingor	1978	2744
128-6/8	20-1/8	20-1/8	17-2/8	5	5	Adams County	OH	Larry David Adams	1981	2744
128-6/8	25-5/8	25-6/8	18-1/8	5	6	Blount County	TN	David Dotson	1981	2744
128-6/8	21-6/8	22-2/8	17-0/8	5	4	Riley County	KS	Dwayne Roepke	1981	2744
128-6/8	22-0/8	22-2/8	16-6/8	4	4	Perice County	WI	Joe Sukowatey	1981	2744
128-6/8	21-3/8	21-2/8	16-4/8	5	5	Muskingum County	OH	P. W. "Bill" Meyer	1982	2744
128-6/8	23-3/8	23-6/8	17-6/8	4	5	Houston County	MN	James P. Finn	1982	2744
128-6/8	21-4/8	21-4/8	17-0/8	5	5	Shelby County	IL	Larry E. Gibson	1982	2744
128-6/8	22-6/8	21-0/8	17-4/8	5	5	Sangamon County	IL	James L. Aebel	1983	2744
128-6/8	23-3/8	24-3/8	19-6/8	4	4	Dodge County	WI	Dale A. Hawkinson	1984	2744
128-6/8	19-6/8	20-3/8	17-0/8	5	5	Robertson County	TN	Terry Louis Carter	1985	2744
128-6/8	22-1/8	20-3/8	19-0/8	5	6	Beaver County	PA	Mark Tallon	1985	2744
128-6/8	18-4/8	20-5/8	17-0/8	4	4	Pittsburg County	OK	Edward P. Martin III	1985	2744
128-6/8	24-1/8	25-5/8	18-1/8	5	4	Buffalo County	WI	Ed Brannen	1985	2744
128-6/8	20-7/8	20-5/8	17-4/8	5	4	Adams County	WI	John Balaine	1986	2744
128-6/8	20-7/8	19-6/8	16-2/8	5	5	Winona County	MN	John R. Micheel	1986	2744
128-5/8	20-6/8	20-2/8	14-7/8	5	5	Mille Lacs County	MN	Milton J. Mattson	1952	2764
128-5/8	14-7/8	26-2/8	20-5/8	5	5	Dodge City	KS	Rod Lies	1966	2764
128-5/8	18-1/8	18-5/8	15-3/8	5	5	Aberdeen	MD	Joseph Egner	1969	2764
128-5/8	20-4/8	20-5/8	18-0/8	6	6	Lawrence County	SD	Ronald Hazledine	1969	2764
128-5/8	21-6/8	22-0/8	17-5/8	4	4	Mercer County	IL	Kenneth E. Yeater	1971	2764
128-5/8	21-3/8	21-0/8	18-5/8	5	5	Delaware County	IA	Jim L. Mahan	1974	2764
128-5/8	22-2/8	22-4/8	15-7/8	5	5	Fond du Lac County	WI	Kevin Clark	1975	2764
128-5/8	23-0/8	23-3/8	17-2/8	8	5	Kendall County	IL	David Martinek	1978	2764
128-5/8	20-4/8	20-1/8	15-1/8	5	5	Ontario County	NY	William Danno	1980	2764

WHITETAIL DEER *(Typical Antlers)*

Minimum Score 125

Score	Length of Main Beam R	L	Inside Spread	Number of Points R	L	Area	State/ Province	Hunter's Name	Date	Rank
128-5/8	21-0/8	20-7/8	14-5/8	5	5	Ionia County	MI	Ronald A. Denney	1980	2764
128-5/8	23-4/8	24-0/8	19-0/8	6	6	Jackson County	WI	John D. Card	1981	2764
128-5/8	22-2/8	21-5/8	16-7/8	5	5	Franklin County	MO	Lance Tyree	1982	2764
128-5/8	21-5/8	23-0/8	17-1/8	8	6	Cedar County	NE	Charles Benertz	1982	2764
128-5/8	19-1/8	19-3/8	15-7/8	5	5	Juneau County	WI	Steve Baker	1982	2764
128-5/8	22-1/8	21-4/8	17-7/8	4	4	Pike County	PA	Joseph V. Caccamo, Jr.	1984	2764
128-5/8	20-2/8	20-2/8	18-5/8	5	5	Kanabec County	MN	Milo L. Carlson	1985	2764
128-5/8	22-1/8	22-1/8	14-5/8	5	5	Kenosha County	WI	Mike Mitten	1985	2764
128-5/8	20-3/8	20-3/8	16-5/8	5	4	Iowa County	WI	Ralph J. Blum	1985	2764
128-5/8	22-5/8	22-5/8	19-0/8	6	4	Green County	WI	Michael G. Martin	1985	2764
128-5/8	21-3/8	21-4/8	18-1/8	4	4	Suffolk County	NY	Richard Kent	1985	2764
128-5/8	23-5/8	24-6/8	18-7/8	6	4	Kandiyohi County	MN	Timothy G. Caven	1986	2764
128-4/8	25-0/8	23-7/8	17-0/8	4	4	Mozart	AR	Alfred Hirt	1959	2785
128-4/8	20-4/8	21-0/8	17-7/8	7	5	Clay County	NE	Rollan Johnson	1961	2785
128-4/8	21-1/8	21-2/8	15-0/8	5	4	Marion County	IA	Thomas Tucker	1968	2785
128-4/8	20-0/8	21-2/8	16-7/8	6	7	Mcleod County	MN	Merlin Eggersgluess	1971	2785
128-4/8	21-6/8	22-3/8	16-6/8	5	5	Jones County	IA	Tom Postel	1971	2785
128-4/8	22-3/8	23-2/8	17-5/8	5	6	Wright County	MN	Elwood Rokala	1971	2785
128-4/8	20-1/8	20-2/8	15-2/8	5	5	Delaware County	OH	Denton O. Baumbarger	1973	2785
128-4/8	25-4/8	23-0/8	15-1/8	5	6	Wapello County	IA	Rick Grooms	1974	2785
128-4/8	22-0/8	21-2/8	13-4/8	5	5	Muskingum County	OH	P. W. "Bill" Meyer	1974	2785
128-4/8	23-1/8	22-0/8	19-0/8	4	6	Henry County	MO	LaVern Rucker	1974	2785
128-4/8	19-5/8	20-3/8	15-4/8	5	5	Ozaukee County	WI	Ronald Mayer	1975	2785
128-4/8	22-0/8	20-4/8	18-2/8	4	4	Rosebud County	MT	Bob Brill	1976	2785
128-4/8	21-0/8	20-6/8	17-4/8	5	5	Kankakee County	IL	Wayne Webber	1983	2785
128-4/8	22-6/8	22-4/8	14-6/8	6	7	Mississippi County	AR	Davy J. Shaw	1983	2785
128-4/8	23-0/8	22-5/8	19-6/8	4	4	Deleware County	PA	Mark Gentry	1984	2785
128-4/8	21-7/8	19-6/8	17-3/8	7	4	Griggs County	ND	Blaine Larson	1984	2785
128-4/8	20-2/8	21-2/8	16-6/8	5	5	Grant County	WI	Jeffery Redfearn	1985	2785
128-4/8	22-7/8	21-5/8	20-4/8	4	5	Platte County	WY	Jayde Allbright	1986	2785
128-4/8	18-6/8	20-3/8	16-2/8	4	4	Plymouth County	IA	Donald F. Pankowski	1986	2785
128-3/8	23-3/8	23-0/8	20-3/8	4	5	Crab Orchard Lake	IL	Don Walker	1959	2804
128-3/8	23-4/8	23-2/8	17-3/8	6	7	Poncil	MT	Bob Samson	1962	2804
128-3/8	19-1/8	19-6/8	15-2/8	6	4	Omaha	NE	Cecil Smith	1962	2804
128-3/8	20-6/8	20-5/8	14-1/8	5	4	Ripley	MN	Ronald Thole	1964	2804
128-3/8	19-6/8	19-7/8	16-7/8	6	5	Columbia County	WI	David D. Luetkens	1965	2804
128-3/8	22-1/8	20-0/8	20-7/8	4	4	Brown County	SD	T. Michael Dunn	1966	2804
128-3/8	21-0/8	22-1/8	18-5/8	5	5	Atterbury	IN	Harold Frye	1966	2804
128-3/8	23-4/8	23-3/8	19-5/8	4	4	Union County	IL	Randy Edmonds	1974	2804
128-3/8	22-0/8	21-7/8	17-7/8	4	4	Switzerland County	IN	Samuel M. Durham	1979	2804
128-3/8	20-4/8	22-1/8	15-1/8	5	5	Highland County	OH	Dean Herschede	1980	2804
128-3/8	21-7/8	22-4/8	18-5/8	5	6	Menominee County	MI	James Saunoris	1980	2804
128-3/8	21-4/8	21-2/8	16-5/8	5	5	Cameron County	TX	Jerry Spencer	1980	2804
128-3/8	24-3/8	23-1/8	20-3/8	4	3	Tazewell County	IL	Jimmy C. Plemmons	1981	2804
128-3/8	20-0/8	19-6/8	16-1/8	4	5	Henry County	KY	Donald Cornett	1982	2804
128-3/8	22-5/8	22-1/8	16-1/8	6	5	Clark County	OH	Rick Rust	1983	2804
128-3/8	23-6/8	23-3/8	20-1/8	4	4	Muskingum County	OH	Mike Spring	1983	2804
128-3/8	20-7/8	21-3/8	17-1/8	5	4	Rock County	WI	Henry W. Holdorf, Jr.	1983	2804
128-3/8	22-2/8	22-6/8	14-7/8	6	6	Clay County	SD	Marlowe Rames	1983	2804
128-3/8	21-1/8	20-5/8	15-3/8	6	6	Anoka County	MN	John Cardinal	1984	2804
128-3/8	23-7/8	22-5/8	20-1/8	4	4	Sheridan County	KS	Tom E. Bowman	1985	2804
128-2/8	22-1/8	21-1/8	15-6/8	5	5	Franklin County	KS	Gary Hunsicker	1966	2824
128-2/8	20-5/8	21-3/8	14-4/8	5	5	Waupaca County	WI	Dennis Arndt	1967	2824
128-2/8	23-0/8	22-5/8	19-1/8	5	5	Lackawanna County	PA	Gary E. Schreck	1971	2824
128-2/8	19-3/8	20-0/8	18-4/8	5	5	Pittsburg County	OK	Pack Giacomo	1972	2824
128-2/8	21-4/8	22-7/8	18-0/8	4	4	Barton County	KS	Nicholas J. Gray	1973	2824
128-2/8	20-5/8	21-4/8	17-0/8	5	5	Buffalo County	NE	Lynn Bombeck	1974	2824
128-2/8	23-1/8	22-7/8	20-3/8	4	5	Jefferson County	OH	Michael W. Brown	1976	2824
128-2/8	21-0/8	21-3/8	17-2/8	4	5	Spokane County	WA	Michael A. Shane	1977	2824
128-2/8	21-1/8	21-4/8	17-0/8	5	5	Green Lake County	WI	Albert G. Slife	1979	2824
128-2/8	19-0/8	19-0/8	14-4/8	5	5	Walworth County	SD	Ronald Arbach	1980	2824
128-2/8	19-0/8	19-1/8	14-4/8	5	5	Travis County	TX	Russell Schmidt	1982	2824
128-2/8	20-4/8	19-6/8	17-6/8	6	5	Floyd County	IA	Johnny Nelson	1982	2824

WHITETAIL DEER *(Typical Antlers)*

(continued)　　　　　　　　　　　　　　　　　　　　　　　　Minimum Score 125

Score	Length of Main Beam R	L	Inside Spread	Number of Points R	L	Area	State/ Province	Hunter's Name	Date	Rank
128-2/8	19-4/8	18-4/8	17-4/8	5	6	Dallas County	IA	Mike Inman	1982	2824
128-2/8	21-7/8	22-4/8	16-6/8	4	4	Todd County	KY	Terry R. Baldwin	1983	2824
128-2/8	22-5/8	22-3/8	17-4/8	3	5	Brown County	KS	Chuck McNally	1983	2824
128-2/8	22-5/8	22-6/8	16-3/8	6	7	Juneau County	WI	Steve Hysell	1984	2824
128-2/8	20-3/8	21-4/8	17-6/8	4	4	Nelson County	ND	Darren Asperheim	1985	2824
128-2/8	22-1/8	22-0/8	17-2/8	6	6	Bleckley County	GA	Wallace Mullis	1985	2824
128-2/8	20-4/8	20-0/8	16-4/8	5	5	Grant County	WI	Robert Govier	1985	2824
128-1/8	20-1/8	21-0/8	17-5/8	5	5	Dorchester County	MD	Powell D. Cook	1964	2843
128-1/8	21-6/8	21-0/8	19-0/8	4	5	Quincy	IL	Clarence Grandt	1972	2843
128-1/8	20-6/8	19-7/8	14-7/8	5	5	Versailles	IN	Sam M. Durham	1978	2843
128-1/8	21-1/8	22-2/8	17-0/8	5	4	South Wayne	WI	W. Grinnell/G. Grinnell	1978	2843
128-1/8	22-6/8	24-0/8	15-1/8	4	4	Chilton County	AL	Dennis Burnett	1980	2843
128-1/8	19-5/8	20-5/8	19-5/8	5	5	Sheboygan County	WI	Mark Kissinger	1980	2843
128-1/8	21-4/8	23-3/8	20-3/8	5	4	Hastings	ONT	Ken McGarrity	1980	2843
128-1/8	22-7/8	22-0/8	19-5/8	5	6	Kingman County	KS	Mark Renollet	1980	2843
128-1/8	20-7/8	19-6/8	18-3/8	4	4	Jefferson County	IL	David R. Darnell	1981	2843
128-1/8	22-7/8	21-7/8	20-1/8	4	4	Carter County	MO	Bill Howe	1981	2843
128-1/8	22-1/8	20-0/8	17-0/8	5	6	Lake County	IL	Donald Schram	1981	2843
128-1/8	21-4/8	22-0/8	17-4/8	4	5	Elgin County	ONT	Peter Hartmann	1982	2843
128-1/8	21-4/8	21-2/8	16-3/8	6	7	Winnebago County	IL	Robert W. Shallenberger, Sr.	1982	2843
128-1/8	21-1/8	21-5/8	16-3/8	4	4	Calhoun County	MI	Clarence Bowers, Jr.	1982	2843
128-1/8	22-1/8	22-1/8	18-3/8	5	5	Marquette County	WI	Newell Easley	1984	2843
128-1/8	22-6/8	19-0/8	16-6/8	5	7	Rock County	WI	Rodger Veneman	1984	2843
128-1/8	22-6/8	23-3/8	17-1/8	5	4	Brown County	SD	Ron Rockwell	1984	2843
128-1/8	20-0/8	20-1/8	16-3/8	5	5	Mower County	MN	John S. Adams	1985	2843
128-1/8	21-5/8	21-2/8	18-5/8	4	4	Washington County	MS	Bobby Ray Woods	1985	2843
128-1/8	21-7/8	21-4/8	15-4/8	6	6	Dallas County	MO	Jay Strain	1985	2843
128-1/8	22-4/8	22-3/8	18-5/8	5	5	Barry County	MI	Ron Rolfe	1985	2843
128-0/8	18-7/8	18-1/8	17-4/8	5	5	Snake Creek	ND	Bennie R. Maytum	1960	2864
128-0/8	22-7/8	23-0/8	19-0/8	6	8	Sibley County	MN	Darwin Grack	1972	2864
128-0/8	22-1/8	22-6/8	17-4/8	5	5	Pine County	MN	Larry Hochmayr	1973	2864
128-0/8	22-3/8	21-2/8	17-0/8	4	4	Macon County	MO	Joe E. McCray	1973	2864
128-0/8	23-2/8	23-0/8	18-2/8	5	5	Jasper County	IA	Paul Casper	1974	2864
128-0/8	19-3/8	19-1/8	15-2/8	5	4	Clearwater County	MN	Warren Nelson	1975	2864
128-0/8	21-5/8	20-5/8	16-0/8	4	4	Vergas	MN	Scott M. Dirks	1978	2864
128-0/8	19-6/8	21-0/8	15-5/8	5	6	Winona County	MN	Martin Szekeresh, Jr.	1978	2864
128-0/8	20-1/8	19-5/8	18-6/8	4	4	Cumberland County	NJ	John J. Newton III	1980	2864
128-0/8	21-5/8	21-7/8	17-6/8	4	5	Towanda	KS	Darrell Wolf	1980	2864
128-0/8	21-1/8	21-6/8	18-0/8	6	8	Allegheny County	PA	Albert Polovich, Jr.	1981	2864
128-0/8	21-2/8	21-1/8	16-4/8	5	6	LaSalle County	IL	Richard Schupp	1983	2864
128-0/8	20-6/8	20-0/8	18-6/8	5	5	St. Charles County	MO	Joseph L. Vincent	1983	2864
128-0/8	22-1/8	22-0/8	15-2/8	5	5	Montgomery County	OH	Gary W. Roberson	1984	2864
128-0/8	22-6/8	22-5/8	17-6/8	4	4	Effingham County	IL	Rick J. Hartke	1985	2864
128-0/8	20-2/8	20-1/8	15-4/8	7	6	Pittsburg County	OK	Everett Laney	1985	2864
128-0/8	21-2/8	21-4/8	16-4/8	5	4	Clark County	OH	Ronald Lockhart	1985	2864
128-0/8	21-7/8	21-0/8	17-7/8	6	5	Rock County	WI	Jerry D. Amundson	1985	2864
128-0/8	21-7/8	22-0/8	19-6/8	4	4	Licking County	OH	Randy D. Ricketts	1985	2864
128-0/8	21-4/8	21-6/8	16-0/8	4	4	Louisa County	IA	Roger Gipple	1985	2864
128-0/8	21-3/8	21-2/8	25-2/8	5	4	Pratt County	KS	C. J. Eifert	1985	2864
128-0/8	19-2/8	20-5/8	17-2/8	5	5	Green County	WI	David R. Covert	1986	2864
127-7/8	21-4/8	20-0/8	18-1/8	4	4	Monroe State Forest	IN	Jerry L. Swafford	1968	2886
127-7/8	21-5/8	21-2/8	15-5/8	6	6	Henderson County	IL	Randy Moore	1971	2886
127-7/8	21-4/8	21-1/8	18-1/8	4	4	Fairfield County	OH	James Munyon	1971	2886
127-7/8	19-2/8	20-3/8	15-7/8	6	5	Jones County	IA	Larry Stewart	1972	2886
127-7/8	20-3/8	20-2/8	18-5/8	4	4	Chadron	NE	Roger Adamson	1975	2886
127-7/8	23-5/8	24-5/8	16-7/8	5	6	Burleigh County	ND	Kevin Hertz	1980	2886
127-7/8	22-7/8	23-1/8	17-1/8	5	5	Scott County	MN	Jim Manuel	1980	2886
127-7/8	18-2/8	18-1/8	15-6/8	6	6	St. Croix County	WI	Larry Williamson	1981	2886
127-7/8	22-1/8	22-0/8	18-1/8	6	5	Boyle County	KY	Carroll Williams	1981	2886
127-7/8	21-7/8	20-4/8	17-7/8	5	5	Robertson County	TN	Walter C. Kirby	1983	2886
127-7/8	21-1/8	21-4/8	16-7/8	4	4	Reno County	KS	Todd Murray	1983	2886
127-7/8	21-0/8	20-7/8	14-6/8	5	5	Genesee County	MI	Bob Bouck	1985	2886
127-7/8	22-4/8	23-5/8	21-4/8	5	6	Lake County	IL	Edward H. Bellmore	1985	2886

WHITETAIL DEER *(Typical Antlers)*

Minimum Score 125   (continued)

Score	Length of Main Beam R	L	Inside Spread	Number of Points R	L	Area	State/ Province	Hunter's Name	Date	Rank
127-7/8	22-0/8	22-0/8	18-1/8	6	8	Nez Perce County	ID	Brad Johnson	1985	2886
127-6/8	21-3/8	22-2/8	16-2/8	4	4	Northfield	MN	David Knutson	1969	2900
127-6/8	24-4/8	23-6/8	18-3/8	6	5	Muskingum County	OH	Charles F. Fineran	1974	2900
127-6/8	20-0/8	19-3/8	17-0/8	4	4	Tucker County	WV	Larry A. Williams	1975	2900
127-6/8	20-2/8	21-2/8	16-0/8	6	5	Rice County	MN	James Caron	1979	2900
127-6/8	21-6/8	21-5/8	15-6/8	4	4	Sawyer	ND	Larry Ziech	1979	2900
127-6/8	23-2/8	23-6/8	18-1/8	5	5	Sumner County	KS	Mark Disney	1980	2900
127-6/8	20-6/8	21-0/8	16-4/8	5	5	Marion County	KY	Hugh Glasscock	1980	2900
127-6/8	21-7/8	21-7/8	17-6/8	5	5	Waupaca County	WI	Bryon Gyldenvand	1981	2900
127-6/8	23-6/8	22-2/8	17-4/8	4	4	Hardin County	IA	Richard Pugh	1981	2900
127-6/8	24-7/8	24-5/8	19-0/8	5	5	Clark County	SD	Jan Buri	1982	2900
127-6/8	24-2/8	23-1/8	20-0/8	4	4	Blue Earth County	MN	Bruce Barrie	1983	2900
127-6/8	23-4/8	24-4/8	20-4/8	4	4	Waukesha County	WI	Max Mollgaard	1983	2900
127-6/8	20-4/8	20-5/8	18-0/8	5	4	Monongalia County	WV	Marshall Ridenour	1984	2900
127-6/8	22-1/8	21-6/8	16-6/8	4	4	Rogers County	OK	Tom Woosley	1984	2900
127-6/8	22-1/8	21-5/8	17-0/8	4	5	St. Albert	ALB	Gary Kieser	1984	2900
127-6/8	23-6/8	22-1/8	17-2/8	5	4	Darke County	OH	Bruce Knick	1985	2900
127-6/8	20-4/8	20-6/8	15-4/8	4	5	Buffalo County	WI	David J. Gard	1985	2900
127-5/8	21-4/8	22-1/8	17-3/8	5	5	Florida	MO	C. R. Jackson	1962	2917
127-5/8	22-3/8	22-3/8	16-5/8	6	5	Vilas County	WI	Carl R. Strauss	1968	2917
127-5/8	21-2/8	21-0/8	18-3/8	5	5	Warren County	NJ	Jerry W. Kauffman	1972	2917
127-5/8	22-0/8	22-6/8	14-7/8	4	4	Winnebago County	IA	Kenneth R. Coe, Jr.	1973	2917
127-5/8	22-6/8	23-0/8	23-7/8	4	4	Broad River	SD	John V. Orr	1973	2917
127-5/8	24-4/8	24-5/8	19-0/8	4	5	Wayne County	OH	Ronald Stine	1975	2917
127-5/8	21-5/8	22-1/8	14-4/8	6	6	Sauk County	WI	Walter S. Jankowski	1976	2917
127-5/8	21-0/8	21-3/8	16-5/8	4	4	Dickson	TN	Andy Jackson	1976	2917
127-5/8	23-2/8	22-4/8	16-1/8	5	5	Tuscarawas County	OH	Jon Scheetz	1976	2917
127-5/8	21-6/8	21-6/8	20-1/8	5	5	Rock County	WI	Jeffrey L. Kersten	1979	2917
127-5/8	20-6/8	21-4/8	15-7/8	5	5	Clark County	WI	James Kleinschmidt	1979	2917
127-5/8	21-7/8	22-4/8	18-5/8	5	5	Tuscarwas County	OH	John H. Raber	1981	2917
127-5/8	19-6/8	19-4/8	17-7/8	5	5	Scott County	KY	Michael A. Fry	1982	2917
127-5/8	22-5/8	23-3/8	17-7/8	4	4	Roane County	TN	William A. "Bill" Simms	1985	2917
127-5/8	21-3/8	23-5/8	14-5/8	5	5	Anoka County	MN	Robert G. Ross	1985	2917
127-5/8	23-7/8	24-4/8	16-7/8	5	5	Licking County	OH	Michael Stumph	1985	2917
127-5/8	21-0/8	21-2/8	20-1/8	5	5	Meigs County	OH	Eric A. Harris	1985	2917
127-5/8	24-2/8	23-4/8	17-3/8	4	4	Kandiyohi County	MN	Mark Harder	1986	2917
127-4/8	20-5/8	20-5/8	16-2/8	5	5	Boone County	MO	Roger Soukup	1978	2935
127-4/8	20-3/8	20-6/8	16-6/8	5	5	Wapello County	IA	Arnold E. Vest	1978	2935
127-4/8	23-5/8	22-5/8	17-2/8	6	5	Muskingum County	OH	Mike Harris	1980	2935
127-4/8	21-4/8	21-5/8	17-1/8	4	7	Trego County	KS	Ron Bain	1981	2935
127-4/8	21-5/8	22-6/8	18-5/8	7	5	Des Moines County	IA	Jim Edwards	1982	2935
127-4/8	19-4/8	18-5/8	16-4/8	5	5	Allen County	KS	Ivan Cooper	1983	2935
127-4/8	21-3/8	22-4/8	17-0/8	4	4	Lake County	IL	Mike Mitten	1983	2935
127-4/8	23-0/8	23-2/8	19-2/8	4	4	Van Buren County	MI	Ken Probst	1983	2935
127-4/8	21-1/8	20-7/8	15-0/8	5	4	Nodaway County	MO	Jeff Davison	1983	2935
127-4/8	19-6/8	20-0/8	16-6/8	5	5	Cherokee County	KS	Larry Thomas	1983	2935
127-4/8	22-4/8	22-5/8	20-3/8	5	4	Nacogdoches County	TX	Harvy Hamby	1984	2935
127-4/8	20-2/8	20-5/8	14-4/8	5	6	Crawford County	WI	Emil H. Loether, Jr.	1984	2935
127-4/8	21-1/8	19-7/8	17-0/8	4	4	Henderson County	KY	Wesley Campbell	1985	2935
127-4/8	23-5/8	23-3/8	19-4/8	4	4	Somerset County	NJ	Steve Kotz	1985	2935
127-4/8	22-2/8	21-5/8	15-2/8	6	6	Lake County	IL	David Mitten	1986	2935
127-4/8	23-2/8	23-3/8	17-2/8	5	4	Waukesha County	WI	Ron Hill	1986	2935
127-3/8	22-0/8	22-1/8	17-3/8	4	4	Lee County	IA	Lewallen Foster	1972	2951
127-3/8	19-5/8	19-7/8	17-1/8	6	5	Scott County	KY	John Farris	1977	2951
127-3/8	20-1/8	20-4/8	16-7/8	4	5	Suffolk County	NY	William R. Quarltere	1979	2951
127-3/8	21-6/8	21-1/8	15-6/8	5	6	Waupaca County	WI	Daniel E. Yaeger	1979	2951
127-3/8	21-6/8	22-0/8	22-0/8	5	5	Hartford Mills	NY	John B. Andrews	1980	2951
127-3/8	22-3/8	22-1/8	17-1/8	5	5	Washington County	KS	Bob Funke	1981	2951
127-3/8	20-5/8	21-7/8	17-1/8	8	7	Sauk County	WI	Roger D. Vondrasek	1981	2951
127-3/8	21-1/8	20-3/8	15-5/8	6	6	Miami County	KS	Tom Wiggin	1982	2951
127-3/8	20-3/8	20-2/8	17-3/8	4	4	Neosho County	KS	John R. Blackburn	1983	2951
127-3/8	20-2/8	20-0/8	15-1/8	5	6	Ferry County	WA	Robert McIntosh	1983	2951
127-3/8	20-0/8	20-0/8	17-7/8	5	5	Waldo County	ME	Debbie A. Small	1984	2951

WHITETAIL DEER *(Typical Antlers)*

(continued)

Minimum Score 125

Score	Length of Main Beam R	L	Inside Spread	Number of Points R	L	Area	State/ Province	Hunter's Name	Date	Rank
127-3/8	21-3/8	22-6/8	13-7/8	5	5	Columbia County	WI	Richard J. Sutter	1985	2951
127-3/8	20-5/8	21-3/8	18-7/8	4	4	Outagamie County	WI	Robert Randerson	1985	2951
127-3/8	22-2/8	22-3/8	16-7/8	5	5	Harris County	GA	Allan Rovig	1986	2951
127-2/8	22-2/8	23-1/8	16-2/8	5	5	Madison County	AR	Johnny Darris	1964	2965
127-2/8	23-5/8	23-7/8	16-4/8	4	3	Lawrence County	IL	Steven R. Tice	1967	2965
127-2/8	22-0/8	21-3/8	17-2/8	4	5	Champaign County	IL	Pete Shepley	1972	2965
127-2/8	20-1/8	20-2/8	16-0/8	5	5	Naples	NY	Robert G. Achter	1973	2965
127-2/8	19-2/8	19-0/8	15-2/8	5	5	Blue Earth County	MN	Stanley R. Defries	1973	2965
127-2/8	21-7/8	21-2/8	15-6/8	5	4	Jefferson County	IN	Robert Pitt	1978	2965
127-2/8	21-7/8	22-3/8	17-2/8	4	4	Latah County	ID	Mike VonLindern	1978	2965
127-2/8	23-6/8	22-4/8	20-2/8	4	4	Bayfield County	WI	Mark Milford	1980	2965
127-2/8	22-4/8	21-6/8	16-4/8	4	5	Oconto County	WI	Don Fullerton	1982	2965
127-2/8	23-3/8	21-3/8	20-3/8	5	5	Hunterdon County	NJ	Wayne Lisehora	1982	2965
127-2/8	22-1/8	21-3/8	17-4/8	4	4	Stanley County	SD	Brad Taylor	1983	2965
127-2/8	22-2/8	22-1/8	17-4/8	5	5	Sauk County	WI	James Byrnes	1983	2965
127-2/8	23-1/8	24-0/8	19-4/8	6	9	Morrison County	MN	Ken Arnzen	1984	2965
127-2/8	18-6/8	18-5/8	21-2/8	7	5	Lake County	MI	James H. Wichman	1984	2965
127-2/8	22-0/8	21-5/8	16-7/8	7	5	Christian County	IL	James Eck	1984	2965
127-2/8	22-6/8	23-2/8	14-6/8	4	4	Grant County	OK	Ronnie B Smart	1985	2965
127-2/8	21-0/8	19-6/8	13-6/8	5	4	Marshall County	KS	Ray Aslin	1985	2965
127-2/8	23-2/8	20-5/8	16-6/8	5	4	Clay County	KS	Jan Kissinger	1985	2965
127-2/8	22-3/8	21-7/8	16-3/8	6	5	Powell County	MT	Sonny Templeton	1985	2965
127-2/8	20-5/8	20-6/8	13-6/8	4	4	Mclean County	ND	Eugene Radke	1986	2965
127-2/8	24-0/8	23-4/8	16-4/8	5	5	Bertie County	NC	Roy Copeland	1986	2965
127-1/8	19-5/8	20-5/8	15-1/8	4	4	Oneida County	WI	Fred Felbab	1961	2986
127-1/8	21-0/8	20-4/8	18-3/8	6	5	Marion County	IA	Donald C. Clark	1970	2986
127-1/8	18-0/8	20-5/8	15-5/8	5	5	Des Moines	IA	Roy Veach	1970	2986
127-1/8	23-0/8	23-0/8	16-7/8	4	4	Union County	IA	Richard Siddens	1971	2986
127-1/8	22-7/8	21-6/8	16-5/8	5	5	Gratiot County	MI	Kim Hagerman	1979	2986
127-1/8	20-6/8	21-4/8	16-5/8	4	4	Keith County	NE	Tom Tietz	1981	2986
127-1/8	21-6/8	23-3/8	18-7/8	4	4	Massac County	IL	John Shelby	1981	2986
127-1/8	19-4/8	20-2/8	16-3/8	5	6	Bon Homme County	SD	John P. Freidel	1982	2986
127-1/8	20-3/8	19-1/8	16-5/8	5	5	Jefferson County	IL	Ed Knaus	1983	2986
127-1/8	20-2/8	21-3/8	18-5/8	5	5	Levenworth County	KS	Albert Lyle Karl	1983	2986
127-1/8	21-3/8	21-4/8	17-0/8	5	5	Bullock County	AL	James D Sims	1984	2986
127-1/8	21-6/8	21-7/8	15-3/8	5	5	Madison County	NY	Louis A Colasanti	1984	2986
127-1/8	23-4/8	21-5/8	18-3/8	5	5	Wyandotte County	KS	Spencer G. Ishmael	1984	2986
127-1/8	19-6/8	21-2/8	14-0/8	5	6	Scott County	MN	Ron Stier	1984	2986
127-1/8	20-2/8	20-0/8	20-3/8	4	4	Towner County	ND	Trent Halberstroh	1984	2986
127-1/8	22-1/8	20-7/8	18-5/8	5	5	Somerset County	NJ	Joe Cotone	1985	2986
127-1/8	23-1/8	24-1/8	19-0/8	8	6	Ogle County	IL	Bifford J. Wyatt	1985	2986
127-0/8	26-1/8	26-3/8	17-6/8	5	5	Boone County	KY	Steve Toles	1976	3003
127-0/8	20-3/8	20-3/8	15-6/8	6	6	Sauk County	WI	Adrian Julson	1979	3003
127-0/8	23-5/8	23-3/8	19-0/8	5	4	Licking County	OH	Curtis W. Price	1979	3003
127-0/8	20-0/8	20-7/8	18-2/8	5	5	Harris County	TX	Daniel Barnes	1980	3003
127-0/8	22-4/8	21-4/8	15-4/8	5	6	Tuscarawas County	OH	David Pappas	1980	3003
127-0/8	22-2/8	22-2/8	14-2/8	8	6	Kittson County	MN	John S. Ritter	1981	3003
127-0/8	19-5/8	18-4/8	18-4/8	5	5	Graham County	KS	Russell Hull	1981	3003
127-0/8	20-7/8	21-4/8	18-4/8	4	4	Miller County	MO	Gary Haupt	1982	3003
127-0/8	21-1/8	20-3/8	14-6/8	5	5	Coahoma County	MS	Charles L. Campassi	1983	3003
127-0/8	21-6/8	20-3/8	17-2/8	4	5	Dane County	WI	Charles F. Hilgendorf	1983	3003
127-0/8	22-6/8	22-6/8	17-2/8	5	5	Spokane County	WA	William J. Lantiegne	1983	3003
127-0/8	22-2/8	22-4/8	15-6/8	5	5	Sauk County	WI	Richard A. Galston	1984	3003
127-0/8	23-1/8	23-1/8	17-6/8	4	5	Litchfield County	CT	Michael Cristillo	1984	3003
127-0/8	19-6/8	18-3/8	16-6/8	5	5	Wayne County	NE	Mike Lutt	1984	3003
127-0/8	19-6/8	19-3/8	16-4/8	5	5	Door County	WI	Wayne Lautenbach	1985	3003
127-0/8	20-0/8	19-4/8	15-0/8	5	5	Audrain County	MO	Marty Bertels	1985	3003
127-0/8	21-5/8	21-1/8	17-0/8	5	4	Powell County	MT	Sonny Templeton	1985	3003
127-0/8	19-6/8	20-3/8	16-0/8	4	4	Dickinson County	KS	Bradley Wayne Whisler	1985	3003
127-0/8	21-0/8	23-6/8	18-4/8	5	5	Lafayette County	WI	Jerod Ray	1985	3003
127-0/8	23-7/8	24-3/8	16-0/8	4	5	Montgomery County	AL	David Barrow	1986	3003
126-7/8	22-5/8	22-6/8	17-4/8	5	4	Dade County	MO	Paul Watson	1970	3023
126-7/8	21-7/8	21-0/8	14-4/8	5	4	Calhoun County	MI	Tom A. Longnecker	1976	3023

WHITETAIL DEER *(Typical Antlers)*

Minimum Score 125

(continued)

Score	Length of Main Beam R	L	Inside Spread	Number of Points R	L	Area	State/ Province	Hunter's Name	Date	Rank
126-7/8	20-0/8	20-4/8	18-3/8	5	5	Muscatine	IA	Ronald W. Crain	1978	3023
126-7/8	22-4/8	22-0/8	17-3/8	6	6	Waukesha County	WI	Daniel J. Hanrahan	1978	3023
126-7/8	21-3/8	21-2/8	16-7/8	6	5	Pine County	MN	Randy Krone	1979	3023
126-7/8	25-5/8	24-6/8	20-3/8	4	4	Washington County	WI	Brent Grensavitch	1980	3023
126-7/8	20-0/8	23-3/8	16-3/8	5	5	Tazewell County	IL	Kenneth Hoback	1981	3023
126-7/8	21-4/8	21-4/8	17-7/8	5	6	Huron County	MI	Greg Talaski	1981	3023
126-7/8	22-7/8	22-2/8	17-3/8	4	4	Brown County	MN	Robert Hertling	1982	3023
126-7/8	22-3/8	22-7/8	16-5/8	4	5	Ogle County	IL	Jerry Taylor	1982	3023
126-7/8	21-5/8	22-2/8	17-3/8	4	5	Vinton County	OH	Mitchell Barnett	1982	3023
126-7/8	22-4/8	23-2/8	18-7/8	4	4	Lake County	IL	Carl H. Spaeth	1983	3023
126-7/8	20-5/8	20-4/8	15-7/8	5	4	Brown County	SD	Jack Ness	1984	3023
126-7/8	17-7/8	18-3/8	14-5/8	5	5	Howard County	IN	James E Taylor	1984	3023
126-7/8	24-0/8	23-1/8	17-7/8	4	4	Isanti County	MN	Gary Lamecker	1985	3023
126-7/8	22-0/8	22-5/8	15-1/8	5	5	Dekalb County	GA	William C. Abernethy	1985	3023
126-7/8	21-7/8	21-4/8	15-5/8	4	5	Polk County	WI	Steve Hischer	1986	3023
126-6/8	22-5/8	22-0/8	17-2/8	6	4	Winneshiek County	IA	Nick Bowlus	1952	3040
126-6/8	20-0/8	19-5/8	13-4/8	5	6	Pine County	MN	Marvin W. Brown	1968	3040
126-6/8	18-1/8	18-2/8	15-6/8	5	5	Todd County	MN	Paul Jenc	1973	3040
126-6/8	22-0/8	20-7/8	17-4/8	5	5	Fulton County	IN	John W. Baker	1974	3040
126-6/8	21-6/8	24-1/8	17-2/8	4	4	Calhoun County	MI	James Birmingham	1976	3040
126-6/8	20-7/8	21-1/8	15-2/8	5	5	Montgomery County	KS	Mike Nixon	1976	3040
126-6/8	21-0/8	21-0/8	16-2/8	5	4	Woodford County	IL	Rick D. Snell	1976	3040
126-6/8	23-0/8	22-5/8	18-4/8	4	4	Grant County	WV	Carl Muth	1977	3040
126-6/8	22-1/8	22-1/8	17-0/8	4	5	Jasper	IN	Gary Shaw	1980	3040
126-6/8	25-0/8	24-0/8	19-2/8	4	4	Auglaize County	OH	Lee Atha	1981	3040
126-6/8	22-2/8	22-5/8	18-6/8	4	5	Genesee County	MI	Bob Bouck	1983	3040
126-6/8	20-0/8	22-0/8	14-6/8	5	5	Licking County	OH	Dana E. Kevelder	1983	3040
126-6/8	20-2/8	20-6/8	16-0/8	5	5	Lee County	IA	Dan Wilcox	1983	3040
126-6/8	24-2/8	22-7/8	17-6/8	6	6	Douglas County	NE	Jim Walter	1985	3040
126-6/8	20-4/8	21-4/8	17-6/8	4	4	Crawford County	WI	Calvin Hendrick	1985	3040
126-6/8	21-4/8	20-4/8	15-7/8	7	5	Bollinger County	MO	Rodney C. Bowling	1985	3040
126-5/8	22-4/8	22-0/8	21-5/8	4	4	Pine County	MN	Buck Doran	1945	3056
126-5/8	22-5/8	23-0/8	19-0/8	5	5	Roberts County	SD	Roland L. Hausmann	1961	3056
126-5/8	21-5/8	21-3/8	19-3/8	4	4	Nineveh	IN	Roger E. Harvey	1975	3056
126-5/8	23-4/8	25-0/8	19-7/8	6	6	Wellington County	ONT	James A. Reid	1976	3056
126-5/8	21-4/8	21-6/8	17-2/8	7	7	Jackson County	MI	Gary A. Dawson	1980	3056
126-5/8	21-0/8	19-7/8	16-5/8	4	4	Boligee	AL	Alvin Pearson	1980	3056
126-5/8	19-7/8	19-3/8	14-1/8	5	4	Owen County	IN	Bill G. Tanner	1980	3056
126-5/8	19-5/8	20-4/8	16-3/8	5	5	Waupaca County	WI	Mark Jahr	1981	3056
126-5/8	18-2/8	18-2/8	12-7/8	6	5	Johnson County	WY	Jerry N. Blossom	1983	3056
126-5/8	21-2/8	21-7/8	14-3/8	4	4	Boone County	IA	Tim Marshall	1983	3056
126-5/8	21-5/8	21-3/8	16-6/8	6	6	Lake County	IL	Mark Fugett	1984	3056
126-4/8	20-4/8	21-2/8	18-6/8	5	5	Warren County	PA	Fred Massa	1967	3067
126-4/8	21-2/8	21-3/8	15-2/8	4	4	Chester County	PA	Joseph R. Yannelli	1967	3067
126-4/8	19-7/8	19-6/8	16-4/8	5	5	Owen County	IN	G. Fred Asbell	1971	3067
126-4/8	22-4/8	21-6/8	17-4/8	4	4	Waupaca County	WI	Arlin Kersten, Jr.	1971	3067
126-4/8	22-1/8	22-0/8	18-2/8	5	4	Cayuga County	NY	John Pardee	1971	3067
126-4/8	21-2/8	21-3/8	12-4/8	4	4	Bayfield County	WI	Del Zwiefelhofer	1972	3067
126-4/8	24-6/8	25-0/8	17-0/8	5	4	Portage County	OH	Burt Thompson, Jr.	1976	3067
126-4/8	23-4/8	24-2/8	17-6/8	4	4	Westchester County	NY	Richard T. Burke	1977	3067
126-4/8	22-3/8	20-7/8	15-6/8	4	4	Phillips County	KS	Orville D. Blubaugh	1977	3067
126-4/8	21-1/8	21-5/8	17-6/8	4	4	Macon	MO	Bruce Hamel	1979	3067
126-4/8	20-4/8	20-3/8	16-2/8	5	5	Harford County	MD	Donald P. Conley	1980	3067
126-4/8	21-7/8	21-0/8	16-0/8	4	5	Edmonton	ALB	Al Schulz	1981	3067
126-4/8	22-6/8	22-0/8	18-7/8	6	5	Clearwater County	ID	J. David Powers	1982	3067
126-4/8	20-4/8	19-6/8	13-2/8	5	5	Olmstead County	MN	Tom Lofgren	1983	3067
126-4/8	20-6/8	21-1/8	15-2/8	4	4	Dane County	WI	Victor H. Mittelstaedt	1983	3067
126-4/8	19-4/8	21-4/8	20-4/8	5	5	Schulyer County	NY	Richard Murphy	1983	3067
126-4/8	21-0/8	21-3/8	15-6/8	5	5	Kent County	MD	Raymond A. Boley	1984	3067
126-4/8	21-6/8	21-6/8	15-4/8	5	5	Somerset County	NJ	Ronald L. Taylor, Sr.	1985	3067
126-4/8	23-4/8	21-2/8	17-5/8	6	5	Menard County	IL	Donald Alwerdt	1985	3067
126-4/8	21-6/8	21-0/8	17-6/8	5	6	Muskingum County	OH	Allen Randal Smith	1985	3067
126-4/8	22-1/8	21-1/8	17-4/8	6	6	Ionia County	MI	Todd E. Peacock	1986	3067

WHITETAIL DEER *(Typical Antlers)*

(continued)

Score	Length of Main Beam R	Length of Main Beam L	Inside Spread	Number of Points R	Number of Points L	Area	State/ Province	Hunter's Name	Date	Rank
126-3/8	23-1/8	23-3/8	17-5/8	4	4	Sussex County	NJ	Jim Ott	1972	3088
126-3/8	21-5/8	20-2/8	17-0/8	5	6	Gallatin	KY	Robert L. Hegge, Jr.	1973	3088
126-3/8	22-4/8	22-4/8	16-3/8	5	5	Augusta	WI	Steven P. Gilbertson	1977	3088
126-3/8	21-0/8	21-5/8	17-7/8	7	6	Clark County	KS	William Rule	1978	3088
126-3/8	25-3/8	25-0/8	18-4/8	5	5	Morris County	NJ	Kurt Carlson	1982	3088
126-3/8	23-3/8	22-4/8	15-3/8	4	4	Cayuaga County	NY	John Pardee	1982	3088
126-3/8	20-0/8	20-5/8	14-1/8	5	5	Shoshone County	ID	Richard J. O'Grady	1983	3088
126-3/8	22-4/8	23-4/8	16-5/8	5	5	Sheboygan County	WI	Ronald Cook	1983	3088
126-3/8	19-3/8	19-4/8	15-5/8	4	4	Polk County	WI	Allen Lunde	1984	3088
126-3/8	22-3/8	21-4/8	18-2/8	6	6	Rock County	WI	John Van Altena	1984	3088
126-3/8	21-2/8	21-1/8	14-6/8	6	6	Washington County	KS	Stan Brustowicz	1984	3088
126-3/8	21-4/8	20-0/8	16-7/8	5	5	Dodge County	WI	Carl Schuett	1985	3088
126-3/8	21-7/8	20-4/8	16-3/8	4	4	Waukesha County	WI	Dale J. Henderson	1985	3088
126-3/8	20-2/8	18-2/8	16-1/8	4	5	Gregory County	SD	Dennis Lengkeek	1986	3088
126-2/8	22-7/8	22-0/8	17-2/8	5	5	Harmon	IL	Edmund R. Braun	1959	3102
126-2/8	22-0/8	20-6/8	17-6/8	4	4	Johnson County	IA	Paul F. Spicer	1963	3102
126-2/8	20-0/8	19-3/8	16-0/8	4	4	Harding County	SD	Gerald Swayze	1965	3102
126-2/8	21-3/8	21-4/8	15-4/8	4	4	Ripley	MN	Frank Hogan	1967	3102
126-2/8	20-6/8	20-2/8	15-6/8	5	5	Long Island	IL	Adrian K. Smith	1967	3102
126-2/8	21-4/8	21-4/8	16-2/8	4	4	Dodge City	KS	Bob Stephenson	1967	3102
126-2/8	20-1/8	20-7/8	14-4/8	5	5	Platte County	NE	Keith Bruhn	1968	3102
126-2/8	23-7/8	23-5/8	17-3/8	5	4	Marathon County	WI	Dan Niehaus	1968	3102
126-2/8	22-1/8	21-5/8	16-0/8	5	5	Dade County	MO	Charles A. Myers	1975	3102
126-2/8	20-0/8	20-0/8	14-6/8	5	5	Washington County	OH	Joe D. Schofield	1977	3102
126-2/8	20-7/8	21-4/8	16-0/8	5	5	Dodge County	WI	Keith Peterson	1977	3102
126-2/8	18-0/8	18-5/8	15-0/8	5	5	Wood County	WI	David Kievet	1978	3102
126-2/8	20-6/8	20-5/8	13-5/8	6	6	Kettle Falls	WA	David B. Muffly	1978	3102
126-2/8	21-4/8	21-7/8	17-2/8	5	5	Waupaca County	WI	Daniel E. Yaeger	1978	3102
126-2/8	22-2/8	22-4/8	16-4/8	4	3	Franklin County	OH	Steven H. Byerly	1979	3102
126-2/8	20-0/8	20-3/8	16-2/8	4	4	Greenwood County	SC	E. Dale Carwile	1980	3102
126-2/8	22-5/8	21-6/8	17-2/8	6	5	Livingston County	MO	Myles Keller	1980	3102
126-2/8	21-5/8	22-4/8	16-4/8	9	4	Jefferson County	NE	Bob Funke	1981	3102
126-2/8	21-5/8	20-7/8	20-2/8	4	5	Lyon County	MN	Wayne Kumm	1981	3102
126-2/8	22-2/8	22-2/8	17-2/8	4	6	Kearney County	KS	David Meyers	1981	3102
126-2/8	21-2/8	21-2/8	15-2/8	4	5	Meigs County	OH	Charles H. Murray	1982	3102
126-2/8	22-1/8	22-2/8	15-4/8	5	5	Live Oak County	TX	Rick Hayley	1983	3102
126-2/8	23-1/8	23-0/8	20-3/8	6	6	Marquette County	WI	Stewart McReath	1983	3102
126-2/8	22-2/8	21-2/8	17-2/8	5	5	Venango County	PA	Jeffrey S. Morrison	1983	3102
126-2/8	22-6/8	22-5/8	13-4/8	5	6	Preble County	OH	Roger D. Dolph	1983	3102
126-2/8	21-0/8	21-1/8	17-4/8	4	4	Lake County	IL	Henry J. Schwarz	1983	3102
126-2/8	19-2/8	20-5/8	17-6/8	6	5	Clay County	MN	Steve Steinhoff	1983	3102
126-2/8	22-6/8	22-1/8	14-4/8	4	5	Dane County	WI	Dennis L. Stiklestad	1983	3102
126-2/8	21-0/8	20-0/8	12-6/8	5	5	Augusta County	VA	Nicholas C. Taylor	1984	3102
126-2/8	19-0/8	20-0/8	18-0/8	5	5	Athens County	OH	Craig Littler	1984	3102
126-2/8	20-3/8	19-6/8	14-4/8	5	5	McKenzie County	ND	Tim Finley	1985	3102
126-2/8	18-4/8	19-6/8	15-2/8	4	4	Pulaski County	IN	Tony Bean	1985	3102
126-2/8	22-2/8	21-2/8	17-2/8	4	5	Pittsburg County	OK	Jim Stith	1985	3102
126-2/8	22-0/8	22-4/8	15-4/8	5	6	Boone County	MO	Tommy Foster	1985	3102
126-1/8	25-2/8	24-5/8	18-5/8	4	4	York County	PA	Gregory E. Smith	1969	3136
126-1/8	22-1/8	21-7/8	16-5/8	5	4	Monmouth County	NJ	Charles C. Lasala	1970	3136
126-1/8	20-4/8	18-6/8	18-1/8	4	4	Pope County	IL	Murray Schuhart	1972	3136
126-1/8	21-4/8	21-4/8	16-3/8	4	5	Newton Hills State Park	SD	Stephen K. Sona	1975	3136
126-1/8	21-3/8	20-5/8	14-4/8	5	4	Oconto County	WI	Rick Moudry	1977	3136
126-1/8	22-0/8	21-1/8	17-1/8	5	5	Gladwin County	MI	Dave Longstreth	1980	3136
126-1/8	18-1/8	18-7/8	15-3/8	5	5	Brown County	SD	Charles Fulker	1980	3136
126-1/8	23-4/8	22-3/8	16-6/8	6	5	Rice County	MN	Jeff Purdie	1981	3136
126-1/8	21-4/8	21-5/8	17-1/8	5	5	Richland County	WI	David P. Berns	1982	3136
126-1/8	22-1/8	21-5/8	18-7/8	4	4	LaMoure County	ND	Rodney W. Peterson	1985	3136
126-0/8	20-3/8	20-3/8	14-0/8	4	4	Cherry County	NE	Dean Bergman	1975	3146
126-0/8	22-1/8	20-4/8	16-2/8	5	4	McMinn County	TN	Wesley B. Snyder	1975	3146
126-0/8	18-4/8	17-5/8	13-6/8	5	5	Delaware County	NY	Alan Beyer	1976	3146
126-0/8	20-4/8	21-6/8	17-0/8	4	4	Dunn County	WI	Richard Paul	1977	3146
126-0/8	20-2/8	18-6/8	15-0/8	4	4	Polk County	IA	Ervin Wagner	1978	3146

WHITETAIL DEER *(Typical Antlers)*

Minimum Score 125

Score	Length of Main Beam R	L	Inside Spread	Number of Points R	L	Area	State/ Province	Hunter's Name	Date	Rank
126-0/8	20-0/8	20-3/8	16-0/8	5	5	Oneida County	WI	Gerald Bonfigt	1980	3146
126-0/8	18-3/8	18-4/8	15-4/8	5	5	Bexar County	TX	James R. Carter	1980	3146
126-0/8	20-4/8	20-4/8	15-4/8	4	5	Iron County	MI	Bill Paiter, Sr.	1980	3146
126-0/8	20-0/8	20-4/8	13-6/8	4	4	Kandiyohi County	MN	Dwayne B. Power	1980	3146
126-0/8	22-1/8	22-6/8	19-0/8	4	4	Westchester County	NY	Thomas Ippolito	1981	3146
126-0/8	19-5/8	19-7/8	15-4/8	4	4	Des Moines County	IA	Doris Hawkins	1981	3146
126-0/8	19-4/8	18-1/8	14-3/8	5	6	Calhoun County	MI	Jerry L. Boggess, Jr.	1981	3146
126-0/8	22-2/8	23-2/8	16-2/8	5	4	Washington County	OH	James D. Boyce	1981	3146
126-0/8	21-4/8	19-6/8	16-4/8	4	4	Reno County	KS	Otto Henning	1982	3146
126-0/8	20-4/8	21-0/8	15-4/8	5	6	Cayuga County	NY	Arthur Quadrini	1982	3146
126-0/8	20-4/8	21-5/8	19-5/8	4	6	Burleigh County	ND	Scott Fairman	1982	3146
126-0/8	20-0/8	20-2/8	18-6/8	4	5	Jo Daviess County	IL	Jerry Smith	1982	3146
126-0/8	20-2/8	19-3/8	13-7/8	6	6	Buffalo County	NE	Richard D. Lange	1983	3146
126-0/8	19-4/8	20-0/8	16-2/8	5	4	Watonwan County	MN	Rory Jensen	1983	3146
126-0/8	21-0/8	20-4/8	15-2/8	5	5	Dallas County	IA	John S. Winslow	1983	3146
126-0/8	20-6/8	20-6/8	16-4/8	4	4	Dawson County	NE	Randy Wilson	1983	3146
126-0/8	21-5/8	21-6/8	16-6/8	4	4	St. Louis County	MO	Huston Martin	1983	3146
126-0/8	22-4/8	20-7/8	15-6/8	5	4	Iowa County	WI	Mark E. Bennett	1984	3146
126-0/8	20-1/8	20-2/8	14-4/8	5	6	Des Moines County	IA	Duane R. Mabry	1984	3146
126-0/8	24-3/8	23-4/8	16-0/8	3	4	Bissett Creek	BC	Mark Siegmueller	1984	3146
126-0/8	22-2/8	22-7/8	19-4/8	4	4	Mackinac County	MI	Kirk A. Radtke	1984	3146
126-0/8	20-2/8	19-7/8	16-6/8	5	5	Monroe County	NY	Gregrey Madison	1985	3146
126-0/8	21-5/8	22-4/8	16-6/8	5	4	Stearns County	MN	Rick Kantor	1985	3146
126-0/8	19-3/8	19-1/8	13-5/8	6	5	Sauk County	WI	Arend Harms	1985	3146
126-0/8	22-4/8	22-4/8	17-1/8	4	5	Westchester County	NY	Louis J. Miceli III	1985	3146
125-7/8	20-0/8	20-0/8	14-5/8	5	5	Oconto County	WI	Chuck Matyska	1972	3176
125-7/8	20-6/8	22-7/8	15-5/8	5	5	Butler County	PA	John Schmiedlin	1976	3176
125-7/8	20-2/8	20-2/8	15-1/8	5	5	Waupaca County	WI	Thomas E. Labisch	1976	3176
125-7/8	20-0/8	20-2/8	16-2/8	5	6	Greene County	IN	Jim Cunningham	1977	3176
125-7/8	21-5/8	22-0/8	15-1/8	4	4	Douglas County	MN	Dan Zinda	1977	3176
125-7/8	24-0/8	22-4/8	14-5/8	7	6	Jones County	GA	William R. Shaw	1979	3176
125-7/8	23-4/8	22-5/8	15-7/8	5	4	Boone County	IA	Max Brower	1980	3176
125-7/8	22-2/8	21-7/8	20-1/8	6	4	Ionia County	MI	David Seidelman	1980	3176
125-7/8	20-4/8	20-7/8	15-1/8	4	4	Lewis and Clark County	MT	Tom Storm	1981	3176
125-7/8	21-7/8	21-7/8	16-1/8	5	5	Dakota County	MN	John M. Lippka	1982	3176
125-7/8	21-0/8	21-0/8	16-3/8	5	4	Lake County	IL	Russell F. Orr	1982	3176
125-7/8	23-0/8	21-7/8	15-5/8	4	4	Sauk County	WI	Dan Cupp	1982	3176
125-7/8	20-7/8	20-7/8	17-7/8	4	4	Marion County	IL	Lavon Doremire, Sr.	1983	3176
125-7/8	21-7/8	22-2/8	18-4/8	4	5	Westchester County	NY	John Cucinella	1983	3176
125-7/8	20-4/8	21-1/8	17-1/8	5	5	Des Moines County	IA	Mark Sivill	1984	3176
125-7/8	19-4/8	18-7/8	14-7/8	5	5	Dodge County	WI	James G. Schoebeck	1984	3176
125-7/8	22-4/8	23-6/8	18-0/8	4	5	Sumner County	KS	Warren C. Townsend	1985	3176
125-7/8	20-1/8	19-2/8	15-3/8	5	5	Green County	WI	David R. Covert	1985	3176
125-7/8	20-4/8	18-4/8	15-5/8	5	5	Johnson County	WY	Jimmy Womble	1986	3176
125-6/8	23-0/8	23-4/8	19-2/8	4	4	Bath County	VA	W. C. Bedall, Jr.	1958	3195
125-6/8	21-4/8	21-5/8	18-6/8	4	5	Martin County	MN	Robert Barnett	1970	3195
125-6/8	20-0/8	21-6/8	20-1/8	6	4	Palo Alto County	IA	Earl J. Gustafson	1971	3195
125-6/8	22-0/8	22-4/8	16-4/8	4	4	Muskingum County	OH	Jim L. Lewis	1976	3195
125-6/8	20-4/8	20-2/8	17-0/8	5	5	Douglas County	MN	Jerry D. Kuhlman	1981	3195
125-6/8	20-2/8	21-2/8	18-2/8	4	5	Sauk County	WI	Hank Lee	1982	3195
125-6/8	22-6/8	22-2/8	15-4/8	4	4	Sedgwick County	KS	Jim Nicholson	1983	3195
125-6/8	21-1/8	21-2/8	17-5/8	6	6	Licking County	OH	Roy L Wilson, Jr.	1984	3195
125-6/8	19-7/8	22-0/8	19-2/8	5	6	Cedar County	MO	Terry Myers	1985	3195
125-6/8	21-5/8	21-5/8	14-4/8	5	4	Vernon County	WI	Thomas Erie	1985	3195
125-6/8	20-2/8	20-4/8	15-2/8	4	4	Branch County	MI	Douglas L. Curey	1985	3195
125-6/8	18-1/8	18-1/8	14-2/8	5	5	Cerro Gordo County	IA	Eric Coe	1985	3195
125-6/8	21-6/8	22-0/8	17-4/8	4	4	Buffalo County	WI	Richard A. Viken	1985	3195
125-5/8	21-4/8	21-3/8	18-3/8	4	4	Brown County	SD	Leo J. Weber	1965	3208
125-5/8	21-5/8	21-4/8	17-5/8	4	4	Lyman County	SD	Dennis Lien	1966	3208
125-5/8	19-2/8	19-3/8	16-3/8	5	5	Sauk County	WI	Andre J. Jestafie	1968	3208
125-5/8	22-1/8	25-0/8	20-1/8	5	6	Meade County	KS	Kent Davis	1971	3208
125-5/8	19-7/8	18-7/8	15-5/8	5	5	Jo Daviess County	IL	Tom Spraetz	1976	3208
125-5/8	21-5/8	21-4/8	16-5/8	5	5	Kent County	MD	Harry A. Weishaar	1977	3208

WHITETAIL DEER *(Typical Antlers)*

(continued)   Minimum Score 125

Score	Length of Main Beam R	Length of Main Beam L	Inside Spread	Number of Points R	Number of Points L	Area	State/ Province	Hunter's Name	Date	Rank
125-5/8	24-6/8	24-2/8	15-5/8	4	4	Fairfield County	SC	Danny Duncan	1978	3208
125-5/8	22-6/8	22-6/8	14-0/8	6	6	Ripley County	IN	Richard Gambrel	1979	3208
125-5/8	22-4/8	22-0/8	17-5/8	4	4	Keokuk County	IA	Roger E. Claypool	1980	3208
125-5/8	23-1/8	23-7/8	14-7/8	5	5	Alpena County	MI	Cameron Cogsdill	1981	3208
125-5/8	21-1/8	21-2/8	17-5/8	4	4	Green Lake County	WI	Raymond E. Golomski	1981	3208
125-5/8	19-7/8	19-3/8	16-1/8	6	6	Jackson County	MN	Rodney Borer	1982	3208
125-5/8	21-2/8	21-1/8	18-7/8	4	4	Clermont County	OH	Claud F. Combs	1982	3208
125-5/8	19-3/8	18-5/8	14-3/8	5	6	Washington County	OH	Ronald G. Boone	1982	3208
125-5/8	23-3/8	22-7/8	15-3/8	5	5	Vernon County	MO	Roger L. Hensley	1982	3208
125-5/8	21-0/8	20-7/8	16-1/8	4	4	Ozaukee County	WI	Thomas G. Bloomingdale	1983	3208
125-5/8	21-5/8	21-1/8	17-3/8	4	4	Will County	IL	Angelo L. Chirban	1983	3208
125-5/8	21-6/8	21-6/8	17-5/8	4	4	Cherokee County	OK	Jon C. Rogers	1983	3208
125-5/8	20-2/8	20-2/8	14-3/8	5	5	Oliver County	ND	Al Zeller	1984	3208
125-5/8	22-6/8	22-3/8	19-3/8	4	5	Lycoming County	PA	Gary A Pennycoff	1985	3208
125-4/8	24-7/8	21-6/8	17-2/8	4	4	Marion County	IA	Thomas Tucker	1962	3228
125-4/8	20-2/8	21-3/8	16-6/8	5	5	Otter Tail County	MN	Terry Tamke	1971	3228
125-4/8	20-7/8	21-0/8	16-0/8	4	5	Meeker County	MN	Chuck Schultz	1978	3228
125-4/8	20-1/8	20-2/8	17-1/8	5	4	Bears Paw Dam	ALB	David R. Coupland	1979	3228
125-4/8	23-0/8	24-1/8	17-4/8	5	4	Murray County	MN	Kerry Ella	1981	3228
125-4/8	20-5/8	20-3/8	17-4/8	5	5	Union County	KY	Brad Tucker	1982	3228
125-4/8	21-3/8	21-5/8	12-6/8	5	5	Oktibbeha County	MS	Stennis Jones	1983	3228
125-4/8	21-7/8	22-5/8	14-2/8	4	4	Knox County	OH	Tom Kayser	1984	3228
125-4/8	21-1/8	21-2/8	15-6/8	4	4	Vernon County	WI	Michael Lang	1985	3228
125-4/8	16-4/8	22-0/8	16-4/8	5	4	Monona County	IA	Larry Couron	1985	3228
125-3/8	20-5/8	21-4/8	16-5/8	5	4	Stevenson County	IL	Vaughn Zimmerman	1969	3238
125-3/8	24-0/8	24-6/8	17-3/8	4	5	Wabasha County	MN	David Mohler	1971	3238
125-3/8	20-7/8	20-3/8	15-3/8	4	4	Ft. Eustis	VA	Dr. Glenn A. Parker	1972	3238
125-3/8	21-7/8	22-6/8	16-3/8	4	5	Warren County	IA	Michael Woolman	1974	3238
125-3/8	22-6/8	23-4/8	18-4/8	7	6	Pawnee County	KS	Don Jensen	1977	3238
125-3/8	19-2/8	19-7/8	14-1/8	5	5	Jasper County	IN	Frank Benka	1978	3238
125-3/8	22-2/8	23-6/8	16-3/8	4	4	Louisa County	IA	Lee Cassabaum	1979	3238
125-3/8	22-0/8	22-2/8	15-5/8	4	4	Saginaw County	MI	James L. Bassett	1980	3238
125-3/8	20-5/8	21-7/8	18-1/8	4	4	Neosho County	KS	Damie Coomes	1982	3238
125-3/8	20-4/8	20-1/8	17-7/8	4	5	Hardin County	IA	Bill Stonebraker	1983	3238
125-3/8	19-4/8	20-1/8	15-5/8	5	5	Watson	SAS	Wayne Dickson	1983	3238
125-3/8	20-7/8	20-1/8	15-5/8	5	5	Suffolk County	NY	Anthony Bernard	1983	3238
125-3/8	21-3/8	21-2/8	18-1/8	4	4	Oconto County	WI	Bob Richardson, Jr.	1984	3238
125-3/8	22-4/8	22-0/8	18-5/8	5	5	Scott County	MN	Bruce Kramer	1984	3238
125-3/8	18-7/8	18-4/8	15-3/8	5	5	Wellington	ONT	Fred Law	1984	3238
125-3/8	21-4/8	20-6/8	15-7/8	5	5	Cheboygan County	MI	Steven Schrauben	1984	3238
125-3/8	22-1/8	21-5/8	18-1/8	4	4	Washington County	WI	Gordon Bell	1985	3238
125-3/8	22-6/8	21-5/8	14-3/8	4	4	Somerset County	ME	Alfred Corson	1985	3238
125-3/8	22-0/8	22-3/8	18-0/8	4	6	Little Falls County	MN	Mike Mitten	1985	3238
125-3/8	18-6/8	18-7/8	16-3/8	5	5	Ramsey County	ND	Charles McGarvey	1985	3238
125-3/8	23-1/8	21-5/8	13-6/8	5	4	St. Charles County	MO	Edgar Ralph Welch	1985	3238
125-2/8	19-3/8	20-0/8	15-0/8	4	4	Missaukee County	MI	Dr. B. P. Garris	1966	3259
125-2/8	26-5/8	25-2/8	22-2/8	4	3	Canton	IL	Arnold C. Hegele	1967	3259
125-2/8	20-6/8	20-7/8	15-6/8	4	4	Sussex County	NJ	Tom Barber	1973	3259
125-2/8	22-6/8	22-2/8	17-2/8	4	3	Washington County	IA	Danny B. Jirsa	1974	3259
125-2/8	21-5/8	21-4/8	17-6/8	5	5	Columbia County	WI	Gary Cahoon	1977	3259
125-2/8	22-2/8	24-7/8	17-6/8	4	4	Guernsey County	OH	Butch Todd	1977	3259
125-2/8	21-7/8	21-7/8	16-2/8	4	4	Jackson County	MI	Bernard Stachowicz	1979	3259
125-2/8	23-2/8	24-6/8	19-2/8	4	4	Baltimore County	MD	Robert E. Arndt	1980	3259
125-2/8	22-3/8	21-6/8	18-6/8	5	6	Goodhue County	MN	John "Jack" Cordes	1981	3259
125-2/8	18-6/8	18-1/8	13-6/8	5	5	Boone County	MO	Jeff Jennings	1981	3259
125-2/8	21-6/8	22-4/8	15-0/8	4	4	Shawano County	WI	David J. Gard	1983	3259
125-2/8	20-6/8	21-4/8	15-2/8	5	5	Calver County	MD	Gary Fillmann	1983	3259
125-2/8	20-0/8	21-0/8	17-6/8	6	5	Cherokee County	KS	Sam F. Lancaster	1984	3259
125-2/8	19-3/8	19-0/8	14-0/8	4	4	Kiowa County	KS	Susan Manwarren	1984	3259
125-2/8	24-1/8	23-4/8	17-4/8	4	4	Blue Earth County	MN	Ray Smothers	1985	3259
125-2/8	21-0/8	21-4/8	19-4/8	8	8	Des Moines County	IA	Rod Waschkat	1985	3259
125-1/8	19-1/8	19-7/8	14-7/8	5	5	Ozaukee County	WI	Don Schwerin	1966	3275
125-1/8	20-7/8	20-6/8	15-3/8	4	4	Graham County	KS	Russell Hull	1975	3275

WHITETAIL DEER *(Typical Antlers)*

Minimum Score 125

Score	Length of Main Beam R	L	Inside Spread	Number of Points R	L	Area	State/ Province	Hunter's Name	Date	Rank
125-1/8	22-3/8	23-5/8	20-0/8	5	5	Vermillion County	IL	Mel Mueller	1976	3275
125-1/8	21-1/8	20-7/8	13-5/8	5	5	Muskogee County	OK	Don Anderson	1979	3275
125-1/8	19-4/8	19-4/8	18-5/8	6	5	Manitowoc County	WI	Peter J. Ording	1982	3275
125-1/8	20-0/8	21-0/8	14-1/8	6	5	Adair County	MO	Terry Findling	1982	3275
125-1/8	21-7/8	22-0/8	17-5/8	5	4	Morrison County	MN	Gordie Rieber	1982	3275
125-1/8	19-7/8	20-1/8	18-6/8	6	7	Des Moines County	IA	David R. Bessine	1983	3275
125-1/8	20-7/8	20-0/8	17-1/8	5	5	Brown County	SD	Jim C. Hill	1983	3275
125-1/8	22-3/8	22-1/8	17-5/8	4	4	Hillsdale County	MI	Andy Keefe	1983	3275
125-1/8	20-2/8	21-2/8	16-3/8	4	4	Dewitt County	IL	Thomas E. Wilson	1984	3275
125-1/8	18-6/8	19-6/8	15-0/8	5	6	Valley County	MT	Leith S Wimmer	1984	3275
125-1/8	21-0/8	21-3/8	19-3/8	5	5	Washington County	WI	Judy Staedler	1986	3275
125-0/8	20-6/8	20-6/8	16-6/8	5	5	Sheboygan Marsh	WI	Earl Uhl	1962	3288
125-0/8	22-4/8	23-0/8	15-4/8	5	5	La Fromboise	SD	Robert A. Clough	1967	3288
125-0/8	20-5/8	20-5/8	17-2/8	4	4	Livingston County	NY	Robert A. Carone	1969	3288
125-0/8	22-0/8	22-0/8	17-4/8	6	6	Dodge County	WI	Charles E. Songstad	1970	3288
125-0/8	24-2/8	24-4/8	17-5/8	8	4	Hollowbend	AR	Tom Quinton	1977	3288
125-0/8	20-5/8	20-6/8	18-2/8	4	4	Freeborn County	MN	Jerry Christenson	1980	3288
125-0/8	23-0/8	21-6/8	17-0/8	4	4	Switzerland County	IN	Barry Scott	1981	3288
125-0/8	19-1/8	20-0/8	16-6/8	5	5	Indiana County	PA	Stephen C. Shesko	1981	3288
125-0/8	21-3/8	20-4/8	16-0/8	5	5	Ontario County	NY	Jim Wicks	1982	3288
125-0/8	23-0/8	22-7/8	16-2/8	5	4	Yates County	NY	Ed O'Dell	1982	3288
125-0/8	20-4/8	21-0/8	16-2/8	5	5	Bexar County	TX	John E. West	1982	3288
125-0/8	23-0/8	23-3/8	21-4/8	4	4	Seneca County	NY	Richard Williamson	1982	3288
125-0/8	19-6/8	19-4/8	15-2/8	7	6	Richland County	MT	Bill Cundiff	1984	3288
125-0/8	20-5/8	20-0/8	17-6/8	4	4	Alfalfa County	OK	Paul E. Keck	1984	3288
125-0/8	20-0/8	20-0/8	17-4/8	4	4	Sauk County	WI	Robert E. McKenna	1984	3288
125-0/8	22-2/8	21-2/8	17-0/8	4	4	Price County	WI	Dennis W. Steinberger	1984	3288
125-0/8	20-2/8	21-2/8	19-6/8	5	4	Kane County	IL	Tom Cousland	1984	3288
125-0/8	21-4/8	21-4/8	15-4/8	5	5	Crow Wing County	MN	Richard Stokke	1985	3288
125-0/8	22-5/8	22-7/8	18-4/8	7	4	Burleigh County	ND	Dave Feist	1985	3288
125-0/8	19-4/8	21-1/8	18-0/8	4	5	Orange County	NY	Richard Powles	1985	3288
125-0/8	21-0/8	21-4/8	14-6/8	5	5	Monroe County	WI	Jeffery S. Oler	1985	3288

WORLD RECORD WHITETAIL DEER
(Non-Typical Antlers)
Score: 279 7/8
Shelton, Nebraska – 1962
Hunter: Del Austin

WHITETAIL DEER *(Non-Typical Antlers)*

Minimum Score 150

Odocoileus virginianus virginianus and certain related subspecies

Score	Length of Main Beam R	L	Inside Spread	Number of Points R	L	Area	State/ Province	Hunter's Name	Date	Rank
279-7/8	27-7/8	28-1/8	21-3/8	21	18	Hall County	NE	Del Austin	1962	1
249-6/8	28-0/8	27-7/8	20-2/8	8	10	Greenwood County	KS	Clifford Pickell	1968	2
245-5/8	29-4/8	29-3/8	20-3/8	16	15	Vermilion County	IL	Robert E. Chesnut	1981	3
241-2/8	25-4/8	26-3/8	18-2/8	19	20	Cochrane	ALB	Dean Dwernuchuk	1984	4
237-5/8	22-4/8	25-4/8	16-5/8	13	12	Wilson County	KS	Gilbert Boss	1986	5
231-5/8	28-1/8	26-5/8	19-2/8	11	11	Dane County	WI	Dennis Shanks	1979	6
230-6/8	26-1/8	27-6/8	19-5/8	11	11	Peoria County	IL	Tophil L. Simon	1984	7
227-6/8	25-5/8	25-4/8	20-6/8	13	20	Fulton County	IL	Richard Keener	1977	8
222-1/8	26-5/8	25-6/8	17-5/8	15	12	Hancock County	IA	J. M. Monson	1977	9
220-6/8	24-6/8	25-2/8	17-6/8	18	16	Rock Island County	IL	John L. Angel	1979	10
218-1/8	26-2/8	25-6/8	17-3/8	10	9	Peterson	IA	Blaine R. Salzkorn	1970	11
217-0/8	28-7/8	28-3/8	21-6/8	9	8	Caroll County	IL	Noel Feather	1982	12
215-6/8	27-4/8	28-7/8	18-6/8	11	14	Meeker County	MN	Steve Turck	1982	13
215-5/8	24-2/8	27-0/8	22-2/8	11	7	Wayne County	IA	Chris Hackney	1983	14
210-7/8	23-1/8	23-2/8	18-6/8	9	9	Teton County	MT	Todd Jensen	1986	15
210-6/8	25-5/8	24-5/8	19-4/8	9	8	Marian County	KS	Bruce Schroeder	1985	16
210-3/8	27-2/8	28-4/8	19-1/8	12	6	Lac Qui Parle County	MN	Steven J. Karels	1974	17
209-2/8	26-5/8	27-6/8	21-4/8	10	10	McPherson County	KS	Lonnie Ensminger	1968	18
208-5/8	26-2/8	26-4/8	22-3/8	9	9	Buffalo County	NE	Carl Clements	1985	19
206-0/8	22-3/8	24-1/8	17-4/8	9	11	Saunders County	NE	Nordean E. Bade	1964	20
205-6/8	25-7/8	25-4/8	21-3/8	14	9	Cottonwood County	MN	Larry Gravely	1975	21
203-7/8	25-7/8	25-1/8	20-2/8	11	9	Union County	OR	Joe Mengore	1982	22
203-4/8	26-6/8	27-6/8	17-0/8	7	13	Dodge County	MN	Lawrence Sowieja	1955	23
203-3/8	24-3/8	24-5/8	20-5/8	10	9	Adams County	IL	Elroy Little	1981	24
203-0/8	25-0/8	25-4/8	19-3/8	12	10	Geauga County	OH	Rudy Grecar	1969	25
202-2/8	23-3/8	25-6/8	19-6/8	12	9	Vermillion	SD	Patrick Hudson	1969	26
202-0/8	29-0/8	27-1/8	22-6/8	9	8	Clark County	KS	Dennis Rule	1982	27
200-5/8	25-1/8	27-0/8	18-7/8	7	7	Clayton County	IA	Dorrance Arnold	1977	28
199-3/8	24-3/8	23-4/8	22-2/8	12	11	Atchison County	KS	Kirby A. Clifton	1973	29
199-3/8	24-3/8	23-1/8	17-6/8	8	8	Comanche County	KS	Phillip L. Kirkland	1981	29
198-5/8	26-2/8	25-0/8	22-6/8	5	5	Waterloo	NE	Ivan Masher	1961	31
198-3/8	24-3/8	24-3/8	20-7/8	10	10	Lyon County	MN	Edward Matthys	1966	32
198-1/8	27-0/8	26-3/8	20-2/8	10	7	Hocking County	OH	Hugh Cox	1964	33
197-4/8	25-0/8	23-7/8	22-2/8	7	7	Johnson County	IA	Dennis R. Ballard	1971	34
197-4/8	25-3/8	26-3/8	16-7/8	6	8	Lyon County	KS	John R. Clifton	1984	34
197-3/8	27-3/8	26-3/8	20-4/8	8	9	Faribault County	MN	Randy Lee Sandt	1982	36
197-1/8	26-4/8	24-2/8	18-5/8	9	12	Linn County	IA	Marsha Fairbanks	1974	37
197-1/8	26-1/8	26-3/8	17-3/8	8	7	Jackson County	MO	Jim Martin	1984	37
197-0/8	26-1/8	26-4/8	21-5/8	8	9	Marshall County	IL	Larry Rowe	1975	39
195-6/8	27-1/8	26-6/8	21-5/8	7	6	Dubuque County	IA	Jim H. Dougherty	1985	40
195-5/8	28-6/8	28-2/8	20-2/8	9	10	Martin County	MN	Ben Johnson	1973	41
195-5/8	24-1/8	24-2/8	19-0/8	9	7	Waushara County	WI	Randy Chamberlain	1984	41
195-4/8	27-2/8	28-1/8	18-2/8	9	7	Putnam County	IN	Chris M. Tanner	1982	43
195-4/8	25-2/8	26-2/8	19-7/8	6	7	Crawford County	IA	Larry Sparks	1985	43
195-0/8	26-6/8	25-0/8	16-3/8	9	13	Juneau County	WI	Maurice Sterba	1955	45
194-7/8	27-7/8	26-1/8	19-0/8	11	10	Warren County	MO	Dennis Jones	1982	46
194-5/8	26-3/8	24-7/8	20-7/8	7	8	Guernsey County	OH	Dick Bayer	1985	47
194-2/8	27-1/8	26-0/8	23-5/8	9	6	Pike County	MO	William E. Knowles	1980	48
193-7/8	25-1/8	27-2/8	18-0/8	11	11	Blaine County	MT	Gene Wensel	1981	49
193-6/8	29-6/8	28-0/8	20-2/8	9	9	Lake County	IN	Walter Sobczak	1979	50
193-3/8	24-3/8	25-3/8	19-3/8	16	9	Roanoke County	VA	Randy Brookshier	1983	51
192-5/8	25-0/8	27-0/8	22-1/8	6	8	Republic County	KS	Don Dejmal	1983	52
192-4/8	21-4/8	20-5/8	15-4/8	11	10	Redwood County	MN	Mark A. Steinle	1973	53
192-1/8	24-3/8	21-1/8	17-3/8	11	10	Gray County	KS	Randall Koehn	1985	54
191-6/8	23-2/8	20-7/8	16-5/8	6	15	Murray County	MN	Delbert Peck	1956	55
191-3/8	22-1/8	22-5/8	20-1/8	9	9	St. Joseph County	IN	Daniel T. Karaszewski	1979	56
191-0/8	23-5/8	24-1/8	20-6/8	13	11	Pope County	MN	Ron Johnson	1985	57
190-7/8	25-0/8	18-4/8	15-1/8	11	13	Douglas County	KS	Leon J. Bidinger	1983	58
190-5/8	23-5/8	22-3/8	21-1/8	13	11	Lee County	IA	Tim Digman	1981	59
190-4/8	29-2/8	28-0/8	18-6/8	8	8	Licking County	OH	John McGee	1982	60
190-3/8	25-4/8	24-1/8	16-5/8	9	9	Saginaw	MI	Robert T. Morey	1975	61
190-2/8	20-0/8	23-4/8	19-7/8	8	9	Isanti County	MN	Johnny J. Williams	1982	62
190-2/8	27-5/8	29-0/8	20-2/8	12	8	Montgomery County	PA	David S. Krempasky	1985	62

WHITETAIL DEER *(Non-Typical Antlers)*

(continued)   Minimum Score 150

Score	Length of Main Beam R	L	Inside Spread	Number of Points R	L	Area	State/Province	Hunter's Name	Date	Rank
190-0/8	24-3/8	24-6/8	18-0/8	8	8	Douglas County	KS	Dan Norris	1977	64
190-0/8	24-4/8	25-2/8	19-1/8	7	8	McHenry County	IL	Edward Schultz	1984	64
189-6/8	24-4/8	23-0/8	16-3/8	9	7	Chisago County	MN	Reinhold L. Lind	1956	66
189-2/8	21-4/8	23-1/8	21-3/8	10	8	Clayton County	IA	Jim Monat	1981	67
189-1/8	21-5/8	24-2/8	17-3/8	13	7	Graham County	KS	Don Berry	1970	68
188-7/8	27-4/8	28-1/8	18-3/8	11	9	Marinette	WI	James Spielvogel	1981	69
188-3/8	24-0/8	24-4/8	18-4/8	9	7	Benton County	IA	Lyle Miller	1977	70
188-1/8	26-5/8	26-0/8	19-4/8	7	10	?	ND	William Cruff	1961	71
188-1/8	26-3/8	26-0/8	19-5/8	10	7	Dane County	WI	Bill Needham	1983	71
188-0/8	23-2/8	22-3/8	17-3/8	8	8	LaSalle County	IL	Gary Tabor	1983	73
187-7/8	24-4/8	24-7/8	20-3/8	8	8	Shiawassee County	MI	Joseph S. Lunkas	1978	74
187-5/8	27-6/8	25-2/8	18-0/8	8	6	Monroe County	IA	Cecil Dicks	1961	75
187-3/8	23-2/8	23-1/8	17-1/8	11	10	Vernon County	WI	Darrell A. Bendel	1986	76
187-2/8	25-3/8	23-6/8	21-0/8	7	9	Merrill County	NE	Glenn Schmidt	1975	77
186-6/8	24-2/8	25-1/8	19-3/8	9	10	Traverse County	MN	Roland L. Hausmann	1964	78
186-5/8	25-3/8	25-0/8	20-7/8	7	9	Scotland County	MO	Charles Lee Smith	1984	79
186-2/8	23-1/8	22-5/8	18-6/8	9	9	Fergus Falls	MN	D. F. Vraspir	1959	80
185-7/8	24-7/8	22-2/8	18-0/8	6	10	Jones County	GA	Wallace Reeves, Jr.	1973	81
185-4/8	29-2/8	28-0/8	22-1/8	8	8	Pickaway	OH	Jerry R. Forson	1979	82
185-3/8	27-6/8	27-4/8	23-5/8	8	8	Allamakee County	IA	LeRoy B. Spiker	1968	83
185-3/8	27-3/8	26-7/8	20-7/8	6	6	Rice County	MN	Wayne Jahnke	1975	83
185-2/8	26-1/8	25-0/8	16-6/8	9	8	Wichita	KS	Alfred Weaver	1965	85
184-5/8	26-1/8	24-7/8	20-4/8	10	11	Vinton County	OH	Dan Davis	1985	86
184-3/8	22-7/8	22-6/8	17-6/8	8	11	Texas County	OK	William E. Miller	1983	87
184-3/8	23-2/8	23-3/8	21-5/8	10	8	Black Hawk County	IA	Paul Hughson	1985	87
184-1/8	24-3/8	26-5/8	19-1/8	8	9	Waushara County	WI	Dwight A. Olson	1979	89
183-5/8	25-1/8	25-0/8	17-7/8	10	10	Lincoln County	SD	Mervin Sterk	1985	90
183-3/8	24-4/8	25-5/8	16-5/8	8	9	Fillmore County	MN	Michael M. Gehrking	1985	91
183-2/8	27-3/8	24-5/8	21-7/8	6	9	Holt County	NE	Lyle Ruff	1967	92
183-2/8	28-4/8	26-6/8	16-4/8	10	9	Christian County	MO	Roger J. Newell	1984	92
183-2/8	27-4/8	26-4/8	20-7/8	7	7	Riley County	KS	Larry Larson	1985	92
182-7/8	24-2/8	25-5/8	19-2/8	9	7	Arkansas County	AR	Tommy Horton	1972	95
182-7/8	24-3/8	25-2/8	18-0/8	11	5	Olmsted County	MN	Dan Matheson	1973	95
182-4/8	19-5/8	26-7/8	17-2/8	11	11	Will County	IL	Richard Heintz	1971	97
182-3/8	29-3/8	27-7/8	20-5/8	6	8	Goodhue County	MN	Jim Danielson	1984	98
182-1/8	22-4/8	22-4/8	17-1/8	10	9	Brown County	KS	Bill Butrick	1985	99
181-6/8	23-2/8	22-6/8	20-1/8	8	7	Quincy	IL	Festal McCarty	1967	100
181-6/8	25-4/8	25-0/8	18-1/8	7	11	Kiowa County	KS	Royce E. Frazier	1985	100
181-4/8	25-6/8	26-0/8	19-7/8	9	8	Wyoming County	WV	Bobby Smith	1985	102
181-3/8	28-0/8	28-0/8	20-5/8	11	6	Hardin County	IA	Howard Nelson	1963	103
181-2/8	22-1/8	24-5/8	19-0/8	12	8	Desha County	AR	John T. Greer	1962	104
181-1/8	24-1/8	24-1/8	17-6/8	9	6	Coles County	IL	Gerald L. Davis	1973	105
181-0/8	24-6/8	25-4/8	19-6/8	11	8	Knox County	OH	Don Quick	1984	106
181-0/8	23-7/8	23-5/8	19-1/8	12	9	Pittsburg County	OK	Harold Jones	1986	106
180-6/8	22-3/8	24-1/8	17-3/8	8	7	Pope County	AR	Johnny Reed	1983	108
180-5/8	28-5/8	28-6/8	24-5/8	7	7	Preble County	OH	James R. Whittaker	1978	109
180-4/8	23-0/8	23-0/8	16-3/8	7	8	Teton County	MT	James Dean	1981	110
180-1/8	24-2/8	23-4/8	18-5/8	10	8	Winnebago County	IA	Jim Orthel	1983	111
179-6/8	24-4/8	24-2/8	21-0/8	7	8	Creek County	OK	Marion Lewis	1975	112
179-6/8	24-7/8	25-7/8	22-0/8	6	7	Hamilton County	OH	Lawrence Ashbrook	1981	112
179-5/8	24-4/8	25-6/8	19-5/8	9	11	Fillmore County	MN	Wayne Pfremmer	1972	114
179-2/8	25-4/8	23-4/8	23-0/8	12	7	Marion County	IA	Roger DeMoss	1982	115
178-6/8	21-2/8	25-3/8	20-5/8	9	8	Lincoln County	SD	H. L. Tuggle	1975	116
178-6/8	22-2/8	23-1/8	13-4/8	10	9	Madison County	IL	Michael B. Fenton	1984	116
178-4/8	22-1/8	23-6/8	17-0/8	12	11	Keokuk County	IA	Ron Turner	1983	118
178-3/8	23-3/8	22-7/8	19-6/8	8	8	Traverse County	MN	Roland L. Hausmann	1953	119
178-3/8	25-1/8	24-4/8	19-6/8	8	10	Mineral County	MT	Gene Wensel	1981	119
178-3/8	22-6/8	24-7/8	17-0/8	11	10	Finney County	KS	Randy Miller	1984	119
177-7/8	28-2/8	27-0/8	18-3/8	6	6	Ross County	OH	Robert L. Elliott	1981	122
177-7/8	26-5/8	25-2/8	18-2/8	8	7	Pott County	KS	Loyd C. Flowers	1983	122
177-6/8	21-4/8	22-2/8	18-1/8	10	9	Pope County	MN	Roger Tollefson	1977	124
177-6/8	23-0/8	21-2/8	16-0/8	6	13	Delaware County	OH	Ronald Eugene Murphy	1983	124
177-4/8	23-4/8	22-6/8	18-1/8	7	8	Flathead County	MT	Jerry Karsky	1972	126

WHITETAIL DEER *(Non-Typical Antlers)*

Minimum Score 150

(continued)

Score	Length of Main Beam R	L	Inside Spread	Number of Points R	L	Area	State/ Province	Hunter's Name	Date	Rank
176-6/8	28-4/8	28-2/8	19-4/8	8	9	Dodge County	WI	Erwin C. Koehler	1957	127
176-3/8	24-6/8	25-4/8	20-3/8	8	8	Greene County	OH	Leroy M. Thompson	1982	128
176-1/8	22-0/8	23-3/8	21-4/8	7	6	Brandon	MAN	Larry J. Pollock	1980	129
175-7/8	27-4/8	28-1/8	23-3/8	8	7	Salt Fork State Park	OH	Jack L. Milligan	1971	130
175-7/8	24-3/8	25-1/8	17-4/8	9	8	Freeborn County	MN	Douglas Swank	1979	130
175-4/8	22-4/8	22-7/8	19-2/8	10	10	Anthon	IA	Everett Gothier	1962	132
175-4/8	28-4/8	27-5/8	20-6/8	7	7	Belmont County	OH	Dan Clutter	1985	132
175-3/8	24-5/8	23-7/8	20-1/8	8	7	Elbow Lake	MN	Lee Offerdahl	1972	134
175-3/8	26-2/8	25-3/8	14-4/8	8	11	Buffalo County	WI	Timothy L. Brommer	1984	134
175-3/8	23-4/8	24-3/8	19-6/8	7	9	Salem County	NJ	Richard Wendt	1985	134
175-1/8	26-4/8	25-1/8	20-0/8	6	7	Dubuque County	IA	Gregory Klein	1983	137
174-7/8	26-6/8	25-3/8	19-7/8	9	9	Waseca County	MN	Robert Barrie	1974	138
174-4/8	24-0/8	25-4/8	22-5/8	5	6	Ottertail County	MN	Don Oelschlager	1976	139
174-4/8	22-1/8	22-3/8	16-4/8	8	8	Benson County	ND	Curtis A. Ehnert	1977	139
174-3/8	26-0/8	25-7/8	18-2/8	9	7	Vinton County	OH	Jack McConnell	1982	141
174-2/8	26-6/8	25-1/8	19-7/8	9	6	Clay County	IA	Darrell Magnussen	1962	142
174-0/8	26-1/8	25-7/8	26-2/8	7	8	Port Tobacco	MD	Robert H. Jones, Sr.	1971	143
174-0/8	26-0/8	27-6/8	26-6/8	7	6	Delaware County	OH	Michael H. Seamster	1983	143
173-6/8	25-4/8	25-2/8	22-0/8	8	9	Tulare	SD	Milton Haag	1959	145
173-6/8	19-3/8	19-5/8	17-1/8	9	9	Douglas County	MN	John Duberowski	1980	145
173-5/8	25-4/8	24-3/8	18-1/8	7	6	Gray County	KS	Allen D. Bailey	1982	147
173-4/8	24-7/8	25-5/8	21-6/8	6	6	Great Bend	KS	Norman Kimber	1967	148
173-4/8	22-4/8	23-7/8	14-1/8	6	8	Hartford	OH	Peter Bradley	1969	148
173-4/8	26-1/8	21-7/8	16-7/8	7	10	Renville County	MN	Larry Godejahn	1973	148
172-7/8	24-0/8	21-4/8	14-4/8	10	10	Checotah	OK	Clark Utley	1976	151
171-6/8	22-3/8	21-5/8	20-5/8	8	9	Dubuque County	IA	Dick Theis	1975	152
171-6/8	26-0/8	26-7/8	19-6/8	9	7	Vermillion County	IL	Gene Maier	1984	152
171-5/8	22-7/8	24-1/8	16-4/8	7	7	Wapello County	IA	Rex Jones	1983	154
171-4/8	24-5/8	24-5/8	19-1/8	7	7	Butler County	KS	Jeff Stevens	1982	155
171-2/8	27-0/8	27-0/8	18-5/8	4	5	Van Buren County	MI	David Anderson	1979	156
171-2/8	23-5/8	24-7/8	14-4/8	6	6	Scottsbluff County	NE	Doug Hauser	1984	156
171-1/8	23-4/8	24-0/8	20-2/8	8	6	Jackson County	MI	Shawn R. Surque	1985	158
171-0/8	24-0/8	24-4/8	18-1/8	7	7	Dodge County	WI	Dallas Johnson	1955	159
170-7/8	24-5/8	25-2/8	15-3/8	6	6	Redwood County	MN	Todd G. Gilbens	1982	160
170-6/8	24-3/8	23-6/8	17-2/8	9	8	Nobles City	MN	David Janssen	1973	161
170-4/8	22-6/8	23-2/8	24-7/8	8	7	Green County	WI	Dean Dilly	1974	162
170-4/8	26-3/8	26-1/8	20-5/8	7	7	Tazewell County	IL	Bret Hamilton	1982	162
169-6/8	24-4/8	25-1/8	17-7/8	6	6	Carter County	KY	Timothy Carter	1974	164
169-5/8	26-5/8	27-6/8	22-0/8	7	7	Dodge County	MN	Lawrence Sowieja	1973	165
169-3/8	22-3/8	22-4/8	17-2/8	8	7	Clearwater County	ID	J. David Powers	1981	166
169-2/8	23-4/8	23-7/8	18-5/8	6	8	Rice County	MN	Vernon J. Kleve	1972	167
169-2/8	25-4/8	26-4/8	19-4/8	7	8	Schuyler County	IL	Robert J. Logsdon	1981	167
168-6/8	24-1/8	25-1/8	20-3/8	9	8	Olmsted County	MN	Jeff Meyer	1974	169
168-0/8	21-3/8	21-2/8	15-6/8	7	9	Martin County	MN	Charles Sutphin	1974	170
167-6/8	24-3/8	24-3/8	19-7/8	9	7	Scott County	IA	Gordon Vrana	1967	171
167-2/8	24-0/8	24-3/8	17-1/8	7	6	Sauk County	WI	Charles Davenport	1969	172
167-0/8	22-2/8	22-1/8	18-3/8	8	5	Dows	IA	Robert Filbrandt	1974	173
166-7/8	25-3/8	25-6/8	18-2/8	6	6	Hubbard County	MN	Jack Smythe	1973	174
166-5/8	28-3/8	26-6/8	15-1/8	8	9	Kirkman	IA	Billy Custer	1968	175
166-3/8	24-5/8	24-5/8	16-2/8	6	6	Brown County	SD	Frank Bauer	1974	176
166-3/8	21-6/8	20-3/8	17-3/8	7	7	Okotoks	ALB	Darren Dale	1980	176
166-0/8	23-0/8	27-0/8	20-1/8	8	7	Ross County	OH	Randy Johnson	1981	178
166-0/8	21-5/8	20-2/8	15-3/8	8	8	Pope County	AR	Donald Alan Barnett	1983	178
165-7/8	24-2/8	22-2/8	17-3/8	6	6	White River N.W.R.	AR	Bruce Wiggins	1959	180
165-7/8	21-1/8	25-6/8	19-3/8	8	8	Gallatin County	KY	John C. Vetter	1977	180
165-7/8	20-6/8	19-7/8	23-1/8	7	8	Washington County	OH	Mike Ferrell	1982	180
164-7/8	20-1/8	22-4/8	16-4/8	7	6	Murray County	MN	Lanny Engler	1975	183
164-6/8	18-0/8	20-4/8	16-1/8	9	9	Chippewa County	MN	Steven P. Ellingson	1975	184
164-1/8	23-5/8	22-1/8	18-5/8	9	8	Winona County	MN	Charles W. Benson	1974	185
164-0/8	20-6/8	21-7/8	15-0/8	7	7	Guthrie County	IA	Dick Rote	1980	186
163-1/8	21-6/8	22-0/8	16-7/8	7	7	Cherry County	NE	Walter Cady	1975	187
162-7/8	20-5/8	20-4/8	17-3/8	7	8	Walsh County	ND	Randy Schuster	1985	188
161-7/8	24-7/8	25-5/8	22-0/8	7	9	Cascade County	MT	Kits Smith	1980	189

WHITETAIL DEER *(Non-Typical Antlers)*
(continued)

Score	Length of Main Beam R	L	Inside Spread	Number of Points R	L	Area	State/ Province	Hunter's Name	Date	Rank
161-1/8	22-2/8	24-4/8	17-3/8	9	8	Marshall County	MN	Richard Hoff	1983	190
160-6/8	20-4/8	21-4/8	18-4/8	7	5	Bremer County	IA	Steven Sims	1983	191
160-5/8	19-6/8	21-6/8	17-0/8	11	9	Quincy	IL	Ray Gedaminski	1967	192
160-3/8	23-1/8	23-1/8	16-1/8	8	13	Winnebago County	WI	John M. Duchatschek	1980	193
160-2/8	23-1/8	23-1/8	15-3/8	6	7	St. Francisville	IL	Mike Deckard	1978	194
160-0/8	27-4/8	26-6/8	18-0/8	7	6	Gallitin County	KY	William J. Epeards	1980	195
159-7/8	22-1/8	24-4/8	19-2/8	9	8	Edmonton	ALB	Brian Bruce	1981	196
159-7/8	23-2/8	24-1/8	18-2/8	5	6	Huron County	OH	Donald W. Howard	1984	196
159-7/8	21-4/8	20-2/8	16-2/8	6	6	Huron County	OH	John R. Gockstetter	1984	196
159-6/8	21-6/8	26-5/8	15-6/8	10	7	Greene County	AR	Randy Ladd	1985	199
159-4/8	20-7/8	20-5/8	15-4/8	6	8	McPherson County	KS	Kenneth L. Vogts	1979	200
159-1/8	21-5/8	21-6/8	13-3/8	8	10	Scott County	KY	Vic Morrison	1972	201
159-0/8	24-0/8	24-4/8	17-3/8	7	5	Lake County	IL	Robert H. Fugett	1976	202
159-0/8	22-5/8	21-5/8	21-1/8	6	8	Merom	IN	Steve Hobbs	1980	202
158-7/8	27-1/8	25-1/8	22-7/8	5	6	Buffalo County	WI	Ted Bauer	1984	204
158-7/8	25-4/8	25-1/8	15-4/8	7	7	Washtenaw County	MI	Larry R. Lange	1984	204
158-4/8	22-6/8	24-1/8	19-4/8	7	4	Winona County	MN	Randy SuPalla	1985	206
158-1/8	19-2/8	21-0/8	17-1/8	6	8	Jackson County	MI	Kim H. Whittman	1982	207
157-7/8	22-6/8	23-2/8	16-7/8	10	8	Dane County	WI	Donald W. Pache	1982	208
157-5/8	25-3/8	25-1/8	17-5/8	8	8	Blackhawk County	IA	Darrell Zacharias	1976	209
157-1/8	23-1/8	22-7/8	16-4/8	8	6	Rock County	WI	Daniel T. Steinke	1982	210
156-6/8	26-7/8	24-7/8	18-4/8	9	7	Beltsville	MD	Anthony C. Malpasso	1979	211
156-4/8	24-6/8	23-3/8	20-2/8	7	9	Winnebago County	IL	Jim Dorney	1975	212
156-2/8	23-2/8	20-0/8	16-4/8	8	5	Page	NE	Darrell Clyde	1963	213
156-1/8	24-4/8	27-7/8	23-3/8	8	9	Dundee	MN	Joe Earl	1959	214
156-1/8	24-5/8	25-5/8	20-3/8	5	5	Lake County	IL	Mike Mitten	1984	214
156-0/8	25-3/8	24-0/8	15-7/8	8	6	Stewart County	TN	Ronald M. Widner	1974	216
155-4/8	25-1/8	25-1/8	16-3/8	9	9	Pottawatomie County	KS	Richard L. Ruetti	1970	217
155-3/8	21-2/8	21-3/8	16-5/8	12	8	Winona County	MN	John W. Zahrte	1974	218
155-3/8	24-2/8	23-6/8	17-6/8	7	8	Morton County	ND	Dennis Simenson	1981	218
155-0/8	24-4/8	23-7/8	17-2/8	8	5	McCreary County	KY	Eddie Howard	1985	220
154-7/8	19-4/8	20-0/8	15-4/8	6	10	Calhoun County	MI	Norman E. Nuding	1982	221
154-6/8	24-5/8	17-1/8	16-6/8	8	10	Marshall County	IN	Sennett Dietl	1965	222
154-4/8	21-4/8	20-0/8	15-3/8	7	7	Marinette County	WI	LeRoy Olson	1974	223
154-3/8	20-6/8	22-5/8	17-2/8	7	7	Morrow County	OH	Nancy Shade	1982	224
153-7/8	21-1/8	21-2/8	11-4/8	12	8	Bayfield County	WI	Claude B. Butler	1954	225
153-7/8	24-3/8	23-4/8	15-6/8	7	6	Branch County	MI	Keith Ackerman	1973	225
153-6/8	22-6/8	22-0/8	17-0/8	8	8	Fairburn	SD	Bennie Spring	1961	227
153-3/8	22-7/8	22-2/8	20-5/8	6	6	Mankato	MN	Maynard L. Nelson	1968	228
153-0/8	23-0/8	23-6/8	19-1/8	5	5	Ripley County	IN	Robert H. Pitt	1970	229
153-0/8	20-4/8	19-7/8	13-2/8	6	12	Lee County	AL	Leonard Hochstedler	1975	229
152-3/8	24-2/8	21-4/8	20-0/8	8	5	Allegan State Forest	MI	Elwood Snell	1947	231
151-6/8	23-1/8	23-0/8	14-1/8	8	8	Van Buren County	MI	Rex S. Millard	1986	232
151-5/8	17-0/8	20-5/8	18-0/8	8	10	Wishek	ND	Craig Lambrecht	1980	233
151-5/8	19-7/8	18-1/8	14-7/8	5	9	Hunterdon County	NJ	Jeff Anderson	1982	233
151-3/8	21-4/8	24-7/8	21-0/8	9	5	Scott County	KY	Johnny Mulberry	1982	235
151-3/8	25-0/8	23-3/8	19-7/8	5	6	Coshocton County	OH	William Randles	1983	235

WORLD RECORD ROOSEVELT *(OLYMPIC)* ELK
Score: 352 1/8
Tillamook County, Oregon – 1985
Hunter: Dale Baumgartner

ROOSEVELT *(OLYMPIC)* ELK

Cervus elaphus roosevelti

Score	Length of Main Beam R	L	Inside Spread	Number of Points R	L	Area	State/ Province	Hunter's Name	Date	Rank
352-1/8	43-5/8	45-6/8	40-0/8	7	8	Tillamook County	OR	Dale Baumgartner	1985	1
347-4/8	51-6/8	53-1/8	38-2/8	7	7	Scappoose County	OR	Ken R. Adamson	1985	2
342-7/8	54-7/8	56-0/8	39-5/8	7	7	Curry County	OR	Kendal Smith	1986	3
311-6/8	52-1/8	49-5/8	36-2/8	6	6	Coos County	OR	Robert Dean Dunson	1982	4
305-6/8	50-2/8	50-4/8	38-6/8	6	6	Polk County	OR	James Wallen	1980	5
300-7/8	48-4/8	48-4/8	42-3/8	6	7	Coos County	OR	Dean Dunson	1986	6
293-5/8	46-6/8	47-0/8	41-3/8	7	7	Long Island	WA	Jess Martin, Jr.	1971	7
291-2/8	48-3/8	49-3/8	33-6/8	5	6	Lane County	OR	Joe Waite	1981	8
290-4/8	41-1/8	42-1/8	41-4/8	6	6	Clallam County	WA	Russ Spaulding	1985	9
289-2/8	50-3/8	47-5/8	37-6/8	5	6	Jefferson County	WA	Ronald E. Ihrig	1984	10
288-6/8	42-3/8	44-1/8	40-0/8	6	7	Curry County	OR	James Atherton	1985	11
282-2/8	44-6/8	44-1/8	38-7/8	7	6	Afognak Island	AK	Edward L. Russell	1980	12
282-0/8	45-0/8	43-6/8	42-0/8	6	6	Jefferson County	WA	Dave Robertson	1970	13
280-5/8	41-0/8	43-1/8	33-5/8	6	7	Pacific County	WA	Dan Free	1983	14
280-2/8	43-2/8	43-0/8	33-0/8	6	6	Lane County	OR	Jeff Sindt	1982	15
280-0/8	45-3/8	45-3/8	34-4/8	6	6	Long Island	WA	Jerry Webster	1979	16
279-7/8	47-4/8	47-2/8	37-2/8	5	6	Grays Harbor County	WA	G. A. "Toby" Hart	1986	17
278-7/8	45-6/8	44-1/8	38-1/8	6	6	Clearwater	WA	Donald N. Morey	1978	18
277-0/8	43-4/8	41-1/8	38-6/8	6	7	Clallum County	WA	Wayne Haag	1982	19
277-0/8	42-0/8	43-0/8	39-2/8	6	5	Jefferson County	WA	Wayne McReynolds	1984	19
275-7/8	46-0/8	42-7/8	29-7/8	6	5	Skamania County	WA	Jerry L. Carter	1973	21
274-1/8	40-4/8	40-1/8	39-7/8	6	6	Clallam County	WA	Clyde E. Graham	1985	22
272-5/8	46-4/8	45-1/8	36-1/8	5	5	Jefferson County	WA	Bryan Mittge	1986	23
272-1/8	39-4/8	40-6/8	33-5/8	5	5	Wahkiakum County	WA	Russ Poppe	1982	24
271-1/8	46-0/8	45-3/8	33-3/8	6	6	Afognak Island	AK	David Harper	1970	25
270-5/8	37-0/8	37-4/8	36-1/8	7	7	Tillamook County	OR	Alan Richardson	1980	26
270-2/8	44-6/8	44-1/8	44-4/8	4	5	Quinalt	WA	Bill Brown	1959	27
268-3/8	44-6/8	45-1/8	38-3/8	6	6	Long Island	WA	Glen Watland	1980	28
268-2/8	43-7/8	43-7/8	41-0/8	5	5	Grays Harbor County	WA	Terry Plato	1984	29
267-2/8	44-3/8	44-3/8	38-0/8	6	5	Grays Harbor County	WA	Scott Bergen	1985	30
266-7/8	40-5/8	41-5/8	35-3/8	6	6	Clatsop County	OR	David M. Jones	1982	31
266-1/8	37-0/8	36-3/8	34-3/8	6	6	Clatsop County	OR	Douglas W. Hamilton	1982	32
265-0/8	40-5/8	41-1/8	34-1/8	5	7	Coos County	OR	Thomas E. Tipton	1986	33
263-6/8	46-3/8	41-6/8	45-0/8	5	6	Grays Harbor County	WA	Mark R. Nieznalski	1984	34
262-0/8	40-1/8	40-0/8	34-0/8	6	6	Coos County	OR	Larry Frost	1985	35
261-6/8	45-4/8	45-5/8	28-6/8	6	6	Douglas County	OR	Dennis Olson	1984	36
261-5/8	41-2/8	42-6/8	29-1/8	6	6	Lane County	OR	Max Lee	1980	37
261-5/8	40-7/8	41-2/8	38-7/8	5	5	Jefferson County	WA	Mark J. Tupper	1986	37
261-0/8	44-7/8	44-7/8	32-4/8	6	6	Long Island	WA	Dan Free	1980	39
260-4/8	41-4/8	41-1/8	34-4/8	6	5	Douglas County	OR	J. B. Hollander	1984	40
259-2/8	42-3/8	42-4/8	37-0/8	5	5	Coos County	OR	James M. Speelman	1974	41
255-2/8	42-1/8	40-2/8	34-2/8	6	6	Clallam County	WA	Frank LaGambina	1980	42
253-5/8	40-4/8	40-0/8	43-1/8	6	6	Columbia County	OR	Randy Jennings	1985	43
252-7/8	40-7/8	42-1/8	31-3/8	6	6	Long Island	WA	John Wall	1979	44
251-4/8	38-2/8	39-5/8	36-4/8	8	6	Clatsop County	OR	James L. Friesz	1981	45
251-0/8	39-1/8	40-4/8	33-2/8	6	6	Jefferson County	WA	Bill Pudell	1982	46
250-0/8	43-1/8	42-0/8	33-6/8	5	6	Pacific County	WA	Bill Egner	1977	47
249-2/8	41-4/8	36-2/8	40-6/8	6	6	Jefferson County	WA	Sanford Windle	1972	48
248-2/8	39-3/8	39-2/8	28-6/8	7	7	Coos County	OR	Craig Matson	1980	49
247-5/8	45-2/8	43-5/8	29-5/8	5	7	Yamhill County	OR	Jerry S. Bailey	1986	50
247-3/8	34-4/8	36-6/8	37-1/8	5	5	Grays Harbor County	WA	Wayne McReynolds	1981	51
247-3/8	43-2/8	44-6/8	30-3/8	6	6	Tillamook County	OR	Steve Pieren	1982	51
247-1/8	35-1/8	36-4/8	36-1/8	6	5	Clatsop County	OR	John C. Bernards	1985	53
247-0/8	39-6/8	38-4/8	39-6/8	5	5	Olympic Peninsula	WA	Lloyd Beebe	1951	54
246-6/8	39-5/8	37-3/8	34-0/8	6	6	Jefferson County	WA	Eugene Wells	1960	55
243-6/8	43-4/8	41-4/8	33-0/8	5	5	Bogachiel River	WA	Glenn St. Charles	1952	56
243-0/8	45-0/8	44-0/8	40-2/8	5	5	Clearwater	WA	James M. Stark	1977	57
241-6/8	39-7/8	39-1/8	34-6/8	6	5	Clatsop County	OR	David Lawrence	1982	58
238-2/8	46-2/8	45-1/8	39-6/8	5	4	Long Island	WA	John R. Martin	1978	59
238-2/8	39-4/8	37-3/8	37-0/8	5	5	Grays Harbor County	WA	Jack McDougall	1986	59
238-0/8	39-7/8	40-4/8	34-2/8	5	5	Jefferson County	WA	Larry Jensen	1985	61
236-6/8	36-5/8	37-6/8	38-0/8	5	6	Grays Harbor County	WA	Richard Mazzei	1984	62
236-6/8	40-3/8	39-3/8	32-4/8	6	6	Lincoln County	OR	Warren Lynch	1986	62

ROOSEVELT *(OLYMPIC)* ELK

(continued)

Minimum Score 210

Score	Length of Main Beam R	L	Inside Spread	Number of Points R	L	Area	State/ Province	Hunter's Name	Date	Rank
236-5/8	39-0/8	37-3/8	31-3/8	6	6	Jefferson County	WA	Mathew Hayvaz	1984	64
235-2/8	38-0/8	39-1/8	34-0/8	5	5	Tillamook County	OR	Smokey Crews	1983	65
234-2/8	39-5/8	38-4/8	33-6/8	5	5	Clallam County	WA	Dean R. Swerin	1985	66
232-6/8	32-4/8	33-1/8	36-2/8	6	6	Clatsop County	OR	Robert J. Wilkie	1984	67
232-0/8	39-1/8	39-2/8	31-2/8	6	5	Josephine County	OR	Joel Robertson	1982	68
231-7/8	35-5/8	37-4/8	32-3/8	5	5	Clallam County	WA	Frank LaGambina	1979	69
231-1/8	37-3/8	38-0/8	29-7/8	5	5	Yamhill County	OR	Curtis C. Altman	1983	70
230-6/8	35-2/8	34-4/8	32-2/8	5	5	Clallam County	WA	Wayne Haag	1980	71
230-2/8	41-4/8	40-3/8	30-0/8	5	6	Curry County	OR	Kendal Smith	1982	72
230-2/8	38-5/8	36-4/8	38-0/8	5	5	Coos County	OR	Thomas Tipton	1984	72
229-0/8	44-3/8	44-3/8	35-6/8	5	4	Clallam County	WA	Pete J. Germeau	1982	74
225-4/8	37-0/8	35-6/8	35-2/8	5	5	Jefferson County	WA	Rodger Squirrel	1984	75
224-6/8	36-6/8	38-7/8	30-4/8	5	5	Sams River	WA	Francis W. Robinson, Jr.	1965	76
224-3/8	36-2/8	31-0/8	29-5/8	5	7	Clatsop County	OR	Randy Jennings	1980	77
223-5/8	40-3/8	38-1/8	34-2/8	6	7	Clatsop County	OR	Ray C Nelson	1985	78
223-3/8	36-5/8	35-7/8	32-7/8	5	5	Tillamook County	OR	Smokey Crews	1985	79
223-1/8	42-1/8	40-6/8	28-3/8	6	5	Clatsop County	OR	David Braem	1982	80
218-7/8	38-5/8	40-4/8	35-1/8	5	5	Jefferson County	WA	Harold Wellan	1985	81
218-0/8	35-7/8	34-6/8	27-0/8	5	6	Polk County	OR	Rand Sether	1984	82
217-7/8	38-1/8	39-3/8	28-1/8	5	5	Long Island	WA	Clyde Kennedy	1975	83
216-3/8	34-0/8	32-5/8	34-3/8	5	5	Clallam County	WA	Arnold LaGambina	1983	84
214-6/8	35-7/8	34-1/8	28-2/8	6	6	Clatsop County	OR	Kurt Klaffke	1986	85
212-0/8	36-6/8	36-4/8	33-0/8	5	5	Grays Harbor County	WA	Dan Boeholt	1985	86

WORLD RECORD YELLOWSTONE *(AMERICAN)* ELK
Score: 393 1/8
Montrose County, Colorado – 1986
Hunter: Wayne Bradley

YELLOWSTONE *(AMERICAN)* ELK

Cervus elaphus nelsoni and certain related subspecies

Score	Length of Main Beam R	L	Inside Spread	Number of Points R	L	Area	State/ Province	Hunter's Name	Date	Rank
393-1/8	61-5/8	63-0/8	43-7/8	7	9	Montrose County	CO	Wayne Bradley	1986	1
389-2/8	63-6/8	63-0/8	42-1/8	7	7	Coconino County	AZ	Jay Elmer	1980	2
386-5/8	53-5/8	53-6/8	41-2/8	8	7	Madison County	MT	Allan Mintken	1986	3
384-6/8	55-2/8	53-4/8	44-2/8	6	7	Coconino County	AZ	Jay Elmer	1979	4
384-4/8	53-4/8	54-6/8	45-4/8	7	7	Meagher County	MT	David Snyder	1981	5
382-2/8	60-0/8	60-0/8	47-2/8	6	6	Coconino County	AZ	Don R. Newton, Jr.	1985	6
380-2/8	56-2/8	54-1/8	45-0/8	7	6	San Francisco Peaks	AZ	Doug Kittredge	1975	7
379-6/8	57-7/8	56-5/8	47-6/8	6	6	Coconino County	AZ	Gregory K. Scott	1986	8
379-3/8	53-4/8	56-0/8	42-7/8	7	8	Coconino County	AZ	Jeff Elmer	1984	9
378-6/8	57-4/8	57-7/8	39-0/8	9	8	Shoshone County	ID	Steven W. Mullin	1981	10
377-0/8	59-2/8	57-1/8	39-4/8	6	6	Coconino County	AZ	Jack Frazier	1981	11
377-0/8	56-1/8	51-1/8	40-3/8	7	8	Coconino County	AZ	Larry Thomas	1985	11
376-6/8	47-2/8	50-3/8	39-2/8	6	7	Adams County	ID	Jack D. Sheppard	1966	13
376-3/8	60-1/8	59-1/8	40-3/8	6	7	Catron County	NM	Wayne K. Curtis	1986	14
375-2/8	56-0/8	55-0/8	38-0/8	6	6	Converse County	WY	Don Stewart	1981	15
375-1/8	53-5/8	55-7/8	46-7/8	6	6	Jackson County	CO	Vincent Kvidera	1976	16
375-0/8	52-3/8	53-7/8	39-1/8	6	7	Sierra County	NM	Jim Wagner	1986	17
372-0/8	52-2/8	52-2/8	44-0/8	7	7	Lincoln County	MT	Jerry Regh	1986	18
371-7/8	52-3/8	53-0/8	46-5/8	6	6	Mineral County	MT	Scott J. Stern	1983	19
371-7/8	59-3/8	57-2/8	42-7/8	6	6	Coconino County	AZ	George Flournoy	1986	19
370-1/8	51-5/8	50-7/8	41-5/8	6	6	Petroleum County	MT	G. L. "Buck" Damone	1985	21
369-6/8	54-6/8	53-0/8	47-6/8	6	6	Greenlee County	AZ	Clifford White	1986	22
369-4/8	53-2/8	51-2/8	39-4/8	7	7	Bonner County	ID	Steve Noort	1986	23
369-4/8	53-0/8	53-0/8	42-4/8	6	7	Catron County	NM	Frank A. Hayes	1986	23
369-2/8	51-0/8	55-4/8	48-4/8	6	6	Madison County	MT	Jeff Engler	1977	25
367-3/8	47-7/8	49-3/8	45-1/8	8	7	Ft. Collins	CO	H. Troxell/B. Alexander	1970	26
367-2/8	55-4/8	57-7/8	46-0/8	6	6	Lemhi County	ID	Ben Fahnholz	1982	27
366-7/8	53-2/8	52-1/8	40-4/8	7	7	Superior	MT	Gerry Lamarre	1977	28
366-5/8	53-0/8	53-2/8	45-3/8	7	7	Shoshone County	ID	D. A. Johnson	1962	29
366-3/8	52-5/8	50-7/8	41-7/8	6	6	Fergus County	MT	J. Douglas Krings	1980	30
366-1/8	52-3/8	51-0/8	43-7/8	6	6	Berland River	ALB	Brad Sidebottom	1986	31
365-1/8	52-3/8	51-2/8	38-5/8	7	7	Sandoval County	NM	John C. McClendon	1985	32
365-0/8	60-6/8	61-4/8	50-2/8	7	7	Fergus County	MT	John Jeide	1983	33
364-6/8	50-3/8	46-2/8	39-2/8	6	6	Grant County	OR	William C. Sanowski	1976	34
363-7/8	50-5/8	47-0/8	41-4/8	7	8	Converse County	WY	David P. Lindman	1986	35
362-2/8	50-2/8	49-4/8	46-2/8	7	7	Jackson County	CO	Alfred H. O'Brien	1972	36
361-2/8	58-4/8	56-4/8	37-0/8	6	6	Coconino County	AZ	Tom Phelps	1986	37
361-0/8	54-0/8	55-0/8	44-4/8	6	6	Coconino County	AZ	Laura Wuertz	1986	38
360-7/8	54-7/8	56-1/8	41-7/8	7	6	Lemhi County	ID	Tony Latham	1983	39
359-7/8	44-4/8	53-5/8	43-0/8	7	8	Caribou County	ID	Calvin Coziah	1973	40
359-5/8	50-4/8	52-0/8	47-1/8	6	6	Pierce County	WA	Doug Nearhood	1985	41
359-3/8	48-1/8	49-2/8	48-1/8	6	6	Love Messa	CO	David W. Christopherson	1978	42
359-2/8	51-0/8	52-5/8	42-0/8	6	9	Coconino County	AZ	Robert Cecrle	1972	43
359-2/8	58-2/8	56-7/8	42-0/8	6	6	Coconino County	AZ	Jim David	1974	43
358-7/8	55-5/8	54-5/8	40-7/8	6	6	Coconino County	AZ	Gary Bills	1986	45
358-6/8	51-7/8	55-0/8	47-6/8	6	6	Sheridan County	WY	Mike Barrett	1986	46
358-5/8	53-0/8	49-7/8	38-3/8	6	6	Cibola County	NM	Moises Perea	1980	47
358-3/8	52-3/8	52-5/8	39-5/8	6	6	Sanders County	MT	Eugene Roesler	1986	48
358-2/8	54-1/8	51-4/8	47-0/8	6	6	Crook County	OR	Oliver Weger	1983	49
357-6/8	50-2/8	50-6/8	40-4/8	6	6	Park County	CO	Donald R. Looper	1975	50
357-4/8	52-5/8	55-0/8	37-6/8	7	6	Fergus County	MT	Michael B. Hedrick	1981	51
357-3/8	56-2/8	49-2/8	37-1/8	6	6	Meagher County	MT	David G. Snyder	1978	52
357-3/8	50-4/8	50-4/8	34-5/8	6	6	Swan River	MAN	Kelly Shykitka	1986	52
357-0/8	54-2/8	56-0/8	41-0/8	6	6	Hole Canyon	ID	Howard F. Johnson	1968	54
357-0/8	56-5/8	56-7/8	46-6/8	6	6	Payson	AZ	David L. Crockett	1973	54
357-0/8	53-5/8	53-6/8	43-2/8	6	7	Strawberry Lake	CO	Frank Fraser	1977	54
356-7/8	54-1/8	53-6/8	53-7/8	6	7	Livingston	MT	Charles Alkire	1964	57
356-7/8	49-6/8	51-0/8	46-3/8	7	6	Flathead County	MT	Terry Krogstad	1984	57
356-6/8	54-2/8	56-1/8	43-4/8	6	6	Lemhi County	ID	Larry Grooms	1986	59
356-4/8	57-3/8	53-1/8	46-4/8	6	6	Catron County	NM	Bill Elmer	1986	60
356-3/8	52-4/8	48-6/8	36-1/8	6	7	Fergus County	MT	Leonard L. Weeks	1984	61
356-0/8	52-1/8	50-1/8	36-4/8	7	6	Linn County	OR	David E. Renoud	1983	62

YELLOWSTONE *(AMERICAN)* ELK
(continued)   Minimum Score 260

Score	Length of Main Beam R	L	Inside Spread	Number of Points R	L	Area	State/ Province	Hunter's Name	Date	Rank
355-4/8	54-7/8	56-5/8	42-6/8	6	6	Anaconda Pintlar Area	MT	Robert B. McKay	1973	63
355-0/8	50-1/8	50-1/8	38-0/8	6	6	Shoshone County	ID	Vern Clary/Ed Oliver	1978	64
354-7/8	51-4/8	51-0/8	41-6/8	6	7	Greenlee County	AZ	David Dickson	1986	65
354-6/8	54-0/8	53-7/8	36-6/8	6	6	Valley County	MT	Kenneth R. Johnson	1986	66
354-4/8	49-1/8	50-4/8	38-6/8	6	6	Happy Jack	AZ	Ron Scherer	1980	67
354-3/8	56-0/8	55-3/8	39-1/8	6	7	Converse County	WY	Edward Coy	1972	68
354-3/8	53-2/8	58-3/8	46-1/8	6	6	Williams	AZ	James M. Frey	1980	68
354-3/8	52-5/8	52-7/8	45-1/8	6	6	Valley County	MT	Gregg Pauley	1985	68
354-3/8	51-3/8	53-1/8	39-7/8	6	6	Lincoln County	MT	Keith Krumbeck	1986	68
354-2/8	55-3/8	53-2/8	41-6/8	6	6	Clearwater River	ID	J. David Powers	1978	72
354-0/8	60-4/8	61-2/8	34-4/8	7	6	Kaibab Nat'l Forest	AZ	Jack Cahill	1982	73
353-0/8	50-4/8	49-6/8	43-2/8	6	6	Blue Ridge	AZ	Richard M. Larsen	1980	74
353-0/8	47-2/8	46-1/8	38-0/8	6	7	Grant County	OR	Kenneth Mills	1983	74
352-7/8	54-4/8	53-4/8	42-0/8	6	7	Bob Marshall Wilderness	MT	Jack Howard	1972	76
352-7/8	51-6/8	52-1/8	41-7/8	6	6	Jemez Mountains	NM	John W. Rose	1981	76
352-5/8	50-1/8	50-0/8	37-5/8	6	6	Woody Ridge	AZ	Oscar Dale Porter	1982	78
352-0/8	51-4/8	53-0/8	38-5/8	6	7	Coconino County	AZ	Bill Elmer	1981	79
351-7/8	50-6/8	50-2/8	40-4/8	7	6	Crook County	OR	Curtis Demaris	1983	80
351-4/8	51-7/8	51-2/8	39-4/8	7	7	E. Clear Creek	AZ	Marvin L. Slaughter	1979	81
351-4/8	50-6/8	49-7/8	40-0/8	6	6	Grant County	OR	Curtis Demaris	1980	81
351-4/8	56-5/8	56-0/8	46-4/8	6	6	Coconino County	AZ	John F. Gurasich	1986	81
351-4/8	43-7/8	45-3/8	40-0/8	6	6	Lincoln County	NM	Terry Arnim	1986	81
351-3/8	49-6/8	54-2/8	48-2/8	8	7	Grant County	OR	Bob Lindsay	1981	85
351-2/8	55-6/8	53-5/8	41-6/8	6	6	Coconino County	AZ	Jay Elmer	1977	86
351-2/8	51-5/8	50-3/8	34-0/8	7	7	Missoula County	MT	James P. Loughran	1986	86
350-6/8	53-5/8	53-0/8	40-2/8	6	6	Sheridan County	WY	Kurt M. Baughman	1980	88
350-3/8	48-7/8	48-5/8	41-7/8	8	7	Fergus County	MT	G. L. "Buck" Damone	1981	89
350-2/8	51-6/8	48-7/8	40-2/8	6	6	Routt County	CO	Mark L. Houslet	1977	90
350-2/8	53-4/8	53-1/8	41-2/8	6	6	Baca Location	NM	Jose Montalvo	1981	90
350-0/8	53-1/8	51-5/8	38-6/8	6	6	Sandoval County	NM	Tom David	1984	92
349-7/8	50-1/8	51-1/8	48-5/8	6	6	Crook County	OR	Dale Shiery	1984	93
349-6/8	53-0/8	52-6/8	41-6/8	6	6	Wheeler County	OR	Dale Shiery	1983	94
349-5/8	46-0/8	44-4/8	37-1/8	6	6	Spanish Peaks	CO	Richard L. Doman	1972	95
349-3/8	52-2/8	51-7/8	36-7/8	6	6	Lewiston	MT	Charles R. Bowman	1966	96
349-3/8	50-4/8	45-6/8	46-1/8	6	6	Park County	CO	Gary Jones	1984	96
349-3/8	53-3/8	54-6/8	43-1/8	6	6	Apache County	AZ	David Sullivan	1986	96
349-2/8	50-6/8	51-0/8	39-4/8	7	6	Clackamas County	OR	Paul Smith	1984	99
349-1/8	56-4/8	60-2/8	45-3/8	6	7	Coconino County	AZ	Alan R. Miller	1975	100
349-0/8	51-1/8	47-6/8	39-2/8	6	6	Los Alamos County	NM	Chuck Adams	1982	101
348-4/8	55-0/8	55-0/8	43-6/8	6	6	San Francisco Peaks	AZ	Bob Jensen	1981	102
348-4/8	45-3/8	44-6/8	41-6/8	6	6	Bonneville County	ID	Ronald L. Mueller	1982	102
348-3/8	50-0/8	51-7/8	34-4/8	7	7	Pierce County	WA	John Lyday	1984	104
348-2/8	30-7/8	47-3/8	34-4/8	6	7	Rio Blanco County	CO	Clark Gallup	1976	105
347-6/8	51-4/8	47-6/8	38-0/8	6	6	Valley County	MT	Greg Zahn	1981	106
347-4/8	50-2/8	49-5/8	45-6/8	7	6	Island Park	ID	Bob Baird	1961	107
347-1/8	54-1/8	53-2/8	37-3/8	6	6	Clackamas County	OR	Bill Lancaster	1986	108
346-7/8	54-1/8	51-4/8	35-5/8	7	7	Lake County	MT	Scott Ganz	1984	109
346-6/8	44-2/8	45-4/8	41-0/8	6	6	Bighorn Mountain	WY	John Yeager	1980	110
346-5/8	52-6/8	53-6/8	44-5/8	7	6	Santa Fe National Forest	NM	Frank C. Sciorilli	1977	111
345-7/8	52-5/8	52-0/8	41-5/8	7	6	Little Wood River	ID	Danny F. Watson	1977	112
345-4/8	52-1/8	52-3/8	37-4/8	7	7	Ravalli County	MT	Howard Nichols	1983	113
344-3/8	52-0/8	52-6/8	45-1/8	6	6	Lincoln County	MT	Lance Sink	1984	114
344-0/8	49-7/8	52-7/8	41-4/8	6	7	Catron County	NM	Wayne Ludington	1985	115
343-7/8	49-0/8	49-4/8	42-3/8	6	6	Union County	OR	Craig Gorham	1983	116
343-5/8	52-4/8	55-3/8	38-7/8	6	7	Anderson Mesa	AZ	J. R. Wilhelmy	1976	117
343-4/8	49-2/8	47-0/8	37-6/8	6	6	Lemhi County	ID	Roger Brockhoff	1985	118
343-4/8	51-4/8	52-1/8	38-4/8	6	7	Socorro County	NM	Richard Dewey	1986	118
343-2/8	52-2/8	51-2/8	40-0/8	6	6	Clearwater River	ID	Mike Schlegel	1978	120
343-1/8	49-2/8	46-6/8	49-5/8	6	6	Grand County	CO	Leon Lambert	1981	121
342-7/8	54-3/8	54-3/8	42-2/8	8	8	Winter Park	CO	G. Fred Asbell	1980	122
342-2/8	49-7/8	49-2/8	37-2/8	6	6	Grant County	NM	Larry M. Sellers	1985	123
342-1/8	52-3/8	52-4/8	45-1/8	6	6	Steamboat Springs	CO	Jerry A. Krueger	1981	124
342-1/8	53-7/8	50-4/8	34-7/8	6	7	Jackson County	OR	J. T. Tepper	1986	124

YELLOWSTONE *(AMERICAN)* ELK

Minimum Score 260   (continued)

Score	Length of Main Beam R	L	Inside Spread	Number of Points R	L	Area	State/ Province	Hunter's Name	Date	Rank
342-0/8	58-6/8	59-0/8	46-6/8	6	6	Cibola County	NM	Dois R. Chesshir	1986	126
341-6/8	54-7/8	53-1/8	44-2/8	6	6	Greenlee County	AZ	Pete Shepley	1983	127
341-6/8	55-3/8	53-3/8	45-6/8	6	6	Garfield County	CO	Gary Frauenkron	1983	127
341-5/8	54-4/8	56-2/8	44-3/8	6	6	Cibolla National Forest	NM	Ross Johnson	1982	129
341-5/8	54-1/8	52-2/8	45-1/8	6	6	Garfield County	MT	Darryl Turner	1985	129
341-4/8	45-6/8	47-5/8	37-4/8	6	6	Stonewall County	CO	Douglas F. Murray	1974	131
341-4/8	53-4/8	54-6/8	36-6/8	6	6	Pitkin County	CO	Nelson Harrington	1977	131
341-4/8	50-5/8	48-5/8	39-4/8	6	6	Adams County	ID	Emery Meeks	1982	131
341-3/8	47-7/8	48-1/8	44-5/8	6	6	Chaffee County	CO	Tom E. Bowman	1979	134
341-3/8	54-0/8	52-3/8	37-7/8	9	7	Missoula County	MT	Ted Miller	1984	134
341-0/8	54-2/8	54-1/8	40-6/8	6	6	Catron County	NM	Ronnie Coburn	1986	136
340-7/8	48-1/8	47-4/8	37-5/8	6	6	Carbon County	WY	Roger Swensen	1977	137
340-6/8	56-6/8	59-5/8	33-6/8	6	6	Morman Lake	AZ	Earnest E. Milton	1976	138
340-6/8	54-0/8	51-7/8	41-2/8	7	6	Petroleum County	MT	John "Rosey" Roseland	1983	138
340-5/8	47-3/8	48-6/8	33-1/8	6	6	Nordegg	ALB	Thaddaus Fenske	1978	140
340-4/8	51-5/8	49-1/8	41-2/8	6	6	Sanders County	MT	Walt Borgmann	1983	141
340-4/8	51-0/8	52-4/8	42-0/8	6	7	Catron County	NM	Brice McWethy	1985	141
340-2/8	53-3/8	54-2/8	40-4/8	6	6	Missoula County	MT	David M. Anderson	1978	143
340-2/8	50-4/8	51-3/8	36-7/8	7	6	Socorro County	NM	Randy B. Furr	1983	143
340-2/8	54-4/8	56-4/8	43-2/8	6	7	Catron County	NM	John Fehrenbacher	1986	143
340-1/8	52-2/8	52-6/8	46-7/8	6	6	Coconino County	AZ	Richard H. Wetnight	1984	146
340-0/8	49-2/8	50-7/8	37-4/8	7	7	Flathead County	MT	Henry Herman	1984	147
339-6/8	47-7/8	46-7/8	41-4/8	6	6	Lewis & Clark County	MT	Doug J. Powell	1983	148
339-5/8	51-6/8	53-5/8	47-1/8	6	6	Coconino National Forest	AZ	Bruce D. Ludeke	1977	149
339-5/8	45-2/8	43-3/8	44-7/8	6	7	Bighorn Mountains	WY	Edward F. Hanlon	1979	149
339-4/8	49-0/8	48-7/8	38-0/8	7	7	Grant County	OR	Dan Dorn	1986	151
339-4/8	51-3/8	50-5/8	39-2/8	6	6	Mineral County	MT	Tom Porter	1986	151
339-3/8	48-4/8	49-5/8	42-1/8	6	6	Mt. Taylor	NM	Delbert Mariano	1980	153
339-2/8	51-7/8	51-0/8	40-6/8	7	6	Fremont County	ID	Gary Skoy	1981	154
338-5/8	50-4/8	53-4/8	42-1/8	6	6	Rio Arriba County	NM	Lee Braudt	1983	155
338-5/8	49-2/8	48-4/8	36-5/8	6	6	Lincoln County	WY	Doug Jenkins	1986	155
338-3/8	55-5/8	54-0/8	36-7/8	6	6	Sheridan County	WY	Mike Barrett	1981	157
337-6/8	45-0/8	46-0/8	37-4/8	6	7	Boulder County	CO	Roger Schuett	1977	158
337-6/8	55-2/8	55-2/8	45-6/8	5	5	Socorro County	NM	Wesley Henderson	1986	158
337-5/8	49-1/8	49-6/8	39-1/8	6	6	Granite County	MT	George E. Wood	1978	160
337-5/8	52-1/8	52-6/8	37-3/8	6	6	Missoula County	MT	Mel Nyman, Jr.	1983	160
337-5/8	49-3/8	51-4/8	36-1/8	6	6	Coconino County	AZ	Danny Eloy Martinez	1985	160
337-4/8	52-3/8	54-5/8	41-4/8	7	6	Knole Lake	AZ	Alan Blanchard	1972	163
337-3/8	53-0/8	49-2/8	42-1/8	6	5	Grand Mesa	CO	Mike Flores	1970	164
337-0/8	52-4/8	51-4/8	38-2/8	6	6	San Mateo Mountains	NM	Ron White	1976	165
337-0/8	57-6/8	57-6/8	36-2/8	7	7	Lewis County	WA	Terry I LaFrance	1984	165
336-7/8	49-3/8	48-0/8	43-1/8	7	7	Apache County	AZ	Eric Penrod	1982	167
336-6/8	50-7/8	51-3/8	34-6/8	6	7	Uinta County	UT	Everett Burson	1981	168
336-3/8	47-7/8	48-2/8	34-1/8	6	6	Little Belt Mountains	MT	Ronald K. Granneman	1973	169
336-3/8	56-0/8	54-5/8	41-3/8	6	6	Custer County	ID	Gregg Welch	1984	169
336-2/8	52-4/8	50-6/8	33-2/8	6	6	Lewis and Clark County	MT	Ronald K. Granneman	1979	171
336-1/8	54-6/8	52-1/8	40-2/8	7	6	Catron County	NM	R. Grant Clawson	1986	172
336-0/8	50-0/8	50-1/8	42-4/8	6	6	Granite County	MT	Tom Storm	1982	173
335-6/8	53-4/8	53-1/8	37-6/8	7	8	Missouri Breaks	MT	John "Rosey" Roseland	1977	174
335-6/8	51-2/8	53-6/8	39-2/8	6	6	Shoshone County	ID	Ernest W. Clanton	1983	174
335-6/8	51-3/8	51-6/8	40-0/8	8	7	Fergus County	MT	Larry L. Schweitzer	1985	174
335-4/8	52-0/8	52-6/8	45-4/8	7	7	Skamonia County	WA	Ted Jaycox	1985	177
335-2/8	47-4/8	48-6/8	49-0/8	6	6	Elk River	ID	Robert J. Kreisher	1958	178
335-0/8	50-7/8	50-5/8	40-0/8	6	6	Soda Springs	ID	Charles Humphreys	1977	179
335-0/8	53 3/8	52-0/8	39-4/8	6	6	Sanders County	MI	Gil Gilbertson	1984	179
334-6/8	51-4/8	51-7/8	44-6/8	6	6	Gore Range	CO	Michael Beckwith	1976	181
334-2/8	52-5/8	49-0/8	38-4/8	6	6	Sweetwater County	WY	Lawrence Branson	1984	182
334-1/8	48-3/8	51-0/8	39-5/8	6	6	Beaver Head N.F.	MT	John Aalto	1979	183
334-0/8	50-1/8	50-1/8	41-2/8	6	6	Fremont County	CO	Dale Vaseen	1984	184
334-0/8	45-5/8	47-6/8	41-2/8	7	6	Boulder County	CO	Gus Roe	1984	184
333-7/8	51-6/8	49-0/8	34-6/8	7	7	Fergus County	MT	Edwin Evans	1983	186
333-6/8	49-4/8	49-4/8	45-0/8	6	6	Sumpter	OR	Russell B. Jones	1946	187
333-6/8	53-4/8	52-2/8	44-2/8	7	6	Sheridan County	WY	Chuck McKenzie	1976	187

YELLOWSTONE *(AMERICAN)* ELK

(continued)   Minimum Score 260

Score	Length of Main Beam R	Length of Main Beam L	Inside Spread	Number of Points R	Number of Points L	Area	State/ Province	Hunter's Name	Date	Rank
333-4/8	45-7/8	47-2/8	40-4/8	6	6	Bighorn County	WY	Chuck Webster	1978	189
333-3/8	45-6/8	47-4/8	39-7/8	6	6	Catron County	NM	Gary A Littauer	1984	190
333-3/8	46-0/8	46-0/8	34-3/8	7	6	Union County	OR	Mark Simmons	1985	190
333-1/8	41-3/8	46-2/8	41-3/8	6	6	Grand County	CO	Dennis Wehling	1981	192
332-7/8	48-4/8	49-3/8	41-3/8	7	7	Grant County	OR	Neil Hinton	1985	193
332-6/8	53-7/8	51-6/8	43-2/8	6	6	Albany County	WY	Pat McAteer	1981	194
332-2/8	52-0/8	49-2/8	37-0/8	6	6	Catron County	NM	John Howard	1984	194
332-1/8	53-4/8	54-6/8	36-7/8	6	6	Long Valley	AZ	James R. Moore	1980	196
332-0/8	49-2/8	50-5/8	38-2/8	7	7	Soda Springs	ID	Joseph M. Hulse	1967	197
332-0/8	52-0/8	51-6/8	42-0/8	7	6	Clearwater County	ID	Don West	1983	197
331-7/8	53-3/8	50-4/8	36-7/8	6	7	Los Alamos County	NM	Robert Barrie	1986	199
331-6/8	48-0/8	49-6/8	45-7/8	7	6	Canmore	ALB	Ken Madsen	1985	200
331-5/8	51-3/8	48-6/8	43-7/8	6	6	Sublette County	WY	Rod Knight	1983	201
331-5/8	49-0/8	47-4/8	41-5/8	6	6	Fremont County	ID	Rick Harris	1986	201
331-1/8	48-3/8	48-1/8	38-3/8	6	6	Sheridan County	WY	Mike Barrett	1984	203
330-7/8	53-5/8	50-4/8	39-5/8	6	6	Coconino County	AZ	Jeff W. Elmer	1985	204
330-4/8	44-6/8	46-4/8	38-1/8	6	6	Bovill	ID	John K. Pell	1964	205
330-3/8	50-6/8	49-1/8	38-5/8	6	6	Madison County	MT	Tom Koelzer	1975	206
330-0/8	53-2/8	53-5/8	45-0/8	6	6	San Mateo Mountains	NM	Ron White	1977	207
330-0/8	48-7/8	49-0/8	37-0/8	7	7	Sanders County	MT	Steve Larson	1981	207
330-0/8	52-7/8	50-4/8	33-4/8	6	6	Petroleum County	MT	John Fleharty	1985	207
330-0/8	46-7/8	49-7/8	43-6/8	6	6	Albany County	WY	Paul Ayotte	1985	207
329-7/8	46-1/8	45-1/8	36-7/8	6	6	White River National	CO	Jeffrey A. Duckworth	1981	211
329-7/8	51-4/8	48-6/8	39-3/8	6	6	Powell County	MT	Marlon J. Clapham	1986	211
329-6/8	49-1/8	49-0/8	37-4/8	6	6	Sleepy Cat Trail	CO	Myles Keller	1974	213
329-6/8	48-1/8	47-6/8	38-0/8	6	6	Coconino County	AZ	Mike Moulton	1983	213
329-5/8	42-1/8	44-7/8	34-2/8	6	7	Adams County	ID	Curtis Lemon	1978	215
329-5/8	54-6/8	52-7/8	40-5/8	6	7	Butte	MT	William E. Bullock	1981	215
329-4/8	47-4/8	47-3/8	43-2/8	6	6	Custer County	ID	Gary Kimball	1979	217
329-4/8	48-2/8	48-4/8	35-2/8	6	6	Catron County	NM	Donald W. Duewall	1982	217
329-2/8	52-3/8	52-4/8	44-4/8	6	6	Cascade	ID	B. C. Cunningham	1969	219
329-2/8	50-1/8	52-4/8	35-6/8	6	6	Valley County	MT	Thomas L. Solem	1981	219
329-2/8	48-6/8	51-1/8	38-2/8	7	6	Palisades	ID	Paul H. Laver	1981	219
329-1/8	47-7/8	49-4/8	40-1/8	6	6	Weiser River	ID	Curt Lemmons	1965	222
329-1/8	51-5/8	53-7/8	44-3/8	7	7	Moffat County	CO	Glenn W. Pritchard	1972	222
329-1/8	44-6/8	44-2/8	37-0/8	6	6	Rio Blanco County	CO	Harold Boyack	1976	222
329-0/8	56-0/8	54-3/8	40-2/8	8	6	Ahtanum	WA	Jerry Harris	1963	225
329-0/8	48-1/8	48-1/8	38-6/8	6	7	Sanders County	MT	Fred Mensik	1983	225
328-7/8	45-6/8	47-0/8	37-7/8	6	6	Caribou County	ID	Calvin Coziah	1970	227
328-6/8	48-5/8	49-0/8	43-6/8	6	6	Crook County	OR	Gary Kiepert	1983	228
328-2/8	48-4/8	49-4/8	40-4/8	6	7	Crook County	OR	Scott Reed	1984	229
328-2/8	52-3/8	50-6/8	43-4/8	6	7	Adams County	ID	Ted Cutler/Craig Keyser	1985	229
328-1/8	44-7/8	44-3/8	41-3/8	6	6	Lewis County	WA	Larry F. Smith	1986	231
328-1/8	45-6/8	47-6/8	37-1/8	6	7	Albany County	WY	Brian L. Biel	1986	231
328-0/8	54-1/8	51-3/8	40-0/8	6	7	Hutch Mountain	AZ	James L. Hyde	1977	233
328-0/8	44-2/8	44-3/8	39-6/8	6	6	Larimer County	CO	J. G. Hamblet, Jr.	1979	233
327-7/8	48-1/8	46-2/8	46-3/8	6	6	Lewis & Clark County	MT	Darrell J. Archey	1984	235
327-4/8	48-4/8	46-6/8	43-6/8	6	6	Dillon	MT	Dave Knudsen	1974	236
327-4/8	49-4/8	47-4/8	40-4/8	6	6	Lewis and Clark County	MT	Richard J. Kornick	1980	236
327-4/8	49-6/8	48-0/8	39-0/8	6	6	Beaverhead County	MT	Roy F. Bach	1984	236
327-1/8	50-3/8	48-2/8	43-3/8	6	6	Livingston	MT	Dale Alt	1968	239
327-0/8	50-6/8	51-7/8	40-4/8	6	6	Clearwater County	ID	C. Randall Byers	1976	240
327-0/8	48-0/8	48-2/8	39-6/8	6	6	Catron County	NM	David Chavez	1981	240
326-6/8	48-5/8	50-3/8	43-0/8	7	6	Bighorn Mountains	WY	Rick Mitchell	1981	242
326-6/8	50-4/8	47-4/8	48-2/8	6	7	Larimer County	CO	Tom Duncan	1983	242
326-6/8	46-6/8	46-4/8	39-4/8	6	6	Colfax County	NM	John L. Chapman	1984	242
326-5/8	52-1/8	53-5/8	42-1/8	6	7	Flagstaff	AZ	Larry Glasson	1975	245
326-4/8	51-5/8	51-0/8	37-6/8	6	6	King County	WA	Leonard L Stolen	1984	246
326-3/8	51-3/8	51-1/8	47-1/8	5	6	San Mateo Mountains	NM	Billy R. Spears	1976	247
326-3/8	55-0/8	55-4/8	39-3/8	6	6	Flathead County	MT	Phil Von Bargen	1976	247
326-1/8	44-6/8	46-6/8	35-5/8	6	6	Lemhi Mountains	ID	Ray Torrey	1967	249
326-1/8	54-2/8	54-5/8	37-5/8	6	6	Grand County	CO	Paul Adams	1977	249
326-0/8	51-1/8	50-6/8	46-2/8	7	6	Boulder County	CO	Duke Prentup	1977	251

YELLOWSTONE *(AMERICAN)* ELK

Minimum Score 260

Score	Length of Main Beam R	L	Inside Spread	Number of Points R	L	Area	State/ Province	Hunter's Name	Date	Rank
326-0/8	51-4/8	51-3/8	38-4/8	6	6	Anaconda Pintlar Area	MT	Scott P. Swan	1978	251
326-0/8	49-3/8	47-4/8	36-4/8	6	6	Catron County	NM	Randall Cooley	1984	251
326-0/8	53-1/8	49-2/8	39-6/8	6	6	Socorro County	NM	Ray Hatfield	1984	251
325-7/8	50-7/8	47-1/8	35-4/8	7	7	Idaho County	ID	Robert C. Mitchell	1978	255
325-7/8	45-3/8	45-1/8	34-5/8	6	6	Canmore	ALB	Douglas A. Parker	1984	255
325-6/8	49-1/8	51-5/8	43-6/8	6	6	Beaverhead County	MT	Bob Helming	1980	257
325-6/8	46-7/8	46-5/8	40-0/8	6	6	Marion County	OR	Ron Bergeron	1983	257
325-5/8	43-6/8	45-0/8	39-1/8	7	7	Beaverhead County	MT	Danny Moore	1983	259
325-4/8	49-6/8	50-3/8	40-4/8	6	6	Uncompahgre Plateau	CO	Carol Cassidy	1973	260
325-3/8	47-3/8	45-2/8	33-3/8	7	6	Benewah County	ID	Tim Chandler	1984	261
325-2/8	49-0/8	49-0/8	36-6/8	6	6	Caribou County	ID	Doug Foss	1986	262
325-0/8	47-1/8	47-3/8	35-6/8	7	7	Fleecer	MT	Bob Gossack	1977	263
325-0/8	52-4/8	49-5/8	39-4/8	6	6	Catron County	NM	Courtney King	1985	263
324-6/8	47-1/8	46-2/8	42-0/8	7	6	Coconino County	AZ	William S. Acheson	1979	265
324-6/8	45-7/8	45-2/8	37-0/8	6	6	Beaverhead County	MT	Tyler Robinson	1983	265
324-3/8	53-2/8	54-7/8	33-7/8	7	6	Summit County	CO	Gordon R. Horn	1986	267
324-2/8	47-5/8	47-4/8	31-0/8	6	6	Hodgson	MAN	Barry Bird	1982	268
324-1/8	47-7/8	48-6/8	46-7/8	6	7	Rio Arriba County	NM	Richard Manwell	1986	269
323-7/8	48-7/8	47-2/8	37-1/8	6	6	Granite County	MT	Clint Carlson	1983	270
323-6/8	48-2/8	51-1/8	43-6/8	6	6	Valley County	ID	Rodney Bremer	1983	271
323-5/8	46-6/8	46-3/8	40-3/8	7	6	Teton County	MT	Ron Granneman	1978	272
323-5/8	52-0/8	53-7/8	42-4/8	6	8	Cascade County	MT	Bill Tesinsky	1983	272
323-4/8	40-7/8	41-2/8	35-6/8	6	6	Phillips County	MT	Buzz Beto	1983	274
323-3/8	50-6/8	50-1/8	37-7/8	7	6	Gallatin Mountain	MT	Rick Jones	1977	275
323-2/8	55-7/8	53-5/8	44-2/8	6	6	Grant County	OR	Andy Day	1982	276
323-2/8	46-7/8	46-4/8	38-7/8	7	8	Catron County	NM	Thomas R. Sansom	1984	276
323-0/8	52-5/8	50-1/8	39-0/8	6	6	Blaine County	ID	Ted Chu	1977	278
323-0/8	54-7/8	50-0/8	45-5/8	6	7	Gallatin County	MT	Tim Wells	1983	278
323-0/8	47-4/8	48-3/8	40-0/8	6	6	Grand County	CO	Russell Gross	1985	278
322-7/8	50-6/8	51-0/8	44-3/8	6	7	Ft. Peck	MT	Ray Hoveskeland	1967	281
322-7/8	48-5/8	46-5/8	36-5/8	6	6	Deer Lodge County	MT	Eddie McGreevey	1977	281
322-7/8	51-3/8	52-2/8	41-4/8	7	7	Coconino County	AZ	Darrell Christensen	1979	281
322-7/8	47-4/8	47-5/8	36-1/8	6	6	Canmore	ALB	David R. Coupland	1982	281
322-6/8	49-2/8	48-5/8	36-4/8	6	6	Rio Arriba County	NM	Santos E. Corriz	1982	285
322-4/8	51-3/8	48-7/8	40-0/8	6	7	Lewis and Clark County	MT	Jerry Biresch	1970	286
322-2/8	51-5/8	53-1/8	33-0/8	6	6	Colfax County	NM	Tom L. Handy	1986	287
322-1/8	50-4/8	50-6/8	37-3/8	6	6	Blue Ridge Reservation	AZ	John F. Schultz	1978	288
322-1/8	50-5/8	50-4/8	37-3/8	6	6	Powell County	MT	Gene Coughlin	1982	288
322-1/8	45-6/8	44-3/8	34-3/8	7	8	Fergus County	MT	Ben Starburg	1985	288
322-0/8	50-3/8	50-6/8	36-2/8	7	8	Coconino County	AZ	Dick Hensley	1979	291
322-0/8	46-3/8	48-0/8	36-2/8	6	6	Sandoval County	NM	John McClendon	1983	291
322-0/8	52-6/8	53-0/8	35-0/8	6	6	Moffat County	CO	Guy Love	1984	291
322-0/8	47-2/8	49-0/8	40-6/8	6	6	Pierce County	WA	Dale Kistenmacher	1985	291
322-0/8	48-4/8	49-0/8	34-4/8	6	7	Boggey Creek	MAN	Tom Nebbs	1986	291
321-7/8	47-7/8	43-6/8	41-7/8	6	6	Taos County	NM	Dr. Dean A. Henbest	1971	296
321-7/8	49-3/8	53-2/8	34-1/8	6	6	Happy Jack	AZ	Mike Burm	1981	296
321-7/8	51-0/8	50-5/8	37-7/8	6	6	Teller County	CO	Harry Rathke	1983	296
321-4/8	45-2/8	56-2/8	39-2/8	5	6	Apache County	AZ	John D. "Jack" Frost	1986	299
321-3/8	45-6/8	45-6/8	43-3/8	6	6	Gallatin County	MT	Ed Tertelgte	1975	300
321-2/8	46-1/8	48-4/8	40-0/8	6	6	Larimer County	CO	Tom Tietz	1981	301
321-1/8	48-6/8	50-6/8	38-1/8	6	6	Lincoln County	NM	Jay H. Henley, Sr.	1985	302
320-3/8	46-1/8	46-6/8	39-3/8	6	6	Summitville	CO	Bing Kemp	1966	303
320-3/8	49-3/8	50-7/8	36-5/8	7	6	Catron County	NM	Randall S. Madding	1986	303
320-2/8	52-0/8	50-6/8	36-0/8	6	6	Meagher county	MT	Ted Hysell	1983	305
320-2/8	49-4/8	49-6/8	47-6/8	6	6	Shoshone County	ID	Tom J. O'Grady	1986	305
320-1/8	46-2/8	47-7/8	41-3/8	6	6	Madison County	MT	Lee J. Poole	1976	307
320-1/8	48-6/8	48-7/8	38-7/8	6	6	Fergus County	MT	J. Douglas Krings	1979	307
320-1/8	48-1/8	45-1/8	44-3/8	6	7	Albany County	WY	Doug Pope	1979	307
320-1/8	50-1/8	48-4/8	37-1/8	6	6	Lemhi County	ID	Joe Fraser	1980	307
320-1/8	52-6/8	51-1/8	41-1/8	6	6	Yellowstone County	MT	Robert M. Labert	1986	307
320-0/8	50-6/8	53-1/8	39-6/8	6	6	Straight Creek	MT	Michael Ruhkala	1980	312
320-0/8	51-4/8	50-5/8	36-6/8	6	6	Huerfano County	CO	Mike Culwell	1984	312
319-7/8	51-7/8	50-2/8	38-1/8	7	8	San Mateo Mountains	NM	David Ryles	1977	314

YELLOWSTONE *(AMERICAN)* ELK
(continued)　　　　　　　　　　　　　　　　　　　　　　　Minimum Score 260

Score	Length of Main Beam R	L	Inside Spread	Number of Points R	L	Area	State/ Province	Hunter's Name	Date	Rank
319-7/8	51-7/8	52-2/8	40-5/8	6	6	Hinton	ALB	Blair D. Crites	1979	314
319-7/8	46-3/8	47-6/8	39-7/8	7	6	Otero County	NM	Simon L. Gomez	1986	314
319-4/8	48-4/8	49-0/8	40-2/8	6	6	Pitkin County	CO	Bob Gulman	1975	317
319-4/8	49-5/8	49-6/8	36-4/8	7	6	Clearwater County	ID	Audie Powers	1979	317
319-4/8	50-6/8	52-0/8	41-2/8	6	6	Soda Springs	ID	Mark Hill	1980	317
319-3/8	44-2/8	43-2/8	35-4/8	7	7	Crook County	OR	Jeff Carver	1985	320
319-1/8	45-2/8	45-0/8	36-3/8	7	7	Rio Arriba County	NM	Dr. O. D. Brown	1986	321
319-0/8	48-7/8	53-2/8	39-6/8	5	6	Catron County	NM	Eddie Howard	1983	322
318-7/8	45-6/8	45-4/8	37-1/8	7	6	Fergus County	MT	Donald R. Hecht	1984	323
318-6/8	48-5/8	48-1/8	42-2/8	6	7	Ft. Collins	CO	Tony Seahorn	1972	324
318-6/8	52-1/8	51-1/8	39-2/8	7	6	Lusk	WY	Donald L. Smith	1973	324
318-6/8	50-1/8	53-6/8	45-0/8	7	6	San Francisco Peaks	AZ	Tom Dalrymple	1980	324
318-6/8	47-4/8	47-4/8	39-4/8	6	6	Sanders County	MT	Wayne L. Haines	1982	324
318-6/8	44-3/8	44-2/8	35-2/8	6	6	Bow Valley	ALB	Pat Leiser	1986	324
318-5/8	44-4/8	44-0/8	34-6/8	6	6	San Juan Mountains	CO	David Powell	1969	329
318-5/8	54-0/8	55-7/8	39-7/8	6	6	Beaverhead County	MT	Greg L. Munther	1981	329
318-5/8	49-3/8	49-7/8	37-7/8	6	6	Missoula County	MT	J. Scott Graham	1982	329
318-4/8	43-7/8	42-6/8	39-4/8	6	6	Bighorn Mountains	WY	Ron Johnson	1975	332
318-3/8	52-4/8	51-5/8	41-0/8	7	6	Anaconda	MT	Dennis Neitzke	1980	333
318-1/8	48-4/8	47-0/8	34-2/8	7	7	Ravalli County	MT	Rick Twardoski	1984	334
318-1/8	49-3/8	47-1/8	36-7/8	6	6	Unita County	UT	Everett Burson	1986	334
318-0/8	45-6/8	45-2/8	44-4/8	7	8	Bighorn Mountains	WY	Henry "Hank" Frey	1977	336
318-0/8	45-6/8	48-4/8	46-6/8	6	6	Medicine Bow	WY	James Blocker	1980	336
317-7/8	45-6/8	45-4/8	45-1/8	6	6	Teton County	MT	Ronald K. Granneman	1974	338
317-7/8	47-6/8	43-3/8	38-5/8	6	6	Park County	WY	Wesley D. Engleman	1983	338
317-5/8	47-6/8	47-7/8	42-3/8	6	6	Lemhi County	ID	Lewis Zane Abbott	1981	340
317-3/8	49-0/8	48-3/8	40-7/8	6	6	Fremont County	ID	Donald M. Sherick	1982	341
317-0/8	46-5/8	47-0/8	42-2/8	6	7	Black River	AZ	Robert H. Warren	1975	342
317-0/8	51-3/8	51-7/8	39-4/8	6	6	Rio Arriba County	NM	Alfred Vigil	1984	342
316-4/8	49-2/8	48-5/8	39-4/8	6	6	Grant County	OR	A. Corey Heath	1984	344
316-3/8	51-0/8	51-0/8	40-5/8	6	6	Missoula County	MT	Ben L. Jennings	1984	345
316-3/8	52-3/8	51-1/8	38-5/8	6	6	Lewis County	WA	Leonard L. Stolen	1986	345
316-2/8	48-2/8	48-2/8	34-6/8	7	7	Flagstaff	AZ	William M. Lanese	1981	347
316-1/8	54-0/8	51-0/8	37-7/8	6	6	Valley County	MT	Dan Sturgis	1981	348
316-0/8	46-4/8	48-2/8	40-0/8	6	6	Pagosa Springs	CO	Loren Hofeldt	1981	349
315-7/8	51-2/8	51-4/8	43-3/8	6	6	Wasco County	OR	Ivan Duncan	1982	350
315-6/8	47-7/8	48-5/8	38-0/8	6	6	Nez Perce County	ID	Alfred J. Gemrich	1984	351
315-5/8	48-6/8	47-6/8	36-3/8	6	6	Gallatin National Forest	MT	Rocky Miller	1981	352
315-4/8	51-7/8	49-0/8	42-6/8	6	6	Minam Unit	OR	Dr. Russell A. Colgan	1976	353
315-2/8	51-0/8	51-1/8	41-2/8	6	6	Teton County	MT	Ronald K. Granneman	1976	354
315-2/8	50-4/8	52-0/8	40-2/8	6	6	Clark County	ID	Ken Vander Linden	1986	354
314-6/8	50-0/8	51-3/8	40-0/8	6	6	Catron County	NM	Wayne K. Curtis	1984	356
314-6/8	46-7/8	45-6/8	42-2/8	6	6	Catron County	NM	Dennis Curtis	1986	356
314-4/8	48-0/8	48-2/8	39-4/8	6	6	Caribou County	ID	Alan E. Christiansen	1982	358
314-3/8	48-4/8	46-1/8	41-3/8	6	6	Soda Springs	ID	Bruce N. Moss	1980	359
314-1/8	51-0/8	51-2/8	41-5/8	6	6	Gallatin County	MT	C. W. Smith	1974	360
314-0/8	47-7/8	48-2/8	44-0/8	6	6	Fremont County	ID	Tom Savage	1981	361
314-0/8	46-1/8	45-6/8	36-4/8	6	7	Missouri Breaks	MT	Mark D. Hughes	1982	361
314-0/8	50-3/8	50-1/8	40-4/8	6	6	Catron County	NM	Randall F. Cooley	1983	361
314-0/8	54-3/8	54-4/8	37-0/8	6	5	Coconino County	AZ	James R. Dreves	1985	361
314-0/8	49-5/8	49-2/8	42-6/8	6	6	Flathead County	MT	Jim Hawkins	1986	361
313-7/8	47-5/8	44-7/8	33-3/8	7	7	Porcupine Hills	ALB	John Archibald	1980	366
313-7/8	49-2/8	47-3/8	44-2/8	7	6	Kaibab National Forest	AZ	Don R. Newton	1980	366
313-4/8	45-0/8	43-4/8	41-4/8	6	6	Evergreen	CO	Charles Cater	1976	368
313-4/8	50-5/8	51-0/8	43-4/8	6	6	Grant County	OR	Andy Day	1980	368
313-2/8	49-2/8	46-0/8	44-2/8	6	6	Albany County	WY	Jerry Bowen	1979	370
313-2/8	43-4/8	44-1/8	30-4/8	7	7	Park County	MT	Robert Wennerstrom	1985	370
313-2/8	51-2/8	51-2/8	39-6/8	6	6	Bonneville County	ID	Ron Mueller	1986	370
313-1/8	46-1/8	49-3/8	34-0/8	8	7	Chaffee County	CO	Rick D. Montgomery	1986	373
313-0/8	48-4/8	47-3/8	46-2/8	6	6	Gardner	MT	Charles Milner	1973	374
312-7/8	46-7/8	50-1/8	43-7/8	6	6	Couer d'Alene	ID	Harry Barker	1962	375
312-6/8	44-3/8	46-1/8	33-4/8	7	6	Clearwater County	ID	Doyle Anderegg	1975	376
312-6/8	55-2/8	54-0/8	40-4/8	5	5	Cibola County	NM	Mark Webber	1982	376

YELLOWSTONE *(AMERICAN)* ELK

Minimum Score 260 (continued)

Score	Length of Main Beam R	L	Inside Spread	Number of Points R	L	Area	State/ Province	Hunter's Name	Date	Rank
312-6/8	53-3/8	53-6/8	39-4/8	6	6	Greenlee County	AZ	Dick Hall	1986	376
312-5/8	47-0/8	47-3/8	39-5/8	6	6	Caribou County	ID	Dean Humphreys	1962	379
312-4/8	51-0/8	51-6/8	42-3/8	9	7	Sanders County	MT	Ron Halvorson	1980	380
312-4/8	46-4/8	49-5/8	40-2/8	6	6	Clearwater County	ID	Steven E. Baxter	1984	380
312-2/8	44-6/8	44-7/8	38-2/8	6	6	Eagle County	CO	Gary D. Allen	1974	382
312-2/8	48-1/8	48-4/8	36-4/8	6	6	Larimer County	CO	Steve Stumbo	1975	382
312-2/8	50-0/8	49-0/8	35-5/8	7	8	Butte County	ID	Floyd L. Collins, Jr.	1982	382
312-2/8	46-4/8	46-2/8	35-0/8	6	7	Catron County	NM	Billy E. Gourley	1984	382
312-1/8	45-5/8	45-3/8	33-3/8	6	6	Garfield County	UT	Russell Peterson	1984	386
312-1/8	45-2/8	44-4/8	35-3/8	6	6	Catron County	NM	Randy Williams	1985	386
312-1/8	50-2/8	50-4/8	34-7/8	6	6	Lehmi County	ID	Mike S. Szekely	1986	386
312-0/8	48-2/8	48-6/8	37-7/8	6	6	Montrose County	CO	Stanley R. Godfrey	1978	389
311-6/8	47-6/8	47-1/8	37-6/8	6	8	Lewis and Clark County	MT	Douglas L. Conrady	1980	390
311-5/8	48-4/8	46-0/8	52-7/8	7	6	Deer Lodge County	MT	Bob Gossack	1976	391
311-4/8	46-4/8	48-4/8	49-2/8	7	7	Ravalli County	MT	Dick Robertson	1973	392
311-4/8	52-3/8	51-6/8	39-4/8	6	6	Coconino County	AZ	Richard Foss	1977	392
311-4/8	48-7/8	45-7/8	37-2/8	6	6	Black Mountain	ID	Gene H. Dressen	1978	392
311-4/8	46-2/8	45-6/8	38-0/8	6	6	Rio Blanco County	CO	Jack Lambert	1980	392
311-4/8	55-6/8	54-4/8	37-4/8	6	6	Archuleta County	CO	Tim Chavez	1983	392
311-3/8	48-4/8	46-5/8	37-3/8	7	7	W. Sanders County	MT	Rus Willis	1981	397
311-2/8	44-5/8	46-2/8	33-6/8	6	6	Park County	CO	Lynn Campbell	1981	398
311-2/8	48-3/8	48-5/8	37-0/8	6	6	Clackamas County	OR	Bill Hensley	1984	398
311-0/8	51-6/8	50-0/8	41-6/8	6	6	Jackson Hole	WY	Fred Bear	1953	400
311-0/8	51-1/8	49-5/8	47-2/8	8	6	Larimer County	CO	H. Mike Palmer	1983	400
311-0/8	47-3/8	47-4/8	43-6/8	6	6	Beaverhead County	MT	Jerry Strodtman	1985	400
310-7/8	55-2/8	53-6/8	53-1/8	6	6	Pitkin County	CO	Bob Gulman	1973	403
310-7/8	45-6/8	45-0/8	36-3/8	6	6	Flathead County	MT	Scott Halama	1986	403
310-6/8	49-5/8	51-2/8	43-4/8	6	6	Panther Creek	ID	Joe Hollifield	1977	405
310-6/8	45-5/8	46-2/8	35-0/8	7	8	Fergus County	MT	Steven J. Nelson	1977	405
310-5/8	51-3/8	51-2/8	38-3/8	6	6	Little Belt Mountain	MT	Jim Ekness	1978	407
310-5/8	47-1/8	44-6/8	39-3/8	7	6	Coconino County	AZ	Rick Brewer	1984	407
310-4/8	49-0/8	49-0/8	43-6/8	6	6	Durango	CO	Tom Price	1967	409
310-4/8	43-2/8	43-6/8	38-2/8	6	6	Baker County	OR	Billy J. Cruise	1970	409
310-4/8	46-7/8	46-6/8	37-4/8	6	6	Orofino	ID	Rory Roby	1981	409
310-4/8	46-1/8	46-3/8	41-0/8	6	6	Valley County	ID	Ron Phillips	1983	409
310-4/8	53-3/8	51-1/8	37-0/8	6	6	Converse County	WY	Dennis Spawn	1986	409
310-3/8	49-0/8	51-0/8	39-2/8	8	6	Tincup	ID	Patrick G. Selfridge	1980	414
310-2/8	49-4/8	50-0/8	30-0/8	6	6	Unit 621	MT	Daniel Tellefson	1981	415
310-2/8	45-0/8	45-4/8	33-4/8	6	6	Canmore	ALB	Cam Wilson	1984	415
310-2/8	48-2/8	49-7/8	34-6/8	6	6	Coconino County	AZ	Russ Warner	1984	415
310-2/8	45-1/8	43-4/8	39-0/8	6	6	Gallatin County	MT	David Burtch	1986	415
310-0/8	51-2/8	50-3/8	38-0/8	6	6	Ravalli County	MT	Bob Sappenfield	1978	419
309-7/8	47-2/8	47-3/8	37-3/8	6	7	Baker County	OR	James D. Ward	1983	420
309-6/8	43-1/8	43-4/8	35-0/8	6	6	Hanns Peak	CO	Steve Gorr	1971	421
309-6/8	50-6/8	51-0/8	40-0/8	7	6	Sanders County	MT	Brad Borden	1984	421
309-6/8	48-6/8	50-6/8	43-2/8	6	6	Coconino County	AZ	Robert L. Smith	1986	421
309-5/8	51-0/8	50-6/8	39-7/8	6	6	Flathead County	MT	Paul Roney	1976	424
309-3/8	47-0/8	47-4/8	35-7/8	6	6	Granite County	MT	Dwayne Garner	1985	425
309-2/8	44-6/8	47-4/8	44-4/8	5	6	Island Park	ID	Larry Bauer	1960	426
309-2/8	45-0/8	45-7/8	34-4/8	6	6	North Powder	OR	Ron Angell	1981	426
309-1/8	44-4/8	46-4/8	34-5/8	6	6	Coconino County	AZ	Les Butters	1981	428
309-1/8	48-0/8	46-6/8	39-7/8	6	6	Missoula County	MT	Chad Spicknall	1984	428
308-5/8	47-5/8	46-3/8	40-1/8	7	6	Wasco County	OR	Gary Paugh	1984	430
308-5/8	50-2/8	51-2/8	37-5/8	6	6	Taos County	NM	Nicholas J Rowley	1985	430
308-4/8	47-7/8	47-7/8	41-2/8	7	6	Socorro County	NM	Jack W. Bruton	1985	432
308-1/8	51-1/8	50-6/8	42-7/8	6	5	Ochoco County	OR	Jim Hodson	1983	433
308-0/8	43-4/8	48-0/8	32-6/8	6	6	Shoshone County	ID	Randy Hammond	1983	434
307-7/8	46-5/8	46-3/8	37-5/8	6	6	Ravalli County	MT	Ray Tlamka	1984	435
307-4/8	45-5/8	42-7/8	37-4/8	7	7	Laveta	CO	Wilbur F. Lay, Jr.	1974	436
307-4/8	47-7/8	48-0/8	40-4/8	5	6	Timothy Creek	ID	Charlie Humphreys	1979	436
307-4/8	54-6/8	54-6/8	46-3/8	7	7	Apache County	AZ	Tom David	1985	436
307-4/8	46-7/8	47-1/8	37-2/8	6	6	Teller County	CO	James M. Strampe	1985	436
307-2/8	49-5/8	50-4/8	35-6/8	6	6	Pine Mountain	AZ	Larry Hines	1981	440

YELLOWSTONE *(AMERICAN)* ELK

(continued)   Minimum Score 260

Score	Length of Main Beam R	L	Inside Spread	Number of Points R	L	Area	State/ Province	Hunter's Name	Date	Rank
307-1/8	54-4/8	52-4/8	40-3/8	6	6	Gallatin National Forest	MT	David Thiry	1981	441
307-1/8	47-0/8	47-5/8	43-1/8	6	6	Grant County	OR	George Schiedler	1983	441
307-1/8	50-4/8	51-0/8	42-3/8	6	6	Park County	MT	Robert Ward	1983	441
307-0/8	51-5/8	50-2/8	35-6/8	6	6	Judith Basin County	MT	Mark A. Petroni	1982	444
307-0/8	49-3/8	50-6/8	37-0/8	6	6	Apache County	AZ	Melvin Edward Norris	1986	444
307-0/8	53-1/8	52-0/8	38-6/8	6	7	Clearwater County	ID	Ralph L. Albright	1986	444
306-5/8	50-2/8	49-1/8	39-7/8	5	5	Granite County	MT	J. Greg Jones	1983	447
306-4/8	43-4/8	44-5/8	40-0/8	6	6	Kelly Creek Drainage	ID	Kim J. Vander Sys	1977	448
306-4/8	46-4/8	47-2/8	37-4/8	6	6	Blaine County	ID	Tom Goicoechea	1982	448
306-3/8	48-4/8	48-5/8	40-6/8	7	6	Summit County	UT	Clifton B. Johnson	1978	450
306-2/8	42-7/8	43-2/8	43-4/8	5	5	Ford Creek	ID	A. LaVerne Hokanson	1974	451
306-2/8	49-3/8	48-3/8	40-2/8	6	6	Garfield County	UT	Bruce E. Carlisle	1985	451
306-1/8	48-6/8	46-0/8	34-1/8	6	7	Wisdom County	MT	Kenneth M. Carlson	1983	453
306-0/8	45-0/8	44-3/8	36-6/8	6	6	Eagle County	CO	Walt Williams	1979	454
306-0/8	49-2/8	48-7/8	34-2/8	6	6	Catron County	NM	William C. Davis	1986	454
305-6/8	46-7/8	47-7/8	34-0/8	6	6	Larimer County	CO	Steve Stumbo	1980	456
305-6/8	45-2/8	46-4/8	38-4/8	6	6	Kootenai County	ID	Brent K. Jacobson	1982	456
305-6/8	47-6/8	47-2/8	33-4/8	6	6	Catron County	NM	Randall S. Madding	1984	456
305-6/8	40-1/8	42-0/8	36-4/8	7	6	Gilpin County	CO	Dennis Myer	1985	456
305-4/8	46-7/8	47-5/8	43-6/8	5	6	Santiam Unit	OR	Bill Lancaster	1981	460
305-4/8	47-4/8	47-5/8	40-2/8	6	6	Catron County	NM	Stan Rauch	1985	460
305-2/8	50-2/8	51-2/8	39-4/8	6	6	Laramie River	CO	Craig Nelson	1968	462
305-2/8	48-7/8	48-6/8	38-0/8	6	6	Catron County	NM	Glen L. Dillehay	1984	462
304-6/8	49-5/8	50-2/8	43-2/8	7	6	Kinnikinnick Lake	AZ	Jerry Carpenter	1979	464
304-4/8	46-7/8	45-4/8	45-2/8	6	6	Grant County	OR	Clayton Severin	1982	465
304-2/8	46-6/8	49-0/8	36-4/8	6	6	Flathead County	MT	Steven C. Street	1980	466
304-2/8	49-5/8	49-6/8	34-4/8	6	6	Sanders County	MT	Ray J. Baenen	1982	466
304-0/8	42-4/8	45-0/8	45-6/8	6	6	Coconino National Forest	AZ	Art Potter	1976	468
304-0/8	47-5/8	46-6/8	39-6/8	6	6	Grant County	OR	James E. Hodson	1981	468
304-0/8	50-1/8	48-4/8	37-0/8	5	5	Park County	CO	Ronald King	1981	468
304-0/8	49-3/8	53-4/8	44-2/8	6	6	Cibola County	NM	Wayne L. Mathews	1986	468
304-0/8	48-5/8	48-7/8	37-2/8	6	6	Chouteau County	MT	K. C. Palagi	1986	468
303-7/8	48-6/8	46-0/8	41-7/8	6	6	Pitkin County	CO	Joseph Mendozza	1980	473
303-7/8	43-3/8	43-4/8	41-3/8	6	6	Fergus County	MT	Carson J. Rife	1984	473
303-6/8	46-2/8	47-7/8	36-2/8	6	6	Eagle County	CO	Tim W. Hulce	1981	475
303-4/8	49-1/8	42-1/8	41-0/8	6	6	Grand County	CO	Jim Cleland	1977	476
303-4/8	44-6/8	45-3/8	36-2/8	6	6	Sierra County	NM	Chuck Wagner	1986	476
303-3/8	44-0/8	43-0/8	42-7/8	5	6	Adams County	ID	Rick Mason	1984	478
303-2/8	47-4/8	45-6/8	38-4/8	6	6	Garfield County	CO	Alan Harbin	1980	479
303-2/8	47-1/8	47-0/8	35-4/8	6	6	Park County	WY	James Dinkins	1983	479
303-0/8	48-7/8	47-6/8	41-0/8	5	6	Las Animas County	CO	David L. Brady	1983	481
302-7/8	44-6/8	45-6/8	38-5/8	6	6	Swan River	MT	Joe Lawrence	1969	482
302-6/8	49-4/8	47-4/8	43-0/8	5	6	Apache County	AZ	Gary Preston	1981	483
302-4/8	47-7/8	47-2/8	38-5/8	6	6	Sweetwater Canyon	CO	Roger Rothhaar	1974	484
302-4/8	46-4/8	46-2/8	37-0/8	6	6	Beaverhead County	MT	Dennis Rehse	1982	484
302-2/8	48-7/8	48-7/8	39-0/8	6	6	Grant County	OR	Randy Bonner	1983	486
302-1/8	51-1/8	49-4/8	37-7/8	6	6	Canmore	ALB	David R. Coupland	1984	487
302-1/8	44-1/8	44-1/8	35-1/8	6	6	Greenlee County	AZ	Timothy Hall	1985	487
302-0/8	45-0/8	46-6/8	40-0/8	6	6	San Juan Mountains	CO	Billy Ellis	1977	489
302-0/8	50-4/8	49-6/8	38-6/8	6	6	Eagle County	CO	John Schell	1980	489
302-0/8	42-3/8	41-6/8	31-0/8	6	6	Routt County	CO	Kevin Stailey	1981	489
301-7/8	44-2/8	44-2/8	38-3/8	6	6	Larimer	CO	Adrian H. Farmer, Jr.	1984	492
301-6/8	47-2/8	46-2/8	36-0/8	6	6	Missoula County	MT	Guy Leibenguth	1976	493
301-5/8	44-1/8	42-2/8	39-2/8	7	7	E. Bitteroot Mountain	MT	Dick Kerr	1977	494
301-4/8	45-1/8	44-6/8	37-0/8	6	6	Lewis & Clark Co.	MT	Doug Conrady	1979	495
301-1/8	45-0/8	41-2/8	38-4/8	7	6	Jackson	WY	Craig Sorenson	1979	496
301-1/8	43-7/8	44-1/8	32-1/8	6	6	Pierce County	ID	Jim Walters	1981	496
301-1/8	47-3/8	45-7/8	37-7/8	6	6	Lincoln County	MT	Paul Buti	1984	496
301-0/8	46-2/8	49-6/8	38-4/8	5	6	Sandoval County	NM	Fred J. McDonald	1985	499
300-7/8	45-6/8	44-5/8	39-1/8	6	5	Teton County	MT	Bill Schenck	1979	500
300-3/8	41-5/8	40-0/8	36-1/8	6	6	Fergus County	MT	Randy Cook	1981	501
300-1/8	45-4/8	47-4/8	39-7/8	6	6	Santa Fe National Forest	NM	Lawrence Stiscak	1977	502
300-1/8	46-3/8	44-2/8	35-7/8	6	6	Clearwater County	ID	Danny Moore	1985	502

YELLOWSTONE *(AMERICAN)* ELK

Minimum Score 260

(continued)

Score	Length of Main Beam R	L	Inside Spread	Number of Points R	L	Area	State/ Province	Hunter's Name	Date	Rank
300-0/8	39-5/8	42-0/8	37-4/8	7	6	Coconino County	AZ	Mike Kentera	1985	504
300-0/8	47-4/8	46-0/8	40-0/8	6	6	Missoula County	MT	Anthony K Nease	1985	504
300-0/8	48-5/8	48-4/8	38-4/8	6	6	Adams County	ID	Robert Dowen	1985	504
299-7/8	51-0/8	54-0/8	41-0/8	6	7	Lewistown	MT	Charles R. Bowman	1966	507
299-3/8	45-2/8	46-2/8	38-3/8	6	6	Gunnison County	CO	Gene Chastain	1985	508
299-2/8	47-2/8	46-1/8	34-4/8	6	6	Tincup	ID	Tex Wolfley	1979	509
299-2/8	51-4/8	49-7/8	37-2/8	6	6	Coconino County	AZ	Larry VanLiew	1983	509
299-1/8	44-2/8	41-2/8	32-5/8	6	6	Lincoln County	WY	Richard Peart	1980	511
299-0/8	42-3/8	43-1/8	33-0/8	6	6	Mineral County	CO	Gary Oden	1976	512
299-0/8	45-5/8	46-4/8	37-2/8	6	6	Ovando	MT	Paul Brunner	1979	512
298-6/8	46-3/8	46-3/8	31-5/8	6	7	Mineral County	MT	James Kingsley	1983	514
298-6/8	44-2/8	45-5/8	38-0/8	6	6	Gallatin County	MT	Steven P Hopkins	1984	514
298-6/8	50-6/8	52-4/8	37-2/8	6	6	Catron County	NM	Wayne Keehart	1986	514
298-5/8	55-0/8	56-5/8	38-3/8	5	6	Red Hills	AZ	Kevin Cox	1979	517
298-5/8	46-0/8	47-5/8	41-7/8	6	6	Coconino County	AZ	Pete Shepley	1986	517
298-0/8	45-6/8	46-4/8	37-0/8	6	6	Caribou County	ID	Dean Monson	1982	519
297-7/8	45-2/8	44-5/8	47-3/8	6	6	Beaverhead County	MT	Greg L. Munther	1980	520
297-7/8	44-5/8	46-7/8	31-1/8	7	8	Coconino County	AZ	Mark Vancas	1980	520
297-7/8	46-4/8	47-0/8	33-5/8	6	6	Lincoln County	MT	Darryl Lien	1985	520
297-6/8	46-4/8	46-5/8	41-4/8	6	6	Allen's Park	CO	Steve Gorr	1969	523
297-6/8	48-6/8	50-0/8	38-6/8	6	7	Caribou County	ID	Doug Cushman, Jr.	1981	523
297-4/8	45-1/8	41-6/8	43-0/8	6	7	King County	WA	Larry L. Sheward	1984	525
297-3/8	46-1/8	45-2/8	42-3/8	5	7	Fremont County	ID	Thomas W. Sauage	1982	526
297-2/8	50-0/8	47-5/8	30-6/8	6	6	Grant County	OR	Joe Copeland	1986	527
297-1/8	46-1/8	44-2/8	42-3/8	6	8	Missoula County	MT	David E. Torrey, Jr.	1977	528
297-1/8	46-0/8	48-0/8	40-6/8	7	8	Coconino County	AZ	Dave Baker	1979	528
297-1/8	43-0/8	42-3/8	39-3/8	6	6	Wainwright	ALB	Norman Hookes	1982	528
297-0/8	46-4/8	46-0/8	36-2/8	6	6	Wallowa County	OR	Martha J Soeth	1985	531
297-0/8	44-4/8	44-3/8	34-0/8	6	6	Rich County	UT	Hugh H. Hogle	1986	531
296-3/8	41-7/8	44-2/8	39-3/8	6	6	Idaho County	ID	Jerry Vega	1985	533
296-2/8	45-7/8	44-6/8	37-0/8	6	7	Clackamas County	OR	Bill Lancaster	1984	534
296-2/8	44-6/8	44-2/8	36-0/8	6	6	Crook County	OR	Rod Curtis	1984	534
296-2/8	48-7/8	45-4/8	37-6/8	6	6	Moffatt County	CO	Robert L Syvertson, Jr.	1984	534
296-1/8	43-2/8	45-3/8	43-1/8	6	6	Sheridan County	WY	Mike Barrett	1982	537
296-0/8	44-2/8	45-0/8	39-4/8	6	6	Gallatin County	MT	Bob Savage	1968	538
296-0/8	48-7/8	46-6/8	37-6/8	6	6	Bighorn Mountains	WY	Dean Fudge	1979	538
296-0/8	40-7/8	41-7/8	28-4/8	8	6	Spruce Woods	MAN	Brian Morash	1981	538
295-7/8	42-5/8	40-5/8	38-2/8	6	7	Larimer County	CO	Ben Alexander	1972	541
295-7/8	44-4/8	43-7/8	38-1/8	6	7	Madison County	MT	Kevin Fogal	1985	541
295-6/8	49-6/8	50-0/8	38-4/8	6	6	Bonneville County	ID	Jim Cox	1976	543
295-6/8	43-7/8	44-6/8	32-6/8	6	6	Powell County	MT	Bryan C. Anderson	1985	543
295-6/8	42-0/8	46-0/8	40-2/8	6	6	Boulder County	CO	Jerry Bryan	1986	543
295-6/8	45-5/8	45-3/8	41-0/8	6	6	Gallatin County	MT	H. C. Tysinger, Jr.	1986	543
295-4/8	48-0/8	47-1/8	37-0/8	6	6	Custer County	ID	A. Lynn Burton	1982	547
295-2/8	45-0/8	46-4/8	38-4/8	6	6	Lincoln County	NM	Bart J. Gillan III	1984	548
295-2/8	51-3/8	51-3/8	37-0/8	7	6	Kittitas County	WA	Kirk Cresto	1984	548
295-2/8	48-4/8	48-4/8	40-6/8	6	6	Catron County	NM	Gary Burnett	1986	548
295-1/8	43-1/8	42-0/8	39-1/8	6	6	Gallatin County	MT	Tom L. Miller	1986	551
295-0/8	51-2/8	49-7/8	38-5/8	7	6	Crook County	OR	Michael Hawkins	1983	552
294-5/8	41-2/8	39-7/8	38-7/8	6	6	Fremont County	CO	William Bowlby	1984	553
294-4/8	46-0/8	45-2/8	40-2/8	6	6	Deer Lodge County	MT	Dale J. Goytowski	1986	554
294-3/8	45-0/8	48-4/8	37-1/8	5	7	Saguache County	CO	David A. Larson	1978	555
294-2/8	50-2/8	45-6/8	37-0/8	7	6	La Plata County	CO	J. Barry Dyar	1983	556
294-2/8	43-5/8	45-4/8	40-2/8	7	6	Apache County	AZ	Fred Clifford	1985	556
294-2/8	42-5/8	46-2/8	42-0/8	6	6	Catron County	NM	Billy Barber	1986	556
294-0/8	41-1/8	42-5/8	33-0/8	6	6	Clearwater County	ID	Don Kubasch	1981	559
293-7/8	46-3/8	48-0/8	40-5/8	6	6	Taylor Park	CO	Robert C. Goodman	1974	560
293-7/8	42-6/8	44-4/8	34-5/8	6	5	Graham County	AZ	Clifford White	1982	560
293-6/8	47-0/8	45-4/8	37-0/8	6	6	Archuleta County	CO	Eddie Claypool	1985	562
293-5/8	42-6/8	43-3/8	39-7/8	6	6	West	MT	Raymond Alt	1962	563
293-4/8	47-4/8	46-6/8	34-6/8	6	6	Beaverhead County	MT	Dennis Rehse	1981	564
293-4/8	50-0/8	46-4/8	33-6/8	6	6	Catron County	NM	Bob Gourley	1984	564
293-3/8	46-0/8	45-5/8	37-5/8	6	6	Boise County	ID	David Hale	1983	566

YELLOWSTONE *(AMERICAN)* ELK
(continued)   Minimum Score 260

Score	Length of Main Beam R	L	Inside Spread	Number of Points R	L	Area	State/ Province	Hunter's Name	Date	Rank
293-3/8	46-0/8	45-5/8	30-5/8	6	7	Lemhi County	ID	William C. Shuster	1986	566
293-2/8	47-2/8	47-6/8	39-2/8	6	6	Musselshell County	MT	Dan Acord	1986	568
293-1/8	44-6/8	39-1/8	32-1/8	6	6	Kelly Creek	ID	T. LeRoy West	1981	569
292-5/8	43-6/8	42-1/8	34-1/8	7	6	Rio Blanco County	CO	James Raetz	1976	570
292-3/8	44-6/8	40-4/8	35-1/8	6	6	Idaho County	ID	Robert C. Mitchell	1979	571
292-3/8	44-6/8	44-2/8	36-3/8	6	6	Ravalli County	MT	Paul Hamilton	1984	571
292-2/8	41-2/8	44-4/8	39-6/8	6	6	Idaho County	ID	Richard C. Nichols	1975	573
292-2/8	47-5/8	46-1/8	31-4/8	6	6	Mineral County	MT	Kenneth D. Verley	1981	573
292-2/8	45-2/8	49-1/8	33-4/8	6	6	Grant County	OR	Robert R. Gedlick	1983	573
292-1/8	44-7/8	47-0/8	34-3/8	6	6	Powell County	MT	Richard W. Malone	1976	576
292-1/8	47-5/8	47-0/8	46-7/8	6	6	Coconino County	AZ	Bryant McGee	1980	576
292-0/8	36-2/8	37-6/8	33-4/8	6	6	Lincoln County	NM	Terence A. Wahlgren	1985	578
291-7/8	45-5/8	45-2/8	38-5/8	6	6	Buena Vista County	CO	Douglas E. Wilson	1982	579
291-6/8	45-2/8	45-5/8	41-0/8	6	6	Blue River Drainage	CO	Howard Moser	1972	580
291-6/8	45-4/8	45-1/8	40-0/8	6	6	Gem County	ID	Larry Holmquist	1986	580
291-4/8	45-7/8	45-0/8	46-2/8	6	6	Coconino County	AZ	Dick & Gary Mendenhall	1974	582
291-4/8	45-4/8	43-7/8	38-4/8	6	6	Dolores	CO	William W. Gurley	1977	582
291-4/8	42-2/8	43-4/8	35-2/8	7	6	Garfield County	MT	Gaylord Johnson	1983	582
291-2/8	44-1/8	48-1/8	27-0/8	6	6	Missouri Breaks	MT	Scott L. Augustine	1980	585
291-2/8	47-5/8	45-0/8	36-6/8	6	6	Albany County	WY	Oliver P. Williamson	1982	585
291-0/8	48-4/8	49-4/8	40-4/8	6	6	Custer County	CO	Douglas R. Jones	1970	587
290-6/8	42-4/8	43-0/8	35-6/8	6	6	Cody	WY	William P. Mastrangel	1955	588
290-6/8	42-6/8	43-6/8	36-2/8	5	5	Larimer County	CO	Tom Tietz	1979	588
290-3/8	49-4/8	48-7/8	36-7/8	6	6	Custer County	ID	Tom Jarvis	1984	590
290-2/8	45-7/8	46-4/8	41-4/8	6	6	Gunnisen County	CO	Jack Allen Rasmusson	1982	591
290-2/8	42-6/8	44-5/8	40-0/8	6	6	Granite County	MT	Dennis Neitzke	1985	591
290-0/8	47-2/8	46-4/8	39-0/8	6	6	Ft. Peck	MT	Cecil I. Tharp	1978	593
289-7/8	43-0/8	41-0/8	40-3/8	6	6	Boulder County	CO	John Powell	1983	594
289-7/8	47-7/8	47-4/8	36-5/8	6	6	Missoula County	MT	Bill Spicknall	1984	594
289-6/8	45-3/8	45-0/8	35-6/8	6	6	Ravalli County	MT	Dan Smith	1980	596
289-5/8	42-2/8	42-2/8	38-3/8	6	6	Ravalli County	MT	Michael S. Mitchell	1985	597
289-4/8	48-0/8	50-3/8	33-2/8	6	6	Clearwater County	ID	LeRoy West	1983	598
289-4/8	48-0/8	46-4/8	41-0/8	6	6	Coconino County	AZ	Fred Searle	1985	598
289-3/8	43-7/8	44-6/8	46-5/8	6	7	Clearwater County	ID	Scott Rabe	1984	600
289-3/8	40-4/8	42-0/8	37-3/8	6	7	Valley County	MT	Erik E. Scarpholt	1986	600
289-1/8	46-0/8	46-1/8	35-1/8	6	6	Catron County	NM	Paul D. Payne	1986	602
288-6/8	53-1/8	52-5/8	34-2/8	5	6	Lane County	OR	Ken Abraham	1986	603
288-4/8	41-6/8	43-5/8	43-5/8	6	7	Canmore	ALB	David R. Coupland	1980	604
288-4/8	50-2/8	49-2/8	34-4/8	6	6	Lemhi County	ID	Ben L. Fahnholz	1984	604
288-2/8	50-6/8	48-3/8	39-2/8	6	6	Lincoln County	MT	Robert L. Burk	1976	606
288-2/8	46-2/8	45-0/8	39-6/8	6	6	Lemhi County	ID	John A. McCarthy	1984	606
288-0/8	46-4/8	44-4/8	35-0/8	6	6	Albany County	WY	Dan Kolb	1981	608
287-7/8	38-1/8	38-4/8	34-7/8	6	6	Trapper Lake	CO	Michael J. Reid	1981	609
287-6/8	44-0/8	44-0/8	35-4/8	6	6	Idaho County	ID	Ronald Ward	1984	610
287-4/8	44-4/8	45-0/8	38-2/8	6	6	Adams County	ID	Gary Kinney	1986	611
287-3/8	45-2/8	43-2/8	29-3/8	6	7	Bighorn Mountains	WY	Don Dvoroznak	1977	612
287-3/8	49-7/8	50-4/8	35-4/8	6	7	Scholz Lake	AZ	William P. Pate	1979	612
287-3/8	51-3/8	50-0/8	44-1/8	6	7	Jackson County	MT	Ronnie Everett	1982	612
287-2/8	41-4/8	41-4/8	29-2/8	6	6	San Isabel N.F.	CO	Richard L. Doman	1977	615
287-2/8	50-0/8	50-6/8	35-4/8	6	6	Grand County	CO	Robert Pitt	1978	615
287-2/8	42-6/8	41-6/8	32-0/8	6	6	Flathead County	MT	Rod Hickle	1982	615
287-1/8	46-0/8	45-6/8	37-3/8	6	7	Valley County	ID	L. Lombard/C. Rukkala	1980	618
287-1/8	44-1/8	44-0/8	32-7/8	6	6	Apache County	AZ	John A. Holcomb	1981	618
287-0/8	46-2/8	47-2/8	42-6/8	6	5	Three Sisters Mtn.	ALB	David R. Coupland	1986	620
286-7/8	42-4/8	42-0/8	40-5/8	6	6	Lewis and Clark County	MT	Stephen Tylinski	1979	621
286-7/8	48-2/8	46-4/8	36-7/8	6	6	Valley County	MT	Jim Seiler	1986	621
286-6/8	46-5/8	47-0/8	36-2/8	6	6	Valley County	ID	Phil VonBargen	1982	623
286-6/8	49-7/8	47-2/8	35-2/8	6	6	Sandoval County	NM	Wilbern Glenn Hitt	1985	623
286-5/8	42-1/8	42-0/8	39-3/8	6	6	Gallatin County	MT	Arnold Marolf	1977	625
286-4/8	43-1/8	44-1/8	39-4/8	6	6	Shoshone County	ID	Donald A. Young	1979	626
286-4/8	41-4/8	43-6/8	39-4/8	6	6	Clackamas County	OR	Larry D. Jones	1983	626
286-4/8	49-0/8	52-2/8	30-6/8	6	6	Coconino County	AZ	Bob Dooley	1984	626
286-1/8	44-6/8	44-6/8	41-7/8	6	6	Mineral County	MT	Ken Drake	1981	629

YELLOWSTONE *(AMERICAN)* ELK

(continued)

Minimum Score 260

Score	Length of Main Beam R	L	Inside Spread	Number of Points R	L	Area	State/ Province	Hunter's Name	Date	Rank
286-1/8	46-6/8	49-5/8	38-3/8	6	6	Yakima County	WA	Raymond Gimlin	1984	629
285-6/8	46-1/8	47-4/8	30-6/8	6	6	Blaine County	ID	Andy Moore	1985	631
285-5/8	45-3/8	45-1/8	37-3/8	6	7	Missoula County	MT	Paul Pasquariello	1982	632
285-3/8	45-4/8	45-7/8	36-1/8	6	6	Umatilla County	OR	Bob Burggraff	1982	633
285-1/8	44-6/8	46-0/8	45-4/8	7	6	Sanders County	MT	Conrad Anderson	1983	634
285-0/8	49-5/8	50-2/8	42-2/8	6	5	Sheridan County	WY	Mike Barrett	1980	635
285-0/8	45-4/8	45-2/8	33-4/8	6	6	Fergus County	MT	James Southworth	1980	635
285-0/8	40-3/8	44-6/8	33-4/8	6	6	Umatilla County	OR	Ray A. Warren	1982	635
284-7/8	44-2/8	44-7/8	35-7/8	6	6	Lewis and Clark County	MT	Ron Granneman	1977	638
284-7/8	44-2/8	43-4/8	32-3/8	6	6	Sanders County	MT	Jim Regh, Jr.	1986	638
284-6/8	47-5/8	47-7/8	37-4/8	6	6	Marion County	OR	Jack Smith	1984	640
284-5/8	44-0/8	45-0/8	33-7/8	5	7	Eagle County	CO	Stan Hunt	1981	641
284-4/8	46-4/8	40-0/8	40-2/8	6	7	Gallatin National Forest	MT	Dennis Fishbaugher	1981	642
284-4/8	38-0/8	40-0/8	38-4/8	6	6	Garfield County	CO	Bruce Easterly	1985	642
284-2/8	45-3/8	45-3/8	41-6/8	6	6	Mineral County	MT	Dwayne Garner	1982	644
284-1/8	50-4/8	49-3/8	37-7/8	5	6	Mt. Evans	CO	Gary Christoffersen	1980	645
284-1/8	42-7/8	39-5/8	44-3/8	6	6	Lemhi County	ID	Larry Cross	1981	645
284-1/8	43-3/8	42-4/8	44-1/8	6	6	Malheur County	OR	Kent Kemble	1982	645
284-1/8	44-1/8	43-1/8	31-1/8	6	6	Sandoval County	NM	Steve Alderete	1986	645
284-0/8	49-4/8	46-7/8	42-2/8	6	6	Grant County	OR	Robert Gedlick	1981	649
283-7/8	47-5/8	47-2/8	33-3/8	6	6	Fort Peck	MT	Doug Quilling	1979	650
283-7/8	52-7/8	51-5/8	46-1/8	5	6	King County	WA	Ty Martin	1984	650
283-6/8	46-0/8	45-4/8	40-6/8	6	6	Cumbres Pass	CO	Arthur M. Davis	1974	652
283-6/8	47-3/8	49-0/8	36-6/8	6	6	Custer County	ID	Donald Johnson	1986	652
283-2/8	44-6/8	40-5/8	32-6/8	6	6	Clearwater County	ID	Jay Deones	1983	654
283-1/8	50-3/8	48-1/8	31-6/8	6	7	Bighorn Mountains	WY	David Shoop	1979	655
283-0/8	42-7/8	44-5/8	41-0/8	6	6	Keating	OR	Don Rajnus	1962	656
283-0/8	45-1/8	47-5/8	43-2/8	6	6	Winter Park	CO	G. Fred Asbell	1973	656
283-0/8	48-4/8	46-4/8	36-2/8	6	6	Crook County	OR	Rick V. Herbst	1985	656
282-5/8	50-0/8	47-2/8	42-1/8	7	6	Gallatin County	MT	Scott L. Koelzer	1979	659
282-5/8	47-1/8	44-7/8	39-7/8	6	6	Little Belt Mountains	MT	Pete Ecker	1980	659
282-5/8	39-2/8	43-7/8	33-3/8	5	6	Valley County	ID	Dennis Gratton	1983	659
282-5/8	42-6/8	43-0/8	42-7/8	6	6	Dolores County	CO	Mike Zion	1985	659
282-4/8	32-6/8	39-2/8	36-4/8	6	6	Judith Basin County	MT	Jerome R. Parsons	1981	663
282-4/8	46-0/8	45-7/8	42-4/8	7	6	Custer County	ID	Joel C. Lenz	1986	663
282-3/8	44-2/8	41-0/8	38-1/8	6	6	Larimer County	CO	Dale E. Wenger	1981	665
282-2/8	42-6/8	43-1/8	39-2/8	6	6	Wallowa County	OR	Neil Summers	1986	666
282-1/8	45-4/8	44-7/8	44-7/8	5	6	Minam River	OR	Dale F. Story	1967	667
282-1/8	43-7/8	43-4/8	33-3/8	6	6	Bob Marshall Wilderness	MT	James Dean	1977	667
282-1/8	43-3/8	44-2/8	32-3/8	6	6	Sheridan County	WY	Mike Barrett	1983	667
282-0/8	44-1/8	43-6/8	46-4/8	7	6	Clearwater County	ID	Neil Hinton	1983	670
282-0/8	53-7/8	53-5/8	34-0/8	6	6	Moffat County	CO	Clark Stokes	1985	670
281-6/8	38-4/8	39-3/8	32-5/8	7	6	Powell County	MT	James L. Tillotson	1980	672
281-6/8	41-7/8	42-4/8	37-0/8	7	7	Lincoln County	MT	Mark Wachsman	1982	672
281-6/8	43-4/8	45-0/8	38-6/8	6	6	Custer County	ID	Vito Palazzolo	1983	672
281-6/8	48-2/8	47-4/8	38-0/8	6	5	Greenlee County	AZ	Joseph Barry	1986	672
281-5/8	44-6/8	45-6/8	39-3/8	6	6	Phillips County	MT	Robert Monhollon	1986	676
281-3/8	40-7/8	42-2/8	42-5/8	6	6	Missoula County	MT	Charles E. Hansen	1982	677
281-2/8	43-4/8	44-4/8	35-2/8	6	6	Powell County	MT	John Bottman	1986	678
281-1/8	42-4/8	44-1/8	35-6/8	6	6	Larimer County	CO	Gary Galloway	1984	679
281-0/8	43-2/8	43-4/8	38-0/8	6	6	Lemhi County	ID	A. Marc Whisler	1980	680
281-0/8	47-0/8	45-5/8	37-0/8	6	6	Baker County	OR	Robert L. Unruh	1982	680
281-0/8	44-4/8	49-0/8	36-6/8	6	6	Moffat County	CO	Lonny Vanatta	1984	680
281-0/8	42-6/8	42-1/8	34-2/8	6	6	Sublette County	WY	George E. Hall	1984	680
281-0/8	42-5/8	41-3/8	39-2/8	6	6	Lemhi County	ID	William Bullock, Sr.	1984	680
280-7/8	43-1/8	42-3/8	32-7/8	6	6	Johnson County	WY	Paul S. Warren	1979	685
280-6/8	48-5/8	47-0/8	38-2/8	6	6	Summit County	UT	John B. Rice, Jr.	1986	686
280-5/8	39-7/8	40-2/8	42-3/8	6	6	Gallatin County	MT	Gregg L. Welch	1982	687
280-3/8	49-7/8	49-1/8	37-5/8	5	5	Rocky Mountain House	ALB	Eugene Lopushinsky	1981	688
280-3/8	47-0/8	46-2/8	36-3/8	6	6	Clearwater County	ID	Tony Hyde	1986	688
280-2/8	39-2/8	37-3/8	33-6/8	6	5	Routt County	CO	D. F. Holt	1981	690
280-1/8	44-0/8	40-2/8	38-7/8	6	7	Coconino County	AZ	Scott Kellner	1983	691
280-0/8	45-4/8	45-3/8	33-6/8	6	6	Meeker	CO	Rolland M. Esterline	1969	692

YELLOWSTONE *(AMERICAN)* ELK

(continued)

Minimum Score 260

Score	Length of Main Beam R	L	Inside Spread	Number of Points R	L	Area	State/ Province	Hunter's Name	Date	Rank
279-7/8	43-6/8	44-0/8	40-2/8	7	6	Valley County	ID	Kenneth A Hyde	1983	693
279-4/8	41-2/8	39-0/8	33-0/8	6	6	Minam River	OR	James R. Brackenbury	1970	694
279-4/8	46-5/8	45-0/8	40-4/8	6	5	S. Clearwater River	ID	Richard C. Nichols	1973	694
279-4/8	41-6/8	40-6/8	33-2/8	6	6	Clearwater County	ID	John Burns, Sr.	1982	694
279-3/8	45-6/8	45-1/8	39-1/8	6	6	Phillips County	MT	Dave Zimmer	1983	697
279-2/8	45-2/8	46-0/8	34-0/8	6	6	Clearwater County	ID	Don West	1981	698
279-2/8	48-7/8	46-5/8	33-6/8	6	5	Clear Creek County	CO	Ken Shelton	1986	698
279-0/8	41-1/8	39-5/8	36-6/8	6	6	Caribou County	ID	Randy J. Stephens	1979	700
278-6/8	43-5/8	43-7/8	35-2/8	6	6	Cascade County	MT	Norman T. Frusti	1979	701
278-6/8	42-3/8	39-0/8	36-4/8	6	6	Park County	MT	George Kamps	1984	701
278-4/8	45-4/8	43-4/8	31-4/8	6	6	Cascade County	MT	David Holloway	1983	703
278-0/8	48-2/8	44-3/8	47-0/8	6	6	Lincoln County	MT	Bud Journey	1978	704
278-0/8	41-2/8	43-1/8	37-2/8	6	6	Grant County	OR	Clayton Severin	1984	704
277-5/8	47-1/8	45-6/8	38-1/8	6	6	Sandoval County	NM	David V. Collis	1983	706
277-4/8	45-2/8	47-4/8	38-0/8	6	6	La Plata County	CO	Andy White	1980	707
277-4/8	43-4/8	45-2/8	37-0/8	6	6	Larimer County	CO	Bruce Bowman	1985	707
277-4/8	44-3/8	43-3/8	30-0/8	7	7	Caribou County	ID	Royce Brown	1986	707
277-3/8	37-7/8	39-2/8	37-3/8	6	6	Greenlee County	AZ	Clifford White	1984	710
277-2/8	47-0/8	47-3/8	40-2/8	6	6	Black Mountain	ID	Jerry Clark	1979	711
277-2/8	41-1/8	39-7/8	40-2/8	6	7	Fergus County	MT	Ray Lundin	1982	711
277-0/8	43-0/8	43-0/8	31-6/8	6	6	Grant County	OR	Andy Day	1981	713
277-0/8	40-4/8	40-3/8	32-0/8	6	6	Cascade County	MT	David Yaeger	1983	713
277-0/8	39-0/8	40-3/8	35-4/8	6	6	Flathead County	MT	Jerry L. Wootan	1984	713
277-0/8	43-1/8	42-4/8	36-0/8	6	6	Sanders County	MT	Chuck Adams	1985	713
276-7/8	46-4/8	46-1/8	38-1/8	6	7	Pitkin County	CO	Byron S. Donahue	1981	717
276-7/8	47-6/8	47-2/8	26-5/8	7	6	Coyote	NM	Michael G. Fierro	1982	717
276-7/8	42-2/8	41-3/8	37-1/8	6	6	Benewah County	ID	Greg DesLaurier	1984	717
276-7/8	46-1/8	45-4/8	33-5/8	6	6	Grant County	OR	Gary Nyden	1984	717
276-6/8	45-0/8	44-1/8	34-4/8	6	6	Lincoln County	MT	Jerry Brown	1982	721
276-6/8	45-2/8	45-0/8	36-2/8	6	6	Taos County	NM	Calvin Farner	1986	721
276-5/8	45-7/8	45-1/8	32-5/8	6	6	Belmont Creek	MT	Max G. Bauer, Jr.	1980	723
276-5/8	46-6/8	45-5/8	35-1/8	6	6	Teton County	MT	William McRae	1982	723
276-5/8	44-4/8	43-4/8	36-5/8	6	6	Bear Lake County	ID	Troy Hymas	1984	723
276-4/8	41-1/8	40-2/8	35-0/8	6	6	Buford	CO	Tom O. Milligan	1976	726
276-4/8	42-3/8	42-2/8	34-0/8	6	6	Gallatin County	MT	George Kamps	1981	726
276-4/8	46-6/8	50-1/8	38-4/8	6	5	Clearwater County	ID	Marvin J. Gerking	1983	726
276-4/8	43-0/8	42-4/8	33-4/8	6	6	Shoshone County	ID	Stephen P. Rapier	1983	726
276-2/8	50-4/8	44-2/8	40-6/8	6	7	Fremont County	ID	Rene' Harrop	1981	730
276-1/8	42-3/8	38-7/8	41-7/8	6	6	San Luis Valley	CO	Jerry Woodland	1977	731
276-1/8	44-4/8	45-7/8	33-1/8	7	6	Caribou County	ID	Irv Wanlass	1981	731
276-0/8	42-2/8	44-6/8	33-4/8	6	6	Teller County	CO	Dr. David B. Johnson	1983	733
275-6/8	45-6/8	44-2/8	34-0/8	6	6	Valley County	ID	David G. Nagelmann	1986	734
275-5/8	42-1/8	43-6/8	38-7/8	6	6	Ravalli County	MT	Rod Osburn	1980	735
275-4/8	35-6/8	40-2/8	33-6/8	6	6	Valley County	MT	Andy Hicks	1983	736
275-4/8	48-5/8	48-7/8	34-2/8	6	6	Clackamas County	OR	Rip H. Caswell	1986	736
275-1/8	42-6/8	39-6/8	39-7/8	6	6	Bonner County	ID	Ren Hone	1980	738
275-1/8	46-6/8	44-6/8	28-7/8	6	6	Idaho County	ID	Hollis Sapp, Jr.	1986	738
275-0/8	43-1/8	44-6/8	33-0/8	7	6	Garfield County	MT	Frank Kasten	1982	740
275-0/8	45-1/8	42-3/8	33-4/8	6	6	Conejos County	CO	Dewey Brown	1982	740
275-0/8	45-3/8	45-5/8	38-3/8	6	7	Madison County	ID	Shayne L. Ard	1982	740
275-0/8	45-2/8	44-6/8	36-6/8	6	6	Missoula County	MT	Terry See	1985	740
274-7/8	43-5/8	43-4/8	37-1/8	6	6	Flathead County	MT	Dean F. Cole	1985	744
274-6/8	42-4/8	41-1/8	29-7/8	7	7	West Rimby	ALB	Clifford Hill	1984	745
274-3/8	41-3/8	42-0/8	31-1/8	6	6	San Luis Valley	CO	Jerry Woodland	1973	746
274-2/8	42-4/8	42-3/8	40-0/8	6	6	Island Park	ID	Clarence A. Frickey	1981	747
274-1/8	42-2/8	43-7/8	38-0/8	7	6	Gallatin County	MT	David F. Gibon	1974	748
274-1/8	48-3/8	48-3/8	34-5/8	6	6	Converse County	WY	Jeffrey Rieker	1979	748
274-0/8	43-3/8	43-4/8	31-2/8	6	6	Clearwater County	ID	Jay Deones	1984	750
274-0/8	43-0/8	41-4/8	36-0/8	6	6	Grant County	OR	Robert D. Coffey	1986	750
273-6/8	48-4/8	49-0/8	33-6/8	6	6	Lemhi County	ID	Greg Munther	1963	752
273-6/8	42-1/8	43-3/8	33-0/8	6	6	Broadwater County	MT	Don Lovely	1978	752
273-6/8	39-3/8	37-6/8	37-6/8	6	6	Grant County	OR	John Bridgewater	1983	752
273-2/8	46-5/8	47-5/8	31-6/8	6	6	Phillips County	MT	Buddy Lundstrom	1981	755

YELLOWSTONE *(AMERICAN)* ELK

(continued)

Minimum Score 260

Score	Length of Main Beam R	Length of Main Beam L	Inside Spread	Number of Points R	Number of Points L	Area	State/ Province	Hunter's Name	Date	Rank
273-2/8	45-5/8	44-3/8	37-6/8	6	6	Coconino County	AZ	Tony W. Zimbaro	1986	755
273-1/8	42-3/8	41-7/8	39-3/8	6	6	Mora County	NM	Michael J. Maes	1986	757
273-0/8	42-2/8	42-1/8	32-6/8	6	6	Sandoval	NM	George Bennett, Jr.	1984	758
272-7/8	39-6/8	40-0/8	37-7/8	6	6	Eagle Creek	OR	Ed Bensel	1959	759
272-7/8	37-1/8	37-1/8	36-0/8	6	6	Meeker	CO	Dr. Charles Leidheiser	1973	759
272-5/8	44-7/8	42-1/8	36-3/8	6	6	Capitol Creek	CO	Robert F. Cutting	1975	761
272-3/8	41-7/8	39-5/8	35-3/8	6	6	Skagit County	WA	Steve Gorr	1982	762
272-2/8	38-6/8	39-4/8	34-4/8	6	6	Elk City	ID	Stanley D. Miles	1976	763
272-2/8	48-0/8	46-5/8	37-2/8	5	5	Saguache County	CO	Kenneth A. Wollermann	1986	763
272-0/8	43-7/8	44-4/8	38-0/8	6	6	San Luis Valley	CO	Buster Mize	1968	765
272-0/8	45-5/8	45-0/8	37-4/8	6	6	Idaho County	ID	Donald M. Martin	1978	765
271-7/8	47-4/8	49-1/8	32-5/8	6	6	Chelan County	WA	Claude E. Gates	1973	767
271-6/8	46-4/8	46-5/8	33-6/8	6	6	Sheridan County	WY	Mike Barrett	1985	768
271-5/8	43-1/8	43-6/8	36-1/8	5	6	Park County	MT	Dennis Vance	1975	769
271-5/8	38-5/8	39-5/8	36-1/8	6	6	Larimer County	CO	Kenneth D. Allen	1981	769
271-5/8	43-5/8	44-4/8	32-7/8	6	6	Lewis County	WA	Keith Heldreth	1985	769
271-4/8	38-4/8	40-6/8	34-2/8	6	6	Mud Creek	ID	Jr. Barnett	1977	772
271-4/8	44-4/8	45-6/8	43-0/8	6	5	Lanes Creek	ID	Preston Phelps	1980	772
271-4/8	46-3/8	47-2/8	36-2/8	6	6	Sweetwater County	WY	Vaughn Cross	1981	772
271-3/8	42-7/8	42-5/8	39-7/8	6	6	Rio Aribba County	NM	Bryan Adair	1984	775
271-2/8	44-2/8	45-7/8	27-0/8	6	6	Gunnison County	CO	Jeff Helming	1984	776
271-2/8	39-5/8	39-5/8	32-2/8	6	6	Rio Arriba County	NM	Lee Braudt	1985	776
271-2/8	42-1/8	43-4/8	39-4/8	6	5	Grant County	OR	Don D. Litts	1986	776
271-2/8	41-0/8	39-3/8	34-4/8	7	7	Rio Arriba County	NM	Greg Harmsen	1986	776
271-0/8	48-0/8	47-7/8	34-2/8	6	5	Park County	CO	Victor B. Hines	1981	780
270-7/8	38-5/8	38-4/8	34-5/8	6	6	Gallatin National Forest	MT	Steve D. Wing	1979	781
270-7/8	37-1/8	42-6/8	31-3/8	6	6	Morgan County	UT	Hugh H. Hogle	1983	781
270-5/8	38-1/8	39-2/8	36-3/8	6	6	Steamboat Springs	CO	Jake Hoeschler	1977	783
270-4/8	50-5/8	48-6/8	42-0/8	5	5	King County	WA	Jon Fuller	1985	784
270-3/8	40-6/8	40-4/8	36-5/8	6	6	Ravalli County	MT	Wayne Buhler	1982	785
270-3/8	46-0/8	46-4/8	36-7/8	6	6	Grant County	OR	Dennis G. Marshall	1986	785
270-2/8	42-6/8	41-6/8	36-2/8	6	6	Mancos	CO	Dwight V. English	1976	787
270-2/8	38-6/8	37-0/8	32-2/8	6	6	Blaine County	ID	John Turner	1977	787
270-2/8	42-7/8	44-4/8	43-6/8	5	5	Shoshone County	ID	Roy Meyer	1979	787
270-1/8	38-1/8	39-1/8	35-5/8	6	6	Powell County	MT	E. Kits Smith	1976	790
270-0/8	45-6/8	46-5/8	31-2/8	6	6	Clints Well	AZ	James H. Hansen	1981	791
270-0/8	48-6/8	47-5/8	32-4/8	6	6	Coconino County	AZ	Wade L. Carstens	1983	791
269-7/8	38-2/8	36-6/8	28-1/8	6	6	Bear Lake County	ID	Dennis Burdick	1969	793
269-7/8	45-4/8	45-4/8	38-5/8	6	5	Park County	MT	Jay Bosma	1984	793
269-6/8	47-4/8	47-5/8	46-2/8	6	5	Idaho County	ID	Edward Keeton	1985	795
269-5/8	41-6/8	42-3/8	35-5/8	6	6	Palisades	ID	Mike Taylor	1980	796
269-5/8	42-0/8	41-1/8	36-1/8	6	6	Caribou County	ID	Chet Hopkins	1985	796
269-5/8	44-4/8	44-1/8	33-1/8	6	6	Park County	MT	George Kamps	1986	796
269-4/8	42-7/8	42-4/8	35-6/8	6	7	Pinal County	AZ	Larry P. Matthews	1985	799
269-3/8	46-1/8	47-2/8	36-5/8	5	6	Cibola County	NM	Deryl Moore	1986	800
269-0/8	48-5/8	44-6/8	39-6/8	5	6	Bighorn Mountains	WY	Dennis A. Phaneuf	1980	801
269-0/8	41-3/8	40-5/8	35-6/8	6	6	Kooskia	ID	Larry A. Youngdell	1980	801
269-0/8	39-2/8	40-6/8	37-2/8	6	6	Lewis & Clark County	MT	Steven E. Miller	1982	801
269-0/8	42-7/8	41-1/8	33-4/8	6	6	Converse County	WY	Jim Young	1982	801
268-7/8	44-0/8	43-4/8	34-7/8	6	6	Judith Basin County	MT	Dan Hassel	1985	805
268-6/8	41-3/8	42-5/8	39-4/8	6	6	Park County	CO	Wayne Helming	1983	806
268-5/8	41-7/8	43-1/8	32-2/8	6	6	San Juan National Forest	CO	Billy R. Spears	1973	807
268-4/8	43-6/8	43-4/8	32-4/8	5	6	Coconino County	AZ	Charles R. Haverin	1984	808
268-2/8	45-6/8	42-6/8	35-2/8	6	6	Navajo County	AZ	Julius Levi	1983	809
268-1/8	39-0/8	40-3/8	30-0/8	7	6	Alpine	WY	Troy Miller	1973	810
268-1/8	45-2/8	46-0/8	36-5/8	5	6	Gallatin County	MT	William L. Anderson	1982	810
268-1/8	44-3/8	44-5/8	34-1/8	6	6	Silver Bow County	MT	Andrew Kuchtyn	1982	810
268-1/8	44-4/8	44-2/8	35-1/8	6	6	Grant County	OR	Gary Persinger	1983	810
268-0/8	42-3/8	40-5/8	32-6/8	6	5	Keating	OR	Les Thoreby	1963	814
268-0/8	41-7/8	42-2/8	33-3/8	7	6	Idaho County	ID	Richard C. Nichols	1974	814
267-7/8	45-2/8	43-5/8	41-3/8	6	6	Valley County	ID	Jack St. Germain	1981	816
267-7/8	44-2/8	43-6/8	32-7/8	6	6	Los Alamos County	NM	Doug Aikin	1983	816
267-6/8	43-3/8	47-0/8	39-6/8	6	6	Caribou County	ID	Jerry Baird	1976	818

YELLOWSTONE *(AMERICAN)* ELK
(continued)   Minimum Score 260

Score	Length of Main Beam R	L	Inside Spread	Number of Points R	L	Area	State/ Province	Hunter's Name	Date	Rank
267-5/8	42-2/8	42-4/8	33-3/8	6	6	Estes Park	CO	Dennis Worrell	1979	819
267-5/8	40-0/8	39-6/8	33-7/8	6	6	Chaffee County	CO	Bruce Long	1985	819
267-3/8	40-4/8	39-3/8	30-3/8	6	6	Southwest	MT	Harold Wilson	1977	821
267-3/8	38-2/8	47-4/8	33-1/8	5	6	San Francisco Peaks	AZ	John C. McClendon	1980	821
267-3/8	43-6/8	45-6/8	35-5/8	6	6	Linn County	OR	Michael Hawkins	1982	821
267-0/8	41-5/8	38-3/8	41-4/8	5	7	Kremling	CO	Noel Feather	1980	824
266-6/8	41-0/8	40-4/8	32-6/8	6	6	Lemhi County	ID	Scott Spaeth	1978	825
266-6/8	45-5/8	43-2/8	37-4/8	6	6	McNary	AZ	Tom David	1980	825
266-5/8	42-1/8	43-7/8	29-5/8	6	6	Mt. Shavano	CO	Frank A. Morminello	1977	827
266-5/8	43-2/8	43-2/8	31-7/8	6	6	Phillips County	MT	Steve Baeth	1985	827
266-4/8	36-7/8	37-0/8	30-4/8	6	6	Lewis and Clark County	MT	Laurence F. Crim	1977	829
266-4/8	41-7/8	43-1/8	35-2/8	6	6	Gem County	ID	Randy L. Wilkins	1985	829
266-2/8	47-3/8	45-6/8	36-4/8	5	6	LaPlata County	CO	Charlie Chrane	1977	831
266-0/8	47-1/8	45-7/8	38-6/8	6	6	Sandoval County	NM	Lloyd Baird	1984	832
265-4/8	43-2/8	42-7/8	32-6/8	6	6	Delta County	CO	Emil C. Frein	1973	833
265-4/8	49-4/8	45-5/8	31-6/8	6	6	San Juan National Forest	CO	Scott Roberts	1975	833
265-1/8	41-2/8	39-2/8	29-1/8	6	7	Goose Creek	CO	Rod Wintz	1968	835
264-7/8	42-5/8	45-5/8	33-1/8	6	6	Coconino County	AZ	Dennis Newman	1973	836
264-7/8	40-0/8	38-2/8	39-7/8	6	6	Union County	OR	Ellis E. Speer	1986	836
264-6/8	38-5/8	37-4/8	32-6/8	6	6	Teton National Forest	WY	Paul Birkholz	1966	838
264-6/8	41-4/8	40-5/8	35-4/8	6	6	Pitkin County	CO	Donald Hanford	1981	838
264-6/8	43-0/8	44-1/8	36-0/8	5	5	Little Belt Mountains	MT	Gary H. Thompson	1981	838
264-6/8	41-3/8	41-0/8	36-4/8	6	6	Meagher County	MT	Gene Clark	1982	838
264-4/8	44-6/8	45-7/8	34-4/8	7	7	Boise	ID	Robert Hiller	1969	842
264-4/8	38-6/8	39-2/8	33-6/8	6	6	Jefferson County	CO	Darrell Kitzman	1986	842
264-2/8	41-5/8	43-5/8	27-6/8	6	6	Coconino County	AZ	Randy Breland	1984	844
264-2/8	39-7/8	39-3/8	39-6/8	5	5	Catron County	NM	Adam Jimenez Jr.	1986	844
264-1/8	40-4/8	39-0/8	39-7/8	5	5	Larimer County	CO	Eric Peterson	1982	846
264-0/8	42-5/8	45-3/8	43-1/8	7	7	Missoula	MT	Will Mitchell	1981	847
263-7/8	46-4/8	46-7/8	39-7/8	6	5	Horseshoe Creek	ID	Jack Brennan	1964	848
263-5/8	40-5/8	39-6/8	34-3/8	6	6	Ouray County	CO	Doug McCauley	1982	849
263-3/8	38-7/8	38-4/8	33-5/8	6	6	Idaho County	ID	John C. Mitchell	1985	850
263-2/8	40-7/8	43-1/8	32-5/8	6	7	Coconino County	AZ	Michael H. Bingham	1982	851
263-1/8	43-5/8	42-6/8	35-5/8	6	5	Lewis County	WA	Keith Heldreth	1984	852
263-0/8	41-0/8	41-3/8	36-2/8	6	6	Clear Creek County	CO	Don Bording	1982	853
263-0/8	41-7/8	42-6/8	35-2/8	6	6	Los Alamos County	NM	Doug Aikin	1984	853
262-7/8	37-7/8	36-7/8	34-3/8	6	6	Garfield County	CO	Clifford White	1977	855
262-7/8	43-4/8	44-1/8	36-5/8	7	6	Coconino County	AZ	Dr. Van Bennett	1985	855
262-6/8	40-5/8	42-1/8	31-6/8	6	6	Archuleta County	CO	David W. Cather	1984	857
262-5/8	39-5/8	39-4/8	36-7/8	6	6	Pierce County	WA	David T. Robertson	1985	858
262-4/8	39-4/8	40-0/8	31-6/8	6	7	Mormon Lake	AZ	Donald L. Kennedy	1977	859
262-4/8	42-6/8	43-4/8	38-4/8	6	6	Flathead County	MT	Chester Fessum	1983	859
262-2/8	45-0/8	45-3/8	32-6/8	5	5	Frasier	CO	G. Fred Asbell	1979	861
262-2/8	41-4/8	40-2/8	37-0/8	5	5	Crook County	OR	Terry A. Luther	1981	861
262-0/8	43-4/8	43-6/8	35-4/8	6	6	Salida	CO	Ray Nelson	1981	863
262-0/8	42-4/8	42-1/8	37-4/8	6	6	Deer Lodge County	MT	Todd R. Zeuske	1982	863
261-7/8	36-6/8	41-3/8	34-7/8	6	6	Leonard Canyon	AZ	Charles Stevenson	1980	865
261-6/8	38-0/8	40-0/8	37-6/8	6	5	Taos County	NM	Dr. D. A. Henbest	1972	866
261-5/8	40-0/8	37-2/8	33-5/8	6	6	Rio Blanco County	CO	H. V. McFarland, Jr.	1974	867
261-4/8	43-0/8	43-2/8	35-0/8	6	6	Caribou County	ID	Randy K. Guinn	1986	868
261-3/8	41-6/8	41-3/8	31-1/8	6	6	Fremont County	ID	Gary Owens	1980	869
261-2/8	42-5/8	42-4/8	31-0/8	5	5	Rio Arriba County	NM	Donald N. Lehman	1983	870
261-2/8	42-4/8	41-3/8	33-4/8	6	6	Costilla County	CO	Timothy L. Walters	1985	870
261-2/8	44-6/8	44-1/8	34-0/8	5	5	Cibola County	NM	Duane T. Corley	1986	870
261-1/8	37-874	36-2/8	37-7/8	6	6	Cowdrey	CO	Knut A. Paulsen	1975	873
261-1/8	44-1/8	43-1/8	36-7/8	6	7	Caribou	ID	Richard T. Vance	1975	873
261-0/8	37-1/8	36-1/8	37-6/8	6	6	Flathead County	MT	Dr. Brad Black	1981	875
260-7/8	37-6/8	37-6/8	34-3/8	6	6	Grant County	OR	Colby Moulton	1986	876
260-6/8	40-4/8	44-6/8	30-2/8	7	7	Coconino County	AZ	James Casady	1978	877
260-6/8	38-0/8	37-3/8	34-0/8	6	6	Converse County	WY	Russell Burghard	1983	877
260-4/8	40-4/8	40-7/8	38-0/8	6	6	Blaine County	ID	Wesley Moore	1986	879
260-3/8	38-4/8	38-7/8	30-7/8	6	6	Madison County	ID	Paul L. Beesley	1979	880
259-6/8	43-0/8	44-0/8	32-0/8	6	6	LaPlata County	CO	Gerald D. Rector	1975	881

YELLOWSTONE *(AMERICAN)* ELK

(continued)

Minimum Score 260

Score	Length of Main Beam R	L	Inside Spread	Number of Points R	L	Area	State/ Province	Hunter's Name	Date	Rank
259-5/8	44-0/8	45-2/8	39-1/8	5	6	Powell County	MT	Dennis Sain	1973	882
259-4/8	41-7/8	42-0/8	33-0/8	6	6	Routt National Forest	CO	Donald E. Hunter	1976	883
259-3/8	42-4/8	41-0/8	32-1/8	6	6	Clear Creek County	CO	Gary Whitten	1984	884
259-2/8	42-1/8	43-0/8	33-0/8	6	6	Flathead County	MT	Bruce E. Parker	1983	885
259-2/8	39-3/8	37-2/8	36-4/8	6	6	Sublete County	WY	Donald Dickerhoof	1984	885
258-7/8	42-1/8	40-6/8	33-1/8	6	6	Kaibab National Forest	AZ	Bobby W. Brewer	1980	887
258-3/8	39-1/8	41-0/8	28-1/8	6	6	Teton County	MT	Ronald K. Granneman	1975	888
258-0/8	39-3/8	39-2/8	36-4/8	5	5	Eagle Cap Wilderness	OR	Gene Macomb	1979	889
257-7/8	40-3/8	40-0/8	36-1/8	6	6	New Castle	CO	Ronald J. Miller	1974	890
257-7/8	40-3/8	38-5/8	39-1/8	5	6	Sand Rock	AZ	Bill L. Wombacker	1980	890
257-6/8	38-4/8	38-6/8	30-0/8	7	7	Nez Perce County	ID	DeWayne Benton	1980	892
257-4/8	36-4/8	36-4/8	37-4/8	6	6	Sheridan County	WY	Vadan L. Scruggs	1983	893
257-0/8	39-2/8	40-1/8	34-2/8	6	6	Teton County	MT	Danny O. Smrdel	1982	894
257-0/8	43-2/8	44-1/8	38-0/8	6	5	Garfield County	CO	Dennis Evancho	1983	894
256-7/8	36-4/8	36-4/8	39-5/8	6	6	Grand County	CO	Kevin O'Connell	1981	896
256-6/8	38-1/8	36-6/8	30-0/8	6	6	Trout Creek Drainage	MT	James M. Monzie	1979	897
256-4/8	40-4/8	39-1/8	33-2/8	6	6	Wallowa County	OR	Gene Macomb	1981	898
256-3/8	39-6/8	40-0/8	29-5/8	6	6	Beaverhead County	MT	Bob Jacobsen	1982	899
256-1/8	42-0/8	41-3/8	36-7/8	6	6	Rio Arriba County	NM	Ronald Madsen	1982	900
256-1/8	45-7/8	45-6/8	35-1/8	6	5	Nez Perce County	ID	J. David Powers	1983	900
256-1/8	46-3/8	44-1/8	33-5/8	6	6	LaPlata County	CO	Malcolm Osbourn	1983	900
255-7/8	37-4/8	37-4/8	34-7/8	6	6	Phillips County	MT	Ed Wolf	1984	903
255-6/8	39-3/8	38-6/8	36-0/8	5	5	Saguache County	CO	Jewell Leadford	1980	904
255-4/8	37-1/8	38-759	31-4/8	6	6	White River N.F.	CO	Walt Krom	1979	905
255-2/8	38-1/8	38-0/8	36-6/8	5	6	Chaffee County	CO	Damon Handley	1984	906
255-1/8	36-3/8	38-6/8	28-5/8	5	5	Clints Well	AZ	Dan Lunde	1979	907
255-0/8	38-5/8	37-2/8	32-4/8	6	6	Mormon Mountain	AZ	Douglas L. Martin	1978	908
254-7/8	42-0/8	40-4/8	35-0/8	5	5	Deschutes County	OR	Jack Coleman	1979	909
254-7/8	38-5/8	38-5/8	34-1/8	6	5	Gallatin County	MT	John M. Berger	1982	909
254-6/8	39-3/8	41-3/8	32-2/8	6	6	Valley County	MT	Herbert W. Weiss	1981	911
254-4/8	38-6/8	39-4/8	35-2/8	6	6	Gallatin County	MT	Duane R. Korthuis	1983	912
254-2/8	39-3/8	41-3/8	36-6/8	6	7	Meagher County	MT	Michael E. Mullens	1983	913
254-0/8	37-5/8	38-0/8	31-4/8	6	6	Saguache County	CO	Russell Hull	1982	914
254-0/8	40-1/8	39-4/8	34-4/8	5	5	San Miguel County	NM	D. B. Thompson	1982	914
253-7/8	39-3/8	39-759	31-0/8	6	6	Elk City	ID	Don D. Seward	1972	916
253-7/8	48-5/8	48-0/8	31-3/8	6	6	Park County	CO	Shari Fraker	1982	916
253-6/8	46-4/8	45-6/8	33-4/8	6	6	Catron County	NM	Randall Madding	1983	918
253-3/8	43-7/8	44-2/8	41-5/8	5	5	Butte	MT	Charles Kaudy	1973	919
253-3/8	44-5/8	45-0/8	34-3/8	6	6	Rio Arriba County	NM	Ronald Madsen	1983	919
253-3/8	34-6/8	34-2/8	32-1/8	5	6	Toole County	MT	Joe Davenport	1984	919
252-6/8	38-3/8	37-5/8	42-1/8	7	7	Sanders County	MT	Bruce Lamkins	1978	922
252-4/8	40-7/8	40-2/8	35-0/8	6	6	Montrose	CO	Charles Waltman	1975	923
252-4/8	38-6/8	39-6/8	36-6/8	5	5	Arapahoe National Forest	CO	Bill Burke	1977	923
252-4/8	40-5/8	40-3/8	39-2/8	6	6	Larimer County	CO	Steve Stumbo	1979	923
252-3/8	38-0/8	40-1/8	33-3/8	6	6	Malta	MT	Gary Olsen	1980	926
252-2/8	35-7/8	37-1/8	36-0/8	6	6	Park County	MT	Jim Schroeder	1983	927
252-2/8	42-2/8	43-0/8	35-4/8	5	5	Ravalli County	MT	Curtis W. Dorroh	1984	927
252-1/8	39-4/8	38-2/8	33-7/8	5	5	Tincup Basin	ID	Patrick G. Selfridge	1978	929
252-0/8	39-1/8	40-2/8	28-6/8	6	6	Catron County	NM	Jerald R. Lopeman	1984	930
251-6/8	39-0/8	39-4/8	32-6/8	6	6	Granite County	MT	Michael Nielsen	1982	931
251-4/8	40-6/8	41-6/8	26-2/8	7	6	Lodgepole	ALB	Warren Witherspoon	1983	932
251-3/8	39-3/8	39-2/8	34-5/8	6	6	Pagosa Springs	CO	Ron Kolpin	1978	933
250-7/8	42-7/8	40-6/8	34-7/8	5	6	Chromo	CO	Dick Ray	1972	934
250-7/8	38-6/8	38-4/8	37-5/8	6	5	Helena National Forest	MT	Thomas M. Parks	1981	934
250-6/8	34-5/8	34-1/8	32-2/8	6	6	Rio Blanco County	CO	Michael L. Lowry	1978	936
250-3/8	39-7/8	41-5/8	41-5/8	6	7	Eagle Creek	OR	Robert J. Bouret	1957	937
250-3/8	37-7/8	37-6/8	33-7/8	6	6	San Juan National Forest	CO	Eddie Howard	1981	937
250-2/8	40-7/8	40-0/8	33-0/8	6	6	Montrose	CO	Don Castrup	1977	939
250-2/8	40-5/8	41-7/8	35-2/8	6	6	Garfield County	CO	Mike Deshazo	1980	939
250-2/8	39-6/8	40-2/8	30-2/8	5	5	Sandoval County	NM	Doug Walker	1982	939
249-7/8	39-6/8	40-5/8	31-1/8	6	6	Meagher County	MT	David Snyder	1977	942
249-7/8	42-3/8	42-0/8	33-1/8	6	6	Mineral County	MT	Tim Hansen	1982	942
249-7/8	35-6/8	38-1/8	37-6/8	7	6	Rio Blanco County	CO	James D. Yuds	1984	942

YELLOWSTONE *(AMERICAN)* ELK

(continued)   Minimum Score 260

Score	Length of Main Beam R	L	Inside Spread	Number of Points R	L	Area	State/Province	Hunter's Name	Date	Rank
249-4/8	38-2/8	39-0/8	34-4/8	6	6	Garfield County	CO	Scott George	1983	945
249-3/8	39-3/8	48-0/8	39-0/8	6	6	Flathead County	MT	Owen Weaver	1981	946
249-3/8	41-2/8	41-7/8	36-5/8	6	6	Pitkin County	CO	Michael Beckwith	1982	946
249-2/8	36-6/8	36-0/8	31-4/8	6	6	Beaverhead County	MT	Scott Leibenguth	1981	948
249-2/8	49-0/8	49-1/8	38-0/8	6	7	Bitterroot N.F.	MT	Jim W. McCrory	1981	948
248-7/8	36-0/8	36-7/8	33-5/8	6	6	Argenteen Pass	CO	Dr. Thomas K. Saville	1973	950
248-6/8	41-1/8	39-4/8	33-6/8	5	6	Starkey	OR	Kenneth R. Davis	1976	951
248-4/8	40-1/8	41-2/8	36-4/8	6	6	Tollgate	OR	Les Scoggin	1981	952
248-4/8	39-2/8	39-1/8	33-0/8	5	5	Garfield County	CO	Steven C. Simpson	1983	952
247-7/8	38-0/8	39-0/8	34-3/8	6	6	Jackson County	CO	Mark Nelson	1923	954
247-7/8	42-2/8	41-4/8	35-5/8	6	6	Pitkin County	CO	Don Minich	1965	954
247-5/8	45-3/8	45-2/8	31-1/8	5	5	Phillips County	MT	David Meehan	1984	956
247-4/8	39-0/8	39-2/8	39-2/8	5	6	Kremmling	CO	Michael K. Ward	1971	957
247-3/8	35-1/8	34-4/8	33-1/8	5	5	Cove	OR	George Cushman	1975	958
247-2/8	36-7/8	37-2/8	37-2/8	6	6	Ravalli County	MT	Dennis Trowbridge	1980	959
247-1/8	40-3/8	41-0/8	36-1/8	5	5	Pitkin County	CO	Terry G. Moore	1983	960
246-7/8	41-0/8	41-6/8	32-6/8	5	6	Cascade County	MT	Ronald K. Granneman	1981	961
246-6/8	39-5/8	39-3/8	43-0/8	6	6	Madison County	MT	Wally Duncan	1978	962
246-5/8	35-1/8	35-6/8	35-6/8	6	6	Baca County	NM	Doug Walker	1981	963
246-3/8	37-7/8	38-1/8	35-7/8	6	6	Jackson County	CO	Roger Stewart	1974	964
246-1/8	41-2/8	41-2/8	40-5/8	6	5	Lasal Mountains	UT	John Chagnovich	1972	965
246-0/8	45-3/8	43-6/8	33-0/8	5	6	Bonner County	ID	Bob Cardinel	1979	966
246-0/8	40-5/8	39-2/8	40-4/8	6	6	Eagle County	CO	Gary Holt	1983	966
246-0/8	38-0/8	39-0/8	31-4/8	6	6	Greenlee County	AZ	Robert W. Johnson	1984	966
245-7/8	38-0/8	37-7/8	34-7/8	6	6	Sandoval County	NM	David E. Crowe	1984	969
245-1/8	40-4/8	38-1/8	31-3/8	6	6	Wallowa County	OR	Roger Fowler	1981	970
245-0/8	40-5/8	39-3/8	31-2/8	5	6	Prichard	ID	Roger Miner	1977	971
244-6/8	36-6/8	36-6/8	32-3/8	6	6	Gore Range	CO	Michael Beckwith	1978	972
244-3/8	37-5/8	39-2/8	41-7/8	5	5	San Juan National Forest	CO	Bobby Gorman	1977	973
244-2/8	38-5/8	38-2/8	32-1/8	6	6	Minam	OR	Jim Young	1977	974
244-2/8	42-0/8	40-1/8	32-2/8	5	5	Jemez Mountains	NM	Santos E. Corriz	1979	974
244-0/8	37-5/8	39-6/8	35-2/8	6	7	Elk City	ID	Jerry E. Burt	1978	976
243-6/8	40-3/8	39-4/8	29-3/8	6	5	Little Belts County	MT	Bill Tesinsky	1981	977
243-5/8	38-3/8	37-3/8	34-5/8	6	6	Bob Marshall Wilderness	MT	Paul Olson	1981	978
243-4/8	42-1/8	42-6/8	34-7/8	8	5	Coconino National Forest	AZ	David Baker	1981	979
243-2/8	33-6/8	34-2/8	32-2/8	6	5	Montrose County	CO	Russell A. Sill	1980	980
243-1/8	39-7/8	39-7/8	31-7/8	6	6	Mineral County	CO	Mike Stenerson	1984	981
242-6/8	38-5/8	37-6/8	36-0/8	5	6	Pagosa Springs	CO	Judd Cooney	1974	982
242-6/8	41-4/8	41-7/8	29-2/8	6	5	Rabbit Ears Peak	CO	Barry J. Smith	1980	982
242-6/8	38-6/8	38-7/8	37-4/8	6	5	Stoner Mesa	CO	Stanley A. Coval	1981	982
242-3/8	36-0/8	36-3/8	35-1/8	6	6	Union County	OR	Don Walsh	1980	985
242-3/8	38-4/8	38-1/8	37-1/8	6	6	Larimer County	CO	Steve Stumbo	1981	985
242-1/8	37-4/8	40-0/8	35-2/8	6	6	Caribou County	ID	Larry Roberts	1978	987
242-1/8	43-3/8	41-7/8	35-5/8	5	5	Valencia County	NM	Mark Webber	1983	987
242-1/8	34-0/8	34-4/8	32-5/8	6	6	Gran County	OR	John Burns	1984	987
241-1/8	39-2/8	37-2/8	38-3/8	6	6	San Miguel County	NM	Louis Baca	1984	990
241-0/8	35-1/8	37-6/8	34-6/8	6	5	San Juan National Forest	CO	Danny Lloyd	1971	991
240-7/8	40-5/8	38-4/8	34-1/8	6	6	Bonneville County	ID	Greg Kretzman	1983	992
240-6/8	38-5/8	37-5/8	34-4/8	6	6	Bonneville County	ID	Frederick W. Sanders	1978	993
240-5/8	35-5/8	37-0/8	32-3/8	5	5	Vermejo Park Ranch	CO	Noel Feather, Jr.	1978	994
240-3/8	38-2/8	42-1/8	34-3/8	6	5	Clackamas County	OR	Ben Munoz	1984	995
240-2/8	35-0/8	35-4/8	34-6/8	6	6	Missoula County	MT	Gene Meyer	1984	996

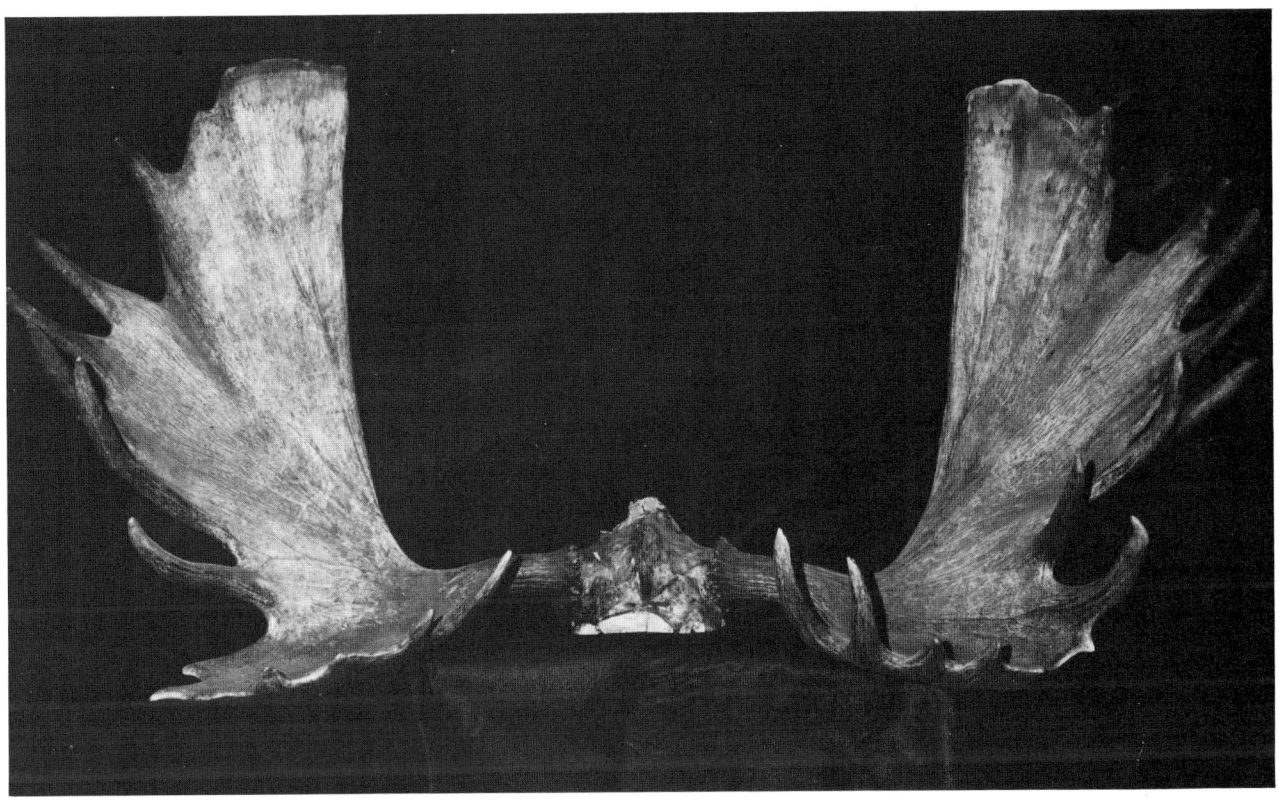

WORLD RECORD ALASKA-YUKON MOOSE
Score: 248 0/8
Bear Creek, Alaska – 1973
Hunter: Dr. Michael Cusack

ALASKA-YUKON MOOSE
Alces alces gigas

Minimum Score 170

Score	Greatest Spread	Width of Palm R	L	Number of Points R	L	Area	State/ Province	Hunter's Name	Date	Rank
248-0/8	74-0/8	18-6/8	19-2/8	11	11	Bear Creek	AK	Dr. Michael L. Cusack	1973	1
224-3/8	59-5/8	17-0/8	16-4/8	15	13	Lake Iliamna	AK	George Faerber	1974	2
223-7/8	73-7/8	14-2/8	16-0/8	12	11	Kugruk River	AK	Rocky Tope	1978	3
220-3/8	57-3/8	16-0/8	16-2/8	12	11	Little Delta River	AK	William Wright	1959	4
219-0/8	61-0/8	14-4/8	8-0/8	13	12	Kichatna River	AK	Ronald N. Kolpin	1974	5
217-4/8	71-2/8	13-2/8	12-6/8	10	12	Ugashik River	AK	Gary Hoffer	1986	6
213-2/8	62-4/8	18-4/8	15-6/8	9	10	Rainy Pass	AK	Rick Tollison	1978	7
212-7/8	65-7/8	13-0/8	17-6/8	9	10	Mulchatna River	AK	Jay Massey	1973	8
212-1/8	58-3/8	15-0/8	14-6/8	16	15	Brooks Range	AK	Roger Stewart	1985	9
211-2/8	66-6/8	15-0/8	14-4/8	9	9	Anchorage	AK	Dr. Rex Hancock	1961	10
211-2/8	66-6/8	21-3/8	16-0/8	7	9	Meshik River	AK	Art Kragness	1970	10
210-1/8	64-5/8	14-1/8	13-6/8	8	9	Nabesna	AK	Bill Ellis	1965	12
209-6/8	69-0/8	13-0/8	14-4/8	9	9	Port Heíden	AK	Margaret Cooley	1966	13
209-1/8	62-7/8	14-6/8	19-4/8	8	9	Susitna River	AK	John D. "Jack" Frost	1981	14
209-1/8	64-7/8	15-0/8	16-0/8	9	10	Tagagawik River	AK	Bill Grahlherr	1984	14
208-1/8	59-7/8	13-5/8	15-2/8	13	13	Brooks Range	AK	Ted Grover	1985	16
208-0/8	65-4/8	13-0/8	12-0/8	9	7	Alaska Peninsula	AK	Jack Niles	1970	17
207-2/8	60-2/8	12-1/8	16-6/8	10	10	Yenlo Mountains	AK	John F. Sumrall	1979	18
206-5/8	62-1/8	12-2/8	13-2/8	12	13	Kotzebue	AK	Bruce A. Moe	1980	19
206-3/8	69-3/8	12-0/8	9-4/8	7	9	Alaska Peninsula	AK	Dr. Charles R. Leidheiser	1974	20
205-7/8	55-1/8	13-1/8	14-0/8	12	10	Inoko River	AK	Jack Smythe	1974	21
205-6/8	70-0/8	15-7/8	13-3/8	9	9	Alaska Peninsula	AK	Dr. Howard Schneider	1982	22
205-4/8	57-6/8	13-4/8	13-3/8	11	13	Horsetrail Lake	AK	Donald Poole	1979	23
205-2/8	64-0/8	14-0/8	12-7/8	8	12	Alaska Peninsula	AK	Donald B. McIntosh	1969	24

ALASKA-YUKON MOOSE

(continued)   Minimum Score 170

Score	Greatest Spread	Width of Palm R	L	Number of Points R	L	Area	State/ Province	Hunter's Name	Date	Rank
204-7/8	60-3/8	14-5/8	15-6/8	10	11	Paxon	AK	Alan Perry	1972	25
204-7/8	68-3/8	14-7/8	14-6/8	7	11	Black Lake	AK	Stanley Winslow	1973	25
204-2/8	61-4/8	13-4/8	12-5/8	10	11	Fairbanks	AK	Keith Jensen	1986	27
203-6/8	66-0/8	11-5/8	12-7/8	13	11	Port Heiden	AK	Jim Dougherty	1968	28
203-3/8	66-7/8	11-0/8	11-7/8	13	12	Seven Mile Lake	AK	Dr. William J. Young, Jr.	1980	29
202-7/8	58-1/8	12-6/8	13-4/8	15	13	Earn Lake	YUK	Dr. R. D. Keeler	1986	30
202-6/8	67-4/8	12-4/8	13-2/8	9	9	Port Heiden	AK	Noel Feather	1973	31
202-4/8	49-6/8	14-2/8	14-4/8	10	12	Brooks Range	AK	Brent Chapman	1978	32
202-4/8	58-2/8	15-2/8	14-1/8	13	12	Chuhtna River Drainage	AK	Rickie V. Snell	1982	32
202-0/8	63-1/8	14-2/8	13-5/8	10	8	Moose John River	AK	Kent Brigham	1985	34
201-6/8	59-0/8	11-7/8	13-0/8	13	12	Brooks Range	AK	Mike Rosetti	1985	35
200-2/8	64-2/8	14-4/8	14-0/8	10	11	Dog Salmon River	AK	Robert C. Keadle	1972	36
200-2/8	62-2/8	13-1/8	12-7/8	12	12	King Salmon	AK	Ken Slaght	1982	36
200-0/8	60-4/8	13-6/8	11-0/8	12	12	Skentna River	AK	David Bailey	1983	36
199-6/8	52-0/8	12-5/8	12-2/8	10	11	Timberline Lk. Kenai	AK	DeWayne Benton	1984	39
199-3/8	56-1/8	11-2/8	11-2/8	9	9	Nelchina	AK	Henry Wichers	1962	40
198-7/8	63-7/8	11-1/8	13-0/8	8	10	Gulkana Basin	AK	Thomas L. A. Pucci	1970	41
198-4/8	60-2/8	16-0/8	15-4/8	9	10	Arctic Wildlife Refuge	AK	William Gardner Rowell	1981	42
198-2/8	52-2/8	17-0/8	13-4/8	8	10	Nenana River	AK	Dr. Harley Scholz	1973	43
198-1/8	63-5/8	11-3/8	11-6/8	10	12	Rainy Pass	AK	Dr. Henry C. McDonald	1970	44
197-6/8	64-0/8	11-4/8	11-2/8	12	11	King Salmon	AK	Gary L. Petty	1976	45
197-4/8	65-4/8	13-0/8	14-5/8	6	9	Ugashik River	AK	Robert Borland	1972	46
197-4/8	61-4/8	10-6/8	12-1/8	8	11	Ugashik Lake	AK	John Wallace	1974	46
197-4/8	59-2/8	11-4/8	15-2/8	12	12	Chulitna River Drainage	AK	Rickie D. Snell	1983	46
197-1/8	62-1/8	14-4/8	11-1/8	12	10	Susitna River	AK	Jake Sonnentag	1969	49
197-0/8	62-6/8	12-0/8	12-3/8	8	11	King Salmon	AK	Brian L. Heise	1977	50
196-6/8	63-6/8	13-2/8	16-4/8	6	6	Alaska Peninsula	AK	Phillip Durr	1969	51
195-4/8	55-6/8	12-6/8	13-6/8	10	10	Bonnet Plume Lake	YUK	Billy Ellis	1981	52
194-7/8	53-1/8	11-7/8	12-4/8	13	14	Tustumena Lake	AK	Lavern Davidhizar	1980	53
194-4/8	64-0/8	17-5/8	15-3/8	11	7	Alaska Peninsula	AK	Jim Dougherty	1962	54
194-2/8	61-6/8	12-7/8	13-7/8	7	12	Koyukuk River Area	AK	Thomas J. Hentrick	1984	55
193-5/8	60-3/8	10-7/8	12-5/8	8	9	Beluga Mountain	AK	Dennis A. Lundine	1984	56
193-3/8	53-7/8	11-6/8	11-6/8	10	10	Kenai Peninsula	AK	Robert LaFollette	1962	57
192-7/8	56-3/8	13-7/8	12-7/8	9	10	Little Tok River	AK	Dennis L. Lattery	1977	58
192-5/8	55-1/8	10-5/8	12-5/8	11	13	Wrangell Mountain	AK	Loren Willey	1973	59
192-4/8	60-6/8	14-2/8	12-4/8	7	9	Kluane Lake	YUK	Eugene A. Tieman	1973	60
192-4/8	51-0/8	10-6/8	9-2/8	14	12	Fort Richardson	AK	Donald D. Roberts	1984	60
192-0/8	52-6/8	14-2/8	16-2/8	8	10	Clarence Lake	AK	John Schoenike	1966	62
191-7/8	57-7/8	16-3/8	14-7/8	8	10	Rainy Pass	AK	Rick Tollison	1977	63
191-6/8	54-6/8	12-3/8	12-2/8	9	12	Brooks Range	AK	Joseph Stanevich	1986	64
191-3/8	57-3/8	14-0/8	14-5/8	8	11	Whitefish Lake	AK	Jim Hoss	1975	65
190-3/8	57-3/8	13-0/8	13-0/8	12	12	Teseland Lake	YUK	Paul Schafer	1977	66
190-2/8	58-4/8	14-0/8	13-2/8	9	14	Yentna River	AK	Dan Hollingsworth	1978	67
190-2/8	57-0/8	11-6/8	13-2/8	13	12	Anchorage	AK	Paul Persano	1981	67
190-1/8	60-5/8	11-2/8	10-6/8	10	12	Alaska Peninsula	AK	Rick W. Simpson	1979	69
190-0/8	57-4/8	12-4/8	15-1/8	11	11	Lime Village	AK	Jerad Dittrich	1976	70
189-0/8	53-6/8	13-1/8	13-1/8	9	13	Alaska Peninsula	AK	Richard T. Vance	1972	71
188-7/8	57-7/8	11-1/8	12-5/8	13	10	Sagaranirktok River	AK	Robert G. Chouinard	1980	72
188-7/8	59-1/8	14-3/8	14-3/8	10	9	Cantwell	AK	John W. Williams	1983	72
188-4/8	63-0/8	11-5/8	12-3/8	8	8	Kenai Peninsula	AK	Dale L. Lofstedt	1969	74
188-2/8	61-2/8	12-3/8	11-0/8	10	9	Upper Dog Salmon River	AK	Robert T. Morgan	1983	75
187-7/8	67-7/8	11-4/8	13-4/8	10	11	Jim River	AK	Ernie Dempsey	1981	76
187-7/8	48-1/8	14-4/8	14-4/8	10	13	Watson Lake	YUK	Pete Shepley	1985	76
186-3/8	52-5/8	13-5/8	14-0/8	10	11	Middle Fork	AK	Glen Williams	1969	78
186-2/8	56-2/8	11-2/8	12-4/8	8	8	Cook Inlet	AK	George Moerlein	1961	79
186-2/8	62-6/8	13-2/8	12-2/8	9	9	Kejulik River	AK	John Crump	1981	79
186-1/8	61-5/8	10-6/8	10-7/8	10	9	Cinder River	AK	Glenn Hisey	1976	81
185-5/8	56-3/8	14-0/8	14-3/8	7	6	Cantwell	AK	John Eilertson	1983	82
185-3/8	57-5/8	10-0/8	9-6/8	10	11	King Salmon	AK	Paul Persano	1982	83
184-6/8	55-6/8	11-3/8	12-4/8	5	10	Cinder River	AK	Francis Hosch	1965	84
184-4/8	55-0/8	12-1/8	12-0/8	10	9	Port Heiden	AK	Frank "Rit" Heller	1974	85
184-4/8	59-6/8	12-0/8	12-2/8	9	15	Eklutna Lake	AK	Steve J. Latz	1986	85
184-3/8	53-5/8	9-4/8	13-4/8	12	13	Palmer	AK	A. H. Stange, Jr.	1962	87
184-3/8	63-3/8	12-4/8	11-0/8	12	8	Mishik River	AK	George Wright	1969	87

ALASKA-YUKON MOOSE
(continued)

Minimum Score 170

Score	Greatest Spread	Width of Palm R	Width of Palm L	Number of Points R	Number of Points L	Area	State/Province	Hunter's Name	Date	Rank
184-0/8	59-6/8	11-0/8	10-6/8	6	7	Whitefish Lake	AK	George A. Mohr	1982	89
183-6/8	50-4/8	12-5/8	12-1/8	8	8	Nabesna	AK	George Moerlein	1962	90
183-0/8	54-6/8	11-1/8	11-2/8	10	10	Alaska Peninsula	AK	Jerry Putnam	1973	91
182-7/8	55-1/8	11-0/8	12-0/8	11	11	Eklutna Lake	AK	K. Edward Atwood	1986	92
182-5/8	57-5/8	11-2/8	16-1/8	10	10	Little Delta River	AK	Keith R. Clemmons	1957	93
182-5/8	54-5/8	13-5/8	13-2/8	9	8	Juniper River	AK	Dennis Faulkenberry	1986	93
182-2/8	57-4/8	12-2/8	12-6/8	7	8	Nome	AK	Erv Plotz	1979	95
182-1/8	56-5/8	9-7/8	12-0/8	7	9	Tolic	AK	Reggie Spiegelberg	1986	96
182-0/8	59-0/8	12-0/8	11-4/8	10	10	Slope Mountain	AK	Roger Wheelock	1980	97
181-4/8	57-2/8	14-3/8	16-6/8	7	9	Port Heiden	AK	Bill L. Carlos	1970	98
181-4/8	55-4/8	12-4/8	12-6/8	6	10	Ft. Yukon	AK	Ron Rockwell	1985	98
181-1/8	57-7/8	9-7/8	10-0/8	10	11	Ugashik Lake	AK	Scott Showalter	1972	100
181-1/8	54-1/8	8-6/8	10-2/8	8	10	King Salmon	AK	Joe Fogleman	1982	100
180-7/8	54-1/8	10-6/8	10-3/8	9	11	Earn Lake	YUK	Glen R. Cousins	1978	102
180-5/8	51-3/8	11-1/8	11-2/8	8	9	Port Heiden	AK	Art Heinze	1973	103
180-4/8	57-6/8	12-7/8	11-3/8	10	8	Middle Fork	AK	Norm Goodwin	1969	104
180-2/8	61-4/8	11-6/8	10-2/8	7	10	Alaska Peninsula	AK	Keith Pilz	1976	105
179-6/8	59-2/8	9-3/8	12-3/8	8	7	Susitna River	AK	Robert Pitt	1968	106
179-6/8	54-2/8	14-3/8	12-6/8	9	9	Tag River	AK	Scott Privette	1986	106
179-5/8	53-3/8	11-0/8	11-2/8	11	12	Berry Creek	AK	Larry Jones	1962	108
179-5/8	53-1/8	9-4/8	13-3/8	10	13	Kenai Peninsula	AK	George Moerlein	1969	108
179-1/8	55-7/8	13-1/8	12-0/8	6	7	Fort Yukon	AK	Barry J. Smith	1985	110
179-0/8	53-0/8	13-6/8	13-3/8	8	10	Ft. Richardson County	AK	Earl G. Brown	1984	111
178-4/8	55-4/8	13-0/8	11-5/8	10	9	Kuskokwim River	AK	Bill Stonebraker	1980	112
178-3/8	53-7/8	9-6/8	7-2/8	13	9	Tustamena Lake	AK	Lowell Thomas	1973	113
178-1/8	59-1/8	10-1/8	9-5/8	9	7	Cheeneetnuk River	AK	H. R. "Rusty" Neely	1982	114
177-2/8	51-6/8	12-4/8	12-0/8	9	9	Kenai Peninsula	AK	Alan Perry	1971	115
177-2/8	55-0/8	13-7/8	12-1/8	7	12	Whitehorse	YUK	Scott Koelzer	1977	115
177-2/8	60-0/8	10-1/8	10-0/8	8	7	Juniper River	AK	Boyd Holley	1986	115
177-0/8	62-0/8	9-0/8	9-2/8	5	7	Port Heiden	AK	James R. Scott	1966	118
176-5/8	57-3/8	10-1/8	11-0/8	11	10	Crow Pass	AK	Michael J. Schneider	1982	119
175-4/8	60-4/8	11-6/8	10-0/8	7	8	Susitna River	AK	David A. Drover	1971	120
175-4/8	50-6/8	11-4/8	11-3/8	9	9	Kuparuk River	AK	Bill Krenz	1984	120
174-6/8	58-6/8	8-0/8	9-6/8	8	8	McCarty Creek	AK	Stanley J. Rogers, Jr.	1972	122
174-3/8	57-5/8	12-5/8	12-0/8	13	8	Tustamena Lake	AK	Gary Wall	1974	123
174-3/8	52-1/8	11-3/8	12-3/8	9	10	Koyukuk River	AK	Roger Stewart	1982	123
174-2/8	54-6/8	10-0/8	10-0/8	12	9	Delta River	AK	Dr. R. Congdon	1960	125
174-2/8	58-0/8	11-3/8	11-6/8	11	9	Kagulik River	AK	Mike Hedrick	1984	125
173-6/8	49-0/8	9-2/8	10-7/8	10	11	Chistochina River	AK	Larry L. Schweitzer	1982	127
173-6/8	53-6/8	10-6/8	10-4/8	7	6	Colville River-North Slope	AK	Bob Gulman	1984	127
173-5/8	57-5/8	12-5/8	11-4/8	12	10	Northway	AK	Chuck Adams	1978	129
173-5/8	55-1/8	12-7/8	12-4/8	8	8	Juniper River	AK	Dr. F. D. Elias	1986	129
173-0/8	50-4/8	33-7/8	32-1/8	12	12	Koyukuk River Area	AK	William E. Lee	1984	131
172-5/8	47-1/8	11-0/8	12-0/8	7	7	Brooks Range	AK	John Ribic	1983	132
171-5/8	57-3/8	10-6/8	9-0/8	13	7	Hayes Creek	AK	Keith R. Clemmons	1962	133
171-4/8	49-4/8	10-2/8	10-6/8	12	9	Delta River	AK	Richard R. Cooper	1959	134
170-7/8	58-1/8	12-0/8	10-6/8	8	5	Port Heiden	AK	John E. Lawson	1970	135
170-7/8	48-5/8	11-0/8	9-2/8	9	10	King Salmon River	AK	Bob Sweisthal	1986	135
170-6/8	56-0/8	10-0/8	12-1/8	9	8	Ugashik Lake	AK	Dr. Von A. Mitton	1978	137
170-4/8	52-6/8	12-1/8	11-4/8	10	9	Unit 13D	AK	Dayle Paulson	1969	138

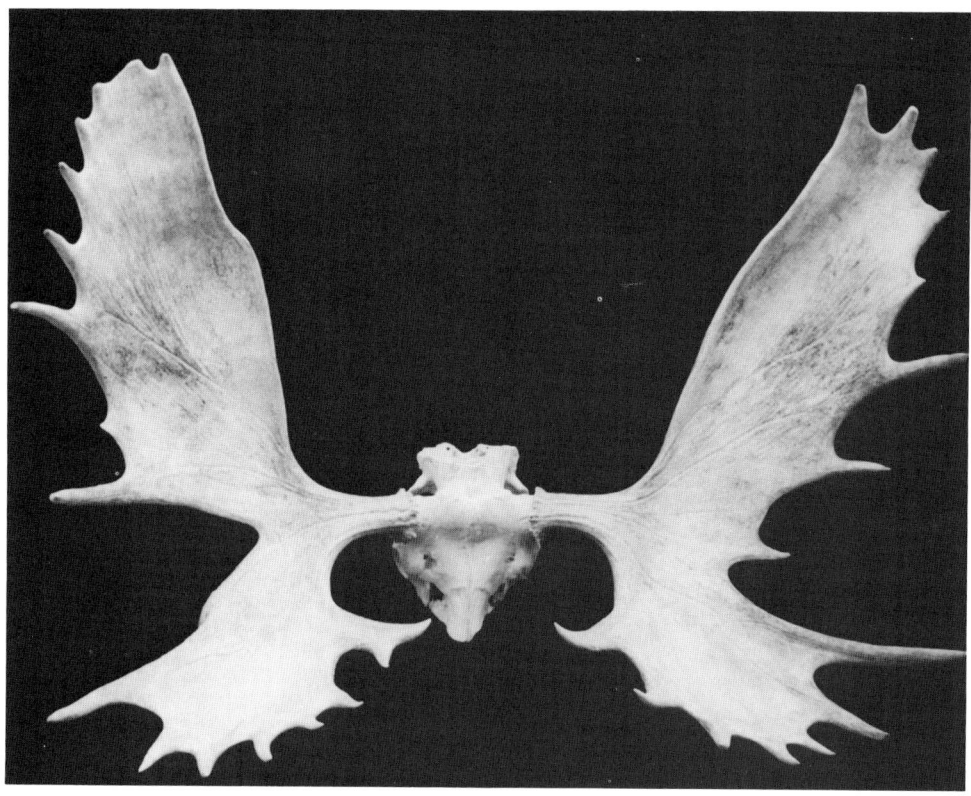

WORLD RECORD CANADA MOOSE
Score: 201 4/8
Mt. Lady Laurier, British Columbia – 1968
Hunter: Peter Halbig

CANADA MOOSE

Alces alces americana and *Alces alces andersoni*   Minimum Score 135

Score	Greatest Spread	Width of Palm R	L	Number of Points R	L	Area	State/ Province	Hunter's Name	Date	Rank
201-4/8	55-2/8	12-4/8	11-4/8	12	12	Mt. Lady Laurier	BC	Peter Halbig	1968	1
198-6/8	56-6/8	16-3/8	16-7/8	15	13	Toad River	BC	Dirk V. Lawyer	1984	2
197-0/8	58-6/8	16-4/8	13-5/8	9	7	Cold Fish Lake	BC	Steve Gorr	1975	3
196-6/8	48-6/8	16-4/8	15-2/8	12	13	Besa River	BC	Edward Flowerdew	1976	4
196-2/8	59-5/8	14-4/8	13-7/8	10	13	Skeena	BC	Larry Garoutte	1972	5
192-6/8	56-6/8	11-5/8	10-5/8	12	13	Cassiar Mountains	BC	Thomas B. Frye	1978	6
187-5/8	57-0/8	13-3/8	12-1/8	11	13	Turnagin River	BC	Glenn Hisey	1978	7
186-2/8	54-0/8	11-2/8	11-2/8	10	11	Ash Mt.	BC	Pink Atkins	1984	8
185-3/8	54-3/8	11-4/8	11-3/8	13	11	Mossy River	SAS	Jerome J. Huseby	1966	9
184-7/8	58-7/8	11-3/8	11-4/8	9	9	Goat Creek	BC	Atley Lovelace	1974	10
184-6/8	55-7/8	11-7/8	11-5/8	13	8	Blanchard Creek	BC	Ron Johnson	1974	11
183-4/8	60-6/8	10-4/8	11-5/8	10	9	Terminus Valley	BC	Paul P. Schafer	1975	12
182-1/8	50-5/8	11-2/8	11-1/8	10	10	Stanley Creek	BC	Donald L. Pahl	1973	13
181-1/8	51-5/8	12-0/8	11-5/8	12	13	Halfway River	BC	Duane L. Scroggins	1977	14
180-1/8	47-3/8	11-6/8	11-1/8	12	13	Unit 23	ONT	Paul F. J. Petrie	1985	15
179-6/8	50-6/8	11-5/8	13-2/8	11	12	Dease Lake	BC	Robert G. Petersen	1985	16
178-5/8	51-2/8	11-1/8	12-6/8	10	10	Kechika River	BC	Scott L. Koelzer	1976	17
177-2/8	52-2/8	10-7/8	9-0/8	10	8	Thrimbal Lake	BC	Chester Schardt	1966	18
176-0/8	55-2/8	13-6/8	14-2/8	9	14	Long Range Mountains	NFL	Waldemar D. Maya	1965	19
175-4/8	50-6/8	11-2/8	9-6/8	10	10	Moose Lake	BC	Dan Martin	1986	20
175-3/8	51-7/8	11-4/8	11-7/8	8	9	Dease Lake	BC	Bill Coburn	1979	21
175-0/8	52-0/8	10-1/8	10-7/8	10	9	Central	BC	Ronald Lauretti	1973	22
175-0/8	53-4/8	10-4/8	12-0/8	8	10	Kechika River	BC	Paul F. Schafer	1974	22
174-5/8	50-5/8	11-3/8	10-7/8	12	11	McConnell Range	BC	Dave Young	1976	24

CANADA MOOSE

(continued)

Minimum Score 135

Score	Greatest Spread	Width of Palm R	Width of Palm L	Number of Points R	Number of Points L	Area	State/ Province	Hunter's Name	Date	Rank
174-3/8	56-1/8	13-0/8	10-2/8	10	7	Algoma District	ONT	Paul Kovich	1981	25
172-0/8	50-6/8	11-4/8	11-7/8	10	10	Thutade Lake	BC	Larry Nirk	1975	26
172-0/8	53-0/8	11-2/8	10-2/8	9	7	Timmins	ONT	Carl Doerner	1976	26
171-6/8	48-4/8	10-4/8	12-2/8	12	11	S. Branch River	NFL	Paul Erdbrink	1966	28
171-5/8	44-1/8	15-5/8	13-1/8	13	11	Cape Anquille Mountains	NFL	Terrance Estes	1966	29
170-7/8	49-3/8	10-2/8	10-6/8	9	9	Graham River	BC	Dr. James Shubert	1979	30
170-4/8	44-4/8	10-7/8	12-4/8	13	12	Quibell	ONT	Fred Bear	1945	31
169-1/8	50-7/8	12-5/8	12-2/8	9	11	Stikine River	BC	Dave Brousseau	1979	32
168-1/8	45-7/8	12-5/8	11-1/8	13	10	Fort St. John	BC	Duane Hicks	1981	33
167-0/8	58-4/8	10-7/8	10-7/8	11	11	Argenteuil	QUE	Richard K. Clark	1983	34
164-3/8	47-7/8	10-2/8	10-3/8	9	12	Fort St. John	BC	Chuck Adams	1976	35
164-1/8	49-3/8	12-5/8	11-2/8	12	10	Tweedsmuir Pk.	BC	Glenn St. Charles	1954	36
163-2/8	45-2/8	9-4/8	10-2/8	10	9	Cassiar Mountains	BC	Harold Boyack	1978	37
163-0/8	50-4/8	10-1/8	11-2/8	6	6	Nakanok Lake	BC	Phil Forte	1984	38
163-0/8	54-0/8	9-1/8	9-0/8	8	8	Sudbury	ONT	Vite Chomicki	1986	38
162-4/8	48-0/8	9-0/8	9-0/8	10	11	Kapakasing	ONT	Ron Alguire	1963	40
161-4/8	50-0/8	6-4/8	9-5/8	7	7	Tatla Lake	BC	Bill Nickerson	1985	41
161-2/8	46-6/8	10-0/8	10-1/8	9	9	Schalze River	BC	Dale Snyder	1983	42
161-1/8	45-5/8	10-5/8	11-6/8	11	11	Lloyds River	NFL	Harold A. Hill	1966	43
160-4/8	46-0/8	10-4/8	10-4/8	10	9	Muskwa River	BC	W. Jay Boynton III	1970	44
159-1/8	51-7/8	9-5/8	8-7/8	9	8	Gogama	ONT	Jack Richard	1984	45
158-7/8	50-7/8	12-1/8	11-7/8	13	11	Kirkland Lake	ONT	Luther Gordon	1963	46
158-0/8	49-0/8	8-0/8	8-5/8	7	8	Williams Lake	BC	Gary Swan	1968	47
158-0/8	47-6/8	10-2/8	9-7/8	11	13	Strathcona	ALB	Darrell Stiles	1985	47
156-2/8	42-0/8	9-6/8	9-5/8	9	9	AK Hwy. Milepost 163	BC	John Zahrte	1978	49
155-6/8	48-6/8	9-5/8	8-7/8	7	9	Maniwaki	QUE	Jay Pitha	1983	50
155-3/8	34-2/8	8-0/8	10-0/8	8	10	Smithers	BC	Chris Vanderhorst	1974	51
155-3/8	48-7/8	8-7/8	9-2/8	9	11	Kapuskasing	ONT	Tom Nowakowski	1980	51
155-1/8	51-5/8	10-3/8	10-4/8	8	9	Algoma District	ONT	Carol Wert	1963	53
154-7/8	49-7/8	10-3/8	11-4/8	8	11	Saddler Pond	NFL	Paul Locey	1982	54
154-1/8	44-3/8	9-7/8	9-7/8	8	11	Thutade Lake	BC	Donald N. Lehman	1973	55
153-5/8	45-3/8	10-6/8	11-2/8	7	12	Lloyds River	NFL	Harold A. Hill	1964	56
153-4/8	45-2/8	9-0/8	7-2/8	8	8	?	QUE	Bruce R. Wilson	1983	57
152-7/8	42-7/8	9-1/8	9-7/8	10	10	Zone 1	NFL	Harold A. Hill	1961	58
152-4/8	49-0/8	8-0/8	8-3/8	6	6	Gilbault Creek	BC	David V. Collis	1977	59
152-2/8	49-6/8	11-2/8	10-6/8	5	6	Naking Lake	BC	Guy Anttila	1982	60
151-6/8	47-6/8	11-5/8	9-6/8	9	10	?	NFL	Bill Hirst	1960	61
151-6/8	44-0/8	10-6/8	9-4/8	9	9	Duti Lake	BC	Walter J. Sawicki	1972	61
151-5/8	53-3/8	8-7/8	9-6/8	8	6	Stikine River	BC	James A. Farnsworth	1973	63
148-3/8	42-1/8	9-2/8	9-2/8	10	10	S. Branch	NFL	W. P. Hirst	1964	64
146-6/8	39-4/8	8-1/8	9-5/8	8	10	King George IV Pond	NFL	Bill Hirst	1966	65
146-0/8	46-0/8	8-4/8	8-0/8	9	8	Tarnasel Lake	BC	Dr. Rex Hancock	1960	66
145-6/8	47-4/8	8-3/8	8-4/8	9	8	Princess Lake	NFL	John Iannuzzo	1967	67
145-4/8	45-4/8	9-1/8	8-3/8	9	8	Tatlatui Lake	BC	G. Fred Asbell	1975	68
145-3/8	48-5/8	9-0/8	8-6/8	9	9	Duck Mtns.	MAN	Richard Hay	1986	69
145-1/8	46-3/8	12-4/8	9-5/8	7	8	Trap Narrows Lake	ONT	John A. Schmidt	1985	70
144-6/8	41-6/8	9-4/8	11-0/8	9	11	Dease Lake	BC	Dave Ramsay	1981	71
144-2/8	50-0/8	8-5/8	10-3/8	8	9	Raith	ONT	Gerald D. Young	1983	72
140-7/8	43-1/8	9-0/8	9-0/8	6	6	Strathcona	ALB	Pat Marek	1985	73
140-2/8	48-2/8	7-0/8	7-2/8	7	7	Princess Lake	NFL	John Musacchia	1966	74
139-5/8	40-7/8	8-0/8	9-0/8	8	8	Fort St. John	BC	Michael R. Traub	1981	75
138-0/8	34-4/8	11-2/8	10-5/8	8	10	St. George Lake	NFL	Bill Carlos	1968	76
137-7/8	41-5/8	8-1/8	10-6/8	7	8	Princess Lake	NFL	Ken Rapp	1966	77
137-5/8	44-7/8	7-7/8	7-0/8	8	9	Thutade Lake	BC	Kim S Ades	1984	78
135-7/8	43-3/8	7-4/8	7-2/8	7	6	Sangudo	ALB	Allan C. Doell	1983	79
135-4/8	47-2/8	8-3/8	9-0/8	4	7	Sheerway Lake	QUE	Richard A. Sawyer	1985	80

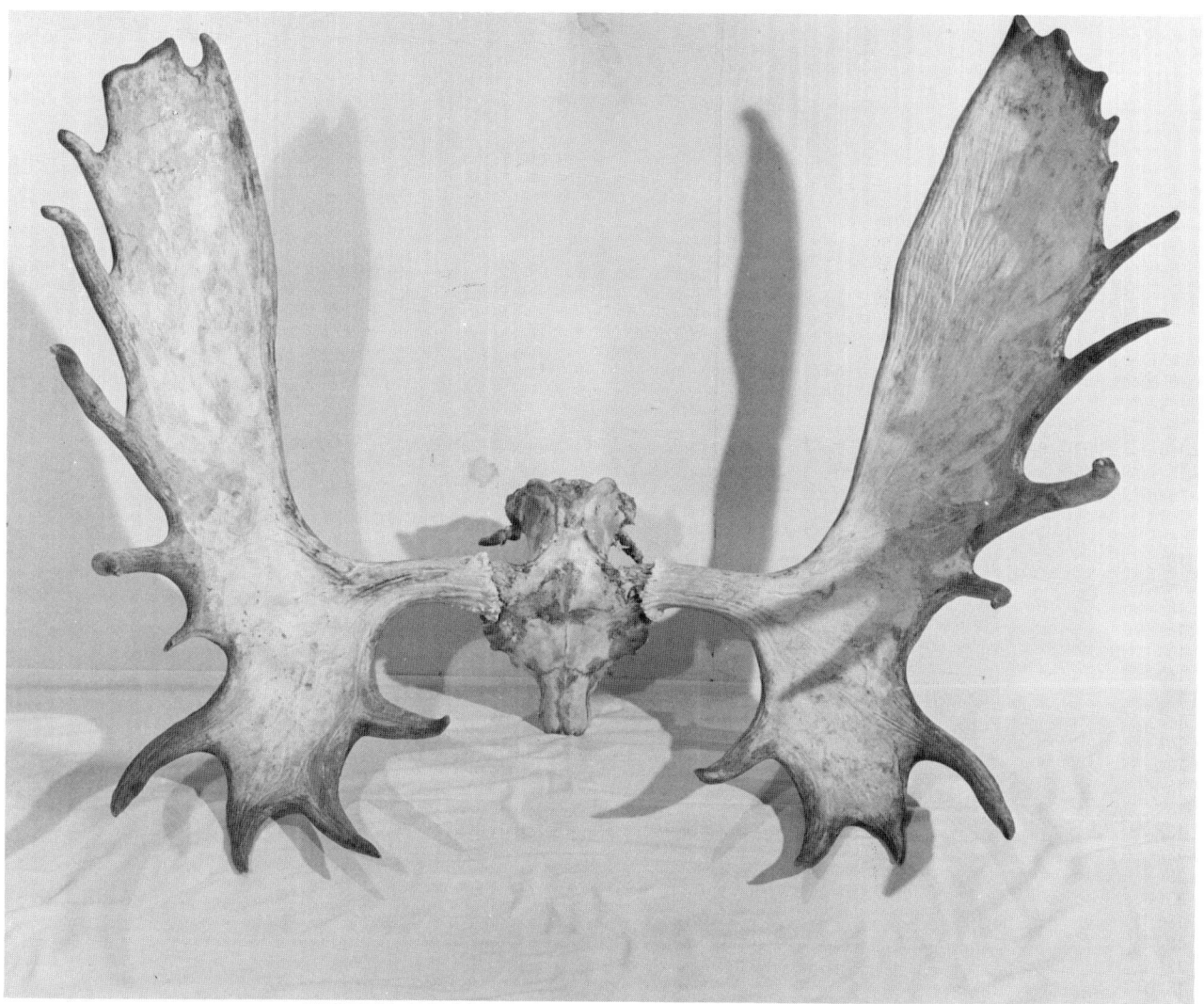

WORLD RECORD SHIRAS *(WYOMING)* MOOSE
Score: 180 3/8
Fremont County, Idaho – 1983
Hunter: Kenneth K. Fordyce

SHIRAS *(WYOMING)* MOOSE

Alces alces shirasi

Score	Greatest Spread	Width of Palm R	Width of Palm L	Number of Points R	Number of Points L	Area	State/ Province	Hunter's Name	Date	Rank
180-3/8	48-1/8	10-4/8	11-0/8	10	10	Fremont County	ID	Kenneth K. Fordyce	1983	1
172-0/8	46-6/8	10-4/8	10-0/8	12	11	Madison County	ID	Trent Wood	1983	2
166-4/8	45-4/8	10-6/8	13-2/8	9	11	Sheridan County	WY	Don Groskopf	1986	3
165-5/8	47-7/8	10-1/8	8-7/8	11	11	Gallatin County	MT	Albert D. Williams	1986	4
164-7/8	49-3/8	8-6/8	9-6/8	9	10	Newsome Creek	ID	Oliver E. Robinett	1980	5
164-1/8	41-3/8	13-4/8	13-2/8	14	12	Gallitan County	MT	Larry Schweitzer	1984	6
163-6/8	44-6/8	13-1/8	13-4/8	12	10	Lincoln County	WY	Walter Walbridge	1980	7
160-6/8	51-6/8	9-3/8	8-0/8	10	8	Bonneville County	ID	Marty George	1986	8
159-6/8	43-0/8	15-4/8	12-0/8	6	7	Teton County	WY	Daniel B. White	1978	9
159-1/8	49-5/8	12-7/8	10-7/8	8	10	Gallatin Canyon	MT	Keith Wheat	1960	10
158-6/8	50-2/8	10-6/8	11-0/8	11	11	Lincoln County	WY	Mike Smith	1976	11
157-1/8	45-3/8	11-6/8	12-1/8	8	8	Bighorn Mountains	WY	Jeffrey L. Welsh	1980	12
154-0/8	49-4/8	9-1/8	8-7/8	8	9	Scott Lake	MT	C. P. Mendenhall	1960	13
154-0/8	45-2/8	9-2/8	9-2/8	10	11	Caribou County	ID	Brett Dee Hymas	1986	13
153-4/8	45-4/8	10-0/8	12-6/8	9	11	Deer Lodge County	MT	Terry L. Button	1986	15
150-7/8	42-3/8	10-7/8	9-7/8	10	10	Spencer	ID	Joseph E. Packer	1981	16
147-4/8	41-2/8	10-0/8	11-3/8	8	10	Sublette County	WY	Michael Beckwith	1985	17
147-1/8	43-5/8	7-5/8	8-3/8	8	9	Summit County	UT	Jerry Cross	1979	18
147-0/8	45-0/8	11-3/8	9-6/8	9	8	Teton County	WY	Jerry Bowen	1982	19
146-4/8	44-4/8	7-3/8	7-5/8	6	6	Absorka Wilderness	MT	Randy Cook	1982	20
145-1/8	45-1/8	9-4/8	8-2/8	5	6	Beaverhead County	MT	Greg L. Munther	1982	21
143-2/8	47-6/8	9-3/8	10-0/8	9	7	Moose Creek	ID	Stanley Leake	1979	22
142-6/8	40-6/8	9-4/8	9-4/8	8	7	Gallatin County	MT	Stuart J. Georgitis	1986	23
141-0/8	41-1/8	9-5/8	9-4/8	8	7	Grey's River	WY	V. Kay Bangerter	1978	24
140-2/8	42-2/8	10-5/8	10-6/8	9	6	Pine Canyon	WY	Keith Dana	1977	25
139-3/8	42-1/8	8-4/8	7-6/8	5	7	Idaho County	ID	Ray Torrey	1968	26
138-2/8	42-0/8	9-6/8	7-6/8	9	7	Libby	MT	Thomas A. DeShazer	1965	27
137-7/8	47-1/8	9-2/8	11-3/8	7	9	Pinedale	WY	R. H. Siegert	1969	28
137-2/8	42-4/8	10-4/8	9-0/8	8	11	Salt River	WY	Robert K. Robinson	1978	29
136-7/8	42-1/8	6-5/8	9-6/8	8	10	Cache County	UT	Larry Cross	1986	30
135-3/8	46-1/8	9-4/8	8-4/8	8	8	Big Piney	WY	Dave Funderburk	1978	31
134-7/8	40-5/8	8-0/8	10-2/8	6	8	Lincoln County	MT	Jerry Brown	1982	32
132-1/8	42-1/8	8-5/8	9-1/8	8	8	Lincoln County	WY	Lee Challinor	1982	33
131-7/8	46-7/8	8-2/8	8-6/8	7	8	White Sand Creek	ID	J. David Powers	1981	34
131-6/8	44-0/8	7-6/8	7-7/8	7	7	Fontenell Creek	WY	Kevin Jackson	1980	35
131-2/8	34-4/8	10-6/8	11-0/8	8	8	Bonneville County	ID	Edward Keller	1986	36
130-7/8	39-5/8	8-6/8	9-1/8	9	8	Lincoln County	WY	Dave Cordes	1982	37
130-6/8	46-2/8	7-2/8	7-5/8	6	6	Lincoln County	WY	Ken Allen	1986	38
130-5/8	38-3/8	8-4/8	8-3/8	7	11	Park County	WY	Greg Deatsman	1985	39
129-2/8	37-2/8	8-6/8	8-5/8	8	8	Big Piney	WY	Jerrold M. Judkins	1979	40
128-1/8	40-5/8	6-4/8	6-0/8	6	6	Teton County	WY	Keith Frick	1984	41
127-4/8	35-0/8	9-6/8	12-0/8	8	8	Lincoln County	WY	Al Bitker	1982	42
127-4/8	36-6/8	7-0/8	7-4/8	7	7	Idaho County	ID	Brad Johnson	1985	42
125-5/8	49-3/8	8-2/8	7-7/8	8	7	Weber County	UT	Clark Stokes	1986	44
124-6/8	40-2/8	10-1/8	10-1/8	5	3	Lincoln County	WY	David H. Boland	1977	45
124-0/8	40-4/8	7-4/8	8-4/8	8	6	Fremont County	WY	John Applegate	1977	46
121-2/8	39-6/8	7-3/8	7-2/8	9	6	Big Piney	WY	Vern A. Butler	1973	47
120-7/8	42-5/8	6-7/8	7-2/8	5	5	Sublette County	WY	Wade L. Carstens	1982	48
120-0/8	49-4/8	3-7/8	5-6/8	5	7	Boulder Lake	WY	Dick Mauch	1959	49
119-4/8	40-4/8	7-3/8	7-4/8	4	4	Idaho County	ID	David Wilken	1986	50
119-0/8	35-4/8	7-0/8	8-6/8	8	9	La Barge	WY	Glen Talbott	1980	51
117-5/8	38-5/8	7-5/8	7-1/8	7	6	Uinta County	WY	David Kaden	1982	52
117-5/8	44-3/8	12-0/8	9-2/8	11	3	Cache County	UT	Mark Wright	1985	52
116-7/8	45-1/8	6-0/8	6-0/8	5	5	Jagg Creek	WY	Robert W. Steller	1975	54
116 6/8	42-0/8	8-1/8	7-2/8	6	6	Lincoln County	WY	Kirt Prestwich	1986	55
116-2/8	41-4/8	8-6/8	9-6/8	5	4	Lincoln County	MT	Lee Lampton	1982	56
116-0/8	33-6/8	8-3/8	7-6/8	8	7	Lincoln County	WY	Glenn Hisey	1982	57
115-5/8	36-1/8	8-6/8	7-5/8	8	8	Lincoln County	WY	Cathy Lee Jordan	1983	58

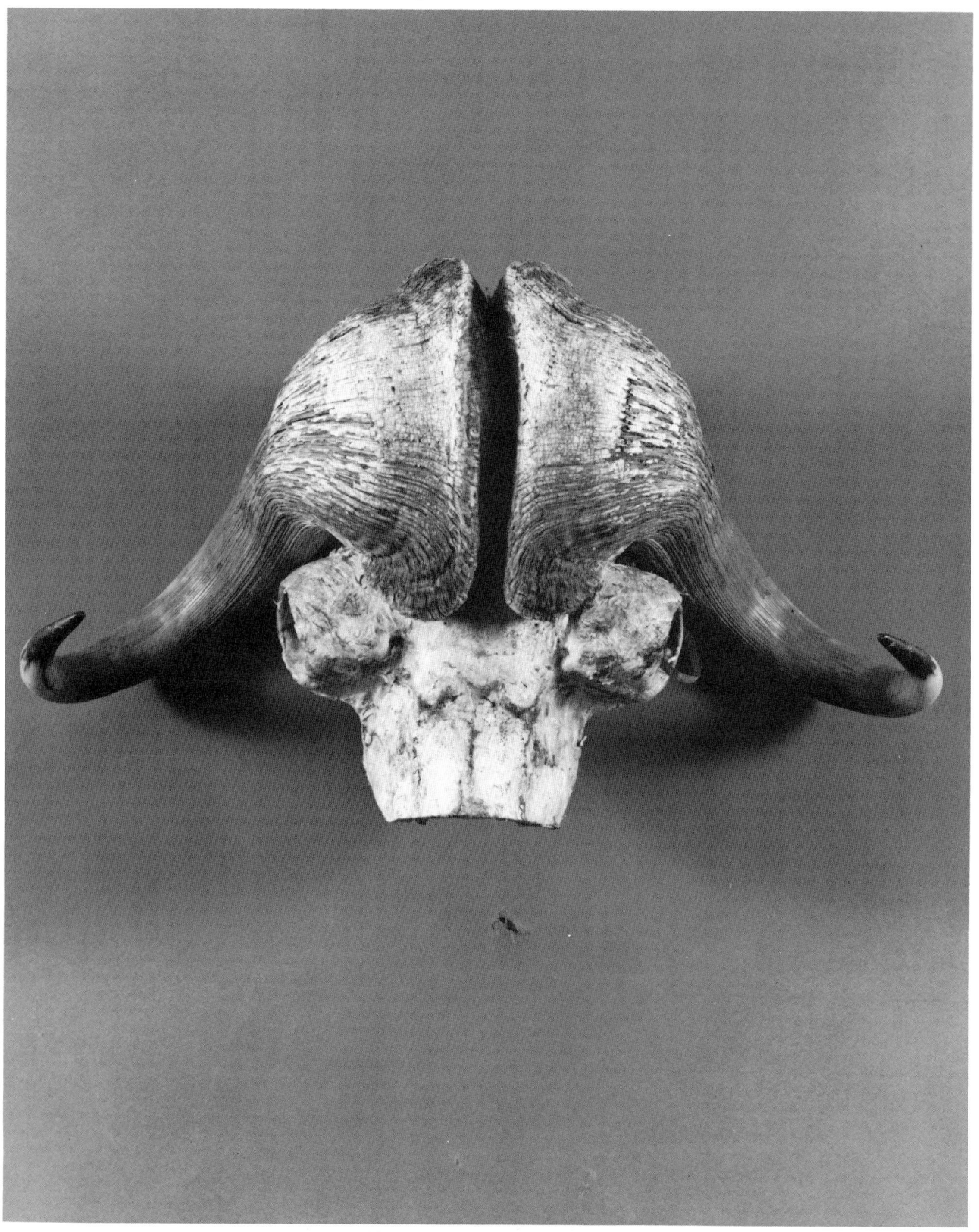

WORLD RECORD MUSKOX
Score: 111 4/8
Banks Island, Northwest Territories – 1985
Hunter: David V. Collis

MUSKOX

Ovibos moschatus moschatus and certain related subspecies

Score	Length of Horn R	L	Circumference of Base R	L	Greatest Spread	Area	State/ Province	Hunter's Name	Date	Rank
111-4/8	26-3/8	26-0/8	9-5/8	9-5/8	25-5/8	Banks Island	NWT	David V. Collis	1985	1
109-4/8	26-2/8	26-5/8	9-5/8	9-5/8	26-7/8	Banks Island	NWT	Roger Anderson	1986	2
109-4/8	26-1/8	26-0/8	9-4/8	9-5/8	25-5/8	Banks Island	NWT	Larry Hoff	1986	2
108-4/8	26-3/8	28-2/8	9-5/8	9-6/8	27-0/8	Paulatuk	NWT	Ron Kolpin	1981	4
108-0/8	27-5/8	28-5/8	8-4/8	8-4/8	25-4/8	Nelson Island	AK	Dexter Lemon	1986	5
108-0/8	26-0/8	25-3/8	9-3/8	9-4/8	26-1/8	Parry Peninsula	NWT	Theodore Dzienis	1986	5
107-4/8	26-3/8	26-0/8	9-5/8	10-0/8	25-7/8	Banks Island	NWT	John McAteer	1986	7
106-6/8	25-5/8	26-2/8	8-5/8	9-0/8	27-6/8	Banks Island	NWT	Billy Ellis	1982	8
106-6/8	25-5/8	25-6/8	8-6/8	8-2/8	27-6/8	Nelson Island	AK	Dexter Lemon	1985	8
106-4/8	24-3/8	24-5/8	8-3/8	8-4/8	27-3/8	Nunivak Island	AK	Joseph O. Fogleman	1976	10
106-4/8	26-7/8	27-3/8	8-0/8	8-0/8	27-4/8	Nunivak Island	AK	John D. "Jack" Frost	1986	10
106-2/8	25-4/8	25-5/8	8-2/8	8-2/8	27-5/8	Kaktovik	AK	Herman Griese	1984	12
105-6/8	25-1/8	25-1/8	9-2/8	9-2/8	26-0/8	Banks Island	NWT	Kirk Westervelt	1986	13
105-0/8	25-1/8	26-4/8	8-7/8	8-6/8	26-2/8	Kaktovik	AK	Bill Petrovish	1984	14
104-6/8	24-5/8	25-0/8	9-4/8	9-2/8	25-0/8	Banks Island	NWT	Suzy Sherer	1986	15
104-4/8	27-2/8	25-4/8	9-2/8	9-2/8	27-2/8	Banks Island	NWT	Dr. Howard Schneider	1985	16
104-4/8	25-4/8	25-2/8	9-0/8	9-1/8	25-4/8	Banks Island	NWT	Ron Sherer	1986	16
104-4/8	24-6/8	25-0/8	9-2/8	9-2/8	26-0/8	Banks Island	NWT	Richard L. Westervelt	1986	16
104-0/8	24-3/8	24-6/8	9-6/8	9-5/8	24-4/8	Banks Island	NWT	Larry Hoff	1986	19
103-2/8	27-0/8	27-0/8	8-1/8	8-2/8	25-5/8	Polatuck	NWT	Erv Plotz	1980	20
103-0/8	22-6/8	23-5/8	8-5/8	8-4/8	26-7/8	Nunivak Island	AK	P.J. Londo	1977	21
102-6/8	25-0/8	27-0/8	8-7/8	8-3/8	29-0/8	Nunivak Island	AK	Jim Voeller	1978	22
101-4/8	24-6/8	25-2/8	8-6/8	8-6/8	27-6/8	Nunivak Island	AK	David A. Widby	1983	23
101-0/8	25-1/8	25-0/8	8-0/8	8-2/8	26-2/8	Nunivak Island	AK	Edward L. Russell	1984	24
100-6/8	24-1/8	25-1/8	7-7/8	7-7/8	24-1/8	Nunivak Island	AK	Dr. Von A. Mitton	1978	25
100-4/8	25-2/8	26-2/8	7-7/8	7-6/8	28-1/8	Nunivak Island	AK	Bruce J. Werba	1977	26
100-4/8	24-5/8	26-4/8	10-2/8	10-1/8	27-2/8	Banks Island	NWT	Dr. Howard Schneider	1985	26
100-2/8	24-5/8	25-5/8	8-3/8	7-7/8	24-0/8	Nunivak Island	AK	Curt Lynn	1984	28
97-0/8	24-4/8	24-1/8	8-3/8	8-4/8	28-0/8	Nunivak Island	AK	Michael J. Schneider	1983	29
95-4/8	21-0/8	20-6/8	8-0/8	8-2/8	26-2/8	Nunivak Island	AK	Dick Gulman	1978	30
94-4/8	24-5/8	23-6/8	6-6/8	6-6/8	26-7/8	Nunivak Island	AK	C. Vernon Humble	1976	31

WORLD RECORD PRONGHORN *(TIE)*
Score: 85 0/8
Moffat County, Colorado – 1983
Hunter: Judd Cooney

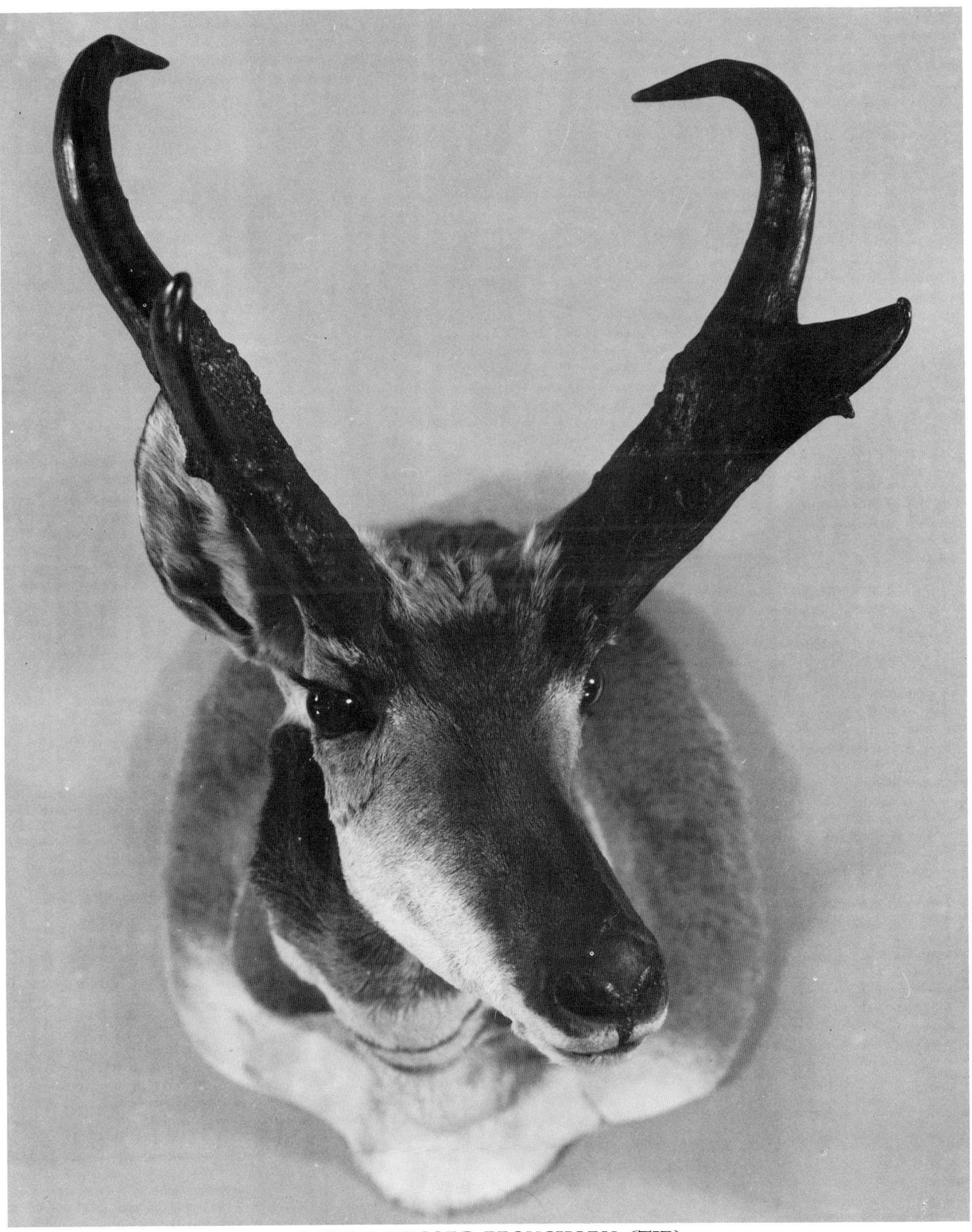

WORLD RECORD PRONGHORN *(TIE)*
Score: 85 0/8
Raleigh, North Dakota – 1958
Hunter: Archie Malm

PRONGHORN

Antilocapra americana americana and related subspecies   Minimum Score 64

Score	Length of Horn		Circumference of Base		Greatest Spread	Area	State/ Province	Hunter's Name	Date	Rank
	R	L	R	L						
85-0/8	15-1/8	15-0/8	6-7/8	6-5/8	12-6/8	Raleigh	ND	Archie Malm	1958	1
85-0/8	17-2/8	17-1/8	6-4/8	6-4/8	10-3/8	Moffat County	CO	Judd Cooney	1983	1
84-0/8	16-2/8	15-5/8	6-7/8	6-7/8	11-6/8	Perkins County	SD	Spike Jorgensen	1964	3
83-6/8	15-4/8	15-2/8	7-3/8	7-3/8	15-2/8	Washoe County	NV	Fred Church	1978	4
83-6/8	15-2/8	15-6/8	6-3/8	6-4/8	11-6/8	Nye County	NV	Rich Sauer	1985	4
83-0/8	17-0/8	17-0/8	6-0/8	6-0/8	12-3/8	Eddy County	NM	Jim Stell	1984	6
83-0/8	16-6/8	16-6/8	6-1/8	6-0/8	13-6/8	Coconino County	AZ	William P Pate	1985	6
82-4/8	15-1/8	16-0/8	6-5/8	6-3/8	6-3/8	Butte	ND	Edward J. Weigel	1966	8
82-0/8	17-4/8	18-2/8	6-6/8	6-2/8	15-6/8	Santa Rosa	NM	C. E. Foster, Jr.	1961	9
82-0/8	16-3/8	16-2/8	6-3/8	6-4/8	9-6/8	Coconino County	AZ	Fred W. Fernow, Jr.	1981	9
81-6/8	16-2/8	16-0/8	7-4/8	7-4/8	8-2/8	Graham County	AZ	Don Lawing	1983	11
81-4/8	15-4/8	15-1/8	7-0/8	6-7/8	13-1/8	Washoe County	NV	Owen K. Mercer, Jr.	1981	12
81-4/8	16-3/8	16-6/8	6-2/8	5-7/8	13-6/8	Yellowstone County	MT	Robert M. Labert	1984	12
81-2/8	15-4/8	15-3/8	7-1/8	7-1/8	6-6/8	Sweetwater County	WY	Clifford Rockhold	1985	14
81-2/8	15-2/8	15-1/8	6-2/8	6-3/8	10-4/8	Sublette County	WY	Ronald J. Clark	1986	14
81-0/8	15-7/8	15-6/8	6-7/8	6-6/8	10-7/8	Mercer	ND	James Lahman	1971	16
81-0/8	15-3/8	15-4/8	7-0/8	6-6/8	12-0/8	Ormsby	WY	Richard L. Huber	1978	16
81-0/8	15-4/8	15-4/8	6-6/8	6-6/8	11-6/8	Elko County	NV	Darcey W. Tate	1979	16
81-0/8	14-6/8	16-4/8	6-3/8	6-4/8	10-0/8	Coconino County	AZ	Jim Scott	1984	16
81-0/8	15-5/8	16-6/8	6-3/8	6-3/8	9-2/8	Yavapai County	AZ	Dan Robbins	1986	16
80-6/8	15-5/8	15-5/8	6-3/8	6-2/8	11-6/8	Corona	NM	Robert W. Davis	1959	21
80-6/8	16-4/8	16-4/8	6-6/8	6-6/8	17-2/8	Jackson County	CO	Steve Jackson	1985	21
80-4/8	16-5/8	17-0/8	5-5/8	5-6/8	10-3/8	Humboldt County	NV	Shane E. Evans	1984	23
80-4/8	15-0/8	15-0/8	6-4/8	6-4/8	9-7/8	Sweetwater County	WY	Christopher J. Cordes	1986	23
80-2/8	14-5/8	14-5/8	7-1/8	7-3/8	8-6/8	Casper	WY	Dr. J. A. Martin	1964	25
80-2/8	14-1/8	13-7/8	7-3/8	7-3/8	10-6/8	Butte County	ID	Danny Owens	1974	25
80-2/8	15-4/8	15-3/8	6-6/8	6-760	8-7/8	Modoc County	CA	Ed Dowling	1982	25
80-2/8	14-5/8	14-7/8	6-6/8	6-7/8	10-4/8	Yuma County	CO	Mark Sievers	1982	25
80-0/8	16-6/8	16-5/8	6-1/8	6-1/8	13-6/8	Laramie	WY	Dave A. Current	1969	29
80-0/8	16-0/8	15-7/8	6-2/8	6-2/8	10-7/8	Washoe County	NV	Kevin S. Wheeler	1983	29
79-6/8	15-4/8	14-6/8	7-1/8	7-3/8	9-3/8	Mellette County	SD	John Anderson	1970	31
79-6/8	15-4/8	15-4/8	6-0/8	6-0/8	10-5/8	Washoe County	NV	Mike J. Ellena	1983	31
79-4/8	14-3/8	14-4/8	5-7/8	5-6/8	11-6/8	Plaza	ND	Bill Kurry	1976	33
79-4/8	16-4/8	16-0/8	6-3/8	6-4/8	9-0/8	Gerber Reservoir	OR	Harold Benson	1977	33
79-4/8	14-4/8	14-4/8	6-3/8	6-3/8	7-5/8	Converse County	WY	Russ Guerndt, Jr.	1985	33
79-4/8	14-1/8	14-0/8	7-2/8	7-2/8	9-2/8	Carbon County	WY	Michael L. Cone	1986	33
79-2/8	14-3/8	14-5/8	6-4/8	6-2/8	9-2/8	Musselshell County	MT	Jon Kowalski	1982	37
79-2/8	15-5/8	15-3/8	6-6/8	6-4/8	9-4/8	Moffat County	CO	Alan Martellaro	1986	37
79-0/8	15-0/8	15-3/8	6-3/8	6-3/8	11-5/8	Washoe County	NV	Tom Thompson	1979	39
79-0/8	15-7/8	15-6/8	6-2/8	6-2/8	12-6/8	Carbon County	WY	Michael Ambur	1982	39
79-0/8	14-7/8	15-0/8	6-3/8	6-2/8	8-5/8	Carbon County	WY	Kim Cooper	1983	39
79-0/8	14-6/8	14-5/8	7-2/8	7-3/8	7-0/8	Sweetwater County	WY	Steve Rueck	1985	39
78-6/8	16-5/8	16-2/8	6-4/8	6-2/8	7-4/8	Sweetwater County	WY	Mike Holmes	1982	43
78-6/8	14-2/8	14-4/8	7-1/8	7-1/8	12-2/8	Buffalo	WY	Steve Winkey	1982	43
78-6/8	15-7/8	15-5/8	6-5/8	6-4/8	9-5/8	Natrona County	WY	Charles Webster	1983	43
78-6/8	16-1/8	16-3/8	6-3/8	6-3/8	15-4/8	Clark County	ID	Dennis R Marshall	1985	43
78-4/8	16-0/8	15-7/8	6-0/8	6-2/8	11-4/8	Roswell	NM	Dr. D. A. Henbest	1957	47
78-4/8	15-1/8	14-7/8	6-5/8	6-5/8	10-0/8	Plaza	ND	Bennie J. Burtts	1967	47
78-4/8	14-4/8	14-1/8	6-3/8	6-2/8	10-6/8	Klamath County	OR	Paul D. Lewis	1976	47
78-4/8	13-7/8	14-0/8	6-4/8	6-2/8	8-2/8	Moffat County	CO	Mike Brezonick	1986	47
78-3/8	14-4/8	14-6/8	6-6/8	6-6/8	15-3/8	Moffat County	CO	Steven J. Lepic	1983	51
78-2/8	17-3/8	17-1/8	5-5/8	5-6/8	14-6/8	Santa Rosa	NM	James L. Henry	1961	52
78-2/8	15-2/8	15-0/8	6-2/8	6-2/8	10-6/8	Wheatland County	MT	Phil Reno	1981	52
78-2/8	16-1/8	16-1/8	6-2/8	6-1/8	6-2/8	Moffat County	CO	Dan Liccardi	1982	52
78-2/8	15-2/8	15-7/8	5-7/8	5-7/8	7-3/8	Moffat County	CO	Ralph L. Albright	1985	52
78-2/8	14-3/8	14-4/8	6-1/8	6-1/8	11-3/8	Cochise County	AZ	Michael John Bylina	1985	52
78-2/8	13-7/8	14-0/8	6-2/8	6-2/8	12-6/8	Sweetwater County	WY	Tom Domson	1986	52
78-0/8	15-0/8	14-7/8	6-3/8	6-2/8	11-5/8	Lemhi County	ID	Eugene J. Ottonello	1980	58
78-0/8	15-1/8	15-2/8	6-2/8	6-1/8	11-3/8	Stanley County	SD	Rick Ray	1980	58
78-0/8	15-3/8	15-2/8	6-7/8	6-4/8	13-7/8	Moffat County	CO	Tony Seahorn	1980	58
78-0/8	14-4/8	14-5/8	5-7/8	6-0/8	12-4/8	Stanley County	SD	George Hipple	1982	58
78-0/8	14-7/8	14-4/8	6-5/8	6-3/8	7-5/8	Fremont County	WY	Joe E. Nelson	1983	58

PRONGHORN

Minimum Score 64

Score	Length of Horn R	L	Circumference of Base R	L	Greatest Spread	Area	State/ Province	Hunter's Name	Date	Rank
78-0/8	16-0/8	16-0/8	6-0/8	6-0/8	12-2/8	Washoe County	NV	Gregg Tanner	1986	58
78-0/8	14-1/8	14-2/8	6-5/8	6-5/8	13-2/8	Moffat County	CO	Calvin Farner	1986	58
77-6/8	15-4/8	15-4/8	6-2/8	6-1/8	11-5/8	Ft. Wingate	NM	Lee Burnett	1975	65
77-6/8	15-7/8	15-0/8	6-0/8	5-6/8	10-4/8	Limon	CO	Steve Winkelman	1978	65
77-6/8	13-7/8	14-1/8	6-4/8	6-4/8	5-6/8	Natrona County	WY	Chuck Webster	1981	65
77-6/8	14-3/8	14-1/8	6-5/8	6-5/8	6-0/8	Moffat County	CO	Phil Hughes	1983	65
77-4/8	15-1/8	15-1/8	6-0/8	6-0/8	8-3/8	Washoe County	NV	Christian J. Coleman	1979	69
77-4/8	15-1/8	15-1/8	6-1/8	6-2/8	13-6/8	Howe	ID	Ron Johnson	1979	69
77-4/8	15-4/8	15-4/8	5-3/8	5-3/8	12-4/8	Casper	WY	Mel Johnson	1981	69
77-4/8	15-7/8	16-1/8	5-7/8	5-7/8	12-0/8	Carbon County	WY	Doug Cringan	1983	69
77-4/8	14-7/8	14-5/8	6-1/8	6-2/8	9-2/8	Unit 32 Graham County	AZ	Scott Kellner	1984	69
77-4/8	16-0/8	16-0/8	6-4/8	6-2/8	12-5/8	Washoe County	NV	James Mason	1985	69
77-2/8	16-3/8	16-4/8	6-0/8	6-0/8	10-0/8	Corona	NM	Charles L. Hughes	1960	75
77-2/8	15-0/8	15-1/8	5-7/8	5-7/8	9-0/8	Treasure County	MT	Tom Grunhuvd	1975	75
77-2/8	14-6/8	15-1/8	6-2/8	6-0/8	12-1/8	Sweetwater County	WY	William Dolenc	1978	75
77-2/8	15-4/8	15-2/8	6-1/8	5-1/8	10-4/8	Seligman	AZ	Tim Pender	1978	75
77-2/8	15-1/8	15-1/8	6-5/8	6-3/8	8-7/8	Moffat County	CO	Tom States	1981	75
77-2/8	15-6/8	15-4/8	6-1/8	6-0/8	14-4/8	Moffat County	CO	Mike Brust	1982	75
77-2/8	14-0/8	14-2/8	6-7/8	6-6/8	14-0/8	Sweetwater County	WY	David L. Price	1983	75
77-2/8	14-4/8	14-3/8	6-0/8	6-0/8	8-7/8	Mesa County	CO	Bob Black	1983	75
77-2/8	16-3/8	16-3/8	6-3/8	6-3/8	14-1/8	Bowman County	ND	Donald C. Hestekin	1983	75
77-2/8	14-4/8	14-4/8	6-3/8	6-1/8	10-6/8	Custer County	MT	Joe Good	1984	75
77-0/8	14-5/8	15-0/8	6-2/8	6-2/8	8-3/8	Natrona County	WY	Chuck Webster	1982	85
77-0/8	14-1/8	15-2/8	6-2/8	6-0/8	9-4/8	Billings County	ND	Jonathan Zieman	1984	85
76-6/8	14-1/8	14-5/8	6-2/8	6-2/8	14-2/8	Atlantic City	WY	Jim Puthoff	1969	87
76-6/8	13-1/8	13-1/8	6-4/8	6-6/8	6-3/8	Bighorn County	WY	Chuck Webster	1978	87
76-6/8	14-6/8	14-6/8	6-3/8	6-3/8	10-5/8	Fremont County	WY	Ron D. Evitt	1982	87
76-6/8	14-2/8	14-2/8	6-1/8	6-0/8	12-4/8	Campbell County	WY	Tony Janssen	1984	87
76-6/8	14-6/8	14-6/8	6-1/8	6-1/8	8-6/8	Converse County	WY	Vito Palazzolo	1984	87
76-6/8	14-0/8	13-6/8	5-5/8	5-6/8	13-4/8	San Miguel County	CO	Stuart Howard	1986	87
76-4/8	14-5/8	14-6/8	5-6/8	5-7/8	10-3/8	Birch Creek	ID	Roger W. Atwood	1977	93
76-4/8	14-6/8	14-6/8	6-1/8	6-1/8	12-3/8	Custer County	ID	Juilan Salutregui	1983	93
76-4/8	16-0/8	15-7/8	6-2/8	6-2/8	9-2/8	McKinley County	NM	Patrick J. Sharp	1984	93
76-4/8	15-1/8	14-6/8	6-0/8	6-0/8	11-3/8	Carter County	MT	Jamie Byrne	1984	93
76-4/8	14-0/8	14-0/8	6-0/8	6-0/8	14-6/8	Garfield County	MT	Paul Schafer	1984	93
76-4/8	13-6/8	13-6/8	6-6/8	6-6/8	10-3/8	Carbon County	WY	Jerry DeCroo	1985	93
76-4/8	15-4/8	15-4/8	6-2/8	6-3/8	12-6/8	Coconino County	AZ	Gary D. Davis	1986	93
76-4/8	13-6/8	14-0/8	6-0/8	5-7/8	11-0/8	Converse County	WY	Scott Wilke	1986	93
76-2/8	14-5/8	14-1/8	6-1/8	6-1/8	10-3/8	Citten	ND	Richard R. Chandler	1972	101
76-2/8	14-1/8	14-2/8	6-4/8	6-2/8	10-6/8	Converse County	WY	Jack Cassidy	1980	101
76-2/8	13-6/8	14-1/8	6-2/8	6-2/8	8-5/8	Converse County	WY	Chris Cassidy	1980	101
76-2/8	14-7/8	14-6/8	5-5/8	5-6/8	8-6/8	Little Wood River	ID	Champ Church	1980	101
76-2/8	16-3/8	16-1/8	6-0/8	6-1/8	8-5/8	Weston County	WY	David M. Nahrgang	1980	101
76-2/8	16-0/8	15-6/8	5-7/8	6-1/8	11-4/8	Glenrock	WY	Jack M. Conner	1981	101
76-2/8	14-3/8	14-3/8	5-6/8	5-7/8	9-2/8	Douglas	WY	Robert R. Vance	1981	101
76-2/8	14-6/8	14-6/8	6-3/8	6-3/8	11-1/8	Carbon County	CO	James Bowerman	1982	101
76-2/8	14-4/8	14-5/8	6-2/8	6-2/8	10-5/8	Sweetwater County	WY	Darrell H. Nations	1982	101
76-2/8	14-4/8	14-5/8	6-0/8	6-0/8	10-2/8	Taos County	NM	Galen G. Roumpf	1983	101
76-2/8	13-4/8	13-7/8	6-4/8	6-2/8	10-6/8	Wallace County	KS	Steve Rugg	1983	101
76-2/8	14-6/8	14-7/8	6-5/8	6-3/8	7-7/8	Sweetwater County	WY	Steve L. Rueck	1984	101
76-2/8	14-6/8	14-7/8	5-7/8	5-6/8	10-6/8	Eddy County	NM	Derek A. Tierney	1986	101
76-0/8	15-0/8	14-7/8	6-0/8	6-0/8	14-6/8	Plaza	ND	Wayne A. Metcalf	1972	114
76-0/8	14-5/8	14-5/8	6-2/8	6-4/8	13-4/8	Medicine Lodge	ID	Kerry Hillman	1977	114
76-0/8	14-7/8	14-3/8	5-6/8	6-1/8	10-0/8	Sweet Water County	WY	John Grady Lee	1983	114
76-0/8	14-2/8	14-2/8	6-1/8	6-1/8	9-3/8	Converse County	WY	Richard Rabe, Jr.	1985	114
75-6/8	14-0/8	14-0/8	6-1/8	6-1/8	12-4/8	Sweetwater County	WY	Gene McFadden	1982	118
75-6/8	14-4/8	14-6/8	6-1/8	5-7/8	10-0/8	Natrona County	WY	Jack M. Conner	1982	118
75-6/8	15-2/8	14-6/8	5-7/8	5-7/8	11-1/8	Moffat County	CO	Judd Cooney	1982	118
75-6/8	15-1/8	15-1/8	6-2/8	6-2/8	10-3/8	Converse County	WY	Lonny G. Herrick	1983	118
75-6/8	15-0/8	15-0/8	5-7/8	5-6/8	14-2/8	Sweetwater County	WY	Marty Martin	1986	118
75-5/8	15-4/8	15-4/8	5-5/8	5-5/8	16-7/8	Halliday	ND	Allan Lynch	1975	123
75-4/8	12-1/8	12-2/8	5-7/8	6-0/8	8-2/8	Gillette	WY	Dr. R. F. Helzerman	1960	124
75-4/8	17-2/8	16-4/8	6-0/8	5-6/8	15-0/8	Santa Rosa	NM	M. K. Vance	1962	124

PRONGHORN

(continued)   Minimum Score 64

Score	Length of Horn R	Length of Horn L	Circumference of Base R	Circumference of Base L	Greatest Spread	Area	State/ Province	Hunter's Name	Date	Rank
75-4/8	14-7/8	14-7/8	6-0/8	6-0/8	12-0/8	Williams County	ND	Terry L. Halgrimson	1970	124
75-4/8	14-3/8	14-2/8	6-0/8	6-2/8	12-6/8	Butte	ND	Don Sorge	1970	124
75-4/8	13-3/8	13-4/8	6-6/8	6-7/8	11-6/8	Ormsby	WY	Richard L. Huber	1979	124
75-4/8	15-3/8	15-2/8	5-6/8	5-6/8	12-5/8	Fergus County	MT	Don Davidson	1981	124
75-4/8	14-5/8	14-7/8	6-2/8	6-2/8	9-6/8	Klamath County	OR	Larry E. Jones	1982	124
75-4/8	16-0/8	16-0/8	6-0/8	5-7/8	11-0/8	Moffat County	CO	John R. Morris II	1983	124
75-4/8	14-4/8	14-4/8	6-4/8	6-4/8	11-6/8	Coconino County	AZ	Gary Warnica	1983	124
75-4/8	14-0/8	14-0/8	6-2/8	6-2/8	10-0/8	Powder River County	MT	Raleigh D. Buckmaster	1983	124
75-4/8	16-2/8	16-2/8	6-0/8	6-0/8	12-0/8	Coconino County	AZ	Harry M. Weeks	1984	124
75-4/8	14-4/8	14-0/8	6-4/8	6-4/8	12-1/8	Weld County	CO	Lorn Barnica	1984	124
75-4/8	14-6/8	14-6/8	6-0/8	6-0/8	11-1/8	Lassen County	CA	Pete Becker	1985	124
75-4/8	15-1/8	15-2/8	6-0/8	5-7/8	9-3/8	Meagher County	MT	Don Babcock	1986	124
75-3/8	15-5/8	15-1/8	6-2/8	6-2/8	18-2/8	Sweetwater County	WY	Don Dvoroznak	1976	138
75-2/8	15-4/8	15-3/8	5-7/8	5-7/8	8-6/8	Coteau	ND	Richard R. Chandler	1971	139
75-2/8	16-1/8	16-6/8	5-6/8	5-5/8	11-2/8	Gerber Reservoir	OR	Steve H. Bell	1973	139
75-2/8	14-3/8	14-4/8	6-2/8	6-1/8	8-7/8	Natrona County	WY	Chuck Webster	1979	139
75-2/8	14-3/8	14-5/8	6-3/8	6-4/8	9-2/8	Rawlins	WY	Duane Caudle	1980	139
75-2/8	14-5/8	14-5/8	6-2/8	6-2/8	10-2/8	Mussel Shell County	MT	John Crump	1980	139
75-2/8	13-0/8	13-0/8	7-0/8	7-1/8	10-6/8	Sweetwater County	WY	Charlene Shaw	1985	139
75-2/8	15-0/8	14-4/8	7-0/8	6-6/8	9-2/8	Sweetwater County	WY	Marlene Bowen	1986	139
75-0/8	14-2/8	14-2/8	6-3/8	6-1/8	10-2/8	Butte County	ID	Ross M. Conlin	1971	146
75-0/8	14-0/8	13-6/8	7-4/8	7-4/8	11-6/8	McClusky	ND	Dave Baumiller	1973	146
75-0/8	13-4/8	13-5/8	6-5/8	6-3/8	10-2/8	Recluse	WY	Mick Larson	1975	146
75-0/8	13-6/8	14-0/8	6-2/8	6-2/8	8-6/8	Bairoil	WY	Mike Ward	1976	146
75-0/8	14-5/8	14-4/8	6-2/8	6-1/8	8-7/8	Little Humboldt River	NV	Robert Mathews	1977	146
75-0/8	14-2/8	14-1/8	6-3/8	6-3/8	10-1/8	Bairoil	WY	Earl Frye	1980	146
75-0/8	14-0/8	14-0/8	5-5/8	5-6/8	9-7/8	Moffat County	CO	Ronald C. Halpin	1980	146
75-0/8	14-0/8	14-0/8	6-1/8	6-0/8	12-6/8	Wheatland County	MT	Phil Reno	1980	146
75-0/8	13-5/8	14-6/8	6-0/8	6-0/8	13-0/8	Craig	CO	Carl Smith	1981	146
75-0/8	15-0/8	14-7/8	6-2/8	6-2/8	9-0/8	Natrona County	WY	Richard A. Schreiber	1982	146
75-0/8	14-5/8	14-5/8	6-0/8	6-0/8	12-1/8	Meagher County	MT	Gene Clark	1984	146
75-0/8	15-5/8	15-3/8	6-0/8	6-0/8	11-6/8	Coconino County	AZ	Jim Scott	1986	146
75-0/8	14-4/8	14-4/8	5-5/8	5-5/8	10-4/8	Converse County	WY	William G. Mason	1986	146
74-6/8	14-3/8	14-3/8	5-5/8	5-5/8	9-5/8	Birch Creek	ID	Kent Merrill	1979	159
74-6/8	13-5/8	13-2/8	7-4/8	7-5/8	11-2/8	Converse County	WY	George A. Zanoni	1980	159
74-6/8	14-4/8	14-5/8	6-3/8	6-1/8	7-0/8	Douglas	WY	Norm Goodwin	1981	159
74-6/8	14-3/8	14-5/8	5-6/8	5-6/8	10-1/8	Fremont County	WY	James R. Mecca	1981	159
74-6/8	14-2/8	14-2/8	6-1/8	6-1/8	9-1/8	Sweetwater County	WY	Pete J Cintorino	1982	159
74-6/8	14-7/8	14-1/8	6-2/8	6-1/8	12-1/8	Moffat County	CO	Richard K. Hess	1982	159
74-6/8	14-1/8	14-1/8	6-0/8	5-7/8	5-7/8	Converse County	WY	Thomas Fleming	1982	159
74-6/8	14-4/8	14-5/8	6-0/8	6-1/8	9-6/8	Converse County	WY	Steve Gorr	1982	159
74-6/8	13-7/8	14-0/8	5-7/8	6-1/8	12-4/8	Rawlins	WY	Len Cardinale	1982	159
74-6/8	14-3/8	14-3/8	6-2/8	6-2/8	8-6/8	Sweetwater County	WY	Mike Denney	1982	159
74-6/8	14-5/8	14-6/8	6-2/8	6-2/8	9-7/8	Campbell County	WY	Arthur Geltz	1984	159
74-6/8	14-4/8	14-4/8	6-2/8	6-2/8	10-3/8	Moffat County	CO	Susan Bingham Syvertson	1985	159
74-6/8	15-3/8	15-4/8	5-7/8	5-6/8	8-0/8	Fremont County	WY	Joe E. Nelson	1985	159
74-6/8	14-1/8	14-0/8	6-1/8	6-0/8	7-3/8	Sweetwater County	WY	Dennis L. Shirley	1986	159
74-6/8	14-2/8	14-1/8	6-4/8	6-3/8	9-6/8	Sweetwater County	WY	Michael Chaffin	1986	159
74-5/8	15-3/8	15-3/8	6-3/8	6-2/8	11-2/8	Corona	NM	Harvey May	1960	174
74-4/8	14-6/8	14-4/8	6-2/8	6-2/8	12-3/8	Gillette	WY	William P. Mastrangel	1957	175
74-4/8	14-2/8	14-6/8	6-0/8	6-1/8	12-0/8	Wand County	ND	Bennie Burtts	1964	175
74-4/8	14-1/8	14-0/8	6-6/8	6-5/8	8-7/8	Bartlett	NE	Lynn M. Briggs	1965	175
74-4/8	13-4/8	13-6/8	7-1/8	7-2/8	8-5/8	Harrison	NE	Bill Carlos	1969	175
74-4/8	14-0/8	14-2/8	6-4/8	6-4/8	11-5/8	Lyman County	SD	Loran Hills	1970	175
74-4/8	15-4/8	15-2/8	5-6/8	5-6/8	9-7/8	Point of Rocks	WY	Clifford White	1977	175
74-4/8	14-4/8	14-4/8	6-0/8	5-6/8	7-2/8	Logan County	KS	Calvin Henry	1980	175
74-4/8	13-3/8	13-3/8	6-1/8	6-0/8	9-0/8	Craig	CO	George Griffiths	1981	175
74-4/8	14-2/8	14-2/8	6-4/8	6-4/8	10-0/8	Baca County	CO	Bill McEndree	1982	175
74-4/8	12-5/8	12-7/8	6-4/8	6-4/8	10-5/8	Arapahoe County	CO	Sid Strzok	1982	175
74-4/8	13-5/8	13-2/8	6-3/8	6-3/8	12-1/8	Moffat County	CO	Dale Drilling	1985	175
74-4/8	14-1/8	14-5/8	6-1/8	6-2/8	14-4/8	Modoc County	CA	George Taylor	1985	175
74-4/8	14-1/8	13-7/8	5-0/8	5-0/8	9-4/8	Douglas County	WY	Ronald M. Cook	1985	175
74-4/8	13-3/8	13-3/8	6-5/8	6-5/8	10-0/8	Sweetwater County	WY	Bill Clink	1986	175

PRONGHORN
(continued)

Minimum Score 64

Score	Length of Horn R	L	Circumference of Base R	L	Greatest Spread	Area	State/ Province	Hunter's Name	Date	Rank
74-4/8	13-3/8	13-3/8	6-4/8	6-4/8	7-4/8	Sweetwater County	WY	Glenn Hisey	1986	175
74-4/8	14-3/8	12-7/8	6-4/8	6-4/8	10-2/8	Carbon County	UT	Don R. Logston	1986	175
74-2/8	13-4/8	13-7/8	5-5/8	5-5/8	8-1/8	Sweetgrass County	MT	Charles Alkire	1964	191
74-2/8	14-5/8	14-6/8	6-3/8	6-2/8	10-3/8	Harrison	NE	Wayne Scherbarth	1969	191
74-2/8	14-1/8	14-0/8	6-0/8	6-0/8	9-2/8	Moffat County	CO	Bret Thomas Atkins	1981	191
74-2/8	13-2/8	13-2/8	6-7/8	6-7/8	10-2/8	Douglas	WY	Arnie Roytek	1981	191
74-2/8	14-0/8	14-0/8	6-1/8	6-1/8	11-4/8	Carbon County	WY	Scott A. Smith	1981	191
74-2/8	14-2/8	14-2/8	5-3/8	5-3/8	8-5/8	Craig	CO	Rich Padula	1982	191
74-2/8	13-1/8	13-0/8	6-2/8	6-2/8	7-6/8	Sweetwater County	WY	Keith Dana	1983	191
74-2/8	14-6/8	14-7/8	6-0/8	5-7/8	9-1/8	Graham County	AZ	Jeran E Montierth	1983	191
74-2/8	14-4/8	14-3/8	5-7/8	5-7/8	9-5/8	Union County	NM	Keith Cheatham	1983	191
74-2/8	13-3/8	13-5/8	6-1/8	6-0/8	11-7/8	Converse County	WY	John Ellas	1983	191
74-1/8	14-6/8	14-4/8	6-0/8	6-1/8	14-7/8	Moffat County	CO	Dennis Heitz	1982	201
74-0/8	14-1/8	13-7/8	6-2/8	6-2/8	9-5/8	Rawlins	WY	James N. Willcox	1977	202
74-0/8	15-2/8	15-5/8	6-2/8	6-3/8	11-4/8	Ft. Wingate	NM	Alfred J. Herrera	1979	202
74-0/8	15-0/8	15-1/8	5-5/8	5-5/8	10-5/8	Wallace County	KS	Mike Gilbert	1980	202
74-0/8	14-3/8	14-0/8	6-3/8	6-1/8	11-3/8	Jefferson County	ID	Earl Peterson	1980	202
74-0/8	16-0/8	15-4/8	5-6/8	5-4/8	8-6/8	Converse County	WY	Frank Moore	1981	202
74-0/8	13-7/8	13-7/8	6-1/8	6-2/8	10-1/8	Craig	CO	Randy Sanburg	1981	202
74-0/8	14-5/8	14-4/8	6-4/8	6-2/8	8-6/8	Valley County	MT	Tom Devlin	1984	202
74-0/8	13-4/8	13-3/8	5-7/8	5-6/8	10-4/8	Sweetwater County	WY	Herb Voyles	1985	202
74-0/8	14-1/8	14-0/8	6-4/8	6-4/8	11-7/8	Billings County	ND	Greg Schafer	1986	202
73-7/8	13-4/8	13-3/8	5-6/8	5-6/8	10-5/8	Rock Springs	WY	Ellen Lewis	1978	211
73-6/8	14-0/8	14-0/8	6-1/8	6-2/8	13-7/8	Epping	ND	Robert Halseth	1967	212
73-6/8	14-2/8	14-0/8	6-2/8	6-2/8	10-4/8	Sweetwater County	WY	Dan Winder	1973	212
73-6/8	14-4/8	15-0/8	6-0/8	6-0/8	10-0/8	Point of Rocks	WY	Clifford White	1978	212
73-6/8	14-2/8	14-1/8	6-1/8	6-0/8	7-7/8	Converse County	WY	Charles Stephens	1980	212
73-6/8	14-2/8	14-1/8	6-5/8	6-4/8	8-5/8	Converse County	WY	Don Schram	1982	212
73-6/8	14-4/8	14-7/8	6-0/8	5-7/8	9-3/8	Sweetwater County	WY	Larry J. Aksamit	1983	212
73-6/8	13-4/8	13-4/8	6-2/8	6-2/8	12-2/8	Carbon County	WY	Willis P. Duhon, Jr.	1983	212
73-6/8	13-3/8	13-4/8	6-3/8	6-1/8	10-1/8	Natrona County	WY	John Priday	1983	212
73-6/8	12-7/8	12-7/8	7-0/8	6-7/8	10-7/8	Natrona County	WY	Pat McAteer	1984	212
73-6/8	14-7/8	15-0/8	5-6/8	5-6/8	14-0/8	Custer County	MT	Marty Penrod	1984	212
73-6/8	15-1/8	15-0/8	5-7/8	5-7/8	10-3/8	Moffat County	CO	Lonny Vanatta	1985	212
73-6/8	14-6/8	14-4/8	6-0/8	6-0/8	10-6/8	Moffat County	CO	Kurt Keskimaki	1986	212
73-6/8	14-1/8	13-6/8	6-3/8	6-3/8	10-7/8	McKinley County	NM	Terry L. Sanders	1986	212
73-4/8	15-4/8	15-1/8	5-6/8	5-7/8	8-3/8	Maybelle	CO	Henry Wichers	1957	225
73-4/8	16-0/8	16-4/8	5-6/8	5-6/8	15-6/8	Santa Rosa	NM	Jack McCaw	1961	225
73-4/8	15-7/8	16-0/8	5-7/8	5-6/8	10-5/8	Round Mountain	AZ	Charles Meriwether	1968	225
73-4/8	13-0/8	12-5/8	6-1/8	6-2/8	9-4/8	Medicine Bow	WY	John Marolt III	1971	225
73-4/8	13-0/8	12-6/8	6-1/8	6-6/8	10-7/8	Cole Harbor	ND	Roy O. Yunker	1971	225
73-4/8	13-2/8	13-2/8	6-7/8	6-6/8	10-0/8	Moffat County	CO	Curtis Lynn	1972	225
73-4/8	14-4/8	14-6/8	6-2/8	6-3/8	8-3/8	Natrona County	WY	Kim S. Ades	1982	225
73-4/8	13-0/8	13-4/8	6-3/8	6-3/8	10-6/8	Sublette County	WY	Terry Reach	1982	225
73-4/8	15-0/8	15-2/8	5-6/8	5-7/8	8-4/8	Val Marie	SAS	Allan Sykes	1982	225
73-4/8	15-4/8	15-4/8	6-0/8	6-1/8	13-2/8	Fremont County	WY	Dan Lookingbill	1983	225
73-4/8	13-7/8	14-1/8	6-2/8	6-3/8	8-6/8	Sweetwater County	WY	Jim Dougherty	1983	225
73-4/8	14-0/8	13-7/8	6-3/8	6-2/8	9-6/8	Weston County	WY	Dick Kinder	1983	225
73-4/8	15-2/8	15-3/8	5-3/8	5-3/8	9-4/8	Prowers County	CO	Lloyd M. Brown	1984	225
73-4/8	15-1/8	15-0/8	5-4/8	5-4/8	9-0/8	Coconino County	AZ	Richard Ball	1985	225
73-4/8	13-7/8	14-2/8	6-1/8	6-0/8	9-7/8	Converse County	WY	Leland E. Scott	1985	225
73-4/8	14-7/8	14-4/8	6-2/8	6-3/8	12-4/8	Garfield County	MT	John Fleharty	1986	225
73-4/8	14-1/8	14-5/8	6-2/8	6-1/8	7-7/8	Moffat County	CO	Roger Gipple	1986	225
73-2/8	13-0/8	13-1/8	6-6/8	6-4/8	11-3/8	Lander	WY	Chuck Kroll	1952	242
73-2/8	11-3/8	11-7/8	6-3/8	6-3/8	11-1/8	Carter County	MT	Benny F. Padden	1960	242
73-2/8	14-2/8	14-2/8	5-2/8	5-2/8	7-5/8	Roy	MT	Wayne Miller	1962	242
73-2/8	14-6/8	14-3/8	6-0/8	6-0/8	9-2/8	Cohagen	MT	Paul Brunner	1976	242
73-2/8	13-5/8	13-3/8	6-2/8	6-1/8	9-5/8	Converse County	WY	Abe White	1980	242
73-2/8	15-2/8	15-2/8	5-5/8	5-5/8	8-3/8	Sweetwater County	WY	Randy Gamble	1982	242
73-2/8	15-2/8	15-0/8	5-4/8	5-5/8	9-4/8	Santa Cruz County	AZ	Tracy G. Hardy	1982	242
73-2/8	13-3/8	13-5/8	6-2/8	6-2/8	13-3/8	Fremont County	WY	Bill Lookingbill	1982	242
73-2/8	13-6/8	13-3/8	6-0/8	6-0/8	12-5/8	Melstone County	MT	Daniel A. Nielsen	1982	242
73-2/8	11-5/8	11-5/8	7-3/8	7-1/8	7-3/8	Macdoel	CA	Mike Domeyer	1982	242

PRONGHORN

(continued)　　　　　　　　　　　　　　　　　　　　　　　　　　　Minimum Score 64

Score	Length of Horn R	L	Circumference of Base R	L	Greatest Spread	Area	State/ Province	Hunter's Name	Date	Rank
73-2/8	13-6/8	13-5/8	6-0/8	5-7/8	9-6/8	Casper	WY	James I. Shipley, Jr.	1982	242
73-2/8	12-7/8	13-2/8	5-7/8	6-0/8	11-0/8	Moffatt County	CO	Jack Cassidy	1983	242
73-2/8	13-2/8	13-3/8	6-3/8	6-2/8	9-3/8	Moffat County	CO	John W. Rose	1983	242
73-2/8	14-2/8	14-4/8	6-1/8	6-1/8	12-1/8	Moffatt County	WY	Paul Locey	1983	242
73-2/8	15-4/8	17-0/8	6-1/8	6-0/8	9-6/8	Coconino County	AZ	Randy Fix	1983	242
73-2/8	13-4/8	14-0/8	5-7/8	6-1/8	10-4/8	Moffatt County	CO	Charles B. Lanzarone	1983	242
73-2/8	13-7/8	14-0/8	6-2/8	6-2/8	13-4/8	Fremont County	WY	John Priday	1984	242
73-2/8	14-4/8	14-3/8	6-4/8	6-3/8	8-7/8	Converse County	WY	Lee Jernigan	1984	242
73-2/8	14-2/8	14-4/8	6-1/8	6-1/8	10-0/8	Rosebud County	MT	Greg Munther	1986	242
73-0/8	13-5/8	13-5/8	5-3/8	5-3/8	9-6/8	Harding County	SD	Ted G. Carter	1961	261
73-0/8	12-7/8	12-6/8	6-2/8	6-3/8	11-7/8	Richardton	ND	Ronald D. Hauck	1970	261
73-0/8	15-1/8	14-6/8	6-1/8	6-1/8	7-1/8	Converse County	WY	Ed Coy	1976	261
73-0/8	14-0/8	14-2/8	5-4/8	5-4/8	11-6/8	Maybell	CO	Fred Cornish	1980	261
73-0/8	14-4/8	13-5/8	6-0/8	5-7/8	8-4/8	Gerber Reservoir	OR	Tom Tipton	1981	261
73-0/8	13-7/8	13-7/8	6-3/8	6-2/8	11-0/8	Rosebud County	MT	Dan Helm	1982	261
73-0/8	14-1/8	13-2/8	6-5/8	6-5/8	9-1/8	Sioux County	NE	Dick Kohles	1983	261
73-0/8	13-5/8	13-7/8	5-6/8	5-6/8	7-6/8	Converse County	WY	Edward Oswald	1983	261
73-0/8	13-4/8	13-4/8	6-1/8	6-0/8	11-2/8	Sweetwater County	WY	Marty Stubstad	1985	261
73-0/8	14-1/8	13-7/8	5-5/8	5-5/8	9-6/8	Yavapai County	AZ	Christopher R. Jackson	1985	261
72-6/8	14-3/8	14-2/8	6-0/8	6-0/8	8-0/8	Vya	NV	Lawrence Heward	1973	271
72-6/8	12-1/8	12-1/8	6-6/8	6-6/8	10-6/8	Natrona	WY	Dennis Spawn	1974	271
72-6/8	15-1/8	14-6/8	5-6/8	5-7/8	9-2/8	Carbon	WY	I. C. Benjamin	1976	271
72-6/8	14-0/8	14-1/8	5-6/8	5-7/8	10-7/8	Duck Flat	NV	Ritchard E. Golden	1977	271
72-6/8	14-7/8	15-0/8	5-7/8	5-7/8	9-1/8	Casper	WY	P. W. "Bill" Meyer	1977	271
72-6/8	12-1/8	11-6/8	6-7/8	6-7/8	9-1/8	Craig	CO	Dwight D. Greenwell	1980	271
72-6/8	13-2/8	13-2/8	6-2/8	6-3/8	12-4/8	Moffat County	CO	Albert Ahlrich	1981	271
72-6/8	13-5/8	13-2/8	5-6/8	5-4/8	7-1/8	Irish Canyon	CO	Lyle Willmarth	1981	271
72-6/8	14-5/8	14-5/8	5-7/8	5-5/8	8-0/8	Washoe County	NV	Gary Furman	1982	271
72-6/8	13-3/8	13-4/8	6-3/8	6-2/8	11-3/8	Moffat County	CO	Thomas H. States	1982	271
72-6/8	13-4/8	13-6/8	5-7/8	5-7/8	9-5/8	Hettinger County	ND	Jeff Watne	1983	271
72-6/8	14-0/8	13-6/8	6-0/8	6-0/8	7-0/8	Moffat County	CO	Jim Dougherty	1983	271
72-6/8	14-0/8	14-0/8	6-2/8	6-1/8	9-0/8	Converse County	WY	Willis Chapman	1983	271
72-6/8	14-6/8	15-1/8	5-6/8	5-6/8	9-0/8	Duchesne County	UT	Delos W. "Sonny" Kempton	1984	271
72-6/8	14-0/8	14-1/8	5-7/8	5-7/8	7-1/8	Natrona County	WY	Dorian Gilbert	1985	271
72-6/8	13-7/8	13-7/8	5-7/8	6-0/8	13-5/8	Yavapai County	AZ	Richard S. Jones	1985	271
72-6/8	13-6/8	13-7/8	6-1/8	6-0/8	11-7/8	Washington County	CO	Randy Fassler	1986	271
72-6/8	14-1/8	14-2/8	6-4/8	6-3/8	10-5/8	Fergus County	MT	Daniel R. Vogl	1986	271
72-4/8	12-4/8	12-5/8	5-4/8	5-4/8	11-6/8	Douglas	WY	Bob Jensen	1976	289
72-4/8	13-6/8	13-5/8	7-0/8	7-3/8	9-4/8	Faith	SD	Wallace C. Neville	1977	289
72-4/8	14-3/8	14-2/8	6-0/8	6-0/8	8-4/8	Jefferson County	ID	Kenny Peterson	1980	289
72-4/8	15-4/8	15-4/8	5-5/8	5-2/8	9-0/8	Converse County	WY	Joseph F. Scheuerman	1982	289
72-4/8	13-6/8	13-3/8	5-7/8	5-7/8	8-1/8	Natrona County	WY	Gilbert Clement	1983	289
72-4/8	13-7/8	13-6/8	5-5/8	5-4/8	10-4/8	Carbon County	WY	Jerome Deaven	1983	289
72-4/8	13-2/8	13-3/8	6-4/8	6-4/8	11-5/8	Natrona County	WY	Tony Lanzarone	1983	289
72-4/8	13-7/8	14-0/8	5-7/8	5-6/8	8-3/8	Converse County	WY	Lee Jernigan	1983	289
72-4/8	13-1/8	13-1/8	6-0/8	5-7/8	8-2/8	Moffat County	CO	Holt Dougherty	1984	289
72-4/8	13-6/8	14-5/8	5-4/8	5-4/8	11-2/8	Converse County	WY	Joe Guth	1984	289
72-4/8	15-2/8	14-0/8	6-1/8	6-1/8	11-3/8	Modoc County	CA	Tim Sayer	1986	289
72-4/8	12-7/8	12-3/8	6-4/8	6-2/8	10-5/8	Lemhi County	ID	Matt March, Jr.	1986	289
72-2/8	13-5/8	13-5/8	6-2/8	6-1/8	11-1/8	Carbon County	WY	William Scoggin	1953	301
72-2/8	14-0/8	14-0/8	6-0/8	5-7/8	10-4/8	Gillette	WY	K. K. Knickerbocker	1954	301
72-2/8	13-1/8	13-2/8	6-1/8	6-1/8	7-3/8	Gillette	WY	Carol Wert	1966	301
72-2/8	13-4/8	13-5/8	5-7/8	5-7/8	10-5/8	Saratoga	WY	Harold Boyack	1972	301
72-2/8	15-1/8	14-7/8	5-5/8	5-4/8	8-6/8	Meade County	SD	John S. Anderson	1973	301
72-2/8	14-3/8	14-3/8	6-0/8	5-7/8	9-5/8	South Valley County	MT	Wayne Anderson	1975	301
72-2/8	13-7/8	13-6/8	6-1/8	5-7/8	8-0/8	Medicine Bow	WY	Arthur Heinze	1977	301
72-2/8	13-7/8	13-6/8	6-0/8	6-0/8	7-2/8	Howe	ID	Dennis A. Gratton	1978	301
72-2/8	14-3/8	14-6/8	5-4/8	5-4/8	13-0/8	Rose Well	AZ	Terry E. Hansen	1981	301
72-2/8	17-0/8	15-5/8	5-4/8	5-5/8	9-0/8	Gerber Reservoir	OR	Richard Howell	1981	301
72-2/8	11-3/8	11-3/8	6-3/8	6-3/8	10-4/8	Humboldt County	NV	Verlyn Owens	1981	301
72-2/8	13-3/8	13-2/8	6-1/8	6-1/8	7-3/8	Moffat County	CO	Wayne A. Jensen	1982	301
72-2/8	13-0/8	12-7/8	6-1/8	6-1/8	6-6/8	Converse County	WY	Thomas Brannagan	1982	301
72-2/8	14-4/8	14-5/8	6-0/8	6-2/8	6-6/8	Carbon County	WY	Kim Cooper	1982	301

Minimum Score 64

Score	Length of Horn R	L	Circumference of Base R	L	Greatest Spread	Area	State/ Province	Hunter's Name	Date	Rank
72-2/8	14-0/8	13-7/8	6-0/8	6-0/8	7-6/8	Morgan County	CO	Barry Smith	1983	301
72-2/8	13-5/8	13-4/8	5-6/8	5-6/8	8-2/8	Moffat County	CO	Dan Liccardi	1983	301
72-2/8	12-7/8	12-7/8	6-3/8	6-1/8	8-0/8	Converse County	WY	Tim Cassidy	1983	301
72-2/8	13-2/8	13-6/8	6-0/8	5-7/8	10-5/8	Carbon County	WY	Paul Persano	1983	301
72-2/8	13-1/8	13-2/8	6-1/8	6-2/8	10-3/8	Carbon County	WY	Larry Hayes	1983	301
72-2/8	13-5/8	13-7/8	5-6/8	5-5/8	11-5/8	Valley County	MT	David Tofte	1983	301
72-2/8	13-0/8	13-0/8	6-1/8	6-2/8	9-3/8	Carbon County	WY	Robert L. Hudman	1984	301
72-2/8	14-7/8	15-0/8	6-0/8	5-7/8	14-1/8	Campbell County	WY	Mike Ballard	1985	301
72-2/8	14-3/8	14-1/8	6-4/8	6-1/8	10-4/8	Lemhi County	ID	Peter Cintorino	1986	301
72-2/8	13-4/8	13-4/8	6-1/8	6-2/8	10-5/8	Natrona County	WY	J. Bruce Ashcroft	1986	301
72-0/8	13-4/8	13-5/8	5-6/8	5-7/8	9-4/8	Perkins	SD	Ben Clark	1974	325
72-0/8	13-3/8	13-3/8	5-6/8	6-0/8	11-2/8	Orella	NE	Richard Koons	1974	325
72-0/8	12-7/8	12-4/8	6-7/8	6-7/8	10-1/8	Bennett County	SD	Donald Pierce	1978	325
72-0/8	13-3/8	13-1/8	5-7/8	5-7/8	10-5/8	Arco	ID	Mike Ellis	1980	325
72-0/8	14-0/8	14-0/8	5-6/8	5-6/8	14-6/8	Converse County	WY	Jack Cassidy	1981	325
72-0/8	13-3/8	13-2/8	6-1/8	5-7/8	6-2/8	Gerber Reservoir	OR	Harold McCraven	1981	325
72-0/8	13-3/8	13-1/8	6-0/8	6-0/8	11-0/8	Casper	WY	E. W. Onken	1981	325
72-0/8	13-3/8	13-3/8	5-7/8	5-7/8	10-4/8	Moffat County	CO	Gary Smith	1981	325
72-0/8	13-4/8	14-0/8	6-3/8	6-3/8	9-3/8	Carbon County	WY	Charles A. Vande Hei	1982	325
72-0/8	13-7/8	14-1/8	5-6/8	5-7/8	11-2/8	Carbon County	WY	Michael Beckwith	1982	325
72-0/8	14-3/8	14-2/8	5-5/8	5-5/8	8-6/8	Moffat County	CO	Augie Nicolas	1983	325
72-0/8	13-1/8	13-1/8	6-1/8	6-1/8	8-2/8	Converse County	WY	Tom Flemming	1983	325
72-0/8	14-1/8	13-6/8	5-7/8	5-6/8	12-3/8	McCone County	MT	Gary Rueh	1983	325
72-0/8	14-2/8	14-1/8	5-6/8	5-7/8	10-2/8	Carter County	MT	Dean Irwin	1983	325
72-0/8	14-6/8	14-6/8	5-3/8	5-3/8	10-6/8	Tide Lake	ALB	Adrian Erickson	1983	325
72-0/8	14-3/8	14-6/8	5-5/8	5-5/8	10-4/8	Washoe County	NV	C. J. Coleman	1984	325
72-0/8	13-2/8	13-1/8	6-0/8	6-0/8	8-7/8	Moffatt County	CO	Lynn Pariso	1985	325
72-0/8	13-6/8	13-3/8	6-2/8	6-2/8	8-1/8	Carbon County	UT	Kenny E. Leo	1986	325
71-6/8	14-2/8	14-1/8	5-6/8	5-7/8	10-5/8	Gerber Reservoir	OR	Jerry Phillips	1977	343
71-6/8	13-5/8	13-3/8	6-1/8	6-0/8	11-0/8	Natrona County	WY	George Kegler	1980	343
71-6/8	14-2/8	14-5/8	5-6/8	5-6/8	10-6/8	Glenrock	WY	Ron Spratling	1981	343
71-6/8	13-0/8	13-0/8	5-5/8	5-4/8	8-7/8	Bowman County	ND	Donald C. Hestekin	1982	343
71-6/8	13-1/8	13-1/8	5-4/8	5-4/8	10-6/8	Douglas	WY	Robert R. Vance	1982	343
71-6/8	13-5/8	14-4/8	5-7/8	5-6/8	10-2/8	Carbon County	WY	Don Carter	1983	343
71-6/8	12-5/8	12-7/8	6-3/8	6-1/8	6-6/8	Converse County	WY	Jim Nielsen	1983	343
71-6/8	14-3/8	14-5/8	5-7/8	5-7/8	11-6/8	Fremont County	WY	Jim Walters	1983	343
71-6/8	14-6/8	14-6/8	5-7/8	5-7/8	10-5/8	Powder River County	MT	Ron Thompson	1983	343
71-6/8	14-5/8	14-1/8	6-2/8	6-1/8	7-4/8	Campbell County	WY	Mike Ingold	1985	343
71-6/8	13-6/8	13-4/8	6-3/8	6-2/8	9-1/8	Sweetwater County	WY	James E. Summerall	1986	343
71-4/8	13-6/8	13-4/8	6-4/8	6-2/8	10-0/8	Carbon County	WY	Bill Scoggin	1957	354
71-4/8	14-7/8	14-7/8	6-0/8	6-2/8	13-5/8	Maybelle	CO	Henry Wichers	1959	354
71-4/8	13-4/8	13-3/8	6-0/8	6-0/8	8-2/8	Tripp County	SD	Dan Smith	1965	354
71-4/8	14-2/8	14-0/8	5-4/8	5-4/8	9-6/8	Carbon County	WY	Jerry Bowen	1976	354
71-4/8	14-1/8	14-0/8	6-2/8	6-3/8	9-1/8	Sweetwater County	WY	Val Jones	1978	354
71-4/8	14-4/8	14-4/8	5-6/8	5-5/8	9-7/8	Albany County	WY	Tom Tietz	1978	354
71-4/8	12-6/8	12-6/8	5-6/8	5-6/8	8-2/8	Rawlins	WY	Ronald J. Wedge	1978	354
71-4/8	13-0/8	13-0/8	6-0/8	5-6/8	9-3/8	Douglas	WY	Mike Burley	1980	354
71-4/8	12-4/8	12-1/8	6-4/8	6-3/8	9-7/8	Carbon County	WY	Bruce Butkiewicz	1980	354
71-4/8	13-1/8	13-6/8	6-1/8	6-2/8	11-4/8	Seligman	AZ	Peter C. Knagge	1980	354
71-4/8	13-6/8	13-6/8	6-0/8	6-0/8	6-6/8	Sheridan County	WY	David Shoop	1980	354
71-4/8	12-6/8	12-5/8	5-7/8	5-6/8	10-0/8	Casper	WY	David Manthei	1981	354
71-4/8	12-7/8	12-4/8	6-7/8	6-4/8	12-7/8	South Ferris County	WY	Dennis Crank	1982	354
71-4/8	15-0/8	15-0/8	5-7/8	5-6/8	10-6/8	Perkins County	SD	H. Melvin Dutton	1982	354
71-4/8	13-0/8	13-0/8	5-6/8	5-7/8	9-4/8	Delta County	CO	Doug McCauley	1983	354
71-4/8	13-3/8	13-4/8	6-2/8	6-1/8	9-2/8	Carbon County	WY	Bob Moore	1983	354
71-4/8	12-6/8	13-0/8	6-0/8	6-1/8	10-0/8	Perkins County	SD	H. Melvin Dutton	1983	354
71-4/8	14-0/8	14-1/8	6-1/8	6-1/8	6-5/8	Grand Forks	ALB	Ian Sangster	1983	354
71-4/8	13-2/8	13-1/8	6-2/8	6-1/8	7-5/8	Converse County	WY	George Hecker	1984	354
71-4/8	12-0/8	14-3/8	6-3/8	6-2/8	8-1/8	Petroleum County	MT	Ben Maughan	1984	354
71-4/8	13-7/8	13-6/8	6-0/8	5-7/8	9-3/8	Beaverhead County	MT	Ron Oswald	1985	354
71-4/8	13-0/8	13-0/8	6-2/8	6-0/8	9-1/8	Moffat County	CO	Terry Weimer	1986	354
71-4/8	14-0/8	14-2/8	5-5/8	5-6/8	9-5/8	Sublette County	WY	Jim Carr	1986	354
71-3/8	12-7/8	12-7/8	6-1/8	6-1/8	12-6/8	Gerlach	NV	Roger Iveson	1980	377

PRONGHORN
(continued)

Minimum Score 64

Score	Length of Horn R	L	Circumference of Base R	L	Greatest Spread	Area	State/ Province	Hunter's Name	Date	Rank
71-2/8	14-4/8	14-2/8	5-7/8	5-7/8	8-1/8	Musselshell County	MT	A. A. Anderson	1960	378
71-2/8	14-3/8	14-5/8	5-4/8	5-4/8	13-1/8	Lodgepole	SD	Elwood Patterson	1961	378
71-2/8	15-0/8	15-3/8	5-3/8	5-2/8	9-7/8	Natrona County	WY	Doug Pope	1976	378
71-2/8	14-5/8	14-7/8	5-2/8	5-2/8	12-0/8	Garrison Dam	ND	Leo N. Patch	1977	378
71-2/8	14-0/8	14-0/8	5-2/8	5-2/8	11-1/8	Meeteese	WY	Fred W. Achilles	1978	378
71-2/8	12-7/8	12-6/8	5-7/8	5-7/8	9-1/8	Converse County	WY	G. Merrill Jones	1980	378
71-2/8	14-2/8	13-4/8	6-1/8	6-2/8	8-3/8	Area 59	WY	Terry Walbridge	1980	378
71-2/8	13-3/8	13-3/8	5-5/8	5-6/8	8-3/8	Natrona County	WY	Hayden Allen, Jr.	1981	378
71-2/8	13-4/8	13-1/8	6-2/8	6-2/8	8-4/8	Green River	WY	Lyle R. Prell	1981	378
71-2/8	12-3/8	12-3/8	6-4/8	6-5/8	9-6/8	Sargent County	ND	Terry Hopewell	1982	378
71-2/8	13-4/8	13-5/8	6-0/8	5-5/8	12-0/8	Natrona County	WY	Rick Landeis	1983	378
71-2/8	13-0/8	13-2/8	6-2/8	6-2/8	10-7/8	Converse County	WY	Jack M. Conner	1983	378
71-2/8	15-0/8	15-1/8	5-7/8	5-6/8	8-4/8	Washoe County	NV	Robert L. Brooks, Jr.	1984	378
71-2/8	12-2/8	12-1/8	6-0/8	6-0/8	9-5/8	Converse County	WY	Jack M. Conner	1984	378
71-2/8	14-4/8	14-6/8	6-1/8	5-6/8	8-0/8	Powder River County	MT	Steve Kramer	1984	378
71-2/8	13-1/8	12-6/8	5-6/8	6-2/8	11-6/8	Johnson County	WY	Glenn Tappen	1984	378
71-2/8	14-3/8	13-2/8	6-0/8	5-7/8	11-6/8	Hot Springs County	WY	Mike Conner	1985	378
71-2/8	13-4/8	13-4/8	6-1/8	6-0/8	11-6/8	Natrona County	WY	Kelley Swift	1985	378
71-1/8	15-2/8	15-0/8	6-0/8	6-1/8	16-3/8	Modoc County	CA	Richard Wormington	1986	396
71-0/8	14-0/8	14-1/8	5-6/8	5-7/8	8-3/8	Converse County	WY	Eugene Smith, Jr.	1980	397
71-0/8	13-2/8	13-0/8	6-0/8	6-0/8	11-5/8	Glenrock	WY	Mike Butler	1981	397
71-0/8	13-7/8	13-5/8	6-0/8	6-0/8	7-3/8	Sweetwater County	WY	Vaughn Cross	1981	397
71-0/8	14-1/8	14-1/8	5-7/8	5-7/8	13-2/8	Craig	CO	Scott Kelley	1981	397
71-0/8	14-7/8	14-7/8	5-6/8	5-6/8	8-1/8	Modoc County	CA	Jeff Scheetz	1982	397
71-0/8	13-5/8	13-4/8	5-6/8	5-6/8	8-4/8	Converse County	WY	Ted J. Jaycox	1982	397
71-0/8	14-4/8	14-5/8	5-5/8	5-4/8	9-3/8	McKenzie County	ND	Mark D. Hughes	1982	397
71-0/8	13-1/8	13-4/8	6-4/8	6-4/8	9-6/8	Moffat County	CO	Lance Cussons	1983	397
71-0/8	13-3/8	13-3/8	5-7/8	5-7/8	8-1/8	Natrona County	WY	Wade L. Carstens	1983	397
71-0/8	14-0/8	14-1/8	6-0/8	6-0/8	9-1/8	Garfield County	MT	Bruce W. Blauvelt	1983	397
71-0/8	13-6/8	13-4/8	5-6/8	5-6/8	10-4/8	Area 11.6 Oldman	NV	Simo O. Ahlgren	1984	397
71-0/8	14-4/8	14-2/8	5-6/8	5-6/8	9-2/8	Sweetwater County	WY	Earl Kennedy	1986	397
70-6/8	14-7/8	15-2/8	5-5/8	5-4/8	10-3/8	S. Duck Flat	NV	Frank M. Davis	1967	409
70-6/8	13-2/8	13-2/8	6-3/8	6-2/8	9-6/8	Duck Flat	NV	Gordon A. Nicholson	1972	409
70-6/8	12-5/8	12-4/8	5-5/8	5-4/8	9-0/8	Casper	WY	Bernard R. Giacoletto	1973	409
70-6/8	11-2/8	11-2/8	6-0/8	6-0/8	10-1/8	Casper	WY	Jerry Zanandrea	1976	409
70-6/8	13-4/8	13-6/8	5-7/8	5-6/8	9-7/8	Lemhi County	ID	Alan Monroe	1979	409
70-6/8	13-0/8	13-3/8	5-6/8	5-5/8	7-4/8	Stanley County	SD	Rick Ray	1979	409
70-6/8	13-6/8	14-0/8	5-4/8	5-3/8	12-1/8	Glen Rock	WY	Russell Hull	1980	409
70-6/8	14-0/8	14-0/8	5-4/8	5-4/8	12-6/8	Converse County	WY	Frank Moore	1980	409
70-6/8	14-3/8	14-1/8	5-4/8	5-3/8	12-5/8	Tillard Ranch	WY	Charles A. Myers	1981	409
70-6/8	13-4/8	13-4/8	6-2/8	6-2/8	10-1/8	Craig	CO	Mike Miller	1981	409
70-6/8	15-0/8	15-1/8	5-5/8	5-4/8	10-4/8	Gerber Reservoir	OR	Paul D. Lewis	1982	409
70-6/8	12-5/8	12-5/8	5-7/8	5-7/8	9-4/8	Glenrock	WY	Steve Woodman	1982	409
70-6/8	13-7/8	13-7/8	6-0/8	6-1/8	10-4/8	Butte County	ID	Larry A. Wilde	1983	409
70-6/8	13-5/8	13-3/8	5-6/8	5-6/8	9-4/8	Converse County	WY	Dan Naccarto	1983	409
70-6/8	13-1/8	13-1/8	6-0/8	5-6/8	11-1/8	Natrona County	WY	Don Wilson	1983	409
70-6/8	16-2/8	15-4/8	5-1/8	5-1/8	9-6/8	Golden Valley County	ND	Thomas S. Lunski	1983	409
70-6/8	13-7/8	13-7/8	5-3/8	5-2/8	9-3/8	Moffat County	CO	Darryl Quidort	1984	409
70-6/8	15-1/8	14-6/8	6-1/8	6-0/8	12-7/8	Lassen County	CA	Wayne Goodrich	1985	409
70-6/8	12-6/8	14-3/8	5-7/8	5-6/8	11-3/8	Slope County	ND	Todd Seymanski	1985	409
70-6/8	14-3/8	14-2/8	5-7/8	5-6/8	11-1/8	Sweetwater County	WY	Craig Boheler	1986	409
70-6/8	13-0/8	13-3/8	6-3/8	6-1/8	10-2/8	Jefferson County	ID	Tony Hyde	1986	409
70-6/8	14-0/8	13-6/8	5-7/8	5-7/8	7-0/8	Moffat County	CO	Mike Ottenbacher	1986	409
70-6/8	13-1/8	13-4/8	6-2/8	6-0/8	11-0/8	Rosebud County	MT	Gary Olsen	1986	409
70-4/8	14-1/8	14-2/8	5-6/8	5-5/8	13-6/8	Miles City	MT	Bob Torgerson	1964	432
70-4/8	12-3/8	12-3/8	5-7/8	5-6/8	7-5/8	Niobe	ND	Bob Torgerson	1964	432
70-4/8	14-0/8	14-0/8	6-0/8	6-0/8	14-4/8	Butte	ND	Don Lawing	1968	432
70-4/8	12-5/8	12-4/8	6-0/8	6-0/8	10-5/8	Flaming Gorge	WY	Vern A. Butler	1973	432
70-4/8	14-2/8	14-1/8	5-5/8	5-4/8	8-2/8	Edgemont	SD	Noel Feather, Jr.	1975	432
70-4/8	13-0/8	13-0/8	6-4/8	6-4/8	9-3/8	Blue Dome	ID	Larry Cross	1977	432
70-4/8	14-5/8	14-0/8	6-4/8	6-1/8	9-6/8	Faith	SD	Floyd McElroy	1977	432
70-4/8	13-6/8	13-4/8	6-1/8	6-1/8	11-6/8	Grant County	NE	Albert Kant	1978	432
70-4/8	13-2/8	13-1/8	5-4/8	5-3/8	7-5/8	Blue Dome	ID	Ron Johnson	1980	432
70-4/8	13-3/8	13-5/8	6-0/8	6-0/8	13-7/8	Sweetwater County	WY	Victor Organ	1980	432

PRONGHORN
(continued)

Minimum Score 64

Score	Length of Horn R	L	Circumference of Base R	L	Greatest Spread	Area	State/ Province	Hunter's Name	Date	Rank
70-4/8	13-0/8	13-1/8	6-1/8	6-1/8	9-1/8	Area 55	WY	Walter Walbridge	1980	432
70-4/8	13-4/8	13-6/8	5-7/8	5-7/8	11-4/8	Bill	WY	James D. Miller	1981	432
70-4/8	15-0/8	15-0/8	5-3/8	5-3/8	8-7/8	Perkins County	SD	John Pollreisz	1981	432
70-4/8	13-7/8	13-5/8	5-6/8	5-6/8	9-1/8	Natrona County	WY	Gordon W. Stone	1981	432
70-4/8	13-3/8	13-0/8	6-1/8	6-1/8	9-3/8	Pierre	SD	Darrel L. Reinke	1982	432
70-4/8	14-2/8	14-3/8	5-5/8	5-5/8	8-6/8	Natrona County	WY	Ray Smith	1982	432
70-4/8	12-4/8	13-1/8	6-3/8	6-3/8	8-6/8	Moffat County	CO	Janet Schreur	1983	432
70-4/8	13-5/8	13-5/8	5-6/8	5-7/8	7-7/8	Converse County	WY	Al Sullivan	1983	432
70-4/8	13-1/8	13-1/8	6-2/8	6-0/8	10-4/8	Converse County	WY	Rick Poe	1983	432
70-4/8	12-7/8	13-1/8	5-6/8	5-6/8	8-3/8	Moffat County	CO	Gary McCain	1983	432
70-4/8	13-4/8	13-4/8	5-7/8	5-6/8	8-2/8	Converse County	WY	Rick Walker	1983	432
70-4/8	13-1/8	13-0/8	5-7/8	6-0/8	8-3/8	Moffat County	CO	H. R. "Rusty" Neely	1984	432
70-4/8	13-2/8	13-3/8	6-0/8	6-0/8	8-3/8	Converse County	WY	Anthony Ruggeri	1984	432
70-4/8	12-4/8	13-0/8	6-4/8	6-4/8	11-1/8	Converse County	WY	Robin Klemme	1984	432
70-4/8	12-1/8	12-3/8	6-0/8	6-0/8	10-6/8	Converse County	WY	John M. McAteer	1984	432
70-4/8	13-2/8	13-2/8	6-1/8	6-1/8	11-6/8	Modoc County	CA	Robert L. Smith	1986	432
70-4/8	15-1/8	15-7/8	5-6/8	5-5/8	15-0/8	Lassen County	CA	Tom Gordon	1986	432
70-4/8	13-6/8	14-0/8	5-4/8	5-4/8	9-5/8	Carbon County	WY	Rod Schmidt	1986	432
70-4/8	13-1/8	13-2/8	6-0/8	6-0/8	8-3/8	Brewster County	TX	Michael M. Reamy	1986	432
70-2/8	15-2/8	15-4/8	5-4/8	5-3/8	11-5/8	Casper	WY	Larry J. Colombo	1970	461
70-2/8	12-7/8	12-7/8	6-1/8	6-1/8	12-5/8	Converse County	WY	Edward Coy	1972	461
70-2/8	14-0/8	14-0/8	5-6/8	5-6/8	13-7/8	Butte County	ID	Dale Dunn	1973	461
70-2/8	12-6/8	13-0/8	6-3/8	6-3/8	9-0/8	Crawford	NE	Bruce Troester	1973	461
70-2/8	12-2/8	12-2/8	5-5/8	5-5/8	9-2/8	Saguache County	CO	Sandra Scheid	1975	461
70-2/8	13-2/8	13-4/8	5-6/8	5-6/8	11-0/8	Saguache County	CO	Tom Tietz	1977	461
70-2/8	13-6/8	13-6/8	6-6/8	6-4/8	10-6/8	Sweetwater County	WY	Vaughn Cross	1980	461
70-2/8	14-2/8	11-7/8	6-1/8	6-1/8	10-0/8	Converse County	WY	Anthony Wells	1980	461
70-2/8	13-7/8	13-4/8	6-1/8	6-0/8	14-1/8	Moffat County	CO	Gene Moore	1981	461
70-2/8	13-1/8	13-2/8	6-2/8	6-1/8	8-1/8	Casper	WY	Jim Plemmons	1981	461
70-2/8	14-2/8	14-3/8	5-5/8	5-5/8	9-6/8	Lassen County	CA	B. Jensen/F. Searle	1981	461
70-2/8	12-6/8	12-7/8	6-0/8	5-7/8	9-6/8	Carbon County	WY	George Raab	1982	461
70-2/8	14-0/8	14-0/8	5-7/8	5-6/8	10-2/8	Douglas County	WY	Brad Johnson	1982	461
70-2/8	13-6/8	14-1/8	6-1/8	6-0/8	12-2/8	Natrona County	WY	Tim Sturm	1982	461
70-2/8	12-4/8	12-4/8	5-5/8	5-7/8	10-6/8	Moffat County	CO	Wendy Decker	1983	461
70-2/8	12-2/8	12-2/8	6-0/8	6-0/8	10-3/8	Converse County	WY	Ron Montross	1983	461
70-2/8	13-0/8	13-4/8	5-6/8	5-7/8	10-6/8	Moffat County	CO	Rick Kralicek	1983	461
70-2/8	13-4/8	13-6/8	5-7/8	5-5/8	9-7/8	Sweetwater County	CO	Judd Cooney	1983	461
70-2/8	13-2/8	13-5/8	5-5/8	5-5/8	10-6/8	Converse County	WY	Rocky Chisholm	1983	461
70-2/8	13-0/8	13-0/8	5-6/8	5-6/8	11-6/8	Sweetwater County	WY	Michael R. Westvang	1984	461
70-2/8	12-6/8	13-2/8	5-7/8	5-7/8	11-1/8	Carbon County	WY	Ken Bean	1984	461
70-2/8	13-5/8	13-6/8	6-1/8	5-7/8	10-3/8	McCone County	MT	Frank Kasten III	1984	461
70-2/8	13-0/8	12-6/8	6-0/8	6-0/8	12-1/8	Sweetwater County	WY	David Wells	1985	461
70-2/8	13-0/8	12-7/8	6-2/8	6-2/8	9-3/8	Converse County	WY	Theodore C. Dzienis	1985	461
70-2/8	13-6/8	14-1/8	6-1/8	6-1/8	8-7/8	Biddle	MT	Stephen J. Jaworski	1985	461
70-2/8	15-0/8	14-7/8	5-1/8	5-1/8	9-6/8	Las Animas County	CO	Bill Swift	1985	461
70-2/8	13-5/8	13-4/8	5-6/8	5-7/8	8-6/8	Sweetwater County	WY	Darren L. Shirley	1986	461
70-0/8	13-1/8	13-1/8	6-1/8	6-1/8	13-1/8	Butte County	SD	Wayne Wanhanen	1961	488
70-0/8	13-6/8	13-7/8	5-6/8	5-6/8	11-4/8	Garfield County	MT	Paul M. Ramsey	1963	488
70-0/8	14-0/8	14-0/8	5-3/8	5-3/8	9-5/8	Harding County	SD	Ira Hilburn	1964	488
70-0/8	13-1/8	13-4/8	5-6/8	5-6/8	9-0/8	Morton County	ND	Paul R. Shannon	1971	488
70-0/8	13-4/8	13-2/8	6-1/8	6-0/8	12-5/8	Pennington	SD	Thomas Huitfeldt	1974	488
70-0/8	13-1/8	13-2/8	5-7/8	5-6/8	8-2/8	Dunlap	NE	Allan Mintken	1974	488
70-0/8	13-4/8	13-7/8	5-4/8	5-5/8	9-0/8	Del Norte	CO	Arthur M. Davis	1975	488
70-0/8	14-5/8	14-6/8	5-6/8	5-5/8	7-1/8	Humboldt County	NV	Wally Lopey	1981	488
70-0/8	12-5/8	12-3/8	5-4/8	5-4/8	7-5/8	Moffat County	CO	Charles A. Nicholas	1981	488
70-0/8	13-7/8	13-6/8	5-5/8	5-5/8	12-5/8	Sweetwater County	WY	Gerri Risley	1981	488
70-0/8	13-2/8	13-2/8	6-0/8	5-7/8	10-5/8	Casper	WY	Mark A. Smith	1981	488
70-0/8	13-6/8	13-6/8	5-4/8	5-4/8	8-7/8	White Pine County	NV	Richard Fillman	1982	488
70-0/8	13-0/8	13-0/8	5-7/8	5-6/8	12-4/8	Converse County	WY	Steven A. Wolff	1982	488
70-0/8	13-6/8	14-1/8	5-7/8	5-7/8	8-1/8	Carbon County	WY	Ron Breitsprecher	1982	488
70-0/8	13-0/8	13-0/8	6-0/8	5-7/8	14-0/8	Carbon County	WY	Ron Stacey	1983	488
70-0/8	13-7/8	13-6/8	5-4/8	5-5/8	10-3/8	Sargent County	ND	Terry Freehauf	1983	488
70-0/8	13-1/8	13-1/8	5-7/8	5-6/8	9-4/8	Douglas County	WY	Dean Taylor	1983	488

PRONGHORN

(continued)   Minimum Score 64

	Length of Horn		Circumference of Base							
Score	R	L	R	L	Greatest Spread	Area	State/ Province	Hunter's Name	Date	Rank
70-0/8	13-5/8	13-5/8	5-7/8	5-5/8	9-2/8	Perkins County	SD	Jeffery Rieker	1983	488
70-0/8	13-3/8	12-5/8	6-1/8	6-1/8	8-0/8	Rosebud County	MT	Daniel A. Nielsen	1983	488
70-0/8	13-2/8	13-2/8	6-0/8	6-0/8	7-2/8	Custer County	ID	Brad Chilton	1984	488
70-0/8	14-5/8	14-0/8	5-6/8	5-6/8	5-7/8	Moffat County	CO	Dale Drilling	1984	488
70-0/8	13-4/8	13-4/8	5-5/8	5-4/8	9-4/8	Moffat County	CO	Todd Clyncke	1984	488
70-0/8	12-4/8	12-4/8	5-7/8	5-7/8	8-3/8	Converse County	WY	Bill Doemland	1984	488
70-0/8	13-4/8	13-4/8	5-4/8	5-3/8	11-6/8	Slope County	ND	Gene D. Davis	1984	488
70-0/8	12-0/8	12-0/8	6-1/8	6-0/8	7-4/8	Elko County	NV	Ted Simpson	1985	488
70-0/8	13-3/8	13-0/8	6-1/8	6-0/8	8-6/8	Converse County	WY	David Stuhr	1985	488
70-0/8	13-0/8	12-7/8	5-4/8	5-3/8	10-1/8	Converse County	WY	Dean Herschede	1985	488
70-0/8	13-2/8	13-4/8	6-0/8	6-0/8	9-7/8	Carter County	MT	James Jessen	1985	488
70-0/8	13-1/8	13-1/8	5-6/8	5-6/8	7-6/8	Converse County	WY	John Unser	1986	488
69-6/8	12-6/8	12-6/8	6-6/8	6-6/8	11-4/8	Copper Basin	ID	Dr. Richard Hagerman	1966	517
69-6/8	13-4/8	13-4/8	6-2/8	6-2/8	10-5/8	Muddy Gap	WY	Maurice Savora	1972	517
69-6/8	13-6/8	13-5/8	5-6/8	5-6/8	9-0/8	Ormsby	WY	Edward Pitchkites	1973	517
69-6/8	14-6/8	14-6/8	5-2/8	5-2/8	10-2/8	Perkins County	SD	Marvin R. Bohnet	1974	517
69-6/8	14-4/8	14-5/8	5-2/8	5-4/8	10-0/8	Faith	SD	David Martin	1976	517
69-6/8	14-0/8	14-2/8	5-2/8	5-0/8	9-0/8	Sublette County	WY	John Kelly	1977	517
69-6/8	13-0/8	12-5/8	5-6/8	5-7/8	9-5/8	Bairoil	WY	John L. Craig	1978	517
69-6/8	14-5/8	14-5/8	5-3/8	5-3/8	13-4/8	Rose Well	AZ	Robin Underdown	1978	517
69-6/8	13-0/8	12-7/8	6-0/8	6-0/8	8-6/8	Arapahoe County	CO	Wayne E. Watson, Sr.	1979	517
69-6/8	13-2/8	13-2/8	5-4/8	5-4/8	10-0/8	Arapahoe County	CO	Steve Cosper	1980	517
69-6/8	13-3/8	13-5/8	5-1/8	5-1/8	10-4/8	Converse County	WY	Rickey Melde	1981	517
69-6/8	13-5/8	13-6/8	5-7/8	5-6/8	9-0/8	Converse County	WY	Jeff Reynolds	1982	517
69-6/8	13-6/8	13-7/8	5-6/8	5-5/8	9-7/8	Moffat County	CO	Albert Ahlrich	1982	517
69-6/8	14-0/8	13-5/8	6-2/8	6-2/8	8-4/8	Siskiyou County	CA	Scott Walker	1983	517
69-6/8	13-6/8	13-6/8	5-4/8	5-3/8	8-4/8	Moffat County	CO	Gary Decker	1983	517
69-6/8	13-2/8	13-2/8	5-4/8	5-3/8	10-7/8	Moffat County	CO	Richard Gearhart	1983	517
69-6/8	11-7/8	11-6/8	6-2/8	6-2/8	9-4/8	Moffat County	CO	Cathy Lee Jordon	1983	517
69-6/8	13-4/8	13-1/8	6-2/8	6-2/8	9-7/8	Moffat County	CO	Galen J. Wertz	1983	517
69-6/8	14-0/8	13-2/8	5-6/8	5-6/8	10-0/8	Converse County	WY	Jeff Davis	1983	517
69-6/8	13-1/8	13-2/8	5-7/8	5-7/8	10-3/8	Sweetwater County	WY	Michael Chaffin	1985	517
69-6/8	14-6/8	15-0/8	5-7/8	6-0/8	13-6/8	Modoc County	CA	Bill Golden	1985	517
69-6/8	14-0/8	14-0/8	5-5/8	5-4/8	10-6/8	Powder River County	MT	David Fitton	1985	517
69-6/8	13-2/8	13-0/8	5-7/8	6-0/8	10-4/8	Moffat County	CO	Howard Tieden	1986	517
69-6/8	13-5/8	13-6/8	5-6/8	5-6/8	10-0/8	McCone County	MT	Mitch Kottas	1986	517
69-5/8	12-4/8	13-0/8	6-4/8	6-3/8	14-1/8	Powder River County	MT	Daryl E. Jennings	1983	541
69-4/8	15-0/8	13-6/8	5-4/8	5-4/8	5-6/8	Forsyth	MT	Glenn Gibson	1958	542
69-4/8	14-4/8	14-2/8	5-2/8	5-2/8	10-6/8	Central	NM	Harold W. Groves	1960	542
69-4/8	14-4/8	14-2/8	5-5/8	5-4/8	9-4/8	L. High Rock Canyon	NV	Kenneth D. Allen	1972	542
69-4/8	13-2/8	13-0/8	6-0/8	6-0/8	10-6/8	Casper	WY	John Benetti	1973	542
69-4/8	13-6/8	14-0/8	5-5/8	5-3/8	9-6/8	Maccacre Lake	NV	Jack S. McCracken	1973	542
69-4/8	12-0/8	12-4/8	6-0/8	6-1/8	9-1/8	Faith	SD	Lelan L. Anderson	1974	542
69-4/8	14-3/8	14-4/8	5-5/8	5-3/8	8-4/8	Park County	CO	Ed Zehner	1974	542
69-4/8	12-6/8	12-3/8	5-7/8	6-0/8	9-4/8	Patterson	ID	Randy J. Stephens	1980	542
69-4/8	12-7/8	12-7/8	6-0/8	6-0/8	9-5/8	Moffat County	CO	Martin James Murrish	1981	542
69-4/8	13-6/8	13-4/8	6-5/8	6-6/8	11-0/8	Carbon County	WY	Mike C. Montgomery	1981	542
69-4/8	11-5/8	11-6/8	6-4/8	6-4/8	10-5/8	Glenrock	WY	Ben Munoz	1981	542
69-4/8	13-5/8	14-3/8	6-1/8	5-7/8	11-5/8	Douglas	WY	Dr. James R. Scott	1981	542
69-4/8	13-0/8	13-0/8	5-5/8	5-5/8	9-5/8	Jefferson County	ID	Ron Stacey	1981	542
69-4/8	12-6/8	12-7/8	5-7/8	5-7/8	9-5/8	Bowman County	ND	Ron Cizek	1982	542
69-4/8	14-1/8	14-2/8	5-4/8	5-3/8	6-5/8	Douglas County	WY	Ronnie Everett	1982	542
69-4/8	13-4/8	13-7/8	5-4/8	5-4/8	8-1/8	Moffat County	CO	Rich Humpal	1982	542
69-4/8	12-2/8	11-7/8	6-0/8	6-0/8	8-0/8	Beaver County	UT	Joey Leko	1982	542
69-4/8	14-0/8	14-0/8	5-6/8	5-5/8	9-6/8	Sweetwater County	WY	Ronnie Williams	1982	542
69-4/8	14-0/8	13-7/8	5-2/8	5-3/8	6-1/8	Converse County	WY	Jim Wilbur	1983	542
69-4/8	13-4/8	12-4/8	6-1/8	6-1/8	10-5/8	Natrona County	WY	Paul Persano	1984	542
69-4/8	12-7/8	13-1/8	5-2/8	5-2/8	7-3/8	Maybell	CO	Roy V. Roig	1984	542
69-4/8	13-6/8	14-7/8	5-7/8	5-7/8	11-6/8	Sweetwater County	WY	Glenn Hisey	1985	542
69-4/8	12-6/8	12-5/8	6-0/8	6-1/8	7-3/8	Sweetwater County	WY	Rod Knight	1985	542
69-4/8	13-5/8	13-2/8	5-2/8	5-2/8	8-3/8	Converse County	WY	Samuel M. Durham	1985	542
69-4/8	13-3/8	13-0/8	5-6/8	5-6/8	13-2/8	Billings County	ND	Pat Caroline	1985	542
69-4/8	12-5/8	12-5/8	5-6/8	5-6/8	8-3/8	Uinta County	UT	Rob Johnston	1986	542

PRONGHORN

Minimum Score 64

Score	Length of Horn R	L	Circumference of Base R	L	Greatest Spread	Area	State/ Province	Hunter's Name	Date	Rank
69-3/8	14-1/8	14-3/8	5-6/8	5-7/8	15-6/8	Pauline	OR	William E. Lancaster	1973	568
69-3/8	12-1/8	12-0/8	5-7/8	5-7/8	8-4/8	Converse County	WY	Larry L. Fies	1985	568
69-2/8	14-2/8	13-7/8	5-4/8	5-4/8	11-6/8	Mackey	ID	Jack Edwards	1960	570
69-2/8	13-5/8	13-4/8	5-3/8	5-2/8	6-2/8	Grindstone	SD	Floyd Hauk	1966	570
69-2/8	12-3/8	12-1/8	5-6/8	5-6/8	8-0/8	Area 25	WY	Bill Martin	1976	570
69-2/8	12-7/8	12-7/8	5-3/8	5-5/8	11-7/8	Douglas	WY	Dr. James L. Emerson	1980	570
69-2/8	12-4/8	12-1/8	6-0/8	6-0/8	9-5/8	Fort Morgan	CO	Filiberto Lopez	1980	570
69-2/8	11-6/8	13-5/8	6-1/8	6-1/8	8-6/8	Custer County	ID	Dick Fleming	1981	570
69-2/8	13-2/8	14-0/8	5-5/8	5-5/8	11-0/8	Converse County	WY	Gene A. Esch	1981	570
69-2/8	13-1/8	13-3/8	5-4/8	5-4/8	7-7/8	Arco	ID	Garry Gunderson	1981	570
69-2/8	12-4/8	13-0/8	5-7/8	5-5/8	11-5/8	Craig	CO	Jim Jarvis	1981	570
69-2/8	14-3/8	13-7/8	5-7/8	5-6/8	10-4/8	Valencia County	NM	Reggie Spiegelberg	1981	570
69-2/8	12-7/8	13-0/8	5-7/8	5-5/8	11-0/8	Sweetwater County	WY	Dean Kendall	1982	570
69-2/8	13-2/8	13-6/8	6-2/8	6-2/8	9-5/8	Albany County	WY	Peter Vasek	1982	570
69-2/8	12-7/8	13-1/8	5-5/8	5-4/8	8-4/8	Maybell	CO	Ross Dieffenbaucher	1982	570
69-2/8	14-3/8	14-0/8	5-7/8	5-7/8	8-0/8	Moffat County	CO	Les Smith	1983	570
69-2/8	14-2/8	13-7/8	6-0/8	6-0/8	8-1/8	Natrona County	WY	Joe M. Skipp	1983	570
69-2/8	12-7/8	12-4/8	5-7/8	5-6/8	9-3/8	Converse County	WY	Bruce H. Sabaini	1983	570
69-2/8	13-7/8	13-4/8	5-4/8	5-4/8	10-6/8	White Pine County	NV	Patrick Fillman	1984	570
69-2/8	14-4/8	14-6/8	5-6/8	5-2/8	10-6/8	Converse County	WY	Donald Jackson	1984	570
69-2/8	13-3/8	13-1/8	5-6/8	5-6/8	10-5/8	Converse County	WY	Bob Frank	1984	570
69-2/8	13-3/8	12-4/8	6-1/8	6-1/8	12-0/8	McKenzie County	ND	Bill Zahradka	1984	570
69-2/8	13-2/8	13-2/8	5-7/8	5-7/8	10-5/8	Carbon County	WY	Steve Bolan	1985	570
69-2/8	12-6/8	12-4/8	6-5/8	6-4/8	9-0/8	Moffat County	CO	Casey Veach	1985	570
69-2/8	13-0/8	12-7/8	5-6/8	5-4/8	11-2/8	Yavapai County	AZ	Tony Zimoaro	1985	570
69-2/8	12-1/8	12-0/8	5-7/8	5-7/8	8-4/8	Converse County	WY	Larry L. Fies	1985	570
69-2/8	13-4/8	13-4/8	6-0/8	6-0/8	9-4/8	Moffat County	CO	Gil Gilbertson	1986	570
69-2/8	13-4/8	13-3/8	5-5/8	5-5/8	10-4/8	Ross County	WY	Don Schram	1986	570
69-2/8	13-4/8	13-5/8	5-5/8	5-5/8	8-3/8	Presidio County	TX	Larry Zimmerman	1986	570
69-0/8	12-7/8	13-0/8	5-6/8	5-7/8	8-4/8	Ardmore	SD	Francis R. Tovar	1968	597
69-0/8	14-0/8	14-2/8	5-2/8	5-3/8	9-1/8	Mercer County	ND	John J. Willoughby	1977	597
69-0/8	13-4/8	13-2/8	5-6/8	5-5/8	8-3/8	Butte County	ID	Larry Roberts	1979	597
69-0/8	14-1/8	13-7/8	5-4/8	5-3/8	10-0/8	Rawlins	WY	Grant Poindexter	1980	597
69-0/8	14-0/8	14-2/8	5-7/8	5-6/8	8-0/8	Converse County	WY	Don Clark	1981	597
69-0/8	13-2/8	13-3/8	5-6/8	5-5/8	11-0/8	Douglas	WY	George Place	1981	597
69-0/8	12-5/8	12-4/8	5-6/8	5-6/8	9-5/8	Fremont County	WY	A. E. "Butch" Whelchel	1981	597
69-0/8	12-6/8	12-6/8	5-6/8	5-6/8	12-5/8	Converse County	WY	Jeff Wright	1981	597
69-0/8	13-5/8	13-6/8	5-7/8	6-0/8	11-6/8	Washoe County	NV	Dr. Ronald H. Thole	1982	597
69-0/8	13-0/8	12-6/8	6-0/8	6-0/8	7-0/8	South Pack County	CO	Greg Brown	1983	597
69-0/8	12-4/8	12-4/8	6-0/8	6-1/8	9-4/8	Moffat County	CO	Burton Arbogast	1983	597
69-0/8	13-2/8	13-3/8	5-6/8	5-6/8	11-4/8	Moffat County	CO	Mike Wallers	1983	597
69-0/8	13-4/8	13-4/8	6-0/8	6-1/8	10-3/8	Converse County	WY	Michael Nimmer	1983	597
69-0/8	13-4/8	12-7/8	5-7/8	5-6/8	9-2/8	Douglas County	WY	James R. Dreves	1983	597
69-0/8	14-1/8	14-0/8	5-4/8	5-4/8	10-1/8	Johnson County	WY	Steve Nolte	1984	597
69-0/8	12-7/8	12-5/8	6-0/8	6-1/8	11-2/8	Converse County	WY	Janice Peterman	1984	597
69-0/8	13-2/8	13-3/8	5-6/8	5-7/8	13-3/8	Converse County	WY	John L Kosharek	1985	597
69-0/8	12-7/8	12-6/8	6-0/8	5-7/8	9-3/8	Campbell County	WY	Bill Heinike	1985	597
68-6/8	14-7/8	14-7/8	5-4/8	5-4/8	12-0/8	Wamsutter	WY	Dr. Fred Mack	1960	615
68-6/8	13-2/8	13-4/8	6-1/8	6-1/8	7-4/8	Gallatin County	MT	Robert Savage	1971	615
68-6/8	12-3/8	12-4/8	6-4/8	6-2/8	11-0/8	Sweetwater County	WY	Keith Dana	1978	615
68-6/8	13-6/8	13-5/8	5-3/8	5-5/8	9-0/8	Park County	MT	George Kamps	1980	615
68-6/8	13-0/8	12-7/8	5-7/8	5-4/8	9-0/8	Casper	WY	Jim L. McCrory	1981	615
68-6/8	12-4/8	12-4/8	5-5/8	5-4/8	7-3/8	Douglas	WY	Donald Schram	1981	615
68-6/8	13-0/8	13-2/8	5-7/8	5-7/8	11-6/8	Weld County	CO	Ron Montross	1983	615
68-6/8	12-4/8	12-0/8	6-4/8	6-3/8	9-4/8	Crook County	WY	Jim P Hallock	1983	615
68-6/8	13-4/8	13-3/8	5-5/8	5-5/8	7-6/8	Converse County	WY	Gary Duncan	1983	615
68-6/8	13-3/8	13-5/8	5-1/8	5-1/8	12-2/8	Garfield County	MT	Darwin Frison	1983	615
68-6/8	14-0/8	14-0/8	5-3/8	5-2/8	10-6/8	Moffat County	CO	Gary Fritzler	1984	615
68-6/8	12-4/8	12-5/8	6-0/8	6-3/8	9-1/8	McKinley County	NM	John W. Rose	1984	615
68-6/8	14-3/8	14-3/8	5-4/8	5-4/8	9-4/8	Butte County	SD	Reginald E. Faber, Jr.	1984	615
68-6/8	12-6/8	12-4/8	6-0/8	5-7/8	8-2/8	Converse County	WY	Eric Bruce	1984	615
68-6/8	14-1/8	14-2/8	6-0/8	5-7/8	15-0/8	Fergus County	MT	James W. Southworth	1984	615
68-6/8	13-4/8	14-0/8	5-6/8	5-4/8	11-1/8	Washoe County	NV	Gary Zunino	1985	615

PRONGHORN

(continued)   Minimum Score 64

Score	Length of Horn R	L	Circumference of Base R	L	Greatest Spread	Area	State/ Province	Hunter's Name	Date	Rank
68-4/8	13-4/8	13-0/8	5-4/8	5-5/8	8-6/8	Tripp County	SD	Spike Jorgensen	1965	631
68-4/8	14-1/8	14-1/8	5-2/8	5-1/8	12-3/8	Corona	NM	James H. Simmons	1966	631
68-4/8	12-6/8	12-2/8	6-5/8	6-5/8	12-1/8	Riverdale	ND	Tom O'Connell	1970	631
68-4/8	14-1/8	14-0/8	5-4/8	5-2/8	10-5/8	Johnson County	WY	David Collis	1975	631
68-4/8	12-6/8	12-7/8	6-0/8	6-0/8	9-4/8	Billings County	ND	Dean Nevland	1975	631
68-4/8	12-6/8	12-4/8	5-6/8	5-7/8	9-3/8	Douglas	WY	Ron Carpenter	1976	631
68-4/8	13-0/8	12-7/8	5-5/8	6-0/8	8-3/8	Kemmer	WY	Preston C. Phelps	1977	631
68-4/8	13-7/8	13-4/8	5-6/8	5-5/8	13-1/8	Sterling	CO	Tony Seahorn	1978	631
68-4/8	13-7/8	14-0/8	6-0/8	5-7/8	12-4/8	Ft. Wingate	NM	James M. Finn	1979	631
68-4/8	14-1/8	14-1/8	5-4/8	5-5/8	10-5/8	Howe	ID	Clifton Robinson	1979	631
68-4/8	13-3/8	13-2/8	5-5/8	5-5/8	13-0/8	Rawlins	WY	Dale Gauthier	1980	631
68-4/8	13-0/8	12-5/8	5-7/8	5-7/8	10-3/8	Moffat County	CO	Ron Bolinger	1981	631
68-4/8	13-6/8	13-5/8	5-0/8	5-0/8	8-4/8	Casper	WY	Dan Skolaski	1981	631
68-4/8	13-5/8	13-4/8	5-4/8	5-3/8	12-1/8	Converse County	WY	Richard Stokke	1981	631
68-4/8	12-6/8	13-3/8	5-7/8	6-0/8	9-1/8	Bill County	WY	Charles O. Boggs	1982	631
68-4/8	14-1/8	13-7/8	5-5/8	5-6/8	8-6/8	Eddy County	NM	Jim Stell	1982	631
68-4/8	13-6/8	14-0/8	5-4/8	5-5/8	13-2/8	Converse County	WY	Harold Leslie	1982	631
68-4/8	13-4/8	13-5/8	5-3/8	5-3/8	13-3/8	Converse County	WY	Kent Brigham	1982	631
68-4/8	12-4/8	13-0/8	6-3/8	6-1/8	8-6/8	Rawlins	WY	Willis Duhon	1982	631
68-4/8	12-7/8	13-0/8	6-0/8	6-0/8	9-6/8	Natrona County	WY	Roger Smith	1982	631
68-4/8	12-3/8	12-1/8	6-2/8	6-3/8	10-3/8	Natrona County	WY	Steve Turck	1982	631
68-4/8	12-7/8	12-7/8	5-5/8	5-4/8	10-6/8	Moffat County	CO	Len Cardinale	1983	631
68-4/8	13-4/8	13-4/8	5-2/8	5-1/8	10-5/8	Sweetwater County	WY	Dean Dolenc	1983	631
68-4/8	13-3/8	13-6/8	5-5/8	5-4/8	7-2/8	Sioux County	NE	Chuck Starr	1983	631
68-4/8	13-6/8	13-6/8	5-2/8	5-3/8	7-6/8	Logan County	KS	Lynn Freese	1984	631
68-4/8	13-6/8	13-6/8	5-6/8	5-4/8	11-2/8	Converse County	WY	Marty Horn	1984	631
68-4/8	12-2/8	12-3/8	6-0/8	6-0/8	10-7/8	Campbell County	WY	John "Jack" Cordes	1984	631
68-4/8	12-0/8	12-0/8	5-5/8	5-5/8	8-2/8	Moffat County	CO	Robert Syvertson, Sr.	1985	631
68-4/8	13-6/8	13-6/8	5-7/8	5-7/8	11-5/8	Coconino County	AZ	Jesse E. Smith	1985	631
68-4/8	12-0/8	11-5/8	5-5/8	5-5/8	9-6/8	Converse County	WY	Steve Woodman	1985	631
68-4/8	12-3/8	12-5/8	5-6/8	5-7/8	10-5/8	Campbell County	WY	Thomas R. Dvorak	1985	631
68-4/8	13-4/8	13-2/8	5-4/8	5-4/8	9-4/8	WMU 151	ALB	Allen Avery	1985	631
68-4/8	13-0/8	13-0/8	5-6/8	5-7/8	10-7/8	Campbell County	WY	Donald Ace Morgan	1986	631
68-4/8	12-0/8	12-4/8	5-7/8	5-7/8	9-0/8	Billings County	ND	Rick Froehlich	1986	631
68-3/8	13-2/8	13-2/8	5-5/8	5-5/8	13-3/8	Medicine Bow	WY	Robert Pitt	1974	665
68-2/8	12-4/8	12-4/8	6-2/8	6-0/8	11-6/8	Maybelle	CO	Burl Duckworth	1958	666
68-2/8	12-6/8	12-6/8	5-7/8	5-5/8	10-5/8	Buffalo	SD	Chet Wohlhueter	1963	666
68-2/8	13-5/8	13-3/8	5-3/8	5-2/8	8-7/8	Morton County	ND	Fred F. Heer	1973	666
68-2/8	13-2/8	13-2/8	5-6/8	6-0/8	9-1/8	Rock Springs	WY	Charles Bartlett	1978	666
68-2/8	13-0/8	12-5/8	5-6/8	5-5/8	8-1/8	Thomas County	NE	Harold L. Bowman	1978	666
68-2/8	13-1/8	13-1/8	5-3/8	5-2/8	9-5/8	San Luis Valley	CO	Doy K. Curtis	1978	666
68-2/8	13-6/8	14-2/8	5-5/8	5-4/8	7-2/8	Lemhi County	ID	Richard Dewey	1978	666
68-2/8	12-4/8	12-5/8	6-2/8	6-3/8	11-4/8	Fremont County	WY	Bob Freese	1978	666
68-2/8	13-5/8	13-2/8	5-6/8	5-4/8	8-4/8	Fremont County	WY	Will Yeates	1978	666
68-2/8	12-1/8	11-7/8	5-6/8	5-7/8	8-0/8	Birch Creek	ID	Larry Cross	1979	666
68-2/8	14-1/8	13-7/8	5-5/8	6-0/8	7-5/8	Rose Well	AZ	Jim Ellis	1979	666
68-2/8	13-6/8	13-7/8	6-2/8	6-2/8	8-6/8	Sweetwater County	WY	Dean Kendall	1980	666
68-2/8	12-6/8	12-6/8	6-0/8	6-1/8	7-3/8	Sweetwater County	WY	Ed Budge	1981	666
68-2/8	13-0/8	13-0/8	6-0/8	5-5/8	9-0/8	Casper	WY	William E. Ehrman	1981	666
68-2/8	12-3/8	12-4/8	5-6/8	5-6/8	8-0/8	Moffat County	CO	Barry J. Smith	1981	666
68-2/8	13-0/8	13-0/8	5-7/8	5-6/8	6-7/8	Natrona County	WY	Rodger Warwick	1981	666
68-2/8	12-6/8	12-6/8	5-4/8	5-5/8	10-0/8	Natrona County	WY	R. G. Williams	1981	666
68-2/8	12-0/8	12-2/8	5-6/8	5-6/8	8-0/8	Douglas County	WY	Butch Crawford	1982	666
68-2/8	14-1/8	13-7/8	5-4/8	5-4/8	13-1/8	Ross	WY	Donald Schram	1982	666
68-2/8	11-7/8	12-1/8	6-1/8	6-1/8	9-3/8	Whitepine County	NV	Tony S. Whitten	1983	666
68-2/8	14-6/8	14-6/8	5-2/8	5-1/8	10-6/8	Saguache County	CO	Steve Van Treese	1983	666
68-2/8	12-7/8	12-6/8	5-4/8	5-4/8	9-4/8	Sublette County	WY	Terry Wright	1983	666
68-2/8	13-3/8	13-1/8	5-4/8	5-4/8	11-1/8	Weld County	CO	Dennis Schweitzer	1983	666
68-2/8	13-5/8	13-5/8	5-4/8	5-4/8	10-4/8	Bingham County	ID	Doug Foss	1983	666
68-2/8	13-1/8	12-7/8	5-7/8	5-6/8	11-7/8	Wallace County	KS	Darren Cullins	1983	666
68-2/8	13-5/8	13-1/8	5-3/8	5-3/8	10-3/8	Hughes County	SD	Darrel L. Reinke	1984	666
68-2/8	13-1/8	13-3/8	5-6/8	5-6/8	11-3/8	Carbon County	WY	Ron Breitsprecher	1984	666
68-2/8	14-3/8	14-6/8	6-1/8	5-7/8	11-1/8	Fremont County	WY	Thomas E. Axthelm	1984	666

PRONGHORN
(continued)

Minimum Score 64

Score	Length of Horn R	L	Circumference of Base R	L	Greatest Spread	Area	State/Province	Hunter's Name	Date	Rank
68-2/8	12-2/8	13-2/8	5-3/8	5-4/8	6-7/8	Converse County	WY	Al Sullivan	1984	666
68-2/8	12-4/8	12-7/8	6-3/8	6-2/8	8-6/8	Natrona County	WY	Ray L. Harbin	1985	666
68-2/8	14-0/8	13-6/8	5-4/8	5-4/8	10-5/8	Carter County	MT	Juanita Byrne	1985	666
68-0/8	13-0/8	13-2/8	5-6/8	5-5/8	10-1/8	Ziebach County	SD	Jim Glines	1934	697
68-0/8	14-1/8	13-0/8	5-4/8	5-6/8	7-7/8	Campbell County	WY	Reinhold L. Lind	1961	697
68-0/8	13-4/8	13-4/8	5-4/8	5-4/8	7-5/8	Medicine Bow	WY	Bill Cunningham	1963	697
68-0/8	14-0/8	13-6/8	5-2/8	5-3/8	8-0/8	Blue Grass	ND	Roy D. Russell, Jr.	1967	697
68-0/8	11-4/8	11-3/8	5-7/8	5-6/8	7-3/8	Burke County	ND	Allen L. Nelson	1974	697
68-0/8	13-0/8	13-0/8	5-7/8	5-7/8	9-6/8	Saguache County	CO	David Scheid	1974	697
68-0/8	12-4/8	12-5/8	5-6/8	5-5/8	10-6/8	Mackey	ID	Gary Schaffner	1975	697
68-0/8	13-0/8	13-3/8	5-5/8	5-4/8	9-7/8	Blue Dome	ID	Ron Parish	1977	697
68-0/8	13-5/8	13-3/8	5-6/8	5-6/8	10-3/8	Humboldt County	NV	Vic Christison	1978	697
68-0/8	13-2/8	12-7/8	6-1/8	6-0/8	10-1/8	Sweetwater County	WY	Jack Riddle	1979	697
68-0/8	12-2/8	12-4/8	5-6/8	5-5/8	8-4/8	Casper	WY	Todd James	1980	697
68-0/8	13-6/8	12-3/8	5-6/8	5-5/8	7-2/8	Moffat County	CO	Judd Cooney	1981	697
68-0/8	14-1/8	14-1/8	5-4/8	5-1/8	6-7/8	Lassen County	CA	Junior Morris	1982	697
68-0/8	13-4/8	13-6/8	5-6/8	5-5/8	13-4/8	Sweetwater County	WY	Sy Gilliland	1982	697
68-0/8	13-2/8	13-3/8	5-5/8	5-4/8	11-0/8	Fremont County	WY	Everett A. Boss	1982	697
68-0/8	13-2/8	13-2/8	5-7/8	5-6/8	10-1/8	Converse County	WY	Bill Frodl	1982	697
68-0/8	12-7/8	12-5/8	4-7/8	4-7/8	14-1/8	Moffat County	CO	Keith R. Hardy	1983	697
68-0/8	12-2/8	12-7/8	5-7/8	6-0/8	6-7/8	Natrona County	WY	E. Michael Onken	1983	697
68-0/8	13-1/8	13-1/8	5-6/8	5-5/8	9-0/8	Converse County	WY	William Kobart	1983	697
68-0/8	13-6/8	13-7/8	5-5/8	5-5/8	12-2/8	Douglas County	WY	David P. Lindman	1983	697
68-0/8	13-1/8	13-2/8	5-7/8	5-6/8	7-5/8	Albany County	WY	Adrian H. Farmer, Jr.	1983	697
68-0/8	14-0/8	14-1/8	5-2/8	5-4/8	12-4/8	Coconino County	AZ	Dean Zuern	1984	697
68-0/8	12-6/8	12-0/8	6-0/8	5-7/8	10-1/8	Converse County	WY	Michael Murphy	1984	697
68-0/8	13-5/8	13-6/8	6-0/8	6-0/8	15-4/8	Sweetwater County	WY	Bill Clink	1985	697
68-0/8	13-4/8	13-5/8	5-6/8	5-5/8	8-6/8	Sweetwater County	WY	Robert L Kampen	1985	697
68-0/8	13-3/8	13-4/8	5-1/8	5-2/8	6-5/8	Natrona County	WY	Joe Brant	1985	697
68-0/8	13-0/8	13-1/8	5-7/8	5-7/8	9-4/8	Natrona County	WY	Dave James	1985	697
68-0/8	14-0/8	13-6/8	6-3/8	6-2/8	14-6/8	Converse County	WY	Frank Moore	1985	697
68-0/8	12-3/8	12-4/8	6-2/8	6-2/8	9-0/8	Converse County	WY	Mark Slaughter	1986	697
67-6/8	12-3/8	12-4/8	5-6/8	5-5/8	9-0/8	Velva	ND	Darryl Ablestad	1967	726
67-6/8	12-6/8	12-4/8	6-2/8	6-0/8	11-3/8	Bergen	ND	Jim Budeau	1968	726
67-6/8	13-4/8	13-4/8	5-5/8	5-5/8	11-2/8	Sterling	CO	Loren Johnston	1968	726
67-6/8	13-3/8	13-2/8	5-2/8	5-5/8	10-1/8	Fremont County	WY	Doris Clark	1970	726
67-6/8	14-0/8	13-1/8	5-0/8	5-0/8	13-4/8	Butte County	ID	Craig L. Hansen	1974	726
67-6/8	12-4/8	12-6/8	5-5/8	5-5/8	11-1/8	Area 62	WY	James Beeson	1976	726
67-6/8	11-2/8	11-2/8	5-6/8	5-5/8	8-1/8	Douglas	WY	Ron Carpenter	1980	726
67-6/8	11-6/8	11-7/8	5-6/8	5-5/8	8-6/8	Rawlins	WY	Bob Funke	1980	726
67-6/8	13-1/8	13-2/8	5-4/8	5-2/8	9-7/8	McKinnon	WY	Jerry Giovannoni	1980	726
67-6/8	13-6/8	13-2/8	5-6/8	5-6/8	11-4/8	Casper	WY	David Stejskal	1980	726
67-6/8	13-5/8	12-6/8	5-5/8	5-4/8	10-4/8	Custer County	ID	Gerard J. Krauth	1981	726
67-6/8	13-7/8	13-6/8	5-6/8	5-5/8	9-2/8	Rio Arriba County	NM	Jose R. Montalvo	1982	726
67-6/8	13-4/8	13-6/8	5-4/8	5-4/8	11-7/8	Moffat County	CO	Robert L. Kinser	1982	726
67-6/8	13-5/8	13-5/8	5-3/8	5-2/8	8-0/8	Beaverhead County	MT	L. C. Trimber	1982	726
67-6/8	12-2/8	12-1/8	5-7/8	5-7/8	11-4/8	Craig County	CO	Mike Ward	1982	726
67-6/8	12-2/8	12-6/8	5-4/8	5-4/8	11-7/8	Douglas County	WY	Joe Ed McCray	1982	726
67-6/8	12-3/8	13-1/8	5-2/8	5-2/8	12-2/8	Larimer County	CO	William Shuster	1983	726
67-6/8	14-0/8	13-6/8	5-3/8	5-2/8	9-5/8	Las Animas County	CO	Edward F. Bryan, Jr.	1983	726
67-6/8	14-2/8	14-3/8	5-7/8	6-0/8	11-1/8	Hettinger County	ND	Mike Schiwal	1984	726
67-6/8	13-0/8	13-0/8	5-6/8	5-6/8	11-5/8	Natrona County	WY	Kirk H. Soulliere	1985	726
67-6/8	14-4/8	14-4/8	5-3/8	5-2/8	8-0/8	Carbon County	WY	Bob Boyle	1985	726
67-6/8	12-6/8	12-6/8	6-1/8	6-1/8	7-6/8	Sweetwater County	WY	Dean Lawyer	1986	726
67-4/8	13-4/8	13-5/8	5-3/8	5-2/8	13-3/8	Cherry County	NE	Marlin Wells	1967	748
67-4/8	13-7/8	13-7/8	5-3/8	5-2/8	10-1/8	Oregon Basin	WY	John Pruszyski	1973	748
67-4/8	13-3/8	13-2/8	5-4/8	5-4/8	9-0/8	Faith	SD	Jim Bohls	1974	748
67-4/8	14-2/8	14-0/8	5-2/8	5-1/8	8-5/8	Cowdrey	CO	Robert Souza	1974	748
67-4/8	13-6/8	13-4/8	5-6/8	5-4/8	11-7/8	Casper	WY	Steve Turck	1976	748
67-4/8	13-1/8	13-5/8	5-4/8	5-4/8	8-2/8	Douglas	WY	James E. Boland	1979	748
67-4/8	13-0/8	13-1/8	5-2/8	5-4/8	13-3/8	Casper	WY	Clifford G. James	1980	748
67-4/8	12-6/8	12-5/8	5-6/8	5-6/8	10-0/8	Douglas	WY	Bruce Sanders	1980	748
67-4/8	12-5/8	12-0/8	6-1/8	5-6/8	9-1/8	Craig County	CO	Robert L. Wright	1981	748

PRONGHORN

(continued)

Score	Length of Horn R	Length of Horn L	Circumference of Base R	Circumference of Base L	Greatest Spread	Area	State/ Province	Hunter's Name	Date	Rank
67-4/8	13-5/8	13-4/8	5-4/8	5-4/8	10-1/8	Converse County	WY	Ron Breitsprecher	1981	748
67-4/8	14-1/8	13-0/8	5-6/8	5-6/8	10-2/8	Lemhi County	ID	Daniel A. Davis	1981	748
67-4/8	14-2/8	14-4/8	5-4/8	5-3/8	7-4/8	Carbon County	WY	Mike Fortman	1982	748
67-4/8	11-6/8	12-6/8	5-5/8	5-4/8	8-1/8	Craig County	CO	Ken Keller	1983	748
67-4/8	13-0/8	13-2/8	5-3/8	5-3/8	6-5/8	Custer County	CO	Rohn L. Garnhart	1983	748
67-4/8	12-3/8	12-4/8	5-4/8	5-4/8	9-1/8	Converse County	WY	Roberta Byerly	1983	748
67-4/8	13-0/8	13-1/8	5-6/8	5-5/8	9-0/8	Converse County	WY	Jon Arneson	1983	748
67-4/8	14-1/8	14-0/8	5-4/8	5-4/8	9-7/8	Converse County	WY	Gary Hunsicker	1983	748
67-4/8	12-4/8	12-6/8	6-3/8	6-1/8	8-4/8	Converse County	WY	Jim Hodson	1984	748
67-4/8	12-3/8	12-4/8	6-0/8	5-7/8	9-0/8	Sweetwater County	WY	Craig Richardson	1984	748
67-4/8	13-0/8	12-6/8	5-6/8	5-6/8	11-0/8	Bowman County	ND	Mark Delong	1984	748
67-4/8	13-4/8	13-3/8	5-4/8	5-4/8	10-3/8	Campbell County	WY	Rick Gilley	1984	748
67-4/8	13-2/8	13-5/8	5-4/8	5-2/8	11-3/8	Johnson County	WY	Edward Carmichael	1984	748
67-4/8	13-4/8	13-4/8	5-4/8	5-4/8	12-0/8	Phillips County	MT	Ken Ruzicka	1984	748
67-4/8	13-1/8	13-1/8	5-6/8	5-6/8	9-2/8	Sweetwater County	WY	Kevin J. Slovak	1985	748
67-4/8	13-0/8	13-0/8	6-2/8	6-3/8	9-4/8	Billings County	ND	Ronald M. Bachmeier	1985	748
67-4/8	13-0/8	12-7/8	5-3/8	5-3/8	8-3/8	Converse County	WY	Len Cardinale	1985	748
67-4/8	12-7/8	12-6/8	5-3/8	5-2/8	9-0/8	Converse County	WY	Burt Thompson, Jr.	1985	748
67-4/8	12-3/8	12-7/8	5-5/8	5-5/8	9-6/8	Converse County	WY	Thomas Vitale	1985	748
67-4/8	12-1/8	12-0/8	5-7/8	6-0/8	9-2/8	Sweetwater County	WY	Chris Switzer	1986	748
67-4/8	13-7/8	12-7/8	5-6/8	5-6/8	8-3/8	McKenzie County	ND	David Tofte	1986	748
67-3/8	13-1/8	13-2/8	5-7/8	5-5/8	13-3/8	Carbon County	WY	Steve Stumbo	1975	778
67-2/8	12-1/8	12-1/8	6-0/8	5-5/8	11-6/8	Medicine Bow	WY	Dennis Behn	1974	779
67-2/8	12-7/8	13-0/8	5-2/8	5-2/8	6-4/8	Musselshell County	MT	Scott L. Koelzer	1976	779
67-2/8	13-7/8	14-0/8	5-4/8	5-4/8	9-2/8	Campbell County	WY	Larry Tiner	1978	779
67-2/8	12-6/8	13-1/8	5-7/8	5-7/8	9-5/8	Sweetwater County	WY	Blair Smith	1978	779
67-2/8	11-5/8	11-5/8	5-0/8	5-0/8	9-2/8	Converse County	WY	Eugene Smith, Jr.	1979	779
67-2/8	13-1/8	13-0/8	5-4/8	5-5/8	9-2/8	Converse County	WY	Ronald J. Collier	1980	779
67-2/8	13-5/8	13-1/8	5-5/8	5-5/8	10-3/8	Button Lake	NV	Jeff Purcell	1980	779
67-2/8	13-3/8	13-4/8	5-5/8	5-4/8	10-2/8	Converse County	WY	John Zawaski	1980	779
67-2/8	12-6/8	12-6/8	5-3/8	5-3/8	12-3/8	Converse County	WY	Al Gross	1981	779
67-2/8	13-7/8	13-7/8	5-4/8	5-4/8	11-2/8	Douglas	WY	Wayne W. Wagner	1981	779
67-2/8	13-1/8	13-2/8	5-2/8	5-1/8	9-4/8	Pueblo County	CO	Mitchell McMahon	1982	779
67-2/8	14-1/8	12-7/8	5-4/8	5-4/8	10-6/8	Craig County	CO	Steven Neal	1982	779
67-2/8	13-4/8	13-4/8	5-4/8	5-3/8	8-2/8	Wallace County	KS	Steve Rugg	1982	779
67-2/8	13-6/8	12-3/8	6-1/8	6-1/8	9-6/8	White Pine County	NV	Larry T. Gilbertson	1983	779
67-2/8	11-7/8	12-0/8	5-7/8	5-7/8	9-4/8	Bowman County	ND	Greg Braun	1983	779
67-2/8	14-3/8	14-2/8	5-4/8	5-4/8	12-0/8	Perkins County	SD	Vilas Schoenfelder	1983	779
67-2/8	13-0/8	12-4/8	6-0/8	5-6/8	7-3/8	Douglas County	WY	Larry Crooks	1983	779
67-2/8	13-1/8	12-7/8	5-5/8	5-6/8	11-5/8	Converse County	WY	Gary Holtz	1983	779
67-2/8	12-5/8	12-3/8	5-3/8	5-4/8	11-7/8	Meade County	SD	Steve D. Krier	1983	779
67-2/8	12-0/8	12-2/8	5-7/8	6-1/8	7-3/8	Campbell County	WY	William Heineke	1984	779
67-2/8	12-0/8	12-1/8	5-6/8	5-5/8	7-7/8	Converse County	WY	Ron Rockwell	1984	779
67-2/8	12-4/8	12-3/8	6-0/8	6-0/8	12-0/8	Sweetwater County	WY	John Cheese	1985	779
67-2/8	13-2/8	13-2/8	5-4/8	5-2/8	7-2/8	Moffat County	CO	John E. Axelson	1985	779
67-2/8	13-3/8	12-6/8	5-4/8	5-4/8	7-6/8	Moffat County	CO	Kurt Keskimaki	1985	779
67-2/8	12-4/8	12-4/8	5-6/8	5-6/8	8-3/8	Moffat County	CO	James A. Davison	1985	779
67-2/8	13-1/8	12-7/8	5-7/8	5-6/8	9-3/8	Carbon County	WY	Richard L. Westervelt	1985	779
67-2/8	13-7/8	13-7/8	5-6/8	5-5/8	11-1/8	Converse County	WY	David Jerome	1985	779
67-2/8	12-5/8	12-5/8	5-3/8	5-3/8	9-0/8	Converse County	WY	William Doemland	1985	779
67-2/8	13-2/8	13-2/8	5-1/8	5-1/8	8-4/8	Cambell County	WY	Richard Andre	1985	779
67-2/8	13-2/8	13-1/8	5-7/8	5-6/8	11-0/8	Converse County	WY	Craig James Stransky	1985	779
67-2/8	12-7/8	12-7/8	6-0/8	5-6/8	8-5/8	Converse County	WY	Gregory White	1986	779
67-0/8	12-7/8	12-7/8	5-6/8	5-4/8	10-2/8	Butte County	SD	David Lind	1961	810
67-0/8	13-0/8	13-2/8	5-5/8	5-5/8	10-6/8	Riverdale	ND	Harold Janssen	1971	810
67-0/8	13-0/8	12-4/8	6-0/8	6-0/8	10-4/8	Spotted Horse	WY	Gerald L. Egbert	1975	810
67-0/8	11-0/8	11-0/8	6-6/8	6-4/8	8-3/8	Douglas	WY	Eddie Hayden	1978	810
67-0/8	12-6/8	12-4/8	6-1/8	6-0/8	11-2/8	Douglas	WY	Kenneth L. Stoneburner	1978	810
67-0/8	12-7/8	12-7/8	5-5/8	5-5/8	7-2/8	Converse County	WY	Alton Gross	1980	810
67-0/8	11-5/8	11-5/8	6-0/8	6-0/8	9-0/8	Weld County	CO	Dennis Schweitzer	1980	810
67-0/8	12-3/8	12-2/8	5-5/8	5-6/8	8-7/8	Sheridan County	WY	Travis Adsit	1981	810
67-0/8	12-6/8	13-0/8	5-5/8	5-6/8	10-7/8	Casper	WY	Robert Arvey	1981	810
67-0/8	11-6/8	11-6/8	5-6/8	5-6/8	9-1/8	Converse County	WY	Richard Smith	1981	810

Minimum Score 64

Score	Length of Horn R	L	Circumference of Base R	L	Greatest Spread	Area	State/ Province	Hunter's Name	Date	Rank
67-0/8	13-7/8	14-0/8	5-7/8	5-7/8	10-5/8	Bill County	WY	Robert A. Christensen	1982	810
67-0/8	12-2/8	12-1/8	5-6/8	5-6/8	9-3/8	Douglas	WY	Howard Holmes	1982	810
67-0/8	13-7/8	14-1/8	5-2/8	5-2/8	10-7/8	Lassen County	CA	Don Rossiter	1983	810
67-0/8	15-0/8	14-7/8	5-2/8	5-2/8	11-2/8	Yauapai County	AZ	Michael John Bylina	1983	810
67-0/8	13-5/8	14-0/8	5-3/8	5-3/8	11-3/8	Natrona County	WY	Charles Lanzarone	1983	810
67-0/8	12-7/8	12-5/8	5-6/8	5-5/8	11-0/8	Broadwater County	MT	Bob A. Closson	1983	810
67-0/8	12-5/8	12-5/8	5-3/8	5-1/8	10-6/8	Converse County	WY	Thomas L. Hughes	1983	810
67-0/8	12-5/8	12-4/8	5-5/8	5-4/8	10-3/8	Custer County	ID	Matt March, Jr.	1984	810
67-0/8	13-4/8	13-3/8	5-2/8	5-3/8	11-2/8	Sweetwater County	WY	Cliff Wiseman	1985	810
67-0/8	13-1/8	12-7/8	5-4/8	5-4/8	7-6/8	Sweetwater County	WY	Chuck Ashton	1985	810
67-0/8	12-5/8	12-5/8	5-4/8	5-3/8	9-2/8	Modoc County	CA	Anthony R. Dipino	1986	810
67-0/8	13-5/8	13-3/8	6-0/8	6-1/8	10-6/8	Mountrail County	ND	Charles LeRohl	1986	810
66-7/8	13-3/8	14-3/8	5-3/8	5-5/8	15-4/8	Gillette	WY	Joseph Strasser, Jr.	1981	832
66-6/8	14-4/8	14-2/8	5-3/8	5-4/8	13-5/8	Douglas	WY	Roland Gravenkemper	1955	833
66-6/8	13-3/8	13-1/8	5-7/8	5-7/8	8-4/8	Campbell County	WY	Pete Erickson	1967	833
66-6/8	13-0/8	13-2/8	5-7/8	5-4/8	12-0/8	Natrona County	WY	Toby Johnson	1972	833
66-6/8	12-4/8	12-4/8	5-6/8	5-6/8	10-3/8	Butte County	SD	Dr. William L. Lee	1974	833
66-6/8	12-6/8	12-6/8	5-6/8	5-5/8	10-0/8	Butte County	SD	Charles C. Tippton, Jr.	1974	833
66-6/8	14-1/8	13-2/8	5-5/8	5-4/8	10-6/8	Wallace County	KS	David Stevenson	1975	833
66-6/8	12-7/8	12-7/8	5-4/8	5-4/8	9-4/8	Casper	WY	Mel Johnson	1978	833
66-6/8	13-1/8	13-0/8	5-4/8	5-2/8	11-6/8	Johnson County	WY	Frederick A. Suran	1978	833
66-6/8	11-6/8	11-3/8	5-4/8	5-3/8	9-6/8	Rawlins	WY	Ed Downard	1980	833
66-6/8	12-5/8	12-7/8	5-6/8	5-6/8	8-0/8	Casper	WY	James R. Kilgore	1980	833
66-6/8	12-2/8	12-2/8	5-7/8	5-7/8	7-4/8	Converse County	WY	Carl W. Van Ryswyk	1980	833
66-6/8	13-0/8	13-0/8	5-3/8	5-4/8	7-4/8	Maybell	CO	Tim Chastain	1981	833
66-6/8	13-0/8	13-0/8	5-7/8	5-6/8	7-7/8	Little Wood River	ID	Champ Church	1981	833
66-6/8	13-3/8	14-3/8	5-3/8	5-3/8	11-4/8	Natrona County	WY	Dean Hamilton	1981	833
66-6/8	14-0/8	11-3/8	5-2/8	5-2/8	10-7/8	Douglas	WY	Lee Jernigan	1981	833
66-6/8	11-7/8	11-5/8	5-5/8	5-6/8	9-0/8	Glenrock	WY	Charlie Kroll	1981	833
66-6/8	12-2/8	12-3/8	5-7/8	5-6/8	8-0/8	Dubois	ID	Richard K. Russell	1981	833
66-6/8	12-1/8	12-0/8	5-4/8	5-5/8	10-4/8	Converse County	WY	John S. Shields	1983	833
66-6/8	14-1/8	14-2/8	5-1/8	5-0/8	12-2/8	Moffat County	CO	Rick Stockburger	1983	833
66-6/8	13-1/8	13-2/8	5-3/8	5-4/8	9-2/8	Converse County	WY	Gene Gilmer	1983	833
66-6/8	12-6/8	12-7/8	5-5/8	5-5/8	11-7/8	Converse County	WY	Spencer Wilker	1983	833
66-6/8	13-2/8	12-6/8	5-7/8	5-6/8	9-2/8	Converse County	WY	Randy Dittmer	1984	833
66-6/8	13-7/8	14-0/8	5-6/8	5-6/8	12-7/8	McKenzie County	ND	Mitch Griebel	1984	833
66-6/8	12-7/8	12-5/8	6-2/8	5-7/8	11-4/8	Campbell County	WY	Robert Finelli	1984	833
66-6/8	12-5/8	12-6/8	6-0/8	5-6/8	10-7/8	Converse County	WY	Jack Leggo	1985	833
66-6/8	12-4/8	12-7/8	5-4/8	5-4/8	9-4/8	Carbon County	WY	Kim Cooper	1985	833
66-6/8	12-7/8	12-7/8	5-5/8	5-5/8	10-4/8	Natrona County	WY	Rickey E. Morse	1986	833
66-6/8	12-4/8	12-6/8	5-6/8	5-5/8	9-4/8	Fergus County	MT	Charles B. Vogl	1986	833
66-6/8	13-7/8	13-1/8	5-4/8	5-4/8	11-5/8	Petroleum County	MT	Stan Colton	1986	833
66-4/8	12-0/8	12-0/8	5-5/8	5-4/8	12-0/8	Lander	WY	Fred Bear	1955	862
66-4/8	13-6/8	13-4/8	5-4/8	5-4/8	11-2/8	?	NM	Paul Link	1962	862
66-4/8	12-6/8	12-2/8	6-0/8	6-0/8	8-2/8	Dickinson	ND	Dennis A. Schneider	1965	862
66-4/8	13-4/8	13-7/8	5-4/8	5-4/8	6-5/8	Harding County	SD	Richard Bolyard	1974	862
66-4/8	13-4/8	13-7/8	5-4/8	5-4/8	8-6/8	Valley County	MT	Tom Solem	1979	862
66-4/8	12-4/8	12-7/8	5-4/8	5-4/8	8-4/8	Dawes County	NE	Jerry Dennis	1980	862
66-4/8	13-0/8	13-0/8	5-6/8	5-4/8	9-0/8	Converse County	WY	Ronald J. Collier	1981	862
66-4/8	13-4/8	13-3/8	5-6/8	6-0/8	9-5/8	Fremont County	WY	Everett A. Boss	1981	862
66-4/8	13-0/8	13-0/8	5-6/8	5-5/8	7-2/8	Glenrock	WY	Andy Tkach	1981	862
66-4/8	12-3/8	12-3/8	5-4/8	5-4/8	12-2/8	Moffat County	CO	Bill Yessa	1981	862
66-4/8	13-1/8	11-7/8	5-7/8	5-7/8	9-0/8	Siskiyou County	CA	Doug Walker	1982	862
66-4/8	12-4/8	12-7/8	5-7/8	5-6/8	10-0/8	Power County	ID	Robert Bennett	1982	862
66-4/8	13-6/8	14-1/8	6-2/8	6-4/8	13-3/8	Bowman County	ND	Curt Wells	1982	862
66-4/8	12-6/8	12-7/8	5-4/8	5-4/8	7-4/8	Moffat County	CO	Dennis J. Erkinger	1982	862
66-4/8	13-1/8	13-1/8	5-5/8	5-5/8	12-6/8	McCone County	MT	Dan Sturgis	1982	862
66-4/8	12-4/8	13-1/8	5-6/8	5-4/8	11-1/8	Moffat County	CO	Chris Cassidy	1983	862
66-4/8	12-3/8	12-4/8	6-1/8	5-7/8	12-4/8	Moffit County	CO	Toni R. Roberts	1983	862
66-4/8	13-0/8	12-6/8	5-6/8	5-6/8	8-4/8	Converse County	WY	Steve Byerly	1983	862
66-4/8	12-1/8	12-1/8	5-7/8	5-4/8	9-1/8	Natrona County	WY	Arthur S. Wert	1983	862
66-4/8	12-5/8	12-3/8	5-6/8	5-4/8	8-1/8	McKensie County	ND	James R. Greutman	1983	862
66-4/8	12-5/8	12-4/8	6-0/8	6-0/8	10-1/8	Carbon County	WY	James D. Davis	1983	862

PRONGHORN

(continued)   Minimum Score 64

Score	Length of Horn R	Length of Horn L	Circumference of Base R	Circumference of Base L	Greatest Spread	Area	State/ Province	Hunter's Name	Date	Rank
66-4/8	12-5/8	12-5/8	5-7/8	5-4/8	9-2/8	Converse County	WY	Gary White	1983	862
66-4/8	11-7/8	12-0/8	5-5/8	5-5/8	6-5/8	Moffat County	CO	Tim Decker	1984	862
66-4/8	12-6/8	13-0/8	5-3/8	5-6/8	9-5/8	Carbon County	WY	Paul Kniss	1984	862
66-4/8	12-2/8	12-3/8	5-7/8	5-6/8	12-1/8	Campbell County	WY	Mark S. Presta	1984	862
66-4/8	13-1/8	13-2/8	5-3/8	5-3/8	12-2/8	Converse County	WY	Charles E Gose	1984	862
66-4/8	13-3/8	13-4/8	5-2/8	5-2/8	10-0/8	Moffat County	CO	Reina Kemp	1985	862
66-4/8	12-7/8	13-4/8	5-4/8	5-3/8	10-0/8	Tooele County	UT	Scott Anderson	1985	862
66-4/8	11-7/8	11-6/8	5-5/8	5-5/8	9-7/8	Musselshell County	MT	Brian Acton	1985	862
66-3/8	12-5/8	13-0/8	5-7/8	5-6/8	13-3/8	Natrona County	WY	Richard Iverson	1981	891
66-3/8	13-0/8	12-6/8	5-7/8	5-6/8	13-1/8	Coconino County	AZ	Scott Kellner	1983	891
66-2/8	12-7/8	13-0/8	5-3/8	5-3/8	8-7/8	McLean County	ND	Robert Freeberg	1967	893
66-2/8	12-5/8	12-6/8	5-5/8	5-4/8	9-2/8	Medicine Bow	WY	Steve Gorr	1971	893
66-2/8	12-1/8	12-1/8	6-3/8	6-4/8	11-5/8	Douglas	WY	Denny Behn	1979	893
66-2/8	13-3/8	13-2/8	5-6/8	5-4/8	11-1/8	Casper	WY	Don Schram	1980	893
66-2/8	11-4/8	11-4/8	5-6/8	5-6/8	8-3/8	Casper	WY	Billy Ellis	1981	893
66-2/8	12-4/8	12-5/8	5-7/8	5-5/8	9-0/8	Campbell County	WY	William F. Heineke	1981	893
66-2/8	13-0/8	12-7/8	5-5/8	5-4/8	8-7/8	Campbell County	WY	Pat Mitchell	1981	893
66-2/8	12-5/8	12-4/8	5-5/8	5-5/8	10-1/8	Lincoln County	WY	Lonnie Smith	1981	893
66-2/8	11-6/8	12-1/8	5-7/8	5-6/8	8-4/8	Maybell	CO	Earl Stout	1981	893
66-2/8	11-7/8	12-0/8	5-5/8	5-5/8	10-7/8	Craig	CO	Warren P. Uhl	1981	893
66-2/8	11-4/8	11-4/8	6-7/8	6-6/8	7-7/8	Converse County	WY	Albert R. Taylor	1982	893
66-2/8	12-4/8	12-4/8	5-7/8	6-0/8	9-2/8	Bowman County	ND	Dean Albertson	1982	893
66-2/8	11-3/8	11-4/8	5-6/8	5-6/8	8-4/8	Converse County	WY	David Hell	1982	893
66-2/8	11-6/8	11-5/8	6-0/8	6-0/8	12-6/8	Sioux County	NE	Melvin L. Rein	1982	893
66-2/8	12-2/8	11-7/8	5-4/8	5-3/8	11-0/8	Moffat County	CO	George T. Kili	1982	893
66-2/8	13-1/8	12-7/8	5-5/8	5-4/8	9-7/8	Meagher County	MT	D. Mitch Kottas	1982	893
66-2/8	12-6/8	13-1/8	5-5/8	5-6/8	9-1/8	Lemhi County	ID	Richard C. Nichols	1982	893
66-2/8	10-7/8	11-0/8	6-3/8	6-2/8	8-6/8	Moffat County	CO	Ray Ryan	1983	893
66-2/8	13-6/8	13-4/8	5-5/8	5-5/8	8-1/8	Weston County	WY	Pat Graham	1983	893
66-2/8	12-6/8	12-4/8	5-5/8	5-3/8	10-0/8	Converse County	WY	Michael Arneson	1983	893
66-2/8	12-3/8	12-3/8	5-4/8	5-4/8	8-5/8	Campbell County	WY	Joseph Strasser, Jr.	1984	893
66-2/8	12-3/8	13-0/8	5-4/8	5-4/8	8-3/8	Crook County	WY	Terry Walton	1984	893
66-2/8	13-3/8	13-3/8	5-4/8	5-4/8	10-2/8	Washoe County	NV	Ralph L Albright	1985	893
66-2/8	13-0/8	12-4/8	5-5/8	5-5/8	11-5/8	Fremont County	WY	David Dickson	1985	893
66-2/8	13-0/8	13-0/8	5-5/8	5-6/8	9-3/8	Moffat County	CO	Randy Lamdin	1986	893
66-1/8	12-6/8	12-4/8	6-0/8	5-7/8	14-3/8	Carbon County	WY	Willis Duhon	1985	918
66-0/8	12-0/8	12-0/8	5-5/8	5-4/8	11-1/8	Rock County	NE	Mac Forbes	1967	919
66-0/8	12-5/8	12-5/8	6-1/8	5-6/8	8-2/8	Big Piney	WY	Frank D. Prentup	1976	919
66-0/8	12-7/8	12-7/8	5-2/8	5-2/8	9-0/8	Stewart Valley	SAS	Daniel N. Rayner	1976	919
66-0/8	12-6/8	12-6/8	6-0/8	6-1/8	11-6/8	Mountrail County	ND	Wade F. Williamson	1976	919
66-0/8	14-4/8	14-3/8	5-5/8	5-3/8	7-6/8	Antelope Creek	ID	Richard B. Harvey	1978	919
66-0/8	13-0/8	12-4/8	5-7/8	5-6/8	8-3/8	Douglas	WY	Pat Walker	1978	919
66-0/8	10-6/8	11-0/8	5-5/8	5-6/8	7-1/8	Stanley County	SD	Brian Fox	1980	919
66-0/8	11-4/8	12-0/8	5-7/8	5-7/8	8-4/8	Maybell	CO	William T. Shoemaker	1980	919
66-0/8	13-0/8	13-2/8	5-3/8	5-3/8	11-6/8	Johnson County	WY	Denny Ennis	1981	919
66-0/8	11-4/8	11-4/8	5-5/8	5-4/8	7-4/8	Douglas	WY	Ronald Grzybowski	1981	919
66-0/8	13-0/8	13-3/8	5-2/8	5-1/8	9-5/8	Natrona County	WY	Dan Kolb	1981	919
66-0/8	11-0/8	10-2/8	5-4/8	5-3/8	7-7/8	Craig	CO	Gail Martin	1981	919
66-0/8	12-3/8	12-2/8	6-0/8	6-2/8	8-7/8	Lassen County	CA	Ronald R. Mayfield	1981	919
66-0/8	12-4/8	11-5/8	5-4/8	5-3/8	8-7/8	Weld County	CO	Mike Nobe	1982	919
66-0/8	12-4/8	12-3/8	6-0/8	5-7/8	14-4/8	Yavapai County	AZ	Jeff W. Elmer	1982	919
66-0/8	13-1/8	13-1/8	5-4/8	5-3/8	11-1/8	Lemhi County	ID	Ben Fahnholz	1983	919
66-0/8	13-4/8	13-5/8	5-7/8	5-6/8	12-2/8	Carbon County	WY	Jim Hodson	1983	919
66-0/8	13-0/8	13-1/8	5-0/8	5-0/8	9-4/8	Moffat County	CO	Jerry Lotspeich	1983	919
66-0/8	13-2/8	12-4/8	5-5/8	5-5/8	10-3/8	Converse County	WY	David S. Bunce	1983	919
66-0/8	12-7/8	12-5/8	5-5/8	5-4/8	6-6/8	Converse County	WY	Roger Wintle	1983	919
66-0/8	13-1/8	13-2/8	5-2/8	5-4/8	11-2/8	Converse County	WY	David Baldwin	1983	919
66-0/8	11-5/8	11-6/8	6-0/8	6-0/8	11-1/8	Converse County	WY	Reggie Spiegelberg	1983	919
66-0/8	12-5/8	13-0/8	5-4/8	5-4/8	7-0/8	Washoe County	NV	Randall T. Harris	1984	919
66-0/8	11-6/8	11-0/8	6-0/8	5-7/8	9-1/8	Converse County	WY	Jeff Wagstaff	1984	919
66-0/8	13-5/8	13-4/8	5-2/8	5-1/8	11-6/8	Carbon County	WY	Kirk Westervelt	1985	919
66-0/8	12-5/8	12-6/8	5-2/8	5-3/8	9-6/8	Garfield County	MT	T. Anthony Brock	1985	919
66-0/8	13-2/8	13-4/8	5-2/8	5-0/8	10-4/8	Perkins County	SD	Michael P. Brust	1985	919

Minimum Score 64

Score	Length of Horn R	L	Circumference of Base R	L	Greatest Spread	Area	State/ Province	Hunter's Name	Date	Rank
66-0/8	13-0/8	13-0/8	6-0/8	6-0/8	10-3/8	Crook County	WY	Pink Atkins	1985	919
66-0/8	12-3/8	12-4/8	5-2/8	5-2/8	9-4/8	Slope County	ND	Tim Belland	1985	919
66-0/8	13-4/8	13-4/8	5-3/8	5-2/8	10-2/8	Converse County	WY	Larry Hesterly	1986	919
65-7/8	13-4/8	13-6/8	5-0/8	5-0/8	13-7/8	Haakon County	SD	Ward McCaughey	1971	949
65-7/8	13-0/8	13-0/8	5-3/8	5-3/8	14-3/8	Natrona County	WY	Dennis Keyser	1978	949
65-6/8	13-2/8	13-5/8	5-1/8	5-1/8	10-6/8	Lovelace Ranch	NM	Frank W. Evans	1960	951
65-6/8	13-0/8	13-0/8	5-4/8	5-3/8	6-7/8	Bassett	NE	Del Austin	1964	951
65-6/8	13-1/8	13-1/8	6-1/8	5-5/8	11-2/8	Gillette	WY	Russell Wright	1966	951
65-6/8	12-5/8	12-2/8	5-6/8	5-7/8	11-0/8	Perkins County	SD	Gerald Bentson	1968	951
65-6/8	11-4/8	11-7/8	5-3/8	5-4/8	9-2/8	McCone County	MT	Charles M. Carlson	1970	951
65-6/8	11-2/8	11-6/8	7-0/8	6-5/8	12-4/8	Casper	WY	Bill Emery	1974	951
65-6/8	12-4/8	12-3/8	5-6/8	5-6/8	10-1/8	Carter County	MT	John Fleharty	1981	951
65-6/8	12-2/8	12-6/8	5-7/8	5-6/8	4-7/8	Seligman County	AZ	Oscar Dale Porter	1981	951
65-6/8	12-1/8	12-0/8	6-1/8	6-0/8	8-3/8	Weld County	CO	Larry Gann	1981	951
65-6/8	11-6/8	11-4/8	5-5/8	5-5/8	12-6/8	Douglas	WY	Tom Kayser	1981	951
65-6/8	11-6/8	11-6/8	8-2/8	8-2/8	10-7/8	Moffat County	CO	Ray Ryan	1982	951
65-6/8	13-4/8	13-2/8	5-5/8	5-4/8	8-5/8	Campbell County	WY	Robert Erickson	1982	951
65-6/8	12-6/8	12-4/8	5-6/8	5-7/8	8-6/8	Johnson County	WY	James Kaszynski	1982	951
65-6/8	13-0/8	12-6/8	5-7/8	6-0/8	11-7/8	Converse County	WY	Steve Miller	1982	951
65-6/8	13-2/8	13-1/8	5-2/8	5-1/8	7-2/8	Converse County	WY	Larry Noland	1982	951
65-6/8	12-6/8	12-6/8	5-4/8	5-4/8	12-1/8	Medicine Lodge	ID	Ron Stacey	1982	951
65-6/8	13-7/8	14-0/8	5-2/8	5-2/8	11-4/8	Sweetwater County	WY	Matt March, Jr.	1983	951
65-6/8	13-2/8	12-7/8	5-4/8	5-2/8	8-0/8	Lemhi County	ID	Larry Cross	1983	951
65-6/8	12-6/8	13-0/8	5-2/8	5-5/8	7-2/8	Carbon County	WY	Mike Schuchard	1983	951
65-6/8	14-6/8	14-4/8	5-1/8	5-1/8	9-7/8	Natrona County	WY	William W. Onken	1983	951
65-6/8	12-3/8	12-3/8	5-2/8	5-1/8	7-0/8	Wright County	WY	Jeff Deline	1983	951
65-6/8	12-5/8	12-3/8	5-1/8	5-2/8	9-7/8	Converse County	WY	Robert M. Sweisthal, Jr.	1983	951
65-6/8	11-6/8	12-2/8	5-4/8	5-4/8	9-0/8	Converse County	WY	Joe Trinceri	1983	951
65-6/8	11-7/8	11-7/8	5-5/8	5-6/8	10-4/8	Sioux County	NE	Kevin Langan	1983	951
65-6/8	12-1/8	12-1/8	5-5/8	5-5/8	10-3/8	Moffat County	CO	Stephen Mikkelsen	1984	951
65-6/8	12-5/8	12-5/8	5-3/8	5-2/8	6-7/8	Converse County	WY	R. Tim Reed	1984	951
65-6/8	12-5/8	12-2/8	5-6/8	5-3/8	8-0/8	Weston County	WY	Gary D. Johansen	1984	951
65-6/8	12-2/8	12-0/8	5-5/8	5-4/8	8-7/8	Natrona County	WY	Kurt Keskimaki	1985	951
65-6/8	11-3/8	11-3/8	6-0/8	6-0/8	8-6/8	Converse County	WY	Dick Gambrel	1985	951
65-6/8	12-2/8	12-4/8	5-5/8	5-5/8	10-0/8	Converse County	WY	Mark Folk	1985	951
65-6/8	11-5/8	11-6/8	5-6/8	5-6/8	7-0/8	Yuma County	CO	Larry Bishop	1986	951
65-6/8	12-6/8	12-5/8	5-4/8	5-5/8	8-5/8	Carbon County	WY	Larry Hayes	1986	951
65-4/8	12-0/8	12-0/8	5-4/8	5-4/8	8-4/8	Belle Buttes	SD	Alden Hobbs	1958	983
65-4/8	12-3/8	12-2/8	5-5/8	5-4/8	7-0/8	Casper	WY	Clarence J. Grandt	1973	983
65-4/8	11-6/8	11-6/8	5-7/8	5-6/8	11-0/8	Casper	WY	Pat Inman	1973	983
65-4/8	12-2/8	12-2/8	5-5/8	5-4/8	9-6/8	Medicine Bow	WY	G. Fred Asbell	1974	983
65-4/8	12-0/8	11-7/8	5-4/8	5-0/8	9-1/8	Kaycee	WY	Charles Jahnke	1979	983
65-4/8	12-1/8	12-1/8	5-3/8	5-2/8	9-4/8	Converse County	WY	Robert V. Anderson	1981	983
65-4/8	13-5/8	13-1/8	5-2/8	5-2/8	11-3/8	Casper	WY	Jack H. Williams	1981	983
65-4/8	13-2/8	12-2/8	5-6/8	5-7/8	8-7/8	Johnson County	WY	Fred Thanel	1982	983
65-4/8	12-6/8	12-7/8	5-4/8	5-2/8	13-5/8	Converse County	WY	Melvin R. Wells	1983	983
65-4/8	12-7/8	13-1/8	5-0/8	5-0/8	6-6/8	Converse County	WY	Terry Wobig	1983	983
65-4/8	12-6/8	12-6/8	5-1/8	5-1/8	8-3/8	Custer County	ID	Dwight Rollins	1984	983
65-4/8	13-4/8	13-3/8	5-5/8	5-5/8	9-2/8	White Pine County	NV	Bob Price	1984	983
65-4/8	12-1/8	12-2/8	5-4/8	5-3/8	9-7/8	Converse County	WY	Don Schram	1984	983
65-4/8	13-3/8	13-4/8	5-2/8	5-3/8	6-7/8	Natrona County	WY	Gregory R. Bonetti	1984	983
65-4/8	11-7/8	11-4/8	5-7/8	5-6/8	9-5/8	Converse County	WY	Ron Hopkins	1984	983
65-4/8	12-5/8	12-4/8	5-7/8	5-6/8	8-5/8	Moffat County	CO	Win Knechtel	1985	983
65-4/8	12-0/8	12-0/8	6-0/8	6-0/8	8-5/8	Moffat County	CO	Randy Lamdin	1985	983
65-4/8	12-7/8	13-1/8	5-0/8	5-0/8	11-1/8	Converse County	WY	Daniel R Sowders	1985	983
65-4/8	13-0/8	13-0/8	5-0/8	5-1/8	8-2/8	Converse County	WY	Gerry Rubalcaba	1985	983
65-4/8	12-5/8	12-3/8	5-4/8	5-4/8	12-0/8	Glasscock County	TX	Courtney King	1985	983
65-4/8	11-6/8	12-4/8	5-2/8	5-3/8	11-2/8	Hettinger County	ND	Bill Clink	1986	983
65-3/8	10-6/8	10-4/8	5-6/8	5-7/8	11-3/8	Wall	SD	Dean Nevland	1970	1004
65-3/8	10-3/8	11-2/8	5-5/8	5-4/8	11-3/8	Moffat County	CO	Harry Campagnola	1982	1004
65-2/8	11-6/8	12-3/8	6-0/8	5-7/8	10-1/8	Maybelle	CO	Henry Wichers	1958	1006
65-2/8	12-0/8	11-7/8	6-2/8	6-2/8	10-3/8	Birch Creek	ID	Larry Cross	1978	1006
65-2/8	13-4/8	13-3/8	4-7/8	4-7/8	11-0/8	Casper	WY	Mark Smith	1978	1006

PRONGHORN
(continued)

Minimum Score 64

Score	Length of Horn R	L	Circumference of Base R	L	Greatest Spread	Area	State/ Province	Hunter's Name	Date	Rank
65-2/8	11-7/8	12-2/8	6-0/8	5-7/8	12-6/8	Natrona County	WY	Greg L. Pope	1979	1006
65-2/8	14-6/8	13-6/8	5-4/8	5-4/8	9-2/8	Johnson County	WY	D. Collis/R. Smith	1979	1006
65-2/8	12-4/8	11-7/8	6-0/8	5-5/8	11-3/8	Petroleum County	MT	Danny Moore	1980	1006
65-2/8	13-0/8	13-1/8	5-5/8	5-3/8	12-1/8	Converse County	WY	Robert King	1980	1006
65-2/8	13-0/8	13-0/8	5-2/8	5-2/8	9-4/8	Converse County	WY	Jim Keim	1981	1006
65-2/8	11-5/8	11-7/8	5-5/8	5-4/8	9-5/8	Bonneville County	ID	J. David Powers	1981	1006
65-2/8	13-3/8	13-4/8	5-6/8	5-6/8	10-7/8	Douglas	WY	William Pyle	1981	1006
65-2/8	12-2/8	12-6/8	5-4/8	5-4/8	9-5/8	Converse County	WY	Hank Sisil	1981	1006
65-2/8	12-4/8	12-1/8	5-5/8	5-5/8	8-3/8	Valley County	MT	Leith S. Wimmer	1982	1006
65-2/8	14-1/8	14-0/8	4-7/8	4-5/8	8-7/8	Fergus County	MT	Don Davidson	1982	1006
65-2/8	13-1/8	13-3/8	5-4/8	5-3/8	10-2/8	Douglas County	WY	Richard C. Martell	1982	1006
65-2/8	11-2/8	11-2/8	6-1/8	6-1/8	9-2/8	Lemhi County	ID	Blair G. Fisher	1982	1006
65-2/8	12-1/8	12-0/8	6-0/8	5-7/8	9-6/8	Butte County	ID	Doug Ramsey	1983	1006
65-2/8	12-0/8	12-1/8	5-6/8	5-6/8	10-5/8	Natrona County	WY	Vincent Cina	1983	1006
65-2/8	12-4/8	12-3/8	5-5/8	5-3/8	10-2/8	Moffat County	CO	Gene E. Smith	1983	1006
65-2/8	11-2/8	11-1/8	5-6/8	5-6/8	9-1/8	Converse County	WY	Ken Horton	1983	1006
65-2/8	12-5/8	12-3/8	6-0/8	6-0/8	10-4/8	Sweetwater County	WY	Bryan Radakovich	1984	1006
65-2/8	12-0/8	12-3/8	5-2/8	5-2/8	8-5/8	Lemhi County	ID	Larry Cross	1984	1006
65-2/8	11-2/8	11-4/8	5-7/8	5-6/8	9-4/8	Carbon County	WY	Dick Bean	1984	1006
65-0/8	13-2/8	13-3/8	5-0/8	4-7/8	10-2/8	Lovelace Ranch	NM	Ben Evans	1962	1028
65-0/8	12-6/8	12-6/8	5-2/8	5-3/8	12-6/8	Butte	ND	John Zahrte	1974	1028
65-0/8	12-4/8	12-2/8	5-4/8	6-1/8	8-3/8	Laramie	WY	Robert Gorge	1979	1028
65-0/8	12-6/8	12-6/8	5-6/8	5-5/8	12-5/8	Converse County	WY	Joseph Hopwood	1980	1028
65-0/8	12-2/8	12-2/8	5-6/8	5-6/8	10-0/8	Moffat County	CO	Lyle Willmarth	1980	1028
65-0/8	11-2/8	11-2/8	6-2/8	6-1/8	7-7/8	Converse County	WY	David E. Smith	1982	1028
65-0/8	12-3/8	12-3/8	5-7/8	6-0/8	9-3/8	Douglas County	WY	Mark R. Mussey	1982	1028
65-0/8	13-2/8	13-0/8	5-5/8	5-4/8	9-5/8	Bowel Tower	ALB	Chris Kearing	1982	1028
65-0/8	11-7/8	12-2/8	5-6/8	5-6/8	10-3/8	Converse County	WY	Darrell A. Bendel	1982	1028
65-0/8	13-4/8	13-0/8	5-3/8	5-3/8	8-6/8	Glenrock	WY	Kathy Kelly	1982	1028
65-0/8	12-4/8	12-6/8	5-2/8	5-2/8	10-6/8	Albany County	WY	Claude Oppegard	1982	1028
65-0/8	13-0/8	13-1/8	5-4/8	5-2/8	9-4/8	Sweetwater County	WY	Joe Dombovy	1983	1028
65-0/8	12-0/8	12-2/8	5-4/8	5-2/8	10-7/8	Carbon County	WY	Steven Bins	1983	1028
65-0/8	12-4/8	12-1/8	5-3/8	5-2/8	11-4/8	Carbon County	WY	Dan McPherson	1983	1028
65-0/8	12-5/8	12-4/8	5-3/8	5-2/8	7-1/8	Slope County	ND	Ed Steidler	1983	1028
65-0/8	12-0/8	12-0/8	6-0/8	6-0/8	11-4/8	Converse County	WY	Gary R. Shields	1983	1028
65-0/8	12-1/8	12-2/8	5-6/8	5-6/8	8-2/8	Moffat County	CO	Reggie Spiegelberg	1983	1028
65-0/8	13-4/8	14-0/8	5-6/8	5-4/8	10-0/8	Sweetwater County	WY	Kevin Jackson	1983	1028
65-0/8	12-3/8	12-3/8	5-2/8	5-2/8	11-6/8	Cochise County	AZ	Dennis R Ward	1984	1028
65-0/8	11-7/8	11-6/8	5-3/8	5-3/8	8-7/8	Garfield County	MT	Loren Blossom	1984	1028
65-0/8	13-7/8	14-2/8	5-0/8	5-1/8	10-4/8	Rosebud County	MT	Daniel A. Nielson	1984	1028
65-0/8	13-3/8	13-5/8	5-4/8	5-4/8	9-0/8	McHenry County	ND	Kevin Ohlhauser	1985	1028
65-0/8	12-0/8	12-2/8	6-1/8	6-0/8	9-0/8	Grassy Lake	ALB	Sam Kadoyama	1985	1028
65-0/8	12-0/8	11-5/8	5-4/8	5-4/8	10-7/8	Converse County	WY	B. J. Higley, Sr.	1986	1028
64-6/8	12-5/8	12-6/8	5-3/8	5-2/8	9-4/8	Perkins County	SD	Richard Bolyard	1975	1052
64-6/8	12-5/8	12-7/8	5-2/8	5-3/8	7-7/8	Area 34	WY	John Dykes	1975	1052
64-6/8	11-3/8	11-4/8	5-6/8	5-6/8	8-7/8	Casey	WY	James E. Taylor	1975	1052
64-6/8	12-3/8	12-4/8	5-3/8	5-2/8	12-2/8	Lemhi County	ID	Dale Johnson	1977	1052
64-6/8	11-6/8	11-6/8	6-0/8	6-1/8	7-3/8	Casper	WY	James E. Hodson	1979	1052
64-6/8	12-0/8	11-6/8	5-7/8	5-7/8	6-6/8	Sweetwater County	WY	Silas Risely	1980	1052
64-6/8	10-5/8	10-5/8	5-5/8	5-6/8	8-0/8	Converse County	WY	Papa Al Walther	1980	1052
64-6/8	12-2/8	12-5/8	5-6/8	5-6/8	8-1/8	Converse County	WY	James H. Cox	1981	1052
64-6/8	12-3/8	12-2/8	5-4/8	5-4/8	11-5/8	Converse County	WY	James K. Keim	1982	1052
64-6/8	12-3/8	12-5/8	5-4/8	5-4/8	9-2/8	Converse County	WY	A. M. Oakes, Jr.	1982	1052
64-6/8	12-1/8	11-4/8	5-3/8	5-3/8	10-3/8	Sweetwater County	WY	Bryan Radakovich	1982	1052
64-6/8	12-6/8	13-1/8	5-0/8	5-2/8	10-5/8	Butte County	ID	William A. Burns	1983	1052
64-6/8	12-0/8	11-6/8	6-0/8	5-6/8	10-0/8	Carbon County	WY	Paul Bowers	1983	1052
64-6/8	13-4/8	13-5/8	5-0/8	5-0/8	8-4/8	Converse County	WY	Robert D Hankins	1984	1052
64-6/8	13-1/8	13-0/8	5-6/8	5-4/8	13-0/8	Glenrock	WY	Steve Woodman	1984	1052
64-6/8	12-2/8	12-3/8	5-2/8	5-2/8	8-5/8	Johnson County	WY	Cecil Benner	1984	1052
64-6/8	11-5/8	12-0/8	5-5/8	5-5/8	11-0/8	Converse County	WY	Rocky Chisholm	1984	1052
64-6/8	11-1/8	11-2/8	6-0/8	6-0/8	8-5/8	Converse County	WY	Roy Goodwin	1984	1052
64-6/8	12-2/8	12-5/8	5-3/8	5-2/8	8-3/8	Converse County	WY	John W. Dillon	1984	1052
64-6/8	12-0/8	11-7/8	5-5/8	5-5/8	9-6/8	White Pine County	NV	Eugene W McNutt	1985	1052

PRONGHORN

Minimum Score 64

Score	Length of Horn R	L	Circumference of Base R	L	Greatest Spread	Area	State/ Province	Hunter's Name	Date	Rank
64-6/8	12-7/8	13-0/8	4-7/8	4-6/8	9-3/8	Moffat County	CO	Gary Oden	1985	1052
64-6/8	12-1/8	12-1/8	5-3/8	5-2/8	9-5/8	Converse County	WY	Leonard J. Emmen	1985	1052
64-6/8	11-7/8	11-7/8	5-7/8	5-6/8	8-5/8	Weston County	WY	Loren J. Liedl	1985	1052
64-6/8	11-4/8	11-3/8	5-7/8	5-7/8	8-0/8	Converse County	WY	John M. Negley	1985	1052
64-6/8	12-5/8	12-5/8	5-2/8	5-2/8	11-4/8	Converse County	WY	Rodney D. Johnson	1985	1052
64-6/8	12-4/8	12-5/8	5-5/8	5-4/8	11-3/8	Rosebud County	MT	Greg L. Munther	1985	1052
64-6/8	11-7/8	11-7/8	5-7/8	5-6/8	9-0/8	Garfield County	MT	John Fleharty	1985	1052
64-6/8	12-0/8	12-1/8	5-3/8	5-3/8	7-3/8	Billings County	ND	Howard Sharp	1985	1052
64-4/8	12-2/8	11-5/8	5-5/8	5-5/8	7-2/8	Harding County	SD	Floyd Hauk	1959	1080
64-4/8	12-1/8	12-0/8	4-7/8	4-7/8	9-3/8	Stanley County	SD	Ned E. Fogle	1965	1080
64-4/8	10-7/8	10-7/8	6-2/8	6-2/8	9-2/8	Valentine	NE	Jack Joseph	1970	1080
64-4/8	13-3/8	13-4/8	5-4/8	5-4/8	9-6/8	Mineral County	NV	Gordon Diehl	1974	1080
64-4/8	11-2/8	12-0/8	5-5/8	5-2/8	7-2/8	Medicine Bow	WY	Art Heinze	1976	1080
64-4/8	13-4/8	13-1/8	5-0/8	5-0/8	12-2/8	Gerlack	NV	Roger O. Iveson	1979	1080
64-4/8	12-7/8	12-3/8	5-1/8	5-1/8	6-0/8	Jefferson County	ID	Doug M. Chase	1980	1080
64-4/8	12-1/8	12-0/8	5-1/8	5-2/8	7-5/8	Douglas	WY	John D. Davis	1980	1080
64-4/8	11-6/8	11-2/8	6-0/8	5-6/8	8-7/8	Jones County	SD	Kenneth Kuchta	1980	1080
64-4/8	13-1/8	13-0/8	5-2/8	5-0/8	9-1/8	Casper County	WY	Carl W. Waggle	1981	1080
64-4/8	12-4/8	12-4/8	5-2/8	5-2/8	13-3/8	Moffat County	CO	Harvey Grady	1981	1080
64-4/8	13-0/8	12-7/8	5-2/8	5-2/8	10-2/8	Casper	WY	Harry A. Ulrich	1981	1080
64-4/8	12-6/8	13-0/8	5-2/8	5-1/8	8-3/8	Douglas	WY	Bob Whitton	1981	1080
64-4/8	12-3/8	12-0/8	5-5/8	5-4/8	10-0/8	Craig County	CO	Mary Ann Madrigal	1982	1080
64-4/8	13-3/8	12-6/8	5-6/8	5-6/8	10-6/8	Klamath County	OR	Richard D. Howell	1982	1080
64-4/8	12-1/8	12-4/8	5-7/8	6-0/8	9-3/8	Casper County	WY	Joseph Guerra	1982	1080
64-4/8	11-5/8	11-5/8	5-5/8	5-5/8	6-6/8	Douglas	WY	Larry Lendman	1982	1080
64-4/8	10-5/8	11-2/8	6-1/8	6-2/8	7-5/8	Wallace County	KS	Doug Wilson	1982	1080
64-4/8	12-1/8	12-3/8	5-5/8	5-4/8	6-3/8	Harding County	SD	Chuck Bame	1983	1080
64-4/8	11-7/8	11-6/8	4-7/8	4-7/8	8-5/8	Butler County	WY	Timmy Glass	1983	1080
64-4/8	12-1/8	12-2/8	5-7/8	5-7/8	10-3/8	Converse County	WY	Randy Rhoads	1984	1080
64-4/8	12-5/8	12-4/8	5-5/8	5-4/8	7-6/8	Converse County	WY	Steve D. Munier	1984	1080
64-4/8	12-4/8	12-6/8	5-7/8	5-6/8	8-4/8	Converse County	WY	Wayne Miller	1984	1080
64-4/8	12-4/8	12-6/8	5-2/8	5-2/8	7-0/8	Washoe County	NV	Michael Davis	1985	1080
64-4/8	12-0/8	11-5/8	5-4/8	5-4/8	9-0/8	Hettinger County	ND	William D. Helphrey	1986	1080
64-3/8	13-5/8	13-3/8	4-7/8	5-0/8	14-2/8	Rawlins	WY	David T. Funderburk	1978	1105
64-2/8	12-0/8	12-2/8	5-6/8	5-7/8	10-6/8	Harding County	SD	Rodney Foster	1965	1106
64-2/8	11-5/8	12-2/8	5-4/8	5-3/8	9-3/8	Butte County	SD	Donald V. Friberg	1968	1106
64-2/8	12-4/8	12-5/8	5-2/8	5-3/8	9-0/8	Stanley County	SD	George Hipple	1971	1106
64-2/8	12-0/8	11-7/8	6-1/8	5-7/8	7-0/8	Ormsby	WY	Frank C. Rathje	1973	1106
64-2/8	12-7/8	12-6/8	5-7/8	5-4/8	10-6/8	Perkins County	SD	Greg Larsen	1977	1106
64-2/8	12-1/8	13-3/8	5-3/8	5-3/8	10-3/8	Casper	WY	Richard Aylward	1980	1106
64-2/8	11-2/8	10-7/8	5-4/8	5-4/8	9-7/8	Craig	CO	Jeff Ollinger	1980	1106
64-2/8	12-2/8	12-3/8	5-4/8	5-7/8	10-4/8	Converse County	WY	David E. Smith	1980	1106
64-2/8	12-3/8	12-4/8	5-6/8	5-6/8	10-6/8	Rollins	WY	Ervin Wagner	1980	1106
64-2/8	11-7/8	11-6/8	5-7/8	5-7/8	10-7/8	Custer County	ID	Robert J. Mayton	1981	1106
64-2/8	13-5/8	13-1/8	5-2/8	5-3/8	15-1/8	Converse County	WY	Michael Smith	1981	1106
64-2/8	12-0/8	11-7/8	5-0/8	5-1/8	6-3/8	Moffat County	CO	Dave Ellis	1982	1106
64-2/8	11-6/8	11-7/8	5-4/8	5-5/8	9-1/8	Natrona County	WY	Douglas R. Parrott	1982	1106
64-2/8	13-1/8	12-0/8	5-4/8	5-4/8	11-1/8	Craig	CO	Gregory White	1982	1106
64-2/8	12-4/8	12-4/8	5-4/8	5-4/8	9-3/8	Jefferson County	ID	C. Eugene Jordan	1983	1106
64-2/8	12-7/8	12-6/8	5-5/8	5-4/8	7-2/8	Converse County	WY	David Arndt	1983	1106
64-2/8	12-6/8	12-2/8	5-3/8	5-3/8	8-5/8	Sublette County	WY	Dennis L. Shirley	1983	1106
64-2/8	11-6/8	11-6/8	5-2/8	5-2/8	11-3/8	Moffat County	CO	Dan Liccardi	1984	1106
64-2/8	12-4/8	12-5/8	5-2/8	5-2/8	9-0/8	Converse County	WY	Donald W Malina	1984	1106
64-2/8	11-2/8	10-7/8	5-6/8	5-4/8	10-6/8	Converse County	WY	Jason S. Miller	1984	1106
64-2/8	12-1/8	12-2/8	5-5/8	5-4/8	6-7/8	Phillips County	MT	Dyrk Eddie	1984	1106
64-2/8	13-0/8	13-0/8	5-2/8	5-2/8	11-2/8	Converse County	WY	Bill Sande	1984	1106
64-2/8	14-0/8	14-3/8	4-6/8	4-6/8	12-0/8	Eddy County	NM	Noble Sinclair	1984	1106
64-2/8	12-5/8	12-6/8	5-4/8	5-4/8	11-4/8	Sweetwater County	WY	Craig Boheler	1985	1106
64-2/8	10-6/8	10-7/8	5-7/8	5-7/8	11-3/8	Dunn County	ND	Scott Lang	1985	1106
64-2/8	12-4/8	13-0/8	5-3/8	5-2/8	6-6/8	Converse County	WY	Dennis Dunn	1985	1106
64-2/8	11-7/8	12-1/8	5-3/8	5-2/8	8-3/8	Campbell County	WY	Richard Sapp	1985	1106
64-2/8	11-7/8	12-3/8	5-4/8	5-4/8	9-7/8	Converse County	WY	Floyd Rettler	1985	1106
64-2/8	12-2/8	11-6/8	5-7/8	5-7/8	9-3/8	Stark County	ND	Scott Borchert	1986	1106

PRONGHORN

(continued)

Score	Length of Horn R	L	Circumference of Base R	L	Greatest Spread	Area	State/ Province	Hunter's Name	Date	Rank
64-0/8	12-4/8	12-4/8	5-0/8	5-0/8	8-6/8	Campbell County	WY	Carol Wert	1964	1135
64-0/8	12-6/8	12-5/8	5-2/8	5-2/8	8-6/8	Corona	NM	Harold Groves	1966	1135
64-0/8	12-6/8	12-6/8	5-3/8	5-4/8	7-1/8	Casper	WY	Bernard Giacoletto	1970	1135
64-0/8	12-1/8	12-1/8	6-1/8	6-0/8	11-3/8	Casper	WY	Mike Massa	1971	1135
64-0/8	12-7/8	12-7/8	5-1/8	5-2/8	9-0/8	Sioux County	NE	Clyde M. Storie	1971	1135
64-0/8	11-6/8	12-4/8	5-5/8	5-5/8	11-7/8	Buffalo	SD	Roger Moul	1972	1135
64-0/8	13-2/8	13-3/8	5-3/8	5-2/8	12-4/8	Harding County	SD	DeWayne Yantes	1973	1135
64-0/8	11-7/8	12-0/8	5-6/8	5-6/8	11-4/8	Maybell	CO	Dennis Behn	1981	1135
64-0/8	12-1/8	12-2/8	5-5/8	5-6/8	8-0/8	Sweetwater County	WY	Mark Chapman	1981	1135
64-0/8	13-0/8	13-1/8	5-1/8	5-1/8	10-7/8	Converse County	WY	Todd Schulz	1981	1135
64-0/8	12-0/8	12-1/8	5-4/8	5-6/8	7-2/8	Natrona County	WY	Jim Smith	1982	1135
64-0/8	12-3/8	12-0/8	5-3/8	5-3/8	10-3/8	Rawlins	WY	Ron Stacey	1982	1135
64-0/8	12-2/8	11-7/8	5-4/8	5-3/8	10-3/8	Converse County	WY	Richard Samson	1983	1135
64-0/8	12-3/8	12-2/8	5-2/8	5-3/8	9-1/8	McCone County	MT	Mike Elsbernd	1983	1135
64-0/8	12-3/8	12-5/8	5-4/8	5-4/8	14-0/8	Carbon County	WY	Kim S. Brockhoff	1984	1135
64-0/8	12-5/8	12-5/8	5-4/8	5-4/8	12-2/8	Converse County	WY	Dicky Newberry	1984	1135
64-0/8	12-4/8	12-5/8	5-1/8	5-1/8	9-4/8	Carson County	SD	Richard D. Hansen	1984	1135
64-0/8	12-7/8	12-0/8	5-6/8	5-5/8	8-1/8	Campbell County	WY	Frank S McClain	1984	1135
64-0/8	12-2/8	12-0/8	5-4/8	5-3/8	9-1/8	White Pine County	NV	David W Taylor	1985	1135
64-0/8	12-6/8	12-6/8	5-1/8	5-0/8	8-1/8	Converse County	WY	Randy Johnson	1985	1135
64-0/8	12-2/8	12-2/8	5-5/8	5-6/8	8-3/8	Natrona County	WY	Gary C. Cargill	1985	1135
64-0/8	13-0/8	13-5/8	5-4/8	5-3/8	9-4/8	Washoe County	NV	David Powning	1986	1135
64-0/8	11-7/8	12-1/8	5-4/8	5-5/8	11-2/8	Converse County	WY	Bill Doemland	1986	1135
63-7/8	11-3/8	11-3/8	5-3/8	5-5/8	11-4/8	Converse County	WY	Mike Lifford	1981	1158
63-7/8	13-0/8	12-4/8	5-6/8	5-5/8	14-1/8	Converse County	WY	Gene Solyntjes	1982	1158
63-6/8	13-3/8	13-6/8	5-3/8	5-2/8	8-6/8	Corona	NM	Robert L. Sullivan	1966	1160
63-6/8	11-7/8	11-7/8	5-4/8	5-3/8	8-0/8	Perkins County	SD	Bill Dunn	1967	1160
63-6/8	10-3/8	10-3/8	5-6/8	5-6/8	10-1/8	Ormsby	WY	Richard L. Huber	1974	1160
63-6/8	12-1/8	12-2/8	5-1/8	5-1/8	11-0/8	Converse County	WY	Richard L. Thrasher	1975	1160
63-6/8	12-1/8	11-2/8	5-4/8	5-4/8	11-3/8	Douglas	WY	Arthur G. Kragness	1978	1160
63-6/8	11-1/8	11-1/8	5-6/8	5-6/8	9-7/8	Weld County	CO	Dennis Behn	1979	1160
63-6/8	12-0/8	12-2/8	6-0/8	5-7/8	8-4/8	Douglas County	WY	Bill Martin	1980	1160
63-6/8	12-1/8	12-1/8	5-0/8	5-1/8	7-4/8	Casper	WY	Gary Rogers	1980	1160
63-6/8	12-7/8	12-7/8	5-2/8	5-3/8	10-4/8	Douglas	WY	Dale Lee	1981	1160
63-6/8	12-6/8	12-4/8	5-1/8	5-1/8	7-7/8	Moffat County	CO	Rudy Marmelo, Jr.	1981	1160
63-6/8	11-2/8	11-2/8	5-2/8	5-3/8	8-4/8	Douglas	WY	Mike Morgan	1982	1160
63-6/8	12-1/8	12-2/8	5-3/8	5-4/8	9-5/8	Douglas	WY	Joseph Trinceri	1982	1160
63-4/8	12-2/8	12-3/8	5-4/8	5-5/8	8-7/8	Albuquerque	NM	Ben Pearson	1956	1172
63-4/8	12-1/8	12-3/8	5-5/8	5-5/8	9-2/8	Harding County	SD	Merle Findeis	1962	1172
63-4/8	10-0/8	10-0/8	5-7/8	5-7/8	9-0/8	Sand Springs	MT	Dick Gulman	1964	1172
63-4/8	12-6/8	12-5/8	5-7/8	5-6/8	10-7/8	Buffalo	SD	Roger Moul	1973	1172
63-4/8	11-6/8	11-7/8	5-7/8	5-7/8	10-3/8	Sinclair	WY	Ron Johnson	1975	1172
63-4/8	13-4/8	13-0/8	5-2/8	5-1/8	8-6/8	Saguache County	CO	Larry Sisemore	1977	1172
63-4/8	10-0/8	9-7/8	6-0/8	6-0/8	7-7/8	Converse County	WY	David E. Smith	1979	1172
63-4/8	11-2/8	11-1/8	6-0/8	6-0/8	7-0/8	Sweetwater County	WY	Silas Risley	1981	1172
63-4/8	12-4/8	11-5/8	5-0/8	5-0/8	8-2/8	Gillette	WY	George E. Wright	1981	1172
63-4/8	13-4/8	13-2/8	5-1/8	5-1/8	11-5/8	Moffat County	CO	Scott Bartosh	1982	1172
63-4/8	12-4/8	12-4/8	5-4/8	5-4/8	7-2/8	Converse County	WY	Mike Miller	1982	1172
63-4/8	11-0/8	11-0/8	5-6/8	5-7/8	8-4/8	Douglas	WY	Woody Nance	1982	1172
63-3/8	12-0/8	12-3/8	5-5/8	5-4/8	13-6/8	Point of Rocks	WY	Mike Gallo	1981	1184
63-2/8	12-4/8	12-6/8	5-0/8	5-3/8	11-2/8	Zeona	SD	Mike Barrett	1972	1185
63-2/8	13-4/8	13-6/8	5-1/8	5-1/8	8-4/8	Slim Buttes	SD	James P. Taylor	1975	1185
63-2/8	11-5/8	10-7/8	5-2/8	5-2/8	7-2/8	Butte County	SD	Mike Barrett	1977	1185
63-2/8	11-0/8	11-1/8	6-0/8	6-0/8	9-4/8	Converse County	WY	Ron Breitsprecher	1977	1185
63-2/8	13-3/8	13-5/8	5-6/8	5-6/8	11-1/8	Sheridan County	WY	Randall A. Smith	1977	1185
63-2/8	11-1/8	11-2/8	5-4/8	5-4/8	9-0/8	Johnson County	WY	Raymond Bitson	1978	1185
63-2/8	11-7/8	11-6/8	5-6/8	5-7/8	9-2/8	Klamath County	OR	Keith R. Dotterer	1980	1185
63-2/8	12-6/8	12-5/8	5-4/8	5-2/8	10-5/8	Douglas	WY	Dennis Behn	1981	1185
63-2/8	12-1/8	11-7/8	5-3/8	5-2/8	9-1/8	Hiawatha Camp	CO	Raymond Dobrosielski	1981	1185
63-2/8	11-4/8	11-6/8	5-5/8	5-5/8	10-3/8	Siskiyou County	CA	Harvey Freetly	1981	1185
63-2/8	12-2/8	12-2/8	4-7/8	4-7/8	10-5/8	Bill County	WY	Charles M. Poppele	1981	1185
63-2/8	11-5/8	11-4/8	6-0/8	5-6/8	9-4/8	Howe	ID	Irv Wanlass	1981	1185
63-2/8	12-7/8	13-0/8	5-0/8	5-0/8	6-6/8	Lemhi County	ID	Larry Cross	1982	1185

PRONGHORN
(continued)

Minimum Score 64

Score	Length of Horn		Circumference of Base		Greatest Spread	Area	State/ Province	Hunter's Name	Date	Rank
	R	L	R	L						
63-2/8	12-3/8	12-5/8	4-7/8	4-7/8	7-1/8	Weld County	CO	Gerald Rasmussen, Jr.	1982	1185
63-2/8	11-5/8	11-6/8	5-6/8	5-6/8	7-7/8	Howe	ID	Clifton Ray Robinson	1982	1185
63-1/8	11-1/8	11-2/8	5-7/8	5-7/8	11-5/8	Williston	ND	Morris Olson	1961	1200
63-0/8	13-4/8	13-3/8	5-4/8	5-4/8	9-5/8	Buffalo	SD	Delvin H. Schweitzer	1957	1201
63-0/8	11-4/8	13-0/8	6-1/8	6-0/8	8-6/8	Buffalo	SD	Lyndell Peterson	1958	1201
63-0/8	11-1/8	11-0/8	5-6/8	5-6/8	5-6/8	Niobe	ND	Glen Watland	1964	1201
63-0/8	11-5/8	12-1/8	5-7/8	5-7/8	10-1/8	Castle Rock	CO	Melvin E. Leverington	1970	1201
63-0/8	11-0/8	11-2/8	6-0/8	6-0/8	8-2/8	Edgemont	SD	John W. Horstman	1971	1201
63-0/8	10-6/8	10-5/8	5-3/8	5-2/8	9-6/8	Ft. Pierre	SD	Charles T. Humphrey	1976	1201
63-0/8	12-4/8	12-4/8	5-4/8	5-4/8	9-1/8	Douglas	WY	Joseph J. Legat	1980	1201
63-0/8	12-2/8	12-2/8	5-0/8	5-1/8	10-7/8	Craig	CO	Ron Scherer	1980	1201
63-0/8	12-0/8	12-0/8	5-6/8	5-5/8	11-7/8	Birch Creek	ID	Larry Cross	1981	1201
63-0/8	11-7/8	11-7/8	5-5/8	5-6/8	8-0/8	Rawlins	WY	James E. Hodson	1981	1201
63-0/8	11-1/8	11-1/8	5-2/8	5-0/8	9-6/8	Converse County	WY	Roland Mantzke	1981	1201
63-0/8	11-6/8	12-0/8	5-6/8	5-6/8	10-7/8	Converse County	WY	Elwood Schultz	1981	1201
63-0/8	12-4/8	12-4/8	5-2/8	5-2/8	11-6/8	Bill	WY	Brian K. Steinhaus	1981	1201
63-0/8	12-6/8	12-5/8	5-3/8	5-2/8	8-1/8	Douglas	WY	Ralph J. Cianciarulo	1982	1201
63-0/8	12-2/8	12-0/8	5-5/8	5-6/8	6-0/8	El Paso County	CO	Dave Martin	1982	1201
63-0/8	11-5/8	11-4/8	5-2/8	5-2/8	9-5/8	Rawlins	WY	David E. Samuel	1982	1201
62-6/8	12-5/8	13-1/8	4-7/8	4-7/8	12-6/8	Spring Valley Range	NV	Ken Ashworth	1975	1217
62-6/8	12-2/8	12-2/8	5-4/8	5-4/8	10-6/8	Weston County	WY	David M. Nahrgang	1977	1217
62-6/8	12-3/8	12-3/8	5-4/8	5-4/8	8-6/8	Douglas	WY	Roger L. Hammond	1979	1217
62-6/8	12-2/8	12-1/8	5-4/8	5-4/8	8-3/8	Newcastle	WY	Larry Arentz	1980	1217
62-6/8	11-5/8	11-2/8	5-2/8	5-2/8	8-5/8	Weld County	CO	Dennis Behn	1980	1217
62-6/8	10-6/8	10-5/8	5-6/8	5-5/8	9-2/8	Carbon County	WY	Mark E. Coy	1980	1217
62-6/8	12-7/8	13-1/8	4-7/8	4-7/8	9-1/8	Converse County	WY	Carolyn S. Zanoni	1980	1217
62-6/8	12-6/8	12-6/8	5-5/8	5-4/8	9-4/8	Sweetwater County	WY	Mike Denney	1981	1217
62-6/8	13-0/8	13-0/8	5-0/8	5-0/8	6-4/8	Sweetwater County	WY	Bryan Radakovich	1981	1217
62-6/8	10-4/8	10-6/8	6-1/8	6-0/8	9-0/8	Redbird	WY	Gene Spinks	1981	1217
62-6/8	11-0/8	11-0/8	6-0/8	6-0/8	7-1/8	Carbon County	WY	Mark Peterson	1982	1217
62-6/8	11-7/8	11-6/8	5-2/8	5-3/8	10-1/8	Douglas	WY	Lola J. Vance	1982	1217
62-5/8	11-7/8	12-0/8	5-4/8	5-5/8	11-7/8	Casper	WY	Brian Poindexter	1980	1229
62-4/8	12-3/8	11-2/8	5-5/8	5-5/8	7-6/8	K-Y Ranch	WY	Douglas Walker	1959	1230
62-4/8	11-3/8	11-4/8	5-2/8	5-1/8	9-5/8	Stanley	ND	Joel D. Yesenko	1975	1230
62-4/8	12-4/8	12-4/8	5-3/8	5-4/8	8-1/8	Casper	WY	Jerry Putnam	1977	1230
62-4/8	11-4/8	11-6/8	5-7/8	5-6/8	11-5/8	Glenrock	WY	Raymond W. Peterman	1978	1230
62-4/8	12-0/8	11-6/8	5-5/8	5-4/8	12-2/8	Casper	WY	Donald Schram	1979	1230
62-4/8	13-6/8	13-3/8	5-2/8	5-1/8	7-0/8	Campbell County	WY	John "Jack" Cordes	1980	1230
62-4/8	11-6/8	12-1/8	5-4/8	5-4/8	8-1/8	Casper	WY	Gary O'Brien	1980	1230
62-4/8	11-1/8	11-2/8	5-3/8	5-3/8	10-3/8	Converse County	WY	Roy S. Marlow III	1981	1230
62-4/8	12-0/8	12-0/8	5-3/8	5-2/8	9-3/8	Douglas	WY	Buddy Warren	1982	1230
62-3/8	11-3/8	11-3/8	6-1/8	6-0/8	6-4/8	Area 54	WY	Steve Gorr	1970	1239
62-2/8	11-3/8	11-2/8	5-6/8	5-7/8	8-3/8	Arco	ID	George Shail	1970	1240
62-2/8	11-4/8	11-6/8	5-5/8	5-5/8	8-2/8	Fall River County	SD	Robert F. Szewc	1971	1240
62-2/8	12-3/8	12-3/8	5-1/8	5-0/8	7-6/8	Sheridan County	WY	David Collis	1976	1240
62-2/8	12-2/8	12-4/8	5-0/8	5-0/8	8-5/8	Converse County	WY	Max A. Smith	1979	1240
62-2/8	11-2/8	11-5/8	5-7/8	5-7/8	12-5/8	Converse County	WY	Jim Ellis	1980	1240
62-2/8	12-7/8	12-7/8	5-2/8	5-4/8	8-4/8	Campbell County	WY	Jack Cooper	1981	1240
62-2/8	10-7/8	10-5/8	5-5/8	5-5/8	9-6/8	Carbon County	WY	Joe Hildreth	1981	1240
62-2/8	11-7/8	11-5/8	5-1/8	5-2/8	9-7/8	Converse County	WY	Howard L. Hill	1981	1240
62-2/8	11-7/8	11-6/8	5-3/8	5-5/8	11-3/8	Douglas	WY	Thomas E. Rothrock	1981	1240
62-2/8	13-2/8	13-3/8	5-1/8	5-1/8	10-1/8	Sweetwater County	WY	Ronnie Williams	1981	1240
62-2/8	10-6/8	10-4/8	5-4/8	5-4/8	9-2/8	Campbell County	WY	John "Jack" Cordes	1982	1240
62-2/8	12-0/8	11-6/8	5-3/8	5-5/8	9-2/8	Douglas	WY	Rudy Edge	1982	1240
62-2/8	12-5/8	12-5/8	5-1/8	4-7/8	9-3/8	Converse County	WY	Dean Hamilton	1982	1240
62-0/8	12-2/8	12-7/8	5-3/8	5-2/8	11-3/8	Buffalo	SD	Roger Moul	1970	1253
62-0/8	12-3/8	12-2/8	4-7/8	5-0/8	8-6/8	Area 23	WY	William Walsh	1975	1253
62-0/8	12-2/8	12-2/8	5-0/8	5-0/8	8-5/8	Pinedale	WY	Robert K. Paulson	1976	1253
62-0/8	10-4/8	10-6/8	5-4/8	5-4/8	12-2/8	Campbell County	WY	Dale H. Bracken	1977	1253
62-0/8	9-5/8	10-0/8	5-1/8	5-0/8	8-0/8	Saguache County	CO	Fred B. Allen III	1978	1253
62-0/8	12-7/8	13-0/8	5-3/8	5-3/8	8-4/8	Bill	WY	James Borman	1980	1253
62-0/8	12-2/8	12-1/8	5-4/8	5-3/8	10-7/8	Moffat County	CO	LeRoy Hartwell	1981	1253
62-0/8	11-4/8	11-2/8	5-2/8	4-6/8	7-6/8	Lander	WY	Joe Wylie	1981	1253

PRONGHORN

(continued)   Minimum Score 64

Score	Length of Horn R	L	Circumference of Base R	L	Greatest Spread	Area	State/ Province	Hunter's Name	Date	Rank
62-0/8	11-5/8	11-5/8	5-0/8	5-0/8	9-1/8	Converse County	WY	Ron Carpenter	1982	1253
62-0/8	11-3/8	11-5/8	6-0/8	5-6/8	9-1/8	Converse County	WY	Robert Paul Casper	1982	1253
62-0/8	11-6/8	12-2/8	5-3/8	5-3/8	9-6/8	Springfield	ID	Dave Schwartz	1982	1253
62-0/8	11-7/8	11-5/8	5-3/8	5-2/8	8-4/8	Converse County	WY	Al Wygant	1982	1253
61-6/8	11-7/8	12-1/8	5-0/8	5-1/8	5-6/8	Mercer County	ND	Dwaine Grimsley	1976	1265
61-6/8	10-6/8	10-6/8	5-3/8	5-3/8	8-7/8	Montrail County	ND	Wade F. Williamson	1976	1265
61-6/8	12-1/8	12-1/8	5-2/8	5-2/8	8-4/8	Douglas	WY	Dennis Behn	1977	1265
61-6/8	13-2/8	13-1/8	5-1/8	5-1/8	9-2/8	Ft. Pierre	SD	Jeff Birdsall	1977	1265
61-6/8	12-4/8	12-6/8	5-0/8	5-1/8	6-4/8	Casper	WY	Ron Styck	1977	1265
61-6/8	10-6/8	10-6/8	5-6/8	5-6/8	8-7/8	Douglas	WY	J. Kelly Choate, Jr.	1978	1265
61-6/8	12-2/8	12-4/8	5-1/8	5-2/8	8-7/8	Haakon County	SD	Wallace C. Neville	1978	1265
61-6/8	12-1/8	12-5/8	5-2/8	5-2/8	9-2/8	Converse County	WY	Joe Sanders	1980	1265
61-6/8	10-3/8	11-1/8	5-6/8	5-6/8	8-2/8	Ft. Wingate	NM	Larry M. Sellers	1980	1265
61-6/8	12-2/8	11-7/8	5-2/8	5-2/8	8-3/8	Natrona County	WY	Jerry Baek	1982	1265
61-6/8	11-4/8	12-2/8	5-3/8	5-3/8	5-6/8	Rawlins	WY	Don Carter	1982	1265
61-6/8	10-7/8	11-0/8	5-4/8	5-3/8	10-4/8	Saratoga	WY	Dennis Fredrickson	1982	1265
61-6/8	11-2/8	11-4/8	5-6/8	5-6/8	7-2/8	Casper	WY	Ted Quillin	1982	1265
61-6/8	11-0/8	11-1/8	5-6/8	5-4/8	9-4/8	Converse County	WY	Andy Tkach	1982	1265
61-6/8	12-4/8	12-4/8	5-0/8	5-0/8	10-6/8	Douglas	WY	Jack H. Williams	1982	1265
61-6/8	11-3/8	11-3/8	5-0/8	4-6/8	10-6/8	Moffat County	CO	Rick Wilson	1982	1265
61-5/8	11-2/8	11-0/8	5-5/8	5-7/8	11-5/8	Douglas	WY	John T. Munson	1978	1281
61-5/8	12-4/8	12-4/8	5-3/8	5-2/8	13-5/8	Bonneville County	ID	Jerry Lyle	1981	1281
61-4/8	10-6/8	10-6/8	5-1/8	5-1/8	7-5/8	Sweetwater County	WY	Vaugh Cross	1974	1283
61-4/8	11-0/8	11-0/8	5-1/8	5-1/8	10-0/8	Campbell County	WY	George Garner	1977	1283
61-4/8	11-5/8	11-7/8	5-2/8	5-3/8	9-3/8	Casper	WY	Donald L. Witt	1978	1283
61-4/8	11-2/8	11-0/8	5-2/8	5-2/8	7-4/8	Cherry Creek Drainage	CO	Chuck Gibbs	1980	1283
61-4/8	11-2/8	12-6/8	5-1/8	5-1/8	9-7/8	Converse County	WY	Ken Horton	1981	1283
61-4/8	9-6/8	10-0/8	6-0/8	5-7/8	8-0/8	Converse County	WY	Dennis Plantenberg	1981	1283
61-4/8	11-7/8	12-0/8	5-2/8	5-1/8	11-6/8	Cole Creek Sheep Co.	WY	Don Tipton	1981	1283
61-4/8	11-3/8	11-1/8	5-7/8	5-6/8	10-2/8	Carbon County	WY	Jewell Leadford	1982	1283
61-4/8	11-1/8	11-1/8	5-2/8	5-2/8	8-6/8	Converse County	WY	Timothy Matheney	1982	1283
61-2/8	12-2/8	12-3/8	5-0/8	5-1/8	11-6/8	Medicine Bow	WY	G. Fred Asbell	1972	1292
61-2/8	11-2/8	11-0/8	5-2/8	5-3/8	11-2/8	Area 26	WY	Jim Burns	1979	1292
61-2/8	11-1/8	11-0/8	5-4/8	5-4/8	11-0/8	Sweetwater County	WY	Dean Kendall	1979	1292
61-2/8	11-0/8	11-0/8	5-4/8	5-3/8	8-3/8	Douglas	WY	Dennis Behn	1980	1292
61-2/8	11-5/8	11-5/8	5-4/8	5-2/8	11-3/8	Douglas	WY	Bob Clenney	1981	1292
61-2/8	11-1/8	11-0/8	5-4/8	5-2/8	8-4/8	Rawlins	WY	Erik William Lippold	1981	1292
61-2/8	12-6/8	12-2/8	5-0/8	5-1/8	11-6/8	Douglas	WY	George A. Moerlein	1981	1292
61-2/8	11-1/8	11-0/8	5-4/8	5-4/8	10-1/8	Johnson County	WY	John Yeager	1981	1292
61-2/8	11-2/8	11-0/8	5-2/8	5-2/8	7-4/8	Douglas	WY	David F. Baldwin	1982	1292
61-2/8	10-7/8	11-1/8	5-4/8	5-5/8	10-3/8	Moffat County	CO	Eugene Ray	1982	1292
61-2/8	11-6/8	11-6/8	5-2/8	5-2/8	11-6/8	Converse County	WY	Carl Spaeth	1982	1292
61-2/8	11-7/8	11-5/8	5-2/8	5-3/8	10-2/8	Johnson County	WY	James E. Taylor	1982	1292
61-0/8	11-7/8	11-7/8	5-3/8	5-2/8	11-4/8	Birch Creek	ID	Lew Reynolds	1978	1304
61-0/8	11-2/8	11-2/8	5-4/8	5-4/8	10-4/8	Birch Creek	ID	Larry Cross	1980	1304
61-0/8	11-5/8	11-4/8	5-2/8	5-3/8	13-1/8	Broadwater County	MT	Audie Anderson	1981	1304
61-0/8	12-3/8	11-7/8	5-0/8	5-0/8	11-1/8	Modoc County	CA	Jim Carr	1981	1304
61-0/8	10-5/8	11-5/8	5-2/8	5-2/8	9-4/8	Craig	CO	Roy Keefer	1981	1304
61-0/8	11-5/8	12-0/8	5-3/8	5-2/8	9-0/8	Douglas	WY	Mike Rybicki	1981	1304
61-0/8	11-7/8	11-7/8	5-4/8	5-2/8	10-2/8	Gill	CO	John G. Stamison	1981	1304
61-0/8	11-1/8	10-7/8	5-7/8	6-1/8	8-6/8	Douglas	WY	Reggie Spiegelberg	1982	1304
60-6/8	11-0/8	10-7/8	5-5/8	5-4/8	9-2/8	Big Timber	MT	Jack Howard	1965	1312
60-6/8	11-1/8	11-0/8	5-5/8	5-4/8	9-6/8	Section 20	WY	Edward C. Coy	1974	1312
60-6/8	11-1/8	11-3/8	5-6/8	5-3/8	12-1/8	Medicine Bow	WY	Jerry Dittrich	1974	1312
60-6/8	11-4/8	11-6/8	5-2/8	5-4/8	8-4/8	Douglas	WY	Joel L. Duncan	1978	1312
60-6/8	11-5/8	12-0/8	5-4/8	5-4/8	9-1/8	Park County	WY	Tim Viner	1978	1312
60-6/8	11-4/8	11-4/8	4-4/8	4-6/8	7-0/8	Craig	CO	Bill Yessa	1980	1312
60-6/8	11-1/8	11-1/8	5-3/8	5-4/8	12-3/8	Craig	CO	Larry J. Arrowood	1981	1312
60-6/8	11-4/8	11-3/8	4-7/8	5-0/8	9-5/8	Moffat County	CO	Dennis Kamstra	1981	1312
60-4/8	11-0/8	11-2/8	5-2/8	5-2/8	10-3/8	Campbell City	WY	Carol Wert	1967	1320
60-4/8	11-2/8	11-5/8	4-7/8	5-5/8	9-2/8	Casper	WY	Joe Adcox	1974	1320
60-4/8	11-0/8	10-7/8	5-2/8	5-2/8	9-2/8	Area 25	WY	Jerry Putnam	1975	1320
60-4/8	11-6/8	12-1/8	5-0/8	5-0/8	5-7/8	Presidio County	TX	Bill Conn, Jr.	1976	1320

Minimum Score 64

Score	Length of Horn R	L	Circumference of Base R	L	Greatest Spread	Area	State/ Province	Hunter's Name	Date	Rank
60-4/8	12-0/8	13-2/8	5-5/8	5-5/8	11-1/8	Moffat County	CO	Neil Peters	1982	1320
60-3/8	11-3/8	11-2/8	5-2/8	5-3/8	11-4/8	Moffat County	CO	Rodney A. York	1975	1325
60-2/8	11-5/8	11-1/8	5-3/8	5-2/8	10-2/8	Gillette	WY	Leon Johnson	1967	1326
60-2/8	13-3/8	13-2/8	5-6/8	5-6/8	14-3/8	Lost Creek	NV	Steve D. Wood	1974	1326
60-2/8	11-7/8	12-4/8	5-5/8	5-3/8	8-0/8	Medicine Bow	WY	Tim Good	1977	1326
60-2/8	11-5/8	11-3/8	5-4/8	5-3/8	10-4/8	Carbon County	WY	Erik Lippold	1977	1326
60-2/8	11-6/8	12-2/8	4-7/8	4-7/8	10-2/8	Johnson County	WY	Gary Olsen	1978	1326
60-2/8	10-3/8	10-3/8	5-1/8	5-1/8	6-4/8	Sweetwater County	WY	Mark Peterson	1978	1326
60-2/8	12-0/8	11-3/8	5-3/8	5-3/8	11-2/8	Moffat County	CO	Tim Anderson	1980	1326
60-2/8	12-1/8	12-1/8	4-7/8	5-1/8	7-7/8	Casper	WY	Richard Lee Kice	1981	1326
60-2/8	10-7/8	10-7/8	6-0/8	5-5/8	9-4/8	Moffat County	CO	Kenny E. Leo	1981	1326
60-2/8	11-3/8	11-2/8	5-2/8	5-2/8	9-3/8	Converse County	WY	Dennis Spawn	1981	1326
60-2/8	11-6/8	11-6/8	5-1/8	5-0/8	9-0/8	Ross	WY	Michael J. Meyers	1982	1326
60-2/8	11-2/8	11-3/8	5-0/8	4-7/8	9-0/8	Douglas	WY	Noble Sinclair	1982	1326
60-1/8	11-5/8	11-5/8	5-2/8	5-1/8	10-1/8	Casper	WY	George Schultz	1980	1338
60-0/8	11-5/8	11-4/8	5-2/8	5-1/8	7-3/8	Saguache County	CO	Jim Jarvis	1978	1339
60-0/8	11-3/8	11-4/8	5-1/8	4-7/8	10-0/8	Converse County	WY	Jim Keim	1979	1339
60-0/8	11-1/8	11-1/8	5-2/8	5-2/8	8-5/8	Casper	WY	Gary Rogers	1979	1339
60-0/8	11-2/8	11-3/8	5-1/8	5-1/8	8-2/8	Campbell County	WY	Walter Seville	1979	1339
60-0/8	10-6/8	11-1/8	5-4/8	5-4/8	10-2/8	Moffat County	CO	Nick Misciagna	1981	1339
60-0/8	11-6/8	12-0/8	5-1/8	5-0/8	8-2/8	Craig	CO	Douglas Mitchell	1981	1339
60-0/8	11-3/8	11-2/8	5-7/8	5-6/8	12-5/8	Douglas	WY	Dennis Behn	1982	1339
60-0/8	11-3/8	10-1/8	5-1/8	5-1/8	8-3/8	Moffat County	CO	Jeff Huth	1982	1339
59-7/8	11-3/8	11-4/8	5-2/8	5-1/8	11-5/8	Douglas	WY	Dennis Behn	1978	1347
59-6/8	11-7/8	12-4/8	5-2/8	5-2/8	10-0/8	Converse County	WY	Edward C. Coy	1973	1348
59-6/8	10-5/8	10-4/8	6-1/8	5-5/8	6-6/8	Butte County	SD	Ronald Glover	1973	1348
59-6/8	11-4/8	11-1/8	5-2/8	5-3/8	9-0/8	Pinedale	WY	Robert McCardell	1976	1348
59-6/8	11-3/8	11-4/8	5-7/8	6-0/8	6-3/8	Pinedale	WY	Dave Baierline	1977	1348
59-6/8	12-1/8	12-1/8	5-1/8	5-1/8	9-4/8	Pinedale	WY	Bill Krenz	1979	1348
59-6/8	10-2/8	10-2/8	5-5/8	5-3/8	9-2/8	Craig	CO	Jim Schmidt	1980	1348
59-4/8	11-7/8	12-4/8	5-1/8	5-0/8	12-4/8	Lander	WY	Fred Bear	1954	1354
59-4/8	11-2/8	11-1/8	5-2/8	5-2/8	7-2/8	Gillette	WY	Gary Landry	1976	1354
59-4/8	11-1/8	10-6/8	5-5/8	5-5/8	10-1/8	Lusk	WY	John Hale	1978	1354
59-4/8	10-3/8	10-4/8	5-2/8	5-1/8	9-0/8	Casper	WY	Donald Witt	1979	1354
59-4/8	11-0/8	10-7/8	5-2/8	5-1/8	9-2/8	Saguache County	CO	William J. McEwen	1980	1354
59-4/8	11-0/8	10-5/8	5-0/8	5-1/8	7-0/8	Douglas	WY	Robert B. Focht	1982	1354
59-3/8	9-6/8	9-5/8	6-0/8	6-0/8	10-3/8	Meade County	SD	Bill Dunn	1974	1360
59-3/8	11-2/8	11-2/8	5-1/8	5-0/8	11-5/8	Converse County	WY	John Savini	1980	1360
59-3/8	12-0/8	11-3/8	5-4/8	5-4/8	13-3/8	Converse County	WY	Clifford Harmon	1981	1360
59-2/8	11-4/8	11-2/8	5-3/8	5-2/8	8-5/8	Butte County	SD	Mike Barrett	1973	1363
59-2/8	11-1/8	11-7/8	5-3/8	5-2/8	7-6/8	Jordan	MT	James Dean	1978	1363
59-2/8	11-1/8	11-4/8	5-1/8	5-1/8	7-7/8	Gillette	WY	Tom David	1979	1363
59-2/8	13-0/8	10-5/8	5-7/8	6-0/8	14-4/8	Converse County	WY	Herbert A. Henderson	1980	1363
59-2/8	10-6/8	11-0/8	4-7/8	5-1/8	10-4/8	Gillette	WY	Steve Scarnato	1980	1363
59-2/8	10-5/8	11-0/8	4-6/8	5-0/8	6-7/8	Campbell County	WY	Dave Cordes	1981	1363
59-2/8	11-0/8	10-6/8	5-1/8	5-2/8	10-0/8	Rawlins	WY	Gerald L. Dowling	1982	1363
59-2/8	10-5/8	10-4/8	5-0/8	4-7/8	6-7/8	MacDoel	CA	Terry W. Sanderson	1982	1363
59-1/8	11-5/8	11-6/8	5-0/8	4-6/8	8-2/8	Douglas	WY	James J. Gardley, Jr.	1981	1371
59-0/8	11-2/8	11-3/8	5-0/8	5-1/8	9-0/8	Villa Grove	CO	Richard Baumfalk	1975	1372
59-0/8	10-7/8	10-7/8	5-2/8	5-2/8	10-4/8	Casper	WY	Gary D. Dunham	1977	1372
59-0/8	10-4/8	10-5/8	4-7/8	4-7/8	10-0/8	Campbell County	WY	Gerald J. McKinney	1979	1372
59-0/8	12-0/8	11-6/8	5-1/8	5-1/8	13-6/8	Douglas	WY	Roy K. Keefer	1982	1372
59-0/8	10-4/8	10-2/8	5-4/8	5-4/8	6-6/8	Natrona County	WY	Barbara Spawn	1982	1372
58-6/8	11-2/8	11-7/8	5-3/8	5-2/8	9-4/8	Cody	WY	Porter Dalton	1972	1377
58-6/8	10-4/8	10-1/8	5-7/8	5-6/8	10-4/8	Casper	WY	Victor Berger	1973	1377
58-6/8	12-3/8	11-5/8	4-1/8	3-4/8	11-7/8	Craig	CO	Bob Yessa	1980	1377
58-6/8	11-5/8	11-6/8	4-7/8	4-6/8	7-3/8	Gillette	WY	Jim Dougherty	1981	1377
58-6/8	11-3/8	11-3/8	5-1/8	5-0/8	6-0/8	Bill	WY	Myron Jochmann	1981	1377
58-6/8	10-1/8	10-1/8	5-5/8	5-4/8	9-5/8	Moffat County	CO	H. R. "Rusty" Neely	1981	1377
58-5/8	11-7/8	11-6/8	5-5/8	5-3/8	15-2/8	Campbell County	WY	Tim Viner	1982	1383
58-4/8	9-6/8	10-0/8	5-3/8	5-2/8	10-0/8	Area 61	WY	Frank "Rit" Heller	1972	1384
58-4/8	11-3/8	11-0/8	5-4/8	5-2/8	10-5/8	Niobrara County	WY	Joe A. Perry, Jr.	1974	1384
58-4/8	11-2/8	10-7/8	5-2/8	5-3/8	12-4/8	Casper	WY	Brian Kragness	1976	1384

PRONGHORN

(continued)   Minimum Score 64

Score	Length of Horn		Circumference of Base		Greatest Spread	Area	State/ Province	Hunter's Name	Date	Rank
	R	L	R	L						
58-4/8	10-7/8	10-6/8	5-2/8	5-2/8	8-5/8	Carbon County	WY	Dr. Jim Aumiller	1978	1384
58-4/8	10-7/8	10-7/8	5-5/8	5-5/8	9-4/8	Douglas	WY	P. W. "Bill" Meyer	1978	1384
58-4/8	10-0/8	11-0/8	5-1/8	5-1/8	6-1/8	Natrona County	WY	Dennis Spawn	1978	1384
58-4/8	12-0/8	11-5/8	4-5/8	4-5/8	7-3/8	Harding County	SD	Paul W. Mammenga	1981	1384
58-4/8	11-2/8	11-2/8	5-0/8	5-0/8	9-4/8	Converse County	WY	Carl Spaeth	1981	1384
58-4/8	12-1/8	11-5/8	4-4/8	4-5/8	8-3/8	Converse County	WY	Jim Thompson	1981	1384
58-4/8	10-6/8	10-6/8	5-2/8	5-3/8	10-0/8	Converse County	WY	James Hampton	1982	1384
58-4/8	11-0/8	11-0/8	5-1/8	5-1/8	9-6/8	Converse County	WY	Dan Zumbro	1982	1384
58-2/8	11-3/8	11-5/8	5-1/8	5-1/8	10-1/8	Campbell County	WY	Don McIntosh	1981	1395
58-2/8	10-3/8	11-4/8	5-4/8	5-3/8	9-1/8	Converse County	WY	Robert D. Platt	1981	1395
58-2/8	10-2/8	10-1/8	5-4/8	5-3/8	10-1/8	Glenrock	WY	Glenn St. Charles	1981	1395
58-1/8	10-6/8	11-0/8	5-4/8	5-5/8	13-1/8	Baggs	WY	Howard A. Goettsch	1976	1398
58-0/8	12-1/8	12-0/8	5-2/8	5-1/8	5-3/8	Buffalo	SD	Floyd Hauk	1957	1399
58-0/8	11-5/8	10-7/8	5-1/8	5-1/8	11-1/8	Carbon County	WY	John Dewar	1964	1399
58-0/8	11-5/8	10-0/8	5-2/8	5-4/8	12-7/8	Garfield County	MT	David Koski	1971	1399
58-0/8	10-6/8	10-6/8	5-6/8	5-5/8	9-7/8	Douglas	WY	Paul Linnell	1973	1399
58-0/8	10-1/8	9-7/8	5-3/8	5-1/8	10-1/8	Johnson County	WY	Calvin Almond	1981	1399
58-0/8	11-5/8	11-6/8	5-2/8	5-2/8	7-7/8	Douglas	WY	Bruce Ladewig	1982	1399
57-6/8	11-1/8	11-2/8	5-1/8	5-1/8	6-7/8	Gillette	WY	Joe Egner	1974	1405
57-6/8	10-4/8	10-2/8	5-3/8	5-3/8	11-6/8	Kaycee	WY	James E. Taylor	1977	1405
57-6/8	11-3/8	11-7/8	5-0/8	5-0/8	5-5/8	Meeteetsa	WY	David Martinek	1978	1405
57-6/8	9-7/8	11-0/8	5-0/8	5-2/8	9-6/8	Moffat County	CO	Kenneth D. Allen	1981	1405
57-6/8	10-6/8	10-4/8	4-7/8	4-7/8	9-1/8	Moffat County	CO	Thomas P. Bartholomew	1981	1405
57-6/8	11-2/8	11-2/8	5-2/8	5-0/8	6-5/8	Converse County	WY	Walt Deyton	1981	1405
57-6/8	11-3/8	11-4/8	4-6/8	5-0/8	10-1/8	Douglas	WY	Reggie Spiegelberg	1981	1405
57-6/8	11-2/8	11-3/8	5-4/8	5-4/8	11-7/8	Converse County	WY	Patrick Cebuhar	1982	1405
57-6/8	10-2/8	10-3/8	5-3/8	5-3/8	5-7/8	Moffat County	CO	Janice Traub	1982	1405
57-4/8	10-2/8	10-0/8	5-0/8	5-1/8	12-6/8	Gillette	WY	Dr. R. F. Helzerman	1964	1414
57-4/8	10-2/8	10-7/8	5-0/8	4-7/8	8-5/8	Jeffrey City	WY	H. R. "Dutch" Wambold	1972	1414
57-4/8	10-6/8	10-4/8	5-2/8	5-1/8	10-2/8	Villa Grove	CO	Rod Wintz	1973	1414
57-4/8	10-3/8	10-2/8	5-3/8	5-1/8	9-0/8	Fremont County	WY	De'ette Pitt	1978	1414
57-4/8	10-4/8	10-6/8	5-5/8	5-4/8	9-6/8	Rawlins	WY	Rick Wilson	1979	1414
57-4/8	11-1/8	11-1/8	4-7/8	4-7/8	7-4/8	Moffat County	CO	Steve Barnhill	1981	1414
57-4/8	9-7/8	10-0/8	5-0/8	5-0/8	8-5/8	Converse County	WY	David S. Bunce	1982	1414
57-4/8	11-0/8	11-3/8	5-1/8	5-3/8	8-2/8	Douglas	WY	Jim Conrad	1982	1414
57-3/8	10-7/8	11-0/8	4-7/8	4-7/8	12-3/8	Douglas	WY	G. Fred Asbell	1979	1422
57-3/8	10-7/8	11-1/8	5-3/8	5-2/8	12-2/8	Rawlins	WY	Al Reay	1982	1422
57-2/8	11-1/8	11-3/8	5-2/8	5-1/8	11-7/8	Ft. Pierre	SD	Rick Ray	1973	1424
57-2/8	10-1/8	10-0/8	5-4/8	5-4/8	8-2/8	Belle Fourche Co.	SD	Jerry Podratz	1977	1424
57-2/8	10-4/8	10-4/8	5-0/8	4-7/8	12-2/8	Converse County	WY	Forrest C. Child	1981	1424
57-2/8	10-5/8	10-4/8	4-7/8	4-7/8	10-0/8	Craig	CO	Suchin Sirsinon	1981	1424
57-2/8	10-6/8	10-4/8	5-3/8	5-3/8	9-5/8	Douglas	WY	David Skiff	1981	1424
57-2/8	10-1/8	10-2/8	5-4/8	5-3/8	8-0/8	Moffat County	CO	Michael R. Traub	1982	1424
57-1/8	10-6/8	10-5/8	5-0/8	5-0/8	11-7/8	Wheatland County	MT	Tom Keating	1982	1430
57-0/8	9-7/8	9-7/8	5-0/8	5-0/8	8-5/8	Jeffrey City	WY	Rolland M. Esterline	1972	1431
57-0/8	10-4/8	10-2/8	5-4/8	5-3/8	8-1/8	Casper	WY	John A. Putnam	1977	1431
57-0/8	11-2/8	10-0/8	5-0/8	5-0/8	8-6/8	Douglas	WY	Robert F. Pool	1978	1431
57-0/8	11-0/8	11-2/8	4-6/8	4-7/8	7-0/8	Craig	CO	Ron Scherer	1981	1431

WORLD RECORD ROCKY MOUNTAIN GOAT
Score: 51 0/8
Terrace, British Columbia – 1982
Hunter: Dave Ramsey

ROCKY MOUNTAIN GOAT

Oreamnos americanus americanus and related subspecies   Minimum Score 40

Score	Length of Horn R	L	Circumference of Base R	L	Greatest Spread	Sex	Area	State/ Province	Hunter's Name	Date	Rank
51-0/8	9-6/8	9-6/8	5-7/8	6-0/8	7-4/8	M	Terrace	BC	Dave Ramsay	1982	1
50-0/8	10-2/8	10-1/8	5-7/8	5-6/8	5-4/8	M	Kittitas County	WA	Bob Haugen	1971	2
50-0/8	10-5/8	10-2/8	5-5/8	5-5/8	7-0/8	M	Snohomish County	WA	Edward M. Beitner	1984	2
49-6/8	9-1/8	9-1/8	5-6/8	5-6/8	7-6/8	M	Tesla Lake	BC	Peter Halbig	1970	4
49-2/8	9-7/8	9-6/8	5-5/8	5-4/8	7-6/8	M	King County	WA	Jerry Solie	1978	5
49-0/8	9-5/8	9-4/8	5-1/8	5-0/8	7-6/8	M	Whatcom County	WA	Courtney Salmonsen	1974	6
49-0/8	9-1/8	9-1/8	5-6/8	5-5/8	7-0/8	M	Snohomish County	WA	Dick Smethurst	1975	6
49-0/8	9-0/8	9-0/8	5-6/8	5-6/8	6-7/8	M	Bennett Lake	BC	Jack Stephen	1982	6
48-6/8	10-0/8	9-4/8	5-5/8	5-5/8	7-6/8	M	Hedley	BC	Ernest Popoff	1981	9
48-4/8	9-5/8	9-5/8	5-5/8	5-5/8	7-3/8	M	Dungeness River	WA	Dr. Charles F. Raab	1967	10
48-4/8	9-6/8	9-7/8	5-4/8	5-4/8	8-2/8	M	Kenai Peninsula	AK	Charles Wirschem	1969	10
48-4/8	9-1/8	9-1/8	5-5/8	5-5/8	5-6/8	M	Terrace	BC	Dave Ramsay	1979	10
48-2/8	9-3/8	9-4/8	5-6/8	5-5/8	6-6/8	M	Seebee	ALB	Chris Kroll	1962	13
48-2/8	9-3/8	9-2/8	5-6/8	5-5/8	7-2/8	M	Crown Mountain	AK	Harold W. Jacobson	1973	13
48-2/8	9-7/8	9-2/8	5-7/8	5-7/8	6-4/8	M	Collegiate Pks.	CO	Marvin Clyncke	1978	13
48-2/8	9-1/8	8-7/8	5-4/8	5-4/8	5-3/8	M	Kittitas County	WA	Jim Pavack	1983	13
48-2/8	9-3/8	9-3/8	5-4/8	5-4/8	6-6/8	M	Kittitas County	WA	L. T. Spring	1986	13
48-0/8	9-4/8	9-7/8	5-5/8	5-5/8	7-4/8	M	Kitchener Lake	BC	Walt Sawicki	1975	18
48-0/8	9-6/8	10-0/8	5-5/8	5-5/8	6-2/8	M	Fire Steel	BC	John H. Kaykendall	1978	18
48-0/8	9-5/8	9-5/8	5-2/8	5-4/8	5-4/8	M	Whitechuck Mountain	WA	Gerry J. Lamarre	1978	18
48-0/8	9-3/8	9-3/8	5-3/8	5-2/8	6-7/8	M	Snohomish County	WA	Greg A. McTee	1986	18
47-6/8	9-2/8	9-2/8	5-5/8	5-4/8	7-0/8	M	Terminus Mountain	BC	Paul P. Schafer	1975	22
47-6/8	9-5/8	9-3/8	5-5/8	5-6/8	6-4/8	M	Thuodadi Lake	BC	Phil Bauer	1978	22
47-6/8	9-5/8	9-7/8	5-3/8	5-3/8	6-6/8	M	Olympic Peninsula	WA	Wayne Haag	1979	22
47-6/8	9-3/8	9-3/8	5-4/8	5-4/8	7-3/8	M	Bonneville County	ID	Darrus D. Martin	1985	22
47-4/8	9-4/8	9-4/8	5-4/8	5-4/8	5-6/8	M	Olympic Peninsula	WA	Bob Dierick	1976	26
47-4/8	9-6/8	9-6/8	7-1/8	5-3/8	5-3/8	M	Stalk Lake	BC	Chester J. Thompson	1977	26
47-4/8	9-5/8	9-3/8	5-4/8	5-4/8	6-2/8	M	Gallatin County	MT	Mark Ness	1984	26
47-3/8	9-2/8	9-3/8	5-2/8	5-2/8	7-0/8	M	Cordova	AK	Dwane J. Sykes	1973	29
47-2/8	9-4/8	9-3/8	5-3/8	5-4/8	6-2/8	M	Kennedy Springs	MT	Don Leondorf	1964	30
47-2/8	8-6/8	8-7/8	5-3/8	5-4/8	6-2/8	M	Cleelum	WA	Arnold L. Deckwa	1969	30
47-2/8	9-2/8	9-2/8	6-2/8	6-2/8	7-5/8	M	Kenai Peninsula	AK	John Moline	1971	30
47-2/8	9-5/8	9-5/8	5-2/8	5-2/8	7-0/8	M	Alsek River	AK	F. Wyatt Cook	1976	30
47-2/8	8-7/8	9-0/8	5-4/8	5-4/8	6-4/8	M	Clear Creek County	CO	Don Stiles	1984	30
47-2/8	9-4/8	9-5/8	5-3/8	5-3/8	6-2/8	M	Lewis & Clark County	MT	Doug Getz	1985	30
47-2/8	10-0/8	9-5/8	5-1/8	5-1/8	7-2/8	M	Ravalli County	MT	Ray Tlamka	1985	30
47-2/8	9-2/8	9-2/8	5-2/8	5-3/8	5-5/8	M	Mitchell Mountain	BC	Vincent Pisani	1986	30
47-0/8	9-3/8	9-3/8	5-3/8	5-4/8	7-2/8	M	Olympic Peninsula	WA	William V. Mishler	1968	38
47-0/8	9-1/8	9-1/8	5-2/8	5-2/8	5-6/8	M	Hayden Creek	ID	Eugene E. Farmer	1972	38
47-0/8	9-1/8	9-1/8	5-5/8	5-5/8	6-4/8	M	Mt. Washington	WA	Bob Brandfas	1976	38
47-0/8	9-3/8	9-0/8	5-5/8	5-5/8	6-6/8	M	Kenai Mountain	AK	Rick Tollison	1978	38
47-0/8	9-2/8	9-3/8	5-5/8	5-4/8	6-0/8	M	Chaffee County	CO	Calvin Farner	1981	38
46-7/8	9-2/8	9-2/8	5-3/8	5-4/8	6-1/8	M	Haines	AK	Lowell Marylin	1962	43
46-6/8	9-2/8	9-3/8	5-4/8	5-4/8	6-2/8	M	Clallam County	WA	Dean Cook	1978	44
46-6/8	9-0/8	9-0/8	5-3/8	5-2/8	6-3/8	M	Stalk Lake	BC	Walt Krom	1979	44
46-6/8	8-2/8	9-5/8	5-6/8	5-6/8	6-3/8	M	Kittitas County	WA	Robert J. Fischer	1981	44
46-6/8	10-0/8	10-1/8	5-3/8	5-4/8	6-0/8	M	Clearwater County	ID	Timothy A. Hyde	1986	44
46-4/8	9-1/8	8-7/8	5-3/8	5-3/8	7-1/8	M	Dungeness	WA	Thos. J. Smith	1969	48
46-4/8	9-6/8	9-0/8	5-4/8	5-4/8	7-2/8	M	Day Harbor	AK	William L. Ruby	1970	48
46-4/8	10-0/8	9-7/8	5-2/8	5-1/8	7-4/8	M	Thuodadi Lake	BC	Gary Petee	1979	48
46-4/8	9-3/8	9-4/8	5-2/8	5-3/8	6-6/8	M	Olympic Peninsula	WA	Gerald Egbert	1980	48
46-4/8	9-2/8	9-1/8	5-4/8	5-4/8	5-6/8	M	Chafee County	CO	Ken McIntosh	1983	48
46-4/8	9-5/8	9-5/8	5-3/8	5-3/8	5-3/8	M	Idaho County	ID	J. David Powers	1983	48
46-2/8	9-2/8	9-5/8	5-2/8	5-3/8	6-5/8	M	Augusta	MT	W. J. Fuller	1958	54
46-2/8	9-1/8	9-1/8	5-2/8	5-3/8	6-2/8	M	Continental Divide	ID	Ray Torrey	1967	54
46-2/8	9-4/8	9-3/8	5-1/8	5-1/8	5-5/8	M	Goat Mountain	WA	Keith E. Anyan	1978	54
46-2/8	8-7/8	8-6/8	5-3/8	5-3/8	6-3/8	M	Terrace	BC	Bill Coburn	1979	54
46-2/8	9-3/8	9-3/8	4-4/8	4-5/8	6-3/8	M	Whitehorse Mountain	WA	Fred Collins	1980	54
46-2/8	9-5/8	9-7/8	5-2/8	5-2/8	7-3/8	M	Berners Bay	AK	Noel Feather	1982	54
46-0/8	9-3/8	9-4/8	5-2/8	5-2/8	6-6/8	M	Whidbey Bay	AK	George Moerlein	1964	60
46-0/8	8-5/8	8-5/8	5-0/8	5-0/8	6-2/8	M	Boise County	ID	Jerry E. Burt	1971	60
46-0/8	8-7/8	9-0/8	5-4/8	5-4/8	7-6/8	M	Kenai Peninsula	AK	Roger D. Morris	1971	60
46-0/8	9-1/8	9-3/8	5-1/8	5-1/8	6-2/8	M	Clear Creek County	CO	Kurt Keskimaki	1979	60
46-0/8	8-7/8	9-0/8	5-4/8	5-4/8	6-5/8	M	Kechika Range	BC	Roger Stewart	1980	60

ROCKY MOUNTAIN GOAT

(continued)

Minimum Score 40

Score	Length of Horn R	L	Circumference of Base R	L	Greatest Spread	Sex	Area	State/ Province	Hunter's Name	Date	Rank
46-0/8	9-2/8	9-2/8	5-2/8	5-2/8	6-6/8	M	Clear Creek	CO	David Skiff	1981	60
46-0/8	9-3/8	9-3/8	5-2/8	5-1/8	5-7/8	M	Chouteau County	MT	Kay Davidson	1984	60
46-0/8	9-0/8	9-0/8	5-2/8	5-1/8	6-5/8	M	Kenai Peninsula	AK	Robert D. Warpack	1985	60
45-6/8	8-5/8	8-5/8	5-3/8	5-3/8	7-3/8	M	Skagway	AK	Rick Furniss	1972	68
45-6/8	8-5/8	8-5/8	5-2/8	5-2/8	6-4/8	M	Quilicene	WA	John Lund	1978	68
45-6/8	9-0/8	8-7/8	5-1/8	5-1/8	5-4/8	M	Stalk Lake	BC	John Stadler	1980	68
45-6/8	8-6/8	9-0/8	5-1/8	5-2/8	6-7/8	M	Cordova	AK	Gary A. Twigg	1980	68
45-6/8	9-1/8	9-1/8	5-2/8	5-2/8	6-4/8	M	Duti Lake	BC	W. C. MacCarty III	1981	68
45-6/8	9-3/8	9-4/8	5-2/8	5-2/8	5-3/8	M	Mount Jeldness	BC	Gerald Bond	1982	68
45-6/8	8-7/8	9-1/8	5-3/8	5-3/8	7-0/8	M	Todagin Mountain	BC	Reggie Spiegelberg	1984	68
45-6/8	9-6/8	9-6/8	5-0/8	5-1/8	6-2/8	M	Clearwater County	ID	Mike VonLindern	1984	68
45-6/8	8-4/8	8-7/8	5-3/8	5-3/8	7-6/8	M	Atlin	BC	Harrison O'Conner	1985	68
45-4/8	9-2/8	9-3/8	5-3/8	5-3/8	6-0/8	M	Lemhi County	ID	A. LaVerne Hokanson	1968	77
45-4/8	8-7/8	8-7/8	5-2/8	5-1/8	8-1/8	M	Kenai Peninsula	AK	Dean Lust	1969	77
45-4/8	8-7/8	8-6/8	5-2/8	5-2/8	6-6/8	M	McCarthy Glacier	AK	John F. Sumrall	1974	77
45-4/8	9-0/8	8-7/8	5-2/8	5-2/8	6-0/8	M	Kilroy	ID	Dean A. Cox	1979	77
45-4/8	8-7/8	9-0/8	5-2/8	5-3/8	6-2/8	M	Kenai Peninsula	AK	Chris Kempf	1981	77
45-2/8	8-6/8	8-7/8	5-5/8	5-4/8	7-4/8	M	Telegraph Creek	BC	Troy M. Miller	1968	82
45-2/8	9-3/8	9-0/8	5-2/8	5-2/8	6-5/8	M	Kenai Mountain	AK	Robert Borland	1970	82
45-2/8	9-5/8	9-4/8	5-0/8	5-0/8	7-1/8	M	Lemhi County	ID	D. Kittredge/R. Torrey	1973	82
45-2/8	8-3/8	8-5/8	5-1/8	5-2/8	6-2/8	M	Ketcheeka River	BC	Paul Brunner	1974	82
45-2/8	8-5/8	8-5/8	5-3/8	5-3/8	5-3/8	M	Kittitas County	WA	Jim Novak	1974	82
45-2/8	8-6/8	8-7/8	5-2/8	5-4/8	6-2/8	M	Jefferson County	WA	Larry Ramsey	1978	82
45-2/8	9-4/8	10-1/8	5-0/8	5-0/8	7-6/8	M	Valdez	AK	Kevin Chelf	1984	82
45-0/8	9-3/8	9-1/8	5-3/8	5-3/8	5-5/8	M	Flathead County	MT	Jack Whitney	1962	89
45-0/8	9-0/8	9-1/8	5-0/8	5-0/8	6-3/8	M	Lowman	ID	Bradley H. Jolley	1972	89
45-0/8	9-4/8	9-3/8	5-0/8	5-0/8	7-1/8	M	Lemhi County	ID	G. Yasuda/R. White	1973	89
45-0/8	8-7/8	8-7/8	4-7/8	5-0/8	5-6/8	M	Tunnel Creek	WA	Edward H. Boyle	1974	89
45-0/8	9-2/8	9-6/8	5-2/8	5-2/8	7-2/8	M	Lemhi County	ID	Donald J. Keady	1976	89
45-0/8	8-6/8	9-0/8	5-2/8	5-2/8	6-4/8	M	Kenai Peninsula	AK	Eugene Smith, Jr.	1976	89
45-0/8	8-2/8	8-2/8	5-4/8	5-3/8	5-3/8	M	Big Sheep Creek	BC	Gerald Bond	1981	89
45-0/8	9-2/8	9-1/8	5-2/8	5-2/8	6-1/8	M	English Bay	AK	Maxallen D. Jackson	1982	89
45-0/8	8-1/8	8-2/8	5-2/8	5-2/8	6-4/8	M	Moricetown	BC	Don St. Jean	1985	89
45-0/8	9-2/8	9-2/8	5-2/8	5-2/8	5-5/8	M	LaPlata County	CO	Jeffrey Yehl	1986	89
44-6/8	8-6/8	8-5/8	5-1/8	5-1/8	-0/8	M	Goat Mountain	WA	Les Turner	1967	99
44-6/8	8-4/8	8-4/8	5-2/8	5-2/8	4-7/8	M	Whitechuck Mountain	WA	Kelly King	1977	99
44-6/8	8-7/8	8-6/8	5-1/8	5-1/8	6-1/8	M	Fox River	AK	John F. Sumrall	1977	99
44-6/8	8-7/8	8-6/8	5-2/8	5-3/8	6-7/8	M	Park County	WY	Scott Steere	1982	99
44-4/8	9-7/8	9-7/8	4-3/8	4-3/8	8-5/8	F	Cold Fish Lake	BC	K. K. Knickerbocker	1957	103
44-4/8	8-7/8	9-0/8	5-1/8	5-1/8	6-4/8	M	Kenai Peninsula	AK	Larry Jones	1969	103
44-4/8	8-5/8	8-5/8	5-1/8	5-2/8	6-1/8	M	Kittitas County	WA	David L. Smartt	1972	103
44-4/8	8-6/8	8-5/8	5-1/8	5-1/8	6-6/8	M	Stalk Lake	BC	Richard J. Crowder	1977	103
44-4/8	10-1/8	10-2/8	4-4/8	4-4/8	8-5/8	F	Stock Lake	BC	Jay Deones	1978	103
44-4/8	9-0/8	9-0/8	4-7/8	4-7/8	6-6/8	M	Murky Lake	BC	Chuck Adams	1979	103
44-4/8	8-1/8	8-2/8	5-2/8	5-1/8	5-7/8	M	Jefferson County	WA	David P. Sanford	1981	103
44-4/8	9-2/8	9-2/8	5-2/8	5-2/8	5-5/8	M	Idaho County	ID	Darrell Howard	1982	103
44-4/8	10-2/8	10-1/8	4-3/8	4-3/8	7-6/8	F	Thatade Lake	BC	Jerry Baek	1984	103
44-4/8	9-2/8	9-3/8	4-6/8	4-5/8	7-7/8	M	Chugach Range	AK	Darryl Quidort	1985	103
44-4/8	9-0/8	9-1/8	5-0/8	5-0/8	6-2/8	M	Atlin	BC	Tom Tietz	1985	103
44-4/8	8-5/8	8-5/8	5-1/8	5-1/8	6-4/8	M	Chugach Mtns.	AK	Gary White	1986	103
44-2/8	8-5/8	8-5/8	5-1/8	5-0/8	5-6/8	M	Kenai Lake	AK	James R. Carr	1973	115
44-2/8	8-6/8	9-0/8	5-1/8	5-1/8	6-5/8	M	Coldfish Lake	BC	Dennis Behn	1975	115
44-2/8	7-7/8	7-6/8	5-1/8	5-2/8	5-2/8	M	King County	WA	Ronald A. Carpenter	1977	115
44-2/8	8-3/8	8-6/8	5-1/8	5-1/8	7-0/8	M	Todagin Lake	BC	Stanley D. Moore	1978	115
44-2/8	9-0/8	8-7/8	5-1/8	5-2/8	6-7/8	M	Custer County	SD	Kent D. Keenlyne	1981	115
44-0/8	7-4/8	9-0/8	5-4/8	5-4/8	6-0/8	M	Tyler Peak	WA	Virgil T. Cole, Jr.	1973	120
44-0/8	8-5/8	8-4/8	5-0/8	5-0/8	5-3/8	M	Rainbow Ridge	WA	Steve Gorr	1975	120
44-0/8	8-4/8	8-3/8	4-6/8	4-6/8	4-0/8	M	Clear Creek	WA	Steve Gorr	1978	120
44-0/8	8-6/8	8-6/8	5-1/8	5-1/8	5-2/8	M	Mt. Evans	CO	Lee Kline	1978	120
44-0/8	7-6/8	7-7/8	5-3/8	5-3/8	5-6/8	M	Duti Lake	BC	Mike Morgan	1981	120
44-0/8	8-5/8	8-6/8	5-2/8	5-1/8	5-7/8	M	Idaho County	ID	Randy Ulmer	1982	120
44-0/8	9-0/8	9-2/8	5-0/8	5-0/8	6-6/8	M	Lake Tatlatui	BC	Rick Gilley	1983	120
44-0/8	9-6/8	6-3/8	5-7/8	5-7/8	7-5/8	M	Kenai Penninsula	AK	Michael R. Traub	1983	120
44-0/8	9-1/8	8-7/8	5-3/8	5-2/8	5-6/8	M	Lincoln County	MT	Jerry Brown	1983	120
44-0/8	8-4/8	8-3/8	4-7/8	4-7/8	6-5/8	M	Cordova	AK	James A. Davison	1985	120

ROCKY MOUNTAIN GOAT
(continued)

Score	Length of Horn R	L	Circumference of Base R	L	Greatest Spread	Sex	Area	State/ Province	Hunter's Name	Date	Rank
44-0/8	8-7/8	8-7/8	5-1/8	5-1/8	6-6/8	M	Clark County	ID	Brent Poulter	1985	120
44-0/8	8-7/8	9-0/8	4-7/8	4-7/8	5-7/8	M	Snohomish County	WA	Stan Hansen	1985	120
43-6/8	8-4/8	8-4/8	5-1/8	5-0/8	5-4/8	M	Goat Mountain	WA	Joe Walker	1967	132
43-6/8	9-3/8	9-4/8	4-6/8	4-4/8	7-3/8	F	Duti River	BC	Walter J. Sawicki	1976	132
43-6/8	8-2/8	8-3/8	5-1/8	5-2/8	6-3/8	M	Park County	WY	Pat McAteer	1979	132
43-6/8	8-7/8	8-7/8	5-0/8	5-0/8	6-7/8	M	Bonner County	ID	Howard W. Holmes	1983	132
43-4/8	8-7/8	8-7/8	4-7/8	4-7/8	6-0/8	M	Lake County	MT	Jack J. Whitney	1969	136
43-4/8	8-7/8	9-1/8	5-1/8	5-1/8	5-1/8	M	Lemhi County	ID	Joe Becker	1977	136
43-4/8	8-7/8	8-6/8	5-0/8	5-0/8	5-1/8	M	Kittitas County	WA	Glen Berry	1979	136
43-4/8	8-0/8	8-2/8	5-0/8	5-0/8	6-5/8	M	Ice Mountain	BC	Larry Streiff	1979	136
43-4/8	8-5/8	8-5/8	4-7/8	4-7/8	6-2/8	M	Kitehewer Lake	BC	James Saunoris	1983	136
43-4/8	8-3/8	8-5/8	5-1/8	5-2/8	5-6/8	M	Chaffee County	CO	Dan Eastin	1983	136
43-4/8	8-6/8	8-6/8	5-1/8	5-1/8	5-6/8	M	Chafee County	CO	Don Bording	1983	136
43-4/8	8-6/8	8-5/8	5-0/8	5-2/8	5-6/8	M	Skagit County	WA	Pat Henley	1983	136
43-4/8	9-0/8	8-7/8	4-7/8	4-7/8	6-1/8	M	Clear Creek County	CO	Daniel L. Tekavec	1986	136
43-2/8	10-0/8	10-0/8	4-2/8	4-2/8	8-0/8	F	Tutaday Lake	BC	Larry Alma	1982	145
43-0/8	10-5/8	8-7/8	5-1/8	5-1/8	4-6/8	M	?	BC	Vic Clarkson	1960	146
43-0/8	10-0/8	10-0/8	4-4/8	4-4/8	6-2/8	F	Davis Mountain	WA	Richard L. Thrasher	1968	146
43-0/8	10-1/8	10-2/8	3-7/8	3-7/8	8-0/8	F	Haines	AK	Roger O. Iveson	1972	146
43-0/8	8-7/8	8-2/8	5-0/8	5-0/8	7-3/8	M	Lemhi County	ID	Gregory D. Dodson	1977	146
43-0/8	9-0/8	9-0/8	5-1/8	5-1/8	5-2/8	M	Lemhi County	ID	Larry Nirk	1977	146
43-0/8	8-4/8	8-5/8	4-7/8	4-7/8	6-5/8	M	Mason County	WA	Andrew E. Appleby	1982	146
43-0/8	9-3/8	9-4/8	4-5/8	4-5/8	5-5/8	M	Custer County	ID	Larry A. Wilde	1983	146
43-0/8	8-0/8	8-1/8	5-0/8	5-1/8	6-6/8	M	Kiittitas County	WA	Lance B. Cussons	1986	146
42-6/8	9-7/8	9-7/8	4-3/8	4-3/8	7-6/8	F	Lake County	MT	Jack Whitney	1965	154
42-6/8	8-2/8	8-7/8	5-0/8	5-0/8	6-0/8	M	Chaffee County	CO	Chuck Hutton	1979	154
42-6/8	9-0/8	7-3/8	5-5/8	5-4/8	6-3/8	M	Collegiate Peaks	CO	Duke Prentup	1979	154
42-6/8	9-7/8	9-7/8	4-0/8	4-0/8	9-2/8	F	Knik Glacier	AK	Gary G. Wall	1985	154
42-4/8	8-4/8	9-0/8	5-2/8	5-1/8	5-0/8	M	Chelan County	WA	G. H. Malinoski	1964	158
42-4/8	8-5/8	8-6/8	4-7/8	4-6/8	4-4/8	M	Goat Area 12	WA	James F. Miller	1977	158
42-2/8	7-6/8	8-2/8	5-0/8	5-0/8	5-4/8	M	Kleena Kleene	BC	William P. Mastrangel	1956	160
42-2/8	8-5/8	9-0/8	4-7/8	4-7/8	5-7/8	M	Terminus Mountain	BC	Paul P. Schafer	1976	160
42-2/8	10-3/8	10-4/8	4-0/8	4-0/8	9-2/8	F	Kenai Peninsula	AK	Gilbert M. W. Smith	1976	160
42-2/8	8-3/8	8-5/8	4-7/8	5-0/8	5-2/8	M	Snohomish County	WA	Eric A. Olson	1979	160
42-2/8	8-1/8	8-1/8	5-1/8	5-0/8	5-1/8	M	Snohomish County	WA	Thomas E. Tipton	1985	160
42-0/8	7-2/8	8-2/8	5-1/8	5-1/8	7-0/8	M	Tayla Lake	BC	Bill Brown	1957	165
42-0/8	8-4/8	8-5/8	5-0/8	5-0/8	5-7/8	F	Swan Range	MT	Jack Whitney	1960	165
42-0/8	8-4/8	8-4/8	4-5/8	4-5/8	6-1/8	M	Lemhi County	ID	Frank N. Hough	1968	165
42-0/8	8-4/8	8-5/8	4-6/8	4-6/8	5-3/8	M	Gates of Mountains	MT	Don Davidson	1978	165
42-0/8	9-4/8	9-4/8	4-0/8	4-0/8	6-1/8	F	Clear Creek	WA	Joseph R. St. Charles	1980	165
42-0/8	9-6/8	9-6/8	4-2/8	4-2/8	6-3/8	F	Square Butte	MT	Terry Albrecht	1981	165
42-0/8	9-3/8	9-4/8	4-0/8	4-1/8	7-3/8	F	Todagin Mtns.	BC	Neil Summers	1985	165
41-6/8	8-1/8	8-0/8	4-7/8	4-7/8	6-3/8	F	Lord River	BC	Dr. R. Congdon	1958	172
41-6/8	8-1/8	8-1/8	4-7/8	4-6/8	5-6/8	M	Anaconda Pintlar Area	MT	Mike Bartz	1976	172
41-6/8	9-1/8	9-1/8	4-3/8	4-3/8	5-3/8	F	Whitechuck Mountain	WA	Scott McDermott	1980	172
41-6/8	9-4/8	9-4/8	4-2/8	4-1/8	6-2/8	F	Snohomish County	WA	Steve Novy	1981	172
41-6/8	8-2/8	8-2/8	4-6/8	4-6/8	5-6/8	M	Heather Creek Basin	WA	Richard Van Calcar	1983	172
41-6/8	7-6/8	7-5/8	4-7/8	4-7/8	5-5/8	M	Lawson Lake	BC	David Baldwin	1984	172
41-6/8	7-3/8	7-6/8	5-1/8	5-1/8	5-0/8	M	Three Fingers	WA	Jack Williams	1984	172
41-4/8	10-2/8	10-2/8	4-0/8	4-0/8	10-1/8	F	Takia Lake	BC	William L. Sullivan	1966	179
41-4/8	8-1/8	8-1/8	4-6/8	4-7/8	5-4/8	M	Gore Range	CO	Wayne Depperschmidt	1979	179
41-4/8	9-5/8	9-6/8	3-6/8	3-5/8	7-2/8	F	Snohomish County	WA	Steve Wait	1981	179
41-4/8	9-3/8	9-1/8	4-1/8	4-1/8	7-1/8	F	Whatcom County	WA	Adam Redford	1981	179
41-2/8	9-7/8	9-6/8	4-2/8	4-2/8	6-4/8	F	Crazy Mountains	MT	Glenn Gibson	1957	183
41-2/8	8-3/8	8-3/8	4-3/8	4-3/8	5-1/8	F	Kittitas County	WA	Dennis Dunn	1973	183
41-2/8	8-3/8	8-2/8	4-6/8	4-6/8	5-3/8	M	Teton County	MT	Edwin Evans	1983	183
41-2/8	9-2/8	9-2/8	4-2/8	4-2/8	6-1/8	F	Rusty Creek	BC	Ronald Montross	1984	183
41-0/8	8-6/8	8-5/8	4-2/8	4-2/8	7-0/8	M	Penticton	BC	Bill Brown	1958	187
41-0/8	8-7/8	9-0/8	4-4/8	4-4/8	5-5/8	F	Snohomish	WA	Bud Peck	1960	187
41-0/8	10-0/8	10-0/8	3-6/8	3-7/8	6-2/8	F	Holly Creek	BC	Jim Jackson	1964	187
41-0/8	9-2/8	9-3/8	3-7/8	3-7/8	10-0/8	F	Valdez	AK	Jim Jarvis	1979	187
41-0/8	8-7/8	9-0/8	4-0/8	3-7/8	5-7/8	F	Whitehorse Mountains	WA	Mark S. Jacobs	1980	187
41-0/8	8-1/8	8-1/8	4-6/8	4-6/8	5-7/8	M	Clallam County	WA	Russ Spaulding	1981	187
41-0/8	8-1/8	7-4/8	4-7/8	4-7/8	6-4/8	M	Bennett Lake	BC	Dave Richardson	1982	187

ROCKY MOUNTAIN GOAT

(continued)

Minimum Score 40

Score	Length of Horn R	L	Circumference of Base R	L	Greatest Spread	Sex	Area	State/ Province	Hunter's Name	Date	Rank
41-0/8	9-1/8	9-1/8	4-0/8	4-0/8	6-1/8	F	Snohomish County	WA	Richard Kobel	1984	187
41-0/8	7-7/8	8-0/8	4-6/8	4-6/8	4-6/8	M	Bonner County	ID	Linda Leake	1984	187
40-6/8	8-3/8	8-3/8	4-6/8	4-6/8	5-2/8	M	Goat Mountain	ID	Ronald Sherer	1970	196
40-6/8	7-3/8	7-2/8	4-7/8	4-6/8	6-1/8	M	Kitchener Lake	BC	Walt Krom	1971	196
40-6/8	8-0/8	7-7/8	4-5/8	4-5/8	6-0/8	M	Kenai Lake	AK	Dennis Lattery	1973	196
40-6/8	8-6/8	8-5/8	4-6/8	4-6/8	5-5/8	M	Park County	WY	Jeff Umphlett	1979	196
40-6/8	9-1/8	9-1/8	4-1/8	4-1/8	5-4/8	F	Goat Mountain	WA	Roger Pitman	1980	196
40-6/8	9-0/8	9-0/8	4-3/8	4-4/8	6-2/8	F	San Juan County	CO	Bill McEwen	1984	196
40-6/8	9-2/8	9-1/8	4-1/8	4-1/8	5-6/8	F	Kittitas County	WA	L. James Bailey	1984	196
40-4/8	9-0/8	8-3/8	4-1/8	4-1/8	7-5/8	F	Little Johnstone Bay	AK	Ray Uhl	1965	203
40-4/8	8-7/8	8-6/8	4-1/8	4-1/8	6-4/8	F	Smithers	BC	Chris Vanderhorst	1974	203
40-4/8	9-4/8	9-5/8	3-7/8	4-0/8	10-3/8	F	Kenai Mountains	AK	David E. Smith	1976	203
40-4/8	8-6/8	8-4/8	4-2/8	4-2/8	4-7/8	F	Roslyn	WA	Kirk Cresto	1981	203
40-2/8	7-6/8	7-3/8	4-5/8	4-5/8	5-5/8	M	Warm Springs Creek	ID	Jack Arbaugh	1975	207
40-2/8	8-5/8	8-4/8	4-0/8	4-0/8	5-7/8	F	Kittitas County	WA	Bob McClure	1977	207
40-0/8	8-7/8	8-7/8	4-2/8	4-2/8	6-6/8	F	Chaffee County	CO	Wayne Spencer	1973	209
40-0/8	8-3/8	8-2/8	4-5/8	4-6/8	6-1/8	M	Lemhi County	ID	Marvin Tye	1973	209
40-0/8	8-3/8	8-3/8	4-1/8	4-1/8	5-1/8	F	Snohomish County	WA	Albert A. Rinaldi, Jr.	1974	209
40-0/8	7-5/8	7-5/8	4-6/8	4-6/8	5-0/8	M	Cordova	AK	Ray P. Noregaard	1975	209
40-0/8	9-1/8	9-1/8	4-1/8	4-1/8	6-7/8	F	Kitchener Lake	BC	John Dmytryka	1976	209
40-0/8	9-4/8	9-2/8	4-2/8	4-1/8	7-5/8	F	Cimari Valley	ID	Robert Frank	1976	209
40-0/8	8-3/8	8-2/8	4-5/8	4-5/8	4-7/8	M	Lemhi County	ID	H. R. "Rusty" Neely	1976	209
40-0/8	8-5/8	8-5/8	4-3/8	4-2/8	6-1/8	F	Gore Range	CO	Michael Beckwith	1978	209
40-0/8	8-7/8	8-5/8	4-1/8	4-1/8	5-5/8	F	Kittitas County	WA	Wilton Viall	1984	209

WORLD RECORD BIGHORN SHEEP
Score: 191 3/8
El Paso County, Colorado – 1983
Hunter: Gene Moore

BIGHORN SHEEP

Ovis canadensis canadensis and certain related subspecies

Score	Length of Horn R	L	Circumference of Base R	L	Greatest Spread	Area	State/ Province	Hunter's Name	Date	Rank
191-3/8	42-3/8	42-2/8	15-5/8	15-4/8	24-0/8	El Paso County	CO	Gene Moore	1983	1
190-2/8	39-4/8	39-4/8	16-4/8	16-3/8	20-4/8	Canmore	ALB	Brian Eloschuk	1982	2
186-1/8	38-2/8	37-1/8	15-5/8	15-3/8	20-7/8	Canmore	ALB	Cornel Yarmoloy	1982	3
184-1/8	38-4/8	38-7/8	15-5/8	15-5/8	21-1/8	Pigeon Mtn.	ALB	Guy Woods	1985	4
183-7/8	38-3/8	38-6/8	15-4/8	15-5/8	24-5/8	Deer Lodge County	MT	Jerry Parsons	1986	5
183-4/8	40-3/8	41-1/8	15-5/8	15-6/8	23-3/8	Libby	MT	Paul Schafer	1983	6
183-4/8	38-4/8	39-0/8	16-1/8	16-0/8	19-6/8	Ravalli County	MT	Jim Chinn	1986	6
183-2/8	40-4/8	39-2/8	14-7/8	14-7/8	21-6/8	Rampart	CO	Bob Renner	1979	8
181-5/8	38-1/8	34-4/8	16-2/8	16-2/8	23-0/8	Canmore	ALB	Paul Inzanti	1984	9
181-1/8	38-1/8	39-0/8	14-3/8	14-3/8	21-6/8	Clear Creek County	CO	Gary Renfro	1982	10
179-3/8	39-4/8	38-3/8	14-4/8	14-2/8	22-1/8	El Paso County	CO	Doy K. Curtis	1977	11
179-3/8	38-1/8	37-4/8	15-7/8	15-7/8	21-0/8	Mineral County	MT	Craig Thomas	1985	11
179-2/8	37-6/8	37-4/8	14-4/8	14-3/8	21-6/8	El Paso County	CO	Thomas H. States	1982	13
178-6/8	35-2/8	35-0/8	16-3/8	16-3/8	19-6/8	Mount Livingston	ALB	Jim Smetaniuk	1982	14
178-5/8	38-4/8	37-5/8	15-4/8	15-3/8	23-0/8	Park County	MT	Mike Mahlman	1983	15
176-3/8	37-3/8	39-0/8	14-6/8	14-4/8	22-0/8	Sweet Grass Area	MT	Ray Alt	1968	16
176-1/8	35-3/8	37-4/8	15-4/8	15-3/8	24-4/8	El Paso County	CO	Tony Seahorn	1977	17
176-0/8	35-2/8	36-2/8	15-2/8	15-2/8	23-5/8	El Paso County	CO	Gary Eastwood	1982	18
175-1/8	39-5/8	39-6/8	15-2/8	15-2/8	19-4/8	Canmore	ALB	Dave Addie	1985	19
174-0/8	35-2/8	35-4/8	16-0/8	16-2/8	21-3/8	Wind Ridge	ALB	Dirk Kieft	1984	20
173-6/8	32-6/8	34-0/8	16-1/8	16-1/8	19-1/8	Canmore	ALB	Michael Ukrainetz	1983	21
173-4/8	38-0/8	38-0/8	15-0/8	15-0/8	23-5/8	Cougar Canyon	ALB	Curt Lynn	1983	22
172-6/8	35-6/8	36-4/8	14-3/8	14-3/8	22-0/8	El Paso County	CO	Duane Imhoff	1982	23
171-7/8	38-3/8	35-2/8	14-5/8	14-5/8	22-0/8	Canmore	ALB	Chuck Adams	1985	24
169-0/8	33-2/8	35-2/8	14-3/8	14-2/8	20-2/8	Cougar Canyon	ALB	Paul Schwengler	1980	25
168-0/8	33-6/8	33-6/8	15-1/8	15-0/8	20-6/8	Sangre De Cristo	CO	Jennings Cress	1977	26
167-6/8	36-3/8	36-1/8	14-6/8	14-6/8	21-1/8	N. Sask. River	ALB	Larry Jones	1962	27
167-6/8	34-4/8	35-0/8	15-4/8	15-4/8	22-2/8	Sanders County	MT	Robert L. Borden	1983	27
167-6/8	32-3/8	35-1/8	14-7/8	15-0/8	20-0/8	Canmore	ALB	Ken Madsen	1984	27
167-1/8	34-1/8	34-4/8	14-2/8	14-5/8	22-4/8	Lincoln County	MT	Ron Bain	1974	30
166-7/8	31-4/8	34-7/8	14-7/8	14-6/8	21-5/8	Clear Creek County	CO	Thomas J. Hoffman	1986	31
166-0/8	33-2/8	32-2/8	14-7/8	14-7/8	19-7/8	Jefferson County	CO	Robert Sorrell	1977	32
165-7/8	36-1/8	37-0/8	13-4/8	13-3/8	19-3/8	Kanamaskis	ALB	Richard G. Perrett	1980	33
165-5/8	31-4/8	36-1/8	14-6/8	14-6/8	21-4/8	Clear Creek County	CO	Kurt Keskimaki	1984	34
164-7/8	38-0/8	37-3/8	14-3/8	14-4/8	20-1/8	Clemans Mountain	WA	Albert Rinaldi, Jr.	1973	35
164-4/8	35-6/8	37-6/8	13-4/8	13-5/8	24-5/8	Columbia County	WA	Jack Sandvig	1981	36
163-6/8	35-3/8	35-3/8	15-2/8	15-3/8	23-1/8	Lincoln County	MT	Paul Brunner	1983	37
163-2/8	34-6/8	34-0/8	15-5/8	15-5/8	22-3/8	Fremont County	WY	Randy Nelson	1984	38
163-1/8	33-4/8	33-1/8	14-7/8	14-7/8	23-0/8	Chaffee County	CO	Roger Stewart	1976	39
163-0/8	36-3/8	36-3/8	13-7/8	13-7/8	22-0/8	Swan Creek	MT	Steve Gorr	1973	40
162-7/8	32-4/8	32-7/8	14-2/8	14-2/8	22-2/8	Clear Creek County	CO	Lyle Willmarth	1982	41
162-7/8	33-3/8	34-2/8	14-7/8	15-0/8	22-3/8	Canmore	ALB	Thomas J. Hoffman	1985	41
162-1/8	30-6/8	33-5/8	15-0/8	15-1/8	23-7/8	Park County	CO	Wayne Depperschmidt	1977	43
161-1/8	33-4/8	33-5/8	15-6/8	15-5/8	20-4/8	Custer County	MT	Joe Frazier	1984	44
161-0/8	36-3/8	33-7/8	13-7/8	13-7/8	24-4/8	Kittitas County	WA	Rick Kobel	1985	45
160-5/8	31-1/8	32-6/8	14-3/8	14-3/8	21-1/8	Fremont County	WY	Daniel S. Fritz	1982	46
160-5/8	35-7/8	34-6/8	14-5/8	14-2/8	21-6/8	Canmore	ALB	John D. "Jack" Frost	1984	46
160-5/8	35-5/8	33-4/8	14-2/8	14-1/8	20-6/8	Catron County	NM	Barry Dyar	1986	46
159-3/8	31-4/8	34-5/8	15-0/8	15-0/8	19-1/8	Canmore	ALB	David R. Coupland	1982	49
158-5/8	30-1/8	30-0/8	15-4/8	15-3/8	21-5/8	Park County	CO	Marvin Clyncke	1977	50
158-3/8	30-2/8	27-3/8	14-4/8	14-4/8	20-4/8	Beaver Creek	CO	John Quick	1974	51
158-3/8	31-7/8	31-0/8	14-4/8	14-2/8	24-2/8	Lake County	CO	Wayne Lucero	1981	51
158-0/8	32-6/8	37-0/8	14-0/8	14-1/8	19-6/8	Canmore	ALB	Jeff Gaudry	1981	53
157-2/8	33-0/8	31-0/8	13-3/8	13-2/8	19-0/8	Texas Creek	CO	Steve Gorr	1973	54
156-5/8	31-1/8	34-2/8	14-5/8	14-5/8	23-4/8	El Paso County	CO	Barry J. Smith	1983	55
155-6/8	33-6/8	33-2/8	13-0/8	13-0/8	17-1/8	Canmore	ALB	William O. Dudley	1985	56
155-4/8	31-0/8	34-4/8	14-2/8	14-2/8	21-0/8	Canmore	ALB	Barry Dyar	1985	57
154-7/8	32-0/8	31-7/8	15-0/8	15-0/8	21-1/8	El Paso County	CO	Lee Kline	1976	58
154-4/8	31-7/8	32-7/8	13-5/8	13-6/8	19-0/8	Kittitas County	WA	Rick Vandergiessen	1984	59
154-3/8	34-5/8	34-4/8	15-0/8	14-6/8	25-0/8	Sander County	MT	John Voelker	1980	60
154-0/8	33-4/8	32-0/8	14-3/8	14-5/8	20-1/8	Waterton Canyon	CO	Dennis Behn	1974	61
153-2/8	28-7/8	26-7/8	14-6/8	15-0/8	20-0/8	Saguache County	CO	Steve Van Treese	1982	62
153-2/8	31-7/8	29-3/8	15-0/8	14-7/8	19-0/8	Park County	WY	William J. Gartland	1982	62

BIGHORN SHEEP

(continued)   Minimum Score 140

Score	Length of Horn		Circumference of Base		Greatest Spread	Area	State/ Province	Hunter's Name	Date	Rank
	R	L	R	L						
151-1/8	31-3/8	31-4/8	15-1/8	15-2/8	21-2/8	Cougar Creek	ALB	Archie Nesbitt	1983	64
151-0/8	34-6/8	33-0/8	13-6/8	13-6/8	22-1/8	Park County	WY	Larry L. Schweitzer	1984	65
150-6/8	29-2/8	29-4/8	14-6/8	14-6/8	19-3/8	Saguache County	CO	David "Jake" Powell	1985	66
150-3/8	31-3/8	33-2/8	13-4/8	13-4/8	18-6/8	Kittitas County	WA	Duane Fink	1984	67
149-3/8	30-0/8	26-5/8	13-6/8	13-6/8	24-6/8	Lake County	OR	Don Rajnus	1982	68
148-2/8	30-6/8	29-6/8	14-5/8	14-5/8	21-4/8	Buffalo Peaks	CO	Roland D. Cameron	1979	69
147-3/8	30-3/8	31-4/8	14-2/8	14-2/8	17-7/8	Canmore	ALB	Don Ferguson	1981	70
147-1/8	29-7/8	30-0/8	13-6/8	13-7/8	19-6/8	Leadville	CO	G. Fred Asbell	1979	71
147-0/8	30-6/8	30-0/8	13-3/8	13-3/8	21-3/8	El Paso County	CO	Sherman Spoelstra	1983	72
145-5/8	29-4/8	30-3/8	13-2/8	13-2/8	19-3/8	Canmore	ALB	Oran Hirsch	1979	73
141-6/8	25-6/8	27-4/8	14-4/8	14-7/8	19-2/8	Chaffee County	CO	Ron Breitsprecher	1978	74
141-4/8	29-1/8	27-3/8	13-3/8	13-3/8	21-0/8	Adams County	CO	Jim Usrey	1976	75
141-2/8	30-7/8	29-1/8	12-6/8	12-5/8	18-6/8	Chafee County	CO	Tom Tietz	1984	76
141-0/8	27-4/8	28-2/8	13-5/8	13-6/8	21-0/8	Park County	CO	Dan Tekavec	1980	77
141-0/8	28-0/8	28-0/8	14-1/8	14-1/8	19-2/8	Fremont County	WY	Jerry W. Mathewes	1983	77
140-7/8	27-6/8	33-3/8	14-1/8	14-0/8	19-6/8	Kittitas County	WA	Stan Hansen	1984	79
134-5/8	29-5/8	29-4/8	12-6/8	12-6/8	20-3/8	Clemans Mountain	WA	Jerry Solie	1982	80
134-4/8	27-7/8	28-3/8	14-2/8	14-3/8	17-6/8	Gibson Lake	MT	Terry Albrecht	1981	81
132-4/8	27-7/8	27-1/8	14-4/8	14-4/8	18-3/8	Idaho County	ID	Jim McLeod	1982	82

WORLD RECORD DALL SHEEP
Score: 164 5/8
Nahanni Butte, Northwest Territories – 1986
Hunter: Gary Laya

DALL SHEEP

Ovis dalli dalli and *Ovis dalli kenaiensis*   Minimum Score 120

Score	Length of Horn		Circumference of Base		Greatest Spread	Area	State/ Province	Hunter's Name	Date	Rank
	R	L	R	L						
164-5/8	40-6/8	41-3/8	13-3/8	13-5/8	28-4/8	Nahanni Butte	NWT	Gary Laya	1986	1
162-3/8	38-7/8	39-0/8	12-4/8	12-4/8	22-6/8	Delta River	AK	Dr. Russell Congdon	1961	2
160-6/8	39-6/8	37-6/8	13-2/8	13-2/8	22-7/8	Nahanni Butte	NWT	Lonny Vanatta	1986	3
157-0/8	35-4/8	35-4/8	13-6/8	14-0/8	21-2/8	Chitina Glacier	AK	Roger Morris	1973	4
155-5/8	36-3/8	35-0/8	12-6/8	12-6/8	19-5/8	McKenzie Mtns.	NWT	Bob Renner	1983	5
155-1/8	37-1/8	37-2/8	13-4/8	13-4/8	25-7/8	Rams Head Mountain	NWT	Ron Breitsprecher	1981	6
154-7/8	35-2/8	34-7/8	14-1/8	14-1/8	21-4/8	McKenzie Mtns.	NWT	Mike Barrett	1983	7
154-6/8	35-6/8	37-2/8	13-0/8	13-2/8	20-6/8	Chugach Mountains	AK	Rick Tollison	1979	8
153-2/8	37-6/8	33-0/8	13-2/8	13-2/8	20-4/8	Rams Head Mountain	NWT	Dennis Schweitzer	1981	9
152-6/8	37-1/8	36-5/8	13-1/8	13-1/8	30-0/8	Wrangell Mountains	AK	Ray Torrey	1973	10
152-5/8	38-6/8	39-3/8	12-3/8	12-4/8	31-2/8	Keel River	NWT	Thomas J. Hoffman	1986	11
152-4/8	33-0/8	34-0/8	12-6/8	12-6/8	18-5/8	Mackenzie Mountains	NWT	Al Reay	1982	12
152-2/8	37-0/8	36-2/8	12-5/8	12-5/8	23-4/8	Kuskokwim Mountains	AK	Kenneth R. Wallenberg	1978	13
152-0/8	37-0/8	37-0/8	12-4/8	12-4/8	27-4/8	Wrangell Mountains	AK	Dr. Rex Hancock	1962	14
151-6/8	35-7/8	35-1/8	13-5/8	13-5/8	28-0/8	Chugach Mts	AK	John D. "Jack" Frost	1984	15
151-2/8	36-6/8	36-6/8	12-6/8	12-6/8	26-4/8	Johnson River	AK	Larry Jones	1963	16
151-2/8	36-4/8	36-4/8	13-7/8	13-6/8	23-4/8	Tonsona Creek	AK	Bruce Stephens	1974	16
151-2/8	35-5/8	36-1/8	13-2/8	13-0/8	25-0/8	Rainy Pass	AK	Roger Stewart	1978	16
151-0/8	35-4/8	34-4/8	13-3/8	13-5/8	27-3/8	Mackenzie Mtns.	NWT	Mike Barrett	1986	19
150-3/8	36-1/8	36-2/8	12-4/8	12-5/8	24-2/8	Mountain River	NWT	George Flournoy	1985	20
150-2/8	37-5/8	33-3/8	12-4/8	12-2/8	19-7/8	Brooks Range	AK	James A. Baker	1971	21
149-3/8	37-1/8	34-4/8	13-2/8	13-2/8	25-7/8	Wrangell Mountains	AK	J. Barry Dyar	1984	22
149-0/8	34-7/8	35-3/8	13-3/8	13-3/8	23-3/8	Keel River	NWT	Thomas J. Hoffman	1985	23
148-6/8	37-6/8	38-0/8	12-2/8	12-2/8	22-5/8	Nahanni Butte	NWT	Bill Grammer	1986	24
148-4/8	35-7/8	35-3/8	13-2/8	13-2/8	26-6/8	Brooks Range	AK	Randy Butler	1979	25
148-4/8	31-4/8	35-4/8	13-6/8	13-6/8	25-0/8	Mackenzie Mtns.	NWT	Dyrk Eddie	1986	25
148-3/8	33-4/8	35-1/8	13-3/8	13-3/8	24-2/8	Atigun Pass	AK	Maxallen D. Jackson	1984	27
147-6/8	35-1/8	35-1/8	12-4/8	12-6/8	19-7/8	Tologotsho	NWT	Archie Nesbitt	1986	28
147-4/8	34-6/8	35-4/8	12-0/8	12-0/8	21-5/8	Mackenzie Mountains	NWT	Paul Brunner	1982	29
146-6/8	35-0/8	34-4/8	12-2/8	12-3/8	23-5/8	Liards Mtns.	NWT	Dennis Dunn	1984	30
146-5/8	36-3/8	35-0/8	11-6/8	11-5/8	21-0/8	Liard Range	NWT	Ron Rockwell	1983	31
146-4/8	33-4/8	34-2/8	12-0/8	12-2/8	25-7/8	Delta River	AK	Elisha Gray	1958	32
145-4/8	33-1/8	37-7/8	11-6/8	11-6/8	21-2/8	Brooks Range	AK	John D. "Jack" Frost	1982	33
145-2/8	35-1/8	35-5/8	12-3/8	12-4/8	25-5/8	Talkeetna Mountains	AK	Jay Deones	1980	34
145-1/8	32-2/8	33-1/8	13-4/8	13-7/8	23-5/8	Wood River	AK	Art Young	1923	35
145-0/8	33-5/8	33-5/8	13-0/8	13-0/8	25-5/8	Mt. Ibex	YUK	Martin Hanson	1957	36
144-5/8	34-5/8	35-2/8	13-0/8	13-0/8	23-1/8	Mt. Hayes	AK	Keith R. Clemmons	1962	37
144-2/8	33-1/8	33-3/8	12-5/8	12-4/8	21-6/8	Liard Range	NWT	Richard W. Sage	1986	38
144-1/8	33-3/8	36-4/8	12-3/8	13-0/8	25-4/8	Delta Management	AK	John W. Williams	1978	39
143-6/8	35-0/8	35-2/8	13-0/8	12-7/8	25-0/8	Chistochina River	AK	Capt. Leonard Mackler	1977	40
143-4/8	35-0/8	34-2/8	12-5/8	12-6/8	22-4/8	Nahanni Butte	NWT	Dirk Lawyer	1985	41
143-3/8	35-0/8	34-5/8	12-0/8	12-2/8	19-4/8	Endicott Mountains	AK	Dwane J. Sykes	1968	42
143-2/8	31-0/8	35-2/8	12-4/8	12-4/8	23-6/8	Mackenzie Mountains	NWT	Paul Schafer	1983	43
143-1/8	32-0/8	32-5/8	13-3/8	13-3/8	21-4/8	Chugach Mountains	AK	Glenn R. L. Schmidt	1977	44
143-0/8	36-0/8	34-6/8	11-4/8	11-4/8	21-2/8	Nahanni Butte	NWT	Lee Veldhouse	1983	45
142-2/8	33-4/8	36-2/8	11-5/8	11-5/8	24-3/8	Post River	AK	Rick Tollison	1978	46
142-0/8	28-1/8	33-5/8	12-1/8	12-0/8	22-1/8	Atigun Pass	AK	Maxallen D. Jackson	1980	47
141-6/8	32-0/8	32-4/8	12-0/8	12-1/8	20-2/8	McKenzie Mtns.	NWT	Reggie Spiegelberg	1982	48
141-5/8	31-7/8	32-0/8	13-0/8	13-0/8	26-2/8	MacKenzie Mountains	NWT	Chuck Adams	1985	49
141-0/8	35-6/8	36-6/8	11-5/8	11-5/8	22-0/8	Ptarmigan Pass	AK	Ralph Ertz	1977	50
140-5/8	32-4/8	31-5/8	12-4/8	12-4/8	23-7/8	Liard River	NWT	Greg Munther	1984	51
139-0/8	37-2/8	32-6/8	11-7/8	12-0/8	26-4/8	Talkeetna Mountains	AK	Rusty Hayes	1975	52
138-4/8	32-6/8	34-0/8	12-6/8	12-5/8	22-6/8	Chitina	AK	Robert Ewers	1972	53
138-0/8	29-3/8	35-5/8	12-4/8	12-4/8	26-7/8	Hula Hula River	AK	Paul Persano	1985	54
133-2/8	32-0/8	31-6/8	11-7/8	11-6/8	21-2/8	Nabesna River	AK	George A. Moerlein	1983	55
133-0/8	30-6/8	30-4/8	12-4/8	12-5/8	27-1/8	Wrangell Mountains	AK	George A. Moerlein	1971	56
132-6/8	30-2/8	30-4/8	12-5/8	12-5/8	18-2/8	Brooks Range	AK	Robert Warpack	1986	57
131-6/8	31-5/8	31-1/8	12-5/8	12-5/8	17-6/8	Wrangell Mountains	AK	John Sarvis	1985	58
130-7/8	32-6/8	28-5/8	12-4/8	12-4/8	20-6/8	Talkeetna Mountains	AK	John L. Wozniak	1984	59
130-0/8	30-2/8	30-6/8	11-4/8	11-4/8	20-6/8	Liard Range	NWT	John Borlang	1986	60
128-0/8	31-2/8	31-4/8	11-2/8	11-3/8	24-0/8	Wrangell	AK	Gilbert M. W. Smith	1977	61
127-0/8	29-7/8	29-3/8	11-2/8	11-1/8	21-2/8	Sheep Creek	AK	Ray Uhl, Jr.	1968	62
125-7/8	31-6/8	31-3/8	10-4/8	10-4/8	21-1/8	Alaska Range	AK	Larry Jones	1969	63
121-1/8	27-3/8	28-2/8	10-7/8	10-6/8	21-4/8	Brooks Range	AK	Thomas Chadwick	1984	64

WORLD RECORD DESERT SHEEP
Score: 167 1/8
Sandtank Mountains, Arizona – 1985
Hunter: Peter C. Knagge

DESERT SHEEP
Ovis canadensis nelsoni and certain related subspecies

Minimum Score 140

Score	Length of Horn R	L	Circumference of Base R	L	Greatest Spread	Area	State/ Province	Hunter's Name	Date	Rank
167-1/8	34-5/8	34-2/8	14-7/8	14-7/8	23-5/8	Sandtank Mountains	AZ	Peter C. Knagge	1985	1
164-2/8	32-4/8	31-6/8	15-3/8	15-3/8	21-1/8	Maricopa County	AZ	Chuck Meacham	1984	2
163-1/8	34-6/8	35-5/8	15-4/8	15-4/8	22-3/8	Clark County	NV	Fred Church	1984	3
157-5/8	32-3/8	33-4/8	13-1/8	13-2/8	21-7/8	Yuma County	AZ	Barry Sopher	1985	4
157-3/8	30-4/8	31-5/8	14-2/8	14-2/8	22-3/8	Lincoln County	NV	James R. Puryear	1984	5
155-7/8	30-5/8	30-2/8	14-4/8	14-4/8	25-7/8	Nye County	NV	David Powning	1984	6
155-5/8	31-6/8	33-7/8	15-1/8	15-2/8	20-0/8	Sonora	MEX	Thomas J. Hoffman	1985	7
154-1/8	30-5/8	31-2/8	14-0/8	14-1/8	22-7/8	Nye County	NV	Richard J. Panelli	1985	8
153-7/8	31-2/8	31-3/8	15-2/8	15-4/8	19-6/8	Maricopa County	AZ	Brad L. Siefarth	1979	9
152-1/8	30-0/8	30-3/8	14-7/8	14-5/8	19-1/8	Mohave County	AZ	Pete Shepley	1986	10
151-3/8	32-3/8	34-6/8	12-6/8	12-1/8	21-2/8	Clark County	NV	Gilbert Hernandez	1985	11
145-1/8	28-6/8	28-3/8	13-7/8	13-7/8	20-4/8	Lincoln County	NV	San Stiver	1980	12
141-2/8	27-0/8	29-2/8	13-2/8	13-2/8	19-0/8	Mohave County	AZ	Chuck Adams	1986	13

WORLD RECORD STONE SHEEP
Score: 158 1/8
Cold Fish Lake, British Columbia – 1957
Hunter: Fred Bear

STONE SHEEP

Ovis dalli stonei   Minimum Score 120

Score	Length of Horn		Circumference of Base		Greatest Spread	Area	State/ Province	Hunter's Name	Date	Rank
	R	L	R	L						
158-1/8	40-4/8	38-3/8	12-4/8	13-1/8	27-0/8	Cold Fish Lake	BC	Fred Bear	1957	1
157-1/8	36-2/8	35-5/8	13-4/8	13-4/8	21-0/8	Trygye Lake	BC	Walt Krom	1979	2
155-2/8	38-1/8	37-1/8	13-1/8	13-2/8	26-6/8	Todagin Mountain	BC	Reggie Spiegelberg	1984	3
154-3/8	35-6/8	36-3/8	13-2/8	13-3/8	25-3/8	Todagin Creek Mtn.	BC	Roy Lynch	1983	4
154-1/8	38-0/8	39-2/8	14-0/8	14-0/8	24-1/8	Ketcheeka River	BC	Paul Brunner	1974	5
154-1/8	35-7/8	34-6/8	13-3/8	13-3/8	23-5/8	Cassiar Mountains	BC	Calvin Farner	1986	5
153-1/8	36-1/8	34-2/8	13-6/8	13-6/8	20-6/8	Kacheeka River	BC	John D. "Jack" Frost	1985	7
152-3/8	30-6/8	37-5/8	13-4/8	13-4/8	24-2/8	Tucho Lake	BC	Chuck Adams	1985	8
151-4/8	33-2/8	33-0/8	13-2/8	13-2/8	20-3/8	Racing River	BC	Pete Shepley	1985	9
149-1/8	35-4/8	35-3/8	13-2/8	13-1/8	21-6/8	Terminus Mountain	BC	Paul P. Schafer	1975	10
148-3/8	34-0/8	35-7/8	13-0/8	13-1/8	28-0/8	Todagin Mountain	BC	Al Klopfenstein	1977	11
147-7/8	35-7/8	30-0/8	13-3/8	13-3/8	28-0/8	Tatoga Lake	BC	Eric Hoglund	1979	12
146-4/8	35-5/8	35-3/8	13-0/8	13-3/8	27-1/8	Atlin	BC	Tom Tietz	1985	13
145-7/8	34-4/8	34-7/8	13-0/8	13-0/8	22-1/8	Todagin Mountain	BC	Lee Kline	1983	14
145-6/8	33-1/8	33-7/8	12-5/8	12-5/8	21-4/8	Todagin Lake	BC	Thomas J. Hoffman	1985	15
142-2/8	33-6/8	34-2/8	12-2/8	12-1/8	22-1/8	Todagin Mountain	BC	David Hooper	1977	16
140-5/8	35-0/8	34-7/8	12-1/8	12-0/8	23-3/8	Turnagin River	BC	Maxallen D. Jackson	1984	17
140-4/8	32-5/8	32-7/8	12-5/8	12-7/8	21-4/8	Todagin Creek Mtn.	BC	Dennis McCarthy	1983	18

APPENDIXES

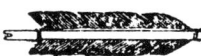

BOWHUNTER'S BIG GAME RECORDS

POPE AND YOUNG CLUB

Under the heading of North American Big Game are included the following with the minimum point score requirements (Boone & Crockett scoring system) as revised effective January 1, 1987.

To be eligible for entry into the Pope and Young Club's Records and Awards, the Trophy must equal or exceed the score listed on the Minimum List and must have been taken by the individual or persons who are entering it, entirely by means of the Bow and Arrow under the Club's Rules of Fair Chase. A Trophy Award Citation will be issued to each qualifying entry.

Cougar taken in any area where a bounty provision of any type is allowed are not eligible for entry in Pope and Young Club Records, or for Record Class Citations.

Southern Boundary of North America to be defined as the Southern Boundary of Mexico.

MINIMUM POINT SCORE REQUIREMENTS

Alaska Brown Bear	20	Mule Deer, Non-Typical	160
Black Bear	18	Whitetail Deer, Typical	125
Grizzly Bear	19	Whitetail Deer, Non-Typical	150
Polar Bear	20	Roosevelt (Olympic) Elk	210
Bison	80	Yellowstone (Wapiti) Elk	260
Barren Ground Caribou	300	Rocky Mountain Goat	40
Mountain Caribou	265	Alaska-Yukon Moose	170
Quebec/Labrador Caribou	300	Canada Moose	135
Woodland Caribou	220	Wyoming Moose	115
Cougar	13 8/16	Muskox	90
Columbian Blacktail Deer	90	Pronghorn	64
Sitka Blacktail Deer	65	Bighorn Sheep	140
Coues Deer, Typical	65	Dall (White) Sheep	120
Coues Deer, Non-Typical	75	Desert Bighorn Sheep	140
Mule Deer, Typical	145	Stone Sheep	120

POPE AND YOUNG CLUB
NORTH AMERICAN BIG GAME TROPHY SCORING FORM
BOWHUNTING

To:
P & Y Records Office
1804 Borah
Moscow, ID 83843

BIG GAME   RECORDS

<u>BEAR</u>   KIND OF BEAR _____

SEX _____

SEE OTHER SIDE FOR INSTRUCTIONS	Measurements
A Greatest Length Without Lower Jaw (Measured in Sixteenths)	
B Greatest Width (Measured in Sixteenths)	
TOTAL and FINAL SCORE	

Exact locality where killed   County   State

Date killed   By whom killed

Present owner

Address

Guide's Name and Address

Remarks. (Mention any abnormalities)

I certify that I have measured the above trophy on _____ 19 _____
at (address) _____ City _____
State _____ Zip Code _____ and that these measurements and data are, to the best
of my knowledge and belief, made in accordance with the instructions given.
Witness: _____
(To Measurer's Signature)

Signature _____
Pope & Young Club Official Measurer

_____
MEASURER (Print)
_____
ADDRESS
_____
CITY   STATE   ZIP

INSTRUCTIONS

All measurements must be made with a flexible steel tape to the nearest one-sixteenth of an inch.

Official measurements cannot be taken for at least sixty days after the animal was killed. Photographs of right side, left side, and front of skull are required.

A. Greatest Length is measured between perpendiculars to the long axis of the skull WITHOUT the lower jaw and EXCLUDING malformations. (Normal teeth are included)

B. Greatest Width is measured between perpendiculars at right angles to the long axis.

All adhering flesh, membrane and cartilage must be completely removed before official measurements are taken.

Photographs: All entries **must** include photographs of the trophy. A right side, left side and front view photograph is required for all skulls. A photograph of the entire animal is requested if at all possible. The photograph should clearly show the cheek bones (zygomatic arches), front and rear portions of the skull.

Drying Period: To be eligible for entry in the Pope & Young Records, a trophy must first have been stored under normal room temperature and humidity for at least 60 consecutive days. No trophy will be considered which has in any way been altered from its natural state.

All flesh and membrane **must** be completely removed from skull prior to measuring.

THIS SCORING FORM MUST BE ACCOMPANIED BY A SIGNED POPE & YOUNG FAIR CHASE AFFIDAVIT, 3 PHOTOS OF SKULL, AND A RECORDING FEE OF $25.00.

Official Scoring
System of the Boone
and Crockett Club

BISON

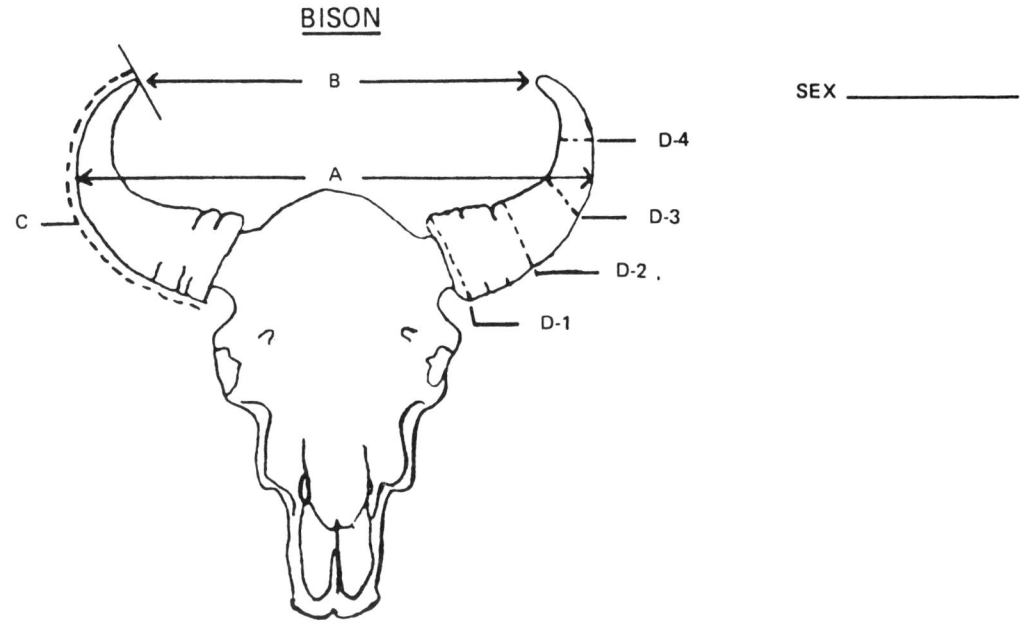

SEX _____

SEE OTHER SIDE FOR INSTRUCTIONS	Supplementary Data	Column 1	Column 2	Column 3
		Right Horn	Left Horn	Difference
A Greatest Spread				
B Tip to Tip Spread				
C Length of Horn				
D-1 Circumference of Base				
D-2 Circumference at First Quarter				
D-3 Circumference at Second Quarter				
D-4 Circumference at Third Quarter				
TOTALS				

ADD	Column 1		Exact locality where killed	
	Column 2		Date killed	By whom killed
TOTAL			Present owner	
SUBTRACT Column 3			Address	
FINAL SCORE			Guide's Name and Address	
			Remarks: (Mention any abnormalities)	

I certify that I have measured the above trophy on _____ 19 _____
at (address)_____City _____
State _____ Zip Code_____ and that these measurements and data are, to the best of my knowledge and belief, made in accordance with the instructions given.

Witness: _____ Signature_____
Pope & Young Club Official Measurer

INSTRUCTIONS

All measurements must be made with a flexible steel tape to the nearest one-eighth of an inch. To simplify addition, please enter fractional figures in eighths.

Official measurements cannot be taken for at least sixty days after the animal was killed. Please submit photographs.

Supplementary Data measurements indicate conformation of the trophy. None of the figures in Lines A and B are to be included in the score. Evaluation of conformation is a matter of personal preference.

A. Greatest Spread measured between perpendiculars at right angles to the center line of the skull.

B. Tip to Tip Spread measured between tips of horns.

C. Length of Horn measured from lowest point on under side over outer curve to a point in line with tip.

D-1. Circumference of Base measured at right angles to axis of horn. DO NOT follow irregular edge of horn.

D-2-3-4. Divide measurement C of LONGER horn by four; mark BOTH horns at these quarters even though the other horn is shorter, and measure circumference at these marks.

Bison: In order to be acceptable the bison must be taken from a free ranging herd on state or federal lands. It must be classed as a game animal in the state or province where taken and a photo copy of the hunting permit must be submitted with the trophy form.

Drying Period: To be eligible for entry in the Pope & Young Records, a trophy must first have been stored under normal room temperature and humidity for at least 60 consecutive days prior to measurement. No trophy will be considered which has in any way been altered from its natural state.

Photographs: All entries must include photographs of the trophy. A right side, left side and front view photograph will be required for all antlers, horns and skulls. A photograph of the entire animal is requested if at all possible.

THIS SCORING FORM MUST BE ACCOMPANIED BY A SIGNED POPE & YOUNG FAIR CHASE AFFIDAVIT AND A RECORDING FEE OF $25.00.

POPE AND YOUNG CLUB
NORTH AMERICAN BIG GAME TROPHY SCORING FORM

BIG GAME RECORDS

CARIBOU

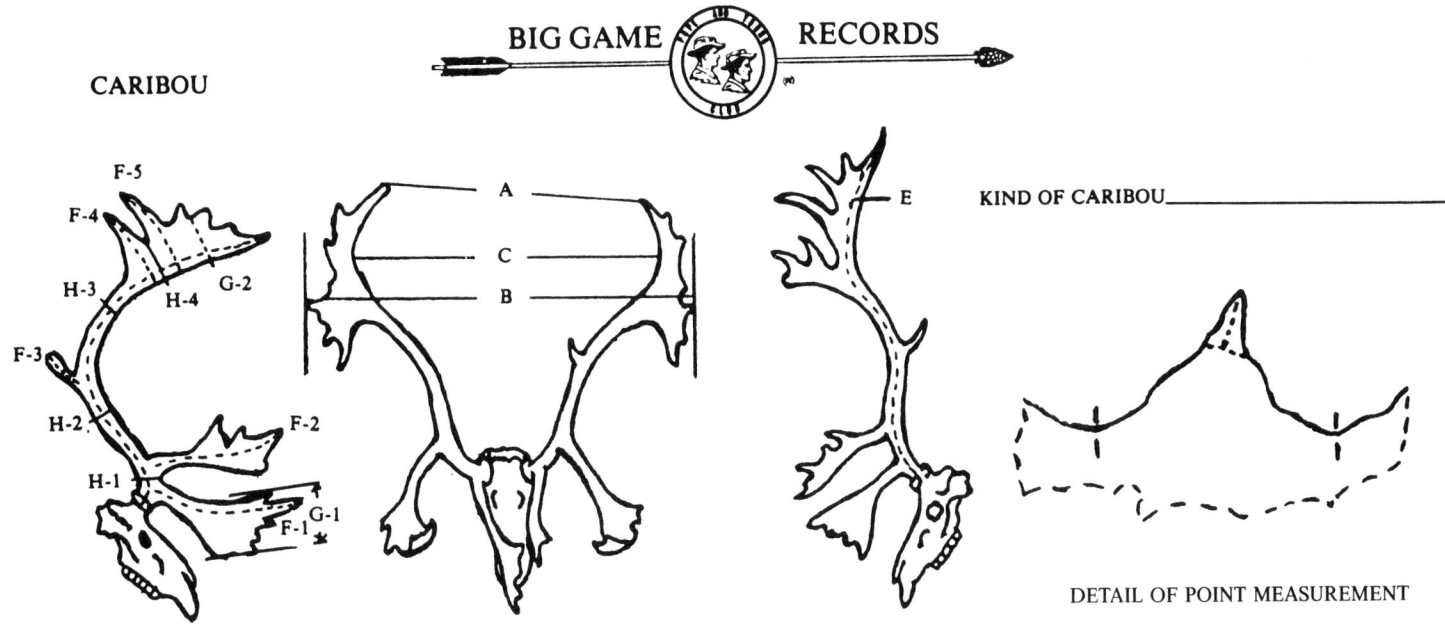

E

KIND OF CARIBOU_____

DETAIL OF POINT MEASUREMENT

SEE OTHER SIDE FOR INSTRUCTIONS			Supplementary Data	Column 1	Column 2	Column 3	Column 4
				Spread Credit	Right Antler	Left Antler	Difference
A.	Tip to Tip Spread						
B.	Greatest Spread						
C.	Inside Spread of MAIN BEAMS		Spread credit may equal but not exceed length of longer antler				
D.	Number of Points on Each Antler excluding brows						
	Number of Points on Each Brow						
E.	Length of Main Beam						
F-1	Length of Brow Palm or First Point						
F-2	Length of Bez or Second Point						
F-3	Length of Rear Point, if present						
F-4	Length of Second Longest Top Point						
F-5	Length of Longest Top Point						
G-1	Width of Brow Palm						
G-2	Width of Top Palm						
H-1	Circumference at Smallest Place Between Brow and Bez Points						
H-2	Circumference at Smallest Place Between Bez and Rear Point, if present						
H-3	Circumference at Smallest Place Before First Top Point						
H-4	Circumference at Smallest Place Between Two Longest Top Palm Points						
	TOTALS						

ADD	Column 1		Exact locality where killed	
	Column 2		Date killed	By whom killed
	Column 3		Present owner	
	TOTAL		Address	
SUBTRACT Column 4			Guide's Name and Address	
	FINAL SCORE		Remarks: (Mention any abnormalities)	

I certify that I have measured the above trophy on_____19_____

at (address)_____City_____

State_____Zip Code_____and that these measurements and data are, to the

best of my knowledge and belief, made in accordance with the instructions given.

Witness:_____   Signature _____
        (To measurer's signature)   Pope & Young Club Official Measurer

_____

MEASURER   (Print)

_____

ADDRESS

_____

CITY   STATE   ZIP

INSTRUCTIONS

Measurements must be made with a flexible steel tape or steel cable to the nearest one-eighth of an inch. To simplify addition, please enter fractional figures in eighths. Official measurements cannot be taken for at least sixty days after the animal was killed. Please submit photographs (see below).

A. Tip to Tip Spread is measured between tips of Main Beams.

B. Greatest Spread is measured between perpendiculars at right angles to the center line of the skull at widest part whether across main beams or points.

C. Inside Spread of Main Beams is measured at right angles to the center line of the skull at the widest point between main beams. Enter this measurement again in "Spread Credit" column if it is less than or equal to the length of longer antler; if longer, enter longer antler length for Spread Credit.

D. Number of points on each antler.   To be counted a point, a projection must be at least one-half inch long and this length must exceed the breadth at the point of measurement. The length may be measured to any location - at least one-half inch from the tip - at which the length of the point exceeds its breadth.   Beam tip is counted as a point but not measured as a point. There are no "abnormal" points on caribou.

E. Length of Main Beam is measured from lowest outside edge of burr over outer curve to the most distant point of what is, or appears to be, the main beam. The point of beginning is that point on the burr where the center line along the outer curve of the beam intersects the burr.

F-1-2-3. Length of Points. The lengths of these points are measured from nearest edge of beam on the shortest line over outer curve to tip. To determine nearest edge (top edge) of beam, lay the tape along the outer curve of the beam so that the top edge of the tape coincides with the tip edge of the beam on both sides of the point. Draw line along top edge of tape. This line will be base line from which point is measured.

F-4-5. The length of these points are measured from the tip of the point to the top of the beam, then at right angle to the LOWER EDGE of beam.   The second longest Top Point **cannot** be a point branch of the Longest Top Point.

G-1. Width of Brow is measured in a straight line from top edge to lower edge, as illustrated, with measurement line at a right angle to main axis of brow.

G-2.Width of Top Palm is measured from midpoint of lower rear edge of main beam to midpoint of a dip between points, at widest part of palm.The line of measurement begins and ends at mid-points of palm edges, which gives credit for palm thickness.

H-1-2-3-4. Circumferences - If rear point is missing, take H-2 and H-3 measurements at smallest place between bez and first top point. A steel tape must be used to take circumference measurements (a cable cannot be used for these measurements).

Photographs: All entries must include photographs of the trophy. A right side, left side and front view photograph will be required for all antlers, horns and skulls. A photograph of the entire animal is requested if at all possible.

Drying Period: To be eligible for entry in the Pope & Young Records, a trophy must first have been stored under normal room temperature and humidity for at least 60 consecutive days. No trophy will be considered which has in any way been altered from its natural state.

THIS SCORING FORM MUST BE ACCOMPANIED BY A SIGNED POPE & YOUNG FAIR CHASE AFFIDAVIT, 3 PHOTOS OF ANTLERS, AND A RECORDING FEE OF $25.00.

POPE AND YOUNG CLUB
NORTH AMERICAN BIG GAME TROPHY SCORING FORM
BOWHUNTING

BIG GAME   RECORDS

COUGAR and JAGUAR

KIND OF ANIMAL _____

SEX _____

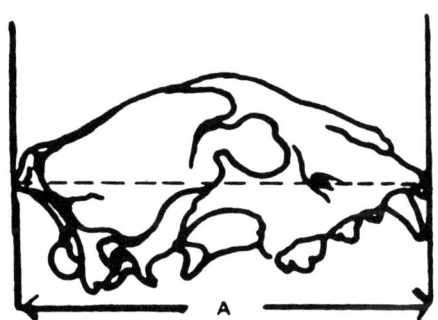

SEE OTHER SIDE FOR INSTRUCTIONS		Measurements
A. Greatest Length Without Lower Jaw (Measured in Sixteenths)		
B Greatest Width (Measured in Sixteenths)		
TOTAL AND FINAL SCORE		

Exact locality where killed	(County)	(State)
Date killed	By whom killed	
Present owner		
Address		
Guide's Name and Address		
Remarks: (Mention any abnormalities)		

I certify that I have measured the above trophy on _____ 19 _____

at (address) _____ City _____

State _____ Zip Code _____ and that these measurements and data are, to the best
of my knowledge and belief, made in accordance with the instructions given.

Witness: _____   Signature _____

(To Measurer's Signature)

Pope & Young Club Official Measurer

MEASURER (Print) _____

ADDRESS _____

CITY   STATE   ZIP

INSTRUCTIONS

All measurements must be made with a flexible steel tape to the nearest one-sixteenth of an inch.

Official measurements cannot be taken for at least sixty days after the animal was killed. Photographs of right side, left side, and front of skull are required.

A. Greatest Length is measured between perpendiculars to the long axis of the skull WITHOUT the lower jaw and EXCLUDING malformations. (Normal teeth are included)

B. Greatest Width is measured between perpendiculars at right angles to the long axis.

All adhering flesh, membrane and cartilage must be completely removed before official measurements are taken.

Photographs: All entries **must** include photographs of the trophy. A right side, left side and front view photograph is required for all skulls. A photograph of the entire animal is requested if at all possible. The photograph should clearly show the cheek bones (zygomatic arches), front and rear portions of the skull.

Drying Period: To be eligible for entry in the Pope & Young Records, a trophy must first have been stored under normal room temperature and humidity for at least 60 consecutive days. No trophy will be considered which has in any way been altered from its natural state.

All flesh and membrane **must** be completely removed from skull prior to measuring.

THIS SCORING FORM MUST BE ACCOMPANIED BY A SIGNED POPE & YOUNG FAIR CHASE AFFIDAVIT, 3 PHOTOS OF SKULL, AND A RECORDING FEE OF $25.00.

POPE & YOUNG CLUB
NORTH AMERICAN BIG GAME TROPHY SCORING FORM
BOWHUNTING

TO:

P & Y Records Office
1804 Borah
Moscow, ID 83843

BIG GAME — RECORDS

KIND OF DEER_____

TYPICAL MULE - BLACKTAIL and SITKA DEER

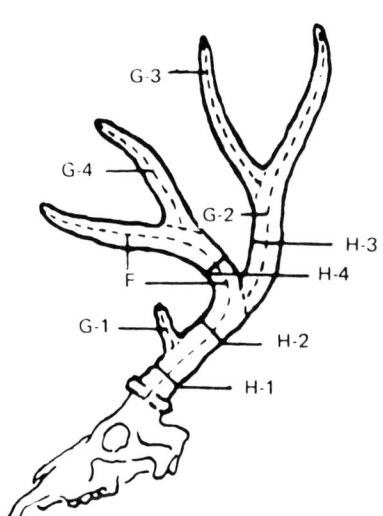

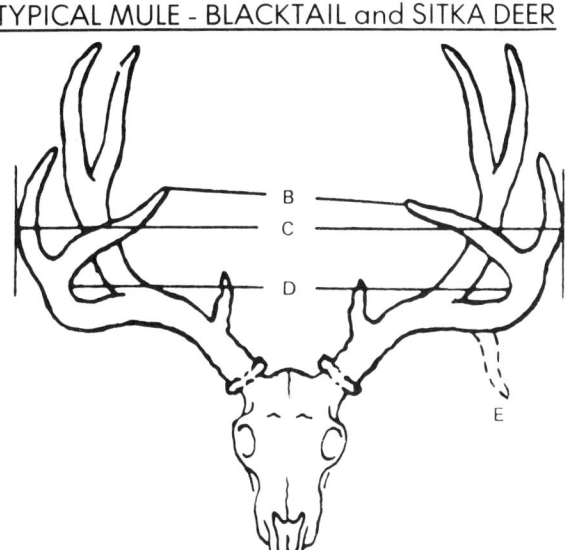

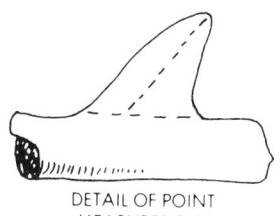

DETAIL OF POINT MEASUREMENT

Abnormal Points	
Right	Left

Total To E	

SEE OTHER SIDE FOR INSTRUCTIONS	Supplementary Data		Column 1	Column 2	Column 3	Column 4
	R	L	Spread Credit	Right Antler	Left Antler	Difference
Number of Points on Each Antler						
Tip to Tip Spread						
Greatest Spread						
Inside Spread of MAIN BEAMS	Spread credit may equal but not exceed length of longer antler					
If Inside Spread of Main Beams exceeds longer antler length, enter difference						
Total of Lengths of all Abnormal Points						
Length of Main Beam						
-1 Length of First Point, if present						
-2 Length of Second Point						
-3 Length of Third Point						
-4 Length of Fourth Point, if present						
-1 Circumference at Smallest Place Between Burr and First Point						
-2 Circumference at Smallest Place Between First and Second Points						
-3 Circumference at Smallest Place Between Main Beam and Third Points						
-4 Circumference at Smallest Place between Second and Fourth Points or half way between Second Point and Beam tip if Fourth Point is missing						
TOTALS						

ADD	Column 1		Exact locality where killed	(County)	(State)
	Column 2		Date killed By whom killed		
	Column 3		Present owner		
	Total		Address		
SUBTRACT Column 4			Guide's Name and Complete Address		
FINAL SCORE			Remarks: (Mention any abnormalities)		

I certify that I have measured the above trophy on _____ 19 _____

at (address) _____ City _____

State _____ Zip Code _____ and that these measurements and data are, to the best

of my knowledge and belief, made in accordance with the instructions given.

Witness: _____ Signature _____
          (To Measurer's Signature)

Pope & Young Club Official Measurer

_____
MEASURER (Print)
_____
ADDRESS
_____
CITY   STATE   ZIP

All measurements must be made with a flexible steel tape or measuring cable to the nearest <u>one-eighth</u> of an inch. Wherever it is necessary to change direction of measurement, mark a control point and swing tape at this point. To simplify addition, please enter fractional figures in **eighths**. Official measurements cannot be take for at least sixty days after the animal was killed. **Photos of left side, right side, and front of antlers are required.**

Supplementary Data measurements indicate conformation of the trophy, and none of the figures in Lines A, B and C are to be included in the score. Evaluation of conformation is a matter of personal preference. Excellent, but nontypical Mule Deer heads with many points shall be placed and judged in a separate class.

A. Number of Points on Each Antler. To be counted a point, a projection must be at least one inch long AND its length must exceed the length of its base. All points are measured from tip of point to nearest edge of beam as illustrated. **Beam tip is counted as a point but not measured as a point.**

B. Tip to Tip Spread measured between tips of main beams.

C. Greatest Spread measured between perpendiculars at right angles to the center line of the skull at widest part whether across main beams or points.

D. Inside Spread of Main Beams measured at right angles to the center line of the skull at widest point between main beams. Enter this measurement again in ''Spread Credit'' column if it is less than or equal to the length of longer antler.

E. Total of Lengths of all Abnormal Points. Abnormal points are generally considered to be those nontypical in shape or location.

F. Length of Main Beam measured from lowest outside edge of burr over outer curve to the tip of the main beam. The point of beginning is that point on the burr where the center line along the outer curve of the beam intersects the burr.

G-1-2-3-4. Length of Normal Points. Normal points are the brow (or first) and the upper and lower forks as shown in illustration. They are measured from nearest edge of beam over outer curve to tip. To determine nearest edge (top edge) of beam, lay the tape along the outer curve of the beam so that the top edge of the tape coincides with the top edge of the beam on both sides of the point. Draw line along top of tape. This line will be base line from which point is measured.

H-1-2-3-4. Circumferences - If first point is missing, take H-1 and H-2 at smallest place between burr and second point. If third point is missing, take H-3 half way between the base and tip of second point. If the fourth is missing, take H-4 half way between the second point and tip of main beam. Circumference measurements must be taken with a steel tape.

Photographs: All entries must include photographs of the trophy. A right side, left side and front view photograph will be required for all antlers, horns and skulls. A photograph of the entire animal is requested if at all possible.

Drying Period: To be eligible for entry in the Pope & Young Records, a trophy must first have been stored under normal room temperature and humidity for at least 60 consecutive days. No trophy will be considered which has in any way been altered from its natural state.

THIS SCORING FORM MUST BE ACCOMPANIED BY A SIGNED
**POPE & YOUNG FAIR CHASE AFFIDAVITT, 3 PHOTOS OF ANTLERS, AND A
RECORDING FEE OF $25.00**

Copyright 1965 by Boone and Crockett Club
(Written request for privilege of complete reproduction is required)

o:
P & Y Records Office
Rt. 1 Box 147
Salmon, Idaho 83467

POPE AND YOUNG CLUB

NORTH AMERICAN BIG GAME TROPHY SCORING FORM

BOWHUNTING

BIG GAME  RECORDS

NON-TYPICAL MULE DEER

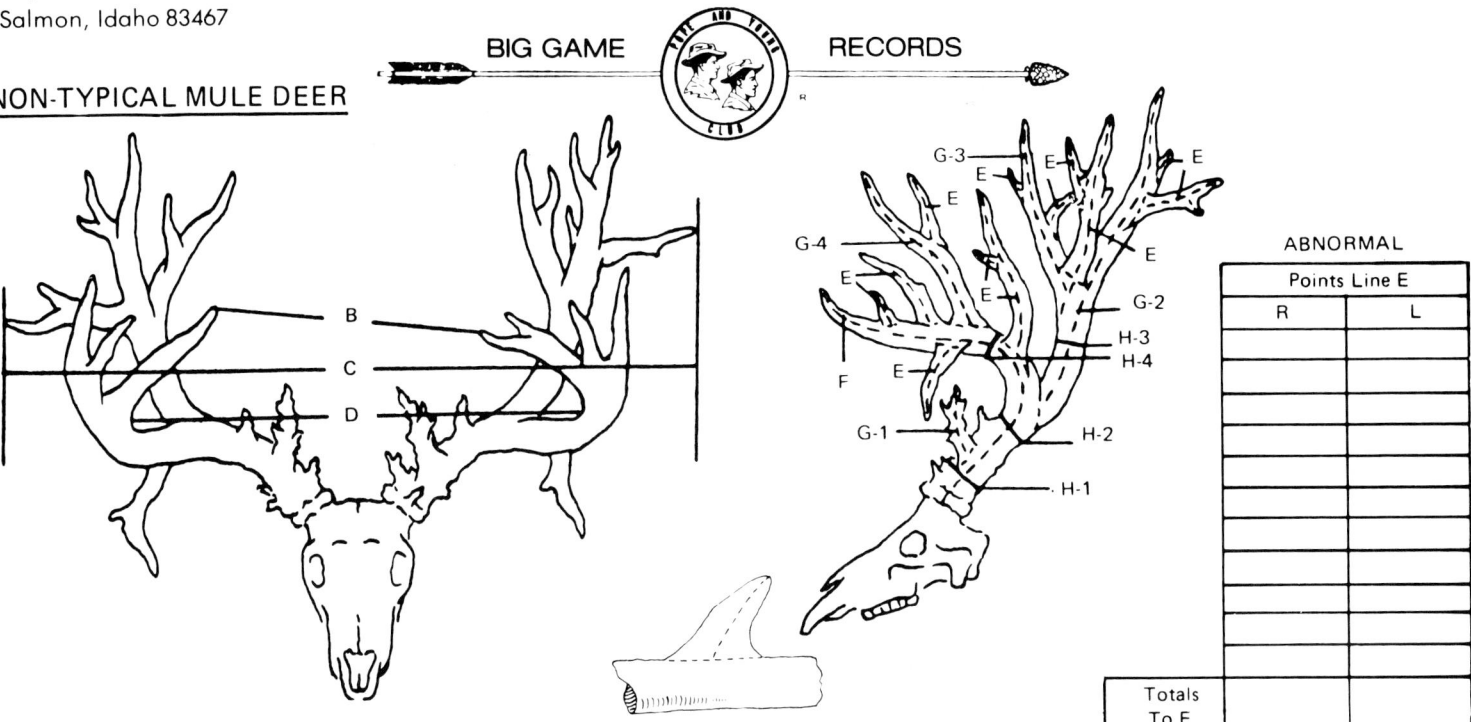

DETAIL OF POINT MEASUREMENT

ABNORMAL		
Points Line E		
	R	L
Totals To E		

E OTHER SIDE FOR INSTRUCTIONS		Supplementary Data		Column 1	Column 2	Column 3	Column 4
		R	L	Spread Credit	Right Antler	Left Antler	Difference
Number of Points on Each Antler							
Tip to Tip Spread							
Greatest Spread							
Inside Spread of MAIN BEAMS		Spread credit may equal but not exceed length of longer antler					
If Inside Spread of Main Beams exceeds longer antler length, enter difference							
Total of Lengths of all Abnormal Points							
Length of Main Beam							
1 Length of First Point, if present							
2 Length of Second Point							
3 Length of Third Point							
4 Length of Fourth Point, if present							
1 Circumference at Smallest Place Between Burr and First Point							
2 Circumference at Smallest Place Between First and Second Points							
3 Circumference at Smallest Place Between Second and Third Points							
4 Circumference at Smallest Place between Third and Fourth Points or half way between Third Point and Beam tip if Fourth Point is missing							
TALS							

ADD	Column 1		Exact locality where killed		(County)		(State)
	Column 2						
	Column 3		Date killed	By whom killed			
	TOTAL		Present owner				
SUBTRACT Column 4			Address				
	Result						
Add Line E Total			Guide's Name and Complete Address				
FINAL SCORE			Remarks: (Mention any abnormalities)				

I certify that I have measured the above trophy on _____ 19 _____
at (address) _____ City _____
State _____ Zip Code _____ and that these measurements and data are, to the best of my knowledge and belief, made in accordance with the instructions given.

Witness: _____ Signature _____

Pope & Young Club Official Measurer

MEASURER (Print)
ADDRESS
CITY   STATE   ZIP

INSTRUCTIONS

All measurements must be made with a flexible steel tape to the nearest one-eighth of an inch. To simplify addition, please enter fractional figures in eighths.

Official measurements cannot be taken for at least sixty days after the animal was killed. Please submit photographs.

Supplementary Data measurements indicate conformation of the trophy, and none of the figures in Lines A, B and C are to be included in the score. Evaluation of conformation is a matter of personal preference.

A. Number of Points on Each Antler. To be counted a point, a projection must be at least one inch long AND its length must exceed the length of its base. All points are measured from tip to point to nearest edge of beam as illustrated. Beam tip is counted as a point but not measured as a point.

B. Tip to Tip Spread measured between tips of antlers.

C. Greatest Spread measured between perpendiculars at right angles to the center line of the skull at widest part whether across main beams or points.

D. Inside Spread of Main Beams measured at right angles to the center line of the skull at widest point between main beams. Enter this measurement again in "Spread Credit" column if it is less than or equal to the length of longer antler.

E. Total of Lengths of all Abnormal Points. Abnormal points are considered to be those nontypical in shape or location. It is very important, in scoring nontypical heads, to determine which points are to be classed as normal and which are not. To do this, study carefully the markings G-1, G-2, G-3 and G-4 on the diagram, which indicate the normal points. On the trophy to be scored, select the points which most closely correspond to these. All others over one inch in length (See A, above) are considered abnormal.

Measure the exact length of each abnormal point, over the outer curve, from the tip to the nearest edge of the beam or point from which it projects. Then add these lengths and enter the total in the space provided.

F. Length of Main Beams measured from lowest outside edge of burr over outer curve to the tip of the main beam.

G-1-2-3-4. Length of Normal Points. Normal points are the brow (or first) and the upper and lower forks as shown in illustration. They are measured from nearest edge of beam over outer curve to tip.

H-1-2-3-4. Circumferences If first point is missing, take H-1 and H-2 at smallest place between burr and second point. If third point is missing, take H-3 half way between the base and tip of second point. If the fourth point is missing take H-4 half way between the second point and tip of main beam.

Photographs All entries must include photographs of the trophy. A right side, left side and front view photograph will be required for all antlers, horns and skulls. A photograph of the entire animal is requested if at all possible.

Drying Period: To be eligible for entry in the the Pope & Young Records, a trophy must first have been stored under normal room temperature and humidity for at least 60 consecutive days. No trophy will be considered which has in any way been altered from its natural state.

THIS SCORING FORM MUST BE ACCOMPANIED BY A SIGNED POPE & YOUNG FAIR CHASE AFFIDAVIT, 3 PHOTOS AND A RECORDING FEE OF $25.00.

POPE & YOUNG CLUB
NORTH AMERICAN BIG GAME TROPHY SCORING FORM
BOWHUNTING

To:

P & Y Records
1804 Borah
Moscow, ID 83843

BIG GAME   RECORDS

KIND OF DEER_____

TYPICAL
WHITETAIL AND COUES DEER

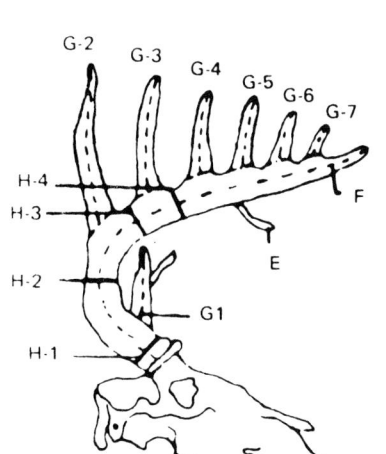

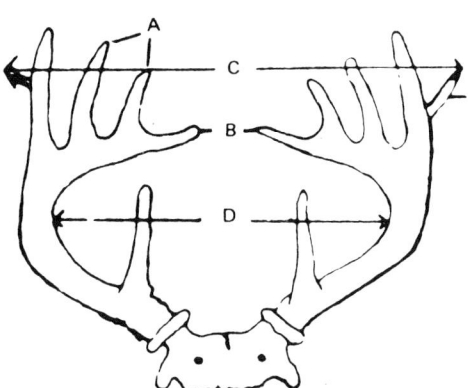

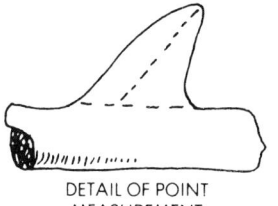

DETAIL OF POINT
MEASUREMENT

Abnormal Points	
Right	Left

Total To E

SEE OTHER SIDE FOR INSTRUCTIONS	Supplementary Data		Column 1	Column 2	Column 3	Column 4
	R	L	Spread Credit	Right Antler	Left Antler	Difference
A. Number of Points on Each Antler						
B. Tip to Tip Spread						
C. Greatest Spread						
D. Inside Spread of MAIN BEAMS	Spread credit may equal but not exceed length of longer antler					
If Inside Spread of Main Beams exceeds longer antler length, enter difference						
Total of Lengths of all Abnormal Points						
Length of Main Beam						
G-1 Length of First Point, if present						
G-2 Length of Second Point						
G-3 Length of Third Point						
G-4 Length of Fourth Point, if present						
G-5 Length of Fifth Point, if present						
G-6 Length of Sixth Point, if present						
G-7 Length of Seventh Point, if present						
H-1 Circumference at Smallest Place Between Burr and First Point						
H-2 Circumference at Smallest Place Between First and Second Points						
H-3 Circumference at Smallest Place Between Second and Third Points						
H-4 Circumference at Smallest Place between Third and Fourth Points or half way between Third Point and Beam tip if Fourth Point is missing						
TOTALS						

ADD	Column 1		Exact locality where killed	(County)	(State)
	Column 2		Date killed By whom killed		
	Column 3		Present owner		
	Total		Address		
SUBTRACT Column 4			Guide's Name and Complete Address		
FINAL SCORE			Remarks: (Mention any abnormalities)		

I certify that I have measured the above trophy on _____ 19 _____
at (address) _____ City _____
State _____ Zip Code _____ and that these measurements and data are, to the
best of my knowledge and belief, made in accordance with the instructions given.

Witness: _____Signature _____
(To Measurer's Signature)

Pope & Young Club Official Measurer

_____
MEASURER (Print)

_____
ADDRESS

_____
CITY   STATE   ZIP

INSTRUCTIONS

All measurements must be made with a flexible steel tape to the nearest one-eighth of an inch. Wherever it is necessary to change direction of measurement, mark a control point and swing tape at this point. To simplify addition, please enter fractional figures in **eighths**. Official measurements cannot be taken for at least sixty days after the animal was killed. Please submit photographs. (see below).

Supplementary Data measurements indicate conformation of the trophy, and none of the figures in line A, B and C are to be included in the score. Evaluation of conformation is a matter of personal preference.

A. Number of Points on each antler. To be counted a point, a projection must be at least one inch long AND its length must exceed the length of its base. All points are measured from tip of point to nearest edge of beam as illustrated. **Beam tip is counted as a point but not measured as a point.**

B. Tip to Tip Spread measured between tips of Main Beams.

C. Greatest Spread measured between perpendiculars at right angles to the center line of the skull at widest part whether across main beams or points.

D. Inside Spread of Main Beams measured at right angles to the center line of the skull at widest point between main beams. Enter this measurement again in "Spread Credit" column if it is less than or equal to the length of longer antler.

E. Total of Lengths of all Abnormal Points. Abnormal points are generally considered to be those nontypical in shape or location. Sketch all abnormal points on antler illustration (front of form) showing location and approximate size.

F. Length of Main Beam measured from lowest outside edge of burr over outer curve to the most distant point of what is, or appears to be, the main beam. The point of beginning is that point on the burr where the center line along the outer curve of the beam intersects the burr.

G-1-2-3-4-5-6-7. Length of Normal Points. Normal points project from main beam. They are measured from nearest edge of main beam over outer curve to tip. To determine nearest edge (top edge) of beam, lay the tape along the outer curve of the beam so that the top edge of the tape coincides with the top edge of the beam on both sides of the point. Draw line along top edge of tape. This line will be base line from which point is measured.

H-1-2-3-4. Circumferences. If first point is missing, take H-1 and H-2 at smallest place between burr and second point.

Photographs: All entries must include photographs of the trophy. A right side, left side and front view photograph will be required for all antlers, horns and skulls. A photograph of the entire animal is requested if at all possible.

Drying Period: To be eligible for entry in the Pope & Young Records, a trophy must first have been stored under normal room temperature and humidity for at least 60 consecutive days after date of kill. No trophy will be considered which has in any way been altered from its natural state.

THIS SCORING FORM MUST BE ACCOMPANIED BY A SIGNED POPE & YOUNG FAIR CHASE AFFIDAVIT, 3 PHOTOS AND A RECORDING FEE OF $25.00.

Copyright 1965 by Boone & Crockett Club
(Written Request for Privilege of Complete Reproduction is Required)

POPE & YOUNG CLUB
NORTH AMERICAN BIG GAME TROPHY SCORING FORM
BOWHUNTING

BIG GAME · RECORDS

To:
P & Y Records Office
1804 Borah
Moscow, Idaho 83843

KIND OF DEER_____

NON-TYPICAL WHITETAIL AND COUES DEER

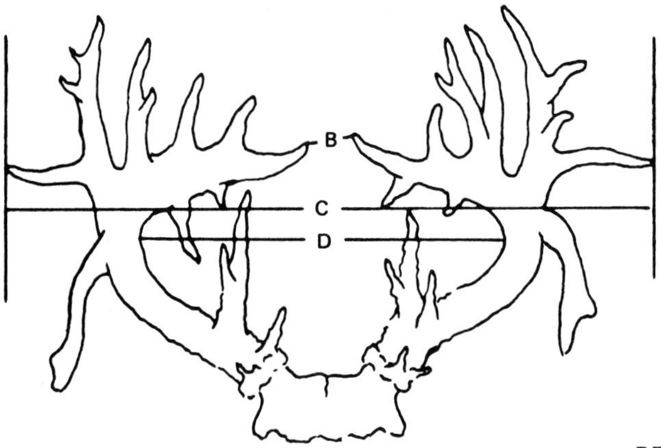

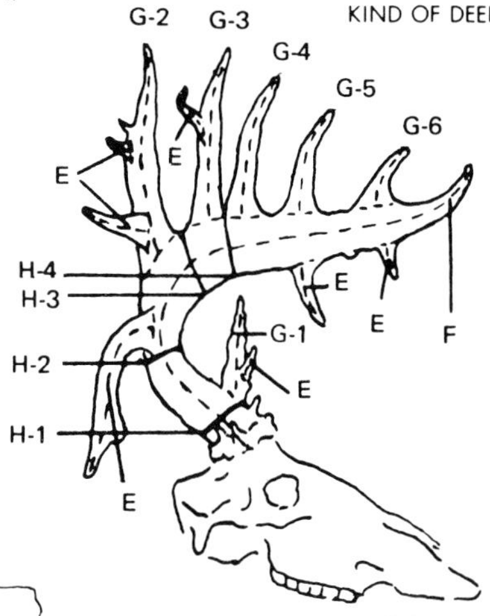

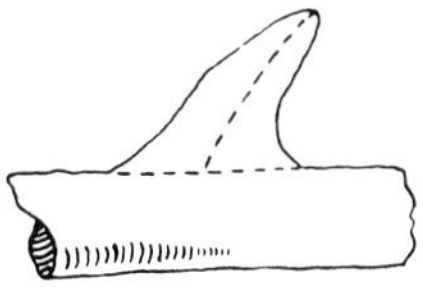

G-2 G-3
G-4
G-5
G-6
E   E
H-4
H-3   E
H-2   G-1
H-1   E   E   F
E
E

DETAIL OF POINT MEASUREMENT

ABNORMAL		
Points Line E		
	R	L
Totals To E		

SEE OTHER SIDE FOR INSTRUCTIONS		Supplementary Data		Column 1	Column 2	Column 3	Column 4
		R	L	Spread Credit	Right Antler	Left Antler	Difference
A.	Number of Points on Each Antler						
B.	Tip to Tip Spread						
C.	Greatest Spread						
D.	Inside Spread of MAIN BEAMS	Spread credit may equal but not exceed length of longer antler					
	If Inside Spread of Main Beams exceeds longer antler length, enter difference						
E.	Total of Lengths of all Abnormal Points						
F.	Length of Main Beam						
G-1	Length of First Point, if present						
G-2	Length of Second Point						
G-3	Length of Third Point						
G-4	Length of Fourth Point, if present						
G-5	Length of Fifth Point, if present						
G-6	Length of Sixth Point, if present						
G-7	Length of Seventh Point, if present						
H-1	Circumference at Smallest Place Between Burr and First Point						
H-2	Circumference at Smallest Place Between First and Second Points						
H-3	Circumference at Smallest Place Between Second and Third Points						
H-4	Circumference at Smallest Place between Third and Fourth Points or half way between Third Point and Beam tip if Fourth Point is missing						
TOTALS							

ADD	Column 1	
	Column 2	
	Column 3	
	TOTAL	
	SUBTRACT Column 4	
	Result	
	Add Line E Total	
	FINAL SCORE	

Exact locality where killed _____ (County) _____ (State)

Date killed _____ By whom killed _____

Present owner _____

Address _____

Guide's Name and Complete Address _____

Remarks: (Mention any abnormalities) _____

I certify that I have measured the above trophy on ————————— 19 —————
at (address)————————————————————————City —————————
State ————————— Zip Code —————— and that these measurements and data are, to the best of my knowledge and belief, made in accordance with the instructions given.

Witness: _____ Signature _____
(To Measurer's Signature)
                                           Pope & Young Club Official Measurer

INSTRUCTIONS

All measurements must be made with a flexible steel tape to the nearest one-eighth of an inch. Wherever it is necessary to change direction of measurement, mark a control point and swing tape at this point. To simplify addition, please enter fractional figures in eighths. Official measurements cannot be taken for at least sixty days after the animal was killed. Please submit photographs.

Supplementary Data measurements indicate conformation of the trophy, and none of the figures in Lines A, B and C are to be included in the score. Evaluation of conformation is a matter of personal preference.

A. Number of Points on each Antler. To be counted a point, a projection must be at least one inch long AND its length must exceed the length of its base. All points are measured from tip of point to nearest edge of beam as illustrated. Beam tip is counted as a point but not measured as a point.

B. Tip to Tip Spread measured between tips of main beams.

C. Greatest Spread measured between perpendiculars at right angles to the center line of the skull at widest part whether across main beam or points.

D. Inside Spread of Main Beams measured at right angles to the center line of the skull at widest point between main beams. Enter this measurement again in "Spread Credit" column if it is less than or equal to the length of longer antler.

E. Total of Lengths of all Abnormal Points. Abnormal points are considered to be those nontypical in shape or location. It is very important, in scoring nontypical heads, to determine which points are to be classed as normal and which are not. To do this, study carefully the character of the normal points on the diagram, which are marked G-1, G-2, G-3, etc. On the trophy to be scored, the points which correspond to these are measured as normal. All others over one inch in length (See A, above) are considered abnormal. Various types of abnormal points are shown (marked with an E) on the diagram. Measure the exact length of each abnormal point, over the outer curve, from the tip to the nearest edge of the beam or point from which it projects. Then add these lengths and enter the total in the space provided.

F. Length of Main Beam measured from lowest outside edge of burr over outer curve to the most distant point of what is, or appears to be, the main beam. The point of beginning is the point on the burr where the center line along the outer curve of the beam intersects the burr.

G-1-2-3-4-5-6-7. Length of Normal Points. Normal points project from main beam They are measured from nearest edge of main beam over outer curve to tip. To determine nearest edge (top edge) of beam, lay the tape along the outer curve of the beam so that the top edge of the tape coincides with the top edge of the beam on both sides of the point. Draw line along top edge of tape. This line will be base line from which point is measured.

H-1-2-3-4. Circumferences - If first point is missing, take H-1 and H-2 at smallest place between burr and second point. If fourth point is missing, take H-4 half way between third point and beam tip.

Photographs: All entries must include photographs of the trophy. A right side, left side and front view photograph will be required for all antlers, horns and skulls. A photograph of the entire animal is requested if at all possible.

Drying Period: To be eligible for entry in the Pope & Young Records, a trophy must first have been stored under normal room temperature and humidity for at least 60 consecutive days. No trophy will be considered which has in any way been altered from its natural state.

THIS SCORING FORM MUST BE ACCOMPANIED BY A SIGNED POPE & YOUNG
FAIR CHASE AFFIDAVIT, 3 PHOTOS OF ANTLERS, AND A RECORDING FEE OF $25.00

BIG GAME RECORDS

ROOSEVELT ELK

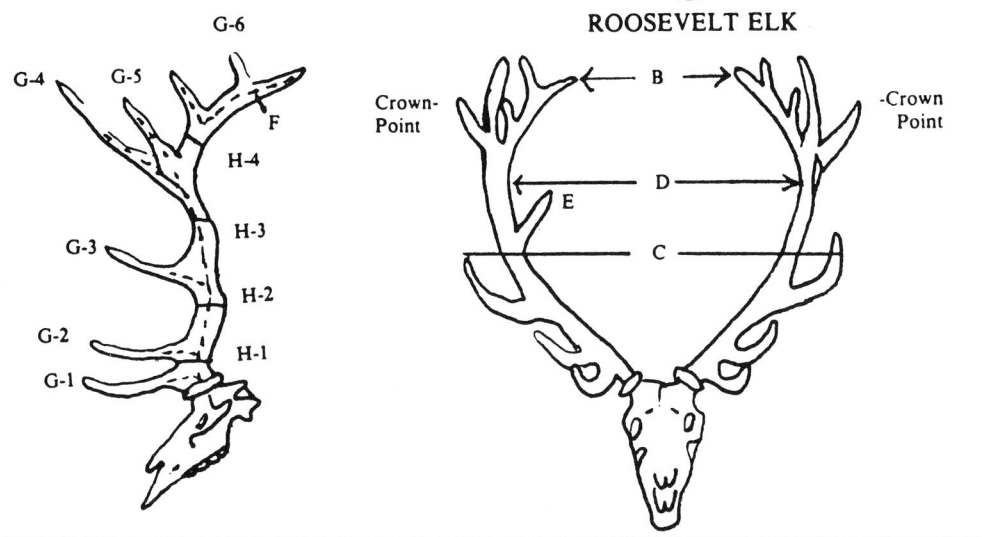

Crown Points	
Right	Left

Abnormal Points	
Right	Left
Total to E	

SEE OTHER SIDE FOR INSTRUCTIONS	Supplementary Data		Column 1	Column 2	Column 3	Column 4
	R	L	Spread Credit	Right Antler	Left Antler	Difference
A. Number of Points on Each Antler						
B. Tip to Tip Spread						
C. Greatest Spread						
D. Inside Spread of MAIN BEAMS — Spread credit may equal but not exceed length of longer antler						
E. Total of Lengths of all Abnormal Points						
F. Length of Main Beam						
G-1. Length of First Point, if present						
G-2. Length of Second Point						
G-3. Length of Third Point						
G-4. Length of Fourth (Royal) Point						
G-5. Length of Fifth Point, if present						
G-6. Length of Sixth Point, if present						
G-7. Length of Seventh Point, if present						
H-1. Circumference at Smallest Place Between First and Second Points						
H-2. Circumference at Smallest Place Between Second and Third Points						
H-3. Circumference at Smallest Place Between Third and Fourth Points						
H-4. Circumference at Smallest Place Between Fourth and Fifth Points						
TOTALS						

ADD	Column 1	
	Column 2	
	Column 3	
TOTAL		
SUBTRACT Column 4		
Result		
Add Crown Point Total		
Final Score		

Exact locality where killed _____ (County) _____ (State)

Date killed _____ By whom killed _____

Present owner _____

Address _____

Guide's Name and Address _____

Remarks: (Mention any abnormalities) _____

I certify that I have measured the above trophy on _____ 19_____
at (address) _____ City _____
State _____ Zip Code _____ and that these measurements and
data are, to the best of my knowledge and belief, made in accordance with the instructions given.

Witness: _____ Signature _____
(To measurer's signature)

Pope and Young Club Official Measurer

INSTRUCTIONS

Measurements must be made with a flexible steel tape or steel cable to the nearest one-eighth of an inch. To simplify addition, please enter fractional figures in **eighths**. Official measurements cannot be taken for at least sixty days after the animal was killed. **Please submit photographs (see below).**
A. Number of Points on each antler. To be counted a point, a projection must be at least one inch long AND at some location, at least one inch from the tip, the length of the projection must exceed its width. **Beam tip is counted as a point but not measured as a point.**
B. Tip to Tip Spread is measured between tips of main beams.
C. Greatest Spread is measured between perpendiculars at right angles to the center line of the skull at widest part whether across main beams or points.
D. Inside Spread of Main Beam is measured at right angles to the center line of the skull at widest point between main beams. Enter this measurement again in "Spread Credit" column if it is less than or equal to the length of longer antler; if longer, enter longer antler length for spread credit.
E. Total of Length of all Abnormal Points. Abnormal points are generally considered to be those non-typical in shape or location on or below G3. Sketch all abnormal points on antler illustration (front of form) showing location and approximate size. Measure in usual manner and enter in appropriate blanks.
Total Length of Crown Points. Crown points are any points projecting from the main beam or from another point on or above G-4 that are NOT typical in shape and location. Sketch these points on the form, enter their individual lengths in the crown point box. Then transfer the total to the score as provided.
F. Length of Main Beam is measured from lowest outside edge of burr over outer curve to the most distant point of the main beam. The point of beginning is that point on the burr where the center line along the outer curve of the beam intersects the burr.
G-1-2-3-4-5-6-7. Length of Normal Points. Normal points project from the top or front of the main beam in the general pattern illustrated. They are measured from the nearest edge of main beam over outer curve to tip. Record point length in appropriate blanks.
H-1-2-3. Circumference. If first point is missing, take H-1 and H-2 at smallest place between burr and second point. A steel tape must be used to take circumference measurements (a cable can not be used for these measurements.)
H-4. Circumference. Take H-4 between G-4 and what appears to be the typical G-5 point. The H-4 score should not be unduly influenced by the presence of crown points. If the typical G-5 points is missing, take H-4 halfway between G-4 and beam tip.

Photographs: All entries must include photographs of the trophy. A right side, left side and front view photograph will be required for all antlers, horns and skulls. A photograph of the entire animal is requested if at all possible.

Drying Period: To be eligible for entry in the Pope & Young Records, a trophy must first have been stored under normal room temperature and humidity for at least 60 consecutive days after date of kill. No trophy will be considered which has in any way been altered from its natural state.

THIS SCORING FORM MUST BE ACCOMPAINIED BY A SIGNED POPE & YOUNG FAIR CHASE AFFIDAVIT, 3 PHOTOS OF ANTLERS AND A RECORDING FEE OF $25.00.

POPE AND YOUNG CLUB
NORTH AMERICAN BIG GAME TROPHY SCORING FORM

To:

P & Y Records
1804 Borah
Moscow, Idaho 83843

BIG GAME   RECORDS

YELLOWSTONE (AMERICAN) ELK

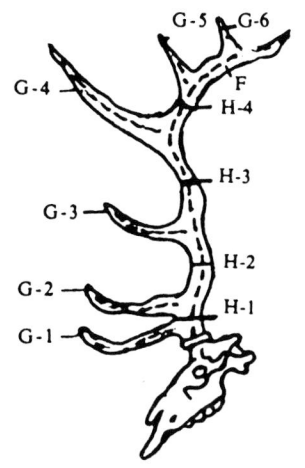

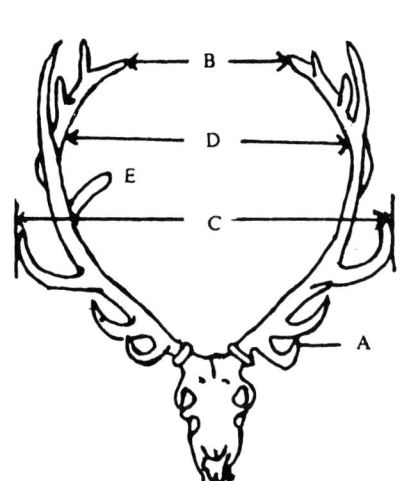

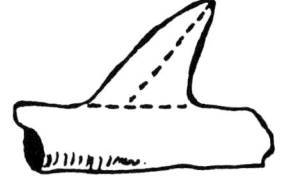

DETAIL OF POINT
MEASUREMENT

Abnormal Points	
Right	Left
	Total to E

SEE OTHER SIDE FOR INSTRUCTIONS	Supplementary Data		Column 1	Column 2	Column 3	Column 4
	R	L	Spread Credit	Right Antler	Left Antler	Difference
A. Number of Points on Each Antler						
B. Tip to Tip Spread						
C. Greatest Spread						
D. Inside Spread of MAIN BEAMS	Spread credit may equal but not exceed length of longer antler					
E. Total of Lengths of all Abnormal Points						
F. Length of Main Beam						
G-1. Length of First Point, if present						
G-2. Length of Second Point						
G-3. Length of Third Point						
G-4. Length of Fourth Point, if present						
G-5. Length of Fifth Point, if present						
G-6. Length of Sixth Point, if present						
G-7. Length of Seventh Point, if present						
H-1. Circumference at Smallest Place Between First and Second Points						
H-2. Circumference at Smallest Place Between Second and Third Points						
H-3. Circumference at Smallest Place Between Third and Fourth Points						
H-4. Circumference at Smallest Place Between Fourth and Fifth Points						
TOTALS						

ADD	Column 1		Exact locality where killed		(County)		(State)
	Column 2		Date killed	By whom killed			
	Column 3		Present owner				
	TOTAL		Address				
SUBTRACT Column 4			Guide's Name and Address				
	FINAL SCORE		Remarks: (Mention any abnormalities)				

I certify that I have measured the above trophy on _____ 19_____

at (address) _____City_____

State _____Zip Code _____and that these measurements and data are, to

the best of my knowledge and belief, made in accordance with the instructions given.

Witness: _____ Signature _____
                        (To Measurer's Signature)

Pope & Young Club Official Measurer

_____

MEASURER   (Print)

_____

ADDRESS

_____

CITY   STATE   ZIP

INSTRUCTIONS

Measurements must be made with a flexible steel tape or steel cable to the nearest one-eighth of an inch. To simplify addition, please enter fractional figures in **eighths**. Official measurements cannot be taken for at least sixty days after the animal was killed. **Please submit photographs (see below).**

A. Number of Points on each antler. To be counted a point, a projection must be at least one inch long AND at some location, at least one inch from the tip, the length of the projection must exceed its width. **Beam tip is counted as a point but not measured as a point.**

B. Tip to Tip Spread is measured between tips of main beams.

C. Greatest Spread is measured between perpendiculars at right angles to the center line of the skull at widest part whether across main beams or points.

D. Inside Spread on Main Beam is measured at right angles to the center line of the skull at widest point between main beams. Enter this measurement again in "Spread Credit" column if it is less than or equal to the length of longer antler; if longer, enter longer antler length for spread credit.

E. Total of Length of all Abnormal Points. Abnormal points are generally considered to be those nontypical in shape or location. Sketch all abnormal points on antler illustration (front of form) showing location and approximate size. Measure in usual manner and enter in appropriate blanks.

F. Length of Main Beam is measured from lowest outside edge of burr over outer curve to the most distant point of the main beam. The point of beginning is that point on the burr where the center line along the outer curve of the beam intersects the burr.

G-1-2-3-4-5-6-7. Length of Normal Points. Normal points project from the top or front of the main beam in the general pattern illustrated. They are measured from the nearest edge of main beam over outer curve to tip. Record point length in appropriate blanks.

H-1-2-3-4. Circumferences. If first point is missing, take H-1 and H-2 at smallest place between burr and second point. IF G-5 is missing, take H-4 halfway between G-4 and beam tip. A steel tape must be used to take circumference measurements (a cable cannot be used for these measurements).

Photographs: All entries must include photographs of the trophy. A right side, left side and front view photograph will be required for all antlers, horns and skulls. A photograph of the entire animal is requested if at all possible.

Drying Period: To be eligible for entry in the Pope & Young Records, a trophy must first have been stored under normal room temperature and humidity for at least 60 consecutive days after date of kill. No trophy will be considered which has in any way been altered from its natural state.

THIS SCORING FORM MUST BE ACCOMPANIED BY A SIGNED POPE & YOUNG FAIR CHASE AFFIDAVIT, 3 PHOTOS OF ANTLERS AND A RECORDING FEE OF $25.00.

MOOSE

KIND OF MOOSE _____

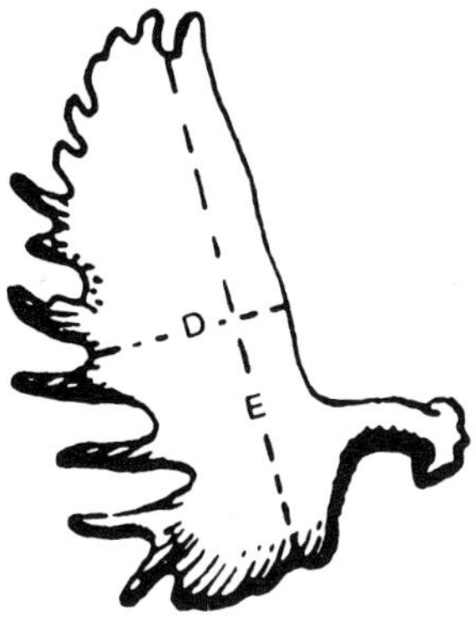

UNDER SURFACE OF ANTLER

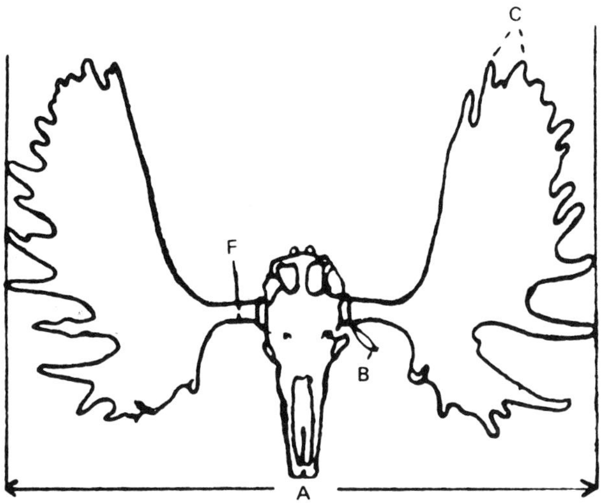

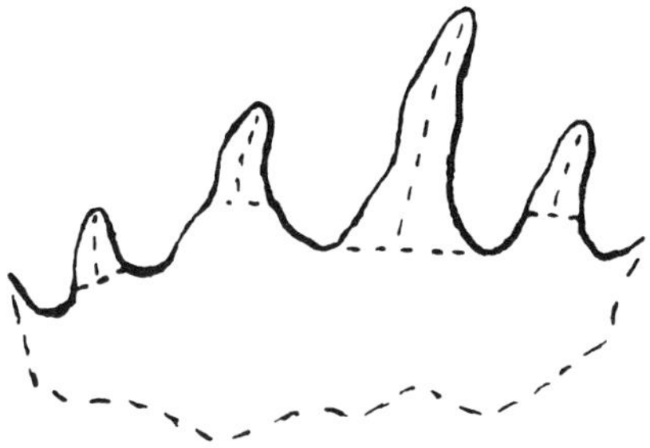

DETAIL OF POINT MEASUREMENT

SEE OTHER SIDE FOR INSTRUCTIONS	Column 1 Greatest Spread	Column 2 Right Antler	Column 3 Left Antler	Column 4 Difference
A. Greatest Spread				
B. Number of Abnormal Points on Both Antlers				
C. Number of Normal Points				
D. Width of Palm				
E. Length of Palm including Brow Palm				
F. Circumference of Beam at Smallest Place				
TOTALS				

ADD	Column 1		Exact locality where killed	(County)	(State)
	Column 2		Date killed	By whom killed	
	Column 3		Present owner		
Total			Address		
SUBTRACT Column 4			Guide's Name and Address		
FINAL SCORE			Remarks: (Mention any abnormalities)		

I certify that I have measured the above trophy on _____ 19 _____

at (address) _____ City _____

State _____ Zip Code _____ and that these measurements and data are, to the best

of my knowledge and belief, made in accordance with the instructions given.

Witness: _____   Signature _____

(To Measurer's Signature)

Pope & Young Club Official Measurer

MEASURER (Print) _____

ADDRESS _____

CITY   STATE   ZIP

INSTRUCTIONS

All measurements must be made with a flexible steel tape or measuring cable to the nearest one-eight of an inch. Wherever it is necessary to change direction of measurement, mark a control point and swing tape at this point. To simplify addition, please enter fractional figures in eighths.

Official measurements cannot be taken for at least sixty days after the animal was killed. **Please submit photographs.**

A. Greatest Spreads - measured in a straight line at right angles to the center line of the skull.

B. Number of Abnormal Points on Both Antlers - Abnormal points are generally considered to be those nontypical in shape or location.

C. Number of Normal Points. Normal points are those which project from the outer edge of the antler. To be counted a point, a projection must be at least one inch long and the length must exceed the breadth of the point's base. The breadth need not be computed from the deepest adjacent dips in the palmation. The length may be measured to any location — at least one inch from the tip — at which the length of the point exceeds its breadth.

D. Width of Palm - taken in contact with the surface across the under side of the palm, at right angles to the inside edge of palm, to a dip between points at the greatest wedge of palm.

E. Length of Palm including Brow Palm - taken in contact with the surface along the under side of the palm, parallel to the inner edge from dips between points at the greatest length of palm. If a deep bay is present in the palm, measure palm length across the open bay if the proper line of measurement crosses the bay.

F Circumference of Beam at Smallest Place - circumference measurements must be taken with a steel tape.

Photographs: All entries must include photographs of the trophy. A right side, left side and front view photograph will be required for all antlers, horns and skulls. A photograph of the entire animal is requested if at all possible.

Drying Period: To be eligible for entry in the Pope & Young Records, a trophy must first have been stored under normal room temperature and humidity for at least 60 consecutive days. No trophy will be considered which has in any way been altered from its natural state.

THIS SCORING FORM MUST BE ACCOMPANIED BY A FULLY COMPLETED AND SIGNED POPE & YOUNG FAIR CHASE AFFIDAVIT PLUS A RECORDING FEE OF $25.00

To:

P & Y Records Office

1804 BORAH

MOSCOW, ID 83843

MUSKOX   SEX _____

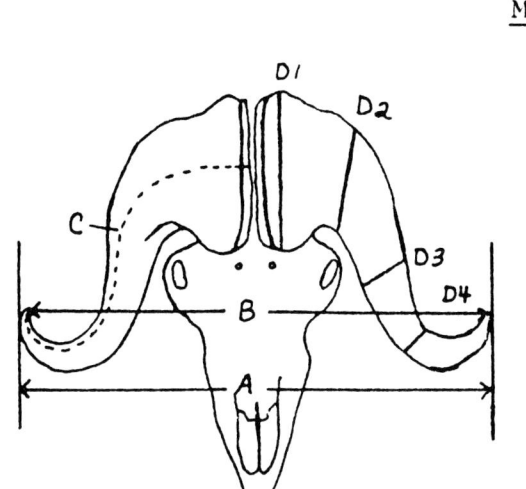

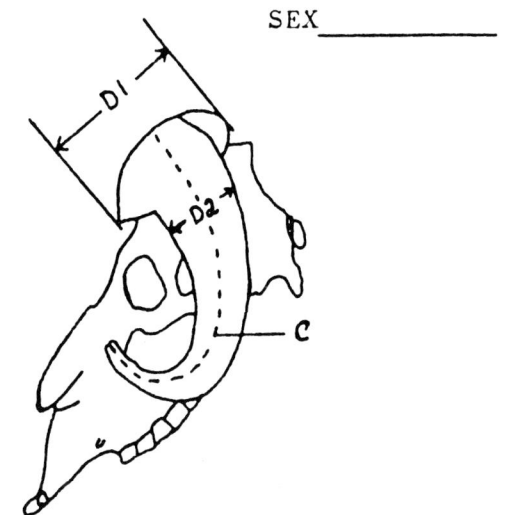

SEE OTHER SIDE FOR INSTRUCTIONS		Column 1	Column 2	Column 3
A. Greatest Spread		Right	Left	
B. Tip to Tip Spread		Horn	Horn	Difference
C. Length of Horn				
D-1. Width of Boss				
D-2. Width at First Quarter				
D-3. Circumference at Second Quarter				
D-4. Circumference at Third Quarter				
TOTALS				

ADD	Column 1		Exact locality where killed
	Column 2		Date killed By whom killed
	Total		Present owner
SUBTRACT Column 3			Address
FINAL SCORE			Guide's Name and Address
			Remarks: (Mention any abnormalities or unique qualities)

I certify that I have measured the above trophy on   19

at (address)   City   State

and that these measurements and data are, to the best of my knowledge and belief, made in accordance with the instructions given.

Witness:_____   Signature: _____

                                                   Official Measurer

INSTRUCTIONS FOR MEASURING MUSKOX

All measurements must be made with a ¼-inch flexible steel tape and adjustable calipers to the nearest one-eighth of an inch. Whenever it is necessary to change direction of measurement, mark a control point and swing tape at this point. Enter fractional figures in <u>eighths</u>, without reduction. Official measurements cannot be taken for at least sixty days after the animal was killed.

A. Greatest Spread is measured between perpendiculars at a right angle to the center line of the skull.

B. Tip to Tip Spread is measured between tips of horns by using large calipers, which are then read against a yardstick.

C. Length of Horn is measured along center of upper horn surface, staying within curve of horn as illustrated, to a point in line with tip. Attempt to free the connective tissue between the horns at the center of the boss to determine the lowest point of horn material on each side, near the top center of the skull. Hook the tape under the lowest point of the horn and measure the length of horn, with the measurement line maintained in the center of the upper surface of horn following the converging lines to the horn tip.

D-1. Width of Boss is measured with calipers at greatest width of base, with measurement line forming a right angle with horn axis. It is often helpful to measure D-1 before C, marking the midpoint of the boss as the correct path of C.

D-2-3-4. Divide measurement C of longer horn by four. Starting at base, mark <u>both</u> horns at these quarters (even though other horn is shorter). Then, using calipers, measure width of boss at D-2, making sure the measurement is at a right angle to horn axis and in line with the D-2 mark. Circumferences are then measured at D-3 and D-4, with measurements being taken at right angles to horn axis.

* * * * * * * * * * * *

BIG GAME **RECORDS**

P & Y Records Office
1804 Borah
Moscow, ID 83843

PRONGHORN

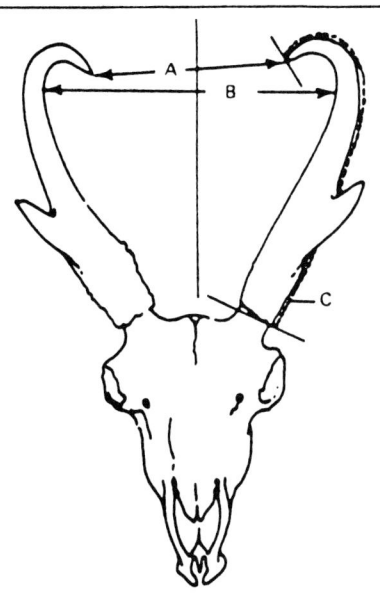

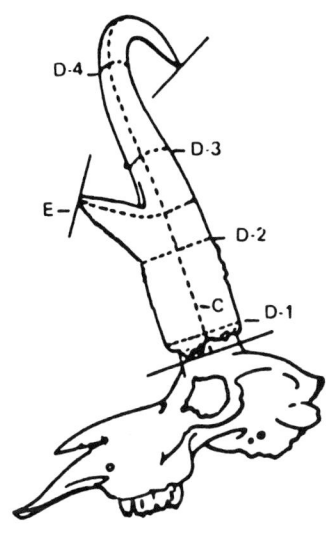

SEE OTHER SIDE FOR INSTRUCTIONS		Supplementary Data	Column 1	Column 2	Column 3
			Right Horn	Left Horn	Difference
A.	Tip to Tip Spread				
B.	Inside Spread of Main Beams		▨▨▨	▨▨▨	▨▨▨
	If Inside Spread of Main Beams exceeds longer horn length, enter difference.		▨▨▨	▨▨▨	
C.	Length of Horn				
D-1.	Circumference of Base				
D-2.	Circumference at First Quarter (this measurement taken at _____ inches from base)				
D-3.	Circumference at Second Quarter (this measurement taken at _____ inches from base)				
D-4.	Circumference at Third Quarter (this measurement taken at _____ inches from base)				
E.	Length of Prong				
	TOTALS				

ADD	Column 1		Exact locality where killed	(County)	(State)
	Column 2		Date killed	By whom killed	
	Total		Present owner		
SUBTRACT Column 3			Address		
FINAL SCORE			Guide's Name and Address		
			Remarks: (Mention any abnormalities)		

I certify that I have measured the above trophy on _____ 19 _____

at (address) _____ City _____

State _____ Zip Code _____ and that these measurements and data are, to the best

of my knowledge and belief, made in accordance with the instructions given.

Witness: _____ Signature _____
(To Measurer's Signature)

Pope & Young Club Official Measurer

_____
MEASURER (Print)

_____
ADDRESS

CITY   STATE   ZIP

INSTRUCTIONS

All measurements must be made with a flexible steel tape or measuring cable to the nearest one-eighth of an inch. Wherever it is necessary to change direction of measurement, mark a control point and swing tape at this point. To simplify addition, please enter fractional figures in eighths.

Official measurements cannot be taken for at least sixty days after the animal was killed. **Please submit photographs, FRONT, RIGHT AND LEFT SIDES are required.**

Supplementary Data measurements indicate conformation of the trophy. None of the figures in Lines A and B are to be included in the score. Evaluation of conformation is a matter of personal preference.

A. Tip to Tip Spread measured between tip of horns.

B. Inside Spread of Main Beams measured at right angles to the center line of the skull at widest point between main beams.

C. Length of horn is measured on the outside curve, so the line taken will vary with different heads, depending on the direction of the curvature. Measure along the center of the outer curve from tip of horn to a point in line with the lowest edge of the base.

D-1 Measure around base of horn at right angles to long axis. Tape must be in contact with the lowest circumference of the horn in which there are no serrations.

D-2-3-4. Divide measurement of LONGER horn by four, mark BOTH horns at these quarters even though one horn is shorter, and measure circumferences at these marks. If any portion of the prong occurs at D-3, take this measurement immediately above prong. Should D-2 land on the swelling of the prong, take D-2 measurement immediately below swelling of prong.

E- Length of Prong — Measure from the tip of the prong along the upper edge of the outer curve to the horn; thence, around the horn to a point at the rear of the horn where a straight edge across the back of both horns touches the horn. This measurement around the horn from the base of the prong should be taken at right angles to the long axis of the horn.

*Note measurement of each quarter from base (i.e. longest horn = 16" — quarters should be noted as D-2 =4, D-3 = 8, D-4 = 12.) If adjustments are made for swelling of prong on D-2 or D-3 measurement, note these adjustments in "remarks" section.

Photographs: All entries must include photographs of the trophy. A right side, left side and front view photograph will be required for all antlers, horns and skulls. A photograph of the entire animal is requested if at all possible.

Drying Period: To be eligible for entry in the Pope & Young Records, a trophy must first have been stored under normal room temperature and humidity for at least 60 consecutive days. No trophy will be considered which has in any way been altered from its natural state.

THIS SCORING FORM MUST BE ACCOMPANIED BY A FULLY COMPLETED AND SIGNED POPE & YOUNG FAIR CHASE AFFIDAVIT PLUS A RECORDING FEE OF $25.00.

ROCKY MOUNTAIN GOAT

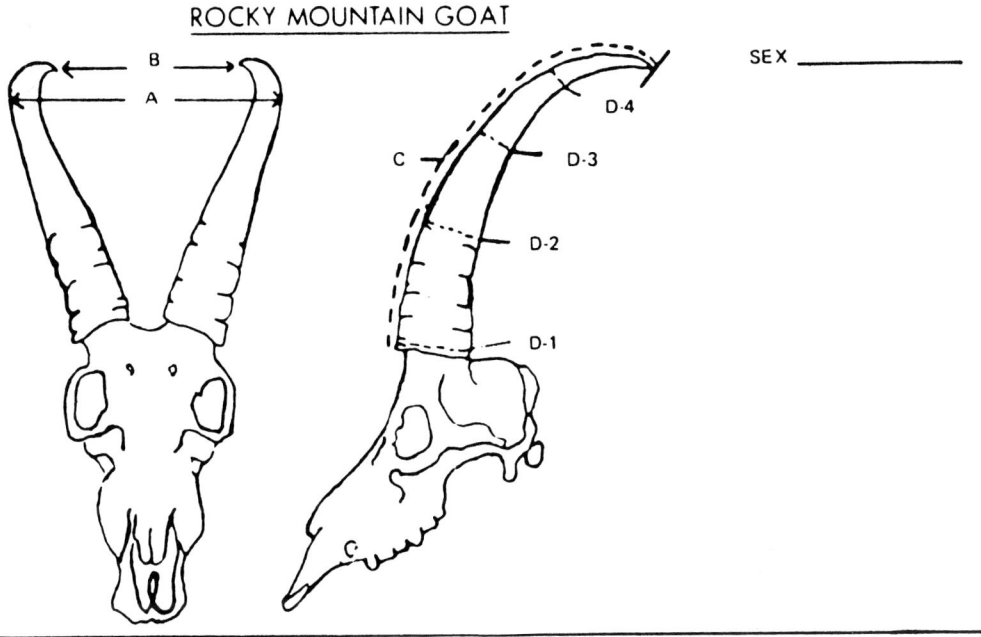

SEX _____

SEE OTHER SIDE FOR INSTRUCTIONS	Supplementary Data	Column 1	Column 2	Column 3
A Greatest Spread		Right Horn	Left Horn	Difference
B Tip to Tip Spread				
C Length of Horn				
D-1 Circumference of Base				
D-2 Circumference at First Quarter (this measurement taken at _____ inches from base)				
D-3 Circumference at Second Quarter (this measurement taken at _____ inches from base)				
D-4 Circumference at Third Quarter (this measurement taken at _____ inches from base)				
TOTALS				

ADD	Column 1		Exact locality where killed (County) (State)	
	Column 2		Date killed By whom killed	
	TOTAL		Present owner	
SUBTRACT Column 3			Address	
FINAL SCORE			Guide's Name and Address	
			Remarks: (Mention any abnormalities)	

I certify that I have measured the above trophy on _____ 19 _____

at (address) _____ City _____

State _____ Zip Code _____ and that these measurements and data are, to the best

of my knowledge and belief, made in accordance with the instructions given.

Witness: _____ Signature _____
         (To Measurer's Signature)

Pope & Young Club Official Measurer

MEASURER (Print) _____

ADDRESS _____

CITY   STATE   ZIP

INSTRUCTIONS

Measurements must be made with a flexible steel tape or steel cable to the nearest one-eighth of an inch. To simplify addition, please enter fractional figures in **eighths.** Official measurements cannot be taken for at least sixty days after the animal was killed. **Please submit photographs (see below).**

A. Greatest Spread is measured between perpendiculars at right angles to the center line of the skull.

B. Tip to Tip Spread is measured between tips of horns.

C. Length of Horn is measured from lowest point in front over outer curve to a point in line with tip.

D-1. Circumference of Base is measured at right angles to axis of horn. **DO NOT** follow irregular edge of horn. Circumference measurements must be taken with a steel tape.

D-1-2-3-4. Divide measurement C of LONGER horn by four, mark **BOTH** horns at these quarters even though other horn is shorter, and measure circumference at these marks. Mark quarters by starting from base only. Circumference measurements must be taken with a steel tape.

Photographs: All entries must include photographs of the trophy. A right side, left side and front view photograph will be required for all antlers, horns and skulls. A photograph of the entire animal is requested if at all possible.

Drying Period: To be eligible for entry in the Pope & Young Records, a trophy must first have been stored under normal room temperature and humidity for at least 60 consecutive days. No trophy will be considered which has in any way been altered from its natural state.

THIS SCORING FORM MUST BE ACCOMPANIED BY A SIGNED POPE & YOUNG FAIR CHASE AFFIDAVIT, 3 PHOTOS OF HORNS, AND A RECORDING FEE OF $25.00.

BIG GAME   RECORDS

SHEEP

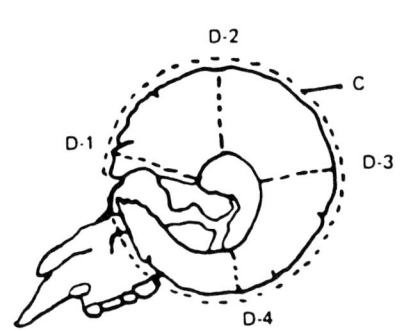

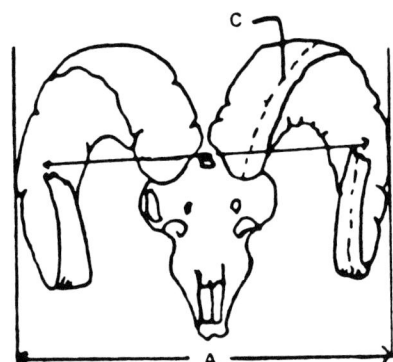

KIND OF SHEEP

_____

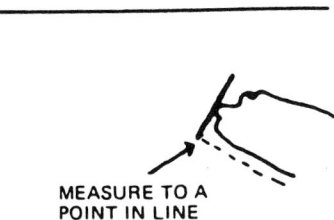

MEASURE TO A
POINT IN LINE
WITH TIP OF
HORN

SEE OTHER SIDE FOR INSTRUCTIONS		Supplementary Data	Column 1	Column 2	Column 3
			Right Horn	Left Horn	Difference
A.	Greatest Spread (Is often Tip to Tip Spread)				
B.	Tip to Tip Spread (If Greatest Spread, Enter again here)				▨
C.	Length of Horn				▨
D-1.	Circumference of Base				
D-2.	Circumference at First Quarter (this measurement taken at _____ inches from base)				
D-3.	Circumference at Second Quarter (this measurement taken at _____ inches from base)				
D-4.	Circumference at Third Quarter (this measurement taken at _____ inches from base)				
	TOTALS				

ADD	Column 1		Exact locality where killed	(County)		(State)
	Column 2		Date killed	By whom killed		
	TOTAL		Present owner			
SUBTRACT Column 3			Address			
FINAL SCORE			Guide's Name and Address			
			Remarks: (Mention any abnormalities)			

I certify that I have measured the above trophy on _____ 19 _____

at (address) _____ City _____

State _____ Zip Code _____ and that these measurements and data are, to the best

of my knowledge and belief, made in accordance with the instructions given.

Witness: _____   Signature _____
(To Measurer's Signature)

Pope & Young Club Official Measurer

_____

MEASURER (Print)

_____

ADDRESS

_____

CITY   STATE   ZIP

INSTRUCTIONS

All measurements must be made with a flexible steel tape or measuring cable to the nearest <u>one-eighth</u> of an inch. Wherever it is necessary to change direction of measurement, mark a control point and swing tape at this point. To simplify addition, please enter fractional figures in eighths.

Official measurements cannot be taken for at least sixty days after the animal was killed.

Please submit photographs. Front, right and left sides of horns.

Supplementary Data measurements indicate conformation of the trophy. None of the figures in Lines A and B are to be included in the score. Evaluation of conformation is a matter of personal preference.

A. Greatest Spread measured between perpendiculars at right angles to the center line of the skull.

B. Tip to Tip Spread measured from outer edge of tips of horns.

C. Length of Horn measured from lowest point in front on outer curve to a point in line with tip. **DO NOT** press tape into depression. The low point of the outer curve of the horn is considered to be the low point of the frontal portion of the horn, situated above and slightly medial to the eye socket, (not on the outside edge of the horn.)

D-1 Circumference of Base measured at right angles to axis of horn. **DO NOT** follow irregular edge of horn. Circumference measurements must be taken with a steel tape.

D-2-3-4. Divide measurement C of LONGER horn by four, mark **BOTH** horns at these quarters even though other horn is shorter, and measure circumferences at these marks. Mark quarters by starting from base only.

Big Horn Sheep: In order to accept trophies in this class, we must have complete documentation. We will require a **photograph** of the complete animal if at all possible; photographs of the front, right and left sides of the horns, photocopy of the hunting permit, and certification from the game department of the state or province hunted as to the authenticity of the kill.

Drying Period: To be eligible for entry in the Pope & Young Records, a trophy must first have been stored under normal room temperature and humidity for at least 60 consecutive days. No trophy will be considered which has in any way been altered from its natural state.

THIS SCORING FORM MUST BE ACCOMPANIED BY A FULLY COMPLETED AND SIGNED POPE & YOUNG FAIR CHASE AFFIDAVIT PLUS A RECORDING FEE OF $25.00

POPE AND YOUNG CLUB OFFICIAL MEASURERS

ALABAMA

Chester Billie, Jr., *Prattville*
Timothy Boyce, *Millbrook*
Dennis C. Campbell, *Adamsville*
Tim Cosby, *Montgomery*
David Crockett, *Birmingham*
Charles Davidson, *Carrollton*
Keith Guyse, *Millbrook*
Cecil Jackson, Jr., *Greensboro*
Kenneth Johnson, *Andalusia*
Dr. Merrill Jones, *Huntsville*
Rett Kelly, *Wetumpka*
Stephen May III, *Safford*
David Nelson, *Forkland*
Douglas Schofield, *Opp*
T. H. Tanner, *Semmes*
James W. Thornhill, Sr., *Montgomery*
Eugene Widder, *Jackson*
Stephen "Joe" Zolczynski, *Spanish Fork*

ALASKA

Ralph V. L. Ertz, *Anchorage*
Dennis Goldbach, *Fairbanks*
Allen L. Grierson, *Juneau*
Richard A. Hemmen, *Fairbanks*
David Klein, *Fairbanks*
Verne L. Landt, *Tok*
Dennis L. Lattery, *Eagle River*
George Moerlein, *Anchorage*
Donald L. Poole, *Soldotna*
Edward L. Russell, *Anchorage*
Dr. James R. Scott, DVM, *Anchorage*

ARIZONA

George S. Blackett, *Mesa*
Harold Boyack, *Tucson*
Rodger L. Bruce, *Phoenix*
Michael C. Cupell, *Glendale*
Thomas L. Dalrymple, *Tucson*
Jay Edward Elmer, *Sedona*
Jimmie E. Engelmann, *Tucson*
James Scott, *Tucson*
Richard D. Tone, *Gilbert*

ARKANSAS

Michael Cartwright, *Fifty Six*
Levi Davis, Jr., *Monticello*
James M. DeSpain, *Manila*
Dave Ensminger, *Little Rock*
Dr. Rex Hancock, *Stuttgart*
James M. Larch, *Mabelvale*

Doyle L. Shook, Jr., *Little Rock*
Carl Turpin, *Clarksville*
Craig K. Uyeda, *Little Rock*
Sandra J. Uyeda, *Little Rock*

CALIFORNIA

Dr. Alfred Adams, *Sacramento*
Dale H. Bracken, *Anaheim*
Jim Cox, *Salinas*
Ron Crouch, *Tulare*
Robert C. Dawson, *Bonita*
David H. Duncan, *Oakhurst*
Steven Dymond, *French Gulch*
Paul W. Farina, *Santa Clara*
Robert E. Frost, *Lincoln*
David A. Graham, *Novato*
Bob Gulman, *Fullerton*
Gary Hoffer, *Fresno*
Ronald D. Hopkins, *Westminster*
Arthur E. Jennings, *Cloverdale*
Jack Kenyon, *San Bruno*
Andy M. Oldfield, *June Lake*
Paul Persano, *Modesto*
David O. Smith, *Anderson*
Naomi J. Torrey, *Placerville*
Doug Walker, *Squaw Valley*
Edward Welch, *Modesto*
Richard L. Westervelt, *Roseville*
Clifford White, *Paradise*
Rodney A. York, *North Fork*

COLORADO

Charles R. Anderson, Jr., *Castle Rock*
G. Fred Asbell, *Longmont*
Dennis Behn, *Thornton*
Albert H. Bellgardt, Jr., *Montrose*
Ronald M. Breitsprecher, *Fort Collins*
Hal Burdick, *Grand Junction*
Marvin Clyncke, *Boulder*
Judd Cooney, *Pagosa Springs*
James M. Finn, *Durango*
Douglas W. Gish, *Denver*
Bill Goosman, *Meeker*
Dr. Nicholas J. Gray, *Woodland Park*
Gary Holtz, *Estes Park*
Jack H. Jonas, *Denver*
Lee Kline, *Loveland*
Ronald J. Laven, *Pueblo West*
J. Kenneth Long, *Durango*
Frank "Duke" Prentup, *Boulder*
Glenn W. Pritchard, *Craig*
Barry J. Smith, *Denver*

Ronald E. Sniff, *Pueblo*
John Jay Verzuh, *Fruita*
Don Waechtler, *Glenwood Springs*
Ed R. Wiseman, *Moffat*

CONNECTICUT

Gary C. Vincent, *Plainville*

FLORIDA

Robert L. Barbee, *Ocala*
Dr. H. Neil Becker, *Gainesville*
Timothy A. Breault, *Panama City*
Donald Lee Francis, *Tallahassee*
William B. Frankenberger, *High Springs*
Stanley H. Kirkland, *Lynn Haren*
Charles Kroll, *Gainesville*
Dale K. Marcy, *Port Richey*
Charles M. Orme, *Ocala*
Phil Palmer, *Tallahassee*
Mikel G. Suelter, *Belleview*
David E. Swindell, *Tallahasse*

GEORGIA

David M. Carlock, *Gainesville*
William L. Cooper, *Tifton*
Jack A. Crockford, *Chamblee*
Oscar H. Dewberry, *Bainbridge*
R. Larry Marchinton, *Athens*
Dan Marshall, *Thomson*
Bob Monroe, *Atlanta*
Richard W. Whittington, *Fort Valley*

HAWAII

W. T. Yoshimoto, *Honolulu*

IDAHO

John E. Anderson, *Boise*
Jack Arbaugh, *Caldwell*
Steven B. Atwood, *Arco*
Roger W. Atwood, *Rexburg*
Gary S. BeVan, *Salmon*
Clyde H. Brothers, *Donnelly*
Dr. C. Randall Byers, *Moscow*
Christian D. Chaffin, *Pocatello*
Larry Cross, *Preston*
Frank N. Hough, *McCammon*
Dr. Brad Johnson, *Lewiston*
Stanley Leake, *Coeur d'Alene*
Michael D. Lewis, *Fruitland*
Matt March, Jr., *Eagle*
Harvey J. "Jack" McNeel, *Coeur d'Alene*
Gary R. "Sam" McNeill, *Lewiston*
Larry D. Merritt, *Bonners Ferry*

Stuart L. Murrell, *Jerome*
Ronald G. Parish, *Monteview*
Ralph V. Pehrson, *Boise*
Michael W. Schlegel, *McCall*
Ronald L. Sherer, *Eagle*
Randy J. Stephens, *Soda Springs*
Ray Torrey, *Salmon*
William R. Vanderhoef, *Boise*

ILLINOIS

Fred W. Achilles, *Oswego*
Thomas J. Beissel, *Dixon*
Patrick A. Cebuhar, *Canton*
Richard Dewey, *Pleasant Hill*
Robert L. Erb, *Rockford*
Jared K. Garver, *Cobden*
Robert "Bob" Gorge, *Elk Grove Village*
Keith J. Graham, *Carlinville*
Arthur A. Heinze, *Rock Falls*
Melvin J. Johnson, *Metamora*
G. Michael Kottkamp, *Irvington*
Art Kragness, *Dolton*
John Kube, *Petersburg*
Thomas R. Micetich, *Olney*
Martin M. Peters, *River Grove*
Dr. James R. Purdue, *Springfield*
Gary S. Rogers, *Deerfield*
Glen C. Sanderson, *Champaign*
Donald E. Schram, *Forest Park*
Carl H. Spaeth, *Zion*
J. James Stewart, *Hebron*
Jeffrey M. Ver Steeg, *Charleston*
Steven A. Wolff, *South Holland*

INDIANA

William F. Bean, *Winamac*
Don Castrup, *Newburgh*
Donald L. Clark, *Fort Wayne*
Bernard R. Giacoletto, *Clinton*
Roy A. Grimes, *Birdseye*
Guy Gustin, *Logansport*
Philip L. Hawkins, *Franklin*
M. R. James, *Fort Wayne*
Larry Eugene Lawson, *Anderson*
Gregory L. Raatz, *Columbia City*
Mark A. Smith, *Crown Point*

IOWA

Larry J. Briney, *Cedar Rapids*
Dr. Raleigh D. Buckmaster, *Lansing*
Kevin Lee Chelf, *Iowa City*
Paul "Buck" Farni, Jr., *Dubuque*
Robert Filbrandt, *Dows*

Lee Gladfelter, *Boone*
Rick Grooms, *Bloomfield*
Guy Hempey, *Sioux City*
Ronald G. Howing, *Wallingford*
Stephen James Manary, *Iowa City*
Joseph B. Meder, *Solon*
Thomas L. Oldfather, *Elk Run*
David W. Schrody, *Clinton*
Thomas L. Tucker, *Knoxville*
Ervin Wagner, *Des Moines*
Laverne E. Woock, *Shell Rock*
Michael R. Woolman, *Des Moines*

KANSAS

Tommie A. Berger, *Dodge City*
Tom E. Bowman, *Wakefield*
Stephen Capel, *Valley Center*
Duane L. File, *Beloit*
Terry L. Funk, *Hays*
Michael R. Gilbert, *Garden City*
Jim Hays, *Ellsworth*
Wally Hayward, *Kansas City*
Bill D. Hlavachick, *Pratt*
Leonard Hopper, *Colby*
Gary Hunsicker, *Topeka*
Ronald J. Little, *Hays*
Don R. McDermott, *Eudora*
Michael McFadden, *Lawrence*
Gerald J. McKinney, *Parsons*
Kent Montei, *Pratt*
Tom Mosher, *Emporia*
Todd A. Murray, *S. Hutchinson*
David R. Rogers, *El Dorado*
Maloy D. Rollins, *Winfield*
Bernard Rottman, *Pittsburg*
Keith Sexson, *Emporia*
Scott M. Showalter, *Garden City*
Mike Sohm, *Otis*
Steven Sorensen, *Concordia*
Charles Lee Stevens, *Cawker City*
Tom Swan, *Mound City*
Charles A. Swank, *Great Bend*
Larry Thomas, *Baxter Springs*
Wayne Van Zwoll, *Pratt*
Greg L. Wright, *Witchita*

KENTUCKY

Roy Wayne Biddle, *Foster*
Joseph E. Bland, *Finchville*
Eugene Culver, *New Haven*
Robert L. Hegge, Jr., *Williamstown*
John Phillips, *Williamstown*
Michael L. Roberts, *Bagdad*

Dr. M. Pete Thompson, *Richmond*
Shirley P. Troublefield, *Munfordville*
Randall B. Webb, *Harrodsburg*
Charles Wilkins, *Kevil*
George A. Wright, *Hopkinsville*

LOUISIANA

J. W. Farrar, *Monroe*
Joe L. Herring, *Baton Rouge*
David E. John, *Metairie*
Robert B. Kimble, *Minden*
David W. Moreland, *Baton Rouge*
Jerald V. Owens, *Tioga*
Tommy L. Ramage, *Bastrop*
John B. Robinette, Jr., *Lake Charles*
Kerney J. Sonnier, *Opelousas*
Reggie Wycoff, *Ferriday*

MAINE

Jean R. Arsenault, *Rumford*
Donald Cote, Sr., *Eustis*
Terrence H. Estes, *Winslow*
Bill Marchand, *Bangor*

MARYLAND

Robert A. Beyer, *Germantown*
Al Sullivan, *Upper Marlboro*
H. W. "Hank" Voight, *College Park*
Paul D. Wigfield, *Salisbury*

MASSACHUSETTS

Richard Christoforo, *Revere*
John Butch Rovedo, *Bellingham*

MICHIGAN

Gary L. Bandrow, *New Baltimore*
Clarence Bowers, Jr., *Albion*
James R. Dean, *Williamsburg*
Craig Engweiler, *Twin Lake*
Ned E. Fogle, *Lansing*
George J. Hronkin, *Crystal Falls*
Lewis H. Johnson, *Grayling*
Lyle C. Kelley, *Drummond Island*
Jack R. Menges, *Three Rivers*
Joseph M. Newmyer, *Union Lake*
Frank J. Rinella, *Twin Lake*
Michael Shaw, *Lawton*
Harry W. "Pete" Squibb, *Grand Ledge*
Glenn J. Williams, *Dearborn*
David E. Wojtas, *Maple City*

MINNESOTA

Dr. Eugene T. Altiere, *Duluth*
Darwin D. Arndt, *Madelia*
Don Bergholm, *Duluth*
Ronald L. Birch, *White Bear Lake*
David H. Boland, *Chatfield*
Steven H. Brasel, *Two Harbors*
Ron Carlson, *Mahtomedi*
Joseph K. Corcoran, *Shoreview*
Glenn E. Hisey, *Chatfield*
M. Dean Holm, *Lynd*
Neil A. Jacobson, *Thief River Falls*
Ronald J. Kienholz, *Dilworth*
Curtis C. Kozitka, *Detroit Lakes*
Sharon R. Larsen, *St. Paul*
Ron Mackedanz, *Kandiyohi*
William C. Peabody, *Alexandria*
Dale A. Pitts, *Crystal*
Dean K. Reidt, *Cottage Grove*
Bob Sandwick, *Sandstone*
Larry L. Streiff, *Rochester*
Walter H. White, *Wayzata*

MISSISSIPPI

Larry Castle, *Kilmichael*
Dan Cotton, *Macon*
Billy Ellis III, *Lexington*
Robert N. Griffin, *Starkville*
Don M. Lewis, *Brookhaven*
Jim L. McCrory, *Greenwood*
Bobby J. Wilson, *Smithville*

MISSOURI

Neal L. Acklie, *Kahoka*
Clay Adams, *Liberty*
Charles "Dwayne" Allen, *Neosho*
Richard L. Flint, *Aurora*
Norb Giessman, *Columbia*
Bill L. Jackson, *Blue Springs*
Dan Krell, *Clinton*
Joe Ed McCray, *Fulton*
Anthony P. Mihalevich, *Kirksville*
Dean A. Murphy, *Hartsburg*
Charles A. Myers, *Greenfield*
Ken Perry, *Holt Summit*
Arthur C. Popham, Jr., *Kansas City*
Wayne R. Porath, *Jefferson City*
Lawrence Redel, *Jefferson City*
Donald P. Roper, *Farmington*
Paul C. Schwarz, *St. Louis*
Carl Schwarz, *St. Louis*

MONTANA

Jerry Brown, *Libby*
Paul B. Brunner, *Ovando*
William Earl Butler, *Billings*
William E. Butler, *Silesia*
Tom Butts, *Roundup*
R. Bruce Campbell, *Kalispell*
Kevin Charles Conners, *Glendive*
James Cross, *Kalispell*
G. L. "Buck" Damone, *Lewiston*
Gary L. Day, *Miles City*
Mark George Delong, *Billings*
Bryan J. Erickson, *Glasgow*
Roger R. Fliger, *Billings*
James A. Ford, *Missoula*
Dwayne Garner, *Missoula*
Bernie D. Hildebrand, *Jordan*
Jerry Kimball, *Miles City*
Fred J. King, *Gallatin Gateway*
Scott L. Koelzer, *Three Forks*
Dale L. Lackner, *Missoula*
James E. Liebelt, *Fort Peck*
L. H. "Vern" Lindquist, *Glendive*
John C. Locke, *Hamilton*
William S. Maloit, *Helena*
Daniel A. Palmisciano, *Bozeman*
Al Rosgaard, *Havre*
Robert R. Savage, *Bozeman*
Thomas L. Solem, *Fort Peck*
David W. Sorensen, *Harlowtown*
Graham S. Taylor, *Belgrade*
Tim Tollett, *Dillon*
Gene Wensel, *Hamilton*
Dr. Barry L. Wensel, *Whitefish*
Philip L. Wright, *Missoula*
Vincent Yannone, *Helena*
Harley W. Yeager, *Great Falls*
Lewis E. Yearout, *Great Falls*

NEBRASKA

Thomas E. Day, *Omaha*
Dennis C. Graham, *Holdredge*
Jack E. Joseph, *Valentine*
Richard L. Mauch, *Bassett*
George W. Nason, *North Platte*
Lyle R. Prell, *North Platte*
Dan Rochford, *North PLatte*
Harvey Y. Suetsugu, *Alliance*
Bruce D. Trindle, *Norfolk*
Steve Woitaszewski, *Scottsbluff*

NEVADA

Fred C. Church, *Reno*
Chris J. Coleman, *Carson City*
Frank H. Dodge, Jr., *Yerington*
Ronald M. Lee, *Pahrump*
Robert Price, *Ely*
David Snyder, *Las Vegas*
George K. Tsukamoto, *Sparks*
Mike Wickersham, *Elko*

NEW HAMPSHIRE

Reginald Moore, *Keene*

NEW JERSEY

Emanuele J. Barone, *Kinnelon*
Len Cardinale, *Belleville*
John Janelli, *Jersey City*
Richard G. Santomavro, *Wall*
Tony Sarlo, Jr., *Moorestown*

NEW MEXICO

Roy Cogburn, Jr., *Albuquerque*
Tom David, *Albuquerque*
Paul R. Engl, *Alamogordo*
VolBarry L. Wensel, *Whitefish*
Philip L. Wright, *Missoula*
Vincent Yannone, *Helena*
Harley W. Yeager, *Great Falls*
Lewis E. Yearout, *Great Falls*

NEW YORK

David F. Baldwin, *Patchogue*
Merritt C. Compton, *Trumansburg*
Roger D. Davis, *New York*
Bob Estes, *Caledonia*
Nelson C. Harrington, *Delmar*
Stephen I. Horn, *Mount Vernon*
Collins F. Kellogg, *Croghan*
John M. McAteer, *Lake Ronkonkoma*
Carl Pepi, *Bronx*
Jon P. Thomas, *Staten Island*

NORTH CAROLINA

Hayden Allen, Jr., *Asheboro*
Denton O. Baumbarger, *Burlington*
Ramon Neil Bell, *Greensboro*
Joffrey W. Brooks, *Waynesville*
John M. Collins, *Morganton*
Jim Edwards, *Colerain*
Earl B. Gillis, *New Bern*
Harlan T. Hall, *Burlington*

Donald Alfred Hayes, *State Road*
Brian D. Hyder, *Otto*
Tom D. Monschein, *New Bern*
J. Scott Osborne, *Sanford*
Jerry D. Powers, *Lansing*
J. Michael Scruggs, *Fountain*
Michael H. Seamster, *Yanceyville*
Terry L. Sharpe, *Hamlet*

NORTH DAKOTA

Warren O. Buss, *Kindred*
Wes Cumings, *Roseglen*
Dane K. Eider, *Grand Forks*
Tim K. Finley, *Oberon*
Scott Lang, *Bismarck*
James V. McKenzie, *Bismarck*
Michael Moline, *Fargo*
John R. Plesuk, *Minot*
Craig Richardson, *Williston*
Paul R. Shannon, *Bismarck*
Cecil I. Tharp, *Williston*
Harold L. Webb, *Bismarck*

OHIO

Dana Robert Booghier, *Springfield*
Barry L. Cooper, *Columbus*
Mike Dickess, *Ironton*
Tom Hentrick, *Kettering*
W. Dean Herschede, *Cincinnati*
Thomas L. Hughes, *Chillicothe*
Jeffrey D. McKnight, *Waterville*
Richard E. Meier, *Columbus*
Paul W. Meyer, *Zanesville*
George R. Mitchell, *Urbana*
John Fred Myers, *Toledo*
Ronald E. Perrine, Sr., *Jamestown*
Elbert "Butch" Todd, *Cambridge*
Thomas F. Wagner, *Bryan*

OKLAHOMA

Edward F. Bryan, Jr., *Goodwell*
Sonny Charboneau, *Wagoner*
Jim C. Dougherty, *Tulsa*
Richard J. Hoar, *Broken Arrow*
David M. Jilge, *Yukon*
Rod W. Smith, *Duncan*

OREGON

Harold Benson, *Lakeside*
Robert J. Bouret, *Portland*
Elvin Hawkins, *Eagle Point*
Larry D. Jones, *Springfield*

Charles R. Lindberg, *St. Helens*
Chuck Lynde, *Clackamas*
Gary Madison, *Prineville*
Stanley D. Miles, *Corvallis*
Donald R. Pritchett, *Medford*
Donald A. Rajnus, *Malin*
Charles B. Sarrett, *LaGrande*
John Stone, *Lebanon*
Thomas E. Tipton, *Roseburg*
Ed Williamson, *Tigard*

PENNSYLVANIA

Thomas P. Bartholomew, *Greenville*
George T. Church, Jr., *Ligonier*
J. E. "Ed" Defibaugh, *Venus*
Phillip Durr, *McKees Rock*
Joseph Egner, *Quakertown*
Frank "Rit" Heller, *Reading*
Chuck Kohler, *Pittsburgh*
Lorraine E. Yocum, *Oil City*

SOUTH CAROLINA

David P. Baumann, *Bonneau*
John E. Davis, *Columbia*
William H. Fleming, *Abbeville*
Robert H. Folk III, *Walterboro*
John E. Frampton, *Union*
Robert W. Gooding, *Greenwood*
David C. Guynn, Jr., *Seneca*
William E. Mahan, *Bonneau*
W. Gerald Moore, *Columbia*
Jimmy F. Rogers, *Williamston*
Lewis O. Rogers, *Garnett*
Sam W. Stokes, *Pickens*
Reggie Thackston, *Union*

SOUTH DAKOTA

Paul A. Anderson, *Crooks*
Wilbur C. Foss, *Watertown*
Larry F. Fredrickson, *Chamberlain*
A. Dean Gretschmann, *Pierre*
Eldon D. Hagen, *Sioux Falls*
Danny H. Havens, *Lead*
Thomas Kuck, *Aberdeen*
Walter A. Larsen, *Redfield*
David A. Linde, *Rapid City*
R. Craig Oberle, *Huron*
Ron Pesek, *Yankton*
Arthur H. Richardson, *Custer*
Joseph John Rieger, *Aberdeen*
Laverne E. Roth, *Mobridge*

TENNESSEE

Lewis "Buddy" Adkisson, *Morristown*
Norman B. Bates, *Thompson Station*
Clarence D. Coffey, *Crossville*
Tom Grimsley, *Jackson*
Jim W. Johnson, *Jackson*
Larry C. Marcum, *Nashville*
Robert C. McGuire, *Johnson City*
Tom W. Pinkston, *Cordova*
Robert D. Ripley, *Morristown*
Curtis S. Williams, *Kingsport*

TEXAS

Viron Barbay, *Lufkin*
Earle W. Bateman III, *Fischer*
Dr. John M. Broadwell, *El Paso*
Randolph Coleman, *San Antonio*
John C. Culpepper, Jr., *College Station*
Paul H. Dickson, *Hillsboro*
Edwin J. Foreman, *Orangefield*
Earl Griffith, *Marble Falls*
James W. Hutcheson, *Springtown*
Jim Jordan, *San Antonio*
James R. Lewis, *Dallas*
Ted A. Low IV, *Houston*
James P. Mitchell, Jr., *Dallas*
L. F. Nowotny, *San Antonio*
A. M. "Mike" Oakes, Jr., *Conroe*
Robert L. "Bob" Oliver, *Abilene*
Dr. Glenn A. Parker, *Houston*
Eugene Smith, Jr., *Austin*
Garth D. Stokes, *Texarkana*
Robert D. Sweisthal, *Spring*
Robert L. West, *San Angelo*
H. A. Yocum, *Austin*

UTAH

Dave Baierline, *West Valley City*
William A. Bradwisch, *Farmington*
Duane R. Brown, *Kearns*
Ruby Drobnick, *Salt Lake City*
Larry W. Gehre, *Fillmore*
Todd Hinkins, *Orangeville*
Merlin L. Killpack, *Ogden*
Bill Krenz, *West Valley City*
Jerry Mason, *Brigham*
Dennis L. Shirley, *Elk Ridge*
Clark P. Warren, *Price*

VIRGINIA

Max Carpenter, *Dayton*
Otto M. Epping, *Winchester*

Ted Grefe, *Fairfax*
Dr. Albert M. Manville II, *Arlington*
Wm. Harold Nesbitt, *Woodbridge*
William J. "Jack" Reneau, *Woodbridge*
Dennis F. Scott, *Hopewell*
C. D. Tarter, *Wytheville*
Frank Whittaker, Jr., *Roanoke*

WASHINGTON

Larry R. Carey, *Spokane*
John O. Cook III, *Redmond*
Dean H. Cook, Jr., *Bremerton*
Jack Davis, *Mt. Vernon*
Mike Davison, *Mt. Vernon*
Gerald L. Egbert, *Vancouver*
Henry T. "Hank" Kohler, *Spokane*
Reginald Lutzvick, *Hoquiam*
Gale Martin, *Walla Walla*
Bob Mayton, *Aberdeen*
Jack Schwabland, *Seattle*
Mike Shane, *Spokane*
Jay G. St. Charles, *Kent*
Glenn St. Charles, *Seattle*
Max Zahn, *Aberdeen*

WEST VIRGINIA

Thomas J. Allen, *Elkins*
Larry A. Berry, *Beckley*
Gregory A. Bonecutter, Sr., *Letart*
James E. Evans, *Fairmont*
Jim Farren, *Malden*
Allan C. Glasscock, *Petersburg*
James R. Hill, *Parkersburg*
Ray W. Knotts, *French Creek*
Gerald E. Lewis, *Romney*
Walt R. Shupe, *Marlington*
Warren T. Stewart, *Sisterville*
Gary D. Strawn, *Romney*

WISCONSIN

Patrick Barwick, *West Allis*
Thomas G. Bloomingdale, *Mequon*
Leo A. Broeckel, *Green Bay*
Jim Carrig, *Limeridge*
Richard A. Case, *Ontario*
Craig A. Cousins, *Milltown*
John F. Davis, *Minocqua*
Clark Gallup, *Stoddard*
Stanley R. Godfrey, *Whitewater*
William "Bill" Grosskreutz, *Plymouth*
Peter Haupt, *Hayward*

David A. Heilmeier, *Whitewater*
James Joseph Hjort, *Deforest*
Craig James Hollman, *Athens*
J. Robert Hults, *Germantown*
Lester W. Jass, *Janesville*
Gunter Lemke, *Onalaska*
Terry A. G. Moline, *Eau Claire*
James Nikolopoulos, *Greenfield*
John Romans, *Cudahy*
Bruce Scheehle, *Milton*
Richard A. Schreiber, *Portage*
Maynard W. Schultz, *Hudson*
Michael Steliga, *Lily*
Dick Strait, *Siren*
Brian J. Tessman, *Milwaukee*
Howard Thelemann, *Wisconsin Rapids*
Gerald M. Weber, *Glidden*

WYOMING

P. Franklin Bays, Jr., *Jackson Hole*
Jerry R. Bowen, *Wheatland*
Thomas Michael Casey, *Laramie*
Mark Chapman, *Rock Springs*
Gary R. Cole, *Newcastle*
Kerry B. Connell, *Lander*
Terry P. Constable, *Sheridan*
Vic R. Dana, *Green River*
Keith Dana, *Rock Springs*
James D. Gay, *Shoshoni*
William G. Hepworth, *Laramie*
Duane Hyde, *Afton*
George B. Johnson, *Buffalo*
G. Richard "Dick" Keeney, *Casper*
Dick Mankin, *Gillette*
Pat A. McAteer, *Casper*
Ricky D. Metz, *Gillette*
Larry M. Pate, *Casper*
Ronell Skinner, *Bedford*
Reg R. Smith, *Clearmont*
Dennis Spawn, *Evansville*
James N. Willcox, *Rawlins*

CANADA

ALBERTA

Ralph L. Cervo, *Milk River*
David R. Coupland, *Calgary*
Jack C. Dezall, *Caroline*
Albert C. England, *Lloydminster*
John M. Graham, *Edmonton*
Duane Hicks, *Beaumont*

Dave Richardson, *Calgary*
Gordon M. Roline, *Edmonton*
Ryk Visscher, *Edmonton*
Fred Walker, *Red Deer*

BRITISH COLUMBIA

Gordon R. Calam, *Comox*
Douglas Clinkenbeard, *Smithers*
Gerald John Deane, *Princeton*
Robert G. Frew, *Montrose*
Peter Halbig, *Mission*
Wilfred W. Klingsat, *Vancouver*
Louis Kratky, *Montrose*
Robert Petrie, *Kamloops*
Albert Rand, *Prince George*

MANITOBA

Delmar E. Bamford, *Foxwarren*
Randall Joseph Bean, *Winnipeg*
Vince Crichton, *Winnipeg*
Dwain Davies, *Dauphin*
Lawrence B. Davison, *Solsgirth*
C. C. Dixon, *Winnipeg*
L. Greg Fehr, *Gladstone*
Lorne Gordon, *Winnipeg*
Jerry C. Hayduk, *Winnipeg*
Hank Hristienko, *Winnipeg*
Cameron Hurst, *Winnipeg*
Ronald A. Larche, *Winnipeg*
Kenneth E. McPhail, *Brendon*
Sam Ransom, *Winnipeg*
Gil A. Rodger, *Brandon*

Eugene Syrotiuk, *St. Martin*
J. Rudolph Turman, *Winnipeg*

NEW BRUNSWICH

William G. Hanson, *Westfield*

NOVA SCOTIA

Allan Joseph Gallant, *Mount Uniacke*
Walter Hingley, *Halifax*

ONTARIO

Grant R. Beattie, *North Bay*
Carl Doerner, *Elmira*
Fred Law, *Guelph*
Herb Scherer, *Sault Ste. Marie*

SASKATCHEWAN

Howard L. Hanson, *Mankota*
Allan R. Hill, *Moose Jaw*
John J. Kuzma, *Norquay*
Archie B. Lovelace, *Pilot Butte*
Keith E. Thue, *Saskatoon*

YUKON TERRITORY

Rick Furniss, *Whitehorse*

MEXICO
CHIHUAHUA

Jose C. Trevino, *Chihuahua*

CANADA

Alberta Fish and Wildlife Division
8th Floor, South Tower
Petroleum Plaza
Edmonton, Alberta T5K 2C9

British Columbia Ministry of Environment
Fish and Wildlife Branch
Parliament Bldgs.
Victoria, British Columbia V8V 1X4

Manitoba Department of Natural Resources
Wildlife Branch
1129 Queens Avenue
Brandon, Manitoba R7A 1L9

New Brunswick Bureau of Natural Resources
Wildlife Division
P.O. Box 6000
Fredericton, New Brunswich E3B 5H1

Newfoundland Department of Culture
Wildlife Division
P.O. Box 8750
St. Johns, Newfoundland A1C 5T7

Nova Scotia Department of Lands and Forests
Wildlife Division
P.O. Box 698
Halifax, Nova Scotia B3J 2T9

Ontario Ministry of Natural Resources
Wildlife Branch
Queen's Park
Toronto, Ontario M7A 1W3

**Prince Edward Island Community and
Cultural Affairs**
P.O. Box 2000
Charlottetown, Prince Edward Island
C1A 7N8

**Quebec Ministere Du Loisir
De la Chasse Et De la Peche**
150 est boul St.-Cyrille
Quebec City, Quebec G1R 4Y1

Saskatchewan Parks and Renewable Resources
3211 Albert Street
Regina, Saskatchewan S4S 5W6

**Northwest Territories Department of
Renewable Resources**
Legislative Bldg.
Yellowknife, N.W.T. X1A 2C6

Yukon Department of Renewable Resources
Wildlife Branch
P.O. Box 2703
Whitehorse, Yukon Territory Y1A 2C6

UNITED STATES

Alabama Game and Fish Division
64 N. Union St.
Montgomery, AL 36130

Alaska Department of Fish and Game
230 S. Franklin
Juneau, AK 99802

Arizona Game and Fish Department
2222 W. Greenway Road
Phoenix, AZ 85023

Arkansas Game and Fish Commission
#2 Natural Resources Dr.
Little Rock, AR 72203

California Department of Game and Fish
1416 9th Street
Sacramento, CA 95814

Colorado Division of Wildlife
6060 Broadway
Denver, CO 80216

Connecticut Wildlife Unit
Department of Environmental Protection
State Office Bldg.
Hartford, CT 06115

Delaware Division of Fish and Wildlife
R & R Bldg. 89 Kings Hwy.
Dover, DE 19903

Florida Game and Fish Commission
620 S. Meridian
Tallahassee, FL 32301

Georgia Fish and Wildlife Division
270 Washington St., S.W.
Atlanta, GA 30334

Hawaii Forestry and Wildlife Division
1151 Punchbowl St.
Honolulu, HI 96813

Idaho Fish and Game Department
600 S. Walnut Street
Boise, ID 83707

Illinois Division of Fish and Wildlife
125 North First St.
Monmouth, IL 61462

Indiana Division Wildlife
608 State Office Bldg.
Indianapolis, IN 46204

Iowa Conservation Commission
Wallace State Office Bldg.
Des Moine, IA 50319

Kansas Fish and Game Commission
832 E. 6th
Emporia, KS 66801

Kentucky Department of Fish and Wildlife
#1 Game Farm Road
Frankfort, KY 40601

**Louisiana Department of Wildlife
and Fisheries**
P.O. Box 15570
Baton Rouge, LA 70895

Maine Department of Fisheries and Wildlife
Wildlife Division
P.O. Box 1298
Bangor, ME 04401

Maryland Wildlife Administration
P.O. Box 68
Wye Mills, MD 21679

Massachusetts Department of Fisheries and Wildlife
Field Headquarters
Westboro, MA 01581

Michigan Wildlife Division
Box 30028
Lansing, MI 48909

Minnesota Division of Wildlife
Box 7, 500 Lafayette
St. Paul, MN 55146

Mississippi Department of Wildlife Conservation
P.O. Box 451
Jackson, MS 39205

Missouri Department of Conservation
1110 College Avenue
Columbia, MO 65201

Montana Department of Fish, Wildlife, and Parks
1420 E. Sixth Street
Helena, MT 59620

Nebraska Game and Parks Commission
P.O. Box 30370
Lincoln, NE 68503

Nevada Department of Wildlife
Box 10678
Reno, NV 89520

New Hampshire Fish and Game Department
34 Bridge St.
Concord, NH 03301

New Jersey Bureau of Wildlife Management
Nacote Creek Research Station
Star Route
Absecon, NJ 08201

New Mexico Fish and Game Department
State Capitol
Santa Fe, NM 87503

New York Department of Environmental Conservation
Wildlife Resources Center
Delmar, NY 12054

North Carolina Wildlife Resources Commission
512 N. Salisbury St.
Raleigh, NC 27611

North Dakota Game and Fish Department
2121 Lovett Ave.
Bismarck, ND 58501

Ohio Division of Wildlife
Fountain Square C-4
Columbus, OH 43224

Oklahoma Department of Wildlife Conservation
1801 N. Lincoln
P.O. Box 53465
Oklahoma City, OK 73105

Oregon Department of Fish and Game
Box 3503
Portland, OR 97208

Pennsylvania Game Commission
P.O. Box 1657
Harrisburg, PA 17105

Rhode Island Division of Fish and Wildlife
Box 37
West Fingsten, RI 02892

South Carolina Wildlife Department
Dennis Wildlife Center
P.O. Box 170
Bonneau, SC 29431

South Dakota Department of Game, Fish, and Parks
Sigurd Anderson Bldg.
445 E. Capitol
Pierre, SD 57501

Tennessee Wildlife Resources Agency
P.O. Box 40747
Nashville, TN 37204

Texas Parks and Wildlife Department
4200 Smith School Road
Austin, TX 78744

Utah State Division of Wildlife Resources
1596 West North Temple
Salt Lake City, UT 84116

Vermont Fish and Game Department
255 N. Main St.
Barre, VT 05641

Virginia Game Commission
Education Division
P.O. Box 11104
Richmond, VA 23230

Washington Department of Game
600 N. Capitol Way
Olympia, WA 98504

West Virginia Department of Wildlife Resources
P.O. Box 67
Elkins, WV 26241

Wisconsin Department of Natural Resources
P.O. Box 7921
Madison, WI 53707

Wyoming Game and Fish Department
5400 Bishop Blvd.
Cheyenne, WY 82002